EVIDENCE

PRINCIPLES AND PROBLEMS

Ninth Edition

by

Ronald Joseph Delisle
B.Sc., LL.B., LL.M.

Faculty of Law
Queen's University

Don Stuart
B.A., LL.B., Dip. Crim., D. Phil.

Faculty of Law
Queen's University

David M. Tanovich
B.A., M.A., LL.B., LL.M.

Faculty of Law
University of Windsor

CARSWELL®

A cataloguing record for this publication is available from Library and Archives Canada.

ISBN 978-0-7798-2707-7

Printed in the United States by Thomson Reuters.

Composition: Computer Composition of Canada Inc.

THOMSON REUTERS

CARSWELL, A DIVISION OF THOMSON REUTERS CANADA LIMITED

One Corporate Plaza	Customer Relations
2075 Kennedy Road	Toronto 1-416-609-3800
Toronto, Ontario	Elsewhere in Canada/U.S. 1-800-387-5164
M1T 3V4	Fax: 1-416-298-5082
	www.carswell.com
	E-mail www.carswell.com/email

To Gloria, Pam and Melanie

Preface to Ninth Edition

In 1984, in the first edition of this book, Ron Delisle sought to depart from the usual casebook format of lengthy case extracts to teach evidence largely by narrative text and consideration of problems. The text throughout aimed to identify the principles of the law, their historical background, their inherent logic or lack of logic, ethical issues and attempts at reform in Canada and other jurisdictions. Another major feature of the first edition was to reflect the reality that in most trials evidence is allowed in rather than excluded. It was therefore important to address the positive part of the law of evidence as to how evidence is adduced rather than to view the law as a briar patch of exclusionary rules.

In 1989, the second edition included, at the urgings of fellow evidence teachers, a careful selection of extracts from leading evidence cases. From this time on the book became partly a text and partly a casebook. The struggle has always been not to overwhelm the original aim by including too many cases.

The Law Reform Commission of Canada in the 70s proposed that Parliament codify the principles of the law of evidence. This view was not well received by the profession who seemed concerned that the new Code would give judges too much discretion. The irony is that with reform left to the courts the unremitting trend over the last 35 years has been to allow judges more discretion as to what evidence to admit and what evidence to exclude. The central issue is how best to provide guidelines for such discretion.

Evidence is a branch of the law where lawyers, judges and those learning the law for the first time must carry a working knowledge in their heads. This can be a daunting challenge given that the principal source is ever-changing case law. We provide a detailed table of contents with many subheadings, and list the major cases to distinguish those in the text that are purely illustrative. To aid the reader we continue to divide the law of evidence into just six broad chapters.

Chapter 1 starts with relating the law of evidence to the common law commitment to an adversarial system of fact adjudication. There is an introductory section on ethics enabling us to directly confront such topical issues as the need for civility in the profession or the controversial issue of whether defence counsel can retain incriminating physical evidence, as counsel did in the *Bernardo* trial. The chapter introduces the reader to the sources of the laws of evidence. We consider views, such as those of Professor Lisa Dufraimont, as to whether the laws of evidence have a unifying purpose. We set out arguments on the controversial issue of whether rules of evidence should be codified. Finally we address their applicability to forums other than courts, such as administrative tribunals.

Chapter 2 considers burdens of proof. Special attention is given to the distinction between persuasive and evidentiary burdens, measures of proof, tests of sufficiency, and the thorny issue of presumptive devices including the presumption of innocence now entrenched in the Canadian Charter of Rights and Freedoms.

In Chapter 3, given their centrality, the topics of relevance and discretion to exclude at common law and now under the Charter are considered in detail. We assess how courts in both criminal and civil cases have recognized a general discretion to exclude evidence where its probative value is exceeded by prejudicial effect. Under the Charter our focus is on the uncertain discretion the Supreme Court now recognizes to exclude evidence to ensure a fair trial. We concentrate less on the Charter discretion in s. 24(2) to exclude evidence obtained in violation of a Charter right. Since one of the central considerations under s. 24(2) is the nature and seriousness of the Charter breach, we are of the view that that topic is better considered in Criminal Procedure courses. See Delisle, Stuart and Quigley, *Learning Canadian Criminal Procedure*, 9th ed., (2010, Carswell). We do summarize the Supreme Court's recent bellwether ruling in *R. v. Grant,* where the Court offers a totally revised template of factors for the exercise of s. 24(2) discretion.

As in previous editions, Chapter 4 on character evidence provides a test case for consideration of principles of relevance and discretion to exclude. The courts remain active and often inconsistent on the issue of good and bad character. We pay particular attention to the decision of the Supreme Court in *Handy* and *Shearing* that similar fact evidence may exceptionally be admitted to show propensity. We focus on the impact of these decisions in the criminal and civil contexts. We explore the topic of rape shield laws, including the Supreme Court's rulings in *Seaboyer* and *Darrach*, and the controversial issue of whether evidence of the complainant's prior sexual conduct *with the accused* should be treated differently.

Chapter 5 addresses the positive side of the laws of evidence – how matters are proved by the admission of evidence. We firstly deal with situations where proof is not required: formal admissions of fact, and the controversial and still evolving doctrine of judicial notice. We focus consideration of the latter topic by comparing the broad views of Justice L'Heureux-Dube with the more cautious recent views of Justice Binnie speaking for the Court in *Spence*. The section on real evidence considers practical topics such as how to file exhibits and how to authenticate. The section on demonstrative evidence reflects growing use of such evidence by the courts, especially in civil cases. The lengthy section on witnesses now includes the current law as to the competency of young witnesses and spouses. We incorporate significant developments relating to the accused's pre-trial and trial Charter rights to silence and the privilege against self-incrimination, recently re-interpreted by Justice Binnie speaking for the Supreme Court in *Henry*. In the general section on cross-examination we include the Supreme Court of Canada's important ruling in *Lyttle* allowing cross-examination on unproven evidence subject to a requirement of good faith. Under the issue of cross-examination of prior inconsistent statements under ss. 10 and 11 of the *Canada Evidence Act* we include advocacy advice. This dimension was also added to the section concerning cross-examination on declarations of adversity under s. 9(1) and (2), using as a hard example the prosecution of domestic assault where the principal witness has recanted.

Chapter 6 covers the major exclusionary principles of hearsay, opinion, privilege and evidence obtained in violation of the Charter. The hearsay chapter focuses on how to identify hearsay and the Supreme Court's principled approach now fully developed with *Khelawon*. In the section on opinion evidence we address the fundamental ruling in *Graat* that lay witnesses may express opinions based on personal knowledge, and also the Supreme Court's "gatekeeper" approach to the admissibility of expert opinion through the controlling authority of *Mohan* and the Court's approach to novel scientific evidence set out in *J. (J.L.)* and *Trochyn*. In the section on privilege we discuss class privileges such as that of client/lawyer, litigation and marital privilege, and the case-by-case privilege according to Wigmore's criteria. We also summarize and consider the effect of major statutory changes substantially expanding state privilege sections of the *Canada Evidence Act*, which were enacted by the Anti-Terrorist Bill C-36 in 2002 and hastily passed by Parliament in the aftermath of the 9/11 attacks. We conclude by examining the approach of the Supreme Court in *O'Connor* and *Mills,* and of Parliament, of balancing Charter rights of complainants in sexual assault cases on the issue of access to their therapeutic records. We compare the Court's controversial allowance of defence cross-examination on a diary in *Shearing*.

In this ninth edition the structure of this text and teaching book remain largely intact. We did carefully re-edit throughout to remove footnotes, text and problems that had grown out of date. We also added new problems and questions to test comprehension of the latest developments and to provoke discussion. The courts have been so active that we found it necessary to add the edited text of more than 30 new cases. We also removed much material and older cases so that the book has not increased in length. In our experience it is impossible to teach every topic and nuance of this case-driven subject in a four hour per week semester course. The subject is too vast and complex, so the teacher must be selective.

Although most of the leading decisions arise in the criminal context we continue to make a special effort to include leading civil cases and also rulings from various tribunals. In this edition we deal with the blockbuster recent ruling of the Supreme Court in *F.H. v. McDougall* that the same balance of probabilities standard applies to all civil cases. We deal with the latest law on motions for non-suit and summary judgments, and with significant differences respecting the admission of evidence of habit and character in civil cases, spousal competence rules and admitting an expert on racial profiling at a Human Rights Commission hearing.

This edition includes and considers the following major new Supreme Court rulings:

- *S. (J.H.) (W.D.* standard for reasonable doubt criticised and not to be used as magical incantation)
- *Griffin* (weighing circumstantial evidence and *Hodge's* case)
- *Stirling, Ellard and Dinardo* (prior consistent statements)
- *Couture* (spousal competency)
- *Khela* (requirements of *Vetrovec* warning)
- *Blackman and Devine* (new applications of principled approach to hearsay)
- *Singh* (right to silence subsumed by voluntary confessions rule)
- *Rojas* (*Duncan* warning not required)
- *Blood Tribe, Goodis* and *Pritchard* (solicitor-client privilege)
- *Blank* (litigation privilege)
- *Named Person* (informer privilege)
- *McNeil* (disclosure and access to third-party records)

These developments necessitated major changes and re-writing of the sections respecting onus of proof and the admissibility of evidence supporting credibility. We also tried to clarify our previous treatment of the notoriously difficult area of character evidence.

Important provincial court decisions are also considered. Special attention is given, for example, to the blockbuster decision of Justice Doherty for the Ontario Court of Appeal in *R. v. Abbey.* This requires a revised approach to the gatekeeper role respecting the admission of expert testimony. We ask whether it is totally consistent with the approach of the Supreme Court in *Mohan, J (J.L.)* and *Trochyn.* We have included Justice Rosenberg's careful approach to the consideration of eyewitness identification evidence in *R. v. Hanemaayer.* The Saskatchewan Court of Appeal's rejection in *R. v. Martin* of a s. 15 equality challenge to the exclusion of common law spouses from spousal competency and privilege rules is considered, as well as contrary rulings of trial judges in Ontario and Quebec.

We address Parliament's comprehensive new scheme which amended the *Canada Evidence Act* passed in 2005 to govern competence and other issues respecting young witnesses. We are grateful to Nick Bala, Katherine Duvall-Antonacopoulos, Rod Lindsay, Kang Lee and Victoria Talwar for permitting us to reproduce their article, "Bill C-2: A New Law for Canada's Child Witnesses", originally published in the Criminal Reports. This describes their interdisciplinary research, which provided the momentum for reform, and also assesses the significance of the new laws.

In our section on rape shield law we thank Dean Michelle Anderson of CUNY for granting us permission to republish her article assessing the rape shield arguments offered in the Kobe Bryant rape trial in Colorado and calling for reform.

We thank Lisa Dufraimont for her permission to re-publish portions of her insightful comments first published in the Criminal Reports and other journals.

We thank Rebecca Duncan of Carswell for her continuing support. We are deeply indebted to Claire Cheverie for so carefully reviewing our manuscript.

R.J. Delisle
Don Stuart
David Tanovich
March 1, 2010

TABLE OF CONTENTS

Preface to Ninth Edition v

Chapter 1 **INTRODUCTION** 1

1. THE ADVERSARY SYSTEM 1
   (a) Not a Scientific Inquiry 1
   (b) Truth and Justice: Competing Goals? 2
       R. v. Mullins- Johnson 7
       Lisa Dufraimont, Evidence Law and the Jury 8
   (c) Role of Trial Judge 10
       R. v. Lawes 11

2. LEGAL ETHICS 14
   R. v. Felderhof 14
   R. v. Murray 19
   Cowles v. Balac 23

3. SOURCES 25
   R. v. Salituro 26

4. CODIFICATION 28
   Arguments for a Comprehensive Statement 28
   Arguments Against a Comprehensive Statement 30

5. APPLICABILITY OF LAWS OF EVIDENCE 31

Chapter 2 **BURDENS OF PROOF AND PRESUMPTIONS** 39

1. BURDENS OF PROOF 39
   (a) Terminology 39
   (b) Allocation of Burdens 41
       (i)   Civil Cases 41
             Fontaine v. Insurance Corp. of British Columbia 42
             Peart v. Peel (Regional Municipality) Police Service 44
       (ii) Criminal Cases 49
             Expediency 50
             Facts Peculiarly Within Knowledge of Accused 51
   (c) Measure of Burden of Persuasion 53
       (i)   Balance of Probabilities Standard for Civil Cases 53
             F.H. v. McDougall 53
       (ii) Reasonable Doubt Standard for Criminal Cases 60
             R. v. Lifchus 60
             R. v. Starr 62
       (iii) Choosing Between Competing Versions 63
             R. v. W. (D.) 64

R. v. S. (J.H.) 64
PROBLEM 69
    (iv) Considering Individual Pieces of Evidence.......................... 70
        R. v. Morin 70
        R. v. White.. 73
    (v) Direct and Circumstantial Evidence 75
        R. v. Munoz 76
        R. v. Whitman 81
        R. v. Hanemaayer.. 85
    (vi) Hodge's Case... 90
        R. v. Cooper 91
        R. v. Tombran 93
        R. v. Griffin 96
    (vii) Preliminary Findings of Facts...................................... 96
        R. v. Evans 96
        R. v. Arp... 97
  (d) Measure of Evidential Burden 97
    (i) Criminal Cases.. 97
        U.S.A. v. Sheppard.. 98
        Monteleone v. R. 98
        R. v. Quercia 100
        R. v. Arcuri... 101
        U.S.A. v. Ferras 104
        Quebec (Ministere du Revenu) v. Buffolino.................. 108
PROBLEM 110
        R. v. Cinous 111
        R. v. Fontaine 115
    (ii) Civil Cases 118
        Canada (A.G.) v. Lameman............................... 118
        FL Receivable Trust v. Cobrand Foods Ltd. 120
        Laufer v. Bucklaschuk 122
PROBLEMS 124

2. PRESUMPTIONS.. 126
  (a) Introduction.. 126
  (b) False Presumptions.. 127
        R. v. Nicholl.. 129
PROBLEMS 133
  (c) True Presumptions... 133
  (d) Presumption of Innocence and Charter 138
        R. v. Oakes 138
        R. v. Chaulk 145
        R. v. Downey 148
        R. v. Laba... 149
        R. v. Curtis 153

PROBLEMS 155

Chapter 3 **RELEVANCE AND DISCRETION TO EXCLUDE** 157

1. RELEVANCE 157
    (a) Tests 157
        R. v. Watson 157
        Morris v. R. 159
    (b) Materiality 162
        R. v. Lavallee 163
    (c) Multiple Relevance.. 164
    (d) Relevance and Social Context 165
        R. v. S. (R.D.).. 166
        R. v. Hamilton... 176

2. DISCRETION AND LAW OF EVIDENCE 183
    (a) Introduction.. 183
    (b) Discretion to Exclude 184
        (i)   Reading in... 185
              Corbett v. R. 185
              R. v. Potvin.. 190
        (ii) Balancing Probative Value and Prejudicial Effect.......... 192
              R. v. Seaboyer.. 192
              R. v. Hunter 195
              Anderson v. Maple Ridge (District) 197
        (iii) Assessing Trial Fairness 200
              R. v. Harrer 200
              R. v. White.. 205
              R. v. Grant.. 206
        PROBLEMS 209

Chapter 4 **CHARACTER EVIDENCE AS TEST CASE OF
             RELEVANCE AND DISCRETION** 213

1. HABIT 213
    Belknap v. Meakes.. 214
    R. v. Watson 215
    Devgan v. College of Physicians & Surgeons (Ontario) 218
    R. v. B. (L.).. 220

2. CHARACTER.. 221
    (a) Admissible as Directly Relevant to Material Issue or As Disposition
        (Propensity)... 221
        R. v. W. (L.) 222

(b) Underlying Assumptions Grounding Character Evidence 223
    R. v. Clarke 223
(c) Character of Parties in Civil Cases 224
    Rawdah v. Evans 225
    Robertson v. Edmonton (City) Police Service 226
(d) Character of Accused in Criminal Cases 228
    (i)   Good Character Evidence 228
          R. v. Profit (Ont. C.A.) 229
          R. v. Profit (S.C.C.) 231
    (ii) When Bad Character Evidence Can be Led by Crown........... 231
    (iii) When Does Accused Put Their Character in Issue?............... 232
          R. v. P. (N.A.) 234
          R. v. A. (W.A.) 236
    (iv) How Character May be Proved... 237
          R. v. Levasseur 238
          R. v. Brown 240
    (v)   Warnings to Jury 242
PROBLEMS 242
(e) Similar Facts 243
    (i)   Need for Connection Between Previous Acts and Accused 247
          Sweitzer v. R. 247
          R. v. Millar 249
    (ii) How are Similar Facts Relevant? 251
          R. v. B. (C.R.) 251
          R. v. Arp 256
          R. v. Handy 261
          R. v. Blake 274
          R. v. Titmus 275
          R. v. Shearing 276
          R. v. Perrier 281
PROBLEMS 285
    (iii) Civil Cases.. 286
          Johnson v. Bugera 286
          S. (R.C.M.) v. K. (G.M.) 289
PROBLEMS 291
(f) Character of Third Party/Co-Accused.. 292
          R. v. Khan 293
(g) Character of Victim 296
    (i)   Self-defence 297
          R. v. Scopelliti 297
    (ii) Sexual Assault 298
          Common Law 300
          Charter of Rights... 303
          R. v. Seaboyer 303
          New Legislation – Bill C-49.. 318
          R. v. Crosby 320

                    R. v. Darrach 323

                    R. v. Temertzoglou 329

                    R. v. A. (No. 2) 332

           Michelle Anderson, Time to Reform Rape Shield Laws .. 335

    PROBLEMS 343

Chapter 5 **MECHANICS OF PROOF** 345

A. **Matters Not Requiring Proof** 345

1. FORMAL ADMISSIONS OF FACT 345

    Castellani v. R. 345

    R. v. Proctor 347

    R. v. Baksh 351

2. JUDICIAL NOTICE 353

    (a) Introduction 353

    (b) Disputed Boundaries of Judicial Notice 354

        Daishowa Inc. v. Friends of the Lubicon 360

        R. v. Lavallee 362

        R. v. Malott 365

        Moge v. Moge 368

        Cronk v. Canadian General Insurance Co. 372

    (c) Spence: Revised Standards 376

        R. v. Spence 376

        CTV Television v. The Queen 384

    PROBLEMS 386

    (d) Judicial Notice of Law 387

        R. v. Smith 389

B. **Real Evidence** 391

1. AUTHENTICATION 391

    R. v. Patterson 393

    R. v. MacPherson 393

    PROBLEMS 394

2. PHOTOGRAPHS AND VIDEOTAPES 395

    R. v. Schaffner 396

    R. v. Nikolovski 398

    PROBLEMS 401

3. DOCUMENTS 402

4. BEST EVIDENCE RULE 404

R. v. Cotroni 405

R. v. Morgan 407

5. ABORIGINAL RIGHTS 409

  Delgamuukw v. British Columbia 409

  Mitchell v. Canada (M.N.R.) 411

6. DEMONSTRATIVE EVIDENCE 412

  R. v. Howard and Trudel 413

  R. v. Macdonald 414

  McCutcheon v. Chrysler Canada Ltd. 419

  R. v. Collins 423

7. VIEWS 424

C. **Witnesses** 426

1. COMPETENCE AND COMPELLABILITY 426

  (a) Introduction 426

  (b) Oath 426

      R. v. Kalever 428

      R. v. Wiebe 430

  (c) Age 432

      R. v. W. (R.) 433

      Ontario Evidence Act 436

      Nick Bala *et al*, Bill C-2: A New Law for Canada's Child

      Witnesses 437

      R. v. Levogiannis 447

  (d) Mental Capacity 449

      Canada Evidence Act, s. 16 450

      R. v. Parrott 451

      R. v. Farley 454

  (e) Interest 455

      Evidence Acts 457

  (f) Spousal Competence and Compellability 458

      (i)   The General Rule 458

            R. v. Couture 458

      (ii) The Common Law Exception 461

            R. v. McGinty 462

            R. v. Moore 464

      (iii) Who Is a Spouse? 466

            R. v. Salituro 467

            R. v. Hawkins 470

            R. v. Martin 472

      (iv) Reform 475

            R. v. Couture 476

(g) Compellability of Accused... 478
  (i)   History of Privilege Against Self-incrimination.................... 478
  (ii)   Canada Evidence Act... 479
  (iii) Sections 11(c) and 13 of Charter... 481
PROBLEMS 483
            Knutson v. Registered Nurses Assn. (Sask.) 484
  (iv) Pre-trial Right to Silence: Charter, s. 7................................ 484
            Hebert 484
  (v)   Principle Against Self-incrimination: Charter, s. 7 488
  (vi) No Adverse Inference from Pre-trial Silence........................ 491
            R. v. Turcotte 491
  (vii) No Adverse Inference from Trial Silence 497
            R. v. Noble.. 498
  (viii) Comments on Accused's Failure to Testify 508
            R. v. Miller 510
PROBLEMS 512
  (ix) Reform 513
(h) Compellability of Corporate Officers 515
            R. v. Amway Corp.... 515

2. MANNER OF QUESTIONING 517
(a) Leading Questions.. 517
            R. v. Rose 520
(b) Refreshing Memory/Past Recollection Recorded......................... 524
            R. v. Wilks.. 524
            R. v. B. (K.G.) 530
            R. v. Mattis 531
PROBLEMS 534
(c) Videotaped Statements by Children.. 535
            R. v. L. (D.O.) 535
            R. v. F. (C.C.) 536
(d) Adoption... 540
            R. v. McCarroll 540
(e) Cross-examination.. 542
            R. v. Lyttle 544
            R. v. R. (A.J.) 547
(f) Duty to Cross-examine (Rule in *Browne v. Dunn*)....................... 552
            R. v. McNeill.. 552
(g) Collateral Facts Rule.. 556
            A.G. v. Hitchcock 557
            R. v. Krause 558
            R. v. Cassibo.. 560
PROBLEMS 561
(h) Examination by Court and Order of Witnesses............................ 562
            Cook.. 563
            R. v. P. (T.L.) 565

3. IMPEACHMENT 565
    (a) Prior Inconsistent Statements 566
            Canada Evidence Act, ss. 10, 11 567
        (i)   Impeaching One's Own Witness... 568
                Anderson v. Flying Saucer Driver – In Ltd. 569
        (ii) Canada Evidence Act, s. 9(1) 571
                R. v. Vivar 571
                R. v. Malik.. 574
        (iii) Canada Evidence Act, s. 9(2) 576
    PROBLEM 578
    (b) Bias... 579
                R. v. Ghorvei 580
        (i)   Motives of Accused and Complainants 583
                R. v. Jackson... 583
                R. v. Ellard 583
                R. v. B. (L.) 585
    (c) Character of Witness... 586
        (i)   Extrinsic Evidence.. 586
                R. v. Clarke 589
        (ii) Evidence Elicited on Cross-examination 591
        (iii) Accused as Witness 592
                R. v. Jones... 593
                Canada Evidence Act, s. 12.. 595
                R. v. McFadyen 599
                Hutton v. Way 600
                R. v. Underwood 602
    (d) Defects in Capacity of Witness... 604

4. SUPPORTING CREDIBILITY... 606
    (a) General Rule Prohibiting 606
                R. c. Beland 607
    (b) Exceptions 614
        (i)   To Rebut Allegation of Recent Fabrication......................... 614
                R. v. Stirling 614
                R. v. Ellard 617
        (ii) Prior Identification 618
                R. v. Tat 619
        (iii) Part of Narrative... 620
                R. c. Dinardo 620
                R. v. Curto.. 622
        (iv) Recent Complaint.. 624
                R. v. O'Connor.. 625

5. DEMEANOUR AS GUIDE TO CREDIBILITY.............................. 628
        R. v. Norman 629

PROBLEMS 631

6. CORROBORATION 633
  (a) When Required? 633
     (i) Treason 634
     (ii) Forgery 634
     (iii) Accomplices 635
         Vetrovec v. R. 635
         R. v. Khela 638
     (iv) Informers 642
         R. v. Brooks 642
     (v) Primary Witnesses in Sex Cases 646
         R. v. S. (F.) 648
     (vi) Unsworn Evidence of Children 648
         R. v. S. (W.) 649
         R. v. G. (A.) 651
     (vii) Miscellaneous Provisions 653
  (b) What is Corroboration? 653
         R. v. B. (G.) 654

Chapter 6 **EXCLUSIONARY RULES** 657

A. **Character** 657

B. **Hearsay** 657

1. THE RULE 657
  (a) History 657
  (b) Reason for Rule 661
  (c) Identifying Hearsay 662
         R. v. Khelawon 665
         R. v. Evans 668
         R. v. Tat 671
         R. v. Starr 674
  PROBLEMS 675
  (d) Approaches to Hearsay 677
         R. v. Khan 680
         R. v. Smith 685
         R. v. Kharsekin 690
         R. v. Cassidy 691
         R. v. B. (K.G.) 693
         R. v. U. (F.J.) 700
         R. v. Chappell 703
         R. v. Khelawon 706
         R. v. Blackman 718

　　　　　R. v. Devine 720
　　(e)　Establishing Necessity 723
　　　　　R. v. Parrott 723
　　　　　Dodge v. Kaneff Homes Inc. 729

2.　EXCEPTIONS... 731
　　(a)　Admissions 732
　　　　(i)　Generally 732
　　　　　　R. v. Phillips 734
　　　　　　R. v. Streu 737
　　　　(ii)　Confessions 740
　　　　(iii)　Statements Adopted by Party's Conduct 740
　　　　(iv)　Statements Authorized by Party.. 742
　　　　　　R. v. Strand Electric Ltd. 742
　　　　(v)　Statements of Person with Common Purpose 746
　　　　　　R. v. Mapara 747
　　　　(vi)　Statements by Representative 753
　　　　(vii)　Statements by those in Privity with Estate or Interest
　　　　　　　with Party... 754
　　(b)　Exceptions where Declarant or Testimony Unavailable (Have
　　　　　Necessity Requirement) 754
　　　　(i)　Declarations Against Interest... 754
　　　　　　R. v. Demeter.. 755
　　　　　　R. v. Lucier 757
　　　　　　R. v. Kimberley 758
　　　　(ii)　Dying Declarations... 761
　　　　(iii)　Declarations in Course of Duty... 763
　　　　　　General.. 763
　　　　　　Business Records 764
　　　　　　　R. v. Martin 766
　　　　　　　R. v. L.(C.).. 769
　　　　　　　R. v. Larsen 772
　　　　(iv)　Former Testimony 774
　　　　　　R. v. Potvin.. 775
　　　　PROBLEM 779
　　(c)　Exceptions Not Dependent on Availability of Declarant (Have No
　　　　　Necessity Requirement) 780
　　　　(i)　Declarations as to Physical Sensation 780
　　　　(ii)　Declarations as to Mental or Emotional State....................... 780
　　　　　　R. v P. (R.).. 783
　　　　　　R. v. Starr... 785
　　　　PROBLEM 788
　　　　(iii)　Spontaneous Statements (Excited Utterances)....................... 789
　　　　　　R. v. Bedingfield.. 789
　　　　　　R. v. Clark 790

C. **Voluntary Confession Rule** 797

1. COMMON LAW PRE-OICKLE 797
   R. v. Wray 801
   R. v. Sweeney 803
   R. v. Hodgson 804

2. REVISED APPROACH IN R. v. OICKLE 812
   R. v Oickle 812

3. THE PRE-TRIAL RIGHT TO SILENCE AND INTERROGATION 825
   R. v. Osmar 825
   R. v. Singh 829
   PROBLEMS 839

4. VIDEOTAPING OF INTERROGATIONS 842
   R. v. Moore-McFarlane 842
   R. v. Wilson 845

5. MIXED INCULPATORY AND EXCULPATORY STATEMENTS 848
   R. v. Rojas 849

D. **Opinion Evidence and Experts** 850

1. OPINION RULE 850
   Graat v. R. 854

2. EXPERT EVIDENCE 858
   (a) Tests 859
        R. v. Mohan 859
        R. v. J. (J.L.) 865
        R. v. Trochym 867
        R. v. Abbey 879
   (b) Examples 893
        R. v. Terceira 893
        R. v. McIntosh 897
        R. v. Olscamp 901
        R. v. Marquard 903
        R. v. D. (D.) 906
        R. v. Talbot 913
        R. v. G.(P.) 917
        R. v. Dimitrov 919
        R. v. Klymchuk 920
        R. v. Osmar 921

R. v. Melaragni 925

Nassiah v. Peel Regional Police Services Board 926

3. ULTIMATE ISSUE RULE... 929

R. v. Bryan 931

4. EXPERT OPINION BASED ON HEARSAY 932

R. v. Jordan 933

R. v. Lavallee 935

R. v. Worrall.. 943

Mizzi v. Debartok 944

5. EXAMINING EXPERT... 945

(a) Hypothetical Questions 945

(b) Use of Textbooks 946

R. v. Marquard... 946

6. APPOINTMENT OF COURT EXPERTS....................................... 949

7. EXCHANGE OF EXPERTS' REPORTS 952

E. **Privilege**... 955

1. PRIVILEGED COMMUNICATIONS 955

(a) Introduction.. 955

R. v. Gruenke.. 955

(b) Solicitor-Client Privilege 959

(i) Generally 959

Descoteaux v. Mierzwinski... 961

Canada (Privacy Commission) v. Blood Tribe Department of Health.. 967

Goodis v. Ontario (Ministry of Correctional Services) 969

Blunk v. Canada (Minister of Justice)........................... 970

(ii) Exceptions 977

Airst v. Airst 977

Smith v. Jones 980

R. v. McClure... 986

R. v. Shirose and Campbell 991

Pritchard v. Ontario (Human Rights Commission) 993

(c) Marital Communications 996

R. v. Zylstra... 1000

(d) Privilege for Without Prejudice Communications....................... 1002

Middelkamp v. Fraser Valley Real Estate Board 1002

R. v. Pabani... 1005

R. v. Lake 1007

2. PUBLIC INTEREST IMMUNITY 1009
   (a) Statutory Provisions... 1009
       (i)   Section 38 – International Relations, National Defence or National
             Security 1010
             Canada (A.G.) v. Ribic 1010
       (ii) Section 39 – Confidential Cabinet Materials....................... 1021
             Babcock v. Canada (Attorney General)....................... 1021
   (b) Identity of Informers.. 1030
       R. v. Leipert.. 1030
       Named Person v. Vancouver Sun 1037

3. CASE-BY-CASE PRIVILEGE 1042

4. BALANCING CHARTER VALUES... 1044
   R. v. Mills.. 1047
   R. v. Shearing 1060
   R. v. McNeil... 1071
   M. (A.) v. Ryan.. 1071

Table of Cases 1079
Index 1109

Chapter 1

Introduction

The law of evidence provides lawyers with the rules and principles that govern the admissibility of material offered by them in an effort to prove or disprove the existence of a material fact. This material most often takes the form of testimony, documents or physical objects.

As the great evidence scholar Rupert Cross was so fond of saying, "evidence of a fact is that which tends to prove it." In most trials, evidence is admitted rather than excluded. However, the law of evidence is sometimes misleadingly viewed as a briar patch of exclusionary rules. In this book, we will first address, before the exclusionary principles, the positive aspects of the law of evidence — how and on what criteria do lawyers get evidence admitted.

This introductory chapter explores the nature and suitability of the adversarial model for fact adjudication, legal ethics, the sources of the law of evidence and the applicability of the rules in different adjudicative contexts.

1. THE ADVERSARY SYSTEM

(a) Not a Scientific Inquiry

A trial, civil or criminal, provides society with the final forum within which a dispute can be settled. Most disputes, civil or criminal, are settled by negotiation between the parties. It is only when they are unable to reach a settlement by themselves that they turn to the courts or administrative tribunals for help. Oftentimes the dispute centres around different appreciations of the applicable law. The parties are agreed as to what happened but cannot agree on the legal significance of those facts. The court or administrative tribunal, operating with agreed facts, provides a legal answer. More often, however, the dispute is caused by different interpretations as to what in fact occurred between the parties. When the parties cannot agree on the historical facts they turn to one of our institutions and ask a third party to make a determination so that the matter can be settled and the parties can get on with their lives. The method of fact determination that we in the Anglo-Canadian common law tradition have adopted is called the "adversary method".

The method of inquiry in our courts is quite distinct from the scientific method; our method of ascertaining the facts is known as adversarial, while the scientific might be labelled inquisitorial. The principal distinguishing characteristic between the two methods resides in the relative passivity of the decision-maker, the judge, in the adversary method. Her function is to make the ultimate finding of facts, but she does not herself investigate; rather, she judges the merits of two positions that are put before her. The tradition in the English-speaking world is to regard the "over-speaking judge [as] no well-tuned cymbal."[1]

A frank description of our method of inquiry is seen in the decision of the Ontario Court of Appeal, *Phillips v. Ford Motor Co.*[2] In *Phillips* the plaintiff sued for damages arising out of an automobile accident. The issue was whether the accident was caused by a defective brake mechanism or driver error. The trial judge appointed an expert pursuant to the rules of court, which then stated:

> The court may obtain the assistance of merchants, engineers, accountants, actuaries or scientific persons, in such way as it thinks fit, the better to enable it to determine any matter of fact in question in any cause or proceeding.

The parties had called their experts but so did the judge. The judge's expert did more than simply interpret the evidence of the other experts; he provided input of his own. The judge also involved himself very much in the conduct of the proceedings. The parties were Nathan Phillips, elderly and retired mayor of Toronto, and the Ford Motor Company. Might it be that the adversaries were seen by the trial judge to be not evenly balanced in resources? Evans J.A. wrote:

> Our mode of trial procedure is based upon the adversary system in which the contestants seek to establish through relevant supporting evidence, before an impartial trier of facts, those events or happenings which form the bases of their allegations. This procedure assumes that the litigants, assisted by their counsel, will fully and diligently present all the material facts which have evidentiary value in support of their respective positions and that these disputed facts will receive from a trial Judge a dispassionate and impartial consideration in order to arrive at the truth of the matters in controversy. A trial is not intended to be a scientific exploration with the presiding Judge assuming the role of a research director; it is a forum established for the purpose of providing justice for the litigants. Undoubtedly a Court must be concerned with truth, in the sense that it accepts as true certain sworn evidence and rejects other testimony as unworthy of belief, but it cannot embark upon a quest for the "scientific" or "technological" truth when such an adventure does violence to the primary function of the Court, which has always been to do justice, according to law.

(b) Truth and Justice: Competing Goals?

Justice Evans appeared to strike the balance in the *Phillips* case in favour of justice over truth. Similarly, in *R. v. Stinchcombe*[3] the Supreme Court of Canada relied on fairness to mandate the Crown's obligation to make disclosure to the defence of all relevant information.

The judgment of the Court was delivered by Sopinka J.:

---

1 Lord Chancellor Bacon, as quoted by Lord Denning in *Jones v. Nat. Coal Bd.*, [1957] 2 Q.B. 55, 64 (C.A.).

2 (1971), 18 D.L.R. (3d) 641, 661 (C.A.). Contrast the remarks of Frankfurter J. in *Johnson v. U.S.*, 333 U.S. 46, 53-54 (1948):

> While a court room is not a laboratory for the scientific pursuit of truth, a trial judge is surely not confined to an account, obviously fragmentary, of the circumstances of a happening. . . . A trial is not a game of blind man's bluff; and the trial judge — particularly in a case where he himself is the trier of the facts upon which he is to pronounce the law — need not blindfold himself by failing to call an available vital witness simply because the parties, for reasons of trial tactics, choose to withhold his testimony. . . . Federal judges are not referees at prize-fights but functionaries of justice.

3 [1991] 3 S.C.R. 326.

Production and discovery were foreign to the adversary process of adjudication in its earlier history when the element of surprise was one of the accepted weapons in the arsenal of the adversaries. This applied to both criminal and civil proceedings. Significantly, in civil proceedings this aspect of the adversary process has long since disappeared, and full discovery of documents and oral examination of parties and even witnesses are familiar features of the practice. This change resulted from acceptance of the principle that justice was better served when the element of surprise was eliminated from the trial and the parties were prepared to address issues on the basis of complete information of the case to be met. Surprisingly, in criminal cases in which the liberty of the subject is usually at stake, this aspect of the adversary system has lingered on. While the prosecution bar has generally co-operated in making disclosure on a voluntary basis, there has been considerable resistance to the enactment of comprehensive rules which would make the practice mandatory. This may be attributed to the fact that proposals for reform in this regard do not provide for reciprocal disclosure by the defence. . . .

It is difficult to justify the position which clings to the notion that the Crown has no legal duty to disclose all relevant information. The arguments against the existence of such a duty are groundless while those in favour, are, in my view, overwhelming. The suggestion that the duty should be reciprocal may deserve consideration by this Court in the future but is not a valid reason for absolving the Crown of its duty. . . .

I would add that the fruits of the investigation which are in the possession of counsel for the Crown are not the property of the Crown for use in securing a conviction but the property of the public to be used to ensure that justice is done. In contrast, the defence has no obligation to assist the prosecution and is entitled to assume a purely adversarial role toward the prosecution. The absence of a duty to disclose can, therefore, be justified as being consistent with this role.[4]

In *R. v. Peruta*,[5] the Crown unsuccessfully maintained that he was entitled to discovery of prior statements of the defence witnesses just as he was obliged to provide prior statements of his witnesses. In denying the thought, Justice Proulx explained:

The discovery of evidence is a constitutional guarantee for the accused which tries fundamentally to balance the forces involved in the trial.[6] . . .

It would be presumptuous to assert that this balance has now been reached and that the two parties, as they do in a civil trial, can mutually claim the total disclosure of the evidence.[7]

Ought there to be reciprocity in disclosure in criminal cases?[8] As is clear from *Stinchcombe* and *Peruta*, procedural or constitutional rights and practices aimed at promoting justice or fairness may impede the search for the truth. In civil litigation, there are rights to full discovery and disclosure of the evidence relied on by your opponent. However, in criminal law the accused has a *Charter* right to disclosure of the Crown's case but the Crown cannot, generally

---

4 *Ibid.*, at pp. 332-33.

5 (1993), 78 C.C.C. (3d) 350 (Que. C.A.), leave to appeal refused, 81 C.C.C. (3d) vi (S.C.C.).

6 "For in criminal cases, the State has in the police, an agency for the discovery of evidence, superior to anything which even the wealthiest defendant could employ": "Devlin Report on Evidence of Identification" (1976), H.C. 338, para. 1.17. [Proulx J.A.'s footnote.]

7 *Supra*, note 5, at p. 370.

8 Compare Tanovich and Crocker, "Dancing with Stinchcombe's Ghost: A Modest Proposal for Reciprocal Defence Disclosure" (1994), 26 C.R. (4th) 333; and Davison, "Putting Ghosts to Rest: A Reply to the Modest Proposal for Defence Disclosure" (1995), 43 C.R. (4th) 105.

speaking, force the accused to reveal its exculpatory evidence or potential defences.

While justice is often referred to as a goal of evidence, the Supreme Court has also held that the search for truth is arguably the primary goal of the law of evidence.

Consider *R. v. Levogiannis*.[9] There an attack was made on the constitutional validity of a Criminal Code provision, section 486(2.1), which permits young complainants to testify behind a screen. The accused challenged the provision on the grounds that it violated his right to a fair trial guaranteed by sections 7 and 11(*d*) of the Canadian Charter of Rights and Freedoms. In deciding that the provision was constitutional Justice L'Heureux-Dubé wrote for the Court. In the course of her judgment she wrote:

> The examination of whether an accused's rights are infringed encompasses multifaceted considerations, such as the rights of witnesses, in this case children, the rights of accused and courts' duties to ascertain the truth. The goal of the court process is truth seeking and, to that end, the evidence of all those involved in judicial proceedings must be given in a way that is most favourable to eliciting the truth. . . . [O]ne cannot ignore the fact that, in many instances, the court process is failing children, especially those who have been victims of abuse, who are then subjected to further trauma as participants in the judicial process.[10]

In *R. v. Darrach*,[11] Gonthier J., for a unanimous court, dealt with rape shield legislation designed to protect the complainants in sexual assault cases. The accused complained that the legislation was unconstitutional as it deprived him of his fair trial rights. Justice Gonthier wrote:

> The current version of s. 276 is carefully crafted to comport with the principles of fundamental justice. It protects the integrity of the judicial process while at the same time respecting the rights of the people involved. The complainant's privacy and dignity are protected by a procedure that also vindicates the accused's right to make full answer and defence. The procedure does not violate the accused's s. 7 *Charter* right to a fair trial nor his s. 11(*c*) right not to testify against himself or his s. 11(*d*) right to a fair hearing.
>
> . . .
>
> while the right to make full answer and defence and the principle against self-incrimination are certainly core principles of fundamental justice, they can be respected without the accused being entitled to "the most favourable procedures that could possibly be imagined". Nor is the accused entitled to have procedures crafted that take only his interests into account. Still less is he entitled to procedures that would distort the truth-seeking function of a trial by permitting irrelevant and prejudicial material at trial. [Citations omitted.]

It is perhaps noteworthy that there are two bronzes in front of the Supreme Court of Canada building. One is entitled Truth and the other Justice. Throughout the materials in this book we will witness the ever present tension in the decision-making process as justice and truth vie for attention.

---

9 [1993] 4 S.C.R. 475.
10 *Ibid.*, at p. 483.
11 [2000] 2 S.C.R. 443, 450, para. 3, 461-462, para. 24

The adversary method has been justified over the years by many lawyers as capable of promoting the finest approximation to the truth. Jerome Frank noted:

> Many lawyers maintain that the best way for the court to discover the facts in a suit is to have each side strive as hard as it can, in a keenly partisan spirit, to bring to the court's attention the evidence favourable to that side. Macauley said that we obtain the fairest decision "when two men argue, as unfairly as possible, on opposite sides" for then "it is certain that no important consideration will altogether escape notice." [12]

Whether the adversary method will more closely approximate truth is certainly open to question. The lawyer is trained to seek success for her client, to win the game. Her goal is to present the best picture of her client's position and not the most complete picture at her disposal. Also, the adversary system presupposes for success some equality between the parties; when this is lacking, the "truth" becomes too often simply the view of the more powerful. Most judges will confess to the frequent temptation to reach out and "even the match" although the system cautions against such practice. Perhaps most importantly, while it is true that in deciding between the validity of two competing theories the decision-maker may be considerably aided by advocates on each side presenting their respective positions in the strongest arguments possible, it is certainly questionable whether such a technique is valuable in ensuring that all of the available evidence has been presented by the parties for examination. As Professor Peter Brett has noted:

> . . . observe the practice of scientists and historians in carrying out their investigations . . . a lengthy search will fail to reveal one competent practitioner in either discipline who will willingly and in advance confine himself, in deciding any question involving factual data, to a choice between two sets of existing data proffered to him by rival claimants. In short, the inquisitorial method is the one used by every genuine seeker of the truth in every walk of life (not merely scientific and historical investigations) with only one exception . . . the trial system in the common-law world. [13]

And Jerome Frank expressed his concern:

> But frequently the partisanship of the opposing lawyers blocks the uncovering of vital evidence or leads to a presentation of vital testimony in a way that distorts it. We have allowed the fighting spirit to become dangerously excessive. . . . In short, the lawyer aims at victory, at winning in the fight, not at aiding the court to discover the facts. He does not want the trial court to reach a sound educated guess, if it is likely to be contrary to his client's interests. Our present trial method is thus the equivalent of throwing pepper in the eyes of a surgeon when he is performing an operation. [14]

A major impediment to our search for truth is that the facts to be discovered by our courts are almost always past facts. Our method of discovering them is normally through the oral testimony of witnesses who have personal knowledge about what happened. This personal "knowledge" might perhaps better be described as personal beliefs about what they now remember of facts which they believe they observed. The trier of fact then has regard to what the witness says,

---

12 *Courts on Trial* (1949), at p. 80.
13 See Brett, "Legal Decision Making and Bias: A Critique of an 'Experiment' " (1973), 45 U. Col. L. Rev. 1 at 23.
14 *Courts on Trial*, (1949) at pp. 81 and 85.

and based on her observations of what the witness said and how he said it, she comes to her own belief as to whether that is an honest belief. She can do no more. She cannot, as the scientist might, duplicate in her laboratory the actual facts and test the hypothesis proposed. Facts as found by the court are really then only guesses about the actual facts. As an illustration:

> When Jack Spratt, as a witness, testifies to a fact, he is merely stating his belief or opinion about that past fact. When he says, "I saw McCarthy hit Schmidt," he means, "I believe that is what happened." When a trial judge or jury, after hearing that testimony, finds as a fact that McCarthy hit Schmidt, the finding means no more than the judge's or jury's belief that the belief of the witness Spratt is an honest belief, and that his belief accurately reflects what actually happened. A trial court's findings of fact is, then, at best, its belief or opinion about someone else's belief or opinion.[15]

Justice Haines in *R. v. Lalonde* described it this way:

> A trial is not a faithful reconstruction of the events as if recorded on some giant television screen. It is an historical recall of that part of the events to which witnesses may be found and presented in an intensely adversary system *where the object is quantum of proof*. Truth may be only incidental.[16]

Besides searching for a different truth than the scientist, our methods are also circumscribed by other considerations, which require our fact-finding to be done in a way which is acceptable to the parties and to society. Our courts provide a forum for the purpose of resolving disputes between parties which they themselves have been unable to resolve in any other way. Our modern form of trial began simply as a substitute for private duels and feuds which had later been dignified by the process of trial by battle. Resolution of conflict now must be done in a way which ensures social tranquility generally, and which is also acceptable to the individual parties. The parties should be able to leave the court feeling that they have had their say, that their case has been presented in the best possible light, and that they have been judged by an impartial trier.[17] In judging the efficacy of the legal system's method of fact-finding we must remember:

> A contested law suit is society's last line of defense in the indispensable effort to secure the peaceful settlement of social conflicts. . . . It is a last-ditch process in which something more is at stake than the truth only of the specific matter in contest. There is at stake also that confidence of the public generally in the impartiality and fairness of public settlement of disputes which is essential if the ditch is to be held and the settlements accepted peaceably.
>
> . . . While it is of course important that the court be right . . . a decision must be made now, one way or the other. . . . To require certainty . . . would be impracticable and undesirable. The law thus compromises.[18]

As we examine the material in the pages that follow, we should ask ourselves whether the compromises we have made are the best that we can do.

---

15 *Ibid.*, at p. 22.

16 (1971), 15 C.R.N.S. 1, 4 (Ont. H.C.) [emphasis added].

17 See authorities described by Brooks, *The Judge and The Adversary System, The Canadian Judiciary* (A. Linden, ed., 1976) at pp. 98 *et seq.*

18 Hart and McNaughton, *Evidence and Inference in the Law* (D. Lerner, ed.); "Evidence and Inference" (Hayden Colloquium, 1958), pp. 52-53.

When the law of evidence speaks of the search for truth, it is, in effect, speaking of legal rather than factual truth. A verdict is the product of what can be proved in the confines of the adjudicative forum applying rules of proof and admissibility. So, for example, in criminal cases there are only two verdicts reached by the trier of fact: not guilty and guilty. A not guilty or acquittal is an example of legal as opposed to factual truth. It is not a verdict of innocence but only that the Crown has not been able to prove its case beyond a reasonable doubt. **Should there be a third verdict of innocence in criminal case?** The Ontario Court of Appeal addressed this issue in the following case involving a wrongful conviction.

R. v. MULLINS-JOHNSON
(2007), 2007 CarswellOnt 6660, 50 C.R. (6th) 265, 228 C.C.C. (3d) 505 (C.A.)

BY THE COURT:

[1] The death of a child is always tragic. In this case, the tragedy of four-year-old Valin Johnson's death is compounded by the fact her uncle, William Mullins-Johnson, was wrongfully convicted of her murder and spent twelve years in prison. It is now clear that there is no evidence that Valin Johnson was assaulted or murdered, and no evidence that Mr. Mullins-Johnson was guilty of any crime in relation to her death.

. . . .

THE DECLARATION OF INNOCENCE

[22] The fresh evidence shows that the appellant's conviction was the result of a rush to judgment based on flawed scientific opinion. With the entering of an acquittal, the appellant's legal innocence has been re-established. The fresh evidence is compelling in demonstrating that no crime was committed against Valin Johnson and that the appellant did not commit any crime. For that reason an acquittal is the proper result.

[23] There are not in Canadian law two kinds of acquittals: those based on the Crown having failed to prove its case beyond a reasonable doubt and those where the accused has been shown to be factually innocent. We adopt the comments of the former Chief Justice of Canada in *The Lamer Commission of Inquiry Pertaining to the Cases of: Ronald Dalton, Gregory Parsons, Randy Druken*, Annex 3, pp. 342:

> [A] criminal trial does not address "factual innocence". The criminal trial is to determine whether the Crown has proven its case beyond a reasonable doubt. If so, the accused is guilty. If not, the accused is found not guilty. There is no finding of factual innocence since it would not fall within the ambit or purpose of criminal law.

[24] Just as the criminal trial is not a vehicle for declarations of factual innocence, so an appeal court, which obtains its jurisdiction from statute, has no jurisdiction to make a formal legal declaration of factual innocence. The fact that we are hearing this case as a Reference under s. 696.3(3)(a)(ii) of the *Criminal Code* does not expand that jurisdiction. The terms of the Reference to this court are

clear: we are hearing this case "as if it were an appeal". While we are entitled to express our reasons for the result in clear and strong terms, as we have done, we cannot make a formal legal declaration of the appellant's factual innocence.

[25] In addition to the jurisdictional issue, there are important policy reasons for not, in effect, recognizing a third verdict, other than "guilty" or "not guilty", of "factually innocent". The most compelling, and, in our view, conclusive reason is the impact it would have on other persons found not guilty by criminal courts. As Professor Kent Roach observed in a report he prepared for the *Commission of Inquiry into Certain Aspects of the Trial and Conviction of James Driskell*, "there is a genuine concern that determinations and declarations of wrongful convictions could degrade the meaning of the not guilty verdict" (p. 39). To recognize a third verdict in the criminal trial process would, in effect, create two classes of people: those found to be factually innocent and those who benefited from the presumption of innocence and the high standard of proof beyond a reasonable doubt.

[26] Nothing we have said in these reasons should be taken as somehow qualifying the impact of the fresh evidence. That evidence, together with the other evidence, shows beyond question that the appellant's conviction was wrong and that he was the subject of a terrible miscarriage of justice. We conclude these reasons by paraphrasing what the president of the panel said to Mr. Mullins-Johnson at the conclusion of the oral argument after entering the verdict of acquittal: it is profoundly regrettable that as a result of what has been shown to be flawed pathological evidence Mr. Mullins-Johnson was wrongly convicted and has spent such a very long time in jail.

[27] We can only hope that these words, these reasons for judgment and the deep apology expressed by Ms. Fairburn on behalf of the Ministry of the Attorney General will provide solace to Mr. Mullins-Johnson, to his mother and to everyone who has been so terribly injured by these events.

DISPOSITION

[28] Accordingly, in accordance with the terms of the Reference and s. 696.3(3)(a)(ii) of the *Criminal Code,* we admit the fresh expert evidence, allow the appeal, quash the conviction for first degree murder and enter an acquittal.

. . . .

Do you agree with the decision?[19]

In her article "Evidence Law and the Jury: A Reassessment"[20] Professor Lisa Dufraimont searches for the purpose of the laws of evidence. She identifies three rationales: fear that jurors may misconstrue evidence (although she finds that empirical evidence for this proposition is weak), to restrain excessive adversarial

---

19 See the discussion by Kent Roach in Beare (ed.) "Do We Need Innocence Hearings" in *Honouring Social Justice: Honouring Dianne Martin* (Toronto: University of Toronto Press, 2008).

20 (2008) 53 *McGill L.J.* 199.

behaviour by lawyers, and to exclude perjured evidence. She concludes that the picture is complex and that none of these rationales can alone explain all the laws of evidence. She concludes that most lawyers, judges and scholars of the laws of evidence identify the jury system as the paradigmatic form of adjudication even though the jury system is in decline. Most trials, civil and criminal, are before judge alone:

> If asked to envision an ideal method for ferreting out the truth about past events, few would imagine a process encumbered by technicalities that conceal relevant information from fact-finders and seek to control their evaluation of the evidence they are allowed to see. But the law of evidence constitutes just such a set of encumbrances. And while some pursue other policies, frequently the rules are directed at serving the search for truth itself. Thus, evidence rules appear apt to impede the very fact- finding they are designed to promote.
>
> Why, then, does our law use evidence rules to advance the search for truth? The classic explanation points to the common law jury, which, it is argued, lacks competence to evaluate certain forms of proof. Unconstrained by evidentiary regulation, it is feared that lay juries would produce an unacceptably high level of error in adjudication. The extent to which the jury in fact accounts for evidence law, either historically or analytically, is a matter of ongoing debate. Other explanations have been offered, the most promising of which focus on two other elements of a common law trial: the adversary nature of the proceedings, and the ever-present risk of witness dishonesty. Like the jury, these trial features are said to explain how the search for historical truth can be facilitated rather than defeated by regulating evidence.

. . . .

C. The Complex Picture

The debate over the explanatory principles of evidence law is largely a debate about whom to mistrust. Is our fear that juries may misconstrue the evidence, that adversaries may obscure the truth, or that witnesses may perjure themselves? Of whom are we afraid, and whom are we trying to control? It seems doubtful that these questions can ever be answered in any decisive way.

Certainly some authors identify one explanatory principle as the primary, underlying principle of evidence law. Thayer, among others, focused on the jury, while recently evidence scholars have suggested that the central rationale for evidence law lies elsewhere. Nance argues that the best evidence principle, which is concerned with advocate control, constitutes a superior explanatory principle to the traditional jury-centred rationale for evidence law. According to Imwinkelried, both of those explanatory principles are inferior to the dishonesty-control rationale, which he claims constitutes "the best explanatory hypothesis for the logical structure of Evidence law. The modem theorists admit forthrightly that no one principle explains the totality of evidence law, an admission that militates in favour of interpreting their claims modestly. But beyond arguing the explanatory power of the various rationales for evidence law, these scholars purport to choose the best, unifying theories, or even to explain the law's "logical structure". Such ambitious claims are difficult to defend.

The search for an "organizing principle" of evidence law is vain because evidence law is not organized around a principle. Given the ad hoc nature of evidentiary regulation, there is no reason to believe that the various possible rationales for evidence rules are mutually exclusive. A more tenable position is to recognize that various factors, including the trial features under consideration, play a role in explaining evidence law. The origins and justifications of evidentiary rules are best uncovered in specific doctrinal contexts. And one could easily add yet more layers of complexity to the picture. Issues that cannot entirely be disentangled from the explanatory principles include extrinsic policy considerations like fairness and due process, as well as concerns about the efficient conduct of the trial process, such as affordability, speed, and finality. [footnotes omitted]

(c) The Role of the Trial Judge

The diligence of the parties in searching out evidence favourable to their side and the vigour with which they attack their opponents' case are seen by many as finer guarantees of approximating the historical truth than giving the problem for resolution to some government official whose motivation can rarely be of the magnitude of the parties.[21] Also, it is believed that the bias of the decision-maker can be minimized if they play a much less active role than is demanded in the inquisitorial method.[22] The judge who conducts the examination of witnesses "descends into the arena and is liable to have his vision clouded by the dust of the conflict. Unconsciously he deprives himself of the advantage of calm and dispassionate observation."[23]

The Supreme Court of Canada ordered a new trial when the trial judge's interruptions were so frequent and of such a nature that justice was not seen to be done. Speaking for the court, Lamer J., in *Brouillard v. R.*,[24] said:

> The role of a trial judge is sometimes very demanding, owing to the nature of the case and the conduct of the litigants (parties). Like anyone, a judge may occasionally lose patience. He may then step down from his judge's bench and assume the role of counsel. When this happens, and, *a fortiori*, when this happens to the detriment of an accused, it is important that a new trial be ordered, even when the verdict of guilty is not unreasonable having regard to the evidence, and the judge has not erred with respect to the law applicable to the case and has not incorrectly assessed the facts.

> The reason for this is well known. It is one of the most fundamental principles of our case-law, the best-known formulation of which is to be found in Lord Hewart C.J.'s judgment in *R. v. Sussex Justices, Ex p. McCarthy*, [1924] 1 K.B. 256 at p. 259: "[it] is of fundamental importance that justice should not only be done, but should manifestly and undoubtedly be seen to be done". . . .

> . . . it is clear that judges are no longer required to be as passive as they once were; to be what I call sphinx judges. We now not only accept that a judge may intervene in the adversarial debate, but also believe that it is sometimes essential for him to do so for justice in fact to be done. Thus a judge may and sometimes must ask witnesses questions, interrupt them in their testimony and if necessary call them to order. . . .

> Finally, prudence and the resulting judicial restraint must be all the greater where the accused is a witness. He must be allowed to proceed, within limits, of course, but always bearing in mind that at the end of the day he is the only one who may be leaving the court in handcuffs.

---

21 See Brooks, *supra*, note 17.

22 See Lind, Thibault and Walker, "Cross-Cultural Comparison of the Effect of Adversary and Inquisitorial Processes on Bias in Legal Decision-Making" (1976), 62 Va. L. Rev. 271.

23 Lord Greene, M.R. in *Yuill v. Yuill*, [1945] 1 All E.R. 183, 189 (C.A.). See also *McFarlane v. Safadi* (2004), 70 O.R. (3d) 599 (C.A.) and *R. v. D'Souza* (2004), 188 C.C.C. (3d) 386 (Ont. C.A.).

24 (1985), 16 D.L.R. (4th) 447, 450, 451, 453 (S.C.C.); the court reproduces instances from the transcript illustrating the nature of the remarks addressed to the accused and to his witness.

In conclusion, although the judge may and must intervene for justice to be done, he must none the less do so in such way that justice *is seen to be done*. It is all a question of manner.

Compare Justice L'Heureux-Dubé in *R. v. L. (D.O.)*,[25] dealing with the accused's complaint that the trial judge had exhibited bias:

The final issue raised by the respondent is whether the trial judge may have acted in such a manner as to raise a reasonable apprehension of bias, as per *R. v. Brouillard*, [1985] 1 S.C.R. 39. In *Brouillard, supra*, Lamer J., for the court held that the judiciary should not be seen as "entering the ring" or acting on behalf of one of the parties. . . .

It is my view that, in the case at hand as well as in other cases involving fragile witnesses such as children, the trial judge has a responsibility to ensure that the child understands the questions being asked and that the evidence given by the child is clear and unambiguous. To accomplish this end, the trial judge may be required to clarify and rephrase questions asked by counsel and to ask subsequent questions to the child to clarify the child's responses. In order to ensure the appropriate conduct of the trial, the judge should provide a suitable atmosphere to ease the tension so that the child is relaxed and calm. The trial judge, in this case, did not prevent the mounting of a proper defence, nor did he demonstrate favouritism toward the witness in such a way as to preclude a fair trial. I find that the trial judge in this instance did nothing more than "intervene for justice to be done".[26]

Should the trial judge be able to comment on the evidence presented by the parties?

R. v. LAWES
(2006), 206 C.C.C. (3d) 15,
37 C.R. (6th) 301, 2006 CarswellOnt 1072 (Ont. C.A.), leave to appeal refused
(2006), 2006 CarswellOnt 8213, 2006 CarswellOnt 8214 (S.C.C.)

The accused was convicted of second degree murder arising out of a bank robbery in Brampton, Ontario. On appeal he argued that the trial judge's comments on the evidence violated his section 11(f) right to be tried by a jury. His appeal was dismissed.

ROULEAU J.A. (MOLDAVER and FELDMAN JJ.A. concurring): —

(a) The common law rule

Courts have long recognized that a trial judge is entitled to comment on the evidence while instructing the jury. The discretion to comment, however, is limited.

The Supreme Court of Canada has recently confirmed the principle that a trial judge is "entitled to give an opinion on a question of fact and express it as strongly as the circumstances permit, so long as it is made clear to the jury that the opinion is given as advice and not direction." [Footnote omitted]

---

25 (1994), 25 C.R. (4th) 285 (S.C.C.).
26 *Ibid.*, at pp. 322-23. See also *R. v. Watson* (2004), 191 C.C.C. (3d) 144 (Ont. C.A.) and *R. v. Palosaari* (2004), 191 C.C.C. (3d) 228 (B.C. C.A.).

There have been various formulations of guidelines to be used by appellate courts in deciding whether a trial judge has gone too far in expressing an opinion. In *R. v. Garofoli*, this court stated that an appellate court may find that the trial judge has crossed the boundary even though the jury was told that they were not bound by his views on the evidence if:

1) the opinion expressed is far stronger than that facts warrant; or

2) the opinion is expressed so strongly that there is a likelihood that the jury would be overawed by it. [Footnote omitted]

Somewhat different formulations of these guidelines appear in other decisions such as *R. v. Muckikekwanate* [Footnote omitted] and *R. v. Valentini*. What can be drawn from all of these cases is that, in this area, everything is a question of degree. The overarching principle is fairness. Within this principle of fairness is the recognition that the jury must remain the arbiter of the facts and that any comments made by the trial judge cannot amount to a rebuttal of the defence address to the jury or unfairly denigrate or undermine the position of the defence.

. . .

ii) Does the common law rule contravene s. 11(f) of the Charter?

The appellant submits that considering the common law's limited "tolerance" of judicial comment in the context of the *Charter* guarantee leads to the conclusion that all judicial comment should be prohibited and, most certainly, that any comment that could influence the jury on a substantial contested factual issue would constitute a breach of the accused's right to a trial by jury.

The right to a trial by jury enshrined in s. 11(f) of the *Charter* was described by this court in *R. v. Finta* as follows:

> It is a basic tenet of our criminal law that in cases tried by a jury, it is the jury which must decide the guilt or innocence of the accused. Findings of facts which are germane to that task must be left to the jury . . . .. Any statutory or judge-made rule which transfers the fact-finding function as it relates to issues going to the culpability of the accused, from the jury to a judge is, at the very least, constitutionally suspect. [Footnote omitted]

The appellant submits that the proposed prohibition on the expression of opinion by trial judges is necessary because trial judges carry such authority and respect with the jury that juries will likely be swayed if a judge expresses any opinion on the facts. This would result in the trial judge usurping the fact finding role of the jury, thereby depriving the accused of the right to the "benefit of trial by jury".

Although I agree that a trial judge cannot usurp the function of the jury, I do not accept the proposition that every expression of opinion on factual issues by a trial judge, even on substantial, contested issues, will invariably lead to this result.

In view of their role, trial judges cannot avoid commenting on the evidence. These comments can be direct and either required or desirable at common law, such as *Vetrovec* warnings, advising a jury that certain previous convictions such as those involving dishonesty may be more important than others in deciding on credibility, or advising the jury of the risks of relying on eyewitness identification evidence. Comments can also be indirect in the sense that, in the charge, when trial judges deal with each element of the offence, they often select and summarize portions of the evidence that they consider relevant and of some significance. Trial judges will, however, take care to tell the jury that, despite any views or opinions on the evidence they may have expressed directly or indirectly and regardless of the cautions given, they, the jury, are the sole arbiters of the facts.

Beyond comments that are required or desirable, it is well recognized that a trial judge has a discretion to comment on evidence during the charge to help the jury focus on the critical issues. The exercise of this discretion is often uncontroversial, for example when, in the present case, the judge told the jury that there was little doubt that Lawes and Rowe formed an intention in common to carry out the unlawful purpose namely, armed robbery. What trial judges cannot do is: assess the evidence and make a determination that the Crown has proven one or more of the essential elements of the offence and to direct the jury accordingly. It does not matter how obvious the judge may believe the answer to be. Nor does it matter that the judge may be of the view that any other conclusion would be perverse. The trial judge may give an opinion on the matter when it is warranted, but never a direction. (*R. v. Gunning*, *supra*, at para. 31).

In my view, a prohibition on the expression of opinion by a trial judge is neither practical nor desirable and such a prohibition is neither explicitly nor implicitly provided for in the words of s. 11(f) of the *Charter*. To seek to limit the prohibition to substantial, contested factual issues is of little assistance. The concern at common law and as expressed in s. 11(f) of the *Charter* is that the trial judge not usurp the function of the jury. By allowing the trial judge to express views and opinions on the evidence "as strongly as the circumstances permit" provided that they do not have the effect of usurping the role of the jury by taking a contested issue away from them or by subverting their independence, the common law recognizes that comments are both a necessary and desirable part of the trial judge's role. The limit is set at the point where the comments interfere with the exercise of the jury's role. Although I firmly believe that judges should avoid unnecessary comments or opinions, the focus of the analysis on appeal is not whether an appellate court views the opinion given by the trial judge as having been necessary or even desirable, but rather whether it interfered with the jury's function or so undermined the defence position that it deprived the accused of a fair trial.

When considering whether a trial judge has gone beyond the limits, the basic assumption is that jurors will abide by their oaths and will accept and follow the judicial instructions they are given. It is assumed, therefore, that when so instructed, jurors will disregard any opinion or statement of the evidence made by the trial judge where it does not accord with their own assessment. This same presumption of juror competence is at the root of the constitutionally protected right to a trial by jury in s. 11(f).

In summary, therefore, the common law rule allows the trial judge to comment on the evidence provided it is made clear to the jury that they are not bound by the judge's views, that the judge's opinions are not stronger than the facts warrant and that the opinions are not overstated to the point where it is likely that the jury will be overawed by them. By setting the limit on judicial comment at the point where the comments might impermissibly erode or threaten the fact finding and ultimate arbiter role of the jury, the common law rule fosters rather than impedes the values underlying s. 11(f) of the *Charter*.

Do you agree with the decision?

2. LEGAL ETHICS

Legal ethics or the norms and values that guide a lawyer's professional judgment and conduct can impact on the law of evidence.[27] In looking for the source of these norms, some find it helpful to distinguish between rules of professional conduct that must be followed to avoid professional discipline and personal ethics which concern the moral code of the individual.[28] A third approach looks to role morality or the profession's conscience to guide ethical reflection. The content of role morality can be found in codes of conduct, legal norms and in the expectations of the profession (i.e., what is the role of lawyers in society).[29]

Some ethical rules, particularly those that are viewed as necessary for the proper functioning of our adversarial process, will often require counsel to act as an investigator or prohibit counsel from disclosing highly relevant evidence that would damage the client's case.[30] **Can you identify what some of these ethical principles might be?**

Notwithstanding the adversarial process and its emphasis on partisanship, zero sum gain and a "sporting theory of justice", we expect that counsel, as officers of the court, will be ethical in the preparation and presentation of their case.

R. v. FELDERHOF
(2003), 180 C.C.C. (3d) 498, 17 C.R. (6th) 20, 2003 CarswellOnt 4943 (C.A.)

ROSENBERG, J.A.:— The respondent to this appeal is facing eight counts of violating the Securities Act, R.S.O. 1990 c. S. 5 arising out of the affairs of Bre-

---

27 See the discussion of using evidence to teach ethics in Joy and McMunigal, "Teaching Ethics in Evidence" (2003), 21 Q.L.R. 961.

28 For a discussion of the relationship between personal morality and legal ethics, see Luban, *Lawyers and Justice: An Ethical Study* (Princeton, N.J.: Princeton University Press, 1998). A variation of Luban's argument which focuses on taking personal responsibility can be found in Hutchinson, *Legal Ethics and Professional Responsibility* (2nd ed.) (Toronto: Irwin Law, 2006).

29 See Tanovich, "Law's Ambition and the Reconstruction of Role Morality in Canada" (2005), 28 Dal. L.J. 267. See also Simon, *The Practice of Justice* (Cambridge, Mass.: Harvard University Press, 1998).

30 The relationship between the adversarial system and legal ethics is discussed in G. MacKenzie, "Breaking The Dichotomy Habit: The Adversarial System and the Ethics of Professionalism" (1996), 9 Can. J. Law and Jurisprudence 33.

X Minerals Ltd. The Ontario Securities Commission charged the respondent, a senior officer in Bre-X, with insider trading and authorizing or acquiescing in misleading press statements. After 70 days of trial, counsel for the prosecution took the unusual step of applying for prohibition and certiorari to halt the prosecution. Counsel for the Ontario Securities Commission, who are conducting the prosecution, seek to prohibit the continuation of the proceedings before Hryn J., to quash rulings he made and ask for an order that the trial begin anew before another judge of the Ontario Court of Justice. The prosecution alleges that the trial judge made a number of serious errors that have deprived him of jurisdiction to proceed and undermined the appellant's right to a fair trial. Fundamental to its position is the allegation that the trial judge has failed in his duty to curb the uncivil conduct of the respondent's counsel. The prosecution also alleges that the trial judge has not made evidentiary rulings when he should have and which were necessary to the presentation of the prosecution case and has improperly interfered in the conduct of the prosecution case. Campbell J. heard the application and in extensive and careful reasons he dismissed the application. He found no jurisdictional error. I agree with that conclusion. The respondent sought costs of the motion. Campbell J. dismissed that application and the respondent appeals from that order. I would dismiss that appeal.

. . . .

It is important that everyone, including the courts, encourage civility both inside and outside the courtroom. Professionalism is not inconsistent with vigorous and forceful advocacy on behalf of a client and is as important in the criminal and quasi-criminal context as in the civil context. Morden J.A. of this court expressed the matter this way in a 2001 address to the Call to the Bar: "Civility is not just a nice, desirable adornment to accompany the way lawyers conduct themselves, but, is a duty which is integral to the way lawyers do their work." Counsel are required to conduct themselves professionally as part of their duty to the court, to the administration of justice generally and to their clients. As Kara Anne Nagorney said in her article, "A Noble Profession? A Discussion of Civility Among Lawyers" (1999), 12 Georgetown Journal of Legal Ethics 815, at 816-17, "Civility within the legal system not only holds the profession together, but also contributes to the continuation of a just society. ... Conduct that may be characterized as uncivil, abrasive, hostile, or obstructive necessarily impedes the goal of resolving conflicts rationally, peacefully, and efficiently, in turn delaying or even denying justice." Unfair and demeaning comments by counsel in the course of submissions to a court do not simply impact on the other counsel. Such conduct diminishes the public's respect for the court and for the administration of criminal justice and thereby undermines the legitimacy of the results of the adjudication. Nothing said here is inconsistent with or would in any way impede counsel from the fierce and fearless pursuit of a client's interests in a criminal or quasi-criminal case. Zealous advocacy on behalf of a client, to advance the client's case and protect that client's rights, is a cornerstone of our adversary system. It is "a mark of professionalism for a lawyer to firmly protect and pursue the legitimate interests of his or her client". As G. Arthur Martin said, "The existence of a strong, vigorous and responsible Defence Bar is essential in a free Society". Counsel have a responsibility to the administration of justice, and as officers of the court, they have a duty to act with integrity, a duty that requires civil conduct. . This was a complex case involving experienced counsel who took very different views about the role of the prosecutor and the rules of evidence. There is nothing in this record that shows that the trial judge was biased against the prosecution. The application judge has catalogued the attempts that the trial judge did make to keep the trial and defence counsel on track. The prosecution says he did not do enough but I think it difficult at this stage to second-guess a trial judge who was faced with what would be a very long and difficult case.

. . . .

In *Marchand*, this court has commented upon the problems caused by incivility in the courtroom. In that case, the court noted that civility in the courtroom is not only the responsibility of counsel but also "very much the responsibility of the trial judge." The failure of counsel and the trial judge in that case to discharge their responsibilities "tarnished the reputation of the administration of justice". Crown counsel have special responsibilities as "ministers of justice". But, as officers of the court and as barristers and solicitors, defence counsel also have responsibilities to the court and to other counsel and they have a duty to uphold the standards of the profession. As I have said, defence counsel's obligation to his or her client to fearlessly raise every legitimate issue is not incompatible with these duties to the court, to fellow counsel and to the profession. See Arthur Maloney, Q.C., "The Role of the Independent Bar", 1979 Law Society of Upper Canada Special Lectures 49 at 63, and G. Arthur Martin, Q.C., "The Role and Responsibility of the Defence Advocate" (1970), 12 C.L.Q. 376 at 385.

Mr. Maloney and Mr. Martin both referred to the well-known passage from *Rondel v. Worsley*, [1969] 1 A.C. 191 at 227-8 where Lord Reid said, in part that, "[c]ounsel must not mislead the court, [and] he must not lend himself to casting aspersions on the other party or witnesses for which there is no sufficient basis in the information in his possession". As the application judge noted, in this case the core problem was that Mr. Groia did not seem to understand the role of the prosecutor. This led him to make his improper allegations against the prosecutor when the prosecutor simply objected to a question or an attempt to introduce a document. I assume Mr. Groia believed in the merit of these submissions and was not deliberately misleading the court and casting aspersions on counsel and the "government" for which there was no foundation; nevertheless, he was bound by the standards of the profession to keep his rhetoric within reasonable bounds. If he was unable to do so, the trial judge had the responsibility referred to in Marchand.

This has nothing to do with trials not being "tea parties". Every counsel and litigant has the right to expect that counsel will conduct themselves in accordance with The Law Society of Upper Canada, Rules of Professional Conduct. Those rules are crystal clear. Counsel are to treat witnesses, counsel and the court with fairness, courtesy and respect. See Rules 4 and 6 and Commentaries. I have set out what seems to have been the genesis for the acrimony between counsel in this case. Even if Mr. Groia honestly believed that the prosecution tactics were excessive and could amount to an abuse of process, this did not give him licence for the kind of submissions he made in this case. As the application judge said, "[a]buse of process and prosecutorial misconduct . . form part of the arsenal of defence tactics". But, motions based on abuse of process and prosecutorial misconduct can and should be conducted without the kind of rhetoric engaged in by defence counsel in this case.[31]

———————

In its 2006 *Code of Professional Conduct*, the Canadian Bar Association included an Appendix entitled "Principles of Civility for Advocates." Part III addresses the conduct of lawyers at trial and offers advice on how to make an objection:

47. During trial, Counsel should not allude to any fact or matter which is not relevant or with respect to which no admissible evidence will be advanced.

48. Counsel should not engage in acrimonious exchanges with opposing Counsel or otherwise engage in undignified or discourteous conduct that is degrading to their profession and to the Court.

49. During trial, Counsel should not make any accusation of impropriety against opposing Counsel unless such accusation is well-founded and without first giving reasonable notice so that opposing Counsel has an adequate opportunity to respond.

50. Objections, requests and observations during trial should always be addressed to the Court, not to other Counsel.

51. Objections during trial are properly made as follows:

(1) Counsel rises and calmly states "Your Honour, I have an objection";
(2) When Counsel rises to make an objection or to address the Judge, other Counsel should be seated until the Judge asks for a response. Under no circumstances should two or more Counsel be addressing the Court at the same time;
(3) The basis for the objection should be briefly and clearly stated. Following a clear statement of the objection, Counsel should present argument in support of it and then sit down;
(4) Counsel opposing the objection shall in turn, or as directed by the Judge, rise and clearly state their position. They will then make their argument, if any, in support and sit down; and

———————

31 The issue of civility was addressed in *Marchand (Litigation Guardian of) v. Public General Hospital Society of Chatham* (2000), 51 O.R. (3d) 97 (C.A.) and *Walsh v. 1124660 Ontario Ltd.* (2002), [2002] O.J. No. 4069, 2002 CarswellOnt 3026 (S.C.J.). See also, S.N. Turner, "Raising The Bar: Maximizing Civility In Alberta Courtrooms" (2003), 41 Alta. L. Rev. 547; The Advocates' Society, *Principles of Civility*, online at www.advocates.ca/civility/principles_tex.htm; and Working Group on the Definition of Professionalism, *Defining Professionalism* (Ontario: Chief Justice of Ontario Advisory Committee on Professionalism (December 2001) online at www.lsuc.on.ca/news/pdf/definingprofessoct2001revdec.pdf.

(5) Usually, Counsel who made the objection will then be given an opportunity to reply. The reply should address only those points raised by opposing Counsel and avoid repetitious re-argument of the issues.

52. When the Court has made a ruling on a matter, Counsel should in no way attempt to re-argue the point or attempt to circumvent the effect of the ruling by other means.

53. In the absence of a jury, a question to a witness by Counsel should not be interrupted before the question is completed for the purposes of objection or otherwise, unless the question is patently inappropriate.

54. Counsel should never attempt to get before the Court evidence which is improper. If Counsel intends to lead evidence about which there may be some question of admissibility, then Counsel should alert opposing Counsel and the Court of that intention.

55. When addressed by the Judge in the courtroom, Counsel should rise. When one Counsel is speaking the other(s) should sit down until called upon. Counsel should never remain with his or her back turned when the Judge is speaking.

56. Counsel cannot condone the use of perjured evidence and, if Counsel becomes aware of perjury at any time, they must immediately seek the client's consent to bring it to the attention of the Court. Failing that, the Counsel must withdraw. Nothing is more antithetical to the role of Counsel than to advance the client's case before the Court, directly or indirectly, on the basis of perjured evidence.

57. Counsel, or any member of their firm, should not give evidence relating to any contentious issue in a trial.

58. In trials where they are acting as Counsel, Counsel should not take part in any demonstrations or experiments in which their own person is involved except to illustrate what has already been admitted in evidence.

_____

In *R. v. Lyttle*,[32] the Supreme Court of Canada observed, in the context of developing a rule of cross-examination (discussed later in Chapter 5, under C. Witnesses), that:

> . . . Counsel . . . bear important professional duties and ethical responsibilities, not just at trial, but on appeal as well. This point was emphasized by Lord Reid in *Rondel v. Worsley*, [1969] 1 A.C. 191 at 227-28, when he said:
>
>> Every counsel has a duty to his client fearlessly to raise every issue, advance every argument, and ask every question, however distasteful, which he thinks will help his client's case. But, as an officer of the court concerned in the administration of justice, he has an overriding duty to the court, to the

_____

32 (2004), 17 C.R. (6th) 1 (S.C.C.) at para. 66. See D. Stuart, "Annotation" (2003), 17 C.R. (6th) 1.

standards of the profession, and to the public, which may and often does lead to a conflict with his client's wishes or with what the client thinks are his personal interests. *Counsel must not mislead the court, he must not lend himself to casting aspersions on the other party or witnesses for which there is no sufficient basis in the information in his possession*, he must not withhold authorities or documents which may tell against his clients but which the law or the standards of the profession require him to produce . . . [Emphasis added].[33]

Consequently, legal ethics can sometimes serve as a shield against the admission of innuendo, prejudicial or otherwise false evidence. On other occasions, it may compel counsel to disclose incriminating evidence. Consider, for example, the classic criminal law dilemma of counsel who knowingly or unwittingly comes into possession of incriminating physical evidence.

R. v. MURRAY
(2000), 144 C.C.C. (3d) 289, 2000 CarswellOnt 1953,
34 C.R. (5th) 290 (S.C.J.)

The accused was charged with attempting to obstruct justice by concealing videotapes which he removed from his client's home on the client's instructions. Shortly after the accused removed the videotapes, his client, Bernardo, was charged with first degree murder and related offences in the deaths of two teenaged girls. The accused retained the tapes for 17 months without disclosing the existence of the tapes to the Crown. The tapes were eventually turned over to the police by counsel who took over the case from the accused. The tapes were used by the Crown at the murder trial. Murray testified he had to retain the critical tapes for Bernardo's defence. Bernardo admitted the crimes shown on the tapes but denied killing Leslie Mahaffy and Kristen French. He blamed his partner Homolka. The tapes, Murray said, supported this position. The Crown was going to portray Homolka as an abused, manipulated victim, while the tapes showed the reverse, that she was not afraid and was an enthusiastic participant in the sexual crimes. He was obliged to keep the existence of the tapes secret so that the Crown could not prepare Homolka for Murray's cross-examination. The accused's explanation as to his use of the two critical tapes in the defence of his client was seen by the Court to be one that might reasonably be true, and he may well have believed under the circumstances that he had no legal duty to disclose the tapes until resolution discussions or trial. The trial judge determined that there was a reasonable doubt as to the accused's intention to obstruct justice. The accused was acquitted.

---

33 *Lyttle* is significant because it represents one of the first cases where the Supreme Court has used ethical principles to develop a common law rule of evidence. For an argument that judges should recognize a right of audience before courts and tribunals and be prepared to exclude counsel who are incompetent or unethical, see Paul Calarco, "Not in My Court You Don't! The Right of Audience and the Enforcement of Unethical Conduct" (2008), 54 *Crim. L.Q.* 130. He argues that leaving these issues to professional discipline by Law Societies is not enough.

PER GRAVELY J.: —

. . . .

Counsel did not suggest that confidentiality of the tapes is protected under the umbrella of solicitor-client privilege and no privilege, in my opinion, attaches to this evidence. Solicitor-client privilege protects communications between solicitor and client: see *R. v. Solosky*, [1980] 1 S.C.R. 821 at p. 829, 50 C.C.C. (2d) 495 at p. 502, 16 C.R. (3d) 294, 105 D.L.R. (3d) 745. These videotapes are not communications. They are, rather, dramatic evidence of crime and pre-existed the solicitor-client relationship. They are not similar, for example, to a sketch, which might be prepared by a client to help explain a point to his counsel, or even a videotape prepared for that purpose. Murray's discussions with his client about the tapes are covered by the privilege; the physical objects, the tapes, are not. Hiding them from the police on behalf of the client cannot be said to be an aspect of solicitor-client communication. The point is expressed well in the "bloody shirt" case. There, a lawyer was confronted with a client, wanted for murder, whose shirt was soaked in blood. Before surrendering the client to the police, the lawyer took possession of the shirt. Having some misgivings about his conduct, he retained counsel who approached the Professional Conduct Committee of the Law Society of Upper Canada for advice. He was told:

> You should not have taken the shirt. It is a piece of physical evidence. Not only that, what you saw with your eyes as opposed to what you heard with your ears, is not privileged so that you may be a witness now in this case. Our advice to you is that you must withdraw from the case and you must turn the shirt over forthwith to the Crown Attorney.

Although Murray had a duty of confidentiality to Bernardo, absent solicitor-client privilege there was no legal basis permitting concealment of the tapes. In this sense Murray had no higher right than any other citizen. Nor, in my opinion, can it be said that concealing the critical tapes was permissible because they may have had some exculpatory value. They were overwhelmingly inculpatory. Some of the United States authorities, including The American Bar Association; Standards for Criminal Justice, Prosecution Function and Defence Function, Third Edition, suggest counsel may retain incriminating physical evidence for a reasonable time for examination and testing. There was no testing contemplated here and, by some time in June 1993, Murray had examined the tapes and knew their contents. He chose to continue to conceal them.

In a line of United States cases beginning with State ex rel. *Sowers v. Olwell*, 64 Wash. (2d) 828 (1964), not only is there recognition that solicitor-client privilege does not protect physical evidence, but there is a suggested obligation on counsel to turn over incriminating physical evidence to a prosecutor. That position appears to have been supported by Canadian commentators, at least with reference to instrumentalities of crime. . . . I am not entirely clear why there exists this almost universal view that incriminating physical evidence must go to the prosecution. In my opinion it does not follow that because concealment of incriminating physical evidence is forbidden there is always a corresponding positive obligation to disclose. In *R. v. P. (M.B.)* (1994), 89 C.C.C. (3d) 289, 113 D.L.R. (4th) 461 (S.C.C.), Lamer C.J.C., said at page 304:

> With respect to disclosure, the defence in Canada is under no legal obligation to co-operate with or assist the Crown by announcing any special defence, such as an alibi, or by producing documentary or physical evidence.

Perhaps the general view that there is a turn-over obligation to the prosecution arises from the dilemma counsel faces once improperly in possession of incriminating physical evidence. At that point, almost any step involves potential risk of criminal liability. For example, in Mr. Martin's address he recounts the difficulty created when the murder weapon is dropped on the lawyer's desk.

What should the lawyer do?

If he says, "Take the gun and come back after you have disposed of it", he has committed a criminal offence unless, of course, he can persuade a jury at his own trial that his intention was merely to instruct the client that he should leave the pistol at his residence so that it would be available to the police under a search warrant. If he takes possession of the pistol and puts it in his desk or vault a serious problem is created. Obviously, if he buried the pistol in his backyard he would be an accessory after the fact. If he puts it in his desk or vault, may it not be argued that he has just as effectively concealed it?

While he had no obligation to assist the police in their investigation or the Crown in its prosecution, Murray could not be a party to concealing this evidence. Having removed the tapes from their hiding place, he could not hide them again. Nor could he implement any instructions from Bernardo that would result in their continued concealment.

Once he had discovered the overwhelming significance of the critical tapes, Murray, in my opinion, was left with but three legally justifiable options:

> (a) Immediately turn over the tapes to the prosecution, either directly or anonymously;
>
> (b) Deposit them with the trial judge; or,
>
> (c) Disclose their existence to the prosecution and prepare to do battle to retain them.
>
> I am satisfied that Murray's concealment of the critical tapes was an act that had a tendency to pervert or obstruct the course of justice.

[The Court then found an absence of the requisite mens rea.[34]]

Had you been the defence counsel, would you have retrieved the tapes? At what point would you have disclosed their existence? In 2002, the Law

---

34 The *Murray* decision is discussed in "Special Issues on Ethics and Criminal Justice"(2003), 47 C.L.Q. 141-223. See also R. Fogl, "Sex, Laws and Videotape: The Ambit of Solicitor-Client Privilege in Canadian Criminal Law as Illuminated in *R. v. Murray*" (2001), 50 U.N.B.L.J. 187.

Society of Upper Canada attempted to reach a consensus for the adoption of the following rule to address the *Murray* issue:

Rule 4 - Relationship to the Administration of Justice

4.01 THE LAWYER AS ADVOCATE

Property Relevant to a Crime or Offence

4.01 (10) A lawyer shall not take or keep possession of **property relevant to a crime or offence**, except in accordance with this rule.

(11) A lawyer may take or keep temporary possession of property relevant to a crime or offence only where:

(a)   it is necessary to do so to prevent the alteration, loss or destruction of the evidence,

(b)   it is necessary to do so to prevent physical harm to any person,

(c)   the client or the person possessing the property instructs the lawyer to promptly arrange for the property to be disclosed or delivered to the Crown or law enforcement authorities,

(d)   the lawyer reasonably believes it is in the interests of justice that the property be examined or tested before it is disclosed or delivered to the Crown or law enforcement authorities, and the property may be examined or tested without altering or destroying its essential characteristics, or

(e)   the lawyer reasonably believes that a wrongful conviction may be prevented if the property is first disclosed at trial, and this use of the property would be significantly diminished if it were disclosed to the Crown or law enforcement authorities before the trial.

(12) A lawyer may take or keep temporary possession under subrule (11) (d) or (e) only if the lawyer has been authorized to do so by a committee of the Law Society established by the Treasurer to decide whether the lawyer may take or keep temporary possession. The lawyer must seek such authorization promptly.

(13) A lawyer who takes or keeps possession of property relevant to a crime or offence shall not

(a)   counsel any alteration, concealment, loss or destruction of the property,

(b)   alter, conceal, lose, or destroy the property, or

(c)   deal with the property in a manner that there are reasonable grounds to believe would (i) obstruct justice, or (ii) risk physical harm to any person.

(14) A lawyer who takes or keeps property relevant to a crime or offence shall give up possession of the evidence as soon as practical and only in accordance with subrules (11)(d) or (e), (15) or (16).

(15) A lawyer in possession of property relevant to a crime or offence may return the evidence to its source only if the lawyer is satisfied on reasonable grounds that the evidence will not be

(a)   altered, concealed, lost or destroyed or

(b)   used to cause physical harm to any person.

(16) Subject to subrules (10) – (15), a lawyer in possession of property relevant to a crime or offence shall disclose or deliver it to the Crown or law enforcement authorities as soon as practicable in all the circumstances. [Emphasis added][35]

---

35   See D. Gambrill, "Physical Evidence Rule Mothballed - Law Society Not Moving Forward On Highly Public Issue" *Law Times* (18 August 2003).

To date, the Law Society of Upper Canada has been unable to reach a consensus on its proposed rule.

Other than Alberta,[36] no other Law Society in Canada has a specific rule to guide counsel in this thorny situation. In Ontario, for example, Rule 4.01(2)(e) of the *Rules of Professional Conduct* prohibits counsel from "suppressing what ought to be disclosed." No guidance is given on "what ought to be disclosed." [37]

What do you think of the Ontario proposal? Does it give counsel too much discretion? Does it create a de facto reciprocal disclosure regime? How would the proposed rule apply, for example, to a corporate lawyer who receives an e-mail with an attachment used to perpetrate a securities fraud? Recently, the Canadian Bar Association decided not to amend its *Code of Professional Conduct* to address the *Murray* issue.[38] The CBA Standing Committee concluded that:

> ... what occurred in the *Bernardo* case is highly exceptional. Moreover, in the Section's view, the adoption of either the Alberta rule or the proposed Ontario rule would potentially impose on an accused person and defence counsel a duty of disclosure that does not now exist in law.

In *R. c. Bédard*[39] a defence lawyer was found guilty of wilfully obstructing justice contrary to s. 139(2) of the Criminal Code for suggesting to the father of an accused in a robbery case that he hide the firearm the son had used. He was sentenced to prison for eight months plus probation for one year. Deterrence and denunciation were held to be the major considerations.

While the Rules of Professional Conduct may, by imposing ethical restrictions on the conduct of counsel, impact on what evidence is introduced by counsel and how it is used, can it serve as a jurisdictional basis for the trial judge to exclude evidence obtained in violation of one of the Rules?

COWLES v. BALAC

(2006), 273 D.L.R. (4th) 596, 83 O.R. (3d) 660 (C.A.), additional reasons at (2006), 2006 CarswellOnt 7936 (Ont. C.A.), leave to appeal refused (2007), 2007 CarswellOnt 1359, 2007 CarswellOnt 1360 (S.C.C.)

The African Lion Safari & Game Farm Ltd (ALS) was sued for injuries resulting from an attack by Bengal tigers at ALS's drive-through safari zoo as the plaintiffs drove through the farm. The trial judge awarded damages in the approximate amounts of $1.7 million and $800,000.

One of the issues at trial was the admissibility of evidence obtained from a private investigator, retained by counsel for ALS. The investigator had maintained

---

36 Rule 20 of Chapter 10 of Alberta's *Code of Professional Conduct* states that a lawyer cannot counsel or participate in either "the destruction of property having potential evidentiary value or the alteration of property so as to affect its evidentiary value" or "the concealment of property having potential evidentiary value in a criminal proceeding."

37 For a further discussion of counsel's obligation to disclose physical evidence of a crime, see Proulx and Layton, *Ethics and Canadian Criminal Law* (Toronto: Irwin Law, 2001) at Chapter 9.

38 See "Modernizing the CBA *Code of Professional Conduct*: Final Report of the Standing Committee on Ethics and Professional Responsibility" (March, 2004).

39 (2005), 38 C.R. (6th) 119 (C.Q.).

surveillance and had spoken to one of the plaintiffs at her place of work. At the time, the plaintiff was represented by counsel who had no knowledge of what the investigator saw and heard until disclosure took place at a pre-trial conference shortly before trial. The trial judge excluded the investigator's testimony on the ground that he had violated rule 4.03(2) of the *Rules of Professional Conduct of the Law Society of Upper Canada*. At paras. 39-42, she said:

> The Rules of Professional Conduct provide:
>
>> 4.03(2) A lawyer shall not approach or deal with a person who is represented by another lawyer, save through or with the consent of that party's lawyer.
>
> Whether the approach is by the lawyer him or himself [*sic*] or an investigator retained by the lawyer it is equally improper and the lawyer bears the responsibility for those to whom he delegates tasks. It is the lawyer's responsibility to insure that those to whom tasks are delegated are aware of the rules and to educate them when they are not. The approach was improper. Any evidence obtained by the investigator and any other evidence obtained as the result or consequence of such information will be excluded from the trial proceeding.

BORINS J.A.: —

Counsel for ALS contends that the trial judge misconstrued the purpose of the rule. It is submitted that the purpose of the rule is to govern the professional conduct of lawyers, and not to govern the admissibility of evidence that may have been obtained consequent to a breach of the rule. I am in agreement with this submission.

Rule 4.03 is entitled "Interviewing Witnesses". The Law Society's commentary to rule 4.03(2) provides, in relevant part, as follows:

> This rule applies to communications with any person, whether or not a party to a formal adjudicative proceeding, contract, or negotiation, who is represented by counsel concerning the matter to which the communication relates. A lawyer may communicate with a represented person or an employee or agent of such a person, concerning matters outside the representation. Also parties to a matter may communicate directly with each other.

> The prohibition on communications with a represented person applies only where the lawyer knows that the person is represented in the matter to be discussed. This means that the lawyer has actual knowledge of the fact of the representation, but actual knowledge may be inferred from the circumstances. This inference may arise whether there is substantial reason to believe that the person with whom communication is sought is represented in the matter to be discussed. Thus, a lawyer cannot evade the requirement of obtaining the consent of counsel by closing eyes to the obvious.

In my view, it is clear from the language of the rule and the commentary that the purpose of the rule is to prevent lawyers from circumventing other lawyers by dealing directly with their clients. There is no evidence that counsel for ALS intended or instructed the investigator to approach Cowles with the intent of "dealing" with her. Had there been evidence that this is what had occurred, counsel might have been in breach of rule 4.03(2). However, this would then be a matter for the Law Society to consider as the court seldom, if ever, becomes involved in such matters.

The Law Society passed *The Rules of Professional Conduct* to ensure that its members maintain the highest standards of professional conduct. Where a member's contravention of a rule is brought to the attention of the Law Society, it may result in the commencement of a disciplinary proceeding against the member. However, the *Rules of Professional Conduct* do not, and could not, affect the admissibility of relevant evidence in civil or criminal proceedings. Thus, even if it could be said that counsel for ALS contravened rule 4.03(2), this would not affect the admissibility of relevant evidence acquired by the investigator.

The record before us does not contain the investigator's complete report of his surveillance of Cowles and what she said to him. What is known from the affidavit of a law clerk in support of Cowles's motion to exclude the investigator's testimony is that the surveillance of Cowles occurred at a "strip club" where she was employed as an exotic dancer before and after the incident with the tigers. Considering the excerpts from the report contained in the affidavit, what the investigator saw and heard would be capable of adversely affecting Cowles's credibility, which is likely why she attacked this admissibility of this evidence. Unfortunately, the trial judge did not consider whether this evidence was relevant but focused only on how it was obtained. There can be no doubt that it is in the public interest to ensure that all relevant evidence is available to the court. This is essential if justice is to be done between the parties.

By commencing this action against ALS, the plaintiff Cowles has placed in issue the cause and extent of her injuries. In my view, having placed these factors in issue, it would be reasonable for Cowles to assume that ALS would investigate her claim, in the course of which it might hire an investigator to make observations of her activity and, if possible, to converse with her if she agreed to do so. Having put in issue her medical condition and the cause of her injuries, Cowles cannot complain where ALS seeks to introduce evidence that its investigator acquired relevant to these issues. *Cf.*, *Cook v. Ip et al* (1985), 52 O.R. (2d) 289 (C.A.), leave to appeal to S.C.C. refused 55 O.R. (2d) 288n.

In their opinion, Associate Chief Justice O'Connor and Justice Rouleau agreed with the reasoning of Justice Borins on the admissibility of the evidence. They disagreed, however, that it was a basis for ordering a new trial. **Why does this Rule not apply to the police in criminal proceedings? Should it?**

3. SOURCES

The law of evidence is primarily judge-made. Numerous procedural reforms were accomplished by statute in England in the 19th century and these were largely copied in Canada. In Canada procedure in criminal matters is entrusted to the federal Parliament[40] and procedure in civil matters to the provincial

---

40 Section 91(27), Constitution Act, 1867.

legislatures.[41] Legislation enacted pursuant to these powers, the *Canada Evidence Act*[42] and the various provincial Evidence Acts, covers only a small portion of the law of evidence, and the bulk of it is still governed by the common law.

R. v. SALITURO
[1991] 3 S.C.R. 654, 9 C.R. (4th) 324, 68 C.C.C. (3d) 289
1991 CarswellOnt 1031, 1991 CarswellOnt 124

The accused was charged with using a forged document. He had signed his wife's name on a cheque payable to them jointly and cashed it. The accused's position was that he was acting under his wife's instructions. The accused's wife testified differently. On appeal the accused argued that his wife was incompetent to testify for the prosecution. The Crown asked the Supreme Court to alter the common law incompetence rule where the spouses were separated at the time of the offence and there was no reasonable prospect of reconciliation. We will return to the ruling on the issue of spousal incompetence in Chapter 5.

IACOBUCCI J.: –

A. *What Are the Limits on the Power of Judges to Change the Common Law?*

(1) Introduction

At one time, it was accepted that it was the role of judges to discover the common law, not to change it. In Book One of his *Commentaries on the Laws of England* (4th ed. 1770), Sir William Blackstone propounded a view of the common law as fixed and unchanging, at p. 69:

> For it is an established rule to abide by former precedents, where the same points come again in litigation; as well to keep the scale of justice even and steady, and not liable to waver with every new judge's opinion; as also because the law in that case being solemnly declared and determined, what before was uncertain, and perhaps indifferent, is now become a permanent rule, which it is not in the best of any subsequent judge to alter or vary from, according to his private sentiments, he being sworn to determine, not according to his own private judgment, but according to the known laws and customs of the land; not delegated to pronounce a new law, but to maintain and expound the old one.

However, Blackstone's static model of the common law has gradually been supplanted by a more dynamic view. This Court is now willing, where there are compelling reasons for doing so, to overturn its own previous decisions. ...

(2) Limits on the Power of the Courts to Change the Common Law

In keeping with these developments, this Court has signalled its willingness to adapt and develop common law rules to reflect changing circumstances in society at large. In four recent cases, *Ares v. Venner*, [1970] S.C.R. 608, *Watkins*

---

41 Section 92(14), Constitution Act, 1867.
42 Section 2 provides that "This part applies to all criminal proceedings and to all civil proceedings and other matters whatsoever respecting which Parliament has jurisdiction."

v. Olafson, supra, R. v. Khan, [1990] 2 S.C.R. 531, and *R. v. Seaboyer*, [1991] 2 S.C.R. 577, this Court has laid down guidelines for the exercise of the power to develop the common law. The common theme of these cases is that, while complex changes to the law with uncertain ramifications should be left to the legislature, the courts can and should make incremental changes to the common law to bring legal rules into step with a changing society. However, a brief review of these cases is warranted.

The issue in *Ares, supra*, was whether it was appropriate to create a new exception to the hearsay rule for hospital records. Speaking for the Court, Hall J. adopted the reasons of Lord Donovan in *Myers v. Director of Public Prosecutions*, [1965] A.C. 1001, and accepted that the proposed new exception was required in consequence of changes in the business environment which could not have been foreseen at the time the hearsay rule was being developed. Hall J. rejected the argument that changes to the common law can only be made by Parliament. In support of his decision making hospital records admissible under a new exception to the hearsay rule, Hall J. quoted the following passage from the reasons of Lord Donovan in *Myers* at p. 1047:

> The common law is moulded by the judges and it is still their province to adapt it from time to time so as to make it serve the interests of those it binds. Particularly is this so in the field of procedural law.

Hall J. followed the minority in *Myers, supra*. However, the majority in *Myers* was not of the opinion that the courts should never change common law rules, but only of the view that a change was not appropriate under the circumstances of the case. In the words of Lord Reid, at p. 1021:

> I have never taken a narrow view of the functions of this House as an appellate tribunal. The common law must be developed to meet changing economic conditions and habits of thought, and I would not be deterred by expressions of opinion in this House in old cases. But there are limits to what we can or should do. If we are to extend the law it must be by the development and application of fundamental principles. We cannot introduce arbitrary conditions or limitations: that must be left to legislation.

. . .

(3) Conclusion

These cases reflect the flexible approach that this Court has taken to the development of the common law. Judges can and should adapt the common law to reflect the changing social, moral and economic fabric of the country. Judges should not be quick to perpetuate rules whose social foundation has long since disappeared. Nonetheless, there are significant constraints on the power of the judiciary to change the law. As McLachlin J. indicated in *Watkins, supra*, in a constitutional democracy such as ours it is the legislature and not the courts which has the major responsibility for law reform; and for any changes to the law which may have complex ramifications, however necessary or desirable such changes may be, they should be left to the legislature. The judiciary should confine itself to those incremental changes which are necessary to keep the common law in step with the dynamic and evolving fabric of our society.

––––––––––

A further source of evidence law, and especially so in criminal law, is the entrenched Charter of Rights and Freedoms. We will in this course address in particular the rule against compellability of accused in section 11(*c*), the principle against self-incrimination in section 7, the right to a fair trial under sections 7 and 11(*d*), the presumption of innocence in section 11(*d*), the ability to exclude evidence in section 24 and equality rights for complainants in sexual assault cases under section 15.

4. CODIFICATION

There was an attempt at codification by the Law Reform Commission of Canada in 1975[43] but this was not well received by the profession.[44] In 1977 the Federal/Provincial Task Force on Uniform Rules of Evidence was established[45] and its product, the proposed *Canada Evidence Act*, 1986, was much more comprehensive than existing legislation. No one has yet enacted this legislation.

In 1975 in the United States the Federal Rules of Evidence were legislated. This was a comprehensive scheme providing for the rules of evidence in federal courts. Since that time the majority of the states has enacted similar schemes patterned on the federal model. In 1995 the Australian Capital Territory enacted a similar comprehensive scheme. Within months Australia' s largest state, New South Wales, copied them for use in its courts. Canada, which in the 19th century had adopted the English Draft Code to cover substantive criminal law and criminal procedure, does not appear ready for a similar venture into the area of evidence.

Arguments for a Comprehensive Statement

1.   The main advantage of a comprehensive statement would be accessibility — bringing together into one document all the evidentiary rules. In Canada today the law of evidence is partly judge-made and partly made by legislation. A comprehensive legislated statement would bring it all together. Obviously this would be preferable to having some evidence rules regarding the use of evidence in judicial decisions while others appear in statutory form.

2.   When an objection is made at trial the judge needs to make an immediate ruling. Wouldn't it be wonderful if we were all on the same page, aiming at the same target? At the very least the comprehensive statement would be, if not the definitive word, a good beginning to the argument. The Federal Rules of Evidence in the United States are available in a 4-inch by 5-inch

––––––––––

43 *Report on Evidence* (1975), Information Canada, Ottawa.

44 See generally Brooks, "The Law Reform Commission of Canada's Evidence Code" (1978), 16 Osgoode Hall L.J. 241; Brooks, "The Common Law and the Evidence Code: Are They Compatible?" (1978), 27 U.N.B.L.J. 27; and Anderson, "A Criticism of the Evidence Code" (1976), 11 U.B.C.L. Rev. 163.

45 See generally *Report of the Federal/Provincial Task Force on Uniform Rules of Evidence* (1982).

pamphlet of about 50 pages. Based on our experience in the courtroom, the present rules are handled, to be kind, unevenly, and a comprehensive, ready-to-hand statement would necessarily improve the present situation. Both the evidentiary arguments and the results would be better based.

3. A comprehensive statement of the rules, written in terms of the underlying principles, would also create a better understanding of how the rules are meant to operate. This is particularly so if the rules were to be accompanied by explanatory notes. Such a rendition would minimize what some have referred to as "rampant conceptualism": the tendency of many lawyers to discuss the rules of evidence in terms of the meanings of the labels attached to them rather than in terms of their underlying rationale.

4. A comprehensive statement of the rules, written in terms of the underlying principles, would recognize a discretion in the judge in the application of the law of evidence, room for choice, room for judgment. The evidence rules are there to promote efficiency, fairness and the best approximation of the truth. Discretion in dealing with each particular case is necessary as it is inherent in the nature of the exercise. Recognizing that within each rule there must exist a fair amount of discretion, by articulating the rule in principled terms you thereby begin the process of describing the guidelines for a sound exercise of discretion. The simplicity of the process makes the law clearer and the discretion of the judge is better brought under control. Counsel then can make arguments based on principle rather than on technical interpretations of a mechanical rule and the judge will similarly be obliged to make decisions based on principle. Indeed, once it is recognized that discretion already exists, and must necessarily exist, we make the law much more certain than it ever was before and the trial more fair.

5. Teaching the beginning student through an examination of a comprehensive statement would better prepare them for the world of practice.

6. Through a comprehensive statement the law becomes more accessible, not only because it is gathered together in one place, but also because it would tend to resolve many of the present ambiguities which give differing results depending on the individual judge. The law becomes more uniform. A comprehensive statement might also encourage uniformity among the various legislatures, easing the burden on the practitioner who goes back and forth between civil and criminal law encountering different pieces of legislation. If uniformity was achieved among the provincial and federal governments, we would all be farther ahead as we generate judicial decisions and academic commentary regarding the rules, such writing coming from a common larger base.

7. Enacting a comprehensive statement of the rules would provide a forum within which reform of the law of evidence would be facilitated. It is true that much of the judge-made law can be reformed by judicial action but such reforms are by their nature piecemeal and also often resisted by the conservatism of the legal profession.

8. A comprehensive statement would also make the law of evidence more accessible to the citizenry. Bentham was moved in his calls for reform in the 19th century to better equip the ordinary man to understand. The present law of evidence is, for many, often unclear and difficult to ascertain. For

those who see the rules as eight volumes of Wigmore with innumerable exceptions, the task is overly complex and daunting. Success often goes to the advocate best equipped with a memory for precedent and the ability to articulate the mechanical rule with precision. For many looking on, the adversary system is seen as too much of a game with the outcome dependent on the skill of the adversaries. If, on the other hand, we recognize precedent as valuable only as a vehicle for the expression of principle and focus on understanding the principle, there will be a more genuine communication between counsel and the judge and a better appreciation by the onlooker as to why a particular piece of evidence was accepted or rejected. Resistance to a comprehensive statement might be partly attributed to the lawyers' self-interest in their wish to keep the law as complicated as possible and thus keep it to themselves.

Arguments Against a Comprehensive Statement

1. The present law of evidence is accessible and known to those who are willing to make the effort. The law of evidence is like any other body of law and can be discovered and learned. It is folly to think that the rules can be made so simple that a lay person would understand without the assistance of a lawyer. A suitable text can inform the profession and the judiciary as well as any legislated statement of the rules.

2. Enacting a comprehensive statute will produce years of extensive litigation with arguments as to whether the legislature intended to effect change in the area or intended to enact the status quo. While there may be some ambiguity in the existing rules, even a restatement will produce argument as to the meaning of the words chosen. Judicial interpretations will vary for a lengthy period of time and uniformity will be an elusive object.

3. A comprehensive statute, which is codification by another name, will freeze the law of evidence and the courts will no longer be vehicles for change. Judges will no longer be able to create a rule or an exception to do justice in an individual case but will be limited to interpreting the legislation. The limits on proper judicial statutory interpretation will strait-jacket the judiciary. Changes will only be available by legislative action and delay will be the natural consequence. In addition, it is the judiciary and the litigation bar who are the experts in the law of evidence; it is they who actually know how the system works, and we ought not to forfeit their expertise.

4. Discretion in the trial judge equates, for many, to greater admissibility of evidence. The trial judge will no longer be as concerned with rejecting evidence as insufficiently reliable and will be moved to leave it to the trier of fact to assess worth given the totality of the evidence. Opponents who voice these concerns are normally found in those members of the bar who do not generally have the burden of proof. As their function is often seen to be preventing evidence being admitted, anything that increases admissibility is to be resisted.

5. A comprehensive legislative scheme runs the risk of being subject to political influence and this will particularly prejudice the accused in criminal cases. Prosecutors in the past, who have had difficulties in certain prosecutions, have been known to lobby, successfully, for changes in admissibility of evidence or changes with respect to the burdens of proof. Criminal lawyers

believe that there is greater protection for an accused from a non-elected judge than from a legislator who feels he must give a fair hearing and respond to concerns of the community toward crime. Given the growing victims' rights movement, defence counsel are increasingly concerned about legislative action. They recognize that accused persons do not have a lobby in the legislature. If changes are to be made to the law of evidence by the legislature, as opposed to the judiciary, the criminal defence bar may feel, with some justification, that the accused's interests will not be well served.

As we explore the laws of evidence you may wish to consider whether you accept this view that legislation is not necessary.[46]

Absent any legislative momentum to re-state or reform the laws of evidence, it has fallen to the Supreme Court to be the major source of new law. The authors of McWilliams[47] have identified six major themes in the Supreme Court's approach to evidence in the last twenty years:

- ensuring fairness in the evidence-gathering process;
- bestowing constitutional status to the organizing principles of the adversarial process;
- the development of a principled approach to admissibility;
- cleansing the law of evidence of stereotypes;
- a recognition of the relevance of social context; and
- protecting against wrongful convictions.

5. APPLICABILITY OF LAWS OF EVIDENCE

The rules of evidence that we will be examining in this book are rules which cover court proceedings, civil and criminal. We will be examining the rules as they are applied when insisted on by the parties to the litigation and when the proceedings are taking place in a courtroom. In other forums, the rules are considerably relaxed. Even in the courtroom there is a relaxation at times: at the sentencing stage in criminal matters, for example, or in custody matters when the best interests of the child are being considered. There are, of course, a number of administrative tribunals functioning in Canada and each, by its enacting legislation and by general legislation referable to all administrative tribunals, must follow its own procedures. More often than not these tribunals are more liberal with respect to what evidence might be received. Understanding the basic rules applicable to the courts will, however, assist in appreciating the process before other tribunals.

For example, the Statutory Powers Procedure Act[48] of Ontario provides:

---

46 For more discussion on the value or not of a comprehensive statement see Delisle, "A Comprehensive Statement of Evidence Rules?" and Paciocco, "The Case Against Legislated Text in Matters of Proof", both pieces to be found in *Towards a Clear and Just Criminal Law: A Criminal Reports Forum* (Carswell, 1999), at pp. 1-84.

47 *Canadian Criminal Evidence* (4th ed., 2003) 3:20. See too Tanovich, "Starr Gazing: Looking into the Future of Hearsay in Canada" (2003) 28 *Queen's L.J.* 371 at 375-383.

48 R.S.O. 1990, c. S.22.

15.(1) Subject to subsections (2) and (3), a tribunal may admit as evidence at a hearing, whether or not given or proven under oath or affirmation or admissible as evidence in a court,

    (*a*)   any oral testimony; and

    (*b*)   any document or other thing,

relevant to the subject matter of the proceeding and may act on such evidence, but the tribunal may exclude anything unduly repetitious.

    (2) Nothing is admissible in evidence at a hearing,

    (*a*)   that would be inadmissible in a court by reason of any privilege under the law of evidence; or

    (*b*)   that is inadmissible by the statute under which the proceeding arises or any other statute.

    (3) Nothing in subsection (1) overrides the provisions of any Act expressly limiting the extent to or purposes for which any oral testimony, documents or things may be admitted or used in evidence in any proceeding.[49]

In *Central Burner Service Inc. v. Texaco Canada Inc.*[50] the defendant to a civil action brought in Provincial Court appealed on the basis that the judge had relied on hearsay evidence with respect to a critical issue. The appeal was dismissed. The court decided:

> Counsel conceded that most, if not all, of the relevant evidence was hearsay. Hearsay evidence is not admissible to prove the truth of its contents in regular court proceedings, particularly where it goes to the root of an issue. However, s. 80(1) of the Courts of Justice Act, S.O. 1984, c. 11, provides as follows:
>
> > 80(1) Subject to subsections (2) and (3), the Provincial Court (Civil Division) may admit as evidence at a hearing, whether or not given or proven under oath or affirmation or admissible as evidence in any other court,
> > (a)   any oral testimony; and
> > (b)   any document or other thing,
> > relevant to the subject-matter of the proceeding and may act on such evidence, but the court may exclude anything unduly repetitious.
>
> Prior to the enactment of s. 80, hearsay evidence was not generally allowed in the Small Claims Court. The question is to what extent has s. 80 changed the law. Counsel for the defendants contends that if hearsay evidence is admitted with respect to critical issues at trial the opposing party will not have the opportunity to test that evidence by cross-examination. While that may be so, the weight to be given to any kind of evidence is for the trial judge to decide. Normally, hearsay evidence should be given less weight than direct evidence.
>
> In my opinion, s. 80 allows hearsay evidence of all oral testimony and all documents or other things, provided they are relevant and not unduly repetitious.

---

49 See, however, the remarks of Reid J. in *Re Northwestern Gen. Hosp. Bd. of Governors and Brown* (1985), 52 O.R. (2d) 591, 600 (Div. Ct.):

    The Board has a wide discretion with respect to evidence pursuant to the *Statutory Powers Procedure Act* . . . it was not entitled, in my opinion, to make a ruling based on some policy it has adopted and without regard to the merits of the issue. Thus, I think that the Board was not only wrong in its given reasons but wrong in its apparent resolution by way of a rigid policy.

50 (1989), 36 O.A.C. 239, 240 (C.A.).

> There is nothing in s. 80 that draws a distinction between critical issues and more peripheral issues. The object of s. 80 is to avoid technical procedures and the additional cost of calling extra witnesses in cases involving small claims.
>
> The trial judge was entitled to rely on hearsay evidence. In the present case the transcript shows that she clearly understood that much of the evidence was hearsay and she stated that she would give it the appropriate weight. Therefore, there was evidence upon which she could come to her conclusion and that she properly weighed it.

In addition, the courts will often take a different attitude toward the rules and procedures if the subject-matter warrants. For example, in *Gordon v. Gordon*,[51] the Ontario Court of Appeal wrote:

> A custody case, where the best interest of the child is the only issue, is not the same as ordinary litigation and requires, in our view, that the person conducting the hearing take a more active role than he ordinarily would take in the conduct of a trial. Generally, he should do what he reasonably can to see to it that his decision will be based upon the most relevant and helpful information available.

The case of *R. v. Barber*[52] is instructive. Section 37(7)(*c*) of the then Ontario Labour Relations Act[53] read:

> An arbitrator or an arbitration board, as the case may be, has power . . . to accept such oral or written evidence as the arbitrator or the arbitration board, as the case may be, in its discretion considers proper, whether admissible in a court of law or not.

The arbitrator, Barber, decided that the clause of the collective agreement under review was ambiguous and received extrinsic evidence consisting of oral evidence as to past practice and a master policy unilaterally secured by the company. The award was quashed on *certiorari* on the basis that the clause was not ambiguous. The Court of Appeal, in dismissing the appeal, wrote about section 37(7)(*c*):

> By that clause the Legislature recognized that arbitrations will frequently be presented before arbitration boards by lay persons. Accordingly, it relaxed the strict rules as to the admissibility of evidence and in particular allowed hearsay evidence to be adduced without objection. However, that provision does not relieve a board from acting only on evidence having cogency in law. For instance, a board may admit evidence which is inadmissible on the ground of irrelevancy, but the section does not permit it to then act illegally by drawing inferences from wholly irrelevant evidence.[54]

In *Re City of Toronto and C.U.P.E., Local 79*,[55] the arbitrator had refused to admit into evidence the report of a Commission of Inquiry. On appeal the union sought to uphold his decision to exclude on the basis that a number of established rules of evidence rendered the report inadmissible; eight or nine rules, including

---

51 (1980), 23 R.F.L. (2d) 266, 271.

52 [1968] 2 O.R. 245 (C.A.).

53 See now S.O. 1995, c. 1, Sched. A, s. 12.

54 *Supra*, note 52, at p. 252.

55 (1982), 133 D.L.R. (3d) 94, 106 (Ont. C.A.); leave to appeal to S.C.C. refused 36 O.R. (2d) 386. See also *C.J.A., Local 579 v. Bradco Construction Ltd.* (1993), 102 D.L.R. (4th) 402 (S.C.C.) and *Greater Niagara Transit Commission v. A.T.U., Local 1582* (1987), 43 D.L.R. (4th) 71 (Ont. Div. Ct.).

the hearsay rule and the best evidence rule, were mentioned. The court referred to the broad discretion conferred by the above section and wrote:

> The argument made to this Court that the Board would have been prevented from doing so by exclusionary rules applicable in the Courts is singularly without merit. It is plain that the Board was not bound by the rules of evidence and the argument addressed to us by the Union and the arbitration board decisions cited by it fly in the face of the statute. A decision by any board to refuse to admit evidence because it was not admissible in the Courts or because the board was bound by decisions of other arbitration boards would constitute an obvious error of law. In addition, the discretion of a board obviously would be improperly exercised if it acted in the belief that these legal rules or prior arbitration decisions were binding upon it. It is beyond question that any board so acting would fetter its discretion.

Presumably, however, an arbitrator could refuse hearsay if he decided, in his discretion, that it was "proper" so to do. The arbitrator could reason that:

> For this Board rejection [of hearsay] is justified by consideration of the effects were hearsay freely used. Free use, at least on central issues, would unfairly disadvantage the opposing party. At the same time, it would reduce the arbitrator's ability to judge the weight of evidence as they determine the facts. Together both would endanger respect for the arbitration process itself. These factors — and not the simple dictates of the Judge-made hearsay rule — justify rejection.[56]

While the legislators may decide that formal rules of evidence may inhibit the inquiry, some of the rules are regarded as so essential to a fair inquiry that administrative tribunals may be moved to follow the example set by the courts.[57]

Rules of evidence applicable in a court proceeding may also be varied by specific legislation. For example, the Child and Family Services Act[58] provides:

> 50.—(1) Despite anything in the *Evidence Act*, in any proceeding under this Part,

---

56 *Re Ont. Jockey Club* (1977), 15 L.A.C. (2d) 273, 276 (Schiff). But compare *Chrysler Can. Ltd. v. U.A.W., Loc. 1285* (1983), 11 L.A.C. (3d) 415 (Palmer), and contrast Lord Denning's acceptance of hearsay by administrative tribunals in *Miller v. Min. of Housing & Loc. Govt.*, [1968] 1 W.L.R. 992 (C.A.). See also *Brewster Transport Co. Ltd. and A.T.U., Local 1374* (1992), 26 L.A.C. (4th) 240 (Alta. Arb. Bd.) (Tettensor). For a detailed discussion of the application of the rules of evidence in labour arbitration proceedings, see Gorsky, Usprich & Brandt, Evidence and Procedure in Canadian Labour Arbitration (2004) and Mitchnick & Etherington, *Labour Arbitration in Canada* (Toronto: Lancaster House, 2006) at Chapter 6; Paciocco, "The Supreme Court of Canada and Hearsay: The Relevance for Arbitration" in Kaplan, Sack & Gunderson, eds., *Labour Arbitration Yearbook 1994-95*, p. 123.

57 See *O.P.S.E.U. v. Min. of Correctional Services* (1984), 2 O.A.C. 351, 358 (Div. Ct.). See generally Adell, "Arbitral Discretion in the Admission of Evidence" in *Labour Arbitration Yearbook 1999-2000*, at pp. 1-38 and see Evans, Janisch and Mullan, *Administrative Law* (4th ed., Emond Montgomery), at pp. 634-5, 637-40. See also R.D. Lunau, "Evidence in Administrative Proceedings: New Issues and Persistent Problems" (2003), 16 C.J.A.L.P. 191.

58 R.S.O. 1990, c. C.11, s. 50(1).

(a)   the court may consider the past conduct of a person toward any child if that person is caring for or has access to or may care for or have access to a child who is the subject of the proceeding; and

(b)   any oral or written statement or report that the court considers relevant to the proceeding, including a transcript, exhibit or finding or the reasons for a decision in an earlier civil or criminal proceeding, is admissible into evidence.

Judicial interpretation of this section and its predecessor, s. 28(4) of the Child Welfare Act,[59] has varied. In *Re C.A.S. Metro Toronto and N.H.B.*[60] the court received various documents from another case involving the same mother and different children: court orders, judgments, clinic reports and transcripts from previous hearings. The court believed the section gave a very wide discretion to admit hearsay. In *Re Jennifer C.*[61] the court, however, refused to admit certain hospital records:

> . . . I can see no reason to permit the society to use s. 28(4) [now s. 46(1)] to prove the very conduct complained of by recorded hearsay, thereby depriving the mother of her right to cross-examine on this pivotal issue.

The debate continues today. In *Catholic Children's Aid Society of Toronto v. L. (J.)*,[62] Justice Jones reviewed the conflicting jurisprudence and concluded:

> In light of the foregoing discussion, I considered whether the historical society records should be admitted under section 50. The society called evidence on the issue of threshold reliability of the records, but did not call evidence on the necessity branch of the test enunciated in *The Queen v. Khan* for the principled admission of hearsay evidence. In these circumstances, must I refuse to admit the evidence? Or is it open to me to exercise my discretion to admit the evidence if I am satisfied that its admission would not, in these circumstances, be contrary to the principles of fundamental justice as guaranteed in section 7 of the Charter? In considering this question, I identified the following factors in determining whether the test in *The Queen v. Khan* is the only test or whether an alternate "reliability test" may be used in certain circumstances.
>
> (1) What is the nature of the evidence? Given the circumstances in which the evidence was created, are there any guarantees or significant indicia of reliability?
>
> (2) What is the purpose for which the evidence is being tendered? To prove current state of affairs or historical backdrop?
>
> (3) What is the importance of the evidence to the issue to be decided? That is, does it go to the very issue to be decided as is the case when a child's sexual abuse statements are being tendered through third party witnesses? In that case, the test in *The Queen v. Khan* would be used.

---

59 R.S.O. 1980, c. 66.

60 (1980), 5 A.C.W.S. 66 (Ont. Prov. Ct.), per Walmsley Prov. J.

61 (1984), 39 R.F.L. (2d) 244 (Ont. Prov. Ct.), per Weisman Prov. J. Compare *Re C.A.S., Metro. Toronto and R. (K.)*, [1983] W.D.F.L. 1320, per Thomson Prov. J. See generally, Bala and Anweiler, "Allegations of Sexual Abuse in a Parental Custody Dispute" (1987), 2 C.F.L.Q. 343. See also *Roman Catholic C.A.S. (Essex) v. H. (L.)*, [1987] O.J. No. 1845 (Ont. Fam. Ct.), dealing with s. 47(7) [now s. 51(7)] of the Child and Family Services Act which provides that in an interim proceeding, "the court may admit and act on evidence that the court considers credible and trustworthy in the circumstances." See too D.A. Thompson, "Are There Any Rules of Evidence in Family Law?" (2003), 21 C.F.L.Q. 245.

62 [2003] O.J. No. 1722, 2003 CarswellOnt 1685 (C.J.).

(4) What limits could be placed on the evidence that would have the effect of buttressing reliability? For example, limiting the admission to first-hand hearsay and discounting second and third-hand hearsay and disregarding opinions.

(5) How extensively were the records used in cross-examination and to what effect?

(6) What effect would the refusal to admit the evidence have on the trial proceedings? Here multiple witnesses would be required to cover the period from 1991 to 1997. Although relevant, would this be a good use of scarce trial time?

In criminal cases, the rules of evidence will often vary depending on who is the proponent and the nature and stage of the proceedings. For example, given the concern for wrongful convictions, our courts have also slowly recognized that there is a need in some cases for a relaxation of the strict application of the rules of evidence in order to ensure that an accused can make full answer and defence. In *R. v. Brown*,[63] a case that we will examine later, Justice Major, for the majority, held:

> . . . [In *R. v. Williams*] Martin J.A. commented that "a court has a residual discretion to relax in favour of the accused a strict rule of evidence where it is necessary to prevent a miscarriage of justice and where the danger against which an exclusionary rule aims to safeguard does not exist" (p. 343 (emphasis added)). This suggests that, where there are some assurances of reliability and where necessary to avoid wrongful conviction, some rules of evidence may be applied with something less than their usual degree of rigour.

In a concurring opinion, Justice Arbour (Justice L'Heureux-Dubé concurring) noted:

> The idea that courts maintain the discretion to relax the rules of evidence when an accused's innocence is at stake has its roots in *Williams*. In that case, Martin J.A. held that an accused's right to make full answer and defence must comply with established rules respecting the admission of evidence (*Williams*, at p. 337; see also *Dersch v. Canada (Attorney General)*, [1990] 2 S.C.R. 1505 at p. 1515, 60 C.C.C. (3d) 132, 77 D.L.R. (4th) 473). Martin J.A. did, however, go on to state that the court had a residual discretion to relax strict rules of evidence in favour of the accused when necessary to prevent a miscarriage of justice (at p. 343). Support for this proposition, as expressed in *Williams*, is also found in the Ontario Court of Appeal decisions of *R. v. Rowbotham* (1988), 41 C.C.C. (3d) 1 at p. 57, and *R. v. Finta* (1992), 73 C.C.C. (3d) 65 at pp. 201-2, 92 D.L.R. (4th) 1, affirmed [1994] 1 S.C.R. 701, 88 C.C.C. (3d) 417, 112 D.L.R. (4th) 513, as well as in this Court's decision in *Finta*, at p. 854.

In *R. v. Zeolkowski*[64] the court was concerned with the rules to be applied when a judge conducted a hearing pursuant to the Criminal Code to determine whether a person should possess firearms. It appeared that a police sergeant was going to testify that a prohibition order should go on the basis that the person's wife had told the sergeant that he had threatened her. The wife would not be called. The Provincial Court judge ruled that hearsay evidence was inadmissible, in that evidence at a hearing under section 98(6) of the Code was limited to that which would be admissible at a criminal trial. Appeals in Manitoba confirmed the ruling. The Supreme Court reversed:

---

63 (2002), 162 C.C.C. (3d) 257 (S.C.C.).

64 (1989), 50 C.C.C. (3d) 566, 572 (S.C.C.).

> The provincial court judge must simply be satisfied that the peace officer had reasonable grounds to believe as he or she did: in other words, that there is an objective basis for the reasonable grounds on which the peace officer acted. . . . Accordingly, I am prepared to hold that hearsay evidence is admissible at a firearm prohibition hearing under s. 98(6).

Finally, the rules of evidence may vary within a court proceeding depending on the stage of the proceedings. For example, in *R. v. Gardiner*[65] the Crown argued that the burden of proof at sentencing should be less than the traditional criminal onus of beyond a reasonable doubt which applies at trial to the determination of guilt. The Supreme Court of Canada decided that the burdens of proof should be the same but also decided that the rules could vary. Justice Dickson wrote:

> One of the hardest tasks confronting a trial judge is sentencing. The stakes are high for society and for the individual. Sentencing is the critical stage of the criminal justice system, and it is manifest that the judge should not be denied an opportunity to obtain relevant information by the imposition of all the restrictive evidential rules common to a trial. Yet the obtaining and weighing of such evidence should be fair. A substantial liberty interest of the offender is involved and the information obtained should be accurate and reliable.
>
> It is a commonplace that the strict rules which govern at trial do not apply at a sentencing hearing and it would be undesirable to have the formalities and technicalities characteristic of the normal adversary proceeding prevail. The hearsay rule does not govern the sentencing hearing. Hearsay evidence may be accepted where found to be credible and trustworthy. The judge traditionally has had wide latitude as to the sources and types of evidence upon which to base his sentence. He must have the fullest possible information concerning the background of the accused if he is to fit the sentence to the offender rather than to the crime. . . .
>
> To my mind, the facts which justify the sanction are no less important than the facts which justify the conviction; both should be subject to the same burden of proof. Crime and punishment are inextricably linked.[66]

Are you satisfied that the burden of proof must be the same but the rules governing admissibility can vary? Why should the hearsay rule govern the determination of the crime but not the punishment?[67]

---

65 (1982), 68 C.C.C. (2d) 477, 513 (S.C.C.). See also the excellent discussion by Grenier J. in *R. v. Alarie* (1980), 28 C.R. (3d) 73 (C.S.P. Qué.). And see *R. v. Albright*, [1987] 2 S.C.R. 383.

66 But see s. 742.6(9) of the Criminal Code where a balance of probabilities standard is used in prosecutions involving a breach of a conditional sentence order. See *R. v. Filippelli* (2002), 12 C.R. (6th) 384, 169 C.C.C. (3d) 217 (Ont. C.A.).

67 Adopting *Gardiner*-like provisions in recent amendments, see ss. 723 and 724 of the Criminal Code.

Chapter 2

Burdens of Proof and Presumptions

1. BURDENS OF PROOF

(a) Terminology

To the confusion of both the student and the profession, the term "burden of proof" is used in the cases to signify different things. Sometimes the term is used to refer to the requirement of satisfying the trier of fact that a certain material proposition has been made out. If the party who has this burden of proof is unable to persuade the trier that his alleged version of the facts actually occurred, that party will lose the case. Sometimes the term is used to signify the obligation of ensuring that there is evidence in the case concerning an issue. Failing to satisfy this burden will prevent the issue from being considered by the trier.

Cases seeking to distinguish the two uses sometimes refer to the former as the "persuasive burden," the "legal burden," the "ultimate," "major," or "primary" burden and to the latter as the "evidential burden," the "tactical burden," the "minor" or "secondary" burden or "the duty of going forward."

Chief Justice Dickson described the chaos and brought order to bear in *R. v. Schwartz*:[1]

> Judges and academics have used a variety of terms to try to capture the distinction between the two types of burdens. The burden of establishing a case has been referred to as the "major burden," the "primary burden," the "legal burden" and the "persuasive burden." The burden of putting an issue in play has been called the "minor burden," the "secondary burden," the "evidential burden," the "burden of going forward," and the "burden of adducing evidence." While any combination of phrases has its advantages and drawbacks, I prefer to use the terms "persuasive burden" to refer to the requirement of proving a case or disproving defences, and "evidential burden" to mean the requirement of putting an issue into play by reference to evidence before the court. The party who has the persuasive burden is required to persuade the trier of fact, to convince the trier of fact that a certain set of facts existed. Failure to persuade means that the party loses. The party with an evidential burden is not required to convince the trier of fact of anything, only to point out evidence which suggests that certain facts existed. The phrase "onus of proof" should be restricted to the persuasive burden, since an issue can be put into play without being proven. The phrases "burden of going forward" and "burden of adducing evidence" should not be used, as they imply that the party is required to produce his or her own evidence

---

1 [1988] 2 S.C.R. 443, 466.

on an issue. As we have seen, in a criminal case the accused can rely on evidence produced by the Crown to argue for a reasonable doubt.

It is important not to identify the evidential burden solely with the accused. The Crown has the evidential burden of leading evidence which, if believed, would prove each element of the offence charged. If the Crown does not even meet this evidential requirement, the case never goes to the trier of fact; the accused has a right to a directed verdict of acquittal.

A leading case which illustrates the damage that can result from confusing the two burdens is *Woolmington v. Director of Public Prosecutions*.[2] The accused was convicted of murdering his bride. The accused admitted the shooting but testified that it was an accident. The trial judge charged the jury:

> If you come to the conclusion that she died in consequence of injuries from the gun which he was carrying, you are put by the law of this country into this position: The killing of a human being is homicide, however he may be killed, and all homicide is presumed to be malicious and murder, unless the contrary appears from circumstances of alleviation, excuse, or justification. "In every charge of murder, the fact of killing being first proved, all the circumstances of accident, necessity, or infirmity are to be satisfactorily proved by the prisoner, unless they arise out of the evidence produced against him; for the law will presume the fact to have been founded in malice, unless the contrary appeareth." That has been the law of this country for all time since we had law. Once it is shown to a jury that somebody has died through an act of another, that is presumed to be murder, unless the person who has been guilty of the act which causes the death can satisfy a jury that what happened was something less, something which might be alleviated, something which might be reduced to a charge of manslaughter, or was something which was accidental, or was something which could be justified.[3]

The Court of Appeal dismissed the accused's appeal as it recognized "ample authority for that statement of law."[4] The House of Lords traced the authority to Sir Michael Foster's text in 1762, written at a time when "the law of evidence was in a very fluid condition."[5] The Lords also noted that there had been many changes in procedure in the intervening two centuries, including the prisoner's right to give evidence, to counsel, to an appeal. Viscount Sankey explained the true meaning of earlier authorities:

> All that is meant is that if it is proved that the conscious act of the prisoner killed a man and nothing else appears in the case, there is evidence upon which the jury may, not must, find him guilty of murder. It is difficult to conceive so bare and meagre a case, but that does not mean that the onus is not still on the prosecution.
>
> . . . Just as there is evidence on behalf of the prosecution so there may be evidence on behalf of the prisoner which may cause a doubt as to his guilt. In either case, he is entitled to the benefit of the doubt. But while the prosecution must prove the guilt of the prisoner, there is no such burden laid on the prisoner to prove his innocence and it is sufficient for him to raise a doubt as to his guilt; he is not bound to satisfy the jury of his innocence.

---

2 [1935] A.C. 462 (H.L.). See also *R. v. Stoddart* (1909), 2 Cr. App. R. 217, 233 and 242 (C.C.A.).
3 *Ibid.*, at pp. 472-73.
4 *Ibid.*, at p. 473.
5 *Ibid.*, at p. 478.

... where intent is an ingredient of a crime there is no onus on the defendant to prove that the act alleged was accidental. Throughout the web of the English Criminal Law one golden thread is always to be seen, that it is the duty of the prosecution to prove the prisoner's guilt subject to what I have already said as to the defence of insanity and subject also to any statutory exception. If at the end of and on the whole of the case, there is a reasonable doubt, created by the evidence given by either the prosecution or the prisoner, as to whether the prisoner killed the deceased with a malicious intention, the prosecution has not made out the case and the prisoner is entitled to an acquittal. No matter what the charge or where the trial, the principle that the prosecution must prove the guilt of the prisoner is part of the common law of England and no attempt to whittle it down can be entertained. When dealing with a murder case the Crown must prove (a) death as the result of a voluntary act of the accused and (b) malice of the accused. It may prove malice either expressly or by implication. For malice may be implied where death occurs as the result of a voluntary act of the accused which is (i) intentional and (ii) unprovoked. When evidence of death and malice has been given (this is a question for the jury) the accused is entitled to show, by evidence or by examination of the circumstances adduced by the Crown that the act on his part which caused death was either unintentional or provoked. If the jury are either satisfied with his explanation or, upon a review of all the evidence, are left in reasonable doubt whether, even if his explanation be not accepted, the act was unintentional or provoked, the prisoner is entitled to be acquitted.[6]

(b) Allocation of Burdens

How do we decide the allocation of responsibility between the parties? Thayer believed we should have regard to the principles of pleading and in attending to these:

> We shall sometimes find ourselves involved in an analysis of the substantive law of the particular case and perhaps in an inquiry into things obsolete, anomolous and forgotten. . . .

> Clearly one has no right to look to the law of evidence for a solution of such questions as these, and I am not proposing to answer them.[7]

Later commentators on the law of evidence have attempted to distill from the cases some general principles, but the furthest they have been able to take us is to note that problems of allocation involve "considerations of policy, fairness and probability."[8]

(i) Civil Cases

In civil cases the burden is normally on the person who asserts, for example the plaintiff in a negligence suit, the defendant on a defence of contributory negligence.

---

6   *Ibid.*, at pp. 480-82.
7   Thayer, *A Preliminary Treatise on Evidence at the Common Law* (1898), p. 355.
8   Cleary, "Presuming and Pleading: An Essay on Juristic Immaturity" (1959), 12 Stan. L. Rev. 5 at 11. To the same effect, and using the same words, see James, "Burdens of Proof" (1961), 47 Va. L. Rev. 51 at 58-61; Morgan, *Some Problems of Proof Under the Anglo-American System of Litigation* (1956), p. 76; and 9 Wigmore, *Evidence* (Chad. Rev.), s. 2486, p. 291. Considerations of policy, fairness and probability can of course change: see, *e.g.*, *R. v. Jackson* (1984), 14 C.R.R. 248 (B.C. Co. Ct.), regarding the presumption that a husband is in possession and control of the premises and their contents.

FONTAINE v. INSURANCE CORPORATION
OF BRITISH COLUMBIA
[1998] 1 S.C.R. 424

The plaintiff claimed damages for negligence with respect to the death of her husband. His body and that of his hunting companion, which was still buckled in the driver's seat, were in the companion's badly damaged truck which had been washed along a flood-swollen creek flowing alongside a mountain highway. No one saw the accident and no one knew precisely when it occurred. A great deal of rain had fallen in the vicinity of the accident the weekend of their hunting trip. The trial judge found that negligence had not been proven against the driver and dismissed the plaintiff's case. An appeal to the Court of Appeal was dismissed.

MAJOR J. (for the court):—This appeal provides another opportunity to consider the so-called maxim of *res ipsa loquitur*. What is it? When does it arise? And what effect does its application have?

. . . .

A. *When does res ipsa loquitur apply?*

Res ipsa loquitur, or "the thing speaks for itself", has been referred to in negligence cases for more than a century. In *Scott v. London and St. Katherine Docks Co.* (1865), 159 E.R. 665 . . . at p. 667 . . ., Erle C.J. defined what has since become known as *res ipsa loquitur* in the following terms:

> There must be reasonable evidence of negligence.
>
> But where the thing is shewn to be under the management of the defendant or his servants, and the accident is such as in the ordinary course of things does not happen if those who have the management use proper care, it affords reasonable evidence, in the absence of explanation by the defendants, that the accident arose from want of care.

. . . .

For *res ipsa loquitur* to arise, the circumstances of the occurrence must permit an inference of negligence attributable to the defendant. The strength or weakness of that inference will depend on the factual circumstances of the case. As described in *Canadian Tort Law* (5th ed. 1993), by Allen M. Linden, at p. 233, "[t]here are situations where the facts merely whisper negligence, but there are other circumstances where they shout it aloud."

As the application of *res ipsa loquitur* is highly dependent upon the circumstances proved in evidence, it is not possible to identify in advance the types of situations in which *res ipsa loquitur* will arise. The application of *res ipsa loquitur* in previous decisions may provide some guidance as to when an inference of negligence may be drawn, but it does not serve to establish definitive categories of when *res ipsa loquitur* will apply. It has been held on numerous occasions that evidence of a vehicle leaving the roadway gives rise to an inference of negligence. Whether that will be so in any given case, however, can only be determined after considering the relevant circumstances of the particular case.

. . . .

B. *Effect of the application of res ipsa loquitur*

As in any negligence case, the plaintiff bears the burden of proving on a balance of probabilities that negligence on the part of the defendant caused the plaintiff's injuries. The invocation of *res ipsa loquitur* does not shift the burden of proof to the defendant. Rather, the effect of the application of *res ipsa loquitur* is as described in *The Law of Evidence in Canada* (1992), by John Sopinka, Sidney N. Lederman and Alan W. Bryant, at p. 81:

> *Res ipsa loquitur*, correctly understood, means that circumstantial evidence constitutes reasonable evidence of negligence. Accordingly, the plaintiff is able to overcome a motion for a non-suit and the trial judge is required to instruct the jury on the issue of negligence. The jury may, but need not, find negligence: a permissible fact inference. If, at the conclusion of the case, it would be equally reasonable to infer negligence or no negligence, the plaintiff will lose since he or she bears the legal burden on this issue. Under this construction, the maxim is superfluous. It can be treated simply as a case of circumstantial evidence.

Should the trier of fact choose to draw an inference of negligence from the circumstances, that will be a factor in the plaintiff's favour. Whether that will be sufficient for the plaintiff to succeed will depend on the strength of the inference drawn and any explanation offered by the defendant to negate that inference. If the defendant produces a reasonable explanation that is as consistent with no negligence as the *res ipsa loquitur* inference is with negligence, this will effectively neutralize the inference of negligence and the plaintiff's case must fail. Thus, the strength of the explanation that the defendant must provide will vary in accordance with the strength of the inference sought to be drawn by the plaintiff.

. . . .

Whatever value *res ipsa loquitur* may have once provided is gone. Various attempts to apply the so-called doctrine have been more confusing than helpful. Its use has been restricted to cases where the facts permitted an inference of negligence and there was no other reasonable explanation for the accident. Given its limited use it is somewhat meaningless to refer to that use as a doctrine of law.

It would appear that the law would be better served if the maxim was treated as expired and no longer used as a separate component in negligence actions. After all, it was nothing more than an attempt to deal with circumstantial evidence. That evidence is more sensibly dealt with by the trier of fact, who should weigh the circumstantial evidence with the direct evidence, if any, to determine whether the plaintiff has established on a balance of probabilities a *prima facie* case of negligence against the defendant. Once the plaintiff has done so, the defendant must present evidence negating that of the plaintiff or necessarily the plaintiff will succeed.

C. *Application to this case*

. . . .

There are a number of reasons why the circumstantial evidence in this case does not discharge the plaintiff's onus. Many of the circumstances of the accident, including the date, time and precise location, are not known. Although this case has proceeded on the basis that the accident likely occurred during the weekend of November 9, 1990, that is only an assumption. There are minimal if any evidentiary foundations from which any inference of negligence could be drawn.

As well, there was evidence before the trial judge that a severe wind and rainstorm was raging at the presumed time of the accident. While it is true that such weather conditions impose a higher standard of care on drivers to take increased precautions, human experience confirms that severe weather conditions are more likely to produce situations where accidents occur and vehicles leave the roadway regardless of the degree of care taken. In these circumstances, it should not be concluded that the accident would ordinarily not have occurred in the absence of negligence.

. . . The trial judge's finding was not unreasonable and should not be interfered with on appeal.

. . . .

The appellant submitted that an inference of negligence should be drawn whenever a vehicle leaves the roadway in a single-vehicle accident. This bald proposition ignores the fact that whether an inference of negligence can be drawn is highly dependent upon the circumstances of each case. . . . The position advanced by the appellant would virtually subject the defendant to strict liability in cases such as the present one.

PEART v. PEEL (REGIONAL MUNICIPALITY) POLICE SERVICES BOARD

(2006), 43 C.R. (6th) 175, 2006 CarswellOnt 6912 (C.A.), leave to appeal refused (2007), 2007 CarswellOnt 1882, 2007 CarswellOnt 1883 (S.C.C.)

The plaintiffs launched a racial profiling law suit against two members of the Peel Regional Police Service. The officers, one of whom was African Canadian, decided to conduct a computer check on the plaintiffs' Honda Prelude. The plaintiffs were African Canadian. The officers testified that computer checks were routine especially at night and that, in addition, this model of vehicle was known to be easily stolen and that car theft was a prevalent problem in the area. They maintained surveillance on the vehicle until they received the results of the computer check. The officers began to follow the vehicle after it had left a gas station as now P was driving in excess of the speed limit. P saw the officers behind him. They had now turned on their lights and siren. He did not stop until he reached his home. He testified that, based on prior experiences with the police, he was afraid for his life. Once he arrived home, he and G were subjected to a high-risk takedown, arrested and taken to the police station where they were strip-searched. Neither of the men were charged with any offence. The trial judge accepted that P had provided some information about a drug dealer he knew in exchange for not being charged with dangerous driving. The lawsuit was dismissed at trial. The plaintiffs appealed. The appeal was dismissed. One of the arguments raised was whether the onus of proof should be shifted to the police in racial profiling cases.

DOHERTY J.A. (GOUDGE and ROULEAU JJ.A. concurring): –

(e) Should the burden of proof be reversed?

The ACLC submits that where racial profiling is alleged against the police in a civil proceeding, the police should bear the onus of demonstrating on a balance of probabilities that improper racial considerations were not a contributing factor to the state action that resulted in the interference with the liberty of a black plaintiff. In short, the ACLC would place the burden of persuasion on the defendant/police.

I do not understand the appellants to have raised the allocation of the burden of proof on the issue of racial profiling as a separate ground of appeal. Presumably, they did not do so because, as in most civil cases, the outcome of this trial did not turn on which party bore the onus of proof. As observed in John Sopinka, Sidney N. Lederman & Allan W. Bryant, *The Law of Evidence in Canada*, 2d ed. (Toronto: Butterworths, 1999) at 58:

> *In civil proceedings, the legal burden does not play a part in the decision-making process if the trier of fact can come to a determinate conclusion on the evidence.* If, however, the evidence leaves the trier of fact in a state of uncertainty, the legal burden is applied to determine the outcome. [Emphasis added.]

This trial judge was not left in any state of uncertainty by the evidence. He made factual findings on all of the contentious issues and from those findings concluded that the officers were not motivated by racial considerations.

I will, however, address the merits of the submission made by the ACLC. In civil proceedings, the burden of persuasion in respect of a fact in issue is generally on the party alleging that fact. The appellants claim that they were the victims of racial profiling at the hands of the police and demand compensation. Applying the normal rule, the appellants must bear the burden of proving racial profiling on the balance of probabilities: *Snell v. Farrell*, [1990] 2 S.C.R. 311 at 320; Kenneth S. Broun *et al.*, *McCormick on Evidence*, 6th ed. (St. Paul, Minn.: Thomson, 2006) vol. II at 473.

In the criminal context, on motions brought by an accused pursuant to s. 24(1) of the *Charter*, this court has followed the general rule and placed the burden on the accused to establish racial profiling on the balance of probabilities: *R. v. Brown, supra*, at para. 45; *R. v. Curry* (2005), 206 C.C.C. (3d) 100 at para. 24 (Ont. C.A.). Placing the onus on the accused to establish racial profiling on a *Charter* motion is consistent with the well established pleading principle that the onus of establishing a *Charter* breach is on the accused where the accused seeks relief under s. 24(1) of the *Charter*: see *R. v. Cobham* (1994), 92 C.C.C. (3d) 333 at 340 (S.C.C.); *R. v. Collins* (1987), 33 C.C.C. (3d) 1 at 13-14 (S.C.C.).

The allocation of the legal burden of proof to the party alleging the fact in issue is not an immutable rule. For example, in some situations, the burden of persuasion will move to the Crown on a motion brought under s. 24(1) of the *Charter* if an accused establishes certain facts. This shifting of the legal burden occurs in cases where the accused alleges an unreasonable search or seizure. If the accused demonstrates that the search was not conducted pursuant to a prior judicial authorization, the burden of establishing the reasonableness of the search on the balance of probabilities moves to the Crown: *R. v. Collins, supra.*

The presumption that warrantless searches are unreasonable unless the Crown establishes that they are reasonable, is a reflection of the fundamental role that prior judicial authorizations have traditionally played in maintaining the delicate balance between state interests in the effective pursuit of criminal investigations and individual rights to personal privacy. At common law and by statute, state intrusion on personal privacy by way of searches or seizures has generally been acceptable only when sanctioned by a prior judicial authorization. Absence of that authorization renders a search or seizure presumptively unreasonable unless the Crown can demonstrate circumstances that overcome that presumption: *Hunter et al. v. Southam Inc.* (1984), 14 C.C.C. (3d) 97 at 109 (S.C.C.).

State interference with individual liberty whether by way of detention or arrest has never been seen as requiring prior judicial authorization. The varied and exigent circumstances in which the police must routinely resort to the use of their powers of detention or arrest defy any presumption that would require prior judicial authorization.

The ACLC does not submit that the onus should fall on the police to disprove racial profiling, because police detention without prior judicial authorization is presumptively unconstitutional. The ACLC makes a very different argument. It contends that the onus should fall on the police where the party who was subjected to detention or arrest is black. In effect, the ACLC submits that any arrest or detention of a black person by the police is as constitutionally suspect as a warrantless search and, therefore, merits the same rebuttable presumption of unconstitutionality.

This contention is based on the argument that racial profiling is so common that where it is alleged, placing the burden on the police to disprove racial profiling is more likely to achieve an accurate result than is leaving the onus on the party alleging racial profiling. As *McCormick*, supra, indicates at 475-76:

> Perhaps a more frequently significant consideration in the fixing of the burdens of proof is the judicial estimate of the probabilities of the situation. *The risk of failure of proof may be placed upon the party who contends that the more unusual event has occurred.* [Emphasis added.]

The reality of racial profiling cannot be denied. There is no way of knowing how common the practice is in any given community. I am not prepared to accept that racial profiling is the rule rather than the exception where the police detain black men. I do not mean to suggest that I am satisfied that it is indeed the exception, but only that I do not know.

In *R. v. Brown, supra*, at para. 45, this court rejected the argument, which was also advanced by the ACLC as intervenor, that the Crown should bear the onus of disproving racial profiling. The court held that a properly informed consideration of the relevant circumstantial evidence – indicators of racial profiling – combined with maintaining the traditional burden of proof on the party alleging racial profiling achieved a proper balancing of the respective interests of the parties. I see no reason to depart from the analysis in *R. v. Brown*. I would add that a sensitive appreciation of the relevant social context in which racial profiling claims must be assessed provides further protection against the failure of meritorious claims as a result of the allocation of the burden of proof.

The ACLC further submits that fairness considerations warrant placing the burden of disproving racial profiling on the police. The ACLC argues that the circumstances relevant to a racial profiling claim are better known to the police who also have better access to the information relevant to those claims. The ACLC submits that as the police are in a much better position to disprove racial profiling than the plaintiffs are to prove racial profiling, fairness dictates that the defendants should bear the legal burden.

Fairness may dictate a reversal of the usual legal burden of persuasion. It is not enough, however, for the party seeking to reverse the burden to demonstrate that the other party is in a better position to disprove the fact in issue. In many civil proceedings where the plaintiffs claim turns on the conduct or state of mind of the defendant, the defendant will be in a better position to prove or disprove the relevant facts. Fairness can justify a reversal of the legal burden in those relatively rare cases where the party who would normally bear the burden of proof has no reasonable prospect of being able to discharge that burden, and the opposing party is in a position to prove or disprove the relevant facts: see *Snell v. Farrell, supra*, at 326-30; *National Trust Co. v. Wong Aviation Ltd.*, [1969] S.C.R. 481 at 489-91.

A review of the caselaw demonstrates that racial profiling claims can and do succeed where the courts adhere to the traditional rule and place the onus of proof on the party alleging racial profiling: see e.g. *R. v. Peck*, [2001] O.J. No. 4581 (S.C.J.); *R. v. Kahn* (2004), 189 C.C.C. (3d) 49 (Ont. S.C.J.); *R. v. Campbell*, [2005] Q.J. No. 394 (Q. C.Q.); *R. v. Nguyen*, [2006] O.J. No. 272 (S.C.J.).

I would emphasize, however, that while the ultimate burden of persuasion remains on the appellants, in any given case there may well be a significant tactical burden on the defendant to introduce evidence negating the inference of racial profiling. In *Snell v. Farrell*, at 328-30, Sopinka J. described the tactical burden in the context of a causation issue in a medical malpractice case in these terms:

> *In many malpractice cases, the facts lie particularly within the knowledge of the defendant. In these circumstances, very little affirmative evidence on the part of the plaintiff will justify the drawing of an inference of causation in the absence of evidence to the contrary.*

. . .

> It is not strictly accurate to speak of the burden shifting to the defendant when what is meant is that evidence adduced by the plaintiff may result in an inference being drawn adverse to the defendant. Whether an inference is or is not drawn is a matter of weighing evidence. *The defendant runs the risk of an adverse inference in the absence of evidence to the contrary.* This is sometimes referred to as imposing on the defendant a provisional or tactical burden. . . . In my opinion, this is not a true burden of proof, and use of an additional label to describe what is an ordinary step in the fact-finding process is unwarranted. [Emphasis added.]

In support of its argument that the onus should fall on the respondents to disprove racial profiling, the ACLC also relies on the line of cases that recognize that a judge may take judicial notice that racism is widespread in the community and use that judicial notice to overcome the presumption that prospective jurors are impartial: see *R. v. Williams* (1998), 124 C.C.C. (3d) 481 (S.C.C.).

The jury selection cases are not helpful. The challenge for cause process involves two distinct steps. At the first step, the trial judge must decide whether to permit any inquiry into the partiality of a prospective juror. A perspective juror is presumed impartial unless the parties seeking to challenge for cause can demonstrate a reasonable possibility of partiality. The Supreme Court in *R. v. Williams, supra*, at para. 32, held that in assessing whether a reasonable possibility of partiality is established, the trial judge should take a generous approach so as to avoid unduly restricting access to challenges for cause: *R. v. Williams* goes on to hold that this generous approach can include taking judicial notice of widespread racism within the community. It must be stressed, however, that at this first stage, a trial judge is not asked to make any findings of bias or partiality. The trial judge is deciding only whether the circumstances warrant an inquiry into partiality.

At the second stage of the challenge for cause process, reached only if the judge decides there is a reasonable possibility of partiality, the triers of the challenge for cause must decide whether the juror is acceptable or not acceptable. They make this decision based on the evidence adduced before them. Usually that evidence consists of the prospective juror's answers to certain agreed upon questions. At this second stage, where the prospective juror's partiality is decided, there is no presumption of impartiality based on the existence of widespread racial bias in the community: see *R. v. Hubbert* (1975), 29 C.C.C. (2d) 279 at 294 (Ont. C.A.), aff'd (1977), 33 C.C.C. (2d) 207 (S.C.C.); *R. v. Li* (2004), 183 C.C.C. (3d) 48 at paras. 26-28 (Ont. C.A.).

In a civil proceeding where an allegation of racial profiling is made, there is no inquiry analogous to the first stage of the challenge for cause inquiry. The party alleging racial profiling in a civil action does not have to demonstrate a reasonable possibility of bias before proceeding to the merits of a bias allegation. In my view, it is one thing to take judicial notice of racism in the community to justify an inquiry into whether a particular individual is biased on account of race, and quite another to use judicial notice to presume that an individual is racially biased unless he or she proves otherwise.

Do you think that Justice Doherty's reasoning is persuasive given the challenges posed when trying to prove systemic issues like unconscious racism?[9]

(ii) *Criminal Cases*

In the criminal law the presumption of innocence normally allocates the persuasive burden of proof to the Crown.

Since 1960, section 2(*f*) of the Canadian Bill of Rights has guaranteed that a person charged with an offence will be "presumed innocent until proved guilty according to law in a fair and public hearing by an independent and impartial tribunal". An identical guarantee is contained in section 11(*d*) of the Charter of Rights and Freedoms. The latter clearly operates irrespective of statutory wording to both federal and provincial legislation. It has long been clear that the *Woolmington* rule applies also to provincial offences.

What values underlie this presumption? The presumption of innocence characterizes most civilized systems of criminal law and is the cornerstone of ours. In the leading interpretation of section 11(*d*), Chief Justice Dickson, for the Supreme Court of Canada in *Oakes*,[10] sees the presumption of innocence as embodying cardinal values lying at the very heart of criminal law which are protected expressly by section 11(*d*) but are also integral to the general protection of life, liberty and security of the person in section 7:

> The presumption of innocence protects the fundamental liberty and human dignity of any and every person accused by the state of criminal conduct. An individual charged with a criminal offence faces grave social and personal consequences, including potential loss of physical liberty, subjection to social stigma and ostracism from the community, as well as other social, psychological and economic harms. In light of the gravity of these consequences, the presumption of innocence is crucial. It ensures that, until the state proves an accused's guilt beyond all reasonable doubt, he or she is innocent. This is essential in a society committed to fairness and social justice. The presumption of innocence confirms our faith in humankind; it reflects our belief that individuals are decent and law-abiding members of the community until proven otherwise.

Our complex and expensive system of police and prosecutors gives the state a powerful advantage against an accused. If we did not presume innocence, an elementary sense of fairness would require us to radically revise our system and give the accused an equivalent fact-finding capability. Before tampering with the presumption of innocence, the whole pattern of present evidential rules would have to be changed. The rules are interrelated. A trial is not just a relentless search for truth. We risk setting some of the guilty free for fear of convicting the innocent. Our universally high conviction rates indicate minimal risk.

Some view the presumption of innocence as legalistic nonsense. Common sense indicates a *de facto* presumption of guilt since the police usually get the

---

9 For an argument that there should be a reverse onus, see Tanovich, *The Colour of Justice: Policing Race in Canada* (Toronto: Irwin Law, 2006) at 144-47.

10 (1986), 50 C.R. (3d) 1, 15 (S.C.C.).

right person. The presumption is unnatural. Our police must have reasonable grounds for their belief in guilt, yet the presumption of innocence requires fact-finders to ignore this and deduce nothing from the workings of the system which brought the accused to court. Brett offers a blunt and persuasive reply:

> Common sense has apparently overlooked that if the police do in fact bring only the guilty to the bar of justice, it may well be because they know that they will have to adduce proof beyond reasonable doubt. Whether they would continue to be so careful if the accused men had to prove their innocence is open to doubt. Moreover, common sense, in assuming that those found guilty are in fact guilty, overlooks the realities of plea bargaining, the cost of defending oneself, the imperfections of the trial process, and so on.[11]

Moreover, common sense is often wrong. Indeed, we are now learning that tunnel vision, a phenomenon whereby the police focus on one suspect and filter all information, including exculpatory evidence, through a lens of guilt is one of the leading causes of wrongful convictions.[12]

Expediency

Even in criminal cases, the allocation of burdens is impacted by matters of expediency. The insanity or mental disorder defence, as it is now known, is one such example. It is true that the judges in *M'Naghten's Case*[13] advised that every person shall be presumed sane until the contrary is proved, and the legislature has followed that lead.[14] Is there anything gained from the imposition of a persuasive burden on the accused that couldn't be equally gained by the lesser evidential burden? According to *Woolmington,* the accused in a murder case is entitled to an acquittal when the trier of fact has a reasonable doubt regarding his intent. Is it not inconsistent or illogical to foreclose an acquittal when the trier has a reasonable doubt regarding the accused's capacity to form the necessary intent and to demand that the trier be satisfied that the accused was incapable? Harlan, J., in *Davis v. U.S.,*[15] rejected the idea that the presumption of sanity must be negatived by a preponderance of evidence in favour of a rule that the presumption simply called for evidence to be introduced to place the matter in issue:

> Upon whom then must rest the burden of proving that the accused, whose life it is sought to take under the forms of law, belongs to a class capable of committing crime? On principle, it must rest upon those who affirm that he has committed the crime for which he is indicted. That burden is not fully discharged, nor is there any legal right to take the life of the accused, until guilt is made to appear from all the

---

11 Brett, "Strict Responsibility: Possible Solutions" (1974), 37 Mod. L. Rev. 417.

12 See also, Susan Bandes, "Loyalty to One's Convictions: The Prosecutor and Tunnel Vision," (2006) 49 Howard L.J. 475. See, for example, the discussion in "The Lamer Commission of Inquiry Pertaining to the Cases of: Ronald Dalton, Gregory Parsons, Randy Druken" (2005).

13 (1843), 8 E.R. 718 (H.L.).

14 Criminal Code, R.S.C. 1985, c. C-46, s. 16.

15 160 U.S. 469, 485-88 (1895). In *Leland v. Oregon,* 343 U.S. 790 (1952), the Supreme Court upheld *state* legislation which imposed a persuasive burden on the accused on the issue of insanity as not violative of due process and noted that the *Davis* case had announced a rule respecting federal cases as opposed to constitutional doctrine. And see Bridge, "Presumptions and Burdens" (1949), 12 Mod. L. Rev. 273, 286-88.

evidence in the case. The plea of not guilty is unlike a special plea in a civil action, which, admitting the case averred, seeks to establish a substantive ground of defense by a preponderance of evidence. It is not in confession and avoidance, for it is a plea that controverts the existence of every fact essential to constitute the crime charged. Upon that plea the accused may stand, shielded by the presumption of his innocence, until it appears that he is guilty; and his guilt cannot in the very nature of things be regarded as proved, if the jury entertain a reasonable doubt from all the evidence whether he was legally capable of committing crime.

In *R. v. Chaulk*[16] it was argued that the presumption of sanity contained in section 16(4) of the Criminal Code, placing the onus of proving the defence of insanity on the accused, was an unconstitutional violation of the presumption of innocence in section 11(*d*). Chief Justice Lamer, writing for himself and four other judges, held that there had been a violation of section 11(*d*) but it could be justified under section 1. The objective of the presumption was to "avoid placing an impossible burden of proof on the Crown." Citing recent judgments of the court indicating that Parliament was not required to adopt the absolutely least intrusive means, Chief Justice Lamer saw the issue as "whether a less intrusive means would achieve the same objective or would achieve the same objective as effectively." The Chief Justice concluded that the alternative of an evidentiary burden requiring that the accused merely raise a reasonable doubt would not be as effective, accepting arguments by Attorneys General that it would be very easy for accused persons to "fake" such a defence.

The sole dissent on this point in *Chaulk* was Madam Justice Wilson, who held that this was not a case for relaxing the minimum impairment test. This might be done where a legislature, mediating between competing groups of citizens or allocating scarce resources, had to compromise on the basis of conflicting evidence. But in *Chaulk* the state was acting as "singular antagonists" of a very basic legal right of an accused and the strict standard of review in *Oakes* should be applied. The government's objective could be quite readily met by a mere burden on the accused to adduce evidence that made insanity "a live issue fit and proper to be left to the jury." Madam Justice Wilson noted the experience in the United States where an evidential burden was the order of the day, and believed the case for the imposition of a persuasive burden had not been made out.

Facts Peculiarly Within Knowledge of Accused

There is a dangerously attractive "doctrine" which is frequently invoked[17] to cast a burden of persuasion on the defendant in a criminal case. Its root is commonly accepted as residing in the judgment of Lord Ellenborough in *R. v. Turner*.[18] The accused in that case was convicted of having game in his possession. The accused argued that the game laws provided a number of exceptions and qualifications and that to support a conviction there must be

---

16 (1990), 2 C.R. (4th) 1 (S.C.C.).

17 See, *e.g.*, Goddard L.J. in *Hill v. Baxter*, [1958] 1 Q.B. 277, 282; and Grove J. in *Abrath v. N.E. Ry. Co.* (1883), 11 Q.B. 79, 82 (C.A.). See also Laidlaw J.A. in *R. v. Roher* (1947), 89 C.C.C. 365 (Ont. C.A.).

18 (1816), 105 E.R. 1026.

evidence led to negative each of the same. The conviction was affirmed and Lord Ellenborough wrote:

> There are, I think, about ten different heads of qualification enumerated in the statute to which the proof may be applied. . . . The (accused's) argument really comes to this, that there would be a moral impossibility of ever convicting upon such an information. . . . Does not, then, common sense shew, that the burden of proof ought to be cast on the person, who, by establishing any one of the qualifications, will be well defended? . . . The proof of (the qualification) is easy on the one side, but almost impossible on the other.[19]

Bayley J. agreed:

> I have always understood it to be a general rule, that if a negative averment be made by one party, which is peculiarly within the knowledge of the other, the party within whose knowledge it lies, and who asserts the affirmative is to prove it, and not he who avers the negative.[20]

In the context of that case there is much to be said for the doctrine. If in present day Ontario a defendant is prosecuted for fishing or hunting without a licence and it is seen that there are 500 persons authorized to issue licences throughout the province, it is relatively simple for the defendant to prove his licence and virtually impossible for the prosecution to negative. But, as MacFarlane, J. said:

> It is obvious that an unrestricted application of the principle would relieve the Crown from the burden of proof that rests on it always of making out a *prima facie* case against the accused and would make the presumption of innocence a mockery.[21]

Reported decisions have invoked the doctrine to place the persuasive burden on the accused to prove that the accused was not driving carelessly,[22] took due diligence in the case of regulatory offences[23] or was relying on an officially induced error of law.[24]

The notion that an accused must prove matters peculiarly within his knowledge was part of the justification provided by Bastarache J. for a 5:4 majority in *Stone*[25] for requiring the accused to prove a defence of sane automatism on a balance of probabilities. The majority also asserted a so-called presumption of voluntariness.[26]

---

19 *Ibid.*, p. 1028.

20 *Ibid.*

21 In *R. v. Billett* (1952), 105 C.C.C. 169 (B.C.S.C.). For further recognition that the proof of a license may have to be reversed see *R. v. Lee's Poultery Ltd.* (1985), 43 C.R. (3d) 289 (Ont. C.A.), which was approved in *R. v. Schwartz* (1988), 45 C.C.C. (3d) 97 (S.C.C.).

22 *R. v. McIver*, [1965] 2 O.R. 475 (C.A.), affirmed (1966), 48 C.R. 4 (S.C.C.).

23 *R. v. Sault Ste. Marie (City)*, [1978] 2 S.C.R. 1299 and *R. v. Wholesale Travel Group Inc.*, [1991] 3 S.C.R. 154.

24 *Lévis (Ville) c. Tétreault*, 207 C.C.C. (3d) 1, 36 C.R. (6th) 215, [2006] 1 S.C.R. 420, 2006 CarswellQue 2911.

25 (1999), 24 C.R. (5th) 1 (S.C.C.).

26 For criticism see Delisle, "*Stone*: Judicial Activism Gone Awry to Presume Guilt" (1999), 24 C.R. (5th) 91; Editorial in (1999), 4 Can. Crim. L. Rev. 119; and Healy, "Automatism Confined" (2000), 45 McGill L.J. 87.

(c) Measure of Burden of Persuasion

(i) *Balance of Probabilities Standard for Civil Cases*

It is commonly said that the burden of persuasion in civil cases requires for satisfaction "a preponderance of evidence," or "proof on the balance of probability." Lord Denning expressed it:

> That degree is well settled. It must carry a reasonable degree of probability, but not so high as is required in a criminal case. If the evidence is such that the tribunal can say: "We think it more probable than not," the burden is discharged, but, if the probabilities are equal, it is not.[27]

It is common then to contrast the civil standard with the criminal standard which requires the trier to be "satisfied beyond a reasonable doubt." This higher standard, according to Phipson,

> . . . dates from the end of the eighteenth century, [and] was due to the reaction then setting in, against the rigours of the penal code, and was originally applied *in favorem vitae* to capital cases only.[28]

F.H. v. MCDOUGGAL

2008 CarswellBC 2041, 2008 CarswellBC 2042, [2008] 3 S.C.R. 41, 61 C.R. (6th) 1

The plaintiff was a resident of an Indian Residential School for some years. The School was operated by a religious organization (of which M was a member) and funded by the federal government. M was the junior and intermediate boys' supervisor during part of the time that H was a resident of the School. Years later, H brought a civil suit alleging that M had sexually assaulted him on four occasions in a washroom when children were brought one by one into the washroom to be inspected for cleanliness.

At trial, the trial judge found that H was a credible witness in spite of certain inconsistencies in his testimony. She held that M had anally raped H on four occasions and physically assaulted him on other occasions, and gave judgment for the plaintiff. The respondents appealed to the British Columbia Court of Appeal, which by a majority partially allowed the appeal and overturned the judgment in respect of the sexual assaults. According to the Court of Appeal, the trial judge had failed to consider serious inconsistencies in H's testimony, that closer scrutiny of the evidence was required in cases where moral blameworthiness was alleged, and that the standard of proof was required to be commensurate with the allegations. H appealed to the Supreme Court of Canada.

---

27 *Miller v. Min. of Pensions*, [1947] 2 All E.R. 372, 374 (K.B.). See also Duff J. in *Clark v. R.* (1921), 61 S.C.R. 608, 616: ". . . such a preponderance of evidence as to shew that the conclusion he seeks to establish is substantially the most probable of the possible views of the facts."

28 Phipson, *Evidence*, 9th ed. (1952), p. 8. Wigmore seems to agree: 9 Wigmore, *Evidence* (Chad. Rev.), s. 2497, p. 405. Compare, however, Thayer, *supra*, note 7, at p. 558 suggesting the rule is an ancient one traceable to the *Corpus Juris* of the fourth century.

ROTHSTEIN J.:

. . . .

III. Analysis

A. The Standard of Proof

(1) *Canadian Jurisprudence*

[26] Much has been written as judges have attempted to reconcile the tension between the civil standard of proof on a balance of probabilities and cases in which allegations made against a defendant are particularly grave. Such cases include allegations of fraud, professional misconduct, and criminal conduct, particularly sexual assault against minors. As explained by L. R. Rothstein, R. A. Centa, and E. Adams, in "Balancing Probabilities: The Overlooked Complexity of the Civil Standard of Proof" in *Special Lectures of the Law Society of Upper Canada 2003: The Law of Evidence* (2003) 455, at p. 456:

> . . . These types of allegations are considered unique because they carry a moral stigma that will continue to have an impact on the individual after the completion of the civil case.

[27] Courts in British Columbia have tended to follow the approach of Lord Denning in *Bater v. Bater*, [1950] 2 All E.R. 458 (C.A.). Lord Denning was of the view that within the civil standard of proof on a balance of probabilities "there may be degrees of probability within that standard" (p. 459), depending upon the subject matter. He stated at p. 459:

> It does not adopt so high a degree as a criminal court, even when it is considering a charge of a criminal nature, but still it does require a degree of probability which is commensurate with the occasion.

[28] In the present case the trial judge referred to *H.F. v. Canada (Attorney General)*, at para. 154, in which Neilson J. stated:

> The court is justified in imposing a higher degree of probability which is "commensurate with the occasion" . . . .

[29] In the constitutional context, Dickson C.J. adopted the *Bater* approach in *R. v. Oakes*, [1986] 1 S.C.R. 103. In his view a "very high degree of probability" required that the evidence be cogent and persuasive and make clear the consequences of the decision one way or the other. He wrote at p. 138:

> Having regard to the fact that s. 1 is being invoked for the purpose of justifying a violation of the constitutional rights and freedoms the *Charter* was designed to protect, a very high degree of probability will be, in the words of Lord Denning, "commensurate with the occasion". Where evidence is required in order to prove the constituent elements of a s. 1 inquiry and this will generally be the case, it should be cogent and persuasive and make clear to the Court the consequences of imposing or not imposing the limit.

[30] However, a "shifting standard" of probability has not been universally accepted. In *Continental Insurance Co. v. Dalton Cartage Co.*, [1982] 1 S.C.R.

164, Laskin C.J. rejected a "shifting standard". Rather, to take account of the seriousness of the allegation, he was of the view that a trial judge should scrutinize the evidence with "greater care". . . .

[31] In Ontario Professional Discipline cases, the balance of probabilities requires that proof be "clear and convincing and based upon cogent evidence" (see *Heath v. College of Physicians & Surgeons (Ontario)* (1997), 6 Admin. L.R. (3d) 304 (Ont. Ct. (Gen. Div.), at para. 53).

(2) *Recent United Kingdom Jurisprudence*

[32] In the United Kingdom some decisions have indicated that depending upon the seriousness of the matters involved, even in civil cases, the criminal standard of proof should apply. In *R (McCann) v. Crown Court at Manchester*, [2003] 1 A.C. 787, [2002] UKHL 39, Lord Steyn said at para. 37:

> . . . I agree that, given the seriousness of matters involved, at least some reference to the heightened civil standard would usually be necessary: In *re H (Minors) (Sexual Abuse: Standard of Proof)*, [1996] AC 563, 586 D H, per Lord Nicholls of Birkenhead. For essentially practical reasons, the Recorder of Manchester decided to apply the criminal standard. The Court of Appeal said that would usually be the right course to adopt. Lord Bingham of Cornhill has observed that the heightened civil standard and the criminal standard are virtually indistinguishable. I do not disagree with any of these views. But in my view pragmatism dictates that the task of magistrates should be made more straightforward by ruling that they must in all cases under section 1 apply the criminal standard.

[33] Yet another consideration, that of "inherent probability or improbability of an event" was discussed by Lord Nicholls in *In re H (Minors) (Sexual Abuse: Standard of Proof)*, [1996] A.C. 563 (H.L.), at p. 586:

> . . . the inherent probability or improbability of an event is itself a matter to be taken into account when weighing the probabilities and deciding whether, on balance, the event occurred. The more improbable the event, the stronger must be the evidence that it did occur before, on the balance of probability, its occurrence will be established.

[34] Most recently in *In re B (Children)*, [2008] 3 W.L.R. 1, [2008] UKHL 35, a June 11, 2008 decision, the U.K. House of Lords again canvassed the issue of standard of proof. Subsequent to the hearing of the appeal, Mr. Southey, counsel for the Attorney General of Canada, with no objection from other counsel, brought this case to the attention of the Court.

[35] Lord Hoffmann addressed the "confusion" in the United Kingdom courts over this issue. He stated at para. 5:

> Some confusion has however been caused by dicta which suggest that the standard of proof may vary with the gravity of the misconduct alleged or even the seriousness of the consequences for the person concerned. The cases in which such statements have been made fall into three categories. First, there are cases in which the court has for one purpose classified the proceedings as civil (for example, for the purposes of article 6 of the European Convention for the Protection of Human Rights and

Fundamental Freedoms) but nevertheless thought that, because of the serious consequences of the proceedings, the criminal standard of proof or something like it should be applied. Secondly, there are cases in which it has been observed that when some event is inherently improbable, strong evidence may be needed to persuade a tribunal that it more probably happened than not. Thirdly, there are cases in which judges are simply confused about whether they are talking about the standard of proof or about the role of inherent probabilities in deciding whether the burden of proving a fact to a given standard has been discharged.

[36] The unanimous conclusion of the House of Lords was that there is only one civil standard of proof. At para. 13, Lord Hoffmann states:

> . . . I think that the time has come to say, once and for all, that there is only one civil standard of proof and that is proof that the fact in issue more probably occurred than not.

However, Lord Hoffmann did not disapprove of application of the criminal standard depending upon the issue involved. Following his very clear statement that there is only one civil standard of proof, he somewhat enigmatically wrote, still in para. 13:

> . . . I do not intend to disapprove any of the cases in what I have called the first category, but I agree with the observation of Lord Steyn in *McCann's* case, at p. 812, that clarity would be greatly enhanced if the courts said simply that although the proceedings were civil, the nature of the particular issue involved made it appropriate to apply the criminal standard.

[37] Lord Hoffmann went on to express the view that taking account of inherent probabilities was not a rule of law. At para. 15 he stated:

> I wish to lay some stress upon the words I have italicised ["to whatever extent is appropriate in the particular case"]. Lord Nicholls [In re H] was not laying down any rule of law. There is only one rule of law, namely that the occurrence of the fact in issue must be proved to have been more probable than not. Common sense, not law, requires that in deciding this question, regard should be had, to whatever extent appropriate, to inherent probabilities.

[38] In *re B* is a child case under the *United Kingdom Children Act 1989*. While her comments on standard of proof are confined to the 1989 Act, Baroness Hale explained that neither the seriousness of the allegation nor the seriousness of the consequences should make any difference to the standard of proof to be applied in determining the facts. At paras. 70-72, she stated:

> My Lords, for that reason I would go further and announce loud and clear that the standard of proof in finding the facts necessary to establish the threshold under section 31(2) or the welfare considerations in section 1 of the 1989 Act is the simple balance of probabilities, neither more nor less. Neither the seriousness of the allegation nor the seriousness of the consequences should make any difference to the standard of proof to be applied in determining the facts. The inherent probabilities are simply something to be taken into account, where relevant, in deciding where the truth lies.
>
> As to the seriousness of the consequences, they are serious either way. A child may find her relationship with her family seriously disrupted; or she may find herself

still at risk of suffering serious harm. A parent may find his relationship with his child seriously disrupted; or he may find himself still at liberty to maltreat this or other children in the future.

As to the seriousness of the allegation, there is no logical or necessary connection between seriousness and probability. Some seriously harmful behaviour, such as murder, is sufficiently rare to be inherently improbable in most circumstances. Even then there are circumstances, such as a body with its throat cut and no weapon to hand, where it is not at all improbable. Other seriously harmful behaviour, such as alcohol or drug abuse, is regrettably all too common and not at all improbable.

(3) *Summary of Various Approaches*

[39] I summarize the various approaches in civil cases where criminal or morally blameworthy conduct is alleged as I understand them:

(1) The criminal standard of proof applies in civil cases depending upon the seriousness of the allegation;

(2) An intermediate standard of proof between the civil standard and the criminal standard commensurate with the occasion applies to civil cases;

(3) No heightened standard of proof applies in civil cases, but the evidence must be scrutinized with greater care where the allegation is serious;

(4) No heightened standard of proof applies in civil cases, but evidence must be clear, convincing and cogent; and

(5) No heightened standard of proof applies in civil cases, but the more improbable the event, the stronger the evidence is needed to meet the balance of probabilities test.

(4) *The Approach Canadian Courts Should Now Adopt*

[40] Like the House of Lords, I think it is time to say, once and for all in Canada, that there is only one civil standard of proof at common law and that is proof on a balance of probabilities. Of course, context is all important and a judge should not be unmindful, where appropriate, of inherent probabilities or improbabilities or the seriousness of the allegations or consequences. However, these considerations do not change the standard of proof. I am of the respectful opinion that the alternatives I have listed above should be rejected for the reasons that follow.

[41] Since *Hanes v. Wawanesa Mutual Insurance Co.*, [1963] S.C.R. 154, at pp. 158-64, it has been clear that the criminal standard is not to be applied to civil cases in Canada. The criminal standard of proof beyond a reasonable doubt is linked to the presumption of innocence in criminal trials.

[42] By contrast, in civil cases, there is no presumption of innocence. As explained by J. Sopinka, S. N. Lederman and A. W. Bryant, *The Law of Evidence* (2nd ed. 1999), at p. 154:

... Since society is indifferent to whether the plaintiff or the defendant wins a particular civil suit, it is unnecessary to protect against an erroneous result by requiring a standard of proof higher than a balance of probabilities.

It is true that there may be serious consequences to a finding of liability in a civil case that continue past the end of the case. However, the civil case does not involve the government's power to penalize or take away the liberty of the individual.

[43] An intermediate standard of proof presents practical problems. As expressed by L. Rothstein et al., at p. 466:

> As well, suggesting that the standard of proof is "higher" than the "mere balance of probabilities" leads one inevitably to inquire what percentage of probability must be met? This is unhelpful because while the concept of "51% probability", or "more likely than not" can be understood by decision-makers, the concept of 60% or 70% probability cannot.

[44] Put another way, it would seem incongruous for a judge to conclude that it was more likely than not that an event occurred, but not sufficiently likely to some unspecified standard and therefore that it did not occur. As Lord Hoffmann explained in *In re B* at para. 2:

> If a legal rule requires a fact to be proved (a "fact in issue"), a judge or jury must decide whether or not it happened. There is no room for a finding that it might have happened. The law operates a binary system in which the only values are zero and one. The fact either happened or it did not. If the tribunal is left in doubt, the doubt is resolved by a rule that one party or the other carries the burden of proof.

> If the party who bears the burden of proof fails to discharge it, a value of zero is returned and the fact is treated as not having happened. If he does discharge it, a value of one is returned and the fact is treated as having happened.

In my view, the only practical way in which to reach a factual conclusion in a civil case is to decide whether it is more likely than not that the event occurred.

[45] To suggest that depending upon the seriousness, the evidence in the civil case must be scrutinized with greater care implies that in less serious cases the evidence need not be scrutinized with such care. I think it is inappropriate to say that there are legally recognized different levels of scrutiny of the evidence depending upon the seriousness of the case. There is only one legal rule and that is that in all cases, evidence must be scrutinized with care by the trial judge.

[46] Similarly, evidence must always be sufficiently clear, convincing and cogent to satisfy the balance of probabilities test. But again, there is no objective standard to measure sufficiency. In serious cases, like the present, judges may be faced with evidence of events that are alleged to have occurred many years before, where there is little other evidence than that of the plaintiff and defendant. As difficult as the task may be, the judge must make a decision. If a responsible judge finds for the plaintiff, it must be accepted that the evidence was sufficiently clear, convincing and cogent to that judge that the plaintiff satisfied the balance of probabilities test.

[47] Finally there may be cases in which there is an inherent improbability that an event occurred. Inherent improbability will always depend upon the circumstances. As Baroness Hale stated in *In re B* at para. 72:

... Consider the famous example of the animal seen in Regent's Park. If it is seen outside the zoo on a stretch of greensward regularly used for walking dogs, then of course it is more likely to be a dog than a lion. If it is seen in the zoo next to the lions' enclosure when the door is open, then it may well be more likely to be a lion than a dog.

[48] Some alleged events may be highly improbable. Others less so. There can be no rule as to when and to what extent inherent improbability must be taken into account by a trial judge. As Lord Hoffmann observed at para. 15 of In re B:

> ... Common sense, not law, requires that in deciding this question, regard should be had, to whatever extent appropriate, to inherent probabilities.

It will be for the trial judge to decide to what extent, if any, the circumstances suggest that an allegation is inherently improbable and where appropriate, that may be taken into account in the assessment of whether the evidence establishes that it is more likely than not that the event occurred. However, there can be no rule of law imposing such a formula.

(5) *Conclusion on Standard of Proof*

[49] In the result, I would reaffirm that in civil cases there is only one standard of proof and that is proof on a balance of probabilities. In all civil cases, the trial judge must scrutinize the relevant evidence with care to determine whether it is more likely than not that an alleged event occurred.

Appeal allowed; conviction of sexual assault restored.

The Supreme Court achieves welcome clarity in holding that in all civil cases there is only the one standard of proof on a balance of probabilities and that in any case the trial judge must scrutinize the relevant evidence with care to determine whether it is more likely than not that an alleged event occurred [para. 40]. The level of scrutiny does not, it is held, depend on the seriousness of the case [para. 45]. The Court does say, borrowing an approach developed in professional malpractice cases, that in all civil cases evidence must be sufficiently clear, convincing and cogent to satisfy the balance of probabilities test [para. 46]. This is the new standard which all judges from now on will be presumed to know. **Does this in fact raise the standard of proof for all civil cases?**

The Court squarely rejects the often-quoted approach of Lord Denning in *Bater v. Bater*, [1950] 2 All E.R. 458 (C.A.) that in civil cases the burden of proof must be "commensurate with the occasion" and within the standard of proof on a balance of probabilities "there may be degrees of probability within that standard depending on the subject matter". The Supreme Court does note that the Denning view was applied by Justice Dickson in *Oakes* to require a high degree of probability to demonstrably justify a Charter breach under s. 1. That particular standard has not been overruled. It was confusing for Lord Denning to use a shifting standard of proof depending on the case. However, was Lord Denning not just being realistic rather than wrongheaded in suggesting that in both civil and criminal cases the degree of proof required is necessarily commensurate with the occasion? **Will jurors not require, as a practical matter, more proof to prove murder than cases of minor assault or shoplifting?**

(ii) *Reasonable Doubt Standard for Criminal Cases*

What does reasonable doubt mean? Should judges define it for juries?

R. v. LIFCHUS

[1997] 3 S.C.R. 320, 9 C.R. (5th) 1, 118 C.C.C. (3d) 1

The accused was charged with fraud. The trial judge told the jury in her charge on the burden of proof that she used the words " 'proof beyond a reasonable doubt' . . . in their ordinary, natural everyday sense", and that the words "doubt" and "reasonable" are "ordinary, everyday words that . . . you understand." The accused was convicted of fraud. On appeal, he contended that the trial judge had erred in instructing the jury on the meaning of the expression "proof beyond a reasonable doubt." The Court of Appeal allowed the appeal and ordered a new trial. The Supreme Court dismissed the Crown's appeal.

CORY J. (LAMER C.J.C., and SOPINKA, MCLACHLIN, IACOBUCCI and MAJOR JJ. concurring):—

. . . .

The phrase "beyond a reasonable doubt", is composed of words which are commonly used in everyday speech. Yet, these words have a specific meaning in the legal context. This special meaning of the words "reasonable doubt" may not correspond precisely to the meaning ordinarily attributed to them. In criminal proceedings, where the liberty of the subject is at stake, it is of fundamental importance that jurors fully understand the nature of the burden of proof that the law requires them to apply. An explanation of the meaning of proof beyond a reasonable doubt is an essential element of the instructions that must be given to a jury. That a definition is necessary can be readily deduced from the frequency with which juries ask for guidance with regard to its meaning. It is therefore essential that the trial judge provide the jury with an explanation of the expression.

. . . .

Perhaps a brief summary of what the definition should and should not contain may be helpful. It should be explained that:

> the standard of proof beyond a reasonable doubt is inextricably intertwined with that principle fundamental to all criminal trials, the presumption of innocence;
>
> the burden of proof rests on the prosecution throughout the trial and never shifts to the accused;
>
> a reasonable doubt is not a doubt based upon sympathy or prejudice;
>
> rather, it is based upon reason and common sense;
>
> it is logically connected to the evidence or absence of evidence;

it does not involve proof to an absolute certainty; it is not proof beyond any doubt nor is it an imaginary or frivolous doubt; and

more is required than proof that the accused is probably guilty, a jury which concludes only that the accused is probably guilty must acquit.

On the other hand, certain references to the required standard of proof should be avoided. For example:

describing the term "reasonable doubt" as an ordinary expression which has no special meaning in the criminal law context;

inviting jurors to apply to the task before them the same standard of proof that they apply to important, or even the most important, decisions in their own lives;[29]

equating proof "beyond a reasonable doubt" to proof "to a moral certainty";

qualifying the word "doubt" with adjectives other than "reasonable", such as "serious", substantial" or "haunting", which may mislead the jury; and

instructing jurors that they may convict if they are "sure" that the accused is guilty, before providing them with a proper definition as to the meaning of the words "beyond a reasonable doubt".

A charge which is consistent with the principles set out in these reasons will suffice regardless of the particular words used by the trial judge. Nevertheless, it may be useful to set out a "model charge" which could provide the necessary instructions as to the meaning of the phrase beyond a reasonable doubt.

Suggested Charge

Instructions pertaining to the requisite standard of proof in a criminal trial of proof beyond a reasonable doubt might be given along these lines:

The accused enters these proceedings presumed to be innocent. That presumption of innocence remains throughout the case until such time as the Crown has on the evidence put before you satisfied you beyond a reasonable doubt that the accused is guilty.

What does the expression "beyond a reasonable doubt" mean? The term "beyond a reasonable doubt" has been used for a very long time and is a part of our history and traditions of justice. It is so engrained in our criminal law that some think it needs no explanation, yet something must be said regarding its meaning.

A reasonable doubt is not an imaginary or frivolous doubt. It must not be based upon sympathy or prejudice. Rather, it is based on reason and common sense. It is logically derived from the evidence or absence of evidence.

Even if you believe the accused is probably guilty or likely guilty, that is not sufficient. In those circumstances you must give the benefit of the doubt to the accused and acquit because the Crown has failed to satisfy you of the guilt of the accused beyond a reasonable doubt.

---

29 In *R. v. Bisson* (1998), 14 C.R. (5th) 1 (S.C.C.), a new trial was ordered in a first degree murder case because the trial judge had erred in giving an example of the every day task of checking oil in a car as the degree of certainty required.

On the other hand you must remember that it is virtually impossible to prove anything to an absolute certainty and the Crown is not required to do so. Such a standard of proof is impossibly high.

In short if, based upon the evidence before the court, you are sure that the accused committed the offence you should convict since this demonstrates that you are satisfied of his guilt beyond a reasonable doubt.

This is not a magic incantation that needs to be repeated word for word. It is nothing more than a suggested form that would not be faulted if it were used. . . . . Further, it is possible that an error in the instructions as to the standard of proof may not constitute a reversible error. It was observed in *R. v. W. (D.)*, [1991] 1 S.C.R. 742, at p. 758, that the verdict ought not to be disturbed "if the charge, when read as a whole, makes it clear that the jury could not have been under any misapprehension as to the correct burden and standard of proof to apply." On the other hand, if the charge as a whole gives rise to the reasonable likelihood that the jury misapprehended the standard of proof, then as a general rule the verdict will have to be set aside and a new trial directed.

R. v. STARR
[2000] 2 S.C.R. 144, 36 C.R. (5th) 1, 147 C.C.C. (3d) 449

The accused had been convicted of two counts of first degree murder. The majority of the court decided that the reasonable doubt instruction given in the case fell prey to many of the same difficulties outlined in *Lifchus*, and likely misled the jury as to the content of the criminal standard of proof. In allowing the accused's appeal they gave further advice.

IACOBUCCI J. (MAJOR, BINNIE, ARBOUR and LEBEL JJ. concurring): —

. . . .

In the present case, the trial judge did refer to the Crown's onus and to the presumption of innocence, and he stated that the appellant should receive the benefit of any reasonable doubt. The error in the charge is that the jury was not told *how a reasonable doubt is to be defined*. As was emphasized repeatedly in *Lifchus* and again in *Bisson*, a jury *must* be instructed that the standard of proof in a criminal trial is higher than the probability standard used in making everyday decisions and in civil trials. Indeed, it is this very requirement to go beyond probability that meshes the standard of proof in criminal cases with the presumption of innocence and the Crown's onus. However, as Cory J. explained in these earlier decisions, it is generally inappropriate to define the meaning of the term "reasonable doubt" through examples from daily life, through the use of synonyms, or through analogy to moral choices. The criminal standard of proof has a special significance unique to the legal process. It is an exacting standard of proof rarely encountered in everyday life, and there is no universally intelligible illustration of the concept, such as the scales of justice with respect to the balance of probabilities standard. Unlike absolute certainty or the balance of probabilities, reasonable doubt is not an easily quantifiable standard. It cannot be measured or described by analogy. It must be explained. However, precisely because it is not quantifiable, it is difficult to explain.

In my view, an effective way to define the reasonable doubt standard for a jury is to explain that it falls much closer to absolute certainty than to proof on a balance of probabilities. As stated in *Lifchus*, a trial judge is required to explain that something less than absolute certainty is required, and that something more than probable guilt is required, in order for the jury to convict. Both of these alternative standards are fairly and easily comprehensible. It will be of great assistance for a jury if the trial judge situates the reasonable doubt standard appropriately between these two standards. The additional instructions to the jury set out in *Lifchus* as to the meaning and appropriate manner of determining the existence of a reasonable doubt serve to define the space between absolute certainty and proof beyond a reasonable doubt. In this regard, I am in agreement with Twaddle J.A. in the court below, when he said, at p. 177:

> If standards of proof were marked on a measure, proof "beyond reasonable doubt" would lie much closer to "absolute certainty" than to "a balance of probabilities". Just as a judge has a duty to instruct the jury that absolute certainty is not required, he or she has a duty, in my view, to instruct the jury that the criminal standard is more than a probability. The words he or she uses to convey this idea are of no significance, but the idea itself must be conveyed. . . .[30]

By suggesting that proof beyond a reasonable doubt falls closer to absolute certainty than to balance of probabilities, has *Starr* moved us closer to thinking about quantifying reasonable doubt? Do you think this would be a good idea?[31]

(iii) *Choosing Between Competing Versions*

In being satisfied to the requisite standard the trier of fact does not "choose" between competing versions of the incident. The plaintiff or the prosecutor makes allegations, seeks to disturb the status quo and bears the burden of satisfying the trier. In *R. v. Nadeau*,[32] the accused was convicted of murder. The accused testified and his version of the incident differed from that of the prosecution's witness. The trial judge told the jury that they had to choose between the two versions. A new trial was ordered and Lamer, J. wrote:

> With respect, this direction is in error. The accused benefits from any reasonable doubt at the outset, not merely if "the two versions are equally consistent with the evidence, are equally valid". Moreover, the jury does not have to choose between two versions. It is not because they would not believe the accused that they would then have to agree with Landry's version. The jurors cannot accept his version, or any part of it, unless they are satisfied beyond all reasonable doubt, having regard to all the evidence, that the events took place in this manner; otherwise, the accused is entitled, unless a fact has been established beyond a reasonable doubt, to the

---

30   See further Patrick Healy, "Direction and Guidance on Reasonable Doubt in the Charge to the Jury" (2001), 6 Can. Crim. L.R. 161.

31   See *United States v. Copeland*, 369 F.Supp.2d 275 (E.D.N.Y., 2005).

32   (1984), 42 C.R. (3d) 305 (S.C.C.).

finding of fact the most favourable to him, provided of course that it is based on evidence in the record and not mere speculation.[33]

R. v. W. (D.)
[1991] 1 S.C.R. 742, 3 C.R. (4th) 302, 63 C.C.C. (3d) 347

The accused was convicted of sexual assault after a trial that pitted the credibility of the accused against that of the complainant. It was objected that the trial judge erred in his recharge in that he characterized the core issue to be determined by the jury as whether they believed the complainant or whether they believed the appellant.

CORY J.:—

A trial Judge might well instruct the jury on the question of credibility along these lines:

First, if you believe the evidence of the accused, obviously you must acquit.

Second, if you do not believe the testimony of the accused but you are left in reasonable doubt by it, you must acquit.

Third, even if you are not left in doubt by the evidence of the accused, you must ask yourself whether, on the basis of the evidence which you do accept, you are convinced beyond a reasonable doubt by that evidence of the guilt of the accused.

If that formula were followed, the oft-repeated error which appears in the recharge in this case would be avoided. The requirement that the Crown prove the guilt of the accused beyond a reasonable doubt is fundamental in our system of criminal law. Every effort should be made to avoid mistakes in charging the jury on this basic principle.[34]

Recently the Supreme Court has recognized various criticisms of the W.(D.) approach and held that it should not be applied as a magical incantation:

R. v. S. (J.H.)
2008 CarswellNS 270, 2008 CarswellNS 271, [2008] 2 S.C.R. 152, 57 C.R. (6th) 79, 231 C.C.C. (3d) 302

A stepfather was charged with sexual assault after the complainant alleged that he had sexually abused her over a number of years, starting when she was approximately four years old. She twice complained to her mother who did not believe her. When the complainant was 15 she went to the police. The accused denied all the allegations and suggested that they were falsely made after he threatened to send her to a Catholic school because of her uncontrollable

---

33 *Ibid.*, at p. 310.

34 *Ibid.*, at p. 310. *W. (D.)* is one of the most frequently cited authorities. For different views as to its wisdom see Gans, (2000) 43 Crim. L.Q. 345 and Plaxton, (2000) 43 Crim. L.Q. 443. For a suggestion that judges are not properly applying *W.(D.)*: see Tanovich, "Testing the Presumption that Trial Judges Know the Law: The Case of W.(D.)" (2001), 43 C.R. (5th) 298.

behaviour. The issue at trial before judge and jury was whether the alleged events had ever happened. The complainant and the accused were the principal witnesses. The trial judge charged the jury on the credibility of the witnesses, instructing them they had to consider all the evidence and that the trial was not a choice between two competing versions of events. The defence raised no objection to the charge. The jury returned a verdict of guilty.

A majority of the Nova Scotia Court of Appeal set aside the conviction and ordered a new trial. According to the Court of Appeal, the trial judge had insufficiently explained the principles of reasonable doubt as they applied to credibility. While the *W.(D.)* phrasing was not a magical incantation, the charge had failed to express the second *W.(D.)* principle that disbelief in the accused's testimony does not amount to proof of his guilt beyond a reasonable doubt. The dissenting judge found that the charge was sufficient.

BINNIE J. (for seven justices):

[8] A series of decisions over at least the past 20 years has affirmed and reaffirmed the proposition that where credibility is a central issue in a jury trial, the judge must explain the relationship between the assessment of credibility and the Crown's ultimate burden to prove the guilt of the accused to the criminal standard. A general instruction on reasonable doubt without adverting to its relationship to the credibility (or lack of credibility) of the witnesses leaves open too great a possibility of confusion or misunderstanding. The so-called *W. (D.)* instruction has long roots: *R. v. Challice* (1979), 45 C.C.C. (2d) 546 (Ont. C.A.), at p. 556; *R. v. Chan* (1989), 52 C.C.C. (3d) 184, (Alta. C.A.), at p. 186; *R. v. Morin*, [1988] 2 S.C.R. 345, at p. 362; *R. v. H. (C.W.)* (1991), 68 C.C.C. (3d) 146 (B.C.C.A.), at p. 155; *R. v. MacKenzie*, [1993] 1 S.C.R. 212, at pp. 219 and 239; *R. v. Levasseur*, [1994] 3 S.C.R. 518 (upholding Fish J.A.'s dissent reported at (1994), 89 C.C.C. (3d) 508 (Que. C.A.), at p. 534). *W. (D.)* has been cited by Canadian courts at all levels in no fewer than 3,743 subsequent reported cases. It has proven to be a fertile source of appellate review. For a recent application, see *R. v. C.L.Y.*, [2008] 1 S.C.R. 5, 2008 SCC 2.

[9] The passage from *W. (D.)* at issue in this case, as in so many others, is found at pp. 757-58, where Cory J. explained:

> Ideally, appropriate instructions on the issue of credibility should be given, not only during the main charge, but on any recharge. A trial judge might well instruct the jury on the question of credibility along these lines:
>
>> First, if you believe the evidence of the accused, obviously you must acquit.
>>
>> Second, if you do not believe the testimony of the accused but you are left in reasonable doubt by it, you must acquit.
>>
>> Third, even if you are not left in doubt by the evidence of the accused, you must ask yourself whether, on the basis of the evidence which you do accept, you are convinced beyond a reasonable doubt by that evidence of the guilt of the accused.
>
> If that formula were followed, the oft repeated error which appears in the recharge in this case would be avoided. The requirement that the Crown prove the guilt of the

accused beyond a reasonable doubt is fundamental in our system of criminal law. Every effort should be made to avoid mistakes in charging the jury on this basic principle.

Nonetheless, the failure to use such language is not fatal if the charge, when read as a whole, makes it clear that the jury could not have been under any misapprehension as to the correct burden and standard of proof to apply . . . .

Essentially, *W. (D.)* simply unpacks for the benefit of the lay jury what reasonable doubt means in the context of evaluating conflicting testimonial accounts. It alerts the jury to the "credibility contest" error. It teaches that trial judges are required to impress on the jury that the burden never shifts from the Crown to prove every element of the offence beyond a reasonable doubt.

[10] The precise formulation of the *W. (D.)* questions has been criticized. As to the first question, the jury may believe inculpatory elements of the statements of an accused but reject the exculpatory explanation. In *R. v. Latimer*, [2001] 1 S.C.R. 3, 2001 SCC 1, the accused did not testify, but his description of the killing of his daughter was put into evidence by way of statements to the police. His description of the event itself was obviously believed. The exculpatory explanation did not amount to a defence at law. He was convicted. The principle that a jury may believe some, none, or all of the testimony of any witness, including that of an accused, suggests to some critics that the first *W. (D.)* question is something of an oversimplification.

[11] As to the second question, some jurors may wonder how, if they believe none of the evidence of the accused, such rejected evidence may nevertheless of itself raise a reasonable doubt. Of course, some elements of the evidence of an accused may raise a reasonable doubt, even though the bulk of it is rejected. Equally, the jury may simply conclude that they do not know whether to believe the accused's testimony or not. In either circumstance the accused is entitled to an acquittal.

[12] The third question, again, is taken by some critics as failing to contemplate a jury's acceptance of inculpatory bits of the evidence of an accused but not the exculpatory elements. In light of these possible sources of difficulty, Wood J.A. in *H. (C.W.)* suggested an additional instruction:

I would add one more instruction in such cases, which logically ought to be second in the order, namely: If, after a careful consideration of all the evidence, you are unable to decide whom to believe, you must acquit. [p. 155]

[13] In short the *W. (D.)* questions should not have attributed to them a level of sanctity or immutable perfection that their author never claimed for them. *W. (D.)*'s message that it must be made crystal clear to the jury that the burden never shifts from the Crown to prove every element of the offence beyond a reasonable doubt is of fundamental importance but its application should not result in a triumph of form over substance. In *R. v. S. (W.D.)*, [1994] 3 S.C.R. 521, Cory J. reiterated that the *W. (D.)* instructions need not be given A word for word as some magic incantation (p. 533). In *R. v. Avetysan*, [2000] 2 S.C.R. 745, 2000 SCC 56,

Major J. for the majority pointed out that in any case where credibility is important A[t]he question is really whether, in substance, the trial judge's instructions left the jury with the impression that it had to choose between the two versions of events (para. 19). The main point is that lack of credibility on the part of the accused does not equate to proof of his or her guilt beyond a reasonable doubt.

[14] In the present case Oland J.A. agreed that the trial judge did not call upon the jury to simply decide which of the complainant or [the accused] it believed (para. 19). Nevertheless, in her view:

> The charge only instructed that probable guilt was not enough to meet the standard of proof beyond a reasonable doubt, that the appellant was to be given the benefit of the doubt, and they did not have to accept or reject all of the testimony of any witness including his, and that they were to consider all of the evidence. Nowhere did it provide any guidance as to how, in the event they were uncertain or unable to resolve the issue of credibility, they were to proceed with their deliberations. *The charge failed to direct that if the jury did not believe the testimony of the accused but were left in a reasonable doubt by that evidence, they must acquit.* [Emphasis added; para. 20.]

In my view, with respect, the reasoning of the majority brushes uncomfortably close to the magic incantation error. At the end of the day, reading the charge as a whole, I believe the instruction to this jury satisfied the ultimate test formulated by Cory J. in *W. (D.)* as being whether the jury could not have been under any misapprehension as to the correct burden and standard of proof to apply (p. 758).

[15] Here the trial judge explained that any reasonable doubt must be resolved in favour of the accused. She also explained that even if they did not accept all of the accused's testimony, they could still accept some of it. She also explained to the jury that they should not see their task as that of deciding between two versions of events. She told them that they could not decide the case simply by choosing between the evidence of the complainant and that of the accused. She reminded them, in that context, that they must consider all of the evidence when determining reasonable doubt. She stated:

> You do not decide whether something happened simply by comparing one version of events with another, or choosing one of them. You have to consider all the evidence and decide whether you have been satisfied beyond a reasonable doubt that the events that form the basis of the crime charged, in fact, took place. [A.R., at p. 54.]

> . . .

> Again, you do not decide whether something happened simply by comparing one version of events with the other, or by choosing one of them. You have to consider all of the evidence and decide whether you have been satisfied beyond a reasonable doubt that the events that form the basis of the crimes charges, in fact, took place. [A.R., at p. 55.]

[16] In my view, the trial judge got across the point of the second *W. (D.)* question without leaving any realistic possibility of misunderstanding. As stated, she told the jury:

It is for the Crown counsel to prove beyond a reasonable doubt that the events alleged in fact occurred. It is not for [the accused] to prove that these events never happened. If you have a reasonable doubt whether the events alleged ever took place, you *must* find him not guilty. [Emphasis added; A.R., at p. 54.]

[17] There was much discussion at the hearing about defence counsel's failure to object. In my view, he correctly ascertained that the jury had been adequately instructed on the relationship between the assessment of credibility and the ultimate determination of guilt beyond a reasonable doubt. Before the recharge was given he told the trial judge he would feel more comfortable if simply the wording that was read previously was re-read to the jury again (A.R., at p. 77). He discharged his duty to the respondent.

Appeal allowed; conviction restored.

Should the Supreme Court have expressly and clearly abandoned the *W.(D.)* **approach?** It has been responsible for many, many prolix appeals and orders of new trials. The main problem is that the second question is potentially confusing and/or too generous to the accused.[35]

In *J.H.S.*, Justice Binnie might have mentioned the remark of McLachlin J. dissenting in *R. v. S. (W.D.)*, [1994] 3 S.C.R. 521:

Certainly if the jury rejected (as opposed to being merely undecided about) all of the evidence of the accused, it is difficult to see how that very evidence, having been rejected, could raise a reasonable doubt.

Should the Supreme Court have considered the disproportionate impact *W.(D.)* **is having in sexual assault cases? Even the most cursory review of the cases reveals that the issue arises most frequently in sexual assault cases and that sexual assault convictions are being frequently reversed on appeal because of a** *W.(D.)* **error. Why is this happening?**

Trials judges are at least now free to reject the complexity of *W.(D.)* as long as they make sure that the jury is warned of the Crown's burden of proof; that it is not just a choice between competing versions and that they may believe some, none or all of any witness, including the accused. These principles, of course, apply equally to judge-alone trials.

In *F.H. v. McDougall* (see above) Justice Rothstein makes it crystal clear that in civil cases, the complex *W.(D.)* approach is NOT an appropriate tool:

[85] The *W. (D.)* steps were developed as an aid to the determination of reasonable doubt in the criminal law context where a jury is faced with conflicting testimonial accounts. Lack of credibility on the part of an accused is not proof of guilt beyond a reasonable doubt.

---

35 See, especially, the late Jack Gibson, "*R. v. W.D.* Revisited: Is Step Two a Misdirection?" (2003) 11 C.R. (6th) 323. His earlier article "The Liars' Defence" (1993) 20 C.R. (4th) 96 led to a spirited debate: see Alan Gold, "The 'Average, Nervous, Inadequate, Inarticulate in Short, Typical' Accused's Defence" (2003) 22 C.R. (4th) 253; Gibson, "Misquote Changes Meaning" (1994) 24 C.R. (4th) 395; and Gold, "Typo Does Not Change Anything" (1994) 24 C.R. (4th) 397.

[86] However, in civil cases in which there is conflicting testimony, the judge is deciding whether a fact occurred on a balance of probabilities. In such cases, provided the judge has not ignored evidence, finding the evidence of one party credible may well be conclusive of the result because that evidence is inconsistent with that of the other party. In such cases, believing one party will mean explicitly or implicitly that the other party was not believed on the important issue in the case. That may be especially true where a plaintiff makes allegations that are altogether denied by the defendant as in this case. *W. (D.)* is not an appropriate tool for evaluating evidence on the balance of probabilities in civil cases.

Do you find this reasoning persuasive? Why does it not equally apply in criminal cases?

A 4-3 majority of the SCC held in *R. v. Y. (C.L.)*[36] that it was not reversible error that the trial judge had considered and weighted the evidence of the complainant before considering that of the accused. The minority held that this had reversed the onus of proof. Similarly, in *R. v. B. (H.S.)*[37] Chief Justice McLachlin, for the Court, affirmed the trial judge's reasons and noted:

[14] The trial judge had to determine whether the evidence as a whole proved the allegations beyond a reasonable doubt. This issue turned largely on the trial judge's findings with respect to the credibility of the complainant and the accused. It is clear from the trial judge's reasons for judgment that his verdict resulted from his acceptance of the complainant's evidence as to whether the incidents occurred, from his rejection of the accused's defence of lack of opportunity from his finding that the accused was not a credible witness and that the evidence as a whole did not leave him with a reasonable doubt. It is also clear that the trial judge found the frailties in the complainant's evidence to be an understandable result of trying to remember events that happened in childhood and were, in any case, related to peripheral, not core, issues.

PROBLEM

The accused was charged with murder. In his charge to the jury, the trial judge defined reasonable doubt in the following passages:

In a criminal case, as I told you before, the accused is presumed to be innocent until the evidence put forth has proven his guilt to you beyond a reasonable doubt. It is not the responsibility of the accused to establish or demonstrate or prove his innocence, if the Crown fails to prove guilt beyond a reasonable doubt, you must acquit the accused. You must, therefore, be satisfied as to his guilt before you can convict and the standard that you use is proof beyond a reasonable doubt, so you have to be satisfied as to guilt and the standard that you use is proof beyond a reasonable doubt. Simply put, a reasonable doubt is just that, Supreme Court of Canada has made a pronouncement in recent—in the last number of months which says we should describe it as a reasonable doubt that is not an imaginary or frivolous doubt, nor is it one based on sympathy or prejudice. A reasonable doubt is a doubt based on reason and common sense which must logically be derived from the evidence or the absence of evidence.

---

36 (2008) 53 C.R. (6th) 207.
37 (2008) 235 C.C.C. (3d) 312 (S.C.C.).

Now the accused gave evidence and he is to be judged as other witnesses in the same way. If you believe him that he did not kill the deceased, then you are to acquit him. If on considering all of the evidence, you are left in a state of reasonable doubt and you are not satisfied as to his guilt, it is your duty to acquit the accused. If, however, upon consideration of all of the evidence and the submissions of counsel, you are satisfied that the accused has been proven guilty beyond a reasonable doubt, it is your duty to convict the accused. I turn to the indictment again and as I've been telling you previously, the obligation and burden upon the Crown is to prove each and every element of the charge as stated in the indictment.

Is this charge in substantial compliance with *Starr* and *W. (D.)*? See *R. v. Squires*, 171 C.C.C. (3d) 226, [2002] 4 S.C.R. 323.

(iv) *Considering Individual Pieces of Evidence*

Some types of evidence raise concerns either because of issues surrounding reliability (e.g., jailhouse informers) or because the evidence is especially incriminating (e.g., after the fact conduct). **Should the reasonable doubt standard apply to individual pieces of evidence?**

R. v. MORIN
[1988] 2 S.C.R. 345, 66 C.R. (3d) 1, 44 C.C.C. (3d) 193

The accused was acquitted on a charge of first degree murder. His position at trial was that he was not the killer, but in the alternative, if he was the killer he was not guilty by reason of insanity. On appeal it was found that the trial judge had misdirected the jury. The trial judge invited the jury to apply the criminal standard of proof beyond a reasonable doubt to individual pieces of evidence. The Court of Appeal allowed the Crown's appeal and directed a new trial. The accused appealed. The Supreme Court confirmed the order of a new trial.

SOPINKA J. (DICKSON C.J.C. and MCINTYRE and LA FOREST JJ. concurring):—

. . . .

The appellant submits that the charge, when read as a whole, did not invite the jury to subject individual pieces of evidence to the criminal standard, but rather the effect of the charge was that during the "fact-finding" stage items of evidence were to be examined in relation to other evidence. The residuum resulting from this process constitutes the "whole of the evidence", from which the jury determines whether guilt has been proved beyond a reasonable doubt.

This argument raises two questions:

(i) Is the appellant's interpretation of the charge correct?

(ii) Assuming that it is, is it misdirection to instruct the jury to apply the criminal standard at two stages as submitted?

. . . .

The following are the relevant excerpts from the charge to the jury set out in the order in which they occurred:

1. *Concerning Evidence*

> You are not obliged to accept any part of the evidence of a witness just because there is no denial of it. If you have a reasonable doubt about any of the evidence, you will give the benefit of that doubt to the accused with respect to such evidence. *Having decided what evidence you consider worthy of belief, you will consider it as a whole, of course, in arriving at your verdict.* [emphasis added]

2. *Concerning Burden of Proof*

> The accused is entitled to the benefit of reasonable doubt on the whole of the case and on each and every issue in the case.

> Proof beyond a reasonable doubt does not apply to the individual items of evidence or the separate pieces of evidence in the case, but to the total body of evidence upon which the Crown relies to prove guilt. Before you can convict you must be satisfied beyond a reasonable doubt of his guilt.

3. *Concerning Hairs and Fibres*

> It seems to me that this evidence does not go beyond proving that Christine could have been in the Honda motor vehicle and that the accused could have been at the scene of the killing, and of course that is not proof beyond a reasonable doubt.

4. *Concerning Appellant's Statements to Hobbs*

> I was going to go on to say that, if you find that the evidence of the accused at trial here represents the correct interpretation of those tapes and transcripts, or parts of the tapes and transcripts, or if you have a reasonable doubt that that might be so, you will give him the benefit of the doubt as to those parts of the tapes or transcripts and adopt his interpretation.

5. *Concerning Appellant's Statement to Inmate May*

> Now, as to that evidence, in relation to that part of the tape that I have just read, if you find the evidence of the accused at trial represents the correct interpretation of that exchange, or if you have a reasonable doubt that that may be so, you will give the benefit of the doubt to the accused and adopt his interpretation.

In my opinion, based on my reading of the charge as a whole, a jury would likely have concluded that in examining the evidence they were to give the accused the benefit of the doubt in respect of *any* evidence. This process of examination and elimination would occur during the so-called "fact-finding" stage, to use the appellant's phrase. The evidence as a whole to which the jury was to apply itself in order to determine guilt or innocence was the residuum after the "fact-finding" stage. There is no other way of reading the first excerpt from the charge.

. . . .

The argument in favour of a two-stage application of the criminal standard has superficial appeal in theory but in my respectful opinion is wrong in principle and unworkable in practice. In principle it is wrong because the function of a standard of proof is not the weighing of individual items of evidence but the determination of ultimate issues. Furthermore, it would require the individual member of the jury to rely on the same facts in order to establish guilt. The law is clear that the members of the jury can arrive at a verdict by different routes and need not rely on the same facts. Indeed, the jurors need not agree on any single fact except the ultimate conclusion: see Wigmore on Evidence, Chadbourn revision, vol. 9 (1981), para. 2497, at pp. 412-14; *R. v. Lynch* (1978), 40 C.C.C. (2d) 7 at 19 (Ont. C.A.); *R. v. Bouvier*, supra, Ont. C.A. at pp. 264-65; *R. v. Moreau* (1986), 51 C.R. (3d) 209, 26 C.C.C. (3d) 359 at 389 (Ont. C.A.); *R. v. Agbim*, [1979] Crim. L. Rev. 171 (C.A.); *R. v. Thatcher*, supra, Sask. C.A. at p. 510, S.C.C. at p. 697.

The matter is summed up in Cross at p. 146:

> It has been held by the Court of Appeal that it is unnecessary for a judge to direct the jury that it must be unanimous with regard to even one item of evidence bearing upon a particular count before convicting on it. It seems to be enough that all members of the jury find the accused guilty upon the basis of some of the facts bearing upon that count.

In practice it is not practical, because the jury would have to agree on not only the same facts but what individual facts prove. Individual facts do not necessarily establish guilt, but are a link in the chain of ultimate proof. It is not possible, therefore, to require the jury to find facts proved beyond a reasonable doubt without identifying *what it is* that they prove beyond a reasonable doubt. Since the same fact may give rise to different inferences tending to establish guilt or innocence, the jury might discard such facts on the basis that there is doubt as to what they prove.

The concern which proponents of the two-stage process express is that facts which are doubtful will be used to establish guilt. The answer to this concern is that a chain is only as strong as its weakest link. If facts which are essential to a finding of guilt are still doubtful notwithstanding the support of other facts, this will produce a doubt in the mind of the jury that guilt has been proved beyond a reasonable doubt.

I conclude from the foregoing that the facts are for the jury to determine, subject to an instruction by the trial judge as to the law. While the charge may and often does include many helpful tips on the weighing of evidence, such as observing demeanour, taking into the account the interest of the witness and so forth, the law lays down only one basic requirement: during the process of deliberation the jury or other trier of fact must consider the evidence as a whole and determine whether guilt is established by the prosecution beyond a reasonable doubt. This of necessity requires that each element of the offence or issue be proved beyond a reasonable doubt. Beyond this injunction it is for the trier of fact to determine how to proceed. To intrude in this area is, as pointed out by North P., an intrusion into the province of the jury.

The reason we have juries is so that lay persons and not lawyers decide the facts. To inject into the process artificial legal rules with respect to the natural human activity of deliberation and decision would tend to detract from the value of the jury system. Accordingly, it is wrong for a trial judge to lay down additional rules for the weighing of the evidence. Indeed, it is unwise to attempt to elaborate on the basic requirement referred to above. I would make two exceptions. The jury should be told that the facts are not to be examined separately and in isolation with reference to the criminal standard. This instruction is a necessary corollary to the basic rule referred to above. Without it there is some danger that a jury might conclude that the requirement that each issue or element of the offence be proved beyond a reasonable doubt demands that individual items of evidence be so proved.

The second exception is that it is appropriate, where issues of credibility arise between the evidence for the prosecution and the defence, that the jury be charged as suggested by Morden J.A. in *Challice*, supra. There is a danger in such a situation that a jury might conclude that it is simply a matter as to which side they believe. The suggested charge alerts them to the fact that, if the defence evidence leaves them in a state of doubt after considering it in the context of the whole of the evidence, then they are to acquit.

Consequently, even if the appellant is correct in his interpretation of the charge to the jury, there was misdirection — although not as serious as the misdirection which I have found occurred.

Morin was convicted on the new trial but later exonerated by D.N.A. evidence.[38]

R. v. WHITE
[1998] 2 S.C.R. 72, 16 C.R. (5th) 199, 125 C.C.C. (3d) 385

The accused were charged with first degree murder. There was evidence that they had fled the jurisdiction after the killing and attempted to dispose of the murder weapon. An issue for the Court was whether the trial judge should have instructed the jury to apply the reasonable doubt standard to the evidence of the accused's post-offence conduct.

MAJOR J. (L'HEUREUX-DUBÉ, GONTHIER, CORY, McLACHLIN, BASTARACHE and BINNIE JJ. concurring):—

. . . .

In cases where the post-offence conduct of an accused is put before the jury, the trial judge should provide an instruction regarding the proper use of that evidence. The purpose of such a charge is to counter the jury's natural tendency to leap from evidence of flight or concealment to a conclusion of guilt, and to ensure that alternative explanations for the accused's conduct are given full consideration. In particular, the trial judge should remind the jury that people sometimes flee or lie for entirely innocent reasons, and that even if the accused was motivated by a feeling of guilt, that feeling might be attributable to some culpable act other than the offence for which the accused is being tried. The jury should be instructed to keep these principles in mind when deciding how much weight, if any, to give such evidence in the final evaluation of guilt or innocence.

---

38 See *R. v. Morin* (1995), 37 C.R. (4th) 395 (Ont. C.A.).

The jury charge in this case complied with those requirements, and the appellants do not claim that there was anything misleading about that charge so far as it went. It is contended, however, that the charge was insufficient because the trial judge did not specifically direct the jury to apply the criminal standard of proof to the evidence of the appellants' post-offence conduct. It is the appellants' submission that the jury should have been told that unless they were satisfied beyond a reasonable doubt that the appellants' post-offence conduct constituted flight or concealment, and moreover that those acts were motivated by the appellants' sense of culpability for Chiu's murder and not by some other explanation, the jury could draw no inference of guilt from the conduct, and must set it aside and proceed to consider the balance of evidence in the case.

It is settled that the criminal standard of proof applies only to the jury's final determination of guilt or innocence and is not to be applied to individual items or categories of evidence. It is improper for the jury to divide their deliberations into separate stages; their verdict must be based on the record as a whole, not merely on items of evidence which have previously been established beyond a reasonable doubt: see *Morin*. The kind of charge argued for by the appellants is facially inconsistent with these principles, and no persuasive reason has been advanced which would justify creating an exception for evidence of post-offence conduct. The trial judge in this case was not required to give such a charge and indeed he would have been in error had he done so. . . . . The inherent difficulty involved in distinguishing between different types of circumstantial evidence only reinforces the holding in *Morin* that jury deliberations are somewhat holistic in nature and should not be broken down in relation to individual pieces or categories of evidence.

. . . .

The appellants concede that as a general rule the criminal standard of proof does not apply to individual pieces of evidence. They contend, however, that because post-offence conduct can give rise to an inference that is tantamount to a finding of guilt itself, such conduct is unlike other kinds of circumstantial evidence and should benefit from an exception to the rule in *Morin*. Specifically, the appellants assert that an act of flight or concealment is not probative of guilt unless the jury is satisfied that the act was motivated by the accused's awareness of having committed the offence in question; but they point out that once the jury has drawn such an inference of "guilty consciousness", it follows as a matter of logic that the accused must in fact be guilty, unless he or she was somehow mistaken or delusional about having committed the crime. Because of this danger, the appellants contend that the jury should be required to apply the same standard of proof to its evaluation of post-offence conduct as it would apply to the ultimate issue of guilt, i.e., proof beyond a reasonable doubt.

That argument is not persuasive. There is no principled basis for the claim that evidence of after-the-fact conduct is substantively different from other kinds of circumstantial evidence, or that it should be accorded special status during jury deliberations. Other types of highly incriminating evidence which present essentially the same kinds of risks do not receive such treatment. In particular, a pretrial oral admission of guilt, which, as the Court of Appeal observed, "goes more directly to the ultimate issue than circumstantial evidence of consciousness of guilt", is not subject to a separate reasonable doubt analysis. As Weiler J.A. observed in *Peavoy*, "[t]here is nothing magical or unique about evidence of after-the-fact conduct." It is simply some evidence which is to be considered and weighed by the jury, together with the rest of the evidence, in deciding whether the accused is guilty or innocent. The fact that such evidence may by its nature be compelling and inculpatory does not have the effect of modifying the evidentiary threshold required by criminal law — namely, that all the evidence, when considered together, must give rise to proof beyond a reasonable doubt.

It is true that a jury may regard an act of flight or concealment as an admission of guilt by conduct, and there is a danger that such evidence could lead a jury to leap erroneously to a conclusion of guilt. As explained below, however, the proper remedy for that danger is not the imposition of a separate burden of proof, but rather an instruction to the jury to be cautious about drawing an incriminatory inference from such evidence and a reminder that all the evidence in the case must be considered.

As a practical matter, if the trial judge invoked the criminal standard of proof as a threshold test for using evidence of post-offence conduct, there would be a risk of confusing the jury and inviting them to short-circuit their deliberations. If the jury determined beyond a reasonable doubt that the accused fled or lied because he or she was aware of having committed the crime charged, they would be less likely to give full consideration to the rest of the evidence. If, on the other hand, the jury failed to determine the motivation of the accused to such a high standard of proof, they would be forced to exclude the evidence of post-offence conduct, which might otherwise be useful in the context of the case as a whole. In either case, the verdict is likely to be reached on the basis of less than all the evidence.

White is also important for discouraging the use of the language of evidence as to "consciousness of guilt". It would be better to refer to "post-offence conduct."[39] See *R. v. Terceira*[40] for a further application of the *Morin* principle in the context of DNA evidence.

(v) *Direct and Circumstantial Evidence*

In its discharge of the persuasive burden, the Crown can tender direct or circumstantial evidence.

In cases of circumstantial evidence, certain facts connected with the material fact are proved and the trier is asked to infer from those facts that the material fact exists. If reason and experience support the connection the evidence led is relevant. John Robinette described it:

---

39 See further Stewart (1999), 43 Crim. L.Q. 17.

40 (1998), 15 C.R. (5th) 359, 123 C.C.C. (3d) 1 (Ont. C.A.), affirmed [1999] 3 S.C.R. 866, 142 C.C.C. (3d) 95, 32 C.R. (5th) 77.

All that circumstantial evidence is, is that you are seeking to prove circumstances, subordinate circumstances, subordinate facts, from which a trial tribunal may draw the inference that a principal issue of fact vital to your case has been established. Therefore, as a matter of logic, if an inference may be drawn from a subordinate fact that the principal fact occurred then evidence is admissible to prove the subordinate fact and that is what is loosely called circumstantial evidence.[41]

R. v. MUNOZ

(2006), 38 C.R. (6th) 376, 205 C.C.C. (3d) 70, 2006 CarswellOnt 673 (S.C.J.)

The accused, M and F, were committed to stand trial on charges including conspiring to kill F's wife. All three men had been housed in the same unit at Maplehurst Detention Centre where the Crown alleged that the conspiracy was hatched. There was no direct evidence implicating the accused. The Crown's sole witness at the preliminary inquiry testified that he and the accused discussed depositing $1,000 with the accused's lawyer. They did not discuss the conspiracy. M brought an application for certiorari to quash the decision. The application was granted.

DUCHARME J.: —

B. The Drawing of Inferences

While the jurisprudence is replete with references to the drawing of "reasonable inferences," there is comparatively little discussion about the process involved in drawing inferences from accepted facts. It must be emphasized that this does not involve deductive reasoning which, assuming the premises are accepted, necessarily results in a valid conclusion. This is because the conclusion is inherent in the relationship between the premises. Rather the process of inference drawing involves inductive reasoning which derives conclusions based on the uniformity of prior human experience. The conclusion is not inherent in the offered evidence, or premises, but flows from an interpretation of that evidence derived from experience. Consequently, an inductive conclusion necessarily lacks the same degree of inescapable validity as a deductive conclusion. Therefore, if the premises, or the primary facts, are accepted, the inductive conclusion follows with some degree of probability, but not of necessity. Also, unlike deductive reasoning, inductive reasoning is ampliative as it gives more information than what was contained in the premises themselves.

A good starting point for any discussion of inference drawing is the definition offered by Justice Watt:

An *inference* is a deduction of fact which may logically and reasonably be drawn from another fact or group of facts found or otherwise established in the proceedings. It is a conclusion that *may*, not must be drawn in the circumstances.[42]

41 *Circumstantial Evidence*, [1955] L.S.U.C. Spec. Lect. 307. For the same author speaking in parables on the subject, see *Charge to the Jury in a Criminal Case*, [1959] L.S.U.C. Spec. Lect. 147 and 153.

42 D. Watt, *Watt's Manual of Criminal Evidence* (Toronto: Carswell, 2005) at p. 108. (Italicized

Equally important is Justice Watt's admonition that, "The boundary which separates permissible inference from impermissible speculation in relation to circumstantial evidence is often a very difficult one to locate."[43] The process of inference drawing was described by Doherty J.A. in *R. v. Morrissey* (1995), 97 C.C.C. (3d) 193 (Ont. C.A.) at p. 209, as follows:

> *A trier of fact may draw factual inferences from the evidence. The inferences must, however, be ones which can be reasonably and logically drawn from a fact or group of facts established by the evidence.* An inference which does not flow logically and reasonably from established facts cannot be made and is condemned as conjecture and speculation. As Chipman J.A. put it in *R. v. White* (1994), 89 C.C.C. (3d) 336 at p.351, 28 C.R. (4th) 160, 3 M.V.R. (3d) 283 (N.S.C.A.):
>
>> These cases establish that there is a distinction between conjecture and speculation on the one hand and rational conclusions from the whole of the evidence on the other. [Emphasis added]

The highlighted sentence suggests that there are two ways in which inference drawing can become impermissible speculation and I will discuss each in turn.

The first step in inference drawing is that the primary facts, i.e. the facts that are said to provide the basis for the inference, must be established by the evidence. If the primary facts are not established, then any inferences purportedly drawn from them will be the product of impermissible speculation. The decision of Lord Wright in *Caswell v. Powell Duffryn Associated Collieries Ltd.*, [1940] A.C. 152 (H.L.) at 169-70, is often cited as authority for this long-standing principle:

> The Court therefore is left to inference or circumstantial evidence. Inference must be carefully distinguished from conjecture or speculation. *There can be no inference unless there are objective facts from which to infer the other facts which it is sought to establish.* In some cases the other facts can be inferred with as much practical certainty as if they had been actually observed. In other cases the inference does not go beyond reasonable probability. *But if there are no positive proved facts from which the inference can be made, the method of inference fails and what is left is mere speculation or conjecture.* [Emphasis added]

While the foregoing point may seem obvious, it can arise in subtle ways. Thus, in *R. v. Portillo* (2003), 176 C.C.C. (3d) 467 (Ont. C.A.), the Crown lead footwear evidence consisting of two primary facts: two partial shoeprints found at the scene were similar to impressions from two shoes found by the police in the course of their investigation, and the shoes were found in the vicinity of the appellant's apartment. The Crown did so in order to support the inference that the appellant had been at the scene of the homicide in close proximity to the body. That conclusion could be drawn only if it could reasonably be inferred that: (a) the shoes found by the police made the prints at the scene; and (b) that the shoes belonged to the appellant. The expert evidence called by the Crown, standing

portions in original) In this passage the phrase "deduction of fact" is not mean to suggest that the process involved is deductive reasoning. Rather, the word is simply used in the sense of a "factual conclusion."

43 Ibid.

alone, could not support the first inference, and the fact that the shoes were found in the vicinity of the appellant's apartment, standing alone, could not support the second inference. While describing the Crown's argument as "seductive," after a careful analysis of the necessary underlying inferences, Doherty J.A. rejected the Crown's reasoning as circular, saying at 476-7:

> The "footwear" evidence could assist in proving either of the factual inferences needed to give the evidence relevance, only if the Crown could first prove the other factual inference for which the "footwear" evidence was offered.

> As indicated above, the evidence connecting Wilfredo Portillo to the homicide scene could not assist the jury in determining whether the shoes made the prints found at the scene unless other evidence established that the shoes belonged to Wilfredo Portillo. The only other evidence connecting Wilfredo Portillo to the shoes was the evidence that they were found in the vicinity of Wilfredo Portillo's apartment. *That fact alone could not reasonably support the inference that the shoes belonged to Wilfredo Portillo as opposed to the many other people who had equal access to that area.* Similarly, the evidence of the prints found at the scene could only assist in identifying Wilfredo Portillo as the owner of the shoes if there was other evidence from which it could be inferred that the prints were made by those shoes. The only other evidence, was the expert's evidence that the treads on the shoes were similar to the partial prints found at the scene. *That evidence, standing alone, could not reasonably support the inference that those shoes made those prints.* This is particularly so given the expert's frank concession that he could not say how many shoes had the same tread pattern. His evidence amounted to no more than an assertion that the shoes found near Wilfredo Portillo's apartment were among an undetermined number of shoes that could have made the prints at the scene of the homicide.

> The "footwear" evidence could not, *absent assumption of facts not proved, or speculation,* support either the inference that the shoes made the prints found at the scene or that the shoes belonged to Wilfredo Portillo. [Emphasis added]

Therefore Justice Doherty concluded that the evidence was not relevant and should have been excluded.

The second way in which inference drawing can become impermissible speculation occurs where the proposed inference cannot be reasonably and logically drawn from the established primary facts. This possibility stems precisely from the fact that an inductive conclusion is not necessarily valid. As McLachlin C.J.C. put it in *Arcuri* at 31-2:

> [W]ith circumstantial evidence, there is, by definition, *an inferential gap between the evidence and the matter to be established*—that is, an inferential gap beyond the question of whether the evidence should be believed... The judge must therefore weigh the evidence, in the sense of assessing *whether it is reasonably capable of supporting the inferences that the Crown asks the jury to draw.* [Emphasis added]

Consequently, one can overreach and draw an inference that should not properly be drawn from the primary facts.

The courts have repeatedly cautioned against confusing a reasonable inference with mere speculation. Where an inferential gap exists, it can only be properly overcome by evidence. This point was powerfully made by Doherty J.A.

in *United States of America v. Huynh* (2005), 200 C.C.C. (3d) 305 (Ont. C.A.). This case involved an appeal of the committal for extradition of an individual on charges of conspiracy and money laundering relating to the designated offence of trafficking in a controlled substance. The material relied on in support of the extradition justified the inference that the appellant had conspired with others to covertly transfer very large amounts of cash from the United States to Canada. He did so by concealing the money in a secret compartment fashioned in the gas tank of his vehicle. While there was no direct evidence as to the source of the cash, the Crown argued that it could be reasonably inferred that the cash was the proceeds of trafficking in a controlled substance based on: (a) the amount of cash involved; (b) the frequency with which cash was being transferred from the United States to Canada; (c) the manner of concealment of the cash suggesting a level of sophistication and a commercial operation; (d) the coded conversations of participants and their obvious concerns about surveillance; and (e) the anticipated evidence of a DEA officer that the modus operandi was consistent with the activities of drug dealers. In rejecting the Crown's contention, Doherty J.A. reasoned as follows:

> The material identified by the respondent certainly permits the inference that the cash was the proceeds of some illicit activity. Drug trafficking comes readily to mind as one possible source. *The process of drawing inferences from evidence is not, however, the same as speculating even where the circumstances permit an educated guess. The gap between the inference that the cash was the proceeds of illicit activity and the further inference that the illicit activity was trafficking in a controlled substance can only be bridged by evidence.* The trier of fact will assess that evidence in the light of common sense and human experience, but neither are a substitute for evidence. The requesting state has not offered any evidence as to the source of the funds even though its material indicates that one of the parties to this conspiracy is cooperating with the police. ... *I do not think there is anything in the material that would reasonably permit a trier of fact to infer that the cash was the proceeds of drug trafficking and not some other illicit activity.*[44] [Emphasis added]

It is difficult, if not impossible, to define with any precision a bright line distinction between the drawing of reasonable inferences and mere speculation. However, in this regard I would adopt the language of Aldisert J. in *Tose v. First Pennsylvania Bank, N.A.*, 648 F.2d 879, 895 (3rd Cir.), cert. denied, 454 U.S. 893 (1981) at 895:

> The line between a reasonable inference that may permissibly be drawn by a jury from basic facts in evidence and an impermissible speculation is not drawn by judicial idiosyncracies. The line is drawn by the laws of logic. If [page84] there is an experience of logical probability that an ultimate fact will follow a stated narrative or historical fact, then the jury is given the opportunity to draw a conclusion because there is a reasonable probability that the conclusion flows from the proven facts. As the Supreme Court has stated, "the essential requirement is that mere speculation be

---

44 In *Rodaro et. al. v. Royal Bank of Canada et. al.* (2002), 59 O.R. (3d) 74 (C.A.) at 94, Doherty J.A. applied the same distinction between legitimate inference drawing and speculation in a civil context.

not allowed to do duty for probative facts after making due allowance for all reasonably possible inferences favoring the party whose case is attacked." *Galloway v. United States*, 319 U.S. 372, 395, 63 S. Ct. 1077, 1089, 87 L. Ed. 1458 (1943).[45]

However, it must be emphasized that this requirement of "logical probability" or "reasonable probability" does not mean that the only "reasonable" inferences that can be drawn are the most obvious or the most easily drawn.[46] This was explicitly rejected in *R. v. Katwaru, supra*, note 6 per Moldaver J.A. at 444:

> [I]n the course of his instructions on the law relating to circumstantial evidence, the trial judge told the jury on numerous occasions that they could infer a fact from established facts but only if the inference flowed "easily and logically from [the] other established facts".
>
> The appellant submits, correctly in my view, that the trial judge erred by inserting the word "easily" into the equation. *In order to infer a fact from established facts, all that is required is that the inference be reasonable and logical. The fact that an inference may flow less than easily does not mean that it cannot be drawn. To hold otherwise would lead to the untenable conclusion that a difficult inference could never be reasonable and logical.* [Emphasis added]

Rather, the requirement of reasonable or logical probability is meant to underscore that the drawing of inferences is not a process of subjective imagination, but rather is one of rational explication. Supposition or conjecture is no substitute for evidence and cannot be relied upon as the basis for a reasonably drawn inference. Therefore, it is not enough simply to create a hypothetical narrative that, however speculative, could possibly link the primary fact or facts to the inference or inferences sought to be drawn. As Fairgrieve J. noted in *R. v. Ruiz*, [2000] O.J. No. 2713 (QL), 47 W.C.B. (2d) 66 (Ont. C.J.), at para. 3, "Simply because a possibility cannot be excluded does not necessarily mean that a reasonable trier could be justified in reaching such a conclusion on the evidence." The inference must be one that can be reasonably and logically drawn and, even where difficult; it cannot depend on speculation or conjecture, rather than evidence, to bridge any inferential gaps.

If a witness is willing to testify that she saw the accused shoot the deceased, this is direct evidence of that fact. The trial judge will first ensure the witness's competence to speak, then the evidence may be evaluated according to the trier of fact's assessment of the witness's credibility. If a witness is willing to testify that she heard the deceased scream and moments later saw the accused standing over the body holding a smoking gun this is circumstantial evidence of

-----

45 Although *Tose* and *Galloway v. United States*, 319 U.S. 372 (1943), dealt with directed verdicts, this language is equally applicable to the assessment of the availability of inferences based on the evidence at a preliminary inquiry.

46 This is especially true at a preliminary inquiry where the judge need only determine whether there is sufficient evidence to permit the trier of fact to draw the inferences necessary to convict.

the accused shooting the deceased. The trial judge will assess the relevance of the evidence led; if received the trier of fact will then assess its sufficiency.

Notice that in the case of direct evidence there is but one source of error. The person who describes a stabbing she witnessed might be mistaken or lying. The witness who says she only saw certain circumstances, the wounds and the blood-stained knife, may also be mistaken or lying about those circumstances, but also, even if she's accurate in her description, the inference that the prosecutor wants the trier to draw may not be the correct one. That is why we say that circumstantial evidence has two sources of error. **This leads some to conclude that circumstantial evidence is weaker than direct, but is it?**

R. v. WHITMAN
35 C.R. (6th) 12, 2005 CarswellBC 2678 (S.C.)

The accused was charged with aggravated assault arising out of a stabbing. The complainant had been stabbed during an altercation on the street, and the stabber had fled the scene. An independent witness (Robertson, a doorman at a local hotel) did not see the stabbing but saw the accused put a knife away and leave the scene. The next day that witness saw the accused on the street and called the police. The accused fled from the police when they arrived. When the police seized his clothing for DNA analysis, he said that they were not the clothes he had been wearing the day before.

At trial, the complainant identified the accused in the dock as the person who had stabbed him. However, the complainant had been under the influence of drugs at the time of the stabbing, and possibly while testifying. The independent witness identified the accused as the person he had seen with a knife leave the scene, but he had not seen the stabbing. The accused testified that he had fled the police because he knew the police had a Canada-wide warrant out for his arrest. He acknowledged having been at the scene, having had a knife, and having left, but denied responsibility for the stabbing. He called a witness who corroborated his version of events in most details, though both the accused and his witness had lengthy criminal records.

ROMILLY J.: —

ii. Identity Issue

Due to the frailties of eyewitness identification, a judge sitting alone should address himself or herself in a manner similar to what a jury as trier of fact would be subject to. The following lines as suggested in *The People v. Casey (No. 2)*, [1963] I.R. 33 at 39 and adopted by Jessup J.A. in *R. v. Sutton*, [1970] 2 O.R. 358 at 368-69 (C.A.) are indicative of a proper approach:

> We are of opinion that juries as a whole may not be fully aware of the dangers involved in visual identification nor of the considerable number of cases in which such identification has been proved to be erroneous; and also that they may be inclined to attribute too much probative effect to the test of an identification parade. In our opinion it is desirable that in all cases, where the verdict depends substantially on the correctness of an identification, their attention should be called in general terms to the fact that in a number of instances such identification has proved erroneous, to the possibilities of mistake in the case before them and to the necessity of caution.

Nor do we think that such warning should be confined to cases where the identification is that of only one witness. Experience has shown that mistakes can occur where two or more witnesses have made positive identifications. We consider juries in cases where the correctness of an identification is challenged should be directed on the following lines, namely, that if their verdict as to the guilt of the prisoner is to depend wholly or substantially on the correctness of such identification, they should bear in mind that there have been a number of instances where responsible witnesses, whose honesty was not in question and whose opportunities for observation had been adequate, made positive identifications on a parade or otherwise, which identifications were subsequently proved to be erroneous; and accordingly that they should be specially cautious before accepting such evidence of identification as correct; but that if after careful examination of such evidence in the light of all the circumstances, and with due regard to all the other evidence in the case, they feel satisfied beyond reasonable doubt of the correctness of the identification they are at liberty to act upon it.

See also *R. v. Howarth* (1970), 1 C.C.C. (2d) 546 (Ont. C.A.); *R. v. Virk* (1983), 33 C.R. (3d) 378 (B.C.C.A.); *R. v. Hang* (1990), 55 C.C.C. (3d) 195 (B.C.C.A.); *R. v. Reitsma*, [1998] 1 S.C.R. 769, (1997), 125 C.C.C. (3d) 1, rev'g [1997] B.C.J. No. 2314, (B.C.C.A.); *R. v. Fengstad* (1994), 27 C.R. (4th) 383 (B.C.C.A.); *R. v. Tam* (1995), 100 C.C.C. (3d) 196 (B.C.C.A.); and *R. v. Field* (1999), 126 B.C.A.C. 103.

The need for a trier of fact to be cautious with respect to the frailties of eyewitness identification has been recognized by the Supreme Court of Canada. In *R. v. Hibbert*, [2002] 2 S.C.R. 445, 2002 SCR 39, the Court was faced with the issue of the adequacy of the trial judge's charge to the jury with respect to the in-court eyewitness identification evidence. Madam Justice Arbour speaking for the seven member majority acknowledged the dangers associated with such evidence at para. 50:

I think it is important to remember that the danger associated with eyewitness in-court identification is that it is deceptively credible, largely because it is honest and sincere. The dramatic impact of the identification taking place in the court, before the jury, can aggravate the distorted value the jury may place on it.

Arbour J. then went on to acknowledge that the dangers of this evidence have been well documented, specifically referring to the recommendations of the Honourable Peter deC. Cory, acting as Commissioner, in The Inquiry Regarding Thomas Sophonow: The Investigation, Prosecution and Consideration of Entitlement to Compensation (Winnipeg: Manitoba Justice, 2001). The following recommendations which can be found at pp. 33-34 of the report relate specifically to the need to provide juries with stronger warnings when confronted with eyewitness identification evidence:

* There must be strong and clear directions given by the Trial Judge to the jury emphasizing the frailties of eyewitness identification. The jury should as well be instructed that the apparent confidence of a witness as to his or her identification is not a criteria of the accuracy of the identification. In this case, the evidence of Mr. Janower provides a classic example of misplaced but absolute confidence that Thomas Sophonow was the man whom he saw at the donut shop.

* The Trial Judge should stress that tragedies have occurred as a result of mistakes made by honest, right-thinking eyewitnesses. It should be explained that a vast majority of the wrongful convictions of innocent persons have arisen as a result of faulty eyewitness identification. These instructions should be given in addition to the standard direction regarding the difficulties inherent in eyewitness identification.

. . .

* The Trial Judge must instruct and caution the jury with regard to an identification which has apparently progressed from tentative to certain and to consider what may have brought about that change.

* During the instructions, the Trial Judge should advise the jury that mistaken eyewitness identification has been a significant factor in wrongful convictions of accused in the United States and in Canada, with a possible reference to the Thomas Sophonow case.

A judge sitting alone as the trier of fact should also be cognizant of the dangers associated with eyewitness identification.

In *R. v. Bullock*, [1999] O.J. No. 3106 (S.C.J.), Hill J. gave a summary of some of the cases that have dealt with the frailties of eyewitness identification. He stated at paras. 49-56:

Eye-witness identification evidence can be notoriously unreliable calling for considerable caution by the trier(s)-of-fact: *The Queen v. Nikolovski* (1997), 111 C.C.C. (3d) 403 (S.C.C.) at 411-412 per Cory J.; *Bardales v. The Queen*, [1996] 2 S.C.R. 461 at 461 per Sopinka J.; *Burke v. The Queen* (1996), 105 C.C.C. (3d) 205 (S.C.C.) at 224 per Sopinka J.; Pretrial Eyewitness Identification Procedures (Law Reform Commission of Canada (1983)) at pages 7-14. Especially where the suspect is unknown to the eye-witness, there is the danger of an honest but inaccurate identification. This is the problem of a mistake by a convinced and convincing witness: *R. v. Menard* (1996), 108 C.C.C. (3d) 424 (Ont. C.A.) at 437 per Arbour J.A. (appeal dismissed (1998), 125 C.C.C. (3d) 416 (S.C.C.)).

Casual acceptance of identification evidence must be avoided: *Burke v. The Queen*, supra at 224.

In The *Queen v. Nikolovski*, supra at 409, 412 Cory J. stated:

The ultimate aim of any trial, criminal or civil, must be to seek and to ascertain the truth. In a criminal trial the search for truth is undertaken to determine whether the accused before the court is, beyond a reasonable doubt, guilty of the crime with which he is charged. The evidence adduced must be relevant and admissible. That is to say, it must be logically probative and legally receivable. The evidence may be that of eyewitnesses or it may be circumstantial . . .

. . .

As a minimum it must be determined whether the witness was physically in a position to see the accused and, if so, whether that witness had sound vision, good hearing, intelligence and the ability to communicate what was seen and heard. Did the witness have the ability to understand and recount what had been perceived? Did the witness have a sound memory? What was the effect of fear or excitement on the ability of the witness to perceive clearly and to later recount the events accurately? Did the witness have a bias or at least a biased perception of the event or the parties involved?

Other judicially formulated checklists provide similar factors for analysis: *Mezzo v. The Queen* (1986), 27 C.C.C. (3d) 97 (S.C.C.) at 129-132 per Wilson J.

In an appropriate case, a trier-of-fact may be justified in convicting on the evidence of a single eye-witness: see *Pelletier v. The Queen*, [1996] 3 S.C.R. 601 at 601 per Lamer C.J.C. (affirming [1995] A.Q. No. 1129 (C.A.)). In this regard, at page 413 of the *Nikolovski* decision, Cory J. stated:

> It is clear that a trier of fact may, despite all the potential frailties, find an accused guilty beyond a reasonable doubt on the basis of the testimony of a single eye-witness.

A fleeting glance of a suspect by an eye-witness is generally unsatisfactory: *Regina v. Carpenter*, [1998] O.J. No. 1819 (C.A.) at para. 1 per Abella J.A..

The courts have shown express preference for the police to conduct pre-trial identification steps to avoid in-court dock identification: *Regina v. Hill*, [1997] O.J. No. 3255 (C.A.) at para 3 per curiam. This will ordinarily take the form of a line-up or other form of prior identification procedure: *Regina v. Grangello*, [1999] O.J. No. 2043 (C.A.). With respect to a suspect unknown to the eye-witness, an in-court, dock identification is, as a general rule, worthless: *Regina v. Izzard* (1990), 54 C.C.C. (3d) 252 (Ont. C.A.) at 255-6 per Morden J.A. (as he then was); *Regina v. Mooney*, [1999] O.J. No. 2793 (C.A.) at para 4 per curiam; *Regina v. Myers*, [1997] O.J. No. 4185 (C.A.) at para. 4, 5 per curiam.

The physical photographic line-up must be fairly structured in terms of its makeup with regard to the number of photographs employed and with a view to the subjects of the photos resembling the suspect at least in terms of age, gender and general appearance including build, height, and complexion: *Rex v. Goldhar; Rex v. Smokler* (1941), 76 C.C.C. 270 (Ont. C.A.) at 271-272 per Robertson C.J.O.; *Regina v. MacKenzie*, [1976] O.J. No. 667 (C.A.) at para. 8 per Martin J.A. While everyone in a forensic line-up cannot be identical, the subjects should be reasonably similar without conspicuous differences even if not all subjects share all of the descriptors advanced by the witness.

As the trier of fact, I have familiarized myself with the law as outlined above on this issue. I am cognizant of the frailties of eyewitness identification evidence, particularly with respect to in court identifications. Therefore, my analysis of the evidence in this case did not rely on the dock identification of the accused made by both the Complainant and Mr. Robertson. I place absolutely no weight whatsoever on the dock identifications made. I also place no weight on the evidence of identification given by the Complainant in his testimony. [Romilly J. found that the complainant was not a very compelling witness. He was possibly under the influence of drugs when he testified and was a volatile witness.]

In assessing the identification evidence, however, I find that although Mr. Robertson did not know the accused by name, he was no stranger to him. Mr. Robertson had seen the accused in the area on about 25 occasions. He knew that the accused was a drug dealer and, as such, he was one of the persons that Mr.

Robertson did not want entering the Savoy and Eaton Hotels to sell drugs there. In his testimony, the accused admitted that he was indeed a drug dealer and that he did sell drugs in the area of the Carnegie Centre. The description given by Mr. Robertson to the police on the night of the incident fit the description of the accused. There was also no tainting of Mr. Robertson's identification due to any faulty procedures on the part of the police. It was Mr. Robertson who saw the accused at the Empress Hotel on the day following the incident, and it was he who reported the accused to the police.

Although no DNA was found on the knife that was on the person of the accused when he was arrested, it was exactly as described by both the Complainant and Mr. Robertson. In addition to all of this, there was the statement made by the accused while in the course of being processed by the police when he was asked to hand over the clothes he was currently wearing. He said, "I don't know why you are taking my clothes anyways. These aren't the clothes that I was wearing yesterday."

Justice Romilly held that the defence evidence was not credible and did not leave him with a reasonable doubt.

For further consideration of the unreliability of eyewitness identification and warning practices in Canada and the United States, see Lisa Dufraimont, "Regulating Unreliable Evidence: Can Evidence Rules Guide Juries and Prevent Wrongful Convictions?"[47]

R. v. HANEMAAYER

(2008), 2008 CarswellOnt 4698, 234 C.C.C. (3d) 3 (Ont. C.A.)

ROSENBERG J.A.:

. . .

[2] Almost twenty years ago, on October 18, 1989, the appellant pleaded guilty to two criminal offences that he did not commit. The story of how that happened is an important cautionary tale for the administration of criminal justice in this province.

THE FACTS OF THE OFFENCES

[3] On September 29, 1987, at about 5:00 a.m., a man broke into a residence in Scarborough and went to the bedroom of the owner's 15-year-old daughter. He jumped on her back, put his hand over her mouth, threatened her, and told her that he had a knife. Fortunately, the homeowner was awakened by the noise in her daughter's room. Thinking that her daughter had fallen out of bed, she went into the hall and turned on the light. She saw a man sitting on her daughter. She yelled at him and he turned around so that she saw his face. She would later testify that she studied the man's face very closely. The man then jumped off the bed

---

47 (2008) 33 *Queen's L.J.* 361.

and confronted the homeowner. He stood inches from her, raised his arms and "roared" at her. He then fled the house.

[4] The homeowner told police that she stared at the intruder for forty seconds to a minute and could identify him again. Her daughter testified that less than thirty seconds passed from the time her mother entered the bedroom to when the intruder fled. The homeowner provided a description of the intruder to the police as follows:

> 6'0", 170 lbs., slim build, 19 years of age with sandy brown, wavy hair, wearing a black leather jacket and blue jeans.

[5] Although the homeowner had never seen the man before she believed that she was particularly adept at remembering faces because her work as a teacher required her to put names to the faces of her students. She decided that the perpetrator must have been keeping watch on her daughter and on the house and likely was working on construction in the area. She drove around and looked at the various construction sites and then telephoned one of the companies working in the area. She provided her description to a woman in the personnel department and the woman gave her the appellant's name as someone who fit the description. She passed on the name to the police.

[6] In the same period of time, the homeowner helped with a composite drawing prepared by a police technician operating a computer. She also viewed about 100 photographs at the police station. She told the police that she remembered two particular characteristics of the man; he had very piercing eyes and small ears. She agreed that the composite sketch did not reflect the small ears but she testified this was because the computer could not get it right. Two months after the break-in, the police showed the homeowner a photo line-up and she picked out the appellant's photograph. The investigating officer told her she had picked out the appellant's picture.

[7] The line-up viewed by the homeowner is no longer available. However, she did testify in cross-examination that the appellant's photograph was the least sharp of all the pictures in the array.

[8] The appellant was arrested on December 18, 1987. He gave a signed statement to the police in which he denied knowing anything of the crime. He confirmed that he had been working on construction in the Scarborough area that summer. It appears that he stopped working with the company five days before the break-in.

THE ORIGINAL COURT PROCEEDINGS

[9] The appellant was originally released on bail but when he failed to appear for his scheduled preliminary inquiry, he was arrested and detained in custody until his trial. His preliminary inquiry was ultimately held in May 1989 and he was committed for trial. His trial commenced on October 17, 1989 before Ferguson J.

[10] The complainant and the homeowner testified on the first day of the trial. On the second day of the trial, after the homeowner had completed her testimony, the appellant changed his plea to guilty. He pleaded guilty to break and enter and committing an assault and assault while threatening to use a weapon. He was convicted on the break and enter charge and the second charge was stayed pursuant to the *Kienapple* doctrine: *R. v. Kienapple* (1974), 15 C.C.C. (2d) 524 (S.C.C.). He was sentenced to two years less one day imprisonment in accordance with a joint submission. The appellant served more than eight months of the sentence before being released on parole.

[11] In an affidavit filed with this court, the appellant explained why he changed his plea. In short, he lost his nerve. He found the homeowner to be a very convincing witness and he could tell that his lawyer was not making any headway in convincing the judge otherwise. Further, since his wife had left him and wanted nothing more to do with him, he had no one to support his story that he was home at the time of the offence. He says that his lawyer told him he would almost certainly be convicted and would be sentenced to six years imprisonment or more. However, if he changed his plea, his lawyer said he could get less than two years and would not go to the penitentiary. The appellant agreed to accept the deal even though he was innocent and had told his lawyer throughout that he was innocent.

THE RE-INVESTIGATION

[12] On October 17, 2005, Paul Bernardo's lawyer sent an e-mail to a police officer with the Toronto Police Sex Crimes Unit listing 18 sexual assaults and other offences that he believed had not been solved. One of the crimes was the break-in to which the appellant had pleaded guilty.

[13] The police interviewed Bernardo in April 2006 and then conducted a further investigation. They are satisfied that Bernardo, not the appellant, committed the crime. At the time, Bernardo lived two blocks from the victim's home. He, of course, was the so-called "Scarborough rapist" and, after his conviction for murder, was convicted of a number of sexual assaults committed in the Scarborough area during this time period. For example, one of the rapes which Bernardo was known to have committed occurred two and one-half months after the attack on this victim and was committed only half a block from the victim's home. It is unnecessary to further detail why there is no doubt of Bernardo's guilt. The fresh evidence is absolutely compelling.

[14] In the course of the re-investigation, the police interviewed the appellant and the homeowner. The appellant reaffirmed his innocence. The homeowner told the investigators that she had been sure at the time that the perpetrator was not the Scarborough rapist because his method of operation was different. She was also sure that the person she saw was not Bernardo. At the hearing of the appeal, counsel informed the court that the homeowner remains convinced that she identified the right person.

THE PROCEEDINGS IN THIS COURT

[15] With the consent of the Crown, the appellant was granted an extension of time to appeal his conviction. The Crown also agreed that fresh evidence in the form of the results of the police re-investigation and the appellant's affidavit should be admitted into evidence and that the appeal should be allowed.

. . .

(2) The Identification Evidence

[21] I wish to make a few comments about the identification evidence in this case. We now know that the homeowner was mistaken. No fault can be attributed to her. She honestly believed that she had identified the right person. What happened in this case is consistent with much of what is known about mistaken identification evidence and, in particular, that honest but mistaken witnesses make convincing witnesses. Even the appellant, who knew he was innocent, was convinced that the trier of fact would believe her. The research shows, however, that there is a very weak relationship between the witness' confidence level and the accuracy of the identification. The confidence level of the witness can have a "powerful effect on jurors": see Manitoba, *The Inquiry Regarding Thomas Sophonow: The Investigation, Prosecution and Consideration of Entitlement to Compensation* (Winnipeg: Manitoba Justice, 2001) at 28; see also *R. v. Hibbert* (2002), 163 C.C.C. (3d) 129 (S.C.C.) at 148.

[22] The homeowner's evidence also reveals a number of concerns that demonstrate the frailties of eyewitness identification. First, there was no circumstantial evidence connecting the appellant with this crime. The fact that he was working in the area around the time is not circumstantial evidence inculpating him, but may possibly explain why the homeowner was able to pick him out of the line-up. Research has shown that witnesses have a difficult time keeping track of where they have seen someone: see *The Inquiry Regarding Thomas Sophonow* at p. 28.

[23] Second, the photographic line-up itself was the kind then in use by the police, that is, presented as an array rather than sequentially. In his report, Commissioner Peter Cory referred at p. 28 to the expert evidence adduced before him that photo line-ups are a form of "multiple choice testing". As I understand it, the danger is that the witness may choose the picture from the array that is the best fit. The witness engages in a process of elimination rather than recognition. Commissioner Cory recommended that the photo pack be presented sequentially.

[24] Third, the appellant's picture was different than the other photographs in the array. In *Hill v. Hamilton-Wentworth Regional Police Services Board* (2005), 76 O.R. (3d) 481 (C.A.), aff'd [2007] 3 S.C.R. 129, Feldman and LaForme JJ.A., in their dissenting opinion, refer at para. 149 to the expert evidence of Professor Roderick Lindsay, adduced in that case concerning structural bias in the presentation of a photo line-up. As Professor Lindsay explained, structural bias results when one person in the line-up is visually distinct from the others in some

way. This bias can cause misidentifications because the person who stands out is more likely to be picked by the identifying witness.

[25] Fourth, the officers conducting the line-up were involved in the investigation and knew the identity of the suspect. There is a danger that the investigating officer may, even if not consciously, convey information to the witness to cause her to select the suspect. Commissioner Cory recommended, at p. 32, that "it is essential that an officer who does not know who the suspect is and who is not involved in the investigation conducts the photo pack line-up".

[26] Fifth, the evidence discloses serious contamination by the investigating officers. They informed the homeowner that she had indeed identified the suspect. This could only serve to increase her confidence in the accuracy of the identification and thus make her a more convincing witness. As Commissioner Cory recommended at p. 32:

> Police officers should not speak to eyewitnesses after the line-ups regarding their identification or their inability to identify anyone. This can only cast suspicion on any identification made and raise concerns that it was reinforced.

[27] Sixth, no permanent record was made of the line-up procedure. Commissioner Cory recommended that the line-up process should be videotaped or at least audio taped. The taped record can provide valuable information for the trier of fact in evaluating the reliability of the identification.

[28] In making these comments, I do not intend any unfair criticism either of the witness or the police. As to the witness, as I have said, she honestly believed she had made a correct identification. That identification was made in difficult circumstances; she was naturally under considerable stress when she encountered the assailant; she only had a brief opportunity to make her observations and she was identifying a stranger. As to the police, they may have been following procedures that were in place at the time. Those procedures and standards have evolved in the last twenty years: see the Supreme Court of Canada's comments in *Hill v. Hamilton Wentworth Police Service* at paras. 78-80.

[29] However, this case represents an example of how flawed identification procedures can contribute to miscarriages of justice and the importance of taking great care in conducting those procedures. Mistaken eyewitness identification is the overwhelming factor leading to wrongful convictions. A study in the United States of DNA exonerations shows that mistaken eyewitness identification was a factor in over 80 per cent of the cases: see *The Inquiry Regarding Thomas Sophonow* at p. 27.

CONCLUSION

[30] I would conclude by reiterating the court's thanks to Mr. Lockyer on behalf of the appellant and Mr. Leibovich on behalf of the Crown for the work they have done to expedite this matter and, so far as can be done, reverse this miscarriage of justice. I also repeat what we said to Mr. Hanemaayer at the conclusion of the hearing:

It is profoundly regrettable that errors in the justice system led to this miscarriage of justice and the devastating effect it has had on Mr. Hanemaayer and his family.

Was it ethical for defence counsel to plead his client guilty in these circumstances?[48]

(vi) *Hodge's Case*

Liverpool Sum. Assizes, 1838
HODGE'S CASE

(Where a charge depends upon circumstantial evidence, it ought not only to be consistent with the prisoner's guilt, but inconsistent with any other rational conclusion.)

The prisoner was charged with murder.

The case was one of circumstantial evidence altogether, and contained no one fact, which taken alone amounted to a presumption of guilt. The murdered party (a woman), who was also robbed, was returning from market with money in her pocket; but how much, or of what particular description of coin, could not be ascertained distinctly.

The prisoner was well acquainted with her, and had been seen near the spot (a lane), in or near which the murder was committed, very shortly before. There were also four other persons together in the same lane about the same period of time. The prisoner, also, was seen some hours after, and on the same day, but at a distance of some miles from the spot in question, burying something, which on the following day was taken up, and turned out to be money, and which corresponded generally as to amount with that which the murdered woman was supposed to have had in her possession when she set out on her return home from market, and of which she had been robbed.

Alderson, B., told the jury, that the case was made up of circumstances entirely; and that, before they could find the prisoner guilty, they must be satisfied, "not only that those circumstances were consistent with his having committed the act, but they must also be satisfied that the facts were such as to be inconsistent with any other rational conclusion than that the prisoner was the guilty person."

He then pointed out to them the proneness of the human mind to look for — and often slightly to distort the facts in order to establish such a proposition — forgetting that a single circumstance which is inconsistent with such a conclusion, is of more importance than all the rest, inasmuch as it destroys the hypothesis of guilt.

The learned Baron then summed up the facts of the case, and the jury returned a verdict of Not guilty.[49]

Would you have convicted based on the evidence presented in this case? How prophetic was Baron Alderson's concern about tunnel vision?[50]

The important question for us is whether Baron Alderson coined a form of words for explaining to the jury how they might be satisfied beyond a reasonable

---

48 See Tanovich, "*Taillefer.* Disclosure, Guilty Pleas and Ethics" (2004), 27 C.R. (6th) 149; and *R. v. K. (S.)* (1995), 99 C.C.C. (3d) 376 (Ont. C.A.).

49 168 E.R. 1136.

50 See the discussion of this in Berger, "The Rule in Hodge's Case: Rumours of Its Death Are Greatly Exaggerated" (2005), 84 Can. Bar Rev. 47.

doubt when the evidence was circumstantial, or whether he intended to erect a new and higher standard of persuasion for such cases.

In 1973 the issue came before the House of Lords in *McGreevy v. Director of Public Prosecutions*[51] on an appeal from Northern Ireland from a conviction for murder. The principal basis for the appeal was that the trial judge in a criminal case dependent on circumstantial evidence should not only direct the jury that they must be satisfied beyond a reasonable doubt but also must charge them in accordance with the so-called rule in *Hodge's Case*. In a unanimous opinion Lord Morris wrote:

> The painstaking research of counsel for the appellant showed that in some countries in the Commonwealth both learned judges and also legal writers have made reference to the "rule" in *Hodge's* case. I do not propose to refer to all the citations which counsel made. The singular fact remains that here in the home of the common law *Hodge's* case has not been given very special prominence: references to it are scant and do not suggest that it enshrines guidance of such compulsive power as to amount to a rule of law which if not faithfully followed will stamp a summing-up as defective. I think that this is consistent with the view that *Hodge's* case was reported not because it laid down a new rule of law but because it was thought to furnish a helpful example of one way in which a jury could be directed in a case where the evidence was circumstantial.[52]

In *R. v. Cooper*[53] the issue again came before the Supreme Court of Canada. The accused was charged that he did confer a benefit on a government employee with respect to dealings between the accused and the government. It was accepted that the evidence from which it was sought to prove that the conferring of the benefit was with respect to accused's dealings with the government, was almost entirely circumstantial. The trial judge charged the jury in accordance with the rule in *Hodge's Case*. The prosecution objected that the question of whether the benefits were with respect to the accused's dealings with the government involved a question of what the accused intended and, therefore, based on earlier jurisprudence, the instruction was not warranted. The trial judge recalled the jury and advised them to disregard his previous charge with respect to circumstantial evidence. On appeal to the Supreme Court of Canada, the accused argued, however, that in recharging the jury in this way the trial judge had diluted his charge as to reasonable doubt as the recharge

> would convey to the jury that his instruction previously given in the language of *Hodge's* case was neither a formula to assist in applying the accepted standard of proof nor a graphic illustration of the principle of reasonable doubt.[54]

The majority of four justices denied that such would be the case and Ritchie J. wrote:

> ... when the charge, as corrected, is read as a whole and in light of this final admonition, I am of opinion that no reasonable juror could have been confused as to the obligation to be satisfied beyond a reasonable doubt before entering a conviction. Nothing was said to suggest any other standard of proof and in my opinion

---

51 [1973] 1 All E.R. 503 (H.L.).
52 *Ibid.*, at p. 508.
53 (1977), 74 D.L.R. (3d) 731 (S.C.C.).
54 *Ibid.*, at p. 745.

the instructions as to reasonable doubt are in no way diluted by charging the jury in accordance with the law established in this Court that the *Hodge's* formula does not apply in determining the "intention" of the accused. The language employed by Mr. Justice Spence in the passage from his reasons in *R. v. Mitchell, supra,* has been reaffirmed in this Court in *R. v. John, supra; R. v. Bagshaw,* (1971), 4 C.C.C. (2d) 303 at p. 307, [1972] S.C.R. at p. 6, and *R. v. Paul* (1975), 27 C.C.C. (2d) 1 at p. 4, 33 C.R.N.S. 328, and must, I think, be taken to have been accepted as confining the application of the *Hodge's Case* formula in the manner there stated. This is not to say that, even where the issue is one of identification, the exact words used by Baron Alderson must necessarily be incorporated in a Judge's charge. It is enough if it is made plain to the members of the jury that before basing a verdict of guilty on circumstantial evidence they must be satisfied beyond a reasonable doubt that the guilt of the accused is the only reasonable inference to be drawn from the proven facts. In this regard it will be seen that I agree with the Chief Justice in his rejection of the *Hodge* formula as an inexorable rule of law in Canada.[55]

Laskin C.J.C., in a dissenting opinion, would go much further:

> There are a few observations I would make on *Hodge's Case* specifically. Intent is no less a question of fact than is identity or the *actus reus* of an offence. I would not condone a situation where a trial Judge may properly charge a jury under *Hodge's Case* in respect of identity, and all other issues except intent, and then in the same case tell them to approach the Crown's burden of proof on a different basis on the question of intent. There must be consistency in a charge where burden of proof is concerned; and to have two different formulae in one case is as unjust to the Crown as it is to an accused.
>
> The judgment of the House of Lords in *McGreevy v. Director of Public Prosecutions,* [1973] 1 All E.R. 503, rejects the notion that there ever was any rule arising from *Hodge's Case* which Judges in England were required to follow where all or most of the evidence in a jury trial was circumstantial. In *R. v. Comba* (1938), 70 C.C.C. p. 237 at p. 238, [1938] S.C.R. 396 at p. 397, this Court referred to the formula in *Hodge's Case* as "the long settled rule of the common law, which is the rule of law in Canada". Notwithstanding this pronouncement, this Court attenuated the rule in its judgment in *R. v. Mitchell, supra,* and manifested its discomfort with *Hodge's Case* in *R. v. John* (1970), 2 C.C.C. (2d) 157, [1971] S.C.R. 781. The time has come to reject the formula in *Hodge's Case* as an inexorable rule of law in Canada. Without being dogmatic against any use of the formula of the charge in *Hodge's Case* I would leave the matter to the good sense of the trial Judge (as was said in *McGreevy*), with the reminder that a charge in terms of the traditional formula of required proof beyond a reasonable doubt is the safest as well as the simplest way to bring a lay jury to the appreciation of the burden of proof resting on the Crown in a criminal case.[56]

In *R. v. Charemski,*[57] Bastarache J., Cory and Iacobucci JJ. concurring, for the majority, wrote:

> In my view, the trial judge should have directed the jury according to the requirement that a finding of guilt could only be made where there was no other rational explanation for the circumstantial evidence but that the defendant committed the crime (*John v. The Queen,* [1971] S.C.R. 781, at pp. 791-92; *R. v. Cooper,* [1978] 1 S.C.R. 860, at p. 881; *Mezzo v. The Queen,* [1986] 1 S.C.R. 802, at p. 843).

---

55 *Ibid.,* at p. 746.
56 *Ibid.,* at p. 735.
57 [1998] 1 S.C.R. 679.

R. v. TOMBRAN

31 C.R. (5th) 349, 142 C.C.C. (3d) 380, 2000 CarswellOnt 231 (C.A.)

The accused was convicted of second degree murder. The Crown's case was entirely circumstantial. The Crown's theory was that the accused was having financial difficulties and killed the deceased to collect on a $400,000 life insurance policy for which he was the beneficiary. The accused testified that he had planned to go into business together with the deceased and that they had taken out joint life insurance policies. He also admitted to having sex with the deceased on the morning that she died. One of the grounds of appeal concerned the adequacy of the charge to the jury on reasonable doubt.

SHARPE J.A. (CARTHY and CHARRON JJ.A. concurring): —

The trial judge did not explain to the jury the difference between direct and circumstantial evidence. After directing the jury on the presumption of innocence and the burden on the Crown to prove the guilt of the accused beyond a reasonable doubt ... [the trial judge] stated as follows:

> In this case the Crown's case is completely circumstantial. There is no direct evidence that the accused killed Ms Lachman. No one saw the accused kill Ms Lachman, and he never admitted that fact. Thus, you must be satisfied that on the basis of the circumstantial evidence that you do accept as credible and reliable, that the only rational and logical conclusion is that the accused is guilty. In other words the Crown must have proven the accused's guilt beyond a reasonable doubt which, conversely put, means the absence of any reasonable doubt whatsoever. The key words of course are "reasonable doubt", not conjectural or speculative doubt.

There is no other specific reference to the words "circumstantial evidence" in the trial judge's charge. While he cautioned the jury against making speculative findings, the trial judge did not specifically instruct the jury on the reasoning process it should follow in assessing circumstantial evidence. The appellant's trial counsel objected to this aspect of the charge and urged the trial judge to instruct the jury on the distinction between direct and circumstantial evidence and the drawing of inferences. The trial judge refused this request.

While the trial judge did not go into the difference between direct and circumstantial evidence, he did review the evidence in detail. He set out in very clear and precise terms the respective positions of the Crown and the appellant as to the conclusions the jury ought to draw.

It is submitted by the appellant that as the Crown's case was entirely circumstantial, the trial judge's treatment of circumstantial evidence amounted to a reversible non-direction. The appellant contends that the trial judge ought to have first explained to the jury the difference between direct and circumstantial evidence, and then to have directed the jury to follow a two-step process of reasoning in relation to the evidence. First, they should decide what evidence they believed and, second, they should determine what inferences should be drawn from that evidence.

It is common ground that the modern starting point on the law relating to circumstantial evidence is *R. v. Cooper* (1977), 34 C.C.C. (2d) 18 (S.C.C.). ...

[25] In *R. v. Fleet* (1997), 120 C.C.C. (3d) 457 at 464-465, this court reviewed the jurisprudence on circumstantial evidence and stated as follows:

> We read the object of both judgments in *Cooper* to be the eradication of any formulaic approach to such cases so long as the jury is clearly made aware of the necessity to find the guilt of the accused to be established beyond a reasonable doubt. This object may be achieved in more ways than one. Thus, the trial judge, reviewing the evidence and setting out the position of the defence and relating the substantial parts of the evidence to that position, may frame the requisite instruction in the manner he or she considers most appropriate in the circumstances, for example, by: "(a) charging the jury in accordance with the traditional language of proof beyond a reasonable doubt (per Laskin C.J.C. in *Cooper*)"(b) charging the jury in accordance with that language and pointing out to the jury the other inferences that the defence says should be drawn from the evidence and the necessity to acquit the accused if any of those inferences raises a reasonable doubt (as the trial judge did in *Cooper* in the final portion of his recharge); or"(c) charging the jury that it must be satisfied beyond a reasonable doubt that the guilt of the accused is the only reasonable inference to be drawn from the proven facts (per Ritchie J. in *Cooper* and Dubin J.A. in *Elmosri*)." The essential requirement is to impress upon the jury the need to find guilt proven beyond a reasonable doubt and to make plain to them the manner in which such a doubt can arise in the context of a case of proof of identity by circumstantial evidence.

In my view, the trial judge's instruction to the jury in the case at bar met the requirements of *Cooper, supra*, and satisfied the standard set out by this court in *Fleet, supra*. Indeed, the trial judge instructed the jury in each of the three ways suggested in that case. First, he charged the jury in accordance with the traditional language of proof beyond a reasonable doubt. Second, he carefully charged the jury on the inferences it was being asked to draw from the evidence and instructed them to acquit the accused if any of those inferences gave rise to a reasonable doubt. Third, he clearly instructed the jury that in order to convict, it must be satisfied beyond a reasonable doubt that the guilt of the accused is the only reasonable inference to be drawn from the facts.

The appellant contends that despite *Cooper, supra* and *Fleet, supra*, the appropriate instruction to be given to the jury in a case based upon circumstantial evidence must now be reassessed in the light of the Supreme Court of Canada's judgment in *R. v. Charemski* (1998), 123 C.C.C. (3d) 225. I disagree. In *Charemski*, the court dealt with the test to be applied on a motion for a directed verdict. The accused was charged with murder. The Crown's case was entirely circumstantial. At the conclusion of the Crown's case, the accused moved for a directed verdict on the ground that there was no evidence on the issue of causation. The trial judge granted the motion and directed a verdict of acquittal. This court allowed the Crown's appeal and set aside the directed verdict. That decision was upheld on appeal to the Supreme Court of Canada. The appellant submits that the effect of the judgment is to resurrect the "rule in *Hodge's Case*" and, by implication, the need to explain the nature of circumstantial evidence and the drawing of inferences from such evidence. ...

... The issue before the court was the respective roles of judge and jury in relation to circumstantial evidence and whether the trial judge was entitled to take the case away from the jury. The entire thrust of the decision is that it is the jury's preserve to draw the appropriate inferences, not the trial judge. The issue presented in the case at bar, namely, the appropriate instruction in law to be given the jury in a case resting upon circumstantial evidence, was not before the court in *Charemski, supra*. It is true that in the second passage quoted above, Bastarache J. referred to the appropriate direction, but in doing so, he specifically cited *R. v. Cooper, supra*, as a governing authority. In light of that reference, and in light of the actual issue presented in the case, I cannot read *Charemski, supra*, as reversing or disturbing what was decided in *Cooper, supra*. Nor do I read the decision as requiring trial judges to deliver abstract lectures to juries on the differences between direct and circumstantial evidence. Moreover, as I have already noted, in the present case, the trial judge did instruct the jury in language very similar to that suggested by Bastarache J. In my view, *Charemski, supra*, does not assist the appellant.

The submission advanced by the appellant on this point runs counter to the steady and unrelenting stream of jurisprudence on circumstantial evidence over the past thirty years. The modern approach to the problem of circumstantial evidence, enunciated clearly in *Cooper, supra*, and reiterated and reinforced by *Fleet, supra*, is to reject a formulaic approach and to deal with all the evidence in terms of the general principles of reasonable doubt. Trial judges are given a degree of latitude to formulate the appropriate instruction as befits the circumstances of the case. Trial judges are not required to adopt any specific language or wording, provided the charge conveys to the jury in a clear fashion the central point, namely, the necessity to find the guilt of the accused beyond a reasonable doubt. In particular, trial judges are not required to deliver to the jury a general, abstract lecture on the nature of circumstantial evidence or on the steps of logic to be followed in assessing circumstantial as distinct from direct evidence. An academic exercise along those lines may well confuse rather than assist the jury. Trial judges are entitled to conclude that the essential message of the need to establish guilt beyond a reasonable doubt can be better conveyed in other ways.

The trial judge's instruction in the case at bar conveyed to the jury in clear and unambiguous terms the respective positions of the Crown and the defence as to the possible inferences to be drawn from the evidence. In his review of the evidence and the possible inferences to be drawn, the trial judge repeatedly conveyed to the jury the need to find that the evidence proved the guilt of the appellant beyond a reasonable doubt. Accordingly, I would dismiss this ground of appeal.

The appeal was dismissed.

Sharpe J.A., in the companion case of *R. v. Roberts*,[58] held that whatever formula was used to explain the drawing of reasonable inferences in circumstantial cases it should not divert from the essential issue of whether there was proof of guilt beyond a reasonable doubt. The trial judge had committed

---

58 (2000) 31 C.R. (5th) 340 (Ont. C.A.).

reversible error in an arson case by using the Hodge's formula to require an explanation from the accused of the proven facts.

Most recently, in *R. v. Griffin*[59] Justice Charron, speaking for a majority of the Supreme Court, wrote:

> We have long departed from any legal requirement for a "special instruction" on circumstantial evidence, even where the issue is one of identification. . . . The essential component of an instruction on circumstantial evidence is to instill in the jury that in order to convict, they must be satisfied beyond a reasonable doubt that the only rational inference that can be drawn from the circumstantial evidence is that the accused is guilty. Imparting the necessary message to the jury may be achieved in different ways.[60]

In her comment on this passage Professor Lisa Dufraimont[61] writes:

> The Supreme Court's rejection of a legal requirement for a special instruction on circumstantial evidence should finally put to rest any lingering notion that a heightened standard of proof applies in circumstantial cases. This passage also clearly and sensibly eliminates any rigid requirement for trial judges to follow a particular form of words in charging the jury on the standard of proof as it applies to circumstantial evidence.

> However, by laying out what it calls an "essential component of an instruction on circumstantial evidence," the judgment in *Griffin* strongly suggests that there must in fact be an instruction on circumstantial evidence. It is not clear what it means that this instruction need not be "special," when the judgment implies that the instruction itself must exist. Trial judges, who take pains to ensure that juries receive all necessary legal instructions, are likely to read *Griffin* as mandating an instruction on circumstantial evidence in every circumstantial case. As long as such a requirement exists, our law remains mired in the legacy of *Hodge's Case*.

> . . . .

> *Griffin* brings some needed clarity to the question of the rule in *Hodge's Case*, but it does not take the rejection of the rule all the way to its logical conclusion. Instead of retaining an emphasis on searching for other rational inferences, the Court might have done better to refocus attention on the ultimate standard of proof beyond a reasonable doubt.

(vii) *Preliminary Findings of Fact*

The persuasive burden also applies where a party has to meet a legal standard in seeking to have evidence admitted. For example, that a piece of real evidence is authentic or that a confession given to a person in authority is voluntary. What standard of proof applies in these circumstances?

R. v. Evans, [1993] 3 S.C.R. 653

SOPINKA J.:

... The general rule is that preliminary questions which are a condition of admissibility are for the trial judge in his or her capacity as the judge of the law rather

---

59 (2009), 67 (6th) 1 (S.C.C.).
60 At para. 33 (citations omitted).
61 "*R. v. Griffin* and the Legacy of *Hodge's Case*", (2009) 67 C.R. (6th) 74.

than as the trier of fact. See *R. v. B. (K.G.), supra,* at pp. 783-84. If factual questions must be resolved, a *voir dire* may be required. The applicable standard of proof in both civil and criminal cases is on a balance of probabilities: *R. v. B.(K.G.),* at p. 800.

R. v. Arp, [1998] 3 S.C.R. 339

CORY J.:

. . . However, the general rule that preliminary findings of fact may be determined on a balance of probabilities is departed from in those certainly rare occasions when admission of the evidence may itself have a conclusive effect with respect to guilt. For example, where the Crown adduces a statement of the accused made to a person in authority, the trial judge must be satisfied beyond a reasonable doubt of the voluntariness of the statement. That evidence may of itself, if accepted as true, provide conclusive proof of guilt. Since doubt about the statement's voluntariness also casts doubt on its reliability, proof beyond a reasonable doubt is warranted. See *Ward v. The Queen,* [1979] 2 S.C.R. 30. If this were not the rule, the jury would be permitted to rely on evidence which it could accept as extremely cogent even though the inherent reliability of that evidence was in doubt.

See further, the discussion of this issue most recently in *R. v. H.(L.T.)*[62] where a majority of the Supreme Court held that the Crown must prove beyond a reasonable doubt that the police properly informed a young person of his or her legal rights in accordance with s. 146 of the *Youth Criminal Justice Act.*

(d) Measure of Evidential Burden

(i) *Criminal Cases*

The evidential burden signifies the duty of going forward in the production of evidence, either at the outset of the trial or during its course. The party who entertains the burden and fails in its discharge not only risks loss at the hands of the trier but also risks loss at the hands of the judge; the party who fails to produce evidence may not get past the judge and into the hands of the jury. While our system is predicated on the right to a jury's verdict, the system has always provided a role for the judge to confine the jury within the parameters of rationality.

Sometimes not meeting the evidential burden can have immediate legal consequences so the measure of the burden may be crucial. Examples are where a trial judge rules that a defence has no air of reality and withdraws it from the jury, on a motion for a directed verdict (motion for non-suit), on whether to discharge or commit following a preliminary inquiry in a criminal trial or on whether to extradite. A series of complex Supreme Court rulings started with the decision in *U.S.A. v. Sheppard.* The Court held that in each of these contexts the basic test is whether a reasonably instructed jury could decide the issue and the judge is not to weigh the evidence. We will see that the Supreme Court has recently modified its position.

---

62 [2008] 2 S.C.R. 739.

U.S.A. v. SHEPPARD

[1977] 2 S.C.R. 1067, 34 C.R.N.S. 207, 30 C.C.C. (2d) 424

The case involved an application for extradition. The affidavit evidence filed on the hearing was that of an admitted drug dealer and alleged accomplice of Sheppard who by his affidavit admitted that he was purchasing immunity for himself by offering his accusation of Sheppard. The extradition judge, Hugessen, J., rejected this evidence as unworthy of belief and refused the extradition. The Supreme Court disagreed. For the 4-3 majority Ritchie J. stated:

> [The test for granting extradition] . . . is the same test which governs a trial Judge in deciding whether the evidence is sufficient to justify him in withdrawing the case from the jury, and this is to be determined according to whether or not there is any evidence upon which a reasonable jury properly instructed could return a verdict of guilty...[It] follows that credibility is not within his sphere....[The extradition judge overlooked] the well established rule that the weighing of evidence is always a matter for the jury.

The Supreme Court first applied its test in *Sheppard* in *R. v. Mezzo*,[63] a case involving direct evidence. Justice McIntyre confirmed that the role of the reviewing judge is not to assess the quality of the evidence and held that the trial judge had erred in directing a verdict of acquittal because of his concerns about the reliability of the identification evidence. One year later, the Court had occasion to consider the test again, this time in a case that turned on circumstantial evidence.

MONTELEONE v. R.

[1987] 2 S.C.R. 154, 59 C.R. (3d) 97, 35 C.C.C (3d) 193

The accused was the proprietor of a men's clothing store which occupied the ground floor of a three-storey building. He was charged with setting a fire which destroyed the building. The fire inspector testified that in his view the fire was set. He admitted that the actual cause of the fire could not be determined, but concluded that the fire was of incendiary origin because the investigation revealed no accidental cause. The accused gave a statement to the inspector that placed him at the scene shortly before the fire; he admitted that he smelled smoke but presumed it was from a defective vacuum cleaner that had overheated. A number of persons had access to the accused's shop. There was no evidence that the accused was in extreme financial difficulty, nor was it shown that he would profit in any substantial degree from the fire. At the close of the Crown's case, before the accused elected whether to call evidence, the trial judge acceded to a defence motion and directed a verdict of acquittal. The Crown appealed to the Court of Appeal, the appeal was allowed, and the accused appealed further.

The judgment of the court was delivered by:

McINTYRE J.:—

. . . .

To reach a conclusion in this case, some consideration of the evidence is

---

63   27 C.C.C. (3d) 97, 52 C.R. (3d) 113, [1986] 1 S.C.R. 802.

involved. The Crown, in seeking to establish its case, tendered evidence which for our purposes may be grouped under four headings:

(1) the nature of the fire;
(2) the motive of the appellant;
(3) the opportunity on the part of the appellant; and
(4) contradictions within the appellant's own statement.

[The Court then examined the evidence that had been led on these matters.]

I do not suggest that the inculpatory evidence is conclusive or even persuasive. That is not the function of an appellate court. The resolution of that question is for the jury upon proper instructions on the law after having heard the evidence. I have made only slight reference to the inculpatory evidence, but I would note that at trial it was strongly challenged on many points. From cross-examination of principal creditors it appeared that the financial obligations of the appellant were not unusual, considering all circumstances and the nature of the business. No creditor expressed any fear as to its security prior to the fire, and the appellant was not being pressed by his creditors. This evidence might very well influence a jury to discount the inculpatory evidence and find in favour of the appellant. This they would do, however, in the exercise of the function imposed upon them by law as the true finders of fact. It is not open to a judge in a jury trial to consider the weight of the evidence. This is the function of the jury and it should be left to them. I am of the view that there was evidence before the trial judge which met the test propounded by Ritchie J. in *U.S. v. Shephard*, supra. I am in substantial agreement with the reasons for judgment of Lacourcière J.A. for the Ontario Court of Appeal and I would dismiss the appeal and confirm the order for a new trial.

Appeal dismissed.

In a companion case, *R. v. Yebes*,[64] handed down the same day as *Monteleone*, the court reviewed the role of an appellate court when a jury's verdict is disputed as "unreasonable or cannot be supported by the evidence" pursuant to section 686(1)(*a*)(i) of the Criminal Code:

> The court must determine on the whole of the evidence whether the verdict is one that a properly-instructed jury, acting judicially, could reasonably have rendered. While the Court of Appeal must not merely substitute its view for that of the jury, in order to apply the test the court must *re-examine* and to some extent *reweigh* and consider the effect of the evidence. [Emphasis added.][65]

Why is it that an appellate court can look back and re-weigh the evidence, and so determine whether the verdict was reasonable, but a trial judge cannot look forward and weigh the evidence to determine whether

---

64 (1987), 59 C.R. (3d) 108, 120 (S.C.C.).
65 R.S.C. 1985, c. C-46.

a verdict based thereon could be reasonable? Are appellate judges more able?

R. v. QUERCIA

(1990), 1 C.R. (4th) 385, 60 C.C.C. (3d) 380 (Ont. C.A.)

The accused was charged with aggravated sexual assault. He denied any involvement in the offence and testified that he was at home with his mother when the assault occurred. His mother testified and corroborated the accused's evidence. The case against the accused rested entirely on the victim's identification of him. The accused was convicted after a trial before a judge and jury. He appealed on the ground that the verdict was unreasonable.

Held, the appeal should be allowed, the conviction quashed and an acquittal entered.

DOHERTY J.A. (GALLIGAN and OSBORNE JJ.A. concurring):—

. . . .

The appellant raises three grounds of appeal:

(1) Did the learned trial judge err in not directing a verdict of not guilty at the close of the Crown's case?
(2) Did the learned trial judge err in failing to instruct the jury as to the reason behind the danger inherent in relying on eyewitness identification?
(3) Was the verdict unreasonable?

We did not call on the Crown on the first two grounds of appeal advanced. The first ground of appeal is determined against the appellant by the judgment of the Supreme Court of Canada in *R. v. Mezzo.* . . . With respect to the alleged non-direction, I cannot agree that the charge to the jury was deficient. The trial judge's instructions pertaining to the manner in which eyewitness identification should be approached and his review of the relevant evidence was marked by both clarity and thoroughness. The instructions to the jury were, at the least, fair to the appellant and were, in some respects, very favourable to him.

The third ground of appeal raises a much more difficult problem. This is a case in which the conviction of the appellant depends entirely on the identification of him by the victim. Where the Crown's case rests on eyewitness identification, one is always very concerned about the reliability of a finding of guilt.

. . . Where the verdict is said to be unreasonable or not supported by the evidence, the appellate court must independently examine and assess the evidence adduced at trial and reach its own conclusion as to the reasonableness of the verdict. In doing so, it must decide whether the totality of the evidence is such that the verdict is one that a "properly instructed jury acting judicially, could reasonably have rendered": *R. v. Yebes.* . . . In deciding whether a jury has exceeded the bounds of reasonableness, the court must give due deference to the advantageous position of the jury, who actually saw and heard the witnesses.

. . . .

Bearing in mind both my duty to weigh and assess the evidence independent of the jury's verdict and the limited scope of my review, I turn to the evidence in the case at bar. I begin by acknowledging that the victim was in every respect an honest witness. Honesty cannot, however, be equated with reliability where identification evidence is concerned.

. . . .

Considering the totality of the evidence describing the attack, and acknowledging the chilling horror of the circumstances in which the victim found herself, I regard this as a case where the victim, in part because of her heroic determination to observe the appellant, had a good opportunity to observe and accurately record in her mind the appearance of her attacker. This was no fleeting encounter. Having made that assessment, I hasten to add that a person in the victim's position could hardly be expected to observe and mentally record all of the salient features of her attacker, nor could she be expected to be completely accurate in her recollection of those observations.

. . . .

I acknowledge the victim's honesty and integrity and I applaud her courage, but I am driven to conclude that her evidence identifying the appellant as her assailant was significantly flawed and could not, standing alone, justify a conviction. There is virtually no other evidence confirming her identification. The weight of the remaining evidence points away from the appellant's involvement in the attack. In my judgment, the verdict is unreasonable and cannot be supported by the evidence. I would allow the appeal, quash the conviction, and enter an acquittal.

R. v. ARCURI
[2001] 2 S.C.R. 828, 44 C.R. (5th) 213, 157 C.C.C. (3d) 21

The accused was charged with first degree murder. At the preliminary inquiry, the Crown's case was entirely circumstantial and the accused called two witnesses whose testimony was arguably exculpatory. The preliminary inquiry judge rejected the accused's contention that he must weigh the evidence and, after viewing the evidence as a whole, determined that the accused should be committed to trial for second degree murder. The accused's certiorari application was dismissed and that decision was affirmed by the Court of Appeal. The issue before the Supreme Court was whether the preliminary inquiry judge, in determining whether the evidence was sufficient to commit the accused to trial, erred in refusing to weigh the Crown's evidence against the allegedly exculpatory direct evidence adduced by the accused.

McLACHLIN C.J. (L'HEUREUX-DUBÉ, GONTHIER, IACOBUCCI, MAJOR, BASTARACHE, BINNIE, ARBOUR and LEBEL JJ. concurring): —

. . . .

The question to be asked by a preliminary inquiry judge under s. 548(1) of the Criminal Code is the same as that asked by a trial judge considering a defence motion for a directed verdict, namely, "whether or not there is any evidence upon which a reasonable jury properly instructed could return a verdict of guilty": *Shephard, supra*, at p. 1080; see also *R. v. Monteleone*, [1987] 2 S.C.R. 154, at p. 160. Under this test, a preliminary inquiry judge must commit the accused to trial "in any case in which there is admissible evidence which could, if it were believed, result in a conviction": *Shephard, supra*, at p. 1080.

The test is the same whether the evidence is direct or circumstantial: see *R. v. Mezzo*, [1986] 1 S.C.R. 802, at p. 842—43; *Monteleone, supra*, at p. 161. The nature of the judge's task, however, varies according to the type of evidence that the Crown has advanced. Where the Crown's case is based entirely on direct evidence, the judge's task is straightforward. By definition, the only conclusion that needs to be reached in such a case is whether the evidence is true: see Watt's *Manual of Criminal Evidence* (1998), at §8.0 ("[d]irect evidence is evidence which, if believed, resolves a matter in issue"); McCormick *on Evidence* (5th ed. 1999), at p. 641; J. Sopinka, S. N. Lederman and A. W. Bryant, *The Law of Evidence in Canada* (2nd ed. 1999), at §2.74 (direct evidence is witness testimony as to "the precise fact which is the subject of the issue on trial"). It is for the jury to say whether and how far the evidence is to be believed: see *Shephard*, supra, at pp. 1086-87. Thus if the judge determines that the Crown has presented direct evidence as to every element of the offence charged, the judge's task is complete. If there is direct evidence as to every element of the offence, the accused must be committed to trial.

The judge's task is somewhat more complicated where the Crown has not presented direct evidence as to every element of the offence. The question then becomes whether the remaining elements of the offence — that is, those elements as to which the Crown has not advanced direct evidence — may reasonably be inferred from the circumstantial evidence. Answering this question inevitably requires the judge to engage in a limited weighing of the evidence because, with circumstantial evidence, there is, by definition, an inferential gap between the evidence and the matter to be established — that is, an inferential gap beyond the question of whether the evidence should be believed. . . . The judge must therefore weigh the evidence, in the sense of assessing whether it is reasonably capable of supporting the inferences that the Crown asks the jury to draw. This weighing, however, is limited. The judge does not ask whether she herself would conclude that the accused is guilty. Nor does the judge draw factual inferences or assess credibility. The judge asks only whether the evidence, *if believed,* could reasonably support an inference of guilt.

. . . .

Notwithstanding certain confusing language in *Mezzo* and *Monteleone* nothing in this Court's jurisprudence calls into question the continuing validity of the common law rule. . . . In *Mezzo*, the issue was whether the Crown had proffered sufficient evidence as to identity. McIntyre J., writing for the majority, stated that a trial judge can direct an acquittal only if there is "no evidence" as to an essential element of the offence. . . . He also stated that the judge has no authority to "weigh and consider the quality of the evidence and to remove it from the jury's consideration". . . . Those statements, taken alone, might be understood to suggest that a preliminary inquiry judge must commit the accused to trial even if the Crown's evidence would not reasonably support an inference of guilt. However, as the dissent in *Charemski* . . . discusses, the remainder of McIntyre J.'s reasons make clear that by "no evidence" McIntyre J. meant "no evidence capable of supporting a conviction," and by "weighing" McIntyre J. was referring to the ultimate determination of guilt (a matter for the jury), as distinguished from the determination of whether the evidence can reasonably support an inference of guilt (a matter for the preliminary inquiry judge). His concern was to reject the argument that the judge must determine whether guilt is the only reasonable inference. His reasons cannot be read to call into question the traditional rule, namely, that the judge must determine whether the evidence can reasonably support an inference of guilt.

In *Monteleone*, the accused was charged with setting fire to his own clothing store. The evidence was entirely circumstantial. The question was whether the trial judge had erred in directing an acquittal on the grounds that the "cumulative effect [of the evidence] gives rise to suspicion only, and cannot justify the drawing of an inference of guilt". . . . In ordering a new trial, McIntyre J. wrote that "[i]t is not the function of the trial judge to weigh the evidence, [or] . . . to draw inferences of fact from the evidence before him". . . . Again, however, the remainder of the reasons make clear that by "weighing" McIntyre J. was referring to the final drawing of inferences from the facts (which task, again, is within the exclusive province of the jury), not to the task of assessing whether guilt could reasonably be inferred. Indeed, the reasons explicitly reaffirm the common law rule that the judge must determine whether "there is before the court any admissible evidence, . . . Whether direct or circumstantial, which, if believed by a properly charged jury acting reasonably, would justify a conviction". . . .

Contrary to the appellant's contention, *Charemski* . . . did not evidence disagreement in this Court as to the proper approach. The appellant in *Charemski* . . . had been charged with the murder of his wife. The trial judge directed a verdict of acquittal, principally because the forensic evidence did not affirmatively suggest that the deceased had been murdered. The question in this Court was whether the Court of Appeal erred in setting aside the trial judge's directed verdict of acquittal. There was no disagreement between the majority and the dissent as to the test that the preliminary inquiry justice must apply. On the contrary, both the majority and the dissent clearly reaffirmed *Shephard* . . . and its progeny. . . . Any disagreement concerned not the test for sufficiency but the question of whether sufficient evidence was led in that case. The majority conceded that forensic evidence had not affirmatively indicated that the deceased had been murdered, but reasoned that a properly instructed jury could reasonably infer guilt from the other evidence that the Crown had led. The dissent argued that, as it had not been established that the deceased had been murdered, it was meaningless to discuss identity and causation, two of the other essential elements of the offence. The dissent also argued that the accused's presence in the deceased's apartment could not reasonably be inferred from the accused's conceded presence in the lobby. The dissenting justices concluded that the circumstantial evidence could not reasonably support an inference of guilt.

. . . .

The question that arises in the case at bar is whether the preliminary inquiry judge's task differs where the defence tenders exculpatory evidence, as is its prerogative under s. 541. In my view, the task is essentially the same, in situations where the defence calls exculpatory evidence, whether it be direct or circumstantial. Where the Crown adduces direct evidence on all the elements of the offence, the case must proceed to trial, regardless of the existence of defence evidence, as by definition the only conclusion that needs to be reached is whether the evidence is true. However, where the Crown's evidence consists of, or includes, circumstantial evidence, the judge must engage in a limited weighing of the whole of the evidence (i.e. including any defence evidence) to determine whether a reasonable jury properly instructed could return a verdict of guilty.

In performing the task of limited weighing, the preliminary inquiry judge does not draw inferences from facts. Nor does she assess credibility. Rather, the judge's task is to determine whether, *if the Crown's evidence is believed*, it would be reasonable for a properly instructed jury to infer guilt. Thus, this task of "limited weighing" never requires consideration of the inherent reliability of the evidence itself. It should be regarded, instead, as an assessment of the reasonableness of the inferences to be drawn from the circumstantial evidence.

. . . .

With those principles in mind, I turn, then, to the question of whether Lampkin Prov. J. properly interpreted and applied the law in this case. . . .

. . . .

Notwithstanding . . . two reservations, I am not persuaded that Lampkin Prov. J. reached the wrong result. Before committing the appellant to trial, the preliminary inquiry justice thoroughly surveyed the circumstantial evidence that had been presented by the Crown. . . . Only after considering "the evidence as a whole" did Lampkin Prov. J. commit the appellant to trial.

. . . .

For the foregoing reasons, I conclude that the appeal should be dismissed.

_____

Arcuri was acquitted at his trial. **Would the result in *Monteleone* have been different if the Court had engaged in the limited weighing permitted by *Arcuri*?**

UNITED STATES v. FERRAS
39 C.R. (6th) 207, 209 C.C.C. (3d) 353, [2006] 2 S.C.R. 77,
2006 CarswellOnt 4450, 2006 CarswellOnt 4451

The accused was charged in the United States with fraud. The extradition proceedings against him was brought by the "record of the case" method under sections 32(1)(a) and 33 of the Extradition Act.[66] In a companion case, *United Mexican States v. Ortega*,[67] the extradition proceedings were brought by the "treaty" method provided in section 32(b) of the Act. The issue was whether these methods violated section 7 of the Charter because of the possibility that a person might be extradited on inherently unreliable evidence. In deciding this issue, the Supreme Court had to confront whether its earlier ruling in *United States v. Sheppard*,[68] which had stood the test of time until the modification made in *Arcuri*, was still good law in extradition cases.

McLACHLIN C.J. (for the Court): —

. . .

On [the *Shephard*] view of the law, the combined effect of the relevant provisions (ss. 29, 32 and 33 of the Act) may be to deprive the person sought of the independent hearing and evaluation required by the principles of fundamental justice applicable to extradition. If the extradition judge possesses neither the ability to declare unreliable evidence inadmissible nor to weigh and consider the sufficiency of the evidence, committal for extradition could occur in circumstances where committal for trial in Canada would not be justified. I take as axiomatic that a person could not be committed for trial for an offence in Canada if the evidence is so manifestly unreliable that it would be unsafe to rest a verdict upon it. It follows that if a judge on an extradition hearing concludes that the evidence is manifestly unreliable, the judge should not order extradition under s. 29(1). Yet, under the current state of the law in *Shephard*, it appears that the judge is denied this possibility. Similarly, I take it as axiomatic that a person could not be committed to trial for an offence in Canada if the evidence put against the person is not available for trial. As Donald J.A., dissenting in *Ortega* stated, at para. 51:

> If evidence is not available for trial it should not be used as a basis for committal. The concern goes well beyond modalities and rules of evidence, it goes to the heart of the question for the judge: whether there is enough evidence to put the requested person on trial.

Yet on the majority view in *Shephard*, committal may be ordered in the absence of certification that the evidence is available for trial. This raises particular concerns in an extradition context because the committal becomes the final judicial determination that sends the subject out of the country.

. . . . .

Section 29(1) of the *Extradition Act*, as discussed, requires the extradition judge to be satisfied that the evidence would justify committal for trial in Canada, had the offence occurred here. Canadian courts in recent decades have adopted

---

66 S.C. 1999, c. 18.
67 [2006] 2 S.C.R. 120, 209 C.C.C. (3d) 387, 39 C.R. (6th) 237, 2006 CarswellBC 1789, 2006 CarswellBC 1790.
68 (1976), [1977] 2 S.C.R. 1067, 30 C.C.C. (2d) 424, 34 C.R.N.S. 207.

the practice of leaving a case or defence to the jury where there is any evidence to support it, and have discouraged trial judges from weighing the evidence and refusing to put a matter to the jury on the basis that the evidence is not sufficiently reliable or persuasive: see *Arcuri*, at para. 30; and *R. v. L. (D.O.)*, [1993] 4 S.C.R. 419, at pp. 454-55. This may explain the conclusion in *Shephard* that the extradition judge has no discretion to refuse to extradite if there is any evidence, however scant or suspect, supporting each of the elements of the offence alleged. This narrow approach to judicial discretion should not be applied in extradition matters, in my opinion. The decision to remove a trial judge's discretion reflects confidence that, given the strict rules of admissibility of evidence on criminal trials, a properly instructed jury is capable of performing the task of assessing the reliability of the evidence and weighing its sufficiency without the assistance of the judge. The accused is not denied the protection of the trier of fact reviewing and weighing the evidence. The effect of applying this test in extradition proceedings, by contrast, is to deprive the subject of any review of the reliability or sufficiency of the evidence. Put another way, the limited judicial discretion to keep evidence from a Canadian jury does not have the same negative constitutional implications as the removal of an extradition judge's discretion to decline to commit for extradition. In the latter case, removal of the discretion may deprive the subject of his or her constitutional right to a meaningful judicial determination *before* the subject is sent out of the country and loses his or her liberty.

It is important as well to note the differences between extradition hearings and domestic preliminary inquiries. Both are pre-trial screening devices and both use the same test of sufficiency of evidence for committal: whether evidence exists upon which a reasonable jury, properly instructed, could return a verdict of guilty: *Shephard*. Previously, the *Extradition Act* cemented the analogy between the two proceedings by directing that an extradition judge "hear the case, in the same manner, as nearly as may be, as if the fugitive was brought before a justice of the peace, charged with an indictable offence committed in Canada": *Extradition Act*, R.S.C. 1985, c. E-23, s. 13. The new Act, however, does not maintain this close parallel in proceedings. Section 24(2) of the Act states: "For the purposes of the hearing, the judge has, subject to this Act, the powers of a justice under Part XVIII of the *Criminal Code*, with any modifications that the circumstances require." This grants the extradition judge the same powers as a preliminary inquiry judge, but requires the judge to exercise those powers in a manner appropriate to the extradition context. The judge no longer follows "as nearly as may be" the procedure of a preliminary inquiry. A second difference comes from the different rules for admitting evidence. Evidence is admitted on a preliminary inquiry according to domestic rules of evidence, with all the inherent guarantees of threshold reliability that those rules entail. In contrast, evidence adduced on extradition may lack the threshold guarantees of reliability afforded by Canadian rules of evidence. A third difference comes from the ability of extradition judges to grant *Charter* remedies. These differences make it inappropriate to equate the task of the extradition judge with the task of a judge on a preliminary inquiry.

I conclude that to deny an extradition judge's discretion to refuse committal for reasons of insufficient evidence would violate a person's right to a judicial hearing by an independent and impartial magistrate — a right implicit in s. 7 of the *Charter* where liberty is at stake. It would deprive the judge of the power to conduct an independent and impartial judicial review of the facts in relation to the law, destroy the judicial nature of the hearing, and turn the extradition judge into an administrative arm of the executive. The process of assessing whether all the boxes are ticked and then ordering committal is not an adjudication, but merely a formal validation. In so far as the majority view in the pre-*Charter* case of *Shephard* suggests a contrary view, it should be modified to conform to the requirements of the *Charter*.

I conclude that s. 32(1)(*a*) and (*b*) and s. 33 of the 1999 Act do not violate the right of a person sought under s. 7 of the *Charter*, because the requirements for committal of s. 29(1), properly construed, grant the extradition judge discretion to refuse to extradite on insufficient evidence such as where the reliability of the evidence certified is successfully impeached or where there is no evidence, by certification or otherwise, that the evidence is available for trial.

Would the result in *Sheppard* have been different applying the *Ferras* approach?

What are the implications of the Chief Justice's observation in *Ferras* that "I take it as axiomatic that a person could not be committed for trial for an offence in Canada if the evidence is so manifestly unreliable that it would be unsafe to rest a verdict upon it"? Does this open the door to some weighing of direct evidence in light of the *Charter*?

As noted in the readings, in criminal cases the sufficiency of the Crown's case is tested before and during a trial. In cases where there is a preliminary inquiry, s. 548(1) of the *Criminal Code* mandates that there be sufficient evidence before the judge will commit the accused for trial. The defence can also challenge the sufficiency of the Crown's case at trial pursuant to the common law application for a directed verdict of acquittal after the close of the Crown's case. A trial judge must rule on the defence's application before the accused elects to call a defence.[69] If the defence successfully challenges the sufficiency of the Crown's case at a jury trial, the trial judge will now withdraw the case from the jury as opposed to directing them to acquit. The trial judge will then enter a verdict of acquittal.[70] Where the evidence is overwhelming and the trial judge is satisfied that the accused is guilty, the judge cannot, however, direct the jury to convict.[71] **Why not?**

---

69 See *R. v. Angelantoni*, (1975) C.R.N.S. 342 (Ont. C.A.); and *R. v. Boissonneault* (1986), 29 C.C.C. (3d) 345 (Ont. C.A.).

70 See *R. v. Rowbotham*, [1994] 2 S.C.R. 463.

71 See *R. v. Krieger* (2007), 41 C.R. (6th) 201 (S.C.C.) and Lisa Dufraimont, "Krieger: The Supreme Court's Guarded Endorsement of Jury Nullification" (2007) 41 C.R. (6th) 209; and *R. v. Gunning* (2005), 29 C.R. (6th) 17.

Should the procedure be different when the directed verdict application is brought in judge-alone trials? This is what Justice Healy had to grapple with in the following case.

QUÉBEC (MINISTÈRE DU REVENU) v. BUFFOLINO
(2009), 2009 CarswellQue 3837, 66 C.R. (6th) 188 (C.Q.)

HEALY J.:

19 According to the orthodox approach, if a judge dismisses a motion for non-suit the defence must then be asked whether it elects to call evidence. A judge would have to do this even if he or she is of the view as that the prosecution case is sufficient in law for the purposes of the test but too weak in fact to sustain a finding of guilt beyond reasonable doubt. In my view this is a self-evident flaw that demands correction. Indeed, it is a flaw that also applies at a preliminary inquiry and trial before jury, but I confine my remarks to motions for non-suit in a criminal trial before judge alone.

20 The motion for non-suit is a practical expression of the presumption of innocence. If the prosecution case is too weak to sustain a finding of guilt beyond reasonable doubt, the case should be stopped and the accused person should be liberated from jeopardy. There is, by definition, no case to meet. In a trial before judge alone, the true test should be: having regard to all of the evidence and to the full meaning of proof beyond reasonable doubt, could a properly-instructed trier of fact find proof to that standard? It is the standard that gives meaning to the test, not the mere presence of evidence.

21 The orthodox approach would force the judge, in a case that is legally sufficient but factually too weak for proof, to dismiss the motion and ask if the defence wishes to call evidence. To sustain a person's jeopardy by dismissing a motion in a "sufficient" but fatally weak case is to create a trap that is also inconsistent with presumption of innocence. Suppose that the judge is compelled to dismiss the motion and put the defence to its election even though he has already determined that on the whole of the evidence the evidence could not come up to proof beyond reasonable doubt. If the defence elects to call evidence in those circumstances, the defence evidence might fill in the deficiencies of the prosecution case. The election put to the defence might serve unwittingly and unintentionally as an invitation to assist in the case against the accused. The election thus becomes an invitation to take a risk of self-incrimination. It becomes an invitation to gamble with the presumption of innocence. There is no justification for this in a trial before judge alone. At the time of the motion the judge should stop the case and acquit the accused if she is satisfied on the whole of the evidence that the case is insufficient for a finding of guilt.

22 When a motion for non-suit is made in a trial before judge alone there is a powerful argument to be made that the judge should fully assess and weigh the evidence, including questions of credibility. That judge is both the trier of law and trier of fact. Throughout the prosecution case he or she must be fully attentive

to all aspects of the evidence in anticipation of a final decision. It is pointlessly artificial to force the judge on the motion for non-suit to apply only the limited test of sufficiency that is applicable in other instances where someone else will make a final determination. In my respectful view the protection afforded by the presumption of innocence in a trial before judge alone requires a full weighing of the evidence against the standard of proof beyond reasonable doubt.

23 The approach that I propose does not imply that dismissal of a motion for non-suit will entail a finding of guilt. It means only that at the time of the motion the judge cannot say definitively that the prosecution case is incapable of coming up to proof beyond reasonable doubt. It means that there is a case to meet. There might still be a reasonable doubt on the whole of the evidence at the end of the case. The defence should be given the opportunity to answer the case if it so elects. If it calls evidence, it assumes the risk of failure. If it calls no evidence, it pins its hopes on the judge's final assessment of the evidence against the standard of proof beyond reasonable doubt.

24 There are three ways to resolve the matter before me. The first is to grant the motion and acquit the defendant. This approach would be sound in principle but inconsistent with the authorities. The second is to grant the motion, wait a few seconds for the defence to repeat that it will call no evidence, wait a few more seconds to see if the parties have anything further to say, and then acquit the defendant. This approach is consistent with the authorities but lacking in principle. The third approach would be to dismiss the motion on the basis that there is some evidence, wait a few seconds for the defence to repeat that it will call no evidence, wait a few more seconds to see if the parties have anything further to say, and then acquit the defendant. I have already rejected the third approach and I will reject the second in favour of the first.

25 The leading authorities are not about the motion for non-suit in a trial before judge alone. Nevertheless, the orthodox view is that the principles expressed in those cases apply in all four relevant contexts. It would seem, however, that the strength of this orthodoxy lies chiefly in repetition rather than analysis. It would also seem that this orthodoxy has become subject to increased scrutiny. There have been important amendments concerning preliminary inquiries that fundamentally change the nature of those committal proceedings. In *Ferras,* the Supreme Court approved in extradition proceedings a more expansive approach to weighing of evidence at committal and sought to distinguish that procedure from committal proceedings at a preliminary inquiry. In short, despite the orthodoxy of the law, there is in this case a welcome opportunity to reconsider the principles that should apply with regard to a motion for non-suit in a trial by judge alone.

26 This case was not argued under the *Charter* with reference to principles of fundamental justice or the presumption of innocence. I will not decide it on that basis but I should say that the approach that I propose in this matter is reinforced by a central and fundamental principle. If, in a trial before judge alone, and taking into account all of the evidence, the evidence is insufficient to find guilt proved

beyond reasonable doubt the judge should make that decision and resolve the general issue by acquitting the accused upon the motion for non-suit. More briefly, if there is in substance no case to meet, the prosecution should be stopped.

27   What distinguishes this situation from others is that it is known from the outset that the person who must decide the motion is also the trier of fact. It is for this reason that it is unnecessary to insist upon subtracting from the decision on the motion any consideration of credibility and more general matters relating to the probative value and weight attributable to the evidence. It cannot be argued that by taking this decision the judge is trespassing upon the functions of the jury and taking away its essential decision-making functions. If anything, forcing the judge to dismiss the motion is to take away her decision-making function as trier of fact, conceal it temporarily and restore it when she officially changes hats.

28   I should note that in this case the defence was not put to its election by the court. At the close of the prosecution evidence the defence spontaneously announced that it would present a motion for non-suit and that it would not call evidence. I attach no significance to the second part of this announcement for the purposes of these reasons because it is well settled that the defence must not be put to its election until a ruling has been made on the motion for non-suit. Thus I have proceeded on the basis that if the motion were dismissed I would have had to put the defence to its election.

29   For these reasons the motion for non-suit is granted and the defendant is acquitted on all counts.

PROBLEM

The accused is charged with second degree murder in the death of his estranged wife. The deceased was found in her bathtub in the early hours of Christmas Day. Her lungs were heavy, which was consistent with drowning. There were no signs of strangulation. There was no evidence of foul play in her apartment. Everything was neat and in order. No fingerprints of the accused were found in the apartment. The forensic evidence failed to establish definitively that the deceased had died from natural causes, or as a result of accident, suicide or homicide. In support of its theory of homicide, the Crown relied on a number of pieces of circumstantial evidence including animus and motive. The accused and the deceased had a difficult marriage marked by periods of separation. During one such period, the deceased began a relationship with another man, which the accused found "shameful" and which had made him feel like an "idiot". On one occasion, the deceased told her doctor that she was afraid of staying with her husband and wanted to move away from him. The deceased also once told a friend that the accused was verbally abusive and that she was afraid of him. There was also evidence of a $50,000 life insurance policy on the deceased. The accused admitted to the police that he was present at the deceased's apartment building on the night she died. He had travelled from Vancouver to London, Ontario. The accused also telephoned her. He asked her whether she was alone. Finally, three days after her death, the accused told the police that the deceased had complained about being short of money, being sick and forgetting things. He also volunteered that the deceased had complained to him about falling asleep in the bathtub sometimes for an hour or two and that she had almost drowned on a couple of occasions.

If you are the preliminary inquiry judge would you commit the accused to stand trial on this evidence? Would you convict? See *R. v. Charemski*, 15 C.R. (5th) 1, [1998] 1 S.C.R. 679, 123 C.C.C. (3d) 225.

As noted earlier, in some cases there will be an evidential burden on the defence to ensure that there is sufficient evidence to put a defence in play.

R. v. CINOUS
[2002] 2 S.C.R. 3, 49 C.R. (5th) 209

The accused was charged with the first degree murder of a criminal accomplice, Mike. The accused testified that he and a friend had been involved in the theft and resale of computers along with Mike and another accomplice, Ice. About one month before the killing, he became convinced that Mike had stolen his gun. He told Mike and Ice that he wanted no more to do with them but they kept calling about doing thefts. He also testified that shortly after the gun went missing he began to hear rumours that Mike and Ice wanted to kill him, and that he was warned by a friend to watch out for them. One morning Mike and Ice called and asked the accused to participate in a computer theft. He agreed to meet with them that evening at his apartment. The accused testified that when they arrived, they kept their jackets on and whispered to one another as they sat in the living room. He saw Ice constantly placing his hand inside his coat. That made him suspect they were armed. The accused said he decided to participate in the theft to see if they really intended to kill him. They left the apartment and got into the accused's van to drive to the location of the theft. The accused said that he knew Mike and Ice wanted to kill him when he saw they had changed their gloves. Neither had changed to the black woollen gloves kept in the van compartment for computer thefts. Mike was wearing surgical latex gloves the accused associated with situations where bloodshed was expected. He had twice before seen them used on "burns" – attacks on criminals by other criminals. The accused drove. Ice sat next to him and Mike sat behind Ice. The accused testified Ice avoided making eye contact with him and kept touching his jacket as if he had a gun. He said he interpreted Ice's hand inside his jacket as a threat. The accused admitted that no other threats were made. The accused testified that he was sure that he was going to be killed and that the shot would more than likely come from behind – from Mike. Since he was driving, he could not get to his own gun quickly enough, were anything to happen. He felt trapped. He pulled into a populated and well-lit gas station to "release the pressure" and get himself out of this bad situation. He bought a bottle of windshield washer after returning to the van to get money from Ice. He poured the fluid in under the hood and brought the bottle back around to the back of the van. He opened the back door, "saw the opportunity", pulled out his gun and shot Mike in the back of the head. The accused testified that this was an instinctive reaction to a situation of danger. It did not occur to him to run away or to call the police.

Per McLACHLIN C.J.C. and BASTARACHE J. (L'HEUREUX-DUBÉ, GONTHIER, BINNIE, LEBEL JJ. concurring):—

Air of Reality

The key issue is whether there was an air of reality to the defence of self-defence in this case. It is our view that there is no air of reality to the defence: a properly instructed jury acting reasonably could not acquit the accused on the ground of self-defence, even if it accepted his testimonial evidence as true. Since the defence should never have been put to the jury, any errors made in the charge to the jury relating to that defence are irrelevant. The curative proviso of s. 686(1)(b)(iii) should be applied, and the conviction upheld. This Court has considered the air of reality test on numerous occasions. The core elements of the test, as well as its nature and purpose, have by now been clearly and authoritatively set out. See *R. v. Osolin*, [1993] 4 S.C.R. 595; *R. v. Park*, [1995] 2 S.C.R. 836; *R. v. Davis*, [1999] 3 S.C.R. 759. Nevertheless, a controversy has arisen in this case concerning the extent of a trial judge's discretion to keep from a jury defences that are fanciful or far-fetched. More narrowly, the contentious issue is the correct evidential standard to be applied in determining whether there is an air of reality to the defence of self-defence on the facts of this case. In our view, the controversy can be resolved on the basis of existing authority, which we consider to be decisive. The correct approach to the air of reality test is well established. The test is whether there is evidence on the record upon which a properly instructed jury acting reasonably could acquit. . . . This long-standing formulation of the threshold question for putting defences to the jury accords with the nature and purpose of the air of reality test. We consider that there is nothing to be gained by altering the current state of the law, in which a single clearly-stated test applies to all defences. . . . There is no need to invent a new test, to modify the current test, or to apply different tests to different classes of cases.

(1) The Basic Features of the Air of Reality Test

The principle that a defence should be put to a jury if and only if there is an evidential foundation for it has long been recognized by the common law. This venerable rule reflects the practical concern that allowing a defence to go to the jury in the absence of an evidential foundation would invite verdicts not supported by the evidence, serving only to confuse the jury and get in the way of a fair trial and true verdict. Following Pappajohn . . . the inquiry into whether there is an evidential foundation for a defence is referred to as the air of reality test. . . . The basic requirement of an evidential foundation for defences gives rise to two well-established principles. First, a trial judge must put to the jury all defences that arise on the facts, whether or not they have been specifically raised by an accused. Where there is an air of reality to a defence, it should go to the jury. Second, a trial judge has a positive duty to keep from the jury defences lacking an evidential foundation. A defence that lacks an air of reality should be kept from the jury. . . . This is so even when the defence lacking an air of reality represents the accused's only chance for an acquittal, as illustrated by *R. v. Latimer*, [2001] 1 S.C.R. 3. It is trite law that the air of reality test imposes a burden on the accused that is merely evidential, rather than persuasive. Dickson C.J. drew attention to the distinction between these two types of burden in *R. v. Schwartz*, [1988] 2 S.C.R. 443. . . . The air of reality test is concerned only with whether or not a putative defence should be "put in play", that is, submitted to the jury for consideration. This idea was crucial to the finding in Osolin that the air of reality test is consistent with the presumption of innocence guaranteed by s. 11(d) of the Canadian Charter of Rights and Freedoms. In applying the air of reality test, a trial judge considers the totality of the evidence, and assumes the evidence relied upon by the accused to be true. . . . The evidential foundation can be indicated by evidence emanating from the examination-in-chief or cross-examination of the accused, of defence witnesses, or of Crown witnesses. It can also rest upon the factual circumstances of the case or from any other evidential source on the record. There is no requirement that the evidence be adduced by the accused. . . . The threshold determination by the trial judge is not aimed at deciding the substantive merits of the defence. That question is reserved for the jury. . . . The trial judge does not make determinations about the credibility of witnesses, weigh the evidence, make findings of fact, or draw determinate factual inferences. . . . Nor is the air of reality test intended to assess whether the defence is likely, unlikely, somewhat likely, or very likely to succeed at the end of the day. The question for the trial judge is whether the evidence discloses a real issue to be decided by the jury, and not how the jury should ultimately decide the issue. Whether or not there is an air of reality to a defence is a question of law, subject to appellate review. It is an error of law to put to the jury a defence lacking an air of reality, just as it is an error of law to keep from the jury a defence that has an air of reality. See *Osolin*, supra; *Park*, supra; *Davis*, supra. The statements that "there is an air of reality" to a defence and that a defence "lacks an air of reality" express a legal conclusion about the presence or absence of an evidential foundation for a defence. The considerations discussed above have led this Court to reject unequivocally the argument that the air of reality test licenses an encroachment by trial judges on the jury's traditional function as arbiter of fact. As Cory J. stated in *Osolin*, supra, at p. 682-3:

> This is no more than an example of the basic division of tasks between judge and jury. . . . The charge to the jury must be directed to the essential elements of the crime with which the accused is charged and defences to it. Speculative defences that are unfounded should not be presented to the jury. To do so would be wrong, confusing, and unnecessarily lengthen jury trials.

This Court has held on many occasions that a single air of reality test applies to all defences..The test has been applied uniformly to a wide range of defences over the years. These include the defence of honest but mistaken belief in consent in sexual assault cases (*Pappajohn*..; *Ewanchuk*, supra; *Davis*, supra), and other defences such as intoxication (*R. v. Robinson*, [1996] 1 S.C.R. 683. . . ., necessity (*Latimer*, supra), duress (*R. v. Ruzic*, [2001] 1 S.C.R. 687), provocation (*R. v.*

Thibert, [1996] 1 S.C.R. 37), and self-defence (*Brisson v. The Queen*, [1982] 2 S.C.R. 227 . . .). Adopting different evidential standards for different classes of cases would constitute a sharp break with the authorities.

BINNIE J.: —

I concur with the Chief Justice and Bastarache J., and with the reasons they have given, that the appeal should be allowed. I add these paragraphs on what I think is the decisive point.

My colleagues have mobilized considerable scholarship for and against all aspects of the issues. When the smoke clears, this appeal comes down to a simple proposition. A criminal code that permitted preemptive killings within a criminal organization on the bare assertion by the killer that no course of action was reasonably available to him while standing outside a motor vehicle other than to put a shot in the back of the head of another member sitting inside the parked vehicle at a well-lit and populated gas station is a criminal code that would fail in its most basic purpose of promoting public order.

The respondent says he did not consider going to the police, although he was outside the car and in a position to flee the scene. He said "I never called the police in my life". Even if the police unexpectedly got there before a shoot-out, they would ask for some information in return for protection. "That's how it works", he said. Accordingly, there was evidence that subjectively, as a self-styled criminal, he felt his only options were to kill or be killed. He wishes the jury to judge the reasonableness of his conduct by the rules of his criminal subculture, which is the antithesis of public order.

A trial judge should be very slow to take a defence away from a jury. We all agree on that. Here, however, the only way the defence could succeed is if the jury climbed into the skin of the respondent and accepted as reasonable a sociopathic view of appropriate dispute resolution.

In dissent Arbour J. (Iacobucci and Major JJ. concurring) sought to revise the approach of the Supreme Court, mainly on her detailed analysis that the air of reality test developed in the context of the mistaken belief defence in sexual assault cases had departed from the common law "no evidence" test for withdrawal from the jury in favour of one of sufficiency of evidence which had usurped the fact-finding function of juries. The "no evidence" test should be adopted for defences such as self-defence especially where there were no special technical or policy considerations, no alternative defences and where it was the accused's only defence.[72]

---

72 See comment by Stuart, "Cinous: The Air of Reality Test Requires Weak Defences to Be Withdrawn from Juries" (2002) 49 C.R. (5th) 392.

R. v. FONTAINE

2004 CarswellQue 814, 2004 CarswellQue 815,
18 C.R. (6th) 203, 183 C.C.C. (3d) 1 (S.C.C.)

The accused was charged with first degree murder of D. The accused worked as a garage mechanic. He received a call from R, a disgruntled former employee, who said, "We're coming to get you, pigs". Two days later the accused heard from a co-worker that D, the victim, had been offered a contract to kill both of them. The accused later felt that he was being watched and followed. He and the co-worker together purchased a gun. That evening, the accused thought he saw R lurking outside his home. He called the co-worker, who came by to check but noticed nothing unusual. During the night, after smoking marihuana, the accused thought he heard someone breaking into his home. He fired the gun at doors and windows and into walls and concluded that he had shot the intruders. The next morning D came to the garage to pay a debt he owed the proprietor. The accused saw him, grabbed his gun and shot him twice. D tried to flee. The accused followed him outside, fired five more shots in his direction and wounded him fatally.

The accused was charged with first degree murder. At his trial before judge and jury his defence was mental disorder automatism. He testified that he had acted involuntarily. Several psychiatrists testified. Two testified that he was suffering from paranoid delusions but one indicated it was difficult to determine whether the story was real or delusional. The main defence psychiatrist was of the opinion he was in a psychotic state at the time triggered by excessive marihuana use such that he was unable to distinguish right from wrong. The Crown psychiatrist testified in reply that the accused had not been and was not psychotic. The judge, applying *R. v. Stone*, refused to put the mental disorder automatism defence to the jury on the ground that there was no evidence that would allow a properly instructed jury to conclude on a balance of probabilities that the accused had acted involuntarily. The accused's evidence contained contradictions and the evidence of the defence psychiatrist was based on the facts recounted by the accused and had been contradicted by the other psychiatrists. The trial judge also refused to charge on the defence of no criminal responsibility on account of mental disorder under section 16 of the Criminal Code.

The Quebec Court of Appeal quashed the conviction on the basis that the trial judge had erred in not putting the defence of mental disorder automatism to the jury. The Crown appealed.

A unanimous Supreme Court dismissed the further appeal.

FISH J.:—

Under our system of trial by judge and jury, the judge decides all questions of law and delimits the issues of fact to be considered and determined by the jury. To avoid manifest unfairness and undue confusion, no issues will be put to the jury in the absence of a sufficient evidential foundation.

In determining whether the required evidential foundation exists, it will be helpful to first consider the incidence and nature of the burden of proof on the issue concerned.

Dealing recently with this issue in the context of directed verdicts of acquittal, McLachlin J. (now C.J.) reaffirmed in the clearest of terms that the evidential burden is a function of the persuasive burden on the issue of guilt and, presumably, on other issues as well. Writing for herself and Major J. in *R. v. Charemski*, [1998] 1 S.C.R. 679, McLachlin J., dissenting on other grounds, stated, at para. 35:

> . . . "sufficient evidence" must mean sufficient evidence to sustain a verdict of guilt beyond a reasonable doubt; merely to refer to "sufficient evidence" is incomplete since "sufficient" always relates to the goal or threshold of proof beyond a reasonable doubt. This must constantly be borne in mind when evaluating whether the evidence is capable of supporting the inferences necessary to establish the essential elements of the case.

. . . .

In some instances, the proponent of an issue bears both the persuasive and the evidential burdens. But this is not invariably the case.

On the ultimate issue of guilt, the Crown bears both burdens. The Crown's persuasive burden on this issue can only be discharged by proof beyond a reasonable doubt. Accordingly, as McLachlin J. explained in Charemski, supra, the case against the accused cannot go to the jury unless there is evidence in the record upon which a properly instructed jury could rationally conclude that the accused is guilty beyond a reasonable doubt.

In the case of "reverse onus" defences, such as mental disorder automatism, it is the accused who bears both the persuasive and the evidential burdens. Here, the persuasive burden is discharged by evidence on the balance of probabilities, a lesser standard than proof beyond a reasonable doubt. Reverse onus defences will therefore go to the jury where there is any evidence upon which a properly instructed jury, acting judicially, could reasonably conclude that the defence has been established in accordance with this lesser standard.

With respect to all other "affirmative" defences, including alibi, duress, provocation and others mentioned in Cinous, at para. 57, the persuasive and the evidential burdens are divided.

As regards these "ordinary", as opposed to "reverse onus" defences, the accused has no persuasive burden at all. Once the issue has been "put in play" (*R. v. Schwartz*, [1998] 2 S.C.R. 443), the defence will succeed unless it is disproved by the Crown beyond a reasonable doubt. Like all other disputed issues, however, defences of this sort will only be left to the jury where a sufficient evidential basis is found to exist. That foundation cannot be said to exist where its only constituent elements are of a tenuous, trifling, insignificant or manifestly unsubstantive nature: there must be evidence in the record upon which a properly instructed jury, acting judicially, could entertain a reasonable doubt as to the defence that has been raised.

From a theoretical point of view, "reverse onus" defences and "ordinary affirmative defences" may thus be thought to be subject to different evidential burdens. But in this as in other branches of the law, pure logic must yield to experience and, without undue distortion of principle, to a more practical and more desirable approach. In determining whether the evidential burden has been discharged on any defence, trial judges, as a matter of judicial policy, should therefore always ask the very same question: Is there in the record any evidence upon which a reasonable trier of fact, properly instructed in law and acting judicially, could conclude that the defence succeeds?

This requirement of a sufficient evidential foundation aims primarily to avoid wrongful convictions and unwarranted acquittals, while at the same time leaving it to the jury to discharge the responsibilities that are by law within its exclusive domain.

It must be remembered in this latter regard that any person charged in Canada with an offence punishable by imprisonment for five years or more is constitutionally entitled, to "the benefit of trial by jury": See s. 11(f) of the Canadian Charter of Rights and Freedoms. And where the accused elects to be tried by a judge alone, the Attorney General may nonetheless require a jury trial if the offence charged is punishable by more than five years' imprisonment: Criminal Code, s. 568.

Like Arbour J., I think it appropriate to underline here the importance of "afford[ing]" the jury the opportunity to pronounce on every factual issue" for which the required evidential foundation has been laid (Cinous, at para. 196). And I agree with her as well (at para. 200) that:

> [T]he cost of risking a wrongful conviction and possibly violating the accused's constitutionally protected rights by inadvisably withdrawing a defence from the jury is a high one.

. . . .

[The Court applied these principles to the facts and held that the trial judge had erred in not putting the defence of mental disorder automatism to the jury.]

Do you consider that *Cinous* and *Fontaine* are consistent on the law and on the application of the air of reality test? Was there an air of reality to the defences in these cases?

The Court in *Fontaine* rejects the language of the majority in *Stone* that the evidentiary burden of establishing mental disorder automatism involves the judge in deciding whether the accused has established the defence on a balance of probability. That muddling of the evidentiary and persuasive burdens was held in *Fontaine* to have been overtaken by the later majority opinion in *Cinous*

The Court in *Fontaine* consistently holds that the evidentiary burden for deciding whether to put a defence, to commit at a preliminary, to extradite or to order a directed verdict, must be measured against the persuasive standard in question. This proposition is derived from the dissenting opinion of McLachlin J. in *Charemski* where the present Chief Justice adopted Ron Delisle's view that this had to be the case as a matter of logic. If the issue is whether a jury could reasonably convict it seems obvious that the question must be asked in relation to the ultimate burden of proof. Yet Justice Fish warns trial judges that it is not their task to assess the likelihood that a defence will succeed (para. 83).This may sometimes involve the drawing of a very fine line. The overall message of *Fontaine* does remain clear: if there is a basis on which the jury could be persuaded, the defence must be put. In contrast the majority message of *Cinous* seemed to be that weak defences should be withdrawn from the jury. One wonders whether, on the new, more generous *Fontaine* approach, the defence of necessity should have been put to the jury in *Latimer*, contrary to the unanimous view of the Supreme Court on that appeal.

The Court in *Fontaine* holds that weighing is not part of assessing whether the evidentiary burden has been met. At one point, the Court relies on *Arcuri* but it says nothing about the Court's ruling in that case, which concerned the test for committal following a preliminary inquiry, of the need for "limited weighing" of circumstantial evidence to see whether reasonable inferences could be drawn by the jury. It seems that that would be a necessary feature wherever an evidentiary burden arises but the Court in *Fontaine* does not expressly say so.

(ii) Civil Cases

In civil cases, there are two stages at which the plaintiff's case is screened. Prior to trial, the defendant can bring a motion for summary judgment.

CANADA (ATTORNEY GENERAL) v. LAMEMAN

2008 CarswellAlta 398, 2008 CarswellAlta 399, [2008] 1 S.C.R. 372

THE COURT:—

. . . .

[10] This appeal is from an application for summary judgment. The summary judgment rule serves an important purpose in the civil litigation system. It prevents claims or defences that have no chance of success from proceeding to trial. Trying unmeritorious claims imposes a heavy price in terms of time and cost on the parties to the litigation and on the justice system. It is essential to the proper operation of the justice system and beneficial to the parties that claims that have no chance of success be weeded out at an early stage. Conversely, it is essential to justice that claims disclosing real issues that may be successful proceed to trial.

[11] For this reason, the bar on a motion for summary judgment is high. The defendant who seeks summary dismissal bears the evidentiary burden of showing that there is "no genuine issue of material fact requiring trial": *Guarantee Co. of North America v. Gordon Capital Corp.*, [1999] 3 S.C.R. 423, at para. 27. The defendant must prove this; it cannot rely on mere allegations or the pleadings: *1061590 Ontario Ltd. v. Ontario Jockey Club* (1995), 21 O.R. (3d) 547 (C.A.); *Tucson Properties Ltd. v. Sentry Resources Ltd.* (1982), 22 Alta. L.R. (2d) 44 (Q.B. (Master)), at pp. 46-47. If the defendant does prove this, the plaintiff must either refute or counter the defendant's evidence, or risk summary dismissal: *Murphy Oil Co. v. Predator Corp.* (2004), 365 A.R. 326, 2004 ABQB 688, at p. 331, aff'd (2006), 55 Alta. L.R. (4th) 1, 2006 ABCA 69. Each side must "put its best foot forward" with respect to the existence or non-existence of material issues to be tried: *Transamerica Life Insurance Co. of Canada v. Canada Life Assurance Co.* (1996), 28 O.R. (3d) 423 (Gen. Div.), at p. 434; *Goudie v. Ottawa (City)*, [2003] 1 S.C.R. 141, 2003 SCC 14, at para. 32. The chambers judge may make inferences of fact based on the undisputed facts before the court, as long as the

inferences are strongly supported by the facts: *Guarantee Co. of North America*, at para. 30.

[12] We are of the view that, assuming that the claims disclosed triable issues and that standing could be established, the claims are barred by operation of the *Limitation of Actions Act*. There is "no genuine issue" for trial. Were the action allowed to proceed to trial, it would surely fail on this ground. . . .

Historically, the role of the trial judge in assessing the evidence on motions for summary judgment was described by the Ontario Court of Appeal in *Aguoine v. Galion Solid Waste Material Inc.*[73] as follows:

> In ruling on a motion for summary judgment, the court will never assess credibility, weigh the evidence, or find the facts. Instead, the court's role is narrowly limited to assessing the threshold issue of whether a genuine issue exists as to material facts requiring a trial. Evaluating credibility, weighing evidence, and drawing factual inferences are all functions reserved for the trier of fact.

Concerns over the delay, access and expense have led to changes to our civil procedures. One such change came into force in Ontario in 2010 with Rule 20.01(2.1) of the *Ontario Rules of Civil Procedure*, which now permits a more expansive role for the judge.

RULE 20 SUMMARY JUDGMENT

WHERE AVAILABLE

To Plaintiff

20.01 (1) A plaintiff may, after the defendant has delivered a statement of defence or served a notice of motion, move with supporting affidavit material or other evidence for summary judgment on all or part of the claim in the statement of claim. R.R.O. 1990, Reg. 194, r. 20.01(1).

. . .

To Defendant

(3) A defendant may, after delivering a statement of defence, move with supporting affidavit material or other evidence for summary judgment dismissing all or part of the claim in the statement of claim. R.R.O. 1990, Reg. 194, r. 20.01(3).

EVIDENCE ON MOTION

20.02 (1) An affidavit for use on a motion for summary judgment may be made on information and belief as provided in subrule 39.01 (4), but, on the hearing of the motion, the court may, if appropriate, draw an adverse inference from the failure of a party to provide the evidence of any person having personal knowledge of contested facts. O. Reg. 438/08, s. 12.

(2) In response to affidavit material or other evidence supporting a motion for summary judgment, a responding party may not rest solely on the allegations or denials in the party's pleadings, but must set out, in affidavit material or other evidence, specific facts showing that there is a genuine issue requiring a trial. O. Reg. 438/08, s. 12.

---

73 (1998), 38 O.R. (3d) 161 (C.A.).

. . .

DISPOSITION OF MOTION

General

20.04 (1) Revoked: O. Reg. 438/08, s. 13(1).

(2) The court shall grant summary judgment if,

    (a) the court is satisfied that there is no genuine issue requiring a trial with respect to a claim or defence; or

    (b) the parties agree to have all or part of the claim determined by a summary judgment and the court is satisfied that it is appropriate to grant summary judgment. O. Reg. 284/01, s. 6; O. Reg. 438/08, s. 13(2).

Powers

(2.1) In determining under clause (2) (a) whether there is a genuine issue requiring a trial, the court shall consider the evidence submitted by the parties and, if the determination is being made by a judge, the judge may exercise any of the following powers for the purpose, unless it is in the interest of justice for such powers to be exercised only at a trial:

    1. Weighing the evidence.

    2. Evaluating the credibility of a deponent.

    3. Drawing any reasonable inference from the evidence. O. Reg. 438/08, s. 13(3).

Oral Evidence (Mini-Trial)

(2.2) A judge may, for the purposes of exercising any of the powers set out in subrule (2.1), order that oral evidence be presented by one or more parties, with or without time limits on its presentation. O. Reg. 438/08, s. 13(3).

A defendant can also bring a motion at trial for non-suit to challenge the sufficiency of the evidence submitted by the plaintiff.

FL RECEIVABLES TRUST v. COBRAND FOODS LTD.

2007 CarswellOnt 3697, 2007 ONCA 425 (C.A.)

LASKIN J.A. (BORINS and FELDMAN JJ.A. concurring:—

. . . .

[12] Before addressing Robert Laba's submission, I want to say a few words about non-suit motions in civil non-jury trials. The term "non-suit" refers to a motion brought by the defendant at the close of the plaintiff's evidence to dismiss the action on the ground that the plaintiff has failed to make out a case for the defendant to answer. Neither the *Courts of Justice Act*, R.S.O. 1990, c. C.43, nor the *Rules of Civil Procedure* specifically provides for non-suit motions, but judges continue to have a recognized jurisdiction to entertain these motions.

[13] Still, I question whether in this province a non-suit motion in a civil non-jury trial has much value. In Ontario, when a defendant moves for a non-suit, the defendant must elect whether to call evidence. See *Ontario v. Ontario Public Service Employees Union (OPSEU)* (1990), 37 O.A.C. 218 at para. 40 (Div. Ct.). If the defendant elects to call evidence, the judge reserves on the motion until the end of the case. If the defendant elects to call no evidence – as Robert Laba elected in this case – then the judge rules on the motion immediately after it has been made.

[14] A non-suit motion adds to the time and expense of a trial. And because of the election requirement, it has little practical value. Perhaps a defendant bringing the motion sees a tactical advantage in being able to argue first. To succeed on the motion, however, the defendant must show that the plaintiff has put forward no case to answer, in most lawsuits an onerous task. Why not simply take on the less onerous task of showing that the plaintiff's claim should fail? It is small wonder that most commentators consider that in civil judge alone trials, non-suit motions gain little and are becoming obsolete. See *Phipson on Evidence*, 16th ed. (London: Sweet & Maxwell, 2005) at 274, and John Sopinka, Donald B. Houston & Melanie Sopinka, *The Trial of an Action*, 2d ed. (Toronto: Butterworths Canada, 1999) at 151-52.

. . . .

[35] On a non-suit motion, the trial judge undertakes a limited inquiry. Two relevant principles that guide this inquiry are these. First, if a plaintiff puts forward some evidence on all elements of its claim, the judge must dismiss the motion. Second, in assessing whether a plaintiff has made out a *prima facie* case, the judge must assume the evidence to be true and must assign "the most favourable meaning" to evidence capable of giving rise to competing inferences. This court discussed this latter principle in *Hall et al. v. Pemberton* (1974), 5 O.R. (2d) 438 at 438-9, quoting *Parfitt v. Lawless* (1872), 41 L.J.P. & M. 68 at 71-72:

> I conceive, therefore, that in judging whether there is in any case evidence for a jury the Judge must weigh the evidence given, must assign what he conceives to be the most favourable meaning which can reasonably be attributed to any ambiguous statements, and determine on the whole what tendency the evidence has to establish the issue.

. . .

> From every fact that is proved, legitimate and reasonable inferences may of course be drawn, and all that is fairly deducible from the evidence is as much proved, for the purpose of a *prima facie* case, as if it had been proved directly. I conceive, therefore, that in discussing whether there is in any case evidence to go to the jury, what the Court has to consider is this, whether, assuming the evidence to be true, and adding to the direct proof all such inferences of fact as in the exercise of a reasonable intelligence the jury would be warranted in drawing from it, there is sufficient to support the issue.

[36] In other words, on a non-suit motion the trial judge should not determine whether the competing inferences available to the defendant on the evidence rebut

the plaintiff's *prima facie* case. The trial judge should make that determination at the end of the trial, not on the non-suit motion. See John Sopinka, Sidney N. Lederman & Alan W. Bryant, *The Law of Evidence in Canada*, 2d ed. (Toronto: Butterworths Canada, 1999) at 139.

As noted in *FL Receivables*, the defendant must elect not to call a defence if he or she wants an immediate ruling on their motion for non-suit. The same is true in cases before administrative tribunals. This is very different from the procedure in criminal cases. **Does it raise any concerns?**

The possibility of the motion for a non-suit being rendered redundant by the existing practice at civil law is bothersome. Although we do not speak of the defendant in a civil case having any right to silence, there seems to be some worth in his ability to have a judicial ruling as to whether the plaintiff has adduced sufficient evidence to warrant calling on the defence for a response. The plaintiff has made certain allegations in his statement of claim and seeks to disturb the status quo. The defendant should have the right to refuse to answer spurious claims.

The courts have evidently created their present practice out of concern that there may be unnecessary effort and expenses flowing from new trials when the trial judge rules incorrectly on a motion. If we posit the thought that trial judges are more often right than wrong, a change in the existing practice would be even more efficient. If there is no case to meet, the defendant is not put to the expense and effort of presenting a defence and the trial tribunal's time is not wasted. The procedure ought to be the same in civil and criminal cases and the plaintiff's claim vetted by a judicial officer before the defendant need determine whether he cares to answer.

So far, we have been speaking about a motion for non-suit that challenges whether the plaintiff has established a prima facie case. There is a more narrow jurisdictional ground where the defendant alleges that there is an absence of evidence (as opposed to insufficient evidence) on an essential element that must be proven. Where this is alleged, it would appear that, generally speaking, there should be no election.

LAUFER v. BUCKLASCHUK

[1999] M.J. No. 553, 1999 CarswellMan 565 (C.A.)

The defendant was an NDP minister in the Manitoba Legislative Assembly responsible for the Manitoba Public Insurance Corporation. The plaintiff was a former general manger of the company. An issue arose about the amount of losses facing the company and public statements were made by the defendant about what he had been told concerning the problem. The plaintiff brought an action for defamation. He succeeded at trial and was awarded two million dollars by the jury, the largest defamation award in Canadian history. One of the grounds of appeal was whether the trial judge had erred in requiring the defendant to make an election on whether he intended to call any evidence before ruling on the motion for non-suit.

Scott C.J.M. and Helper J.A. (Monnin J.A. concurring): —

... The general practice of requiring counsel to make an election before ruling on a defendant's non-suit application is a well-settled rule and need not be further explained. While this general rule is well known, few decisions have discussed the fact that a non-suit motion can emerge in two separate and distinct forms. These two forms were discussed in *Petit Trucking* by Huband J.A. at p. 140 and Twaddle J.A. at p. 143. Twaddle J.A., after referring to Lord Goddard's judgment in *Parry v. Aluminium Corpn. Ltd.*, went on to observe at para. 30:

> The exceptions noted by Goddard L.J. do not stand alone. They are merely illustrative of those cases in which the submission of no case is based on a total lack of evidence to prove an essential ingredient of the plaintiff's claim.

In such circumstances, the judge is in effect being asked to decide as a matter of law rather than fact whether any case has been made out. This can be contrasted to the usual type of non-suit motion, where (*Petit Trucking* at para. 34):

> Save perhaps in exceptional circumstances, any submission which is based on the alleged insufficiency of evidence should not be permitted without an election being required. Any doubt as to whether a submission is based on no evidence or on its alleged insufficiency should be resolved in favour of putting counsel to his election.

Although the dichotomy between the two forms of non-suit have not often been addressed, there is clearly in our opinion a distinction between a non-suit based on the failure of the plaintiff to call evidence on an essential ingredient or element of his case - where the defendant accepts the plaintiff's evidence and argues no case has been established in law - and a motion founded on the "probative insufficiency" of the plaintiff's case: G. L. Bladon, NonSuit - Heads I Win, Tails I Don't Lose, (1993), 15 *Advocates' Quarterly* 425, or where the argument is that the evidence led on behalf of the plaintiff is so "unsatisfactory or unreliable that the court should find that the burden of proof has not been discharged," per Allan Rock, The Principles of Non-Suit in Ontario, Eric Gertner, *Studies in Civil Procedure* (Toronto: Butterworths, 1979) at p. 169. In the latter instance, counsel for the defendant should always be put to an election. In the former, which tends very much to be the exception rather than the rule, counsel should normally not be put to an election, although even here, in our opinion, the trial judge has an overriding discretion to be exercised judicially to require an election if in the court's opinion the facts and circumstances make it just and proper to do so. See *Surfwood Supply Ltd. v. General Alarms Ltd.*, [1976] 3 W.W.R. 93 (B.C.S.C.) and *Roberge v. Huberman et al.* (1999), 121 B.C.A.C. 28. The distinction between the two forms of non-suit has also been identified in a number of Commonwealth decisions: *Copper Industries v. Hill* (1975), 12 S.A.S.R. 292 (S.C.); *Compaq Computer Australia Ltd. v. Howard Merry, David & Ors*, [1998] 968 F.C.A. (14 August 1998); and *Residues Treatment & Trading Co. Ltd. and Another v. Southern Resources Ltd. and Others* (1989), 52 S.A.S.R. 54 (S.C.).

. . .

Part of the difficulty in this case undoubtedly arose from the way in which the motion for non-suit was argued at trial. Counsel for the defendant (not counsel on appeal) seemed to accept the proposition that the trial judge had a discretion whether to put the defendant to an election where "there is an essential ingredient missing" (otherwise the usual practice is to call for an election), but then invited the trial judge on the facts to exercise his discretion in favour of not requiring the defendant to make an election, which the trial judge declined to do.

Counsel, advancing an application for non-suit, clearly have an obligation to make it clear which of the two types of motions for non-suit is being advanced so there can be no confusion as to the type of application the court is adjudicating upon. What happened here is illustrative of what can occur when this distinction is not clearly made. While counsel for the defendant purported to be dealing with a true "no evidence" motion based on a legal argument, he was also inviting the court to consider and weigh the evidence before it. He urged the court to exercise its discretion against requiring an election, and did not seem to appreciate that, assuming the motion was truly confined in its scope as he had initially stated, ordinarily the discretion should be exercised against requiring an election. In such circumstances the trial judge can hardly be faulted for exercising his discretion in favour of requiring the defendant to elect.

The appeal was allowed on other grounds.

PROBLEMS

Problem 1

The accused is charged with breach of probation. A term of his probation was that he be in his residence from 11:00 pm to 7:00 am. Evidence was led that the accused was found at 1234 Donwoods Avenue when a search warrant was executed at 1:00 a.m. on September 15, 2006. At trial, the Crown filed a copy of his probation order, dated March 15, 2006, which indicated a residence of 1245 Donwoods Avenue. There was also a term requiring that the accused notify his probation officer and the Court of a change of address. The Crown called the accused's probation officer who testified that he was not notified at any time between April 12, 2006, and September 14, 2006, of a change of address. The defence moved for a directed verdict of acquittal. In granting the motion, the trial judge held:

> I quite understand the submissions made by the Crown, and I agree that is it not the law that in every case the Crown must prove that no bail variation was sought or obtainod.

> However, I distinguish that case, which is plainly right, from this case in which there is a statutory provision requiring the accused to notify the court of any change of name or address before moving. To my mind that clearly distinguishes the two different situations, and the Crown therefore is obliged to prove that he did not notify the Court.

Now, it is certainly not the case the Crown never has to prove a negative. The Crown has to prove a great many negatives, for example that an accused person did not act in self defence. There is a clear case of a Crown having to prove a negative.

So I see nothing in this case, given the statutory provision to take it out of the normal role, which is the Crown must prove the elements of the offence beyond a reasonable doubt.

But in this case, because the Crown has not proved that evidence, and I note quite frankly I do not know how the Crown could prove that, because I have no idea how at least in Ontario a person notifies the court of a change of address.

Be that as it may, the fact is that the Crown has not proved it ... therefore there must be a failure of proof on that key point and I will grant the application for a directed verdict and find the accused not guilty.

Grounds for appeal? See *R. v. Gibbons*, [2009] O.J. No. 2295 (S.C.J.).

Problem 2

The accused is charged with robbery, using an imitation firearm and unlawful confinement arising out of a home invasion. At the preliminary inquiry, the Crown led evidence that three men gained entry to the complainant's apartment on the pretext that one of them required treatment for back pain. The complainant is an acupuncturist. The purported patient who identified himself as Stan gained entry to the complainant's apartment building without using the buzzer. He arrived at her apartment at 3:35 p.m. After an initial consultation, Stan left her apartment to purportedly pick up an x-ray from his car. Minutes later, he returned with two other men.

A copy of the security surveillance tapes was entered as an exhibit. It showed three men, including the accused, standing outside an initial door leading to the intercom area of the apartment building lobby. The video shows the men entering the apartment building at 3:31 p.m. by following another tenant with a pass. The three men then wait for the elevator. Approximately 12 minutes later (consistent with the period of time the complainant believed the intruders were present with her), they are seen leaving the apartment complex by a back stairwell. The accused is seen wearing gloves and putting his hand to his face as he got closer to the video camera. One of the three men resembled the description the complainant gave of Stan. The other was the accused's co-accused who conceded at the preliminary inquiry that the evidence was sufficient to warrant his committal to stand trial. Counsel for the accused argued that while there was evidence that he was in the apartment complex at the time of the home invasion, there was insufficient evidence connecting him to the complainant's apartment. Do you agree? See *R. v. Raja*, [2009] O.J. No. 3193 (S.C.J.); *R. v. Muir*, [2008] O.J. No. 3418 (C.A.).

2. PRESUMPTIONS

(a) Introduction

> Every writer of sufficient intelligence to appreciate the difficulties of the subject-matter has approached the topic of presumptions with a sense of hopelessness and has left it with a feeling of despair.[74]

Stanley presumed from certain basic facts that the man he was addressing was Dr. Livingstone. So, too, all presumptions in the law of evidence describe a process or a legal consequence whereby we infer the existence of a presumed fact when certain other basic facts have been established by evidence; the inference from the evidentiary fact is usually taken as a result of our own sense of logic or our own sense of experience but at times it may be statutorily or judicially directed to accommodate some extrinsic policy consideration.

The literature on the subject of presumptions is extensive and much of it is devoted to attempts to minimize the confusion by demonstrating the misuse or overuse of the term "presumption."[75]

Professor Thayer, on whose thesis all other writers have built,[76] described presumptions as follows:

> Presumptions are aids to reasoning and argumentation, which assume the truth of certain matters for the purpose of some given inquiry. They may be grounded on general experience, or probability of any kind; or merely on policy and convenience. On whatever basis they rest, they operate in advance of argument or evidence, or irrespective of it, by taking something for granted; by assuming its existence. When the term is legitimately applied it designates a rule or a proposition which still leaves open to further inquiry the matter thus assumed. The exact scope and operation of these *prima facie* assumptions are to cast upon the party against whom they operate, the duty of going forward, in argument or evidence, on the particular point to which they relate. . . . Presumption, assumption, taking for granted, are simply so many names for an act or process which aids and shortens inquiry and argument. . . . Such is the nature of all rules to determine the legal effect of facts as contrasted with their logical effect. To prescribe and fix a certain legal equivalence of facts, is a very different thing from merely allowing that meaning to be given to them. A rule of presumption does not merely say that such and such a thing is a permissible and usual inference from other facts, but it goes on to say that this significance shall always, in the absence of other circumstances, be imputed to them, — sometimes passing first through the stage of saying that it *ought to be* imputed.[77]

---

74 Morgan, "Presumptions" (1937), 12 Wash. L. Rev. 255.
75 Among the classic expositions on the subject are Cleary, "Presuming and Pleading: An Essay on Juristic Immaturity" (1959), 12 Stan. L. Rev. 5; Stone, "Burden of Proof and the Judicial Process" (1944), 60 L.Q.R. 262, Morgan, "Some Observations Concerning Presumptions" (1931), 44 Harv. L. Rev. 906; McBaine, "Burden of Proof: Presumptions" (1955), 2 U.C.L.A. Law Rev. 13; Bohlen, "The Effect of Rebuttable Presumptions of Law Upon the Burden of Proof" (1920), 68 U. Pa. L. Rev. 307; Denning, "Presumptions and Burdens" (1945), 61 L.Q.R. 379. And see Helman, "Presumptions" (1944), 22 Can. Bar Rev. 117.
76 Interestingly, Wigmore refers to him simply as "the master in the law of evidence": 9 Wigmore, *Evidence* (Chad. Rev.), s. 2511, p. 533.
77 Thayer, *supra*, note 7, at pp. 314-17.

Later writers interpreted the Thayerian view of presumptions as the "bursting bubble theory" by which was meant that the effect of any presumption was spent when the opponent led any evidence.[78] But Thayer never suggested that all presumptions should have this minimal effect, and he recognized that, depending on the need or purpose which gave rise to a recognition of the particular presumption, the onus on the opponent would vary. Later in his *Treatise* he wrote:

> How much evidence shall be required from the adversary to meet the presumption, or, as it is variously expressed, to overcome it or destroy it, is determined by no fixed rule. It may be merely enough to make it reasonable to require the other side to answer; it may be enough to make out a full *prima facie* case, and it may be a great weight of evidence, excluding all reasonable doubt. A mere presumption involves no rule as to the weight of evidence necessary to meet it. When a presumption is called a strong one, like the presumption of legitimacy, it means that it is accompanied by another rule relating to the weight of evidence to be brought in by him against whom it operates.[79]

From this framework we can profitably limit the use of the term presumption and so minimize the confusion.

(b) False Presumptions

Professor Thayer notes that the term "presumption" is legitimately used only when the matter presumed is left open to further inquiry. It is sometimes said that given certain facts other facts shall be "conclusively presumed." For example, at common law it was said that a child under seven years of age was conclusively presumed to be incapable of the commission of a crime; he was *doli incapax*.The Criminal Code provides that "a place that is found to be equipped with a slot machine shall be conclusively presumed to be a common gaming house."[80] In truth these are not presumptions apportioning burdens of proof, but rather rules of substantive law; a "conclusive presumption" is a contradiction in terms. On proof of the basic fact the so-called "presumed fact" in such a case is actually immaterial; if the prosecution proves that the place was equipped with a slot machine the substantive law provides for conviction and whether the place is a common gaming house or not is immaterial.[81] It would be best then, in our quest to minimize confusion, to discard the use of the term "conclusive presumption." The above section could simply be reworded to provide that "a place that is found to be equipped with a slot machine is a common gaming house."

At the other end of the scale, we note that Thayer would deny the use of the term presumption to describe simply the permissible inference which flows from the logical effect of certain facts. For him a presumption *demands* an effect unless the opponent does something. When a material fact *may* be inferred from basic facts proved, as opposed to *must,* it would be best to label such simply as a justifiable inference. The cases sometimes refer to this process as a presumption of fact as opposed to a presumption of law, or a permissive

---

78 Cleary points out that this was due to "tearing his statement from its context, and popularized by Wigmore," *supra*, note 76, at p. 18. And see Helman, *supra*, note 75, at p. 122.
79 Thayer, *supra*, note 7, at pp. 575-76.
80 Section 198(2). For other examples of conclusive presumptions, see ss. 163(8), 356(2), 421(2), 436(2) and 588.
81 See 9 Wigmore, *Evidence* (Chad. Rev.), s. 2492.

presumption as opposed to a compelling presumption, but this is misleading and can be dangerous. Let us take two examples: the presumption that persons intend the natural consequences of their acts, and the "doctrine" of recent possession.

When a criminal offence requires the mental element of intention, the prosecution will need to establish the same, barring a confession, by proof of the accused's actions, asking the jury to infer from such actions that the requisite state of mind existed. The best statement of the process is by Lord Goddard in *R. v. Steane*:[82]

> No doubt, if the prosecution prove an act, the natural consequence of which would be a certain result and no evidence or explanation is given, then a jury may, on a proper direction, find that the prisoner is guilty of doing the act with the intent alleged, but if on the totality of the evidence there is room for more than one view as to the intent of the prisoner, the jury should be directed that it is for the prosecution to prove the intent to the jury's satisfaction, and if, on a review of the whole evidence, they either think that the intent did not exist or they are left in doubt as to the intent, the prisoner is entitled to be acquitted.

To explain this to the jury, judges have occasionally advised them that persons are presumed to intend the natural consequences of their acts. Lord Denning explained, however:

> When people say that a man must be taken to intend the natural consequences of his acts, they fall into error: there is no "must" about it; it is only "may." The presumption of intention is not a proposition of law but a proposition of ordinary good sense. It means this: that, as a man is usually able to foresee what are the natural consequences of his acts, so it is, as a rule, reasonable to infer that he did foresee them and intend them. But, while that is an inference which may be drawn, it is not one which must be drawn. If on all the facts of the case it is not the correct inference, then it should not be drawn.[83]

In *R. v. Ortt*,[84] a murder prosecution, the trial judge instructed the jury in terms of the presumption and Jessup J.A., delivering the opinion of the Ontario Court of Appeal, wrote:

> It has been held by this Court that it is error in law to tell a jury it is a presumption of law that a person intends the natural consequences of his acts. . . . Moreover the word "presumption" alone creates a difficulty in that it may suggest an onus on the accused. I agree with the comment of the authors of *Martin's Annual Criminal Code* (1968), p. 195:
>
> > The difficulty would not arise if the use of the word "presumption" were avoided. A presumption requires that a certain conclusion must be drawn, unless the accused takes steps to make that conclusion unwarranted. An inference, however, is no more than a matter of common sense and merely indicates that a certain conclusion may be drawn if warranted by the evidence. . . .
>
> In my opinion, therefore, the word "presumption" is to be avoided in this context and juries simply told that generally it is a reasonable inference that a man intends the natural consequences of his acts so that when, for instance, a man points a gun at another and fires it the jury may reasonably infer that he meant

---

82 [1947] 1 K.B. 997, 1004 (C.C.A.).

83 *Hosegood v. Hosegood* (1950), 66 T.L.R. 735, 738 (C.A.).

84 [1969] 1 O.R. 461 (C.A.) applied by the Supreme Court in the context of the defence of intoxication: *R. v. Robinson* (1996), 105 C.C.C. (3d) 97 (S.C.C.).

> either to cause his death or to cause him bodily harm that he knew was likely to cause death reckless of whether death ensued or not.[85]

In *Stapleton v. R.,*[86] Dixon C.J. of the Australian High Court was also critical of such a direction:

> The introduction of the maxim or statement that a man is presumed to intend the reasonable consequences of his act is seldom helpful and always dangerous. For it either does no more than state a self evident proposition of fact or it produces an illegitimate transfer of the burden of proof of a real issue of intent to the person denying the allegation.

The so-called legal doctrine of recent possession is, also on analysis, a matter of common sense and not of law.[87] An analysis of the early cases involving charges of theft or possession of stolen goods shows the courts applying common sense to an evaluation of a piece of circumstantial evidence, namely, possession in the accused of the recently stolen goods. The early case of *Clement*[88] has no need for the language of presumption or doctrine. The entire report of the case reads:

> Prisoner was indicted for horse-stealing. The evidence was, that he had the horse in his possession in Kirkcudbright, three days after it had been stolen, in the county of Cumberland.

Parke J. held this to be sufficient evidence of a stealing by the prisoner in Cumberland.

R. v. NICHOLL
25 C.R. (6th) 192, 190 C.C.C. (3d) 549, 2004 CarswellOnt 4289 (Ont. C.A.)

CRONK J.A. (LABROSSE and MACPHERSON JJ.A. concurring): —

The appellant was charged with seven offences on a single information: two counts of possession of stolen property, one count of break and enter, two counts of failing to comply with a probation order and two counts of failing to comply with an undertaking. He entered a plea of guilty to breach of an undertaking to inform the police of any change in his place of residence and not guilty to the remaining six charges.

On July 28, 2004, following a trial before Hachborn J. of the Ontario Court of Justice, the appellant was convicted on all counts and sentenced to one year imprisonment concurrent on all counts. He appeals his convictions on the first six counts and his sentence on all counts. If his appeal against conviction is dismissed, he seeks to have his overall sentence reduced to one of time served in light of the time that he has already served in custody.

---

85 *Ibid.*, at p. 463. And see *R. v. Berger* (1975), 27 C.C.C. (2d) 357, 383 (B.C.C.A.) per McIntyre J.A.

86 (1952), 86 C.L.R. 358, 365 (H.C.).

87 See *R. v. Smythe* (1980), 72 Cr. App. R. 8, 11 (C.A.): "Nearly every reported case of recent possession is merely a decision of fact as an example of what is no more than a rule of evidence."

88 (1830), 168 E.R. 980.

The trial proceeded on the basis of an agreed statement of facts. No witnesses were called. The first six charges arose from the theft of a motor vehicle and a break and enter on the same day at a nearby high school where several cellos were stolen from the music department. Two weeks after the theft of the vehicle, municipal parking lot authorities reported the vehicle to the police as abandoned. When the police recovered the vehicle, the stolen cellos and a parking stub bearing a date five days after the date of the vehicles theft were inside the car. Three of the cellos were marked with the name of the high school from which the cellos had been stolen. The record does not establish whether the vehicle was locked or whether the windows of the vehicle were open or closed when the vehicle was recovered by the police.

At the time of the offences, the appellant was subject to probation and bail orders requiring that he keep the peace and abide by a curfew. He was also subject to an undertaking requiring that he notify the police of any change in his address.

Apart from the breach of undertaking charge to which the appellant pled guilty, the only evidence connecting the appellant to the offences was the presence of a single can of Coca Cola discovered by the police inside the stolen vehicle. The appellants thumb print was found on the can. The owner of the stolen vehicle confirmed that the pop can was not inside the vehicle prior to its theft.

The Crown asserted at trial that the doctrine of recent possession applied to the agreed facts and that, in the absence of any explanation from the appellant, the Crown had proven its case beyond a reasonable doubt based on the agreed facts. The Crown maintained that the presence of the pop can inside the stolen vehicle was sufficient to connect the appellant to the break and enter at the high school and the thefts of the cellos and the motor vehicle. In brief reasons, the trial judge accepted the Crown's argument and found the appellant guilty on all charges.

The appellant argues that the trial judge erred in relying on the doctrine of recent possession to convict him on the first six counts. I agree.

The unexplained recent possession of stolen goods permits, but does not require, an inference to be drawn that the possessor stole the goods: *R. v. Kowlyk*, [1988] 2 S.C.R. 59 at 71-72. Before such an inference may be drawn, however, the Crown must satisfy the trier of fact that: (i) the accused is in possession of the goods; (ii) the goods were stolen; and (iii) the theft was recent: *R. v. Cuming*, [2001] O.J. No. 3578 (C.A.). There is no question here that the motor vehicle and the cellos were stolen. The issue is whether the Crown met its burden to satisfy the remaining two prerequisites for invocation of the doctrine of recent possession.

Neither of these prerequisites was satisfied in this case. On the record before the trial judge, there was no evidence establishing that the appellant ever had possession of the vehicle or the cellos; nor was there any evidence to indicate when or how, during the two weeks that the car was missing, the pop can was placed inside the stolen car. As well, there was no demonstration that the appellant had been in recent possession of the coke can or how he had come to dispose of it. Importantly, the appellant's thumb print was found on the pop can – not on any of the stolen property.

. . . .

In ... this case, the pop can bearing the respondent's thumb print was not discovered until two weeks after the theft of the vehicle. During that time, the pop can could have been placed in the vehicle by a variety of means. As well, the respondent's thumb print may have been placed on the pop can before or after the offences in question, or while the respondent was a passenger in the vehicle. In addition, the Crown failed to establish that the pop can had any connection with the theft of the motor vehicle or the cellos.

Thus, the evidence relied upon by the Crown as establishing the respondent's culpability was compatible with explanations other than those involving the respondent's guilt. The presence of the respondent's thumb print on the pop can establishes that he handled the pop can, but this does not prove possession of the stolen vehicle in which the can was found, or of the cellos contained in the vehicle: see *Poirier v. The Queen* (1971), 16 C.R.N.S. 174 (Que. C.A.) and *R. v. Sweezey* (1974), 20 C.C.C. (2d) 400 (Ont. C.A.).

In all the circumstances, there was an insufficient evidentiary footing at trial to support an inference of guilt based on the doctrine of recent possession. The appellant's convictions on counts one to six are unsustainable.

The appeal was allowed and acquittals were entered.[89]

Just as relevance is dictated by common sense and experience, so too is sufficiency.[90] These matters vary with the fact situation under review. Certain fact situations regularly recur and appellate opinions are produced expressing their concurrence that particular facts are relevant and that a certain measure of circumstantial evidence is sufficient to pass the judge and support a reasonable verdict. From an early time our courts have recognized that possession of goods recently stolen is relevant to the issue of whether the possessor is the thief, or knowing receiver, and sufficiently probative to permit the finding. The reasoning which underlies this finding of relevance and sufficiency is perhaps best expressed in *Wills on Circumstantial Evidence:*[91]

> Since the desire of dishonest gain is the impelling motive to theft and robbery, it naturally follows that the possession of the fruits of crime recently after it has been committed, affords a strong and reasonable ground for the presumption that the party in whose possession they are found, was the real offender, unless he can account for such possession in some way consistent with his innocence. The force of this presumption has been recognized from the earliest times; and it is founded on the obvious consideration, that if such possession had been lawfully acquired, the party would be able, at least shortly after its acquisition, to give an account of the manner

---

89 See also *R. v. Dionne*, 198 C.C.C. (3d) 159, 29 C.R. (6th) 32, [2005] 1 S.C.R. 665.

90 *Que. (A.G.) v. Hamel* (1987), 60 C.R. (3d) 174 (Que. C.A.); leave to appeal to S.C.C. refused (1988), 89 N.R. 80n (up to preliminary magistrate to draw inferences), applying *Dubois v. R.*, [1986] 1 S.C.R. 366.

91 6th ed. (1912), pp. 82-83.

in which it was obtained; and his unwillingness or inability to afford such explanation is justly regarded as amounting to strong self-condemnatory evidence.

As the factual situation of theft and possession[92] regularly occurred and the practice of drawing the inference became standard, the courts, perhaps unfortunately, began speaking of the "presumption" which arises from the possession of recently stolen goods;[93] from there it was a short step to talk of the "doctrine" of recent possession. This is unfortunate as the clothing of legal language often serves to distract from the simplicity and common sense of the proposition and may place too heavy a burden on the accused. Viewed against this background the classic and oft-quoted statement on recent possession by Reading C.J.C. in *R. v. Schama*,[94] is seen not as a technical treatise but rather as a simple statement on reasonable doubt:

> Where the prisoner is charged with receiving recently stolen goods, when the prosecution has proved the possession by the prisoner, and that the goods had been recently stolen, the jury should be told that they may, not that they must, in the absence of any reasonable explanation, find the prisoner guilty. But if an explanation is given which may be true, it is for the jury to say on the whole of the evidence whether the accused is guilty or not; that is to say, if the jury think the explanation may reasonably be true, though they are not convinced that it is true, the prisoner is entitled to an acquittal, because the Crown has not discharged the onus of proof imposed upon it of satisfying the jury beyond reasonable doubt of the prisoner's guilt.[95]

The process which permits, but does not demand, a finding does not deserve the label presumption.[96] Laskin J., in *R. v. Graham*,[97] wrote:

> The use of the term "presumption", which has been associated with the doctrine (of recent possession), is too broad, and the word which properly ought to be substituted is "inference". . . . The inference of guilty knowledge which may be made upon proof of unexplained recent possession ought not to be magnified as some iniquity which necessarily stands out above all other evidence in the case. The misuse, in my opinion, of the term "presumption" in this connection may lead to injustice because of its strong connotation.[98]

---

92 In *R. v. Langmead* (1864), 169 E.R. 1459, it was urged that evidence of recent possession was only evidence of stealing and not of receiving or possession but Pollock C.B. denied any such distinction: the evidence was sufficient and the jury would determine on the facts.

93 Kellock J. in *R. v. Suchard* (1956), 114 C.C.C. 257, 263 (S.C.C.) commented: "The presumption is merely an inference of fact which has become crystallized into a rule of law."

94 (1914), 11 Cr. App. R. 45.

95 *Ibid.*, at p. 49.

96 See 9 Wigmore, *Evidence* (Chad. Rev.), s. 2513(4) for numerous citations indicating a proper trend toward repudiating presumptive language.

97 (1972), 7 C.C.C. (2d) 93 (S.C.C.).

98 *Ibid.*, at pp. 108, 110. See also *R. v. Raviraj* (1987), 85 Cr. App. R. 93, 103 (C.A.):

> The doctrine is only a particular aspect of the general proposition that where suspicious circumstances appear to demand an explanation and no explanation, or an entirely incredible explanation, is given, the lack of explanation may warrant an inference of guilty knowledge in the defendant. This again is only part of a wider proposition that guilt may be inferred from unreasonable behaviour of a defendant when confronted with facts which seem to accuse.

PROBLEMS

Problem 1

The accused is charged with possession of stolen property. The property was stolen two years before the accused was found in possession. The accused has testified that he didn't know the property was stolen and was simply holding it as bailee for another. The accused's counsel has asked you as trial judge to direct the jury that if the accused's explanation was one that could reasonably be true, a verdict of not guilty should be rendered. Will you accede to his request? Compare *R. v. Palmer*, [1970] 3 C.C.C. 402 (B.C. C.A.).

Problem 2

There were three break-ins in the neighbourhood during the summer in each of which the owners of the burgled houses had recently died and the burglaries took place during the time of the pre-advertised funeral service. The accused's brother was arrested in the act of committing a theft. During questioning by the investigating officers, he admitted that he committed the three break and enters in question. He then led the officers to a house that he shared with the accused. Here the officers found seventy-six items stolen during the break and enters described above. The accused was found in his bedroom. The door was closed and the police officer demanded that the accused come out. The accused stated that he would do so after he got dressed. Five minutes later the accused emerged from his bedroom. A police officer who had been stationed outside testified that the accused had opened the curtains, unlocked the window and attempted to lift the window, but upon seeing the officer had stopped these activities. Fourteen of the stolen items were found in the accused's bedroom. The items were grouped according to the separate break-ins. The accused was arrested and charged with three counts of break, enter and theft. When questioned by the police about his involvement in the burglaries the accused replied "All you got me for is possession. I'm not saying anything". He made no further comment and did not testify at his trial. You are sitting as a judge alone. Would you convict? Compare *R. v. Kowlyk*, [1988] 2 S.C.R. 59.

(c) True Presumptions

If satisfied that the language of conclusive and permissive presumptions should be discarded, we can then examine the true presumptions: devices which leave open to inquiry the matters presumed but which demand a finding if the opponent does nothing.

A true presumption compels the trier of fact to find a fact, the presumed fact, to be proved against a party when another fact, the basic fact, is proved. The trier is compelled to find the presumed fact unless the party against whom the presumption operates does something. That "something" depends on the language of the particular presumptive device. It may be to ensure that there is evidence in the case contrary to the presumed fact or it may actually require the party to disprove the presumed fact. The former "something" imposes an evidential burden on the party and the latter a persuasive burden.

There are many true presumptions scattered throughout the cases and statutes created out of considerations of probabilities or substantive law policy.

We will examine a few, as Professor Thayer cautioned that "any detailed consideration of the mass of legal presumptions [would be] an unprofitable and monstrous task."[99]

A good example of a presumptive device placing an evidential burden may be seen in the criminal case of *R. v. Proudlock.*[100] The accused was charged with break and enter with intent to commit an indictable offence contrary to section 306(1)(*a*) of the Criminal Code. The Code provided:

> **306.**(2) For the purposes of proceedings under this section, evidence that an accused
>
> (*a*)   broke and entered a place is, in the absence of any evidence to the contrary, proof that he broke and entered with intent to commit an indictable offence therein.[101]

The crime charged required proof of an act and proof of an intention. An evidentiary assist was given to the prosecution with respect to the latter element. In *R. v. Proudlock,* the trial judge summarized the accused's evidence:

> When he testified, Proudlock said that he did not have an explanation and did not know what his motives had been. He acknowledged that it was "possible" he had told the janitor he was looking for soup, but said that would not have been a true statement of his purpose. He resolutely denied any intention to steal. . . . I did not find Proudlock's evidence, when he was asked why he broke and entered the restaurant to be convincing in the least degree. To put the matter simply, I did not believe him. . .
>
> In my opinion, Proudlock broke and entered the restaurant purposefully, and I do not believe that purpose has escaped his memory. . . . I do not believe Proudlock.[102]

Nevertheless, the trial judge acquitted the accused. He reasoned that evidence to the contrary was present, the presumption of intent was rebutted, and as the prosecution led no evidence of intent a material ingredient of the crime had not been established. The Supreme Court of Canada held that "evidence disbelieved by the trier of fact is not 'evidence to the contrary' "[103] and Pigeon J. for the majority reasoned:

> The accused does not have to "establish" a defence or an excuse, all he has to do is to raise a reasonable doubt. If there is nothing in the evidence adduced by the Crown from which a reasonable doubt can arise, then the accused will necessarily have the burden of adducing evidence if he is to escape conviction. . . . The accused may remain silent, but, when there is a *prima facie* case against him and he is, as in the instant case, the only person who can give "evidence to the contrary" his choice really is to face *certain conviction* or to offer in testimony whatever explanation or excuse may be available to him. [Emphasis added.][104]

---

99 Thayer, *supra*, note 7, at p. 313. Regarding the unfortunate and confusing phrase "*prima facie* evidence," see *R. v. Pye* (1984), 38 C.R. (3d) 375 (N.S.C.A.).

100 (1979), 43 C.C.C. (2d) 321 (S.C.C.).

101 This phrasing is repeated in a number of sections of the Criminal Code: see ss. 198(1), 212(3), 215(4), 338(3), 339(4), 349(2), 364(2), 396(2), 414, 421(1) and 446(4).

102 *Supra*, note 100, at p. 329.

103 *Ibid.*, at p. 323.

104 *Ibid.*, at pp. 325 and 327. And see *R. v. Vanegas* (1987), 60 C.R. (3d) 169 (B.C.C.A.).

Since there had been no "evidence to the contrary" the accused had failed to discharge his evidential burden and the Supreme Court entered a conviction.

With respect to a prosecution for an over 80 offence, s. 258 enables the Crown to establish two facts by means of presumptions. The "presumption of identity" arising from s. 258(1)(c), is that the blood alcohol concentration of the accused at the time of driving is the same as that indicated by the Intoxilyzer tests. According to MacDonnell J. in *R. v. Snider*,[105] this presumption enables the Crown to bridge the temporal gap between the occurrence of the alleged offence and the administration of the breath tests without calling expert evidence. It presumes that in the interval between those two events nothing has changed in relation to the accused's blood alcohol concentration. The second "presumption of accuracy" that s. 258(1)(g) enables the Crown to establish is that the Intoxilyzer readings recorded in the certificate of a qualified technician are an accurate reflection of the accused's blood alcohol concentration at the time of the Intoxilyzer tests. Both presumptions are only available to the Crown in the absence of "evidence to the contrary." According to MacDonnell J. in *Snider*, where evidence to the contrary is offered in relation to the presumption of accuracy, a trial judge cannot take the breath test results into account in assessing the credibility of the evidence to the contrary. That would amount to circular reasoning. However, where the qualified technician gives evidence in relation to the breath tests results there is no presumption of accuracy. Whether the qualified technician's testimony is sufficient to establish the accused's blood alcohol concentration at the time of testing is simply an issue of fact to be resolved in the way all issues of fact are resolved. Here testimony of the qualified technician with respect to the blood alcohol concentrations revealed by the Intoxilyzer tests could be taken into account in assessing the credibility of the evidence of the accused and his friend and in determining whether the Crown has proved its case beyond a reasonable doubt.[106]

An example of a presumptive device placing an evidential burden on the opponent in a civil case is the presumption of testamentary capacity. Lord Dunedin, in *Robins v. National Trust*,[107] explained:

> Those who propound a will must show that the will of which probate is sought is the will of the testator, and that the testator was a person of testamentary capacity. In ordinary cases if there is no suggestion to the contrary any man who is shown to have executed a will in ordinary form will be presumed to have testamentary capacity,

---

105 (2006), 37 C.R. (6th) 61, 2006 CarswellOnt 1321 (C.J.).

106 Justice MacDonnell was interpreting a complex ruling of the Supreme Court in *R. v. Boucher*, [2005] 3 S.C.R. 499. See also *R. v. Gibson*, (2008) 55 C.R. 201 (S.C.C.), where the majority of the Supreme Court further narrows the 'straddle evidence' defence. In 2008, by amendment to ss. 258(1)(c) and (d) by s. 24 of the *Tackling Violent Crime Act*, S.C. 2008, c. 6, Parliament made the presumption of accuracy virtually irrebuttable. For an argument that these amendments violate the right to full answer and defence guaranteed by s. 7 of the Charter, see Joseph Neuberger and Stacey Nichols, "The Rise and Fall of Evidence to the Contrary: A Brief History" (2009) 13 *Can. Crim. L.R.* 159.

107 [1927] A.C. 515, 519 (P.C.). And see *Smith v. Nevins*, [1925] S.C.R. 619, 638. See also generally, Wright, "Testamentary Capacity" (1938), 16 Can. Bar Rev. 405. Other presumptions of validity of marriage, presumption of validity of a foreign divorce decree and the presumption in favour of the domicile of origin: *Powell v. Cockburn* (1976), 68 D.L.R. (3d) 700, 706 (S.C.C.).

but the moment the capacity is called in question then at once the onus lies on those propounding the will to affirm positively the testamentary capacity.

As an example of a presumptive device shifting a persuasive burden on a material ingredient to the accused in a criminal case, consider the case of *R. v. Appleby.*[108] The accused was charged with having the care and control of a motor vehicle while his ability to drive was impaired by alcohol. There was no question of the accused's impairment, and the only question was whether he had care and control. The Crown relied on a statutory presumption which provided:

224A(1) [now s. 258(1)(a)] In any proceedings under section 222 or 224,

> (a) where it is proved that the accused occupied the seat ordinarily occupied by the driver of a motor vehicle, he shall be deemed to have had the care or control of the vehicle unless he establishes that he did not enter or mount the vehicle for the purpose of setting it in motion.[109]

The trial judge convicted though he did make the finding of fact:

> That the Defendant sought to rebut the presumption under Section 224A(1)(a) by testifying that he entered the driver's seat of the taxi to use the radio to summon a wrecker, rather than for the purpose of driving the vehicle and, although this evidence was unsupported by any other witness, it did raise a reasonable doubt in my mind.[110]

The conviction was entered then on the basis that the judge was not satisfied by a preponderance of evidence "that he did not enter or mount the motor vehicle for the purpose of setting it in motion." The British Columbia Court of Appeal found the trial judge had erred and that the presumptive effect was to cast only an evidential burden on the accused. The Supreme Court of Canada reversed and restored the conviction, holding that there had been an express enactment exceptionally[111] placing a persuasive burden on the accused. Ritchie J., for the majority, reasoned:

---

108 (1971), 3 C.C.C. (2d) 354 (S.C.C.).

109 *Ibid.*, at p. 356.

110 *Ibid.*

111 As to whether it is presently "exceptional" to place a persuasive burden on the accused in Canada, consider the fact that over 60 sections in the Criminal Code have language akin to that canvassed in *Appleby:*

> "Until the contrary is proved, be presumed," s. 16(4); "without lawful excuse, the proof of which lies upon him," ss. 57(3), 82, 104(3), 145(1)(b), 177, 215(2), 276(5), 349(1), 351(1), 352, 376(1)(b), (c); "without lawful authority, the proof of which lies upon him," ss. 125(c), 294(a), 417(1), (2), 419; "without lawful authority or excuse, the proof of which lies upon him," ss. 369, 405; "without lawful justification or excuse, the proof of which lies upon him," ss. 450, 451, 452, 458, 459; "unless the accused establishes," ss. 50(1)(a), 394(1); "unless he has consent . . . the proof of which lies upon him," s. 110(1)(*b*), (*c*); "no accused shall be convicted . . . where he proves," ss. 409(2), 429(2); "the burden of proving . . . is upon the accused," ss. 338(4), 339(5), 383(2), 794(2); "the onus of proving . . . is on the accused," s. 197(3); "no person shall be convicted . . . if he establishes," ss. 163(3), 420(2); "shall be deemed to have committed . . . unless he proves," s. 210(4); "shall be deemed to have committed . . . unless he establishes," ss. 255(1)(a), 290(4); "no person shall be deemed . . . where he proves," s. 311; "it shall be presumed . . . unless the court is satisfied," s. 362(4); "no person shall be convicted . . . where, to the satisfaction of the court or judge, he accounts . . . and shows," s. 402(2); "the burden of proof of which lies upon

With all respect, it appears to me that if the Court of Appeal of British Columbia were correct in holding that it is enough, to rebut the presumption created by the words "shall be deemed" as they occur in s. 224A(1)(a), for the accused to raise a reasonable doubt as to whether or not he entered the motor vehicle for the purpose of setting it in motion, then it would, in my view follow, that if the Crown has established the basis of the presumption beyond a reasonable doubt, it must also give similar proof of the facts which the statute deems to exist and expressly requires the accused to negate. This is exactly the burden which the Crown would have to discharge if the section had not been enacted, and in my view such a construction makes the statutory presumption ineffective and the section meaningless.[112]

Could the section have meaning by imposing an evidential burden?[113] That is, commanding a result if no contrary evidence was given?

An example of a presumptive device having the effect of shifting a persuasive burden to the opponent in a civil case is the presumption of legitimacy.[114] In *Welstead v. Brown*[115] the plaintiff was successful at trial in his claim for damages for criminal conversation. The wife had given birth to a child and blood tests indicated it was *impossible* for the husband to be the father. The Supreme Court of Canada decided that on such evidence the presumption of legitimacy could be rebutted. But Cartwright J. wrote:

Had the doctors testified that the result of the tests indicated that it was in the highest degree improbable, but not impossible that the appellant be the father of the child it would, in my opinion, have been the duty of the trial Judge to direct the jury that as a matter of law such evidence could not avail against the presumption.[116]

And Kellock J. wrote:

In my view, a child born in lawful wedlock is still presumed to be a legitimate child, and *the presumption is to be overborne only by evidence excluding reasonable doubt.* [Emphasis added.][117]

---

the accused," s. 440. Of course, many sections in other Acts in the Revised Statutes of Canada contain these operative words. The best known are s. 8 of the Narcotic Control Act, R.S.C. 1985, c. N-1, and s. 38 of the Food and Drugs Act, R.S.C. 1985, c. F-27. Although all of these sections have not, of course, been interpreted in the courts, they would all appear to place the burden of persuasion on the accused since the cases, in interpreting the words of the various sections, have not distinguished between the purpose of the section or whether the section required the accused to assert a positive or negative averment.

112 (1971), 3 C.C.C. (2d) 354, 360 (S.C.C.).
113 The court also denied that the legislation was in conflict with the Bill of Rights guarantee of a "presumption of innocence."
114 Another presumption having such an effect in civil cases is the presumption of death of a person not heard of for seven years: *Middlemiss v. Middlemiss*, [1955] 4 D.L.R. 801 (B.C.C.A.); *Re Bell*, [1946] O.R. 854 (C.A.). And see Treitel, "The Presumption of Death" (1954), 17 Mod. L. Rev. 530. The adversary must also persuade on the balance of probabilities to rebut the presumption of advancement to show that no gift was intended: see *Dagle v. Dagle* (1990), 81 Nfld. & P.E.I.R. 245 (P.E.I.C.A.).
115 [1952] 1 D.L.R. 465 (S.C.C.). See also *Hiuser v. Hiuser*, [1962] O.W.N. 220 (C.A.) and *S. v. McC.*, [1972] A.C. 24 (H.L.).
116 *Ibid.*, at pp. 475-76.
117 *Ibid.*, at p. 483.

(d) Presumption of Innocence and Charter

In *R. v. Appleby*[118] the accused argued that the reverse onus provision requiring him to establish the lack of an essential ingredient of the offence contravened the Canadian Bill of Rights, which provides that no law of Canada shall be construed or applied so as to

> 2(f) deprive a person charged with a criminal offence of the right to be presumed innocent until proved guilty according to law. . . .

The Supreme Court of Canada reasoned that this provision had not been contravened since the accused had been "proved guilty according to law" since the law was stated as stated in *Woolmington v. Director of Public Prosecutions.*[119] Viscount Sankey had there written:

> . . . it is the duty of the prosecution to prove the prisoner's guilt subject to what I have already said as to the defence of insanity *and subject also to any statutory exception.* [Emphasis added.][120]

Of course, on this thesis, Parliament could enact any reverse onus provision and never contravene the Bill of Rights!

R. v. OAKES
[1986] 1 S.C.R. 103, 50 C.R. (3d) 1, 24 C.C.C. (3d) 321

The Supreme Court was called on to deal with the constitutionality of section 8 of the Narcotic Control Act, which provided that a person found in possession of a narcotic was presumed to be in possession for the purpose of trafficking unless he established the contrary.

DICKSON C.J.C. (CHOUINARD, LAMER, WILSON and LE DAIN JJ. concurring):—

. . . .

[O]ne cannot but question the appropriateness of reading into the phrase "according to law" in s. 11(*d*) of the Charter the statutory exceptions acknowledged in *Woolmington*, supra, and in *Appleby*, supra. The *Woolmington* case was decided in the context of a legal system with no constitutionally-entrenched human rights document. In Canada, we have tempered Parliamentary supremacy by entrenching important rights and freedoms in the Constitution. Viscount Sankey L.C.'s statutory exception proviso is clearly not applicable in this context and would subvert the very purpose of the entrenchment of the presumption of innocence in the Charter. I do not, therefore, feel constrained in this case by the interpretation of s. 2(*f*) of the Canadian Bill of Rights presented in the majority judgment in *Appleby*. Section 8 of the Narcotic Control Act is not

---

118 (1971), 3 C.C.C. (2d) 354 (S.C.C.); Canadian Bill of Rights, R.S.C. 1985, App. III.
119 [1935] A.C. 462 (H.L.).
120 *Ibid.*, at p. 481.

rendered constitutionally valid simply by virtue of the fact that it is a statutory provision.

. . . .

In general one must, I think, conclude that a provision which requires an accused to disprove on a balance of probabilities the existence of a presumed fact which is an important element of the offence in question violates the presumption of innocence in s. 11(*d*). If an accused bears the burden of disproving on a balance of probabilities an essential element of an offence, it would be possible for a conviction to occur despite the existence of a reasonable doubt. This would arise if the accused adduced sufficient evidence to raise a reasonable doubt as to his or her innocence but did not convince the jury on a balance of probabilities that the presumed fact was untrue.

The fact that the standard is only the civil one does not render a reverse onus clause constitutional. As Sir Rupert Cross commented in the Rede lecture "The Golden Thread of the English Criminal Law: The Burden of Proof", delivered in 1976 at the University of Toronto, at p. 11:

> It is sometimes said that exceptions to the Woolmington rule are acceptable because, whenever the burden of proof on any issue in a criminal case is borne by the accused, he only has to satisfy the jury on the balance of probabilities, whereas on issues on which the Crown bears the burden of proof the jury must be satisfied beyond a reasonable doubt.

And at p. 13:

> The fact that the standard is lower when the accused bears the burden of proof than it is when the burden of proof is borne by the prosecution is no answer to my objection to the existence of exceptions to the Woolmington rule as it does not alter the fact that a jury or bench of magistrates may have to convict the accused although they are far from sure of his guilt.

As we have seen, the potential for a rational connection between the basic fact and the presumed fact to justify a reverse onus provision has been elaborated in some of the cases discussed above and is now known as the "rational connection test". In the context of s. 11(*d*), however, the following question arises: if we apply the rational connection test to the consideration of whether s. 11(*d*) has been violated, are we adequately protecting the constitutional principle of the presumption of innocence? As Professors MacKay and Cromwell point out in their article "*Oakes*: A Bold Initiative Impeded by Old Ghosts" (1983), 32 C.R. (3d) 221, at p. 233:

> The rational connection test approves a provision that *forces* the trier to infer a fact that may be simply rationally connected to the proved fact. Why does it follow that such a provision does not offend the constitutional right to be proved guilty beyond a reasonable doubt?

A basic fact may rationally tend to prove a presumed fact, but not prove its existence beyond a reasonable doubt. An accused person could thereby be convicted despite the presence of a reasonable doubt. This would violate the presumption of innocence.

I should add that this questioning of the constitutionality of the "rational connection test" as a guide to interpreting s. 11(*d*) does not minimize its importance. The appropriate stage for invoking the rational connection test, however, is under s. 1 of the Charter. This consideration did not arise under the Canadian Bill of Rights because of the absence of an equivalent to s. 1. At the Court of Appeal level in the present case, Martin J.A. sought to combine the analysis of s. 11(*d*) and s. 1 to overcome the limitations of the Canadian Bill of Rights jurisprudence. To my mind, it is highly desirable to keep s. 1 and s. 11(*d*) analytically distinct.

To return to s. 8 of the Narcotic Control Act, I am in no doubt whatsoever that it violates s. 11(*d*) of the Charter by requiring the accused to prove on a balance of probabilities that he was not in possession of the narcotic for the purpose of trafficking. Mr. Oakes is compelled by s. 8 to prove that he is *not* guilty of the offence of trafficking. He is thus denied his right to be presumed innocent and subjected to the potential penalty of life imprisonment unless he can rebut the presumption. This is radically and fundamentally inconsistent with the societal values of human dignity and liberty which we espouse, and is directly contrary to the presumption of innocence enshrined in s. 11(*d*). Let us turn now to s. 1 of the Charter.

V. Is S. 8 of the Narcotic Control Act a Reasonable and Demonstrably Justified Limit Pursuant to S. 1 of the Charter?

The Crown submits that, even if s. 8 of the Narcotic Control Act violates s. 11(*d*) of the Charter, it can still be upheld as a reasonable limit under s. 1, which, as has been mentioned, provides:

> 1. The *Canadian Charter of Rights and Freedoms* guarantees the rights and freedoms set out in it subject only to such reasonable limits prescribed by law as can be demonstrably justified in a free and democratic society.

The question whether the limit is "prescribed by law" is not contentious in the present case, since s. 8 of the Narcotic Control Act is a duly-enacted legislative provision. It is, however, necessary to determine if the limit on Mr. Oakes' right, as guaranteed by s. 11(*d*) of the Charter, is "reasonable" and "demonstrably justified in a free and democratic society" for the purpose of s. 1 of the Charter, and thereby saved from inconsistency with the Constitution.

It is important to observe at the outset that s. 1 has two functions: first, it constitutionally guarantees the rights and freedoms set out in the provisions which follow; and second, it states explicitly the exclusive justificatory criteria (outside of s. 33 of the Constitution Act, 1982) against which limitations on those rights and freedoms must be measured. Accordingly, any s. 1 inquiry must be premised on an understanding that the impugned limit violates constitutional rights and freedoms — rights and freedoms which are part of the supreme law of Canada. As Wilson J. stated in *Singh v. Min. of Employment & Immigration*, supra, at p. 218:

. . . it is important to remember that the courts are conducting this inquiry in light of a commitment to uphold the rights and freedoms set out in the other sections of the *Charter*.

A second contextual element of interpretation of s. 1 is provided by the words "free and democratic society". Inclusion of these words as the final standard of justification for limits on rights and freedoms refers the court to the very purpose for which the Charter was originally entrenched in the Constitution: Canadian society is to be free and democratic. The court must be guided by the values and principles essential to a free and democratic society, which I believe embody, to name but a few, respect for the inherent dignity of the human person, commitment to social justice and equality, accommodation of a wide variety of beliefs, respect for cultural and group identity, and faith in social and political institutions which enhance the participation of individuals and groups in society. The underlying values and principles of a free and democratic society are the genesis of the rights and freedoms guaranteed by the Charter and the ultimate standard against which a limit on a right or freedom must be shown, despite its effect, to be reasonable and demonstrably justified.

The rights and freedoms guaranteed by the Charter are not, however, absolute. It may become necessary to limit rights and freedoms in circumstances where their exercise would be inimical to the realization of collective goals of fundamental importance. For this reason, s. 1 provides criteria of justification for limits on the rights and freedoms guaranteed by the Charter.

These criteria impose a stringent standard of justification, especially when understood in terms of the two contextual considerations discussed above, namely, the violation of a constitutionally-guaranteed right or freedom and the fundamental principles of a free and democratic society.

The onus of proving that a limit on a right or freedom guaranteed by the Charter is reasonable and demonstrably justified in a free and democratic society rests upon the party seeking to uphold the limitation. It is clear from the text of s. 1 that limits on the rights and freedoms enumerated in the Charter are exceptions to their general guarantee. The presumption is that the rights and freedoms are guaranteed unless the party invoking s. 1 can bring itself within the exceptional criteria which justify their being limited. This is further substantiated by the use of the word "demonstrably", which clearly indicates that the onus of justification is on the party seeking to limit: *Hunter v. Southam Inc.*, supra.

The standard of proof under s. 1 is the civil standard, namely, proof by a preponderance of probability. The alternative criminal standard, proof beyond a reasonable doubt, would, in my view, be unduly onerous on the party seeking to limit. Concepts such as "reasonableness", "justifiability" and "free and democratic society" are simply not amenable to such a standard. Nevertheless, the preponderance of probability test must be applied rigorously. Indeed, the phrase "demonstrably justified" in s. 1 of the Charter supports this conclusion. Within the broad category of the civil standard, there exist different degrees of probability depending on the nature of the case: see Sopinka and Lederman, The Law of

Evidence in Civil Cases (Toronto, 1974), at p. 385. As Denning L.J. explained in *Bater v. Bater*, [1950] 2 All E.R. 458 at 459 (C.A.):

> The case may be proved by a preponderance of probability, but there may be degrees of probability within that standard. The degree depends on the subject-matter. A civil court, when considering a charge of fraud, will naturally require a higher degree of probability than that which it would require if considering whether negligence were established. It does not adopt so high a standard as a criminal court, even when considering a charge of a criminal nature, but still it does require a degree of probability which is commensurate with the occasion.

This passage was cited with approval in *Hanes v. Wawanesa Mut. Ins. Co.*, [1963] S.C.R. 154 at 161, [1963] 1 C.C.C. 321 [Ont.]. A similar approach was put forward by Cartwright J. in *Smith v. Smith*, [1952] 2 S.C.R. 312 at 331-32, [B.C.]:

> I wish, however, to emphasize that in every civil action before the tribunal can safely find the affirmative of an issue of fact required to be proved it must be satisfied, and that whether or not it will be so satisfied must depend on the totality of the circumstances on which its judgment is formed including the gravity of the consequences . . .

Having regard to the fact that s. 1 is being invoked for the purpose of justifying a violation of the constitutional rights and freedoms the Charter was designed to protect, a very high degree of probability will be, in the words of Denning L.J., "commensurate with the occasion". Where evidence is required in order to prove the constituent elements of a s. 1 inquiry, and this will generally be the case, it should be cogent and persuasive and make clear to the court the consequences of imposing or not imposing the limit: see *L.S.U.C. v. Skapinker*, supra, at p. 384; *Singh v. Min. of Employment & Immigration*, supra, at p. 217. A court will also need to know what alternative measures for implementing the objective were available to the legislators when they made their decisions. I should add, however, that there may be cases where certain elements of the s. 1 analysis are obvious or self-evident.

To establish that a limit is reasonable and demonstrably justified in a free and democratic society, two central criteria must be satisfied. First, the objective, which the measures responsible for a limit on a Charter right or freedom are designed to serve, must be "of sufficient importance to warrant overriding a constitutionally protected right or freedom": *R. v. Big M Drug Mart Ltd.*, supra, at p. 352. The standard must be high in order to ensure that objectives which are trivial or discordant with the principles integral to a free and democratic society do not gain s. 1 protection. It is necessary, at a minimum, that an objective relate to concerns which are pressing and substantial in a free and democratic society before it can be characterized as sufficiently important.

Second, once a sufficiently significant objective is recognized, then the party invoking s. 1 must show that the means chosen are reasonable and demonstrably justified. This involves "a form of proportionality test": *R. v. Big M Drug Mart Ltd.*, supra, at p. 352. Although the nature of the proportionality test will vary depending on the circumstances, in each case courts will be required to balance the interests of society with those of individuals and groups. There are, in my view, three important components of a proportionality test. First, the measures adopted must be carefully designed to achieve the objective in question. They must not be arbitrary, unfair or based on irrational considerations. In short, they must be rationally connected to the objective. Second, the means, even if rationally connected to the objective in this first sense, should impair "as little as possible" the right or freedom in question: *R. v. Big M Drug Mart Ltd.*, supra, at p. 352. Third, there must be a proportionality between the *effects* of the measures which are responsible for limiting the Charter right or freedom and the objective which has been identified as of "sufficient importance".

With respect to the third component, it is clear that the general effect of any measure impugned under s. 1 will be the infringement of a right or freedom guaranteed by the Charter; this is the reason why resort to s. 1 is necessary. The inquiry into effects must, however, go further. A wide range of rights and freedoms are guaranteed by the Charter, and an almost infinite number of factual situations may arise in respect of these. Some limits on rights and freedoms protected by the Charter will be more serious than others in terms of the nature of the right or freedom violated, the extent of the violation, and the degree to which the measures which impose the limit trench upon the integral principles of a free and democratic society. Even if an objective is of sufficient importance, and the first two elements of the proportionality test are satisfied, it is still possible that, because of the severity of the deleterious effects of a measure on individuals or groups, the measure will not be justified by the purposes it is intended to serve. The more severe the deleterious effects of a measure, the more important the objective must be if the measure is to be reasonable and demonstrably justified in a free and democratic society.

Having outlined the general principles of a s. 1 inquiry, we must apply them to s. 8 of the Narcotic Control Act. Is the reverse onus provision in s. 8 a reasonable limit on the right to be presumed innocent until proven guilty beyond a reasonable doubt as can be demonstrably justified in a free and democratic society?

The starting point for formulating a response to this question is, as stated above, the nature of Parliament's interest or objective which accounts for the passage of s. 8 of the Narcotic Control Act. According to the Crown, s. 8 of the Narcotic Control Act is aimed at curbing drug trafficking by facilitating the conviction of drug traffickers. In my opinion, Parliament's concern that drug trafficking be decreased can be characterized as substantial and pressing. The problem of drug trafficking has been increasing since the 1950s, at which time there was already considerable concern: see Report of the Special Committee on Traffic in Narcotic Drugs, Appendix to Debates of the Senate of Canada, session of 1955, pp. 690-700; see also Final Report, Commission of Inquiry into the Non-Medical Use of Drugs (Ottawa, 1973). Throughout this period, numerous measures were adopted by free and democratic societies, at both the international and national levels.

At the international level, on 23rd June 1953, the Protocol for Limiting and Regulating the Cultivation of the Poppy Plant, the Production of, International and Wholesale Trade in, and Use of Opium, to which Canada is a signatory, was adopted by the United Nations Opium Conference held in New York. The Single

Convention on Narcotic Drugs (1961), was acceded to in New York on 30th March 1961. This treaty was signed by Canada on 30th March 1961. It entered into force on 13th December 1964. As stated in the preamble, "addiction to narcotic drugs constitutes a serious evil for the individual and is fraught with social and economic danger to mankind".

At the national level, statutory provisions have been enacted by numerous countries which, inter alia, attempt to deter drug trafficking by imposing criminal sanctions: see, for example, Misuse of Drugs Act, 1975 (New Zealand), no. 116; Misuse of Drugs Act, 1971 (Eng.), c. 38.

The objective of protecting our society from the grave ills associated with drug trafficking is, in my view, one of sufficient importance to warrant overriding a constitutionally-protected right or freedom in certain cases. Moreover, the degree of seriousness of drug trafficking makes its acknowledgement as a sufficiently important objective for the purposes of s. 1 to a large extent self-evident. The first criterion of a s. 1 inquiry, therefore, has been satisfied by the Crown.

The next stage of inquiry is a consideration of the means chosen by Parliament to achieve its objective. The means must be reasonable and demonstrably justified in a free and democratic society. As outlined above, this proportionality test should begin with a consideration of the rationality of the provision: Is the reverse onus clause in s. 8 rationally related to the objective of curbing drug trafficking? At a minimum, this requires that s. 8 be internally rational; there must be a rational connection between the basic fact of possession and the presumed fact of possession for the purpose of trafficking. Otherwise the reverse onus clause could give rise to unjustified and erroneous convictions for drug trafficking of persons guilty only of possession of narcotics.

In my view, s. 8 does not survive this rational connection test. As Martin J.A. of the Ontario Court of Appeal concluded, possession of a small or negligible quantity of narcotics does not support the inference of trafficking. In other words, it would be irrational to infer that a person had an intent to traffic on the basis of his or her possession of a very small quantity of narcotics. The presumption required under s. 8 of the Narcotic Control Act is overinclusive and could lead to results in certain cases which would defy both rationality and fairness. In light of the seriousness of the offence in question, which carries with it the possibility of imprisonment for life, I am further convinced that the first component of the proportionality test has not been satisfied by the Crown.

As I have concluded that s. 8 does not satisfy this first component of proportionality, it is unnecessary to consider the other two components.

VI. CONCLUSION

The Ontario Court of Appeal was correct in holding that s. 8 of the Narcotic Control Act violates the Canadian Charter of Rights and Freedoms and is therefore of no force or effect. Section 8 imposes a limit on the right guaranteed by s. 11(*d*) of the Charter which is not reasonable and is not demonstrably justified in a free and democratic society for the purpose of s. 1. Accordingly, the constitutional question is answered as follows:

Question: Is s. 8 of the Narcotic Control Act inconsistent with s. 11(*d*) of the Canadian Charter of Rights and Freedoms and thus of no force and effect?

Answer: Yes.

I would therefore dismiss the appeal.

Appeal dismissed.

In *R. v. Whyte*,[121] the Court amplified on its reasons in *Oakes* and Dickson C.J. provided:

> The distinction between elements of the offence and other aspects of the charge is irrelevant to the s. 11(*d*) inquiry. The real concern is not whether the accused must disprove an element or prove an excuse, but that an accused may be convicted while a reasonable doubt exists. When that possibility exists, there is a breach of the presumption of innocence. The exact characterization of a factor as an essential element, a collateral factor, an excuse, or a defence should not affect the analysis of the presumption of innocence. It is the final effect of a provision on the verdict that is decisive. If an accused is required to prove some fact on the balance of probabilities to avoid conviction, the provision violates the presumption of innocence because it permits a conviction in spite of a reasonable doubt in the mind of the trier of fact as to the guilt of the accused.

Section 16(4) of the Criminal Code, amended in 1991, formerly read:

16(4) Every one shall, until the contrary is proved, be presumed to be and to have been sane.

R. v. CHAULK
[1990] 3 S.C.R. 1303, 2 C.R. (4th) 1, 62 C.C.C. (3d) 193

LAMER C.J. (DICKSON C.J.C., and LA FOREST and CORY JJ., concurring):—

. . . .

In my view, the principles enunciated in *Whyte* are applicable to this case and establish that the presumption of sanity embodied in s. 16(4) violates the presumption of innocence. If an accused is found to have been insane at the time of the offence, he will <u>not</u> be found guilty; thus the "fact" of insanity precludes a verdict of guilty. Whether the claim of insanity is characterized as a denial of *mens rea*, an excusing defence or, more generally, as an exemption based on criminal incapacity, the fact remains that sanity is essential for guilt. Section 16(4) allows a factor which is essential for guilt to be <u>presumed</u>, rather than proven by the Crown beyond a reasonable doubt. Moreover, it requires an accused to disprove sanity (or prove insanity) on a balance of probabilities; it therefore violates the presumption of innocence because it permits a conviction in spite of a reasonable doubt in the mind of the trier of fact as to the guilt of the accused.

---

121 (1988), 64 C.R. (3d) 123 (S.C.C.).

. . . .

Is s. 16(4) a Reasonable Limit Under s. 1 of the Charter?

. . . .

2. *As Little as Possible*

... In my view, the question to be addressed at this stage of the s. 1 inquiry is whether Parliament could reasonably have chosen an alternative means which would have achieved the identified objective as effectively.

Recent judgments of this Court (*R. v. Edwards Books and Art Ltd.*, [1986] 2 S.C.R. 713; *Irwin Toy Ltd. v. Quebec (Attorney General)*, [1989] 1 S.C.R. 927; and *Reference re ss. 193 and 195.1(1)(c) of the Criminal Code (Man.)*, [1990] 1 S.C.R. 1123) indicate that Parliament is not required to search out and to adopt the absolutely least intrusive means of attaining its objective. Furthermore, when assessing the alternative means which were available to Parliament, it is important to consider whether a less intrusive means would achieve the "same" objective or would achieve the same objective as effectively.

. . . .

It is true that s. 16 will be seldom raised, given the substantial constraint on liberty which follows a successful insanity plea. Nonetheless, I have concluded that the objective of the current provision is "pressing and substantial", given the next to impossible burden which would be placed on the Crown if s. 16(4) did not exist. If insanity were easier for an accused to establish, the defence would be successfully invoked *more* often (even if, statistically, it is still infrequently raised). Thus, putting a lesser burden on the accused would *not* have achieved the objective which is achieved by s. 16(4).

. . . .

WILSON J.:—

. . . .

The issue under this part of the *Oakes* test is whether some other legislative provision could achieve the desired objective while impairing the *Charter* right "as little as possible". Lamer C.J. is of the view that Parliament is not required to seek and adopt "the absolutely least intrusive means of attaining its objective" (p. 1341). He indicates that he is unwilling to embark on a course of "second-guessing" the wisdom of Parliament's choice of legislative means and cites some recent decisions of this Court as authority for this deferential attitude. In my view, this is not a case for deference. In one of the cases on which the Chief Justice relies, *Irwin Toy Ltd. v. Quebec (Attorney General)*, [1989] 1 S.C.R. 927, this Court indicated that there might be exceptions to the stringent review called for under this part of the *Oakes* test. Whether or not such an exception was warranted would depend upon the role Parliament was fulfilling in enacting the impugned legislation.

As I understand this aspect of *Irwin Toy*, an exception may be made where the legislature mediating between the competing claims of groups of citizens or allocating scarce resources among them is forced to strike a compromise on the basis of conflicting evidence. In such cases there will be a substantial policy component to the choice of means selected by the legislature and that choice should be respected even if it cannot be said to represent the "least intrusive means". In my view, *Irwin Toy* does not stand for the proposition that in balancing the objective of government against the guaranteed right of the citizen under s. 1 different levels of scrutiny may be applied depending upon the nature of the right. The prerequisite for the exception to the minimal impairment test in *Oakes*, as I understand *Irwin Toy*, is that the guaranteed right of different groups of citizens cannot be fully respected; to respect to the full the right of one group will necessarily involve an infringement upon the right of the other. In such a circumstance *Irwin Toy* holds that it is appropriate for the government to fashion a compromise on the basis of policy considerations.

. . . .

For these reasons, I am not persuaded that s. 16(4) impairs the accused's right to be presumed innocent as little as is reasonably possible. Rather, I am of the view that the government's objective could be quite readily met by imposing a purely evidentiary burden on the accused. The infringement on s. 11(*d*) of the *Charter* resulting from s. 16(4) is accordingly not saved by s. 1.

Justices Gonthier, McLachlin and L'Heureux-Dubé found the provision did not violate the presumption of innocence as section 16 "should be read as relating to the fundamental pre-condition for the assignment of criminal responsibility rather than to the elements of an offence or to particular defences." Justice Sopinka dissented, but he agreed that section 16(4) of the Criminal Code was valid for the reasons expressed by the Chief Justice.

In 1991, the Code was amended to provide:

16(3) The burden of proof that an accused was suffering from a mental disorder so as to be exempt from criminal responsibility is on the party that raises the issue.

In *Re Boyle*,[122] the issue before the Ontario Court of Appeal concerned presumptions created by language of the Criminal Code "in the absence of any evidence to the contrary proof," a frequently-used legislative device. The Court held that, although such presumptions can be displaced merely by evidence which raises a reasonable doubt rather than proof on a balance of probabilities, there was a common feature in the mandatory nature of the conclusion required to be drawn. The trier of fact must find the presumed fact; there was no may about it. The obligation on the accused required mandatory presumptions to also receive protection under the Charter presumption of innocence. In *Boyle*, the Court held that the presumption that arises under section 354(2) on possession of a motor vehicle with an obliterated identification number, that the motor vehicle

---

122 (1983), 35 C.R. (3d) 34 (Ont. C.A.).

or part thereof was at some time obtained by the commission of an indictable offence, was entirely reasonable and constitutionally valid. However, the second presumption under section 354(2), that the person found in possession knows that the vehicle or part thereof was obtained by the commission of an indictable offence, was not constitutionally valid, since it was arbitrary and hence unreasonable.

R. v. DOWNEY
[1992] 2 S.C.R. 10, 13 C.R. (4th) 129, 72 C.C.C. (3d) 1

The accused was charged with two counts of living on the avails of prostitution. The accused answered the agency's telephones, made up the receipts and did the banking. He knew the calls were for sexual services. Throughout the period he had no other employment. During the course of the trial an application was made for a declaration that section 195(2) of the Criminal Code was of no force or effect because of section 11(d) of the Charter. Section 195(2) [now section 212(3)] provides that "[e]vidence that a person lives with or is habitually in the company of a prostitute . . . is, in the absence of evidence to the contrary, proof that the person lives on the avails of prostitution. . . ." The application was dismissed. The accused was convicted and his appeals to the Court of Appeal and the Supreme Court of Canada were dismissed.

CORY J. (L'HEUREUX-DUBÉ, SOPINKA and GONTHIER JJ. concurring):—

. . . .

The presumption contained in s. 195 infringes s. 11(d) of the *Charter* since it can result in the conviction of an accused despite the existence of a reasonable doubt. For example consider the situation of a spouse or companion of a prostitute, who is working, self-supporting and not dependent or relying upon the income garnered by the spouse or companion from prostitution. There is nothing parasitical about such a relationship. Neither being a prostitute nor being a spouse of a prostitute constitutes a crime. Yet as a result of the presumption, the spouse could be found guilty despite the existence of a reasonable doubt. The fact that someone lives with a prostitute does not lead inexorably to the conclusion that the person is living on avails. The presumption therefore infringes s. 11(d).

Downey is welcome in its extension of Charter protection to mandatory presumptions. However, its reasoning may be suspect. The *Oakes* case dealt with a persuasive burden being imposed on the accused. Is the test there formulated for determining a violation of section 11(d) appropriate to a similar determination of the validity of an evidential burden? Can a trier have a reasonable doubt as to whether the accused is living on the avails if there has been no evidence led on the matter? On the other hand, if there was evidence led that the accused was working, self-supporting and not dependent on the prostitute's earnings, the presumptive device would disappear and a result would not be mandated. Perhaps a different test would be more suitable:

> Any presumptive device which compels the trier of fact to find an essential element, or the absence of any material justification or excuse, to be proved beyond a

reasonable doubt, though no direct positive evidence was led concerning the existence of either, must violate the presumption of innocence in section 11(*d*).

The majority of four justices, having found a section 11(d) violation, determined that the provision should be saved under section 1. The three dissenters (La Forest, McLachlin and Iacobucci JJ.), agreeing there was a violation, decided the section could not be saved.

R. v. LABA
[1994] 3 S.C.R. 965, 34 C.R. (4th) 360, 94 C.C.C. (3d) 385

The accused were charged under section 394(1)(*b*) of the Criminal Code, which provided:

(1) Every one is guilty of an indictable offence and liable to imprisonment for a term not exceeding five years who

. . . .

(*b*) sells or purchases any rock, mineral or other substance that contains precious metals or unsmelted, untreated, unmanufactured or partly smelted, partly treated or partly manufactured precious metals, unless he establishes that he is the owner or agent of the owner or is acting under lawful authority.

They brought a pre-trial motion challenging the constitutional validity of the section. The motions judge declared that section 394(1)(*b*) violated the presumption of innocence in section 11(*d*) of the Charter, was not saved by section 1 of the Charter, and so was of no force or effect. He granted the accused's application for a stay of proceedings. On appeal the Crown conceded that there was an infringement of section 11(*d*) but sought to reverse the ruling on the ground that the provision should have been saved under section 1. The Court of Appeal concluded that the Crown had not met the onus of proving that the reverse onus clause was a reasonable limit within the meaning of section 1. In its order it stated that the appeal was allowed to the extent that, with the exception of the words "he establishes that", which were struck out, the validity of the remainder of section 394(1)(*b*) was upheld.

SOPINKA J. (CORY, McLACHLIN, IACOBUCCI and MAJOR JJ. concurring):—

. . . .

Both in this Court and in the Court of Appeal the Crown conceded that the reverse onus in s. 394(1)(*b*) violates s. 11(*d*) of the *Charter* because it is open for a person to be convicted under that provision even if there is a reasonable doubt as to whether he or she was entitled to buy or sell the precious metal. There is no doubt in my mind that this concession was properly made and that the parties were correct in proceeding on the basis that the only point in issue is whether s. 394(1)(*b*) of the *Criminal Code* constitutes a reasonable limit on the s. 11(*d*) *Charter* right pursuant to s.1 of the *Charter*.

. . . .

. . . Does s. 394(1)(b) pass the Oakes test?

. . . Taking into account the modification suggested by the Chief Justice in his reasons in *Dagenais v. Canadian Broadcasting Corp.*, [1994] 3 S.C.R. 835, released concurrently herewith, the test can be stated as follows:

> 1) In order to be sufficiently important to warrant overriding a constitutionally protected right or freedom the impugned provision must relate to concerns which are pressing and substantial in a free and democratic society;

> 2) The means chosen to achieve the legislative objective must pass a three-part proportionality test which requires that they (a) be rationally connected to the objective, (b) impair the right or freedom in question as little as possible and (c) have deleterious effects which are proportional to both their salutary effects and the importance of the objective which has been identified as being of "sufficient importance".

(i) *Pressing and Substantial Objective*

I agree with the Attorney General of Canada that the objective of s. 394(1)(b) is the deterrence of theft of precious metal ore. In furtherance of this general objective, the specific objective of the reverse onus clause is to facilitate the prosecution of offenders given the special problem of proof to which I have referred above. I also agree that s. 394(1)(b) creates a "true criminal offence" and that like other true criminal offences involving activity bereft of social utility, it is an expression of society's repugnance to the conduct proscribed. In these circumstances, the Court can conclude, in the absence of extrinsic evidence as to the importance of the objective, that the subsection meets the first branch of the *Oakes* test.

. . . .

(ii) *Rational Connection*

Parliament has chosen to achieve the objective of deterring theft of ore by proscribing trade in stolen ore and placing the onus upon the accused to show that the ore is not stolen. Both these measures strike me as rational responses to the problem posed by theft of precious metal ore. The criminalization of trade in stolen goods is a common and eminently sensible method of deterring theft. Where there is good reason to believe that it would be difficult for the Crown to prove that goods have been stolen it is rational to place some kind of burden of proving that they have not been stolen upon the accused. . . .

Before moving on to consider the next step in the *Oakes* test I would like to address the respondents' argument that s. 394(1)(b) fails the rational connection test because it creates an unreasonable presumption that any ore which has been purchased or sold was stolen. This argument is premised upon the notion that in order for a legislatively created presumption to pass this portion of the *Oakes* test it must be internally rational in the sense that there is a logical connection between the presumed fact and the fact substituted by the presumption. This argument was made by the appellant in *R. v. Downey*, [1992] 2 S.C.R. 10. It was contended that a presumption which is not internally rational unduly enmeshes the innocent in the criminal process. This argument was not accepted by the majority. Consequently, I regard it as settled that there is no general requirement that a presumption be internally rational in order to pass the rational connection phase of the proportionality test. The only relevant consideration at this stage of the analysis is whether the presumption is a logical method of accomplishing the legislative objective. Later in these reasons, I will consider the relevance of this factor in connection with the final phase of the proportionality test.

(iii) *Minimal Impairment*

. . . .

The legislature is entitled to some deference in choosing the means of attaining a given objective. As Lamer C.J. stated in *R. v. Chaulk*, [1990] 3 S.C.R. 1303 at p. 1341, "Parliament is not required to search out and to adopt the absolutely least intrusive means of attaining its objective". . . . However, it is also important to remember that this is not a case in which the legislature has attempted to strike a balance between the interests of competing individuals or groups. Rather it is a case in which the government (as opposed to other individuals or groups) can be characterized as the singular antagonist of an individual attempting to assert a legal right which is fundamental to our system of criminal justice. As the majority wrote in *Irwin Toy Ltd. v. Quebec (Attorney General)*, [1989] 1 S.C.R. 927 . . . , in such circumstances the courts are in as good a position as the legislature to assess whether the least drastic means of achieving the governmental purpose have been chosen, especially given the inherently legal nature of the rights in question and the courts' accumulated experience in dealing with such matters.

In drafting s. 394(1)(*b*) Parliament could have chosen merely to place an evidentiary burden rather than a full legal burden of proving ownership, agency or lawful authority upon the accused. Under such a provision the accused would simply be required to adduce or point to evidence which, if accepted, would be capable of raising a reasonable doubt as to whether he was the owner or agent of the owner or was acting under lawful authority. If he or she succeeded in raising such a doubt the burden would shift to the Crown to prove the contrary beyond a reasonable doubt. If the Crown failed to dispel a reasonable doubt, the accused would be acquitted. Knowledge of the availability of this option must be imputed to Parliament since evidentiary burdens of this kind are and were commonly used to relieve the Crown of the burden of proving that an accused did not legitimately acquire possession of property.

The appellant has not demonstrated to my satisfaction that Parliament has chosen the alternative which impairs s. 11(*d*) as little as is reasonably possible. . . . In my opinion, Parliament's purpose will be effectively served by the imposition of an evidential burden. A seller will have to testify or produce documents tending to show that he or she was either the owner or agent of the owner, or is duly authorized. A purchaser may be required to adduce *viva voce* evidence or produce a document tending to show that the person from whom he or she purchased the material was the owner, agent of the owner or duly authorized. In either case, the matter will have been narrowed to identify the basis of the seller's claim in the one case and the identity of the seller in the other. This will in most cases enable the Crown to produce testimony or documents disproving the claim that the seller or alleged seller is the owner or agent or is duly authorized.

. . . .

Remedy

. . . .

In view of the conclusion that I have reached on the s. 1 issue, the available alternative remedies are: (i) striking down the offending words, a remedy adopted by the Court of Appeal and supported in this Court by the respondents; and (ii) striking down the offending words coupled with reading in appropriate words to substitute an evidentiary burden.

. . . .

In *R. v. Holmes*, [1988] 1 S.C.R. 914, this Court acknowledged that the words "without lawful excuse, the proof of which lies upon him" were capable of creating a legal burden but interpreted them to require the accused to raise a reasonable doubt. This is an interpretation which could be adopted in this case but I would hesitate to do so in view of the many provisions in the *Criminal Code* and other statutes employing the same wording, some of which may validly create a legal burden. I do, however, conclude from the foregoing and the fact that there are many provisions in the *Criminal Code* and other federal statutes that place an evidentiary burden on the accused, that it is safe to assume that Parliament would have enacted the subsection in question in this appeal but restricted to an evidentiary burden, if the option of a legal burden had not been available.

. . . .

In the result I would allow the appeal in part by affirming the lifting of the stay but varying the Court of Appeal's order to state that, pursuant to s. 52 of the *Constitution Act, 1982*, s. 394(1)(*b*) should be read as follows:

> 394. (1) Every one is guilty of an indictable offence and liable to imprisonment for a term not exceeding five years who

> . . . .

> (*b*) sells or purchases any rock, mineral or other substance that contains precious metals or unsmelted, untreated, unmanufactured or partly smelted, partly treated or partly manufactured precious metals, in the absence of evidence which raises a reasonable doubt that he is the owner or agent of the owner or is acting under lawful authority.

[Lamer C.J. and La Forest, Gonthier, L'Heureux-Dubé JJ. agreed with Sopinka J. on the substantive issues.]

The evidentiary device in *Laba* was seen to impose a persuasive burden on the accused to prove that he was the owner of the minerals when he sold them. The Court of Appeal had found the evidentiary device violative of section 11(*d*) and not salvageable under section 1 because it failed the first part of the *Oakes* test in that the objective was not sufficiently pressing to permit the violation of the presumption of innocence. The Ontario Court decided that removing the offending words, "he establishes that", would make the provision constitutional. Then the normal rules of a criminal case would apply. The Crown would have to prove that the accused was not the owner of the minerals and any evidence in the case, led by the Crown or by the defence, that created a reasonable doubt in that regard would enure to the benefit of the accused. If there was no evidence as to ownership the accused would have to be acquitted. The Supreme Court also decided that the section was violative of section 11(*d*) and could not be saved under section 1. The Supreme Court decided that the section was not salvageable because the section did not impair the constitutionally protected right as little as reasonably possible. The Supreme Court decided, however, that simply striking out the offending words was not sufficient. The court decided to write into the provision that guilt would be mandated "in the absence of evidence which raised a reasonable doubt" that he is the owner. If there was no evidence as to ownership the accused would have to be convicted. That result would be mandated by the words written in.

R. v. CURTIS
(1998), 14 C.R. (5th) 328, 123 C.C.C. (3d) 178 (Ont. C.A.)

The accused were charged under section 215(2) of the Criminal Code with failing to provide the necessaries of life. That section provides that everyone commits an offence who, being under a legal duty within the meaning of section 215(1) of the Code, fails without lawful excuse, "the proof of which lies upon him", to perform that duty in certain specified circumstances. The accused applied for a declaration that section 215(2) was unconstitutional in that it requires a person to prove the defence of lawful excuse on the balance of probabilities. The trial judge found that section 215(2) violated the presumption of innocence guaranteed by section 11(*d*) of the Canadian Charter of Rights and Freedoms and that the section could not be saved under section 1 of the Charter. He declared the entire section unconstitutional and stayed the proceedings. The Crown's appeal was allowed.

On appeal, the Crown conceded that the reverse onus clause rendered section 215(2) in violation of section 11(*d*) of the Charter but sought to justify it under section 1. The Court decided there was a rational connection but found that the provision did not impair the accused's right "as little as possible." Observe the Court's solution.

GOUDGE J.A. (DOHERTY and CARTHY JJ.A. concurring):—

. . . .

In my view, the fundamental question for the minimal impairment analysis is whether, if s. 215(2) simply permitted an accused to escape responsibility by raising a reasonable doubt as to a lawful excuse for not doing his duty, the Crown could show that the section would less effectively achieve Parliament's objective than it does now with the reverse onus language.

If the impugned language were removed, the section would merely require that, to take advantage of the defence of lawful excuse, the accused point to evidence which could leave a reasonable doubt as to his having a lawful excuse for not performing his duty. If such evidence existed, the Crown would have to prove beyond a reasonable doubt the absence of lawful excuse for there to be a conviction. In my view, the section changed in this way would not compromise at all the right of the accused to the presumption of innocence. Would the Crown, however, be able to demonstrate that the changed section would less effectively achieve its objective?

The Crown put forward no factual basis to suggest that without the reverse onus clause it would be easy for an accused to point to evidence sufficient to raise a reasonable doubt as to a lawful excuse for non-performance, when no such excuse actually existed. Nor did it demonstrate that if the accused attempted to raise a reasonable doubt as to lawful excuse the Crown would be handicapped in proving the absence of such an excuse.

. . . .

I would therefore conclude that the Crown has not shown that if s. 215(2) were shorn of the reverse onus clause, accused persons would more easily be excused for not doing their duty than under the section as presently worded. The Crown has thus not shown that s. 215(2), if it were changed in this way, would less effectively meet Parliament's objective. The reverse onus clause cannot, therefore, clear the minimal impairment hurdle.

. . . .

What remains, then, is the question of remedy. The trial judge, having concluded as I have, simply declared the entirety of s. 215 unconstitutional and of no effect pursuant to s. 52 of the *Constitution Act, 1982* and, as well, granted the accused a stay of proceedings.

In my opinion, he erred in doing so. In this case, the offending portion of s. 215(2) is clearly defined. It is the reverse onus clause, "the proof of which lies upon him". This language constitutes the extent to which the section is inconsistent with the provisions of the *Constitution*. The declaratory remedy available under s. 52 thus extends only to the impugned provision, not to the entire section. . . . I therefore agree with the remedy proposed by the Crown, namely that the reverse onus clause, "the proof of which lies upon him", be declared of no force or effect. Given that with this excision, s. 215(2) does not violate the presumption of innocence, there is no basis for a stay of proceedings of a charge under the section shorn of this language. I would therefore allow the appeal, declare the words "the proof of which lies upon him" in s. 215(2) to be of no force or effect, and otherwise set aside the order declaring s. 215 to be unconstitutional and of no effect. I would further set aside the order staying the proceedings and direct that this matter be remitted for trial.

Do you see the difference in the solution in *Curtis* from that arrived at in *Laba*? Which is preferable?

PROBLEMS

Problem 1

The accused is charged with possession of counterfeit money contrary to section 450 of the Criminal Code:

> **450**(*b*) Every one who, without lawful justification or excuse, the proof of which lies on him, has in his custody or possession counterfeit money is guilty of an indictable offence. . . .

The accused was found to have four counterfeit $10 bills in his wallet. He advises you he didn't know they were counterfeit. What onus? He advises you he collects counterfeit money as a hobby. What onus? See *R. v. Santeramo* (1976), 32 C.C.C. (2d) 35 (Ont. C.A.) and *R. v. Freng* (1993), 86 C.C.C. (3d) 91 (B.C.C.A.).

Problem 2

The accused was convicted of driving while prohibited contrary to the Motor Vehicle Act. The Crown relied upon a certificate of the superintendent. The Act provides that such a certificate proves the prohibition and is proof that the defendant had knowledge of the prohibition unless the accused proves the contrary. Construct an argument for appeal. Compare *R. v. Alston* (1985), 36 M.V.R. 67 (B.C.C.A.).

Problem 3

The accused is charged with kidnapping contrary to section 279 of the Criminal Code. Section 279(3) provides:

> In proceedings under this section, the fact that the person in relation to whom the offence is alleged to have been committed did not resist is not a defence unless the accused proves that the failure to resist was not caused by threats, duress, force or exhibition of force.

Constitutional? Compare *R. v. Gough* (1985), 43 C.R. (3d) 297 (Ont. C.A.), *R. v. Grift* (1986), 43 Alta. L.R. (2d) 365 (Q.B.) and *R. v. Pete* (1998), 131 C.C.C. (3d) 233 (B.C. C.A.).

Problem 4

The accused is charged with leaving the scene of an accident with intent to escape liability contrary to section 252(1) of the Criminal Code. Section 252(2) provides that evidence that an accused failed to stop and give his name and address is, in the absence of evidence to the contrary, proof of an intent to escape liability. What is the burden on the accused? Is it constitutional? Compare *R. v. S.D.T.* (1985), 33 M.V.R. 148 (N.S.C.A.) and *R. v. Gosselin* (1988), 45 C.C.C. (3d) 568 (Ont. C.A.).

Problem 5

The accused is charged with obtaining goods by false pretences. Section 362(4) of the Criminal Code provides that goods shall be presumed to have been obtained by a false pretence if obtained by a cheque that was dishonoured unless the court is satisfied that when the accused issued the cheque he reasonably believed it would be honoured. Burden on the accused? Rational connection? Constitutional? Compare *Bunka v. R.*, [1984] 4 W.W.R. 252 (Sask. Q.B.), *R. v. Driscoll* (1987), 49 Alta. L.R. (2d) 383; affirmed [1987] 6 W.W.R. 748 (C.A.) and *R. v. Ferguson* (1992), 70 C.C.C. (3d) 330 (P.E.I. T.D.).

Chapter 3

Relevance and Discretion to Exclude

1. RELEVANCE

(a) Tests

Professor Thayer described the function and limitations of the law of evidence created by the English common law:

> There is a principle — not so much a rule of evidence as a presupposition involved in the very conception of a rational system of evidence, as contrasted with the old formal and mechanical system — which forbids receiving anything irrelevant, not logically probative. How are we to know what these forbidden things are? Not by any rule of law. The law furnishes no test of relevancy. For this, it tacitly refers to logic and general experience, — assuming that the principles of reasoning are known to its judges and ministers, just as a vast multitude of other things are assumed as already sufficiently known to them.[1]

Thayer later explained that by "logic" he was not referring to the deductive logic of the syllogism, but the inductive logic of knowledge or science. He noted that his book used:

> . . . the word relevancy merely as importing a logical relation, that is to say, a relation determined by the reasoning faculty. . . . The law has no orders for the reasoning faculty, any more than the perceiving faculty, — for the eyes and ears.[2]

In *R. v. Watson*,[3] Doherty J.A. explained:

> Relevance . . . requires a determination of whether as a matter of human experience and logic the existence of "Fact A" makes the existence or non-existence of "Fact B" more probable than it would be without the existence of "Fact A." If it does then "Fact A" is relevant to "Fact B". As long as "Fact B" is itself a material fact in issue or is relevant to a material fact in issue in the litigation then "Fact A" is relevant and prima facie admissible.

Relevancy of evidence must be distinguished from sufficiency of evidence and we need to recognize that to be receivable as relevant the piece of evidence

---

1 Thayer, *Preliminary Treatise on Evidence at the Common Law* (1898), pp. 264-69 [footnotes omitted].
2 "Law and Logic" (1900), 14 Harv. L. Rev. 139 in reply to a criticism by Fox at p. 39 of the same volume. Interestingly, Thayer's earlier version of the material in his "Treatise in Presumptions and the Law of Evidence" (1889-1890), 3 Harv. L. Rev. 141 at 144, refers only to logic as the test rather than to logic and general experience.
3 (1996), 50 C.R. (4th) 245, 257 (Ont. C.A.).

being tendered need not by itself be compelling. Also, evidence objected to as irrelevant may need to be received on counsel's undertaking to link up the same with other expected evidence and so later demonstrate relevance. The trier may need to be advised to disregard such evidence conditionally received if the connection fails to materialize.[4] McCormick explained:

> This is the distinction between relevancy and sufficiency. The test of relevancy, which is to be applied by the trial judge in determining whether a particular item or group of items of evidence is to be admitted is a different and less stringent one than the standard used at a later stage in deciding whether all the evidence of the party on an issue is sufficient to permit the issue to go to the jury. A brick is not a wall.
>
> What is the standard of relevance or probative quality which evidence must meet if it is to be admitted? We have said that it must "tend to establish" the inference for which it is offered. How strong must this tendency be? Some courts have announced tests, variously phrased, which seem to require that the evidence offered must render the inference for which it is offered more probable than the other possible inferences or hypotheses, that is, the chances must appear to preponderate that the inference claimed is the true one.
>
> . . . .
>
> . . . It is believed that a more modest standard better reflects the actual practice of the courts, and that the most acceptable test of relevancy is the question, does the evidence offered render the desired inference *more probable than it would be without the evidence*?[5]

We know that evidence is relevant if it has any tendency to make the proposition for which it is tendered more probable than that proposition would be without the evidence. For evidence to have any value there must be a premise, a generalization that one makes, allowing the inference to be made. Borrowing from Professors Binder and Bergman,[6] evidence that roses were in bloom, when tendered to prove that it was then springtime, has meaning only if we adopt the premise or generalization that roses usually bloom in the spring. The tendency of evidence to prove a proposition, and hence its relevance, depends on the validity of the premise which links the evidence to the proposition. The probative worth of the relevant evidence depends on the accuracy of the premise which supports the inference. Sometimes the premise will be indisputable, sometimes always true, sometimes often true and sometimes only rarely true. But a premise there must be. The next time someone says to you that the evidence is *clearly* relevant ask the proponent of the evidence to articulate for you what premise she is relying on. If she has no premise the evidence is irrelevant. If she has a premise you can debate with her the validity of the premise. What experience does she base it on? Is there contrary experience? Is the premise based on myth? Is the premise always true, sometimes or only rarely? These latter parameters do not affect relevance since relevance has a very low threshold but may affect the probative worth which may cause rejection of the evidence if the probative value is outweighed by competing considerations. Approaching

---

4 See *R. v. Dass* (1979), 47 C.C.C. (2d) 194, 203 (Man. C.A.); or a new trial may be necessary, *R. v. Spence* (1979), 47 C.C.C. (2d) 167 (Ont. C.A.).

5 McCormick, *Evidence* (2d ed.), pp. 436-38.

6 *Fact Investigation* (West Publishing, 1984), p. 82.

discussions of relevance in this way may yield a more intelligent discussion than the oftentimes typical exchange of conclusory opinions.

In *Morris v. R.*[7] the Supreme Court of Canada adopted the Thayerian view of relevance and rejected the Wigmore view that a piece of information must have a minimum probative value before it can be considered relevant.

MORRIS v. R.
[1983] 2 S.C.R. 190, 36 C.R. (3d) 1, 7 C.C.C. (3d) 97

McINTYRE J. (RITCHIE, BEETZ and ESTEY JJ. concurring):—I have had the opportunity of reading the reasons for judgment prepared in this case [an appeal from (1982), 68 C.C.C. (2d) 115] by my brother Lamer. I agree with his observation on the subject of the relevancy of evidence. I also agree with his exposition of the reason for and the development of the exclusionary rule which applies to evidence in criminal cases dealing only with the question of disposition and character of the accused. I am unable, however, to agree with his characterization of the newspaper clipping in this case as evidence indicating only a disposition on the part of the appellant.

In my view, an inference could be drawn from the unexplained presence of the newspaper clipping among the possessions of the appellant that he had an interest in and had informed himself on the question of sources of supply of heroin, necessarily a subject of vital interest to one concerned with the importing of the narcotic.

. . . .

I agree that the probative value of such evidence may be low, especially since the newspaper article here concerns the heroin trade in Pakistan rather than in Hong Kong, which was apparently the source of the heroin involved in this case. However, admissibility of evidence must not be confused with weight. If the article had concerned the heroin trade in Hong Kong, it would of course have had greater probative value. If the article had been a manual containing a step-by-step guide to importing heroin into Vancouver from Hong Kong, the probative value would have been still greater. The differences between these examples, however, and the facts at bar are differences in degree, not kind. In other words, the differences go to weight and not to admissibility.

The weight to be given to evidence is a question for the trier of fact, subject of course to the discretion of the trial judge to exclude evidence where the probative value is minimal and the prejudicial effect great: see *R. v. Wray*, [1971] S.C.R. 272. In the present case the trial judge did not consider that the evidence should be thus excluded. In my opinion it would not be proper in the circumstances of this case for this court to substitute its view on this matter of discretion for that of the trial judge. In my opinion the trial judge made no error in law in admitting evidence of the newspaper clipping, and I would therefore dismiss the appeal.

---

7 (1983), 7 C.C.C. (3d) 97, 104, 106 (S.C.C.).

LAMER J. (dissenting) (DICKSON and WILSON JJ. concurring):— The appellant, one Gary Robert Morris, was convicted in Vancouver, by a County Court Judge sitting without a jury, of having conspired with others to import and traffic heroin. He appealed from his conviction to the British Columbia Court of Appeal. His appeal was heard by a panel of three judges and was dismissed [(1982), 68 C.C.C. (2d) 115]. One of the judges, Anderson J.A., dissented and would have allowed the appeal and ordered a new trial on the following ground of law, namely:

> That the learned trial judge erred in admitting into evidence and in taking into consideration a newspaper clipping entitled, 'The Heroin Trade Moves to Pakistan', being Exhibit 26 at the Appellant's trial.

. . . .

THE LAW

While I agree with Anderson J.A. that the clipping should not have been admitted in evidence, it is not because I believe the clipping irrelevant, but because it was, in my view, not admissible. His reference to the clipping as having "no probative value in proving the offence charged" is understandable given the language this court resorted to when dealing with analogous evidence in the case of *Cloutier*. Cloutier was charged with importing a narcotic into Canada, namely, 20 pounds of cannabis (marihuana). The evidence was that the merchandise was concealed in the false bottom of a dresser arriving from South America, which the appellant asked his mother to store in her home, and it was there that the police made the seizure.

One of the grounds of appeal in this court was that the trial judge refused to admit in evidence certificates of analysis to establish that the items seized at the accused's home, a cigarette butt, a pipe and a green substance, indicated that the accused was a user of marihuana.

Pratte J., writing for a majority of this court, stated the following, at p. 731:

> For one fact to be relevant to another, there must be a connection or nexus between the two which makes it possible to infer the existence of one from the existence of the other. One fact is not relevant to another if it does not have real probative value with respect to the latter (Cross, *On Evidence*, 4th ed. [1974], at p. 16).
>
> Thus, apart from certain exceptions which are not applicable here, evidence is not admissible if its only purpose is to prove that the accused is the type of man who is more likely to commit a crime of the kind with which he is charged; such evidence is viewed as having no real probative value with regard to the specific crime attributed to the accused: there is no sufficient logical connection between the one and the other.

It has been said that some might read in these comments (see Report of the Federal/Provincial Task Force on Uniform Rules of Evidence (1982), at p. 62 et seq.) a pronouncement by this court indicating a departure from Thayer's premise in A Preliminary Treatise on Evidence at the Common Law, of relevancy, logic and experience, and an adoption of Wigmore's concept of "legal relevancy" of which "the effect is to require a generally *higher degree of probative value for all evidence to be submitted to a jury"* and that "legal relevancy denotes, first of all, *something more than a minimum of probative value.* Each single piece of evidence must have a plus value.": Wigmore on Evidence, 3rd ed., vol. 1 (1940), para. 28, pp. 409-10. I do not think that it was intended by the majority in this court in *Cloutier,* supra, that such a departure be made. All agreed that the evidence could not be admitted to prove the accused's propensity, including the dissenting judges. In fact, the whole case, in my view, turned upon whether the evidence was relevant and admissible as tending to establish motive.

. . . .

Thayer's statement of the law, which is still the law in Canada, was as follows (p. 530):

> (1) that nothing is to be received which is not logically probative of some matter requiring to be proved; and (2) that everything which is thus probative should come in, unless a clear ground of policy or law excludes it.

To this general statement should be added the discretionary power judges exercise to exclude logically relevant evidence (p. 266):

> . . . as being of too slight a significance, or as having too conjectural and remote a connection; others, as being dangerous, in their effect on the jury, and likely to be misused or overestimated by that body; others, as being impolitic, or unsafe on public grounds; others, on the bare ground of precedent. It is this sort of thing, as I said before, — the rejection on one or another practical ground, of what is really probative, — which is the characteristic thing in the law of evidence; stamping it as the child of the jury system.

It was through the exercise of this discretionary power that judges developed rules of exclusion. As said by Thayer at p. 265, when speaking of the rule of general admissibility of what is logically probative:

> . . . in an historical sense it has not been the fundamental thing, to which the different exclusions were exceptions. What has taken place, in fact, is the shutting out by the judges of one and another thing from time to time; and so, gradually, the recognition of this exclusion under a rule. These rules of exclusion have had their exceptions; and so the law has come into the shape of a set of primary rules of exclusion; and then a set of exceptions to these rules.

Thus came about, as a primary rule of exclusion, the following: disposition, i.e., the fact that the accused is the sort of person who would be likely to have committed the offence, though relevant, is not admissible. As a result, evidence adduced *solely* for the purpose of proving disposition is itself inadmissible, or, to put it otherwise, evidence the sole relevancy of which to the crime committed is through proof of disposition is inadmissible.

. . . .

Now to consider the "clipping". The presence of the clipping in the room tends to prove that the accused either clipped it or received it and kept it for future reference. Had the article referred to movement of drugs in Hong Kong, to a laxity in that colony on the part of the customs officials, and so forth, it would have found its relevancy as proving the accused's participation in the conspiracies through his possession of a document that might have been instrumental to the commission of the crimes. But such is not the case. Its sole relevancy is through proof of the accused's disposition, the reasoning being as follows, that, because persons who are traffickers are more likely to keep such information than not, people who keep such information are more likely to be traffickers than people who do not, and that a person who trafficks is more likely to have committed the alleged offence than a person who does not. The ultimate purpose of placing the accused in the first category (people who keep such information for future reference) is to put him in a category of people the character of which indicates a propensity to commit the offences of which he was charged. This is clearly inadmissible evidence.

. . . .

I have read the evidence and agree with Anderson J.A. that this is not the proper case for the application of s. 613(1)(*b*)(iii). I cannot say, however, that, once the clipping and the answers of the accused when cross-examined as to the reasons for its presence in his room are excluded, there is left no evidence upon which a trier of fact might reasonably convict. As a result, I would allow the appeal, quash the conviction and order a new trial.

Appeal dismissed.

Are you satisfied with the way in which the majority articulated the relevance of the newspaper clipping? Do you think that Justice Lamer got it right when he concluded that its relevance was only in revealing the accused's disposition for criminality?

(b) Materiality

Not only must the evidence tendered be rationally probative of the fact sought to be thereby established; the fact sought to be established must concern a matter in issue between the parties, *i.e.*, it must be material. Another way of saying this is that the evidence must be relevant to a legal issue in the case. With this concept as well the law of evidence does not dictate the parameters, but rather the same is set down by the substantive law and the pleadings.

In civil cases the statements of claim and defence narrow the issues between the parties. In criminal cases the prosecution sets out in the information or indictment what is intended to be established. In our system of fact-finding the parties select a particular slice of life to be litigated and test their rights in that context against their understanding of the substantive law; they do not litigate all of history.[8]

The accused is charged with possession of undersized lobsters. Defence counsel tenders in evidence a witness who will testify that the accused didn't know that there were undersized lobsters in his catch. What do you, as prosecutor, say? "The evidence is immaterial".[9] Notice that by objecting that the evidence is immaterial the prosecutor is not arguing that the evidence would fail

---

8 See 1 Wigmore, *Evidence* (3d ed.), s. 2, at p. 6.
9 See *R. v. Pierce Fisheries Ltd.*, [1970] C.C.C. 193 (S.C.C.).

to rationally persuade a trier of fact regarding the accused's state of mind but rather that the accused's state of mind doesn't matter. It's immaterial. Our courts decided, as a matter of substantive law, that there is no *mens rea* requirement for the offence of possession of undersized lobster; the offence was decided to be one of absolute liability. The evidence tendered was relevant to the matter sought to be established but what was sought to be established was beside the point; it was immaterial.

R. v. LAVALLEE

[1990] 1 S.C.R. 852, 76 C.R. (3d) 329, 55 C.C.C. (3d) 97

The accused, a battered woman in a volatile common law relationship, killed her partner late one night by shooting him in the back of the head as he left her room. A psychiatrist described the accused's terror and her inability to escape the relationship. The psychiatrist opined that the shooting was the final desperate act of a woman who sincerely believed that she would be killed that night. The accused was acquitted at trial. The court had to decide whether the psychiatric evidence was properly received. Was the evidence relevant to a material issue?

WILSON J.:—

. . . .

Expert evidence on the psychological effect of battering on wives and common law partners must, it seems to me, be both relevant and necessary in the context of the present case. How can the mental state of the appellant be appreciated without it? The average member of the public (or of the jury) can be forgiven for asking: Why would a woman put up with this kind of treatment? Why should she continue to live with such a man? How could she love a partner who beat her to the point of requiring hospitalization? We would expect the woman to pack her bags and go. Where is her self-respect? Why does she not cut loose and make a new life for herself? Such is the reaction of the average person confronted with the so-called "battered wife syndrome". We need help to understand it and help is available from trained professionals.

. . . .

The feature common to both s. 34(2)(*a*) and s. 34(2)(*b*) [the self-defence sections of the Criminal Code] is the imposition of an objective standard of reasonableness on the apprehension of death and the need to repel the assault with deadly force. . . .

If it strains credulity to imagine what the "ordinary man" would do in the position of a battered spouse, it is probably because men do not typically find themselves in that situation. Some women do, however. The definition of what is reasonable must be adapted to circumstances which are, by and large, foreign to the world inhabited by the hypothetical "reasonable man".

. . . .

It will be observed that subsection 34(2)(*a*) does not actually stipulate that the accused apprehend *imminent* danger when he or she acts. Case law has, however, read that requirement into the defence. ... The sense in which "imminent" is used conjures up the image of "an uplifted knife" or a pointed gun. The rationale for the imminence rule seems obvious. The law of self-defence is designed to ensure that the use of defensive force is really necessary. It justifies the act because the defender reasonably believed that he or she had no alternative but to take the attacker's life. If there is a significant time interval between the original unlawful assault and the accused's response, one tends to suspect that the accused was motivated by revenge rather than self-defence. In the paradigmatic case of a one-time bar room brawl between two men of equal size and strength, this inference makes sense. How can one feel endangered to the point of firing a gun at an unarmed man who utters a death threat, then turns his back and walks out of the room? One cannot be certain of the gravity of the threat or his capacity to carry it out. Besides, one can always take the opportunity to flee or to call the police. If he comes back and raises his fist, one can respond in kind if need be. These are the tacit assumptions that underlie the imminence rule.

All of these assumptions were brought to bear on the respondent in *R. v. Whynot* (1983), 37 C.R. (3d) 198 (C.A.).

. . . .

Where evidence exists that an accused is in a battering relationship, expert testimony can assist the jury in determining whether the accused had a "reasonable" apprehension of death when she acted by explaining the heightened sensitivity of a battered woman to her partner's acts. Without such testimony I am skeptical that the average fact-finder would be capable of appreciating why her subjective fear may have been reasonable in the context of the relationship. After all, the hypothetical "reasonable man" observing only the final incident may have been unlikely to recognize the [batterer's] threat as potentially lethal. Using the case at bar as an example, the "reasonable man" might have thought, as the majority of the Court of Appeal seemed to, that it was unlikely that Rust would make good on his threat to kill the appellant that night because they had guests staying overnight.

_____

(c) Multiple Relevance

The same piece of evidence may be relevant to different matters. An awareness of the underlying policies for our rules will assist us in dealing with the problems that arise when the evidence has multiple relevance. We will then appreciate that though evidence may be inadmissible when tendered for one purpose as violative of a certain policy it may nevertheless be admissible when tendered for another purpose. For example, evidence of character may be relevant to both credibility and disposition; rules of evidence could exclude such evidence if tendered to prove that the person acted in conformity with that character on the occasion under review, but admit the same if tendered to impact on the credibility of a witness. If we keep in mind the policy underlying the rule we should then be better able to judge whether the evidence ought to be received, with a limiting instruction to the trier of its limited utility, or rejected.

(d) Relevance and Social Context

The concept of relevancy is ordered by our present insistence on a rational method of fact-finding and its substance, we say, is dictated by our common sense and experience. The law furnishes no test for relevancy and therefore, in the final analysis, the decision rests with the individual judge to value the probabilities in the particular case.[10] This decision, this judicial finding of relevance, is a question of law reviewable on appeal.[11] While we cannot legally define relevance, and we, of necessity, must therefore leave it to the trial judge's sound exercise of discretion, subject to review, we need to recognize that "common sense and experience," and hence relevance, will vary depending on the judge's culture, age, sexual orientation, gender, racial or ethnic background, and socio-economic status. The judge's intuition that fact X frequently accompanies fact Y, making X's presence relevant to Y's, may not accord with another's and counsel may need to be provided with the opportunity to encourage the judge that the hunch is incorrect, and deserves to be rethought in light of the other's experience.[12]

In order to guard against this and to ensure a rational, fair and inclusive system of fact adjudication, should judges be able to use social context evidence, for example, evidence of the existence of systemic bias such as racism or sexism in assessing relevance and later when engaging in fact-finding? Justice Doherty certainly thinks so. In *Peart v. Peel (Regional Municipality) Police Services Board,*[13] he noted that:

> I do not pretend that the hypothetical, reasonable person is purely objective. The reasonable person is an analytical device that will inevitably reflect the world view of the judge applying that device: see Richard F. Devlin, "We Can't Go On Together

---

10 In his classic article "Relevancy, Probability and the Law" (1941), 29 Cal. L. Rev. 689, 696, Professor James explained that relevancy is a tendency to prove and commented:

> This tendency to prove can be demonstrated only in terms of some general proposition, based most often on the practical experience of the judge and jurors as men, sometimes upon generalizations of science introduced into the trial to act as connecting links.

Professor McCormick wrote: "The answer must filter through the judge's experience, his judgment, and his knowledge of human conduct and motivation."

11 See, *e.g.*, *R. v. Driver* (1984), 39 C.R. (3d) 297 (Ont. Dist. Ct.); *Parke, Davis & Co. v. Empire Laboratories Ltd.*, [1964] S.C.R. 351; and *R. v. Borg*, [1969] S.C.R. 551. See also *R. v. Hewitt* (1986), 55 C.R. (3d) 41 (Man. C.A.), regarding admission of irrelevant evidence being a violation of the principles of fundamental justice contrary to s. 7 of the Charter.

12 See Weyrauch, "Law as Mask — Legal Ritual and Relevance" (1978), 66 Cal. L. Rev. 699; and Weinstein, "Some Difficulties in Devising Rules for Determining Truth in Judicial Trials" (1966), 66 Cal. L. Rev. 223. See also D.M. Tanovich, "Relevance, Social Context and Poverty" (2003), 9 C.R. (6th) 348; A. Mewett, "Secondary Facts, Prejudice and Stereotyping" (1999), 42 Crim. L.Q. 319 and M. MacCrimmon, "Developments in the Law of Evidence: The 1995-96 Term: Regulating Fact Determination and Common Sense Reasoning" (1997), 8 Supreme Ct. L. Rev. 367.

13 (2006), [2006] O.J. No. 4457, 43 C.R. (6th) 175, 2006 CarswellOnt 6912 (C.A.), leave to appeal refused (2007), 2007 CarswellOnt 1882, 2007 CarswellOnt 1883 (S.C.C.).

With Suspicious Minds: Judicial Bias and Racialized Perspective in R. v. R.D.S."
(1995), 18 Dal. L.J. 408 at 419-21. The realization that the hypothetical, reasonable
person is to some degree reflective of the judge's own preconceptions is what makes
an appreciation of social context so important. An understanding of how others
legitimately view the circumstances serves to counteract the subjectivity of the judge's
own view of the world.

Social context evidence can be admitted by taking judicial notice (discussed
in Chapter 5) or by expert evidence (discussed in Chapter 6). The extent to which
a judge may rely on social context evidence acquired from personal knowledge
and judicial experience has proved highly controversial and produced sharp
divisions in *S. (R.D.)*.

R. v. S. (R.D.)
[1997] 3 S.C.R. 484, 10 C.R. (5th) 1, 118 C.C.C. (3d) 353

The accused was charged with a series of offences involving an encounter
with a police officer. The relevant evidence is summarized, on behalf of the Court,
by Justice Cory:

I. Facts

R.D.S. is an African-Canadian youth. When he was 15 years of age he was charged
with three offences: unlawfully assaulting Constable Donald Stienburg;
unlawfully assaulting Constable Stienburg with the intention of preventing the
arrest of N.R.; and unlawfully resisting Constable Stienburg in the lawful
execution of his duty.The Crown proceeded with the charges by way of summary
conviction. There were only two witnesses at the trial: R.D.S. himself and
Constable Stienburg. Their accounts of the relevant events differed widely. The
credibility of these witnesses would determine the outcome of the charges.

A. Constable Stienburg's Evidence

Constable Stienburg testified that he was in his police cruiser with his partner
when a radio transmission alerted them that other officers were in pursuit of a
stolen van. In the car was a "ride-along", Leslie Lane, who was unable to testify
at the trial. The occupants of the stolen van were described as "non-white" youths.
When Constable Stienburg and his partner arrived at the designated area they saw
two black youths running across the street in front of them. Constable Stienburg
detained one of the individuals, N.R., while his partner pursued the other. He
testified that there were a number of other people standing around at the time.

N.R. was detained outside the police car since the "ride-along" was in the back
seat. While Constable Stienburg was standing by the side of the road with N.R.,
the accused, R.D.S., came towards Constable Stienburg on his bicycle. Constable
Stienburg testified that R.D.S. ran into his legs, and while still on the bicycle,
yelled at him and pushed him. R.D.S. was then arrested for interfering with the
arrest of N.R., and Constable Stienburg called for back-up. Constable Stienburg
stated that he put both R.D.S. and N.R. in "a neck restraint". When R.D.S. was

finally brought to the police station, he was read his rights, and charged with the three offences.

In cross-examination, it was suggested to Constable Stienburg that R.D.S. had been overcharged. It was pointed out that R.D.S. had no prior record and it was suggested, although not particularly clearly, that R.D.S. had been singled out because he was black.

B. Testimony of R.D.S.

R.D.S. testified that he remembered that the weather on the particular day was misty and humid. While riding his bike from his grandmother's to his mother's house he saw the police car and the crowd standing beside it. A friend told him that his cousin N.R. had been arrested. R.D.S. approached the crowd, and stopped his bike when he saw N.R. and the officer. R.D.S. then tried to talk to N.R. to ask him what had happened and to find out if he should tell N.R.'s mother. Constable Stienburg told him: "Shut up, shut up, or you'll be under arrest too". When R.D.S. continued to ask N.R. if he should call his mother, Constable Stienburg arrested R.D.S. and put him in a choke hold. R.D.S. indicated that he could not breathe, and that he heard a woman tell the officer to "Let that kid go . . . ." He also heard her ask for his phone number. He could not talk so N.R. gave the number to her. R.D.S. indicated that the crowd standing around were all "little kids" under the age of 12. He denied that he ran into anyone or that he intended to run into anyone on his bike. He also testified that his hands remained on the handlebars, and he did not push the officer. In cross-examination, he indicated that the reason he approached the crowd was because he was "being nosey". He remembered that N.R. was handcuffed when he arrived. Both R.D.S. and N.R. were placed in a choke hold at the same time. He repeated his denial that he touched the officer either with his bicycle or his hands. He also denied that he said anything to Constable Stienburg prior to his arrest. He indicated that all his questions were directed to N.R.

The trial judge weighed the evidence and determined that the accused should be acquitted. Her reasons are described by Justice Cory as follows:

> In her oral reasons, Judge Sparks reviewed the details of Constable Stienburg's testimony, and noted that R.D.S.'s evidence was directly opposed to it. In describing R.D.S.'s testimony, she observed that she was impressed with his clear recollection of the weather conditions on that day, and his candour in pointing out that he was simply being nosey in approaching the crowd. She also noted that his description of being placed in the choke hold was vivid. R.D.S. stated clearly that when he was placed in the choke hold, he could not speak and had difficulty breathing. In fact, he was unable to respond when a woman asked him for his phone number so she could notify his mother.
>
> The Youth Court Judge paid particular attention to R.D.S.'s testimony that N.R. was handcuffed when R.D.S. arrived on the scene. This aspect of R.D.S.'s testimony suggested that N.R. was not a threat to the officer. Significantly, Constable Stienburg did not mention that N.R. was handcuffed, and gave the Court the distinct impression that he had difficulty restraining N.R. In Judge Sparks' view, R.D.S.'s testimony that

N.R. was handcuffed had "a ring of truth" to it, which raised questions in her mind about the divergence between R.D.S.'s evidence and the evidence of Constable Stienburg on this point.

In general, Judge Sparks described R.D.S's demeanour as "positive", even though he was not particularly articulate. She found him to be a "rather honest young boy". In particular, she was struck by his openness in acknowledging his own "nosiness" and by his surprise at the hostility of the police officer. Judge Sparks indicated that she was not saying that she accepted everything that R.D.S. said, but noted that "certainly he has raised a doubt in my mind". She still had queries about "what actually transpired on the afternoon of October the 17th". As a result, she concluded that the Crown had not discharged its evidentiary burden to prove all the elements of the offence beyond a reasonable doubt.

At the end of her reasons, the trial judge, who is African-Canadian, remarked:

The Crown says, well, why would the officer say that events occurred the way in which he has relayed them to the Court this morning? I am not saying that the Constable has misled the court, although police officers have been known to do that in the past. I am not saying that the officer overreacted, but certainly police officers do overreact, particularly when they are dealing with non-white groups. That to me indicates a state of mind right there that is questionable. I believe that probably the situation in this particular case is the case of a young police officer who overreacted. I do accept the evidence of [R.D.S.] that he was told to shut up or he would be under arrest. It seems to be in keeping with the prevalent attitude of the day. At any rate, based upon my comments and based upon all the evidence before the court I have no other choice but to acquit.

In her later written reasons for judgment, Justice Sparks also observed:

On cross-examination by defence counsel the police officer admitted that his police department routinely refers to African-Canadian persons, at least back in October 1993, the date of these alleged offences, as "non-white." At this point in his viva voce evidence, the officer became ruffled; and in my view became tense. The line of questioning by defence counsel was that this labelling of "non-white" was a pejorative categorization of African-Canadians. As well, on cross-examination, the witness admitted that the accused had no police record. Generally the court observed that this witness appeared nervous when he commenced giving evidence. It was not unnoticed by the Court that this may have been due to the racial configuration in the court which consisted of the accused, the defence counsel, the court reporter and the judge all being of African-Canadian ancestry. . . .

Apart from the above, the general demeanour of the accused was pleasant, honest and forthright. Here the Court notes that the police officer is a full bodied man while the young person is slight and slender and was probably lighter in weight when the incident occurred as the incident happened over one year ago. The Court questioned the necessity of choke-holding a young person of such a slight and slender build. Also, in my mind, was the fact that, from other proceedings, it is not routine for a police officer to place a 15 year old youngster in a choke-hold.[14]

---

14 *R. v. S. (R.D.)*, [1994] N.S.J. No. 629 (Fam. Ct.). Justice Sparks' oral reasons were delivered on December 2, 1994. The Crown filed its Notice of Appeal on December 22, 1994. These written reasons were released January 13, 1995.

On appeal, the Crown challenged these comments as revealing an actual "racial bias" and "bias" against the police. Chief Justice Glube of the Summary Conviction Appeal Court concluded that Justice Sparks' oral reasons revealed an apprehension of bias and ordered a new trial. Her decision was affirmed by the Nova Scotia Court of Appeal. The accused appealed further. The Supreme Court of Canada first concluded that Justice Sparks' supplementary written reasons could not be considered on the bias issue because they had been produced after the Crown had filed their notice of appeal. **Do you agree that these reasons should not have been considered?** The Supreme Court went on to determine whether the oral reasons raised a reasonable apprehension of bias.

A majority of the Supreme Court held that there was no reasonable apprehension of bias in this case, allowed the appeals and restored the acquittals. The division in the court on the law is complex. **What is the majority ratio of the decision for future cases?**

CORY J. (IACOBUCCI J. concurring):—

. . . .

In some circumstances it may be acceptable for a judge to acknowledge that racism in society might be, for example, the motive for the overreaction of a police officer. This may be necessary in order to refute a submission that invites the judge as trier of fact to presume truthfulness or untruthfulness of a category of witnesses, or to adopt some other form of stereotypical thinking. Yet it would not be acceptable for a judge to go further and suggest that all police officers should therefore not be believed or should be viewed with suspicion where they are dealing with accused persons who are members of a different race. Similarly, it is dangerous for a judge to suggest that a particular person overreacted because of racism unless there is evidence adduced to sustain this finding. It would be equally inappropriate to suggest that female complainants, in sexual assault cases, ought to be believed more readily than male accused persons solely because of the history of sexual violence by men against women.

If there is no evidence linking the generalization to the particular witness, these situations might leave the judge open to allegations of bias on the basis that the credibility of the individual witness was prejudged according to stereotypical generalizations. This does not mean that the particular generalization — that police officers have historically discriminated against visible minorities or that women have historically been abused by men —- is not true, or is without foundation. The difficulty is that reasonable and informed people may perceive that the judge has used this information as a basis for assessing credibility instead of making a genuine evaluation of the evidence of the particular witness' credibility. As a general rule, judges should avoid placing themselves in this position.

. . . .

The Crown contended that the real problem arising from Judge Sparks' remarks was the inability of the Crown and Constable Stienburg to respond to the remarks. In other words, the Crown attempted to put forward an argument that the trial was rendered unfair for failure to comply with "natural justice". This cannot be accepted. Neither Constable Stienburg nor the Crown was on trial. Rather, it is essential to consider whether the remarks of Judge Sparks gave rise to a reasonable apprehension of bias. This is the only basis on which this trial could be considered unfair.

. . . .

However, there was no evidence before Judge Sparks that would suggest that anti-black bias influenced this particular police officer's reactions. Thus, although it may be incontrovertible that there is a history of racial tension between police officers and visible minorities, there was no evidence to link that generalization to the actions of Constable Stienburg. The reference to the fact that police officers may overreact in dealing with non-white groups may therefore be perfectly supportable, but it is nonetheless unfortunate in the circumstances of this case because of its potential to associate Judge Sparks' findings with the generalization, rather than the specific evidence. This effect is reinforced by the statement "[t]hat to me indicates a state of mind right there that is questionable" which immediately follows her observation.

There is a further troubling comment. After accepting R.D.S.'s evidence that he was told to shut up, Judge Sparks added that "[i]t seems to be in keeping with the prevalent attitude of the day". Again, this comment may create a perception that the findings of credibility have been made on the basis of generalizations, rather than the conduct of the particular police officer. Indeed these comments standing alone come very close to indicating that Judge Sparks predetermined the issue of credibility of Constable Stienburg on the basis of her general perception of racist police attitudes, rather than on the basis of his demeanour and the substance of his testimony.

The remarks are worrisome and come very close to the line. Yet, however troubling these comments are when read individually, it is vital to note that the comments were not made in isolation. It is necessary to read all of the comments in the context of the whole proceeding, with an awareness of all the circumstances that a reasonable observer would be deemed to know.

The reasonable and informed observer at the trial would be aware that the Crown had made the submission to Judge Sparks that "there's absolutely no reason to attack the credibility of the officer". She had already made a finding that she preferred the evidence of R.D.S. to that of Constable Stienburg. She gave reasons for these findings that could appropriately be made based on the evidence adduced. A reasonable and informed person hearing her subsequent remarks would conclude that she was exploring the possible reasons why Constable Stienburg had a different perception of events than R.D.S. Specifically, she was rebutting the unfounded suggestion of the Crown that a police officer by virtue of his occupation should be more readily believed than the accused. Although her remarks were inappropriate they did not give rise to a reasonable apprehension of bias.

. . . .

A high standard must be met before a finding of reasonable apprehension of bias can be made. Troubling as Judge Sparks' remarks may be, the Crown has not satisfied its onus to provide the cogent evidence needed to impugn the impartiality of Judge Sparks. Although her comments, viewed in isolation, were unfortunate and unnecessary, a reasonable, informed person, aware of all the circumstances, would not conclude that they gave rise to a reasonable apprehension of bias. Her remarks, viewed in their context, do not give rise to a perception that she prejudged the issue of credibility on the basis of generalizations, and they do not taint her earlier findings of credibility.

. . . .

I must add that since writing these reasons I have had the opportunity of reading those of Major J. It is readily apparent that we are in agreement as to the nature of bias and the test to be applied in order to determine whether the words or actions of a trial judge raise a reasonable apprehension of bias. The differences in our reasons lies in the application of the principles and test we both rely upon to the words of the trial judge in this case. The principles and the test we have both put forward and relied upon are different from and incompatible with those set out by Justices L'Heureux-Dubé and McLachlin.

MAJOR J. (LAMER C.J.C. and SOPINKA J. concurring):— The trial judge stated that "police officers have been known to [mislead the court] in the past" and that "police officers do overreact, particularly when they are dealing with non-white groups" and went on to say "[t]hat to me indicates a state of mind right there that is questionable." She in effect was saying, "sometimes police lie and overreact in dealing with non-whites, therefore I have a suspicion that this police officer may have lied and overreacted in dealing with this non-white accused." This was stereotyping all police officers as liars and racists, and applied this stereotype to the police officer in the present case. The trial judge might be perceived as assigning less weight to the police officer's evidence because he is testifying in the prosecution of an accused who is of a different race. Whether racism exists in our society is not the issue. The issue is whether there was evidence before the court upon which to base a finding that this particular police officer's actions were motivated by racism. There was no evidence of this presented at the trial.

. . . .

Trial judges have to base their findings on the evidence before them. It was open to the appellant to introduce evidence that this police officer was racist and that racism motivated his actions or that he lied. This was not done. For the trial judge to infer that based on her general view of the police or society is an error of law. For this reason there should be a new trial.

. . . .

The life experience of this trial judge, as with all trial judges, is an important ingredient in the ability to understand human behaviour, to weigh the evidence, and to determine credibility. It helps in making a myriad of decisions arising during the course of most trials. It is of no value, however, in reaching conclusions for which there is no evidence. The fact that on some other occasions police officers have lied or overreacted is irrelevant. Life experience is not a substitute for evidence. There was no evidence before the trial judge to support the conclusions she reached.

. . . .

Canadian courts have, in recent years, criticized the stereotyping of people into what is said to be predictable behaviour patterns. If a judge in a sexual assault case instructed the jury or him or herself that because the complainant was a prostitute he or she probably consented, or that prostitutes are likely to lie about such things as sexual assault, that decision would be reversed. Such presumptions have no place in a system of justice that treats all witnesses equally. Our jurisprudence prohibits tying credibility to something as irrelevant as gender, occupation or perceived group predisposition. . . . It can hardly be seen as progress to stereotype police officer witnesses as likely to lie when dealing with non-whites. This would return us to a time in the history of the Canadian justice system that many thought had past. This reasoning, with respect to police officers, is no more legitimate than the stereotyping of women, children or minorities.

. . . .

I agree with the approach taken by Cory J. with respect to the nature of bias and the test to be used to determine if the words or actions of a judge give rise to apprehension of bias. However, I come to a different conclusion in the application of the test to the words of the trial judge in this case. It follows that I disagree with the approach to reasonable apprehension of bias put forward by Justices L'Heureux-Dubé and McLachlin.

L'HEUREUX-DUBÉ J. (McLACHLIN J. concurring):—

. . . .

In our view, the test for reasonable apprehension of bias established in the jurisprudence is reflective of the reality that while judges can never be neutral, in the sense of purely objective, they can and must strive for impartiality. It therefore recognizes as inevitable and appropriate that the differing experiences of judges assist them in their decision-making process and will be reflected in their judgments, so long as those experiences are relevant to the cases, are not based on inappropriate stereotypes, and do not prevent a fair and just determination of the cases based on the facts in evidence. We find that on the basis of these principles, there is no reasonable apprehension of bias in the case at bar. Like Cory J. we would, therefore, overturn the findings by the Nova Scotia Supreme Court (Trial Division) and the majority of the Nova Scotia Court of Appeal that a reasonable apprehension of bias arises in this case, and restore the acquittal of R.D.S. This said, we disagree with Cory J.'s position that the comments of Judge

Sparks were unfortunate, unnecessary, or close to the line. Rather, we find them to reflect an entirely appropriate recognition of the facts in evidence in this case and of the context within which this case arose — a context known to Judge Sparks and to any well-informed member of the community.

. . . .

Cardozo recognized that objectivity was an impossibility because judges, like all other humans, operate from their own perspectives. As the Canadian Judicial Council noted in Commentaries on Judicial Conduct (1991), at p. 12, "[t]here is no human being who is not the product of every social experience, every process of education, and every human contact". What is possible and desirable, they note, is impartiality:

> The wisdom required of a judge is to recognize, consciously allow for, and perhaps to question, all the baggage of past attitudes and sympathies that fellow citizens are free to carry, untested, to the grave.

> True impartiality does not require that the judge have no sympathies or opinions; it requires that the judge nevertheless be free to entertain and act upon different points of view with an open mind.

. . . .

As discussed above, judges in a bilingual, multiracial and multicultural society will undoubtedly approach the task of judging from their varied perspectives. They will certainly have been shaped by, and have gained insight from, their different experiences, and cannot be expected to divorce themselves from these experiences on the occasion of their appointment to the bench. In fact, such a transformation would deny society the benefit of the valuable knowledge gained by the judiciary while they were members of the Bar. As well, it would preclude the achievement of a diversity of backgrounds in the judiciary. The reasonable person does not expect that judges will function as neutral ciphers; however, the reasonable person does demand that judges achieve impartiality in their judging.

. . . .

An understanding of the context or background essential to judging may be gained from testimony from expert witnesses in order to put the case in context: *R. v. Lavallee, R. v. Parks*, and *Moge v. Moge*, from academic studies properly placed before the Court; and from the judge's personal understanding and experience of the society in which the judge lives and works. This process of enlargement is not only consistent with impartiality; it may also be seen as its essential precondition. A reasonable person far from being troubled by this process, would see it as an important aid to judicial impartiality.

. . . .

It is important to note that having already found R.D.S. to be credible, and having accepted a sufficient portion of his evidence to leave her with a reasonable doubt as to his guilt, Judge Sparks necessarily disbelieved at least a portion of the conflicting evidence of Constable Stienburg. At that point, Judge Sparks made reference to the submissions of the Crown that "there's absolutely no reason to attack the credibility of the officer", and then addressed herself to why there might, in fact, be a reason to attack the credibility of the officer in this case. It is in this context that Judge Sparks made the statements which have prompted this appeal. [The trial judge's] remarks do not support the conclusion that Judge Sparks found Constable Stienburg to have lied. In fact, Judge Sparks did quite the opposite. She noted firstly, that she was not saying Constable Stienburg had misled the court, although that could be an explanation for his evidence. She then went on to remark that she was not saying that Constable Stienburg had overreacted, though she was alive to that possibility given that it had happened with police officers in the past, and in particular, it had happened when police officers were dealing with non-white groups. Finally, Judge Sparks concluded that, though she was not willing to say that Constable Stienburg did overreact, it was her belief that he probably overreacted. And, in support of that finding, she noted that she accepted the evidence of R.D.S. that "he was told to shut up or he would be under arrest".

At no time did Judge Sparks rule that the probable overreaction by Constable Stienburg was motivated by racism. Rather, she tied her finding of probable overreaction to the evidence that Constable Stienburg had threatened to arrest the appellant R.D.S. for speaking to his cousin. At the same time, there was evidence capable of supporting a finding of racially motivated overreaction. At an earlier point in the proceedings, she had accepted the evidence that the other youth arrested that day, was handcuffed and thus secured when R.D.S. approached. This constitutes evidence which could lead one to question why it was necessary for both boys to be placed in choke holds by Constable Stienburg, purportedly to secure them. In the face of such evidence, we respectfully disagree with the views of our colleagues Cory and Major JJ. that there was no evidence on which Judge Sparks could have found "racially motivated" overreaction by the police officer.

. . . .

While it seems clear that Judge Sparks did not in fact relate the officer's probable overreaction to the race of the appellant R.D.S., it should be noted that if Judge Sparks had chosen to attribute the behaviour of Constable Stienburg to the racial dynamics of the situation, she would not necessarily have erred. As a member of the community, it was open to her to take into account the well-known presence of racism in that community and to evaluate the evidence as to what occurred against that background. That Judge Sparks recognized that police officers sometimes overreact when dealing with non-white groups simply demonstrates that in making her determination in this case, she was alive to the well-known racial dynamics that may exist in interactions between police officers and visible minorities.

. . . .

Judge Sparks' oral reasons show that she approached the case with an open mind, used her experience and knowledge of the community to achieve an understanding of the reality of the case, and applied the fundamental principle of proof beyond a reasonable doubt. Her comments were based entirely on the case before her, were made after a consideration of the conflicting testimony of the two witnesses and in response to the Crown's submissions, and were entirely supported by the evidence. In alerting herself to the racial dynamic in the case, she was simply engaging in the process of contextualized judging which, in our view, was entirely proper and conducive to a fair and just resolution of the case before her.

GONTHIER J. (LA FOREST J. concurring):—I agree with Cory J. and L'Heureux-Dubé and McLachlin JJ. as to the disposition of the appeal and with their exposition of the law on bias and impartiality and the relevance of context. However, I am in agreement with and adopt the joint reasons of L'Heureux-Dubé and McLachlin JJ. in their treatment of social context and the manner in which it may appropriately enter the decision-making process as well as their assessment of the trial judge's reasons and comments in the present case.

If we accept that we must rely on informed generalizations to draw links between two facts in order to conclude that a fact is relevant or when assessing credibility, how is what Justice Sparks did in _S. (R.D.)_ different from a trier of fact who concludes that a witness is not credible because they have a criminal record or have provided inconsistent statements or that a witness' flight from the scene is evidence of a guilty mind?[15]

Professor Connie Backhouse, "Bias in Canadian Law: A Lopsided Precipice",[16] observes:

> . . . the initial finding of apprehension of bias against Canada's first African-Canadian judge, Corrine Sparks, is far from anomalous. An all-white bench of the Ontario Divisional Court had removed African-Canadian adjudicator, Frederica Douglas, from the tri-partite Ontario Police Complaints Board in 1994, also on the basis of reasonable apprehension of bias. The complaint involved a case in which an African-Canadian woman had alleged that she had been strip-searched by white police officers. The African-Canadian vice-president of the Toronto chapter of the Congress of Black Women had commented publicly to the media about the case. Douglas was removed from the board because she was the president of the Mississauga chapter of the same organization. Derrick Bell, an outstanding African American scholar of critical race issues, describes the phenomenon as "a widespread assumption that blacks, unlike whites, cannot be objective on racial issues and will favor their own no matter what." Bell notes that in the American context: "Black judges hearing racial cases are eyed suspiciously and sometimes asked to recuse themselves in favor of a white

---

15 For competing views on _S. (R.D.)_, see Archibald, "The Lessons of the Sphinx: Avoiding Apprehensions of Judicial Bias in a Multi-racial, Multi-cultural Society" (1998), 10 C.R. (5th) 54 and Delisle, "An Annotation to _S. (R.D.)_" (1998), 10 C.R. (5th) 7. See also David M. Paciocco, "The Promise of R.D.S.: Integrating the Law of Judicial Notice and Apprehension of Bias", (1998) 3 _Can. Crim. L.Rev._ 319, R.F. Devlin, "We Can't Go On Together With Suspicious Minds: Judicial Bias and Racialized Perspective in _R. v. R.D.S._ (1995), 18 Dal. L.J. 408; C.A. Alyward, "Take The Long Way Home: R.D.S. v. R. The Journey" (1998), 47 U.N.B.L.J. 249.

16 (1997) 10 _C.J.W.L. 170._

judge – without those making the request even being aware of the paradox in their motions.

Since there are still very few judges who are drawn from racially distinct groups, it is useful to expand this analysis to encompass female adjudicators who have been challenged on the basis of gender bias. Here, too, it is noteworthy how many challenges of bias have emerged against a numerically small group of female adjudicators. The Honourable Maryka Omatsu has outlined the allegations of bias made against Ontario law professor Mary Jane Mossman, feminist litigators Mary Eberts, Lillian Pan, and Mayo Moran, and myself in an earlier issue of the *Canadian Women and the Law*. The thrust of these allegations seems to have been aimed at our reputations as feminist advocates. In addition, in *Great Atlantic & Pacific Co. of Canada v. Ontario* . . . the Ontario Court General Division concluded that the fact that I was one of 121 female law students, law professors, and lawyers who maintained an outstanding human rights complaint against Osgoode Hall Law School and York University was sufficient to disqualify me from adjudicating on "the same issues."

Earlier in Chapter 1, we examined the role of the trial judge in the adversarial process and the extent to which he or she can interfere in the proceedings (e.g. in questioning witnesses or commenting on the evidence). In the following case, the Crown argued that the trial judge had stepped over the line in raising issues of racial and gender bias on his own motion. Another issue was whether the trial judge had relied on generalizations about how drug couriers act in the absence of any evidence linking those generalizations to the accused.

R. v. HAMILTON
[2004] O.J. No. 3252, 2004 CarswellOnt 3214, 186 C.C.C. (3d) 129, 241 D.L.R. (4th) 490 (Ont. C.A.)

The accused H and M were each charged with importing cocaine. Each had swallowed pellets of cocaine in order to smuggle them into Canada from Jamaica. H imported 349 grams in November, 2000 while M imported 489 grams in May, 2001. Both accused were black single mothers supported entirely or in part by social assistance. Neither had any prior criminal record, and both had pleaded guilty to the charges laid. Each accused spent four days in custody on arrest, apologized in court for her behaviour, and received a pre-sentence report stating she was a suitable candidate for community supervision. M was not a Canadian citizen and faced the risk of deportation. At the sentencing hearings before Justice Hill, conducted over 13 separate days, extensive social context evidence concerning poverty, gender bias, systemic racism and rates of incarceration in Canada and other countries was filed. The judge himself provided 700 pages of materials. Based, in part, on this evidence, the trial judge concluded that the accused should not receive the usual sentence of imprisonment but should receive conditional sentences. In his opinion, the background factors of race, gender, and poverty were linked to the commission of the offence because they made these accused particularly vulnerable targets to those who sought out individuals to act as cocaine couriers. H was sentenced to a 20-month conditional sentence of imprisonment. M was sentenced to a 24-month-less-a-day conditional sentence of imprisonment. The Crown appealed.

The Ontario Court of Appeal dismissed the sentence appeal given the time that had passed but made it clear that in their view the trial judge had acted inappropriately.

DOHERTY J.A. (O'CONNOR A.C.J.O. AND GILLESE J.A. concurring):

. . . .

Having read and reread the transcripts, I must conclude that the trial judge does appear to have assumed the combined role of advocate, witness, and judge. No doubt, the trial judge's extensive experience in sentencing cocaine couriers had left him with genuine and legitimate concerns about the effectiveness and fairness of sentencing practices as applied to single poor black women who couriered cocaine into Canada for relatively little gain. The trial judge unilaterally decided to use these proceedings to raise, explore, and address various issues which he believed negatively impacted on the effectiveness and fairness of current sentencing practices as they related to some cocaine importers. Through his personal experience and personal research, the trial judge became the prime source of information in respect of those issues. The trial judge also became the driving force pursuing those issues during the proceedings.

No one suggests that a trial judge is obliged to remain passive during the sentencing phase of the criminal process. Trial judges can, and sometimes must, assume an active role in the course of a sentencing proceeding. Section 723(3) of the Criminal Code provides that a court may, on its own motion, require the production of evidence that "would assist in the determination of the appropriate sentence." Quite apart from that statutory power, the case law has long recognized that where a trial judge is required by law to consider a factor in determining the appropriate sentence and counsel has not provided the information necessary to properly consider that factor, the court can, on its own initiative, make the necessary inquiries and obtain the necessary evidence: *R. v. Wells* (2000), 141 C.C.C. (3d) 368 at 390-91 (S.C.C.); *R. v. Gladue*, [1999] 1 S.C.R. 688 at paras. 84-85.

Recognition that a trial judge can go beyond the issues and evidence produced by the parties on sentencing where necessary to ensure the imposition of a fit sentence does not mean that the trial judge's power is without limits or that it will be routinely exercised. In considering both the limits of the power and the limits of the exercise of the power, it is wise to bear in mind that the criminal process, including the sentencing phase, is basically adversarial. Usually, the parties are the active participants in the process and the judge serves as a neutral, passive arbiter. Generally speaking, it is left to the parties to choose the issues, stake out their positions, and decide what evidence to present in support of those positions. The trial judge's role is to listen, clarify where necessary, and ultimately evaluate the merits of the competing cases presented by the parties.

The trial judge's role as the arbiter of the respective merits of competing positions developed and put before the trial judge by the parties best ensures judicial impartiality and the appearance of judicial impartiality. Human nature is such that it is always easier to objectively assess the merits of someone else's argument. The relatively passive role assigned to the trial judge also recognizes that judges, by virtue of their very neutrality, are not in a position to make informed decisions as to which issues should be raised, or the evidence that should be led.

Judicial intrusion into counsel's role can cause unwarranted delay and bring unnecessary prolixity to the proceedings.

Judges must be very careful before introducing issues into the sentencing proceeding. Where an issue may or may not be germane to the determination of the appropriate sentence, the trial judge should not inject that issue into the proceedings without first determining from counsel their positions as to the relevance of that issue. If counsel takes the position that the issue is relevant, then it should be left to counsel to produce whatever evidence or material he or she deems appropriate, although the trial judge may certainly make counsel aware of materials known to the trial judge which are germane to the issue. If counsel takes the position that the issue raised by the trial judge is not relevant on sentencing, it will be a rare case where the trial judge will pursue that issue.

It is also important that the trial judge limit the scope of his or her intervention into the role traditionally left to counsel. The trial judge should frame any issue that he or she introduces as precisely as possible and relate it to the case before the court. This will avoid turning the sentencing hearing into a de facto commission of inquiry.

The manner in which the proceedings were conducted created at least four problems. First, by assuming the multi-faceted role of advocate, witness, and judge, the trial judge put the appearance of impartiality at risk, if not actually compromising that appearance. For example, the trial judge introduced the issues of race and gender bias into the proceedings, and then, through the material he produced and the questions he addressed to Crown counsel, the trial judge appeared to drive the inquiry into those matters towards certain results. Those results are reflected in his reasons. Looking at the entirety of the proceedings, there is a risk that a reasonable observer could conclude that the trial judge's findings as to the significance of race and gender bias in fixing the appropriate sentences had been made before he directed an inquiry into those issues. At the very least, the conduct of the proceedings produced a dynamic in which the trial judge became the Crown's adversary on the issues introduced by the trial judge.

Although the appearance of impartiality was put at risk by the conduct of these proceedings, the trial judge did take steps to try and preserve the appearance of fairness. He gave counsel clear indications of his concerns and any tentative opinions he had formed. He also provided the material to counsel to which he planned to refer in considering the issues he had raised. This procedure was much fairer to the parties and much more likely to produce an accurate result than had the trial judge simply referred to the material without giving counsel any notice: *R. v. Paul* (1998), 124 C.C.C. (3d) 1 (N.B. C.A.); *Cronk v. Canadian General Insurance Co.* (1995), 25 O.R. (3d) 505 at 518 (C.A.); Ian Binnie, "Judicial Notice: How Much is Too Much?" in Law Society of Upper Canada, Special Lectures 2003: The Law of Evidence (Toronto: Irwin Law, 2004) 543 at 564-65. Much of the material produced by the trial judge was not suggestive of any particular answer to the questions raised by the trial judge in the course of the proceedings. The scrupulous fairness with which the trial judge conducted the proceedings went some way towards overcoming the potentially adverse effects of the extraordinary role he assumed in the conduct of the proceedings.

The second problem arising from the trial judge's approach is that it produced a fundamental disconnect between the case on sentencing presented by counsel for the respondents and the case of the paradigmatic cocaine courier constructed by the trial judge. From the time he first introduced race and gender into the proceedings, the trial judge spoke in terms of poor black single women who were "targeted" and "conscripted" by drug overseers to act as couriers. The trial judge referred to these couriers as "virtue-tested" by drug overseers and as living "in the despair of poverty". The trial judge also described these couriers as using the small compensation they received from the drug overseers to pay rent, feed children, and support a subsistence level-existence.

Counsel for the respondents chose to provide next to no information about the respondents' involvement in these crimes. Ms. Hamilton indicated she acted out of financial need. Ms. Mason offered no explanation. There was no evidence that these respondents were conscripted, virtue-tested, or paid minimal compensation, nor was there evidence that such compensation was used to pay for the necessaries of life. The reasons for sentence indicate to me that the trial judge based his sentences more on his concept of the typical drug courier than on the evidence pertaining to these two individuals.

A third problem with the trial judge's conduct of the proceedings is that it created a real risk of inaccurate fact-finding. The trial judge introduced a veritable blizzard of raw statistical information. He also produced various forms of opinion on a wide variety of topics. None of this material was analyzed or tested in any way.

. . . .

I do not think the meaning of the statistics introduced by the trial judge or the inferences that could be properly drawn from them is self-evident. There were real risks that these statistics could be misunderstood and misused absent proper expert evidence. Instead of being treated with the caution that all statistics deserve, these statistics – probably because they were introduced by the trial judge – took on a strong aura of reliability and were treated as if they were self-explanatory.

A fourth difficulty with the way the trial judge conducted these proceedings is evident from his introduction of the "certainty of detection" issues. These issues consumed a good deal of time and effort. In the end, quite properly, they played virtually no role in determining the appropriate sentence. . . .

The trial judge made several findings of fact which were specific to the respondents' involvement in their offences. He relied on these findings to support his conclusion that their personal culpability was significantly reduced. He found as a fact that:

- the respondents were "conscripted" by the "drug distribution hierarchy" to participate in their crimes (para. 198);

- the involvement of the respondents was the result of "virtue-testing" by "drug operation overseers" (para. 195);

- the respondents were paid relatively minimal amounts and used those amounts to provide the bare necessities for their families (para. 191); and

• the respondents' children would be "effectively orphaned" if the respondents were incarcerated (para. 198).

Although the rules of evidence are substantially broadened on the sentencing inquiry, factual findings that are germane to the determination of the appropriate sentence and are not properly the subject of judicial notice must be supported by the evidence. There was no evidence to support the findings of fact outlined immediately above.

The respondents chose not to offer any explanation for, or description of, their involvement in the crimes, apart from Ms. Hamilton's indication that she acted out of financial need. The trial judge had no information as to how the respondents came to be involved in this scheme, what their prior association or relationship was with the individuals who may have hired them, when or where the importation plans were formed, what amount of compensation was paid to the respondents, or how the respondents proposed to use that compensation. He also had no information concerning the care of the children if the respondents went to jail. All of this information was uniquely within the knowledge of the respondents. If the respondents were conscripted – that is, compelled to engage in this activity – they could have said so. If they agreed to be involved in the crimes only after repeated requests, they could have said so, just as they could have provided other details concerning their involvement in the scheme and the compensation they received. Similarly, if the effect of the respondents' imprisonment on the children was as drastic as the trial judge held it to be, I would have expected the respondents to have led evidence to that effect.

The Crown's concession that the respondents were couriers did not constitute an admission that they possessed every characteristic that the trial judge ascribed to couriers. Nor do I accept the contention that requiring the respondents to lead the kind of evidence described above works any hardship on them. This kind of evidence has been given in other cases... Safety concerns rising out of implicating others in the scheme can be addressed if and when they arise. In any event, concerns about the potential safety of the offender should he or she provide certain evidence, do not justify assumptions that have no basis in the evidence.

The trial judge did not purport to base the findings of fact outlined above on any material that actually related to these respondents. Instead, he relied on his experiences in sentencing other individuals who couriered cocaine from Jamaica. He applied those generalizations to these respondents. In doing so, he relied on *R. v. S. (R.D.)* (1997), 118 C.C.C. (3d) 353 (S.C.C.). I read that authority as prohibiting the very kind of fact-finding made by the trial judge.

. . . The majority of the Supreme Court of Canada rejected the bias allegation. In the course of doing so, the court addressed the extent to which trial judges can use personal judicial experience and judicial understanding of the applicable social context in the course of the fact-finding process. Major J., in dissent, speaking for the three members of the court who would have accepted the bias argument, observed at para. 13:

The life experience of this trial judge, as with all trial judges, is an important ingredient in the ability to understand human behaviour, to weigh evidence, and to determine credibility. It helps in making a myriad of decisions arising during the course of most trials. It is of no value, however, in reaching conclusions for which there is no evidence. The fact that on some other occasions police officers have lied or overreacted is irrelevant. *Life experience is not a substitute for evidence. There was no evidence before the trial judge to support the conclusions she reached* [emphasis added].

Cory J., speaking for himself and Iacobucci J., joined the majority in rejecting the bias argument. However, he approached the use of judicial experience and social context in a manner that was consistent with that applied by Major J. In referring to trial judges' credibility assessments, Cory J. said at para. 129:

> *On one hand, the judge is obviously permitted to use common sense and wisdom gained from personal experience in observing and judging the trustworthiness of a particular witness on the basis of factors such as testimony and demeanour. On the other hand, the judge must avoid judging the credibility of the witness on the basis of generalizations or upon matters that were not in evidence* [emphasis added].

Cory J. then addressed the trial judge's reasons at para. 150:

> However, there was *no* evidence before Judge Sparks that would suggest that anti-black bias influenced *this particular police officer's reactions.* Thus, although it may be incontrovertible that there is a history of racial tension between police officers and visible minorities, there was no evidence to link that generalization to the actions of Constable Stienburg. The reference to the fact that police officers may overreact in dealing with non-white groups may therefore be perfectly supportable, but it is nonetheless unfortunate in the circumstances of this case because of its potential to associate Judge Sparks' findings with the generalization, rather than the specific evidence [underline added, italics in original].

I think the trial judge fell into the error described by Cory J. While his generalizations concerning the way in which persons like the respondents come to be involved in couriering cocaine from Jamaica, the amounts they are paid for that service, and the use to which they put those amounts may be true as generalizations, there was no evidence that they had any application to the facts of this case.

Justices L'Heureux-Dubé and McLachlin, speaking for four members of the majority on the bias issue, took a somewhat wider view of the use that trial judges could make of information garnered through personal judicial experience and judicial understanding of applicable social context. Their view is the minority view on this issue. However, even on their analysis, fact-finding has to ultimately have some basis in the evidence. They observed at para. 56:

> While it seems clear that Judge Sparks *did not in fact* relate the officer's probable overreaction to the race of the appellant R.D.S., it should be noted that if Judge Sparks *had* chosen to attribute the behaviour of Constable Stienburg to the racial dynamics of the situation, she would not necessarily have erred. As a member of the community, it was open to her to taken into account the well-known presence of racism in that community and to evaluate the evidence as to what occurred against that background [underline added, italics in original].

R. v. S. (R.D.) draws a distinction between findings of fact based exclusively on personal judicial experience and judicial perceptions of applicable social context, and findings of fact based on evidence viewed through the lens of personal judicial experience and social context. The latter is proper; the former is not.

The proper use of personal experience and social context can be demonstrated by reference to Ms. Hamilton's evidence concerning the motive for her crime. She testified that she acted out of dire financial need. The fact that a crime was committed for financial gain can, in some circumstances, mitigate personal responsibility, and, in different circumstances, it can increase personal responsibility. The trial judge was required to determine what weight should be given on sentencing to Ms. Hamilton's admitted financial motive for committing the crime. In making that assessment, he was entitled to put her statement as to her motive in its proper context by recognizing, based on his experiences and the operative social context, that individuals in the circumstances of Ms. Hamilton often find themselves in very real financial need for reasons that include societal factors, like racial and gender bias, over which those individuals have no control. Used in this way, the tools of personal judicial experience and social context help illuminate the evidence. This use can be contrasted with the trial judge's use of his experience in other cases to make the specific finding of fact that these respondents were conscripted – that is, compelled by drug overseers to engage in this criminal activity – when there was no evidence as to how the respondents came to be involved.

The limits on judicial fact-finding based on prior judicial experience and social context are necessary for at least two reasons. First, fact-finding based on a judge's personal experience can interfere with the effective operation of the adversary process. It is difficult, if not impossible, to know, much less explore or challenge, a trial judge's perceptions based on prior judicial experiences or his or her appreciation of the social issues which form part of the context of the proceedings. Second, fact-finding based on generalities developed out of personal past experience can amount to fact-finding based on stereotyping. That risk is evident in this case. The trial judge appears to have viewed all poor black single women who import cocaine into Canada from Jamaica as essentially sharing the same characteristics. These characteristics describe individuals who, because of their difficult circumstances, have virtually no control over their own lives and turn to crime because they are unable to otherwise provide for their children. While this may be an apt description of some of the individuals who turn to cocaine importing, it is stereotyping to assume that all single black women who import cocaine into Canada fit this description.

. . . .

Do you agree with the Ontario Court of Appeal's interpretation of *R.D.S.*? Do you agree that the trial judge overstepped his sentencing role?[17]

---

17 Academic commentary on the Ontario Court of Appeal has been highly critical: see comments by Song and Boyle, Tanovich and Kaiser, (2004) 22 C.R. (6th) 45, 57 and 86.

2. DISCRETION AND LAW OF EVIDENCE

(a) Introduction

Recognizing a discretion in the trial judge recognizes room for choice, room for judgment. It's inherent in the nature of the exercise. We should not fear it nor should we insist on certainty in all our rules of evidence. The so-called "rules" of evidence were designed largely by trial judges seeking justice in their individual cases and were not meant to be a calculus rigidly applied. The best that we can do is to catalogue factors which are important to the sound exercise of discretion. Nor should discretion be feared as some form of palm-tree justice which is unreviewable. Protection against a trial judge's abuse of discretion should always be available by appeal.[18] Appellate court judges at the same time should recognize, however,

> . . . the vantage point of the trial judge, the superiority of his position. It's not that he knows more. It's that he sees more, and sometimes smells more.[19]

What do we mean by "discretion"? Consider these contrasting views:

> The discretion of a Judge is the Law of Tyrants; it is always unknown; it is different in different men; it is casual and depends on constitution, temper and passion. In the best it is often times caprice, in the worst it is every vice, folly and passion to which human nature is liable.[20]

> Discretion when applied to a court of justice means sound discretion guided by law. It must be governed by rule not by humour; it must not be arbitrary, vague and fanciful, but legal and regular.[21]

No one would speak in favour of the former type of discretion; no one however can deny the necessity of the latter. Discretion is endemic to the law of evidence and essential to any model of adjudication. There is a need to recognize that fact and to get on with the task of articulating the guidelines necessary to exercise the judicial function.

It is somewhat odd to see resistance to discretion in the application of the rules of evidence when we remind ourselves that in bench trials we regularly equip the trial judge with the ultimate discretion of finding guilt or innocence. When a judge seeks to reach a conclusion of fact from the evidence of witnesses, he discriminates as to weight and cogency. Jerome Frank referred to this exercise as "fact discretion."[22] A witness describes a past event. On analysis, the witness is stating his present recall of what he believes he then saw. The trier of fact observes the demeanour of the witness, sees him tested on cross-examination, and expresses his opinion regarding the correctness of the witness's belief. We

---

18 See *R. v. B. (C.R.)*, 55 C.C.C. (3d) 1, 76 C.R. (3d) 1, [1990] 1 S.C.R. 717, at 23-24 [C.C.C.] (similar fact evidence); *R. v. Litchfield*, 86 C.C.C. (3d) 97, 25 C.R. (4th) 137, [1993] 4 S.C.R. 333, at 113-114 [C.C.C.] (severance applications); *R. v. M. (T.E.)*, 114 C.C.C. (3d) 436, [1997] 1 S.C.R. 948, 6 C.R. (5th) 231, at 445-448 [C.C.C.] (sentencing); and, *R. v. Stillman*, 113 C.C.C. (3d) 321, 5 C.R. (5th) 1, [1997] 1 S.C.R. 607, at 350 [C.C.C.] (s. 24(2)).

19 Rosenberg, "Judicial Discretion" (1965), 38 The Ohio Bar 819.

20 Lord Camden in *Doe d. Hindson v. Kersey* (1765).

21 Lord Mansfield in *R. v. Wilkes* (1770), 4 Burr 2527, 2539 (H.L.).

22 *Courts on Trial*, 1949, p. 57.

have "subjectivity piled on subjectivity"; guesses upon guesses.[23] In this exercise, which is the best we can do, we trust in the judge to exercise her discretion in a sound manner and to discriminate wisely.[24]

A sound exercise of discretion is absolutely essential to the proper application of the rules of evidence and recognition of that fact will likely produce greater actual certainty at the sacrifice only of apparent certainty. In answer to those who fear discretion, listen to Professor Rosenberg:

> Discretion need not be, as Lord Camden said, a synonym for lawlessness or tyranny, if those who created it wield it and review its use are sensitive to the risks and responsibilities it raises, and if they play fair with the system; for the difference between government of law and government of man is not that the lawyers decide cases in one and fools in the other. Men, that is the judges, always decide. The difference is in whether judges are aware of their power, sensitive to their responsibilities and true to the tradition of the common law.[25]

We, properly, trust our judges to make all manner of preliminary and final decisions affecting the outcome of a case. It would be incongruous then to deny them the right to exercise discretion in judging how, and what evidence will be heard by the trier of fact. We should always then be conscious of the policy on which the rule is based, so that we may gauge whether that policy is actually being advanced in the particular application of the rule and whether the policy that gave birth to the rule continues as a viable support.

In the proposed Code of Evidence,[26] the most important sections, indeed the Code's heart and soul, were:

> 4.(1) All relevant evidence is admissible except as provided in this Code or any other Act.
> (2) "Relevant evidence" means evidence that has any tendency in reason to prove a fact in issue in a proceeding.
> 5. Evidence may be excluded if its probative value is substantially outweighed by the danger of undue prejudice, confusing the issues, misleading the jury, or undue consumption of time.

The Code was not accepted by the profession. The profession expressed great concern with equipping trial judges with discretion in the application of the law of evidence. Antonio Lamer was the Vice-Chairman of the Law Reform Commission at the time and G.V. La Forest was the Commissioner in charge of the Evidence Project. We shall discover that the Supreme Court was able to effectively establish judicially what these two jurists were unable to accomplish legislatively.

(b) Discretion to Exclude

Even though evidence is relevant to a legal issue in the case and therefore admissible, we will discover that the courts have over the past 20 years developed

---

23 *Ibid.*, Ch. III, Facts are Guesses.
24 See H.L. Krongold, "A Comparative Perspective on the Exclusion of Relevant Evidence: Common Law and Civil Law Jurisdictions" (2003), 12 Dal. J. Leg. Studies.
25 Rosenberg, *supra*, note 19, at p. 826.
26 Law Reform Commission of Canada, 1975.

various forms of discretions to exclude. Sometimes exclusion occurs because of a canon of exclusion, such as the Hearsay Rule (to which there are a number of exceptions), where judicial tradition has been established favouring exclusion.

Here we consider the more general discretions available to judges to exclude otherwise admissible evidence. We will discover that:

1. In criminal cases, a discretion to exclude can be read into a statute.

2. In civil and criminal cases, there is now a discretion, at common law, to exclude where probative value is exceeded by prejudicial effect. Probative value refers to the strength of the inference that can be drawn.[27] By prejudicial effect, the concern is not that the evidence is unfavourable to the party's case but that the evidence will generate unfairness either by its misuse, the undue consumption of time or the confusion it creates.[28]

3. In criminal cases where evidence is tendered by the accused, the evidence may only be excluded where the probative value is substantially exceeded by its prejudicial effect (see especially *R. v. Seaboyer*, below).

4. In criminal cases there is also an uncertain discretion developed under the Charter to exclude evidence to ensure a fair trial.

(i) *Reading In*

CORBETT v. R.
[1988] 1 S.C.R. 670, 64 C.R. (3d) 1, 41 C.C.C. (3d) 385

The accused was convicted of murder. He appealed, arguing that he was deprived of his right to a fair hearing by reason of the introduction of evidence of his earlier conviction of another murder. The accused had sought a ruling that, if he was called as a witness, section 12 of the *Canada Evidence Act* would not apply to him because of section 11(*d*) of the Charter and he could not be cross-examined as to his prior criminal record. Under section 12 "A witness may be cross-examined as to whether the witness has been convicted of any offence. . . .". The evidence of his previous conviction was elicited after a negative ruling by the trial judge. When the matter reached the Supreme Court, the Court was divided. The Court held 4-2 that a discretion should be read into section 12 to make it constitutional. The four majority judges (see below) further divided 3-1 on the correct application of the discretion to the facts of the case. The sole dissent of La Forest on the facts was however accepted as properly stating the factors relevant to the exercise of the discretion.

27 See *R. v. B. (L.)* (1997), 35 O.R. (3d) 35, 9 C.R. (5th) 38, 116 C.C.C. (3d) 481 (C.A.), at p. 45, *per* Charron J.A.

28 See Delisle, "Three Recent Decisions of the Supreme Court of Canada Affecting the Law of Similar Fact Evidence" (1992), 16 *Prov. Judges J.* 13 at 15 as cited by Justice Charron in *B.(L.), supra* at para. 22.

DICKSON C.J.C. (LAMER J. concurring and BEETZ J. concurring separately):—

. . . .

I agree with La Forest J. that there is a discretion to exclude evidence of prior convictions of an accused. However, as I take a different view as to the manner in which the trial judge's discretion should have been exercised, it will be necessary for me to deal with the constitutional validity of s. 12 of the Canada Evidence Act.

. . . .

Before calling any evidence, Corbett's counsel sought a ruling that, if the accused were called, s. 12 of the Canada Evidence Act would not apply to him because of s. 11(*d*) of the Charter, and therefore that Corbett could not be cross-examined as to his prior criminal record. The trial judge ruled against Corbett on this issue, following the decision of the British Columbia Supreme Court in *R. v. Jarosz* (1982), 3 C.R.R. 333. The accused was then called, and in order "to soften the blow" his own counsel put to him his criminal record, which Corbett admitted. The record is as follows:

— 23 April 1954   armed robbery, receiving stolen property, breaking, entering and theft (four counts)
— 12 May 1954   escaping custody
— 6 Dec. 1954   theft of auto, breaking and entering
— 8 Nov. 1971   non-capital murder

In his evidence, Corbett denied shooting Pinsonneault and swore that he left his hotel room only once during the night, to get some liquor and cigarettes from his car, the hotel clerk having testified that he had let Corbett back into the hotel at 3:10 a.m.

In charging the jury, the trial judge stated as follows with regard to the relevance of Corbett's criminal record:

> There was evidence tendered by the accused that he was previously convicted of a number of Criminal Code offences, including the offence of non-capital murder, which conviction was registered on November 8th 1971. Evidence of previous convictions is admissible only in respect to the credibility of the witness. It can only be used to assess the credibility of the accused, and for no other purpose. Because the accused was previously convicted of murder, it must not be used by you, the jury, as evidence to prove that the accused person committed the murder of which he stands charged. You, the jury, must not take the person's previous convictions into account in your deliberations when determining whether the Crown has proven beyond a reasonable doubt that the accused committed the murder with which he is charged.

This warning could hardly have been more explicit.

. . . .

It is my view that on the facts of the present case a serious imbalance would have arisen had the jury not been apprised of Corbett's criminal record. Counsel for Corbett vigorously attacked the credibility of the Crown witnesses and much was made of the prior criminal records of Marcoux and Bergeron. What impression would the jury have had if Corbett had given his evidence under a regime whereby the Crown was precluded from bringing to the jury's attention the fact that Corbett had a serious criminal record? It would be impossible to explain to the jury that one set of rules applies to ordinary witnesses, while another applies to the accused, for the very fact of such an explanation would undermine the purpose of the exclusionary rule. Had Corbett's criminal record not been revealed, the jury would have been left with the quite incorrect impression that, while all the Crown witnesses were hardened criminals, the accused had an unblemished past. It cannot be the case that nothing short of this entirely misleading situation is required to satisfy the accused's right to a fair trial.

There is perhaps a risk that, if told of the fact that the accused has a criminal record, the jury will make more than it should of that fact. But concealing the prior criminal record of an accused who testifies deprives the jury of information relevant to credibility, and creates a serious risk that the jury will be presented with a misleading picture.

In my view, the best way to balance and alleviate these risks is to give the jury all the information, but at the same time give a clear direction as to the limited use they are to make of such information. Rules which put blinders over the eyes of the trier of fact should be avoided except as a last resort. It is preferable to trust the good sense of the jury and to give the jury all relevant information, so long as it is accompanied by a clear instruction in law from the trial judge regarding the extent of its probative value. . . .

In my view, it would be quite wrong to make too much of the risk that the jury *might* use the evidence for an improper purpose. This line of thinking could seriously undermine the entire jury system. The very strength of the jury is that the ultimate issue of guilt or innocence is determined by a group of ordinary citizens who are not legal specialists and who bring to the legal process a healthy measure of common sense. The jury is, of course, bound to follow the law as it is explained by the trial judge. Jury directions are often long and difficult, but the experience of trial judges is that juries do perform their duty according to the law. We should regard with grave suspicion arguments which assert that depriving the jury of all relevant information is preferable to giving them everything, with a careful explanation as to any limitations on the use to which they may put that information. So long as the jury is given a clear instruction as to how it may and how it may not use evidence of prior convictions put to an accused on cross-examination, it can be argued that the risk of improper use is outweighed by the much more serious risk of error should the jury be forced to decide the issue in the dark. . . .

I agree with La Forest J. that the trial judge has a discretion to exclude prejudicial evidence of previous convictions in an appropriate case.

However, I respectfully disagree with my colleague La Forest J. that this discretion should have been exercised in favour of the appellant in the circumstances of the present case. In his reasons, La Forest J. provides a useful catalogue of factors to which reference may be had in determining how this discretion is to be exercised. In my view, however, my colleague gives too little weight to the fact that in this case the accused appellant made a deliberate attack on the credibility of Crown witnesses, largely based upon their prior records.

LA FOREST J. (dissenting):—

. . . .

GENERAL PRINCIPLES

As is true with respect to the resolution of most, if not all, issues relating to the law of evidence, resort must be had first and foremost to its animating or first principles, for it is only with reference to these that the more specific rules of evidence can be understood and evaluated. Failure to so reference discussion often results in the unhappy divorce of legal reasoning from common sense, with the consequence that rules of evidence are apt to be viewed as both self-sustaining and self-justifying. The present case further illustrates that statutory rules of evidence must also be interpreted in light of these guiding principles.

The organizing principles of the law of evidence may be simply stated. All relevant evidence is admissible, subject to a discretion to exclude matters that may unduly prejudice, mislead or confuse the trier of fact, take up too much time, or should otherwise be excluded on clear grounds of law or policy. Questions of relevancy and exclusion are, of course, matters for the trial judge, but over the years many specific exclusionary rules have been developed for the guidance of the trial judge, so much so that the law of evidence may superficially appear to consist simply of a series of exceptions to the rules of admissibility, with exceptions to the exceptions, and their sub-exceptions. . . .

I agree with Professor Friedland that the law's sedulously fostered position, that the character of an accused may not be considered unless he first raises the issue or unless the Crown meets the criteria of similar fact evidence, ought not to easily yield to what a Law Reform Commission of Canada paper has described as "the fallacy [in s. 12] that it is rational to treat the accused like an ordinary non-party witness" (Evidence Study Paper 3, Credibility (1972), at p. 8). Furthermore, I think it self-evident that the law cannot profess to learn from common sense and experience and yet selectively ignore such lessons. I also think it significant that I have not unearthed any academic or empirical evidence tending to undermine these observations. Indeed, quite the contrary is true: see Wissler and Saks, "On the Inefficacy of Limiting Instructions: When Jurors Use Prior Conviction Evidence to Decide on Guilt" (1985), 9 L. & Human Behavior 37; also Ratushny and Friedland.

. . . .

Having satisfied myself that the risk of prejudice is by no means speculative or illusory, I now turn to the question whether s. 12 admits of a discretion in the trial judge to prevent such prejudice materializing.

[Having found that there was a discretion, he continued.]

It is impossible to provide an exhaustive catalogue of the factors that are relevant in assessing the probative value or potential prejudice of such evidence, but among the most important are the nature of the previous conviction and its remoteness or nearness to the present charge.

. . . .

. . . [T]he more similar the offence to which the previous conviction relates to the conduct for which the accused is on trial, the greater the prejudice harboured by its admission.

. . . .

I think that a court should be very chary of admitting evidence of a previous conviction for a similar crime, especially when the rationale for the stringent test for admitting "similar fact" evidence is kept in mind. . . .

. . . .

As I indicated in my earlier comments respecting the admission into evidence of previous convictions for offences similar to that for which the accused is on trial, I think it self-evident that the prejudicial potential harboured by the admission at a trial for murder of a previous conviction for non-capital murder is manifestly profound. Furthermore, the probative value of this item of evidence in relation to credibility (which is the only use to which it legitimately could be put) is, at best, trifling, certainly in this case. The foregoing alone appears to satisfy a narrow reading of the test in *Wray*.

However, as I mentioned earlier, discretion cannot be judicially exercised in a vacuum; it is only with reference to the circumstances of the case that its exercise becomes meaningful. The circumstances of the present case, however, rather than "indicat[ing] strong reasons for disclosure" (*Gordon*, supra, at p. 940), militate strenuously for exclusion. It is true that the appellant had assailed the credibility of Crown witnesses, and indeed that credibility was the vital issue at trial. However, the circumstances of the case itself, indicating a violation by the appellant of his parole conditions, and the substance of the appellant's defence, indicating clearly the appellant's involvement in cocaine transactions, would have served to bring home to the jury the unsavoury criminal character of the appellant and, on the theory that such evidence affects credibility, this objective would have been fulfilled. This, along with the evidence of the appellant's previous convictions for theft and breaking and entering, amply served the purpose of impeaching his credibility. Indeed, the convictions for theft and breaking and entering, though quite remote in time, would appear far more probative of a disposition for dishonesty than a conviction for murder. The latter, in the circumstances of the case, added very little, if anything, to the jury's perception of the appellant's character for veracity; on the other hand, in the words of Hutcheon J.A. in the court below [p. 230], "it might well be that the fact that he had been convicted some years before of a similar offence might have been the last ounce which turned the scales against him". The jury's actions at trial in this case in no way diminish this possibility.

CONCLUSION

I conclude, therefore, that s. 12 of the Canada Evidence Act, when read in conjunction with the salutary common law discretion to exclude prejudicial evidence, does not violate an accused's right to a fair trial or deprive him of his liberty except in accordance with the principles of fundamental justice. Here, the trial judge erred in law in failing to recognize the existence of the exclusionary discretion described above, and consequently in admitting into evidence the previous conviction for murder. Given my belief that the introduction of this evidence was, in the circumstances of the case, unjustifiably prejudicial to the fairness of the appellant's trial, I am unable to conclude that no substantial wrong or miscarriage of justice was occasioned thereby. I would therefore allow the appeal, quash the conviction and order a new trial pursuant to s. 613(2)(b) of the Criminal Code. I would answer the first constitutional question in the negative, and consequently find it unnecessary to answer the second constitutional question.

Appeal dismissed.[29]

Where cross-examination of an accused under s. 12 is allowed the Supreme Court in *Corbett* requires a warning to the jury that the evidence can only be used to assess credibility rather than to show the accused is the type of bad character likely to have committed this crime. **Can the jury make and act on such a distinction?**[30]

In *R. v. Potvin*[31] the Supreme Court had to deal with the admissibility at trial of former testimony. The accused and two others, D. and T., were charged with murder. The Crown proceeded against the accused first, and called D. as a witness. Although D. had testified at the preliminary inquiry, he refused to testify at the trial. The transcript of D.'s testimony at the preliminary was received into evidence at trial pursuant to section 643 [now section 715] of the Criminal Code, and the accused was convicted. An appeal from his conviction was dismissed, and the accused appealed further. The Supreme Court allowed the appeal and ordered a new trial. The court decided that the statutory provision did not violate section 7 or section 11(d) of the Charter. All five judges concluded, however, that a trial judge has a discretion to exclude former testimony, even though the statutory conditions have been met, and determined that the trial judge in this case had failed to exercise that discretion. Madam Justice Wilson, Justices Lamer and Sopinka concurring, wrote:

> ... In my view there are two main types of mischief at which the discretion might be aimed. First, the discretion could be aimed at situations in which there has been unfairness in the manner in which the evidence was obtained. ... An example of unfairness in obtaining the testimony might be a case in which, although the witness

---

29 See generally Delisle, "Case Note to *Corbett v. R.*" (1988), 67 Can. Bar Rev. 706.
30 See Knazan, "Putting Evidence Out of Your Mind" (1999), 42 Crim. L.Q. 501. For how the discretion under section 12 of the *Canada Evidence Act* has been exercised, see Chapt. 7, 3(c) Character of the Witness, *infra*.
31 (1989), 68 C.R. (3d) 193 (S.C.C.).

was temporarily absent from Canada, the Crown could have obtained the witness's attendance at trial with a minimal degree of effort. Another example might be a case in which the Crown was aware at the time when the evidence was initially taken that the witness would not be available to testify at the trial but did not inform the accused of this fact so that he could make best use of the opportunity to cross-examine the witness at the earlier proceeding. . . .

A different concern at which the discretion might have been aimed is the effect of the admission of the previously-taken evidence on the fairness of the trial itself. This concern flows from the principle of the law of evidence that evidence may be excluded if it is highly prejudicial to the accused and of only modest probative value.

. . . .

In my view, . . . s. 643(1) of the Code should be construed as conferring a discretion on the trial judge broader than the traditional evidentiary principle that evidence should be excluded if its prejudicial effect exceeds its probative value.[32]

Madam Justice Wilson stressed that even evidence of high probative value could be excluded if admission would render the trial unfair. She noted that the credibility of the witness in this case was critical, the jury had no opportunity to observe the witness's demeanour, and the trial judge had failed to consider this possible lack of fairness.[33]

Similar discretionary treatment was accorded the reception of videotaped interviews under section 715.1 in the Criminal Code. In *R. v. L. (D.O.)*[34] the Supreme Court dealt with the admissibility of videotaped statements of young complainants in sexual assault cases pursuant to section 715.1 of the Criminal Code. The question was whether the statutory provision was consistent with principles of fundamental justice. The court of appeal had held that section 715.1 contravened sections 7 and 11(*d*) of the Charter and could not be sustained under section 1. The Supreme Court decided that the statutory provision did not violate the Charter as there was discretion in the trial judge in the application of the section. Lame, C.J., La Forest, Sopinka, Cory, McLachlin and Iacobucci JJ., concurring, wrote:

[T]he incorporation of judicial discretion into s. 715.1, which permits a trial judge to edit or refuse to admit videotaped evidence where its prejudicial effect outweighs its probative value, ensures that s. 715.1 is consistent with fundamental principles of justice and the right to a fair trial protected by ss. 7 and 11(*d*) of the *Charter.*[35]

L'Heureux-Dubé J. (Gonthier J. concurring), wrote:

[T]he wording of s. 715.1 itself supports the interpretation that such a provision accommodates traditional rules of evidence and judicial discretion. Thus, in addition to the power to expunge or edit statements where necessary, the trial judge has discretion to refuse to admit the videotape in evidence if its prejudicial effect outweighs its probative value. Properly used, this discretion to exclude admissible evidence

---

32 *Ibid.*, at pp. 236-37.
33 See *R. v. Lewis,* 2009 CarswellOnt 7685, 2009 ONCA 874 (Ont. C.A.) for an application of *Potvin* in the context of the non-disclosure of evidence prior to the testimony of a witness at the preliminary inquiry.
34 [1993] 4 S.C.R. 419.
35 *Ibid.*, at p. 429.

ensures the validity of s. 715.1 and is conversant with fundamental principles of justice necessary to safeguard the right to a fair trial enshrined in the *Charter*.[36]

Notice that in both *Potvin* and in *L. (D.O.)* the statutory provisions say nothing about discretion in the trial judge. The judges in the Supreme Court of Canada, to ensure a fair trial, read the requirement in.

(ii) *Balancing Probative Value and Prejudicial Effect*

R. v. SEABOYER
[1991] 2 S.C.R. 577, 7 C.R. (4th) 117, 66 C.C.C. (3d) 321

The accused were charged with sexual assault. They argued that section 276 of the Criminal Code, commonly known as the "rape shield provision" was unconstitutional because it deprived them of the ability to introduce relevant evidence. We will address the constitutional arguments in the next chapter. In this part of the judgment, the Supreme Court over-ruled its earlier decision in *R. v. Wray* (1970), 4 C.C.C. 1, 11 C.R.N.S. 235, [1971] S.C.R. 272 on the scope of a trial judge's discretion to exclude evidence. It also established a more narrow discretion for defence evidence.

McLACHLIN J. (LAMER C.J.C., LA FOREST, SOPINKA, CORY, STEVENSON and IACOBUCCI JJ. concurring): —

... The precept that the innocent must not be convicted is basic to our concept of justice. One has only to think of the public revulsion felt at the improper conviction of Donald Marshall in this country or the Birmingham Six in the United Kingdom to appreciate how deeply held is this tenet of justice. Lamer J. (as he then was) put it this way in *Re B.C. Motor Vehicle Act, supra*, at p. 513:

> It has from time immemorial been part of our system of laws that the innocent not be punished. This principle has long been recognized as an essential element of a system for the administration of justice which is founded upon a belief in the dignity and worth of the human person and on the rule of law.

· · ·

The right of the innocent not to be convicted is dependent on the right to present full answer and defence. This, in turn, depends on being able to call the evidence necessary to establish a defence and to challenge the evidence called by the prosecution. As one writer has put it:

> If the evidentiary bricks needed to build a defence are denied the accused, then for that accused the defence has been abrogated as surely as it would be if the defence itself was held to be unavailable to him. (Doherty, *supra*, at p. 67).

· · ·

It is fundamental to our system of justice that the rules of evidence should permit the judge and jury to get at the truth and properly determine the issues.

---

36 *Ibid.*, at p. 461.

This goal is reflected in the basic tenet of relevance which underlies all our rules of evidence: see *Morris v. The Queen*, [1983] 2 S.C.R. 190, and *R. v. Corbett*, [1988] 1 S.C.R. 670. In general, nothing is to be received which is not logically probative of some matter requiring to be proved and everything which is probative should be received, unless its exclusion can be justified on some other ground. A law which prevents the trier of fact from getting at the truth by excluding relevant evidence in the absence of a clear ground of policy or law justifying the exclusion runs afoul of our fundamental conceptions of justice and what constitutes a fair trial.

The problem which arises is that a trial is a complex affair, raising many different issues. Relevance must be determined not in a vacuum, but in relation to some issue in the trial. Evidence which may be relevant to one issue may be irrelevant to another issue. What is worse, it may actually mislead the trier of fact on the second issue. Thus the same piece of evidence may have value to the trial process but bring with it the danger that it may prejudice the fact-finding process on another issue.

The law of evidence deals with this problem by giving the trial judge the task of balancing the value of the evidence against its potential prejudice. Virtually all common law jurisdictions recognize a power in the trial judge to exclude evidence on the basis that its probative value is outweighed by the prejudice which may flow from it.

Professor McCormick, in McCormick's Handbook of the Law of Evidence (2nd ed. 1972), put this principle, sometimes referred to as the concept of "legal relevancy", as follows at pp. 438-40:

> Relevant evidence, then, is evidence that in some degree advances the inquiry, and thus has probative value, and is prima facie admissible. But relevance is not always enough. There may remain the question, is its value worth what it costs? There are several counterbalancing factors which may move the court to exclude relevant evidence if they outweigh its probative value. In order of their importance, they are these. First, the danger that the facts offered may unduly arouse the jury's emotions of prejudice, hostility or sympathy. Second, the probability that the proof and the answering evidence that it provokes may create a side issue that will unduly distract the jury from the main issues. Third, the likelihood that the evidence offered and the counter proof will consume an undue amount of time. Fourth, the danger of unfair surprise to the opponent when, having no reasonable ground to anticipate this development of the proof, he would be unprepared to meet it. Often, of course, several of these dangers such as distraction and time consumption, or prejudice and surprise, emerge from a particular offer of evidence. This balancing of intangibles—probative values against probative dangers—is so much a matter where wise judges in particular situations may differ that a leeway of discretion is generally recognized.

This Court has affirmed the trial judges' power to exclude Crown evidence the prejudicial effect of which outweighs its probative value in a criminal case, but a narrower formula than that articulated by McCormick has emerged. In *Wray*, *supra*, at p. 293, the Court stated that the judge may exclude only "evidence gravely prejudicial to the accused, the admissibility of which is tenuous, and whose probative force in relation to the main issue before the court is trifling". More recently, in *Sweitzer v. The Queen*, [1982] 1 S.C.R. 949, at p. 953, an appeal involving a particularly difficult brand of circumstantial evidence offered by the Crown, the Court said that "admissibility will depend upon the probative effect of the evidence balanced against the prejudice caused to the accused by its admission". In *Morris, supra*, at p. 193, the Court without mentioning *Sweitzer* cited the narrower *Wray* formula. But in *R. v. Potvin*, [1989] 1 S.C.R. 525, La Forest J. (Dickson C.J. concurring) affirmed in general terms "the rule that the trial judge may exclude admissible evidence if its prejudicial effect substantially outweighs its probative value" (p. 531).

I am of the view that the more appropriate description of the general power of a judge to exclude relevant evidence on the ground of prejudice is that articulated in *Sweitzer* and generally accepted throughout the common law world. It may be noted that the English case from which the *Wray* formula was adopted has been superseded by more expansive formulae substantially in the language of *Sweitzer*.

The Canadian cases cited above all pertain to evidence tendered by the Crown against the accused. The question arises whether the same power to exclude exists with respect to defence evidence. Canadian courts, like courts in most common law jurisdictions, have been extremely cautious in restricting the power of the accused to call evidence in his or her defence, a reluctance founded in the fundamental tenet of our judicial system that an innocent person must not be convicted. It follows from this that the prejudice must substantially outweigh the value of the evidence before a judge can exclude evidence relevant to a defence allowed by law.

These principles and procedures are familiar to all who practise in our criminal courts. They are common sense rules based on basic notions of fairness, and as such properly lie at the heart of our trial process. In short, they form part of the principles of fundamental justice enshrined in s. 7 of the *Charter*. They may be circumscribed in some cases by other rules of evidence, but as will be discussed in more detail below, the circumstances where truly relevant and reliable evidence is excluded are few, particularly where the evidence goes to the defence. In most cases, the exclusion of relevant evidence can be justified on the ground that the potential prejudice to the trial process of admitting the evidence clearly outweighs its value.[37]

---

37 The Supreme Court affirmed this more narrow exclusionary discretion for defence evidence in *R. v. Shearing* (2002), 165 C.C.C. (3d) 225 (S.C.C.) but it has not been consistent in such recognition: see, for example, *Lyttle*, below Chapter 5, C. Witnesses. See also *R. v. Humaid* (2006), 37 C.R. (6th) 347, 208 C.C.C. (3d) 43, 2006 CarswellOnt 2278 (C.A.), leave to appeal refused (2006), 2006 CarswellOnt 7132, 2006 CarswellOnt 7133 (S.C.C.) and *R. v. L. (R.I.)* (2005), 29 C.R. (6th) 330, 197 C.C.C. (3d) 166 (B.C. C.A.).

R. v. HUNTER

(2001), 155 C.C.C. (3d) 225, 45 C.R. (5th) 345, 2001 CarswellOnt 2164 (C.A.)

The accused was charged with attempted murder of a police officer. At trial, the Crown sought to call Lorenzo DiCecco whose evidence was that on the day of the accused's preliminary hearing he was walking past the accused and his lawyer who were standing together in an open area of the Old City Hall. Mr. DiCecco said that he overhead the accused say "I had a gun, but I didn't point it." He acknowledged that he just caught that part of the conversation. He agreed that there might have been conversation between the accused and his lawyer both before and after the overheard utterance. He could not give the Court the context of the utterance. After a *voir dire* the trial judge held this evidence to be admissible.

GOUDGE J.A. (MOLDAVER and ROSENBERG JJ.A. concurring):—

The appellant's first ground of appeal is that the trial judge erred in admitting the evidence of the appellant's utterance overheard by Mr. DiCecco. Relying on *R. v. Ferris* (1994), 34 C.R. (4th) 26 (S.C.C.) affirming (1993), 27 C.R. (4th) 141 (Alta. C.A.), the appellant argued that the utterance cannot meet the threshold of relevance required for admissibility because its meaning cannot be determined without its context or alternatively its meaning is so speculative that it ought to have been excluded because its prejudicial effect outweighed its tenuous probative value. I agree.

The facts in *Ferris* closely parallel this case. The accused was arrested for murder and taken into police custody. He was permitted to telephone his father from the police station. A police officer walked past the accused on two occasions while he was on the phone. On the first occasion the accused was overheard to say "I've been arrested" and on the second occasion, shortly thereafter, "I killed David". The police officer heard the appellant talking before, after and in between the two sets of words but, apart from the quoted utterances, he could not tell what was said. The trial judge ruled that the officer could give evidence of the two overheard utterances.

Conrad J.A., writing for the majority in the Alberta Court of Appeal, turned first to whether, in the circumstances, it was possible to ascertain the meaning of these words so that they could be said to meet the relevance requirement for admissibility. She pointed out that the only possible relevance of these words was if they could be found to constitute an admission by the accused that he killed David. However, the Crown had no evidence of the words preceding or following the overheard phrases and Conrad J.A. cited examples of possible surrounding words that would make the full statement innocuous rather than an admission of guilt and hence not probative of any fact in issue. Given that there was a verbal context for the overheard phrases but no evidence of what that context was, Conrad J.A. found that a properly instructed jury could not determine from the fragmented utterance which was overheard the meaning either of the whole thought or of the overheard words themselves. Hence she concluded that these words could not be said to be probative of a fact in issue and were therefore irrelevant and inadmissible.

Conrad J.A. went on to find that since the utterance "I killed David" had no probative value (given that the court did not know the words surrounding it) and since the utterance was extremely prejudicial its exclusion must be favoured. On this basis as well she found that the overheard words should not have been admitted.

The Supreme Court of Canada dismissed the appeal from this judgment. The reasons of the court by Sopinka J. are as follows:

> In our opinion, with respect to the evidence that the respondent was overheard to say "I killed David", if it had any relevance, by reason of the circumstances fully outlined by Conrad J.A. [reported at (1994), 27 C.R. (4th) 141 (Alta. C.A.)], its meaning was so speculative and its probative value so tenuous that the trial judge ought to have excluded it on the ground its prejudicial effect overbore its probative value.

The appeal is therefore dismissed.

In my view, Sopinka J.'s reasoning is anchored in the important role that context can play in giving meaning to spoken words. Where an overheard utterance is known to have a verbal context, but that context is itself unknown, it may be impossible to know the meaning of the overheard words or to otherwise conclude that those words represent a complete thought regardless of context. Even if the overheard words can be said to have any relevance, where their meaning is speculative and their probative value therefore tenuous yet their prejudicial effect substantial, the overheard words should be excluded.

When the principles derived from *Ferris* are applied to this case, I think the evidence must be excluded as it was in *Ferris*. The only possible relevance of the overheard utterance is if it could be found to constitute an admission by the appellant that he had a gun. Here, as in *Ferris,* the trial judge found that the overheard utterance had a verbal context, which is unknown and that it was part of a fuller statement. That statement may have been a statement such as "I could say I had a gun, but I didn't point it, but I won't because it is not true" or "What if the jury finds I had a gun but I didn't point it — is that aggravated assault?" Neither would constitute an admission. Indeed, given the reasoning of the trial judge, had these possibilities been pointed out to him he might well have reached a different conclusion.

In my view, without the surrounding words, it would be impossible for a properly instructed jury to conclude that the overheard utterance was an admission or perhaps even what it meant. Clearly its meaning remains highly speculative. The trier of fact would have to guess at the words that came before and after to fix on a meaning. Since its meaning is highly speculative, its probative value is correspondingly tenuous. However, the substantial prejudicial effect is obvious. This balance clearly favours exclusion of the overheard utterance and, as in *Ferris,* that should have been the result.

ANDERSON v. MAPLE RIDGE (DISTRICT)

(1992), [1993] 1 W.W.R. 172, 1992 CarswellBC 250 (C.A.)

The negligence alleged against the defendant municipality had to do with the placement of a stop sign and the nature of road markings at an intersection within its corporate limits, which were said to have contributed to the cause of a motor vehicle accident in which Anderson was seriously injured. Some months after the accident, the municipality moved the stop sign in question to a different location. A local resident, who testified to a frequency of accidents at that intersection before the sign was moved, was said to be able to give evidence that there had been no accidents since it was moved. The trial judge refused to admit any evidence relating to either the relocation of the sign or its apparent consequences. The plaintiff appealed.

Per WOOD J.A. (SOUTHIN and LEGG JJ.A. concurring):—

. . . .

I begin with the fundamental proposition that evidence which is relevant, and which is not excluded by any rule of evidence, is admissible.

(a) Was the evidence relevant?

Evidence is relevant if it is logically probative of either a fact in issue or a fact which itself is probative of a fact in issue. Evidence which tends to make the existence of a fact in issue either more or less probable is logically probative of that fact. . . . Here, as an essential first step in his case, the appellant had to establish that the stop sign facing east bound traffic on Chigwell Street approaching Princess Street was, at the time, of the accident, positioned so as to be either difficult to see or easily overlooked by the very traffic it was meant to serve. Without proof of that there was no point moving on to consider what duty of care, if any, was owed by the municipality to the plaintiff, or whether that duty was breached.

In support of that essential fact the plaintiff offered the evidence of his expert, and the evidence of the police constable who attended at the scene of the accident. Mr. Arcand's evidence of the accident history of the intersection in question before the appellant's accident, and the evidence which he would have given if permitted, of what happened after the stop sign was moved, was offered for the same purpose. In my view that evidence would have been logically probative of the fact sought to be proved, in the sense that it could reasonably support the inference the sign was less visible to east bound drivers on Chigwell Street in its pre-accident location than it was after it was moved. Thus I am satisfied that the evidence which the trial judge excluded was relevant.

(b) Was the evidence inadmissible by virtue of any exclusionary rule?

At different times throughout the course of argument, both in the court below and in this Court, at least two different "rules" were relied upon by the defendant as a basis. The first was that to which reference has already been made, namely the policy, which Wigmore discusses at para. 283 of Vol II of the Chadbourn Revision, which is said to exclude evidence of acts of "repair" or "improvement" undertaken by a defendant subsequent to the occurrence giving rise to the cause of action.

This policy is said by Wigmore to have two distinct rationales. The first is the fact that such acts of repair or improvement, by themselves, will most often support nothing more than an inference that the owner believed the prior condition was capable of causing injury such as that alleged, a state of mind which is equally consistent with a belief that the injury was in fact caused in some other way. Thus there is no "probable" inference to draw from such acts and they should be excluded. The other rationale is that evidence of such acts would likely be overemphasized by juries, thus inhibiting all owners, the careful as well as the negligent, from undertaking repairs or improvements which would enure to the benefit of all. While the learned editor concedes that the first rationale is theoretically weak, it is suggested that when combined with the second "policy" rationale, the impropriety of admitting such evidence is clear.

With respect I do not agree with the first rationale. In my view it is the product of Wigmore's concept of "legal relevance" which requires that "[e]ach single piece of evidence must have a plus value" before it can be received in evidence. But as Lamer, J. (as he then was) made clear in *Morris v. The Queen*, [1983] 2 S.C.R. 190, at pp.199-201, the law in Canada has never adopted that supercharged view of relevance. Instead, we have adhered to Thayer's analysis which applies principles of logic and common sense to determine relevance, and which, subject to recognized exclusionary rules, admits all evidence logically probative of a fact in issue, reserving for the court only a narrow discretion to exclude for reasons of policy or fairness.

As for the second rationale described by Wigmore, Seaton, J.A. in *Cominco Ltd. v. Westinghouse Canada Limited et al* (1979), 11 B.C.L.R. 142 noted the following at p. 157:

> No case binding on us supports an exclusionary rule based on policy and I am not inclined to introduce such a rule. In my view a defendant will not expose other persons to injury and himself to further lawsuits in order to avoid the rather tenuous argument that because he has changed something he has admitted fault.

The fact is that the argument advanced by the respondent goes further than even Wigmore would attempt to take the exclusionary rule which he describes, for after reviewing several authorities, the following appears in para. 283 in the latter's work at p. 185:

> Accordingly, it is conceded by almost all courts that no act in the nature of repairs, improvements, substitution, or the like, done after the occurrence of an injury, is receivable as evidence of a consciousness (or an "implied admission"), on the part of the owner, of his negligence, connivance, or other culpability in causing the injury.

The learned editor then goes on to point out:

> There may of course be other evidential purposes for which the acts in question may be relevant; in that event they are to be received, subject to a caution restricting their use to a specific proper purpose.

As I have noted, the evidence at issue in this case, as it was described in argument, was relevant to the question whether the pre-accident location of the stop sign made it difficult to see. The exclusionary rule described in Wigmore does not purport to limit its admissibility for that purpose, so long as the Jury are instructed that standing by itself the evidence can not be taken as an admission of liability.

The other "exclusionary rule" relied upon by the respondent, both here and in the court below, was a general discretion which a trial Judge is said to have, in a civil case, to exclude evidence the relevance of which is overshadowed by its prejudicial effect. This was, in fact, the "rule" relied upon by the trial judge when he held the evidence to be inadmissible.

There is no doubt that a Judge trying a civil case in Canada has a discretion to exclude relevant evidence on the ground that its prejudicial effect outweighs its probative value; *Draper v. Jacklyn et al*, [1970] S.C.R. 92, per Spence, J. What is less clear is under what circumstances that discretion should be exercised. There is a paucity of jurisprudence on the subject. Counsel did refer us to a 1975 English Court of Appeal decision in *Mood Music Publishing Co. Ltd. v. De Wolfe Ltd.*, [1976] 1 All E.R. 763, where Lord Denning, M.R. said this at p. 766 in connection with the admissibility of similar fact evidence in that case:

> The admissibility of evidence as to 'similar facts' has been much considered in the criminal law. Some of them have reached the highest tribunal, the latest of them being *Boardman v. Director of Public Prosecutions*. The criminal courts have been very careful not to admit such evidence unless its probative value is so strong that it should be received in the interests of Justice: and its admission will not operate unfairly to the accused. In civil cases the courts have followed a similar line but have not been so chary of admitting it. In civil cases the courts will admit evidence of similar fact evidence if it is logically probative, that is if it is logically relevant in determining the matter which is in issue; provided that it is not oppressive or unfair to the other side; and also that the other side has fair notice of it and is able to deal with it.

To the extent that this passage suggests there is a more narrow discretion to exclude prejudicial evidence in civil cases than exists in criminal cases, it would appear to be at odds with the situation in this country where the broad scope of the discretion suggested by Spence, J. in *Draper v. Jacklyn et al.*, stands in contrast to the very narrow discretion to exclude described in the decision of the Supreme Court of Canada a year later in *Regina v. Wray*, [1971] S.C.R. 272.

The exact scope of the discretion of the court trying a civil case, to exclude otherwise relevant evidence because of its prejudicial effect, is a complex question that can be left for another day. I am satisfied that whatever that scope may be, it was exceeded in this case. The only potential prejudice to the defendant, resulting from the admission of the evidence in question, was that already discussed, namely that the jury might improperly draw the inference that by changing the position of the stop sign the municipality was admitting negligence. But the jury could, and should, have been told that standing alone the evidence could not be used for that purpose, and I have every confidence that if such instruction had been given it would have been followed. In my view, in the absence of evidence to suggest that it would be impossible for a reasonable jury to follow such an instruction, there could be no basis for the exercise of the discretion to exclude otherwise relevant evidence.

In the result, I am of the view that the trial judge erred when he excluded the evidence that the stop sign in question was moved by the defendant municipality some months after the appellant's accident, and that, so far as Mr. Arcand knew, no further accidents had occurred at that intersection since that date.

———————

Subsequent civil cases have identified the discretion broadly. For example, in *Monks v. ING Insurance Co. of Canada*,[38] the trial judge observed, after citing *Anderson*, that "[a] judicial discretion to exclude admissible evidence in civil cases is undertaken, if in the judge's view its prejudicial effect outweighs its probative value." However, in *Homolka v. Harris*,[39] Justice Saunders observed that "[w]hile the extent to which evidence in a civil case will be excluded on the basis of prejudice may not coincide always with the experience in criminal cases, an issue which is unresolved as Mr. Justice Wood pointed out in *Anderson v. Erickson...*" **Should the discretion in civil cases be narrower than in criminal cases? What policy arguments support such an argument?**

(iii) *Assessing Trial Fairness*

R. v. HARRER
[1995] 3 S.C.R. 562, 42 C.R. (4th) 269, 101 C.C.C. (3d) 193

The accused's boyfriend escaped from custody in Vancouver while awaiting extradition to the United States. The United States immigration officers began an investigation which led them to the accused. The accused was herself suspected of being illegally in the United States. The accused was arrested and she was given the "Miranda" warning against self-incrimination. She was later taken to a State Police post. The immigration officers left her with U.S. Marshals and advised that the Marshals wanted to question her. At some point the interview shifted to the accused's alleged criminal participation in her boyfriend's escape, but she was not given another warning as would be required under the Canadian Charter of Rights. American law does not require a second warning. The accused was returned to Canada, the Marshals forwarded her statements to police in Vancouver, and she was charged with assisting in an escape from custody, contrary to section 147(*a*) of the Criminal Code. At trial, the Crown attempted to adduce the statement to the United States Marshals but the judge ruled that the interrogation violated section 10(*b*) of the Charter, which guarantees the right of a person arrested or detained to retain and instruct counsel without delay. The evidence was rejected on the basis that its admission would bring the administration of justice into disrepute. Accordingly, the accused was acquitted.

———————

38 (2005), 76 O.R. (3d) 146 (S.C.J.). Cronk J.A. in *Landolfi v. Fargione*, (2006) 79 O.R. (3d) 767 (Ont. C.A.) is content to hold that the test for exclusion in both civil and criminal cases is whether the probative value is outweighed by its prejudicial effect.
39 [2002] B.C.J. No. 831, 2002 CarswellBC 821 (C.A.).

On appeal, a new trial was ordered on the ground that the Charter has no application to interrogations conducted in the United States. The accused appealed. The appeal was dismissed. The Supreme Court decided that the rights flowing from section 10(*b*) to persons arrested or detained had no application in this case. The Charter applied when the Canadian police began proceedings against the accused. If the admission of crucial evidence, such as the out-of-court self-incriminatory statement, would violate the principles of fundamental justice, the trial would not be fair. Although dicta, the following excerpt emphasizes the trial judge's role in conducting a fair trial.

LA FOREST J. (LAMER C.J.C., L'HEUREUX-DUBÉ, SOPINKA, GONTHIER, CORY and IACOBUCCI JJ. concurring):—

. . . .

I would be inclined to think that evidence obtained following a *Miranda* warning should ordinarily be admitted in evidence at a trial unless in the light of other circumstances the court has reason to think the admission of the evidence would make the trial unfair.

There were no such circumstances here — quite the opposite. As I mentioned, not only was the *Miranda* warning given at the outset of the questioning by the Immigration agents; it was also later recalled to the appellant when the police began their questioning. As well, before the relevant statements were made, the interrogating Marshal impressed upon the appellant the seriousness of her situation and his knowledge that she was involved in the escape. On a reading of the judge's findings, it is abundantly clear that the appellant (whom the trial judge, despite her age, described as a "cagey witness" and as "a street wise and sophisticated young woman" intimately associated with a fugitive sought on charges of high level cocaine trafficking) knew full well that she was being questioned in relation to the very matter in respect of which it is argued a second warning should have been given. Under these circumstances, I am at a loss to understand how these statements would, if admitted, result in the trial being unfair.

I should add that, had the circumstances been such that the admission of the evidence would lead to an unfair trial, I would have had no difficulty rejecting the evidence by virtue of the *Charter*. I would not take this step under s. 24(2), which is addressed to the rejection of evidence that has been wrongfully obtained. Nor would I rely on s. 24(1), under which a judge of competent jurisdiction has the power to grant such remedy to a person who has suffered a *Charter* breach as the court considers just and appropriate. Rather, I would reject the evidence on the basis of the trial judge's duty, now constitutionalized by the enshrinement of a fair trial in the *Charter*, to exercise properly his or her judicial discretion to exclude evidence that would result in an unfair trial.

I shall, however, attempt to put more flesh on this approach because the argument was strongly advanced that since there was no breach of the *Charter* in obtaining the evidence, a prerequisite to the power to exclude evidence under s. 24(2) of the *Charter*, there was no *Charter* based jurisdiction to exclude evidence. The difficulty with this contention is that it fails to appreciate the full nature of a fair trial. As I mentioned, while s. 24(2) is directed to the exclusion of evidence obtained in a manner that infringed a *Charter* right, it does not operate until there is a *Charter* breach. What we are concerned with here is not the remedy for a breach but with the manner in which a trial must be conducted if it is to be fair.

The law of evidence has developed many specific rules to prevent the admission of evidence that would cause a trial to be unfair, but the general principle that an accused is entitled to a fair trial cannot be entirely reduced to specific rules. In *R. v. Corbett*, [1988] 1 S.C.R. 670, a majority of this court made it clear that a judge has a discretion to exclude evidence that would, if admitted, undermine a fair trial; see also *R. v. Potvin*, [1989] 1 S.C.R. 525. . . . In *Thomson Newspapers*, supra, I attempted to explain that this approach is a necessary adjunct to a fair trial as guaranteed by s. 11(*d*) of the Charter in the following passage:

> There can really be no breach of the *Charter* until unfair evidence is admitted. Until that happens, there is no violation of the principles of fundamental justice and no denial of a fair trial. Since the proper admission or rejection of derivative evidence does not admit of a general rule, a flexible mechanism must be found to deal with the issue contextually. That can only be done by the trial judge.

I went on to further explain, as I had in *Corbett*, supra, that the common law principle had now been constitutionalized by the *Charter's* guarantee of a fair trial under s. 11(*d*) of the *Charter*. I continued:

> The fact that this discretion to exclude evidence is grounded in the right to a fair trial has obvious constitutional implications. The right of an accused to a fair hearing is constitutionalized by s. 11(*d*), a right that would in any event be protected under s. 7 as an aspect of the principles of fundamental justice.

The effect of s. 11(*d*), then, is to transform this high duty of the judge at common law to a constitutional imperative. As I noted in *Thomson Newspapers*, judges must, as guardians of the Constitution, exercise this discretion where necessary to give effect to the *Charter's* guarantee of a fair trial. In a word, there is no need to resort to s. 24(2), or s. 24(1) for that matter. In such circumstances, the evidence is excluded to conform to the constitutional mandate guaranteeing a fair trial, i.e., to prevent a trial from being unfair at the outset.

McLachlin J. (Major J. concurring):—

. . . .

[T]he argument [is] that the conduct of the American police prior to the taking of the statement requires its exclusion from evidence to preserve a fair trial in Canada. The argument is simply put. Every person charged in Canada has a right to a fair trial. The Canadian courts are bound to provide this fair trial, and to this end may exclude evidence which would render a trial unfair. Admission of Harrer's second statement would render her trial unfair. Therefore the trial judge correctly excluded it.

The first premise of this argument does not permit of dissent. Every person tried in Canada is entitled to a fair trial. The right to a fair trial is the foundation upon which our criminal justice system rests. It can neither be denied nor compromised. The common law has for centuries proclaimed it, and the Canadian

Charter confirms it. Section 11(d) provides that "Any person charged with an offence has the right . . . to be presumed innocent until proven guilty according to law in a fair and public hearing by an independent and impartial tribunal". The right to a fair trial is also a "principle of fundamental justice" which s. 7 of the Charter requires to be observed where the liberty of the subject is at stake.

The second premise of the argument, that judges have the power to exclude evidence where its admission would render the trial unfair, while less obvious, is readily resolved. At common law, a trial judge has a discretion to exclude evidence "if the strict rules of admissibility would operate unfairly against the accused": *Kuruma v. The Queen*. Similarly, in Canada, the discretion allows exclusion of evidence that "would undermine the right to a fair trial": *R. v. Corbett*, considering s. 12 of the Canada Evidence Act. . . .

In addition to the common law exclusionary power, the Charter guarantees the right to a fair trial (s. 11(d)) and provides new remedies for breaches of the legal rights accorded to an accused person. Evidence obtained in breach of the Charter may only be excluded under s. 24(2): *R. v. Therens*, [1985] 1 S.C.R. 613. Evidence not obtained in breach of the Charter but the admission of which may undermine the right to a fair trial may be excluded under s. 24(1), which provides for "such remedy as the court considers appropriate and just in the circumstances" for Charter breaches. Section 24(1) applies to prospective breaches, although its wording refers to "infringe" and "deny" in the past tense: *Operation Dismantle Inc. v. The Queen*, [1985] 1 S.C.R. 441. It follows that s. 24(1) permits a court to exclude evidence which has not been obtained in violation of the Charter, but which would render the trial unfair contrary to s. 11(d) of the Charter.

. . . .

Whether a particular piece of evidence would render a trial unfair is often a matter of some difficulty. . . .

At base, a fair trial is a trial that appears fair, both from the perspective of the accused and the perspective of the community. A fair trial must not be confused with the most advantageous trial possible from the accused's point of view: *R. v. Lyons*, [1987] 2 S.C.R. 309, at p. 362, per La Forest J. Nor must it be conflated with the perfect trial; in the real world, perfection is seldom attained. A fair trial is one which satisfies the public interest in getting at the truth, while preserving basic procedural fairness to the accused.

Evidence may render a trial unfair for a variety of reasons. The way in which it was taken may render it unreliable. Its potential for misleading the trier of fact may outweigh such minimal value it might possess. Again, the police may have acted in such an abusive fashion that the court concludes the admission of the evidence would irremediably taint the fairness of the trial itself. In the case at bar, police abuse or unfairness is the only ground raised, and hence the only one with which we need concern ourselves.

. . . .

The question is whether the failure of the foreign police to comply with the procedures required under the Charter in Canada so taints the evidence that its admission would result in an unfair trial. In my view, it does not. This is because the police conduct of which Harrer complains was, viewed in all the circumstances of this case, including the expectations of Harrer in the place where the evidence was taken, neither unfair or abusive. Since the police conduct was not unfair, it follows necessarily that its admission cannot render the trial unfair.

What are the implications of *Harrer* for using discretion to protect against wrongful convictions? At first blush, *Harrer* appears to state the obvious. A trial judge has a duty to protect the fairness of an accused's trial and has a jurisdiction to exclude evidence in furtherance of that duty. Statements to this effect can be found in the common law dating back to the early to mid part of this century. In the classic case of *Noor Mohamed v. R.*, Lord du Parcq noted that the decision to exclude evidence "must then be left to the discretion and the sense of fairness of the judge."[40] The problem, of course, was that what was considered fair depended on the eye of the beholder. Consequently, unfair, at common law, has not historically meant admitting evidence improperly or unfairly obtained no matter how serious the police misconduct.[41] Nor has it meant admitting putatively unreliable evidence.[42]

By recognizing a common law jurisdiction to exclude evidence because of the manner in which it was obtained, *Harrer* has effectively overhauled the common law and freed it from the constraints of its past. It has empowered trial judges to use discretion to ensure fairness regardless of the origins of the unfairness. In other words, there is no policy or principled basis to suggest that reliability should not be factored into the exercise of the *Harrer* discretion. Of course, the relevant question becomes: what do we mean by reliability? In his recommendations at the Guy Paul Morin Inquiry, Commissioner Kaufman urged the adoption of the following approach to the admissibility of jailhouse informers, a category of evidence traditionally linked with wrongful convictions:

> It is my strongly held belief that the dangers associated with jailhouse informant evidence, together with its great potential to mislead, should make such evidence presumptively inadmissible. A trial judge should determine whether the evidence, together with the surrounding circumstances, meets a threshold of reliability sufficient to justify its reception as evidence. If admissible, the jury would determine its ultimate reliability.[43]

---

40 [1949] A.C. 182 (British Guyana P.C.) at 192. Similarly in *Kuruma v. R.*, [1955] A.C. 197 (East Africa P.C.) at 204, Lord Goddard held "[n]o doubt in a criminal case the judge always has a discretion to disallow evidence if the strict rules of admissibility would operate unfairly against an accused."

41 See *R. v. Wray*, [1970] 4 C.C.C. 1 (S.C.C.) at 13, 17, 19.

42 See for example *R. v. Mezzo* (1986), 27 C.C.C. (3d) 97 (S.C.C.); *R. v. Monteleone* (1987), 35 C.C.C. (3d) 193 (S.C.C.). See also *R. v. Wang* (2001), 153 C.C.C. (3d) 321 (Ont. C.A.) (identification evidence); *R. v. Chenier* (2001), [2001] O.J. No. 4708, 2001 CarswellOnt 4354 (S.C.J.); *R. v. Murrin* (1999), [1999] B.C.J. No. 3131, 1999 CarswellBC 3051 (S.C.) and *R. v. Dickins* (1999), [1999] A.J. No. 331, 1999 CarswellAlta 267 (Q.B.) (jailhouse informers). See also the discussion in *McWilliams Canadian Criminal Evidence* (4th edition) (Toronto: Canada Law Book, 2009) at 5-10 to 5-14.2

43 Ontario, *Report of the Commission on Proceedings Involving Guy Paul Morin*, (Kaufman

This kind of approach which focuses on threshold rather than ultimate reliability could be adopted under *Harrer* with respect to any type or class of evidence that has historically been linked to wrongful convictions.[44]

R. v. WHITE

[1999] 2 S.C.R. 417, 24 C.R. (5th) 201, 135 C.C.C. (3d) 257

The accused was charged under the Criminal Code with leaving the scene of an accident. Provincial legislation required persons involved in a traffic accident to complete an accident report. The Court needed to decide whether the accused's statements made under compulsion in the traffic report were admissible in criminal proceedings.

IACOBUCCI J. (LAMER C.J. and GONTHIER, McLACHLIN, BASTARACHE and BINNIE, JJ. concurring):—

. . . .

Although I agree with the majority position in *Harrer* that it may not be necessary to use s. 24(1) in order to exclude evidence whose admission would render the trial unfair, I agree also with McLachlin J.'s finding in that case that s. 24(1) may appropriately be employed as a discrete source of a court's power to exclude such evidence. In the present case, involving an accused who is entitled under s. 7 to use immunity in relation to certain compelled statements in subsequent criminal proceedings, exclusion of the evidence is required. Although the trial judge could have excluded the evidence pursuant to his common law duty to exclude evidence whose admission would render the trial unfair, he chose instead to exclude the evidence pursuant to s. 24(1) of the Charter. I agree that he was entitled to do so.

[Justice L'Heureux-Dubé dissented on the basis that there was evidence to conclude that the third statement, which was made after the police officer had

---

Report) (Toronto: Ontario Ministry of the A.G. 1998) at Volume 1, page 623. It is interesting to note that Justice Cory went further in his Sophonow recommendations and suggested that courts should rarely, in ever, permit the introduction of evidence from jailhouse informers. "Jailhouse Informants, Their Unreliability and the Importance of Complete Crown Disclosure Pertaining to Them - Recommendations" Manitoba, Manitoba Justice, *Report on the Inquiry Regarding Thomas Sophonow* (Winnipeg: Queen's Printer, 2001) (Chair: P. Cory). Available on-line at www.gov.mb.ca/justice/sophonow/.

44 As we will see the Supreme Court has adopted this kind of an approach in determining the admissibility of presumptively inadmissible evidence such as hearsay, similar act and expert opinion evidence. Developing an approach which focuses on threshold reliability should also serve to distinguish the short endorsement of the Supreme Court of Canada in *R. v. Buric* (1997), 114 C.C.C. (3d) 95 (S.C.C.) which is often cited to defeat reliability based admissibility arguments. In *Buric*, Justice Labrosse of the Ontario Court of Appeal concluded that the trial judge had no jurisdiction to exclude the testimony of a witness because his evidence may have been tainted by the police. Applying the traditional common law approach, Justice Labrosse held that the reliability of evidence is for the jury to decide. The Supreme Court adopted Justice Labrosse's opinion in a four line endorsement. It would appear that Justice Labrosse was speaking about ultimate reliability rather than threshold reliability.

informed the accused of her section 10(b) *Charter* rights and her right to silence, was admissible, since it was voluntary and freely made.]

––––––––––––

In addition to the discretion witnessed above we should recognize of course that there is given in the *Charter* an express discretion to exclude evidence obtained in violation of an accused's rights. Section 24 provides:

> 24. (1) Anyone whose rights or freedoms, as guaranteed by this Charter, have been infringed or denied may apply to a court of competent jurisdiction to obtain such remedy as the court considers appropriate and just in the circumstances.

> (2) Where, in proceedings under subsection (1), a court concludes that evidence was obtained in a manner that infringed or denied any rights or freedoms guaranteed by this Charter, the evidence shall be excluded if it is established that, having regard to all the circumstances, the admission of it in the proceedings would bring the administration of justice into disrepute.

Under s. 24(2), the focus is on whether admission of the evidence at trial will bring the administration of justice into disrepute, but the decision will depend on "all the circumstances". As we explain in the preface, this topic is better explored in Criminal Procedure courses since one of the main factors is the seriousness of the Charter violation and this requires a full assessment of each *Charter* right. What follows here is a brief discussion of major Supreme Court rulings on s. 24(2).

In *R. v. Collins*,[45] Chief Justice Lamer identified as a "matter of personal taste" three groups of factors to be considered. Under the first grouping, where an accused had been conscripted against himself, the trial would be rendered unfair and the evidence should generally be excluded. The second factor was the seriousness of the breach and the third, the effect of admission or exclusion on the administration of justice. Ten years later Justice Cory, speaking for a 5-4 majority, in *R. v. Stillman*,[46] refused to change course and held that conscriptive evidence is generally inadmissible — because of its presumed impact on trial fairness — unless it would have been independently discovered. For several years the effect of *Stillman* was the drawing of a bright line: conscripted evidence was almost always excluded and non-conscripted evidence almost always included. A satisfactory definition of conscription also proved elusive. In *Stillman*, Justice Cory described conscription broadly as a process in which the accused is "compelled to participate in the creation or discovery of the evidence," and also as a narrow category approach of compelled incrimination "by means of a statement, the use of the body or the production of bodily samples". Courts tended to rely on the category test when defining conscription, which sometimes led to strange results.

In *R. v. Grant*,[47] a 6-1 majority of the current Supreme Court, having reserved for 15 months, asserted a discretionary approach with revised criteria and emphasis. The *Collins/Stillman* distinction between conscripted and non-conscripted evidence was abandoned. Much of the voluminous prior

––––––––––––

45 [1987] 1 S.C.R. 265 at para. 36.
46 [1997] 1 S.C.R. 607 at para. 80.
47 (2009) 66 C.R. (6th) 1 (S.C.C.).

jurisprudence on s. 24(2) over the past 27 years will now be of little moment. The Court has arrived at a revised discretionary approach to s. 24(2), free of rigid rules but placing special emphasis on the factor of seriousness of the breach rather than the seriousness of the offence or the reliability of the evidence. The same criteria are to be applied to all Charter breaches.

McLachlin C.J. and Charron J. (Binnie, LeBel, Fish and Abella JJ. concurring) settled on the following revised template:

> When faced with an application for exclusion under s. 24(2), a court must assess and balance the effect of admitting the evidence on society's confidence in the justice system having regard to: (1) the seriousness of the Charter-infringing state conduct (admission may send the message the justice system condones serious state misconduct), (2) the impact of the breach on the Charter-protected interests of the accused (admission may send the message that individual rights count for little), and (3) society's interest in the adjudication of the case on its merits. The court's role on a s. 24(2) application is to balance the assessments under each of these lines of inquiry to determine whether, considering all the circumstances, admission of the evidence would bring the administration of justice into disrepute.

According to the Chief Justice and Justice Charron, the words of s. 24(2) capture its purpose: to maintain the good repute of the administration of justice. Viewed broadly, the term "administration of justice" embraces maintaining the rule of law and upholding Charter rights in the justice system as a whole. The phrase "bring the administration of justice into disrepute" must be understood in the long-term sense of maintaining the integrity of, and public confidence in, the justice system.

Whether there will be more or less exclusion in the future will likely only become evident after several years of applying *Grant*. The Court has clearly decided that evidence can no longer be excluded simply because it was conscripted — which may well result in less exclusion in breathalyser and bodily sample cases, for example.

However, favouring exclusion is the Court's important rulings that the seriousness of Charter violation is the first consideration and that the same analysis is to be applied whatever the seriousness of the offence. This is made especially clear by Chief Justice McLachlin speaking for the 6-1 majority in the companion case of *R. v. Harrison*:[48]

> As Cronk J.A. [dissenting in the Ontario Court of Appeal in the Court below] put it, allowing the seriousness of the offence and the reliability of the evidence to overwhelm the s. 24(2) analysis "would deprive those charged with serious crimes of the protection of the individual freedoms afforded to all Canadians under the *Charter* and, in effect, declare that in the administration of the criminal law 'the ends justify the means'" (para. 150). *Charter* protections must be construed so as to apply to everyone, even those alleged to have committed the most serious criminal offences. [The] ... trial judge seemed to imply that where the evidence is reliable and the charge is serious, admission will always be the result. As *Grant* makes clear, this is not the law.

> Additionally, the trial judge's observation that the *Charter* breaches "pale in comparison to the criminality involved" in drug trafficking risked the appearance of turning the s. 24(2) inquiry into a contest between the misdeeds of the police and

---

48   (2009) 66 C.R. (6th) 105 (S.C.C.).

those of the accused. The fact that a *Charter* breach is less heinous than the offence charged does not advance the inquiry mandated by s. 24(2). We expect police to adhere to higher standards than alleged criminals.

Exclusion is also favoured by the Court's determination that although reliability of the evidence and that it is essential to the Crown's case are relevant considerations for admission, they are not trump cards. This is very evident in the Court's decision in the companion case of *R. v. Harrison*[49] to exclude 35 kilograms of cocaine found in a vehicle search in violation of search and seizure and arbitrary detention rights in ss. 8 and 9.[50]

In addition to section 24, there may now also be a jurisdiction at common law to exclude evidence whose admission would bring the administration of justice into disrepute. In *R. v. Buhay*,[51] Justice Arbour, for the Court, observed:

> . . . I wish to stress that even if the reasoning of the Court of Appeal were sound and that there had been no search and seizure triggering s. 8 of the *Charter*, remedies other than under the *Charter* might be available in such a case to an accused seeking exclusion of the impugned evidence. Indeed, even in the absence of a *Charter* breach, judges have a discretion at common law to exclude evidence obtained in circumstances such that it would result in unfairness if the evidence was admitted at trial, or if the prejudicial effect of admitting the evidence outweighs its probative value (see, in the context of confessions: *R. v. Rothman*, [1981] 1 S.C.R. 640, at p. 696, per Lamer J., as he then was; *R. v. Oickle*, [2000] 2 S.C.R.3, 2000 SCC 38, at para. 69, per Iacobucci J.; see also J. Sopinka, S. N. Lederman and A. W. Bryant, *The Law of Evidence in Canada* (2nd ed. 1999), at pp. 339-40); see also, in other contexts, *R. v. Harrer*, [1995] 3 S.C.R. 562, per La Forest J.; Caucci, *supra*, at paras. 13 and 17; Sopinka, Lederman and Bryant, *supra*, at pp. 30-33). Such an argument was not advanced in this case as the appellant maintained throughout that he was entitled to a *Charter* remedy for a s. 8 violation. In light of my conclusion on the s. 8 issue, it is not necessary to explore further whether this common law discretion could have extended to the exclusion of real evidence in circumstances such as here. Rather, we must turn to whether the marijuana illegally seized by the police should be excluded under s. 24(2) because its admission "would bring the administration of justice into disrepute."[52]

---

49 (2009) 66 C.R. (6th) 105 (S.C.C.).

50 Early Canadian commentary has been largely favourable: see, especially, Professors David Paciocco, Revisions to David Paciocco and Lee Stuesser, *The Law of Evidence* (5th ed., 2008, Irwin Law) (2009); Tim Quigley, "Was it Worth the Wait? The Supreme Court's Approaches to Detention and Exclusion of Evidence", (2009) 67 C.R. (6th) 88; and Don Stuart, "Welcome Flexibility and Better Criteria for Section 24(2)", (2009) 66 C.R. (6th) 82. See further, Stuart, *Charter Justice in Canadian Criminal Law* (5th ed., 2010), ch. 11, "Charter Remedies". However, Professor Hamish Stewart in "The *Grant* Trilogy and the Right Against Self-incrimination" (2009) 67 C.R. (6th) 97 expresses concerns that the Court has diminished the right against self- incrimination.

51 (2003), 10 C.R. (6th) 205 (S.C.C.).

52 For criticism see Michael Plaxton, "Who Needs Section 24(2)? Or Common Law Sleight-of-Hand" (2005) 23 C.R. (6th) 229. In *P.(D.) v. Wagg* (2004) 184 C.C.C. (3d) 312 (Ont. C.A.), involving discovery in a civil suit for sexual assault, the Court accepted that section 24 of the Charter could be applied to give a just remedy given that the Charter had been breached by an agent of the State.

PROBLEMS

Problem 1

In a civil suit for negligent injury arising out of a motor vehicle collision counsel wants the jury to see pictures of the plaintiff's injuries soon after her emergency surgery. Her face is bruised and disfigured with bones showing and also medical pins to hold her fractured skull together. Relevant? Receivable? Does it matter that the photographs are in colour? What if counsel for the plaintiff wants to wheel in the plaintiff in her hospital bed where she has been confined for a year? Relevant? Receivable? See *Draper v. Jacklyn*, [1970] S.C.R. 192 and compare *R. v. Wade* (1994), 18 O.R. (3d) 33 (C.A.), *R v. S-R (J.)*, (2008) 236 C.C.C. (3d) 486 (Ont. S.C.) and *R. v. Teerhuis-Moar*, (2009) C.R. (6th) (Man. Q.B.).

Problem 2

In a prosecution for assault causing bodily harm the accused argued self-defence. The incident occurred at Joe's Bar. The accused wants to lead evidence that the alleged victim had a reputation as a bully. That the alleged victim regularly beat on newcomers to the bar. Relevant? Receivable? Does it matter whether the accused was aware of the alleged victim's reputation prior to the incident? Why? If you say the evidence is relevant, what is the premise that rationally connects the evidence offered with the proposition sought to be established? Is that premise indisputable? Usually true? Sometimes true? Rarely true?

Problem 3

The accused was charged with speeding. He allegedly travelled 30 K.P.H. in a school zone that prescribed a limit of 20 K.P.H. The prosecutor wants to call a witness who will testify that he saw the accused, a block away from the school zone, travelling at 40 K.P.H. in a 30 K.P.H. zone. Relevant? Why? Premise? Always or sometimes true? Suppose the observation was made three blocks away? A mile away? Accused wants to tender evidence that the police officer who gave him the speeding ticket had been told by his superior that week that if he didn't issue his quota of speeding tickets he'd be suspended. Relevant? Prejudicial? Receivable?

Problem 4

The accused is charged with the theft of a rare stamp. The Crown wants to lead evidence that the accused is a stamp collector. Relevant? Premise? Receivable? Sufficient?

Problem 5

Smith sues Jones for damages arising out of a motor vehicle accident. Jones earlier pleaded guilty to a charge of dangerous driving arising out of the same incident and Smith seeks to tender this fact in evidence. No conviction was entered. Relevant? Receivable? See *Pollard v. Simon*, [2009] B.C.J. No. 1258 (P.C.). If Jones had pleaded not guilty would that fact be relevant? Receivable when tendered by Jones? If he was acquitted would that fact be receivable? If convicted? See *Toronto (City) v. C.U.P.E., Local 79*, [2003] 3 S.C.R. 77. What if the trial judge in the criminal case concluded that not only was there reasonable doubt but she was satisfied that Jones was innocent? See *Polgrain Estate v. Toronto East General Hospital* (2008), 60 C.R. (6th) 67 (Ont. C.A.).

Problem 6

The accused is charged with possession of a weapon for a purpose dangerous to the public peace. In his bedroom the police found a loaded .25 calibre pistol. From a kitchen cupboard they seized notes handwritten in Italian. The notes have been translated and an expert has testified that they are a constitution of a secret Italian criminal organization related to the Mafia and that anyone in possession of them almost certainly had to belong to the organization. Are the notes relevant? Receivable? Compare *R. v. Caccamo* (1975), 29 C.R.N.S. 78 (S.C.C.).

Problem 7

Plaintiff sues defendant bus company for personal injuries sustained as the result of negligent operation of a bus claimed to belong to the defendant. On the facts presented the defendant concedes that the evidence warranted the submission to the jury of the question of the operator's negligence in the management of the bus. The accident occurred on Main Street at 1:00 a.m. and the only description of the bus came from the plaintiff who was able to describe the bus simply as "a great big, long, wide affair." Records at City Hall indicate that the defendant bus company was the only bus company licensed to operate on that street. The defendant's timetable shows its buses scheduled to leave North Square for South Square via Main Street at 12:15 a.m., 12:45 a.m., 1:15 a.m., and 1:45 a.m. Are these records relevant? Receivable? Sufficient? Compare *Smith v. Rapid Transit Inc.*, 58 N.E. 2d 754 (Mass. Sup. Ct., 1945). See also *People v. Collins*, 438 P. 2d 33 (Cal. Sup. Ct., 1968).

Problem 8

In a civil suit for negligence plaintiff seeks to tender evidence that the defendant is insured. Relevant? Plaintiff argues that it is rational to infer that a person who is insured is less apt to careful, as he is fully protected against loss, and to then infer that he was careless on the particular occasion under review. Defendant argues that being insured marks him as one of those careful and wise individuals who take all appropriate precautions against risk. If the evidence is relevant ought it to be received? See *Hamstra v. BC Rugby Union*, [1997] 1 S.C.R. 1092.

Problem 9

The accused is charged with the murder of his wife. Following the discovery of the body and upon informing his children that their mother was dead, the accused unsuccessfully took his own life. Is the evidence admissible? On what basis? Is the strength of the Crown's case relevant to the question of admissibility? See *R. v. Sodhi* (2003), 179 C.C.C. (3d) 60 (Ont. C.A.).

Problem 10

The accused was arrested at Pearson International Airport after returning to Toronto following a trip to Ghana. Customs officers discovered 1.038 kilograms of heroin secreted in the insoles of three pairs of shoes that were found in his possession. The only disputed issue at trial was knowledge. The accused testified that a former girlfriend who lives in Ghana gave him the shoes and that he was not aware that they contained heroin. Apart from the evidence relating to the discovery of the heroin, the Crown relied on evidence of its value and of the accused's poor financial situation in an effort to demonstrate a motive to import narcotics into Canada.

The accused was convicted and appealed against his conviction and sentence. It was argued that the evidence as to his financial status had been wrongly admitted. It had been designed to exploit stereotypical views about the economically disadvantaged and amounted to a form of propensity reasoning. The evidence was not only prejudicial, but was also of minimal probative value, offensive, and unfair. Was this evidence properly admitted?

See *R. v. Mensah* (2003), 9 C.R. (6th) 339 (Ont. C.A.), leave to appeal refused (2003), 2003 CarswellOnt 3640, 2003 CarswellOnt 3641 (S.C.C.). See comments by Michael C. Plaxton, "Poverty and Motive", (2003) 9 C.R. (6th) 345 and David Tanovich, "Relevance, Social Context and Poverty" (2003), 9 C.R. (6th) 348. See further, *R. v. Phillips*, [2008] O.J. No. 4194 (C.A.).

Problem 11

A police officer shot to death a man stopped as a robbery suspect. The officer testified that he did so because the victim made a quick movement with his hand to his coat as if going for a gun. The officer was sued for a civil rights violation. The jury found against the officer and awarded $ 1.6 million in damages. The officer appeals on the basis that the trial judge erred in placing before the jury that the victim was in fact unarmed. Relevant? Premise? Receivable? See *Sherrod v. Berry*, 856 F.2d 002 (U.S. 7th Cir., 1988).

Problem 12

The accused was charged with murder after his 22-year-old girlfriend, a student at the Scarborough campus of the University of Toronto, disappeared in circumstances suggesting foul play. The victim's body was never found. The accused was convicted of the murder in 1992, but the Court of Appeal quashed the conviction and ordered a new trial in 2004.

At the opening of the second trial, the accused applied to introduce third-party suspect evidence suggesting that the victim may have been murdered by Paul Bernardo. The proffered evidence was of two kinds. First, there was evidence of Bernardo's proven crimes of sexual assault and murder. Second, there was other evidence linking Bernardo to the victim's murder, including evidence that Bernardo had met the victim, evidence that the victim had been seen with a man matching Bernardo's general description, evidence that Bernardo was seen acting suspiciously on the Scarborough campus around the time of the victim's disappearance, and evidence of other crimes admitted by Bernardo but not established by independent investigation. Rule.

Compare *R. v. Baltovich* (2008) 56 C.R. (6th) 369 (Ont. S.C.).

Chapter 4

Character Evidence
as Test Case
of Relevance and Discretion

1. HABIT

Evidence of how a person acted on another occasion is evidence of a circumstance from which we ask the trier of fact to infer that the person acted in a similar fashion on the occasion being litigated. If the evidence is that the person always, invariably, acted in a certain way, the circumstantial evidence is very probative and deserves to be received. We label this as evidence of Habit but see it for what it is — a piece of circumstantial evidence, more specific than evidence of the person's general character but differing only in degree and not in kind. If the circumstantial evidence indicates invariable habit the evidence is very powerful. If the evidence is that the person normally acted in that way the circumstantial evidence is less powerful. If the evidence is that he acted in that way occasionally the court may have concerns that the time necessary to hear the evidence may not be justified given the low probative value. If the evidence is of the person's general character or personality trait, the court recognizes that, even though the person' s character or trait has relevance, the probative value may be outweighed by competing considerations and should be excluded. The court recognizes that even so-called "good people" sometimes do bad things and "bad people" do good things. Plumbing the depths of their character may not be worth the time and trouble. Determining receivability is thus seen to be a matter for the trial judge's discretion where she weighs probative value against the dangers of consumption of time, confusion of the issues and prejudice to the proper outcome of the trial.

McCormick distinguished between habit and character:

> Although the courts frown on evidence of traits of character when introduced to prove how a person or organization acted on a given occasion, they are more receptive to evidence of personal habits or of the customary behaviour of organizations. To understand this difference one must appreciate the distinction between habit and character. The two are easily confused. People sometimes speak of a habit for care, a habit for promptness, or a habit of forgetfulness. They may say that an individual has a bad habit of stealing or lying. Evidence of these "habits" would be identical to the kind of evidence that is the target of the general rule against character evidence. Character is a generalized description of a person's disposition, or of the disposition in respect to a general trait, such as honesty, temperance or peacefulness. Habit, in the present context, is more specific. It denotes one's regular response to a repeated

situation. If we speak of a character for care, we think of the person's tendency to act prudently in all the varying situations of life – in business, at home, in handling automobiles and in walking across the street. A habit, on the other hand, is the person's regular practice of responding to a particular kind of situation with a specific type of conduct. Thus, a person may be in the habit of bounding down a certain stairway two or three steps at a time, of patronizing a particular pub after each day's work, or of driving his automobile without using a seatbelt. The doing of the habitual act may become semi-automatic, as with a driver who invariably signals before changing lanes.

Evidence of habits that come within this definition has greater probative value than does evidence of general traits of character. Furthermore, the potential for prejudice is substantially less. By and large, the detailed patterns of situation-specific behaviour that constitute habits are unlikely to provoke such sympathy or antipathy as would distort the process of evaluating the evidence.

As a result, many jurisdictions accept the proposition that evidence of habit is admissible to show an act. These courts only reject the evidence categorically if the putative habit is not sufficiently regular or uniform, or if the circumstances are not sufficiently similar to outweigh the dangers of prejudice, distraction and time-consumption.[1]

BELKNAP v. MEAKES
(1989), 64 D.L.R. (4th) 452 (B.C.C.A.)

The Court allowed an appeal from a finding of negligence.

SEATON J.A. (HUTCHEON and WALLACE JJ.A. concurring):—

. . . .

The defence had a difficult time putting its case. Dr. Meakes was prevented from saying what he did before the operation. He could not specifically remember it. That is understandable. Nearly three years elapsed between the operation and the trial, and two and one-half years elapsed between the operation and the time the allegation of negligent blood pressure management was raised. Dr. Meakes said that his "pre-operative assessment is a very standard part of my practice" and that he could say what had happened "because this is a habit from which I do not waiver". The trial judge said that he did not think the evidence was admissible unless the witness could "remember what he said to Mr. Belknap" and that if the evidence of Dr. Meakes's practice from which he did not waiver was admitted it carried so little weight that it would be "not much help to me at all".

If a person can say of something he regularly does in his professional life that he invariably does it in a certain way, that surely is evidence and possibly convincing evidence that he did it in that way on the day in question.

Wigmore on Evidence, vol. IA (Tillers rev. 1983), states that there is no reason why habit should not be used as evidence either of negligent action or of careful action (para. 97), and that habit should be admissible as a substitute for present recollection. *Phipson on Evidence*, 13th ed. (1982), paras. 9-22, reaches a similar conclusion.

---

1 McCormick, *Evidence* (5th ed., 1999), pp. 686-90.

Similar reasoning admits evidence of a general course of business, a question dealt with by the New Brunswick Court of Appeal in *Medical Arts Ltd. v. Minister of Municipal Affairs* (1977), 17 N.B.R. (2d) 147 at p. 152:

> The evidence adduced on behalf of the Minister of the usual course of business in the district office together with the certificate of the post office employee date stamped September 3, 1974 were admissible to prove the sending to the respondent of the documents referred to in s. 25(4) of the Act. *Phipson on Evidence*, 7th ed. states at p. 102:
>
>> To prove that an act has been done, it is admissible to prove any general course of business or office, whether public or private, according to which it would ordinarily have been done; there being a probability that the general course will be followed in the particular case.

R. v. WATSON
(1996), 50 C.R. (4th) 245, 108 C.C.C. (3d) 310 (Ont. C.A.)

The accused was charged with murder. The Crown took the position that the accused, with Headley and Cain, went to the deceased's premises, armed, with the intention of killing the deceased. The deceased went to the rear of the premises while the accused remained near the front office. The Crown took the position that the accused remained on guard in the front area and was guilty as an aider and abetter. The accused took the position that the shooting was the result of a dispute which arose in the context of a private drug transaction between the deceased and Headley. According to the accused, the deceased was hit five times by Headley, and the deceased shot Cain, who was standing some distance away, unarmed. The accused claimed to have panicked, then fled the scene with Headley and Cain.

The accused wanted to introduce the evidence of Mair, a good friend of the deceased, to demonstrate that the deceased had a habit of carrying a gun. In a statement to the police, Mair had said that the deceased always carried a gun; in fact, the gun was like a credit card for the deceased, since he never left home without it. The trial judge found that this evidence was irrelevant. He concluded that there was no viable issue of self-defence, that there was no evidence that the deceased had a gun on the day in question, and that there was no evidence that he fired a gun, if he did have a gun in his possession on that date.

The accused was convicted of manslaughter and successfully appealed.

DOHERTY J.A. (MORDEN A.C.J.O. and ARBOUR J.A. concurring): —

. . . .

Where a person's conduct in given circumstances is in issue, evidence that the person repeatedly acted in a certain way when those circumstances arose in the past has been received as circumstantial evidence that the person acted in conformity with past practice on the occasion in question: *Cross and Tapper on Evidence*, 8th ed. (1995) at pp. 25-26; *Wigmore on Evidence*: Tillers Rev. (1983) Vol. 1A, pp. 1607-1610; R. Delisle, *Evidence Principles and Problems,* 4th ed. (1996) at p. 38; *McCormick on Evidence*, 4th ed. (1992), Vol. I, pp. 825-830. For example, in *McCormick* at p. 826 it is said:

> Surely any sensible person in investigating whether a given individual did a particular act would be greatly helped in his inquiry by evidence as to whether that individual was in the habit of doing it.

The position taken in these authorities is, in my opinion, consistent with human experience and logic. The fact that a person is in the habit of doing a certain thing in a given situation suggests that on a specific occasion in which those circumstances arose the person acted in accordance with established practice. It makes the conclusion that the person acted in a particular way more likely than it would be without the evidence of habit. Evidence of habit is therefore properly viewed as circumstantial evidence that a person acted in a certain way on the occasion in issue.

Evidence of habit is closely akin to, but not identical to, evidence of disposition. Evidence of habit involves an inference of conduct on a given occasion based on an established pattern of past conduct. It is an inference of conduct from conduct. Evidence of disposition involves an inference of the existence of a state of mind (disposition) from a person's conduct on one or more previous occasions and a further inference of conduct on the specific occasion based on the existence of that state of mind. Evidence of habit proceeds on the basis that repeated conduct in a given situation is a reliable predictor of conduct in that situation. Evidence of disposition is premised on the belief that a person's disposition is a reliable predictor of conduct in a given situation.

The distinction between evidence of habit and evidence of disposition is demonstrated by a comparison of this case and the facts in *Scopelliti*. Here the defence wanted to show that the deceased habitually carried a gun in the past and to invite the jury to infer from that prior conduct that he had a gun when he was shot. In *Scopelliti*, the defence wanted to show that the deceased had on occasions in the past been the aggressor in physical confrontations with others and to invite the jury to infer, first that the deceased was a physically aggressive person (his disposition), and second that the deceased's actions at the relevant time were in keeping with his physically aggressive nature. Like evidence of habit, evidence of disposition can constitute circumstantial evidence of conduct on a specific occasion. The inferences necessary to render disposition evidence relevant to prove conduct on a specific occasion may be more difficult to draw than those required where evidence of habit is tendered.

The recognition that evidence of habit is relevant to prove conduct on a specific occasion begs the more fundamental question — what is a habit? *McCormick* at p. 826 describes habit as:

> the person's regular practice of responding to a particular kind of situation with a specific type of conduct.

Habit therefore involves a repeated and specific response to a particular situation.

Mair's graphic assertion that the deceased carried a gun "like a credit card. He never left home without it" strongly suggests repeated and specific conduct. Mair's statement does not suggest that the deceased's possession of a weapon was limited to any particular situation. To the contrary, Mair indicated that the deceased always carried a gun. The general nature of the habit described by Mair does not affect the relevance of the evidence, but would, along with other aspects of the evidence (e.g., the duration and regularity of the habit), go to the weight to be given to the evidence by the jury.

Having concluded that evidence that the deceased always carried a gun was relevant to the question of whether he had a gun when he was shot, I turn to the second level of the relevance inquiry. Mair's evidence may put the deceased in possession of a gun at the material time, but standing alone it cannot support the inference that he fired the gun at that time. In fact, Mair's evidence did not suggest that the deceased had ever used his gun. The further inference from possession to use of the weapon is essential to make Mair's evidence relevant to any issue in the trial. The availability of that inference requires a consideration of the rest of the evidence.

There were at most three people at the back of the warehouse. The deceased and Cain were shot and the evidence does not suggest that Cain shot himself. He must have been shot by either Headley or the deceased. Headley definitely shot the deceased and at least two of the bullets which hit the deceased came from a different gun than the one used to shoot Cain. There were, therefore, two possibilities. Either Cain was shot by the deceased or Headley fired two different guns hitting the deceased with one and Cain with the other. In my opinion, a jury, having concluded that the deceased was armed, could have inferred that Cain was shot not by his friend Headley, but by the deceased who was the target of Headley's assault.

I am further satisfied, had the jury inferred that the deceased was armed and fired a weapon, that those inferences could logically have influenced the jury's conclusion as to the origins of the shooting. If the deceased was unarmed, the circumstances strongly suggest a preconceived plan to shoot the deceased. If the deceased was armed and used his weapon, then the possibility that the shooting was a result of a spontaneous confrontation between Headley and the deceased, both of whom were armed, becomes a viable one. If the shooting was the product of an armed confrontation between the two men it could reasonably be inferred that the confrontation arose during the discussion involving Headley and the deceased. If the confrontation arose in this manner, it offered strong support for the appellant's contention that he was not party to any plan to kill or do harm to the deceased. Therefore, evidence supporting the inferences that the deceased was armed and used a weapon during the confrontation made the defence position as to the appellant's non-involvement in any plan to kill or do harm to the deceased more viable than it would have been if those inferences were not available. Mair's proposed evidence, which provided the basis for those inferences, was, therefore, relevant to a material fact in issue. In so concluding, I do not pass on the cogency of the inferences relied on by the defence or attempt to measure the effect of the proposed evidence on the jury's assessment of the appellant's liability. I limit myself to the inquiry demanded by our concept of relevancy.[2]

---

2 *Watson* was applied in *R. v. Pilon,* (2009) 64 C.R. (6th) 356 (Ont. C.A.) to evidence that the victim had a violent disposition and had a habit of carrying a gun. Doherty J.A. held that the

How many occurrences are necessary to infer habit?

DEVGAN v. COLLEGE OF PHYSICIANS & SURGEONS (ONTARIO)
[2005] O.J. No. 306, 2005 CarswellOnt 342 (Div. Ct.)

Dr. Devgan was charged with professional misconduct in his treatment of three terminally ill cancer patients. The Discipline Committee of the College of Physicians and Surgeons concluded that he charged exorbitant fees for the treatments and failed to fairly and accurately explain the likelihood of success. On appeal, Devgan argued that the Committee had erred in excluding evidence of what he told other cancer patients about a cure as this was relevant to the issue of what he told these three patients. The appeal was dismissed.

THEN J. (GRAVELY and WHALEN JJ. concurring): —

... [T]he exclusion of the evidence of the representations made by the Appellant to other cancer patients is more problematic if, as the Appellant submits, the excluded evidence was admissible as evidence of habit or routine. Although counsel for either parties had not supplied the court nor the Committee with any authority on this issue, evidence of habit or routine has been ruled to be admissible both in a criminal and civil context.

[The Court discusses *R. v. Watson.*]

It is also useful to refer to the observations of Professors Delisle and Stuart in Evidence. Principles and Problems, 6th edition, Carswell, where they explain with their customary clarity the basis of admissibility and the probative value of evidence of habit at p. 125:

> Evidence of how a person acted on another occasion is evidence of a circumstance from which we ask the trier of fact to infer that the person acted in a similar fashion on the occasion being litigated. If the evidence is that the person always, invariably, acted in a certain way, the circumstantial evidence is very probative and deserves to be received. We label this as evidence of Habit but see it for what it is - a piece of circumstantial evidence, more specific than evidence of the person's general character but differing only in degree and not in kind. If the circumstantial evidence indicates invariable habit the evidence is very powerful. If the evidence is that the person normally acted in that way the circumstantial evidence is less powerful. If the evidence is that he acted in that way occasionally the court may have concerns that the time necessary to hear the evidence may not be justified given the low probative value.

In the civil context, the decision of the British Columbia Court of Appeal in *Belknap v. Meakes* (1980) 64 D.L.R. (4th) 452 is instructive as there is some factual similarity to the instant case.

[The Court quotes from the decision.]

---

trial judge had rightly excluded some of this evidence tendered by the defence in this first degree murder trial on the basis that its prejudicial effect substantially outweighs its probative value.

In the instant case there was no issue as to the admissibility of the evidence of the Appellant as to the representations he routinely claimed to have made to all of his cancer patients. It is of some importance to consider the Appellant's own evidence of what he routinely told his patients before considering the admissibility of the proffered evidence of the 3 or 4 other cancer patients as to what the Appellant represented to them. The Appellant's evidence was that he never told any patient that his treatments would cure them because to do so was improper. What he did tell them was that he could not promise a cure but that only God could do that. He told them that his treatments would not harm them but would help them feel better and to become stronger to fight the cancer and might prolong life and that while his treatments had helped some patients his treatments did not help all patients.

In my view, the terse outline by counsel of the proffered evidence of the 3 or 4 other cancer patients simply amounts to this: 1) the Appellant did not say anything about a cure; 2) the Appellant did say that his treatment did "work" on other patients. In the context of the Appellant seeing four to five cancer patients a week over a number of years the proffered evidence that he did not mention a cure on 3 or 4 specific occasions which are not even identified by means of a timeline does not amount to evidence of any habit or routine on the part of the Appellant to never mention a cure within any of the authorities to which I have referred or have been able to find. In my view, at its highest this evidence may be minimally supportive of the credibility of the Appellant that he never mentioned a cure to his cancer patients. Even if the evidence could have been used for that limited purpose its probative value is so slight that it was properly excluded in the exercise of its discretion by the Committee.

In *McCormick on Evidence* (5th ed.) Practitioner Treatise Series Vol. 1 (1999) West Group, the authors state that there must be enough instances to permit the finding of habit and provide a helpful example to demonstrate how evidence of specific instances may result in admissibility of evidence of routine conduct or exclusion at the discretion of the court. At p. 690 in footnote 22 the authors state:

> 22. See, e.g., *Strauss v. Douglass Aircraft Co.*, 404 F.2d 1152, 1158 (2d Cir. 1968); *Wilson v. Volkswagen of America*, 561 F.2d 494, 511-12 (4th Cir. 1977); *Coats & Clark, Inc. v. Gay*, 755 F.2d 1506, 1511 (11th Cir. 1985) ("the methods employed by a single warehouser at a single location are not sufficiently probative of the custom of the warehouse industry generally"); *State v. Mary*, 368 N.W.2d 166, 168-169 (Iowa 1985) (10-12 observations of nurse drawing blood samples adequate to show habitual features of her procedure); *Weisenberger v. Senger*, 381 N.W.2d 187, 191 (N.D. 1986) (insufficient number of observations to establish habit of driving on extreme right of narrow country roads); *Steinberg v. Arcilla*, 535 N.W.2d 444 (Wis.Ct.App.1995) (anesthesiologist's regular response of positioning arms of patients in certain way during each of 65 to 70 cases per month); *Lewan*, supra note 1; Mode Code Evid. R. 307(3) ("many instances"); supra note 10.

And footnote 24 contains the following example:

> See supra ss. 185. Thus, citing illustrations to the Model Code of Evidence Rule 307, the Federal Advisory Committee mentions the possibility of admitting testimony by

W that on numerous occasions he had been with X when X crossed a railroad track and that on each occasion X had first stopped and looked in both directions, but that offers of ten witnesses, each testifying to a different occasion, might be excluded in the discretion of the court. Note to Fed.R.Evid. 406(b).

It will be evident that in this case evidence of 3 or 4 witnesses who can testify only that the Appellant did not mention anything about a cure but do not purport to testify about anything the Appellant states he routinely or habitually did tell his patients about a cure does not rise to the probative value of the evidence mentioned in the example. In my view, the Committee was not unreasonable in excluding this evidence in its discretion nor was the Appellant deprived of natural justice or unfairly impeded in establishing his defence.

In considering whether the bad character exclusionary rule applies in criminal cases, what matters is not whether the evidence can be characterized as habit but whether it is discreditable.

R. v. B. (L.)
(1997), 116 C.C.C. (3d) 481, 9 C.R. (5th) 38 (Ont. C.A.)

CHARRON J.A. (McMURTRY C.J. and DOHERTY J.A. concurring): —

... Where the Crown seeks to introduce evidence of the conduct of an accused other than which forms the subject-matter of the charge, it is the adverse reflection that this evidence may have on the accused's character that signals the need for further investigation. One should ask, is the prior conduct discreditable? If it is not, the rationale underlying the similar fact evidence rule will not apply. Unless the proposed evidence, which does not discredit the accused, triggers the application of some other exclusionary rule of evidence, it is admissible. However, where the other conduct is sufficiently discreditable that it may prejudice the trier of fact against the accused, the similar fact evidence rule does apply and its probative value must outweigh its prejudicial effect before it will be admitted.

Professors Paciocco and Stuesser set out an example that distinguishes will between discreditable conduct and other conduct which does not discredit the accused:

> So, evidence that the accused was in the habit of carrying a concealed, illegal weapon should be inadmissible unless it conforms to the similar fact evidence rule. By contrast, the similar fact evidence rule does not apply to evidence that the accused was in the habit of smoking a particular brand of cigarette that was found at the scene of a crime. . . .

The authors in fact start off by saying that "[i]t is important in applying these rules to distinguish between 'character' and 'habit'." (Other authors have drawn such a distinction as well: see, for example, Strong, ed., McCormick on Evidence, 4th ed., vol. 1 (1992), at pp. 825-30.) However, Paciocco and Stuesser, in explaining why the distinction must be made, identify discreditability as the distinguishing feature that will trigger the application of the similar fact evidence rule, regardless of whether the evidence can be categorized as character or habit. I agree with that conclusion.

2. CHARACTER

(a) Admissible as Directly Relevant to Material Issue or as Evidence of Disposition (Propensity)

Before examining the evidence rules concerning character we need to recognize that character evidence may be relevant in different ways. A person's conduct or reputation previous to the event being litigated may be relevant to a material issue in the case without the necessity of the trier of fact inferring that the person acted in conformity with his or her previous conduct or reputation on the occasion under review. For example, in a case of assault, a claim of self-defence might be founded on the accused's belief, based on his understanding of the victim's previous conduct or reputation, that the victim had a disposition towards violent behaviour; such a belief, if honestly held, could cause the accused to view the victim's conduct with apprehension and so cause the accused to strike out at the victim. The chain of reasoning which we ask the trier of fact to follow in these cases does not involve the necessity of inferring that the person acted in conformity with his or her character. The evidence of character is led, and the trier is asked simply to infer from it that the accused's belief was genuine.

Occasionally the character of a person is not just relevant to a fact in issue but rather is itself a material point in the case; an operative fact which dictates rights and liabilities. For example, in an action for defamation in which justification is pleaded, the plaintiff's reputation or character is the determining matter. An action for wrongful dismissal might include as a material issue the lack of fitness or competency of the employee.

When the character of a person is relevant to a fact in issue other than by inferring from the character to the conduct of the person, or when the substantive law makes the character material as the very core of the inquiry, evidence of it must be admitted.[3] For example the Ontario Court of Appeal in *R. v. Kruge*[4] admitted evidence of threats and spying by the accused on a former girlfriend as character evidence of motive directly at issue where he was charged with her murder.[5] In such cases courts have usually[6] held that there need be no warning as to the limited use to be made of character evidence.

Consider the broad approach to admissibility in the following endorsement judgment:

---

3 See *R. v. G. (S.G.)*, 8 C.R. (5th) 198, [1997] 2 S.C.R. 716, 116 C.C.C. (3d) 193; *R. v. Lepage*, 95 C.C.C. (3d) 385, 36 C.R. (4th) 145, [1995] 1 S.C.R. 654; *R. v. Hinchey*, 111 C.C.C. (3d) 353, 3 C.R. (5th) 187, [1996] 3 S.C.R. 1128 and *R. v. Davison* (1974), 20 C.C.C. (2d) 424 (Ont. C.A.).

4 (2000), 31 C.R. (5th) 314 (Ont. C.A.).

5   See too *R. v. Escobar-Benavidez*, 200 C.C.C. (3d) 287, [2005] 3 S.C.R. 386; *R. v. G. (S.G.)* (1997), 8 C.R. (5th) 198 (S.C.C.), *R. v. Merz* (1999), 140 C.C.C. (3d) 259 (Ont. C.A.) and *R. v. Sandhu*, (2009) 63 C.R. (6th) 1 (Ont. C.A.); and *R. v. D.(D.)*, (2005) 203 C.C.C. (3d) 6 (B.C. C.A.) (criminal harassment to establish context as to whether complainant fearful or accused reckless)

6 See, recently, *Sandhu*, *supra*, note 5. However, sometimes courts require a warning against use to show general propensity (e.g. *D.(D.)*, above note; *R. v. Rodrigues*, (2007) 223 C.C.C. (3d) 53 (Yuk. C.A.); and *R. v. Seck*, (2007) 52 C.R. (6th) 300 (Que. C.A.)).

R. v. W. (L.)
2004 CarswellOnt 4138, [2004] O.J. No. 4163 (C.A.)

THE COURT (LABROSSE, MACPHERSON and CRONK JJ.A.):

1 The appellant appeals his conviction for sexual assault by Byers J. of the Superior Court of Justice.

2 The complainant met the appellant over the telephone in December 2000. . . . She sponsored the appellant to join her in Canada and he arrived in August 2002. Thereafter, the complainant alleged that their previously good relationship changed and the appellant became extremely domineering and controlling. Over the next few months, she alleged that he assaulted her, both physically and sexually, on several occasions. The appellant was convicted of assault in March 2003, but the couple got back together after he vowed to change his ways.

3 The complainant alleged that he began to abuse her again and, in June 2003, he was charged with assault and sexual assault. . . . .

4 At the trial, the appellant challenged the complainant's allegations, suggesting that she had a motive to fabricate the offences and that the sex between them was consensual. The appellant did not testify. He was acquitted of the assault charge and convicted of sexual assault.

. . .

6 In our view, the circumstances of the present case support the admissibility of the . . . prior discreditable conduct evidence. This evidence related to the history of domestic abuse in the relationship between the appellant and the complainant and it had probative value regarding the material issues in the prosecution.

7 The evidence demonstrated how the relationship had progressed from the appellant lecturing about his strict rules to abusive conduct. It also demonstrated the appellant's domineering and possessive behaviour in his attempt to control the complainant.

8 The evidence was admissible as part of the narrative, as evidence of motive or animus and it was relevant in assessing the complainant's credibility, particularly on the questions why she did not leave the relationship or disclose the abuse earlier. Its probative value outweighed its prejudicial effect.

9 It is important to keep in mind that the risk of prejudice was much reduced because of the fact that this was a trial by judge alone. When the trial judge decided to admit the evidence, he noted that this was not a jury case and when the complainant's testimony extended past her relationship with the appellant, he immediately stopped Crown counsel. The trial judge saw the prior discreditable conduct as relevant to the relationship between the appellant and the complainant and used it to assist him in understanding and explaining the actions of the parties.

. . .

15 Accordingly, the appeal is dismissed.

Was this evidence really directly relevant to a material fact in issue or was it really admitted to show the accused's bad disposition, which evidence we shall see below is normally excluded? Some see resort to

words such as animus, motive, context or part of the narrative as glib devices to avoid the exclusionary rule.[7] If this is true, does this matter? Do you agree that such evidence should be admitted?

Notice that the Court of Appeal indicated they were less concerned about the prejudicial effect of the evidence because this was a judge alone trial.[8] Do you agree?

This part of the chapter is concerned, however, with the canons of exclusion which the law of evidence has created for the reception of character as circumstantial evidence of how a person acted during the material incident; character evidence of this sort is seen to be relevant on the premise that character reflects disposition and a person's disposition to act, think or feel in a particular way is evidence from which it might be inferred that he or she behaved in conformity with that character on the particular occasion.

(b) Underlying Assumptions Grounding Character Evidence

The common law assumes that character evidence is predictive of behaviour; that a person's behaviour is governed by personality traits. The common law assumes, for example, that if there is evidence that the accused has behaved aggressively in the past, that evidence has probative worth in determining if he committed the assault with which he is now charged. Some disagree:

> Empirical research, however, has not only failed to validate trait theory but has generally rejected it. As Walter Mischel notes: "The initial assumptions of trait-state theory were logical, inherently plausible, and also consistent with common sense and intuitive impressions about personality. Their real limitation turned out to be empirical — they simply have not been supported adequately." Instead, the research shows that behaviour is largely shaped by specific situational determinants that do not lend themselves easily to predictions about individual behaviour. ... From this psychological perspective, evidence that a witness has been convicted of a felony involving dishonesty or has cheated on his taxes may or may not tell us anything about whether he was truthful on the stand. Likewise, evidence that the accused was engaged in an altercation after a New Year's Eve party may tell us nothing about his behaviour during a peace demonstration. These findings threaten the common law's basic assumptions about the probative value of character evidence.[9]

While empirical findings may threaten, the common law nevertheless continues with its assumptions.

R. v. CLARKE
(1998), 18 C.R. (5th) 219, 129 C.C.C. (3d) 1 (Ont. C.A.)

The issue concerned the admissibility of evidence of a witness's reputation for veracity. It was resolved that questions could be put to an impeaching witness

---

7 See Stuart, Annotation to *Sandhu* ((2009) 63 C.R. (6th) 3) and Nowlin, "Narrative Evidence: A Wolf in Sheep's Clothing" (2006) 51 *Crim. L.Q.* 238 and 271.

8 See also *R. v. B.(T)* (2009), 63 C.R. (6th) 197 (Ont. C.A.), and comment by Lisa Dufraimont, discussed below under similar fact evidence.

9 Mendez, "California's New Law on Character Evidence: The Impact of Recent Psychological Studies" (1984), 31 U.C.L.A. Law Rev. 1003, 1052.

concerning a witness's reputation, or character, for truth-telling. In the course of approving such evidence the court offered the following advice.

ROSENBERG J.A. (MCMURTRY C.J.O. and LABROSSE J.A. concurring): —

The theory upon which the admissibility of this evidence is based, the "trait or generality theory" has been criticized. It has been argued that there is no such thing as stable personality traits from which one could reasonably predict how a person would act in a given situation. To the contrary, it is argued that a theory of "situationism" provides a more reasonable basis for predicting behaviour. According to this theory, behaviour is determined almost exclusively by environmental factors, by the situation in which the actors find themselves. However, even this theory has been found to be flawed and trait theory has come back into its own. Susan M. Davies describes the understanding of social scientists, S.M. Davies, "Evidence of Character to Prove Conduct: A Reassessment of Relevancy" (1991), 27 Crim. L.B. 504 at 516-17:

> Using improved methodology, trait theorists are now able to demonstrate the existence in individuals of consistent behavioral tendencies over a sample of situations, and to predict average behaviour accurately. In fact, the usefulness of trait information in predicting behaviour is no longer controverted by members of the psychology community. The most outspoken critic of trait theory has conceded that traits exist and that trait theorists 'can predict many things about people at levels of confidence that are reasonable for various goals and purposes.' Even more significant for the forensic consideration of character is the fact that most psychologists now recognize that, as a general matter, a lay person, given information about a subject's past behaviour, can predict the subject's future behaviour with a significant degree of accuracy.

(c) Character of Parties in Civil Cases

A person's character or disposition is commonly taken into account when we seek to forecast how the person will respond to a future situation or to judge how he did respond to a past situation. From our common sense and experience we view his character as rationally probative and hence his character may be regarded as relevant in judicial proceedings.

Generally speaking, the character of the plaintiff or defendant in a civil case is not receivable for the purpose of proving that the litigant acted in conformity therewith on the occasion under review. In the old case of *A.G. v. Radloff*,[10] Baron Martin "reasoned":

> In criminal cases evidence of the good character of the accused is most properly and with good reason admissible in evidence, because there is a fair and just presumption that a person of good character would not commit a crime; but in civil cases such evidence is with equal good reason not admitted, because no presumption would fairly arise, in the very great proportion of such cases, from the good character

---

10 (1854), 156 E.R. 366, 371.

of the defendant, that he did not commit the breach of contract or of civil duty alleged against him.[11]

This reasoning seems strained. If character is relevant in one context, can it really be said that it is not relevant in the other? Perhaps the distinction is to be justified on the basis that, in a criminal case, with the disparity in resources between the litigants and the consequences for the accused, the accused is entitled to lead any evidence that could possibly affect the result. In civil cases, the court may be more concerned that the probative value of the character evidence, whether it be good or bad character, is outweighed by the prejudice it causes by confusing the issues, prolonging the proceedings or unfairly surprising the opposing litigants.

As you read the next two cases, are you satisfied with how the court deals with the character evidence? Was the evidence really excluded because it was not relevant or because of some other concern(s)?

In *McArthur v. Prudential Insurance Co. of America*[12] a widow was suing on a life insurance policy following her husband's death. The insurance company would not pay on the basis that he had misled the company as to his state of health. The plaintiff wanted to lead evidence as to his reputation for honesty. The evidence was disallowed. **Defensible?**

RAWDAH v. EVANS
(February 1, 1995), Clarke J., [1994] O.J. No. 3322 (Gen. Div.)

CLARKE J.: —

In this action before judge and jury for damages arising from a motor vehicle accident, liability was admitted. The plaintiff moved to call three friends to testify with respect to his general reputation in the community for honesty. The motion raised the issue of character evidence in a civil proceeding. ...

... [C]ounsel for the defendant ... cross-examined the plaintiff on his lack of candour, with respect to pre-accident history and also attempted to demonstrate that he was exaggerating pain and disability ... I find such evidence of good character has little probative value here. No compelling inference could be drawn from it that the plaintiff was not deliberately exaggerating injuries and disability for secondary economic gain because other rational explanations exist, apart from dishonesty, to explain the shortcomings of the plaintiff's testimony. The plaintiff claimed memory loss related to the accident for his faulty disclosure. Further, it is widely recognized that where as here there is scant objective pathology to support injuries, litigants often entertain sincere, but mistaken beliefs as their gravity and cause. ...

---

11 See further *Gentles v. Toronto (City) Non-Profit Housing Corp.* (2006), [2006] O.J. No. 1013, 2006 CarswellOnt 1543 (S.C.J.); *Tsoukas v. Segura*, [2001] B.C.J. No. 2418, 2001 CarswellBC 2562 (C.A.) at paras. 47-54; and, *Deep v. Wood* (1983), 143 D.L.R. (3d) 246 (Ont. C.A.).

12 (1969), 6 D.L.R. (3d) 477 (Ont. H.C.).

... [E]xcept in restricted circumstances where character is directly in issue, the law holds that evidence of a litigant's character is inadmissible.

> The exclusionary rule prevails also in civil cases, where there is no exception in favour of one party. Thus, where a will was impeached for fraud, the defendant was not allowed to prove his good character in answer, nor, in divorce cases, can a husband, in disproof of a particular act of cruelty, tender evidence of his general character for humanity. So, to rebut a charge of cowardice on a particular occasion, both general evidence of courage and specific acts of bravery on other occasions are inadmissible." (Phipson on Evidence, 12ed, p. 217.)

This is not a civil assault or defamation case where the character of one of the parties for peacefulness or violence or some other moral quality may be germane. Nor is this a case where the reputation of a third party is at stake. The sole issues here are the extent of the plaintiff's injuries and the compensation to which he is entitled. In sum general evidence of good character is irrelevant.

For these reasons, the plaintiff's motion is dismissed.

ROBERTSON v. EDMONTON (CITY) POLICE SERVICE
[2005] A.J. No. 840, 2005 CarswellAlta 949 (Q.B.)

The plaintiff was an Edmonton detective who alleged that the Edmonton Police Service had been infiltrated by the Outlaw Motorcycle Gang. A police investigation determined that, outside of one civilian of the Police Service who had bought drugs from the Outlaws, the dozens of other incidents reported by Robertson involved innocent contact or were unfounded. Robertson was then charged with disciplinary offences including breach of confidence, deceit, discreditable conduct and insubordination. Robertson argued that the disciplinary proceeding was biased. The motion was dismissed. The Chief of Police then sought costs against Robertson's lawyer for the aggressive way in which he litigated the bias motion and other interlocutory motions. To respond to this allegation, the lawyer wanted to call evidence about his legal practice.

SLATTER J.: —

The general rule is that only the parties to the litigation are liable for costs, although in exceptional circumstances counsel may be liable as well. Rule 602 provides:

> 602 In any proper case any barrister and solicitor who has acted for any of the parties to any proceeding, may be ordered to pay any of the costs thereof.

In recognition of the special role that counsel play in the legal process, and in recognition of the need for counsel to strenuously put forward even unpopular arguments, this Rule is only invoked in the most extreme cases. ...

Counsel for Mr. Engel attempted to refer to a number of previous cases in which Mr. Engel had been involved to demonstrate how "fearless" he has been, how well he represents his clients' interests, and therefore why he should be entitled to conduct litigation in an aggressive manner without fear of a costs award against himself. Counsel also noted that Mr. Engel had been awarded the 2004

Harradence Prize for "exceptional commitment to protecting the rights of the accused and others who have suffered at the hands of government". ...

It should first be noted that general evidence of good character is rarely admissible in civil cases unless it amounts to similar fact evidence. This is simply because such evidence is rarely probative. The fact that a litigant may have done good deeds on a prior occasion is little evidence that they did not do a bad deed on this particular occasion: *Attorney-General v. Radloff* (1854), 10 Exch. 84, 156 E.R. 366. For example, the fact that a litigant did not drive through a red light on a previous occasion does not mean that he or she stopped at the red light on this occasion. On the other hand, the fact that a defendant did drive through a red light on a previous occasion is no evidence that he or she also drove through the red light on this occasion. Where it is clear someone went through a red light, even proving that the defendant had a "habit" of stopping for red lights is not probative of much, as all motorists have that habit. Evidence tending to show that Mr. Engel had conducted himself in a proper manner on previous occasions is no evidence of what he did on this occasion.

[As noted in] ... *R. v. Hector* (2000), 146 C.C.C. (3d) 81, 132 O.A.C. 152 (C.A.), at para. 21:

> This quasi-similar act evidence is representative of a practice, all too prevalent in my opinion, of inviting the court to venture into a parallel investigation of what, superficially, appears to be a similar situation, only to find after an extended hearing that it is every bit as contentious as the primary issue in the case and most unlikely to be dispositive of it. . . . The complaints of another client in an unrelated case are of little or no probative value and simply extend and confuse the investigation into the main issue.

These comments, which have been approved in *R. v. Dunbar*, 2003 BCCA 667, 191 B.C.A.C. 223, at para. 39, were made in response to an argument that because counsel had acted incompetently in previous cases, he probably acted in an incompetent manner in the appeal presently before the Court. For the same reason that previous instances of incompetence are inadmissible, so are previous instances of good conduct. Simply because Mr. Engel may have prosecuted other cases properly, does not mean that he prosecuted this case properly. ...

A "habit" of responding in a regular mechanical way to a particular set of circumstances may have probative value. For example, a doctor may testify that he routinely did a medical procedure in a particular way. But to attempt to show that someone was in the "habit" of acting "reasonably and properly" provides no probative evidence. This is merely evidence of general good character.

As the Court pointed out in *Hector, supra*, proof of prior deeds invites a parallel investigation into all sorts of collateral issues. Citing previous cases in which Mr. Engel was counsel in support of his aggressive style of litigation invites the citation of other cases in which Mr. Engel arguably went over the line. For example, in *Libo-on v. Fort Saskatchewan Correctional Centre*, 2004 ABQB 416, 32 Alta. L.R. (4th) 128, 362 A.R. 231, at para. 15, Mr. Engel made the impossible argument that an inmate with morphine concealed in his rectum was not in possession of that morphine. In *R. v. Jarema* (1996), 43 Alta. L.R. (3d) 345, 187

A.R. 194 (C.A.) the accused had pleaded guilty to raping three young girls. He then retained Mr. Engel and attempted to withdraw the guilty pleas. In support of that application Mr. Engel issued a Statement of Claim against the three victims, claiming general damages of $1 million. As the Court of Appeal stated at para. 11: "Needless to say, we were not impressed with this tactic". Counsel for the Respondent cited *Ilnicki v. McLeod*, 2003 ABQB 676, 20 Alta. L.R. (4th) 78, at para. 13, and *Munoz v. Alberta (Edmonton Remand Centre)*, 2004 ABQB 769, at paras. 96-99 for the same purpose.

It will be readily apparent from citing these few examples that the attempt to use general evidence of good character simply invites a public inquiry into Mr. Engel's entire career. ... [T]he system simply cannot devote the resources necessary to conduct proceedings in that way. See also Sopinka, *The Law of Evidence in Canada*, 2d ed. (Markham: Butterworths, 1999) at para. 10.27. In any event, even if such an inquiry was conducted, the resulting conclusions will not be sufficiently probative to be of any use. Even if the inquiry should conclude that Mr. Engel was in some instances a good advocate, and in other instances a bad advocate, but that overall in his entire career he was good (or bad), that does not provide any probative evidence as to whether in the particular case before the Court he misconducted himself or not. I have accordingly disregarded all this "evidence". ...

While this litigation was conducted in a wholly unacceptable way, ... [t]here is no overt evidence of bad faith, and while this is a borderline case, I am not prepared to draw an inference of bad faith, given all the circumstances.

The plaintiff was convicted on 14 of the 15 disciplinary charges.[13] **Do you agree with the conclusions in the driving illustrations provided by the Court?**

We shall see later that bad character evidence is, however, sometimes admitted in civil cases under the head of similar fact evidence.

(d) Character of Accused in Criminal Cases[14]

(i) *Good Character Evidence*

Shortly stated, the accused is entitled to lead evidence of his own good character but, generally speaking, the prosecution is not entitled to lead evidence of the accused's bad character.

In criminal prosecutions from an early period, the prosecutor has had the right to the last word with the jury unless the accused calls no evidence. In *R. v. Stannard*[15] the accused called no evidence directly bearing upon the facts of the case, but did call witnesses to his good character and the court was asked

---

13 Rusnell, "Judge Flays Engel For Legal Tactics" *Edmonton Journal* (12 July 2005) at B.2.
14 See generally Matthew Shuber, "Evidence of the Accused's Character: A Road Map for Young Counsel", (2000) 43 Crim.L.Q. 489.
15 (1837), 173 E.R. 295 (N.P.); and see *R. v. McMillan* (1975), 23 C.C.C. (2d) 160, 167 (Ont. C.A.); affirmed [1977] 2 S.C.R. 824.

to rule whether the prosecutor had the right to address the jury last. Patterson, J. ruled:[16]

> I cannot in principle make any distinction between evidence of facts, and evidence of character: the latter is equally laid before the jury as the former, as being relevant to the question of guilty or not guilty: the object of laying it before the jury is to induce them to believe, from the improbability that a person of good character should have conducted himself as alleged, that there is some mistake or misrepresentation in the evidence on the part of the prosecution, and it is strictly evidence in the case.

It was at one time thought that character evidence was only useful in borderline cases. Martin J.A., in *R. v. Tarrant*,[17] wrote:

> Evidence of good character is evidence which has a bearing on the improbability of the accused committing the offence and also is relevant to his credibility. The effect of the charge by the learned trial Judge was to deprive character evidence of any use unless the jury was in doubt or the scales were evenly balanced. It need scarcely be pointed out that if the jury were in doubt or if the scales were equally balanced it would be their duty to acquit whether or not there was evidence of good character. The evidence of good character may, along with all the other evidence, create or result in the jury having a reasonable doubt.[18]

How probative is good character evidence in sexual assault cases?

R. v. PROFIT
(1992), 16 C.R. (4th) 332, 85 C.C.C. (3d) 232 (Ont. C.A.)

The accused, a school principal, was convicted of sexual offences involving students. The accused appealed.

GOODMAN J.A. (BLAIR J.A. concurring):—

. . . .

Twenty-two character witnesses testified on behalf of the appellant. Fifteen were colleagues or school board employees who had worked either for or with the appellant. Three were associated with the appellant through volunteer or church organizations. Two were independent businessmen from the appellant's community and two were personal friends. Some of them had, as children, attended camps where the appellant was a director and in later years had acted as counsellors in the camp under the appellant's supervision. All of these witnesses had seemingly impeccable backgrounds and were well qualified to give evidence

---

16 *Ibid.*, at p. 296.
17 (1982), 63 C.C.C. (2d) 385, 388 (Ont. C.A.).
18 In *R. v. Flis* (2006), 205 C.C.C. (3d) 384 , 2006 CarswellOnt 698 (C.A.), leave to appeal refused (2006), 2006 CarswellOnt 5926, 2006 CarswellOnt 5927 (S.C.C.), Moldaver J.A., in affirming a conviction of a police officer for assault, held that the trial judge had properly admitted evidence of his professionalism and unblemished career respecting his credibility and (impliedly) to prove that he was less likely guilty. See also *R. v. H. (S.E.)* (1994), [1994] B.C.J. No. 3057, 1994 CarswellBC 1721 (C.A.), and *R. v. Molnar* (1990), 55 C.C.C. (3d) 446, 76 C.R. (3d) 125 (Ont. C.A.).

with respect to the reputation of the appellant in the community with respect to honesty, integrity and morality.

A fair résumé of their evidence with respect to their personal knowledge was that they had never seen the appellant conduct himself in a sexually inappropriate manner, nor had they ever heard the appellant make a statement that they would consider sexually inappropriate. None of them had ever received a complaint about the appellant's conduct.

. . . .

The trial judge, however, made no reference whatsoever to the use of character evidence as a basis of an inference that the appellant was unlikely to have committed the crime charged.

. . . .

[W]here the character witnesses have given evidence as to the moral behaviour of an accused with respect to children in cases alleging sexual offences against children and have given evidence with respect to the general reputation of an accused for not only honesty and integrity but also morality, in the broader sense, such evidence has the same degree of relevance and weight to establish the improbability that the accused committed the offence, as evidence of general reputation with respect to honesty has in the case of an alleged offence involving a theft or a fraudulent transaction. In each case it is only one part of the evidence to be considered by the finder of fact along with all other evidence in determining the culpability of an accused and its weight will no doubt vary with the circumstances of each case. . . . . [T]he character evidence in the case at bar dealt specifically with the appellant's behaviour with his students and his general reputation with respect to morality.

. . . .

Accordingly, I would allow the appeal and quash the convictions.

GRIFFITHS J.A. (dissenting):—

. . . .

[W]hile such evidence may be relevant in cases involving crimes of commercial dishonesty, it has little probative value in cases involving sexual misconduct against children by persons in positions of trust or control.

Recently there have been a number of cases involving persons who enjoyed impeccable reputations in the community for honesty, integrity and morality, such as teachers, scout leaders, priests and others who, in breach of their positions of trust, have committed acts of sexual assault. In these cases, the sexual assaults were generally shrouded in secrecy, and the flaw in the character of the offender frequently did not come to light until he had been charged and convicted.

R. v. PROFIT
[1993] 3 S.C.R. 637, 24 C.R. (4th) 279, 85 C.C.C. (3d) 232

SOPINKA J.:—We agree with the conclusion of Griffiths J.A. in his dissenting reasons. When the reasons of the trial judge are considered as a whole, we are satisfied that he dealt with the character evidence tendered in this case adequately. The reasons of the trial judge must be viewed in light of the fact that as a matter of common sense, but not as a principle of law, a trial judge may take into account that in sexual assault cases involving children, sexual misconduct occurs in private and in most cases will not be reflected in the reputation in the community of the accused for morality. As a matter of weight, the trial judge is entitled to find that the propensity value of character evidence as to morality is diminished in such cases.

Accordingly, the appeal is allowed and the convictions restored.

With whom do you agree on this issue?

(ii) *When Bad Character Evidence Can Be Led By Crown*

Just as good character is relevant, so too evidence of the accused's bad character is relevant to whether he committed the complained of act. We might rationally infer that on the occasion under review the accused may have acted in conformity with his character, his disposition. While it is relevant, the law has created a canon of exclusion lest the trier of fact give it more probative force than it warrants or be diverted from judging the action to judging the man. In the leading case of *R. v. Rowton*[19] Willes J. wrote of character evidence:

It is strictly relevant to the issue; but such evidence is not admissible upon the part of the prosecution . . . because if the prosecution were allowed to go into such evidence we should have the whole life of the prisoner ripped up, and as has been witnessed in the proceedings of jurisdictions where such evidence is admissible upon a charge preferred, you might begin by showing that when a boy at school he had robbed an orchard and so read the rest of his conduct and the whole of his life; and the result would be that a man on his trial would be overwhelmed by prejudice instead of being convicted on affirmative evidence, which the law of this country requires. The prosecution is prevented from giving such evidence for reasons rather of policy and humanity than because proof that the prisoner was a bad character is not relevant to the issue, — it is relevant to the issue, but it is expedient for the sake of letting in all the evidence which might possibly throw light upon the subject; you might arrive at justice in one case and you might do injustice in ninety-nine.

And Baron Parke in *Attorney General v. Hitchcock*:[20]

We cannot enter into a collateral question as to the man's having committed a crime on some former occasion, one reason being, that it would lead to complicated issues and long inquiries; and another, that a party cannot be expected to be prepared to defend the whole of the actions of his life.

---

19 (1865), 10 Cox. C.C. 25, 38. See the description of French trials where character evidence was freely used.
20 (1847), 1 Ex. 91.

There are a number of exceptions to the general rule that the prosecution cannot lead evidence of bad character as disposition evidence. They include where:

1. The accused puts his or her character in issue (discussed in the next section);

2. The evidence constitutes similar act evidence (see *R. v. Handy, below*); and,

3. The accused leads propensity evidence to suggest that a third party committed the offence (see *R. v. Parsons, below*).

(iii) *When Does an Accused Put Their Character in Issue?*

When does the accused put their character into issue and thereby open the door for the prosecution to rebut? In *R. v. Shrimpton* [21] the accused maintained that he had not given evidence of good character as he had not called witnesses to that fact but rather elicited the same in cross-examination of a prosecution witness. It was held:

> If, either by calling witnesses on his part, or by cross-examination of the witnesses for the Crown, the prisoner relies upon his good character, it is lawful for the prosecutor to give the previous conviction in evidence.

At that time, of course, the accused was incapable of giving evidence. When he now takes the stand and denies the charge, does he open the door to character evidence being led by the prosecution? Let us compare three cases.

In *R. v. McFadden* [22] the accused was charged with first degree murder. The Crown's theory was that the accused had killed the deceased in the course of an indecent assault. In cross-examination of the accused it was suggested that he had gone to the deceased's place to satisfy his sexual urge and that he had stabbed her when she resisted. The accused replied: "I have the most beautiful wife in the world. I worship the ground that girl walks on." The British Columbia Court of Appeal held that the accused had thereby placed his character for sexual morality in issue because he meant to convey that he would not get sexually involved with any other woman. Craig J.A. said:

> The purpose of evidence of good character is to show the accused is a person who is not likely to have committed the act with which he is charged and, also, to enhance his credibility. An accused may adduce evidence of good character (1) by calling witnesses; (2) by cross-examining Crown witnesses on the subject; (3) by giving testimony. Normally, he may lead evidence of good character by adducing evidence only of his general reputation, not by adducing evidence of specific acts which might tend to establish his character. The Crown may call evidence of bad character in rebuttal, but such evidence, also, must relate only to general reputation: *R. v. Rowton* (1865), 169 E.R. 1497. An accused may put his character in issue in the course of giving his testimony, not by giving evidence of his general reputation, but by making assertions which tend to show that he is a person of good character, particularly with regard to the aspect of his character which is in issue. Obviously, the Crown may

---

21 (1851), 5 Cox. C.C. 387.
22 (1981), 65 C.C.C. (2d) 9 (B.C.C.A.).

rebut this testimony by calling evidence of bad character, but may the Crown call evidence only of general reputation or may the Crown call evidence other than the evidence of general reputation? In some circumstances, the Crown may call evidence of specific incidents in rebutting evidence of good character. For example, under the provisions of s. 593 of the *Criminal Code*, the Crown could prove previous convictions as evidence of bad character. The Crown may, also, adduce similar fact evidence to rebut evidence of good character: *Guay v. The Queen* (1979), 42 C.C.C. (2d) 536, [1979] 1 S.C.R. 18.[23]

R. v. McNamara[24] was a prosecution of a number of companies and individuals for conspiracy to defraud by agreeing on who should bid the successful bid on dredging contracts. A principal Crown witness, Rindress, was the president of two companies, J.P. Porter and Richelieu, which were part of a corporate structure of which the accused Jean Simard was a director. Rindress testified that he assumed he had a mandate from Simard to bid-rig. In Simard's examination-in-chief he was asked as to the mandate he had given Rindress:

> Q.   Mr. Rindress in giving his evidence has told us that what he considered his mandate was in connection with the operation of the Porter Company and the Richelieu Company, what did you consider was the mandate of Mr. Rindress in connection with operating the company?
>
> A.   The mandate that Mr. Rindress had is to run the company like a company should be run, legally.
>
> Q.   I am sorry?
>
> A.   Like any company should be run, legally.

The trial judge ruled that the accused had put his character into issue, and the Crown was permitted to cross-examine Simard with respect to an otherwise unrelated building transaction which inpugned Simard's character for honesty. The Ontario Court of Appeal held:

> Manifestly, an accused does not put his character in issue by denying his guilt and repudiating the allegations made against him, nor by giving an explanation of matters which are essential to his defence. An accused is not entitled, however, under the guise of repudiating the allegations against him to assert expressly or impliedly that he would not have done the things alleged against him because he is a person of good character; if he does, he puts his character in issue.
>
> The difficult question is whether the appellant crossed over the line of permissible repudiation of the charge and asserted that he was an honest man. . . .
>
> The appellant Jean Simard in response to his counsel's question as to the scope of Rindress' mandate did not confine himself to saying that the mandate was to run the company legally. The appellant said that Rindress' mandate was to run the company like a company should be run, legally. He followed that answer by repeating that Rindress' mandate was to run the company "like any company should be run, legally". The appellant's evidence is consistent only with his intention to assert that he would not knowingly permit a Simard company to be operated other than legally. If there were any doubt whether the appellant, by these answers, intended to project the image of a law-abiding citizen, these answers, when taken together with his subsequent evidence, make it clear that the appellant intended to project the image of a man of integrity and of an ethical businessman.[25]

---

23 *Ibid.*, at p. 13.
24 (1981), 56 C.C.C. (2d) 193, 343 (Ont. C.A.).
25 *Ibid.*, at pp. 346-47.

In *R. v. Shortreed*[26] the accused was charged with a number of sexual assaults. He testified in chief that he never sexually assaulted anyone. The accused later explained that what he meant by that was that he had not attacked any of the victims in this case. The court held that the accused had not placed his character in issue and the Crown should not therefore have been permitted to cross-examine the accused as to facts underlying a prior conviction for wounding:

> Having regard to the qualification of his general statement when he was asked in-chief to explain its meaning, it is apparent that the appellant was not attempting to rely on his non-violent nature, but merely intended to deny having assaulted any of the five complainants. He was not adducing evidence of good character within the meaning of s. 666 of the *Criminal Code*. . . .

> . . . .

> An accused person does not place his character in issue by denying his guilt and repudiating the allegations made against him. Neither do the introductory routine questions as to education, marital status, religious affiliation have the effect of rendering the accused's character relevant.[27]

Do you agree with the Court of Appeal that questions about education, marital status and religious affiliation do not put character in issue? If not, what is their relevance?

R. v. P. (N.A.)
(2002), 171 C.C.C. (3d) 70, 8 C.R. (6th) 186 (Ont. C.A.)

The accused was charged with offences of violence against his wife and daughter.

DOHERTY J.A. (AUSTIN and ARMSTRONG JJ.A. concurring): —

The vexing question of when an accused can be said to put his or her character in issue through his answers during examination-in-chief was considered by this court in *R. v. McNamara (No. 1)*, *supra*, at p. 346:

> Manifestly, an accused does not put his character in issue by denying his guilt and repudiating the allegations made against him, nor by giving an explanation of matters which are essential to his defence. An accused is not entitled, however, under the guise of repudiating the allegations against him to assert expressly or impliedly that he would not have done the things alleged against him because he is a person of good character; if he does, he puts his character in issue. The difficult question is whether the appellant crossed over the line of permissible repudiation of the charge and asserted that he was an honest man.

---

26 (1990), 54 C.C.C. (3d) 292 (Ont. C.A.).
27 *Ibid.*, at p. 307. In *R. v. Farrant*, 4 C.C.C. (3d) 354, [1983] 1 S.C.R. 124, 32 C.R. (3d) 289, the accused put his character in issue when he testified that "It's not my character to be violent." An opposite conclusion was reached in *R. v. Turpin*, [2005] B.C.J. No. 490, 2005 CarswellBC 871 (S.C.) where the accused testified that "It's not my style to kill people." The trial judge distinguished *Farrant* on the basis that the testimony was elicited during the Crown's cross-examination and the accused seemed to regret the fact that he had made the utterance.

The line between permissible repudiation of the Crown's case and putting one's character in issue can be particularly difficult to draw in cases where the prosecution is allowed to lead evidence of a lengthy marital and family relationship so as to provide a proper context in which the jury can assess the specific allegations made against an accused. The importance of context and background in this kind of case is beyond doubt: *R. v. F. (D.S.)* (1999), 132 C.C.C. (3d) 97 (Ont. C.A.) at 106-107. In my view, however, the accused must be able to repudiate the charges by presenting his or her version of that context without suffering the disadvantage of putting character in issue. For example, where the Crown is allowed to lead evidence to demonstrate that an accused was a controlling and dominating spouse in order to give context to the allegations, I do not think that an accused should be said to have put his character in issue when he describes himself as a loving and caring spouse.

That is not to say that where the Crown is allowed to introduce evidence of the dynamics within a family to provide context or narrative, an accused has free rein and can never be said to put his character in issue during examination-in-chief. In *R. v. W. (L.K.), supra*, the accused was charged with having assaulted five of his children on many occasions over many years. The Crown led evidence that throughout those many years, the accused systematically abused and intimidated his wife and children. After reviewing the substance of the accused's examination-in-chief, Moldaver J.A. said at pp. 465-66:

> Having reviewed the appellant's examination-in-chief, I have no doubt that he placed his character in issue, thereby opening the door to being questioned about prior acts of discreditable conduct, including the details surrounding the 1956 assault upon his sister. Throughout his examination-in- chief, the appellant availed himself of every opportunity to extol his moral and ethical virtues in an effort to portray himself as the kind of person who would not abuse anyone physically or sexually, let alone those people, such as his immediate family members, whom he cared for and loved. Having adopted that posture, he placed his character in issue.. . . . . Once the appellant placed his character in issue, the Crown was entitled to lead evidence designed to level the playing field and provide the jury with a yardstick against which to measure the clear and unmistakable impression that the appellant sought to convey, namely, that he was not the type of person to commit the offences in question.

Drawing the line between repudiation of the Crown's case and putting character in issue requires that an evaluation of the accused's evidence-in- chief be informed by the nature of the case he or she had to meet. .. A review of the Crown's evidence demonstrates that a large part of the Crown's case consisted of a detailed description of the relationship between M.P. and the respondent. He was entitled to give his version of that relationship during his examination-in-chief without being said to have put his character in issue. ...

The Crown chose to make the entire family history and the relationships within the family the focal point of its case against the respondent. In so commenting, I do not suggest any criticism of Crown counsel. The Crown, quite properly, took the position that the charges could only be properly understood in the context of the marital and family relationships involving the respondent, M.P., N.P., and the rest of her family. On the Crown's evidence, the family picture was not a pretty one. In that picture, the respondent was painted as a terrible husband and father. To repudiate this part of the Crown's case, the respondent had to put forward his version of those relationships. Given the scope of the evidence led by the Crown, repudiation of that case extended to a description of the respondent's relationship with M.P., N.P. and his other children. To the extent that the respondent's evidence adopted a moral tone, it was directly responsive to the many allegations of immorality made against him during the Crown's case.

...

I do not think that the respondent put his character in issue. Section 666 was not engaged.

Will the accused be deemed to have put their character in issue when the evidence emerges from a Crown cross-examination of a defence witness?

R. v. A. (W.A.)
(1996), 3 C.R. (5th) 388, 112 C.C.C. (3d) 83 (Man. C.A.)

The accused was charged with sexually assaulting his stepdaughter. At trial, the stepdaughter's long cross-examination attacked her character and truthfulness. The accused's wife, who was the stepdaughter's natural mother, gave evidence for the accused as to her daughter's bad behaviour, and the accused's lack of opportunity to commit the crime. During the Crown's cross-examination as to why she considered her daughter a liar, the wife said, "I know my husband." The trial judge then let the Crown cross-examine the wife as to the family's dynamics. Under further cross-examination, the wife admitted that the accused had once assaulted her, that he had committed himself to a mental health centre, and that he had had an angry meeting with the stepdaughter's teacher. The trial judge cautioned the members of the jury that the cross-examination evidence was useful only to give them a balanced insight into the accused's temperament and that it was not relevant as to the accused's propensity to commit the offence charged. The accused was convicted, and he appealed.

SCOTT C.J.M. (HUBAND and MONNIN JJ.A. concurring): —

. . . .

In my opinion, the accused did not put his "character" in issue through answers given by Mrs. A. during cross-examination by Crown counsel. The line of questioning pursued by Crown counsel that led Mrs. A. to make the response "I know my husband" was directly attributable to Crown counsel's persistence in cross-examination in querying why she was supportive of the accused and not her daughter, the complainant.

In any event there is clear authority that, while the accused may put his own character in issue by introducing such evidence himself, when dealing with defence witnesses it is only through their examination-in-chief that an accused's character may be put in issue. . . . In my opinion, limiting the ways of putting character in issue through defence witnesses to evidence-in-chief makes eminent good sense as illustrated by the very facts of this case where the approbation by Mrs. A. of her husband's "character" was not volunteered, but was elicited as a direct response to a line of questioning only pursued during cross-examination. If it were otherwise, the Crown could put the accused's character in issue through clever cross-examination of defence witnesses and thus frustrate the rule against it.

The evidence brought out during the cross-examination of Mrs. A. is simply incapable of constituting character evidence introduced by or on behalf of the accused. Indeed, the point is so obvious that I have not been able to find any authorities directly on point. See, for example, *R. v. Valeanu* (1995), 97 C.C.C. (3d) 338 (Ont. C.A.), where the Crown conceded on appeal that questioning such as occurred here was clearly improper cross-examination.

Since it is not now strictly necessary to review the scope of character evidence once the accused has put it in issue, I simply note that authorities of many years' standing make it clear that it ordinarily refers to evidence of reputation and not to evidence of disposition. This is normally attested to by evidence as to the accused's general reputation within the community. Thus the evidence brought out during cross-examination is not character evidence in the traditional sense since it deals with specific incidents involving the accused and members of his household during the period relevant to the indictment.

(iv) *How Character May be Proved*

Having examined *when* the character of the accused may be evidenced, we turn now to the separate question of *how* that character may be shown. Three methods suggest themselves as rational: first, by reports of the accused's reputation in the community for the pertinent character trait; second, by the opinion of one who knows the accused's character; and, finally, by description of specific acts of conduct or misconduct from which his general disposition or character might be inferred. The last method was viewed by the courts as of little probative value and carried the danger of multiplicity of issues and unfair surprise. Willes J. explained:

> You exclude particular facts on the part of the prisoner because a person who is a robber may do an act or acts of generosity, and the proof of such acts are, therefore, irrelevant to the question whether he was likely to have committed the particular act of robbery or not; and, on the one hand, I agree that particular acts must be excluded on the part of the prosecution partly for the reason that excludes them in the first instance, and partly for the reason that no notice has been given to the prisoner that you are going into an inquiry as to particular facts.[28]

Prior to the landmark decision of *Rowton* the normal technique of informing the trier of the accused's character was by the opinions of those who knew him, bolstered at times by their reports of his reputation. Curiously, this practice was there suddenly reversed.[29] Rowton was charged with having committed an

---

28 *R. v. Rowton* (1865), 10 Cox. C.C. 25, 39.
29 See 7 Wigmore, *Evidence* (3d ed.), s. 1981, at p. 210 for a description of how *Rowton* surprised the legal profession.

indecent assault upon a 14-year-old boy. The accused called several witnesses who gave him an excellent character as a moral and well-conducted man. The prosecution called in reply a witness who knew the accused and when asked:

> What is the defendant's general character for decency and morality of conduct?

He replied:

> I know nothing of the neighbourhood's opinion, because I was only a boy at school when I knew him; but my own opinion, and the opinion of my brothers who were also pupils of his, is, that his character is that of a man capable of the grossest indecency and the most flagrant immorality.

This evidence was received over the objections of the accused, the accused was convicted, and the question was reserved for the opinion of 12 judges. The majority[30] held this to be error and the conviction was quashed. Since that time evidence of character was usually limited to evidence of reputation, and character witnesses are commanded that they are not to speak from their own experience of the accused but rather to report on the rumours in the community. As Wurtele J. later summarized:

> In criminal prosecutions evidence respecting the general character of the defendant is admissible for the purpose of raising a presumption of innocence or of guilt, but the party who tenders such evidence must restrict himself to evidence of mere general reputation, and the question to be put to a witness to character is: What is the defendant's reputation for honesty, morality or humanity? as the case may be. The Crown has no right, however, in making out its case to put in evidence of bad character, but, on the other hand, the defendant is at liberty to give evidence of his general good character; and then the counsel for the Crown can cross-examine the witnesses as to particular or isolated facts and as to the ground of their belief, and may also call witnesses to prove the general bad reputation of the defendant, and thus to contradict his witnesses.[31]

The character witness must have knowledge of the person's reputation in the community. Our jurisprudence reflects the fact, however, that the nature of the community changes with the times.

R. v. LEVASSEUR
(1987), 56 C.R. (3d) 335, 35 C.C.C. (3d) 136 (Alta. C.A.)

The accused was charged with break, enter and theft. The defence sought to introduce evidence of the accused's good character through testimony of her employer, who had discussed the accused's general reputation with 15 of their business acquaintances. The trial judge ruled the evidence was inadmissible because the evidence was not of her reputation in the community in which she lived.

---

30 Willes J. and Erle C.J. dissented.

31 *R. v. Barsalou* (1901), 4 C.C.C. 347, 348 (Que. K.B.). And see *Michelson v. U.S.*, 335 U.S. 469 (1948). See also *R. v. Grosse* (1983), 9 C.C.C. (3d) 465 (N.S.C.A.); leave to appeal to S.C.C. refused 61 N.S.R. (2d) 447n.

HARRADENCE J.A.:—

. . . .

Scrutiny by a modern appellate court can only result in the conclusion that the neighbourhood requirement is no longer justifiable. While it may have been appropriate in the days of the redoubtable Duke of Wellington, who regretted the advent of the British railroad system because it would allow the lower classes to move about, it is not appropriate to a society which has supersonic transport available to it.

The laws of evidence must not continue to reflect this parochial attitude; as Lord Ellenborough pointed out, "The rules of evidence must expand according to the exigencies of society" (*Pritt v. Fairclough* (1812), 170 E.R. 1391 at 1392).

. . .

Credibility is crucial to the issue of whether the appellant committed the offence of breaking and entering. The appellant claims that she was told to remove the vehicles from the warehouse bay and therefore had colour of right. Had the jurors heard evidence of her good character, their conclusion might have differed.

[A new trial was ordered.]

Levasseur was applied in *R. v. Clarke*[32] where Justice Rosenberg held that:

> ... I should point out that, in my view, the trial judge was in error in holding that the character witnesses could only give evidence about reputation if they were aware of the accused's or complainant's reputation in a particular city or town where they lived, such as Trenton. With the increasing urbanization of society, a person's community will not necessarily coincide with a particular geographic location. Thus, in this case, it would seem to me that it was open to the defence to lead evidence of the respondent's reputation in the Caribbean community in the area.[33]

An accused can, generally speaking, lead good character evidence in one of three ways:

1. Cross-examining witnesses called by the Crown;
2. Calling defence witnesses;
3. Testifying him/herself as to their character.

While the first two are limited to general reputation evidence, the accused can testify about specific acts that reveal their good character (see *R. v. Brown*, below).

An exception to the general rule forbidding the evidencing of character by specific acts of the accused was created by the legislature in England[34] and now finds itself exampled in section 666 of the *Criminal Code*, which provides:

---

32 (1998), 129 C.C.C. (3d) 1, 18 C.R. (5th) 219 (Ont. C.A.) at 10 [C.C.C.].
33 See further *R. v. Soikie*, [2004] O.J. No. 2902, 2004 CarswellOnt 8840 (S.C.J).
34 See An Act to Prevent the Fact of a Previous Conviction being given on Evidence to the Jury, 1836 (6 & 7 Will. 4, c. 111), and An Act for the Better Prevention of Offences, 1851 (14 & 15 Vict., c. 19), s. 9. See also *R. v. Nealy* (1987), 17 O.A.C. 164 (C.A.).

> Where, at a trial, the accused adduces evidence of his good character, the prosecutor may, in answer thereto, before a verdict is returned, adduce evidence of the previous conviction of the accused for any offences, including any previous conviction by reason of which a greater punishment may be imposed.

The legislation was enacted

> . . . to defeat the scandalous attempt often made by persons, who had been repeatedly convicted of felony, bringing witnesses, or cross-examining the witnesses for the prosecution, to prove that the prisoner had previously borne a good character for honesty.[35]

Note that the legislation allows for proof of specific acts to be called in reply only when the act resulted in a conviction.

Note that section 666 only applies where the accused puts his character in issue. Recall that section 12 of the *Canada Evidence Act* allows any witness including the accused to be cross-examined on a criminal record whether or not the accused has put his character in issue. This evidence can only be used to assess credibility. Under *Corbett* we have seen that there is a discretion to prevent such cross-examination in the case of the accused.

In *R. v. P. (N.A.)*,[36] it was observed that:

> If an accused puts his or her character in issue during examination-in- chief, the scope of cross-examination on the criminal record permitted by s. 666 goes beyond that allowed under s. 12 of the *Canada Evidence Act*. Since the cross-examination under s. 666 is predicated on the accused having put his or her character in issue, the accused may also be questioned about the specifics underlying the criminal convictions: *R. v. W. (L.K.)* (1999), 138 C.C.C. (3d) 449 (Ont. C.A.) at 465, leave to appeal to S.C.C. refused [2000] S.C.C.A. No. 383 (QL) [148 C.C.C. (3d) vi]; *R. v. Deyardin* (1997), 119 C.C.C. (3d) 365 (Que. C.A.) at 375-77. The wide ambit of cross-examination contemplated by s. 666 could have been significant in this case. If cross-examination had been allowed, the jury would have heard not only about the respondent's conviction for attempted murder but also that it involved a brutal beating administered in the course of a robbery.

Where an accused has put his character in issue, the Ontario Court of Appeal has recently recognised a discretion to allow evidence of specific acts, apart from s. 666, to level the playing field.

R. v. BROWN
(1999), 27 C.R. (5th) 151, 1999 CarswellOnt 2443,
137 C.C.C. (3d) 400 (C.A.)

The accused was charged with aggravated assault. The Crown case was that he had violently shaken the 14-month-old baby causing him severe brain injury. The accused, who was unrepresented, denied the shaking and called witnesses to testify as to his good character. He testified himself that he had never abused a child in his life. After the accused closed his case, the Crown

---

35 *R. v. Shrimpton* (1851), 5 Cox. C.C. 387. Consider the legislative history of s. 666 as prior to the 1955 revision. It apparently was limited to prosecutions for offences which called for a greater penalty on a second conviction.

36 (2002), 171 C.C.C. (3d) 70, 8 C.R. (6th) 186 (Ont. C.A.), at 83 [C.C.C.].

called one of the accused's sons who testified that as a child he was assaulted on many occasions by the accused. The accused was convicted. The Ontario Court of Appeal allowed the appeal and ordered a new trial.

ROSENBERG J.A.:—

In my view, the trial judge erred in permitting Stewart to give evidence of specific bad acts by the appellant.

In this case, the appellant put his character in issue by calling a character witness. He also put his character in issue by asserting in his own testimony that he had never abused a child and, indeed, that he had rescued children on prior occasions. By testifying in this way, the appellant was attempting to show that he was not the type of person who would have abused the infant.

Where an accused puts his character in issue, as this appellant clearly did, he may be cross-examined on prior specific acts of misconduct: *R. v. McNamara et al. (No. 1)* (1981), 56 C.C.C. (2d) 193 (Ont. C.A.) at 346-49; *R. v. Farrant*, [1983] 1 S.C.R. 124 at 145. Thus, it would have been open to Crown counsel to cross-examine the appellant on the specific acts of misconduct by the appellant against Stewart and his brother. Crown counsel did not do so in this case. Rather, she chose to put these allegations before the trial judge by calling Stewart in reply.

The law as it has developed to date is that where the Crown proposes to call extrinsic evidence in reply, solely to rebut evidence of the accused's good character, the Crown may not lead evidence of specific acts of bad conduct. The only established exception to this rule is for acts that would also constitute evidence of similar facts. Otherwise, the Crown is limited to leading evidence of general reputation, the accused's criminal record pursuant to s. 666 of the Criminal Code, or s. 12 of the Canada Evidence Act if the accused testifies, or possibly expert evidence of disposition. *See R. v. McNamara et al.* (No. 1) at 348-49; *R. v. Tierney* (1982), 70 C.C.C. (2d) 481 (Ont. C.A.) at 485-86; *R. v. Donovan* (1991), 65 C.C.C. (3d) 511 (Ont. C.A.) at 534-5.

In my view, Stewart's evidence does not come within the exception that permits evidence of good character to be rebutted by similar fact evidence. The incidents to which Stewart testified bore no resemblance to the allegation in this case. . . .

A more difficult question is whether the appellant in this case, by not asserting simply that he was a person of good character, but by expressly stating in direct examination that he had never abused a child and – implicitly - that he had never abused his own children and grandchildren, should be open to contradiction on that point. . . . In my view, . . . where an accused does not simply lead evidence of his good character generally, but relies upon specific acts that bear a direct relationship to the offence charged, he or she should be open to contradiction on those narrow points to avoid permitting the accused to leave the trier of fact with a distorted picture. However, because of the potentially prejudicial nature of the evidence when called in reply, before the Crown would be entitled to lead such evidence, it should have to demonstrate that resort to the traditional rules of evidence will not suffice to prevent a distorted picture. That did not occur here.

. . . .

Moreover, even if Stewart's evidence was otherwise admissible, a careful balancing was required to ensure that the rebuttal evidence did not "overcompensate for the imbalance sought to be offset" Or, put another way, the trial judge was required to exercise his discretion carefully to ensure that the prejudicial effect of the evidence did not outweigh its probative value.

. . . .

Moreover, I also have some concern that the trial judge may have misused that evidence. Where the Crown is permitted to adduce evidence of bad character, to rebut evidence of good character, and that evidence does not constitute similar fact evidence, the reply evidence can only be used to neutralize the evidence of good character and to assess the accused's credibility. This court held in *R. v. McNamara et al.* No. (1), supra, at pp. 352-53, that it cannot be used as affirmative evidence of the accused's disposition to commit the offence charged.

(v) *Warnings to Jury*

Where character evidence is admitted courts usually insist on a warning to the jury as to the permissible use of the evidence. In the case of good character evidence the jury must be advised that they can use the evidence to show that the accused was unlikely to have committed the crime see, for example, *R. v. Millar*[37] (see below). However in the case of bad character evidence the jury must be warned that the jury cannot use the evidence merely to show the accused was the type of person to commit the crime. For example in *R. v. Dunn*[38] a new trial was ordered on an appeal against a conviction for living off the avails of prostitution because the jury were not warned that they could not infer from evidence that the accused was a drug dealer that he was the type of person who was likely to exploit a prostitute.[39]
Do these warnings make sense?

PROBLEMS

Problem 1

The accused is charged with manslaughter in the death of his wife. The defence is accident. He does not testify but his statement to the police is introduced by the Crown. In it, he states that he is a loving husband and father and that he is not a violent person. Will the Crown be permitted to introduce evidence of the accused's criminal record for assault? What if he had testified that his wife had assaulted him in the past and threatened him with a gun before she was killed? He further testifies that the gun went off accidentally when he tried to grab it from his wife. See *R. v. Wilson* (1999), 136 C.C.C. (3d) 252 (Man.

---

37 (1989), 71 C.R. (3d) 78 (Ont. C.A.). See also *R. v. McNamara* (1981), 56 C.C.C. (2d) 193 (Ont. C.A.), affirmed 45 C.R. (3d) 289, 19 C.C.C. (3d) 1, [1985] 1 S.C.R. 662. (1989), 71 C.R. (3d) 78 (Ont. C.A.)
38 (1993), 22 C.R. (4th) 344 (Ont. C.A.).
39 See also *R. v. N. (R.K.)* (1996), 114 C.C.C. (3d) 40 (Ont. C.A.).

C.A.) at 265-269 and *R. v. Truscott* (2006), 213 C.C.C. (3d) 183 (Ont. C.A.) at 192.

Problem 2

A nurse is charged with three counts of sexual assault arising out of the course of his duties at Toronto East General Hospital. In his examination-in-chief, the accused testified that "he had never been involved with the police." Provide a ruling as to whether he has put his character in issue. See *R. v. Cocchio*, [2003] O.J. No. 780, 2003 CarswellOnt 767 (S.C.J.) and *R. v. Morris* (1978), 43 C.C.C. (2d) 129, [1979] 1 S.C.R. 405, 6 C.R. (3d) 36, at 157-158 [C.C.C.].

Problem 3

The accused is on trial for perjury and threatening death. The charges relate to false statements made on a Legal Aid application and a phone call to the Area Director in which he said "I'm going to knock you off." The accused has a lengthy criminal record including convictions for making threatening or harassing phone calls. During his examination-in-chief, the accused admitted that he had a criminal record but not the details. During cross-examination, the accused stated that he believed in honesty and fairness. The trial judge concluded that he put his character in issue:

> In so far as the issue of character, I think it has been put in issue on the basis of your direct examination. You indicated, and got an affirmative answer from the accused, that he had a criminal record and I believe the issue of character evidence is germane to what is before the court. I think having indicated that he is a firm believer in honesty and forthrightness, he has put his character on the line, and on that basis I am prepared to hear further evidence as it relates to the record.

Is there a basis to appeal? See *R. v. Bricker* (1994), 90 C.C.C. (3d) 268 (Ont. C.A.).

Problem 4

The accused is charged with first degree murder. The only issue is identity. The theory of the Crown is that the accused killed the victim because of an unpaid drug debt. The defence is alibi. The defence also vigorously challenged the integrity of the police investigation including the failure to investigate other potential suspects. To respond, the Crown wants to lead evidence of the accused's involvement in the drug trade. Admissible? Has the accused put his character in issue? See *R. v. Dhillon* (2002), 166 C.C.C. (3d) 262, 5 C.R. (6th) 317 (Ont. C.A.). But see: *R. v. Truscott* (2006), 213 C.C.C. (3d) 183 (Ont. C.A.).

(e) Similar Facts

So far, we have seen that disposition evidence led by the Crown is most commonly admissible as an exception to the bad character exclusionary rule when the Crown is responding to something the defence has done, such as putting their character in issue. In other words, it is largely rebuttal evidence which can only be used to rebut propensity evidence led by the accused. We now come to the controversial case of similar fact evidence. Here, the Crown is permitted to go on the offensive and lead propensity evidence to prove the commission of the offence. You will see as you read the cases that it is only recently that courts accepted this view of similar fact evidence. Courts for many years in England and Canada would only admit similar fact evidence if it was relevant to some issue other than propensity.

The classic and oft-repeated statement of the rule regarding the reception in evidence of similar facts was that of Lord Herschell L.C. in *Makin v. Attorney-General for New South Wales*:[40]

> It is undoubtedly not competent for the prosecution to adduce evidence tending to shew that the accused has been guilty of criminal acts other than those covered by the indictment, for the purpose of leading to the conclusion that the accused is a person likely from his criminal conduct or character to have committed the offence for which he is being tried. On the other hand, the mere fact that the evidence adduced tends to shew the commission of other crimes does not render it inadmissible if it be relevant to an issue before the jury, and it may be so relevant if it bears upon the question whether the acts alleged to constitute the crime charged in the indictment were designed or accidental, or to rebut a defence which would otherwise be open to the accused. The statement of these general principles is easy, but it is obvious that it may often be very difficult to draw the line and to decide whether a particular piece of evidence is on the one side or the other.

This statement, however, has been the cause of considerable confusion and difficulty both for the law student and the courts as it seeks to distinguish between different kinds of relevance. If the evidence is relevant only as showing the accused to be by his nature or disposition a person likely to commit the crime alleged, the evidence is inadmissible. If, on the other hand, the evidence is relevant in some other way to an issue before the jury, it is admissible. This approach led to the judicial creation over the years of categories of relevance[41] which would admit similar facts if the evidence "rebutted the defence of accident," "rebutted a defence of legitimate association for honest purpose," "demonstrated system," "went to identity," and so on. While this pigeon-hole method of analysis can be used to explain most of the similar fact cases, some cases continued to be troubling[42] and after repeated attempts at resolution the House of Lords opted for a quite different approach.

In *R. v. Boardman*[43] the accused was charged and convicted of buggery and incitement to commit buggery. The victims, pupils at the accused's school,

---

40 [1894] A.C. 57, 65.

41 See the numerous categories detailed in Cross, *Evidence* (5th ed.), pp. 378-93. See the pigeon-hole approach in *Leblanc v. R.*, [1977] 1 S.C.R. 339.

42 Cases such as *R. v. Straffen*, [1952] 2 Q.B. 911 (C.C.A.); *Thompson v. R.*, [1918] A.C. 221; and *R. v. Ball*, [1911] A.C. 47 (C.C.A.); the opinions profess to follow *Makin*, but on analysis the only relevance of the similar facts lies in showing the accused to be one "likely from his criminal conduct or character to have committed the offence for which he is being tried." See analysis by Hoffman, "Similar Facts after Boardman" (1975), 91 L.Q. R. 193.

43 [1975] A.C. 421 (H.L.). For commentaries see also: Williams, "The Problem of Similar Fact Evidence" (1979), 5 Dalhousie L. Rev. 281; Turcott, "Similar Fact Evidence: The Boardman Legacy" (1978), 21 Crim. L.Q. 43; Tapper, "Similar Facts; Peculiarity and Credibility" (1975), 38 Mod. L. Rev. 206; Eggleston, *Evidence, Proof and Probability* (1978); Sklar, "Similar Fact Evidence — Catchwords and Cartwheels" (1977), 23 McGill L.J. 60; Cross, "Fourth Time Lucky — Similar Fact Evidence in the House of Lords", [1975] Crim. L.R. 62; Killeen, "Recent Developments in the Law of Evidence" (1975), 18 Crim. L.Q. 103 at 120; Cross, *Evidence*, 5th ed. (1979), pp. 374-76; Piragoff, *Similar Fact Evidence* (1981), p. 161.

testified concerning the particular acts committed on each, and the trial judge ruled that the evidence of each could be taken as corroborative of the other as the acts were similar. The Court of Appeal dismissed the accused's appeal but certified the following question of law:

> Whether, on a charge involving an allegation of homosexual conduct there is evidence that the accused person is a man whose homosexual proclivities take a particular form, that evidence is thereby admissible although it tends to show that the accused has been guilty of criminal acts other than those charged.[44]

In answering that question, the House of Lords were unanimous in declining to create, or recognize, a "category of relevance" giving "automatic admissibility to evidence where proclivities take a particular form."[45] Rather the approach was to be based on principle and the trial judge in each case was to assess the probative worth of the evidence compared to the possibilities of prejudice and confusion of issues. The Law Lords followed the lead of Lord Simon in *Director of Public Prosecutions v. Kilbourne* when he interpreted the classic passage from Lord Herschell's opinion in *Makin*:

> That what was declared to be inadmissible in the first sentence of this passage is nevertheless relevant (i.e., logically probative) can be seen from numerous studies of offences in which recidivists are matched against first offenders. . . . All relevant evidence is prima facie admissible. The reason why the type of evidence referred to by Lord Herschell L.C. in the first sentence of the passage is inadmissible is, not because it is irrelevant, but because its logically probative significance is considered to be grossly outweighed by its prejudice to the accused, so that a fair trial is endangered if it is admitted; the law therefore exceptionally excludes this relevant evidence: whereas in the circumstances referred to in the second sentence the logically probative significance of the evidence is markedly greater.[46]

Lord Wilberforce in *Boardman* wrote:

> The basic principle must be that the admission of similar fact evidence (of the kind now in question) is exceptional and requires a strong degree of probative force. This probative force is derived, if at all, from the circumstance that the facts testified to by the several witnesses bear to each other such a striking similarity that they must, when judged by experience and common sense, either all be true, or have arisen from a cause common to the witnesses or from pure coincidence. The jury may, therefore, properly be asked to judge whether the right conclusion is that all are true, so that each story is supported by the other(s).[47]

Lord Cross agreed:

> the reason for this general rule is not that the law regards such evidence as inherently irrelevant but that it is believed that if it were generally admitted jurors would in many cases think that it was more relevant than it was, so that, as it is put, its prejudicial effect would outweigh its probative value. Circumstances, however, may arise in which such evidence is so very relevant that to exclude it would be an affront to

---

44 *Boardman, ibid.*, at p. 437.
45 *Ibid.*, at p. 441 per Lord Morris of Borth-y-Gest.
46 [1973] A.C. 729, 757. But see the opinion of Lord Hailsham in *Boardman, supra*, note 43, at p. 451, that adds, as "another" reason or theory for excluding similar fact evidence, that it is irrelevant!
47 *Supra*, note 43, at p. 444.

common sense. Take, for example, *Reg. v. Straffen* [1952] 2 Q.B. 911. There a young girl was found strangled. It was a most unusual murder for there had been no attempt to assault her sexually or to conceal the body though this might easily have been done. The accused, who had just escaped from Broadmoor and was in the neighbourhood at the time of the crime, had previously committed two murders of young girls, each of which had the same peculiar features. It would, indeed, have been a most extraordinary coincidence if this third murder had been committed by someone else and though an ultra-cautious jury might still have acquitted him it would have been absurd for the law to have prevented the evidence of the other murders being put before them although it was simply evidence to show that Straffen was a man likely to commit a murder of that particular kind. . . . The question must always be whether the similar fact evidence taken together with the other evidence would do no more than raise or strengthen a suspicion that the accused committed the offence with which he is charged or would point so strongly to his guilt that only an ultra-cautious jury, if they accepted it as true, would acquit in face of it. In the end — although the admissibility of such evidence is a question of law, not of discretion — the question as I see it must be one of degree.[48]

Lord Morris of Borth-y-Gest similarly opined:

where what is important is the application of principle, the use of labels or definitive descriptions cannot be either comprehensive or restrictive. . . . Evidence of other occurrences which merely tend to deepen suspicion does not go to prove guilt: so evidence of "similar facts" should be excluded unless such evidence has a really material bearing on the issues to be decided. . . . There may be cases where a judge, having both limbs of Lord Herschell's famous proposition in mind, considers that the interests of justice (of which the interests of fairness form so fundamental a component) make it proper that he should permit a jury when considering the evidence on a charge concerning one fact or set of facts also to consider the evidence concerning another fact or set of facts if between the two there is such a close or striking similarity or such an underlying unity that probative force could fairly be yielded.[49]

Viewed in this way, the so-called similar fact evidence rule may be stated in terms of its underlying rationale. Previous misconduct of the accused which is similar to the activity presently charged is relevant thereto but in our concern for a fair trial we erect a canon of exclusion lest the accused be prejudiced by its reception. Prejudice in this context does not mean that the evidence might increase the chances of conviction but rather that the evidence may be improperly used by the trier of fact. The trier who learns of the accused's previous misconduct may then view the accused as a bad man, one who deserves punishment regardless of his guilt of the instant offence and may be less critical of the evidence presently marshalled against him. The only true relevance of the previous activity follows a chain of reasoning through the accused's disposition and the law recognizes that frequently such chain is tenuous in its nature as people can change and dispositions vary. The law then erects a canon of exclusion for similar fact evidence which is tenuous in nature when viewed against the possibility of prejudice. If, however, the similar fact evidence is *not* tenuous in nature, if it has sufficient relevance, if it has genuine probative worth when taken together with the other evidence and is not then outweighed by

---

48 *Ibid.*, at p. 456.
49 *Ibid.*, at pp. 439-41.

considerations of prejudice, the reason for the canon of exclusion disappears. The first principle of rational fact-finding, that all relevant evidence should be received, then controls.

The classic statement of Lord Herschell continues to be troublesome. While Lords Cross and Wilberforce did not even mention *Makin* in their opinions, Lord Hailsham, in *Boardman*, sought to continue its force and "*explained*" the rule:

> It is perhaps helpful to remind oneself that what is *not* to be admitted is a chain of reasoning and not necessarily a state of facts. If the inadmissible chain of reasoning is the *only* purpose for which the evidence is adduced as a matter of law, the evidence itself is not admissible. If there is some other relevant, probative purpose than for the forbidden type of reasoning, the evidence is admitted, but should be made subject to a warning from the judge that the jury must eschew the forbidden reasoning.[50]

As Hoffman[51] points out, while this may be an accurate paraphrase of the *Makin* rule, it is impossible to reconcile it with many of the other classic cases on similar fact evidence.

Whether similar fact act evidence can be admitted in some cases to show propensity as in *Boardman* or whether some other purpose must be found as in *Makin* has been one of the most hotly contested issues in the Canadian law of evidence.

(i) *Need for Connection Between Previous Acts and Accused*

Before similar facts can be considered as evidence in the case there must be seen to be a connection between the previous acts and the accused. If the previous acts cannot be tied to the accused they have no relevance at all. Canadian courts have recognized this fact but have not clearly articulated an appropriate test.

Should the prosecution have to establish beyond a reasonable doubt that the accused committed the earlier acts? On a balance of probabilities? To whose satisfaction? The judge as a preliminary condition of admissibility? The jury who decides everything at the end of the case?[52]

The following two cases provide some guidance.

SWEITZER v. R.
[1982] 1 S.C.R. 949, 29 C.R. (3d) 97, 68 C.C.C. (2d) 193

The accused had originally been committed to trial on 15 counts of (what is now) sexual assault. The various counts were severed prior to trial. At the trial of the first count, the circumstances surrounding the 14 other offences were admitted into evidence. In 11 of these offences, including count 1, the victims were unable to identify their assailant. The only evidence of identification was to

---

50 [1975] A.C. 421, 453 (H.L.).

51 See "Similar Facts After Boardman" (1975), 91 L.Q. Rev. 193 at 198.

52 See generally, Tanovich, "Probative Value and the Issue of Proof in Similar Fact Evidence Cases" (1994), 23 C.R. (4th) 157, and more recently, Tanovich, "Revisiting the *Sweitzer* Issue of Proof" (1997), 9 C.R. (5th) 74.

be found in the fact that the conduct of the assailant in the episodes where he was unidentifiable was similar to his conduct where he was identified and in one episode caught at the scene. The Court of Appeal dismissed the accused's appeal against conviction. Before ordering a new trial, McIntyre J., for the full court, reviewed the law on similar fact evidence.

The question of the admissibility of similar fact evidence has been the subject of much legal writing to be found in the decided cases and textbooks and in the academic articles and commentaries. The general principle stated by Lord Herschell L.C. in *Makin and Makin v. A.-G. for New South Wales*, [1894] A.C. 57 at p. 65, has been largely accepted as the basis for the admission of this evidence. . . .

Over the years in seeking to apply this principle judges have tended to create a list of categories or types of cases in which similar fact evidence could be admitted, generally by reference to the purpose for which the evidence was adduced. Evidence of similar facts has been adduced to prove intent, to prove a system, to prove a plan, to show malice, to rebut the defence of accident or mistake, to prove identity, to rebut the defence of innocent association and for other similar and related purposes. This list is not complete.

This approach has been useful because similar fact evidence by its nature is frequently adduced for its relevance to a single issue in the case under trial. It has however involved, in my opinion, a tendency to overlook the true basis upon which evidence of similar facts is admissible. The general principle described by Lord Herschell may and should be applied in all cases where similar fact evidence is tendered and its admissibility will depend upon the probative effect of the evidence balanced against the prejudice caused to the accused by its admission whatever the purpose of its admission. This approach finds support in *Boardman v. Director of Public Prosecutions*, [1974] 3 All E.R. 887, and is implicit in the words of Lord Herschell in the *Makin* case.

· · · ·

The general principle enunciated in the *Makin* case by Lord Herschell, should be borne in mind in approaching this problem. The categories, while sometimes useful, remain only as illustrations of the application of that general rule.

Before evidence may be admitted as evidence of similar facts, there must be a link between the allegedly similar facts and the accused. In other words there must be some evidence upon which the trier of fact can make a proper finding that the similar facts to be relied upon were in fact the acts of the accused for it is clear that if they were not his own but those of another they have no relevance to the matters at issue under the indictment.

· · · ·

Dealing with the 11 episodes I say at once that in my view evidence relating to them was inadmissible and ought not to have been admitted. I put that proposition simply upon the footing that they afford no evidence of identification of the appellant, because, despite the existence of varying degrees of similarity between the acts revealed in the evidence and the facts of the case under trial, there is no evidence which connects the appellant with any of those episodes.

Appeal allowed; new trial ordered.

R. v. MILLAR
(1989), 71 C.R. (3d) 78, 49 C.C.C. (3d) 193 (Ont. C.A.)

The accused was charged with manslaughter. The victim was his nine-week-old son. The cause of death was subdural haemorrhage as a result of the child having been shaken by the accused. It was the theory of the Crown that the accused had shaken the baby excessively using more force than was necessary to assist the infant, or that he shook the infant in anger. The defence maintained that the accused shook the infant because he had stopped breathing. The Crown adduced evidence of a number of other injuries including fractures to the child's ribs. These injuries had occurred some weeks before. On appeal, objection was taken to the admissibility of the evidence of other injuries to the child. This ground of appeal failed. The appeal was allowed on the basis that the trial judge had not properly directed the jury as to the proper use of the evidence of these other injuries and as to expert evidence suggesting that they pointed to abuse. A new trial was ordered.

MORDEN J.A. (GRIFFITH and CARTHY JJ. concurring):—

· · · ·

2. *The admission of the evidence of other injuries*

The appellant's basic submission with respect to this evidence is that it was inadmissible because it had little probative value and strong prejudicial effect. The appellant concedes that evidence of other injuries to the victim is potentially relevant. . . . Evidence of this kind is potentially relevant to the state of mind with which the accused person kills the victim and, where relevant, to the fact that he killed him. The appellant, however, submits that notwithstanding its potential relevance this evidence should have been excluded because it was incapable of supporting two inferences:

(1) that the injuries were not the result of mere accident, but were the consequence of aggression towards the victim; and

(2) that the injuries were inflicted by the appellant.

With respect to (1), although there was evidence to the contrary — that is, that the other injuries could have been the result of accidents — it is clear that there was evidence sufficient for consideration by the jury that the injuries were not the result of accidents but were intentionally inflicted.

With respect to (2), there is, however, more difficulty. Because there was no objection to the admissibility of this evidence at the trial we do not have the benefit of the trial judge's consideration of this issue. It is clear that there must, at least, be some evidence capable of reasonably supporting a finding that the appellant was implicated in the other injuries.

. . . .

The only evidential basis for considering that the appellant was implicated in the earlier injuries is that the deceased was in the appellant's custody for the whole of his short life. This was not, however, exclusive custody. No doubt he spent more time alone with his mother than with the appellant alone. There is really no evidence of the deceased's being in the care of anyone else apart from the appellant's sister for one night at the Millar residence and Mrs. Chouinard, the grandmother, from time to time at the campsite. Both of these persons gave evidence and I do not think it could be said from a reading of the record as a whole that there was a reasonable possibility that either of these persons caused the injuries. Mrs. Millar testified that after Michael had been with his grandmother there never was any indication that he could have been hurt and, further, that she never saw any mishap when other people were holding the child that could have caused the injuries.

When the Crown had completed its case I do not think that there was any basis on which the jury could more reasonably conclude, assuming that the injuries were intentionally caused, that it was the appellant rather than Mrs. Millar who had caused the injuries. When, however, all of the evidence at the trial had been given I think that the picture changed.

Mrs. Millar gave evidence that she had been charged with manslaughter with respect to the death of the child. Although it is not stated clearly in the record it may be inferred that she was discharged following the preliminary inquiry. Mrs. Millar was never asked point blank whether she had caused the injuries. However, at more than one point in her evidence she testified that she had had no idea of the injuries that Michael was subsequently discovered to have suffered. She speculated in her evidence that the rib injuries could have occurred during birth, and also that the injuries could have occurred on the two occasions when Sean carried the baby or when the baby had apparently fallen out of bed. She also referred to the occasion when the baby fell out of the appellant's arms.

Although, certainly, there is no positive suggestion in Mrs. Millar's evidence that the appellant caused the injuries, if the jury accepted her evidence that she was ignorant of the injuries before August 1st and rejected the appellant's evidence that he had not caused the injuries, then there was an evidentiary basis which could reasonably support a finding that the appellant had caused the other injuries.

The Crown, at the end of the case, was entitled to rely upon all of the evidence in the record. Accordingly, I think that this ground of appeal should fail.

. . . .

It should be emphasized that the evidence of the other injuries was before the jury solely on the issue of the accused's state of mind at the time he shook the baby; it could not be used to support a general inference that the appellant was the sort of person likely to have committed the crime in question: *Makin v. A.-G. N.S.W.*, [1894] A.C. 57 at p. 65 (P.C.).

We will return to this difficult issue of linkage when we later consider the Supreme Court's judgment in *R. v. Arp.*

(ii) *How are Similar Facts Relevant?*

R. v. B. (C.R.)
[1990] 1 S.C.R. 717, 76 C.R. (3d) 1, 55 C.C.C. (3d) 1

The accused was charged with sexual offences against a young child, his natural daughter. The daughter testified that the acts of sexual misconduct by the accused began in 1981 when she was 11 years old and continued for almost two years. In support of the child's testimony, the Crown sought to introduce evidence that the accused had had sexual relations in 1975 with a 15-year-old girl, the daughter of his common law wife, with whom he had enjoyed a father-daughter relationship. The trial judge admitted the evidence and convicted the accused. The majority of the Court of Appeal held that the similar fact evidence was properly admitted and upheld the conviction. The accused appealed further.

McLachlin J. (Dickson C.J.C. and Wilson, L'Heureux-Dubé and Gonthier JJ. concurring):—

. . . .

The common law has traditionally taken a strict view of similar fact evidence, regarding it with suspicion. In recent years, the courts have moved to loosen the formalistic strictures which had come to encumber the rule. The old category approach determining what types of similar fact evidence is admissible has given way to a more general test which balances the probative value of the evidence against its prejudice.

Despite the apparent simplicity of the modern rule for the admission of similar fact evidence, the rule remains one of considerable difficulty in application. The problems stem in part from a tendency to view the modern formulation of the rule in isolation from the historical context from whence it springs. While the contemporary formulation may permit a more flexible, less restricted analysis, the dangers which it addresses and the principles upon which it rests remain unchanged.

. . . .

Problems with the category approach to similar fact evidence became increasingly apparent in the less formalistic 20th century. On the one hand, the effect of the categories and the frequently referred to requirement of "striking similarity" was that similar fact evidence, which from the point of view of common sense had great relevance, might be excluded — a result which provoked one judge to declaim (*R. v. Hall* (1987), 5 N.Z.L.R. 93 at 108-10 (C.A)):

> Viewed in the light of science . . . or common sense, there is without doubt a nexus . . . The common law must often result in what the public may regard as a failure of justice. That is really not our concern.

Other judges reacted to the tendency of the rule to exclude probative evidence by drawing distinctions that were fundamentally unworkable or imaginary in order to admit evidence which common sense told them should be admitted. On the other hand, the rule sometimes permitted reception of evidence of doubtful worth.

Provided it fell within one of the accepted categories, evidence of prior misconduct or inclination might be admitted even though its relevance was suspect.

From the point of view of theory too, the category approach associated with *Makin* was subject to criticism. The categories focussed attention on the *purpose* for which the similar fact evidence was adduced, rather than the real question — its *relevance*: see J.A. Andrews and M. Hirst, Criminal Evidence (1987), para. 15.34. As Sklar stated ("Similar Fact Evidence — Catchwords and Cartwheels" (1977), 23 McGill L.J. 60 at 62), "Whether the evidence was really *relevant* to the issue by whatever the rationale and whether, if it was, it was *relevant enough* to justify its reception despite its nearly uncontrollable tendency to damn the accused in the minds of the jury, was lost in the shuffle" (emphasis added in original). If the evidence fell within a recognizable category, it was admitted even if its relevance may have been suspect. Moreover, the emphasis on the need for the evidence to relate to an issue other than disposition was arguably artificial. As Professor Andrews and Mr. Hirst have commented at pp. 342-43:

> 15.37 Although the courts made a great show of relying on the categories of relevance and of avoiding the forbidden chain of reasoning [guilt from propensity], their whole approach was really based upon a fundamental misconception. In reality, similar fact evidence can hardly ever show design or rebut a defence except by encouraging the court or jury to utilise the forbidden chain of reasoning. Whether the judges realised this or not, the undeniable fact is that in many of the leading cases evidence was admitted where it could only have been relevant because it showed disposition or propensity.

Provided some element, however small, other than disposition could be found to which the evidence related, it went in, although the effect might be almost entirely related to disposition.

Difficulties such as these led the House of Lords to readdress the question of similar fact evidence in *D.P.P. v. Boardman*, [1975] A.C. 421. On its face, *Boardman* constitutes no great departure from *Makin*, with three of the five Law Lords (Lords Morris, Hailsham and Salmon) expressly affirming the validity of *Makin*. However, all five judges rejected the category approach that had become associated with *Makin*, emphasizing that similar fact evidence is not automatically admissible merely because it fits into a prescribed category. The admissibility of similar fact evidence was to be based on general principle, not categories and catch phrases. That general principle was relevance.

While the five separate and sometimes conflicting opinions delivered in *Boardman* may not provide a comprehensive picture of the various ways in which cogency may be found, the ratio decidendi of the case is clear: the admissibility of similar fact evidence depends on its bearing a very high degree of probative value — sufficient to outweigh the inherent prejudice likely to flow from its reception.

. . . .

The Canadian jurisprudence since *Boardman* is generally consistent with the approach advocated in that case. It has followed *Boardman* in rejecting the category approach to the admission of similar fact evidence. At the same time, cases in Canada have on the whole maintained an emphasis on the general rule that evidence of mere propensity is inadmissible, and have continued to emphasize the necessity that such evidence possess high probative value in relation to its potential prejudice.

. . . .

While our courts have affirmed the general exclusionary rule for evidence of disposition and propensity, they have for the most part cast it in terms of *Boardman* rather than *Makin*. It is no longer necessary to hang the evidence tendered on the peg of some issue other than disposition. While the language of some of the assertions of the exclusionary rule admittedly might be taken to suggest that mere disposition evidence can *never* be admissible, the preponderant view prevailing in Canada is the view taken by the majority in *Boardman* — evidence of propensity, while generally inadmissible, may exceptionally be admitted where the probative value of the evidence in relation to an issue in question is so high that it displaces the heavy prejudice which will inevitably inure to the accused where evidence of prior immoral or illegal acts is presented to the jury.

. . . .

Catchwords have gone the same way as categories. Just as English courts have expressed doubts about the necessity of showing "striking similarity" . . . , so in *Robertson* Wilson J. rejected the validity of this phrase as a legal test.

A third feature of this court's treatment of the similar fact rule since *Boardman* is the tendency to accord a high degree of respect to the decision of the trial judge, who is charged with the delicate process of balancing the probative value of the evidence against its prejudicial effect. . . . This deference to the trial judge may in part be seen as a function of the broader, more discretionary nature of the modern rule at the stage where the probative value of the evidence must be weighed against its prejudicial effect.

. . . .

. . . In a case such as the present, where the similar fact evidence sought to be adduced is prosecution evidence of a morally repugnant act committed by the accused, the potential prejudice is great and the probative value of the evidence must be high indeed to permit its reception. The judge must consider such factors as the degree of distinctiveness or uniqueness between the similar fact evidence and the offences alleged against the accused, as well as the connection, if any, of the evidence to issues other than propensity, to the end of determining whether, in the context of the case before him, the probative value of the evidence outweighs its potential prejudice and justifies its reception.

Against this background, I turn to the facts in this case and the ruling of the trial judge.

. . . .

The main similarity is that in each case the accused, shortly after establishing a father-daughter relationship with the victim, is alleged to have engaged her in a sexual relationship. Additionally, the trial judge detailed similarities relating to the place and manner in which the relations occurred in the two situations. The age of the girls was different; one was sexually mature, the other only a child when the acts began. One girl was a blood relation, the other was not. . . .

That said, it cannot be concluded that the evidence necessarily fails the test indicated by the authorities to which I earlier referred. The fact that in each case the accused established a father-daughter relationship with the girl before the sexual violations began might be argued to go to showing, if not a system or design, a pattern of similar behaviour suggesting that the complainant's story is true. The question then is whether the probative value of the evidence outweighs its prejudicial effect. While I may have found this case to have been a borderline case of admissibility if I had been the trial judge, I am not prepared to interfere with the conclusion of the trial judge, who was charged with the task of weighing the probative value of the evidence against its prejudicial effect in the context of the case as a whole.

I would dismiss the appeal and affirm the conviction.

SOPINKA J. (LAMER J. concurring), dissenting:—

. . . .

There is no special rule with relation to similar fact evidence in sexual offences. . . . There is no support in the cases in our court for the theory that the rule has special application in sexual offences. Accordingly, evidence that the accused has a propensity to molest children or his or her own children is never admissible solely for that purpose.

. . . .

To have probative value the evidence must be susceptible of an inference relevant to the issues in the case other than the inference that the accused committed the offence because he or she has a disposition to the type of conduct charged: *Morris v. R.*, supra, . . . As in the case of relevance, evidence can be logically probative but not legally probative. When the term "probative value" is employed in the cases, reference is made to legally probative value.

The principal reason for the exclusionary rule relating to propensity is that there is a natural human tendency to judge a person's action on the basis of character. Particularly with juries there would be a strong inclination to conclude that a thief has stolen, a violent man has assaulted and a pedophile has engaged in pedophilic acts. Yet the policy of the law is wholly against this process of reasoning. This policy is reflected not only in similar acts cases, but as well in the rule excluding evidence of the character of the accused unless placed in issue by him. The stronger the evidence of propensity, the more likely it is that the forbidden inference will be drawn and, therefore, the greater the prejudice.

I am unable therefore to subscribe to the theory that in exceptional cases propensity alone can be the basis for admissibility. To say that propensity may have probative value in a sufficiently high degree to be admissible is a contradiction in terms. It is tantamount to saying that when the danger of the application of the forbidden line of reasoning is the strongest, the evidence can go in. The view has been expressed that this change in the principles outlined above was made in *Boardman*, supra (see Hoffmann, "Similar Facts after *Boardman*" (1975), 91 L.Q. Rev. 193 at 202).

The suggestion that *Boardman* effected a radical change in the law is not borne out by an analysis of the respective speeches in the House of Lords. . . .

. . . .

In considering the admissibility of the evidence in this case, I observe that no attempt appears to have been made to negative the possibility of collaboration. No questions were directed to Crown witnesses to determine whether this possibility existed. The Crown, who must persuade the trial judge that the evidence has probative value, has the burden of proof. . . . In my view, the Crown must negative conspiracy or collaboration in accordance with the criminal standard. This is a requirement that applies whenever a preliminary finding of fact is a precondition to the admissibility of evidence tendered by the Crown. . . .

There is then the further question of coincidence. Are the common characteristics in the evidence of the two girls so unusual that it would be against common sense to conclude that they are not both telling the truth? In this connection, the observation of Lord Cross in *Boardman*, quoted above, is helpful. We have only two instances and should proceed with caution. They are separated by a considerable passage of time and as well there are material differences which are detailed in the reasons of Harradence J.A. in the Court of Appeal. McLachlin J. stresses that in each case the appellant established a father relationship. As her statement of the facts indicates, the appellant was the father of one child and he enjoyed a father-daughter relationship with the other. These are not unusual facts and indeed are neutral. In any case, where it is alleged that a father has had an incestuous relationship with two of his children, this fact will be common to both. If one or both girls are not telling the truth, is it unlikely that they would both have said that the appellant established a father relationship with them? Obviously not, because that happened irrespective of whether the balance of their evidence is true.

. . . .

. . . I am unable to say what would have occurred if the similar fact evidence had been rejected by the trial judge. Accordingly, I would direct a new trial. The appeal is therefore allowed and a new trial directed.[53]

Why has, as Justice McLachlin writes, the common law "traditionally taken a strict view of similar fact evidence, regarding it with suspicion?"

---

53 For several years after *B. (C.R.)*, the Supreme Court and courts below vacillated between the focus on propensity and that requiring a purpose other than propensity: see analysis by R.J. Delisle, "The Direct Approach to Similar Fact Evidence", (1996) 50 C.R. (4th) 286.

Do you think that this concern is linked to the nature of the offences where similar act evidence is most likely to be tendered by the Crown?[54]

R. v. ARP
[1998] 3 S.C.R. 339, 20 C.R. (5th) 1, 129 C.C.C. (3d) 321

Two women, U and B, were murdered some two-and-a-half years apart in the same city and in similar circumstances. The accused was charged with first degree murder of both women. Defence counsel unsuccessfully applied to sever the two murder counts in the indictment. The Crown opposed the application and asserted that even in the case of severance, it would seek to adduce the evidence of each offence in the other trial as similar fact evidence. The Crown conceded that unless the evidence concerning the one murder was admissible to establish that the accused committed the other murder, there should be a severance of the two counts. However, the Crown argued that there were many similarities between the two events indicative of pattern and design.

The trial judge charged the jury that, if they concluded both counts were likely committed by the same person, they could use the evidence on each count to assist in deciding the accused's guilt on both counts. He stated that the evidence on the B killing was admissible in proving the guilt of the accused for the U killing and vice versa. When examining the evidence on both counts, they were instructed not to conclude that the appellant was a person whose character or disposition was such that he likely committed the offences. The trial judge stated that they could infer from the evidence, although they were not required to do so, that the incident mentioned in the B count and the incident mentioned in the U count had characteristics in common that were so strikingly similar that it was likely that they were committed by one person.

The trial judge reviewed the evidence related to the murder of U. The trial judge noted that the Crown submitted the crimes were similar in that the victims were young single females who were vulnerable and who were without funds or transportation in the early morning hours; there was evidence that each was picked up by the accused in a grey pickup truck; the U case clearly involved sexual intercourse, while in the B murder a sexual purpose could be inferred; the victims were left in isolated but accessible areas outside Prince George; the victims' clothes were found discarded nearby; there was evidence that in both cases a sharp-edged instrument, such as a knife, was used.

The accused was convicted and his appeal dismissed.

Cory J. (Lamer C.J. and L'Heureux-Dubé, Gonthier, McLachlin, Iacobucci, Major, Bastarache and Binnie JJ. concurring): —

. . . .

Admissibility of Similar Fact Evidence

Probative Value

This appeal concerns the proper charge to a jury on the use of similar fact evidence. This issue necessarily requires a careful review of the role of the trial

---

54 See Hanson, "Sexual Assault and the Similar Fact Rule" (1993), 27 U.B.C.L. Rev. 51.

judge in considering the admission of similar fact evidence. This is necessary in order to place the function of the jury in weighing similar fact evidence in its proper context.

. . . .

Evidence of propensity or disposition (e.g., evidence of prior bad acts) is relevant to the ultimate issue of guilt, in so far as the fact that a person has acted in a particular way in the past tends to support the inference that he or she has acted that way again. Though this evidence may often have little probative value, it is difficult to say it is not relevant. In this regard, I disagree in part with Lord Hailsham's judgment in *Director of Public Prosecutions v. Boardman*, [1975] A.C. 421. He wrote, at p. 451, that "[w]hen there is nothing to connect the accused with a particular crime except bad character or similar crimes committed in the past, the probative value of the evidence is nil and the evidence is rejected on that ground". I think this statement may go too far. . . .

Thus evidence of propensity or disposition may be relevant to the crime charged, but it is usually inadmissible because its slight probative value is ultimately outweighed by its highly prejudicial effect. As Sopinka J. noted in *R. v. D. (L.E.)*, [1989] 2 S.C.R. 111, at pp. 127-28, there are three potential dangers associated with evidence of prior bad acts: (1) the jury may find that the accused is a "bad person" who is likely to be guilty of the offence charged; (2) they may punish the accused for past misconduct by finding the accused guilty of the offence charged; or (3) they may simply become confused by having their attention deflected from the main purpose of their deliberations, and substitute their verdict on another matter for their verdict on the charge being tried. Because of these very serious dangers to the accused, evidence of propensity or disposition is excluded as an exception to the general rule that all relevant evidence is admissible.

However, as Lord Hailsham stated in *Boardman*, *supra*, at p. 453, "what is *not* to be admitted is a chain of reasoning and not necessarily a state of facts" (emphasis added). That is, disposition evidence which is adduced *solely* to invite the jury to find the accused guilty because of his or her past immoral conduct is inadmissible. However, evidence of similar past misconduct may exceptionally be admitted where the prohibited line of reasoning may be avoided.

[Justice Cory then reviewed the majority opinion of McLachlin J. in *R. v. B. (C.R.)* and concluded.]

It can be seen that in considering whether similar fact evidence should be admitted the basic and fundamental question that must be determined is whether the probative value of the evidence outweighs its prejudicial effect. As well it must be remembered that a high degree of deference must be given to the decision of a trial judge on this issue. . . .

It follows that where identity is at issue in a criminal case and the accused is shown to have committed acts which bear a striking similarity to the alleged crime, the jury is not asked to infer from the accused's habits or disposition that *he is the type of person* who would commit the crime. Instead, the jury is asked to infer from the degree of distinctiveness or uniqueness that exists between the commission of the crime and the similar act that *the accused is the very person* who committed the crime. This inference is made possible only if the high degree of similarity between the acts renders the likelihood of coincidence objectively improbable. See *Hoch v. The Queen* (1988), 165 C.L.R. 292 (Aust. H.C.). That is, there is always a possibility that by coincidence the perpetrator of the crime and the accused share certain predilections or that the accused may become implicated in crimes for which he is not responsible. However, where the evidence shows a distinct pattern to the acts in question, the possibility that the accused would repeatedly be implicated in strikingly similar offences purely as a matter of coincidence is greatly reduced.

. . . .

[A] principled approach to the admission of similar fact evidence will in all cases rest on the finding that the accused's involvement in the alleged similar acts or counts is unlikely to be the product of coincidence. This conclusion ensures that the evidence has sufficient probative force to be admitted, and will involve different considerations in different contexts. Where, as here, similar fact evidence is adduced on the issue of identity, there must be a high degree of similarity between the acts for the evidence to be admitted. For example, a unique trademark or signature will automatically render the alleged acts "strikingly similar" and therefore highly probative and admissible. In the same way, a number of significant similarities, taken together, may be such that by their cumulative effect, they warrant admission of the evidence. Where identity is at issue ordinarily, the trial judge should review the manner in which the similar acts were committed — that is to say, whether the similar acts involve a unique trademark or reveal a number of significant similarities. This review will enable him or her to decide whether the alleged similar acts were all committed by the same person. This preliminary determination establishes the objective improbability that the accused's involvement in the alleged acts is the product of coincidence and thereby gives the evidence the requisite probative force. Thus, where the similar fact evidence is adduced to prove identity, once this preliminary determination is made, the evidence related to the similar act (or count, in a multi-count indictment) may be admitted to prove the commission of another act (or count).

. . . .

In summary, in considering the admissibility of similar fact evidence, the basic rule is that the trial judge must first determine whether the probative value of the evidence outweighs its prejudicial effect. In most cases where similar fact evidence is adduced to prove identity it might be helpful for the trial judge to consider the following suggestions in deciding whether to admit the evidence:

    (1) Generally where similar fact evidence is adduced to prove identity a high degree of similarity between the acts is required in order to ensure that the similar fact evidence has the requisite probative value of outweighing its prejudicial effect to be admissible. The similarity

between the acts may consist of a unique trademark or signature on a series of significant similarities.

(2) In assessing the similarity of the acts, the trial judge should only consider the manner in which the acts were committed and not the evidence as to the accused's involvement in each act.

(3) There may well be exceptions but as a general rule if there is such a degree of similarity between the acts that it is likely that they were committed by the same person then the similar fact evidence will ordinarily have sufficient probative force to outweigh its prejudicial effect and may be admitted.

(4) The jury will then be able to consider all the evidence related to the alleged similar acts in determining the accused's guilt for any one act.

Once again these are put forward not as rigid rules but simply as suggestions that may assist trial judges in their approach to similar fact evidence.

. . . .

Link to the Accused

Where the similar fact evidence adduced to prove identity suggests that the same person committed the similar acts, then logically this finding makes the evidence linking the accused to each similar act relevant to the issue of identity for the offence being tried. Similarly, in a multi-count indictment, the link between the accused and any one count will be relevant to the issue of identity on the other counts which disclose a striking similarity in the manner in which those offences were committed.

A link between the accused and the alleged similar acts is, however, also a precondition to admissibility. This requirement was set forth in *R. v. Sweitzer*, [1982] 1 S.C.R. 949, at p. 954. . . .

. . . .

Should the trial judge be required to conclude *not only* that the evidence suggests that the acts are the work of one person with sufficient force to outweigh the prejudicial effect of the evidence, but that they also are likely the acts of the accused? This is the approach advocated by Professor R. Mahoney in "Similar Fact Evidence and the Standard of Proof", [1993] Crim. L. Rev. 185, at pp. 196-97, and is implicitly favoured by those courts which have endorsed the "anchor" or "sequential" approach to similar fact evidence. See, e.g., *R. v. Ross*, [1980] 5 W.W.R. 261 (B.C. C.A.); *R. v. J.T.S.*, [1997] A.J. No. 125 (C.A.).

The suggestion that the evidence linking the accused to the similar acts must also link the acts to the accused goes too far. Once the trial judge has concluded that the similar acts were likely the work of one person and that there is some evidence linking the accused to the alleged similar acts, it is not necessary to conclude that the similar acts were likely committed by the accused. The answer to this question may well determine guilt or innocence. This is the very question which the trier of fact must determine on the basis of all the evidence related to the similar acts, including of course the accused's involvement in each act. The standard set out in *Sweitzer* should be maintained. This only requires that the trial judge be satisfied that there is some evidence which links the accused to the similar acts.[55]

. . . .

The general principles enunciated in these cases indicate that the jury should determine, on a balance of the probabilities, whether the similarities between the acts establishes that the two counts were committed by the same person. If that threshold is met, the jury can then consider all the evidence relating to the similar acts in determining whether, beyond a reasonable doubt, the accused is guilty.

However, the general rule that preliminary findings of fact may be determined on a balance of probabilities is departed from in those certainly rare occasions when admission of the evidence may itself have a conclusive effect with respect to guilt. For example, where the Crown adduces a statement of the accused made to a person in authority, the trial judge must be satisfied beyond a reasonable doubt of the voluntariness of the statement. That evidence may of itself, if accepted as true, provide conclusive proof of guilt. Since doubt about the statement's voluntariness also casts doubt on its reliability, proof beyond a reasonable doubt is warranted. See *Ward v. The Queen*, [1979] 2 S.C.R. 30. If this were not the rule, the jury would be permitted to rely on evidence which it could accept as extremely cogent even though the inherent reliability of that evidence was in doubt.

Similar fact evidence, on the other hand, as circumstantial evidence, must be characterized differently, since, by its nature, it does not carry the potential to be conclusive of guilt. It is just one item of evidence to be considered as part of the Crown's overall case. Its probative value lies in its ability to support, through the improbability of coincidence, other inculpatory evidence. As with all circumstantial evidence, the jury will decide what weight to attribute to it. The mere fact that in a particular case, similar fact evidence might be assigned a high degree of weight by the trier is entirely different from the concept that, by its very nature, the evidence has the potential to be decisive of guilt.

One of the curiosities of *Arp* is that it would appear that there was no need for similar facts evidence to establish identity. At the time of the first murder, the accused was released by police because hair samples could not be linked to the accused. However, two and one half years later, DNA evidence linked the accused to cigarette samples and semen found at the second murder scene and also to the hair samples seized in the earlier case.

Cory J. emphasized that where similar fact evidence is admitted to prove identity in a multi-count indictment the jury must be warned

---

55 For a recent discussion of the linkage requirement see *R. v. MacCormack*, (2009) 64 C.R. (6th) 137 (Ont. C.A.) and annotation by Lisa Dufraimont.

that they are not to use the evidence on one count to infer that the accused is the person whose character or disposition is such that he or she is likely to have committed the offence or offences charged in the other count or counts"(para. 80).

In *Arp*, Cory J. also remarks in *obiter* that normally a prior acquittal cannot be relied on for similar fact evidence in a subsequent trial of the same accused. He speaks of a fundamental principle that an accused not repeatedly defend himself against the same allegations (para. 31). The House of Lords in *R. v. Z.*[56] specifically rejected this aspect of *Arp*. However, the Supreme Court of Canada recently endorsed this aspect of *Arp*.[57] **With whom do you agree?**[58]

R. v. HANDY

[2002] 2 S.C.R. 908, 1 C.R. (6th) 203, 2002 CarswellOnt 1968, 2002 CarswellOnt 1969, 164 C.C.C. (3d) 481

The accused was charged with sexual assault. His defence was that the sex was consensual. The complainant's position was that she had consented to vaginal sex but not hurtful or anal sex. The Crown sought to introduce similar fact evidence from the accused's former wife to the effect that the accused had a propensity to inflict painful sex, including anal sex, and when aroused would not take no for an answer. The similar fact evidence concerned seven alleged prior incidents. The accused denied committing any of the alleged assaults on his ex-wife. The trial judge admitted the similar fact evidence.

The ex-wife testified that she had met the complainant a few months before the alleged sexual assault took place. She had told the complainant at that time about the accused's criminal record and her allegations of his abuse of her during their marriage. The ex-wife told the complainant that she had received $16,500 from the Criminal Injuries Compensation Board and agreed when it was put to her in cross-examination that all she had to do to get the money was say that she had been abused. The trial judge ruled that it was not for him to resolve the possibility of collusion between the complainant and the ex-wife.

The jury convicted. The Court of Appeal held that the former wife's testimony had been wrongly admitted and ordered a new trial.

Held: Appeal dismissed.

Per BINNIE, J. (McLACHLIN C.J. and L'HEUREUX-DUBÉ, GONTHIER, IACOBUCCI, MAJOR, BASTARACHE, ARBOUR and LEBEL JJ. concurring):

. . . .

I. Facts

The complainant's evidence was that on the evening of December 6, 1996, she went out drinking with some friends. The respondent, whom she had met six

---

56 [2002] 1 A.C. 483.

57 See *R. v. Mahalingan* (2008), 61 C.R. (6th) 207 (S.C.C.) at paras. 66-69.

58 For differing views to this question see Lee Stuesser, "Admitting Acquittals as Similar Fact Evidence", (2002) 45 Crim. L.Q. 488 and Richard Mahoney, "Acquittals as Similar Fact Evidence: Another View", (2003) 47 Crim. L.Q. 265. See also *R. v. Akins* (2002), 5 C.R. (6th) 400 (Ont. C.A.) and *R. v. Mahalingan* (2006), 208 C.C.C. (3d) 515 (Ont. C.A.).

months earlier, was also at the bar. The two spent the evening drinking and flirting with one another. After leaving the bar, they went to the home of one of the complainant's friends to smoke marijuana. The respondent and the complainant left the house together and drove to a nearby motel intending to have sex. In the course of vaginal intercourse, she became upset because the respondent was hurting her, forcing himself into her. She told him that it was painful but he continued. He then brusquely switched to anal intercourse. She said, "Stop that, it hurts". She tried to get him off her or to make him stop but he would not. She slapped his face. She says he hit her on the chest, he grabbed her arms, squeezed her stomach and choked her, and he punched her. She says she was pleading and crying. She had consented to vaginal sex but she did not consent to and did not want anal sex. After the incident, she told the respondent that he had made [page 915] her bleed. He allegedly responded to her by saying, "What the hell am I doing here? Why does this keep happening to me?"

A number of witnesses testified that they had seen bruises on her throat, chest and arms in the days following the incident. The complainant was diagnosed with post-traumatic stress.

A. The Similar Fact Evidence

The respondent's defence was that the sex was consensual. The issue thus came down to credibility on the consent issue. The Crown sought to introduce similar fact evidence from the respondent's former wife to the effect that the respondent has a propensity to inflict painful sex and when aroused will not take no for an answer. It was thus tendered to explain why the complainant should be believed when she testified that the assault proceeded despite her protest.

(1) Incident One

In March 1990, a few weeks after their first child was born, the ex-wife says the respondent wanted to have sexual intercourse with her to "see what it would feel like". She did not want to do so because she thought that it would be painful. The respondent insisted that they have vaginal intercourse. Once they started she told the respondent that she was in pain but he did not stop.

(2) Incident Two

Five or six months later she and the respondent visited her sister and brother-in-law in their mobile trailer. After everyone went to bed, the respondent wanted to have sexual intercourse. She told the respondent that she did not want to have sex because her sister and her husband were at the other end of the trailer. She tried to move away from him. The respondent told her to shut up and had vaginal intercourse with her anyway.

(3) Incident Three

She returned home one day to find that the respondent had invited a number of people to their apartment for a party. After seeing the respondent tickle two women on the couch, she got angry and told everyone to leave. After most of the guests departed, she went into the bedroom. The respondent followed her. He was upset that she had broken up his party. He tried to have intercourse with her. She tried to get away but he blocked the door with a dresser. She then attempted to flee through the second floor bedroom window, but he pulled her back in. He then forced her to have vaginal intercourse and passed out.

(4) Incident Four

Sometime early in 1992, the respondent came home drunk and wanted to have anal intercourse. She told him that she did not want to do so because it had hurt her on previous occasions. The respondent initiated anal intercourse nonetheless. She kept moving and tried to get away. Eventually, he grabbed a bottle of baby oil from underneath the bed and applied the oil to his penis and her anus. He initiated anal intercourse. They were interrupted by a crying baby, and she used the distraction to escape to the basement but the respondent followed her. He told her that if she did not stop running, he would tie her up with a rope. She ran naked from the house and over to the neighbour's house. The police were called but she did not lay charges.

(5) Incident Five

The respondent was imprisoned from 1992 until 1995 for sexual assaults on two other women (although the fact they were "other" women was withheld from the jury by agreement of counsel). In that period he placed a threatening phone call to his then wife, which precipitated their divorce. They resumed living together soon after he was released. Shortly thereafter, she became upset because the respondent had gone out with a woman he had once dated. The respondent became angry, grabbed her by the throat, threw her around, pinned her against the wall and broke their glass coffee table. He did not, however, sexually assault her on that occasion.

(6) Incident Six

One night during the summer of 1996, she and the respondent were returning home after dropping off their friends. The respondent told her that instead of going home, they were going to a gravel pit where she "was going to get it up the ass". She testified that he had forced her to have sex with him at the gravel pit in the past. She told him that she was willing to do anything other than anal intercourse because it hurt too much. The respondent, however, insisted on anal intercourse. Once at the gravel pit he attempted anal intercourse, but was unsuccessful because there was insufficient room in the back seat of the car. The respondent took her out of his car and put her face down on the hood. He attempted anal intercourse again. He eventually turned her over onto her back and had vaginal intercourse.

(7) Incident Seven

In October 1996, her grandfather passed away. She and the respondent were alone in her mother's home. She was crying and upset. She testified that her crying "turned [the respondent] on" and that he wanted to have sexual intercourse on her mother's new couch. She told him that she did not want to. The respondent put her on the couch and commenced vaginal intercourse. She cried. While they were having intercourse, he punched her a number of times in the stomach to make her cry louder.

B. The Respondent's Testimony

The respondent denied committing any of the alleged assaults on his ex-wife. With respect to the complainant's allegations, he testified that he [page 918] met her at the bar, that they were both intoxicated and that they left the bar together. Eventually they went to a motel room. He testified that once inside the room, the complainant straddled him while he lay on his back and they engaged in approximately 15 to 20 minutes of vaginal intercourse. He denied that she had complained or told him to stop. He also denied hitting her and choking her. He testified that she drove him home at approximately 6:40 a.m. He did not see her again.

C. The Evidence of Collusion

The ex-wife testified that she had met the complainant a few months before the alleged sexual assault took place. She had told the complainant at that time about the respondent's criminal record and her allegations of his abuse of her during their marriage. The ex-wife told the complainant that she had received $16,500 from the Criminal Injuries Compensation Board and agreed when it was put to her in cross-examination that "[a]ll you had to do [to get the money] was say that you were abused". The ex-wife's cross-examination was, in part, as follows:

Q.   You knew [the complainant]?

A.   Yes, I did.

Q.   You had met her in the summer of '96?

A.   That's correct.

Q.   She had come over and visited with you, right?

A.   That's correct.

Q.   At one point, she actually said to you that she thought that [the respondent] loved you very much?

A.   Yes, she did.

Q.   And you straightened her out?

A.   That's correct.

Q. And you told her that he had been to jail?

A. Yes, I did.

Q. You told her that he abused you?

A. Yes, I did.

Q. And you told her that you collected $16,500 from the government. All you had to do was say that you were abused.

A. Yes.

Q. So she knew all of that before December of 1996?

A. Yes. [Emphasis added.]

Subsequently, on December 6, 1996, the complainant met up with the respondent at the bar and, after sharing some marijuana, agreed to accompany him to a motel for sex.

. . . .

A. The Disputed Inferences

The ex-wife's testimony related to incidents removed in time, place and circumstances from the charge. It was thus only circumstantial evidence of the matters the jury was called on to decide and, as with any circumstantial evidence, its usefulness rests entirely on the validity of the inferences it is said to support with respect to the matters in issue. The argument for admitting this circumstantial evidence is that the jury may infer firstly that the accused is an individual who derives pleasure from sex that is painful to his partner, and will not take no for an answer, and secondly, that his character or propensity thus established gives rise to the further inference that he proceeded wilfully in this case knowing the complainant did not consent.

. . . .

B. The General Exclusionary Rule

The respondent is clearly correct in saying that evidence of misconduct beyond what is alleged in the indictment which does no more than blacken the accused's character is inadmissible. . . . The exclusion thus generally prohibits character evidence to be used as circumstantial proof of conduct. The danger is that the jury might be confused by the multiplicity of incidents and put more weight than is logically justified on the ex-wife's testimony (reasoning prejudice) or might convict based on the accused's bad personhood (moral prejudice). . . . The dangers of propensity reasoning are well recognized. Not only can people change their ways but they are not robotic. . . .

The policy basis for the exclusion is that while in some cases propensity inferred from similar facts may be relevant, it may also capture the attention of the trier of fact to an unwarranted degree. Its potential for prejudice, distraction and time consumption is very great and these disadvantages will almost always outweigh its probative value. It ought, in general, to form no part of the case which the accused is called on to answer. It is excluded notwithstanding the general rule that all relevant evidence is admissible. . . .

If propensity evidence were routinely admitted, it might encourage the police simply to "round up the usual suspects" instead of making a proper unblinkered investigation of each particular case. One of the objectives of the criminal justice system is the rehabilitation of offenders. Achievement of this objective is undermined to the extent the law doubts the "usual suspects" are capable of turning the page and starting a new life.

It is, of course, common human experience that people generally act consistently with their known character. We make everyday judgments about the reliability or honesty of particular individuals based on what we know of their track record. If the jurors in this case had been the respondent's inquisitive neighbours, instead of sitting in judgment in a court of law, they would undoubtedly have wanted to know everything about his character and related activities. His ex-wife's anecdotal evidence would have been of great interest. Perhaps too great, as pointed out by Sopinka J. in *B. (C.R.)*, *supra*, at p. 744:

> The principal reason for the exclusionary rule relating to propensity is that there is a natural human tendency to judge a person's action on the basis of character. Particularly with juries there would be a strong [page 927] inclination to conclude that a thief has stolen, a violent man has assaulted and a pedophile has engaged in pedophilic acts. Yet the policy of the law is wholly against this process of reasoning.

The policy of the law recognizes the difficulty of containing the effects of such information which, once dropped like poison in the juror's ear, "swift as quicksilver it courses through the natural gates and alleys of the body": Hamlet, Act I, Scene v, ll. 66-67.

C. The Narrow Exception of Admissibilty

While emphasizing the general rule of exclusion, courts have recognized that an issue may arise in the trial of the offence charged to which evidence of previous misconduct may be so highly relevant and cogent that its probative value in the search for truth outweighs any potential for misuse. . . .

The "common sense" condemnation of exclusion of what may be seen as highly relevant evidence has prompted much judicial agonizing, particularly in cases of alleged sexual abuse of children and adolescents, whose word was sometimes unfairly discounted when opposed to that of ostensibly upstanding adults. The denial of the adult, misleadingly persuasive on first impression, would melt under the history of so many prior incidents as to defy innocent explanation. That said, there is no special rule for sexual abuse cases. In any case, the strength of the similar fact evidence must be such as to outweigh "reasoning prejudice" and "moral prejudice". The inferences sought to be drawn must accord with common sense, intuitive notions of probability and the unlikelihood of coincidence. Although an element of "moral prejudice" may be introduced, it must be concluded by the trial judge on a balance of probabilities that the probative value of the sound inferences exceeds any prejudice likely to be created.

. . . .

Canadian case law recognizes that as the "similar facts" become more focussed and specific to circumstances similar to the charge (i.e., more situation specific), the probative value of propensity, thus circumscribed, becomes more cogent. As the differences and variables that distinguish the earlier "similar facts" from the subject matter of the charge in this type of case are reduced, the cogency of the desired inferences is thought to increase. Ultimately the policy premise of the general exclusionary rule (prejudice exceeds probative value) ceases to be true.

D. The Test of Admissibilty

. . . .

Although evidence relating solely to the accused's disposition will generally be excluded, exceptions to this rule will arise when the probative value of the evidence outweighs its prejudicial effect. . . . Evidence classified as "disposition" or "propensity" evidence is, exceptionally, admissible. . . . Similar fact evidence is thus presumptively inadmissible. The onus is on the prosecution to satisfy the trial judge on a balance of probabilities that in the context of the particular case the probative value of the evidence in relation to a particular issue outweighs its potential prejudice and thereby justifies its reception.

E. Difficulties in the Application of the Test

. . . .

It is one thing to talk about so general a test as balancing probative value against prejudice, and a different and much more difficult thing to apply the test in a practical way. In an attempt to provide more precise guidance. . . . Canadian appellate courts have from time to time advocated, amongst others, a "categories" approach, a multi-step "purpose" approach and a "conclusiveness" approach. Each of these attempts, helpful as they were in practice, were ultimately thought to obfuscate and detract from the principled approach eventually adopted.

(1) Propensity Evidence by Any Other Name Is Still Propensity Evidence

. . . .

While identification of the issue defines the precise purpose for which the evidence is proffered, it does not, and cannot, change the inherent nature of the propensity evidence, which must be recognized for what it is. By affirming its true character the Court keeps front and centre its dangerous potential.

(2) Identification of the "Issue in Question" is an Important Control

. . . .

Whether or not probative value exceeds prejudicial effect can only be determined in light of the purpose for which the evidence is proffered. . . . The requirement to identify the material issue in question, i.e., the purpose for which the similar fact evidence is proffered, does not detract from the probative value/ prejudice balance, but is in fact essential to it. Probative value cannot be assessed in the abstract. The utility of the evidence lies precisely in its ability to advance or refute a live issue pending before the trier of fact. . . . It is therefore incumbent on the Crown to identify the live issue in the trial to which the evidence of disposition is said to relate. . . . The relative importance of the issue in the particular trial may also have a bearing on the weighing up of factors for and against admissibility. Similar fact evidence that is virtually conclusive of a minor issue may still be excluded for reasons of overall prejudice. The "issues in question" are not however, categories of admissibility. Their identification is simply an element of the admissibility analysis which turns on weighing probative value against prejudice.

(3) Identification of the Required Degree of Similarity

The principal driver of probative value in a case such as this is the connectedness or nexus that is established between the similar fact evidence and the offence alleged. . . . The issue in the present case is not identification but the actus reus of the offence. The point is not that the degree of similarity in such a case must be higher or lower than in an identification case. The point is that the issue is different, and the drivers of cogency in relation to the desired inferences will therefore not be the same. . . . If, for example, the complainant in this case had not been able to identify the accused as the perpetrator of the alleged offence, the conduct described by the ex-wife was not so particular and distinctive as to amount to a signature that would safely differentiate him from other possible assailants. On the other hand, in a case where the issue is the animus of the accused towards the deceased, a prior incident of the accused stabbing the victim may be admissible even though the victim was ultimately shot, the accused says accidentally. The acts could be said to be dissimilar but the inference on the issue in question would nonetheless be compelling.

(4) Identification of Connecting Factors

The decided cases suggest the need to pay close attention to similarities in character, proximity in time and frequency of occurrence. . . . The trial judge was called on to consider the cogency of the proffered similar fact evidence in relation to the inferences sought to be drawn, as well as the strength of the proof of the similar facts themselves. . . . On the other hand, countervailing factors which have been found helpful in assessing prejudice include the inflammatory nature of the similar acts and whether the Crown can prove its point with less prejudicial evidence. In addition the court was required to take into account the potential distraction of the trier of fact from its proper focus on the facts charged and the potential for undue time consumption. These may be collectively described as moral prejudice and reasoning prejudice.

(5) Differentiating Admissible from Inadmissible Propensity Evidence

Part of the conceptual problem with similar fact evidence is that words like "disposition" or "propensity" are apt to describe a whole spectrum of human character and behaviour of varying degrees of potential relevance. At the vague end of the spectrum, it might be said that the respondent has a general disposition or propensity "for violence". . . . At a more specific level, it is alleged here that the propensity to violence emerges in this accused in a desire for hurtful sex. This formulation provides more context, but the definition of so general a propensity is still of little real use. . . . Cogency increases as the fact situation moves further to the specific end of the spectrum. . ... References to "calling cards" or "signatures" or "hallmarks" or "fingerprints" similarly describe propensity at the admissible end of the spectrum precisely because the pattern of circumstances in which an accused is disposed to act in a certain way are so clearly linked to the offence charged that the possibility of mere coincidence, or mistaken identity or a mistake in the character of the act, is so slight as to justify consideration of the similar fact evidence by the trier of fact. The issue at that stage is no longer "pure" propensity or "general disposition" but repeated conduct in a particular and highly specific type of situation. At that point, the evidence of similar facts provides a compelling inference that may fill a remaining gap in the jigsaw puzzle of proof, depending on the view ultimately taken by the jury.

. . . .

(6) Similar Fact Evidence Need Not Be Conclusive

Some authorities urge adoption of a further refinement that has been accepted in some common law jurisdictions in the balancing of prejudice against probative value, namely that similar fact evidence should only be admitted if its probative value is so great as to be virtually conclusive of guilt. . . . (But) we are dealing here with admissibility, not adjudication. The conclusiveness test does not sit well with the balancing model set out in *B. (C.R.)*. If the evidence were truly "conclusive", its probative value would ex hypothesi outweigh prejudice.

Application of the Test to the Facts of this Case

(1) The Probative Value of the Evidence

The issue at this stage is to determine whether the similar fact evidence is indeed strong enough to be capable of properly raising in the eyes of the jury the double inferences contended for by the Crown.

(a) *The Potential for Collusion*

If collusion is present, it destroys the foundation on which admissibility is sought, namely that the events described by the ex-wife and the complainant, testifying independently of one another, are too similar to be credibly explained by coincidence. . . . The trial judge cannot assess "the objective improbability of coincidence" without addressing the issue of whether the apparent coincidence is in fact the product of collusion. Admissibility is a question of law for the judge alone. . . . The trial judge held that he ought not to reach even a preliminary view of the likelihood of collusion. . . . If the evidence amounts to no more than opportunity, it will usually best be left to the jury. Here there is something more. It is the whiff of profit. The ex-wife acknowledged that she had told the complainant of the $16,500 she received from the Criminal Injuries Compensation Board on the basis that all you had to do was say that you were abused. A few days later the complainant, armed with this information, met the respondent and went off with him to have sex in a motel room. Where, as here, there is some evidence of actual collusion, or at least an air of reality to the allegations, the Crown is required to satisfy the trial judge, on a balance of probabilities, that the evidence of similar facts is not tainted with collusion. That much would gain admission. It would then be for the jury to make the ultimate determination of its worth. The trial judge erred in law in deferring the whole issue of collusion to the jury.

(b) Identification of the Issue in Question

The Crown says the issue generally is "the credibility of the complainant" and more specifically "that the accused has a strong disposition to do the very act alleged in the charges against him", but this requires some refinement. Care must be taken not to allow too broad a gateway for the admission of propensity evidence or, as it is sometimes put, to allow it to bear too much of the burden of the Crown's case (Sopinka, Lederman and Bryant, supra, at s. 11.26). Credibility is an issue that pervades most trials, and at its broadest may amount to a decision on guilt or innocence.

Anything that blackens the character of an accused may, as a by-product, enhance the credibility of a complainant. Identification of credibility as the "issue in question" may, unless circumscribed, risk the admission of evidence of nothing more than general disposition ("bad personhood").

. . . .

If the jury could legitimately infer sexual intransigence in closely comparable circumstances from the accused's past behaviour and refusal to take his wife's no for an answer, the present complainant's testimony that intercourse occurred despite her lack of consent gains in credibility. The issue broadly framed is credibility, but more accurately and precisely framed, the issue in question in this trial was the consent component of the actus reus and in relation to that issue the accused's alleged propensity to refuse to take no for an answer.

(c) Similarities and Dissimilarities Between the Facts Charged and the Similar Fact Evidence-The Connecting Factors

(i) Proximity in Time of the Similar Acts

The charge against the accused relates to December 6, 1996. The ex-wife's seven alleged incidents occurred between March 1990 and October 1996. The evidence of the accused's inability to take no for an answer gains cogency both from its repetition over many years and its most recent manifestation a couple of months before the offence charged.

(ii) Extent to Which the Other Acts Are Similar in Detail to the Charged Conduct

The learned trial judge paid insufficient attention to the dissimilarities. . . . None of the incidents described by the ex-wife began as consensual, then allegedly became non-consensual. Each of the incidents recounted by the ex-wife were bound up with the intimacy of a long-term relationship. The dynamic of these situations is not the same as the motel scene. . . . The search for similarities is a question of degree. Sexual activity may not show much diversity or distinctiveness. Not every dissimilarity is fatal, but for the reasons already mentioned, substantial dissimilarities may dilute probative strength and, by compounding the confusion and distraction, aggravate the prejudice.

(iii) Number of Occurrences of the Similar Acts

An alleged pattern of conduct may gain strength in the number of instances that compose it. . . . The ex-wife's evidence here, if believed, established a pattern over many years that the jury might think showed that the respondent's pleasure in not taking no for an answer in sexual encounters was a predictable characteristic of general application.

(iv) Circumstances Surrounding or Relating to the Similar Acts

Perhaps the most important dissimilarity lies not in the acts themselves but in the broader context. The "similar fact" evidence occurred in the course of a long-term dysfunctional marriage whereas the charge relates to a one-night stand following a chance meeting of casual acquaintances in a bar.

(v) Any Distinctive Feature(s) Unifying the Incidents

It is not alleged that the sex acts themselves or the surrounding circumstances were highly distinctive. Cogency was said to derive from repetition rather than distinctiveness.

(vi) Intervening Events

If the similar facts were sufficient to raise the inferences suggested by the Crown, there were no intervening events as such to undermine their probative value.

(d) Strength of the Evidence that the Similar Acts Actually Occurred

The respondent did not admit the prior misconduct, and, "quite apart from the issue of collusion", a vigorous attack was made in cross-examination on the ex-wife's credibility. . . . In the usual course, frailties in the evidence would be left to the trier of fact, in this case the jury. However, where admissibility is bound up with, and dependent upon, probative value, the credibility of the similar fact evidence is a factor that the trial judge, exercising his or her gatekeeper function is entitled to take into consideration. Where the ultimate assessment of credibility was for the jury and not the judge to make, this evidence was potentially too prejudicial to be admitted unless the judge was of the view that it met the threshold of being reasonably capable of belief.

(2) Assessment of the Prejudice

(a) Moral Prejudice

Prejudice in this context is not the risk of conviction. It is, more properly, the risk of an unfocussed trial and a wrongful conviction. The forbidden chain of reasoning is to infer guilt from general disposition or propensity. The evidence, if believed, shows that an accused has discreditable tendencies. In the end, the verdict may be based on prejudice rather than proof, thereby undermining the presumption of innocence.

The inflammatory nature of the ex-wife's evidence in this case cannot be doubted. It is, to the extent these things can be ranked, more reprehensible than the actual charge before the court. The jury would likely be more appalled by the pattern of domestic sexual abuse than by the alleged misconduct of an inebriated lout in a motel room on an isolated occasion. . . . This evidence has a serious potential for moral prejudice.

(b) Reasoning Prejudice

The major issue here is the distraction of members of the jury from their proper focus on the charge itself aggravated by the consumption of time in dealing with allegations of multiple incidents involving two victims in divergent circumstances rather than the single offence charged. Distraction can take different forms. In *R. v. D. (L.E.)*, McLachlin, J. observed that the similar facts may induce in the minds of the jury sentiments of revulsion and condemnation which might well deflect them from the rational, dispassionate analysis upon which the criminal process should rest.

Further, there is a risk, evident in this case, that where the similar facts are denied by the accused, the court will be caught in a conflict between seeking to admit what appears to be cogent evidence bearing on a material issue and the need to avoid unfairness to the right of the accused to respond. The accused has a limited opportunity to respond. Logistical problems may be compounded by the lapse of time, surprise, and the collateral issue rule, which will prevent trials within trials on the similar facts. Nor is the accused allowed to counter evidence of discreditable conduct with similar fact evidence in support of his or her credibility. Thus the practical realities of the trial process reinforce the prejudice inherent in the poisonous nature of the propensity evidence itself.

(3) Weighing Up Probative Value Versus Prejudice

As probative value advances, prejudice does not necessarily recede. On the contrary, the two weighing pans on the scales of justice may rise and fall together.

Nevertheless, probative value and prejudice pull in opposite directions on the admissibility issue and their conflicting demands must be resolved. . . . Justice is achieved when relevant evidence whose prejudice outweighs any probative value is excluded and where evidence whose probative value exceeds its prejudice, albeit an exceptional circumstance, is admitted. Justice includes society's interest in getting to the truth of the charges as well as the interest of both society and the accused in a fair process. A criminal justice system that has suffered some serious wrongful convictions in part because of misconceived notions of character and propensity should not, and does not, take lightly the dangers of misapplied propensity evidence.

In this case, the similar fact evidence was prima facie inadmissible and the Crown did not discharge the onus of establishing on a balance of probabilities that its probative value outweighed its undoubted prejudice. The probative value of the evidence, especially with respect to potential collusion, was not properly evaluated. The potential of such evidence for distraction and prejudice was understated. The threshold for admission of this sort of evidence was set too low.

. . . .

A trial judge's decision to admit similar fact evidence is entitled to substantial deference. In this case, however, quite apart from the other frailties of the similar fact evidence, the trial judge's refusal to resolve the issue of collusion as a condition precedent to admissibility was an error of law. A new trial is required.

The Crown decided subsequently not to re-prosecute.

We now have a unanimous nine-person decision of our highest court clearly stating that the test for the admissibility of similar fact evidence is assessing probative value against the possibility of prejudice and that reasoning through propensity is, exceptionally, permissible, if specific and not just general disposition. The test is now easier to articulate. The Court also spells out various factors that trial judges need to take into account. The principled approach adopted, and the clear statement of values deserves our applause. What had been a most confusing area in the law of evidence is now clearer. The approach taken in *Handy* now applies to the admissibility of all character evidence not just similar fact evidence.[59]

On *Handy* it is not necessary to find a purpose other than propensity, as appeared to be the approach of Justice Sopinka in judgments such as that in *D. (L.E.)*. The Court has expressly returned to the position of McLachlin J. in *C.R.B.* This is a very welcome development and one long preferred by the Ontario Court of Appeal.[60]

---

59 See *R. v. Kirk* (2004), 188 C.C.C. (3d) 329, 22 C.R. 13 (6th) 231 (Ont. C.A.) and *R. v. S.(P.)* (2007), 221 C.C.C. (3d) 56 (Ont. C.A.).

60 See its leading pronouncements in *R. v. B. (L.)* (1997), 9 C.R. (5th) 38 (Ont. C.A.) (giving practical advice on how to weigh probative value and prejudicial effect) and *R. v. Batte* (2000), 145 C.C.C. (3d) 498, 34 C.R. (5th) 263 (Ont. C.A.) (where Doherty J.A. adopts the general/specific propensity distinction adopted in *Handy*).

Are you satisfied with the manner in which the Court applied the test to the facts of the case? Did the Court apply too narrow a view about sexual assault in distinguishing between marital and date rape?

It remains to be seen whether similar fact evidence will now be more or less readily admitted. The Supreme Court in *Handy* rejects the Australian limit that the evidence must be "conclusive" (para.93). On the other hand, less favourable to admission, the Court stands firmly against general propensity evidence and expressly indicates that propensity evidence is presumptively inadmissible (para.55).

It also rules that the issue in question cannot be framed as broadly as "credibility" (paras. 115-116), which has often in the past been the basis for the admission of similar fact evidence.[61] Consider the following two cases on the issue of identifying credibility as the issue in question.

R. v. BLAKE
(2003), 68 O.R. (3d) 75, 181 C.C.C. (3d) 169 (C.A.)

The accused was charged with sexual assault and sexual interference alleging touching of the vagina of an eight-year-old girl in a bedroom. The trial judge admitted as similar fact evidence details of the accused's two previous convictions involving genital touching of a girl aged 10 and a boy aged 8. In both cases the accused had lured them to a private space. The jury returned a verdict of guilty. Noting that the decision was pre-*Handy,* the majority of the Ontario Court of Appeal ordered a new trial on the basis that the similar fact evidence ought not to have been admitted.

SIMMONS J.A. (ARMSTRONG JJ.A.) (concurring): —

... the cumulative effect of five aspects of the trial judge's reasoning led her to set the threshold for admissibility of the discreditable conduct evidence too low:

    i)   she framed the issue in question too widely allowing too broad "a gateway" for the admission of discreditable conduct evidence;

    ii) she did not identify the degree of connection to the alleged offence required to make the discreditable conduct evidence admissible;

    iii) in assessing the cogency of the discreditable conduct evidence, she relied primarily on generic similarities between it and the evidence of the complainant;

    iv) in assessing the cogency of the discreditable conduct evidence, she did not identify the features of proposed evidence that distinguished it from the evidence of the complainant; and

    v) she failed to recognize the significant moral prejudice arising from the generic quality of the similarities she identified.

[On the issue of framing the issue, the majority held that the trial judge had relied too heavily on the issue of credibility.]

---

61 See also generally, Hamish Stewart, "Rationalizing Similar Facts: A Comment on R. v. Handy", (2003) 8 Can. Crim. L. Rev. 113 and Mahoney, "Similar Fact Evidence" (2009), 55 Crim. L.Q. 22 (applauding *Handy* for its cautious approach to similar fact evidence, in contrast to a trend of admission in New Zealand, Australia, the United Kingdom and United States).

ii. Identification of the Issue in Question

Initially, the trial judge framed the issue in question as "whether the incident alleged by T.D. occurred". However, she later found that the discreditable conduct evidence was probative of several issues "other than [the appellant's] propensity to sexually assault young children". Those issues were the credibility of the complainant, the credibility of the allegations, B.'s credibility and character, a pattern of behaviour on the part of B., and rebuttal of the defence of innocent association.

As noted by my colleague, at paras. 116 and 117 of *Handy*, Binnie J. cautioned that framing "the issue in question" as credibility may result in "too broad a gateway for the admission of propensity evidence" therefore "risk[ing] the admission of evidence of nothing more than general disposition ("bad personhood")". In particular, he noted that when the issue in question is framed as the complainant's credibility, "anything that blackens the character of the accused" tends to enhance the credibility of the complainant.

In dissent Abella J.A. (as she then was) expressed the opinion that although this was not a "clear cut" case for admissibility, strong deference should be paid to the trial judge. The further appeal to the Supreme Court was dismissed in a brief oral judgment expressing agreement with the majority in the Court below.[62]

A different approach was taken by the British Columbia Court of Appeal in *R. v. Titmus*.

R. v. TITMUS
(2004), 27 C.R. (6th) 77, 191 C.C.C. (3d) 468 (B.C.C.A.)

1. Identifying the Issue

The Crown tendered the similar fact evidence as relevant to the *actus reus* of the offences (para. 98) and the trial judge treated the evidence of both complainants concerning the shower incidents as admissible on that issue (para. 105). In the case of each complainant, the only evidence of the acts alleged against the appellant came from their own testimony. So the credibility of each complainant was central to the Crown's case, and the similar fact evidence was therefore relevant to their credibility, as well as to the *actus reus* of the offences alleged.

The trial judge held that the similar fact evidence enhanced the credibility of both complainants and tipped the scales beyond a balance of probability in establishing the *actus reus* of the shower incidents (paras. 140-141). I see no error by the trial judge in her identification of the issues to which the similar fact evidence was relevant.

As in this case, where it is the conduct element of the *actus reus* and not the accused's identity that is in issue, "similar fact evidence may be admitted to prove

---

62 (2004) 23 C.R. (6th) 63, [2004] 3 S.C.R. 503, 188 C.C.C. (3d) 428. The analysis in *Blake* was recently applied in *R. v. Candale* (2006), 205 C.C.C. (3d) 167, 2006 CarswellOnt 659 (C.A.).

that the accused committed the offence or offences in question": *R. v. Arp*, [1998] 3 S.C.R. 339, 129 C.C.C. (3d) 321, at para. 48, see also *R. v. P.*, [1991] 3 All E.R. 337 (H.L), cited at para. 44 of *Arp*, supra, and *R. v. Handy*, supra, at paras. 78, 118-120. For sexual assault cases in particular, Madam Justice McLachlin (as she then was) said that where identity is not an issue, the credibility of a complainant is an issue in which similar fact evidence might be received: *B. (C.R.), supra*, at paras. 38-41 [p. 27]. In *Handy, supra*, while warning against the admissibility of similar fact evidence on the issue of credibility because of the risk that the evidence might go only to the appellant's general disposition or propensity, Mr. Justice Binnie said that where the similar fact evidence is relevant to an element of the *actus reus*, the fact that it is also relevant to the complainants' credibility will not render the evidence inadmissible.

In the case at bar the issue of both complainants' credibility was inextricably tied to proof of the *actus reus*. In my view, in admitting the similar fact evidence as relevant to both credibility and to the *actus reus*, the trial judge made no error of law.

Which approach do you prefer?[63]

Should there be a special rule in sexual assault cases for the admission of similar fact evidence?[64] How would you articulate and justify such a rule? Would such an approach create a slippery slope for admission of other types of bad character evidence?

In *Handy*, the Court also makes it clear that admission should not occur where there is an air of reality to the issue of collusion amongst witnesses.[65] **Are you satisfied with the Court's conclusion that there was collusion in *Handy*?**

The issue of collusion was further addressed by Binnie J. in *Shearing* where he applied his *Handy* approach to admit similar fact evidence.

R. v. SHEARING
[2002] 3 S.C.R. 33, 165 C.C.C. (3d) 225, 2 C.R. (6th) 213,
2002 CarswellBC 1661, 2002 CarswellBC 1662

The accused was charged with 20 counts of sexual offences alleged to have occurred between 1965 and 1989. The accused was the leader of a cult. He preached that sexual experience was a way to progress to higher levels of consciousness and that he, as cult leader, could be instrumental in enabling young girls to reach these higher levels. Two of the complainants were sisters who lived in a group home while the others, adherents to the cult, did not. The

---

63 See Tanovich, "Annotation" (2004), 27 C.R. (6th) 78. See also, *R. v. C. (T.)* (2005), 27 C.R. (6th) 94 (Ont. C.A.).

64 See Tanovich, "Why Equality Demands that Prior Sexual Misconduct Evidence be Presumptively Admissible in Sexual Assault Cases" in Sheehy (ed.), *Sexual Assault Law, Practice & Activism in a Post-Jane Doe Era* (Ottawa: University of Ottawa Press, 2010).

65 For commentary on this aspect of the case, see Schreck, "*Handy*: Raising the Threshold for the Admission of Similar Fact Evidence" (2002), 1 C.R. (6th) 245 and Morris, "The Possibility of Collusion as a Bar to the Admission of Similar Fact Evidence.".

counts were tried together and each was admitted as similar fact evidence for the others. We consider here the unanimous ruling that the similar fact evidence had been properly admitted. We will consider later another controversial aspect of *Shearing* in which the majority of the Supreme Court decided that the trial judge ought to have allowed cross-examination of a complainant as to the absence of mention of abuse in her diary.

BINNIE J.:—

. . . .

As the test of admissibility weighs probative value against prejudice, a question that quickly emerges is whether the Crown is able to lead cogent evidence of the alleged similar acts. In this case, the similar acts are all the subject of distinct charges. They are therefore, in any event, before the jury for a verdict. Apart from the usual issues of credibility, the appellant says there is evidence of collusion.

The theory of similar fact evidence turns largely on the improbability of coincidence. Collusion, by offering an alternative explanation for the "coincidence" of evidence emanating from different witnesses, destroys its probative value, and therefore the basis for its admissibility.

In *Handy* we held that where there is an air of reality to the allegation of collusion, the trial judge, in assessing the admissibility of the similar fact evidence, must be satisfied on a balance of probabilities that the evidence is not the product of concoction. This is inherent in deciding whether, as a matter of law, the evidence has sufficient probative value to overcome the prejudice.

If this threshold test is passed, the jury must determine for itself what weight, if any, to assign to the similar fact evidence.

There was evidence of some communication among the complainants. With respect to the G sisters, this was almost inevitable. They had also kept in touch with JV. Other complainants were in touch with each other prior to trial. Civil proceedings had been commenced by the G sisters for compensation and to close down the Kabalarians. KWG expressed the hope that the appellant would "rot in Hell".

The evidence here is far more speculative than in *Handy*. In that case, there was consultation between the complainant and the similar fact witness prior to the alleged offence about the prospect of financial profit. Here, there is some evidence of opportunity for collusion or collaboration and motive, but nothing sufficiently persuasive to trigger the trial judge's gatekeeper function. There is no reason here to interfere with the trial judge's decision to let the collusion issue go to the jury. He instructed the jury to consider "all of the circumstances which affect the reliability of that evidence including the possibility of collusion or collaboration between the complainants". He defined collusion as the possibility that the complainants, in sharing their stories with one another, intentionally or accidentally allowed themselves to change or modify their stories in order that their testimony would seem more similar or more convincing. It was for the jury to make the ultimate determination whether the evidence was "reliable despite the opportunity for collaboration" or that "less weight or no weight should be given to evidence which may have been influenced by the sharing of information".

While the trial judge did not specifically link the potential of collusion to the issue of admissibility, he appears to have thought collusion (as distinguished from contact) was not a serious danger. The evidence supports his decision. He was justified in letting the collusion issue go to the jury with an appropriate warning.

. . . .

The cogency of the similar fact evidence in this case is said to arise from the repetitive and predictable nature of the appellant's conduct in closely defined circumstances. There must therefore be shown a persuasive degree of connection between the similar fact evidence and the offence charged in order to be capable of raising the double inferences. The degree of required similarity is assessed in relation to the issue sought to be established and must be evaluated in relation to the other evidence in the case. If the cumulative result is simply to paint the appellant as a "bad person", it is inadmissible.

The Crown's position is that the appellant utilized a distinctively bizarre modus operandi which runs like a common thread through the incidents charged.

While the sexual acts themselves were not particularly distinctive, the underlying unity lies in the alleged abuse of a cult leader's authority. It is the fantastic sales pitch and rationale developed by the appellant that could be considered "particular and distinctive" *Handy, supra*, at paras. 77-79). While it is not necessary to reach for these epithets or insert catch words into the test—as explained in *B. (C.R.)*—such distinctiveness enhances probative value.

. . . .

Similarity does not lie in the physical sexual acts themselves (the G counts are far more serious). The incidents occurred in private places on Kabalarian premises and sexual touching began in the majority of cases when the complainants were under 18. . . . The similarities really lay in the *modus operandi* employed by the appellant to create sexual opportunities. . . .

The surrounding circumstances are united by the allegation of gross abuse of power by a cult leader. The spiritual theme is more dominant in the non-G counts because "spiritualism" was the source of the appellant's power over the complainants who did not live under his roof. Nevertheless, the "spiritual" theme surfaced in the testimony of KWG ("removing disembodied planes of mind") and SG (being made an "instrument"). . . . . .

The combination of spiritualist imagery (achieving higher states of awareness) and horror stories (invasion of young girls by disembodied minds), and the supposed prophylactic power of the appellant's sexual touching to ward off these horrific threats is, to say the least, distinctive.

. . . .

In my view, the similar act evidence has significant potential to create moral prejudice. The appellant's defence to the non-G complainants (religiously inspired consent) becomes more delicate when the jury is told that he also had sexual relations with two sisters from the age of 13 who were not Kabalarian disciples but simply residents of his Kabalarian household. The atmosphere of the case is redolent of quack spiritualism and this would clearly disturb a Canadian jury. Similarly, the appellant's denial of abuse of the G sisters may lose much of its force in light of the admitted sexual touching of other adolescent girls, to which the only defence is consent (vitiated, so the jury must have found, by the abuse of authority).

. . . .

In the weighing up of probative value versus prejudice, a good deal of deference is inevitably paid to the view of the trial judge: B. (C.R.), supra, at p. 733. This does not mean that the trial judge has a discretion to admit similar fact evidence whose prejudicial effect outweighs its probative value, but it does mean that the Court recognizes the trial judge's advantage of being able to assess on the spot the dynamics of the trial and the likely impact of the evidence on the jurors. These are evidentiary issues on which reasonable judges may differ and, absent error in principle, the decision should rest where it was allocated, to the trial judge. In this case the trial judge's view has been endorsed by a unanimous Court of Appeal.

The trial judge concluded that both the prejudicial effect and the probative value of the similar fact evidence were "significant", but that in the end the probative value prevailed. I see no reason to interfere with that conclusion.

Once the Court in *Handy* agreed that propensity is the true basis for the admission of similar fact evidence it seemed to follow, as it did for Doherty J.A. in *R. v. Batte*[66] that the jury need not be warned that they cannot use this to show that the accused was the type of person who could have committed the crime. Yet the Supreme Court has persisted with the need for a warning, as it did in *Arp* and *Shearing*.

This seems unfortunate as the lack of a warning has often necessitated a new trial and seems superfluous if the jury can indeed rely on propensity. Furthermore warnings have often been so tortuous as to be arguably perverse. In *R. v. Peterffy*[67] for example, evidence by several witnesses as to acts of prior physical abuse by a husband to his common law wife were held to have been properly admitted in a murder case to show a violent and threatening attitude, a motive of anger at the deceased's taunting and disobedience and the type of relationship. However the Court confirmed that this was only so because the trial judge had properly warned the jury that they could not conclude from the bad character evidence that he was the sort of person likely to have committed the murder!

In *R. v. B. (C.)*[68] a case alleging sexual assault against a daughter and a granddaughter the judge had admitted as similar fact evidence of sexual conduct

---

66 (2000), 34 C.R. (5th) 197 (Ont. C.A.). See, however, concerns expressed by Michael Plaxton and Glen Luther, "Limiting Instructions and Similar Facts" (2009), 63 C.R. (6th) 12.

67 (2000), 30 C.R. (5th) 297 (B.C. C.A.).

68 (2003), 7 C.R. (6th) 3 (Ont. C.A.).

with other daughters. One of the reasons for ordering a new trial and as a violation of the *Handy* approach was an improper warning . Although the judge warned the jury not to use the evidence of prior sexual conduct with other daughters to show the accused was a bad character such that they could infer that he was more likely to have committed the offences charged, there had not been a direction as to the distinction between general and specific propensity. The Court was also concerned about the issue of collusion.[69]

However, in *R. v. B.(R.T.)*,[70] where the accused was charged with several sexual offences against his two teenaged step-nieces, the Court held that the trial judge had erred in dismissing the Crown's application to have evidence across counts considered as similar fact evidence. Justice Borins reasoned that this was a judge-alone trial and moral prejudice is not a significant risk. In her Criminal Reports annotation, Lisa Dufraimont has severely criticised this assumption. She argues that this view overlooks the key danger identified in *Handy* from reasoning from general propensity to guilt. She concludes as follows:

> If one focuses on this general propensity reasoning, it is far from clear that trial judges are invulnerable to moral prejudice. To be sure, courts frequently state that jurors are especially prone to this type of faulty reasoning; for example, in *B. (C.R.)*, [1990] 1 S.C.R. 717, Sopinka J. identified "a natural human tendency to judge a person's action on the basis of character. Particularly with juries there would be a strong inclination to conclude that a thief has stolen, a violent man has assaulted and a pedophile has engaged in pedophilic acts" (at 744, cited in *Handy, supra* at para. 39). Of course, judges have an advantage over lay jurors because their training and experience help them achieve an accurate understanding of which inferences are permitted, and which forbidden, in the context of similar fact evidence. On the other hand, there is little basis for any confident assertion that judges are immune to the "natural human tendency" Sopinka J. described. Psychological research suggests that people have difficulty mentally cabining off information and using it only for limited purposes (see, *e.g.*, Owen M. Rees, "The Jury's Propensity for Prohibited Reasoning: *Corbett* Revisited" (2002) 7 Can. Crim. L. Rev. 333, 344-47; Roselle L. Wissler & Michael J. Saks (1985) "On the Inefficacy of Limiting Instructions" 9 Law & Hum. Behav. 37, 43-47). No doubt judges, like juries, can be affected by moral prejudice when they hear evidence of the accused's bad character (see Mirjan R. Damaska, *Evidence Law Adrift* (New Haven: Yale University Press, 1997) at 31-32).
>
> To recognize that judges may be vulnerable to moral prejudice arising from similar fact evidence is not to deny that the potential for prejudice is typically unavoidable. Often, as in *B. (R.T.)*, the similar facts relate to the various counts of a multi-count indictment, and in even in cases where the similar facts alleged lie outside the indictment, the trial judge will normally hear the evidence in order to determine its admissibility. Thus, as Borins J.A. points out in *B. (R.T.)*, the potential for prejudice that flows from the fact finder's exposure to evidence of the accused's bad character exists whether or not the evidence is ruled admissible. Trial judges are routinely asked to do what may well be impossible: to remain unaffected by the prejudicial material they hear. What the Court of Appeal may have overlooked in *B. (R.T.)* is the way in which the admissibility inquiry surrounding similar fact evidence can help

---

69 See further N. Harris, "Limiting Instructions: Preventing Wrongful Conviction or Causing Juror Confusion?" (2004), 20 C.R. 6th 117. See also *R. v. Thomas* (2004), 26 C.R. (6th) 274, 190 C.C.C. (3d) 31 (Ont. C.A.).

70 (2009) 63 C.R. (6th) 197 (Ont. C.A.); and see earlier, *R. v. Vrdoljak* (2002), 1 C.R. (6th) 250 (Ont. C.J.).

judges rise to this challenge. Surely a judge who has grappled with the prejudicial effect of similar fact evidence and perhaps even ruled it inadmissible on that basis is more likely to resist the influence of moral prejudice than one who relies on the easy assumption that moral prejudice is not an issue in bench trials.

Where there is more than one count and evidence on one count is not admissible as similar fact evidence on other counts, the jury must be instructed to consider each charge separately and not to use evidence relating to one count as evidence on any other count.[71]

In *Perrier* the Supreme Court announced a special, very complex approach to similar fact evidence in gang trials:

R. v. PERRIER
22 C.R. (6th) 209, [2004] 3 S.C.R. 228, 188 C.C.C. (3d) 1, 28 2004 CarswellBC 2116, 2004 CarswellBC 2117

Over the course of a month, on three separate days, a gang of men invaded the homes of three families in the Vancouver area. The method of operation adopted by the gang was distinctive. One of its members, disguised as a postman carrying a package, in daylight hours, would ring the doorbell of the targeted home. The "postman" and two accomplices would then overpower the person who answered the door. In each case the person answering the door was a middle-aged Asian woman. Once inside the home, the intruders contacted, by cell phone or walkie-talkies, others who were to enter the home. On each occasion the occupant or occupants of the home were bound with duct tape while members of the gang searched the home for valuables. According to the victims, up to five or six people were involved in each incident. The accused P was charged with a number of counts of breaking and entering, robbery, unlawful confinement and possession of stolen property in relation to two of the incidents. Prior to trial he had been convicted of robbery and break and enter in relation to the third incident. C was charged with offences relating to each home invasion.

The sole issue at trial was identity. The theory of the Crown was that, while membership in the gang rotated, P and C were involved in all three incidents. It was alleged that P's role varied, dressing as the postman in one incident and assisting in overpowering the victims in the others. The Crown's case consisted largely of the evidence of an accomplice W who implicated the accused in each incident and circumstantial evidence that linked the accused to some of the incidents and to W. At the beginning of the trial, the Crown sought and obtained a ruling from the trial judge that P's involvement in the third incident could be led as similar fact evidence. The accused was convicted by a jury on all counts.

The accused's appeal to the B.C. Court of Appeal was dismissed. The majority held that the trial judge had not erred in admitting the similar fact evidence. The Supreme Court of Canada allowed the appeal, holding that the similar fact evidence ought not to have been admitted. A new trial was ordered.

---

71 *R. v. Farler*, (2006) 131 C.C.C. (3d) 134 (N.S. C.A. (per Cromwell J.A., in ordering a new trial)).

MAJOR J. (BASTARACHE, BINNIE, DESCHAMPS and FISH JJ. concurring):—

The law governing the admissibility of similar fact evidence is well established. It is presumptively inadmissible as it is propensity reasoning: see *Handy...,Shearing...,Arp..., B. (C.R.).*

The onus falls on the prosecution to satisfy the trial judge, on a balance of probabilities, that the probative value of the evidence in relation to a particular issue outweighs its prejudicial effect. Where the similar fact evidence is relevant only to support the prohibited inference (that the accused is the type of person who, because of past conduct or character, is predisposed to commit the type of crime for which he is being tried), it will not outweigh the prejudice caused.

The rationale for the admission and use of similar fact evidence where identity is in issue is the improbability that two persons would display the same configuration of matching characteristics in committing a crime. Thus a jury is not being asked to infer that the accused is the type of person who would commit the offence but to conclude that he is exactly the person who did commit the offence. This inference is made possible only if the high degree of similarity between the acts renders the likelihood of coincidence objectively improbable: see *Arp,* per Cory J.:

> Where, as here, similar fact evidence is adduced on the issue of identity, there must be a high degree of similarity between the acts for the evidence to be admitted. For example, a unique trademark or signature will automatically render the alleged acts "strikingly similar" and therefore highly probative and admissible. In the same way, a number of significant similarities, taken together, may be such that by their cumulative effect, they warrant admission of the evidence.

In *Arp*, Cory J. stated that a high degree of similarity was required in order to establish the objective improbability that the accused's involvement in the alleged acts was the product of coincidence. This point was considered in *Handy*, at para. 91, where Binnie J. equated the possibility of coincidence with mistaken identity or a mistake in the character of the act. The point is that we must be cautious when using propensity evidence in the context of identity. We want to be sure, on a balance of probabilities, that the same person committed the acts in question such that we can safely say it is not a coincidence nor a case of mistaken identity.

In determining whether the acts are similar enough to admit, the focus should first be on the acts themselves and not on evidence of the accused's involvement in those acts. A high degree of similarity between the acts is required in order to be admissible. The greater the similarity between the acts, the greater the probative value of the similar fact evidence.

The similarity between the acts must be determined on a case-by-case basis after considering all relevant factors. Such factors include, but are not limited to: proximity in time and place, number of occurrences of the similar acts and similarities in detail and circumstances: see *Handy*, para. 82.

Once the trial judge has determined that the crime charged and the similar act were likely committed by the same person, the judge must then consider whether there is evidence linking the accused to the similar act. A link between the accused and the similar acts is a precondition to admissibility: see *Sweitzer* . . . as cited with approval in *Arp* :

> Before evidence may be admitted as evidence of similar facts, there must be a link between the allegedly similar facts and the accused. In other words there must be some evidence upon which the trier of fact can make a proper finding that the similar facts to be relied upon were in fact the acts of the accused for it is clear that if they were not his own but those of another they have no relevance to the matters at issue under the indictment.

If the similar facts relied upon were not in fact the acts of the accused, then they have no probative value.

The threshold is not particularly high. The trial judge must determine whether there is "some evidence" linking the accused to the similar acts. However, evidence of mere opportunity or possibility is not sufficient.

In the group context, the link between an accused and the similar acts of a group is particularly important. Where a group commits a series of crimes with a distinct modus operandi, such as in the case before the Court, the "signature" of the offence is the "signature" of the group only. If the Crown can prove that membership in the gang never changed and that all members were present and participating in all offences, then the signature of the group will be the signature of the accused such that a similar fact instruction will likely be justified (provided that the overall probative value of the evidence outweighs its prejudice). However, where group membership was not constant, the fact that an individual may have been a member of the gang on one occasion proves nothing more than a mere possibility that he was a member on another occasion. In this case the evidence of group activity must be accompanied by evidence linking the individual to each of the group's offences for which he has been charged, either by virtue of the distinctiveness of his role or by other independent evidence. Without this additional link, the required nexus between the similar fact evidence and the acts of a particular accused is absent, and the similar fact evidence will not have sufficient probative value to outweigh the prejudice caused.

B. Application of Similar Fact Evidence to Crimes Committed by Groups

Where it is highly improbable that two different groups employing the same *modus operandi* committed the crimes at issue, the evidence may be used to support the inference that the same gang committed all the acts. . . . It would be illogical to infer individual liability without further evidence of individual participation. . . .

The proper approach to the case of similar fact evidence as it pertains to groups or gangs is to adopt a framework that goes one step beyond the basic prejudice versus probative value assessment. Similar fact evidence of group activities should be admissible in order to identify a group or gang responsible for a particular crime. Where, as here, you have several crimes committed with a unique *modus operandi*, and the objective improbability of coincidence is high, the trier of fact should be permitted to draw an inference that the same gang committed the acts. At this first stage, identification of the group, the trier of fact may rely on the factors outlined by Binnie J. in *Handy* to assess, according to the test in *Arp*, whether the evidence of one group activity can be used to identify the group responsible for another. Once the trier of fact has determined that the same group was involved, a second step or assessment is needed in order to determine if the evidence has enough probative value with regard to the individual accused to outweigh the prejudice it will cause.

Where evidence of similar offences committed by a gang is being introduced not just to identify the gang itself but to identify a particular member, a sufficient connection between the individual and the crimes of the group must be established. This can be done in two ways:

(1) If the Crown can prove that group membership never changed, that the gang always remained intact and never committed the criminal acts unless all were present, and that the accused was a member of the group, and present, at the relevant time, that will be sufficient to connect the individual to the crimes of the group, and the evidence will usually have sufficient probative value to be admitted as similar fact.

(2) Where membership in the group is not constant, as in this case, then an additional "link" or "connection" must be made in order to use evidence of group activity against a particular accused. This additional requirement will be satisfied where

(a) the accused's role was sufficiently distinctive that no other member of the group or person could have performed it; thus he necessarily must have participated in all offences; or

(b) there is independent evidence linking the accused to each crime. Without this second stage of analysis, there is a risk that the net will be cast too broadly and members of a group who participated in some crimes will be improperly convicted of other crimes by virtue of their association with the group alone.

Group similar fact evidence can be used to identify groups, but not to assign liability to particular members. Identifying the group will facilitate prosecution where it can be shown that membership in the group was constant and the individual members can be identified. Identifying the group will not likely facilitate prosecution where membership in the group was not constant, unless the role played by a particular accused was sufficiently distinct that he can be identified as having been involved in all the offences.

. . . .

[Major J. concluded that where, as in this appeal, membership in the group varied, and the roles played by a particular accused were not distinctive, similar fact evidence could only be introduced against this accused once he has been linked to each individual crime. Here the Court held that there was no independent evidence linking the accused to each crime.]

———————————

The Supreme Court's decision in *Perrier* and in the companion case of *Chan* appear to be commendably concerned about the risk of false identification and the particular dangers of guilt by association in gang cases.

The rulings are significant for being clear that *Arp* rather than *Handy* is the controlling authority where similar fact evidence is tendered to establish identity. The key tests for admission are striking similarity and no possibility of coincidence.

It announces stringent new tests of linkage where the membership of the gang has fluctuated. Indeed, given that those tests were held not to have been met in the case before the Court, it is difficult to see how the Court's new standards will ever be satisfied in such cases. The accused appear to have been linked to each crime by independent evidence, notably by the testimony of an accomplice.[72]

PROBLEMS

Problem 1

A is charged with the murder of B, a woman with whom he was then living. The cause of B's death was arsenical poisoning. The prosecution seeks to tender evidence that A's wife died of arsenical poisoning two years earlier. Relevant? Receivable? Compare *Noor Mohammed v. R.*, [1949] A.C. 182 (P.C.).

Problem 2

The accused is charged with sexual assault. The victim, a 12-year-old girl, was sleeping in an eastern Ontario campsite in a small pup tent. She was with her brother while with her parents slept in a larger tent nearby. After midnight, a man entered her tent by cutting it and attempted to fondle her. She fought him off by biting him and he ran off. Identification is an issue at trial because she only saw him for seconds and it was dark. She did not identify him until more than two years after the attack from police photographs. The Crown seeks to enter similar act evidence from six years earlier. In the dark of night, the accused unzipped the small pup tent of a 12-year-old girl in a different Eastern Ontario campsite where she was sleeping with a group of Girl Guides. Adult supervisors were sleeping near by. The offense also involved fondling. A number of other tents were slashed that night. The accused pled guilty to sexual assault in relation to that incident. Would you admit the evidence applying *Handy*? See *R. v. Harvey* (2001) 48 C.R. (5th) 247, 160 C.C.C. (3d) 52 (Ont. C.A.), affirmed 7 C.R. (6th) 1, 169 C.C.C. (3d) 576, [2002] 4 S.C.R. 311.

Problem 3

The accused is charged with second-degree murder in the death of his former girlfriend. She was found dead in her bedroom with a cord wrapped around her neck. A detached part of the cord was wrapped around the outside bedroom doorknob. A kitchen chair was found nearby. The defence position was that the death was a suicide. The theory of the Crown was that the accused could not accept that the relationship was over and, as had happened in the past, he

---

72 See comment by Lou Strezos (2004), 22 C.R. (6th) 222.

became violent. The Crown wants to introduce evidence from the accused's former girlfriend. She will testify that the accused could not accept that she wanted to end the relationship and during an argument, the accused bound her hands with a telephone cord and then wrapped it around a doorknob and then around a bannister. Admissible? See *R. v. Watkins* (2003), 181 C.C.C. (3d) 78 (Ont. C.A.) and *R. v. Trochym*, 43 C.R. (6th) 217, 216 C.C.C. (3d) 225, [2007] 1 S.C.R. 239, [2007] S.C.J. No. 6, 2007 CarswellOnt 400 (S.C.C.).

Problem 4

The accused is charged with murder. The victim was one of his children, aged three, and there is no doubt from the evidence that the child died as the result of external violence. Two prosecution witnesses have testified in graphic detail the manner in which the accused allegedly beat the child into unconsciousness. The defence is an outright denial. The prosecution wishes to tender in evidence descriptions of other occasions on which the accused beat the child. Relevant? Receivable? Of other occasions when the accused beat the other children. Of occasions when he abused the family dog. Relevant? Receivable? Compare *R. v. Drysdale*, [1969] 2 C.C.C. 141 (Man. C.A., 1968), *R. v. Roud* (1981), 58 C.C.C. (2d) 226 (Ont. C.A.), *R. v. Speid* (1985), 46 C.R. (3d) 22 (Ont. C.A.), and *R. v. Gottschall* (1983), 10 C.C.C. (3d) 447 (N.S. C.A.).

Problem 5

The accused is charged with several counts of assault causing bodily harm and sexual assault of S, his male common law partner. The allegation is that the accused one particular night came home somewhat drunk and in a grumpy mood. After a fight over washing the dishes the accused beat S twice with a broom and chased him up to the bedroom where he had anal sexual intercourse with S despite S's protests that he did not want that.

The Crown seeks to tender evidence of the accused's violent relationship towards two previous male common law partners. In both cases the evidence will be that the accused was often moody and quick-tempered and often accused them of sleeping with others. Each former partner will detail incidents when this jealousy lead to the accused attacking them with his fists, causing bruises. With reference to appropriate authority, consider whether this evidence is admissible?

Compare *R. v. K. (C.P.)* (2002), 7 C.R. (6th) 16 (Ont. C.A.).

(iii) *Civil Cases*

There are far fewer reported civil cases involving the problem of similar facts than criminal cases.

JOHNSON v. BUGERA
(1999), 172 D.L.R. (4th) 535 (B.C. C.A.)

Statton, Johnson, and Robertson were involved in a single car accident. The accident resulted in Robertson's death, and left Statton in a coma for several weeks. Statton had virtually no recall of the events several days before the accident and several weeks thereafter. Statton appealed against the trial judge's determination that he was the driver of the vehicle at the time of the accident. Although he was thrown from the vehicle as a result of the accident, Johnson did not suffer any major injuries, and he said that he had a clear memory of the events. The vehicle involved in the accident was owned by Statton's common law wife, Bugera. Johnson claimed that Statton was driving at the time of the accident. It was determined that the accident occurred as a result of the vehicle being driven at a remarkable rate of speed. While Johnson had a remarkable record for speeding, this was not taken into account by the trial judge.

Per HALL J.A. (GOLDIE and DONALD JJ.A. concurring):

. . . .

In his reasons for judgment His Lordship said this concerning the respondent Johnson:

His prior driving record was tendered in regard to his credibility. It is not suggested there is any basis for a similar act analysis and indeed there is none.

With respect, it seems to me that there does exist a very substantial basis for a similar act analysis on the facts of this case.

It must be remembered that what was at the heart of this case and the issue being litigated was the question of who, on a balance of probabilities, was the driver of the car that was involved in the fatal accident. In other words, the central issue was a question of identity. "Similar facts" or "similar acts" is a much discussed principle in the law of evidence, particularly in its application in the criminal law. A case often referred to as a starting point in such an analysis is *Makin v. Attorney- General for New South Wales*, [1894] A.C. 57. Although Makin, often referred to as the baby farming case, is perhaps the most well known and a leading case in the area, the principle upon which it is based is older and lies much deeper in the law. One starts with the proposition that all relevant evidence is admissible. Of course, some "relevant evidence" may be rather marginal and such evidence can also be highly prejudicial. The rule of evidence preventing rebuttal of collateral fact evidence is one device employed by courts to avoid the admission of evidence that may be tangentially relevant but would lead to a great expansion of time taken in trials. The courts have also exercised a jurisdiction to avoid the introduction of highly prejudicial but marginally probative evidence, especially in jury trials, in order to prevent the misuse of evidence by the trier of fact.

But I return to the proposition that evidence is adduced in a trial to prove a fact or facts in issue. In assessing the admissibility of evidence, lawyers and judges ask themselves the question, is this evidence probative of a fact in issue and hence relevant? Subject to other exclusionary rules like the hearsay rule, if those queries be answered in the affirmative, then the evidence is prima facie admissible at a trial.

. . . .

I doubt that there is any difference between admissibility of evidence in civil and criminal cases, with the possible exception that in the latter class of case, particularly cases tried before a jury, there may be a heightened concern that potentially prejudicial evidence not be placed before the trier of fact unless it has significant probative value. In the case of *Anderson v. Maple Ridge* (1992), 71 B.C.L.R. (2d) 68 at p. 75, Wood J.A., giving the judgment of the court, briefly adverted to the subject:

> There is no doubt that a judge trying a civil case in Canada has a discretion to exclude relevant evidence on the ground that its prejudicial effect outweighs its probative value: *Draper v. Jacklyn*, [1970] S.C.R. 92, 9 D.L.R. (3d) 264, per Spence J. at pp. 96-97 [S.C.R.]. What is less clear is under what circumstances that discretion should be exercised. There is a paucity of jurisprudence on the subject. Counsel did refer us to a 1975 English Court of Appeal decision in *Mood Music Publishing Co. v. De Wolfe Ltd.*, [1976] Ch. 119, [1976] 1 All E.R. 763, where Lord Denning M.R. said this at p. 766 [All E.R.] in connection with the admissibility of similar fact evidence in that case:
>
>> The admissibility of evidence as to "similar facts" has been much considered in the criminal law. Some of them have reached the highest tribunal, the latest of them being Boardman v. Director of Public Prosecutions. The criminal courts have been very careful not to admit such evidence unless its probative value is so strong that it should be received in the interests of justice: and its admission will not operate unfairly to the accused. In civil cases the courts have followed a similar line but have not been so chary of admitting it. In civil cases the courts will admit evidence of similar facts if it is logically probative, that is if it is logically relevant in determining the matter which is in issue; provided that it is not oppressive or unfair to the other side; and also that the other side has fair notice of it and is able to deal with it.
>
> To the extent that this passage suggests there is a more narrow discretion to exclude prejudicial evidence in civil cases than exists in criminal cases, it would appear to be at odds with the situation in this country where the broad scope of the discretion suggested by Spence J. in *Draper v. Jacklyn*, supra, stands in contrast to the very narrow discretion to exclude described in the decision of the Supreme Court of Canada a year later in *R. v. Wray*, [1971] S.C.R. 272, 11 C.R.N.S. 235, [1970] 4 C.C.C. 1, 11 D.L.R. (3d) 673.

In this case, a combination of speeding infractions admitted by the respondent Johnson in cross-examination at trial coupled with a transcript of his driving record that was filed establish that he had amassed a great number of speeding convictions between 1989 and 1997. As I counted them, there are over 25 of these infractions. The great majority of these occurred between 1989 and 1994. A large number of the offences involved highway speeding. As noted by the trial judge, Johnson was under a driving suspension at the time of the accident. This accident occurred as a result of a vehicle being driven at a very excessive rate of speed. The respondent Johnson has a remarkable record for this sort of conduct. I do not overlook the fact that Statton had some speeding convictions as well but his record is of a different order entirely from that of Johnson. It seems to me that it could justly be said that this very substantial history of speeding on the part of Johnson could be found to have probative force and be a highly relevant matter for a trier of fact to assess in deciding the question at issue in this case, namely, who was the driver of the Dodge car at the time of the accident? I find it impossible to say as a matter of logic that this would not be a matter potentially probative on this matter. While the record is one arguably demonstrating "bad conduct" of Johnson as a driver, it also could be reckoned to be highly probative of the fact that he was more probably the driver of the Dodge at the relevant time. I believe that a trial judge could and should undertake a similar act analysis in deciding this case.

. . . .

S. (R.C.M.) v. K. (G.M.)
2005 CarswellSask 447, [2005] S.J. No. 443, 266 Sask. R. 31 (Q.B.)

This was an application for custody. One of the issues was the admissibility of evidence that the father was abusive in a previous relationship.

RYAN-FROSLIE J.: —

When family relationships break down, children are hurt. This is particularly true when parents, obsessed with their own battles, lose sight of the needs and interests of their children. It is against such a backdrop that this Court must determine the appropriate parenting arrangements for two young girls. Their mother, Jane, wants sole custody with no, or limited, access to their father. Their father, John, wants joint custody with specified parenting time. The only thing these two parents appear to agree upon is that their relationship is an acrimonious one and the only thing they appear to have in common is love for their daughters.

...

During the course of the trial, counsel for Jane proffered as a witness the former common-law spouse of John who testified that during her relationship with John she was subjected to physical and emotional abuse. Counsel for John objected to the admission of this evidence, arguing that it is evidence of bad character, that it is extremely prejudicial and irrelevant to the issues before this Court. Counsel for Jane argued the evidence is relevant, that domestic violence and spousal abuse are matters that relate directly to an individual's ability to parent and that the evidence proffered corroborates Jane's claims of spousal abuse and thus bolsters her credibility. After a voir dire, this Court ruled the evidence was admissible. What follows are the reasons for that decision.

The leading case on similar fact evidence is the Supreme Court of Canada in *R. v. Handy*, [2002] 2 S.C.R. 908, 2002 SCC 56. As a general rule, similar fact evidence is inadmissible. The rationale is that individuals should not be judged on past conduct but rather on conduct that is in issue. People can and do change. If they are judged on past conduct, no allowance is made for that ability. The exception to the rule is when the probative value of the evidence tendered outweighs its prejudicial effect. The Supreme Court of Canada in *R. v. Handy* set out the framework within which a court could make that determination. The court must look at a number of factors including whether the evidence is relevant to an issue before the court, the similarity of the evidence in time and circumstance to the case in issue and whether there is prejudice to the party against who the evidence was tendered.

Section 16(9) of the *Divorce Act* provides that in making orders with regard to custody and access "... the court shall not take into consideration the past conduct of any person unless the conduct is relevant to the ability of that person to act as a parent of a child."

Abuse is conduct that is relevant to a person's ability to act as a parent. This is so for a number of reasons. The negative effect on children who witness domestic violence is well-documented. Moreover, spousal abuse affects the dynamics of decision-making as it relates to the children and the milieu in which exchanges of the children occur. It is also an important consideration in determining parenting arrangements - whether sole or joint custody is appropriate, where the child should reside, whether the parenting time should be supervised or unsupervised, flexible or inflexible. Issues of abuse may directly impact the psychological and emotional needs of the children as well as their physical safety. It also relates to the type of "role model" a parent is for a child. Whether John abused Jane during their relationship is therefore relevant to his ability to parent.

Jane also alleges John sexually abused her and the parties' daughter, Sally. An individual's sexual appetites or proclivities may or may not be relevant to parenting. If an individual is discreet and they do not act inappropriately in the children's presence, what they do behind closed doors may very well have no bearing on ability to parent. The only way a court can make this determination, however, is to hear the evidence.

How does a victim of spousal abuse prove that abuse when they and their spouse and/or their infant children are the only witnesses to the altercations? Spousal abuse is a pattern of conduct. Human experience tells us that generally people act consistently. Counsel for Jane put forward the evidence in issue to show that John was abusive in the spousal relationship he had immediately prior the relationship with Jane and that, true to form, he continued that abuse with Jane.

The evidence in issue relates to circumstances which are removed in time and place from the spousal abuse alleged by Jane. As such, it is only circumstantial evidence. Its usefulness rests in the validity of the inference it is said to support, that is, that John engaged in spousal abuse in the relationship he had immediately prior to his relationship with Jane and thus Jane's evidence that he abused her is more credible.

The rules relating to the admissibility of similar fact evidence apply in civil cases but as Lord Denning pointed out in *Mood Music Publishing Co. Ltd. v. De Wolfe Ltd.*, [1976] 1 All E.R. 763 (C.A.), the rule in civil cases is not as rigidly applied as in criminal ones.

> ... The criminal courts have been very careful not to admit [similar fact] evidence unless its probative value is so strong that it should be received in the interests of justice; and its admission will not operate unfairly to the accused. In civil cases the courts have followed a similar line but have not been so chary of admitting it. In civil cases the courts will admit evidence of similar facts if it is logically probative, that is if it is logically relevant in determining the matter which is in issue; provided that it is not oppressive or unfair to the other side; and also that the other side has fair notice of it and is able to deal with it. ...

This Court has examined the differences between the criminal standard and the civil standard in the recent cases of *C.M. v. A.G. (Canada)*, 2004 SKQB 174, (2004), 248 Sask.R. 1 (Q.B.) and *K.M. v. A.G.* (Canada), 2004 SKQB 287, (2004), 251 Sask.R. 12 (Q.B.). Both those cases indicate the bar for the admission of similar fact evidence in civil cases is lower than in criminal cases. They both found similar fact evidence relating to credibility admissible.

While the fact John may have been abusive in a prior spousal relationship does not necessarily mean he was abusive to Jane, it does support her credibility on this issue. There are strong similarities between the evidence of John's former common-law spouse and Jane. Both of them had spousal relationships with John. Both of them testified that during their relationships John was controlling and that he was emotionally, physically and sexually abusive to them. While the extent of the abuse does vary, for example John's former common-law spouse testified that John ground his open hand into her face, while Jane testified he hit her with his fist, there is sufficient similarity in the conduct to form the necessary nexus. In addition, there is considerable similarity in the emotional abuse alleged - the name-calling and control. The evidence proffered is relevant as it relates to spousal abuse, an important factor in determining parenting arrangements. It is of sufficient probative value to warrant its admission.

The admission of this evidence does not unduly prejudice John. While he had no prior notice that this evidence was to be tendered, the fact that this Court adjourned for a considerable length of time afforded him the opportunity to examine and fully meet the evidence presented.

———————

The judge granted sole custody to the mother and specified parenting time to the father. She was satisfied that while the father had physically abused the mother, including in front of the children, he had never physically or sexually assaulted his children.

PROBLEMS

Problem 1

Two individuals entered into a franchise agreement for the sale of flowers under the plaintiff's name. The relationship broke down after less than two years. The plaintiff alleges that the defendant breached the agreement by purchasing flowers from non-authorized suppliers. The defendant did not dispute this but responded that the quality of flowers provided by the plaintiff was of such low quality that it deprived the defendant of the benefit of the agreement. The defendant wanted to call three franchisees to testify that they experienced similar problems with the product they received from the plaintiff. Is this evidence admissible? On what theory of relevance? See *Jardin Direct Inc. v. Floradin Florists Ltd.*, [2006] N.J. No. 195, 2006 CarswellNfld 200 (T.D.).

Problem 2

Plaintiff is suing for damages for injuries received when struck by defendant's plane during a low pass made by defendant. Plaintiff proposes to call witnesses who will describe defendant's reputation for carelessness. Plaintiff also proposes to call evidence that on two previous occasions the defendant violated the Aeronautics Act by flying too low, and that on one of these occasions a person was injured and the defendant settled the matter out of court. Is the evidence receivable? See *Leblanc v. R.*, [1977] 1 S.C.R. 339. See also *Rock v. Canadian Northern Railway Co.*, [1922] 1 W.W.R. 496 (Sask. C.A.), *R. v. Royal Bank*, [1920] 1 W.W.R. 198 (Man. C.A.), and *Brown v. Eastern & Midlands Railway Co.* (1889), 22 Q.B.D. 391.

(f) Character of Third Party/Co-Accused

An accused is entitled to lead bad character evidence of a third party to suggest, for example, that the third party's propensity for violence makes it more likely that he committed the offence. There is a requirement, however, that there be some evidence of a link between the third party and the offence: see most recently the discussion in *R. v. Grandinetti*.[73] Once the defence leads this evidence, it opens the door for the Crown to rebut by calling propensity evidence in relation to the accused.

In *R. v. Parsons*[74] Finlayson J.A. addressed the propriety of propensity evidence by the Crown to counter a defence raised by the accused based on the alleged propensity of another person. He said at pp. 237-38:

> In my opinion, Mercier J. was correct in ruling that if the evidence relating to Miller's propensity to commit robberies was introduced into evidence, fairness dictated that the very similar evidence that the Crown possessed relating to the appellant could also be introduced. *I would go further and suggest that if the appellant chose to throw sticks at Miller, the Crown should be able to counter this evidence with any similar evidence relating to the propensity to commit robbery, not only of the appellant, but of the other suspects arrested with the appellant....To rule otherwise would leave the jury with the highly misleading impression that Miller alone of those arrested had a propensity to commit robberies, whereas in truth he was part of a gang that committed robberies and the appellant was part of that gang* [emphasis added].[75]

In addition to fairness concerns, courts have held that when third party propensity evidence is called, the accused impliedly puts his own character in issue.[76]

Recently, the Ontario Court of Appeal limited the "tit for tat" principle to cases where it is general propensity evidence led by the accused. In *R. v. Vanezis*,[77]

---

73 191 C.C.C. (3d) 449, [2005] 1 S.C.R. 27, 25 C.R. (6th) 1.

74 (1993), 84 C.C.C. (3d) 226, 24 C.R. (4th) 112 (Ont. C.A.).

75 See also *R. v. Dhillon* (2002), 166 C.C.C. (3d) 262, 5 C.R. (6th) 317 (Ont. C.A.) at 277 [C.C.C.]; *R. v. Woodcock* (2003), 177 C.C.C. (3d) 346, 14 C.R. (6th) 155 (Ont. C.A.) at 381-382 [C.C.C.]; *R. v. Rodgers* (2000), 144 C.C.C. (3d) 568 (Ont. C.A.); *R. v. B. (C.)* (1997), 118 C.C.C. (3d) 43 (Ont. C.A.) at 56-57; *R. v. McMillan* (1975), 23 C.C.C. (2d) 160, 29 C.R.N.S. 191 (Ont. C.A.), affirmed 33 C.C.C. (2d) 360, [1977] 2 S.C.R. 824.

76 See the discussion in *R. v. Truscott* (2006), 213 C.C.C. (3d) 183 (Ont. C.A.) and *R. v. M.(M.)* (2003), [2003] O.J. No. 5949, 2003 CarswellOnt 6194 (S.C.J.).

77 (2006), 213 C.C.C. (3d) 449, 43 C.R. (6th) 116 (Ont. C.A.).

the defence wanted to call evidence of a third party's threats to kill the victim and assaults directed at her. Justice Moldaver held that the trial judge had erred in concluding that this opened the door for the Crown to lead evidence of the accused's propensity for violence towards third parties. As he put it, this evidence was "not being led to show that he was the kind of person likely to have killed her but that he was in fact the person who killed her."

An accused can also lead bad character evidence in relation to a co-accused: see *R. v. Suzack*.[78] However, recently in *R. v. Pollock*,[79] Justice Rosenberg recognized that "there must be some evidentiary foundation to support" the assertion that the evidence is necessary to make full answer and defence. When admitted, a trial judge has the difficult task of providing a careful limiting instruction, namely, that this evidence cannot be used as part of the Crown's case against the co-accused.

R. v. KHAN
(2004), 189 C.C.C. (3d) 49, 24 C.R. (6th) 48 (Ont. S.C.J.)

The accused was charged with possession of one kilogram of cocaine for the purpose of trafficking. The police found the drugs in a vehicle being driven by the accused. The accused alleged that he was the victim of racial profiling. He was African-Canadian and the vehicle was a Mercedes. The accused wanted to rely on evidence of another individual who had been stopped by the same officer as similar act evidence of racial profiling.

MOLLOY J.: —

. . .

(ii) Similar Fact Evidence and Racial Profiling

On the other hand, if as Mr. Khan alleges, he was targeted by these officers because of racial profiling, this would constitute an improper purpose and would invalidate the stop, and everything that flowed from the stop. A finding that a police officer was motivated by racism, whether consciously or unconsciously, is a serious matter. It ought not to be made lightly. Knowledge of the existence of racial profiling by police of young black males driving expensive cars, even knowledge that such profiling exists in Metro Toronto, is not sufficient to establish that it actually occurred in this particular case. It would be improper to infer racist motivation in the absence of evidence that the particular officer or officers involved actually had that intent: *R. v. S.(R.D.)*, [1997] 3 S.C.R. 484.

In *R. v. Brown* (2003), 173 C.C.C. (3d) 23 (Ont. C.A.) the Court of Appeal noted that racial profiling will rarely be proven by direct evidence, as officers are not likely to admit their motivation was overtly racist. The Court held that one way racial profiling can be proven is by circumstantial evidence where: (a) the circumstances relating to the detention correspond to the phenomenon of racial

---

78 (2002), 141 C.C.C. (3d) 449 (Ont. C.A.).
79 (2004), 187 C.C.C. (3d) 213, 23 C.R. (6th) 98 (Ont. C.A.).

profiling (as is the case here); and (b) the circumstances provide a basis for the court to infer that the police officer is lying about why the police officer singled out the accused person for attention: *R. v. Brown* at paras. 44 and 45.

As I noted in my earlier ruling on the production motion in this case [reported at [2004] O.J. No. 3811 (S.C.J.)], that is only one of the ways in which racial profiling may be proven. I ruled that an accused could also rely on evidence that the officer in question had acted in a similar manner in the past or on evidence of bias. In the case before me, evidence was called by the defence with respect to the detention and arrest of Sheldon Jackson by these same two officers in March 2001 (about 7 months before Mr. Khan's arrest). The officers testified they were driving along St. Clair Avenue and passed Mr. Jackson who was driving in the opposite direction in an expensive BMW. Mr. Jackson is also a young black male. Officer Asselin noticed that when Mr. Jackson saw the police, he gave a strange look, as if he looked guilty. The officers made a U-turn and followed Mr. Jackson's vehicle which, they testified, was being driven in an erratic manner suggestive of an attempt to avoid the police. A CPIC check disclosed the owner of the vehicle was a suspended driver. The officers pulled Mr. Jackson over. As Officer Asselin was approaching the car, he said he could see Mr. Jackson frantically trying to put a white powdered substance wrapped in clear plastic into a hand-held single bottle beer cooler with a zipper on it. Mr. Jackson was asked to step out of the car and he accompanied Officer James to the police cruiser. Officer Asselin then went to Mr. Jackson's car and retrieved the beer cooler, which did in fact turn out to have cocaine in it.

Mr. Jackson's version of events was quite different. He said he was driving along St. Clair Avenue going toward a restaurant to meet a friend. He did not notice the police car on St. Clair and did not make eye contact with the officers. He turned off St. Clair and travelled a number of one-way side streets to find a parking spot. He then noticed the police lights and siren behind him and pulled over. He was asked to step out of the car, which he did. He was also asked to unlock the doors, which he also did. Officer James then took him back to the police cruiser while Officer Asselin proceeded to search his car. Mr. Jackson acknowledged there were drugs in the car and that they were inside a zipped up red single-bottle beer cooler. However, he said he put the drugs in the bottle cooler earlier that day, and then hid it in a space at the back of his headrest, which, he said, is where Officer Asselin actually found it.

As I have already ruled, evidence of discreditable conduct, bad character or bias is admissible against a mere witness in a trial even in circumstances where it might not be admissible against an accused. The strictures surrounding the admission into evidence of similar fact evidence against an accused do not apply with the same rigour against a non-accused witness. That said, many of the same considerations apply to the weight that can be given to the similar fact evidence and its degree of probative value.

In *R. v. Handy* (2002), 164 C.C.C. (3d) 481 at paras. 102-136, the Supreme Court of Canada held that in assessing the probative value of similar fact evidence it is relevant to consider: (a) the potential for collusion; (b) identification of the issue in question; (c) the degree of similarity or dissimilarity between the allegations in the case and the similar fact evidence (otherwise referred to as "connecting factors"); and (d) the strength of the evidence that the similar acts actually occurred. Within category (c), the trial judge should consider any factor connecting the similar facts to the circumstances being alleged, including:

(i)   proximity in time of the similar acts;
(ii)   extent to which the other acts are similar in detail to the conduct alleged;
(iii) number of occurrences of the similar acts;
(iv)   circumstances surrounding or relating to the similar acts;
(v)   any distinctive features unifying the incidents;
(vi)   intervening events;
(vii) any other factor which would tend to support or rebut the underlying unity of the similar events.

(*R. v. Handy* at para. 82)

As a preliminary matter, I am satisfied that collusion between Mr. Jackson and Mr. Khan can be ruled out. They did not know each other. Each, coincidentally, happened to retain the same criminal defence counsel and it was their lawyer who noted the similarity between the two arrests and the fact that the same two officers were involved.

Other factors enhancing the probative value of the similar fact evidence in this case are their proximity in time and the degree of similarity between them. In both situations, the targeted individuals were young black men driving expensive vehicles. The officers' initial reasons for curiosity were slightly different in each case. Mr. Khan was staring straight ahead, and he failed to take the right-of-way; Mr. Jackson had a look of guilt on his face. However, both Mr. Khan and Mr. Jackson allege that the police followed them for no reason and then pulled them over without there having been any traffic infraction. In both cases, the police allege a traffic infraction in full view of the police as an initial reason for the stop. In both cases, the police allege that as they approached the stopped vehicle they could see the driver attempting to hide something. Both Mr. Khan and Mr. Jackson allege that they were first removed from their cars and detained by Officer James while Officer Asselin searched their vehicles and that they were not arrested until his search turned up drugs.

There are also dissimilarities between the two events, as one would expect. Further, the circumstances in which the incidents arose (a routine traffic stop) are so similar that there will almost inevitably be some degree of similarity between the two events. For example, when police pull over any vehicle for an alleged traffic violation and then find drugs, it is not uncommon for the driver to deny the traffic violation. There will always be some similarities between cases of this nature.

I do not propose to dwell at length on these and other connecting factors because in my opinion there are two critical factors that completely undermine the probative value of the similar fact evidence. The first, and lesser in importance, is the fact that there is only one incident. That is not necessarily fatal. However, the fact that a person has done something once before is not nearly as compelling as the fact he has done it, say, twenty times before. If there is only one other similar incident, its probative strength in other areas would need to be greater. For example, I would be less concerned about attaching weight to one prior incident if it was so similar in detail as to be almost a "fingerprint." Conversely, in the absence of striking similarity, I would be reluctant to conclude that one prior incident was a coincidence so compelling as to be highly probative.

The second, and most persuasive, negative factor is the strength of the evidence that the similar act actually occurred. Sheldon Jackson is not the most credible of witnesses. He is an admitted drug dealer. He has a criminal record, including a drug-related offence. He was a suspended driver, but was driving. He was using a fabricated driver's license with false identification, and had used it with success in the past. He attempted to flee the scene. He had a motive to fabricate, as he is himself facing charges of possession for the purposes of trafficking in relation to that same event. Of course, none of this means he is not telling the truth about this particular incident. However, since proof that this incident occurred depends entirely on Mr. Jackson's credibility, I am driven to the conclusion that this evidence is frail, at best, and possibly unproven.

I have a discretion in determining the weight and admissibility of evidence of this nature. Having heard the evidence, I am of the view that its probative value is too weak to attach any weight to it. That means, as is undoubtedly often the case, Mr. Khan is in the difficult position of having to prove racial profiling by showing that the police have lied.

The trial judge ultimately found that the officers had lied about the reason they stopped the accused and that he was the victim of racial profiling. Khan was acquitted. The charges against Mr. Jackson were ultimately stayed.

(g) Character of Victim

Chief Justice Cardozo sought to justify a difference in treatment of character evidence depending on whether it was of the accused or the victim:

> In a very real sense a defendant starts his life afresh when he stands before a jury, a prisoner at the bar. There has been a homicide in a public place. The killer admits the killing, but urges self-defence and sudden impulse. Inflexibly the law has set its face against the endeavour to fasten guilt upon him by proof of character or experience predisposing to an act of crime. At times, when the issue has been self-defence, testimony has been admitted as to the murderous propensity of the deceased, the victim of the homicide, but never of such a propensity on the part of the killer. The principle back of the exclusion is one, not of logic, but of policy. There may be cogency in the argument that a quarrelsome defendant is more likely to start a quarrel than one of a milder type, a man of dangerous mode of life more likely than a shy recluse. The law is not blind to this, but equally it is not blind to the peril of the innocent if character is accepted as probative of crime. "The natural and inevitable tendency of the tribunal — whether judge or jury — is to give excessive weight to the vicious record of crime thus exhibited, and either to allow it to bear too strongly on the present charge, or to take the proof of it as justifying a condemnation irrespective of guilt of the present charge."[80]

---

80 *People v. Zackowitz*, 172 N.E. 466 (1930). The quotation in this excerpt is from 1 Wigmore, *Evidence*, s. 194.

Are you satisfied with this justification?

(i) *Self-defence*

The accused is charged with murder and he offers self-defence as a justification. The accused testifies that he viewed the deceased's actions as threatening since he believed him to be a violent man. The accused offers in evidence the deceased's character, his reputation and his violent acts to support his defence.

Earlier in this chapter we discussed character evidence as admissible for a non-character purpose. We used this example to show that the evidence would be relevant not to establish that the deceased is a violent person but instead for the purpose of assessing the reasonableness of the accused's state of mind.

Suppose, however, that in the manslaughter case the deceased's character or disposition towards violence was not known to the accused at the time of the incident.

In this case we ask the trier to infer that the persons acted in conformity with their character. Since here we are offering the character evidence as circumstantial evidence from which we ask the trier of fact to infer that the victim acted in conformity with their character, a problem of relevance arises. The law provides no answer to such a problem. Rather, we must rely on our common sense and experience to guide us.

In *R. v. Scopelliti*[81] the accused was charged with two counts of murder. The principal defence was self-defence. The accused testified to his apprehension caused by the deceased's actions. The trial judge allowed the defence to intoduce evidence of three prior acts of violence or threats of violence, *not known to the accused*, committed by the deceased and directed at other persons. On appeal from the acquittal the Ontario Court of Appeal, presented with no authorities on the issue, reasoned from basic principles:

> . . . the admission of such evidence accords in principle with the view expressed by this Court that the disposition of a person to do a certain act is relevant to indicate the probability of his having done or not having done the act. The law prohibits the prosecution from introducing evidence for the purpose of showing that the *accused* is a person who by reason of his criminal character (disposition) is likely to have committed the crime charged, on policy grounds, not because of lack of relevance. There is, however, no rule of policy which excludes evidence of the disposition of a third person for violence where that disposition has probative value on some issue before the jury.[82]

Interestingly, the court, following Wigmore,[83] saw "no substantial reason against evidencing the character by particular instances of violent or quarrelsome conduct." While not necessary to its decision, the court went on to hold that in

---

81 (1981), 63 C.C.C. (2d) 481 (Ont. C.A.). *Scopelliti* was first followed in *R. v. DeLong* (1989), 47 C.C.C. (3d) 402, 69 C.R. (3d) 147 (Ont. C.A.), and *R. v. Ryan* (1989), 49 C.C.C. (3d) 490 (Nfld. C.A.). For more recent authority, see *R. v. Hamilton* (2003), 180 C.C.C. (3d) 80 (B.C. C.A.); *R. v. Varga* (2001), 159 C.C.C. (3d) 502, 48 C.R. (5th) 387 (Ont. C.A.) and *R. v. Cameron* (1995), 96 C.C.C. (3d) 346 (Ont. C.A.). For academic commentary, see Alvaro, "Emerging Issues in the Area of *Scopelliti* Evidence" (1994), 36 Crim. L.Q. 372.

82 *Scopelliti, ibid.*, at p. 493.

83 1 Wigmore, *Evidence* (3d ed.), s. 198.

a case such as this the Crown would be entitled to rebut the defence evidence by character evidence showing the deceased to be of a peaceable disposition.[84]

Recognizing that evidence of the victim's character for violence is relevant to whether he was the aggressor on the occasion under review, is there any policy presented that might argue for exclusion?

In *Scopelliti* the court recognized the need for a weighing by the trial judge of the probative worth of the evidence against the possibility of an irrational decision by the jury:

> Since evidence of prior acts of violence by the deceased is likely to arouse feelings of hostility against the deceased, there must inevitably be some element of discretion in the determination whether the proferred evidence has sufficient probative value for the purpose for which it is tendered to justify its admission.[85]

The Crown in *Scopelliti* argued that there was insufficient probative value as none of the prior acts were life-threatening, and the acts simply tended to show a general disposition toward violence which would make it likely that the deceased were the aggressors. This attempt to provide a limitation on such evidence akin to the limitation on the introduction of similar facts against an accused was rejected by the court.

(ii) *Sexual Assault*

When dealing with evidence of the alleged victim's character in sexual assault cases there are hazards. Professor Estrich describes the difficulties of teaching in this area.[86] She writes:

> I know many students, and even a few professors, who believe that the women are always right and the men are always wrong; that if she didn't consent fully and voluntarily, it is rape, no matter what she said or did, or what he did or did not realize. Everything about his past should be admitted, and nothing about hers. And that's what they want to hear in class.
>
> This kind of orthodoxy is not only bad educationally but, in the case of rape, it also misses the point. Society is not so orthodox in its views. There is a debate going on in courthouses and prosecutors' offices, and around coffee machines and dinner tables, about whether Mike Tyson was guilty or not, and whether William Kennedy Smith ever should have been prosecuted; about when women should be believed, and what counts as consent. There's a debate going on in America as to what is reasonable when it comes to sex. Turn on the radio and you will hear it. To silence that debate in the classroom is to remove the classroom from reality, and to make ourselves irrelevant. It may be hard for some students, but ultimately the only way to change things — and that's usually the goal of those who find the discussions

---

84 See the discussion of this issue, including whether evidence of a victim's peaceable disposition is admissible in self-defence cases not involving an attack on the victim's character, in cases such as *R. v. Diu* (2000), 144 C.C.C. (3d) 481, 33 C.R. (5th) 203 (Ont. C.A.) at 498-503 [C.C.C.]; *R. v. Dejong* (1998), 125 C.C.C. (3d) 302, 16 C.R. (5th) 372 (B.C. C.A.) at 323-326 [C.C.C.]; *R. v. Soares* (1987), 34 C.C.C. (3d) 403 (Ont. C.A.) at 429-431 and *R. v. Johnson* (1965), 49 C.R. 176 (N.S. S.C.). See too, Uniform Law Conference of Canada, Report of the Federal/Provincial Task Force on Uniform Rules of Evidence (Toronto: Carswell, 1982) at 91.

85 *Supra*, note 81, at p. 496. See also *R. v. Yaeck* (1991), 10 C.R. (4th) 1, 23 (Ont. C.A.).

86 Susan Estrich, "Teaching Rape Law" (1992), Yale L.J. 509. See also Tomkovicx, "Teaching Rape: Reasons, Risks and Rewards" (1992), Yale L.J. 481.

most difficult — is to confront the issues squarely, not to pretend that they don't exist. Besides, the purpose of education, in my classes anyway, is to prepare our students to participate in the controversies that animate the law, not to provide them with a shelter from reality.

. . . .

Judges and juries these days are less inclined to accept male conduct that only a few years ago was tolerated as understandably macho. I don't find as many students in my classes these days who believe that a man has the right to ignore the fact that a woman is saying no. And I don't think the reason for this change is that feminists have defined what is "politically correct" in the classroom; I think instead that most of my students, male and female, actually believe that a man should listen to a woman's words, and take her at her word.

This shift in our thinking about the elements of culpability leaves credibility as the only defense game in town. After all, rapes rarely take place in front of witnesses. If no doesn't mean yes, if bruises aren't necessary, and if no unusual force is required, then in many cases there's not going to be much physical evidence to rely on. She gives her version and he gives his. If you are the defense attorney, your job is to convince the jury not to believe what she says — which means that the only way to defend may be to destroy the credibility of the victim.

The key question in many acquaintance rape cases today thus becomes not what counts as rape but rather what we need to know about the victim, and the defendant, in order to decide who is telling the truth.

. . . .

It is one thing to exclude evidence of a woman's sexual past or of psychiatric treatment when she has been beaten and burned; it is easy to argue there that admitting such evidence does almost nothing except to deter legitimate prosecutions and to victimize the victim. But it is surely a harder case when there have been no weapons and no bruises, and when the man's liberty depends on convincing a jury not to believe a woman who appears at least superficially credible.

Many of the traditional rules of rape liability were premised on the notion that women lie; Wigmore went so far as to view rape complainants as fundamentally deranged. I don't buy that for a moment nor, I expect, do most of my students. Yet even if only one of a hundred men, or one of a thousand, is falsely accused, the question is still how we can protect that man's right to disprove his guilt. Assume for a moment, I tell my students, that it was you, or your brother, or your boyfriend or your son, who was accused of rape by a casual date with a history of psychiatric problems, or by a woman he met in a bar who had a history of one-night stands. Would you exclude that evidence? What else can the man do to avoid a felony conviction and a ruined life? Where do you draw the line? But if you don't exclude the evidence, will some women as a result become unrapable, at least as a matter of law? That is, will women who have histories of mental instability or of "promiscuity" ever be able to convince juries who know those histories that they really were raped?

Similar issues arise with respect to the man's credibility. The first question many people asked when Anita Hill charged that Clarence Thomas had harassed her was whether there were other women who had been similarly mistreated. The first significant ruling in the Smith case, indeed the decisive ruling, was the judge's pretrial decision to exclude the testimony of three other women who claimed that they had been sexually abused by the defendant. If the testimony of only one woman cannot be believed — unless she is a Sunday school teacher, camera in hand, as Desiree Washington was, and the defendant is a black man who has made a host of inconsistent statements, as Mike Tyson did — is it fair to exclude the testimony of the other women? And if the testimony is not excluded, do we risk convicting a defendant for being a bad man, indeed being a rapist, rather than committing the particular act charged?

One answer is to say that we need symmetry: exclude all the evidence about both of them. That's the approach the judge followed in the William Kennedy Smith case. On the surface, it is neat and appealing. The only problem is that it's a false symmetry that is being enforced. After all, evidence that a man has abused other women is much more probative of rape than evidence that a woman has had consensual sex with other men is probative of consent. Most women have had sexual experiences, and unless those experiences fall into some kind of unusual pattern, the mere fact that a woman has had lovers tells us almost nothing about whether she consented on the particular occasion that she is charging as rape. But won't we all look at a defendant differently if three other women have also come forward to say they were abused? The danger with such evidence is not that it proves so little, but that it may prove too much. Symmetry won't get you out of this hole, at least not in my classroom.

Thus, even if most students can agree these days that no means no, and that force can be established if you push a woman down, there's very little agreement about what we need to know about her or him before deciding whether she in fact said yes or no, and whether he actually pushed her down or just lay down with her. The consensus on what counts as rape is more apparent than real. These days, society's continued ambivalence towards acquaintance rape is increasingly being expressed in evidentiary rules and standards of credibility rather than in the definitions of force and consent. The questions have shifted; answering them is no easier.[87]

Historically, prior sexual history was characterized as character evidence because as we will see in the next section, triers of fact were invited to use it to make an evaluative or moral judgment about the complainant. Is it still appropriate today to refer to prior sexual history as character evidence? If so, would other human functions such as sleeping or eating be classified as character evidence? **Is it now more appropriate to refer to prior sexual history evidence as conduct or circumstantial evidence from which relevant inferences may possibly be drawn?**

Common Law

The position at common law regarding evidence of the character of the alleged victim in sexual assault cases was summarized by the English Court of Appeal in *R. v. Krausz*:[88]

> It is settled law that she who complains of rape or attempted rape can be cross-examined about (1) her general reputation and moral character, (2) sexual intercourse between herself and the defendant on other occasions, and (3) sexual intercourse between herself and other men; and that evidence can be called to contradict her on (1) and (2) but that no evidence can be called to contradict her denials of (3).

The common law regarded evidence of (1) and (2) as relevant to the material issue of consent[89] but evidence of (3) as irrelevant to the issue of consent but

---

87 Estrich, *ibid.*, at pp. 515-20.
88 (1973), 57 Cr. App. R. 466, 472. See *R. v. Finnessey* (1906), 11 O.L.R. 338, 341 (C.A.) for a similar outline of the common law. And see *R. v. Basken* (1974), 21 C.C.C. (2d) 321, 337 (Sask. C.A.) approving this description. See also *Gross v. Brodrecht* (1897), 24 O.A.R. 687 (C.A.).
89 For examples of cases where evidence of the complainant's reputation and general habits

relevant to credit. As (3) was only relevant to credit the matter was collateral and the witness could not be contradicted. Osler J.A. in the Ontario Court of Appeal remarked:

> . . . she may be asked, but, inasmuch as the question is one going strictly to her credit, she is not generally compellable to answer whether she has had connection with persons other than the prisoner. This seems to rest to some extent in the discretion of the trial Judge. Whether, however, she answers it or not that is an end of the matter, otherwise as many collateral, and therefore irrelevant issues might be raised as there were specific charges of immorality suggested, and the prosecutrix could not be expected to come prepared to meet them, though she might well be prepaared to repel an attack upon her general character for chastity.[90]

While most of the older authorities state that sexual history with persons other than the accused is irrelevant to the issue of consent, can it be argued that on our understanding of the meaning of the term "relevant," i.e., "does the evidence offered render the desired inference more probable than it would be without the evidence?", the evidence may, in exceptional cases, be relevant? Though relevant the evidence could nevertheless still be excluded because of considerations of fairness to the victim-witness and because of prejudice to the outcome of the trial through improper use of the evidence. Cardozo J. deplored the existence of the inflexible rule based on "irrelevancy" and argued for a discretion in the trial judge, who could assess probative worth against the dangers in his particular case.[91]

Arguments have been advanced, however, that prior sexual history with others is not relevant to the issue of consent. In a speech given on sexual harassment, Professor Catherine MacKinnon stated:

> The question of prior sexual history is one area in which the issue of sexual credibility is directly posed. Evidence of the defendant's sexual harassment of other women in the same institutional relation or setting is increasingly being considered admissible, and it should be. The other side of the question is whether evidence of a victim's prior sexual history should be discoverable or admissible, and it seems to me it should not be. Perpetrators often seek out victims with common qualities or circumstances or situations — we are fungible to them so long as we are similarly accessible — but victims do not seek out victimization at all, and their nonvictimized sexual behavior is no more relevant to an allegation of sexual force than is the perpetrator's consensual sex life, such as it may be.
>
> So far the leading case, consistent with the direction of rape law, has found that the victim's sexual history with other individuals is not relevant, although consensual history with the individual perpetrator may be.[92]

---

for promiscuity was received, see *R. v. Krausz* (1973), 57 Cr. App. R. 466; *R. v. Barker* (1829), 172 E.R. 558 (N.P.); and *R. v. Bashir*, [1969] 3 All E.R. 692 (Q.B.).

90 In *R. v. Finnessey, supra*, note 88, at p. 341. The historical development of the common law position is concisely presented in Julie Taylor, "Rape and Women's Credibility: Problems of Recantations and False Accusations Echoed in the Case of Cathleen Crowell Webb and Gary Dotson" (1987), 10 Harvard Women's L.J. 59 at 74-81.

91 Cardozo, *The Nature of the Judicial Process* (1921), p. 156. Wigmore argued for admissibility of the particular acts: 1 Wigmore, *Evidence* (3d ed.), s. 200. See also Scutt, "Admissibility of Sexual History Evidence and Allegations in Rape Cases" (1979), 53 Aust. L.J. 817 and Bohmer Blumberg, "Twice Traumatized: The Rape Victim and the Court" (1975), 58 Judicature 391.

92 MacKinnon, *Feminism Unmodified: Discourses on Life and Law* (1987), at p. 113.

Professor Christine Boyle has argued:[93]

The tendency in this area has been, unfortunately, simply to assert or deny the relevance of the sexual activity of the complainant. One can appreciate the reluctance of those concerned about the abuse of such evidence in the past to concede its relevance in any context, but the problems have arisen with respect to the introduction of the evidence to suggest consent or to undermine the credibility of the complainant. Its use for these purposes is unjustifiable since the tests of relevance, common sense and human experience, suggest that people exercise choice over each sexual partner. Moreover, there is no evidence to suggest that sexual activity has any link with credibility.

An intermediate approach to this issue focuses on the assumptions underlying findings of relevance of the victim's prior sexual history. The position advanced is that though evidence of prior sexual acts may be relevant in certain limited circumstances, the identification of those circumstances must be based on a reevaluation of the assumptions upon which findings of relevance have traditionally been based.

Professor Adler explains the premise upon which the intermediate approach is based:

According to one authority on evidence, "relevant" means that "any two facts to which it is applied are so related to each other that according to the common course of events one either taken by itself or in connection with other facts proves or renders probable the past, present or future existence or non-existence of another." Thus, if one "fact" is the complainant's sexual experience, and the other, her consent to intercourse on the occasion of the alleged rape, there must be a link of some sort between the two for evidence of the former to be relevant and hence admissible in court. In practice, such a link almost invariably involves some alleged or actual aspect of the complainant's past sexual behaviour which is argued to bear some similarity to the incident involved in the trial. The similarity may be in the mere fact of her having had sexual intercourse in the past, or additional factors inherent in the situation may be drawn upon to imply greater relevance.

The main question currently open to judicial interpretation concerns the nature, logic and strength of such links. Few would wish to argue that a woman's past experience of consensual intercourse with her husband makes her more likely to have consented to another defendant. But where the line is to be drawn is far from clear, and without explicit guidelines, decisions in individual cases remain diverse and uneven.[94]

Professor Adler notes that one difficulty with leaving determinations of relevance of previous sexual history to the discretion of the trial judge is the subjectivity inherent in the exercise of discretion.

Compare the remarks of Susan Brownmiller in *Against Our Will:*[95]

Not only is the victim's response during the act measured and weighed, her past sexual history is scrutinized under the theory that it relates to her "tendency to consent," or that it reflects on her credibility, her veracity, her predisposition to tell the truth or to lie. Or so the law says. As it works out in practice, juries presented with evidence concerning a woman's past sexual history make use of such information

---

93 *Sexual Assault* (1984), at p. 137.
94 Adler, "The Relevance of Sexual History Evidence in Rape: Problems of Subjective Interpretation", [1985] Crim. L. Rev. 769, 772.
95 (New York: Simon & Schuster, 1975), pp. 385-86.

to form a moral judgment on her character, and here all the old myths of rape are brought into play, for the feeling persists that a virtuous woman either cannot get raped or does not get into situations that leave her open to assault. Thus the questions in the jury room become "Was she or wasn't she asking for it?"; "If she had been a decent woman, wouldn't she have fought to death to defend her 'treasure'?"; and "Is this bimbo worth the ruination of a man's career and reputation?"

The crime of rape must be totally separated from all traditional concepts of chastity, for the very meaning of chastity presupposes that it is a woman's duty (but not a man's) to refrain from sex outside the matrimonial union. That sexual activity renders a woman "unchaste" is a totally male view of the female as *his* pure vessel. The phrase "prior chastity" as well as the concept must be stricken from the legal lexicon, along with "prosecutrix," as inflammatory and prejudicial to a complainant's case.

A history of sexual activity with many partners may be indicative of a female's healthy interest in sex, or it may be indicative of a chronic history of victimization and exploitation in which she could not assert her own inclinations; it may be indicative of a spirit of adventure, a spirit of rebellion, a spirit of curiosity, a spirit of joy or a spirit of defeat. Whatever the reasons, and there are many, prior consensual intercourse between a rape complainant and other partners of her choosing should not be scrutinized as an indicator of purity or impurity of mind or body, not in this day and age at any rate, and it has no place in jury room deliberation as to whether or not, in the specific instance in question, an act of forcible sex took place. Prior consensual intercourse between the complainant and *the defendant* does have some relevance and such information probably should not be barred.

An overhaul of present laws and a fresh approach to sexual assault legislation must go hand in hand with a fresh approach to enforcing the law. The question of who interprets and who enforces the statutes is as important as the contents of the law itself. At present, female victims of sexual crimes of violence who seek legal justice must rely on a series of male authority figures whose masculine orientation, values and fears place them securely in the offender's camp.

Charter of Rights

R. v. SEABOYER
[1991] 2 S.C.R. 577, 7 C.R. (4th) 117, 66 C.C.C. (3d) 321

The accused were each charged with sexual assault. At their preliminary hearings they sought to cross-examine the respective complainants with respect to their previous sexual conduct. In each case the judge ruled that such cross-examination was foreclosed by the Criminal Code. Each accused applied to the Supreme Court for an order quashing their committals for trial on the ground that the judge, in enforcing the then existing sections 276 and 277 of the Criminal Code, had exceeded his jurisdiction and deprived the accused of his right to make full answer and defence. The orders were granted on the ground that sections 276 and 277 violated the Charter of Rights and Freedoms. The cases were remitted to the preliminary inquiry judges for a ruling on the evidentiary issues unhampered by the statutory provisions. An appeal to the Court of Appeal was allowed on the ground that the preliminary inquiry judges lacked the jurisdiction to determine the constitutional validity of the impugned sections and accordingly had not erred in applying the sections. The Court of Appeal went on however to consider the constitutional validity of the sections. The majority of the court held that section 276 was capable of contravening an accused's rights under the Charter in some circumstances. The majority held that the section would generally be operative and the appropriate course was for the trial judge to decline to apply it in those limited and rare instances where it could lead to a Charter breach. The accused appealed. On the appeal, constitutional questions were stated putting in issue the constitutional validity of sections 276 and 277.

McLACHLIN J. (LAMER C.J.C., LA FOREST, SOPINKA, CORY, STEVENSON and IACOBUCCI JJ. concurring):—

. . . .

These cases raise the issue of the constitutionality of ss. 276 and 277 of the *Criminal Code*, . . . commonly known as the "rape-shield" provisions. The provisions restrict the right of the defence on a trial for a sexual offence to cross-examine and lead evidence of a complainant's sexual conduct on other occasions. The question is whether these restrictions offend the guarantees accorded to an accused person by the *Canadian Charter of Rights and Freedoms*.

My conclusion is that one of the sections in issue, s. 276, offends the *Charter*. While its purpose—the abolition of outmoded, sexist-based use of sexual conduct evidence—is laudable, its effect goes beyond what is required or justified by that purpose. At the same time, striking down s. 276 does not imply reversion to the old common law rules, which permitted evidence of the complainant's sexual conduct even though it might have no probative value to the issues on the case and, on the contrary, might mislead the jury. Instead, relying on the basic principles that actuate our law of evidence, the courts must seek a middle way that offers the maximum protection to the complainant compatible with the maintenance of the accused's fundamental right to a fair trial.

. . . .

I deal first with *Seaboyer*. The accused was charged with sexual assault of a woman with whom he had been drinking in a bar. On the preliminary inquiry the judge refused to allow the accused to cross-examine the complainant on her sexual conduct on other occasions. The appellant contends that he should have been permitted to cross-examine as to other acts of sexual intercourse which may have caused bruises and other aspects of the complainant's condition which the Crown had put in evidence. While the theory of the defence has not been detailed at this early stage, such evidence might arguably be relevant to consent, since it might provide other explanations for the physical evidence tendered by the Crown in support of the use of force against the complainant.

The *Gayme* case arose in different circumstances. The complainant was 15, the appellant 18. They were friends. The Crown alleges that the appellant sexually assaulted her at his school. The defence, relying on the defences of consent and honest belief in consent, contends that there was no assault and that the complainant was the sexual aggressor. In pursuance of this defence, the appellant at the preliminary inquiry sought to cross-examine and present evidence of prior and subsequent sexual conduct of the complainant. . . .

. . . .

It should be noted that the admissibility of the evidence sought to be tendered in the two cases is not at issue. In neither case did the preliminary inquiry judge consider whether the evidence would have been relevant or admissible in the absence of ss. 276 or 277 of the *Criminal Code.*

Relevant Legislation

Criminal Code, s. 276:

276. (1) In proceedings in respect of an offence under section 271, 272 or 273, no evidence shall be adduced by or on behalf of the accused concerning the sexual activity of the complainant with any person other than the accused unless

(*a*) it is evidence that rebuts evidence of the complainant's sexual activity or absence thereof that was previously adduced by the prosecution;

(*b*) it is evidence of specific instances of the complainant's sexual activity tending to establish the identity of the person who had sexual contact with the complainant on the occasion set out in the charge; or

(*c*) it is evidence of sexual activity that took place on the same occasion as the sexual activity that forms the subject-matter of the charge, where that evidence relates to the consent that the accused alleges he believed was given by the complainant.

(2) No evidence is admissible under paragraph (1)(*c*) unless

(*a*) reasonable notice in writing has been given to the prosecutor by or on behalf of the accused of his intention to adduce the evidence together with particulars of the evidence sought to be adduced; and

(*b*) a copy of the notice has been filed with the clerk of the court.

(3) No evidence is admissible under subsection (1) unless the judge, provincial court judge or justice, after holding a hearing in which the jury and the members of the public are excluded and in which the complainant is not a compellable witness, is satisfied that the requirements of this section are met.

Criminal Code, s. 277:

277. In proceedings in respect of an offence under section 271, 272 or 273, evidence of sexual reputation, whether general or specific, is not admissible for the purpose of challenging or supporting the credibility of the complainant.

. . . .

Everyone, under s. 7 of the *Charter*, has the right to life, liberty and security of person and the right not to be deprived thereof except in accordance with the principles of fundamental justice.

. . . .

The real issue under s. 7 is whether the potential for deprivation of liberty flowing from ss. 276 and 277 takes place in a manner that conforms to the principles of fundamental justice.

. . . .

All the parties agree that the right to a fair trial—one which permits the trier of fact to get at the truth and properly and fairly dispose of the case—is a principle of fundamental justice. Nor is there any dispute that encouraging reporting of sexual offences and protection of the complainant's privacy are legitimate goals provided they do not interfere with the primary objective of a fair trial. Where the parties part company is on the issue of whether ss. 276 and 277 of the *Criminal Code* in fact infringe the right to a fair trial. The supporters of the legislation urge that it furthers the right to a fair trial by eliminating evidence of little or no worth and considerable prejudice. The appellants, on the other hand, say that the legislation goes too far and in fact eliminates relevant evidence which should be admitted notwithstanding the possibility of prejudice.

. . . .

[Here the Supreme Court set out the scope of a trial judge's discretion to exclude evidence including defence evidence. In the latter case, the prejudicial effect of the evidence must substantially outweigh its probative value. This was reviewed in Chapter 3.]

. . . .

Section 277 excludes evidence of sexual reputation for the purpose of challenging or supporting the credibility of the plaintiff. The idea that a complainant's credibility might be affected by whether she has had other sexual experience is today universally discredited. There is no logical or practical link between a woman's sexual reputation and whether she is a truthful witness. It follows that the evidence excluded by s. 277 can serve no legitimate purpose in the trial. Section 277, by limiting the exclusion to a purpose which is clearly illegitimate, does not touch evidence which may be tendered for valid purposes, and hence does not infringe the right to a fair trial.

I turn then to s. 276. Section 276, unlike s. 277, does not condition exclusion on use of the evidence for an illegitimate purpose. Rather, it constitutes a blanket exclusion, subject to three exceptions—rebuttal evidence, evidence going to identity, and evidence relating to consent to sexual activity on the same occasion as the trial incident. The question is whether this may exclude evidence which is relevant to the defence and the probative value of which is not substantially outweighed by the potential prejudice to the trial process. To put the matter another way, can it be said *a priori*, as the Attorney General for Ontario contends, that any and all evidence excluded by s. 276 will necessarily be of such trifling weight in relation to the prejudicial effect of the evidence that it may fairly be excluded?

In my view, the answer to this question must be negative. The Canadian and American jurisprudence affords numerous examples of evidence of sexual conduct which would be excluded by s. 276 but which clearly should be received in the interests of a fair trial, notwithstanding the possibility that it may divert a jury by tempting it to improperly infer consent or lack of credibility in the complainant.

Consider the defence of honest belief. It rests on the concept that the accused may honestly but mistakenly (and not necessarily reasonably) have believed that the complainant was consenting to the sexual act. If the accused can raise a reasonable doubt as to his intention on the basis that he honestly held such a belief, he is not guilty under our law and is entitled to an acquittal. The basis of the accused's honest belief in the complainant's consent may be sexual acts performed by the complainant at some other time or place. Yet section 276 would preclude the accused leading such evidence.

Another category of evidence eliminated by s. 276 relates to the right of the defence to attack the credibility of the complainant on the ground that the complainant was biased or had motive to fabricate the evidence. In *State v. Jalo*, 557 P.2d 1359 (Or. Ct. App. 1976), a father accused of sexual acts with his young daughter sought to present evidence that the source of the accusation was his earlier discovery of the fact that the girl and her brother were engaged in intimate relations. The defence contended that when the father stopped the relationship, the daughter, out of animus toward him, accused him of the act. The father sought to lead this evidence in support of his defence that the charges were a concoction motivated by animus. Notwithstanding its clear relevance, this evidence would be excluded by s. 276. The respondent submits that the damage caused by its exclusion would not be great, because all that would be forbidden would be evidence of the sexual activities of the children, and the father could still testify that his daughter was angry with him. But surely the father's chance of convincing the jury of the validity of his defence would be greatly diminished if he were reduced to saying, in effect, "My daughter was angry with me, but I can't say why or produce any corroborating evidence." As noted above, to deny a defendant the building blocks of his defence is often to deny him the defence itself.

Other examples abound. Evidence of sexual activity excluded by s. 276 may be relevant to explain the physical conditions on which the Crown relies to establish intercourse or the use of force, such as semen, pregnancy, injury or disease—evidence which may go to consent: . . . In the case of young complainants where there may be a tendency to believe their story on the ground that the detail of their account must have come from the alleged encounter, it may be relevant to show other activity which provides an explanation for the knowledge: . . .

Even evidence as to pattern of conduct may on occasion be relevant. Since this use of evidence of prior sexual conduct draws upon the inference that prior conduct infers similar subsequent conduct, it closely resembles the prohibited use of the evidence and must be carefully scrutinized: . . . Yet such evidence might be admissible in non-sexual cases under the similar fact rule. Is it fair then to deny it to an accused, merely because the trial relates to a sexual offence? . . .

. . . .

These examples leave little doubt that s. 276 has the potential to exclude evidence of critical relevance to the defence. Can it honestly be said, as the Attorney General for Ontario contends, that the value of such evidence will always be trifling when compared with its potential to mislead the jury? I think not. The examples show that the evidence may well be of great importance to getting at the truth and determining whether the accused is guilty or innocent under the law—the ultimate aim of the trial process. They demonstrate that s. 276, enacted for the purpose of helping judges and juries arrive at the proper and just verdict in the particular case, overshoots the mark, with the result that it may have the opposite effect of impeding them in discovering the truth.

. . . .

2. *Is s. 276 Saved by s. 1 of the Charter?*

Is s. 276 of the *Criminal Code* justified in a free and democratic society, notwithstanding the fact that it may lead to infringements of the *Charter*?

The first step under s. 1 is to consider whether the legislation addresses a pressing and substantial objective: . . .

The second requirement under s. 1 is that the infringement of rights be proportionate to the pressing objective. . . . In creating exceptions to the exclusion of evidence of the sexual activity of the complainant on other occasions, Parliament correctly recognized that justice requires a measured approach, one which admits evidence which is truly relevant to the defence notwithstanding potential prejudicial effect. Yet Parliament at the same time excluded other evidence of sexual conduct which might be equally relevant to a legitimate defence and which appears to pose no greater danger of prejudice than the exceptions it recognizes. To the extent the section excludes relevant defence evidence whose value is not clearly outweighed by the danger it presents, the section is overbroad.

I turn finally to the third aspect of the proportionality requirement — the balance between the importance of the objective and the injurious effect of the legislation. The objective of the legislation, as discussed above, is to eradicate the erroneous inferences from evidence of other sexual encounters that the complainant is more likely to have consented to the sexual act in issue or less likely to be telling the truth. The subsidiary aims are to promote fairer trials and increased reporting of sexual offences and to minimize the invasion of the complainant's privacy. In this way the personal security of women and their right to equal benefit and protection of the law are enhanced. The effect of the legislation, on the other hand, is to exclude relevant defence evidence, the value of which outweighs its potential prejudice. As indicated in the discussion of s. 7, all parties agree that a provision which rules out probative defence evidence which is not clearly outweighed by the prejudice it may cause to the trial strikes the wrong balance between the rights of complainants and the rights of the accused. The line must be drawn short of the point where it results in an unfair trial and the possible conviction of an innocent person. Section 276 fails this test.

I conclude that s. 276 is not saved by s. 1 of the Charter.

. . . .

4. *What Follows From Striking Down s. 276?*

The first question is whether the striking down of s. 276 revives the old common law rules of evidence permitting liberal and often inappropriate reception of evidence of the complainant's sexual conduct. . . .

The answer to this question is no. The rules in question are common law rules. Like other common law rules of evidence, they must be adapted to conform to current reality. As all counsel on these appeals accepted, the reality in 1991 is that evidence of sexual conduct and reputation in itself cannot be regarded as logically probative of either the complainant's credibility or consent. Although they still may inform the thinking of many, the twin myths which s. 276 sought to eradicate are just that—myths—and have no place in a rational and just system of law. It follows that the old rules which permitted evidence of sexual conduct and condoned invalid inferences from it solely for these purposes have no place in our law.

The inquiry as to what the law is in the absence of s. 276 of the *Code* is thus remitted to consideration of the fundamental principles governing the trial process and the reception of evidence. Harking back to Thayer's maxim, relevant evidence should be admitted, and irrelevant evidence excluded, subject to the qualification that the value of the evidence must outweigh its potential prejudice to the conduct of a fair trial. Moreover, the focus must be not on the evidence itself, but on the use to which it is put. As Professor Galvin puts it, our aim is "to abolish the outmoded, sexist-based use of sexual conduct evidence while permitting other uses of such evidence to remain": *supra*, at p. 809.

This definition of the problem suggests an approach which abolishes illegitimate uses and inferences, while preserving legitimate uses. There is wide agreement that the approach of a general exclusion supplemented by categories of exceptions is bound to fail because of the impossibility of predicting in advance what evidence may be relevant in a particular case: see Galvin, *supra*, Doherty, *supra*, and Elliott, *supra*. On the other hand, judges are not free to act on whim. As Professor Vivian Berger puts it in her article "Man's Trial, Woman's Tribulation: Rape Cases in the Courtroom" (1977), 77 *Colum. L. Rev.* 1, at p. 69:

> The problem is to chart a course between inflexible legislative rules and wholly untrammelled judicial discretion: The former threatens the rights of defendants; the latter may ignore the needs of complainants.

. . . .

Galvin's proposal, with some modification, reflects an appropriate response to the problem of avoiding illegitimate inferences from evidence of the complainant's sexual conduct, while preserving the general right to a fair trial. It is, moreover, a response which is open to trial judges in the absence of legislation. It reflects, in essence, an application of the fundamental common law notions which govern the reception of evidence on trials. The general prohibition on improper use of evidence of sexual conduct reflects the fact that it is always open to a judge to warn against using a particular piece of evidence for an inference on an issue for which that evidence has no probative force. Similarly, the mandate to the judge to determine when the evidence may be properly receivable is a reflection of the basic function of the trial judge of determining the relevance of evidence and whether it should be received, bearing in mind the balance between its probative value and its potential prejudice.

As for the procedures which should govern the determination of whether the sexual conduct evidence should be admitted, Galvin proposes a written motion followed by an in camera hearing. The devices of a preliminary affidavit and an in camera hearing are designed to minimize the invasion of the complainant's privacy. If the affidavit does not show the evidence to be relevant, it will not be heard at all. Where this threshold is met, the evidence will be heard in camera so that, in the event the judge finds its value is outweighed by its potential prejudice, it will not enter the public domain. Such procedures do not require legislation. It has always been open to the Courts to devise such procedures as may be necessary to ensure a fair trial. The requirements of a voir dire before a confession can be admitted, for example, is judge-made law.

While accepting the premise and the general thrust of Galvin's proposal, I suggest certain modifications. There seems little purpose in having separate rules for the use of sexual conduct evidence for illegitimate inferences of consent and credibility in the Canadian context. Again, I question whether evidence of other sexual conduct with the accused should automatically be admissible in all cases; sometimes the value of such evidence might be little or none. The word "complainant" is more compatible with the presumption of innocence of the accused than the word "victim". Professor Galvin's reference to the defence of "reasonable belief in consent must be adapted to meet Canadian law, which does not require reasonableness. And the need to warn the jury clearly against improper uses of the evidence should be emphasized, in my view.

In the absence of legislation, it is open to this Court to suggest guidelines for the reception and use of sexual conduct evidence. Such guidelines should be seen for what they are—an attempt to describe the consequences of the application of the general rules of evidence governing relevance and the reception of evidence—and not as judicial legislation cast in stone.

In my view the trial judge under this new regime shoulders a dual responsibility. First, the judge must assess with a high degree of sensitivity whether the evidence proffered by the defence meets the test of demonstrating a degree of relevance which outweighs the damages and disadvantages presented by the admission of such evidence. The examples presented earlier suggest that while cases where such evidence will carry sufficient probative value will exist, they will be exceptional. The trial judge must ensure that evidence is tendered for a legitimate purpose, and that it logically supports a defence. The fishing expeditions which unfortunately did occur in the past should not be permitted. The trial judge's discretion must be exercised to ensure that neither the *in camera* procedure nor the trial become forums for demeaning and abusive conduct by defence counsel.

The trial judge's second responsibility will be to take special care to ensure that, in the exceptional case where circumstances demand that such evidence be permitted, the jury is fully and properly instructed as to its appropriate use. The jurors must be cautioned that they should not draw impermissible inferences from evidence of previous sexual activity. While such evidence may be tendered for a purpose logically probative of the defence to be presented, it may be important to remind jurors that they not allow the allegations of past sexual activity to lead them to the view that the complainant is less worthy of belief, or was more likely to have consented for that reason. It is hoped that a sensitive and responsive exercise of discretion by the judiciary will reduce and even eliminate the concerns which provoked legislation such as s. 276, while at the same time preserving the right of an accused to a fair trial.

I would summarize the applicable principles as follows:

1. On a trial for a sexual offence, evidence that the complainant has engaged in consensual sexual conduct on other occasions (including past sexual conduct with the accused) is not admissible solely to support the inference that the complainant is by reason of such conduct:

   (*a*) more likely to have consented to the sexual conduct at issue in the trial;

   (*b*) less worthy of belief as a witness.

2. Evidence of consensual sexual conduct on the part of the complainant may be admissible for purposes other than an inference relating to the consent or credibility of the complainant where it possesses probative value on an issue in the trial and where that probative value is not substantially outweighed by the danger of unfair prejudice flowing from the evidence.

   By way of illustration only, and not by way of limitation, the following are examples of admissible evidence:

   (A) Evidence of specific instances of sexual conduct tending to prove that a person other than the accused caused the physical consequences of the rape alleged by the prosecution;

   (B) Evidence of sexual conduct tending to prove bias or motive to fabricate on the part of the complainant;

   (C) Evidence of prior sexual conduct, known to the accused at the time of the act charged, tending to prove that the accused believed that the complainant was consenting to the act charged (without laying down absolute rules, normally one would expect some proximity in time between the conduct that is alleged to have given rise to an honest belief and the conduct charged);

   (D) Evidence of prior sexual conduct which meets the requirements for the reception of similar act evidence, bearing in mind that such evidence cannot be used illegitimately merely to show that the complainant consented or is an unreliable witness;

   (E) Evidence tending to rebut proof introduced by the prosecution regarding the complainant's sexual conduct.

3. Before evidence of consensual sexual conduct on the part of a victim is received, it must be established on a *voir dire* (which may be held *in camera*) by affidavit or the testimony of the accused or third parties, that the proposed use of the evidence of other sexual conduct is legitimate.

4.   Where evidence that the complainant has engaged in sexual conduct on other occasions is admitted on a jury trial, the judge should warn the jury against inferring from the evidence of the conduct itself, either that the complainant might have consented to the act alleged, or that the complainant is less worthy of credit.

[L'Heureux-Dubé J., Gonthier J. concurring, decided that section 276 did not violate sections 7 or 11(*d*) and, if it did, it would be saved by section 1.]

L'HEUREUX-DUBÉ J. (GONTHIER J. concurring), dissenting in part:—

. . . .

Sexual assault is not like any other crime. In the vast majority of cases the target is a woman and the perpetrator is a man. . . . Unlike other crimes of a violent nature, it is for the most part unreported. Yet, by all accounts, women are victimized at an alarming rate and there is some evidence that an already frighteningly high rate of sexual assault is on the increase. The prosecution and conviction rates for sexual assault are among the lowest for all violent crimes. Perhaps more than any other crime, the fear and constant reality of sexual assault affects how women conduct their lives and how they define their relationship with the larger society. Sexual assault is not like any other crime.

. . . .

There are a number of reasons why women may not report their victimization: fear of reprisal, fear of a continuation of their trauma at the hands of the police and the criminal justice system, fear of a perceived loss of status and lack of desire to report due to the typical effects of sexual assault such as depression, self-blame or loss of self-esteem. Although all of the reasons for failing to report are significant and important, more relevant to the present inquiry are the numbers of victims who choose not to bring their victimization to the attention of the authorities due to their perception that the institutions with which they would have to become involved will view their victimization in a stereotypical and biased fashion. . . .

. . . .

The woman who comes to the attention of the authorities has her victimization measured against the current rape mythologies, i.e., who she should be in order to be recognized as having been, in the eyes of the law, raped; who her attacker must be in order to be recognized, in the eyes of the law, as a potential rapist; and how injured she must be in order to be believed. If her victimization does not fit the myths, it is unlikely that an arrest will be made or a conviction obtained. As prosecutors and police often suggest, in an attempt to excuse their application of stereotype, there is no point in directing cases toward the justice system if juries and judges will acquit on the basis of their stereotypical perceptions of the "supposed victim" and her "supposed" victimization. . . .

. . . .

More specifically, police rely in large measure upon popular conceptions of sexual assault in order to classify incoming cases as "founded" or "unfounded". It would appear as though most forces have developed a convenient shorthand regarding their decisions to proceed in any given case. This shorthand is composed of popular myth regarding rapists (distinguishing them from men as a whole), and stereotype about women's character and sexuality. Holmstrom and Burgess, *supra*, at pp. 174-99, conveniently set out and explain the most common of these myths and stereotypes:

> 1. *Struggle and Force: Woman As Defender of Her Honor.* There is a myth that a woman cannot be raped against her will, that if she really wants to prevent a rape she can.
>
>   The prosecution attempts to show that she did struggle, or had no opportunity to do so, while the defence attempts to show that she did not.

Women know that there is no response on their part that will assure their safety. The experience and knowledge of women is borne out by the *Canadian Urban Victimization Survey: Female Victims of Crime* (1985). At page 7 of the report the authors note:

> Sixty percent of those who tried reasoning with their attackers, and 60% of those who resisted actively by fighting or using weapon [*sic*] were injured. Every sexual assault incident is unique and so many factors are unknown (physical size of victims and offenders, verbal or physical threats, etc.) that no single course of action can be recommended unqualifiedly.

> 2. *Knowing the Defendant: The Rapist As a Stranger.* There is a myth that rapists are strangers who leap out of bushes to attack their victims. . . . the view that interaction between friends or between relatives does not result in rape is prevalent.

The defence uses the existence of a relationship between the parties to blame the victim. . . .

> 3. *Sexual Reputation: The Madonna-Whore Complex.* . . . women . . . are categorized into one-dimensional types. They are maternal or they are sexy. They are good or they are bad. They are madonnas or they are whores.

The legal rules use these distinctions.

> 4. *General Character: Anything Not 100 Percent Proper and Respectable.* . . . Being on welfare or drinking or drug use could be used to discredit anyone, but where women are involved, these issues are used to imply that the woman consented to sex with the defendant or that she contracted to have sex for money.

> 5. *Emotionality of Females.* Females are assumed to be 'more emotional' than males. The expectation is that if a woman is raped, she will get hysterical during the event and she will be visibly upset afterward. If she is able to 'retain her cool,' then people assume that "nothing happened". . . .

> 6. *Reporting Rape.* Two conflicting expectations exist concerning the reporting of rape. One is that if a woman is raped she will be too upset and ashamed to report it, and hence most of the time this crime goes unreported. The other is that if a woman is raped she will be so upset that she will report it. Both expectations exist simultaneously.

7. *Woman as Fickle and Full of Spite.* Another stereotype is that the feminine character is especially filled with malice. Woman is seen as fickle and as seeking revenge on past lovers.

8. *The Female Under Surveillance: Is the Victim Trying to Escape Punishment?* . . . It is assumed that the female's sexual behavior, depending on her age, is under the surveillance of her parents or her husband, and also more generally of the community. Thus, the defense argues, if a woman says she was raped it must be because she consented to sex that she was not supposed to have. She got caught, and now she wants to get back in the good graces of whomever's surveillance she is under.

9. *Disputing That Sex Occurred.* That females fantasize rape is another common stereotype. Females are assumed to make up stories that sex occurred when in fact nothing happened. . . . Similarly, women are thought to fabricate the sexual activity not as part of a fantasy life, but out of spite.

10. *Stereotype of the Rapist.* One stereotype of the rapist is that of a stranger who leaps out of the bushes to attack his victim and later abruptly leaves her. . . . stereotypes of the rapist can be used to blame the victim. She tells what he did. And because it often does not match what jurors think rapists do, his behavior is held against her.

. . . .

This list of stereotypical conceptions about women and sexual assault is by no means exhaustive. Like most stereotypes, they operate as a way, however flawed, of understanding the world and, like most such constructs, operate at a level of consciousness that makes it difficult to root them out and confront them directly. This mythology finds its way into the decisions of the police regarding their "founded"/"unfounded" categorization, operates in the mind of the Crown when deciding whether or not to prosecute, influences a judge's or juror's perception of guilt or innocence of the accused and the "goodness" or "badness" of the victim, and finally, has carved out a niche in both the evidentiary and substantive law governing the trial of the matter.

. . . .

Absolutely pivotal to an understanding of the nature and purpose of the provisions and constitutional questions at issue in this case is the realization of how widespread the stereotypes and myths about rape are, notwithstanding their inaccuracy.

The appellants argue that we, as a society, have become more enlightened, that prosecutors, police, judges and jurors can be trusted to perform their tasks without recourse to discriminatory views about women manifested through rape myth. Unfortunately, social science evidence suggests otherwise. Rape myths still present formidable obstacles for complainants in their dealings with the very system charged with discovering the truth. Their experience in this regard is illustrated by the following remarks of surprisingly recent vintage:

> Women who say no do not always mean no. It is not just a question of saying no, it is a question of how she says it, how she shows and makes it clear. If she doesn't want it she has only to keep her legs shut and she would not get it without force and

there would be marks of force being used. (Judge David Wild, Cambridge Crown Court, 1982, quoted in Elizabeth Sheehy, "Canadian Judges and the Law of Rape: Should the Charter Insulate Bias?" (1989), 21 *Ottawa L. Rev.* 741, at p. 741.)

Unless you have no worldly experience at all, you'll agree that women occasionally resist at first but later give in to either persuasion or their own instincts. (Judge Frank Allen, Manitoba Provincial Court, 1984, quoted in Sheehy, *supra*, at p. 741.)

. . . it is easy for a man intent upon his own desires to mistake the intentions of a woman or girl who may herself be in two minds about what to do. Even if he makes no mistake it is not unknown for a woman afterwards either to take fright or for some other reason to regret what has happened and seek to justify herself retrospectively by accusing the man of rape. (Howard, *Criminal Law* (3rd ed. 1977), at p. 149.)

Modern psychiatrists have amply studied the behavior of errant young girls and women coming before the courts in all sorts of cases. Their psychic complexes are multifarious, distorted partly by inherent defects, partly by diseased derangements or abnormal instincts, partly by bad social environment, partly by temporary physiological or emotional conditions. One form taken by these complexes is that of contriving false charges of sexual offenses by men. (Wigmore, *Evidence in Trials at Common Law*, vol. 3A (1970), at p. 736.)

Regrettably, these remarks demonstrate that many in society hold inappropriate stereotypical beliefs and apply them when the opportunity presents itself.

. . . .

Traditional definitions of what is relevant include "whatever accords with common sense" (McWilliams, *Canadian Criminal Evidence* (3rd ed. 1990), at p. 3-5); " 'relevant' means that any two facts to which it is applied are so related to each other that according to the common course of events one either taken by itself or in connection with other facts proves or renders probable the past, present or future existence or non-existence of the other" (Stephens, *A Digest of the Law of Evidence* (12th ed. 1946), art. 1), and finally Thayer's "logically probative" test with relevance as an affair of logic and not of law, a test adopted by this Court in *Morris*, *infra*.

Whatever the test, be it one of experience, common sense or logic, it is a decision particularly vulnerable to the application of private beliefs. Regardless of the definition used, the content of any relevancy decision will be filled by the particular judge's experience, common sense and/or logic. For the most part there will be general agreement as to that which is relevant and the determination will not be problematic. However, there are certain areas of inquiry where experience, common sense and logic are informed by stereotype and myth. As I have made clear, this area of the law has been particularly prone to the utilization of stereotype in determinations of relevance and again, as was demonstrated earlier, this appears to be the unfortunate concomitant of a society which, to a large measure, holds these beliefs. It would also appear that recognition of the large role that stereotype may play in such determinations has had surprisingly little impact in this area of the law. . . .

. . . .

Once the mythical bases of relevancy determinations in this area of the law are revealed (discussed at greater length later in these reasons), the irrelevance of most evidence of prior sexual history is clear. Nevertheless, Parliament has provided broad avenues for its admissibility in the setting out of the exceptions to the general rule in s. 246.6 (now s. 276). Moreover, all evidence of the complainant's previous sexual history with the accused is *prima facie* admissible under those provisions. Evidence that is excluded by these provisions is simply, in a myth- and stereotype-free decision-making context, irrelevant.[96]

Most would agree that receiving evidence of the complainant's previous sexual history on a trial of sexual assault will so prejudice the trial that the same should rarely be admitted. **Has the court drawn the proper line?**

While striking down the complainant's statutory protection, the court recognized the possibility that the then existing common law rules could permit the inappropriate reception of evidence of the complainant's sexual conduct and the majority therefore changed the common law. The majority said it was suggesting "guidelines for the reception of sexual conduct evidence" and these were not to be seen as "judicial legislation cast in stone". Rather they were "an attempt to describe the consequences of the application of the general rules of evidence governing relevance and the reception of evidence". While the majority wrote that it was not legislating but only offering "guidelines", if the "guidelines" are the Supreme Court of Canada's thoughts on the common law of today, their expression differs little from the exercise of legislating. There will surely be no different result waiting for the trial judge who decides not to follow the guidelines.

The new regime announced in *Seaboyer* offers greater protection to the complainant than did the legislative provision that was struck down. The old section 276 forbade the introduction of evidence "concerning the sexual activity of the complainant with any person other than the accused". The common law had always recognized that previous sexual conduct with the accused was relevant to the issue of whether the complainant consented on the occasion under review. The majority's opinion "question[ed] whether evidence of other sexual conduct with the accused should automatically be admissible in all cases; sometimes the value of such evidence might be little or none". While sometimes the value of such evidence will be little or none the majority decided to exclude it in all cases: "evidence that the complainant has engaged in consensual sexual conduct on other occasions (including past sexual conduct with the accused) is not admissible solely to support the inference that [she] is more likely to have consented".

Suppose A and B have been living together for a year. The evidence is clear and undisputed that the parties regularly engaged in consensual

---

96 For comments on *Seaboyer* see Christine Boyle and Marilyn MacCrimmon, "*R. v. Seaboyer:* A Lost Cause?" (1992), 7 C.R. (4th) 225 and a reply by Anthony Allman in (1992), 10 C.R. (4th) 153. See too Paciocco, "Techniques for Eviscerating the Concept of Relevance" (1995), 33 C.R. (4th) 365.

sexual intercourse. On the evening brought into question before the court sexual intercourse occurred. A says it was consensual and B says it was not. The relationship continued for another year where A and B continued to have consensual sex. The court in *Seaboyer* says that evidence of the previous consensual activity is not admissible. Such evidence cannot come in if the sole purpose is to show consent. No one, of course, would suggest that such previous conduct would be determinative of the issue, but is it relevant and at least worth considering along with the other evidence? Is the post-incident sexual activity relevant?

The commonly accepted meaning of relevance, we noted earlier, bespeaks a very low threshold: does the evidence offered render the desired inference more probable than it would be without the evidence? Consider the absolute nature of the prohibition which operates regardless of whether the probative value of the evidence outweighs the potential prejudice to the proper outcome of the trial. There is no discretion in the trial judge to receive the evidence if, in her opinion, the probative value outweighs the prejudice.

The majority in *Seaboyer* cited frequently and quoted heavily from Professor Galvin's article, "Shielding Rape Victims in the State and Federal Courts: A Proposal for the Second Decade". Galvin's proposed rape shield law, however, was confined to the exclusion of evidence of sexual conduct with persons other than the accused. The majority in *Seaboyer* wrote "Galvin's proposal, with some modification, reflects an appropriate response to the problem . . ." One "modification" eliminates the distinction regarding sexual conduct with the accused. This is a major modification. Professor Galvin wrote:

> Even the most ardent reformers acknowledged the high probative value of past sexual conduct in at least two instances. The first is when the defendant claims consent and establishes prior consensual relations between himself and the complainant. . . . Although the evidence is offered to prove consent, its probative value rests on the nature of the complainant's specific mindset toward the accused rather than on her general unchaste character. . . . All 25 statutes adopting the Michigan approach (to rape shield laws) allow the accused to introduce evidence of prior sexual conduct between himself and the complainant. The high probative value and minimal prejudicial effect of this evidence have been discussed.

But see research which suggests that "as the sexual intimacy of the couple increases, people are more likely to be focussed on the behaviour of the woman and question the validity of her claim.[97]

Another article quoted by the majority in *Seaboyer* is Professor Vivian Berger's "Man's Trial, Woman's Tribulation". Professor Berger justified the reception of evidence of sexual conduct with the accused in this way:

> The inference from past to present behaviour does not, as in cases of third party acts, rest on highly dubious beliefs about "women who do and women who don't" but rather relies on common sense and practical psychology. Admission of the proof supplies the accused with a circumstance making it probable that he did not obtain by violence what he might have secured by persuasion.

---

97 Schuller and Klippenstine, "The Impact of Complaint Sexual History Evidence on Juror's Decisions: Considerations for a Psychological Perspective" (2004), 10 Psych. Pub. Pol. and Law 321.

Another major modification to Galvin's proposal is with respect to so-called similar fact evidence. Galvin proposed that "evidence of a pattern of sexual conduct so distinctive and so closely resembling the accused's version of the alleged encounter with the victim as to tend to prove that the victim consented to the act charged" could be received. The majority in *Seaboyer* wrote that "similar fact evidence cannot be used illegitimately merely to show that the complainant consented" and where evidence of sexual conduct on other occasions is admitted, the trial judge should warn the jury against this prohibited use. Why? This major modification of Galvin's proposal is not explained unless we are to take it as a given that previous sexual conduct of the complainant can never be indicative of a specific propensity to have sexual intercourse, from which a trier could infer that she acted in conformity with that character.

Suppose the evidence is that the accused and complainant met in Sam's Bar one Saturday night and left to go to her apartment. It's agreed that sexual intercourse occurred but the parties disagree on the issue of consent. The accused's evidence is that he was sitting at the bar when the complainant approached him, offered him a drink and propositioned him. Should the accused be able to call Sam to testify that every Saturday night for the previous four weeks the complainant came into his bar, offered a stranger a drink, propositioned him and left in his company? Should Sam be permitted to testify that the complainant had been picking up these men because she is a working prostitute? He knows because he is her pimp and has been receiving a portion of her fees.

On the issue of receiving similar fact evidence tendered by the accused, Professor Berger wrote:

> What if the accused were offering to show that the victim habitually goes to bars on Saturday nights, picks up strangers and takes them home to bed with her, and that over the past 12 months she has done so on more than 20 occasions. Now could one assert with assurance that this particular sexual record does not substantially reinforce the defendant's version of the night's events? And if it does, should he not be permitted as a matter of constitutional right to place this evidence before the jury?

New Legislation — Bill C-49

Seaboyer produced an immediate outcry on the basis that it would mean that women and children would be even less likely to pursue charges of sexual assault given that there would be unrestricted cross-examination of their prior sexual history. Such comments were quite unfair to the majority of the Supreme Court of Canada. For the majority, Madam Justice McLachlin had been quite alive to the dangers of leaving this crucial issue to unfettered judicial discretion and had crafted what she considered to be careful guidelines as to the admissibility of such evidence. She had also extended the protection to prior sexual conduct with the accused. One of the sources of the vehement reaction was that the majority took but a line to hold that, although victims might have equality rights, these had to give way to the accused's right to make full answer and defence.

The response from the Minister of Justice, the Honourable Kim Campbell, was swift. She announced that Parliament would better respond to protect women and children. She called a meeting of national and regional women's groups and thereafter worked very closely with them in drafting and revising a Bill. The coalition of some 60 women's groups reached unanimity at each point and agreed to oppose any attempt to water down the Bill.

Bill C-49 was tabled on December 12, 1991. It was referred to committee after second reading on April 16, 1992. It quickly passed through the House of Commons and Senate and received Royal Assent on June 23, 1992. Bill C-49 was proclaimed to be in force on August 15, 1992.[98] The new section 276, regarding the admissibility of evidence of the complainant's sexual activity, provides:

> **276.**(1) In proceedings in respect of an offence under section 151, 152, 153, 155 or 159, subsection 160(2) or (3) or section 170, 171, 172, 173, 271, 272 or 273, evidence that the complainant has engaged in sexual activity, whether with the accused or with any other person, is not admissible to support an inference that, by reason of the sexual nature of that activity, the complainant
>
> > (*a*)   is more likely to have consented to the sexual activity that forms the subject-matter of the charge; or
> >
> > (*b*)   is less worthy of belief.
>
> (2) In proceedings in respect of an offence referred to in subsection (1), no evidence shall be adduced by or on behalf of the accused that the complainant has engaged in sexual activity other than the sexual activity that forms the subject-matter of the charge, whether with the accused or with any other person, unless the judge, provincial court judge or justice determines, in accordance with the procedures set out in sections 276.1 and 276.2, that the evidence
>
> > (*a*)   is of specific instances of sexual activity;
> >
> > (*b*)   is relevant to an issue at trial; and
> >
> > (*c*)   has significant probative value that is not substantially outweighed by the danger of prejudice to the proper administration of justice.
>
> (3) In determining whether evidence is admissible under subsection (2), the judge, provincial court judge or justice shall take into account
>
> > (*a*)   the interests of justice, including the right of the accused to make a full answer and defence;
> >
> > (*b*)   society's interest in encouraging the reporting of sexual assault offences;
> >
> > (*c*)   whether there is a reasonable prospect that the evidence will assist in arriving at a just determination in the case;
> >
> > (*d*)   the need to remove from the fact-finding process any discriminatory belief or bias;
> >
> > (*e*)   the risk that the evidence may unduly arouse sentiments of prejudice, sympathy or hostility in the jury;
> >
> > (*f*)   the potential prejudice to the complainant's personal dignity and right of privacy;
> >
> > (*g*)   the right of the complainant and of every individual to personal security and to the full protection and benefit of the law; and
> >
> > (*h*)   any other factor that the judge, provincial court judge or justice considers relevant.

---

98 See Sheila McIntyre, "Redefining Reformism: The Consultations that Shaped Bill C-49" in J. Roberts and R. Mohr (eds.), *Confronting Sexual Assault. A Decade of Legal and Social Change* (1994), chapter 12.

The new section 276.1 imposes a requirement of written notice for a hearing to determine admissibility under section 276(2). Section 276.2 provides for the exclusion of the public at the hearing and the non-compellability of the complainant at the hearing. The new section 276.4 requires the trial judge to instruct the jury as to the proper use of the evidence received.

Does the new legislation give more or less discretion to judges than did *Seaboyer*? What are the differences?

At the time Parliament enacted these revised rape shield provisions, it also imposed limits to the defence that the accused mistakenly believed that the complainant consented. Under s. 273.2(a) there is no defence of the belief arising from self-induced drunkenness, recklessness or wilful blindness. The most significant new limit under s. 273.2(b) is that there is no defence if the accused "did not take reasonable steps, in the circumstances known to the accused at the time, to ascertain that the complainant was consenting." Later in *R. v. Ewanchuk*,[99] the Supreme Court imposed further common law limits on the mistaken belief defence. These include that there must be belief that consent was communicated, that belief that silence, ambiguity or passivity constitutes consent is a mistake of law and will not excuse, and finally that proceeding after a "no" is reckless conduct. The practical effect of these developments is that the defence of mistaken belief will very seldom pass the air of reality test and will rarely succeed.

The Court in *Ewanchuk* also decided that consent is to be determined subjectively. In determining whether the complainant consented, the Court held that there was no such thing as implied consent to sexual assault but the Court did say that consent may be inferred from words or conduct.

Given the above substantive law, as a practical matter the admissibility of prior sexual history will often relate to the issue of consent. Sometimes the issue will be whether the Crown has charged the right accused.

R. v. CROSBY
[1995] 2 S.C.R. 912, 39 C.R. (4th) 315, 98 C.C.C. (3d) 225

The accused was charged with sexual assault. The complainant testified that she had been attacked by the accused and another man and forced to engage in non-consensual sexual acts with both. The accused testified that the complainant had consented throughout. In a *voir dire* before the commencement of the trial, the defence sought permission from the trial judge to lead evidence or cross-examine the complainant on certain statements which referred in some way to sexual activity other than that which formed the subject matter of the charge. This application triggered section 276 scrutiny.

In her original statement to police, the complainant admitted to having engaged in consensual sexual intercourse with the accused three days before the alleged assault. She also admitted that when she visited the accused on the day of the alleged assault she did so with the intention of having sexual intercourse with him again. At the preliminary hearing, the complainant testified that she did not visit the accused with the intention of having sex with him. The

---

99 [1999] 1 S.C.R. 330, 131 C.C.C. (3d) 481, 22 C.R. (5th) 1

material inconsistency was inextricably linked in the police questioning to a reference to the earlier, consensual sexual contact between the complainant and the accused. Relying upon section 276 of the Code, the trial judge prohibited defence counsel from cross-examining the complainant on her original statement made to police. The accused was convicted of sexual assault. He appealed on the basis that the trial judge erred in excluding the evidence of the statements. The majority in the Court of Appeal upheld his conviction.

Held: Appeal allowed; new trial ordered.

L'HEUREUX-DUBÉ J. (LAMER C.J., LA FOREST, and GONTHIER JJ. concurring):—

. . . .

In her original statement to police, the complainant admitted to having engaged in consensual sexual intercourse with Crosby on November 1, 1991, three days before the alleged assault. She also admitted that when she visited Crosby on November 4, she did so with the intention of having sexual intercourse with him again:

Q: Have you had sex with Scott before?
A: The Friday night before I did.
Q: Is that the reason you went there on Monday?
A: Yup.
Q: Why did you change your mind?
A: Because I didn't feel right with John there and I didn't want to have to have sex with him.

By contrast, at the preliminary hearing, the complainant testified that she did not visit Crosby on November 4, 1991 with the intention of having sex with him:

Q: O.K. Were you hoping to have sex with Scott again that night?
A: No.

There was an apparent inconsistency between these two statements.

Ordinarily, nothing would prevent defence counsel from cross-examining the complainant on an inconsistency which related to her intentions in going to the accused's house on the day of the alleged assault. Material inconsistencies are relevant to the complainant's credibility. Unfortunately for the accused in this case, however, the material inconsistency was inextricably linked in the police questioning to a reference to the earlier, consensual sexual contact between the complainant and the accused. Defence counsel (and apparently the trial judge) thought that it was necessary to place into evidence the actual excerpts from the interview between the complainant and the police.

This created a dilemma. If the actual questions and answers were placed before the jury, then the jury would also have been alerted to the prior sexual activity between the complainant and Crosby on November 1. Relying upon s. 276 of the Code, the trial judge therefore prohibited defence counsel from cross-examining the complainant on this entire portion of her original statement made to police. When the complainant was cross-examined at trial, the following exchange occurred between defence counsel and the complainant:

Q: Now when you went to Mr. Crosby's home on November 7th, did you want to have sex with Mr. Crosby?
A: November 7th?
Q: Or sorry, November 4th, the day this happened with you and Rines . . .
A: No.
Q: You didn't?
A: No.

As a result of the s. 276 ruling, counsel for the appellant was precluded from pursuing this inconsistency between the complainant's trial testimony and her original statement to the police.

With respect, the trial judge erred in excluding this statement, and therefore in preventing defence counsel from cross-examining the complainant on this material inconsistency in her statements.

Where the defence of honest but mistaken belief is not realistically advanced by the accused at trial, then evidence of prior, unrelated sexual activity between the complainant and the accused will seldom be relevant to an issue at trial. . . . However, although the defence of honest but mistaken belief in consent was not realistically at issue in the present case, the circumstances were nonetheless somewhat exceptional. In particular, it appears from the transcripts that the only reason the unrelated sexual activity of November 1 was at all implicated was because it was directly referred to *by police* while posing a question which did, indeed, bear on the sexual activity which formed the subject matter of the charge. The effect of the trial judge's invocation of s. 276 in this case was therefore to exclude otherwise admissible evidence (the complainant's prior statement as to her original intention in going to Crosby's house) by piggybacking it atop otherwise *prima facie* inadmissible evidence (the evidence of the unrelated sexual activity). In my view, it would be unfair for an accused person to be denied access to evidence which is otherwise admissible and relevant to his defence if the prejudice related to admitting that evidence is uniquely attributable to the authorities' conduct. I do not believe that s. 276 was ever designed or intended to be employed to prevent cross-examination in a situation such as this.

. . . Section 276 cannot be interpreted so as to deprive a person of a fair defence. This is not its purpose. This does not mean, of course, that the accused is entitled to the most beneficial procedures possible. . . . Rather, it is evident from the majority's remarks in *Seaboyer* and from the criteria enumerated in s. 276(3) that judges must undertake a balancing exercise under s. 276 that is sensitive to many differing, and potentially conflicting, interests.

In the present case, however, consideration of those factors favoured admission of the complainant's earlier statement. The versions told by the complainant and the accused were diametrically opposed in every material respect, and credibility was consequently the central issue at trial. An inconsistency on a material and pertinent issue is highly relevant in such circumstances. The interests of justice, including the right of the accused to make full answer and defence, therefore militated in favour of admitting the evidence (s. 276(3)(*a*)). So, too, did the fact that there was a reasonable prospect that the evidence would have assisted the jury in arriving at a just determination in the case (section 276(3)(*c*)).

[Sopinka J., Iacobucci and Major JJ. concurring, agreed with the reasons for judgment of Justice L'Heureux-Dubé with respect to the admissibility of the complainant's statement to the police.]

In *Crosby* all the justices agreed that evidence of the statement to the police should have been admitted as it was necessary to ensure a fair trial for the accused. This was despite the fact that the first statement referred to previous sexual activity with the accused. The Court read a discretion into s. 276.

Section 276(1) seems to contain an express blanket prohibition on what is commonly referred to as the "twin myths" reasoning. It prohibits the use of prior sexual history of the complainant on the issue of consent or to show that the complainant was less worthy of belief. This seemed to make it unconstitutional because *Seaboyer* had called for discretion.[100]

However, Professor David Paciocco, "The New Rape Shield Provisions in Section 276 Should Survive Charter Challenge" (1993), 21 C.R. (4th) 223, suggested that the legislation could be read down. Section 276(1) only prohibited general stereotypical inferences. Evidence of prior sexual history with the accused could be admitted under section 276(2) where the defence could establish that a specific inference can be drawn from such evidence to an issue relevant in the trial. In Charter challenges in lower courts the Paciocco position carried the day and was increasingly relied on as the proper interpretation.[101]

When the Supreme Court finally considered the constitutionality of the "new" statutory scheme in *Darrach* a unanimous court had little difficulty in declaring the "new" rape shield provisions constitutional.

R. v. DARRACH
[2000] 2 S.C.R. 443, 36 C.R. (5th) 223, 148 C.C.C. (3d) 97

The accused was charged with sexual assault and, at his trial, attempted to introduce evidence of the complainant's sexual history. He unsuccessfully challenged the constitutionality of section 276.1 (2)(*a*) of the Criminal Code (which requires that the affidavit contain "detailed particulars" about the evidence), sections 276(1) and 276(2)(*c*) (which govern the admissibility of sexual conduct evidence generally), and section 276.2(2) (which provides that the complainant is not a compellable witness at the hearing determining the admissibility of evidence of prior sexual activity). After a *voir dire*, the trial judge refused to allow the accused to adduce the evidence of the complainant's sexual history. The accused was convicted and the Court of Appeal dismissed the accused's appeal,

---

100 See Delisle, "Potential Charter Challenges to the New Rape Shield Law" (1992), 13 C.R. (4th) 390.

101 See, for example, *R. v. Ecker* (1995), 96 C.C.C. (3d) 161 (Sask. C.A.) and *R. v. Darrach* (1998), 122 C.C.C. (3d) 225 (Ont. C.A.).

concluding that the impugned provisions did not violate the accused's right to make full answer and defence, his right not to be compelled to testify against himself or his right to a fair trial as protected by sections 7, 11(c) and 11(d) of the Canadian Charter of Rights and Freedoms. Here we consider the accused's argument that section 276(1) was unconstitutional.

GONTHIER J. (MCLACHLIN C.J.C., L'HEUREUX-DUBÉ, IACOBUCCI, MAJOR, BASTARACHE, BINNIE, ARBOUR and LEBEL JJ. concurring): —

. . . .

The current s. 276 categorically prohibits evidence of a complainant's sexual history only when it is used to support one of two general inferences. These are that a person is more likely to have consented to the alleged assault and that she is less credible as a witness by virtue of her prior sexual experience. Evidence of sexual activity may be admissible, however, to substantiate other inferences. . . .

. . . .

The current version of s. 276 is in essence a codification by Parliament of the Court's guidelines in *Seaboyer.*

. . . .

[T]he Court's jurisprudence . . . has consistently held that the principles of fundamental justice enshrined in s. 7 protect more than the rights of the accused. . . . One of the implications of this analysis is that while the right to make full answer and defence and the principle against self-incrimination are certainly core principles of fundamental justice, they can be respected without the accused being entitled to "the most favourable procedures that could possibly be imagined" (*R. v. Lyons*, [1987] 2 S.C.R. 309, at p. 362; cited in *Mills, supra*, at para. 72). Nor is the accused entitled to have procedures crafted that take only his interests into account. Still less is he entitled to procedures that would distort the truth-seeking function of a trial by permitting irrelevant and prejudicial material at trial.

In *Seaboyer,* the Court found that the principles of fundamental justice include the three purposes of s. 276 identified above: protecting the integrity of the trial by excluding evidence that is misleading, protecting the rights of the accused, as well as encouraging the reporting of sexual violence and protecting "the security and privacy of the witnesses" (p. 606). This was affirmed in *Mills, supra*, at para. 72. The Court crafted its guidelines in *Seaboyer* in accordance with these principles, and it is in relation to these principles that the effects of s. 276 on the accused must be evaluated.

The Court in *Mills* upheld the constitutionality of the provisions in the Criminal Code that control the use of personal and therapeutic records in trials of sexual offences. The use of these records in evidence is analogous in many ways to the use of evidence of prior sexual activity, and the protections in the Criminal Code surrounding the use of records at trial are motivated by similar policy considerations. L'Heureux-Dubé J. has warned that therapeutic records should not become a tool for circumventing s. 276: "[w]e must not allow the defence to do indirectly what it cannot do directly" (*R. v. O'Connor*, [1995] 4 S.C.R. 411, at para. 122, and *R. v. Osolin*, [1993] 4 S.C.R. 595, at p. 624). Academic commentators have observed that the use of therapeutic records increased with the enactment of s. 276 nonetheless (see K. D. Kelly, "'You must be crazy if you think you were raped': Reflections on the Use of Complainants' Personal and Therapy Records in Sexual Assault Trials" (1997), 9 C.J.W.L. 178, at p. 181).

. . . .

(T)he test for admissibility in s. 276(2) requires not only that the evidence be relevant but also that it be more probative than prejudicial. *Mills* dealt with a conflict among the same three Charter principles that are in issue in the case at bar: full answer and defence, privacy and equality (at para. 61). The Court defined these rights relationally: "the scope of the right to make full answer and defence must be determined in light of privacy and equality rights of complainants and witnesses" (paras. 62-66 and 94). The exclusionary rule was upheld. The privacy and equality concerns involved in protecting the records justified interpreting the right to make full answer and defence in a way that did not include a right to all relevant evidence.

. . . .

In the case at bar, I affirm the reasons in *Seaboyer* and find that none of the accused's rights are infringed by s. 276 as he alleges. *Seaboyer* provides a basic justification for the legislative scheme in s. 276, including the determination of relevance as well as the prejudicial and probative value of the evidence. *Mills* and *White* show how the impact of s. 276 on the principles of fundamental justice relied on by the accused should be assessed in light of the other principles of fundamental justice that s. 276 was designed to protect. The reasons in *Mills* are apposite because they demonstrate how the same principles of equality, privacy and fairness can be reconciled. I shall show below how the procedure created by s. 276 to protect the trial process from distortion and to protect complainants is consistent with the principles of fundamental justice. It is fair to the accused and properly reconciles the divergent interests at play, as the Court suggested in *Seaboyer*.

. . . .

Section 276(1) — The Exclusionary Rule

The accused objects to the exclusionary rule itself in s. 276(1) on the grounds that it is a "blanket exclusion" that prevents him from adducing evidence necessary to make full answer and defence, as guaranteed by ss. 7 and 11(d) of the Charter. He is mistaken in his characterization of the rule. Far from being a "blanket exclusion", s. 276(1) only prohibits the use of evidence of past sexual activity when it is offered to support two specific, illegitimate inferences. These are known as the "twin myths", namely that a complainant is more likely to have consented or that she is less worthy of belief "by reason of the sexual nature of the activity" she once engaged in.

This section gives effect to McLachlin J.'s finding in *Seaboyer* that the "twin myths" are simply not relevant at trial. They are not probative of consent or credibility and can severely distort the trial process. Section 276(1) also clarifies *Seaboyer* in several respects. Section 276 applies to all sexual activity, whether with the accused or with someone else. It also applies to non-consensual as well as consensual sexual activity, as this Court found implicitly in *R. v. Crosby*, [1995] 2 S.C.R. 912, at para. 17. Although the *Seaboyer* guidelines referred to "consensual sexual conduct" (pp. 634-35), Parliament enacted the new version of s. 276 without the word "consensual". Evidence of non-consensual sexual acts can equally defeat the purposes of s. 276 by distorting the trial process when it is used to evoke stereotypes such as that women who have been assaulted must have deserved it and that they are unreliable witnesses, as well as by deterring people from reporting assault by humiliating them in court. The admissibility of evidence of non-consensual sexual activity is determined by the procedures in s. 276. Section 276 also settles any ambiguity about whether the "twin myths" are limited to inferences about "unchaste" women in particular; they are not (as discussed by C. Boyle and M. MacCrimmon, "The Constitutionality of Bill C-49: Analyzing Sexual Assault As If Equality Really Mattered" (1999), 41 Crim. L.Q. 198, at pp. 231-32).

The Criminal Code excludes all discriminatory generalizations about a complainant's disposition to consent or about her credibility based on the *sexual nature* of her past sexual activity on the grounds that these are improper lines of reasoning. This was the import of the Court's findings in *Seaboyer* about how sexist beliefs about women distort the trial process. The text of the exclusionary rule in s. 276(1) diverges very little from the guidelines in *Seaboyer*. The mere fact that the wording differs between the Court's guidelines and Parliament's enactment is itself immaterial. In *Mills*, *supra*, the Court affirmed that "[t]o insist on slavish conformity" by Parliament to judicial pronouncements "would belie the mutual respect that underpins the relationship" between the two institutions (para. 55). In this case, the legislation follows the Court's suggestions very closely.

The phrase "by reason of the sexual nature of that activity" in s. 276 is a clarification by Parliament that it is inferences from the *sexual nature* of the activity, as opposed to inferences from other potentially relevant features of the activity, that are prohibited. If evidence of sexual activity is proffered for its non-sexual features, such as to show a pattern of conduct or a prior inconsistent statement, it may be permitted. The phrase "by reason of the sexual nature of that activity" has the same effect as the qualification "solely to support the inference" in *Seaboyer* in that it limits the exclusion of evidence to that used to invoke the "twin myths" (p. 635).

. . . .

An accused has never had a right to adduce irrelevant evidence. Nor does he have the right to adduce misleading evidence to support illegitimate inferences: "the accused is not permitted to distort the truth-seeking function of the trial process" (*Mills*, *supra*, at para. 74). Because s. 276(1) is an evidentiary rule that only excludes material that is not relevant, it cannot infringe the accused's right to make full answer and defence. Section 276(2) is more complicated, and I turn to it now.

Section 276(2)(c) — "Significant Probative Value"

If evidence is not barred by s. 276(1) because it is tendered to support a permitted inference, the judge must still weigh its probative value against its prejudicial effect to determine its admissibility. This essentially mirrors the common law guidelines in *Seaboyer* which contained this balancing test (at p. 635). The accused takes issue with the fact that s. 276(2)(c) specifically requires that the evidence have "significant probative value". The word "significant" was added by Parliament but it does not render the provision unconstitutional by raising the threshold for the admissibility of evidence to the point that it is unfair to the accused.

. . . .

The context of the word "significant" in the provision in which it occurs substantiates this interpretation. Section 276(2)(c) allows a judge to admit evidence of "*significant* probative value that is not *substantially* outweighed by the danger of prejudice to the proper administration of justice" (emphasis added). The adverb "substantially" serves to protect the accused by raising the standard for the judge to exclude evidence once the accused has shown it to have significant probative value. In a sense, both sides of the equation are heightened in this test, which serves to direct judges to the serious ramifications of the use of evidence of prior sexual activity for all parties in these cases.

In light of the purposes of s. 276, the use of the word "significant" is consistent with both the majority and the minority reasons in *Seaboyer*. Section 276 is designed to prevent the use of evidence of prior sexual activity for improper purposes. The requirement of "significant probative value" serves to exclude evidence of trifling relevance that, even though not used to support the two forbidden inferences, would still endanger the "proper administration of justice". The Court has recognized that there are inherent "damages and disadvantages presented by the admission of such evidence" (*Seaboyer, supra*, at p. 634). As Morden A.C.J.O. puts it, evidence of sexual activity must be significantly probative if it is to overcome its prejudicial effect. The Criminal Code codifies this reality.

By excluding misleading evidence while allowing the accused to adduce evidence that meets the criteria of s. 276(2), s. 276 enhances the fairness of trials of sexual offences. Section 11(d) guarantees a fair trial. Fairness under s. 11(d) is determined in the context of the trial process as a whole *(R. v. Stoddart* (1987), 37 C.C.C. (3d) 351 (Ont. C.A.), at pp. 365-66). As L'Heureux-Dubé J. wrote in *Crosby, supra*, at para. 11, "[s]ection 276 cannot be interpreted so as to deprive a person of a fair defence." At the same time, the accused's right to make full answer and defence, as was held in *Mills, supra*, at para. 75, is not "automatically breached where he or she is deprived of relevant information". Nor is it necessarily breached when the accused is not permitted to adduce relevant information that is not "significantly" probative, under a rule of evidence that protects the trial from the distorting effects of evidence of prior sexual activity.

. . . .

Thus the threshold criteria that evidence be of "significant" probative value does not prevent an accused from making full answer and defence to the charges against him. Consequently his Charter rights under ss. 7 and 11(d) are not infringed by s. 276(2)(c).

The Procedural Sections to Determine Relevance: The Affidavit and Voir Dire

The constitutionality of the procedure that must be followed to introduce evidence of prior sexual activity has also been challenged. It requires that whoever seeks to introduce it "by or on behalf of the accused" must present an affidavit and establish on a voir dire that the evidence is admissible in accordance with the criteria in the Criminal Code.

[The Court determined that the procedural provisions were not violative of the accused's constitutional rights. In the course of its analysis the court later commented on relevance and probative value of evidence of previous sexual activity.]

———————

Although the Supreme Court has determined the issue of constitutionality, it seems very likely that *Darrach* has not resolved the question of the proper application of sections 276(1) and (2), especially in the context of prior sexual history with the accused where the issue is consent. The Court does not refer to the views of David Paciocco. **Has the Court implicitly accepted his approach?** We have seen that the Court in *Darrach* at one point says that such evidence is not relevant, then in the next breath it says it may be admitted. Towards the end of the judgment this is put in yet another way:

> Evidence of prior sexual activity will rarely be relevant to support a denial that sexual activity took place or to establish consent (C.R., para. 58).

That judges have different views on the issue of the relevance and probative value of evidence of prior sexual history with the accused on the issue of consent is reflected in the views of the Ontario Court of Appeal in the court below in *Darrach*, which were not addressed in the Supreme Court. According to Morden, A.C.J.O.[102] for the court:

> It will likely be that evidence of previous sexual activity with the accused will satisfy the requirements of admissibility in s. 276(2) more often than that relating to sexual activity with others. This does not mean that this evidence should always be admissible (C.R. at 299).

Trial judges appear to regularly admit evidence of a prior or ongoing relationship where there is a viable issue of consent. Otherwise the trial would

———————

102 (1998), 13 C.R. (5th) 283, 122 C.C.C. (3d) 225 (Ont. C.A.) (Osborne and Doherty JJ.A. concurring).

be devoid of context and potentially unfair to accused. That is not to say that such evidence is determinative.[103]

R. v. TEMERTZOGLOU
(2002), 11 C.R. (6th) 179, 2002 CarswellOnt 4225 (S.C.J.)

After spending an evening in a motel room with a young woman, C, the accused, aged 40, was charged with sexual assault. It was alleged that he had sexual intercourse with her without her consent. Following a preliminary inquiry the accused was committed for trial. He re-elected to be tried by judge without a jury. His defence counsel brought an application under s. 276 of the Criminal Code, to adduce evidence of the complainant's prior consensual sexual activity with the accused. According to the accused he had met three times with the complainant and they had engaged in sexual touching. They had spoken about going to a motel. She had indicated that she was allergic to latex condoms. That is why he had brought a lambskin condom to the motel. The judge granted the defence an in camera hearing pursuant to s. 276.2. On the hearing, defence called the viva voce evidence of the accused and a detective who gave evidence about statements made to him by C which appeared inconsistent with her videotaped statement to police and her testimony at the preliminary inquiry.

FUERST J.:—

Subsection 276(2) provides that in a prosecution for, inter alia, sexual assault, no evidence shall be adduced by or on behalf of the accused that the complainant has engaged in sexual activity other than that forming the subject-matter of the charge, whether with the accused or with any other person, unless the judge determines in accordance with the specified procedure that the evidence

(a)   is of specific instances of sexual activity;

(b)   is relevant to an issue at trial; and

(c)   has significant probative value that is not substantially outweighed by the danger of prejudice to the proper administration of justice.

Subsection 276(1) specifies that evidence of other sexual activity is not admissible to support an inference that, by reason of the sexual nature of that activity, the complainant is more likely to have consented to the sexual activity that forms the subject-matter of the charge, or is less worthy of belief. These illegitimate inferences have been referred to as the "twin myths".

Subsection 276(3) requires that in determining the admissibility of evidence of other sexual activity, the trial judge must take into account eight enumerated factors.

---

103 See recently the full analysis of Heeney J. in *R. v. Strickland*, [2007] O.J. 517 (S.C.J.). Gotell, "When Privacy is Not Enough: Sexual Assault Complainants, Sexual History Evidence and the Disclosure of Personal Records" (2006), 43 Alta. L. Rev. 743. For a comprehensive review of case law on s. 276 see Chapman, "Section 276 of the Criminal Code and the Admissibility of Sexual Activity Evidence" (1999), 25 Queen's Law Journal 121. See also Christine Boyle and Marilyn MacCrimmon, "The Constitutionality of Bill C-49: Analyzing Sexual Assault as if Equality Really Mattered", (1998) 41 Crim. L.Q. 198.

In *R. v. Darrach*, [2000] 2 S.C.R. 443 the Supreme Court of Canada held that s. 276 does not function as a blanket exclusion of evidence of other sexual activity, but prohibits the admission of such evidence solely to support the inference that a complainant is more likely to have consented, or is less worthy of belief, by virtue of that other sexual activity. The exclusion of evidence is limited under ss. 276(1) to that used to invoke the twin myths, and under ss. 276(2)(c), to relevant information that is more prejudicial to the administration of justice than it is probative.... The Supreme Court of Canada agreed with the interpretation given to the term "significant" in ss. 276(2)(c), by the Ontario Court of Appeal. It means that the evidence is not to be so trifling as to be incapable, in the context of all the evidence, of raising a reasonable doubt, but it is not necessary for the defence to demonstrate strong and compelling reasons for admission of the evidence.

The principle was stated by Cory J. in *R. v. Osolin*, *supra*, as follows: "Generally a complainant may be cross-examined for the purpose of eliciting evidence relating to consent and pertaining to credibility when the probative value of that evidence is not substantially outweighed by the danger of unfair prejudice which might flow from it. Cross-examination for the purposes of showing consent or impugning credibility which relies upon "rape myths" will always be more prejudicial than probative. Such evidence can fulfil no legitimate purpose and would therefor be inadmissible to go to consent or credibility".

In *R. v. Seaboyer* (1991), 66 C.C.C. (3d) 321 (S.C.C.) McLachlin J. gave as an example of admissible evidence, prior sexual conduct known to the accused at the time of the alleged offence, tending to prove that the accused believed that the complainant was consenting to the act charged. In *R. v. Crosby*, [1995] 2 S.C.R. 912 (S.C.C.) evidence of other sexual activity was held to be admissible where the complainant's credibility was the central issue at trial, and she had made a prior inconsistent statement to the police that was inextricably linked to an admission of prior sexual activity with the accused. The Ontario Court of Appeal held in *R. v. Harris*, [1997] O.J. No. 3560 that where the complainant testified in examination-in-chief that she was shocked when the accused asked her if they were going to have sex, because prior to that there had been nothing sexual between them, evidence of their prior sexual activity became admissible to contradict her. The court pointed out that the jury otherwise was left with the misleading impression that the relationship had been platonic, and could not fairly assess the conduct of the parties and the believability of their respective positions on the issue of consent. The court was aware that the complainant would have denied the accused's version of their prior contact. In *R. v. M.(M.)*, [1999] O.J. No. 3943 (Ont. Sup. Ct.) evidence of prior sexual activity between the parties was admitted because the development of the relationship between the parties was necessary to provide context, without which the alleged sexual assault would be assessed in a vacuum and the testimony of the accused in support of his position that the contact was consensual would appear improbable. . . .

I am satisfied that the preconditions set out in ss. 276(2) have been met. The evidence the defence seeks to adduce is evidence of specific instances of sexual activity.

Further, as the Supreme Court of Canada pointed out in *R. v. Ewanchuk*, once the complainant asserts that she did not consent, it will be open to the defence to raise a reasonable doubt about that element of the offence, by adducing relevant evidence. In that sense, consent and Ms. M.C.'s credibility will be issues at the trial. I am satisfied that the evidence of other sexual activity is relevant to those issues, in particular ways that do not involve twin myth reasoning. The inferences to be drawn from the evidence are not the general inferences that solely by reason of the other sexual activity, Ms. M.C. is more likely to have consented on November 24, or should not be believed. Specifically, the evidence of other sexual activity has relevance in that it shows the development of a relationship between the parties which is more than platonic, notwithstanding an age difference that might otherwise engender a presumption against the defence; it provides necessary context to the motel visit on November 24, without which aspects of Mr. Temertzoglou's account such as the obtaining of lambskin condoms would be untenable; it is necessary in order to make sense of prior inconsistent statements that will be put to Ms. M.C., which can impact on her credibility; and it demonstrates the complainant's involvement in planning the evening of November 24, which tends to support the defence position.

I also find that the evidence of other sexual activity has significant probative value that is not substantially outweighed by the danger of prejudice to the proper administration of justice.

In determining whether the evidence of other sexual activity is admissible, I have considered all of the factors in ss. 276(3). The evidence bears on Mr. Temertzoglou's right to make full answer and defence to a very serious allegation that he had forcible sexual intercourse with a teenaged girl. There is a reasonable prospect that the evidence will assist in arriving at a just determination of the case, given its relevance to the issues. It is not in the interests of justice that Mr. Temertzoglou be prevented from making full answer and defence, or that I as the trier of fact not receive relevant evidence that will assist in arriving at a just determination. The evidence cannot and will not be used to support illegitimate inferences. This is not a case where discriminatory belief or bias will form part of the fact-finding process. There is no jury involved, and there is no risk that sentiments of prejudice, sympathy or hostility will be unduly aroused by the evidence. Any potential prejudice to Ms. M.C.'s personal dignity and right of privacy is minimized, given that the nature of the other sexual activity is less intrusive than the acts involved in the offence alleged, and given that she spoke to the police about some of this other activity in her videotaped interview. Further, her anonymity can be achieved through a publication ban concerning her identity. Society's interest in encouraging the reporting of sexual assault offences cannot prohibit an accused from making full answer and defence by adducing relevant evidence that has significant probative value. The right of Ms. M.C. and of every individual to personal security and to the full protection and benefit of the law is not infringed in the circumstances of this case, where the evidence to be adduced is limited to that of her prior contact with Mr. Temertzoglou on occasions proximate in time to the alleged offence, and does not involve an intrusion into other aspects of her life.

In *R. v. S.(L.R.)*[104] the trial judge admitted evidence of post-charge sexual conduct between the parties but instructed the jury that this could not be used to assess credibility. The New Brunswick Court of Appeal ordered a new trial. They held that the jury ought to have been instructed that the evidence could have been used to assess the complainant's credibility in relation to the specific events charged but not to support the inference that by reason of the sexual nature of the later incident she was more likely to have consented or was less worthy of belief. **How is the evidence relevant to credibility?**[105]

<h1 style="text-align:center">R. v. A. (No. 2)</h1>
[2001] 2 W.L.R. 1546 (H.L.)

On a charge of rape the trial judge had ruled that the accused could not cross-examine the complainant as to her previous sexual relationship with the accused. The Court of Appeal reversed the accused's conviction. The Court of Appeal certified the following question:

> May a sexual relationship between a defendant and complainant be relevant to the issue of consent so as to render its exclusion under section 41 of the Youth Justice and Criminal Evidence Act 1999 a contravention of the defendant's right to a fair trial?

The House of Lords dismissed the Crown's appeal.

LORD SLYNN OF HADLEY: —

The need to protect women from harassment in the witness box is fundamental. It must not be lost sight of but I suspect that the man or woman in the street would find it strange that evidence that two young people who had lived together or regularly as part of a happy relationship had had sexual acts together, must be wholly excluded on the issue of consent unless it is immediately contemporaneous. The question whether such evidence should be believed and whether it is sufficient to establish consent or even belief in consent are different matters. The man and woman in the street might also find it strange that evidence may be given and cross examination allowed as to belief in consent but not to consent itself when the same evidence was being relied on. That distinction has been recognised in the cases but without in any way resiling from a strong insistence on the need to protect women from humiliating cross examination and prejudicial but valueless evidence. It seems to me clear that these restrictions in section 41 prima facie are capable of preventing an accused person from putting forward relevant evidence which may be evidence critical to his defence, whether it is as to consent or to belief that the woman consented. If thus construed section 41 does prevent the accused from having a fair trial then it must be declared to be incompatible with the Convention.

---

104 (2005) 40 C.R. (6th) 180 (N.B. C.A.).

105 For differing views on this case see annotations in the C.R.'s by Janine Benedet and Don Stuart.

LORD STEYN: —

As a matter of common sense, a prior sexual relationship between the complainant and the accused may, depending on the circumstances, be relevant to the issue of consent. It is a species of prospectant evidence which may throw light on the complainant's state of mind. It cannot, of course, prove that she consented on the occasion in question. Relevance and sufficiency of proof are different things. The fact that the accused a week before an alleged murder threatened to kill the deceased does not prove an intent to kill on the day in question. But it is logically relevant to that issue. After all, to be relevant the evidence need merely have some tendency in logic and common sense to advance the proposition in issue. It is true that each decision to engage in sexual activity is always made afresh. On the other hand, the mind does not usually blot out all memories. What one has been engaged on in the past may influence what choice one makes on a future occasion. Accordingly, a prior relationship between a complainant and an accused may sometimes be relevant to what decision was made on a particular occasion.

. . . .

Following *R v Seaboyer* section 276 of the Criminal Code was amended. Subsequently the Supreme Court held that section 276 as amended was valid. As amended it was not viewed as a blanket exclusion: *R v Darrach* (2000) 191 DLR (4th) 539. Unfortunately, the Secretary of State's understanding of the Canadian position was flawed. *R v Seaboyer* is largely concerned with the irrelevance of sexual experience between the complainant and third parties. In her leading judgment McLachlin J placed general reliance upon an article of Galvin, who emphasises the probative value of prior sexual conduct between a complainant and an accused to the issue of consent: "Shielding Rape Victims in the State and Federal Courts: A Proposal for the Second Decade" (1986) 70 Minn L Rev 763. Moreover, McLachlin J made a telling comment on prior sexual history with the accused. It is to the following effect, at 83 DLR (4th) 193, 280D:

> I question whether evidence of other sexual conduct with the accused should automatically be admissible in all cases; sometimes the value of such evidence might be little or none.

R v Seaboyer does not justify the breadth of the exclusionary provisions of section 41 in respect of previous sexual experience between a complainant and a defendant.

LORD HOPE OF CRAIGHEAD: —

It is plain a balance must be struck between the right of the defendant to a fair trial and the right of the complainant not to be subjected to unnecessary humiliation and distress when giving evidence. The right of the defendant to a fair trial has now been reinforced by the incorporation into our law of article 6 of the European Convention for the Protection of Human Rights and Fundamental Freedoms by the Human Rights Act 1998. But the principles which are enshrined in that article have for long been part of our common law. The common law recognises that a defendant has the right to cross-examine the prosecutor's witnesses and to give and lead evidence. The guiding principle as to the extent of that right is that prima facie all evidence which is relevant to the question whether the defendant is guilty or innocent is admissible. As the fact that the act of sexual intercourse was without the consent of the complainant is one of the essential elements in the charge which the prosecutor must establish, the defendant must be given an opportunity to cross-examine the prosecutor's witnesses and to give and lead evidence on that issue. That is an essential element of his right to a fair trial.

. . . .

While section 41(3) imposes very considerable restrictions, it needs to be seen in its context. I would hold that the required level of unfairness to show that in every case where previous sexual behaviour between the complainant and the accused is alleged the solution adopted is not proportionate has not been demonstrated. I emphasise the words "every case", because I believe that it would only be if there was a material risk of incompatibility with the article 6 Convention right in all such cases that it would be appropriate to lay down a rule of general application as to how, applying section 3 of the Human Rights Act 1998, section 41(3) ought to be read in a way that is compatible with the Convention right or, if that were not possible, to make a declaration of general incompatibility. I do not accept that there is such a risk.

LORD CLYDE: —

The Canadian experience shows how important it is to secure a proper balance between the necessity to provide sufficient protection for the victim of a sexual offence at the trial of the person accused of the offence and the corresponding necessity to secure that the accused has the opportunity to present any relevant defence which he has to the charge. It is right that the victim be protected. But it is also right that an accused should be allowed a fair trial.

. . . .

But there is one vital distinction which must be recognised among the generalities which are sometimes adopted in this context, and that is the distinction between a history of intercourse with the defendant and a history of intercourse with other men. To an extent that distinction has been recognised in the past. While questions could be asked in cross-examination of the complainant about someone other than the defendant evidence could not be called to contradict her answer since that would open the way to an inquiry into a multitude of collateral issues (*R v Holmes* (1871) LR 1 CCR 334). On the other hand evidence could be led to counter an answer where the question had been asked in relation to intercourse with the defendant (*R v Riley* (1887) 18 QBD 481). But the distinction should be recognised as going further. It may readily be accepted that some evidence at least relating to sexual behaviour with the defendant outside the particular event which is the subject of the trial may be relevant as casting light on the question of the complainant's consent. But I do not consider that evidence of her behaviour with other men should now be accepted as relevant for that purpose.

LORD HUTTON: —

My Lords, in a criminal trial there are two principal objectives of the law. One is that a defendant should not be convicted of the crime with which he is charged when he has not committed it. The other is that a defendant who is guilty of the crime with which he is charged should be convicted. But where the crime charged is that of rape, the law must have a third objective which is also of great importance: it is to ensure that the woman who complains that she has been raped is treated with dignity in court and is given protection against cross-examination and evidence which invades her privacy unnecessarily and which subjects her to humiliating questioning and accusations which are irrelevant to the charge against the defendant. The need to protect a witness against unfair questioning applies, of course, to all trials but it is of special importance in a trial for rape. Linked to the third objective is the further consideration that allegations relating to the sexual history of the complainant may distort the course of the trial and divert the jury from the issue which they have to determine.

It is the need to achieve both the objective of protecting an innocent defendant and the objective of protecting a woman complainant which gives rise to the difficult and important issue before the House on this appeal. The issue is difficult because in some cases where an innocent defendant wishes to give evidence that prior to the sexual intercourse which gives rise to the charge against him he had had consensual sexual intercourse with the complainant on previous occasions, it may be necessary to permit him to give such evidence and the complainant to be cross-examined on the matter in order to enable the jury to come to a just verdict. On the other hand there will be other cases where the adducing of evidence of the complainant's past sexual conduct and cross-examination about it will be unnecessary to ensure that justice is done and may prevent the conviction of a guilty defendant.[106]

Time To Reform Rape Shield Laws.
Kobe Bryant Case Highlights Holes in the Armor
(2004) Criminal Justice 14-19[107]

by
Michelle J. Anderson[108]

Attorney Pamela Mackey is fighting two battles on behalf of her client, NBA superstar Kobe Bryant and the man accused of sexually assaulting a 19-year-old

---

106 For discussion of *R. v. A.*, see P. Mirfield, "Human Wrongs" (2002), 118 L.Q.R 20; Jennifer Temkin, "Sexual History Evidence—Beware the Backlash", [2003] Crim. L. Rev. 217 and Di Birch, "Untangling Sexual History Evidence: A Rejoinder to Professor Temkin", [2003] Crim. L. Rev. 370.
107 © Michelle Anderson.
108 Dean and Professor of Law, CUNY.

hotel employee in Eagle County, Colorado. The first battle is in the media, the second is in the courtroom. Strategic arguments in pre-trial motions and in the press have already largely won her the first battle. Soon, in what may be the most closely watched criminal trial since the O.J. Simpson case, Mackey may win the second.

One reason underlies Mackey's probable success in both arenas. Despite three decades of legal and social reform on behalf of rape victims, the American public remains deeply distrustful of sexually active women who report having been raped by people they know. In the pretrial litigation and publicity, Mackey and the rest of Bryant's public relations team focused on the young woman's lack of sexual chastity. Mackey asked the police detective at the preliminary hearing if the lacerations on the teenager's vagina were "consistent with a person who had sex with three different men in three days." Mackey also asked the detective, "The accuser arrived at the hospital wearing panties with someone else's semen and sperm in them, not that of Mr. Bryant, correct?" Focusing attention on her sexual activity with third parties puts her sexual virtue on trial and, predictably, finds her guilty.

Mackey's aggressive defense tactics derive from centuries of sexism in rape law that allowed invasive scrutiny of victims' private sexual lives. Until about three decades ago, courts in the United States routinely allowed a rape defendant to elicit evidence regarding a complainant's unchaste reputation or unchaste conduct in an effort to show that she was unworthy of the law's protection.

Lack of chastity was not itself a defense to a rape charge. However, a woman's lack of chastity was thought to speak to two important issues: credibility and consent. Courts believed that unchaste women lie. If a complainant had broken societal mores already by being promiscuous, she was assumed to be more likely to continue to defy those mores by lying as a witness under oath. As a Texas appellate court noted, the possibility that the complainant "was in the habit of bestowing carnal favors indiscriminately upon men ... would certainly have had a very strong bearing upon her credibility as a witness."[109]

A similar lack of chastity in a man, however, did not imply corruption of his credibility. As the Missouri Supreme Court explained:

> It is a matter of common knowledge that the bad character of a man for chastity does not even in the remotest degree affect his character for truth when based upon that alone while it does that of a woman. It is no compliment to a woman to measure her character for truth by the same standard that you do that of man's predicated upon character for chastity. What destroys the standing of the one in all the walks of life has no effect whatever on the standing for truth of the other.[110]

When the corruption of character rationale fell out of favor, courts persisted in admitting a complainant's sexual history under the theory that a complainant who consented to sexual intercourse with others was more likely to have consented to sexual intercourse with the defendant. As the Iowa Supreme Court explained:

---

109 *Calhoun v. State*, 214 S.W. 335, 339 (Tex. Crim. App. 1919).
110 *State v. Sibley*, 33 S.W. 167, 171 (1895).

"Of course, a common prostitute may be raped and one may rape a woman although she be his mistress; but it was not so likely that his act is by force and against her will."[111] Likewise, the Tennessee Supreme Court wrote: "although the body of a harlot may, in law, no more be ravished than the person of a chaste woman. Nevertheless it is true that the former is more likely than the latter voluntarily to have yielded."[112] As the Illinois Supreme Court explained: "In order to show the probability of consent, the general reputation of the prosecutrix for immorality and unchastity is of extreme importance and may be shown."[113]

A woman's lack of sexual purity

Never underestimate the continuing grip of Puritanism on the American heart. Americans are, as a whole, schizophrenic about female sexuality. On the one hand, we appear to celebrate it. On the other hand, we punish it. We want to see females writhing nearly nude on MTV. We just don't think the criminal law should protect the kind of women who would writhe nearly nude on MTV when they are raped, and often we doubt if they even can be raped.

Study after study reveals that the average juror does not like promiscuous women or girls. As David Bryden and Sonja Lengnick discovered, when rape complainants are found to have acted in ways that are contrary to a retrograde model of feminine sexual propriety, jurors acquit their accused rapists by importing the tort doctrines of assumption of the risk and contributory negligence, although neither is a defense to a criminal charge of rape.[114] In an empirical study of jury decision making in rape trials, Douglas Koski pointed out that when small groups are required to render unanimous decisions, as jurors are required to do, they tend to rely on stereotypes to generate consensus.[115] One stereotype available to jurors in rape trials is that the woman is to blame because of her sexual past, so an assessment of the alleged victim's character affects the jury's decision on the guilt or innocence of a defendant accused of rape.[116]

[Here Professor Anderson reviews the different approaches taken to the admissibility of prior sexual history in the United States.]

Holes in the armor. Rape shield laws have repeatedly failed to deflect character attacks on women who allege rape. Although most rape shield laws appear to bar the admission of a complainant's sexual history except under carefully limited circumstances, their exceptions - both legislated and judicially improvised - bore holes in the armor, rendering them ineffective protection devices.

---

111 *State v. Johnson*, 133 N.W. 115, 116 (Iowa 1911).
112 *Lee v. State*, 179 S.W. 145, 146 (Tenn. 1915).
113 *People v. Fryman*, 122 N.E.2d 573, 576, 4ILL. 2d 224, 229 (Ill. 1954).
114 *"Rape in the Criminal Justice System"*, 87 J. Crim. L. & Criminology 1194,1257_62 (1997).
115 *"Jury Decisionmaking in Rape Trials: A Review & Empirical Assessment"*, 38 Crim. L. Bull. 21, 128 (2002).
116 *Id.*

Evidence passes through holes created by state legislators who mandate a variety of exceptions in their shield laws. Evidence also passes through holes created by judges who employ the flexibility afforded them by constitutional catch-all, evidentiary purpose and judicial discretion laws. Even in legislated exceptions jurisdictions, judges have found cause for new exceptions that the legislature did not authorize. Courts have also exaggerated the scope of the defendants' constitutional rights to admit evidence of complainants' sexual history. To evaluate the number and width of the holes in rape shield laws, one place to start is the arguments Pamela Mackey and the rest of Bryant's defense team made on his behalf in their pretrial motions. The Bryant team advanced multiple theories for the admission of evidence of the young woman's sexual history, and many of those theories mirror the holes in rape shield laws.

A pattern of sexual conduct with third parties. The first type of analysis the defense team advanced to admit evidence of the young woman's sexual history was that her sexual interaction with Bryant was part of a pattern of similar consensual sexual interactions with other men. They argued, "Acts of prior and subsequent sexual activity of the accuser are relevant because of the factual similarity between those acts and the circumstances of the accuser's sexual intercourse with Mr. Bryant."[117] They also argued, "Acts of prior and subsequent sexual activity of the accuser are relevant to show the accuser's knowledge, intent, common plan, pattern, and modus operandi with respect to whether she consented to have sexual intercourse with Mr.Bryant." [118] These two claims were, in fact, one: the teenager was engaged in a pattern of consensual sexual conduct of which her interaction with Bryant was but one example. Five state rape shield laws (in Florida, Minnesota, Nebraska, North Carolina and Tennessee) contain a legislated exception for a pattern of sexual conduct with third parties. Additionally, as I will discuss below, judges in a number of other jurisdictions have created a pattern exception to their states' rape shield laws.

This argument amounts to the same old saw: She consented to sex before; this was sex: therefore, she consented again this time. That syllogism may sound odd to modern ears, so it has been updated to: She consented to a lot of sex before: this was sex, therefore, she consented again this time. In other words, it is her modus operandi to be sexually loose. This is exactly the kind of character assassination that rape shield laws should prevent. The trial judge in the Bryant case has the discretion to admit this evidence if he is convinced it is relevant because Colorado's rape shield law bars nothing.

Credibility. The second type of analysis the Bryant defense team advanced to admit evidence of the young woman's sexual history was that she was less than forthcoming when questioned about her sexual past and so is less credible as a witness. Bryant's team alleged, "False, inconsistent and/or deceptive statements and omissions by prosecution witnesses -including the accuser -

---

117 Def. 's Mar. 1 Response to Motion to Limit Questioning at 7.
118 *Id.*

concerning their sexual relationships are relevant to their credibility." [119] The attorneys continued, "Certain evidence of the accuser's subsequent sexual activity is also relevant to the accuser's credibility, because she made statements that are inconsistent with the physical evidence." [120] To the extent that this argument was different than the outdated notion that promiscuous women lie more under oath, the difference appeared to lie here: Even if the teenager's prior or subsequent sexual history itself was ordinarily irrelevant, her attempt to conceal it when questioned now make it relevant to her credibility. If the evidence of her sexual past was presumptively irrelevant, however, her answers to questions about her sexual past were also irrelevant and her attempt to guard herself from those inquiries was but an expression of what the law suggested she was entitled to.

The credibility argument appeared to be a bald attempt to circumvent the presumption of irrelevance that Colorado's rape shield law establishes. It reminds one of the many other arguments defense attorneys have used to try to bootstrap the admission of otherwise excludable evidence of a complainant's sexual history, including mistaken belief in consent. This argument usually begins by conceding that the complainant's sexual history is ordinarily irrelevant. It argues, however, that the defendant heard that the complainant had a reputation for promiscuity and, based on his belief in her loose sexual character, he believed that she consented to sex with him, too. The defendant then argues that he must be able to prove his mistaken belief in her consent and the only way for him to do so is to admit evidence of the complainant's reputation for promiscuity. Four state rape shield laws (in Georgia, New Jersey, North Carolina, and Tennessee) contain an explicit legislated exception for evidence of the complainant's sexual history when the defendant claims a reasonable but mistaken belief in her consent shows up. Additionally, judges in other jurisdictions have imposed a mistaken belief as to consent exception to the prohibition on evidence of sexual history. By this exception the law constructs the unreasonable man - who believes that a woman consents to sex with him because she has a reputation for promiscuity with third parties - as reasonable.

Res gestae evidence. The third type of analysis the Bryant defense team advanced to admit evidence of the young woman's sexual history was that the evidence was res gestae. Bryant's team alleged. "Evidence that the accuser engaged in sexual intercourse within the two days preceding and within less than 15 hours following her encounter with Mr. Bryant is relevant and admissible as res gestae evidence, because it is 'necessary to complete the story of the [alleged] crime for the jury' and 'is admissible to provide the fact-finder with a full and complete understanding of the events surrounding the [alleged] crime.' "[121] The defense argues:

> [M]ultiple acts of consensual intercourse within 72 hours preceding the physical examination is evidence the jury must have to render a fair and informed decision.

---

119 *Id.*
120 *Id.* at 8.
121 *Id.*

This is particularly true when the conduct of the accuser is likely to be outside the normal experience for the jury in this case. It is safe to say that sexual intercourse with multiple partners during a 72 hour period is outside the norm.[122]

The young woman's promiscuity was argued to be so unusual that the jurors would be unable to render an impartial decision on guilt or innocence unless they were fully informed of her sexual history. This argument implied that she was actually the one on trial and her lack of sexual innocence was important to assessing her guilt. One cannot deny that evidence of the young woman's alleged frequent sex with third parties is interesting. Nor can one deny that the average juror would want to know about it. Rape shield laws, however, are designed to exclude tremendously interesting facts upon which jurors are likely to fixate because those facts are of little probative value to the incident in question and yet are prejudicial to the truth-seeking process.

Judges in some jurisdictions have made new exceptions to their rape shield laws for what they consider to be a complainant's unusual sexual conduct with third parties. In New Hampshire, for example, Justice Souter (then on the New Hampshire Supreme Court) reversed a rape conviction on the basis of an erroneous jury instruction that the "evidence of the complainant's behavior with men other than the defendant in the hours preceding the incident was immaterial, or irrelevant, to the question of the defendant's guilt or innocence."[123] Souter explained "the jury could have taken evidence of the complainant's openly sexually provocative behavior toward a group of men as evidence of her probable attitude toward an individual within the group."[124]

In New York, an appellate court reversed a trial judge's decision to exclude some evidence of a complainant's sadomasochistic conduct with third parties[125].The reviewing court echoed the res gestae argument that Bryant's lawyers advanced. It held that the admission of evidence of this sexual history with third parties would have "permitted Jovanovic to effectively place the complainant in a somewhat less innocent, and possibly more realistic light."[126]

Source of semen or injury. The fourth type of analysis the Bryant defense team advanced for the admission of the young woman's sexual history was that it proved another source for the semen or injury found. Bryant's team first alleged that "the accuser was wearing panties, at the time of her examination, containing the semen and sperm of an (as yet) unidentified male compellingly suggests an intervening sexual event."[127] This evidence "of the accuser's subsequent sexual activity is relevant ... to show the source or origin of semen."[128] If Bryant admitted having had sexual intercourse with the young woman, however, the presence of another man's semen appeared to be irrelevant.

---

122 Def.'s Jan. 12 Response to Motion in Limine at 14.
123 *State v. Colbath*, 540 A.2d 1212, 1214 (N.H. 1988).
124 *Id.* at 1217.
125 *People v. Jovanovic*, 700 N.Y.S.2d 156 (N.Y. App. Div. 1999).
126 *Id.* at 1 71.
127 Def.'s Jan. 2 Response at 10.
128 Def.'s Mar. 1 Response at 8.

More to the point, Bryant's team argued, "Evidence that the accuser engaged in multiple acts of sexual intercourse in the 72 hours preceding the sexual assault physical examination is relevant to test and rebut the prosecution's expert opinion that the minor abrasions observed on the accuser's posterior fourchette are 'diagnostic' of sexual assault."[129] This was the best argument the defense team advanced. Many states include an exception to their rape shield laws for evidence that the defendant did not cause the injury alleged to prove force. For example, Connecticut's statute says, in a sexual assault trial, "no evidence of the sexual conduct of the victim may be admissible unless such evidence is (1) offered by the defendant on the issue of whether the defendant was, with respect to the victim, the source of semen, disease, pregnancy or injury." [130]

As I have argued elsewhere, this kind of exception is appropriate and may be constitutionally mandated. Defendants should be able to rebut the claim that they caused the injuries or other evidence of sexual assault on which the prosecution relies. However, judges must be careful to circumscribe the kind of evidence admitted under such a rule. The defendant should have to proffer evidence that the prior sexual act happened during a relevant time frame and that this type of sexual act could have actually caused the injury in dispute.

Sexual conduct with the defendant. Bryant's team also pointed out that the young woman willingly engaged in sexual contact with Bryant in the form of kissing and hugging. Bryant's team argued:

> The evidence will show that ... the accuser accepted Kobe Bryant's invitation to enter his room. The undisputed evidence will show that the accuser expected Kobe Bryant "to put a move on her" before she accepted the invitation into his hotel room. The undisputed evidence will show that once inside Kobe Bryant's hotel room, the accuser engaged in conversation about tattoos (hers and the lack of his) and the Jacuzzi. During and after such conversation, she willingly kissed and hugged Kobe Bryant. The evidence will show that all of this conduct was completely consensual. Thus ... based on the accuser's own account, there is substantial evidence of the accuser consenting to sexual contact with Defendant.[131]

It was a fair argument and a place of legitimate dispute. The prosecution will insist the young woman had a right to say no to sex after kissing him. The defense will argue that she did not say no.

Whereas evidence of flirting and kissing on the incident in question should be admitted to show context, rape shield laws routinely allow for the admission of all prior sexual history with the defendant, no matter how remote in time or unrelated to the incident in question. The exception to rape shield laws for prior sexual conduct with the defendant himself appears in all laws in the legislated exceptions and constitutional catch-all categories. Where it is not an exception by statute, judges have created it. The Department of Justice estimates that 62 percent of adult rapes are committed by prior intimates – spouses, ex-spouses,

---

129   *Id.*
130   CONN. GEN. STAT. § 54_86f (2003).
131   Def.'s Jan. 12 Response to Motion in Limine at 6_7.

boyfriends, or ex-boyfriends.[132] For women raped by prior intimates, shield laws provide little protection. Many believe that rapes that occur after a man and a woman have been previously intimate are less injurious. In fact, however, research indicates that rape by a prior intimate tends to inflict more psychological damage on a victim than does stranger rape.[133]

I have argued elsewhere that all aspects of the complainant's conduct and communication with the defendant on the instance in question should be admissible; however prior sexual acts between the parties should not always be admissible. Only prior negotiations between the complainant and the defendant regarding the specific acts at issue or customs and practices about those acts should be admissible. These negotiations, customs and practices between the parties reveal their legitimate expectations on the incident in question.

Mental health history. Finally, the Bryant defense team advanced the argument that the teenager's mental health history was relevant to her propensity to fabricate an allegation of sexual assault. Bryant's legal team argued that the young woman's prior attempts at suicide and her prior use of an antipsychotic drug made "it more probable that the accuser's allegations are false and are merely a continuation of her pattern of engaging in extreme, dangerous, attention-seeking behavior without regard to its effects on those around her."[134] They continue: "Her behavior and treatment with an antipsychotic drug also makes it more probable that she is not to be believed."[135]

A deep cultural bias exists that women who come forward with allegations of sexual abuse must be "a little bit nutty and a little bit slutty," as David Brock accused in his 1993 book *The Real Anita Hill*. The notion that women who allege sexual abuse are mentally unstable derives from Sigmund Freud who asserted in 1901 that women who claim sexual abuse may unconsciously desire it because they are masochistic.

A number of people have asked me how rape shield laws protect the complainant from fishing expeditions in her mental health history. Answer: They do not. Despite the cultural bias surrounding allegations of sexual abuse and mental instability, rape shield laws do not prevent defense attorneys from attempting to subpoena rape crisis records, therapist records, mental health records and other evidence of a complainant's mental health history. These kinds of requests have increased lately as defense teams seek new ways to tarnish the credibility of those who come forward to report having been raped.

During Bryant's trial, when Pamela Mackey tries to trawl through the young woman's sexual history, Colorado's rape shield law, which grants the judge discretion to admit any evidence, may not preclude her from doing so. Whatever

---

132 Patricia Tjaden & Nancy Thoennes, Full Report of the Prevalence, Incidence, and Consequences of Violence against Women 44 (2000).

133 Bonnie L. Katz, *"The Psychological Impact of Stranger Versus Nonstranger Rape on Victims'Recovery"*, ACQUAINTANCE RAPE: THE HIDDEN CRIME 267 (Andrea Parrot & Laurie Bechhofer. eds. 1991).

134 Def.'s Dec. 11 Mot. to Admit Evidence at 10_11.

135 *Id.* at 1.

salacious information Mackey nets will undermine the claimant's credibility on the stand and may turn the jury against her. It is this legalized fishing expedition that deters most rape victims from reporting their experiences to the police. To be sure, Mackey has had substantial help from Internet snoops and supermarket tabloids that have disseminated the young woman's name, address, telephone number, educational history, alleged sexual proclivities, alleged mental instability, and likeness in the form of multiple photographs. But few women could bear even the average amount of scrutiny of their own imperfect sexual lives that occurs in many routine rape trials without substantial pain. The Bryant case is a signal that it is time to reform rape shield laws to provide victims with real protection at trial.

After extensive publicity of the complainant's sexual activity with other men within 72 hours of the alleged rape by Kobe Bryant, she declined to testify and the charge was dismissed. A civil action is proceeding. Bryant issued the following apology:

> First, I want to apologize directly to the young woman involved in this incident. I want to apologize to her for my behaviour and the consequences she has suffered in the past year. Although this year has been incredibly difficult for me personally, I can only imagine the pain she has had to endure. I also want to apologize to her parents and family members and to my family and friends and supporters, and to the citizens of Eagle, Colorado. I also want to make it clear that I do not question the motives of this young woman. No money has been paid to this woman. She has agreed that this statement will not be used against me in the civil case. Although I truly believe this encounter between us was consensual, I recognise now that she did not and does not view this incident the same way I did. (*Globe and Mail*, Sept. 2, 2004).

PROBLEMS

Problem 1

The accused was convicted of two counts of indecent assault, which incidents occurred some 20 years before. On appeal he argued that the trial judge had erred in not permitting his counsel to cross-examine the complainant with respect to other alleged sexual assaults committed upon her by other male persons in the small community in which she lived during the same period of time and with respect to which she had made complaints. The complainant had made statements to the police officer investigating the matter that seven men, including the accused, had sexually assaulted her while she was in her sub-teens and teens. Counsel at trial had received copies of the statements made by the complainant to the police during the police investigation of the matter and the allegations made in each of these statements were, according to counsel, strikingly similar to the allegations made against the accused. Counsel submitted that it was highly improbable that the seven individuals would have committed strikingly similar offences against the same complainant and that he should be permitted to cross-examine the complainant with respect to these similar acts because the similarity of these statements reflected on the complainant's credibility. Should the evidence have been allowed. *See R. v. Anstey* (2002), 2

C.R. (6th) 203 (Nfld. C.A.) and *R. v. G. (S.)* (2007), 2007 CarswellOnt 2591, 219 C.C.C. (3d) 549, [2007] O.J. No. 1645 (S.C.J.), but see *R. v. Riley* (1992), 11 O.R. (3d) 151 (C.A.), leave to appeal refused [1993] 2 S.C.R. x and *R. v. B. (A.R.)* (1998), 128 C.C.C. (3d) 457 (Ont. C.A.), affirmed (2000), 146 C.C.C. (3d) 191 (S.C.C.).

Problem 2

The accused is charged with sexual assault. His defence is consent and the defence counsel wants to lead evidence that the act occurred in the course of the complainant's work as a prostitute. What if the defence is that the charge was laid because the complainant was a prostitute attempting to extort more money by laying a false charge?

See *R. v. Sauve* (1997), 13 C.R. (5th) 391 (B.C.C.A.) and Boyle and McCrimmon, above at note 96.

Problem 3

The accused is charged with sexual assault based on allegation of hurtful acts of sadomasochistic acts. The defence counsel wishes to introduce email messages to the accused from the complainant prior to the day in question in which the accused indicates her desire for, and experience in, participating in sadomasochistic sexual acts.

People v. Jovanovic, 263 A.D.2d 182 (U.S. N.Y.A.D. 1st Dept.) (discussed in (2001) 51 Syracuse L. Rev. at 529-530.

Problem 4

The complainant in a sexual assault trial testifies that she had ceased a sexual relationship with the accused because she now preferred women. Can the defence introduce evidence of her subsequent relationships with other men?

See *R. v. Morden* (1991), 69 C.C.C. (3d) 123 (B.C. C.A.).

Chapter 5

Mechanics of Proof

A. *MATTERS NOT REQUIRING PROOF*

1. FORMAL ADMISSIONS OF FACT

In civil cases pleadings are designed to narrow issues and determine facts not in dispute. Failure to admit facts can result in an award of costs. Admissions of fact, law or mixed law and facts can occur in a number of ways such as in pleadings, a failure to respond, an agreed statement in a signed letter, or orally at trial.

In criminal trials section 655 of the Criminal Code allows the accused or his counsel to admit any fact alleged against him thereby dispensing with the need for proof.

CASTELLANI v. R.
[1970] S.C.R. 310, 9 C.R.N.S. 111, [1970] 4 C.C.C. 287

Cartwright C.J.C.:— This is an appeal from the unanimous judgment of the Court of Appeal for British Columbia, pronounced on July 19, 1968, dismissing the appellant's appeal from his conviction before Dryer J. and a jury on October 6, 1967, of the capital murder of his wife.

. . . .

The grounds of appeal relied upon by the appellant in the Court of Appeal are accurately summarized as follows in the reasons of Norris J.A. and of Bull J.A.:

1. The learned trial Judge erred in refusing to allow the appellant or his counsel to admit at the trial certain facts under Section 562 (now s. 655) of the *Criminal Code*.

. . . .

As to the first of these grounds, it appears that on September 25, 1967, the first day of the trial, after the evidence of one Crown witness had been heard, counsel for the appellant tendered a formal written admission of facts "for the purpose of freeing the Crown of the responsibility for proving same" and asked that this be received pursuant to s. 562 of the *Criminal Code* which reads as follows:

562. Where an accused is on trial for an indictable offence he or his counsel may admit any fact alleged against him for the purpose of dispensing with proof thereof.

The document tendered consisted of eight paragraphs; following the style of cause it read as follows:

> Pursuant to the provisions of section 562 of the *Criminal Code* of Canada, Counsel for Rene Emile Castellani hereby admit the following facts:
>
> 1. That at the Vancouver General Hospital, in the City of Vancouver in the County of Vancouver, in the Province of British Columbia, on July 12th, 1965, an autopsy was performed by Dr. Frank H. Anderson on the body of Esther Castellani, deceased.
>
> 2. That on July 14th, 1965, at Forest Lawn Memorial Park in the Municipality of Burnaby, in the Province of British Columbia, the body of Esther Castellani, deceased, was buried in a casket placed in a closed cement crypt.
>
> 3. That on August 3rd, 1965, the body of Esther Castellani, deceased, was exhumed from the cement crypt of Forest Lawn Memorial Park in the Municipality of Burnaby, and delivered to the morgue in the City of Vancouver where a post-mortem examination was conducted by Dr. Thomas Redo Harmon.
>
> 4. That control specimens of embalming fluid from the same source as were used by the undertakers who embalmed the body of Esther Castellani, deceased and who buried her, namely Simmons & McBride Ltd. of the City of Vancouver, were delivered to Eldon Rideout at the City of Vancouver on August 3rd, 1965.
>
> 5. That on July 28th, 1965, at the Broadway and Cambie Branch of the Canadian Imperial Bank of Commerce in the City of Vancouver, Rene Emile Castellani signed a certain application for a loan from from the Kinross Mortgage Corporation, in the presence of Mr. R.S. Keyes.
>
> 6. That no action or proceeding for dissolution of the marriage between Rene Emile Castellani and Esther Castellani, which marriage was solemnized on July 16th, 1946, was ever commenced in any Court having jurisdiction to hear such an action.
>
> 7. That scientific tests known as X-ray diffraction procedures were done by Mrs. Thompson at the Ontario Attorney-General's Crime Detection Laboratory, in an effort to determine from the hair samples removed from the body of Esther Castellani what salt or compound the arsenic had originated from, but the results were inconclusive because there was not a sufficient quantity of hair.
>
> 8. That Rene Emile Castellani and Adelaide Miller mutually engaged in an extra-marital sexual relationship from approximately the Fall of A.D., 1964 to the Spring of A.D., 1966.

It was dated September 25, 1967, and signed by both the counsel who appeared for the appellant at the trial.

Counsel for the Crown objected and the question was adjourned to the following day for argument. During the adjournment counsel for both parties agreed that the first seven paragraphs should be admitted but Crown counsel objected to the inclusion of para. 8 while counsel for the appellant insisted that under s. 562 he had the right to make that admission and intended to do so.

Following argument in the absence of the jury the learned trial Judge, after expressing regret that counsel for the Crown had not seen fit to accept the admissions as tendered, ruled that while the Crown's case was being put in the defence did not have the right to make an admission unless the Crown were willing to accept it. Later the admission consisting of the seven paragraphs was signed and filed with the consent of both parties but counsel for the appellant maintained that they had the right to insist on also making the admission contained in para. 8.

The Court of Appeal were of the view that the learned trial Judge should have permitted the admission set out in para. 8 to be made, interpreting the words of s. 562 as giving the accused an unqualified right to make an admission of any fact alleged against him. They held therefore that the learned trial Judge had erred in law but went on to hold that the error had caused no prejudice to the appellant and that no substantial wrong or miscarriage of justice had occurred. If I were in agreement with the Court of Appeal that the learned trial Judge had erred in law in the manner stated I would also have agreed with their conclusion that this occasioned no substantial wrong or miscarriage of justice; but, with respect, I do not agree that the learned trial Judge was in error in the ruling which he made.

In a criminal case, there being no pleadings, there are no precisely worded allegations of fact which are susceptible of categorical admission. An accused cannot admit a fact alleged against him until the allegation has been made. When recourse is proposed to be had to s. 562 it is for the Crown, not for the defence, to state the fact or facts which it alleges against the accused and of which it seeks admission. The accused, of course, is under no obligation to admit the fact so alleged but his choice is to admit it or to decline to do so. He cannot frame the wording of the allegation to suit his own purposes and then insist on admitting it. To permit such a course could only lead to confusion. The idea of the admission of an allegation involves action by two persons, one who makes the allegation and another who admits it.

. . . .

It seems reasonably clear that before the enactment of s. 690 in the *Criminal Code*, 1892, the predecessor of s. 562, an accused on his trial for felony could not be allowed to make an admission in court although he desired to do so and counsel for the Crown was willing to accept it.

. . . .

In my opinion the purpose of enacting s. 562 and its predecessors was to alter the common law rule by eliminating the necessity, on the trial of an indictable offence, of proof by the Crown of any fact which it desires to prove and which the accused is prepared to admit at his trial.

R. v. PROCTOR
(1991), 11 C.R. (4th) 200, 69 C.C.C. (3d) 436 (Man. C.A.)

The accused was charged with first degree murder. The victim, a 21-year-old woman, had been raped and strangled. The trial began with the Crown's argument that he should be permitted to tell the jury in his opening address about similar attacks made by the accused on two teenagers a few weeks after the killing. Crown counsel argued that the evidence was probative of the killer's identity but defence counsel argued that identity was not in issue. Defence counsel said the only issue was the accused's sanity at the time of the killing. The evidence was led as relevant to state of mind. The conviction was set aside.

TWADDLE J.A.:—

Counsel had previously agreed to the proof of some facts by admission. Although these facts consisted mainly of minutiae, they were probably enough when added together to enable the jury to infer that the accused was the killer. In any event, defence counsel made it crystal clear that the accused did not dispute his role as the killer: the only issue was his sanity at the time of the killing.

. . . .

The usual practice where the admissibility of similar fact evidence is in dispute is for Crown counsel to refrain from mentioning it in his opening address. Then, as the case develops, and the nature of the defence is known, the relevance of the disputed evidence can better be determined by the trial judge. This practice avoids the necessity of relying upon the mere statement of the accused's counsel as to what his client's defence will be and enables the judge to determine the admissibility of the similar fact evidence on the basis of its relevance to an issue which is really in dispute.

. . . .

The *Criminal Code* contains provision enabling an accused person to admit facts for the purpose of dispensing with proof of them. Whilst it is true that such admissions must first be accepted by the Crown (*Castellani v. R.*, [1970] S.C.R. 310, I do not think the Crown is entitled to refuse acceptance where its purpose in doing so is to keep an issue alive artificially. In my opinion, evidence which shows the accused to have committed another crime of moral turpitude should not ordinarily be admitted where its only relevance is to an issue which the accused does not dispute. The accused must, of course, make all necessary admissions. But, if the accused is willing to make them, the Crown should not be allowed to gain entry for prejudicial evidence by refusing to accept the admissions.

If the admissions made by the accused in the case at bar had been read into the record before the application with respect to the teenagers' evidence had been made, it would have been apparent that the accused's identity as the killer was not in dispute. The absence of an express admission to that effect was clearly due to the refusal of the Crown to accept it. The learned trial judge, correctly in my view, recognized this fact and found that identity was not an issue on which the teenagers' evidence should be admitted.

. . . .

In view of the disposition I propose, further comments on how much of the teenagers' evidence should have been admitted in rebuttal of the insanity defence should not be made. The extent to which such evidence should be admitted, at the proper time, is a matter for the trial judge to decide. He will no doubt be aware of the evidence which the teenagers will be expected to give and of the fact that such evidence, detailing as it does their harrowing encounter with the accused, is enough to make a petrified mummy cry. In that circumstance, he will no doubt give much thought to the words of McLachlin J. in *R. v. B. (C.R.)*, [1990] 1 S.C.R. 717, where she said (at p. 735):

> In a case such as the present, where the similar fact evidence sought to be adduced is prosecution evidence of a morally repugnant act committed by the accused, the potential prejudice is great and the probative value must be high indeed to permit its reception.

· · · ·

The role of prosecuting counsel in Canada is to promote the cause of justice. It is not his function to persuade a jury to convict other than by reason. His function is to ensure that all the proper evidence, and all the proper inferences that may be drawn from it, are placed before the jury, together with a reasoned argument as to the conclusion to which such evidence and inferences lead.

In *R. v. MacDonald*[1], the Ontario Court of Appeal held that the trial judge in a murder trial did not err in failing to instruct the jury that "not guilty" was a possible verdict. On appeal, the defence relied on the decision of the Supreme Court in *R. v. Krieger*[2] that a trial judge cannot direct a jury to convict. Doherty J.A. held that *Krieger* could not be extended to prevent admissions. At trial, experienced defence counsel repeatedly indicated that the accused was admitting liability for manslaughter. Given this express and unequivocal admission, acquittal was properly removed from the jury as a possible verdict. This respected both the accused's Charter s. 11(f) right to trial by jury and his s. 7 right, within limits, to control his defence.

Admissions can also be made at common law. As Justice Watt observed in *R. v. Fatima and Khan*[3]

> Section 655 of the *Criminal Code* is not the only authority that permits admissions of fact. The common law retains its vitality as a sponsor of admissions. For example, an accused or counsel representing an accused may waive a voir dire into the voluntariness of a statement allegedly made to a person in authority. See, *R. v. Park* (1981), 59 C.C.C. (2d) 385, 390-1 (S.C.C.) per Dickson J.; and *R. v. Dietrich* (1970), 1 C.C.C. (2d) 49, 58 (Ont. C.A.) per Gale C.J.O., leave to appeal refused (1970), 1 C.C.C (2d) 68n (S.C.C.).

> The common law authority to make admissions of fact, invoked in *Park* and *Dietrich*, both above, related to the primary facts underlying a determination of voluntariness of a statement made to a person in authority. This finding, essential to the admissibility of the statement, is for the trial judge, not the jury. See also, *R. v. Fong* (1994), 92 C.C.C. (3d) 171 (Alta. C.A.).

Where the admission is in writing and entered as an exhibit, should the jury be permitted to have it during their deliberations? What are the concerns raised by such a practice?[4]

---

1 (2008) 59 C.R. (6th) 339 (Ont. C.A.).
2 (2006) 41 C.R. (6th) 201 (S.C.C.).
3 [2004] O.J. No. 6155 (S.C.J.).
4 See *Fatima and Khan, supra*, note 3 at paras. 47-50.

The issue of formal admissions and the ethical obligations of counsel to use them to shorten the length of criminal trials was the subject of comment by two experienced criminal law participants in their report *"Report of the Review of Large and Complex Criminal Cases Procedures"*,[5] who issued the following two recommendations:

> **Recommendation 18:**
> **Counsel for the Crown and for the defence are both under ethical duties to make reasonable admissions of facts that are not legitimately in dispute. The court should encourage and mediate efforts to frame reasonable admissions. When the defence fully admits facts alleged by the Crown, the court has the power to require the Crown to accept a properly framed admission and to exclude evidence on that issue.**

> **Recommendation 19:**
> **Federal, Provincial and Territorial Justice Ministers ought to instruct their officials to consider expanding s. 657.1 of the *Criminal Code* to include other routine factual issues that can properly be proved by way of affidavit, subject to a right to cross-examine the affiant where some live issue exists.**

Another type of formal admission of fact is a plea of guilt.
Section 606 of the Criminal Code provides:

Pleas permitted

(1) An accused who is called on to plead may plead guilty or not guilty, or the special pleas authorized by this Part and no others.

Conditions for accepting guilty plea

(1.1) A court may accept a plea of guilty only if it is satisfied that the accused

(a)   is making the plea voluntarily; and

(b)   understands

(i)   that the plea is an admission of the essential elements of the offence,

(ii)   the nature and consequences of the plea, and

(iii) that the court is not bound by any agreement made between the accused and the prosecutor.

Validity of plea

(1.2) The failure of the court to fully inquire whether the conditions set out in subsection (1.1) are met does not affect the validity of the plea.

What is the purpose of section (1.2)? Is it not preferable for a trial judge to inquire to ensure that an innocent person does not plead guilty to an offence he or she did not commit?

A formal admission in a civil or criminal case is normally admissible in a subsequent legal proceeding.[6]

---

5 The Honourable Patrick Lesage and Professor Michael Code (November, 2008) (Ministry of the Attorney General of Ontario).

6 In *R. v. Hurry* (2002), 4 C.R. (6th) 358, 165 C.C.C. (3d) 182 (Alta. Q.B.) it was held that, because of the accused's right to silence, admissions made by accused at a *voir dire* on a Charter motion are not admissible at trial.

R. v. BAKSH
(2005), 199 C.C.C. (3d) 201, 2005 CarswellOnt 3106 (S.C.J.)

HILL J.: —

A statement of facts signed by an accused and provided to the prosecution in an effort to have a charge withdrawn, or to have the Crown agree to an acquittal, constitutes a statement or admission by the accused. Where the tendered statement of facts is not subject to an express or implied limitation as to its use, the informal admission is properly receivable as evidence against the declarant in a subsequent legal proceeding. An admission may be oral, written or by conduct: *Phipson on Evidence* (15th ed.), at p. 715. An express waiver or judicial admission made in court conceding for the purposes of the trial the truth of some alleged fact, "has the effect of a confessory pleading" with the fact then taken for granted requiring no further proof by the party benefitting from its admission, and, immune from contradiction by its maker: Wigmore, *Evidence at Common Law* (Chadbourn ed.), vol. 9, s. 2588. In the same paragraph, Wigmore described a judicial admission as "a substitute for evidence, in that it does away with the need for evidence".

. . . .

An admission validly made in the context of s. 655 of the *Code* is an acknowledgement that some fact alleged by the prosecution is true. Such an admission dispenses with proof of that fact by testimony or ordinary exhibit and the accused is not entitled to set up competing contradictory evidence in an attempt to disprove the judicial or formal admission. In other words, the formal admission is conclusive of the admitted fact. Assuming that parties in a criminal trial, as occurred in the earlier trial, can agree to waive the necessity of testimonial proof on certain matters in issue by jointly tendering an agreed statement of facts going beyond the narrow scope of s. 655 of the Code, such a statement, in my view, also amounts to a solemn, formal or judicial admission and is conclusive against contradiction by both parties.

Though the weight of a declaration or admission will vary with the circumstances, its weight "will, no doubt, be greater if against interest at the time, than the contrary", and the weight to be afforded an admission generally "increases with the knowledge and deliberation of the speaker, or the solemnity of the occasion on which it was made": *Phipson on Evidence*, at pp. 709, 712-3.

As well, in the civil context, formal admissions, for example, "an agreed statement of facts filed at the trial", is considered conclusive in the original proceeding as described in *The Law of Evidence* (2nd ed.), Sopinka et al., at para. s. 19.1:

> A formal admission in civil proceedings is a concession made by a party to the proceedings that a certain fact or issue is not in dispute. Formal admissions made for the purpose of dispensing with proof at trial are conclusive as to the matters admitted. As to these matters, other evidence is precluded as being irrelevant but, if such evidence is adduced, the court is bound to act on the admission even if the evidence contradicts it. A formal admission should be distinguished from an informal admission. The latter is admitted into evidence as an exception to the hearsay rule

and does not bind the party making it, if it is overcome by other evidence. (footnotes omitted)

See also Wigmore, at s. 1064.87

The Crown here likened an agreed statement of facts to a guilty plea. In criminal proceedings, a guilty plea constitutes an admission of all the essential elements of the offence charged in the indictment necessary to be proven by the prosecution: *R. v. Adgey* (1973), 13 C.C.C. (2d) 177 (S.C.C.), at pp. 183, 191; *R. v. Gardiner* (1982), 68 C.C.C. (2d) 477 (S.C.C.), at p. 514; *R. v. Ford* (2000), 145 C.C.C. (3d) 336 (Ont. C.A.), at p. 346. An accused's legally valid guilty plea is admissible in subsequent criminal proceedings at the behest of the Crown as an informal or evidentiary admission: *R. v. Pentiluk and MacDonald* (1974), 21 C.C.C. (2d) 87 (Ont. C.A.), at pp. 90-2 (affirmed (1977), 34 C.C.C. (2d) 1 (S.C.C.)); *R. v. Ford, supra*, at pp. 346-7; *R. v. Dobson* (1985), 19 C.C.C. (3d) 93 (Ont. C.A.), at pp. 94-5.

. . . .

To like effect, in *R. v. Ford, supra*, at pp. 346-7, the court stated:

A plea of guilty is an admission of the facts in issue and a waiver of strict proof of the charge. In a number of pre-Charter cases, courts have held that such a plea may be used against an accused person at a subsequent criminal or civil trial ...

The appellant submits that this rule must be re-evaluated in light of s. 7 of the Canadian Charter of Rights and Freedoms. Before the trial judge, the appellant relied on both ss. 7 and 13 of the Charter. The trial judge held that, by definition alone, s. 13 did not preclude the admission of a guilty plea because a plea is not "testimony" or "evidence". The appellant does not appeal this component of the trial judge's ruling. The appellant's contention is that the admission of a guilty plea in subsequent criminal proceedings infringes the protection of a broadened notion of self-incrimination (beyond testimonial compulsion) anchored in the principles of fundamental justice in s. 7 of the Charter.

I do not agree with this submission. Absent evidence to the contrary, a plea of guilty must be assumed to be voluntary and informed: see *R. v. T.(R.)* (1992), 10 O.R. (3d) 514 (C.A.). Once such a plea is made, the conviction which is entered is part of the public record. It works no injustice on the accused to permit the guilty plea and conviction to be admitted as evidence of the truth of the facts for which they stand at a subsequent criminal trial: see *R. v. Duong* (1998), 108 O.A.C. 378, 124 C.C.C. (3d) 392. It remains open to the accused to challenge or explain previous conviction if he so desires. No challenge or explanation was made in this case.

That said, a guilty plea in a former proceeding is not inevitably admissible in a successive proceeding, for example, where in the discretion of the first court the guilty plea was withdrawn for good cause (*R. v. Thibodeau*, [1955] S.C.R. 646, at pp. 653-6) or the plea struck for cause: *R. v. B. (D.M.)* (2005), 193 C.C.C. (3d) 409 (Ont. C.A.), at pp. 410-1.

. . . .

Where a judicial admission is withdrawn or otherwise exists from an earlier civil proceeding, it is nevertheless admissible in evidence as an evidentiary admission at the instance of the adversary opposed in interest:

> Where an admission in a pleading has been withdrawn it can no longer be used as a conclusive judicial admission, but it is admissible in evidence at the instance of the adversary as an evidentiary admission, with the party who made the admission free to explain why it was made and withdrawn: McCormick, Evidence s. 242 (1954). In *Donnison v. Donnison* (1984), 35 Sask. R. 183 (C.A.), the court held that generally admissions contained in a pleading may be read as evidence against a party at trial, but where an order has permitted the withdrawal of an admission because of error or inadvertence, the withdrawn admission may not be read in evidence against that party; the party may be cross-examined on the pleading and such evidence will form part of the total evidence which the trial judge must consider. (Holmested and Watson, *Ontario Civil Procedure*, at pp. 51-26, 27).

In civil cases, where an order has permitted the withdrawal of a formal admission because of error or inadvertence, the admission is not directly admissible against the party who made it (Holmested and Watson, *Ontario Civil Procedure*, at pp. 51-26-7) but may constitute evidence upon which that party may be cross-examined: Holmested, at pp. 51-26-7; *Donison v. Donison*, [1984] S.J. No. 686 (QL) (C.A.), at para. 7; *Capital Distributing Co. v. Blakey et al.* (1997), 33 O.R. (3d) 58 (Gen. Div.), at pp. 61-2. An admission in the superseded or amended pleading continues to exist "as an utterance once deliberately made by the party": Wigmore, at s. 1067. An admission in a pleading which is struck out, while it can no longer be relied upon as a formal admission, might still be adduced as an informal admission: *The Law of Evidence (2nd)*, Sopinka et al., at s. 19.4 citing *O'Kelly v. Downie* (1924), 17 D.L.R. 395 (Man. C.A.), at p. 396-97. Recognizing a conflict of authority in civil cases, as to whether an admission in a first trial continues to bind when a new trial is ordered, Sopinka et al., at s. 19.5 of their text, conclude:

> Formal admissions are only binding for the purposes of the particular case in which they are made. However, there is a conflict of authority as to whether an admission made at the first trial continues to bind when a new trial is ordered. We think that an admission for the purpose of dispensing with evidence is generally intended to apply only to the trial which is in progress or imminent and not in the differing circumstances that may prevail at a new trial. Accordingly, the admission is no longer binding at the new trial in the formal sense, but may be introduced as an informal admission. The party who made the admission may, therefore, lead evidence to explain or contradict the previous statement.[7]

2. JUDICIAL NOTICE

(a) Introduction

> . . . [T]o require that a judge should affect a cloistered aloofness from facts that every other man in Court is fully aware of, and should insist on having proof on oath of

---

7 An appeal of the trial judge's ruling was dismissed. See *R. v. Baksh*, [2008] O.J. No. 538 (C.A.).

what, as a man of the world, he knows already better than any witness can tell him, is a rule that may easily become pedantic and futile. . . . Judicial notice . . . involves that, at the stage when evidence of material facts can be properly received, certain facts may be deemed to be established, although not proved by sworn testimony, or by the production, out of the proper custody, of documents, which speak for themselves. Judicial notice refers to facts, which a judge can be called upon to receive and to act upon, either from his general knowledge of them, or from inquiries to be made by himself for his own information from sources to which it is proper for him to refer. . . .[8]

The judicial process cannot construct every case from scratch, like Descartes creating a world based on the postulate Cogito, ergo sum.[9]

We do not prove by evidence, indeed we cannot prove by evidence, all the facts that are necessary to a judicial decision. Certain matters are so well known in the community or so easily determinable as to be indisputable.

Consider a civil suit for damages for injuries sustained in an automobile accident. The defendant describes his speed and handling of the car. He maintains that the accident was unavoidable as he was unable to bring his vehicle to a stop. The plaintiff maintains that the defendant was negligent in that he was driving too fast for the conditions of the road at the time of the accident. The evidence indicates that it was raining at the time of the accident. To resolve the issue of liability, do we need evidence to be led to establish that rain makes road surfaces wet, that the coefficient of friction between tires and asphalt is thereby reduced, that such a fact is known to most drivers, and that careful drivers lower their speed in such conditions? Such matters are so well known in the community as to be indisputable. This material need not be proved according to the normal rules of evidence. This knowledge is assumed to be already possessed by the judge and the party who has the burden on the issue may simply call on the judge to judicially notice those facts which are necessary to the determination of the question. The judge, at times, may not herself have the knowledge and may need to be informed, but when the judge is informed about such matters it is not through material filtered through the various rules of evidence. Dictionaries, atlases and the like are ready at hand and may freely be consulted by her. In some cases she may even need to be informed by testimony on the matter; but in such cases the testimony is to inform the judge and the fact is decided by her, is judicially noticed by her, and is not left open for a contrary decision by the jury.

(b) Disputed Boundaries of Judicial Notice

Illustrations from reported cases give us a notion of what is traditionally described as judicial notice. For example, we see court rulings that evidence is not necessary to establish that Victoria is in British Columbia,[10] that Toronto is in Canada,[11] that L.S.D. can be a mind destroying drug,[12] that Colonel By Drive

---

8 *Commonwealth Shipping Representative v. P. & O. Branch Service*, [1923] A.C. 191, 211-12 (H.L.) per Lord Sumner.
9 Advisory Committee's Note to Rule 201 of the U.S. Federal Rules of Evidence.
10 *R. v. Kuhn* (1970), 1 C.C.C. (2d) 132 (B.C. Co. Ct.).
11 *R. v. Cerniuk* (1948), 91 C.C.C. 56 (B.C.C.A.).
12 *R. v. Shaw* (1977), 36 C.R.N.S. 358 (Ont. C.A.).

in Ottawa is National Commission property,[13] that big horn sheep are mountain sheep,[14] that a pizza costs less than $200,[15] that "O.D.'d" means overdosed on a drug,[16] or that the incidence of a particular crime has reached such a high level that deterrence is mandated.[17] All these things can be judicially noticed. The judge does not need to be informed about these matters by evidence.

Judicially noticing geographic locations and the meaning of words presents few real problems. When the facts are indisputable, no one has a basis to object. But suppose a judge notices or assumes something about which there are different opinions. Is this also judicial notice? Is it permissible?

There are different schools of thought concerning the boundaries of judicial notice. Professor Thayer regarded judicial notice not as belonging peculiarly to the law of evidence, but rather

> to the general topic of legal or judicial reasoning. It is, indeed, woven into the very texture of the judicial function. In conducting a process of judicial reasoning, as of other reasoning, not a step can be taken without assuming something which has not been proved; and the capacity to do this, with competent judgment and efficiency, is imputed to judges and juries as part of their necessary mental outfit. . . . What are the things of which judicial tribunals may take notice, and should take notice, without proof? It is possible to indicate with exactness only a part of these matters. Some things are thus dealt with by virtue of express statutory law; some in a manner that is referable merely to precedent — to the actual decision, which have selected some things and omitted others in a way that is not always explicable upon any general principle; others upon a general maxim of reason and good sense, the application of which must rest mainly with the discretion of the tribunal, and, in any general discussion, must rather be illustrated than defined.[18]

Cross on Evidence similarly concludes:

> The tacit applications of the doctrine of judicial notice are more numerous and more important that the express ones. A great deal is taken for granted when any question of relevance is considered or assumed. For example, evidence is constantly given that persons accused of burglary were found in possession of jemmies or skeleton keys, that the accused became confused when charged; these are relevant only provided there is a common practice to use such things in the commission of crime, or provided that guilty people tend more to become confused when charged, but no one ever thinks of calling evidence on such a subject.[19]

---

13 *R. v. Potts* (1982), 134 D.L.R. (3d) 227 (Ont. C.A.).

14 *R. v. Quinn* (1975), 27 C.C.C. (2d) 543 (Alta. S.C.). See also *Sigeareak v. R.*, [1966] S.C.R. 645.

15 *Re Livingstone and R.* (1975), 29 C.C.C. (2d) 557 (B.C.S.C.).

16 *R. v. MacAulay* (1975), 25 C.C.C. (2d) 1 (N.B.C.A.).

17 See, *e.g.*, *R. v. McNicol*, [1969] 3 C.C.C. 56 (Man. C.A.) and *R. v. Adelman*, [1968] 3 C.C.C. 311 (B.C.C.A.). But see *R. v. Priest* (1996), 1 C.R. (5th) 275 (Ont. C.A.) where the trial judge was criticised by Rosenberg J.A. for relying too heavily on general deterrence for a youthful first offender based on the prevalence of break and enter cases. It was noted that the judge had no statistics before him and see, similarly, *R. v. Mallory*, (2004) 25 C.R. (6th) 182 (B.C. C.A.).

18 Thayer, *A Preliminary Treatise on Evidence at the Common Law* (1898), pp. 279 and 299.

19 *Cross and Tapper on Evidence*, 8th ed., p. 79.

Professor Morgan, on the other hand, in his classic article on the subject, so viewed the purpose of judicial notice that he limited its application to those facts which were indisputable:

> Just as the court cannot function unless the judge knows the law and unless the judge and jury have the fund of information common to all intelligent men in the community as well as the capacity to use the ordinary processes of reasoning, so it cannot adjust legal relations among members of society and thus fulfil the sole purpose of its creation if it permits the parties to take issue on, and thus secure results contrary to, what is so notoriously true as not to be the subject of reasonable dispute, or what is capable of immediate and accurate demonstration by resort to sources of indisputable accuracy easily accessible to men in the situation of members of the court. This, it is submitted, is the rock of reason and policy upon which judicial notice of facts is built. . . . To warrant judicial notice the probability must be so great as to make the truth of the proposition notoriously indisputable among reasonable men.[20]

It has been noted that the Morgan thesis thrived in an era dominated by a mood of judicial restraint.[21] How the particular judge views his role will probably dictate how much he or she will rely on materials not introduced by the parties. It depends on "whether he will play an affirmative or quiescent role in the performance of his duties."[22]

While we see that in many instances the judicially noticed facts are indisputable, and the court then *must* notice them, Professor Thayer believed that there were other instances when a court, in its discretion, might judicially notice facts which could not be demonstrated as being indisputable. While Professor Morgan saw the purpose of judicial notice as ensuring that courts did not make decisions contrary to nature, and therefore would confine it to instances where the facts were notoriously indisputable, Professor Thayer saw another purpose for the doctrine: efficiency. Professor Thayer wrote:

> Taking judicial notice does not import that the matter is indisputable. It is not necessarily anything more than a *prima facie* recognition, leaving the matter still open to controversy. . . . Courts may judicially notice much which they cannot be required to notice. That is well worth emphasizing, for it points to a great possible usefulness in this doctrine, in helping to shorten and simplify trials; it is an instrument of great capacity in the hands of a competent judge; and is not nearly as much used, in the region of practice and evidence, as it should be.[23]

Professor Kenneth Culp Davis, also disagreeing with Morgan's thesis, wrote:

> The plain fact is, however, that judges and administrative officers necessarily use extra-record facts which are neither indisputable nor found in sources of indisputable accuracy. A human being is probably unable to consider a problem — whether of fact, law, policy, judgment or discretion — without using his past experience, much of which may be factual and much highly disputable. Judges and administrators are

---

20 Morgan, "Judicial Notice" (1944), 57 Harv. L. Rev. 269, 273-74.

21 Roberts, "Preliminary Notes Toward a Study of Judicial Notice" (1966-67), 52 Cornell Law Q. 210, 230.

22 Weinstein's Evidence, 200-04. The authors note that this phrase was termed "the most important decision the judge makes for himself" by Judge Breitel, "Ethical Problems in the Performance of the Judicial Function" (Chicago University Conference of Judicial Ethics) 65.

23 *Supra*, note 18 at pp. 308-09.

at their best when they are well informed; their understanding and information must be used to the full if their decisions are to be wise and sound. Fact finding, law making, and policy formulation should be guided by experience and understanding, not limited to wooden judgments predicated upon the literal words of witnesses.[24]

In his textbook, Davis later emphasized that judicial notice was *not* based simply on ensuring that courts were protected from making findings which did not accord with reality, but that

the basic principle is that extra-record facts should be assumed whenever it is convenient to assume them, except that convenience should always yield to the requirement of procedural fairness that parties should have an opportunity to meet in the appropriate fashion all facts that influence the disposition of the case.[25]

Professor Roberts commented:

The Davis theory of judicial notice is just as much a product of the times as was the Morgan theory. Courts seen as super-legislatures must be allowed to roam far and wide and must at all costs not be inhibited by any requirement that the facts with which they deal must be either found in the record or attributable to common knowledge or sources of indisputable accuracy. The law, in short, must be seen as a creative process and the rules of judicial notice recast to expedite this creativity.[26]

In *R. v. Zundel*, Zundel was charged with the Criminal Code offence of spreading false news in his denial of the Holocaust. One of his publications was entitled "Did Six Million Jews Really Die?" He was convicted. On his appeal an issue was whether the trial judge had erred in not taking judicial notice of the Holocaust. The Court of Appeal responded as follows:[27]

It is well established that the court may take judicial notice of an historical fact. The court may, on its own initiative, consult historical works or documents, or the court may be referred to them: see *Read v. Lincoln (Bishop)*, [1892] A.C. 644 (P.C.); *R. v. Bartleman*, 55 B.C.L.R. 78, [1984] 3 C.N.L.R. 114, 13 C.C.C. (3d) 488 at 491-

---

24 Davis, "Judicial Notice" (1955), 55 Col. L. Rev. 945, 948-49. In Davis, *A System of Judicial Notice Based on Fairness and Convenience, Perspectives of Law* (1964), 69, 74, Davis explained that the boundaries of judicial notice coincide with those of judicial reasoning: When the judge reads a pleading or listens to a witness testify, he cannot know the meaning of the words used except through extra-record information, and apart from the meaning of words, he cannot understand the significance of the ideas expressed unless he uses his general background of knowledge — knowledge that cannot conceivably be captured and penned up within the pages of a formal record. As judges go about their workaday tasks, they assume facts all along the line without either thinking or speaking in terms of judicial notice. They assume facts without mentioning that they do so, and when they mention that they do so, they are more likely to say that they "assume" the facts than that they "take judicial notice" of them. Nothing hinges — and nothing should hinge — on the form of words that happen to be used. Compare Carter, "Do Courts Decide According to the Evidence?" (1988), 22 U.B.C.L. Rev. 51, 363: When assessing any evidence given in court, the trier of fact must obviously draw upon a vast mass of previously acquired factual information, knowledge and experience. The use of the terminology of judicial notice to describe this may be confusing. This is not a question of judicial notice, but of the tribunal relying on its own experience as to the ordinary course of human affairs.
25 Davis, *Administrative Law*, 3d ed. (1972), p. 314.
26 Roberts, *supra*, note 21, at p. 233.
27 (1987), 56 C.R. (3d) 1, 56.

92, 12 D.L.R. (4th) 73 (C.A.). The court may even hear sworn testimony before judicial notice is taken: see *McQuaker v. Goddard*, [1940] 1 K.B. 687, [1940] 1 All E.R. 471 (C.A.).

As Professor Cross points out, the distinction between the process of taking judicial notice and the reception of evidence begins to fade when the judge makes inquiries before deciding to take judicial notice of a matter. He points out that if learned treatises are consulted it is not easy to say whether evidence is being received under an exception to the hearsay rule or whether the judge is equipping himself to take judicial notice. The resemblance of taking judicial notice to the reception of evidence is even more marked when sworn testimony is heard before judicial notice is taken. He concludes, however, that, even where the processes of taking judicial notice and receiving evidence approximate most closely, they are essentially different: see Cross on Evidence, pp. 67-68. The essential difference is that, when the judge is equipping himself to take judicial notice, the hearsay rule does not apply.

The court recognized that it was fitting and proper to judicially notice historical facts. The court in *Zundel* recognized that the fact of the Holocaust was generally known and accepted and that the trial judge would be entitled, therefore, to judicially notice it. The court decided, however, that judicial notice was a discretionary matter and that the trial judge was right to refuse the Crown's application for judicial notice and to insist that the Crown prove it. The court exhibited concern that judicially noticing that the Holocaust occurred would be "gravely prejudicial" to the accused's defence. Ask yourself whether it is proper to refuse to judicially notice that which is generally known and accepted. **Should the accused be provided an opportunity to try to prove, in a courtroom, the opposite of what everyone knows, and accepts as true?** Professor Thayer had written: "Courts may judicially notice much which they cannot be required to notice." The court relied on this sentence for saying that a judge had a discretion whether or not to judicially notice. But Thayer was saying that besides noticing things that they were required to notice, things which were indisputable, judges could also judicially notice other things. He never said that a judge could refuse to notice things that were indisputable! The court repeated this "error" when sitting on appeal from the second *Zundel* trial: *R. v. Zundel* (1990), 53 C.C.C. (3d) 161 (Ont. C.A.).

Professor Davis drew a distinction between judicially noticing adjudicative facts and legislative facts. He wrote:

When a court or an agency finds facts concerning the immediate parties — who did what, where, when, how, and with what motive or intent — the court or agency is performing an adjudicative function, and the facts so determined are conveniently called adjudicative facts. When a court or an agency develops law or policy, it is acting legislatively; the courts have created the common law through judicial legislation, and the facts which inform the tribunal's legislative judgment are called legislative facts.[28]

These legislative facts, by their nature, are generally known or discovered by the judge from sources outside the formal proof offered by the parties. Unlike

---

28 Davis, "Judicial Notice", *supra*, note 24. The distinction was coined in an earlier article: Davis, "An Approach to Problems of Evidence in the Administrative Process" (1942), 55 Harv. L. Rev. 364.

adjudicative facts they can seldom be indisputable and knowledge of them is more properly labelled belief:

> The bulk of social science probably cannot be called "clearly indisputable". Even though anyone would prefer to found lawmaking upon clearly indisputable facts, the practical choice is often between proceeding in ignorance and following the uncertain, tentative, and far from indisputable searchings of social science such as they are, for the simple reason that clearly indisputable facts are unavailable.[29]

These legislative facts are necessary, however, to an informed policy choice between competing rules or interpretations and also decisions on constitutional validity.[30] Judge Weinstein explains why consultation with the parties concerning notice of legislative fact is appropriate:

> In taking judicial notice of legislative facts, courts frequently take cognizance of matter which is neither indisputable nor easily verifiable. . . . Is such power compatible with our adversary system, which presupposes that disputed facts must be brought into the open, subject to cross-examination? . . . Legislative facts . . . relate to substantive law, and if the judge is to exercise the function of shaping the law he must have discretion to consider those factors essential to the process. Limitations in the form of indisputability or rigid and formal requirements of notice are inappropriate. . . . Once the court decides to advise itself in order to make new law, it ought not to add to the risk of a poor decision by denying itself whatever help on the facts it can with propriety obtain. Informal consultation with the parties enables the court to enlist their aid in obtaining further information, guarantees that differing points of view will be consulted, and is especially appropriate in those cases where the facts the judge is noticing may have adjudicative as well as legislative implications.[31]

Problems of fairness to the parties are generated in the silent use of legislative facts, as the parties must frequently guess at the judge's appreciation of the legislative facts and may not be given the opportunity of displaying contrary data to support a competing view. A notorious example from the cases is seen in *Hersees of Woodstock Ltd. v. Goldstein*.[32] In that case, the plaintiff sought an injunction to restrain the secondary picketing of his premises. The Ontario Court of Appeal reasoned:

> But even assuming that the picketing carried on by the respondents was lawful in the sense that it was merely peaceful picketing for the purpose only of communicating information, I think it should be restrained. Appellant has a right lawfully to engage in its business of retailing merchandise to the public. In the City of Woodstock where that business is being carried on, the picketing for the reasons already stated, has caused or is likely to cause damage to the appellant. *Therefore*, the right, if there be such a right of the respondents to engage in secondary picketing of appellant's premises must give way to appellant's right to trade; the former, assuming it to be a legal right, is exercised for the benefit of a particular class only

---

29 Davis, *A System of Judicial Notice Based on Fairness and Convenience*, *supra*, note 24, at pp. 69 and 87, quoted in Weinstein's Evidence, at pp. 200-16.

30 When a court is involved in determining an appropriate remedy or penalty it frequently goes outside the record for assistance and notices the legislative facts that condition deterrence and rehabilitation. See Davis, "Judicial Notice", *supra*, note 24 at p. 960. And for examples of Canadian courts using such legislative facts, see *R. v. McNicol*, [1969] 3 C.C.C. 56 (Man. C.A.); *R. v. Adelman*, [1968] 3 C.C.C. 311 (B.C.C.A.).

31 Weinstein's Evidence, pp. 200-17.

32 (1963), 2 O.R. 81 (C.A.); leave to appeal to S.C.C. refused.

while the latter is a right far more fundamental and of far greater importance, in my view, as one which in its exercise affects and is for the benefit of the community at large. If the law is to serve its purpose then in civil matters just as in matters within the realm of the criminal law, the interests of the community at large must be held to transcend those of the individual or a particular group of individuals. [Emphasis added.][33]

Is the "therefore" self-evident?[34] Are property interests clearly more important than the community's interest in free speech? Is the property interest protected here clearly of benefit to the community at large? Is the picketing right here restrained only of benefit to this "particular class"? Must individual rights always bow to the community? Perhaps the court silently addressed all these questions before giving its answer. The record does not tell us. If the legislative facts believed in by the court were made known to the parties and the parties were given the opportunity to present competing legislative facts, the parties would probably be more satisfied with the decision and the court would be better informed.[35]

DAISHOWA INC. v. FRIENDS OF THE LUBICON
(1998), 39 O.R. (3d) 620 (Ont. Gen. Div.)

The plaintiff sought an injunction to restrain the activities of the defendants. When discussions between the plaintiff and the Lubicon Cree failed to produce any agreement that the company not log the property until land rights were settled, the Friends of the Lubicon began a boycott campaign in Ontario, which was aimed both at customers of the plaintiff's paper products and at the consumers of the customers' goods and services, such as Pizza Pizza. The latter was carried out by picketing at the stores and businesses of the plaintiff's customers. The campaign was remarkably successful and the plaintiff brought an action seeking a permanent injunction against the Friends' consumer boycott activities. The application was dismissed.

MacPherson J.:—

. . . .

The first and most important case cited by Daishowa on the picketing issue is *Hersees of Woodstock Ltd. v. Goldstein*. Daishowa relies heavily on this case because, as it puts it at para. 76 of its factum, "the Ontario Court of Appeal clearly established that the common law of Ontario prohibits secondary picketing as does the common law of other Canadian jurisdictions".

---

33 *Ibid.*, at p. 86.
34 See the case comment by Arthurs (1963), 41 Can. Bar Rev. 573, 580. Compare the opinions in *Harrison v. Carswell*, [1976] 2 S.C.R. 200.
35 See the solution of Frank, J., in *Repouille v. U.S.*, 165 F. 2d 152 (2d Cir., 1947). And see Laskin, J. in *A.G. Man. v. Manitoba Egg & Poultry Assn.* (1971), 19 D.L.R. (3d) 169, 181 (S.C.C.) deploring the absence of legislative facts in assessing the constitutional validity of legislation. See also the inclusion of such data in *Reference re Anti-Inflation Act, 1975 (Canada)*, [1976] 2 S.C.R. 373.

. . . .

In the passage from Aylesworth J.A.'s judgment set out earlier, he refers explicitly to a "right to trade". Moreover, he states that this right "is for the benefit of the community at large" and contrasts it with the union's speech through their picketing which he describes as being "exercised for the benefit of a particular class only". Without quarrelling with the ratio of *Hersees* and its continuing applicability in cases dealing with secondary picketing in a labour relations context, it strikes me that this component of Aylesworth J.A.'s reasoning is anachronistic today. The fact that freedom of expression is protected in the Canadian Charter of Rights and Freedoms, coupled with the absence of any economic rights, except for mobility to pursue the gaining of a livelihood, in the same document, is a clear indication that free speech is near the top of the values that Canadians hold dear. As expressed by MacIntyre J. in *Dolphin Delivery, supra*, at p. 583 S.C.R.:

> Freedom of expression . . . is one of the fundamental concepts that has formed the basis for the historical development of the political, social and educational institutions of western society. Representative democracy, as we know it today, which is in great part the product of free expression and discussion of varying ideas, depends upon its maintenance and protection.

Additionally, even if one accepts Aylesworth J.A.'s description of unions as representing "a particular class only", namely their own membership interested in their own economic well-being, this description does not apply to the Friends. They are interested in an issue, the plight of the Lubicon Cree, that presents an amalgam of historical, political, social, economic and even moral factors. The plight of the Lubicon is precisely the type of issue that should generate widespread public discussion. Moreover, there is not one penny of economic self-interest in the Friends' campaign.

With the advent of the Charter of Rights and the new task of determining the constitutional validity of legislation, the courts are, of necessity, called on to judicially notice legislative facts. For example, in *R. v. Oakes*[36] the government had the task of justifying a violation of a constitutional right under section 1: to establish that the violation of the accused's right to be presumed innocent was justified as a reasonable limit in a free and democratic society. In that case, the court noted:

> Where evidence is required in order to prove the constituent elements of a s. 1 inquiry, *and this will generally be the case*, it should be cogent and persuasive and make clear to the court the consequences of imposing or not imposing the limit. [Emphasis added.][37]

Nevertheless, the court, in deciding that the legislative objective was of sufficient importance to warrant overriding a constitutionally protected right relied on all manner of material to inform itself regarding the legislative facts. The court noted:

---

36 (1986), 50 C.R. (3d) 1 (S.C.C.).
37 *Ibid.*, at pp. 29-30.

In my opinion, Parliament's concern that drug trafficking be decreased can be characterized as substantial and pressing. The problem of drug trafficking has been increasing since the 1950s, at which time there was already considerable concern: see Report of the Special Committee on Traffic in Narcotic Drugs, Appendix to Debates of the Senate of Canada, session of 1955, pp. 690-700; see also Final Report, Commission of Inquiry into the Non-Medical Use of Drugs (Ottawa, 1973). Throughout this period, numerous measures were adopted by free and democratic societies, at both the international and national levels.

At the international level, on 23rd June 1953, the Protocol for Limiting and Regulating the Cultivation of the Poppy Plant, the Production of, International and Wholesale Trade in, and Use of Opium, to which Canada is a signatory, was adopted by the United Nations Opium Conference held in New York. The Single Convention on Narcotic Drugs (1961), was acceded to in New York on 30th March 1961. This treaty was signed by Canada on 30th March 1961. It entered into force on 13th December 1964. As stated in the preamble, "addiction to narcotic drugs constitutes a serious evil for the individual and is fraught with social and economic danger to mankind".

At the national level, statutory provisions have been enacted by numerous countries which, inter alia, attempt to deter drug trafficking by imposing criminal sanctions: see, for example, Misuse of Drugs Act, 1975 (New Zealand), no. 116; Misuse of Drugs Act, 1971 (Eng.), c. 38.

The objective of protecting our society from the grave ills associated with drug trafficking is, in my view, one of sufficient importance to warrant overriding a constitutionally-protected right or freedom in certain cases. Moreover, the degree of seriousness of drug trafficking makes its acknowledgement as a sufficiently important objective for the purposes of s. 1 to a large extent self-evident. The first criterion of a s. 1 inquiry, therefore, has been satisfied by the Crown.[38]

Judicial notice of social facts or social context evidence has also arisen in cases attempting to address inequality or gender bias.

R. v. LAVALLEE
[1990] 1 S.C.R. 852, 76 C.R. (3d) 329, 55 C.C.C. (3d) 97

The accused, a battered woman in a volatile common law relationship, killed her partner, Rust, late one night by shooting him in the back of the head as he left her room. The shooting occurred after an argument where the accused had been physically abused. She was fearful for her life after being taunted with the threat that either she kill him or he would get her. She had frequently been a victim of his physical abuse and had concocted excuses to explain her injuries to medical staff on those occasions. A psychiatrist with extensive professional experience in the treatment of battered wives prepared a psychiatric assessment of the appellant which was used in support of her defence of self-defence. The jury acquitted the accused but its verdict was overturned by a majority of the Manitoba Court of Appeal. The Supreme Court allowed the accused's appeal

---

38 *Ibid.*, at pp. 31-32. See also *R. v. Clayton*, [2007] 2 S.C.R. 725; *R. v. Edwards Books & Art Ltd.*, [1986] 2 S.C.R. 713; *R. v. Thomsen* (1988), 63 C.R. (3d) 1 (S.C.C.) and *R. v. Hufsky* (1988), 63 C.R. (3d) 14 (S.C.C.). And see generally, Maybank, "Proof of Facts Under S. 1 of the Charter" (1990), 77 C.R. (3d) 260 and Morgan, "Proof of Facts in Charter Litigation" in Sharpe, ed., *Charter Litigation* (1987). See also McEachern, "Viva Voce Evidence in Charter Cases" (1989), 23 U.B.C. Law Rev. 591.

deciding that the expert's opinion was admissible as relevant to her claim of self-defence.

Notice the court's reasoning. Notice how it judicially notices legislative facts; how it decides; how it reforms the law to fit society's attitude. Notice the literature relied on which was not proved in evidence.

WILSON J. (DICKSON C.J.C and LAMER, L'HEUREUX-DUBÉ, GONTHIER and CORY JJ. concurring):—

. . . .

The gravity, indeed, the tragedy of domestic violence can hardly be overstated. Greater media attention to this phenomenon in recent years has revealed both its prevalence and its horrific impact on women from all walks of life. Far from protecting women from it, the law historically sanctioned the abuse of women within marriage as an aspect of the husband's ownership of his wife and his "right" to chastise her. One need only recall the centuries old law that a man is entitled to beat his wife with a stick "no thicker than his thumb".

Laws do not spring out of a social vacuum. The notion that a man has a right to "discipline" his wife is deeply rooted in the history of our society. The woman's duty was to serve her husband and to stay in the marriage at all costs "till death do us part" and to accept as her due any "punishment" that was meted out for failing to please her husband. One consequence of this attitude was that "wife battering" was rarely spoken of, rarely reported, rarely prosecuted, and even more rarely punished. Long after society abandoned its formal approval of spousal abuse, tolerance of it continued and continues in some circles to this day.

Fortunately, there has been a growing awareness in recent years that no man has a right to abuse any woman under any circumstances. Legislative initiatives designed to educate police, judicial officers and the public, as well as more aggressive investigation and charging policies all signal a concerted effort by the criminal justice system to take spousal abuse seriously. However, a woman who comes before a judge or jury with the claim that she has been battered and suggests that this may be a relevant factor in evaluating her subsequent actions still faces the prospect of being condemned by popular mythology about domestic violence. Either she was not as badly beaten as she claims or she would have left the man long ago. Or, if she was battered that severely, she must have stayed out of some masochistic enjoyment of it.

. . . .

. . . Was the appellant "under reasonable apprehension of death or grievous bodily harm" from Rust as he was walking out of the room? The second is the assessment in s. 34(2)(b) of the magnitude of the force used by the accused. Was the accused's belief that she could not "otherwise preserve herself from death or grievous bodily harm" except by shooting the deceased based "on reasonable grounds"?

. . . .

If it strains credulity to imagine what the "ordinary man" would do in the position of a battered spouse, it is probably because men do not typically find themselves in that situation. Some women do, however. The definition of what is reasonable must be adapted to circumstances which are, by and large, foreign to the world inhabited by the hypothetical "reasonable man".

. . . .

The cycle described by Dr. Shane conforms to the Walker Cycle Theory of Violence named for clinical psychologist Dr. Lenore Walker, the pioneer researcher in the field of the battered wife syndrome. Dr. Shane acknowledged his debt to Dr. Walker in the course of establishing his credentials as an expert at trial. Dr. Walker first describes the cycle in the book The Battered Woman, (1979). In her 1984 book, The Battered Woman Syndrome, Dr. Walker reports the results of a study involving 400 battered women. Her research was designed to test empirically the theories expounded in her earlier book. At pp. 95-96 of The Battered Woman Syndrome she summarizes the Cycle Theory as follows:

[There follows a lengthy extract from the book.]

Dr. Walker defines a battered woman as a woman who has gone through the battering cycle at least twice. As she explains in her introduction to The Battered Woman, at p. xv, "Any woman may find herself in an abusive relationship with a man once. If it occurs a second time, and she remains in the situation, she is defined as a battered woman."

. . . .

Another aspect of the cyclical nature of the abuse is that it begets a degree of predictability to the violence that is absent in an isolated violent enounter between two strangers. This also means that it may in fact be possible for a battered spouse to accurately predict the onset of violence before the first blow is struck, even if an outsider to the relationship cannot. Indeed, it has been suggested that a battered woman's knowledge of her partner's violence is so heightened that she is able to anticipate the nature and extent (though not the onset) of the violence by his conduct beforehand. In her article "Potential Uses for Expert Testimony: Ideas Toward the Representation of Battered Women Who Kill" (1986), 9 Women's Rights Law Reporter 227, psychologist Julie Blackman describes this characteristic, at p. 229:

[Another lengthy quote.]

. . . The requirement imposed in *Whynot* that a battered woman wait until the physical assault is "underway" before her apprehensions can be validated in law would, in the words of an American court, be tantamount to sentencing her to "murder by instalment": *State v. Gallegos*, 719 P.2d 1268 (N.M. 1986), at p. 1271. I share the view expressed by Willoughby in "Rendering Each Woman Her Due: Can a Battered Woman Claim Self-Defense When She Kills Her Sleeping Batterer" (1989), 38 Kan. L. Rev. 169, at p. 184, that "society gains nothing, except perhaps the additional risk that the battered woman will herself be killed, because she must wait until her abusive husband instigates another battering episode before she can justifiably act".

. . . .

R. v. MALOTT
[1998] 1 S.C.R. 123, 12 C.R. (5th) 207, 121 C.C.C. (3d) 456

The accused was charged with murder. The accused and the deceased had lived as common law spouses for almost 20 years. The deceased abused the accused physically, sexually, psychologically and emotionally. The jury found her guilty of second degree murder in the death of the deceased and of the attempted murder of his girlfriend. A majority of the Court of Appeal affirmed the convictions. The accused appealed, complaining about the adequacy of the trial judge's charge to the jury on the murder charge with regard to the issue of battered woman syndrome as a defence. The appeal was dismissed. Concurring in the result, Justice L'Heureux-Dubé, McLachlin J. concurring, noted that concerns had been expressed that the treatment of expert evidence on battered woman syndrome, admissible in order to combat the myths and stereotypes which society has about battered women, had led to a new stereotype of the battered woman.

L'HEUREUX-DUBÉ J. (McLACHLIN J. concurring):— I have read the reasons of my colleague Justice Major, and I concur with the result that he reaches. However, given that this Court has not had the opportunity to discuss the value of evidence of "battered woman syndrome" since *R. v. Lavallee*, [1990] 1 S.C.R. 852, and given the evolving discourse on "battered woman syndrome" in the legal community, I will make a few comments on the importance of this kind of evidence to the just adjudication of charges involving battered women.

. . . .

. . . Concerns have been expressed that the treatment of expert evidence on battered women syndrome, which is itself admissible in order to combat the myths and stereotypes which society has about battered women, has led to a new stereotype of the "battered woman": see, e.g., Martha Shaffer, "The battered woman syndrome revisited: Some complicating thoughts five years after *R. v. Lavallee*" (1997), 47 *U.T.L.J.* 1, at p. 9; Sheila Noonan, "Strategies of Survival: Moving Beyond the Battered Woman Syndrome", in Ellen Adelberg and Claudia Currie, eds., *In Conflict with the Law: Women and the Canadian Justice System* (1993), 247, at p. 254; Isabel Grant, "The 'syndromization' of women's experience", in Donna Martinson et al., "A Forum on *Lavallee v. R.*: Women and Self-Defence" (1991), 25 *U.B.C. L. Rev.* 23, 51, at pp. 53-54; and Martha R. Mahoney, "Legal Images of Battered Women: Redefining the Issue of Separation" (1991), 90 *Mich. L. Rev.* 1, at p. 42.

It is possible that those women who are unable to fit themselves within the stereotype of a victimized, passive, helpless, dependent, battered woman will not have their claims to self-defence fairly decided. For instance, women who have demonstrated too much strength or initiative, women of colour, women who are professionals, or women who might have fought back against their abusers on previous occasions, should not be penalized for failing to accord with the stereotypical image of the archetypal battered woman. See, e.g., Julie Stubbs and

Julia Tolmie, "Race, Gender, and the Battered Woman Syndrome: An Australia Case Study" (1995), 8 *C.J.W.L.* 122. Needless to say, women with these characteristics are still entitled to have their claims of self-defence fairly adjudicated, and they are also still entitled to have their experiences as battered women inform the analysis. Professor Grant, *supra*, at p. 52, warns against allowing the law to develop such that a woman accused of killing her abuser must either have been "reasonable 'like a man' or reasonable 'like a battered woman'". I agree that this must be avoided. The "reasonable woman" must not be forgotten in the analysis, and deserves to be as much a part of the objective standard of the reasonable person as does the "reasonable man".

How should the courts combat the "syndromization", as Professor Grant refers to it, of battered women who act in self-defence? The legal inquiry into the moral culpability of a woman who is, for instance, claiming self-defence must focus on the *reasonableness* of her actions in the context of her personal experiences, and her experiences as a woman, not on her status as a battered woman and her entitlement to claim that she is suffering from "battered woman syndrome". This point has been made convincingly by many academics reviewing the relevant cases: see, e.g., Wendy Chan, "A Feminist Critique of Self-Defense and Provocation in Battered Women's Cases in England and Wales" (1994), 6 *Women & Crim. Just.* 39, at pp. 56-57; Elizabeth M. Schneider, "Describing and Changing: Women's Self-Defense Work and the Problem of Expert Testimony on Battering" (1992), 14 *Women's Rts. L. Rep.* 213, at pp. 216-17; and Marilyn MacCrimmon, "The social construction of reality and the rules of evidence", in Donna Martinson et al., *supra,* 36, at pp. 48-49. By emphasizing a woman's "learned helplessness", her dependence, her victimization, and her low self-esteem, in order to establish that she suffers from "battered woman syndrome", the legal debate shifts from the objective rationality of her actions to preserve her own life to those personal inadequacies which apparently explain her failure to flee from her abuser. Such an emphasis comports too well with society's stereotypes about women. Therefore, it should be scrupulously avoided because it only serves to undermine the important advancements achieved by the decision in Lavallee.

. . . .

My focus on women as the victims of battering and as the subjects of "battered woman syndrome" is not intended to exclude from consideration those men who find themselves in abusive relationships. However, the reality of our society is that typically, it is women who are the victims of domestic violence, at the hands of their male intimate partners. To assume that men who are victims of spousal abuse are affected by the abuse in the same way, without benefit of the research and expert opinion evidence which has informed the courts of the existence and details of "battered woman syndrome", would be imprudent.

Alan Gold, in response to *Malott*[39], highlights an article by Faigman and Wright, "The Battered Woman Syndrome in the Age of Science".[40] The article begins with a scathing denunciation of Lenore Walker's book, *The Battered Woman* (New York: Harper Collins, 1980), which figured so prominently in Justice Wilson's judgment in *R. v. Lavallee:*

> The battered woman syndrome illustrates all that is wrong with the law's use of science. The working hypothesis of the battered woman syndrome was first introduced in Lenore Walker's 1979 book, *The Battered Woman*. When it made its debut, this hypothesis had little more to support it beyond the clinical impressions of a single researcher. Five years later, Walker published a second book that promised a more thorough investigation of the hypothesis. However, this book contains little more than a patchwork of pseudo-scientific methods employed to confirm a hypothesis that its author and participating researchers never seriously doubted. Indeed, the 1984 book would provide an excellent case study for psychology graduate students on how not to conduct empirical research. Yet, largely based upon the same political ideology driving the researchers, judges have welcomed the battered woman syndrome into their courts. Because the law is driven by precedent, it quickly petrified around the original conception of the defense. Increasingly, observers are realizing that the evidence purportedly supporting the battered woman syndrome is without empirical foundation, and, perhaps more troubling, that the syndrome itself is inimical to the political ideology originally supporting it. In short, in the law's hasty effort to use science to further good policy, it is now obvious that the battered woman syndrome is not good science nor does it generate good policy.

In *Lavallee*, the Court announced a major change in the law. It was informed partly by the expert opinion given at the trial, but also by books and articles which the Court read for itself. The Court judicially noticed legislative facts outlined in Lenore Walker's books, and formed the law to fit the Court's view of society's present attitude. But the literature, before and after *Lavallee*, is replete with research disagreeing with Walker's description of battered woman syndrome, which description was adopted in *Lavallee*. Some are mentioned in Justice L'Heureux-Dubé's opinion in *Malott*. For citations to literature disagreeing with the court's description of battered woman syndrome, see Fischer, Vidmar & Ellis, "The Culture of Battering and the Role of Mediation in Domestic Violence Cases".[41]

It is a welcome advance that the Court in *Malott*, or at least two members of the Court, are now prepared to admit that the Court's reliance on the battered woman's syndrome was in error and too restrictive for developing appropriate sensitivity to the situation of the abused partner. Justice L'Heureux-Dubé in *Malott* speaks of courts having been informed by expert opinion evidence. In truth the Supreme Court frequently informs itself through its own research, judicially noticing facts found in the literature, and not by expert witnesses. Using expert witnesses has the advantage that their opinions can be challenged by cross-examination and by competing experts and a truer picture will then emerge. Also it would be fairer to the parties. To use *Lavallee* as but one example, the Court would have been better off, before issuing its opinion, had it advised counsel that it was about to rely on this book by Lenore Walker so that the parties might

---

39 ADGN/98-075 (QUICKLAW database Gold).

40 (1997), 39 Ariz. L. Rev. 67.

41 (1993), 46 S.M.U. L. Rev. 2117.

have had the opportunity to inform the court of other sources. When the courts decide to use science to inform the law they will be better informed if the parties are engaged. The joint endeavour will improve the court's ability to recognize junk science when it comes across it.

MOGE v. MOGE
[1992] 3 S.C.R. 813

The parties were married in the mid-50's in Poland and moved to Canada in 1960. They separated in 1973 and divorced in 1980. The wife had a grade seven education and no special skills or training. During the marriage, she cared for the house and their three children and, except for a brief period, also worked six hours per day in the evenings cleaning offices. After the separation, she was awarded custody of the children and received $150 per month spousal and child support and continued to work cleaning offices. The husband remarried in 1984 and continued to pay support to his former wife. She was laid off in 1987 and, as a result of an application to vary, her spousal and child support was increased to $400. She was later able to secure part-time and intermittent cleaning work. In 1989, the husband was granted an order terminating support. The trial judge found that the former wife had had time to become financially independent and that her husband had supported her as long as he could be required to do. The Court of Appeal set aside the judgment and ordered spousal support in the amount of $150 per month for an indefinite period. The appeal to the Supreme Court of Canada was then to determine whether the wife was entitled to ongoing support for an indefinite period of time or whether spousal support should be terminated. The Court decided to reverse a series of cases that had been based on a self-suffiency model of spousal support. Justice L'Heureux-Dubé noted the heavy costs that would be involved if expert evidence was necessary and decided the answer lay in judicial notice. She was influenced by a number of writings.

L'HEUREUX-DUBÉ J. (LA FOREST, GONTHIER, CORY and IACOBUCCI JJ. concurring):—

. . . .

In Canada, the feminization of poverty is an entrenched social phenomenon. Between 1971 and 1986 the percentage of poor women found among all women in this country more than doubled. During the same period the percentage of poor among all men climbed by 24 percent. The results were such that by 1986, 16 percent of all women in this country were considered poor: M. Gunderson, L. Muszynski and J. Keck, *Women and Labour Market Poverty* (1990), at p. 8.

Given the multiplicity of economic barriers women face in society, decline into poverty cannot be attributed entirely to the financial burdens arising from the dissolution of marriage: J.D. Payne, "The Dichotomy between Family Law and Family Crises on Marriage Breakdown" (1989), 20 *R.G.D.* 109, at pp. 116-17. However, there is no doubt that divorce and its economic effects are playing a role. Several years ago, L.J. Weitzman released her landmark study on divorce, The Divorce Revolution: The Unexpected Social and Economic Consequences for Women and Children in America (1985), and concluded at p. 323:

On a societal level, divorce increases female and child poverty and creates an ever-widening gap between the economic well-being of divorced men, on the one hand, and their children and former wives on the other.

. . . .

One proposal put forth by Professor Rogerson would be for Parliament to consider enacting a set of legislative guidelines. . . .

One possible disadvantage of such a solution lies in the risk that it may impose a strait-jacket which precludes the accommodation of the many economic variables susceptible to be encountered in spousal support litigation.

Another alternative might lie in the doctrine of judicial notice. The doctrine itself grew from a need to promote efficiency in the litigation process and may very well be applicable to spousal support. One classic statement of the content and purpose of the doctrine is outlined in *Varcoe v. Lee*, 181 P. 223 (Cal. 1919), at p. 226:

> The three requirements . . . — that the matter be one of common and general knowledge, that it be well established and authoritatively settled, be practically indisputable, and that this common, general, and certain knowledge exist in the particular jurisdiction — all are requirements dictated by the reason and purpose of the rule, which is to obviate the formal necessity for proof when the matter does not require proof.

As E.M. Morgan noted in "Judicial Notice" (1944), 57 Harv. L. Rev. 269, at p. 272:

> . . . the judge . . . must be assumed to have a fund of general information, consisting of both generalized capacity to relate it to what he has perceived during the proceeding, as well as the ability to draw reasonable deductions from the combination by using the ordinary processes of thought. That fund of general information must be at least as great as that of all reasonably well-informed persons in the community. He cannot be assumed to be ignorant of what is so generally accepted as to be incapable of dispute among reasonable men.

. . . .

Based upon the studies which I have cited earlier in these reasons, the general economic impact of divorce on women is a phenomenon the existence of which cannot reasonably be questioned and should be amenable to judicial notice. More extensive social science data are also appearing. Such studies are beginning to provide reasonable assessments of some of the disadvantages incurred and advantages conferred post-divorce. . . . While quantification will remain difficult and fact related in each particular case, judicial notice should be taken of such studies, subject to other expert evidence which may bear on them, as background information at the very least. . . .

In all events, whether judicial notice of the circumstances generally encountered by spouses at the dissolution of a marriage is to be a formal part of the trial process or whether such circumstances merely provide the necessary background information, it is important that judges be aware of the social reality in which support decisions are experienced when engaging in the examination of the objectives of the Act.

In an article written by L'Heureux-Dubé which had justified her decision in *Moge v. Moge,* Justice L'Heureux-Dubé discussed the propriety of bringing social reality into the courtroom by way of judicial notice and concluded:

> Judicial notice of evidence of a general character has the potential to simplify the judges' task of assessing the true consequences flowing from the relationship and its breakup and of formulating a more accurate picture of the realistic needs of the parties, particularly when self-sufficiency, market conditions and real estate situations are at issue. It promotes judicial awareness of the context in which support awards are experienced, rather than merely contemplated.
>
> Though judicial notice as a proper device in family law is not new, its use appears to have escalated since it received the Court's blessing in *Moge.* It has been taken of many different facts in Canadian matrimonial cases. A recent article itemizes fifty-nine cases where judicial notice was taken in Canadian family law cases on subjects such as the following: the employment market for women; the impairment of the economic ability of a woman at the end of a relationship; the increase in the cost of raising children as they grow older; the effects of inflation on the parties; the tax implications to the parties; changes in the value of property, including changes in the real estate market; and the costs of disposition of property. *Moge* has acknowledged that as much as laws are not enacted in a Judicial vacuum, judicial decisions should not be made in isolation, particularly of the socio-economic research and data of the time. It is now up to courts in support and custody disputes to take the baton and run with it.
>
> Judicial notice of the general economic impact of divorce on women and children and of studies providing social science data on related matters also serves important ends of judicial efficiency. Specifically, it helps to moderate the high cost of family law litigation by reducing the need for experts, and frees for more important matters court time that would otherwise be required in order to deal with evidence on socio-economic context. Moreover, it reduces the burden on many spouses (most often women) who do not have the resources necessary to bring to the court's attention the studies and expert evidence which might demonstrate such context. In other cases, the small sums involved simply would not justify the expenditure of such resources. Finally, requiring that such facts be proven in each individual case would undoubtedly spawn needless duplication. The value of judicial notice, responsibly exercised, as a practical and economic measure to increase judicial consciousness on the social realities of support should therefore not be underestimated.
>
> In parting, it should be evident that I do not mean to suggest that judicial notice can take the place of effective counsel and situation-specific evidence. It cannot. Moreover, whenever possible, I think that , participation of counsel in determinations of what is to be noticed judicially should be encouraged. I do think it important to emphasize, however, that courts should be willing to join hands with the legislature in promoting family law legislation that truly and effectively addresses the needs and concerns of those individuals falling within its ambit. By recognizing that exclusive reliance on the adversarial framework, and all of its accompanying legal baggage, may not be the best means by which to address family law concerns, we open the door for more innovative and co-operative solutions that should ultimately improve both the interpretation and application of family law in Canada.[42]

---

42 L'Heureux-Dubé, "Re-examining the Doctrine of Judicial Notice in the Family Law Context" (1994), 26 Ottawa L. Rev. 551.

But not all agree! *Willick v. Willick*[43] was concerned with an application to vary the amount of child support which had been set in a separation agreement later incorporated into a divorce judgment. The Court was unanimous that the conditions necessary for a variation had been satisfied. There was a difference of opinion regarding the propriety of judicial notice. Justice Sopinka, La Forest, Cory and Iacobucci JJ. concurring, decided that he was able to arrive at the same result as Justice L'Heureux-Dubé on the basis of the rules of statutory construction as to the proper statutory interpretation of s. 17(4) of the Divorce Act, without resort to extensive extrinsic materials. He wrote:

> A contextual approach to the interpretation of the statutory provisions is appropriate but does not require an examination of the broad policy grounds to which my colleague refers. Following that course would require us to resolve the thorny question of the use of extraneous materials such as studies, opinions and reports and whether it is appropriate to take judicial notice of them and what notice to counsel, if any, is required. We would also have to consider the extent to which our approach is different in a case such as this from a constitutional case in which wider latitude is allowed.

Justice L'Heureux-Dubé, Gonthier and McLachlin JJ. concurring, wrote:

> Social science research and socio-economic data are longstanding judicial tools in both Canada and the United States. The judiciary's long-recognized function as a policy finder sometimes compels it to consider social authority even when the parties do not, themselves, present relevant evidence on relevant questions of public policy. In the course of Charter interpretations, this Court has often taken judicial notice of reliable social research and socio-economic data in order to assist its contextual s. 1 analysis of a rights violation. Social authority can be an indispensable element to this approach and this Court has accepted its value in non-constitutional contexts which nonetheless raise broad questions of public policy. See *R. v. Lavallee*.

Justice L'Heureux-Dubé then went on to consider a variety of studies.

A trial judge, Judge Williams, was critical of Justice L'Heureux-Dubé's willingness to use judicial notice without informing the parties and seeking their involvement.[44] Recently Justice L'Heureux-Dubé has responded and maintained her position:

> In his view, judicial notice of social framework evidence should not be undertaken without providing the parties with the opportunity to make submissions at trial on this evidence or other evidence which refutes it. I, on the other hand, believe that, while desirable in certain cases, strict procedural requirements applied uniformly to all cases may too readily ignore the very reasons for which judicial notice is both needed and appropriate in the family law context. I have already underlined the significance of cost and the unfairly onerous burden a lengthy trial may place on the spouse with more limited resources. I have also demonstrated the need for tempering the adversarial process in family law matters.[45]

But consider the concerns of Professor Peggy Davis, herself a former judge:

> The absence of traditions and procedures for regulating judicial notice of legislative facts provides the sitting judge with a dangerous freedom. As a former judge who

---

43 [1994] 3 S.C.R. 670.
44 Williams, "Grasping a Thorny Baton" (1996), 14 C.F.L.Q. 179.
45 L'Heureux-Dubé, "Making Equality Work in Family Law" (1997), 14 Can. J. Fam. Law 103, 119.

has experienced the freedom granted by this permissive view, I have had cause to doubt its wisdom.[46]

Davis calls for some legislative response to encourage litigants and judges to address the issues directly and to ensure, as far as possible, a fair procedure and informed deliberation. There needs to be a procedure for the judge to solicit briefs, depositions of experts or to conduct hearings as to whether the judge should take notice of a disputable fact. No one presently denies the necessity of judges sometimes making law. To change the common law, to interpret a statute, to make a constitutional decision. Everyone recognizes as well that the decision should be informed by the facts. It is not too much to ask however that the judges, when they recognize that they are relying on extra-record disputable facts, advise the litigants so that they have an opportunity to agree or disagree.

Perhaps something along the lines of what was proposed in "Study Paper No. 6, Judicial Notice", published by the Law Reform Commission of Canada in 1973 could be used. The Evidence Project recommended legislation dealing with the subject:

> 2 (3) A judge may take judicial notice of scientific, economic and social facts in determining the law or in determining the constitutional validity of a statute.

> . . . .

> 4 (2) With respect to any fact referred to in subsection 2(3)

>> (a) if the judge has been requested to take, or proposes to take, or has taken judicial notice, he shall, if requested, afford each party reasonable opportunity to make representations as to the fact or matter of law involved and as to the propriety of taking judicial notice; and

>> (b) if the judge resorts to any source of information, including the advice of persons learned in the subject matter, that is not received in open court, that information and its source shall be made a part of the record in the proceedings and the judge shall, if requested, afford each party an opportunity to make representations as to the validity of that information.

CRONK v. CANADIAN GENERAL INSURANCE CO.
(1995), 25 O.R. (3d) 505 (Ont. C.A.)

The plaintiff was employed as a clerk-stenographer. In 1993, as a result of internal reorganization by the defendant, the plaintiff's employment was terminated. She brought an action for damages for wrongful dismissal and moved for summary judgment, seeking damages based on a notice period of 20 months. The plaintiff was awarded damages of 20 months' salary and the defendant appealed.

---

46 Commenting on the absence of any restrictions in the Federal Rules, see Davis, "There is a Book Out . . ." (1987), 100 Harv. L. Rev. 1539, 1541.

LACOURCIÈRE J.A.:—

. . . .

In granting judgment in her favour, MacPherson J. noted that "the factors to be considered in determining reasonable notice have remained more or less constant for over 30 years", having been enunciated by McRuer C.J.H.C. in *Bardal v. Globe & Mail Ltd.*, [1960] O.W.N. 253 (H.C.J.) at p. 255:

> There could be no catalogue laid down as to what was reasonable notice in particular classes of cases. The reasonableness of the notice must be decided with reference to each particular case, having regard to the character of the employment, the length of service of the servant, the age of the servant and the availability of similar employment, having regard to the experience, training and qualifications of the servant.

. . . .

Addressing the role played by the character of employment in determining the requisite notice period, MacPherson J. observed that the length of notice requested by the respondent had traditionally been reserved for persons with positions more senior to hers. Having said that, he could find no principled reason why this should be so. He rejected the proposition that senior employees are more stigmatized by the loss of employment than are their underlings. Likewise, he could find no support for the notion, frequently articulated in the case-law, that senior, specialized employees have greater difficulty in securing new employment. Apart from the fact that the appellant had not provided any evidence to that effect, and the fact that the respondent was still out of work eight months after her dismissal, MacPherson J. found another basis on which to dismiss the proposition (at p. 25):

> Third, the reality is — as we are all told by our parents at a young age — that education and training *are* directly related to employment. The senior manager and the professional person are better, not worse, positioned to obtain employment, both initially and later in a post-dismissal context. Higher education and specialized training correlate directly with *increased* access to employment.

In support of this assertion, the learned motions court judge cited two studies published by the Council of Ontario Universities, as well as a May 21, 1994 article in the *Economist* magazine. He discovered these materials through his own research. For those reasons, he refused to accept the defendant's argument based on a managerial-clerical distinction.

. . . .

In my opinion, the learned motion court judge's reasons do not justify departing from the widely accepted principle. He erred in doing so on the basis of his own sociological research without providing counsel an opportunity to challenge or respond to the results of the two studies relied upon. I agree with the appellant that the factual conclusions which he drew from these studies are beyond the scope of proper judicial notice.

. . . .

The conclusion of the motions court judge based on the studies prepared by the Council of Ontario Universities are obviously not so generally known or accepted as to challenge the validity of an established principle which has found judicial acceptance for over three decades. It is not, as the respondent contended, an undisputed "social reality" as was the background information concerning the circumstances encountered by spouses at the dissolution of a marriage, in *Moge v. Moge*, [1992] 3 S.C.R. 813 at p. 874.

Before taking new matters into account based on statistics which have not been considered in the judgment under appeal, the adversarial process requires that the court ensure that the parties are given an opportunity to deal with the new information by making further submissions, oral or written, and allowing, if requested, fresh material in response.

The result arrived at has the potential of disrupting the practices of the commercial and industrial world, wherein employers have to predict with reasonable certainty the cost of downsizing or increasing their operations, particularly in difficult economic times. As well, legal practitioners specializing in employment law and the legal profession generally have to give advice to employers and employees in respect of termination of employment with reasonable certainty. Adherence to the doctrine of *stare decisis* plays an important role in that respect: *Cassell & Co. v. Broome*, [1972] 1 All E.R. 801 at p. 809, [1972] A.C. 1027 (H.L.).

. . . .

In my opinion, the character of the employment of the respondent does not entitle her to a lengthy period of notice.

. . . .

For these reasons, I would vary the judgment of MacPherson J. so that the plaintiff respondent will recover damages based on a salary calculation covering 12 months from September 9, 1993.

WEILER J.A. (dissenting in part):—

. . . .

The justification for placing less weight on the factor of character of employment in the case of a clerical employee is based on several factual propositions or assumptions put forward by the appellant. Lacourcière J.A. does not find it necessary to deal with the validity of these propositions because they were not challenged in argument before MacPherson J. MacPherson J. did, however, question the validity of these factual propositions. In my opinion he was not prevented from doing so although he erred in not giving the parties an opportunity to lead evidence and to make submissions respecting his rejection of these factual propositions.

. . . .

A trial is a search for the truth. When a trial judge reviews jurisprudence and finds it rests on a factual assumption, that may no longer be true or which may not apply in all cases, the judge is not obliged to continue to accept this assumption as a fact. Naturally, the judge wishes to avoid the expense and delay of requiring counsel to re-attend for further argument concerning the material he has discovered and upon which he seeks to rely. However, where a judicial approach rests on a factual proposition with which the judge disagrees, and counsel are unaware that the judge is considering a break with the past, I can see no alternative but for the judge to allow counsel an opportunity to call evidence and to make submissions. The reason for this is two-fold. The general studies or material that the judge sees as rebutting the factual proposition may, as a result of expert evidence, be susceptible to other interpretation. In addition, the parties have a right to expect that if a judge disagrees with a factual assumption, which has found its way into the jurisprudence and which has gone unchallenged, the judge will give the parties an opportunity to make submissions concerning the studies he sees as rebutting this assumption. MacPherson J. erred in not doing so. The parties should have been recalled.

. . . .

I would allow the appeal, set aside the judgment of MacPherson J. respecting reasonable notice, and in its place, substitute an order pursuant to rule 20.04(3) directing the trial of an issue as to the amount that Ms. Cronk is entitled to be paid in lieu of notice.

MORDEN A.C.J.O.:— I have had the benefit of reading the reasons of Lacourcière J.A. and Weiler J.A. I agree with Lacourcière J.A.'s proposed disposition of this appeal and agree, generally, with his reasons. I shall state my particular reasons briefly.

. . . .

The parties were content to have MacPherson J. and this court dispose of Ms. Cronk's motion for summary judgment on the basis of the materials which they had filed with the court. They were satisfied that the court could come to a just conclusion on what was a reasonable notice period on these materials. Although this would involve the court's consideration of the parties' competing contentions on the application of the reasonable notice standard to differing views of the facts, a trial was not required for this purpose. There was no genuine issue requiring a trial: see *Ron Miller Realty v. Honeywell, Wotherspoon* (1991), 4 O.R. (3d) 492 (Gen. Div.). I think that the parties are to be commended for adopting this approach. In the light of this and, also, the consideration that character of employment is not commensurate with availability of other employment, and, even if it were, my doubt that this would necessarily result in the upward adjustment of notice periods for clerical employees (rather than the downward adjustment of those for senior employees), I do not think, with respect, that a trial should be directed.

Do you see why it was undisputed social reality in *Moge v. Moge* and therefore amenable to judicial notice, but not in *Cronk*?

(c) *Spence*: Revised Standards

R. v. SPENCE
33 C.R. (6th) 1, [2005] 3 S.C.R. 458, 202 C.C.C. (3d) 1

A black accused was charged with robbery of a South Asian pizza deliveryman in the hallway of an apartment block. The trial judge permitted the defence to challenge potential jurors for cause on the basis of potential bias against a black accused, but refused to allow a question addressing the interracial nature of the crimes. He held that the "interracial" element was irrelevant on the facts of this case. The accused was convicted.

On appeal, the accused argued that he was deprived of his right to an impartial jury and therefore to a fair trial. The majority of the Ontario Court of Appeal set aside the conviction. The trial judge had misinterpreted the ruling in *R. v. Parks*[47] entitling Black accused to challenge prospective jurors for cause on the basis of race. The majority held that where an accused entitled to challenge the jury for cause on the basis of race wishes to include the interracial nature of the crime in the question for potential jurors, he is entitled to have the question posed in that way.

On further appeal, the Supreme Court allowed the appeal and restored the conviction. Justice Binnie wrote the unanimous judgment of the Court. He held it was up to the defence to show an "air of reality" to the assertion that the complainant's South Asian origin had the realistic potential of aggravating jurors' prejudice against the black accused because of natural sympathy for the victim by jurors who might be South Asian. This burden was not met. While it was open to the trial judge to include the "interracial" aspect of the crime in the challenge for cause, neither the case law, nor the studies on which case law was based, supported the need for a broad entitlement in every case to challenge for cause based on racial sympathy as distinguished from potential racial hostility. The majority in the court below had pushed judicial notice beyond its proper limits. It was within the trial judge's discretion to allow the interracial question but it was not an error of law for the trial judge to draw the line where he did. This had not resulted in an unfair trial. In the course of the judgment the Court revised its approach to judicial notice.

BINNIE J. (MAJOR, LEBEL, DESCHAMPS, FISH, ABELLA and CHARRON JJ. concurring): —

It is not to be doubted that evidence of *how* and *to what extent* racial discrimination affects the behaviour of jurors is difficult to come by, as noted by Finlayson J.A. in *Koh* (paras. 28 and 41). The intervener, African Canadian Legal Clinic, in a useful submission that went beyond the more case law oriented argument of the respondent, urged the Court to fill the evidentiary gap with the taking of judicial notice that where the complainant is also a member of a visible minority:

> [r]acial bias can affect the fairness of the trial process ... for example affecting juror assessment of credibility and weight of the evidence, shaping information received

---

47 (1993) 24 C.R. (4th) 81 (Ont. C.A.), later adopted in *R. v. Williams*, [1998] 1 S.C.R. 1128.

during the trial, consideration of the accused's propensity for criminality, and favouring of the Crown or witnesses. During the trial process stereotypes relating to both the complainant and the accused may interact and affect a potential juror. The operation of biases in this context is potentially harmful, unpredictable, and can skew the outcome in innumerable ways.

Juror impartiality may arise from a favouring of the victim over the accused because the victim is from the same racialized group as the juror. [paras. 34-35]

In taking this broad approach to judicial notice, the intervener was perhaps invoking the work of the great American expert on the law of evidence, Professor James Thayer, who wrote in 1890 that "courts may and should notice without proof, and assume as known by others, whatever, as the phrase is, everybody knows" (emphasis added) (J.B. Thayer, "Judicial Notice and the Law of Evidence" (1889-90), 3 *Harv. L. Rev.* 285, at p. 305.) In taking this view, he is largely supported by Dean Wigmore. (See J.H. Wigmore, *Evidence in Trials at Common Law* (Chadbourn rev. 1981), vol. 9, at p. 732.) From time to time, similarly broad statements have issued from this Court. No less strict a judge than Duff C.J.C. was prepared in 1938 to take judicial notice of "facts which are known to intelligent persons generally": *Reference re Alberta Statutes*, [1938] S.C.R. 100 at p. 128, [1938] 2 D.L.R. 81 *sub nom. Reference re Alberta Legislation.* More recently Beetz J. in *Montréal (City of) v. Arcade Amusements Inc.*, [1985] 1 S.C.R. 368, 18 D.L.R. (4th) 161, took judicial notice of a number of "facts" dealing with the habits and lifestyles of children and adolescents on the basis that judges "cannot disregard" such obvious things that are part of our everyday experience:

The courts cannot be unaware that children and adolescents generally have limited financial resources. . . .The courts cannot disregard the attraction which amusement machines and amusement halls are likely to exert on children and adolescents,... both while they have money and when they run out of it. [pp. 382-83]

Professor Thayer's view was that "[i]n conducting a process of judicial reasoning, as of other reasoning, not a step can be taken without assuming something which has not been proved" (pp. 287-88). I would add the comment of Scrutton L.J.:

It is difficult to know what judges are allowed to know, though they are ridiculed if they pretend not to know. (*Tolley v. Fry*, [1930] 1 K.B. 467 (Eng. C.A.) at p. 475)

This is true, so far as it goes. The Court's judgment in *Whirlpool Corp. v. Camco Inc.*, [2000] 2 S.C.R. 1067, 2000 SCC 67, 194 D.L.R. (4th) 193, for instance, talked at length about the functioning of clothes washing machines, even though no washing machine had been filed as a trial exhibit, and no special instruction about their general operations was offered through the expert witnesses. It was just that "everyone" knew.

Thayer's approach to judicial notice has its role but I do not think it helps us to solve the issue posed by the African Canadian Legal Clinic. There are at least three difficulties standing in its way. Firstly what "everybody knows" may be wrong. Until *Parks*, "everybody" knew the solemnity of a criminal trial and careful jury instructions from the judge meant there was little possibility that potential jurors in Toronto would be influenced by racial prejudice (Doherty J.A., at p. 360 of *Parks*, cites a number of trial decisions where race-based challenges for cause were rejected for that reason). Common law judges in early Tudor England would presumably have taken judicial notice of the "fact" that the sun revolves around the earth. Secondly, there is the problem of trial fairness. Where do these facts come from and how are the parties going to address them? How can parties who are prejudiced by the taking of judicial notice rebut what "everybody" knows unless a plausible source is put to them for their comment and potential disagreement? (See *R. v. Parnell* (1995), 98 C.C.C. (3d) 83 (Ont. C.A.) at p. 94.) A third problem is that judges occasionally contradict each other about some "fact" that "everybody" knows, even on the same court in the same case. Thus, in *Campbell v. Royal Bank of Canada*, [1964] S.C.R. 85, 43 D.L.R. (2d) 341, Martland and Ritchie JJ., dissenting, pointed out, at p. 91, that the majority and dissenting judges in the court below had taken judicial notice of flatly contradictory facts, namely whether it was usual or unusual to find water in substantial quantities on the floor of a Manitoba bank in wintertime. More dramatically, in *Clinton v. Jones*, 520 U.S. 681 (1997), where the issue before the Supreme Court of the United States was whether a sitting President is entitled to automatic immunity during his term of office with respect to private conduct prior to his election to the presidency, the court stated with confidence with respect to the Paula Jones affair that "it appears to us highly unlikely to occupy any substantial amount of petitioner's time" (p. 702).

While courts have accepted the widespread existence of racism, and the likelihood that anti-black racism is aggravated when the alleged victim is white, there is no similar consensus that "everybody knows" a juror of a particular race is likely to favour a complainant or witness of the same race, despite the trial safeguards and the trial judge's instruction to the contrary.

Still less can it be said that such favouritism satisfies the more stringent test of judicial notice adopted by this Court in *Find*, at para. 48, per McLachlin C.J.C.:

> Judicial notice dispenses with the need for proof of facts that are clearly uncontroversial or beyond reasonable dispute. Facts judicially noticed are not proved by evidence under oath. Nor are they tested by cross-examination. Therefore, the threshold for judicial notice is strict: a court may properly take judicial notice of facts that are either: (1) so notorious or generally accepted as not to be the subject of debate among reasonable persons; or (2) capable of immediate and accurate demonstration by resort to readily accessible sources of indisputable accuracy.

This stricter formulation adopted in *Find* was originally put forward by Professor E.M. Morgan in "Judicial Notice" (1943-1944), 57 *Harv. L. Rev.* 269. Morgan, in common with other critics, took the view that the Thayer formulation of judicial notice was too broad. It allowed the courts to make too much use of out-of-court information, and did not sufficiently recognize the limitations on a judge imposed by the adversarial process and fair trial considerations. The narrower Morgan view is found in J. Sopinka, S.N. Lederman and A.W. Bryant, *The Law of Evidence* (2nd ed. 1999), p. 1055, and D.M. Paciocco and L. Stuesser, *The Law of Evidence* (2nd ed. 1999), at p. 285. I do not think the African Canadian

Legal Clinic's view of race-based sympathy for victims (or partiality in favour of certain witnesses) is so notoriously correct as "not to be the subject of debate among reasonable persons". Nor is it capable of immediate demonstration by resort to "readily accessible sources of indisputable accuracy" (*Find*, at para. 48).

Unlike Professor Thayer, for whom judicial notice created a rebuttable presumption of accuracy, Professor Morgan (p. 273) necessarily concluded that if certain facts were properly made subject to judicial notice, they were, by definition, not open to rebuttal. In this, he was supported by Professor C.T. McCormick, who wrote that "a ruling that a fact will be judicially noticed precludes contradictory evidence"; see "Judicial Notice" (1951-1952), 5 Vand. L. Rev. 296, at p. 322. In *R. v. Zundel* (1987), 31 C.C.C. (3d) 97, 35 D.L.R. (4th) 338 (Ont. C.A.), the court said that "[t]he generally accepted modern view ... is that where the court takes judicial notice of a matter, the judicial notice is final" (p. 150). On this view, acceptance through judicial notice of the broad race-based thesis of the intervener African Canadian Legal Clinic would not only stretch the elasticity of judicial notice, it would create a set of irrebuttable presumptions about how individuals called to jury duty can be expected to think. If there is one thing most of the social science studies agree upon, it is that much work remains to be done in Canada within the limits imposed by s. 649 of the *Criminal Code* to clarify our working assumptions about jury behaviour.

It could be argued that the requirements of judicial notice accepted in Find should be relaxed in relation to such matters as laying a factual basis for the exercise of a discretion to permit challenges for cause. These are matters difficult to prove, and they do not strictly relate to the adjudication of guilt or innocence, but rather to the framework within which that adjudication is to take place. Such non-adjudicative facts are now generally called "social facts" when they relate to the fact-finding process and "legislative facts" in relation to legislation or judicial policy. Juror partiality is a question of fact, and what the African Canadian Legal Clinic invites us to do is to take judicial notice of the "social facts" of different aspects of racism.

"Social fact" evidence has been defined as social science research that is used to construct a frame of reference or background context for deciding factual issues crucial to the resolution of a particular case: see, e.g., C. L'Heureux-Dubé "Re-examining the Doctrine of Judicial Notice in the Family Law Context" (1994), 26 *Ottawa L. Rev.* 551, at p. 556. As with their better known "legislative fact" cousins, "social facts" are general. They are not specific to the circumstances of a particular case, but if properly linked to the adjudicative facts, they help to explain aspects of the evidence. Examples are the Court's acceptance of the "battered wife syndrome" to explain the wife's conduct in *R. v. Lavallée*, [1990] 1 S.C.R. 852, 55 C.C.C. (3d) 97, or the effect of the "feminization of poverty" judicially noticed in *Moge v. Moge*, [1992] 3 S.C.R. 813 at p. 853, 99 D.L.R. (4th) 456, and of the systemic or background factors that have contributed to the difficulties faced by aboriginal people in both the criminal justice system and throughout society at large in *R. v. Wells*, [2000] 1 S.C.R. 207, 2000 SCC 10, 141 C.C.C. (3d) 368, 182 D.L.R. (4th) 257, at para. 53, and in *R. v. Gladue*, [1999] 1 S.C.R. 688, 133 C.C.C. (3d) 385, 171 D.L.R. (4th) 385, at para. 83.

No doubt there is a useful distinction between adjudicative facts (the where, when and why of what the accused is alleged to have done) and "social facts" and "legislative facts" which have relevance to the reasoning process and may involve broad considerations of policy: Paciocco and Stuesser, at p. 286. However, simply categorizing an issue as "social fact" or "legislative fact" does not license the court to put aside the need to examine the trustworthiness of the "facts" sought to be judicially noticed. Nor are counsel encouraged to bootleg "evidence in the guise of authorities": *Public School Boards' Assn. of Alberta v. Alberta (Attorney General)*, [1999] 3 S.C.R. 845, 180 D.L.R. (4th) 670, at para. 3.

The distinction between legislative and adjudicative facts was formulated by the astute administrative law expert, Kenneth Culp Davis, who thought it important to distinguish for purposes of judicial notice between "adjudicative" fact (where he thought the Morgan criteria should apply) and "legislative" fact (where he tended to side with Thayer): K.C. Davis, *Administrative Law Treatise* (2nd ed. 1980), vol. 3, at p. 139. The proof of facts about widespread racism in the community, and whether or not it is so strong as to create a "realistic possibility" of overcoming a juror's presumed impartiality, has to do with juries in general and judicial policy towards their composition. Such matters, according to Sopinka J., "are subject to less stringent admissibility requirements": (*Danson v. Ontario (Attorney General)*, [1990] 2 S.C.R. 1086 at p. 1099, 73 D.L.R. (4th) 686. The "less stringent" standard was not defined.

Professor Davis' useful distinction between adjudicative facts and legislative facts is part of his larger insight, highly relevant for present purposes, that *the permissible scope of judicial notice should vary according to the nature of the issue under consideration*. For example, more stringent proof may be called for of facts that are close to the center of the controversy between the parties (whether social, legislative or adjudicative) as distinguished from background facts at or near the periphery.

To put it another way, the closer the fact approaches the dispositive issue, the more the court ought to insist on compliance with the stricter Morgan criteria. Thus in *Find*, the Court's consideration of alleged juror bias arising out of the repellant nature of the offences against the accused did not relate to the issue of guilt or innocence, and was not "adjudicative" fact in that sense, but nevertheless the Court insisted on compliance with the Morgan criteria because of the centrality of the issue, which was hotly disputed, to the disposition of the appeal. While some learned commentators seek to limit the Morgan criteria to adjudicative fact (see, e.g., Paciocco and Stuesser, at p. 286; McCormick, at p. 316), I believe the Court's decision in Find takes a firmer line. I believe a review of our jurisprudence suggests that the Court will start with the Morgan criteria, whatever may be the type of "fact" that is sought to be judicially noticed. The Morgan criteria represent the gold standard and, if satisfied, the "fact" will be judicially noticed, and that is the end of the matter.

If the Morgan criteria are not satisfied, and the fact is "adjudicative" in nature, the fact will not be judicially recognized, and that too is the end of the matter.

It is when dealing with social facts and legislative facts that the Morgan criteria, while relevant, are not necessarily conclusive. There are levels of notoriety and indisputability. Some legislative "facts" are necessarily laced with supposition, prediction, presumption, perception and wishful thinking. Outside the realm of adjudicative fact, the limits of judicial notice are inevitably somewhat elastic. Still, the Morgan criteria will have great weight when the legislative fact or social fact approaches the dispositive issue. For example, in *R. v. Advance Cutting & Coring Ltd.*, [2001] 3 S.C.R. 209, 2001 SCC 70, 205 D.L.R. (4th) 385, LeBel J. observed:

> The fact that unions intervene in political social debate is well known and well documented and might be the object of judicial notice. ... Taking judicial notice of the fact that Quebec unions have a constant ideology, act in constant support of a particular cause or policy, and seek to impose that ideology on their members seems far more controversial. It would require a leap of faith and logic, absent a proper factual record on the question. [paras. 226-27]

See also *Gladue*, at para. 83.

The reality is that in many *Charter* cases (for example), the adjudicative facts are admitted. It is the legislative facts or social facts that are likely to prove dispositive (e.g., *R. v. Sharpe*, [2001] 1 S.C.R. 45, 2001 SCC 2, 150 C.C.C. (3d) 321, 194 D.L.R. (4th) 1; *R. v. Butler*, [1992] 1 S.C.R. 452, 70 C.C.C. (3d) 129, 89 D.L.R. (4th) 449; *Little Sisters Book and Art Emporium v. Canada (Minister of Justice)*, [2000] 2 S.C.R. 1120, 2000 SCC 69, 150 C.C.C. (3d) 1, 193 D.L.R. (4th) 193). The Court in those cases was rightly careful to keep judicial notice on a relatively short leash, while at the same time acknowledging that facts cannot be demonstrated with greater precision than the subject matter permits.

When asked to take judicial notice of matters falling between the high end already discussed where the Morgan criteria will be insisted upon, and the low end of background facts where the court will likely proceed (consciously or unconsciously) on the basis that the matter is beyond serious controversy, I believe a court ought to ask itself whether such "fact" would be accepted by reasonable people who have taken the trouble to inform themselves on the topic as not being the subject of reasonable dispute for the particular purpose for which it is to be used, keeping in mind that the need for reliability and trustworthiness increases directly with the centrality of the "fact" to the disposition of the controversy. Thus, for example, journalists claim that "everybody knows" some important news sources will dry up unless their identity can be kept secret. On that basis, some courts have been prepared to refuse (or delay) compelling journalists to disclose confidential sources for the purpose of defamation proceedings, e.g., *Hays v. Weiland* (1918), 43 D.L.R. 137 (Ont. C.A.); *Reid v. Telegram Publishing Co.*, [1961] O.R. 418, 28 D.L.R. (2d) 6 (H.C.); *Drabinsky v. Maclean-Hunter Ltd.* (1980), 28 O.R. (2d) 23, 108 D.L.R. (3d) 390 (H.C.J.); *McInnis v. University Students' Council of University of Western Ontario* (1984), 14 D.L.R. (4th) 126n (Ont. H.C.), leave to appeal to Divisional Court refused, at p. 127. However, when the issue of compelled disclosure of confidential sources became dispositive in *Moysa v. Alberta (Labour Relations Board)*, [1989] 1 S.C.R. 1572, 60 D.L.R. (4th) 1, the Court declined to recognize any Charter entitlement for journalists to refuse to disclose "secret" sources before an administrative tribunal, at p. 1581, per Sopinka J.:

> While judicial notice may be taken of self-evident facts, I am not convinced that it is indisputable that there is a direct relationship between testimonial compulsion and a "drying-up" of news sources as alleged by the appellant. The burden of proof that there has been a violation of s. 2(b) rests on the appellant. Absent any evidence that there is a tie between the impairment of the alleged right to gather information and the requirement that journalists testify before the Labour Relations Board, I cannot find that there has been a breach of s. 2(b) in this case.

Both of these examples dealt with the "legislative facts" underlying a claimed rule giving effect to journalistic privilege. For the purposes of regulating procedures in defamation proceedings, the courts were prepared to accept as a reasonable generalization that failure to respect confidential sources would "chill" the gathering of news, which would not be in the public interest. In *Moysa*, however, for the very different purpose of considering whether the underlying "legislative fact" was sufficiently beyond controversy to support a claim to entrenchment as a *Charter* privilege, the generalization was subjected to closer scrutiny.

Here, the respondent and the African Canadian Legal Clinic are asking the Court to make some fundamental shifts in the law's understanding of how juries function and how the selection of their members should be approached. Their submissions carry us well beyond the specific context in which *Williams* and *Parks* were decided. The facts of which they ask us to take judicial notice would be dispositive of the appeal; yet they are neither notorious nor easily verified by reference to works of "indisputable accuracy". We are urged to pile inference onto inference. To take judicial notice of such matters for this purpose would, in my opinion, be to take even a generous view of judicial notice a leap too far. We do not know whether a favourable predisposition based on race—to the extent it exists—is any more prevalent than it is for people who share the same religion, or language, or national origin, or old school. On the present state of our knowledge, I think we should decline, at least for now, to proceed by way of judicial notice down the road the African Canadian Legal Clinic has laid out for us.

I would add this comment: in *R. v. Malmo-Levine*, [2003] 3 S.C.R. 571, 2003 SCC 74, 179 C.C.C. (3d) 417, 233 D.L.R. (4th) 415, a majority of our Court expressed a preference for social science evidence to be presented through an expert witness who could be cross-examined as to the value and weight to be given to such studies and reports. This is the approach that had been taken by the litigants in *Sharpe*, *Little Sisters*, *Malmo-Levine* itself and subsequently in *Canadian Foundation for Children, Youth and the Law v. Canada (Attorney General)*, [2004] 1 S.C.R. 76, 2004 SCC 4, 180 C.C.C. (3d) 353, 234 D.L.R. (4th) 257. We said in *Malmo-Levine* that

... courts should nevertheless proceed cautiously to take judicial notice even as "legislative facts" of matters ... are reasonably open to dispute, particularly where they relate to an issue that could be dispositive. [para. 28]

The suggestion that even legislative fact and social "facts" should be established by expert testimony rather than reliance on judicial notice was also made in cases as different from one another as *Find*, *Moysa*, *Danson*, at p. 1101, *Symes v. Canada*, [1993] 4 S.C.R. 695, 110 D.L.R. (4th) 470, *Waldick v. Malcolm*, [1991] 2 S.C.R. 456 at pp. 472-73, 83 D.L.R. (4th) 114, *Stoffman v. Vancouver General Hospital*, [1990] 3 S.C.R. 483 at pp. 549-50, 76 D.L.R. (4th) 700, *R. v. Penno*, [1990] 2 S.C.R. 865 at pp. 881-82, 59 C.C.C. (3d) 344, and *MacKay v. Manitoba*, [1989] 2 S.C.R. 357, 61 D.L.R. (4th) 385. Litigants who disregard the suggestion proceed at some risk.

Spence is now the controlling authority on judicial notice. Justice Binnie is clearly at pains to establish principles upon which all issues of judicial notice are to be based. On the one hand, the Court is cautious. The closer any issue is to the dispositive issue, the less scope there is for judicial notice. If the matter relates to adjudicative issues, the strict *Morgan* criteria of notorious or indisputable govern. When it comes to social or legislative facts, the Court opens the door a little wider. However a judge must still ask whether the alleged fact would be accepted by a properly informed reasonable person as not subject to reasonable dispute. This latter test is new. Binnie J. clearly prefers notice to counsel before judicial notice is taken and prefers that social science evidence be presented through experts who can be cross-examined.

These views appear to diverge considerably from those of L'Heureux-Dubé J. we examined earlier. She championed the need for a wide approach to judicial notice to bring social context into the courtroom, saw no distinction between the role of trial or appeal judges, did not stress the distinction between adjudicative and other facts and indicated that it is not necessary to alert counsel as to when judicial notice may be taken. She also wrote that family law matters require an especially generous approach to judicial notice. **Which view do you prefer and why?**

It will be interesting to see whether the Supreme Court extends its new approach to judicial notice to contexts other than criminal matters and whether it will be able to satisfactorily distinguish between adjudicative facts, where there is to be a strict standard for judicial notice, and social and legal facts where there is now a slightly relaxed standard.

In the meantime, trial judges in particular would be well advised to alert counsel as to matters seen to be subject to judicial notice. Alerting counsel requires a delicate balance that must avoid taking on the role of a research director.[48]

---

48 See Doherty J.A. in *R. v. Hamilton* (2004), 186 C.C.C. (3d) 129, 22 C.R. (6th) 1 (Ont. C.A.)..
    Hamilton has been considered earlier in Chapter 3 under "Relevance and Social Context".

CTV TELEVISION v. THE QUEEN [R. v. Hogg]
(2006), 214 C.C.C. (3d) 70, 2006 CarswellMan 372 (C.A.)

The accused pleaded guilty to a vicious and unprovoked aggravated assault that garnered public and media attention. He was sentenced to a conditional sentence. On appeal, the sentenced was varied to three years imprisonment. Given the public and political debate surrounding conditional sentences, W-Five intended to use the case in an upcoming episode. It attempted to obtain a copy of the videotaped statement. Its application was denied. CTV successfully appealed.

MONNIN J.A. (SCOTT C.J.M. and STEEL J.A. concurring): —

The judge's conclusion that the releasing of the videotape would hamper the process of obtaining videotaped statements generally, and therefore hinder the administration of justice, is based, as he himself states, on common sense and logic or judicial experience. He bases his authority for doing so on the decisions of *Harper v. Canada (Attorney General)*, 2004 SCC 33, [2004] 1 S.C.R. 827, and *RJR-MacDonald Inc. v. Canada (Attorney General)*, [1995] 3 S.C.R. 199, 100 C.C.C. (3d) 449.

With respect, I am of the view that in the circumstances of this case, the judge erred when he based his conclusion on common sense and logic alone, without the benefit of real and substantial evidence.

I distinguish the cases that the judge relied on because they only place reliance on common sense and logic after considering some social science evidence. That type of evidence was lacking in the present case. In fact, in this case, the judge had no evidence, let alone social science evidence on which to apply logic and common sense.

Furthermore, the cases on which the judge relied are cases dealing with legislative enactments as opposed to common law rights, and in each case there existed bodies of work or commission reports that the Legislature relied upon prior to enacting the legislation being challenged.

A court in and of its own, without anything further, should not be relying on simple common sense and logic when the effect of a decision is to limit a *Charter* right. The analysis that the judge conducted with respect to the difficulty in having videotaped statements presented in court cannot be the justification for the conclusion that the judge arrives at absent some evidence. That requires a speculative leap of faith that cannot be countenanced.

To a certain degree, the judge could be said to have taken judicial notice of facts he found central to the resolution of the controversy, and in doing so, he erred. This is even more so since the decision of the Supreme Court of Canada in *R. v. Spence*, 2005 SCC 71, [2005] 3 S.C.R. 458, 202 C.C.C. (3d) 1, a case dealing with the racial makeup of juries.

In *Spence*, Binnie J. proceeds to an all-encompassing review of the application of the concept of judicial notice. In his analysis he goes back to the work of Professor James Thayer, who in 1890 laid down a broad approach to judicial notice ("Judicial Notice and the Law of Evidence" (1889-1890), 3 *Harv.*

L. Rev. 285). The analysis encompasses the 2001 Supreme Court decision in *R. v. Find*, 2001 SCC 32, [2001] 1 S.C.R. 863, 154 C.C.C. (3d) 97, which adopted a stricter approach to the reliance on judicial notice. This approach, according to Binnie J. is based on the writings of Professor Edmund M. Morgan, "Judicial Notice" (1943-44), 57 *Harv. L. Rev.* 269.

. . .

In an annotation by Professor Don Stuart published along with *Spence* the decision is summarized in these words (2005 CarswellOnt 6824):

> *Spence* is now the controlling authority on judicial notice. Justice Binnie is clearly at pains to establish principles upon which all issues of judicial notice are to be based. On the one hand the Court is cautious. The closer any matter is to the dispositive issue, the less scope there is for judicial notice. If the matter relates to adjudicative issues, the strict Morgan criteria of notorious or indisputable fact govern. When it comes to social or legislative facts, the Court opens the door a little wider. However, a judge must still ask whether the alleged fact would be accepted by a properly informed reasonable person as not subject to reasonable dispute. This latter test is new.

[The Court quotes from *Spence* where Justice Binnie expresses the Court's preference for social science evidence to be presented even for legislative and "social" facts.]

In the present case, when the judge speaks of "compelling common sense and logic" and "judicial experience" he can only be referring to judicial notice under another name. His reasoning, therefore, must be subject to the restrictions that the Supreme Court has expressed in *Spence*, as well as the evidentiary requirements referred to therein. In this case, there was no evidence that could permit him to link the difficulty courts have had in convincing police services to videotape statements of accused persons with the release of the respondent's videotaped statement, sufficient to displace the presumption of openness of the courts.

The simple fact of this appeal and the Crown's argument in support of the appellant's position demonstrate that reasonable people are debating the accuracy of what the judge concluded as being a fact. As such, that fact cannot be taken judicial notice of, based on the first prong of the Morgan criteria.

Furthermore, if readily accessible sources were available, they were not advanced before the judge. Satisfaction of this criterion would have required the judge to take judicial notice of the existence of such sources, and then make a further inference that these sources confirmed that releasing the videotape would create reluctance to consenting to future videotaping. Simply piling inference upon inference does not satisfy the second prong of the Morgan criteria.

When the judge took judicial notice of the fact that the releasing of the videotape would hinder the producing of videotaped statements before the courts, that conclusion became determinative of the application. Being so central to the issue at hand, the dicta of *Spence* should have been applied and the Morgan criteria should have been adhered to strictly. Neither prong of the Morgan criteria being satisfied, the social fact that releasing the respondent's videotaped statement would deter the producing of videotaped statements before the courts should not have been a fact accepted without proof.

I conclude, therefore, that in the case before us, the judge simply did not have the proper factual foundation or evidence that would have permitted him to come to the conclusion that he did. He was in error when he denied the appellant access to the videotape.

PROBLEMS

Problem 1

How would the *Zundal* case, discussed earlier at note 27, be decided under *Spence*?

Problem 2

In May of 1997, a trial judge listens to a lecture by a psychologist to Family Court judges respecting a "compelling cultural disinclination" for aboriginals to "relive past events of an unpleasant nature." Presiding at a sexual assault trial, he notes that the aboriginal complainant has difficulty in responding to questions. In the course of convicting, he puts the complainant's difficulty down to "cultural disinclination." The accused appeals on the basis that there was no evidence of this put before the Court and the judge was relying on personal knowledge he did not share. Applying *Spence*, should the accused receive a new trial? Compare *R. v. S.(W.)* (1991), 6 C.R. (4th) 373 (Ont. C.A.).

Problem 3

The accused is charged with the wilful promotion of hatred arising from his participation in a demonstration to protest against the entry of Roma refugee claimants into Canada. At the end of the Crown's case, the defence called no evidence and argued that the Crown had failed to prove that there was hatred promoted against "Roma." Counsel argued that the evidence only showed that the actions of the demonstrators were directed toward "gypsies" and that there was no evidence that Roma is the same as "gypsies." The Crown presented the trial judge with five dictionaries that linked "Roma" and "gypsy." The trial judge refused to take judicial notice and acquitted the accused. Is there a ground of appeal? See *R. v. Krymowski*, [2005] 1 S.C.R. 101, 26 C.R. (6th) 207, 193 C.C.C. (3d) 129.

Problem 4

In a sexual assault trial, the only issue was whether the accused was wearing a condom. It was common ground that the accused was not wearing a condom when he ejaculated and that the complainant would never have consented to unprotected sex. The accused maintained that he was wearing a condom but that it had slipped off as he had lost his erection shortly before ejaculating. The trial judge convicted, in part, on the basis that "A virile young man with a full erection bound on having a climax would not lose his erection." Is this a matter of the judge taking judicial notice? If so, did the judge comply with *Spence*? Compare *R. v. Perkins* (2007), 51 C.R. (6th) 116 (Ont. C.A.).

Problem 5

The accused was convicted of breaking and entering into a dwelling house in a small community. He was sentenced to 30 months imprisonment. In her reasons, the trial judge stated:

> This week and last I have had to sentence many young people for break and entries and break and entries are on the rise and it is a very serious matter in King's County. It is a really big problem and people do not seem to understand the significance of other person's property and people who are inclined to commit these kinds of offences need to be deterred. We have a problem with this . . .

Neither the Crown nor defence had made submissions with respect to the issue of prevalence and deterrence. Are there any grounds of appeal? See *R. v. Mallory* (2004), 25 C.R. (6th) 182, 189 C.C.C. (3d) 345 (N.B. C.A.); and *R. v. Priest* (1996), 110 C.C.C. (3d) 289, 1 C.R. (5th) 275 (Ont. C.A.). But see also the reasoning in *R. v. Knoshnow*, [2005] A.J. No. 1812, 2005 CarswellAlta 1944 (Q.B.); and *R. v. Calderwood*, [1995] B.C.J. No. 625, 1995 CarswellBC 2543 (C.A.). Are these cases still good law after *Spence*?

(d) Judicial Notice of Law

Professor Morgan well described the process of judicially noticing law and distinguished it from judicially noticing fact:

> In any lawsuit the litigants may be in disagreement as to the tenor of an applicable rule of domestic law, or as to the applicability of an unquestioned rule, or as to the facts, or as to two or more of these. A dispute as to the tenor or applicability of a rule of domestic law must be resolved by the judge; a dispute as to the facts is ordinarily decided by the jury in a court of common law, by the judge in a court of equity. The process of resolving the former is quite different from that of deciding the latter.
>
> The judge is charged with the duty of knowing the domestic law. If he does not have the requisite knowledge, he must acquire it. Knowledge of the domestic law, or the capacity to acquire it, is part of his equipment for the office. The same is true as to his knowledge of the applicability of a rule of law to a given state of facts. The assumption that he has such knowledge is imperative. If he lacks it, or any element of it, what he has must serve for what he ought to have. The defects, if any, of a trial judge may be cured or corrected by the judges of the appellate courts; those of the judges of the court of last resort must be assumed not to exist.
>
> In determining the content or applicability of a rule of domestic law, the judge is unrestricted in his investigation and conclusion. He may reject the propositions of either party or of both parties. He may consult the sources of pertinent data to which they refer, or he may refuse to do so. He may make an independent search for persuasive data or rest content with what he has or what the parties present. He may reach a conclusion in accord with the overwhelming weight of available data or against it. If he is a trial judge, his conclusion is subject to review. If he is a judge of a court of last resort and the majority of its members agree with him, his conclusion is final though contrary to the contentions of the parties and to theretofore accepted postulates, principles, and rules. In all this he is entitled to the assistance of the parties and their counsel, for he is acting for the sole purpose of reaching a proper

solution of their controversy. But the parties do no more than to assist; they control no part of the process.

In describing the exercise of the judge's functions as to domestic law, it is commonly said that the judge takes judicial notice of the law, and, subject to the operation of the doctrine of invited error, is bound to do so. No fault can be found with this phraseology. It describes the qualification of a judge, distinguishing what he must be assumed to know from what he may actually know. It connotes the process by which he may make the assumption a fact. Both the assumption and the process are necessary concomitants of our system of administering justice. The judicial office in our system cannot be rationally administered on any other premise.[49]

The common law position requiring the court to judicially notice domestic common and statute law has been supplemented by a variety of statutory enactments and some examples follow:

Canada Evidence Act[50]

17. Judicial notice shall be taken of all Acts of the Imperial Parliament, of all ordinances made by the Governor in Council, or the lieutenant governor in council of any province or colony that, or some portion of which, now forms or hereafter may form part of Canada, and of all the Acts of the legislature of any such province or colony, whether enacted before or after the passing of the *British North America Act, 1867*.

18. Judicial notice shall be taken of all Acts of the Parliament of Canada, public or private, without being specially pleaded.

Criminal Code[51]

781.(1) No order, conviction or other proceeding shall be quashed or set aside, and no defendant shall be discharged, by reason only that evidence has not been given

(a) of a proclamation or order of the Governor in Council or the lieutenant governor in council;

(b) of rules, regulations or by-laws, made by the Governor in Council under an Act of the Parliament of Canada or by the lieutenant governor in council under an Act of the legislature of the province; or

(c) of the publication of a proclamation, order, rule, regulation or by-law in the *Canada Gazette* or in the official gazette for the province.

(2) Proclamations, orders, rules, regulations and by-laws mentioned in subsection (1) and the publication thereof shall be judicially noticed.

The Interpretation Act (Ontario)[52]

7.(1) Every Act shall be judicially noticed by judges, justices of the peace and others without being specially pleaded.

(2) Every proclamation shall be judicially noticed by judges, justices of the peace and others without being specially pleaded.

---

49 Morgan, "Judicial Notice" (1944), 57 Harv. L. Rev. 269 at 270-72.
50 R.S.C. 1985, c. C-5, ss. 17,18.
51 R.S.C. 1985, c. C-46, s. 781.
52 R.S.O. 1980, c. 219, s. 7.

Delegated legislation will frequently not have the notoriety or accessibility needed for judicial notice and will need to be proved as a fact.[53] Statutory provisions in each of the provinces and in the federal sphere ease the manner of their proof. For example, in Ontario, the Municipal Act[54] provides:

> **129.**(4) A copy of a by-law purporting to be certified by the clerk, under the seal of the corporation, as a true copy, shall be received in evidence in all courts without proof of the seal or signature.

And in the *Canada Evidence Act*:[55]

> **33.**(1) No proof shall be required of the handwriting or official position of any person certifying, in pursuance of this Act, to the truth of any copy of or extract from any proclamation, order, regulation, appointment, book or other document.

R. v. SMITH
[1988] O.J. No. 2551

Harris Prov. Ct. J. (orally):—

The short issue here is whether a municipal by-law, or a certified copy thereof, must be an Exhibit at a trial or may the party propounding it merely refer to it, or to a certified copy thereof, and ask the Court to take judicial notice thereof.

The argument in favour of judicial notice is as follows:

> Section 7, subsection (1) of the Interpretation Act, R.S.O. 1980, c. 219, provides that every Act shall be judicially noticed by judges, justices of the peace and others without being specially pleaded.

Section 30, subsection (1) of the Interpretation Act provides that in every Act the word "Act" includes "enactment. . . . So, a municipal by-law is an "enactment"; an "enactment" is included within the meaning of the term "Act"; judicial notice shall be taken of an Act, and therefore of an enactment, and therefore of a municipal by-law.

The argument in favour of entering as an Exhibit is as follows:

> Rogers on Municipal Law, paragraph 82 says it must be so entered and refers to Snelling; [1952] O.W.N. 2142, unless a statute otherwise directs: Priest (1955), 16 W.W.R. 556, at 558. The judicial notice proponents say that there is such statutory direction.

Mr. Justice Barlow in Snelling says, briefly, only that he has carefully perused the case law and is satisfied judicial notice cannot be taken. Unfortunately, he does not cite any of the case law to which he refers, nor does it appear that the Interpretation Act was argued to him.

---

53 See *R. v. Snelling*, [1952] O.W.N. 214 (H.C.). Compare *R. v. Clark* (1974), 3 O.R. (2d) 716 (C.A.). See also *R. v. Jahn*, [1982] 3 W.W.R. 684 (Alta. C.A.) and *R. v. Lum*, [1982] 3 W.W.R. 694 (B.C. Co. Ct.).

54 R.S.O. 1980, c. 302. See also, regarding the currency of the certificate, *R. v. Bleta*, [1966] 2 O.R. 108 (C.A.). And see *R. v. Clark* (1974), 1 O.R. (2d) 210 (H.C.).

55 R.S.C. 1985, c. C-5, s. 33(1).

I have concluded that the case law notwithstanding, the section 7 statutory argument is compelling, even though accepting it means a departure from long established practice. In my opinion that practice rests on flimsy foundations unsupported by ascertainable authority, whereas the statutory authority is clear and unambiguous.

However, because of the absence of any authoritative and easily available printed by-laws, similar to the R.S.O. or the R.R.O., it would be well if counsel for the prosecuting municipality would file with the Court at the trial, not the whole by-law but a certified copy of the relevant section or sections of the by-law, as amended, together with the enacting clause, penalty clause or clauses, and date or dates of passage — whether this be marked as an Exhibit or not, or merely become part of the record, should be left to the ruling of the trial judge or justice.

But contra, *Grand Central Ottawa Ltd. v. Ottawa (City).*[56]

The court must judicially notice domestic law because the court is expected to have knowledge of the same by the nature of the office. The court is not expected to know foreign law and the same must therefore be proved by evidence, by the testimony of experts. In *Lazard Brothers & Co. v. Midland Bank Ltd.*[57] the issue was whether by Soviet law a certain bank, on a certain day, was an existing juristic person. Lord Wright wrote:

> What the Russian Soviet Law is in that respect is a question of fact, of which the English Court cannot take judicial cognizance, even though the foreign law has already been proved before it in another case. The Court must act upon the evidence before it in the actual case. . . . The evidence it is clear must be that of qualified experts in the foreign law. If the law is contained in a code or written form, the question is not as to the language of the written law, but what the law is as shown by its exposition, interpretation and adjudication. . . . if there be a conflict of evidence of the experts, "you (the judge) must decide as well as you can on the conflicting testimony, but you must take the evidence from the witnesses." Hence the Court is not entitled to construe a foreign code itself: it has not "organs to know and to deal with the text of that law." . . . The text of the foreign law if put in evidence by the experts may be considered, if at all, only as part of the evidence and as a help to decide between conflicting expert testimony.[58]

In an earlier decision in the Supreme Court of Canada, Duff J. wrote with regard to the expert witnesses:

> . . . if the evidence of such witnesses is conflicting or obscure the Court may go a step further and examine and construe the passages cited for itself in order to arrive at a satisfactory conclusion.[59]

But in *Drew Brown Ltd. v. The Orient Trader,*[60] Laskin, J., relying on *Allen v. Hay,* wrote:

---

56 (1998), 39 O.R. (3d) 47 (Ont. Prov. Div.).

57 [1933] A.C. 289 (H.L.).

58 *Ibid.,* at pp. 297-98.

59 *Allen v. Hay* (1922), 69 D.L.R. 193, 195 (S.C.C.). See also *Bondholders Securities Corp. v. Manville (No. 2),* [1935] 1 W.W.R. 452 (Sask. C.A.).

60 (1972), 34 D.L.R. (3d) 339, 366 (S.C.C.).

[The expert's] evidence was that the weight of authority accorded with the view he expressed, and I do not think it is open to me to re-examine all the authorities to see if they, on balance . . . support his evidence. At the most, I may look to his sources to see if his reliance on them is borne out.

An example of the strictness with which Canadian courts demand proof of foreign law may be seen in *Walkerville Brewing Co. v. Mayrand.*[61] The trial judge had dismissed plaintiff's action and in doing so had found that there existed in Ontario the business of exporting liquor from Canada to the United States "in contravention of the constitution and laws of that country." The Ontario Court of Appeal set the judgment aside, saying:

One country does not take judicial notice of the laws of another, but, like any other fact, they must be proved. In this case there is no evidence of any law making the importation of liquor into the United States unlawful. There may be no moral doubt of the existence of such a law, and every one may know — or thinks he knows — of its existence, but Courts require legal evidence of material facts.[62]

B. *REAL EVIDENCE*

1. AUTHENTICATION

Wigmore distinguished the three modes by which a trier may acquire knowledge: testimonial evidence, circumstantial evidence, and real evidence:

If, for example, it is desired to ascertain whether the accused has lost his right hand and wears an iron hook in place of it, one source of belief on the subject would be the testimony of a witness who had seen the arm; in believing this testimonial evidence, there is an inference from the human assertion to the fact asserted. A second source of belief would be the mark left on some substance grasped or carried by the accused; in believing this circumstantial evidence, there is an inference from the circumstance to the thing producing it. A third source of belief remains, namely, the *inspection by the tribunal* of the accused's arm. This source differs from the other two in omitting any step of conscious inference or reasoning, and in proceeding by direct self-perception, or autopsy. . . . From the point of view of the litigant party furnishing the source of belief, it may be termed *autoptic proference.*[63]

His term "autoptic proference" has not gained much acceptance and the third source of belief is commonly referred to in England and Canada as real evidence.[64] The types or kinds of real evidence are infinitely variable and may affect any of the senses. Here we are content to explore some general principles applicable to all.

To be receivable, real evidence must of course be relevant and it will only be relevant to the matters in issue if the item proffered is identified as genuine, i.e., if the item tendered as an exhibit is authenticated to be what it is represented

---

61 [1929] 2 D.L.R. 945 (Ont. C.A.).

62 *Ibid.*, at p. 946. Compare *Saxby v. Fulton*, [1909] 2 K.B. 208, 221 (C.A.) where the English Court of Appeal was prepared to assume that playing roulette was lawful in Monte Carlo.

63 4 Wigmore, *Evidence* (Chad. Rev.), s. 1150, p. 322.

64 See generally Nokes, "Real Evidence" (1949), 65 L.Q.R. 57. McCormick, *Evidence* (2d ed., 1972), at p. 524 notes that "it will be seen variously referred to as real, autoptic, demonstrative, tangible, and objective.".

to be by its proponent. In a prosecution for assault causing bodily harm, a blood-stained shirt is not relevant evidence unless it is identified as having been worn by the victim on the evening of the altercation. There are functions here for both the judge and the jury. The judge must be satisfied that there is sufficient evidence introduced to permit a rational finding by the jury that the item is as claimed; the jury then weighs the evidence and determines whether the item is authentic.

This process, and the division of labours, may be illustrated by *R. v. Parsons*.[65] The accused were charged with conspiracy to use forged documents as if they were genuine. The prosecution's case was entirely dependent upon evidence obtained by the interception of private telephone communications. The interception was purportedly in accord with an authorization given by a judge pursuant to the provisions of the Criminal Code. For such evidence to be received, the trial judge must be satisfied that the authorization was valid, that the investigation authorized was carried out in the manner provided therein, that the authorization allowed the intercept of the parties to the particular conversation and that notice of an intention to introduce such evidence was given to the opponent; these conditions are set by statute and the trial judge must be satisfied with their compliance on a *voir dire*. The trial judge in this case was persuaded as well that he must also be satisfied that the voice was that of the party. On appeal, Dubin J.A. for the court wrote:

> The determination of whether the statutory conditions precedent have been fulfilled rests exclusively with the trial Judge and are properly determined in a *voir dire*.
>
> Once the statutory conditions have been met, what the Crown must show is that the intercepted private communications are those of the person against whom it is tendered and accurately reproduce his words. The Crown's proof as to the integrity of the tape, its accuracy, its continuity, and voice identification, and that there has been no tampering nor alterations in any way all relate to the proof that the evidence tendered is an accurate reproduction of what it is alleged the person against whom it is tendered said. The weight to be given to that evidence is for the jury, and the admissibility of such evidence is not subject to any statutory conditions precedent, and should be dealt with in the same manner as any other issues of fact, which arise in every jury trial.
>
> In *Cross on Evidence,* 4th ed., p. 61, the following appears:
>
>> The question whether the maker of a dying declaration was under a settled hopeless expectation of death, a condition precedent to its admissibility at a trial for homicide, should on principle be decided by the judge. By way of contrast, the question whether a tape-recording was the original, being one which must ultimately be determined by the jury, *the judge need do no more than decide whether there is sufficient evidence to leave the issue to it.* [Emphasis added].
>
> Counsel for the respondent Charette forcefully urged that the issue of voice identification went to the lawfulness of the interception, a view apparently shared by the trial Judge. He submitted that the lawfulness of an intercepted private communication, and hence the admissibility of evidence of an intercepted private communication, depended, *inter alia,* on whether those persons identified in the authorization are those same persons who are identified as having been intercepted,

---

65 (1977), 37 C.C.C. (2d) 497 (Ont. C.A.); affirmed (*sub nom. Charette v. R.*) (1980), 51 C.C.C. (2d) 350 (S.C.C.).

and hence (voice identification) is not simply a question of fact for the trier of fact, but is part of the larger question, *i.e.*, the lawfulness of the interception. It followed, in his submission, that it was a matter initially for the trial Judge who had to be satisfied on this issue beyond a reasonable doubt before the evidence could be left with the jury. With respect, however, I do not agree.[66]

The court was properly critical of the extent of the *voir dire* conducted as it tended to usurp the function of the jury. The Evidence Code proposed by the Law Reform Commission of Canada suggested:

> When the relevancy of evidence depends upon its authenticity or identity, the requirement of authentication or identification is satisfied by evidence sufficient to support a finding that the matter in question is what its proponent claims.[67]

In the absence of agreement of counsel, real evidence, whether this be the gun, the drugs, a photograph or a letter, must be tendered through witnesses and be authenticated. There is no set procedure or questions that must be asked. The usual steps for counsel seeking to tender a piece of real evidence are:

1. call a witness with personal knowledge of the object,
2. ask the witness to describe the object before showing it to the witness,
3. allow the witness to examine and identify it as genuine, and
4. task that the object be entered as an exhibit, with an appropriate stamp applied by the clerk.

Sometimes the witness will not be able to identify the object as that previously seen. In such cases the accepted practice is to have it marked as an "exhibit for identification". Hopefully there will be a later witness to call who can properly authenticate it so that it can then be marked as an exhibit as a piece of evidence in the case. If entered as an exhibit in jury trials the jury is usually allowed to take the exhibits into the jury room during their deliberations.[68] In *R. v. Patterson,*[69] Gillese J.A. held that it is within the trial judge's discretion as to whether exhibits go to the jury:

> It was open to the trial judge to permit the videotape to go to the jury room during deliberations. This was a matter within his discretion and there is no basis to suggest he erred in law. The trial judge was not required to depart from the general practice of giving the jury all exhibits whenever feasible. He heard submissions on the issue and declined to adopt the suggestion that the video go to the jury only if they requested it. He was entitled to reach this decision. The trial judge was correct in his assessment that any concern about potential misuse of the video could be avoided by clear cautionary instructions and he gave those instructions. *R. v. Pleich* (1980), 55 C.C.C. (2d) 13 at 32-33 (Ont. C.A.).

An important part of authentication, particularly in drug cases, is the issue of continuity. **Is this an issue of weight or admissibility?** The current law respecting proof of continuity was reviewed by Owen-Flood J. in *R. v. MacPherson:*[70]

---

66 *Ibid.*, at p. 502 (37 C.C.C.).
67 1975, s. 46.
68 See further Lee Stuesser, *An Advocacy Primer* (3rd ed., 2005) pp. 227-232.
69 (2003), 174 C.C.C. (3d) 193 (Ont. C.A.).
70 [2005] B.C.J. No. 575, 2005 CarswellBC 610 (S.C.).

There were a number of problems relating to the continuity of the evidence in this case. Unfortunately, Cst. Banky, the exhibits officer assigned to this case, died unexpectedly in October 2003. Because Cst. Banky could not testify at trial, there is a break in the continuity of the evidence. No alternate evidence as to the chain of custody of the real evidence was proferred by the Crown.

The extent to which the Crown proves the continuity of real evidence in a narcotics case, and whether or not breaks in continuity makes evidence inadmissible are questions of fact for the trier of fact to decide. Breaks in the chain of continuity reduce the weight which can be given to the proferred evidence: *R. v. Andrade* (1985), 18 C.C.C. (3d) 41 (Ont. C.A.). In *R. v. Larsen*, [2001] B.C.J. No. 824, 2001 BCSC 597, aff'd on other grounds, [2003] B.C.J. No. 45, 2003 BCCA 18, Romilly J. held as follows:

> It is important to appreciate what the Crown must prove in a narcotics-related case. In essence, the Crown must show beyond a reasonable doubt that the material seized from an accused was a prohibited substance. To that end, the Crown must prove that the substance dealt with by, or in the possession of, the accused is the same substance that is alleged in the information or indictment (and prohibited by law). Undoubtedly, then, continuity of possession of the substance from the accused to the law enforcement officer to the analyst is crucial. However, Canadian case law makes it clear that proof of continuity is not a legal requirement and that gaps in continuity are not fatal to the Crown's case unless they raise a reasonable doubt about the exhibit's integrity. See *R. v. Dawdy and Lamoureaux* (1971), 4 C.C.C. (2d) 122 (Ont. C.A.); *R. v. Oracheski* (1979), 48 C.C.C. (2d) 217 (Alta. C.A.), *R. v. DeGraaf* (1981), 60 C.C.C. (2d) 315 (B.C.C.A.); and *R. v. Taylor* (1988), 93 N.B.R. (2d) 246 (N.B.Q.B.). These cases establish there is no duty upon the Crown to show detailed continuity of the location and handling of the exhibits from the time of their seizure by law enforcement officers to their deposit with analysts.[71]

PROBLEMS

Problem 1

The plaintiff is suing a manufacturer for damages. Plaintiff claims that a tool manufactured by defendant was defective in its design and as a result plaintiff was hurt. Plaintiff seeks to tender into evidence the tool so that the jury might examine the same and observe first hand the design. How should plaintiff go about authenticating the tool?

Problem 2

RCMP officers commenced a drug investigation known as "Project Entomology" in Surrey, B.C. It was very successful and ended with the arrest of a number of individuals, and the seizure of 69 kilograms of cocaine and 33.5 pounds of marijuana. One of the accused is charged with trafficking cocaine on four occasions to Constable Robertson. According to the evidence, Constable S received four cocaine exhibits from Constable R that were purportedly the drugs sold to her by the accused. Sidh weighed each one and put each into a plastic baggie and then put his number and date on the baggie. He then put the baggies

---

71 See also *R. v. Wilder*, [2002] B.C.J. No. 2110, 2002 BCSC 1333.

into a standard "H" envelope. What happened next was set out in the following trial testimony of S:

> A. Once it's placed in the exhibit locker it's the responsibility of the exhibit custodians to further those exhibits, if they are deemed necessary, for analysis.
>
> Q. And is that the standard procedure?
>
> A. That is my understanding of the procedure.
>
> Q. And you placed these in the exhibit locker on what day?
>
> A. On the 25th.
>
> Q. Okay. And you subsequently received back a corresponding certificate of analysis, right?
>
> A. That's correct.
>
> Q. And them some time later, you were requested to resubmit the exhibit; is that correct?
>
> A. That's correct.
>
> Q. And you did so at the request of the Crown; is that right?
>
> A. I did so, yes.
>
> Q. And do you recall the reason for the request to resubmit the exhibits?
>
> A. I believe there was some form of discrepancy with the individual that actually performed the original analysis.

Constable S then described taking "the contents or what was remaining of the contents" from the original envelopes, and weighing them and resubmitting them in new "H" envelopes. The test results revealed that the baggies contained cocaine. You are defence counsel. What submissions will you make? See *R. v. Fehr*, [2000] B.C.J. No. 2660 (S.C.J.), aff. [2000] B.C.J. No. 2660 (C.A.); and *R. v. DeGraaf* (1981), 60 C.C.C. (3d) 315 (B.C. C.A.).

Problem 3

The accused is charged with murder. The Crown proposes to introduce certain letters allegedly written by the accused while he was remanded in custody; these letters are highly incriminating. The Crown has sought your advice as to how he might authenticate these letters. Advise. Are there alternative techniques? See *Pitre v. R.*, [1933] 1 D.L.R. 417 (S.C.C.) and *R. v. Adam*, [2006] B.C.J. No. 2615 (S.C.).

2. PHOTOGRAPHS AND VIDEOTAPES

Professor Wigmore preferred to regard photographs and recordings as a form of non-verbal testimony.[72] He wrote:

> . . . a document purporting to be a map or diagram is, for evidential purposes, simply *nothing, except so far as it has a human being's credit to support it.* It is mere waste paper — testimonial nonentity. . . . We must somehow put a testimonial human being

---

72 See 4 Wigmore, *Evidence* (Chad. Rev.), s. 1156.

behind it (as it were) before it can be treated as having any testimonial standing in court. It is *somebody's testimony*, or it is nothing. . . . But whenever such a document is offered as proving *a thing to be as therein represented*, then it is offered testimonially and it *must be associated with a testifier*. . . . Upon like principles a photograph may be admissible as the testimony of a qualified witness who instead of verbalizing his knowledge of what the picture portrays, adopts it as a substitute for description with words.[73]

He relied on the early English decision of *R. v. Tolson*,[74] where Willes, J. described the process:

The photograph was admissible because it is only a visible representation of the image or impression made upon the minds of the witnesses by the sight of the person or the object it represents; and, therefore is, in reality, only another species of the evidence which persons give of identity, when they speak merely from memory.

For Wigmore two consequences followed:

On the one hand, the mere picture or map itself cannot be received except as a nonverbal expression of the *testimony of some witness* competent to speak to the facts represented. On the other hand, it is *immaterial whose hand prepared the thing*, provided it is presented to the tribunal by a competent witness as a representation of his knowledge.[75]

R. v. SCHAFFNER
(1988), 44 C.C.C. (3d) 507 (N.S.C.A.)

MATTHEWS J.A. (PACE and CHIPMAN JJ.A. concurring):— After a lengthy trial, on February 2, 1988, His Honour Judge John R. Nichols found the appellant guilty of stealing moneys between February 27, 1987 and April 10, 1987, the property of the Nova Scotia Liquor Commission, of a value not exceeding $1,000.00, contrary to s. 294(*b*)(ii) of the *Criminal Code*.

. . . .

Between May, 1986 and April 10, 1987, the appellant was employed as a clerk at the Middleton store of the Liquor Commission. Due to inordinately high shortages there, the Commission conducted an internal investigation and then the matter was turned over to the Middleton town police. They requested that the Commission use its video surveillance equipment. During the *voir dire* in respect to the admissibility of the videotapes John Nield, in charge of security for the commission, testified that he directed the installation of that equipment in the attic of the store immediately above one of the cash registers. Prior to joining the Commission Nield was a member of the R.C.M.P. and had used such equipment while with the force.

The evidence disclosed that attached to the video cassette recorder were a time/date generator and a tape stacker. The generator imprinted directly on the videotape the date in day, month and year, and the time in hour, minute and

---

73 3 Wigmore, *Evidence* (Chad. Rev.), s. 790. Regarding x-ray photographs see *id.*, at s. 795.
74 (1864), 176 E.R. 488 (Surrey Assizes).
75 4 Wigmore, *Evidence* (Chad. Rev.), s. 1156, p. 218.

second. The stacker held three tapes, each of which provided four and a half hours of recording and automatically ejected a recorded tape and inserted another tape in the machine. There was no operator present during the filming, the procedure was automatic. Once installed Nield determined that it was functioning properly. Frank Cress, the manager of the store, was instructed in the use of the equipment and to keep accurate notations of the videotapes. The equipment was operated during business hours between February 23 and April 10, 1987. When a day's recording had been completed, the tapes were collected by Cress and forwarded to Kenneth Cole, the regional supervisor for the commission. They were then viewed by Nield, Cole and Detective Brown. During the *voir dire* Nield showed and commented upon four tapes depicting irregularities on the part of the appellant in conjunction with the detailed cash-register tape for each particular day under study. Nield was able to match a particular transaction recorded on videotape with its corresponding notation on the cash register tape. He was able to properly identify the appellant and pointed out four separate irregularities in the handling of cash by the appellant amounting to a total of $23.

It was over the objection of appellant's counsel that the trial judge ruled that the tapes were admissible in evidence. The appellant now says that the trial judge erred in law in doing so. Briefly put, the appellant's submission is that a photograph is not admissible by itself. It must be verified on oath by a witness as to its accuracy and fairness. He urges that the same principles should apply in determining the admissibility of films or videotapes. He quoted from the interesting and informative article by Elliott Goldstein, "Photographic and Videotape Evidence in the Criminal Courts of England and Canada", [1987] Crim. L.R. 384, p. 386:

> A photograph may be authenticated by
>
> > (a) the photographer;
> > (b) a person present when the photograph was taken;
> > (c) a person qualified to state that the representation is accurate; or,
> > (d) an expert witness.
>
> Witnesses in categories one and two, who see the event as it is being photographed, are eye-witnesses. An eye-witness testifies to two things: (a) what he saw, from memory, and (b) whether what he sees in a courtroom in the photograph, is the same as what his memory tells him he saw at the scene. Witnesses in categories three and four are not eye-witnesses, but can still authenticate a photograph either because of their familiarity with its subject matter or their knowledge of the operation of the equipment that produced it.

The issue of the admissibility of evidence at trial is a question of law and thus properly before us.

A photograph is admissible in evidence if it accurately represents the facts, is not tendered with the intention to mislead and is verified on oath by a person capable to do so. . . . I agree with Judge O Hearn that "This can be proved by anybody who is able to attest to those qualities . . .": *R. v. Lorde and Johnson* (1978), 33 N.S.R. (2d) 376 at p. 378 (N.S. Co. Ct.).

Here Nield described the equipment used, where it was located, the reasons why it was so located, that it was operating properly, and how the detailed cash register tape matched the video. As earlier mentioned he testified that he had used similar equipment as a member of the R.C.M.P.

The trial judge in determining the admissibility of the videotapes considered the appropriate factors, and was satisfied as to the quality of the tapes. We are unanimously of the opinion that those tapes were properly "authenticated" and that the trial judge did not err in law in admitting them into evidence.

R. v. NIKOLOVSKI
[1996] 3 S.C.R. 1197, 3 C.R. (5th) 362, 111 C.C.C. (3d) 403

The accused was convicted of robbing a convenience store. The sole witness, the store clerk, could not identify the accused with any certainty and, when shown a videotape of the robbery during his testimony, did not identify the person in the videotape as the accused. The Crown called no other identification evidence. The trial judge relied on her own comparison between the accused and the robber in the videotape to conclude that the accused was the robber.

CORY J. (LAMER C.J. and LA FOREST, L'HEUREUX-DUBÉ, GONTHIER, MCLACHLIN and IACOBUCCI JJ. concurring):—

Can a videotape alone provide the necessary evidence to enable the trier of fact to identify the accused as the perpetrator of the crime? That is the question that must be resolved on this appeal.

. . . .

The courts have long recognized the frailties of identification evidence given by independent, honest and well-meaning eyewitnesses. This recognized frailty served to emphasize the essential need to cross-examine eyewitnesses. So many factors come into play with the human identification witness. As a minimum it must be determined whether the witness was physically in a position to see the accused and, if so, whether that witness had sound vision, good hearing, intelligence and the ability to communicate what was seen and heard. Did the witness have the ability to understand and recount what had been perceived? Did the witness have a sound memory? What was the effect of fear or excitement on the ability of the witness to perceive clearly and to later recount the events accurately? Did the witness have a bias or at least a biased perception of the event or the parties involved? This foreshortened list of the frailties of eyewitness identification may serve as a basis for considering the comparative strengths of videotape evidence.

It cannot be forgotten that a robbery can be a terrifyingly traumatic event for the victim and witnesses. Not every witness can have the fictional James Bond's cool and unflinching ability to act and observe in the face of flying bullets and flashing knives. Even Bond might have difficulty accurately describing his would be assassin. He certainly might earnestly desire his attacker's conviction and be biased in that direction.

The video camera on the other hand is never subject to stress. Through tumultuous events it continues to record accurately and dispassionately all that comes before it. Although silent, it remains a constant, unbiased witness with instant and total recall of all that it observed. The trier of fact may review the evidence of this silent witness as often as desired. The tape may be stopped and studied at a critical juncture.

So long as the videotape is of good quality and gives a clear picture of events and the perpetrator, it may provide the best evidence of the identity of the perpetrator. It is relevant and admissible evidence that can by itself be cogent and convincing evidence on the issue of identity. Indeed, it may be the only evidence available. For example, in the course of a robbery, every eyewitness may be killed yet the video camera will steadfastly continue to impassively record the robbery and the actions of the robbers. Should a trier of fact be denied the use of the videotape because there is no intermediary in the form of a human witness to make some identification of the accused? Such a conclusion would be contrary to common sense and a totally unacceptable result. It would deny the trier of fact the use of clear, accurate and convincing evidence readily available by modern technology. The powerful and probative record provided by the videotape should not be excluded when it can provide such valuable assistance in the search for truth. In the course of their deliberations, triers of fact will make their assessment of the weight that should be accorded the evidence of the videotape just as they assess the weight of the evidence given by viva voce testimony.

It is precisely because videotape evidence can present such very clear and convincing evidence of identification that triers of fact can use it as the sole basis for the identification of the accused before them as the perpetrator of the crime. It is clear that a trier of fact may, despite all the potential frailties, find an accused guilty beyond a reasonable doubt on the basis of the testimony of a single eyewitness. It follows that the same result may be reached with even greater certainty upon the basis of good quality video evidence. Surely, if a jury had only the videotape and the accused before them, they would be at liberty to find that the accused they see in the box was the person shown in the videotape at the scene of the crime committing the offence. If an appellate court, upon a review of the tape, is satisfied that it is of sufficient clarity and quality that it would be reasonable for the trier of fact to identify the accused as the person in the tape beyond any reasonable doubt then that decision should not be disturbed. Similarly, a judge sitting alone can identify the accused as the person depicted in the videotape.

. . . .

Once it is established that a videotape has not been altered or changed, and that it depicts the scene of a crime, then it becomes admissible and relevant evidence. Not only is the tape (or photograph) real evidence in the sense that that term has been used in earlier cases, but it is to a certain extent, testimonial evidence as well. It can and should be used by a trier of fact in determining whether a crime has been committed and whether the accused before the court committed the crime. It may indeed be a silent, trustworthy, unemotional, unbiased and accurate witness who has complete and instant recall of events. It may provide such strong and convincing evidence that of itself it will demonstrate clearly either the innocence or guilt of the accused.

The weight to be accorded that evidence can be assessed from a viewing of the videotape. The degree of clarity and quality of the tape, and to a lesser extent the length of time during which the accused appears on the videotape, will all go towards establishing the weight which a trier of fact may properly place upon the evidence. The time of depiction may not be significant for even if there are but a few frames which clearly show the perpetrator that may be sufficient to identify the accused. Particularly will this be true if the trier of fact has reviewed the tape on several occasions and stopped it to study the pertinent frames.

Although triers of fact are entitled to reach a conclusion as to identification based solely on videotape evidence, they must exercise care in doing so. For example, when a jury is asked to identify an accused in this manner, it is essential that clear directions be given to them as to how they are to approach this task. They should be instructed to consider carefully whether the video is of sufficient clarity and quality and shows the accused for a sufficient time to enable them to conclude that identification has been proven beyond a reasonable doubt. If it is the only evidence adduced as to identity, the jury should be reminded of this. Further, they should be told once again of the importance that, in order to convict on the basis of the videotape alone, they must be satisfied beyond a reasonable doubt that it identifies the accused.

The jury or trial judge sitting alone must be able to review the videotape during their deliberations. However, the viewing equipment used at that time should be the same or similar to that used during the trial. I would think that very often triers of fact will want to review the tape on more than one occasion.

A trial judge sitting alone must be subject to the same cautions and directions as a jury in considering videotape evidence of identification. It would be helpful if, after reviewing the tape, the trial judge indicated that he or she was impressed with its clarity and quality to the extent that a finding of identity could be based upon it. This courtesy would permit Crown or particularly defence counsel to call, for example, expert evidence as to the quality of the tape or evidence as to any changes in appearance of the accused between the taking of the videotape and the trial and to prepare submissions pertaining to identification based on the tape.

I viewed the tape and it is indeed of excellent quality and great clarity. The accused is depicted for a significant period of time. At one point, it is almost as though there was a close-up of the accused taken specifically for identification purposes. There is certainly more than adequate evidence on the tape itself from which the trial judge could determine whether or not the person before her was the one who committed the robbery. The fact that the store clerk could not identify the accused is not of great significance. When the tape is viewed, it is easy to appreciate that the clerk might not have been able to properly focus upon the identity of the robber. The violent and savagely menacing jab made by the robber with a large knife directed towards the clerk suggests that self-preservation, not identification, may very reasonably have been the clerk's prime concern at the time of the robbery. Yet, the tape remained cool, collected, unbiased and accurate. It provides as clear a picture of the robbery today as it did when the traumatic events took place. The evidence of the tape is of such clarity and strength that it was certainly open to the trial judge to conclude that the accused before her was the person depicted on the tape. The trial judge was aware of the difficulties and frailties of identification evidence and acknowledged them in her reasons. Nonetheless, she was entitled on the evidence before her to conclude beyond a reasonable doubt that the accused was guilty. There was no need for corroboration of this tape.

SOPINKA J. and MAJOR J. dissenting:—

. . . .

It is significant that the judge's observations are entirely untested by cross-examination. Cross-examination in identification is of special importance. Here, not only was there no opportunity to cross-examine, but the substance of the judge's observations was unknown until the case for both the Crown and defence was closed. Not only are the judge's subjective observations not tested by cross-examination but they cannot be tested on appeal. In order to evaluate the reasonableness of the evidence upon which a trier of fact relies, the Court of Appeal must be able to examine all the evidence. All we can do is see one side of a coin that has two sides. All the assurances about the clarity of the video are of no avail if we cannot see the person with whom the comparison is being made.

In summary, this conviction was based on evidence that amounted to no more than the untested opinion of the trial judge which was contradicted by other evidence that the trial judge did not reject. This included evidence that the victim, a few days after the robbery, identified a person other than the accused as the more likely perpetrator of the crime. The trial judge simply relied on her own observations, the accuracy of which we are not in a position to assess. Having regard for the inherent frailties in identification evidence, I conclude that the conviction rests on a shaky foundation and is unsafe and unsatisfactory. I am satisfied that the verdict is unreasonable and cannot be supported by the evidence.[76]

Which opinion do you find more compelling?

PROBLEM

Problem 1

The accused is charged with assault causing bodily harm arising out of an altercation during a hockey game. The prosecution seeks to introduce a videotape taken of the game. Portions of the tape depict the action in slow motion and there are also stop-action shots of the accused striking the victim with his hockey stick.

---

76 In *R. v. K. (T.A.)* (2006), 207 C.C.C. (3d) 547, 2006 CarswellBC 483 (C.A.), a new trial was ordered because of the failure of the trial judge to permit defence counsel an opportunity to make submissions about the quality and content of the videotape.

Defense counsel objects that the tape should not be received as it does not accord with reality. Rule on the objection. Compare *R. v. Maloney (No. 2)* (1976), 29 C.C.C. (2d) 431 (Ont. Co. Ct.).

3. DOCUMENTS

Documents are the most common form of real evidence. Their authenticity may be established by calling the suggested writer, by calling one who saw him write the document or who has an awareness of his handwriting, by direct comparison of the handwriting in dispute with handwriting known to be that of the suggested writer, by the testimony of experts, or by admission of authenticity by the party against whom the document is tendered.

Section 8 of the *Canada Evidence Act* provides:

> Comparison of a disputed writing with any writing proved to the satisfaction of the court to be genuine shall be permitted to be made by witnesses, and such writings, and the evidence of witnesses respecting those writings, may be submitted to the court and jury as proof of the genuineness or otherwise of the writing in dispute.

In *R. v. Abdi*[77] it was held that s. 8 did not preclude a common law option of allowing a jury to compare writing samples without witness testimony. The Court relied on *Nikoloski* but also decided that the jury should be warned to be cautious in reaching a conclusion without expert or witness testimony as to the handwriting. In addition, there are some documents which so regularly have significance in legal proceedings that the common law has developed rules allowing the documents to authenticate themselves because of the circumstances in which they are generated or kept in custody.

Two examples of such rules allowing authentication by circumstantial evidence are those affecting ancient documents and reply letters. If a document is over 30 years old, there are no circumstances indicating fraud, and it is produced from a place where its custody is natural, the circumstances call for it to be presumed authentic; the courts were also moved by the fact that circumstantial evidence would often be necessary as the maker or witnesses might no longer be available.[78] If a letter is received purportedly signed by Smith, the law will presume the letter authentic if it was received in response to an earlier letter; the reply indicates knowledge in the signer which, relying on the habitual accuracy of the mails, could only have come from the earlier letter addressed to Smith.[79] In addition to the rules developed at common law, the various Evidence Acts in Canada and the Criminal Code are filled with provisions to aid the authentication of documents. For example, the *Canada Evidence Act*[80] provides:

> **19.** Every copy of any Act of Parliament, public or private, published by the Queen's Printer, is evidence of that Act and of its contents, and every copy purporting

---

77 (1997), 116 C.C.C. (3d) 385, 11 C.R. (5th) 197 (Ont. C.A.).
78 See *Stevenson v. Dandy*, [1920] 2 W.W.R. 643, 661 (Alta. C.A.).
79 See *Montgomery v. Graham* (1871), 31 U.C.Q.B. 57 (C.A.). Note that the document though authenticated as genuine may still be held inadmissible as violative of the hearsay rule. A hearsay exception for ancient writings deserves further consideration.
80 R.S.C. 1985, c. C-5. And when statutory provisions cannot be satisfied, do not forget the common law: see *R. v. Tatomir* (1989), 51 C.C.C. (3d) 321 (Alta. C.A.).

to be printed by the Queen's Printer shall be deemed to be so printed, unless the contrary is shown.

20. Imperial proclamations, orders in council, treaties, orders, warrants, licences, certificates, rules, regulations, or other Imperial official records, Acts or documents may be proved

(a)   in the same manner as they may from time to time be provable in any court in England;

(b)   by the production of a copy of the *Canada Gazette*, or a volume of the Acts of Parliament purporting to contain a copy of the same or a notice thereof; or

(c)   by the production of a copy thereof purporting to be published by the Queen's Printer.

21. Evidence of any proclamation, order, regulation or appointment, made or issued by the Governor General or by the Governor in Council, or by or under the authority of any minister or head of any department of the Government of Canada and evidence of a treaty to which Canada is a party, may be given in all or any of the following ways:

(a)   by the production of a copy of the *Canada Gazette*, or a volume of the Acts of Parliament purporting to contain a copy of the treaty, proclamation, order, regulation or appointment, or a notice thereof;

(b)   by the production of a copy of the proclamation, order, regulation or appointment, purporting to be published by the Queen's Printer;

(c)   by the production of a copy of the treaty purporting to be published by the Queen's Printer;

(d)   by the production, in the case of any proclamation, order, regulation or appointment made or issued by the Governor General or by the Governor in Council, of a copy or extract purporting to be certified to be true by the clerk or assistant or acting clerk of the Queen's Privy Council for Canada; and

(e)   by the production, in the case of any order, regulation or appointment made or issued by or under the authority of any minister or head of a department of the Government of Canada, of a copy or extract purporting to be certified to be true by the minister, by his deputy or acting deputy, or by the secretary or acting secretary of the department over which he presides.

22. (1) Evidence of any proclamation, order, regulation or appointment made or issued by a lieutenant governor or lieutenant governor in council of any province, or by or under the authority of any member of the executive council, being the head of any department of the government of the province, may be given in all or any of the following ways:

(a)   by the production of a copy of the official gazette for the province purporting to contain a copy of the proclamation, order, regulation or appointment, or a notice thereof;

(b)   by the production of a copy of the proclamation, order, regulation or appointment purporting to be published by the government or Queen's Printer for the province; and

(c)   by the production of a copy or extract of the proclamation, order, regulation or appointment purporting to be certified to be true by the clerk or assistant or acting clerk of the executive council, by the head of any department of the government of a province, or by his deputy or acting deputy, as the case may be.

(2) Evidence of any proclamation, order, regulation or appointment made by the Lieutenant Governor or Lieutenant Governor in Council of the Northwest Territories, as constituted prior to September 1, 1905, or by the Commissioner in Council of the Yukon Territory, the Commissioner in Council of the Northwest Territories or the legislature for Nunavut, may be given by the production of a copy of the *Canada Gazette* purporting to contain a copy of the proclamation, order, regulation or appointment, or a notice thereof.

23. (1) Evidence of any proceeding or record whatever of, in or before any court in Great Britain, the Supreme Court, Federal Court or Tax Court of Canada, any court in any province, any court in any British colony or possession or any court of record of the United States, of any state of the United States or of any other foreign country, or before any justice of the peace or coroner in any province, may be given in any action or proceeding by an exemplification or certified copy of the proceeding or record, purporting to be under the seal of the court or under the hand or seal of the justice or coroner or court stenographer, as the case may be, without any proof of the authenticity of the seal or of the signature of the justice, coroner or court stenographer or other proof whatever.

(2) Where any court, justice, coroner or court stenographer referred to in subsection (1) has no seal, or so certifies, the evidence may be given by a copy purporting to be certified under the signature of a judge or presiding provincial court judge or of the justice or coroner or court stenographer, without any proof of the authenticity of the signature or other proof whatever.

It must be borne in mind that these provisions merely authenticate the writing, merely establish that in fact the statement was made. If the statement is to be introduced to establish the truth of the matter stated, its receivability will be conditioned by the hearsay rule which will be examined later.[81]

4. BEST EVIDENCE RULE

In contrast to the above rules which *facilitate* the proof of a document there is an ancient rule which *requires* that, when the terms of a document are material, proof of the terms of the document must be by production of the original. The documentary originals rule, sometimes called the best evidence rule, existed even before witnesses were called to testify before a jury,[82] but as the new system of inquiry took hold, the rule was retained, as it was seen to be beneficial; production of the original avoided possible errors in copying or in oral evidence regarding the contents. Some text-writers in the 19th century spoke of a wider best evidence rule applicable to *all* forms of evidence which *required* the best evidence that could be given and also *allowed* the best evidence that could be given. Thayer described this as "an old principle which had served a useful purpose for the century while rules of evidence had been forming and . . . was no longer fit to serve any purpose as a working rule of exclusion."[83] Restricting the rule's use to documents, perhaps jettisoning its use completely in favour of the name "documentary originals rule," would bring needed clarity. As opposed to a general rule of exclusion for the other forms of real evidence, we would have then simply

---

81 See Lester, "The Rules of Evidence Governing Cross-Examination Based on Documents: A Practical Guide" (1996), 18 Advocates' Quarterly 261.

82 Thayer, *A Preliminary Treatise on Evidence at the Common Law* (1898), p. 503.

83 *Ibid.*, at p. 495.

the application of common sense that the failure to produce the best evidence available to the proponent might yield a distrust for the evidence that was produced. As Lord Denning put it:

> . . . the old rule that a party must produce the best evidence that the nature of the case will allow, and that any less good evidence is to be excluded. That old rule has gone by the board long ago. The only remaining instance of it that I know is that if an original document is available in one's hands, one must produce it. One cannot give secondary evidence by producing a copy. Nowadays we do not confine ourselves to the best evidence. We admit all relevant evidence. The goodness or badness of it goes only to weight, and not to admissibility.[84]

The documentary originals rule requires production of the original unless the proponent is unable to do so. Secondary evidence may be introduced if the proponent can satisfy the court that the original is lost or destroyed or is in the possession of another and cannot be obtained.[85]

In *R. v. Betterest Vinyl Manufacturing Ltd.*[86] Justice Taggart wrote for the B.C. Court of Appeal:

> As I read the textwriters and the authorities we are no longer bound to apply strictly the best evidence rule as it relates to copies of documents and especially photocopies of them. . . An over-technical and strained application of the best evidence rule served only to hamper the inquiry without at all advancing the cause of truth.[87]

In addition, various statutory provisions have been enacted to provide for the introduction of copies when to require the original would produce great inconvenience. For example, section 29 of the *Canada Evidence Act*[88] provides for the receipt of copies of entries in bankers' books, section 30(3) for copies of records made in the usual and ordinary course of business, and section 31(2)(*c*) for copies of records belonging to or deposited with any government or corporation there defined.

R. v. COTRONI

(1977), 37 C.C.C. (2d) 409 (Ont. C.A.), affirmed (*sub nom. Papalia v. R.*)
[1979] 2 S.C.R. 256, 45 C.C.C. (2d) 1, (*sub nom. R. v. Swartz*) 7 C.R. (3d)
185, 11 C.R. (3d) 150

The accused were charged with conspiracy to possess money obtained by extortion.

---

84   *Garton v. Hunter*, [1969] 1 All E.R. 451, 453 (C.A.). Followed in *Kajala v. Noble* (1982), 75 Cr. App. R. 149, 152 (C.A.) per Arkner, L.J.: "In our judgment the old rule is limited and confined to written documents in the strict sense of the term, and has no relevance to tapes or films." See also *R. v. Donald* (1958), 121 C.C.C. 304, 306 (N.B.C.A.) and *R. v. Galarce* (1983), 35 C.R. (3d) 268 (Sask. Q.B.).

85   See, *e.g.*, *R. v. Wayte* (1983), 76 Cr. App. R. 110.

86   (1989) 52 C.C.C. (3d) 441.

87   At 447-448.

88   R.S.C. 1985, c. C-5.

JESSUP J.A. (ARNUP and ZUBER JJ.A. concurring):—

. . . .

The only evidence incriminating Violi and Cotroni, and essential evidence against Swartz and Papalia, consisted of the tape recordings of three conversations which took place in premises at Montreal. The recordings proffered in evidence were re-recordings. The explanation for this was that, after re-recording, the original recordings had been erased and the tapes of them reused. The reason was that at that time it was not the practice of the Montreal police to use tape recordings as evidence in Court. The further reason was that electronic surveillance of the premises in Montreal had extended over a protracted period and the storage of the many resultant tapes presented a problem. As a result, a record only of significant conversations was kept by re-recording such significant parts on fresh tapes which were preserved.

It was argued that the re-recordings proffered were inadmissible as not being the best evidence of the conversations they reproduced. However, counsel made the significant admission that no question was raised as to the authenticity of the re- recordings.

Of the "best evidence" rule Halsbury states in 17 Hals., 4th ed., pp. 8-9, para. 8:

> That evidence should be the best that the nature of the case will allow is, besides being a matter of obvious prudence, a principle with a considerable pedigree. However, any strict interpretation of this principle has long been obsolete, and the rule is now only of importance in regard to the primary evidence of private documents. The logic of requiring the production of an original document where it is available rather than relying on possibly unsatisfactory copies, or the recollections of witnesses, is clear, although modern techniques make objections to the first alternative less strong.

The rule itself, in its relatively modern form, did not absolutely exclude evidence. It is stated by Lord Esher, M.R., in *Lucas v. Williams & Sons*, [1892] 2 Q.B. 113 at p. 116:

> "Primary" and "secondary" evidence mean this: primary evidence is evidence which the law requires to be given first; secondary evidence is evidence which may be given in the absence of the better evidence which the law requires to be given first, when a proper explanation is given of the absence of that better evidence.

Lord Denning would remove the question of secondary evidence entirely from the area of admissibility to that of weight. In *Garton v. Hunter*, [1969] 2 Q.B. 37 at p. 44 he said:

> It is plain that Scott L.J. had in mind the old rule that a party must produce the best evidence that the nature of the case will allow, and that any less good evidence is to be excluded. That old rule has gone by the board long ago. The only remaining instance of it that I know is that if an original document is available in your hands, you must produce it. You cannot give secondary evidence by producing a copy. Nowadays we do not confine ourselves to the best evidence. We admit all relevant evidence. The goodness or badness of it goes only to weight, and not to admissibility.

However, the counsel of prudence mentioned by Halsbury accords with the principle stated by McCormick's Handbook of the Law of Evidence, 2nd ed. (1972), p. 571:

> If the original document has been destroyed by the person who offers evidence of its contents, the evidence is not admissible unless, by showing that the destruction was accidental or was done in good faith, without intention to prevent its use as evidence, he rebuts to the satisfaction of the trial judge, any inference of fraud.

The same principle should apply to tape recordings.

. . . .

. . . In my opinion, the learned trial Judge properly received in evidence in the present case the re-recordings proffered.

The notion of "best evidence" has arisen again with the admissibility regime in the Canada Evidence Act concerning electronic evidence.

R. v. MORGAN
(January 10, 2002), Flynn Prov. J., [2002] N.J. No. 15 (N.L. Prov. Ct.)

1 FLYNN PROV. CT. J.:

1. Wayne Morgan and Edward Morgan were each charged in a separate information that he

> Did on or about the 21st day of May A.D. 2001 at or near Port De Grave, Conception Bay, Newfoundland unlawfully violate a condition of a licence, namely, fail to have a Dockside Observer supervise the offloading of fish, namely Crab, from a vessel contrary to section 22(7) of the Fishery (general) Regulations, as amended, thereby committing an offence punishable under Section 78(a) of the Fisheries Act, R.S.C. 1985 c. F-14 as amended.

6 . . . . Recent amendments to the Canada Evidence Act S.C. 2000 c. 5 s. 56 have dealt specifically with the criteria necessary for the admissibility of computer generated documents. These amendments are a major step forward in allowing the admissibility of such documents, while maintaining the reliability of such documents and the information contained within those documents.

. . . .

21 Enacted in the year 2000, the general purpose of section 31.1 and Section 31.2 as gleaned from the statutory provisions themselves is to allow the use of computerized information as either business, public documents or other types of documents provided the reliability of such documents can be established. It is a legislative attempt to grapple with the realities of modern business practice.

22 To comply with these Sections, the Crown must first satisfy the general provisions of Section 31.1 of the Act. That section states:

> Any person seeking to admit an electronic document as evidence has the burden of proving its authenticity by evidence capable of supporting a finding that the electronic document is that which it is purported to be.

There was oral evidence submitted from the one witness called by the Crown that the document the Crown wished to tender was what it was purported to be - a fishery licence issued by the department of Fisheries and Oceans. There was no objection taken by the defence to the fact it was what it was purported to be. As well, a review of the document as provided shows that it is titled Licenses/Conditions, and the upper left hand corner has the Canadian flag and the words "Fisheries and Oceans" engraved on the document. The bottom of the document contains in bold letters the word "CANADA". The other documents forming the package are entitled Schedules and are in Schedules 1 through 5. Therefore, without reviewing the content of the documents themselves, they are what they are purported to be - a fishing licence, conditions and schedules relating to Wayne Morgan. Therefore, it is clear to me that the documents are what they are purported to be - a fishing licence, conditions and Schedules relating to Mr. Wayne Morgan.

23 The next hurdle for the Crown is to establish that the electronic documents satisfy the best evidence rule and are therefore admissible. The Crown must comply with either Section 31.2(1) or Section 31.2(2) for that purpose. These sections state:

> 31.2(1) The best evidence rule in respect of an electronic document is satisfied
>
> > (a) on proof of the integrity of the electronic documents system by or in which the electronic document was recorded or stored; or
> > (b) if an evidentiary presumption established under section 31.4 applies.
>
> (2) Despite subsection (1), in the absence of evidence to the contrary, an electronic document in the form of a printout satisfies the best evidence rule if the printout has been manifestly or consistently acted on, relied on or used as a record of the information recorded or stored in the printout

I am of the view that the affidavit evidence provided by Ms. Karen Snook satisfies both of these criteria.

24 The affidavit evidence attests to the integrity of the computer system. The affidavit discloses that the computer system that held the data respecting the documents was operating properly, as set out in paragraph 6 and 7 of the first affidavit. It also establishes in paragraph 4 of the affidavit that the documents were made from computer records.

25 The affidavit evidence as set out in paragraph 5 also satisfies the requirements of Section 31.2(2) of the *Canada Evidence Act*. That is, a printout satisfies the best evidence rule if the printout has been manifestly or consistently acted on, relied on or used as a record of the information recorded or stored in the printout.

26 The result of compliance with Section 31.2(1) and Section 31.2 (2) of the *Canada Evidence Act* is that the computer generated documents comply by operation of statute, with the best evidence rule. That is, they are considered in law to be the best evidence available.

27 The best evidence rule allows the admission into evidence of the best evidence available provided all other criteria for admissibility have been met. Since I have

already concluded that the criteria of Section 30(1) have been met, and the documents presented from their electronic format are the best evidence available, therefore the license with the conditions and schedules attached to the license are admissible under section 30(1) of the *Canada Evidence Act*. . . .

5. ABORIGINAL RIGHTS

In two decisions, the Supreme Court has provided guidance on the relationship between the rules of evidence and the use of oral histories in Aboriginal rights cases.

DELGAMUUKW v. BRITISH COLUMBIA
[1997] 3 S.C.R. 1010, 1997 CarswellBC 2358

The appellants, all Gitksan or Wet'suwet'en hereditary chiefs, claimed Aboriginal title over 58,000 square kilometres of territory in British Columbia. This landmark case which addressed issues including the content of Aboriginal title and how it is protected under section 35(1) of the Constitution Act, 1982, also examined the trial judge's use of oral histories as part of his fact-finding mission. The Court held that the trial judge had erred in refusing to admit or give no independent weight to these histories. A new trial was ordered.

LAMER C.J. (CORY, MCLACHLIN and MAJOR JJ. concurring): —

This appeal requires us to . . . adapt the laws of evidence so that the aboriginal perspective on their practices, customs and traditions and on their relationship with the land, are given due weight by the courts. In practical terms, this requires the courts to come to terms with the oral histories of aboriginal societies, which, for many aboriginal nations, are the only record of their past. Given that the aboriginal rights recognized and affirmed by s. 35(1) are defined by reference to pre-contact practices or, as I will develop below, in the case of title, pre-sovereignty occupation, those histories play a crucial role in the litigation of aboriginal rights.

A useful and informative description of aboriginal oral history is provided by the Report of the Royal Commission on Aboriginal Peoples (1996), vol. 1 (Looking Forward, Looking Back), at p. 33:

> The Aboriginal tradition in the recording of history is neither linear nor steeped in the same notions of social progress and evolution [as in the non-Aboriginal tradition]. Nor is it usually human-centred in the same way as the western scientific tradition, for it does not assume that human beings are anything more than one—and not necessarily the most important—element of the natural order of the universe. Moreover, the Aboriginal historical tradition is an oral one, involving legends, stories and accounts handed down through the generations in oral form. It is less focused on establishing objective truth and assumes that the teller of the story is so much a part of the event being described that it would be arrogant to presume to classify or categorize the event exactly or for all time.

> In the Aboriginal tradition the purpose of repeating oral accounts from the past is broader than the role of written history in western societies. It may be to educate the

listener, to communicate aspects of culture, to socialize people into a cultural tradition, or to validate the claims of a particular family to authority and prestige.

. . .

Oral accounts of the past include a good deal of subjective experience. They are not simply a detached recounting of factual events but, rather, are "facts enmeshed in the stories of a lifetime". They are also likely to be rooted in particular locations, making reference to particular families and communities. This contributes to a sense that there are many histories, each characterized in part by how a people see themselves, how they define their identity in relation to their environment, and how they express their uniqueness as a people.

Many features of oral histories would count against both their admissibility and their weight as evidence of prior events in a court that took a traditional approach to the rules of evidence. The most fundamental of these is their broad social role not only "as a repository of historical knowledge for a culture" but also as an expression of "the values and mores of [that] culture": Clay McLeod, "The Oral Histories of Canada's Northern People, Anglo-Canadian Evidence Law, and Canada's Fiduciary Duty to First Nations: Breaking Down the Barriers of the Past" (1992), 30 Alta. L. Rev. 1276, at p. 1279. Dickson J. (as he then was) recognized as much when he stated in *Kruger v. The Queen*, [1978] 1 S.C.R. 104, at p. 109, that "[c]laims to aboriginal title are woven with history, legend, politics and moral obligations." The difficulty with these features of oral histories is that they are tangential to the ultimate purpose of the fact-finding process at trial—the determination of the historical truth. Another feature of oral histories which creates difficulty is that they largely consist of out-of-court statements, passed on through an unbroken chain across the generations of a particular aboriginal nation to the present-day. These out-of-court statements are admitted for their truth and therefore conflict with the general rule against the admissibility of hearsay.

Notwithstanding the challenges created by the use of oral histories as proof of historical facts, the laws of evidence must be adapted in order that this type of evidence can be accommodated and placed on an equal footing with the types of historical evidence that courts are familiar with, which largely consists of historical documents. This is a long-standing practice in the interpretation of treaties between the Crown and aboriginal peoples: *Sioui, supra*, at p. 1068; *R. v. Taylor* (1981), 62 C.C.C. (2d) 227 (Ont. C.A.), at p. 232. To quote Dickson C.J., given that most aboriginal societies "did not keep written records", the failure to do so would "impose an impossible burden of proof" on aboriginal peoples, and "render nugatory" any rights that they have (*Simon v. The Queen*, [1985] 2 S.C.R. 387, at p. 408). This process must be undertaken on a case-by-case basis.[89]

89 See Napoleon, "*Delgamuukw*: A Legal Sraightjacket for Oral Histories?" (2005), 20 No. 2 *Can. J.L. & Soc'y* 123.

MITCHELL v. MINISTER OF NATIONAL REVENUE
[2001] 1 S.C.R. 911, 2001 CarswellNat 873

The respondent was a Mohawk of Akwesasne and a descendant of the Mohawk nation, one of the polities of the Iroquois Confederacy prior to the arrival of the Europeans. In 1988, he brought goods across the St. Lawrence River from the United States. He asserted that Aboriginal and treaty rights exempted him from paying duty. In concluding that the claimed Aboriginal right had not been established, the Supreme Court once again addressed the issue of evidence in Aboriginal rights cases.

MCLACHLIN C.J. (GONTHIER, IACOBUCCI, ARBOUR and LEBEL JJ. concurring): —

Courts render decisions on the basis of evidence. This fundamental principle applies to aboriginal claims as much as to any other claim. *Van der Peet* and *Delgamuukw* affirm the continued applicability of the rules of evidence, while cautioning that these rules must be applied flexibly, in a manner commensurate with the inherent difficulties posed by such claims and the promise of reconciliation embodied in s. 35(1). This flexible application of the rules of evidence permits, for example, the admissibility of evidence of post-contact activities to prove continuity with pre-contact practices, customs and traditions (*Van der Peet, supra*, at para. 62) and the meaningful consideration of various forms of oral history (*Delgamuukw, supra*).

The flexible adaptation of traditional rules of evidence to the challenge of doing justice in aboriginal claims is but an application of the time-honoured principle that the rules of evidence are not "cast in stone, nor are they enacted in a vacuum" (*R. v. Levogiannis*, [1993] 4 S.C.R. 475, at p. 487). Rather, they are animated by broad, flexible principles, applied purposively to promote truth-finding and fairness. The rules of evidence should facilitate justice, not stand in its way. Underlying the diverse rules on the admissibility of evidence are three simple ideas. First, the evidence must be useful in the sense of tending to prove a fact relevant to the issues in the case. Second, the evidence must be reasonably reliable; unreliable evidence may hinder the search for the truth more than help it. Third, even useful and reasonably reliable evidence may be excluded in the discretion of the trial judge if its probative value is overshadowed by its potential for prejudice.

In *Delgamuukw*, mindful of these principles, the majority of this Court held that the rules of evidence must be adapted to accommodate oral histories, but did not mandate the blanket admissibility of such evidence or the weight it should be accorded by the trier of fact; rather, it emphasized that admissibility must be determined on a case-by-case basis (para. 87). Oral histories are admissible as evidence where they are both useful and reasonably reliable, subject always to the exclusionary discretion of the trial judge.

Aboriginal oral histories may meet the test of usefulness on two grounds. First, they may offer evidence of ancestral practices and their significance that would not otherwise be available. No other means of obtaining the same evidence may exist, given the absence of contemporaneous records. Second, oral histories may provide the aboriginal perspective on the right claimed. Without such evidence, it might be impossible to gain a true picture of the aboriginal practice relied on or its significance to the society in question. Determining what practices existed, and distinguishing central, defining features of a culture from traits that are marginal or peripheral, is no easy task at a remove of 400 years. Cultural identity is a subjective matter and not easily discerned: see R. L. Barsh and J. Y. Henderson, "The Supreme Court's Van der Peet Trilogy: Naive Imperialism and Ropes of Sand" (1997), 42 McGill L.J. 993, at p. 1000, and J. Woodward, Native Law (loose-leaf), at p. 137. Also see Sparrow, supra, at p. 1103; *Delgamuukw, supra*, at paras. 82-87, and J. Borrows, "The Trickster: Integral to a Distinctive Culture" (1997), 8 Constitutional Forum 27.

The second factor that must be considered in determining the admissibility of evidence in aboriginal cases is reliability: does the witness represent a reasonably reliable source of the particular people's history? The trial judge need not go so far as to find a special guarantee of reliability. However, inquiries as to the witness's ability to know and testify to orally transmitted aboriginal traditions and history may be appropriate both on the question of admissibility and the weight to be assigned the evidence if admitted.

In determining the usefulness and reliability of oral histories, judges must resist facile assumptions based on Eurocentric traditions of gathering and passing on historical facts and traditions. Oral histories reflect the distinctive perspectives and cultures of the communities from which they originate and should not be discounted simply because they do not conform to the expectations of the non-aboriginal perspective. Thus, *Delgamuukw* cautions against facilely rejecting oral histories simply because they do not convey "historical" truth, contain elements that may be classified as mythology, lack precise detail, embody material tangential to the judicial process, or are confined to the community whose history is being recounted.

In this case, the parties presented evidence from historians and archaeologists. The aboriginal perspective was supplied by oral histories of elders such as Grand Chief Mitchell. Grand Chief Mitchell's testimony, confirmed by archaeological and historical evidence, was especially useful because he was trained from an early age in the history of his community. The trial judge found his evidence credible and relied on it. He did not err in doing so and we may do the same.

6. DEMONSTRATIVE EVIDENCE

One needs to recognize a distinction between real evidence and demonstrative evidence. Demonstrative evidence, charts, models and the like are tools to assist the trier in understanding the evidence. Real evidence, the gun, the narcotics, the bloodstained shirt, tendered as an object within the courtroom is not a helpful aid but rather is evidence itself. Real evidence needs to be authenticated. With demonstrative evidence their worth depends on whether they are accurate representations of what happened. The judge needs to be satisfied that the demonstration will genuinely assist the trier of fact and not distort the fact finding process. There is concern that the demonstration might overpower the trier. In the end we can do little more than trust the discretion of the trial judge.

R. v. HOWARD AND TRUDEL
(1983), 3 C.C.C. (3d) 399, 1983 CarswellOnt 1332 (Ont. C.A.)

The accused were charged with first degree murder. Over a period of some four days at the trial, expert evidence was called with respect to four footprints. Nineteen feet five inches south of the body a complete shoe impression was located. Twelve feet west and four feet north there was a partial heel print. Two inches from the victim's head two partial heel impressions were found with one superimposed upon the other. Both inked and plastic impressions of the heels of the accused T's shoes were obtained. In addition a rubber silicone mould of the heel was obtained and photographed. Expert witnesses called by the Crown testified that T's right shoe had made the impression. The expert called by the defence disagreed with the evidence of the Crown's experts that Trudel's heel had made the impression.

HOWLAND C.J.O. (BROOKE and LACOURCIERE JJ.A concurring):—

. . . .

The trial judge refused to permit Dr. Watt, [the defence expert], when he was giving evidence, to make an impression of Trudel's heel in plasticine so that he could demonstrate that the shoe could not make the right angle mark that appeared in the photograph (of the footprint impression). The trial judge refused to permit the demonstration. He stated:

> Court room demonstrations are normally not acceptable, they are subject to distortion, the exact conditions under which comparisons are made cannot be duplicated, it involves confusion and delay, and in this particular one the material with which he would work is highly susceptible to transformation in the handling of it in the jury room, and it really amounts to the creation of evidence in court which in my view unless it is a very simple matter is not permissible and this is certainly a discretionary matter and in my discretion I refuse to permit the witness to make the cast which you requested him to make.

Bearing in mind the importance of the footprint evidence and the fact that the Crown had had the opportunity to make ink and plastic impressions and a rubber silicone mould to assist its witnesses in presenting its evidence, the defence expert should have been given equal latitude in presenting the defence. It is true that what he wanted to do was somewhat different. It was not merely a case of producing a plasticine mould in advance of the heel of Trudel's shoe, but of demonstrating to the jury when he was giving evidence that the heel of Trudel's shoe could not make the right angle mark that appeared in the photograph. Counsel for the Crown stated that the Crown never disputed that Trudel's right shoe could not make a right angle turn; in his view the real dispute was whether the photograph of the footprint showed the corner of the heel, and the demonstration would not have been of assistance on this point. In *McCormick's Handbook of the Law of Evidence*, 2nd ed. 1972, it is stated at p. 536:

> Whether demonstrations in the form of experiments in court are to be permitted is also largely subject to the discretion of the trial judge. Unlike experiments performed out of court, the results of which are generally communicated testimonially, in-court experimentation may involve considerable confusion and delay, and the trial judge is viewed as in the best position to judge whether the game is worth the candle. Simple demonstrations by a witness are usually permitted, and may be strikingly effective in adding vividness to the spoken word.

While such courtroom demonstrations are only permitted in rare cases, in my opinion this was such a case. It was a demonstration which Dr. Watt had always performed in such cases and it seems appropriate that he should have been permitted to undertake it. However, I am not prepared to say that the trial judge proceeded on any wrong principle. In the last analysis the decision whether to permit the demonstration was within his discretion and his refusal to permit it was not reversible error.[90]

R. v. MACDONALD
(2000), 35 C.R. (5th) 130, 146 C.C.C. (3d) 525 (Ont. C.A.)

The accused M was a fugitive from justice. He and his co-accused V were the targets of a police "takedown" which did not go smoothly. As a result, M was charged with two counts of aggravated assault and one count of dangerous driving, and V was charged with possession of a restricted weapon, possession of a weapon for a purpose dangerous to the public peace and assault with a weapon. Twenty months after the attempted takedown, the police made a video in which they attempted to reconstruct and re-enact the takedown. The finished product reflected the recollections of four police officers. Defence counsel objected to the admissibility of the video at trial on the ground that it was more prejudicial than probative. The trial judge ruled that the video was admissible. The Crown played the video twice during the examination-in-chief of one of the police officers.

PER CURIAM:—

. . . .

We will first describe how the video was made and its contents, then discuss the applicable principles governing its admissibility and, finally, apply the principles to this case.

The evidence on the *voir dire* explained how the video re-enactment was produced and what it showed. The police acquired a car similar to the car MacDonald was driving and another car to be positioned behind the "suspect car". During the takedown, the car behind had been a large sport-utility vehicle, a Ford Explorer; its replacement in the video was much smaller, a 1987 Toyota. The location chosen for the video, apparently a deserted sand quarry, differed from the location of the actual incident, a controlled intersection with a traffic light in the town of Markham. The video lasted 20 seconds. Officer Brown testified

---

90 The Supreme Court overturned the decision of the Ontario Court of Appeal on other grounds: *R. v. Howard*, [1989] 1 S.C.R. 1357. It did not address the issue of in-court identification.

that it showed the cars moving "much slower" than they did during the actual incident and, therefore, the length of the video was also longer than the time of the incident.

The video re-enacts the police's version of what occurred during the attempted takedown. Four police officers — Brown, Wright, Rodgers and Giangrande — played themselves, recreating what each claimed to have done during the incident. The video shows the four officers getting out of the emergency response unit van, which is partly blocking the suspect car. Three officers take up positions several feet in front of the car with their guns aimed at the occupants. All three are shouting loudly: "Police, don't move." Four seconds elapse between the police first shouting and the suspect car backing up. The camera shows the police from behind facing the suspect car. The camera is then set inside the car to show the driver's perspective looking out at the officers through the windshield. The police are clearly visible to the driver of the suspect car.

After the suspect car backs up a considerable distance, the camera shows the car from the outside, advancing on the officers. Brown, the officer nearest the passenger side, shoots twice into the windshield on that side of the car. Rodgers, the officer at the driver's window, fires four shots in rapid succession at the windshield on the driver's side. Red lines were added to the video to show the trajectory of the bullets but the trial judge ruled they be deleted before the video was shown to the jury. As the car moves forward on the video it hits Brown, who rolls onto the hood in a fetal position. The video ends with the car driving away, Brown still on the hood.

The video re-enactment took two hours to make. The finished product reflected the recollections of the four officers. Although each officer tried to recreate his own actions, the four discussed the incident among themselves before making the video.

We turn now to the applicable legal principles. A serious concern with videotaped re-enactments, particularly those created without the participation of the accused, is their potential to unfairly influence the jury's decision-making. Because a video re-enactment has an immediate visual impact, jurors may be induced to give it more weight than it deserves and, correspondingly, to discount less compelling or less vivid evidence which is nonetheless more probative of the facts in dispute. Several commentators and courts have warned against this danger. Dean Wigmore adverted to it in his classic treatise on evidence, *Wigmore, Evidence in Trials at Common Law* (1970), at s. 798a:

> In so far as such a [motion] picture has any value beyond a still picture, this value depends on the correctness of the *artificial reconstruction* of a complex series of movements and erections, usually involving several actors, each of them the paid agent of the party and acting under his direction. Hence its reliability, as identical with the original scene, is decreased and may be minimized to the point of worthlessness.

> Where this possibility is serious, what should be done? Theoretically, of course, the motion picture can never be assumed to represent the actual occurrence: what is seen in it is merely what certain witnesses say was the thing that happened. And, moreover, the party's hired agents may so construct it as to go considerably further in his favor

than the witnesses' testimony has gone. And yet, any motion picture is apt to cause forgetfulness of this and to impress the jury with the convincing impartiality of Nature herself . . .

So too did Professor McCormick in his evidence text, *McCormick on Evidence*, 4th ed. (1992), vol. 2, at pp. 3-4:

It has already been noted that evidence from which the trier of fact may derive his own perceptions, rather than evidence consisting of the reported perceptions of others, possesses unusual force. Consequently, demonstrative evidence is frequently objected to as prejudicial, a term which is today generally defined as suggesting "decision on an improper basis, commonly, though not necessarily, an emotional one." A great deal of demonstrative evidence has the capacity to generate emotional responses such as pity, revulsion, or contempt, and where this capacity outweighs the value of the evidence on the issues in litigation, exclusion is appropriate. Again, even if no essentially emotional response is likely to result, demonstrative evidence may convey an impression of objective reality to the trier. Thus, the courts are frequently sensitive to the objection that the evidence is "misleading", and zealous to insure that there is no misleading differential between objective things offered at trial and the same or different objective things as they existed at the time of the events or occurrences in litigation.

This danger increases when the videotape depicts not just the undisputed positions of persons and things, but one side's version of disputed facts. McCormick makes this point in discussing the admissibility of photographs, at p. 17:

A somewhat . . . troublesome problem is presented by posed or artificially reconstructed scenes, in which people, automobiles, and other objects are placed so as to conform to the descriptions of the original crime or collision given by the witnesses. When the posed photographs go no further than to portray the positions of persons and objects as reflected in the undisputed testimony, their admission has long been generally approved. Frequently, however, a posed photograph will portray only the version of the facts supported by the testimony of the proponent's witness. The dangers inherent in this situation, i.e., the tendency of the photographs unduly to emphasize certain testimony and the possibility that the jury may confuse one party's reconstruction with objective fact, have led many courts to exclude photographs of this type . . . the current trend would appear to be to permit even photos of disputed reconstructions in some instances [e.g., if pressing necessity].

In a comprehensive article on the subject, "Manufacturing Evidence for Trial: The Prejudicial Implications of Videotaped Crime Scenery Re-enactments" (1994), 142 *U. Pa. L. R.* 2125, David B. Hennes examined the high sensory impact of video images and their tendency to stay at the front of the viewer's mind. He summarized why admitting videotaped re-enactments may be unfair at pp. 2179-80:

The danger of unfair prejudice presented by the videotaped re-enactment is a function of both the manner of the presentation and the content of the presentation. That danger is only accentuated by its stark lack of probative value. The availability heuristic suggests that the re-enactment will be readily recalled and heavily relied upon during the decision-making process. Individuals learn more readily through sight, and a key component of the learning process comes through the use of the television, an everyday source of entertainment and information. A television videotape, much more than other forms of demonstrative visual evidence, leaves a lasting impression on jurors' mental processes, since its vividness dictates that it will be readily available for cognitive recall. The videotaped re-enactment, because of its mental impressionability, is exactly the type of vivid information to which the availability heuristic grants cognitive priority during decision-making.

Mr. Hennes approved of the majority opinion of the Texas Court of Appeals in *Lopez v. State*, 651 S.W. 2d 413 (1983) at p. 416, banning video re-enactments. Burdock J. wrote:

> . . . We find that any staged, re-enacted criminal acts or defensive issues involving human beings are impossible to duplicate in every minute detail and are therefore inherently dangerous, offer little in substance and the impact of re-enactments is too highly prejudicial to insure the State or the defendant a fair trial.

In addition to the concerns about video re-enactments discussed by courts and commentators, we cannot ignore the reality that usually only the Crown has the resources to produce a video and thus, in many cases, the re-enactment will be an "extra witness for the state".

Despite these concerns, however, we think it would be unwise to lay down rigid rules governing the admissibility of video re-enactments. In an era of rapidly changing technology we would take a step backward were we to prohibit the use of video re-enactments in the courtroom. Further, an outright prohibition would hinder the efforts of today's advocates to devise new and creative ways to promote their clients' causes.

In our view, the preferable approach recognizes the dangers of video re-enactments but adopts a case-by-case analysis. As with the admissibility of other kinds of evidence, the overriding principle should be whether the prejudicial effect of the video re-enactment outweighs its probative value. If it does, the video re-enactment should not be admitted. In balancing the prejudicial and probative value of a video re-enactment, trial judges should at least consider the video's relevance, its accuracy, its fairness, and whether what it portrays can be verified under oath: see *R. v. Creemer*, [1968] 1 C.C.C. 14 at p. 22 (N.S. C.A.). Other considerations may be material depending on the case. And as with rulings on the admissibility of other kinds of evidence, the trial judge's decision to admit or exclude a video re-enactment is entitled to deference on appeal.

The appellants contend that another consideration should be necessity, whether the video is needed in the light of the other evidence in the case. According to the appellants, if a taped re-enactment merely repeats what witnesses have already testified to, it adds nothing new and accordingly should not be admitted. This argument, however, applies equally to other kinds of demonstrative evidence — charts, graphs, diagrams and photographs — that courts routinely admit to help the trier of fact understand the testimony of witnesses. The question of necessity is, therefore, better dealt with as yet another aspect of evaluating the prejudicial effect and probative value of a video re-enactment in a given case.

With these principles in mind, we consider the use of the video by the Crown in this case. We accept that the video was relevant because it sought to portray the incident that gave rise to the charges against the appellants. We also accept that Officer Rodgers testified under oath about the video and explained it to the jury. In our view, however, the trial judge erred in admitting the video for two main reasons: first, he failed to appreciate that its many inaccuracies undermined its probative value; and, second, he was not sensitive enough to the prejudice caused by re-enacting one side's version of events.

A video's probative value rests on the accuracy of its re-enactment of undisputed facts. This video failed to meet this requirement. It did not accurately represent the undisputed facts and even ventured into the realm of disputed facts. Variation from the actual facts may be permissible but only if the variation can be fully explained to and properly understood by the trier of fact. No explanation was given to the jury in this case.

Accuracy imports many different factors. LeSage J. observed in *R. v. Maloney (No. 2)* (1976), 29 C.C.C. (2d) 431 (Ont. Co. Ct.) at p. 436 that accuracy means "consistent with facts, agreeing with reality . . . reality therefore includes not only material objects but also the immaterial such as light, sound, and the dimensions of space and *time*". Discrepancies in various factors may affect the accuracy of a videotaped re-enactment, including time of day, time of year, weather conditions, lighting or visibility, speed of action, distance, location, physical characteristics of the individuals portrayed, physical characteristics of the "props", and complexity of the events depicted. Many of these factors are inaccurately represented in this video re-enactment. The following table shows how the undisputed evidence at trial about the attempted takedown differed from the video re-enactment of it:

Facts	*Actual Takedown*	*Video Re-enactment*
Time of year	June 20	February
Time of day	4:00 p.m.	Morning
Location	Markham intersection at stop light	Deserted sand quarry
Speed	Actual	Slower
Distance (of suspect's car from Officer Rodgers)	3 – 4 feet	Inches
Type of car behind the suspect car	Ford Explorer	Toyota

These inaccuracies distorted the reality of the takedown. The jurors were given a powerful and misleading image of what occurred, which could only have undermined their ability to fairly determine the crucial fact in the case, whether MacDonald could see that those who surrounded his car were police officers. Moreover, the video re-enactment was superfluous. The jury heard ample evidence from the Crown and the defence about what happened during the takedown. They were also given maps and diagrams of the scene. Overall, in our view, the video re-enactment had little or no probative value.

In contrast, the video was highly prejudicial. The trial judge dismissed the claim of prejudice by stating that the video re-enactment "is not more prejudicial than oral testimony". This is surely wrong. All of the authorities say the opposite. The video permitted the prosecution to put before the jury its own version of what occurred, distilled into a neatly packaged, compressed, and easily assimilated sight and sound bite. The violent, visual, highly impressionistic imagery gave the Crown an unfair advantage in this trial. Courts must be sensitive to how a video re-enactment that depicts only the Crown's version of disputed facts may distort the jury's decision-making and thus prejudice an accused's right to a fair trial.

In this case, the Crown's video re-enactment contradicted in material ways not just MacDonald's testimony but even the evidence of the Crown's ballistics expert. For example, the video depicts the police van cutting off MacDonald's car; MacDonald testified that he did not see the van. In the video the police are yelling loudly; MacDonald testified that he did not hear the police announce their presence. In the video the police are plainly visible in front of the car; MacDonald said that he did not see the police at first and then mistook them. On the video MacDonald's car backs up; MacDonald testified that the unmarked police car bumped him from behind. The video showed two shots fired into the front windshield on the passenger's side and four shots into the windshield on the driver's side; MacDonald's evidence, supported by the Crown's ballistics expert, was that shots were fired through the window on the driver's door.

These examples demonstrate how one-sided the video re-enactment was. This one-sided depiction of what occurred, presented in vivid and forceful imagery, was highly prejudicial. The distortion of even undisputed facts only added to the prejudice.

. . . .

[Appeals against conviction were allowed, the convictions were set aside and a new trial was ordered.]

McCUTCHEON v. CHRYSLER CANADA LTD.
[1998] O.J. No. 5818, 1998 CarswellOnt 5091 (Gen. Div.)

PER SHAUGHNESSY J.: —

On the second day of this trial a Voir Dire has been conducted to determine the admissibility of a computer generated animated video detailing the premorbid and post accident gait of the Plaintiff, Dr. Larry McCutcheon. There appears to be some controversy as to the admissibility of such evidence. The obvious objection is that such evidence has the appearance of authenticity which may not exist.

Filed as exhibits on the voir dire are the computer video animation depicting the premorbid and post accident gait of the Plaintiff; a further VHS home video taken of the Plaintiff in or about the Spring of 1995 which was viewed but not used by the video animator; photographs of Larry McCutcheon pre and post accident which were viewed by the video animator and there was also filed as an exhibit the curriculum vitae of the video animator, as well as a further video made by the animator, Mr. Lenartowich, which details the Plaintiff walking to and fro, as well as on stairs and without his leg brace in a locked position, as well as in a locked position.

The computer generated video which the Plaintiff proposes to introduce details a computer humanoid figure which visually presents the gait of the Plaintiff before the accident, as well as after the accident. The scene changes at various times to show the bone structure of the legs and feet pre and post accident and also, at one point, shows an actual picture of the Plaintiff walking with his brace on. There are also on the screen split scene comparisons showing the humanoid in gaits pre and post accident.

The Plaintiff, Larry McCutcheon, and his wife, Marilyn, were called to give evidence on the voir dire. It was their evidence that the computer video was an accurate depiction of the Plaintiff's gait both before and after the accident. In particular the change of pace in his gait as well as a change in the positioning of his leg in order to enable the swing of his leg above the ground with the brace on is stated to be an accurate depiction on the video.

Mr. Brian Lenartowich gave evidence on the voir dire. His curriculum vitae was filed as Exhibit #5 and he was qualified to give expert opinion evidence as a professional animator. While he has no medical training, his assignment was to provide animation of a gait, premorbid and post accident. His evidence was that he met with the Plaintiff and Dr. Anthony Newall to establish how a computer generated animation would illustrate the differences in the gait before and after the accident. The technical detail concerning the hardware and software used the 3D models employed in the animation are detailed in his report dated November 6, 1998, which was also filed as an exhibit. If I understand the submissions of Defence counsel he has really no serious objection concerning the technical aspects of the evidence and he accepted that the equipment and software used was what is described as the high end of the state of art for computer generated animation.

. . . .

The position of counsel for the Plaintiff is that while this technology is somewhat new, nevertheless this type of demonstrative evidence should be entered into evidence in accordance with the Rules of Evidence governing same. The Plaintiff refers to two fairly recent decisions. . . . Essentially, the Plaintiff's argument is that the evidence would be helpful and relevant to the issues in this case. It is argued that the animator has provided evidence relating to the technical requirements of the hardware and software and the method of computer animation and that the animator employed reliable software and hardware to the application of the information provided to him. Finally, the Plaintiff argues that the animator, to a tolerable level, accurately produced a computer animation which reasonably represents what it is intended to illustrate.

The Defendant's position is that the animation is far too subjective a depiction in which the animator solely relied on information provided to him by the Plaintiff. Counsel for the Defendant argues that the animation depicts something that is not entirely accurate. His principal objection is that the video animation is extremely prejudicial to his client. He argues that the video presentation is not accurate in that it does not clearly delineate a premorbid leg shortage of three-quarters of an inch – relating to the Plaintiff's polio condition and it does not depict the hardware in the hip joint. Counsel for the Defendant further argues that the depiction is prejudicial because it can mislead the Jury and it is not an objective assessment of the Plaintiff's pace or his tiring at the end of the day. In fairness to counsel for the Defence, there are subjective components to the animation which I noted and it was clear that the Plaintiff had direct input in terms of the information provided to the animator. In particular, decisions were made by the Plaintiff's counsel to display only a post accident gait with the knee brace locked and as well, it was subjectively decided that the pace of the Plaintiff's gait was one-half of the pre-accident pace. The Defendants referred me to *Draper v. Jacklyn* (1970), 9 D.L.R. (3d) 264. At p. 270 there is cited the case of *Noor Mohamed v. The King*, [1949] A.C. 182 where it is stated:

> It is right to add, however, that in all such cases the judge ought to consider whether the evidence which it is proposed to adduce is sufficiently substantial, having regard to the purpose to which it is professedly directed, to make it desirable in the interest of justice that it should be admitted. If, so far as that purpose is concerned, it can in the circumstances of the case have only trifling weight, the judge will be right to exclude it. To say this is not to confuse weight with admissibility. The distinction is plain, but cases must occur in which it would be unjust to admit evidence of a character gravely prejudicial to the accused even though there may be some tenuous ground for holding it technically admissible. The decision must then be left to the discretion and the sense of fairness of the judge."

Therefore Defence counsel argues that although the video may be technically admissible, nevertheless, its prejudicial value outweighs its probative value. I should indicate that counsel for the Defence stated on the Record that he was not challenging the introduction of the evidence based on Rule 53.04 of the Ontario Rules of Civil Procedure. Ultimately the matter has to be determined by the trial judge exercising his discretion judicially and the test applicable in terms of judicial discretion is whether the prejudicial effect of demonstrative evidence outweighs its probative value. The Supreme Court of Canada in *Draper v. Jacklyn, supra*, held that demonstrative evidence is admissible where it is relevant to the issues in dispute and where it would assist the jury to better understand the conditions alleged so long as its prejudicial value does not outweigh its probative value.

. . . .

I find the following:

The computer generated video animation will assist the Jury and will provide some evidence by which to compare the premorbid and post traumatic gait of the Plaintiff. The only other home video of the Plaintiff is not adequate or sufficient in the circumstances for the reasons which I have outlined previously.

I further find the video animation is relevant to the issues in this proceeding. It is the Plaintiff's position in this proceeding that the change in the Plaintiff's gait has caused the thigh muscle to weaken and which has resulted in the onset of fatigue, reduced and deteriorating function, including the ability to walk. This accordingly has affected his enjoyment of life as well as requiring future care. I further find that the hardware and software methods employed by the animator have been verified by the witness Mr. Lenartowich. I have viewed the video and it does not contain any editorial comments, other than the usual headings one might expect, detailing premorbid, versus post traumatic viewings of the humanoid figure and there are some isolated measurements involving the foot.

I find that the evidence adduced before me establishes that the video animation accurately represents the Plaintiff's premorbid and post traumatic gaits. The objection raised by Defence counsel concerning the leg shortening and hip hardware are, in my opinion, not relevant in these proceedings as these conditions remained the same before and after the accident and have no real value or effect on the fairness of the video animation. However, it is not enough to end my consideration at this point. I have also considered whether the prejudicial value outweighs the probative value and as well, the considerations that Morin J. put forward, namely whether the evidence is relevant and necessary.

I have provided my findings concerning relevancy. As to the matter of whether the evidence is necessary, I have considered that it is difficult for a witness to describe a person's gait or limp. It is ever more difficult, as in the present case, to describe a change in the gait. The Plaintiff had a noticeable limp before this accident occurred. The gait has, to some degree, become more pronounced since the accident and it is the Plaintiff's case that his pace and manner of walking has changed as depicted on the animation with resultant serious consequences. I find the animations are helpful, not only in relationship to the medical evidence that will be forthcoming in this trial, but also in helping the jury to understand the evidence of other witnesses. I believe the Jury's understanding of the issues will be greatly assisted by the use of the computer animation. Therefore, I find that the computer animation is necessary.

Finally, even though I may have found that the evidence is relevant and necessary I still have directed my mind to a determination as to whether the prejudicial value outweighs the probative value. Again, as I stated, I have reviewed the video on the Voir Dire. It is presented in a very simple, straightforward manner. There is no sound. There were few headings and no editorializing. It lasts approximately ten minutes. In essence, it depicts a humanoid with a very clear limp premorbid and a gait that is different but still a limp, post accident. I do not find that it is inflammatory. Nor do I think that the presentation is much different than any member of this jury might see on any television commercial. I find that it will not inflame the Jury, nor will it negatively impact on the fairness of this trial. I do not find that the presentation is misleading, or unfair to the Defendant.

While there are perceived frailties in the evidence, in particular the subjective component in the information and involvement of the Plaintiff before the production of the video, nevertheless I find that these are all matters that counsel for the Defendant may adequately pursue on cross-examination and go to the weight of the evidence.

My Ruling is that the computer video animation shall not be excluded as evidence in this case and I expect that Mr. Oatley will follow the proper procedure in terms of introducing that evidence before the Jury.

R. v. COLLINS
(2001), 160 C.C.C. (3d) 85, 2001 CarswellOnt 3462 (C.A.)

The accused was charged with criminal negligence causing death. The victim was a seven-year-old boy who was camping with his father, two siblings and the accused. The accused shot a number of rounds from a rifle into the lake, close to where the victim was sitting on a log, about 45 metres away. The victim was hit by one bullet and died from his injury. The Crown lead evidence of a police officer who was qualified as an expert in handling firearms. He testified to an experiment he conducted whereby he shot the accused's rifle 16 times aiming at the water at various distances from where the victim was positioned. All but one of the bullets struck a large target placed in the area where the victim was sitting. The trial judge ruled that the evidence was admissible to show what happened when a gun was fired in the way suggested by the witnesses. The accused was convicted. His appeal was dismissed.

CHARRON J.A. (SHARPE J.A. concurring): —

. . . .

The Law on the Admissibility of Experiment Evidence

Despite the fact that experiment evidence is often, and at times routinely, admitted at trials, there is a paucity of Canadian jurisprudence relating to this kind of evidence. Perhaps this is explained by the fact that experiment evidence often goes unrecognized for what it is: in some cases, it consists of mere factual evidence, much like any other sworn testimony; in other cases, it is a combination of factual and opinion evidence. In either situation, its admissibility is governed by well-established rules of evidence.

. . . .

A witness's testimony as to observed facts is, of course, subject to the general principles governing the admissibility of any evidence: relevance and materiality. Relevance is established at law if, as a matter of logic and experience, the evidence tends to prove the proposition for which it is advanced. The evidence is material if it is directed at a matter in issue in the case. Hence, evidence that is relevant to an issue in the case will generally be admitted. Indeed, it is a fundamental principle of our law of evidence that any information that has any tendency to prove a fact in issue should be admitted in evidence unless its exclusion is justified on some other grounds. [Citations omitted.]

. . . .

These general principles apply to experiment evidence. A pre-trial experiment can be as simple as driving from one location to another to determine the time it takes to cover the distance in order to substantiate or disprove an alibi, or driving along a particular stretch of road to determine at what point a stop sign becomes visible. The evidence in such cases, provided that it is relevant to an issue in the case, will usually be admitted without argument. It is entirely factual, and its admissibility is only subject to the general principles of relevance, materiality and discretion as discussed earlier.

. . . .

In a nutshell, experiment evidence, if it is relevant to an issue in the case, should generally be admitted, subject to the trial judge's residuary discretion to exclude the evidence where the prejudice that would flow from its admission clearly outweighs its value.

. . . .

In most cases, the relevance of the experiment evidence will depend on the degree of similarity between the replication and the original event. Consider the example given earlier where the experiment consists of the driving along a particular stretch of road to determine at what point a stop sign becomes visible. If the distance at which the stop sign becomes visible is in issue at trial, the experiment evidence will be material, but will only be relevant if the replication bears some similarity to the original event. For example, if the original event occurred in the summer when vegetation partly obstructed the driver's view but the experiment was conducted in winter after all the leaves had fallen, the relevance of the evidence will be greatly diminished. Depending on all the circumstances, it may not be worth receiving.

Simmons, J.A. concurred in a separate opinion.

Collins was applied as the "leading case" in *R. v. Nikitin*[91] to admit into evidence a videotaped re-enactment of a school bus crossing accident in which a five-year-old child was killed. The accused was convicted of manslaughter.

In *Nikitin,* the re-enactment was made an exhibit and this was not discussed in the Court of Appeal judgment which upheld the decision of the trial judge to admit the videotape. **Are there dangers in making the demonstration an exhibit?**[92]

7. VIEWS

If it is physically impossible to bring the real evidence into the courtroom, the courtroom may have to go to the evidence and take a view. Statutory authority for taking a view in criminal cases is found in the Criminal Code:

> **652.**(1) The judge may, where it appears to be in the interests of justice, at any time

---

91 (2003), 176 C.C.C. (3d) 225, 2003 CarswellOnt 2360 (C.A.).

92 For a discussion of the recent developments in using computer animation to demonstrate a litigant's position see D'Angelo, "The Snoop Doggy Dogg Trial: A Look at How Computer Animation Will Impact Litigation in the Next Century" (1998), 32 Univ. of San. Fran. Law Rev. 561. See also B.S. Fiedler, "Are Your Eyes Deceiving You?: The Evidentiary Crisis Regarding The Admissibility Of Computer Generated Evidence" (2004), 79 New York Law School Law Review 295; E.E. Weinreb, "'Counselor Proceed With Caution'. The Use Of Integrated Evidence Presentation Systems And Computer-Generated Evidence In The Courtroom" (2001), 23 Cardoza L. Rev. 393, and N. Wiebe, "Regarding Digital Images: Determining Courtroom Admissibility Standards" (2000), 28 Manitoba L.J. 61; Legate, "The Admissibility of Demonstrative Evidence in Jury Trials: Applying the Principled Approach to the Law of Evidence" (2006), 31 Advocates' Quarterly 316.

after the jury has been sworn and before it gives its verdict, direct the jury to have a view of any place, thing or person, and shall give directions respecting the manner in which, and the persons by whom, the place, thing or person shall be shown to the jury, and may for that purpose adjourn the trial.

(2) Where a view is ordered under subsection (1), the judge shall give any directions that he considers necessary for the purpose of preventing undue communication by any person with members of the jury, but failure to comply with any directions given under this subsection does not affect the validity of the proceedings.

(3) Where a view is ordered under subsection (1) the accused and the judge shall attend.

and in civil cases is located in the various rules of court. For example, the Ontario Rules[93] provide:

52.05 The judge or judge and jury by whom an action is being tried or the court before whom an appeal is being heard may, in the presence of the parties or their counsel, inspect any property concerning which any question arises in the action, or the place where the cause of action arose.

The decision as to whether a view will be taken is properly within the discretion of the judge, who will assess the importance of the evidence against the disruption of the trial necessitated by the adjournment.[94]

On the question of whether a view is evidence or is only a device for better understanding the evidence the courts have divided. In *Chambers v. Murphy* [95] the trial judge had taken a view of the motor vehicle accident scene. He rejected the defendant's evidence as to how the accident had taken place:

When the defendant Peter Murphy told me that he stopped, that his vision was obstructed, and that he started into Tashmoo Avenue so that he could see, he told me what was not so.[96]

A new trial was ordered as the Ontario Court of Appeal believed it was

. . . well settled and beyond all controversy that the purpose of a view by a Judge or jury of any place is "in order to understand better the evidence". . . .

I have no doubt that the learned Judge proceeded quite innocently in taking the course he did, and indeed counsel assented to that course and were present at the time of the making of the tests. Nevertheless the facts ascertained from those tests were evidence that might properly have been received from a witness at the trial, but was not so given. The learned Judge in reality supplied that evidence himself and erroneously acted upon it.[97]

The decision of the English Court of Appeal[98] relied on for this holding was, however, later regarded by that court, per Lord Denning, as

unduly restrict[ive of] the function of a view. Everyday practice in these courts shows that, where the matter for decision is one of ordinary common sense, the judge of

---

93 Rules of Civil Procedure, R.R.O. 1990, Reg. 194.
94 See generally 4 Wigmore, *Evidence* (Chad. Rev.), s. 1164.
95 [1953] 2 D.L.R. 705 (Ont. C.A.).
96 *Ibid.*, at p. 706.
97 *Ibid.* See criticism of this case by Milner (1953), 31 Can. Bar Rev. 305.
98 *London Gen. Omnibus Co. v. Lavell*, [1901] 1 Ch. 135 (C.A.).

fact is entitled to form his own judgment on the real evidence of a view, just as much as on the oral evidence of witnesses.[99]

This approach to views was adopted by the Manitoba Court of Appeal in *Meyers v. Govt. of Man.*[100] It seems preferable to regard the view as evidence and allow all reasonable inferences to be drawn therefrom as

> it is unreasonable to assume that jurors, however they may be instructed, will apply the metaphysical distinction suggested and ignore the evidence of their own senses when it conflicts with the testimony of the witnesses.[101]

Nevertheless, in Canada some appeal courts continue to apply the *Chambers* approach.[102]

C. WITNESSES

1. COMPETENCE AND COMPELLABILITY

(a) Introduction

Competence deals with the ability of a witness to testify. Compellability deals with compelling a witness who is competent to testify when that witness does not wish to.

The testimonial qualifications of any witness are to be gauged according to that witness's ability, first, to observe, second, to accurately recall her observation, and, third, to communicate her recollection to the trier of fact. The witness's ability to communicate has two aspects: the *intellectual* ability to understand questions and to give intelligent answers, and the *moral responsibility* to speak the truth.[103]

Each of these qualifications provides fertile ground for the cross-examiner to explore, for the benefit of the trier of fact, the credibility of the testimony offered.

The early common law also erected rules which completely forbade testimony from those witnesses who were seen from the outset as incapable of exercising the necessary powers of observation, recollection and communication. These witnesses were regarded as incompetent, and their incompetency was determined not by the jury but by the trial judge. As the common law matured the blanket rules were refined.

(b) Oath

At common law, a person was obliged to take an oath in order to be a competent witness. In the earlier modes of trial, the oath was a direct appeal to the Almighty to witness the justness of the party's claim, and since it was then

---

99 *Buckingham v. Daily News Ltd.*, [1956] 2 All E.R. 904, 914 (C.A.).

100 (1960), 26 D.L.R. (2d) 550 (Man. C.A.).

101 McCormick, *Evidence* (1972), p. 539.

102 See *R.v. Welsh* (1997), 120 C.C.C. (3d) 68 (B.C. C.A.); *Triple A Invt. Ltd. v. Adams Bros. Ltd.* (1985), 56 Nfld. & P.E.I.R. 272 (Nfld. C.A.), and *Swadron v. North York* (1985), 8 O.A.C. 204 (Div. Ct.).

103 See 2 Wigmore, *Evidence* (Chad. Rev.), s. 506, approved in *R. v. Kendall* (1962), 132 C.C.C. 216, 220 (S.C.C.).

believed that a false appeal would be immediately visited with punishment, the claim would be upheld if the party survived the oath. As the mode of trial changed and witnesses informed the trier, the oath was given to the witnesses to guard against false evidence; the witnesses were advised that they were undertaking a solemn obligation, and it was hoped that bringing to their mind the threat of retribution from some Superior Being would cause the witnesses to be truthful:

> The object of the law in requiring an oath is to get at the truth by obtaining a hold on the conscience of the witness.[104]

Since this is the purpose of the oath it must be determined what form, if any, would act as an assurance of trustworthiness. Although in Canada a fear of divine retribution may no longer be necessary,[105] there must be some belief in the witness of something sacred called to witness his evidence. The form of the oath must then vary according to the witness. This was recognized in 1744 in *Omychund v. Barker*:[106]

> But oaths are as old as the creation. . . .
> The nature of an oath is not at all altered by Christianity, but only made more solemn from the sanction of rewards and punishments being more openly declared.
>
> . . . .
>
> The form of oaths varies in countries according to different laws and constitutions, but the substance is the same in all.
>
> . . . .
>
> There can be no evidence admitted without oath, it would be absurd for him to swear according to the Christian oath, which he does not believe; and therefore, out of necessity, he must be allowed to swear according to his own notion of an oath.
>
> . . . .
>
> I found my opinion upon the certificate, which says, the *Gentoos* believe in a God as the Creator of the universe, and that He is a rewarder of those who do well, and an avenger of those who do ill.

As emphasis that there is no "correct" form of oath, see the *Ontario Evidence Act* which provides:

> **16.** Where an oath may be lawfully taken, it may be administered to a person while such person holds in his or her hand a copy of the Old or New Testament without requiring him or her to kiss the same, or, when the person objects to being sworn in this manner or declares that the oath so administered is not binding upon the person's conscience, then *in such manner and form and with such ceremonies as he or she declares to be binding.* [Emphasis added.][107]

The *Canada Evidence Act* prescribes no particular form of oath. The traditional form of oath which developed in England, and which will be normally

---

104 Best, *Evidence* (1849), s. 161 as quoted in 6 Wigmore, *Evidence* (Chad. Rev.), s. 1816.
105 See below, respecting child witnesses.
106 (1744), 26 E.R. 15, 30, 31 (C.A.) per Willes, L.C.J. See *R. v. Lai Ping* (1904), 11 B.C.R. 102 (C.A.), paper oath administered wherein witness writes his name on paper which is then burned, and *R. v. Lee Tuck* (1912), 4 Alta. L.R. 388 (S.C.). See also *R. v. Ah Wooey* (1902), 8 C.C.C. 25 (B.C.S.C.), chicken oath administered. And see generally Silving, *Essays on Criminal Procedure* (1964), for a thorough description of many forms of oaths.
107 R.S.O. 1990, c. E-23.

administered in Canada unless the witness requests otherwise, varies slightly between criminal and civil cases. In criminal cases the witness is addressed:

> You swear that the evidence to be given by you to the Court (and jury sworn between our Sovereign Lady the Queen and the prisoner at the Bar) shall be the truth, the whole truth, and nothing but the truth. So help you God.[108]

And in civil cases:

> You swear that the evidence to be given by you to the Court (and jury sworn) touching the matters in question, shall be the truth, the whole truth, and nothing but the truth. So help you God.

R. v. KALEVAR
(1991), 4 C.R. (4th) 114 (Ont. Gen. Div.)

The accused was charged with theft under $1,000. He represented himself at his trial. When he came forward to testify he objected to the Bible that was offered to him for taking the oath. The court instructed that he be affirmed. The accused sought to give notice that he wished to raise a constitutional question. The court admonished him that he was to give his evidence under oath or affirmation. In the result the accused gave no evidence. A conviction was entered and the accused appealed.

HALEY J.: —

. . . .

. . . [T]he appellant gave no evidence and the matter was put over for submissions. On the subsequent hearing the Crown suggested to the Judge that the wording of the *Canada Evidence Act*, . . . dealing with oaths was such that an oath need not be taken on the Bible, and that some other religious oath could bind the appellant as a solemn oath so that he could give evidence in the proceedings. The Judge held that the appellant had refused to be affirmed, and there was no other course now open to him to permit him to give evidence except to give unsworn evidence as a "dock statement" from the body of the Court. The appellant refused and a conviction was entered.

On this appeal, the Crown took the position that the Judge had erred in not giving the appellant the right to a religious oath other than on the Bible and, accordingly, the appellant had not had the opportunity to make full answer and defence. In those circumstances the Crown agreed that the appeal should be allowed, the conviction set aside and an acquittal entered. This was done as I was in agreement that a solemn oath was not limited to one taken on the Bible.

Section 13 of the *Canada Evidence Act* reads as follows:

> Every court and judge, and every person having, by law or consent of parties, authority to hear and receive evidence, has power to administer an oath to every witness who is legally called to give evidence before that court, judge or person.

---

108 See *R. v. Budin* (1981), 58 C.C.C. (2d) 352, 354 (Ont. C.A.). See also 6 Wigmore, *Evidence* (Chad. Rev.), s. 1818 and Crankshaw's *Criminal Code of Canada*, 7th ed. (1959), p. 622.

The *Shorter Oxford Dictionary* . . . defines oath as "a solemn appeal to God (or something sacred) in witness that a statement is true, or a promise binding."

The use of oaths other than those taken on the Bible are not unknown in this country. *R. v. Ah Wooey* (1902), 8 C.C.C. 25 (S.C.) was a case in the Supreme Court of British Columbia in which the following decision was taken [p. 25 C.C.C.]:

> For taking the evidence of a Canton Chinaman not a believer in Christianity, the oath known as the 'chicken oath' should be administered instead of the less solemn 'paper oath', if the trial is for a capital offence.

In those circumstances an oath in writing to the King of Heaven was signed by the witness. "The oath was then read out loud by the witness, after which he wrapped it in Joss-paper as used in religious ceremonies, then laid the cock on the block and chopped its head off, and then set fire to the oath from the candles and held it until it was consumed" [pp. 26-27].

Clearly, Canada's emerging multi-cultural society requires an acknowledgement in the courts that the Judaic-Christian form of oath is not necessarily the only form of religious oath to be administered, and that persons of other religious persuasions should not automatically be given affirmation as the only alternative.

The appellant wishes to go further and have me decide his appeal on the ground that his right to freedom of conscience and religion under the *Canadian Charter of Rights and Freedoms* has been breached by the offering to him of an oath on the Bible. He argues strenuously that this freedom has been offended by the presence of the Bible in the courtroom to the exclusion of all other holy books, and that steps should be taken to remove any suggestion of paramountcy of the Bible in the court process.

It is perhaps disappointing from the appellant's point of view that this ground is not necessary to the success of his appeal. Throughout the transcripts it is plain that his main concern was the making of the constitutional argument. However, in the circumstances anything I might decide on the *Charter* issue would be only obiter dicta as unnecessary for the appeal, and the argument must wait until a new case with the proper factual basis can be found to place the argument before the Court for decision.

Rather than automatically proffering a Bible to every witness who comes forward, it might be better to ask each witness whether he or she wishes to be sworn and, if so, in what manner. A witness is normally frightened attending court and the court taking this initiative would avoid yet another burden on the witness of objecting to the oath. Or, counsel might best inquire of the witness what he prefers and make the announcement for him as he goes to the witness stand. Or, one might see the wisdom of the "oath ceremony" devised by His Honour Judge Peter Nasmith.[109] His Honour described the way in which witnesses in his

---

109 See "High Time for One Secular Oath" (1990), L. Soc. Gaz. 230.

court, over the age of 12, had been treated. His clerk addressed the witness as follows:

> Do you know that it is a criminal offence to intentionally give false evidence in a judicial proceeding?
> Do you solemnly promise to tell the truth in this proceeding?

His Honour noted that the answers were invariably "Yes" and the witness was then considered to be under oath.

Though the common law developed some flexibility in the form of the oath, there were people still excluded as witnesses though they were competent in all other respects: those who were children and had not yet formed any religious beliefs, those who had religious beliefs which forbade taking an oath, for example Quakers, and those who were atheists or agnostics. These groups were accommodated by legislation enacted during the 19th century. See now section 14 of the *Canada Evidence Act*,[110] which provides:

> **14.**(1) A person may, instead of taking an oath, make the following solemn affirmation:
>
> > I solemnly affirm that the evidence to be given by me shall be the truth, the whole truth and nothing but the truth,
>
> (2) Where a person makes a solemn affirmation in accordance with subsection (1), his evidence shall be taken and have the same effect as if taken under oath.

The *Ontario Evidence Act* provides:

> **17.**(1) Where a person objects to being sworn from conscientious scruples, or on the ground of his or her religious belief, or on the ground that the taking of an oath would have no binding effect on the person's conscience, he or she may, in lieu of taking an oath, make an affirmation or declaration that is of the same force and effect as if the person had taken an oath in the usual form.[111]

Should the distinction between an oath and solemn affirmation be abolished?

R. v. WIEBE
(2006), 205 C.C.C. (3d) 326 (Ont. C.A.)

ENDORSEMENT

[The accused was convicted at trial of sexual assault.]

. . .

The affirmation and the e-mails

[2] The appellant, who the evidence disclosed was an active member of a congregation, testified under an affirmation that he would tell the truth. During his examination-in-chief, the jury asked the judge what the difference was between swearing an oath on the Bible and affirming. With the agreement of both counsel,

---

110 R.S.C. 1985, c. C-5; am. S.C. 1994, c. 44, s. 87.
111 R.S.O. 1990, c. E-23.

the trial judge told the jury that, for their purposes, there was no difference and that both are methods by which evidence is given in courts.

[3] When the appellant was recalled, his counsel asked him why he had chosen to affirm instead of swearing on the Bible; the judge remarked that he thought the matter had been dealt with. In the absence of the jury, the Crown objected, taking the position the jury had already been instructed they could not draw any inference from the fact that the appellant had affirmed. The Crown further argued that defence counsel had defied the Court by raising the issue after the Court had dealt with it.

[4] Before the judge ruled on the objection, the trial adjourned for the day. The next morning, defence counsel advised the Court that he had received copies of two e-mails that had been sent to the appellant from an excluded defence witness in the trial. One offered a rationale for why a devout Christian would choose to affirm rather than swear an oath. Defence counsel explained that he considered he had an ethical duty to disclose the e-mails to the Court.

[5] Crown and defence counsel disputed what use could be made of the e-mails at trial. The trial judge accepted the Crown's submission that cross-examination of the appellant and other defence witnesses about the e-mails was relevant to the credibility and reliability of those witnesses. The judge directed defence counsel to file the e-mails as lettered exhibits and dismissed the defence's application for a mistrial.

[6] The trial judge also ruled that the appellant could explain why he had chosen to affirm instead of swearing an oath.

[7] In our view, the trial judge was unable to accede to the defence request that he exclude the e-mails from the trial and prohibit any reference to them. The e-mails were closely related to real trial issues. Cross-examination of the appellant on the e-mails was relevant to his credibility, because they raised the issue of whether some of his evidence may have been coached. Cross-examination of the excluded defence witness who sent the e-mails was relevant to his credibility as a witness, because it was apparent that he knew about the jury's question and had provided advice on how the question could be answered if it arose again. In particular, it was relevant to the question of his objectivity or impartiality as a witness.

[8] We do not agree that requiring production of the e-mails and permitting cross-examination on them, in effect, made defence counsel a witness against his own client. Defence counsel did indeed have an ethical duty to advise the Court of the e-mails. The trial judge, in turn, had the responsibility of ensuring the integrity of the trial process, and he permitted cross-examination on the e-mails in order to do so.

[9] Nor are we persuaded that the appellant's affirmation, when combined with the e-mail issue, became such a significant issue that it rendered the trial unfair and that the judge erred by dismissing the defence's application for a mistrial. An

appellate court will not interfere with the discretion of a trial judge to grant or refuse an application for a mistrial absent an error of principle. The trial judge refused to grant a mistrial because he was not satisfied that the jury had heard anything to "tilt its deliberations at this point." The judge left it open for counsel to bring a further motion after hearing what the witnesses had said.

[10] When the trial proceeded and the appellant was questioned about the e-mails, he explained that he had not received them, because he had not opened his computer during the course of the trial. He also explained that his religious beliefs prevented him from swearing an oath. The person who sent the e-mails testified that he was attempting to provide support to the appellant and, while he knew the issue had arisen in Court, that he was not aware that the question would be raised again. There was no renewal of the defence application for a mistrial.

[11] The judge's charge to the jury, read as a whole, and his review of the evidence pertaining to the credibility of the particular witnesses, including that of the sender of the e-mails, would have made clear to the jury that it could use evidence about the e-mails only in relation to the credibility of the sender.

The appeal was dismissed.

(c) Age

The evidence of children (defined as a person under the age of 14) has traditionally been regarded with some circumspection. In *Horsburgh v. R.*,[112] Spence J. said:

> The view expressed by the learned trial Judge is not only that the evidence of children, once sworn, must be received, but it must be treated as that of a competent adult witness. In my opinion, this is a serious misdirection, as the witnesses, despite the fact that it was determined, in my opinion properly, that they were capable of being sworn, were nevertheless child witnesses and their testimony bore all the frailties of testimony of children, such frailties as Judson, J., in this Court referred to in *R. v. Kendall* . . . . The evidence of such children was, as Judson, J., pointed out, subject to the difficulties related to (1) capacity of observation, (2) capacity to recollect, (3) capacity to understand questions put and frame intelligent answers, and (4) the moral responsibility of the witness. It is this fourth difficulty which is very marked in the present case.

We should note, however, that the difficulties enumerated as particularly referable to the evidence of children are, on reflection, the difficulties inherent in the testimony of all witnesses, including adults!
Dr. Haka-Ikse explained:

> Children are not necessarily incompetent morally or cognitively to testify as implied by the present legal system. The assumptions about the testimonial limitations of children do not as an example take into consideration the significant differences between pre-school and adolescent children just under 14 years of age. Conversely, the law considers as competent witness any individual after his or her 14th birthday, which is a totally arbitrary division. Also, the law fails to consider the very wide range of verbal, cognitive and perceptual abilities between children of the same age. The

---

112 [1968] 2 C.C.C. 288, 320 (S.C.C.).

assumption that every individual of older age has the necessary moral judgement, impartiality, objectivity and rationality to give competent testimony is at best questionable. Long pediatric experience in interviewing and coming to know sufficiently close large numbers of pre-latency and latency age children and their parents, indicate that children are able to talk about events that are important to them with simplicity, candor and without excursions to fantasy. The normal pre-schooler or young school age child may have fears about ghosts or the boogey man (and so do some adults by the way) but he or she does not mistake the parent, the babysitter or the teacher as the ghost or the monster. Many children have imaginary companions but they only play with or talk to them in the privacy of their room. The memory of children is often surprising. I have seen 4 and 5 year olds returning to the clinic for a visit after several months and remember where they had sat or where the toys were kept. Conversely the memory of some parents I interview is subjective, bound to interpretation rather than facts, indicating poor recall or understanding of events and often being colored by the parents' emotional status and wishful thinking. The competence of a person to present facts either in giving medical history or in testifying in court, depends on the particular individual's qualities and is not a function of age. I recall many situations when parents interviewed in the presence of their child turn to the child for assistance in answering some questions they ignore or cannot recall the answers. In other instances I recall children interrupting parents to correct or clarify what the parents are reporting. In terms of moral judgement although it is true that the younger the individual is the more he or she relies on authority figures to define or set moral standards rather than to absolute moral imperatives, and their actions are not perceived as "bad" as long as nobody knows about them. The same is true for a good number of adults. Discrimination against children by the law on such grounds is developmentally unfounded and unconstitutional.[113]

To what extent have the rules governing the competency of children and the assessment of their evidence evolved to give effect to the concerns expressed by Dr. Haka-Ikse?

R. v. W. (R.)
[1992] 2 S.C.R. 122, 13 C.R. (4th) 257, 74 C.C.C. (3d) 134

The accused was charged with indecent assault, gross indecency and sexual assault against three young girls. The evidence of the oldest child, S.W., was internally consistent. The evidence of the two younger children, however, revealed a number of inconsistencies and was contradicted in some respects. The accused was convicted on all counts and appealed. The convictions were set aside on the basis that there was no confirmatory evidence and the evidence of the younger children was fraught with inaccuracy. The Crown appealed.

McLACHLIN J. (LA FOREST, L'HEUREUX-DUBÉ, GONTHIER, CORY, and IACOBUCCI JJ. concurring):—

. . . .

The following is the text of the Court of Appeal's endorsement:

---

113 Haka-Ikse, "The Child as Witness in Sexual Abuse Cases: A Developmental Perspective," unreported paper delivered September 10, 1985, University of Toronto. See also Goodman, "The Child Witness" (1984), 40 J. of Social Issues 157; Wehrspann and Steinhauer, "Assessing the Credibility of Young Children's Allegations of Sexual Abuse" (1987), 32 Can. J. of Psychiatry 610, 615.

This case has caused us very great concern. The case has been carefully argued. We recognize the advantage of the trial judge, but also the responsibility of this court. . . . Giving the matter our best consideration, we are all of the opinion that on this evidence these convictions cannot safely stand. There was really no confirmatory evidence, the evidence of the two younger children was fraught with inaccuracy and in the case of the older children [it was] perfectly clear that neither was aware or concerned that anything untoward occurred which is really the best test of the quality of the acts. The appeal is allowed, the conviction is set aside and an acquittal is entered.

. . . .

. . . I pause to consider the general question of how courts should approach the evidence of young children. The law affecting the evidence of children has undergone two major changes in recent years. The first is removal of the notion, found at common law and codified in legislation, that the evidence of children was inherently unreliable and therefore to be treated with special caution. Thus, for example, the requirement that a child's evidence be corroborated has been removed. . . . The repeal of provisions creating a legal requirement that children's evidence be corroborated does not prevent the judge or jury from treating a child's evidence with caution where such caution is merited in the circumstances of the case. But it does revoke the assumption formerly applied to all evidence of children, often unjustly, that children's evidence is always less reliable than the evidence of adults. So if a court proceeds to discount a child's evidence automatically, without regard to the circumstances of the particular case, it will have fallen into an error.

The second change in the attitude of the law toward the evidence of children in recent years is a new appreciation that it may be wrong to apply adult tests for credibility to the evidence of children. One finds emerging a new sensitivity to the peculiar perspectives of children. Since children may experience the world differently from adults, it is hardly surprising that details important to adults, like time and place, may be missing from their recollection. Wilson J. recognized this in *R. v. B. (G.)*, [1990] 2 S.C.R. 30, at pp. 54-55, when, in referring to submissions regarding the court of appeal judge's treatment of the evidence of the complainant, she said that:

> . . . it seems to me that he was simply suggesting that the judiciary should take a common sense approach when dealing with the testimony of young children and not impose the same exacting standard on them as it does on adults. However, this is not to say that the courts should not carefully assess the credibility of child witnesses and I do not read his reasons as suggesting that the standard of proof must be lowered when dealing with children as the appellants submit. Rather, he was expressing concern that a flaw, such as a contradiction, in a child's testimony should not be given the same effect as a similar flaw in the testimony of an adult. I think his concern is well founded and his comments entirely appropriate. While children may not be able to recount precise details and communicate the when and where of an event with exactitude, this does not mean that they have misconceived what happened to them and who did it. In recent years we have adopted a much more benign attitude to children's evidence, lessening the strict standards of oath taking and corroboration,

and I believe that this is a desirable development. The credibility of every witness who testifies before the courts must, of course, be carefully assessed but the standard of the 'reasonable adult' is not necessarily appropriate in assessing the credibility of young children.

As Wilson J. emphasized in *B. (G.)*, these changes in the way the courts look at the evidence of children do not mean that the evidence of children should not be subject to the same standard of proof as the evidence of adult witnesses in criminal cases. Protecting the liberty of the accused and guarding against the injustice of the conviction of an innocent person require a solid foundation for a verdict of guilt, whether the complainant be an adult or a child. What the changes do mean is that we approach the evidence of children not from the perspective of rigid stereotypes, but on what Wilson J. called a "common sense" basis, taking into account the strengths and weaknesses which characterize the evidence offered in the particular case.

It is neither desirable nor possible to state hard and fast rules as to when a witness's evidence should be assessed by reference to "adult" or "child" standards — to do so would be to create anew stereotypes potentially as rigid and unjust as those which the recent developments in the law's approach to children's evidence have been designed to dispel. Every person giving testimony in court, of whatever age, is an individual, whose credibility and evidence must be assessed by reference to criteria appropriate to her mental development, understanding and ability to communicate. But I would add this. In general, where an adult is testifying as to events which occurred when she was a child, her credibility should be assessed according to criteria applicable to her as an adult witness. Yet with regard to her evidence pertaining to events which occurred in childhood, the presence of inconsistencies, particularly as to peripheral matters such as time and location, should be considered in the context of the age of the witness at the time of the events to which she is testifying.

Against this background, I turn to a more particular consideration of the Court of Appeal's treatment of the evidence in this case. First, the Court referred to the fact that "there was really no confirmatory evidence". This suggests that the Court may have been applying the old rule that the evidence of a child could not found a conviction unless it was confirmed or corroborated by independent evidence. It may be that in considering the whole of the evidence in accordance with the *Yebes* test, a court of appeal will take into account, along with other factors, the presence or absence of confirmatory evidence. So the reference to lack of confirmatory evidence is not in itself an error of law. But standing as it does as a bald proposition unrelated to a detailed examination of the evidence, it does support the submission that the Court of Appeal was treating the evidence of the children as being inherently less reliable than adult evidence might be.

. . . .

The Court of Appeal next referred to the fact that the evidence of the younger children was fraught with inaccuracy. This is true, particularly with respect to B.W.'s evidence. Some of the inconsistencies are minor, for example an error on the distance from a van to a ball game many years ago. Others are more significant, relating to the sleeping arrangements of the three children, the location of bedrooms in the house and possibly the respondent's nighttime attire. While it was the proper task of the Court of Appeal to consider such inconsistencies, one finds no mention of the fact that the trial judge was alive to them and resolved them to his satisfaction in his reasons for judgment, nor of the fact that many of the inconsistencies may be explained by reference to the fact that a young child might not be paying particular attention to sleeping arrangements or clothing or that the children had lived in a variety of different arrangements, which might well have given rise to confusion on such details.

Finally, the Court of Appeal relied on the fact that neither of the older children was "aware or concerned that anything untoward occurred which is really the best test of the quality of the acts." This reference reveals reliance on the stereotypical but suspect view that the victims of sexual aggression are likely to report the acts, a stereotype which found expression in the now discounted doctrine of recent complaint. In fact, the literature suggests the converse may be true; victims of abuse often in fact do not disclose it, and if they do, it may not be until a substantial length of time has passed. . . .

In summary, the Court of Appeal was right to be concerned about the quality of the evidence and correct in entering upon a re-examination and reweighing, to some extent, of the evidence. It went too far, however, in finding lacunae in the evidence which did not exist and in applying too critical an approach to the evidence, an approach which appears to have placed insufficient weight on the trial judge's findings of credibility, influenced as the Court of Appeal appears to have been by the old stereotypes relating to the inherent unreliability of children's evidence and the "normal" behaviour of victims of sexual abuse.

Placing myself, as I must, in the position of the Court of Appeal . . . I conclude that we are here concerned with verdicts which "a properly instructed jury [or judge], acting judicially, could reasonably have rendered", to repeat the words of *Yebes*. I would allow the appeal and restore the convictions.[114]

Both the *Ontario Evidence Act* and *Canada Evidence Act* have been amended over the last twenty years to remove barriers to the evidence of children (e.g., abolishing the presumption of incompetency for witnesses under the age of 14) and to facilitate their testimony. We begin with looking at the current provincial regime, which came into effect in 1995.

---

114 For commentary on *W. (R.)*, see Bala, "More Sensitivity to Child Witnesses" (1992), 13 C.R. (4th) 270 and Rauf, "Questioning the New Orthodoxy of the Proper Approach to Child Witnesses" (1993), 17 C.R. (4th) 305. Consider the Martensville cases involving several false charges of child abuse: see *R. v. S. (T.)* (1995), 40 C.R. (4th) 1 (Sask. C.A.). See also David Paciocco, "The Evidence of Children: Testing the Rule Against What We Know" (1996), 21 Queen's L.J. 345 and Nick Bala, "Developmentally Appropriate Questions for Child Witnesses" (1999), 25 Queen's L.J. 252 and "A Legal and Psychological Critique of the Present Approach to the Assessment of the Competence of Child Witnesses" (2001), 38 Osgoode Hall L.J.

18.4(1) A witness under the age of 18 may testify behind a screen or similar device that allows the witness not to see an adverse party, if the court is of the opinion that this is likely to help the witness give complete and accurate testimony or that it is in the best interests of the witness, and if the condition set out in subsection (4) is satisfied.

(2) The court may order that closed-circuit television be used instead of a screen or similar device if the court is of the opinion that,

(a)   a screen or similar device is insufficient to allow the witness to give complete and accurate testimony; or

(b)   the best interests of the witness require the use of closed-circuit television.

(3) If the court makes an order under subsection (2), the witness shall testify outside the courtroom and his or her testimony shall be shown in the courtroom by means of closed-circuit television.

(4) When a screen or similar device or closed-circuit television is used, the judge and jury and the parties to the proceeding and their lawyers shall be able to see and hear the witness testify.

18.5(1) During the testimony of a witness under the age of 18, a support person chosen by the witness may accompany him or her.

(2) If the court determines that the support person chosen by the witness is not appropriate for any reason, the witness is entitled to choose another support person.

(3) The following are examples of reasons on the basis of which the court may determine that the support person chosen by a witness is not appropriate:

1.   The court is of the opinion that the support person may attempt to influence the testimony of the witness.
2.   The support person behaves in a disruptive manner.
3.   The support person is also a witness in the proceeding.

18.6(1) The court may prohibit personal cross-examination of a witness under the age of 18 by an adverse party if the court is of the opinion that such a cross-examination,

(a)   would be likely to affect adversely the ability of the witness to give evidence; or

(b)   would not be in the best interests of the witness.

(2) If the court prohibits personal cross-examination by the adverse party, the cross-examination may be conducted in some other appropriate way (for example, by means of questions written by the adverse party and read to the witness by court).

Bill C-2 (S.C. 2005, c. 32) came into effect at the start of 2006. It amended the competency provisions in the *Canada Evidence Act* and introduced a range of protective measures for young witnesses in the Criminal Code. Professor Nick Bala of Queen's University served as an expert consultant to the Department of Justice with respect to Bill C-2. The following is an article co-written by Nick Bala, Katherine Duvall-Antonacopoulos, R.C.L. Lindsay, Kang Lee and Victoria Talwar.

Bill C-2: A New Law for Canada's Child Witnesses
(2006), 32 C.R. (6th) 48

Bill C-2 . . . introduces significant procedural and substantive amendments that are intended to increase protections for children, women and vulnerable adults from various forms of exploitation. . . . This article deals with the procedural and evidentiary reforms in Bill C-2, and considers their effect on Canada's criminal justice system. . . . [T]he procedural and evidentiary provisions which amend the Criminal Code and Evidence Act apply to trials held after the law is in force, even if the offences occurred earlier.[115]

Overview and Context

Historically, the common law regarded children as inherently unreliable. In 1893, Canada enacted its first statutory provisions concerning child witnesses, permitting children to give unsworn evidence, provided a court found that the child "possessed sufficient intelligence" and understood "the duty to speak the truth."[116] A child's unsworn evidence was viewed with suspicion, and there was a statutory requirement for corroboration of a child's unsworn testimony. Further, no steps were taken to accommodate children when they testified in court, and children did not frequently testify. In the 1980s there was an increased awareness of the under-reporting of child abuse, and a growing body of research about child witnesses. There is a large body of psychological research which establishes that children as young as four years of age can provide important, reliable evidence about events that they have experienced or observed.[117]

In 1988, there were significant amendments to the procedural and evidentiary law governing child witnesses, allowing the use of such testimonial aids as videotaped statements, screens and closed circuit television.[118] The Canada Evidence Act was also amended to permit a child who was able to "communicate the evidence" to testify on a promise to tell the truth. In 1993, the Supreme Court of Canada upheld the constitutional validity of a number of these provisions, emphasizing that these reforms facilitated the truth-seeking function of the criminal justice process without compromising the rights of the accused to a fair trial.[119]

While prior reforms have been significant, there remained substantial concerns about the treatment of vulnerable persons in the justice system, and the difficulty in prosecuting cases in which they are witnesses. Even after the 1988 reforms, in some important respects the justice system failed to treat child witnesses fairly. The Preamble to Bill C-2 states that Parliament "wishes to facilitate the participation of children and other vulnerable witnesses" in the

---

115 See R. Sullivan, *Statutory Interpretation* (Toronto: Irwin Law, 1997), 190.

116 For a discussion of the history and development of Canada's child witness laws, see Bala, "Child Witnesses in the Canadian Criminal Justice System: Recognizing Their Needs & Capacities" (1999), 5 (2) Psychology, Public Policy and the Law 323.

117 See e.g. Carole Peterson, "Children's long-term memory for autobiographical events" (2002), 22 Developmental Review 370; and S.J. Ceci & M.Bruck, Jeopardy in the Courtroom: A Scientific Analysis of Children's Testimony (Washington, DC: American Psychological Association, 1995).

118 R.S.C. 1985, c. 19 (3rd Supp.).

119 *R. v. L. (D.O.)*, [1993] 4 S.C.R. 419, 85 C.C.C. (3d) 289, 25 C.R. (4th) 285; *R. v. Levogiannis*, [1993] 4 S.C.R. 475, 85 C.C.C. (3d) 327, 25 C.R. (4th) 325. See also *R. v. F. (C.)*, [1997] 3 S.C.R. 1183, 154 D.L.R. (4th) 13, 120 C.C.C. (3d) 225, 11 C.R. (5th) 209.

criminal justice system "while ensuring that the rights of accused persons are respected." The court system requires a fair and balanced approach to witnesses, one that recognizes that children have different needs and capacities than adults, and that, like adults, they can provide reliable evidence, as well as lie or make mistakes in their recollection of events.

Bill C-2 changes the approach for determining if child witnesses are competent to testify, allowing children to testify if they are able to understand and respond to questions. The new legislation will facilitate use of testimonial aids, including support persons, screens and closed circuit television, in cases involving children and vulnerable adults. It also facilitates the use in court of video recorded statements made by a child or disabled adult, if the witness adopts the content of the recording when he or she testifies. . . .

The Competency Requirement: Section 16 of the *Canada Evidence Act*

The competency inquiry (or *voir dire*) has long been a critical, initial challenge for child witnesses. For young children these inquiries could be confusing and intimidating, and sometimes resulted in children who were capable of giving important evidence being prevented from testifying.

Under the 1988 version of s.16 of the *Canada Evidence Act*, before a child under the age of fourteen can testify, the court is required to conduct an inquiry to determine if the child understands "the nature of an oath" or solemn affirmation. Those without religious beliefs relating to an oath or who choose not to testify under oath may solemnly affirm, which has the same legal effect as testimony under oath. Interestingly, it seems that judges rarely ask children to affirm, and there are no reported Canadian cases in which children have been asked questions about their understanding of the solemn affirmation.

Historically, in order to demonstrate an understanding of the oath, children were required to state that they expected "divine sanctions" if they told a lie under oath. More recently, it has been accepted that the focus of the inquiry about the oath should be whether the child understands the moral significance of making a commitment to tell the truth, and appreciates the importance of telling the truth in court proceedings, and not on the spiritual significance of an oath.[120] However, many trial judges have continued to ask children intrusive questions about religious beliefs and observances as part of the inquiry about the oath.[121]

If the child cannot demonstrate an understanding of the nature of an oath, s. 16(3) permits a child to testify if the child is "able to communicate in court. . .on promising to tell the truth." While the 1988 legislation did *not* state that there

---

120 *R. v. Fletcher* (1982), 1 C.C.C. (3d) 370 (Ont. C.A.) at 380, leave to appeal to S.C.C. refused (1983), 48 N.R. 319 (S.C.C.). In *R. v. F. (W.J.)*, [1999] 3 S.C.R. 569, 27 C.R. (5th) 169, 138 C.C.C. (3d) 1, at 591 [S.C.R.]. McLachlin J. commented on the "absurdity of subjecting children to examination on whether they understood the religious consequences of the oath."

121 N. Bala, K. Lee, R.C.L. Lindsay & V. Talwar, "A Legal & Psychological Critique of the Present Approach to the Assessment of the Competence of Child Witnesses" (2000), 38(3) Osgoode Hall L.J. 409.

should be an inquiry into a child's understanding of such concepts as "truth," "lie" or "promise," the courts have interpreted s. 16(3) to mean that a child could only give unsworn testimony if the court conducts an inquiry to satisfy itself that the child can *demonstrate* an understanding of the duty to speak the truth.[122] This involves inquiring into the child's understanding of the nature of a "promise," and into the child's understanding of the meaning of "truth" and "lie." [123] Adults are not asked these challenging questions before being asked to testify, and laboratory based psychological research has established (not surprisingly) that a child's ability to correctly answer questions about the meaning of various such abstract concepts as "truth" and "promise" is not related to whether a child will actually tell the truth.[124]

The final requirement for competency to testify under the 1988 *Canada Evidence Act* is that a child, giving either sworn or unsworn testimony, must be "able to communicate the evidence." In *R. v. Marquard,* McLachlin J. indicated a relatively brief inquiry could satisfy the "ability to communicate" test, stating that the judge should explore "in a general way whether the witness is capable of perceiving events, remembering events and communicating events to the court."[125] This is usually done by asking the child questions about a past event, like a previous birthday, that is not the subject of the proceedings.

The New Competency Standard: s. 16.1 of the *Evidence Act*

Bill C-2 leaves s.16 of the *Canada Evidence Act* essentially unchanged for proposed witnesses fourteen or older whose mental capacity is challenged. A new s. 16.1 establishes a completely new approach for qualifying children under the age of fourteen, and securing their commitment to telling the truth to the best of their ability.

Person under fourteen years of age

16.1 (1) A person under fourteen years of age is presumed to have the capacity to testify.

No oath or solemn affirmation

(2) A proposed witness under fourteen years of age shall not take an oath or make a solemn affirmation despite a provision of any Act that requires an oath or a solemn affirmation.

---

122 See *R.* v. *McGovern* (1993), 82 C.C.C. (3d) 301, 22 C.R. (4th) 359 (Man C.A.) at 304-5 [C.C.C.], leave to appeal to S.C.C. refused (1993), 84 C.C.C. (3d) vi (S.C.C.); and *R.* v. *Ferguson* (1996), 112 C.C.C. (3d) 342 (B.C. C.A).

123 N. Bala, J. Lee & R.C.L Lindsay, "*R v M. (M.A.)*: Failing to Appreciate the Testimonial Capacity of Children" (2001), 40 C.R. (4th) 93.

124 V. Talwar, K. Lee, N. Bala & R.C.L. Lindsay, "Children's Conceptual Knowledge of Lying and its Relation to their Actual Behaviors: Implications for the Court Competence Examination" (2002), 26 Law & Human Behavior 395.

125 *R.* v. *Marquard,* [1993] 4 S.C.R. 223, 25 C.R. (4th) 1, 85 C.C.C. (3d) 193, at paras. 236-237.

Evidence shall be received

(3) The evidence of a proposed witness under fourteen years of age shall be received if they are able to understand and respond to questions.

Burden as to capacity of witness

(4) A party who challenges the capacity of a proposed witness under fourteen years of age has the burden of satisfying the court that there is an issue as to the capacity of the proposed witness to understand and respond to questions.

Court inquiry

(5) If the court is satisfied that there is an issue as to the capacity of a proposed witness under fourteen years of age to understand and respond to questions, it shall, before permitting them to give evidence, conduct an inquiry to determine whether they are able to understand and respond to questions.

Promise to tell truth

(6) The court shall, before permitting a proposed witness under fourteen years of age to give evidence, require them to promise to tell the truth.

Understanding of promise

(7) No proposed witness under fourteen years of age shall be asked any questions regarding their understanding of the nature of the promise to tell the truth for the purpose of determining whether their evidence shall be received by the court.

Effect

(8) For greater certainty, if the evidence of a witness under fourteen years of age is received by the court, it shall have the same effect as if it were taken under oath.

The new provision begins with the statement in s 16.1 (1) that children are "presumed to have the capacity to testify," while s. 16.1(4) places a burden on the "party who challenges the capacity" of a child to "satisfy the court that there is an issue as to the capacity" of the child "to understand and respond to questions." Subsection 16.1(4) might suggest that there is an onus on the party not calling the child as a witness (usually the accused) to raise the issue of competence. However, s. 16.1(5) provides that if the judge "is satisfied that there is an issue" as to a child's capacity to "understand and respond to questions," then before permitting the child to testify, the judge "shall conduct an inquiry" to determine whether the child is "able to understand and respond to questions." The words of s. 16.1(5) clearly suggest that the court itself or the party calling the child witness (usually the Crown), may also raise the issue of a child's competence, though the effect of ss. 16.1 (1) and (4) is that there will be a presumption of competence at the inquiry.

It is clearly preferable for the child for any issues about competency to be dealt with prior to the child giving evidence; further, there might be some risk of a mistrial if a child is called as a witness and begins to testify without an inquiry and then proves unable to answer most of the questions posed. The practice of taping of investigative interviews with the child by police or social workers and disclosure to defence counsel of the tapes should minimize these risks, as defence counsel should be in a position to have assessed whether the child is competent to answer questions prior to the child being called to the stand. It would also be a good practice for judges to ascertain at the time that a child is called to the stand whether the defence is challenging the competence of the witness, or accepts the child's competence.

The words of the new s. 16.1(5) are different from the words of the inquiry carried out under the 1988 provisions, which focused on whether the child "is able to communicate the evidence." The former competence inquiry concerned the capacity of the child to communicate about past events in general.[126] A child was required to be capable of giving more than "yes" or "no" responses to straightforward questions.[127] The courts also required that the child demonstrate an ability to distinguish between fact and fiction, and a capacity and a willingness to relate to the court the essence of what happened to her.[128]

Given the new test of "ability to understand and respond to questions," the issue under the new test is whether the child has basic cognitive and language abilities. The ability to observe and recollect now will be dealt with as matters of evidentiary weight. Whether a child witness is able to understand and respond to questions will be a matter for the judge to determine, and expert testimony will not normally be required.[129] In "exceptional circumstances," where the child would be so traumatized by the experience of appearing in court even for the limited purpose of establishing the inability to understand and respond to questions, an expert might be called to establish that the child is *not* able to testify.[130] If the inability to testify is established to the satisfaction of the court, this may be a ground for establishing the "necessity" for the admission of hearsay evidence instead of having the child testify.

In theory, the new words suggest a somewhat less onerous inquiry, but in practice the application of the test is likely to be very similar to the part of the old inquiry that focused on the child's capacity to meaningfully communicate evidence in court. It is submitted that, as required by the Supreme Court in applying the test in the 1988 *Evidence Act* in *R. v. Marquard*,[131] there should be a relatively brief inquiry into whether the child has the capacity to remember events and answer questions about those events. The inquiry into the child's capacity should be conducted by having the judge or counsel ask the child questions about a non-contentious past event. The judge has a duty to ensure that

---

126 *R. v. Marquard, ibid.*
127 *R. v. Caron* (1994), 94 C.C.C. (3d) 466 (Ont. C.A.).
128 *Ibid.* at 471.
129 *R. v. Parrott*, [2001] 1 S.C.R. 178, 39 C.R. (5th) 255, 150 C.C.C. (3d) 449.
130 *Ibid.*
131 *R. v. Marquard*, [1993] 4 S.C.R. 223, 25 C.R. (4th) 1, 85 C.C.C. (3d) 193, at paras. 236-237.

the questions that are posed to the child during this inquiry, and later in the proceedings, are appropriate to the child's stage of development, with age appropriate vocabulary and sentence structure.[132]

Prior to the 1988 amendments, trial judges always took the lead in actually asking the child questions, and counsel would then be given the opportunity to ask further questions. As with the 1988 provisions, Bill C-2 specifies that "the court shall conduct" an inquiry, if necessary because the capacity of a child witness has been challenged. It has been held that under the 1988 provisions it is sufficient for the judge to control the process and make the determination of competency to testify, but it is not necessary for the judge to take the lead in asking the questions.[133]

Judges increasingly appreciate that the counsel who calls the child as a witness (almost always the prosecutor) is a more suitable person to take the lead in questioning the child. The prosecutor should have met the child before court and the child will be more familiar with that counsel, and more comfortable in answering questions from that person during the invariably stressful first minutes in the courtroom.[134] This approach continues to be appropriate under the new provisions in s.16.1.

Subsection 16.1(2) and (6) provide that a child under fourteen years of age shall not testify under oath or solemn affirmation, but rather shall give a "promise to tell the truth." These provisions remove the possibility that a judge or counsel might want to attempt to determine whether a child might be permitted to testify under oath by requiring the child to answer questions about the nature of an oath, or intrusive questions about religious understandings or observance. This will ensure that all child witnesses receive the same treatment.

Subsection 16.1(6) specifically requires a child to make a "promise to tell the truth" before testifying. The process of a witness, whether a child or adult, making a commitment to tell the truth has symbolic importance for all of those involved in the justice process. Further, psychological research suggests that children who have promised to tell the truth may be more likely to tell the truth,

---

132 See J. Schuman, N. Bala & K. Lee, "Developmentally Appropriate Questions for Child Witnesses" (1999), 25 Queen's Law Journal 251. In *R. v. L. (D.O.)*, [1993] 4 S.C.R. 419, 25 C.R. (4th) 285, 85 C.C.C. (3d) 289 L'Heureux-Dubé J., writing for the entire Supreme Court of Canada on this point, gave judges the authority to intervene whenever a child is asked inappropriate questions (at 471, emphasis added):

   in . . . cases involving fragile witnesses such as children, *the trial judge has a responsibility to ensure that the child understands the question being asked and that the evidence given by the child is clear and unambiguous. To accomplish this end, the trial judge may be required to clarify and rephrase questions asked by counsel and to ask subsequent questions to the child to clarify the child's responses. In order to ensure the appropriate conduct of the trial, the judge should provide a suitable atmosphere to ease the tension so that the child is relaxed and calm.*

133 *R. v. F. (R.G.)* (1997), [1997] A.J. No. 409, 1997 CarswellAlta 336 (Alta. C.A.), at paras. 24-26.

134 *R. v. Peterson* (1996), 106 C.C.C. (3d) 64, 27 O.R. (3d) 739, 47 C.R. (4th) 161 (C.A.); leave to appeal to S.C.C. refused [1996] S.C.C.A. no. 202, 109 C.C.C. (3d) vi, [1996] 3 S.C.R. xii.

even if they are not able to provide a *definition* of "promise" or "truth."[135] (Interestingly, there is no comparable research for the effect of an oath, solemn affirmation or promise on adults.)

However, in a very significant change from practice under the 1988 law, s.16.1(7) specifies that "[n]o proposed witness under fourteen years of age shall be asked any questions regarding their understanding of the nature of the promise to tell the truth for the purpose of determining whether their evidence shall be received by the court." This provision is clearly intended to preclude the judge or counsel from asking a child questions about the meaning of such abstract concepts as "promise", "truth" and "lie" as a condition of being permitted to testify. Under the new provision, it is clear that children are not expected to demonstrate that they understand the duty to speak the truth or can define abstract concepts. These changes to the competency inquiry reflect the psychological research which demonstrates that the previous cognitively based inquiry might exclude children who were in fact competent to give honest, reliable answers to questions.

A result of the changes to the competency test for children is that children and adults are now treated in a more similar manner. By requiring children to demonstrate that they understood the "nature of an oath or solemn affirmation," judges were requiring more of children than of adults. Adults are not asked to define abstract concepts like "oath" before they are permitted to testify, even though a significant portion of adult witnesses are not able to give a good definition of this abstract concept. Children (and often adults) often understand and correctly use words without being able to answer questions that require them to provide a definition. For both adults and children, the process of promising or swearing an oath may serve to impress on the witness and others in the court the solemnity of the occasion. While having a child promise to tell the truth provides no guarantee of the honesty of the witness, it does no harm, and may do some good.

Though Bill C-2 does not provide detailed directions about how a judge is to deal with a child who is called as a witness, the language used in the new s.16.1 suggests that when the child takes the stand, after initial introductions, the judge, or counsel who has called the child as a witness, should ask the child preliminary questions about name, and such matters as age, school, and residence, and then about one or two past events, such as a holiday, not related to the matters at issue.[136] This initial questioning is intended to allow the court to ascertain whether the child is "able to understand and respond to questions." This questioning about non-contentious matters may also help the court to understand the child's speech

---

135 V. Talwar, K. Lee, N. Bala, & R.C.L. Lindsay, "Children's conceptual knowledge of lie-telling and its relation to their actual behaviors: Implications for court competence examination,"(2002) *26* Law & Human Behavior 395; V. Talwar, K. Lee, N. Bala, & R.C.L. Lindsay, "Children's lie-telling to conceal a parent's transgression: Legal implications" (2004), 8 Law & Human Behavior 411.

136 For a discussion of the type of "pre-interview" questioning that should be carried out to allow for the best "interview", see J. Schuman, N. Bala & K. Lee, "Developmentally Appropriate Questions for Child Witnesses" (1999) 25 Queen's Law Journal 251; and M.E. Lamb, K.K. Sternberg & P.W. Esplin, "Conducting Investigative Interviews of Alleged Sexual Abuse Victims" (1998) 22 Child Abuse and Neglect 813, at 818-19.

and vocabulary, and will help the child feel less uncomfortable in court and hence able to be a more effective witness.

While s. 16.1(7) makes clear that the answering of questions about the promise is not to be a condition of the child testifying, it is submitted that the judge may give the child simple instructions about the role of a witness in court.[137] This might include brief instructions about the importance of telling the truth.[138] The child could also be encouraged and instructed during this initial period about the need to give responses that are as detailed as possible. Children should also be reminded that if there are questions which they do not understand, that they should indicate this to the court, and if there are questions that they cannot answer, they should not guess at answers, but rather should respond "I don't know."[139]

Section 16.1 (8) makes clear that if a child testifies after giving a promise to tell the truth, this "shall have the same effect" as if the child testified under oath; that is, there is to be no discounting of the evidence of a child merely because the child has not given an oath. This new provision addresses a common judicial view that, under the 1988 *Act*, there was a distinction between the sworn and unsworn testimony of a child. It has not been uncommon, in the charge to the jury, for the judge to advert to the fact that a child did not testify under oath as a possible reason for discounting the child's testimony,[140] even though there is no legislative authority for this practice and no research to support it. This practice should no longer occur, since all children will testify on the basis of a promise to

---

137 It is submitted that this is as an aspect of the inherent obligation and power of the presiding judge to control the court process. See *R. v. A. (A.),* [2003] O.J. No. 4, 2003 CarswellOnt 16, 170 C.C.C. (3d) 449 (C.A.) on the inherent powers of a presiding judge, including a justice of the peace, to control the court process, and in the context of a youth court proceeding to ensure that a young person understands the significance of the charges that he faces, even if his counsel waives the reading of the charges.

138 The Youth Criminal Justice Act, S.C. 2002, c. 1, s. 151 provides that a youth justice court judge shall "instruct" a child witness under twelve "as to the duty to speak the truth and the consequences of failing to do so," and may give such instructions to a young person who testifies.

139 Young children often do not understand all that an adult questioner asks, but have been socially trained to "guess" at what is being asked and "respond." They will usually try to provide an answer to a question even if they did not understand it, or do not know how to answer it. It is appropriate for the judge to remind a child of the importance of saying that they did not understand a question, and to not guess at answers.

140 See *R. v. Demerchant* (1991), 66 C.C.C. (3d) 49 (N.B. C.A.). In G.A. Ferguson & J.C. Bouck, *Canadian Criminal Jury Instructions*, 3rd ed. (Vancouver, Continuing Legal Education Society of British Columbia, 2002), vol. 1, p. 4-65-2 , it is suggested that a judge should charge the jury in the following way:

   Despite the fact that [the child witness" did not testify under oath. . .to tell the truth, you may still accept or reject (his/her) evidence in the same way you accept or reject the evidence of any other witness.

   They go on to propose a further "discretionary instruction that may be given in appropriate circumstances" that would summarize the specific concerns about a particular child's testimony, and then conclude that "there is a dangerous risk of relying on (his/her) unsworn evidence standing alone without some other supporting or confirming evidence.

the truth. While a judge might caution a jury about inconsistencies or frailties in the testimony of any individual witness, including a child, there should not be a warning for classes of witnesses, such as children.

In the past, the intrusive inquiry required by s.16 was upsetting to children, a waste of court time and did nothing to promote the search for the truth. Some children who could give honest, reliable evidence were precluded from testifying, potentially resulting in miscarriages of justice. The changes created with the passage of Bill C-2 should address those concerns, by making it simpler for child witnesses to testify, through the introduction of a more logical competency test. Social science research establishes that the old practice of requiring children to "correctly" answer cognitive questions about the meaning of such abstract concepts as "oath", "truth", or "promise" did not increase the likelihood that a child would give honest or reliable testimony. Examining a child witness' ability to meaningfully understand and answer questions is a more realistic criterion to use to determine whether a child is competent to testify. If the child is found "able to understand and respond to questions" about past events, the child will invariably have sufficient basic understanding of the concepts involved to give the child some appreciation for the significance of "promising to tell the truth." Asking the child to promise to tell the truth, but not expecting the child to explain the significance of this undertaking is similar to how adults are treated.

Conclusion

While the justice system at one time operated on the basis of erroneous stereotypes about the inherent unreliability of children, psychological research conducted over the past two decades has led to a better understanding of children as witnesses. Research also has examined the experience of children as witnesses, and the changes enacted by the passage of Bill C-2 reflect the increased awareness of the capacities and needs of children and other vulnerable witnesses. Some of the changes, such as the new competency test in s. 16.1 of the *Canada Evidence Act,* will permit children to serve as witnesses who previously would have been prevented from testifying. Other changes in Bill C-2 will enable children and other vulnerable witnesses to testify in a more effective manner, while experiencing less trauma and anxiety. While children will continue to feel a great deal of stress, and in some cases suffer emotional trauma, from the testifying, the new provisions are a clear improvement. The changes in Bill C-2 should both enhance the truth-seeking function of the criminal justice system and reduce the stress on children and other vulnerable witnesses from their involvement in the legal process.

The constitutionality of section 16.1 was upheld by the Supreme Court in *R. v. S.(J.).*[141] In *R. v. I.D.*[142] the Ontario Court of Appeal held that section 16.1 and

---

141 January 19, 2010. The Court was content to adopt the judgment of the B.C. Court of Appeal: (2008) 61 C.R. 282 - see laudatory C.R. annotation to that ruling by Lisa Dufraimont.
142 February 19, 2010.

its philosophy could not be applied to a developmentally challenged adult whose competency was to be determined by section 16 tests (discussed below).

The *Ontario Evidence Act* has arguably not yet caught up to its federal counterpart. Section 18.1 reads:

Evidence of witness under 14

18.1 (1) When the competence of a proposed witness who is a person under the age of 14 is challenged, the court may admit the person's evidence if the person is able to communicate the evidence, understands the nature of an oath or solemn affirmation and testifies under oath or solemn affirmation.

Same

(2) The court may admit the person's evidence, if the person is able to communicate the evidence, even though the person does not understand the nature of an oath or solemn affirmation, if the person understands what it means to tell the truth and promises to tell the truth.

Further discretion

(3) If the court is of the opinion that the person's evidence is sufficiently reliable, the court has discretion to admit it, if the person is able to communicate the evidence, even if the person understands neither the nature of an oath or solemn affirmation nor what it means to tell the truth.

Bill C-2 also added to the procedures in the Criminal Code that were enacted in 1988 to accommodate the evidence of children. As a result of both amendments, witnesses under the age of 18 can testify with a support person (section 486.1), and behind a screen or with the aid of a closed circuit television (section 486.2). There is also a requirement that an accused must apply to the judge to personally cross-examine the complainant (section 486.3).

The constitutionality of the 1988 amendments was upheld in the following case:

R. v. LEVOGIANNIS
[1993] 4 S.C.R. 475, 25 C.R. (4th) 325, 85 C.C.C. (3d) 327

The accused was charged with touching a child for a sexual purpose. The Crown requested that the 12-year-old complainant be allowed to testify behind a screen pursuant to section 486(2.1) of the Code. The trial judge granted the Crown's motion following the testimony of a clinical psychologist who indicated that the complainant was experiencing a great deal of fear about testifying. The accused challenged the constitutional validity of section 486(2.1) on the grounds that it violated his right to a fair trial guaranteed by sections 7 and 11(*d*) of the Charter. Both the trial judge and the Court of Appeal held that section 486(2.1) of the Code did not infringe sections 7 and 11(*d*). The Court of Appeal added that even if section 486(2.1) infringed these sections, the infringement would be justified under section 1 of the Charter.

L'HEUREUX-DUBÉ J.:—

. . . .

The examination of whether an accused's rights are infringed encompasses multifaceted considerations, such as the rights of witnesses, in this case children, the rights of accused and courts' duties to ascertain the truth. The goal of the court process is truth seeking and, to that end, the evidence of all those involved in judicial proceedings must be given in a way that is most favourable to eliciting the truth. In ascertaining the constitutionality of s. 486(2.1) of the *Criminal Code*, one cannot ignore the fact that, in many instances, the court process is failing children, especially those who have been victims of abuse, who are then subjected to further trauma as participants in the judicial process.

. . . .

The plight of children who testify and the role courts must play in ascertaining the truth must not be overlooked in the context of the constitutional analysis in the case at hand. As this Court has said, children may require different treatment than adults in the courtroom setting.

. . . .

An order under s. 486(2.1) simply blocks the complainant's view of the accused and not vice versa. The wording of s. 486(2.1) merely provides that the screen "would allow the complainant not to see the accused". The screen does not obstruct the view of the complainant by the accused, his counsel, the Crown or the judge. All are present in court. The evidence is given and the trial is conducted in the usual manner, including cross-examination. As a result, the issue before this Court, is, simply put, whether a witness's obstructed view of an accused, infringes the rights of such accused under s. 7 or 11(*d*) of the *Charter*.

. . . .

In my view, the main objective pursued by the legislative enactment presently challenged is to better "get at the truth", by recognizing that a young child abuse victim's evidence may, in certain circumstances, be facilitated if the child is able to focus his or her attention on giving testimony, rather than experiencing difficulties in facing the accused. Section 486(2.1) of the *Criminal Code* recognizes that a child may react negatively to a face-to-face confrontation and, as a result, special procedures may be required to alleviate these concerns.

. . . .

The appellant submits that his right to "be presumed innocent until proven guilty according to law in a fair and public hearing by an independent and impartial tribunal" is violated, as the screen undermines the presumption of innocence, operates unfairly against the accused and hampers cross-examination. . . .

According to the appellant, the use of a screen lends an air of credence to the witness' testimony and, since the courtroom has been altered for the protection of the young complainant, the accused may appear guilty. In the case at bar, the appellant was tried before a judge sitting alone and, as a result, the issue of appearance to the jury is not relevant. Had a jury been present, however, I suggest that, properly informed, they would not have been swayed by the use of the screen. As Dickson C.J. said in *R. v. Corbett*, [1988] 1 S.C.R. 670, at p. 692:

In my view, it would be quite wrong to make too much of the risk that the jury might use the evidence for an improper purpose.

In a similar vein, I suggest that one should assume that a jury will follow judicial instruction and will not be biased by the use of such a device. In fact, in contrast to the perspective raised by the appellant, it has been remarked that Crown prosecutors are reluctant to request the use of screens because they are concerned that the young complainant may not come across as credible or the child's testimony may have less of an impact. . . . The use of a screen could very well be held against a child complainant, who might be judged to be an unreliable witness, because she or he is unable to look the accused in the eye, rather than against the accused. If screens were used more regularly as part of the courtroom procedure, as recommended by the Family Court Clinic in London, these perceptions may well be totally eliminated. Finally, while it is true, as the appellant contends, that s. 486(2.1) of the *Criminal Code*, similar in this regard to most sections of the *Code*, does not contain prescribed jury instructions, such instructions are routinely given by judges and such a caution is no more a constitutional prerequisite with respect to this section than with respect to any other section of the *Criminal Code*. Such caution may not be necessary or, if it is, it will be a function of the circumstances of the case.

(d) Mental Capacity

In *R. v. Hill*[143] the accused, an attendant at what was then called a lunatic asylum, was convicted for the manslaughter of one of the patients. It was objected that the chief prosecution witness was incompetent. Evidence was given that the witness did suffer the delusion that spirits spoke to him, but he was also described as having a good memory and ability to give an account of events observed. The precedents at the time were in conflict over whether there should be a blanket rule of inadmissibility and the court answered:

Lord Campbell, C.J.:

> It has been argued that any particular delusion, commonly called monomania, makes a man inadmissible. This would be extremely inconvenient in many cases in the proof either of guilt or innocence: it might also cause serious difficulties in the management of lunatic asylums. I am, therefore, of opinion that the Judge must, in all such cases, determine the competency, and the jury the credibility. Before he is sworn, the insane person may be cross-examined, and witnesses called to prove circumstances which might shew him to be inadmissible; but, in the absence of such proof, he is *prima facie* admissible, and the jury must attach what weight they think fit to his testimony.

In the course of argument Lord Campbell spoke of the judge determining

> whether the insane person has the sense of religion in his mind, and whether he understands the nature and sanction of an oath,[144]

---

143 (1851), 169 E.R. 495 (Crown Cases Reserved). Followed in *R. v. Dunning*, [1965] Crim. L.R. 372 (C.C.A.).
144 *Ibid.*, at p. 498.

and concluded that the trial judge was right in swearing the witness as the uncontradicted evidence showed that the witness was able to give a rational account of matters observed. Although the witness had described his awareness of the consequences of a false oath, eternal damnation, and so demonstrated moral responsibility, the bulk of the evidence led on his testimonial qualifications concerned the quite separate aspects of his ability to accurately observe, recollect and rationally communicate.

Although, generally, the competency of a witness should be challenged before the witness is sworn, if the incompetency only becomes manifest later, the trial judge may stop the examination and order the evidence stricken.[145] The mental capacity of the witness will initially be presumed, but when challenged the offering party will be put to proof on a *voir dire* and the trial judge must then make an express finding.[146] The *voir dire* should be in the presence of the jury "since the dispute would be for their use and their instruction."[147] The trial judge is advised

> that the derangement or defect, in order to disqualify, must be such as *substantially negatives trustworthiness* upon the specific subject of the testimony.[148]

Commentators have long argued for an abandonment of the present rule leaving it to the jury to consider what weight, if any, it will attach to the testimony of such a witness. In 1853 the Common Law Practice Commissioners recommended:

> Plain sense and reason would obviously suggest that any living witness who could throw light upon a fact in issue should be heard to state what he knows, subject always to such observations as may arise as to his means of knowledge or his disposition to tell the truth.[149]

Following Bill C-2, section 16 of the *Canada Evidence Act* now reads:

Witness whose capacity is in question
16. (1) If a proposed witness is a person of fourteen years of age or older whose mental capacity is challenged, the court shall, before permitting the person to give evidence, conduct an inquiry to determine

---

145 See *R. v. Steinberg*, [1931] O.R. 222, 257 (C.A.) per Grant, J.A., quoted with approval in *R. v. Hawke* (1975), 22 C.C.C. (2d) 19, 43 (Ont. C.A.). And see *R. v. Deol* (1981), 58 C.C.C. (2d) 524 (Alta. C.A.) rejecting such an objection raised for the first time on a non-suit application as not timely. See also *R. v. Clark* (1983), 35 C.R. (3d) 357 (Ont. C.A.).

146 See 2 Wigmore, *Evidence* (3d ed.), s. 497, approved as accurately reflecting the duty of the trial judge in *R. v. Hawke, ibid.,* at p. 27.

147 *Toohey v. Metro. Police Commr.*, [1965] 1 All E.R. 506, 512 (H.L.).

148 2 Wigmore, *Evidence* (3d ed.), s. 492, adopted in *R. v. Hawke, supra,* note 145, at p. 27.

149 As quoted in 2 Wigmore, *Evidence* (Chad. Rev.), s. 501, note 2. See *R. v. Spencer; R. v. Smails*, [1986] 2 All E.R. 928 (H.L.) re duty to warn of danger of convicting on the uncorroborated evidence of a mental patient. See *R. v. Thurlow* (1994), 34 C.R. (4th) 53 (Ont. Gen. Div.), where Weekes, J. dealt with the difficult problem of the competency of a witness with multiple personalities. While giving evidence at the preliminary hearing she took the oath identifying herself as M.B. During cross-examination she explained that the person who was testifying was not M.B. but was, in fact, a persona she identified as "Me". Subsequently she purportedly transformed into a different persona, a male, who identified himself as "Alex". "Alex" gave evidence but, during this time, neither M. nor "Me" was present in the court. The witness appeared to the court to be in a dissociative state.

(a) whether the person understands the nature of an oath or a solemn affirmation; and

(b) whether the person is able to communicate the evidence.

Testimony under oath or solemn affirmation

(2) A person referred to in subsection (1) who understands the nature of an oath or a solemn affirmation and is able to communicate the evidence shall testify under oath or solemn affirmation.

Testimony on promise to tell truth

(3) A person referred to in subsection (1) who does not understand the nature of an oath or a solemn affirmation but is able to communicate the evidence may, notwithstanding any provision of any Act requiring an oath or a solemn affirmation, testify on promising to tell the truth.

Inability to testify

(4) A person referred to in subsection (1) who neither understands the nature of an oath or a solemn affirmation nor is able to communicate the evidence shall not testify.

Burden as to capacity of witness

(5) A party who challenges the mental capacity of a proposed witness of fourteen years of age or more has the burden of satisfying the court that there is an issue as to the capacity of the proposed witness to testify under an oath or a solemn affirmation.

Does the witness have to be called on the s. 16 competency hearing?

R. v. PARROTT
[2001] 1 S.C.R. 178, 39 C.R. (5th) 255, 150 C.C.C. (3d) 449

The accused was charged with offences in relation to a woman who suffered from Down's Syndrome. The complainant was considered to be mildly to moderately retarded and had been in institutional care for almost 20 years. The complainant made statements to the police when she was found, and to the doctor who first examined her. The police also conducted a videotaped interview the following day. We will see later, in the chapter dealing with Hearsay, that out-of-court statements may be received for their truth if there are grounds of necessity and the statements were made in circumstances that indicated they were reliable. This case deals with the requirement of necessity.

BINNIE J. (MAJOR, BASTARACHE and ARBOUR JJ. concurring): —

This appeal tests the limits of the principled hearsay exception that allows the Crown in exceptional circumstances to lead the out-of-court evidence of a complainant at a criminal trial without having him or her present in court and available for cross-examination by the defence.

In this case, the complainant in a kidnapping and sexual assault case was a mature woman who had suffered since birth from Down's Syndrome. She was considered mildly to moderately retarded and had been in institutional care for almost 20 years. Expert evidence was called to establish that her mental development was equivalent to that of a three- or four-year-old child and that her memory of events was poor. Her response to even the simplest questions was said to be not very coherent. The complainant herself was never called into the presence of the trial judge so that these attributes could be verified even though she was available and there was no suggestion that she would suffer any trauma or other adverse effect by appearing in court. Instead the court received evidence of out-of-court statements that she had earlier made to the police and to a doctor.

. . . .

Analysis

While in this country an accused does not have an absolute right to confront his or her accuser in the course of a criminal trial, the right to full answer and defence generally produces this result. In this case, unusually, the Crown precipitated an inquiry under s. 16 of the Canada Evidence Act not for the purpose of establishing the testimonial competence of "a proposed witness", namely the complainant, but to lay an evidentiary basis to keep her out of the witness box. Having satisfied the trial judge entirely through expert evidence that the complainant neither understood the nature of an oath nor could communicate her evidence, the Crown used the *voir dire* as a springboard to establish the admissibility of hearsay evidence of her out-of-court statements under the principles established in *Khan*.

This procedure raises two distinct though related issues, firstly the admissibility of the expert evidence at the *voir dire*, and secondly the admissibility of the complainant's out-of-court statements at the trial. In my view, these issues ought to have been resolved in favour of the respondent, as held by the majority judgment of the Newfoundland Court of Appeal, for the following reasons:

1. The expert evidence was improperly admitted at the *voir dire*. Trial judges are eminently qualified to assess the testimonial competence of a witness. The trial judge, after all, was to be at the receiving end of the complainant's communication, and could have determined whether or not she was able to communicate her evidence to him. If she had been called and it became evident that the trial judge required expert assistance to draw appropriate inferences from what he had heard her say (or not say), or if either the defence or the Crown had wished to pursue the issue of requiring an oath or solemn affirmation, expert evidence might then have become admissible to assist the judge. At the time the expert testimony was called, it had not been shown that expert evidence as such was necessary, and the testimony of Drs. Gillespie, Morley and Parsons was therefore inadmissible: *R. v. Mohan*, [1994] 2 S.C.R. 9.

2. Consequently, the trial judge erred in ruling at the conclusion of the *voir dire* that the complainant's out-of-court statements would be admissible at trial. Having dispensed with hearing from the complainant, and the expert medical testimony having been improperly admitted, the trial judge had no admissible evidence on which to exercise a discretion to admit the complainant's out-of-court statements.

. . . .

At the threshold stands the question of why expert evidence was admitted in the first place to establish the competency of a witness, a task which is specifically assigned by s. 16 of the Canada Evidence Act to the trial judge. In *R. v. Abbey*, [1982] 2 S.C.R. 24, the Court adopted as correct the statement that "[i]f on the proven facts a judge or jury can form their own conclusions without help, then the opinion of the expert is unnecessary".

The key and undisputed facts of this case are that the complainant was available to testify and there was no suggestion by anybody that she might be harmed thereby. She was not called simply because the Crown made the tactical decision to proceed without calling her. The medical experts were not called to assist the judge to interpret what he had seen or heard from the complainant in the witness box, but in substitution for any such opportunity of direct observation.

The special role of the expert witness is not to testify to the facts, but to provide an opinion based on the facts, to assist the trier of fact to draw the appropriate inferences from the facts as found "which the judge and jury, due to the technical nature of the facts, are unable to formulate" (*Abbey, supra.*)

. . . .

Whether a complainant "is able to communicate the evidence" in this broad sense is a matter on which a trial judge can (and invariably does) form his or her own opinion. It is not a matter "outside the experience and knowledge of a judge or jury" (*Mohan, supra*, at p. 23). It is the very meat and potatoes of a trial court's existence.

LeBel J. (L'Heureux-Dubé and Gonthier JJ. concurring) dissenting: —

. . . The question at issue in this appeal is whether, on the *voir dire* to determine necessity, the Crown was *obliged* to put the complainant forward as a witness in order for the trial judge to evaluate her testimonial capacity. While I agree with my colleague, Binnie J., that it is generally a prudent practice to have the Crown do so, I would not elevate it to an absolute legal requirement in every case. In my view, the evidence before the trial judge in the present case amply supports his findings of necessity and reliability. . . .

Under s. 16(1), the critical inquiries will be whether the witness is able to (a) communicate the evidence; and (b) understands the nature of an oath or solemn affirmation or promises to tell the truth. In *R. v. Fletcher*,[150] the Ontario Court of Appeal established that a witness understands the nature of an oath where they appreciate the moral obligation to tell the truth and, in particular, the solemnity of a court of law and the added responsibility of telling the truth above the duty to tell the truth which is an ordinary duty of normal social conduct. This jurisprudence, which concerned the evidence of children, is still relevant under s. 16(1). In the case that follows, the Ontario Court of Appeal sets out the tests to be applied in determining whether the witness has the ability to communicate and understands what it means to promise to tell the truth. Again, although the case was decided before Bill C-2, it is still applicable today in cases involving challenges to mental capacity.

---

150 (1982), 1 C.C.C. (3d) 370 (Ont. C.A.).

R. v. FARLEY
(1995), 40 C.R. (4th) 190, 99 C.C.C. (3d) 76

DOHERTY J.A. (ROBINS and WEILER JJ.A. concurring):—

The appellant was convicted of sexual assault and sentenced to three years in the penitentiary. . . .

The complainant was 26 years of age at the time of the trial. He is severely intellectually handicapped and has, according to one of his caregivers, the comprehension of a three-year-old child. Before the complainant testified, the trial judge conducted the inquiry required under s. 16 of the *Canada Evidence Act*, R.S.C. 1985, c. C-5. She determined that the complainant could not testify under oath or affirmation, but could testify upon promising to tell the truth.

· · · ·

The appellant contends that the complainant should not have been found competent to give evidence. Apart from that contention, I see no error in the trial proceedings.

· · · ·

Section 16(3) has two components. Before the prospective witness can testify pursuant to that section, he or she must:

- be able to communicate the evidence
  AND
- promise to tell the truth.

The phrase "able to communicate the evidence" refers to the cognitive and communicative capacity of the proposed witness. . . .

In *R. v. Caron* (1994), 94 C.C.C. (3d) 466 at 471 (Ont. C.A.), Arbour J.A. considered the above passage from *Marquard* and said:

> In order to be found capable of communicating his or her evidence, a witness must demonstrate some ability not only to distinguish between fact and fiction, as this child did with respect to colour for instance, but also a capacity and a willingness, limited as it may be in the case of a young child, to relate to the court the essence of what happened to her.

In my opinion, the capacity to perceive entails not only an ability to perceive events as they occur, but also an ability to differentiate between that which is actually perceived and that which the person may have imagined, been told by others, or otherwise have come to believe. Similarly, the capacity to remember refers to the person's capacity to maintain a recollection of his or her actual perceptions of a prior event, and the ability to distinguish those retained perceptions from information provided to the person from other sources, such as statements made to the person by others. The capacity to communicate refers to the ability to understand questions and to respond to them in an intelligible fashion.

The cognitive and communicative components of the competence test found in s. 16(3) refer to capacity and not to the proposed witness's actual perception, recollection, and narration of the relevant events. A person may have the capacity to perceive, recall, and recount and yet be unable to perform one or more of those functions in a given situation. For example, a witness who genuinely has no recollection of the relevant events is not thereby rendered incompetent unless that inability to recall is a reflection of the absence of the capacity to recall. It must also be stressed that the cognitive and communicative components of s. 16(3) set a relatively low threshold for testimonial competence. Once the capacity to perceive, remember, and recount is established, any deficiencies in a particular witness's perception, recollection, or narration go to the weight of that witness's evidence and not the witness's competence to testify: *R. v. Marquard, supra*, at p. 220.

. . . .

If a proposed witness is able to communicate the evidence in the sense described above, s. 16(3) provides that the witness may testify only upon promising to tell the truth. Unless a promise to tell the truth is a meaningless formalism, it must impose a further prerequisite to testimonial competence beyond the above-described capacity to communicate the evidence.

. . . .

There is clearly a close relationship between an understanding of the duty to speak the truth and the making of a meaningful promise to tell the truth. The latter assumes the existence of the former.

. . . .

A proposed witness who can communicate the evidence should be allowed to testify under s. 16(3) only if he or she "understand[s] the duty to speak the truth in terms of . . . everyday social conduct." In the context of a witness called to describe a prior event, an understanding of the duty to speak the truth entails an appreciation by the witness that he or she must answer all questions in accordance with the witness's recollection of what actually happened.

. . . .

In holding that an understanding of the duty to tell the truth remains a precondition to giving unsworn or unaffirmed evidence, I do not mean to suggest that a proposed witness must make an actual commitment to tell the truth before being allowed to testify under s. 16(3). A witness who understands the duty to speak the truth, but is nonetheless prepared to ignore that obligation, is not thereby rendered an incompetent witness. A willingness to lie goes to credibility and not to competence.

Appeal dismissed. Accused competent to testify on promise to tell truth.

(e) Interest

When witnesses first began informing the jury in the 15th century, there was no bar against witnesses who were interested in the outcome. Indeed, witnesses who were disinterested were regarded as meddling and unless summoned by the court or the jury they might risk a maintenance prosecution.[151] Originally witnesses were interested in the outcome and as a result distinctly partisan. To this there was one major exception: the parties themselves. The party could plead or argue but could not be sworn since to do so would be to mix two kinds of proof; during the fifteenth century, and indeed continuing into the sixteenth, the party could elect trial by wager of law rather than by jury, and in that mode of proceeding he was entitled to the use of his own oath. Later, as trial by witnesses before a jury became the predominant mode of proceeding in civil cases, the disqualification of parties was extended, by analogy, to include other persons interested in the outcome and by 1650 the disqualification was firmly established. One particular group of readily identifiable interested persons were the spouses of the parties. Curiously, while the disqualification was extended to cover the spouse, the common law did not go further and extend it to children or other relatives; perhaps the extension to spouses was grounded on the then current notion of identity or merger of the two spouses into a single person. In criminal trials the accused had been entitled, like a party in a civil case, to plead and argue orally, by himself, and later, through his counsel. The accused then presented his own "evidence" and was questioned though he was not sworn. By analogy to the civil cases his statements were not to be regarded as testimony since he was disqualified as a witness from his own interest in the outcome.[152]

As in civil cases, the spouse was incompetent in criminal trials:

> . . . except in case of necessity, and that necessity is not a general necessity, as where no other witness can be had, but a particular necessity, as where, for instance, the wife would otherwise be exposed without remedy to personal injury.[153]

Inspired by Bentham, the reformers in the mid to late 19th century gradually discarded these disqualifications for interest, preferring that the proposed witness' interest be displayed to, and taken into account by, the trier of fact, who could then evaluate to what particular extent the interest may have impaired credibility. As Bentham noted:

> Any interest, interest of any sort and quantity, sufficient to prove mendacity? As rational would be it to say, any horse, or dog, or flea, put to a wagon, is sufficient to move it . . .

---

151 See Thayer, *Preliminary Treatise on Evidence at the Common Law* (1898), pp. 125-29. At p. 128 quoting Paston, J. in 1442: "If one who has no reason to meddle in the matter and is not learned in the law shows the jury, or the party himself, or his counsel, the truth of the matter and opens evidence of it as well and as fully as one who was learned in the law could, yet this is a maintenance in his person."

152 The detailed history of the development here briefly described may be seen in 2 Wigmore, *Evidence* (Chad. Rev.), ss. 575, 601. See also *Coleman's Trial* (1678), 7 Howell's State Trials 1, 65: the prosecution witness maintained the prisoner's treasonous act was done about the 21st of August and the prisoner said to the court:
- Prisoner: I went out of town on the 10th of August, it was the latter end I came home.
- L.C.J.:   Have you any witness to prove that?
- Prisoner: I cannot say I have a witness.
- L.C.J.:   Then you say nothing. . . . You say you went out of town the 10th and came home the last of August; you say it is impossible that he should say right, but yet you do not prove it.

153 *Bentley v. Cooke* (1784), 99 E.R. 729, per Lord Mansfield.

... In the eyes of the English lawyer, one thing, and one thing only, has a value: that thing is money. On the will of man, if you believe the English lawyer, one thing, and one thing only, has influence: that thing is money. Such is his system of psychological dynamics. If you will believe the man of law, there is no such thing as the fear of God; no such thing as regard for reputation; no such thing as fear of legal punishment; no such thing as ambition; no such thing as the love of power; no such thing as filial, no such thing as parental, affection; no such thing as party attachment; no such thing as party enmity; no such thing as public spirit, patriotism, or general benevolence; no such thing as compassion; no such thing as gratitude; no such thing as revenge.[154]

The reforming legislation enacted in England was copied in Canada. The incremental nature of the change in England by individual statutes over a period of years is seen reflected in the provincial legislation, which in its present form consequently appears duplicative. For example, the *Ontario Evidence Act*[155] provides:

> 6. No person offered as a witness in an action shall be excluded from giving evidence by reason of any alleged incapacity from crime or interest.
>
> 7. Every person offered as a witness shall be admitted to give evidence notwithstanding that he has an interest in the matter in question or in the event of the action and notwithstanding that he has been previously convicted of a crime or offence.
>
> 8.(1) The parties to an action and the persons on whose behalf it is brought, instituted, opposed or defended are, except as hereinafter otherwise provided, competent and compellable to give evidence on behalf of themselves or of any of the parties, and the spouses of such parties and persons are, except as hereinafter otherwise provided, competent and compellable to give evidence on behalf of any of the parties. R.S.O. 1990, c. E.23, s. 8 (1); 2005, c. 5, s. 25 (2).
>
>   . . . .
>
> 10.(1) The parties to a proceeding instituted in consequence of adultery and the spouses of such parties are competent to give evidence in such proceedings, but no witness in any such proceeding, whether a party to the suit or not, is liable to be asked or bound to answer any question tending to show that he or she is guilty of adultery, unless such witness has already given evidence in the same proceeding in disproof of his or her alleged adultery. R.S.O. 1990, c. E.23, s. 10; 2005, c. 5, s. 25 (4).

The Canada Evidence Act[156] provides:

> 3. A person is not incompetent to give evidence by reason of interest or crime.
>
> 4.(1) Every person charged with an offence, and, except as otherwise provided in this section, the wife or husband, as the case may be, of the person so charged, is a competent witness for the defence, whether the person so charged is charged solely or jointly with any other person.
>
> (2) The wife or husband of a person charged with an offence against subsection

---

154 Bentham, *Rationale of Judicial Evidence* (1827), cited in 2 Wigmore, *Evidence* (Chad. Rev.), s. 576.
155 R.S.O. 1990, c. E-23.
156 R.S.C. 1985, c. C-5 [s. 4 am. 1987, c. 24, s. 17].

50(1) of the Young Offenders Act or with an offence against any of sections 151, 152, 153, 155 or 159, subsection 160(2) or (3), or sections 170 to 173, 179, 212, 215, 218, 271 to 273, 280 to 283, 291 to 294 or 329 of the Criminal Code, or an attempt to commit any such offence, is a competent and compellable witness for the prosecution without the consent of the person charged.

. . . .

(4) The wife or husband of a person charged with an offence against any of sections 220, 221, 235, 236, 237, 239, 240, 266, 267, 268 or 269 of the Criminal Code where the complainant or victim is under the age of fourteen years is a competent and compellable witness for the prosecution without the consent of the person charged.

(5) Nothing in this section affects a case where the wife or husband of a person charged with an offence may at common law be called as a witness without the consent of that person.

(f) Spousal Competence and Compellability[157]

(i) *General Rule*

R. v. COUTURE
2007 CarswellBC 1365, 2007 CarswellBC 1366, [2007] 2 S.C.R. 517, 47 C.R. (6th) 1, 220 C.C.C. (3d) 289

CHARRON J. (McLachlin C.J. and Binnie, LeBel and Fish JJ. Concurring): —

1. Overview

1   David Couture was convicted of two counts of second degree murder in respect of the 1986 killings of his ex-girlfriend Darlinda Lee Ritchey and her friend Karen Ann Baker. His convictions were based, in part, on two out-of-court statements made by his spouse Darlene Couture to the police in 1997. In her statements, Darlene Couture disclosed that in 1989, some time before their marriage, she had been Mr. Couture's Christian volunteer counsellor in prison where he was serving time on unrelated offences and that during the course of the counselling, he had confided in her that he had murdered the two women. This appeal turns on the admissibility of the spouse's out-of-court statements under the principled exception to the hearsay rule.

[This issue will be addressed later in the book when we come to hearsay.]

2   At the time Mrs. Couture gave the two statements to the police she was living estranged from Mr. Couture. The couple reconciled shortly after and, at the time of trial, their marriage was valid and subsisting.

[The accused was convicted at trial. His convictions were overturned by the Supreme Court of Canada.]

---

157 Where the spouse is an accused other special rules apply, as discussed below.

. . .

3. Analysis

3.1 *The Law Respecting Spousal Testimony*

37 Before dealing with the evidentiary issue that occupies us, I will do a brief overview of the current law respecting spousal testimony. Spousal testimony raises issues of competence, compellability, and privilege that are governed by a combination of common law principles and statutory provisions.

38 At common law, in civil cases, the parties and their spouses were incompetent to testify. The same rule applied in criminal cases to accused persons and their spouses, save in cases that involved the witness spouse's person, liberty or health. The rule has been abolished in civil cases and, in criminal cases, it has been modified by statute.

. . .

39 The statute implicitly preserves the common law, subject to the exceptions that it creates. Section 4(5) makes it clear that the common law exception to spousal incompetency is unaffected and the spouse is therefore both competent and compellable to testify for the prosecution in cases involving the spouse's person, liberty or health. Further exceptions are created for specified offences under ss. 4(2) and 4(4). None of these exceptions apply here. Therefore, because the marriage between Darlene Couture and the accused was valid and subsisting, at the time of the trial, Darlene was neither competent nor compellable to testify for the Crown.

40 Under s. 4(1) of the *Canada Evidence Act*, the accused and his or her spouse are both competent to testify for the defence. The words of the section address only competence and not compellability, leaving the question whether the spouse can also be *compelled* by her spouse to testify still somewhat unsettled. The provision has been interpreted differently in respect of the accused and the spouse. This Court in *Gosselin v. The King* (1903), 33 S.C.R. 255, held that, under the provisions of the *Canada Evidence Act, 1893* (which did not include the words "for the defence"), the spouse of an accused was not only a competent but a compellable witness for or against the accused person on a trial for an indictable offence. However, Sopinka J., in *R. v. Amway Corp.*, [1989] 1 S.C.R. 21, expressed the view that s. 4(1) only deals with competence and not compellability. He concluded in that case that the provision left intact the common law with respect to the non-compellability of an accused at the instance of the Crown. While it is unnecessary to settle this issue, I will assume for the purpose of this appeal that Darlene Couture, although not compellable by the Crown, could be compelled to testify for the defence. Quite apart from any issue of statutory interpretation, it is well-established at common law that a competent witness is a compellable witness: see review of the relevant law in *R. v. McGinty* (1986),1 Y.R. 27 (C.A.), *per* McLachlin J.A., as she then was.

41 Section 4(3) creates a spousal privilege in respect of marital communications. The question of privilege was not really an issue at common law because spouses,

with few exceptions, were not competent to testify. The concept of spousal privilege was therefore created by statute after legislation in the 19th century made spouses competent witnesses. The privilege is testimonial in nature, giving a right to withhold evidence but the communications themselves are not privileged. The privilege belongs to the spouse receiving the communication and can be waived by him or her. See *Lloyd v. The Queen*, [1981] 2 S.C.R. 645, at pp. 654-55. The question of privilege does not arise in this case with respect to the alleged confessions made by Mr. Couture to Darlene in 1989 since these communications were made prior to their marriage on February 14, 1996. It would arise in respect of any later communications made during the marriage. The question of spousal privilege must be kept in mind in considering broader implications that may result from any modification to the law respecting spousal testimony.

42 Historically, different rationales were advanced to support and justify the rule of spousal incompetency, some of which have been overcome in the more modern era with the legal recognition of spouses as being two separate entities. However, two rationales have survived to this day. They were explained in *R. v. Salituro*, [1991] 3 S.C.R. 654, at p. 672, and reiterated in *Hawkins*, at para. 38.

43 The first justification for the rule is that it promotes conjugal confidences and protects marital harmony. The second is that the rule prevents "the indignity of conscripting an accused's spouse to participate in the accused's own prosecution" (*Hawkins*, at para. 38). Wigmore describes this second justification as the "*natural repugnance* in every fair-minded person to compelling a wife or husband to be the means of the other's condemnation, and to compelling the culprit to the humiliation of being condemned by the words of his intimate life partner" (*Wigmore on Evidence* (McNaughton rev. 1961), vol. 8, at §2228, p. 217, cited in part in *Salituro*, at p. 672). The disruption to marital harmony and "natural repugnance" resulting from one spouse testifying against the other has been aptly described, in words that somewhat reflect the sentiments expressed by Darlene Couture in her statements to the police, by Professor Hamish Stewart in his article "Spousal Incompetency and the *Charter*" (1996), 34 *Osgoode Hall L.J.*, 411, as follows (at p. 417):

> [O]ne can easily envisage that both the accused and his spouse would feel considerable resentment and distrust arising from the mere fact of the spouse's testifying for the Crown and from cross-examination of the spouse by counsel or indeed by the accused himself, quite apart from the resentment that would arise if the accused were actually convicted as a result of his spouse's testimony. There is more than mere sentiment at work in the marital harmony justification. If the marital relationship deserves protection — and most people would agree that it does — then at times other social goals, including even truth-finding, may have to give way before it.

The marital privilege in s. 4(3) reviewed her by Charron J. will be considered later under the chapter on Privilege. Although the *Ontario Evidence Act* abolishes the spousal incompetency rules in civil cases (see s. 8(1)), we will see that the marital privilege is retained.

(ii) *Common Law Exception*

Section 4(5) maintains the common law exception to the general rule which is vaguely described as involving those cases wherein the spouse's "person, liberty or health" were affected. In the early case of *Lord Audley's Trial*,[158] in 1631, the accused was charged with the rape of his own wife in assisting one of his servants to have intercourse with her against her will. The accused objected to his wife's evidence as incompetent, but it was held that she was competent "for she was the party wronged; otherwise she might be abused."[159] This exception was then founded on necessity but as Professor Wigmore criticized:

> The notion of necessity, indeed, might commendably have been a broader one; the necessity of doing justice to other persons in general, when the spouse's testimony was indispensable, would have been at least as great. But the common lawyers here kept their eyes upon the ground, and did not allow their survey to exceed the range of immediate and unavoidable vision. Anyone could see that an absolute privilege in a husband to close the mouth of the wife in testimony against him would be a vested license to injure her in secret with complete immunity. This much the common lawyers saw, and were willing to concede. Just how far the concession went, in concrete cases, was never precisely settled. It was given varying definitions at different times. It certainly extended to causes involving corporal violence to the wife, and it certainly did not extend to all wrongs done to the wife.[160]

The breadth of the common law exception was extended in the case of *R. v. McPherson*.[161] The accused had been convicted of assaulting his six-year-old son, the principal Crown witness being the accused's wife. In extending the exception the court reasoned:

> In this day and age the principal reasons for spousal non-competency in child abuse cases, namely, the unity of husband and wife and a desire to avoid discord and dissension between them and to protect the legal relationship of marriage as one of full confidence and affection, must, in my opinion, take a subservient position to that of the welfare and protection of the child. This cannot be accomplished unless the criminal law can be enforced. The need of children to be protected calls out for an extension of the common law exceptions to spousal disqualification to allow one spouse to testify against the other in cases of child abuse.[162]

---

158 (1631), 3 Howell's State Trials 401.

159 *Ibid.*, at pp. 402 and 414.

160 8 Wigmore, *Evidence* (McNaughton Rev.), s. 2239. Compare *R. v. Bowles* (1967), 60 W.W.R. 276 (Alta. Mag. Ct.) and *R. v. Comiskey* (1973), 12 C.C.C. (2d) 410 (Ont. Prov. Ct.) for different views re the nature of the crime necessary to qualify. See also the trial judge's view (OHearn, Co. Ct. J.) in *R. v. Marchand* (1980), 55 C.C.C. (2d) 77, 85 (N.S.C.A.) that the subsection extended to "crimes of forgery and uttering forged documents as coming within the ambit of 'person and liberty' of the wife." See also *R. v. Giroux* (1985), 38 Sask. R. 172 (Q.B.) and *R. v. Wood* (1982), 8 C.C.C. (3d) 217 (Ont. Prov. Ct.).

161 (1980), 52 C.C.C. (2d) 547 (N.S.C.A.). In a strong dissenting opinion, Jones J.A. recognized the need for an exception but believed it to be a case for Parliament to create. See also *R. v. McNamara* (1979), 48 C.C.C. (2d) 201 (Ont. Co. Ct.) and *R. v. Fellichle* (1979), 12 C.R. (3d) 207 (B.C.S.C.).

162 *Ibid.*, at p. 557. See also *R. v. Czipps* (1979), 48 C.C.C. (2d) 166 (Ont. C.A.) and *R. v. Sillars* (1978), 45 C.C.C. (2d) 283 (B.C.C.A.) that the charge itself need not allege interference with the spouse's person, liberty or health, but rather that it is sufficient if the evidence of the surrounding circumstances discloses a threat to her person, liberty or health.

In 1982, section 4 of the *Canada Evidence Act* was amended[163] to provide for the compellability of spouses where the victim was a young child.

R. v. McGINTY
(1986), 52 C.R. (3d) 161, 27 C.C.C. (3d) 36 (Y.T.C.A.)

The accused was charged with assault causing bodily harm. Three weeks before the trial she married the alleged victim. At the trial the victim said that he would rather not testify. The judge ruled that he was both a competent and a compellable witness for the prosecution. The victim testified, the accused was convicted and appealed.

McLACHLIN J.A.: —

. . . .

It emerges clearly from a review of the authorities that policy plays a large part in resolving the question of the compellability of a wife or husband to testify against his or her spouse in a case arising from an act of violence against the witness spouse. On the one hand, it is desirable that persons who commit crimes of violence against their spouses be effectively prosecuted. On the other, it is contended, compelling a husband or wife to testify against his spouse will disturb marital harmony and is repugnant to fair-minded persons. The issue is succinctly stated in the Criminal Law Revision Committee's Eleventh Report, Evidence (General), Cmnd. 4991 (1972), at p. 93:

> How far the wife of the accused should be competent and compellable for the prosecution, for the accused and for a co-accused is in these days essentially a question of balancing the desirability that all available evidence which might conduce to the right verdict should be before the court against (i) the objection on social grounds to disturbing marital harmony more than is absolutely necessary and (ii) what many regard as the harshness of compelling a wife to give evidence against her husband.

The interest of society in securing proper prosecution of persons who commit crimes of violence against their spouses is vital. Such crimes are common. Their consequences are frequently grave. Because they tend to be committed in the privacy of the home, very often it is impossible to prosecute them unless the victim-spouse testifies. And very often when the trial date arrives the spouse declines to testify, whether out of fear of further brutality or blandishments or a combination of the two. As Dean Weir noted in his comment on *Lapworth* at p. 221:

> Cases are frequently reported in the press in which a wife who has laid a charge against her husband for an offence involving injuries to her person, has later had a change of heart and has refused to give evidence when the time came. In such cases, if the prosecution is dependent on the spouse's evidence, the magistrate, probably with reluctance because he realizes that the wife's change of attitude may have been

---

163 S.C. 1980-81-82-83, c. 125, s. 29(2).

brought about by the 'kicks or kisses' or curses of her husband, has frequently considered himself as having no power to compel the recalcitrant wife to give evidence and has dismissed the case.

Unfortunately, these words are as true now as they were in 1931. If the victim spouse is given the option of whether to testify or not, the result is frequently that the guilty spouse is acquitted. It thus becomes possible for a spouse who has brutalized his or her mate to continue to commit crimes of violence with impunity. On the other hand, if the offending spouse knows that the victim has no choice but to testify, he or she is more likely to be deterred from committing crimes of violence or from inflicting further threats or violence to prevent him or her from testifying.

What then of the competing interests? The first is the disruption to matrimonial harmony which may be caused by compelling the spouse to testify; the second the "natural repugnance" to fair-minded persons of compelling him or her to testify. These interests were discussed by Craig J.A. in *R. v. Sillars, supra*, in the context of competence. In my view his comments are equally applicable to the issue of compellability. After referring to Wigmore on Evidence (McNaughton Revision, 1961), vol. 8, para. 2228, Craig J.A. stated at p. 286:

> The most common view for not permitting such evidence [Wigmore] suggests, is the 'danger of causing dissention and of disturbing the peace of families.' Wigmore opines that there is no merit whatsoever in this particular view. At p. 216 he says:
>
>> But if we are to ignore the futility of appealing to a reason which is never allowed in practice to be logically applied and are to treat it as a serious argument, the answer is, first, that the peace of families does not essentially depend on this immunity from compulsory testimony, and next, that so far as it might be affected, that result is not to be allowed to stand in the way of doing justice to others.
>
> A second reason which is sometimes advanced for not permitting a spouse to testify against the other spouse is 'that there is a *natural repugnance* to every fair-minded person to compelling a wife or husband to be the means of the other's condemnation . . .' p. 217. With regard to these views, Wigmore says at pp. 217-8:
>
>> . . . that the state and the complainant have a right to the truth; and that this high and solemn duty of doing justice and of establishing the truth is not to be obstructed by considerations of sentiment . . .

I adopt these comments with the following additional remarks. In my opinion, a rule which leaves to the husband or wife the choice of whether he or she will testify against his aggressor-spouse is more likely to be productive of family discord than to prevent it. It leaves the victim-spouse open to further threats and violence aimed at preventing him or her from testifying, and leaves him or her open to recriminations if he or she chooses to testify. It seems to me better to leave the spouse no choice and to extend to married persons the general policy of the law that victims are compellable witnesses against their aggressor.

With respect to the contention that fair-minded persons find it naturally abhorrent to require one spouse to testify against another, it must also be remembered that fair-minded persons generally find it abhorrent that persons who commit crimes go unprosecuted. A crime committed against a spouse is as much a crime as a crime against a stranger, and should bear the same consequences. Crimes of violence are particularly abhorrent, raising as they do the state's duty to protect the safety of its citizens, married and unmarried. Presumably it was for such reasons that the common law centuries ago concluded that a spouse ought to be permitted to testify against her spouse where the latter had inflicted violence upon her. The same reasons dictate that such spouses should be compellable.

For these reasons I conclude that as a matter of policy husbands and wives should be competent and compellable witnesses against each other in cases of crimes of violence perpetrated by the one upon the other.

Conclusion

On the basis of the authorities and policy, I conclude that the trial judge was correct in ruling that under s. 4(4) [now s. 4(5)] of the Canada Evidence Act spouses are competent and compellable witnesses against their spouses in cases involving violence against them. The husband in this case was properly required to testify. I would dismiss the appeal.

Appeal dismissed.

[Taggart J.A. concurred with McLachlin J.A.; Lambert J.A. concurred in the result for somewhat different reasons.]

What possible unintended consequences have there been from zero tolerance policies and compelling the complainant to testify in domestic violence prosecutions?

R. v. MOORE
(1986), 30 C.C.C. (3d) 328 (N.W.T. T.C.)

Judy Moore was found in contempt of court. She was a witness at the trial of her common law husband who was charged with assault against her. After being sworn, she refused to testify concerning the events.

BOURASSA TERR. CT. J.:—

Judy Moore's current problems with the law may be traced to a policy of the Government of Canada made applicable to the Northwest Territories as set out in a government news release dated the 21st of December, 1983:

> All complaints of domestic violence involving spousal assault should be investigated immediately and thoroughly with a criteria of charges being laid for court prosecution, irrespective of whether the assaulted spouse wishes to proceed with the charges.

> An early object of the investigation should be the protection and assistance of victims. It is the purpose of this directive to require the prosecution of spousal assault cases where there is sufficient evidence.

. . . .

[T]he defendant's choice not to testify was clear and unambiguous, polite and determined. The State's case against the accused Jack Storr was thereby totally frustrated and the State's valid interest in the protection of society and the prevention of violence was foreclosed in this case — the search for juridical truth terminated.

. . . .

The policy of "prosecution regardless", has, for a significant number of people not had the beneficial effect originally anticipated. In fact, its effect has been noticeably detrimental to certain people and institutions and in a number of ways. The problems created in trying to replace an imperfect system (police discretion) by another imperfect system may even be more severe than the problems that were to be originally eliminated. This has in fact been recognized in this jurisdiction, appropriately enough, in the report by the "Task Force on Spousal Assault", February 5, 1985, Government of the Northwest Territories, which observes at p. 44:

> Two years ago the R.C.M.P. were directed to lay charges in spousal assault cases without requiring a complaint from the victim. This was an important policy change because it signaled the determination of the Parliament of Canada to have spousal assaults be treated as a crime. The policy change has led to problems, however, and is being used in the North in a discretionary way, though not consistently. The problems are:— when victims know the R.C.M.P. will lay charges they are sometimes reluctant to call the R.C.M.P. even to act as Peace Officers to break-up the incident.

> — Victims now fear greater retribution when the R.C.M.P. are called than they did formerly. R.C.M.P. may lay charges which can not be successfully prosecuted because the victim is reluctant, sometimes afraid, to testify and will refuse to give evidence or decline to tell the truth where a batterer knows he can, by threats or promises to the victim, prevent her from giving evidence, his disrespect for the law and the court grows.

> *Recommendations*

> The Task Force therefore recommends:— because it appears to be more important to the victim that the R.C.M.P. investigate and restore the peace than whether batterers can be prosecuted, that the policy be reviewed.

Too often this court has presided over spousal assault cases where the witness takes the stand and through swollen lips and with eyes bruised shut suddenly becomes reticent and unable to recall when and how her injuries occurred.

Perversely, in some incidents spouses have conspired together to concoct a story to defeat the State's case and indeed the whole process of law — conspirators against the court and the rule of law. . . .

In a sense, the defendant is a victim, and a deterrent sentence would only serve to increase the degree of victimization. Rather than offering protection, peace and order, the courts become an institution to avoid, to subvert and denigrate.

However, from another perspective a deterrence sentence is called for: The criminal law of Canada applies to all persons equally which application does not depend upon the individual's consent. The State has a valid and continuing interest in maintaining peace between its citizens and intervening when the laws of the land are ignored or broken. This defendant's refusal to testify and contempt was deliberate, calculated, premeditated and without apology. No one person should be allowed, nor can they be allowed, to stand above the law of the land. This attitude, were the court dealing with sentencing on another matter, would be a most aggravating factor.

The defendant apparently does not want the protection of the law with respect to any difficulties she may experience in her personal relationship with her spouse. That relationship is such that it is more important to her than the possible or potential injury she may sustain within it. It would be perverse if the defendant should end up in jail as a result of these proceedings while it is equally unjust the alleged offender . . . should escape the consequences of his actions and it is not just, or right, that people should come to court and refuse to testify. There is no easy answer or resolution to this Gordian knot.

One may refer to the position taken by the Law Reform Commission in effect that people are not going to use the laws if they don't agree with them, in the result the laws will not function. It would appear, at least in this defendant's situation, that the existence of the criminal court, the police and the law by itself and with the well reasoned intentions behind a policy which ultimately brought this woman to court will not prevent spousal assaults, and will not resolve the problem of spousal assault. In my view there is nothing this court can do with respect to this matter before it, this criminal court cannot resolve all of society's problems, one of which being a witness who does not want to testify against her spouse.

There will be a fine of one dollar.

(iii) *Who Is a Spouse?*

What is the meaning of "wife or husband of a person charged"? It is for the trial judge to determine if the witness is a spouse,[164] that is, whether the witness has entered into a legal marriage relationship[165] with the accused. Should the witness's status change if the marriage is dissolved before the trial? For some years it was believed the status remained insofar as the witness's right to speak to matters which arose during the marriage,[166] but the Nova Scotia Supreme Court has expressed the view that there is no reason not to simply follow the plain grammatical meaning of the legislation and terminate incompetency after dissolution.[167]

---

164 See *R. v. Mann*, [1971] 5 W.W.R. 84 (B.C.S.C.).

165 See, *e.g.*, *R. v. Coté* (1972), 22 D.L.R. (3d) 353 (Sask. C.A.). See also *R. v. Junaid Khan* (1987), 84 Cr. App. R. 44 (C.A.).

166 See *R. v. Algar*, [1954] 1 Q.B. 279 (C.C.A.) per Lord Goddard, and *R. v. Cooper (No. 1)* (1974), 51 D.L.R. (3d) 216 (Ont. H.C.). Marriage after the material incident but prior to trial makes the spouse incompetent: see *R. v. Lonsdale* (1973), 15 C.C.C. (2d) 201 (Alta. C.A.). But see *R. v. Bailey* (1983), 32 C.R. (3d) 337 (Ont. C.A.): divorced person permitted to testify about events occurring during marriage.

167 *R. v. Marchand* (1980), 55 C.C.C. (2d) 77 (N.S.C.A.).

R. v. SALITURO
[1991] 3 S.C.R. 654, 9 C.R. (4th) 324, 68 C.C.C. (3d) 289

The accused was charged with the forgery of his wife's signature on a cheque payable jointly to her and to him. The wife testified against her husband. There was evidence that at the time of the trial the accused and his wife were separated without any reasonable possibility of reconciliation. The trial judge accepted the wife's evidence and convicted. Without the wife's testimony the accused would not have been convicted. The accused's appeal was dismissed and he appealed further.

IACOBUCCI J. (LAMER, C.J.C. AND GONTHIER, CORY, and MCLACHLIN JJ. concurring):—

. . . .

A. *What Are the Limits on the Power of Judges to Change the Common Law?*

(1) *Introduction*

At one time, it was accepted that it was the role of judges to discover the common law, not to change it. In Book One of his *Commentaries on the Laws of England* (4th ed. 1770), Sir William Blackstone propounded a view of the common law as fixed and unchanging. . . .

. . . .

However, Blackstone's static model of the common law has gradually been supplanted by a more dynamic view. . . .

. . . .

In keeping with these developments, this Court has signalled its willingness to adapt and develop common law rules to reflect changing circumstances in society at large. In four recent cases, *Ares v. Venner*, [1970] S.C.R. 608, *Watkins v. Olafson, supra, R. v. Khan*, [1990] 2 S.C.R. 531, and *R. v. Seaboyer*, [1991] 2 S.C.R. 577, this Court has laid down guidelines for the exercise of the power to develop the common law. The common theme of these cases is that, while complex changes to the law with uncertain ramifications should be left to the legislature, the courts can and should make incremental changes to the common law to bring legal rules into step with a changing society. . . .

. . . .

These cases reflect the flexible approach that this Court has taken to the development of the common law. Judges can and should adapt the common law to reflect the changing social, moral and economic fabric of the country. Judges should not be quick to perpetuate rules whose social foundation has long since disappeared. Nonetheless, there are significant constraints on the power of the judiciary to change the law. . . . The judiciary should confine itself to those incremental changes which are necessary to keep the common law in step with the dynamic and evolving fabric of our society.

B. *The Policy of the Rule that a Spouse Is an Incompetent Witness for the Prosecution*

From an examination of the history of the rule making a spouse an incompetent witness for the prosecution, it is apparent that any policy justification which may at one time have existed in support of the rule has now disappeared in the context of divorced or irreconcilably separated spouses. The rule reflects a view of the role of women which is no longer compatible with the importance now given to sexual equality. In particular, the rule making an irreconcilably separated spouse an incompetent witness is inconsistent with the values enshrined in the *Canadian Charter of Rights and Freedoms*, and preserving the rule would be contrary to this Court's duty to see that the common law develops in accordance with the values of the *Charter*.

. . . .

The most important justification is that the rule protects marital harmony. . . . A second reason sometimes mentioned is what Wigmore called the "*natural repugnance* to every fair-minded person to compelling a wife or husband to be the means of the other's condemnation". . . .

The two justifications which have not survived are that a spouse is an incompetent witness because husband and wife are in law a single person, . . . and that husband and wife are disqualified from being witnesses for or against each other because their interests are identical.

. . . .

In the study paper "Competence and Compellability" by the Evidence Project of the Law Reform Commission of Canada, the rule was characterized as more a product of history than the reflection of any clear policy decision:

> . . . the rule, rather than the reflection of a clear-cut fundamental policy decision, appears to be simply a product of history. This is confirmed when we note that a fundamental policy decision surely would be based on concern not only for the married couple but for the family unit as a whole, and yet no one has suggested legislation making fathers and sons or mothers and daughters incompetent witnesses for the prosecution against their parents or children.

. . . .

There is in my opinion a more fundamental difficulty with the reasons for the rule. The grounds which have been used in support of the rule are inconsistent with respect for the freedom of all individuals, which has become a central tenet of the legal and moral fabric of this country particularly since the adoption of the *Charter*. In *R. v. Big M Drug Mart Ltd.*, [1985] 1 S.C.R. 295, Dickson J. (as he then was) defined freedom in this way (at p. 336): "Freedom must surely be founded in respect for the inherent dignity and the inviolable rights of the human person." The common law rule making a spouse an incompetent witness involves a conflict between the freedom of the individual to choose whether or not to testify and the interests of society in preserving the marriage bond. It is unnecessary for me to consider the difficult question of how this conflict ought to be resolved, because in this appeal we are concerned only with spouses who are irreconcilably separated. Where spouses are irreconcilably separated, there is no marriage bond to protect and we are faced only with a rule which limits the capacity of the individual to testify.

To give paramountcy to the marriage bond over the value of individual choice in cases of irreconcilable separation may have been appropriate in Lord Coke's time, when a woman's legal personality was incorporated in that of her husband on marriage, but it is inappropriate in the age of the *Charter*. . . .

. . . .

Where the principles underlying a common law rule are out of step with the values enshrined in the *Charter*, the courts should scrutinize the rule closely. If it is possible to change the common law rule so as to make it consistent with *Charter* values, without upsetting the proper balance between judicial and legislative action that I have referred to above, then the rule ought to be changed. The common law rule making an irreconcilably separated spouse an incompetent witness for the prosecution against the other spouse is inconsistent with the values in the *Charter*. Subject to consideration of the limits on the judicial role, the rule ought therefore to be changed. Society can have no interest in preserving marital harmony where spouses are irreconcilably separated because there is no marital harmony to be preserved.

The facts of this case do not raise the issue of whether a spouse who is a competent witness for the prosecution will also be compellable. That question is for another day. However, were it necessary to decide this question, the possibility that a competent spouse would be found also to be compellable is a real one, in light of the reasons in *R. v. McGinty* (1986), 27 C.C.C. (3d) 36 (Y.T.C.A.), *R. v. Marchand, supra, R. v. Czipps, supra*, and *R. v. Lonsdale* (1973), 15 C.C.C. (2d) 201 (Alta. S.C., App. Div.), although I would note that in the U.S., a spouse is a competent but not a compellable witness for the prosecution: *Trammel v. United States*, 445 U.S. 40 (1980).

. . . .

Concerns were raised before us that making an irreconcilably separated spouse a competent witness would increase the risk of violence to women. Violence against women is a very grave problem in our society, and any possibility of an increase in the risk of violence must be taken most seriously. But I find it difficult to accept that the proper response to the threat of violence is to limit the capacity of women in the hope that preventing women from testifying will decrease the risk of violence against them. If our expectations for a society founded on respect for the dignity of the human person are to have meaning, we must encourage and protect everyone in the exercise of their rights and responsibilities as equal members of our society. Furthermore, if a competent spouse is also compellable, I would note that McLachlin J.A. (as she then was) suggested in *McGinty, supra*, at p. 60, that making a spouse compellable may in fact reduce the risk of violence by giving the spouse no choice but to testify. The same argument was made by the Evidence Project of the Law Reform Commission of Canada in their study paper "Competence and Compellability", *supra*, at pp. 6-7.

. . . .

Absent parliamentary intervention, I would conclude that changing the common law rule to make spouses who are irreconcilably separated competent witnesses for the prosecution would be appropriate. . . .

. . . .

I would conclude that in appropriate cases, judges can and should change the common law. This is such a case. The common law should be the servant of society. While there are changes to the common law that are best left to the legislature, the change made by the Court of Appeal in the present case to the rule that a spouse is an incompetent witness for the prosecution is not an example of such a change.

Has the Court changed the common law or has it changed the statutory law? Both?

————————————

In *R. v. Jeffrey*,[168] the accused was convicted of two counts of breaking and entering the unoccupied home of his estranged wife's parents and stealing. The trial judge held that she was a competent witness for the Crown on the principle that irreconcilably separated spouses were competent witnesses against each other in a criminal trial. On appeal the sole issue was the standard of proof of irreconcilable separation required to render a spouse a competent witness. The accused argued that the Crown's burden of proof was that beyond a reasonable doubt as against the standard of balance of probabilities adopted by the convicting judge. It was held that the proof of irreconcilable separation was to be decided under the civil standard of balance of probabilities.

What if the marriage is a sham?

R. v. HAWKINS
[1996] 3 S.C.R. 1043, 2 C.R. (5th) 245, 111 C.C.C. (3d) 129

The accused, H. and M., were charged with conspiracy to obstruct justice. The investigation with respect to H. and M. was commenced after H.'s then girlfriend G. provided information to the police. G. testified as a Crown witness at the preliminary inquiry and originally implicated the accused. However, at the end of her testimony at the preliminary inquiry, G. indicated that she had obtained advice from independent counsel. Her counsel informed the presiding judge that she wished to be recalled as a witness, and substantially recant her initial testimony. She was permitted to do so. Shortly after the preliminary inquiry was concluded, G. married H. At trial, the Crown nevertheless sought to call G. as a

————————————

168 (1993), 25 C.R. (4th) 104 (Alta. C.A.).

Crown witness. On the motion, the Crown adduced evidence tending to show that H.'s motivation for marrying G. was to render her an incompetent witness for the Crown. The trial judge held that G. was not a competent witness for the Crown. The trial judge also refused to admit G.'s evidence under s. 715 of the Criminal Code, or as an exception to the hearsay rule.

LAMER C.J.C. and IACOBUCCI J. (GONTHIER and CORY JJ. concurring):—

. . . .

In our view, the circumstances of this case do not warrant modifying the common law rule of spousal incompetence. Both the trial judge and the Court of Appeal were correct in holding that Graham was not a competent witness for the Crown at the trial, as she had entered into a valid and genuine marriage with the co-appellant Hawkins.

. . . .

Numerous justifications for the rule have been advanced over the history of the common law, but only two appear to have survived to the modern era. As originally noted by Lord Coke, in his *Institutes of the Laws of England* (1832), the first justification for the rule is that it promotes conjugal confidences and protects marital harmony. The second justification is that the rule prevents the indignity of conscripting an accused's spouse to participate in the accused's own prosecution. However, as this Court recognized in *Salituro*, serious criticisms have been levelled against these two surviving justifications of the traditional rule. It has been called arbitrary for excluding other familial relationships, and antiquated, because it is based on outmoded notions of marriage. Perhaps most importantly, rendering a person incapable of testifying solely on the basis of marital status does strip an individual of key aspects of his or her autonomy.

. . . .

Some have suggested an alternative approach whereby a spouse could be declared competent against his or her spouse, but not compellable. The United Kingdom recently endorsed such a rule with the passage of s. 80 of the *Police and Criminal Evidence Act 1984* (U.K.), 1984, c. 60. The United States Supreme Court adopted a similar modification of the common law rule. The court held that under the Federal Rules of Evidence, a spouse is a competent but not compellable witness for the prosecution, with the witness spouse having the privilege to refuse to testify adversely: *Trammel v. United States*, 445 U.S. 40 (1980). While such alternative approaches to the rule of spousal incompetency may serve to promote the autonomy and dignity of an individual spouse, it is our opinion that any significant change to the rule should not be made by the courts, but should rather be left to Parliament.

The common law rule of spousal incompetence has remained largely unchanged for some 350 years. The respondent has submitted that there is ample scope for judicial development of the rule. While it is true that this Court has signalled its willingness to adapt and develop common law rules to reflect changing circumstances in society at large it is clear that the courts will only make incremental changes to the common law. So, for example, the change implemented in *Salituro*, did not strike at the original justifications of marital harmony and repugnance which animated the substance of the common law rule.

. . . .

In this instance, the Crown has conceded that the marriage of Hawkins and Graham is genuine. At the time of this Court's hearing, the couple were approaching their seventh wedding anniversary. There was no evidence that either of the two partners had failed to fulfil their reciprocal obligations of care and support. Under the circumstances, making Graham compellable by the Crown would threaten the couple's genuine marital harmony and undermine the purpose of the spousal incompetency rule. . . . Absent evidence that the marriage was a sham, we fail to see how the court can begin to inquire into the reasons for the marriage. There is no justification for such an inquiry unless there should be concrete evidence that the marriage was legally invalid. . . . We emphasize that the matter may be different if the evidence clearly established that the only purpose of the marriage was to avoid criminal responsibility by rendering a key witness uncompellable and that the partners had no intention of fulfilling their mutual obligations of care and support. In such circumstances, the marriage would be a "sham", and the court may be willing to take this into account. However, this is not the case in the Hawkins-Graham marriage.

[La Forest, L'Heureux-Dubé, Major, Sopinka and McLachlin JJ. agreed with the above position on competence and compellability.]

Lower courts have refused to extend the current spousal incompetency protections to common law relationships. Do you agree or think that the protection should be extended?

R. v. MARTIN
(2009), 64 C.R. (6th) 378 (Sask. C.A.)

KLEBUC C.J.S.:—

. . .

[15] Whether the spousal incompetency rule applies or should apply to persons in common-law relationships and other *de facto* spousal arrangements has been considered in numerous cases before and after the *Charter* came into force. In *R. v. Coffin*, the Québec Court of Appeal held that a common-law spouse is not a spouse within the meaning of the *Act*, and therefore, is a competent witness against the accused spouse. In 1971, this Court held in *R. v. Cote* that a woman who was in a long term "aboriginal customary marriage" was not a "wife" within the meaning of the *Act*. A similar view was expressed by the Nova Scotia Court of Appeal in *R. v. Jackson*, although the view may be *obiter* because the common-law husband had been charged with intent to cause bodily harm to the common-law wife, and therefore, she would have been a competent witness pursuant to the person, liberty or health exception to the spousal incompetency rule as carried forward in s. 4(5) of the *Act*.

[16] In the post-*Charter* case of *R. v. Duvivier*, Ms. Johnson, the common-law spouse of the accused, applied for an order under s. 24(1) of the *Charter* quashing a subpoena which required her to testify at the accused's trial on the ground that her relationship with the accused was equivalent to a legal marriage. She consequently maintained she was being treated differently than if she had been married to the accused, in violation of s. 15 of the *Charter*. The Chambers judge dismissed the application on the basis that Ms. Johnson was not a "wife" within the meaning of s. 4 of the *Act* and her exclusion from the spousal incompetency provisions did not violate s. 15 of the *Charter*. His reasons regarding s.15 are instructive:

> Johnson is not a spouse. However, it is not just members of the *quasi*-marital relationship who are compellable. A daughter is compellable against her mother; a father against his son; a mother-in-law against her son-in-law—all no matter whether they live together in the same household or not.
>
> . . .
>
> Is the group to which Johnson belongs those who live together in a relationship of some permanence? What would be the logical reason for excluding homosexual lovers who cohabit as a couple from the exemption if they asserted that they had a *quasi*-marital relationship. Neither does it seem to me that the test involves the question of living together. It appears to me that the true group of which Johnson is a member in this context are all those persons who are non-spouses and therefore compellable to testify. In this regard, Johnson is not a member of a "discreet and insular minority". . . .

[17] The Ontario Court of Appeal dismissed the appeal by Ms. Johnson on the basis her *Charter* issues arose in the context of a criminal proceeding and should be dealt with by the trial court in the absence of a compelling reason not to follow the Court's non-interventionist policy.The trial was to begin shortly and Ms. Johnson had not testified at the preliminary inquiry.

[18] In *R. v. Thompson*, the Alberta Court of Appeal considered an argument similar to the one raised in *Duvivier* and ruled:

> It could hardly be asserted that the burdens endured by "persons choosing to live in a common law relationship" are analogous to persons suffering discrimination on the basis of race, religion or gender. The group is not one which has suffered historical disadvantage, or political prejudice. The group is not "discrete and insular", but in fact is highly fluid, with participants constantly flowing in and out of it. Persons living in such relationships do so by choice, and it has not been shown to us that this choice is for reasons so fundamental to their human dignity that they cannot forsake that association. In short, none of the traditional indicia of discrimination have been exhibited, which merit the creation of a new s. 15(1) category.

[19] The Court of Quebec in *R. v. Campeau* arrived at substantially the same conclusion, namely: s. 4 of *Act* does not apply to *quasi*-marital spouses and the distinction between married spouses as non-compellable witnesses and common-law spouses as compellable witnesses does not violate s. 15 of the *Charter*.

[20] I have considered civil cases such as *Winik v. Wilson Estate* and *Armstrong v. McLaughlin Estate*, both cited by the appellant in support of his argument that the spousal incompetence rule applies to spouses in a common-law relationship. However, both cases concerned the definition of "spouse" provided in provincial legislation relevant to specific civil matters, and thus, are of no assistance in interpreting the spousal incompetency rule as applied in the area of criminal law.

[21] Based on the authorities reviewed, I am satisfied that neither the spousal incompetency rule nor the provisions of s. 4 of the *Act* apply to persons in a common-law relationship. Thus, the learned trial judge's ruling must be viewed as a decision on his part to materially change the traditional rule by extending its provisions to common-law spouses, contrary to the cautious approach for developing the common law outlined in *Salituro*. . . .

[22] In my view, the expansion of the spousal incompetency rule by the learned trial judge is far more than an incremental change required to keep the common law in step with the changing social, moral and economic fabric of Canada. Rather, it is a major change that should be left to Parliament. . . .

[23] I would add that while there is considerable debate amongst jurisprudential writers as to whether the spousal incompetency rule should be extended in its application or completely abolished, there appears to be no support by the proponents of either approach for the courts to undertake such reforms. Sopinka, Lederman & Bryant agree that the spousal incompetency rule is not applicable to common-law spouses or to persons cohabiting with no permanent commitment to each other, but question the validity of such a distinction in today's society, and suggest the rule should be abolished altogether. A similar position is taken by Lee Stuesser. He argues all spousal exemptions from giving testimony against a spouse should be abolished in Canada.

[24] The contrary position is taken by Hamish Stewart. He maintains the exclusion of common-law couples from the protection of the spousal incompetency rule amounts to a violation of the *Charter*. However, he concedes that, "any reform in this direction should be left to the legislature."

[25] In conclusion, I am satisfied the learned trial judge erred when he implemented a major change to the spousal incompetency rule in a manner inconsistent with *R. v. Hawkins, Salituro* and *Couture*. Nevertheless, his ultimate conclusion that Ms. Stevens was a competent and compellable witness is correct in law.

[26] Given that my conclusion is dispositive of the appeal I need not consider the remaining issue. Thus, I would dismiss the appeal.

[All footnotes excluded.][169]

---

169 The exclusion of common law spouses from s. 4(3) was recently held to violate the s. 15 equality guarantee in *R. v. Masterson* (2009), 245 C.C.C. (3d) 400 (Ont. S.C.J.) and *R. v. Bordo* (Que. S.C.) (July 11, 2009). In *Masterson,* common law spouses were read into s.

(iv) *Reform*

Is it time to abolish or further amend restrictions on spousal competence and compellability in criminal cases?

Finally, one is driven to ask whether these rules, fashioned in the 16th century, have any place in present day society. Professor Wigmore was clear in his views:

> This privilege has no longer adequate reason for retention. In an age which has so far rationalized, depolarized and dechivalrized the marital relation and the spirit of femininity as to be willing to enact complete legal and political equality and independence of man and woman, this marital privilege is the merest anachronism in legal theory and an indefensible obstruction to truth in practice. It is unfortunate that the United States Supreme Court, when handed the opportunity in 1958, failed to eliminate this relic from the impediments to justice in the federal courts.[170]

In 1980 the United States Supreme Court reversed itself, and abolished the spousal competence rule.

> The ancient foundations for so sweeping a privilege have long since disappeared. Nowhere in the common-law world — indeed in any modern society — is a woman regarded as chattel or demeaned by denial of a separate legal identity and the dignity associated with recognition as a whole human being. Chip by chip, over the years those archaic notions have been cast aside . . .
>
> The contemporary justification for affording an accused such a privilege is also unpersuasive. When one spouse is willing to testify against the other in a criminal proceeding — whatever the motivation — their relationship is almost certainly in disrepair; there is probably little in the way of marital harmony for the privilege to preserve. In these circumstances, a rule of evidence that permits an accused to prevent adverse spousal testimony seems far more likely to frustrate justice than to foster family peace.[171]

In *R. v. Schell*[172] Paperny J.A. (Picard and Wittmann JJ.A. concurring) voiced considerable dissatisfaction with the present law:

> The law on spousal competence has been the subject of sustained judicial criticism for over 25 years. Judgments from several provincial courts of appeal and the Supreme Court of Canada have urged a major legislative overhaul to what has been labelled as anachronistic, paternalistic and an anomalous rule of common law, namely, that spouses are not competent to give testimony against one another. . . .
>
> Commentators and academics writing on the point share the view that the law requires reconsideration and reform. For example, the editor of *Wigmore on Evidence* (McNaughton rev., 1961) vol. 8 at p. 217, states:
>
> > We behold the fantastic spectacle of a fundamental rule of evidence, which had only questionable reasons for existence surviving nonetheless through two centuries (now almost three) upon the strength of certain artificial dogmas – pronouncements wholly irreconcilable with each other, with the facts of life and

---

4, while in *Bordo* the discrimination was held to be demonstrably justified under s. 1. Respective C.R. comments by Lisa Dufraimont and Anne-Marie Boisvert call for review by Parliament.

170 8 Wigmore, *Evidence* (McNaughton Rev.), s. 2228, p. 221.

171 *Trammel v. U.S.*, 445 U.S. 40, 52 (1980); overturning *Hawkins v. U.S.*, 358 U.S. 74 (1958).

172 (2004), 20 C.R. (6th) 1 (Alta. C.A.).

with the rule itself, and yet repeatedly invoked, with smug judicial positiveness, like magic formulas to still the spectre of forensic doubt.

Sopinka, Lederman and Bryant, *The Law of Evidence in Canada*, 2d ed. (Toronto: Butterworths, 1999), echo the concerns that the law in this area is in disarray and disconnected from prevailing social and legal realities. They state at p. 698, s. 13.61, "The general law relating to spousal competency is marked with significant inconsistencies and is in serious need of rationalization at the legislative level".

The current state of the law, as suggested above, is a hodgepodge of common law, statutory exceptions and common-law exceptions. As previously noted, the genesis of the rule stemmed from the lack of independent legal status of a married person. A married couple had but one legal personality. A married woman, devoid of legal persona, could not testify for or against her husband and vice versa. This rationale became untethered when the legal personalities of married women were ultimately untied from their spouses.

Thus, the only remaining rationale, and arguably the only legitimate societal value supporting the rule, is the "preservation of marital harmony". It appears the loss of probative evidence is still considered a fair price to pay to preserve marital harmony. Whether there is any genuine linkage between marital accord and the rule has never been seriously explored, either in the case law or the academic commentary, but is assumed.

R. v. COUTURE
2007 CarswellBC 1365, 2007 CarswellBC 1366, [2007] 2 S.C.R. 517, 47 C.R. (6th) 1, 220 C.C.C. (3d) 289

CHARRON J.:

44   There is no question that the spousal incompetency rule and its underlying rationales have been the subject of significant criticism. The various bases for this criticism has been discussed at some length in *Salituro* and again in *Hawkins* and need not be repeated here. However, while there seems to be a growing consensus that the rules should be changed, it is less clear how they should be changed. On the one hand, there would be sound reasons for giving the spouse the choice whether to testify or not. As Iacobucci J. noted in *Salituro* (at p. 673):

> The grounds which have been used in support of the rule are inconsistent with respect for the freedom of all individuals, which has become a central tenet of the legal and moral fabric of this country particularly since the adoption of the *Charter*. . . .The common law rule making a spouse an incompetent witness involves a conflict between the freedom of the individual to choose whether or not to testify and the interests of society in preserving the marriage bond.

La Forest J. made similar comments about a spouse's liberty and equality interests in *Hawkins* (para. 101).

45   On the other hand, there are sound reasons for not giving the spouse the choice whether to testify or not. As aptly noted by McLachlin J.A., in *McGinty*, giving the spouse a choice "is more likely to be productive of family discord than to prevent it. It leaves the victim-spouse open to further threats and violence aimed at preventing him or her from testifying, and leaves him or her open to recriminations if he or she chooses to testify" (p. 40). Based on this rationale, the

options for reform appear to be between leaving the rule as it is, or abolishing it altogether making spouses competent and compellable by both the Crown and defence in all cases.

46 However, it is far from clear that the question is an "all or nothing" proposition. Other options would be available. For example, in some Australian states, the spouse is a compellable witness for the prosecution but the trial judge has a discretion to exempt the witness from testifying: *Crimes Act 1958* (Vic.), s. 400. In the United States, the accused's spouse is competent but the testimony is subject to various privileges, including the spouse's privilege not to testify against the accused: see, for example, *Hawkins v. United States*, 358 U.S. 74 (1958), and *Trammel v. United States*, 445 U.S. 40 (1980), at p. 44. (See Law Commission of Canada, *Beyond Conjugality: Recognizing and supporting close personal adult relationships* (2001); A. Manson, *Spousal Testimony in Criminal Cases in Canada* (September 2001); and Stewart.

47 The recurring question before the courts is the extent to which any reform of the rule can or should be made by the courts as opposed to the legislator. Although recognized, at least implicitly, by statute, the spousal incompetency rule is grounded in common law and hence its scope subject to interpretation by the courts. For example, this Court held in *Salituro* that spousal incompetency did not apply where the spouses, although still legally married, were irreconcilably separated because, in such cases, "there is no marital harmony to be preserved". However, there are constraints on the power of courts to change the common law. In *Salituro*, Iacobucci J. reflected on the limits of the judiciary's power in this area:

> Judges can and should adapt the common law to reflect the changing social, moral and economic fabric of the country. Judges should not be quick to perpetuate rules whose social foundation has long since disappeared. Nonetheless, there are significant constraints on the power of the judiciary to change the law. As McLachlin J. indicated in *Watkins, supra*, in a constitutional democracy such as ours it is the legislature and not the courts which has the major responsibility for law reform; and for any changes to the law which may have complex ramifications, however, necessary or desirable such changes may be, they should be left to the legislature. The judiciary should confine itself to those incremental changes which are necessary to keep the common law in step with the dynamic and evolving fabric of our society.

We are now closely approaching the twentieth anniversary of *Salituro* and there is no evidence that Parliament is prepared to engage in a reform of s. 4. How much longer should the Supreme Court wait? If you were the Minister of Justice, would you recommend action or inaction?

(g) Compellability of Accused

(i) *History of Privilege Against Self-incrimination*[173]

Prior to the 13th century, criminal procedure was basically accusatorial. Both on the continent and in England, a private person accused another, provided details of the complaint, conducted the prosecution and led the proof. The resultant trial might be by compurgation, battle, or ordeal. By the 13th century, trials by battle and compurgation had fallen into disfavour as they were increasingly seen as irrational and untrustworthy. In 1215, the church forbade its clergy from participating in trials by ordeal and new methods of proceeding became necessary. England retained the accusatorial method and gave its grand jury of presentment the additional task of finding a verdict. In England the perceived lack of partiality in the trier gradually gave birth to a separate, petit jury for the latter task. The ecclesiastical courts and the continental civilian courts on the other hand embraced the inquisitorial method as a replacement.

The inquisitorial method allowed the judge to fill all the roles; he was accuser, prosecutor and trier. The judge, and not a jury of presentment, decided whether there were sufficient grounds to call the individual to answer. The method also provided for a new oath to be taken by the accused at the beginning of the inquiry whereby he promised to answer all questions put to him though he be given no information regarding the charges against him nor the evidence, if any, which supported them. This type of oath became known as the oath *ex officio* as it was administered by the judge by virtue of his office.

The oath *ex officio* was introduced into the ecclesiastical courts in England in 1236, and was adopted by the judicial arm of the King's Council, the Court of Star Chamber, in 1487. In the common law courts at this time the accused was interrogated but he was not sworn. On taking the oath *ex officio* the accused was compelled to choose between offending his God and risking punishment for perjury or accusing himself of crime; failing to take the oath was regarded by the court as a confession of guilt. Placing an individual in such a dilemma was regarded by many as more cruel than physical torture. With no requirement of a charge in advance, much less a demonstrated basis for the same, the individual became his own accuser and his own means of destruction.

During the 16th and 17th centuries the *ex officio* oath was used in England by the Court of Star Chamber and the Court of the High Commission in Causes Ecclesiastical for the purposes of stamping out non-conforming political and religious views. Opposition to this method of inquiry, wide ranging and without benefit of accusation, steadily grew and reached its culmination in 1638 in the trial in the Court of Star Chamber of a young Puritan named John Lilburne. The offence was importing seditious books into England, and while it would appear that he knew the nature of the charge against him, no bill of complaint was preferred before he was requested to take the oath. Lilburne denied the charges against him but refused to take the oath. Rather than taking this as a confession

---

173 See Levy, *Origins of the Fifth Amendment* (1968, Oxford). But compare Langbein, "The Historical Origins of the Privilege" (1994), 92 Mich. L. Rev. 1047. And note the comment of Frankfurter, J.: "The privilege against self-incrimination is a specific provision of which it is peculiarly true that 'a page of history is worth a volume of logic'," in *Ullman v. U.S.*, 350 U.S. 422, 438 (1956). See also Morgan, "The Privilege Against Self-Incrimination" (1949), 34 Minn. L. Rev. 1; and 8 Wigmore, *Evidence* (McNaughton Rev.), s. 2250.

of guilt, the court found him guilty of contempt and sentenced him to a fine, corporal punishment and imprisonment until he conformed by taking the oath. Lilburne's martyrdom, and his numerous pamphlets against the excesses of the High Commission and Star Chamber smuggled out of his prison caused others to follow his example, public discontent to swell, and the way to be paved for radical reforms. In 1641 the High Commission and Star Chamber were abolished and the *ex officio* oath outlawed. The opposition had been to the far ranging inquiry on oath without benefit of accusation or bill of complaint; but such was the depth of emotion over the excesses of those courts that anything akin to their procedures was regarded as odious. Gradually, in the common law courts, accused persons, even though properly charged, began to resist their questioning on the basis that no man is bound to incriminate himself. By 1700 it was firmly recognized that no person, in any court, whether he be accused or merely witness, could be compelled to answer if the answer would tend to incriminate. The common law privilege was born.

It should be noted, however, that accused persons continued being questioned by examining justices of the peace prior to trial, although that examination was not on oath. The normal criminal trial would begin with a reading of the accused's earlier compulsory examination.[174] The privilege against self-incrimination, at least in its formative years, was confined to foreclose only compulsory examination at trial. It was not until *Jervis's Act* of 1848[175] that we see the accused being advised that he need not make a statement to the examining justices prior to committal.

Until the end of the 19th century the accused was not able to give testimony on oath for two reasons. First, he was regarded as incompetent because of his obvious interest in the outcome of the proceedings. Second, it was regarded as a violation of his privilege against self-incrimination to place him on the horns of a dilemma: should he choose to testify falsely gaining temporal relief but everlasting damnation or testify truthfully and forfeit his liberty? Perhaps a trilemma in that should he choose not to testify, and it being known that he was able, he risked an inference of guilt being drawn from his silence.

(ii) *Canada Evidence Act*

By the end of the 19th century statutory reforms made the accused competent for the defence. The common law position of non-compellability at the instance of the prosecution remained. Section 4 of the *Canada Evidence Act* provides:

> (1) Every person charged with an offence, and, except as otherwise provided in this section, the wife or husband, as the case may be, of the person so charged, is a competent witness for the defence, whether the person so charged is charged solely or jointly with any other person.

It is important to recognize that this privilege, in its origins and as later interpreted in Canada, operated to protect a person from being compelled to give

---

174 The compulsory examination was provided for by statute: (1554), 1 & 2 Phil. & Mar., c. 13, s. 4.

175 11 & 12 Vict., c. 42, s. 18, the predecessor to the present Canadian provision used in the preliminary hearing: see Criminal Code, R.S.C. 1985, c. C-46, ss. 540, 541.

evidence before a court or like tribunal. It was also restricted to testimonial evidence. Taking bodily samples, fingerprints or photographs were not seen as captured by the privilege.[176] In short, the privilege in Canada was seen to be reflected simply, and solely, in the accused's non-compellability at trial. The accused, pursuant to the legislation, was a competent witness for the defence. It was up to the accused to decide whether he would go into the box.

In Canada, the legislation also provided that no witness, including the accused who chose to become a witness, could refuse to answer a question on the grounds that the answer might tend to criminate. Rather, the legislation provided that he was obliged to answer but the answer could not be used against him in later proceedings. For example, the *Canada Evidence Act* provides:

> 5.(1) No witness shall be excused from answering any question on the ground that the answer to the question may tend to criminate him, or may tend to establish his liability to a civil proceeding at the instance of the Crown or of any person.

> (2) Where with respect to any question a witness objects to answer on the ground that his answer may tend to criminate him, or may tend to establish his liability to a civil proceeding at the instance of the Crown or of any person, and if but for this Act, or the Act of any provincial legislature, the witness would therefore have been excused from answering the question, then although the witness is by reason of this Act or the provincial Act compelled to answer, the answer so given shall not be used or admissible in evidence against him in any criminal trial or other criminal proceeding against him thereafter taking place, other than a prosecution for perjury in the giving of that evidence or for the giving of contradictory evidence.

Similar provisions exist in provincial legislation.[177]

In *R. v. Mottola*[178] Morden J.A. explained the proper procedure to be followed:

> An accused person who is a witness and any other witness is not excused from answering incriminating questions. However, if the witness objects to answering a question upon the ground that his answer may tend to incriminate him and he then answers it as he is bound by the Act to do, the answer shall not be used in evidence against him in any criminal proceedings against him thereafter taking place with the necessary exception for a perjury charge in the giving of such evidence. The objection must be taken by the witness to the question. In practice when a witness is being examined upon an incident or series of incidents and he thinks that all or any of his answers might tend to incriminate him, the Judge might of course permit a general objection to the series of such questions and not require a specific objection to each and every question. But the objection cannot be taken before the witness is sworn and before he is asked any questions. Any protection the witness has if he objects to the question, as provided by s. 5(2), is against the use of his answer in independent, contemporaneous or subsequent prosecutions. This protection is conferred by the Act and not by any ruling of the Judge when objection is taken to a question. The procedure followed in the case under appeal was unwarranted. The Magistrate had no authority to confer or withhold "the protection of the Court" upon the witness Boule

---

176 *Marcoux v. R.* (1975), 24 C.C.C. (2d) 1 (S.C.C.).

177 For similar provincial and territorial provisions. see: R.S.A. 1980, c. A-21, s. 6; R.S.B.C. 1979, c. 116, s. 4; R.S.M. 1987, c. E-150, s. 6; R.S.N.B. 1973, c. E-II, s. 6; R.S.N. 1970, c. 115, s. 3A; R.S.N.W.T. 1974, c. E-4, s. 8; R.S.N.S. 1989, c. 154, s. 59; R.S.O. 1990, c. E.23, s. 9; R.S.P.E.I. 1988, c. E-11, s. 6; R.S.S. 1978, c. S-16, s. 37; and R.S.Y.T. 1986, c. 57, s. 7.

178 (1959), 124 C.C.C. 288, 295 (Ont. C.A.).

or upon the appellant Vallee. Both these witnesses could at any time during their examination object to answer questions — they had no right to refuse to answer — but if they would have been excused at common law from answering such questions, their answers could not be used against them in other criminal proceedings. The accused has the same rights in this regard as any other witness at his trial.

(iii) *Sections 11(c) and 13 of Charter*

The Charter of Rights provides:

11. (*c*) Any person charged with an offence has the right. . . not to be compelled to be a witness in proceedings against that person in respect of the offence.

13.   A witness who testifies in any proceedings has the right not to have any incriminating evidence so given used to incriminate that witness in any other proceedings, except in a prosecution for perjury or for the giving of contradictory evidence.

Section 11 (c) confirms that the Crown or co-accused cannot compel an accused to testify. Section 13 entrenches a privilege against incrimination which results in use immunity. Note that s. 13 provides for blanket exclusion without the necessity of objection. **Is this a welcome advance?**

In *R. v. Dubois*[179] the Supreme Court held that "in any other proceeding" in s. 13 included a second trial. The Crown could not adduce into evidence statements made by the accused at his first trial for murder into the second trial. Otherwise this would allow the accused to indirectly compel the accused to testify contrary to s. 11(c). This was extended in *R. v. Mannion*[180] to prevent cross-examination by the Crown on the accused's testimony from the first trial, although this ruling was on the narrow footing that the purpose of the cross-examination was to incriminate Mannion. Then, in *R. v. Kuldip*[181] the Supreme Court held that cross-examination on the accused's previous voluntary testimony is permitted if the purpose is to impugn her credibility, rather than to incriminate her. The policy behind *Kuldip* was laudable—to prevent an accused from advancing conflicting versions without being faced with the inconsistency—but the distinction between an incriminating purpose and impugning credibility was sometimes difficult to draw and to explain clearly to a jury. In *R. v. Noel*[182] the Supreme Court decided that under s. 13 of the Charter, when an accused testifies at trial he or she cannot be cross-examined on prior testimony from an earlier trial unless the trial judge is satisfied that there is no realistic danger that the prior testimony could be used to incriminate the accused.

With this background of complex rulings, the Supreme Court in *R. v. Henry*[183] attempted to simplify the Court's interpretation of s. 13. In *Henry*, the two accused had voluntarily testified at their first trial and then, after a new trial was ordered, provided quite different testimony at their second trial. The s. 13 issue arose because the Crown cross-examined them on their prior inconsistent testimony. On the previous jurisprudence, *Mannion* would have barred the cross-examination. However, the Supreme Court departed from its previous position

---

179 [1985] 2 S.C.R. 350.
180 (1986), 53 C.R. (3d) 193 (S.C.C.).
181 (1990), 1 C.R. (4th) 285 (S.C.C.).
182 [2002] 3 S.C.R. 433.
183 [2005] 3 S.C.R. 609.

and overruled *Mannion* and modified *Kuldip*. The focus has shifted to whether or not the accused voluntarily testified at the other proceeding. If so, the Crown may cross-examine on the prior testimony, regardless of whether the purpose is to impeach credibility or to incriminate. As Justice Binnie, for the Court, held:

> 60 The result of a purposeful interpretation of s. 13 is that an accused will lose the *Mannion* advantage in relation to prior *volunteered* testimony but his or her protection against the use of prior *compelled* testimony will be strengthened. The two different situations will be treated differently instead of homogenized, and the unpredictability inherent in sorting out attacks on credibility from attempts at incrimination will be avoided.

> 61 For the foregoing reasons, I conclude that the s. 13 *Charter* rights of the appellants (who were volunteers at both trials) were not violated by the Crown's cross-examination. Their appeals must therefore be dismissed.

Like the majority judges in the B.C. Court of Appeal, the Supreme Court could not see why s. 13 should protect an accused from cross-examination where he chose to testify one way at his first trial then differently on the re-trial.

Some had thought that the Court might have been prepared to reverse the *Dubois* ruling so that when a new trial is ordered the trial does not constitute "other proceedings" to trigger any s. 13 protection. Justice Binnie did not accept this view. The Court declined, however, to overrule *Dubois*, with the result that the Crown may not introduce the prior testimony as a part of its case in chief even if the accused voluntarily testified at the previous trial.

On the other hand, where the accused has been compelled to testify in the previous proceeding, usually at the trial of another person, the Supreme Court now gives the accused greater s. 13 protection. The prior testimony may not be used by the Crown to incriminate or attach credibility. Thus, the decision leaves *Noël* intact as well.[184] The courts will now be spared the task of trying to draw a distinction that the Supreme Court now says has been, in this context, too difficult to draw.

The issue of what constitutes compulsion to testify may lead to uncertainty. Clearly a subpoena would amount to such compulsion but Justice Binnie makes it express that a finding of compulsion may not turn on the existence of a subpoena. Out of an abundance of caution it may be advisable for counsel to establish compulsion by insisting on subpoenas or claiming the protection of s. 5(2) of the *Canada Evidence Act*. Do you think that the Court should have simply declared that s. 13 does not apply at a re-trial where the accused testifies as a matter of policy rather than focus on the issue of voluntariness?

Henry is also significant because it confirms that s. 13 does not require an objection to be compelled as does s. 5(2), and that its use immunity extends to all other proceedings and not just criminal. As Justice Binnie observed:

> 22 The consistent theme in the s. 13 jurisprudence is that "the purpose of s. 13 . . . is to protect individuals from being indirectly compelled to incriminate themselves" (*Dubois*, at p. 358, and reiterated in *Kuldip*, at p. 629). That same purpose was

---

184 For comments on *Henry*, see: Stuart, "Annotation" (2005), 33 C.R. (6th) 215 and Hamish Stewart, "*Henry* in the Supreme Court of Canada: Reorienting the s. 13 Right against Self-incrimination" (2006), 34 C.R. (6th) 112, especially at 119.

flagged in *Noël*, the Court's most recent examination of s. 13, by Arbour J., at para. 21: Section 13 reflects a long-standing form of statutory protection against compulsory self-incrimination in Canadian law, and is best understood by reference to s. 5 of the *Canada Evidence Act*. Like the statutory protection, the constitutional one represents what Fish J.A. called a *quid pro quo*: when a witness who is compelled to give evidence in a court proceeding is exposed to the risk of self-incrimination, the state offers protection against the subsequent use of that evidence against the witness in exchange for his or her full and frank testimony. [Emphasis added.]

23 There is thus a consensus that s. 13 was intended to extend s. 5 of the *Canada Evidence Act* to give further and better effect to this purpose. As McIntyre J. pointed out in *Dubois*, in reasons that dissented in the result but not on this point, s. 13 "does not depend on any objection made by the witness giving the evidence. It is applicable and effective without invocation, and even where the witness in question is unaware of his rights" (p. 377). Further, s. 13 "is not limited to a question in respect of which a witness would have been entitled to refuse to answer at common law and its prohibition against the use of incriminating evidence is not limited to criminal proceedings. It confers a right against incrimination by the use of evidence given in one proceeding in any other proceedings" (p. 377).

PROBLEMS

Problem 1

At his friend's trial, the accused agrees to testify. He admits that he committed the offence. His friend is acquitted. The accused is now charged with the very same offence based on evidence the police had prior to his testimony. At his trial, he testifies that he did not commit the offence. Can the Crown confront him with his earlier admission?

Problem 2

The accused is charged with a bank robbery in Windsor. At his trial, he testifies that he didn't commit the offence. His defence is alibi. He was in Kingston at the time of the robbery committing an armoured car robbery. The accused is acquitted. The Kingston police are unaware of the accused's testimony and are independently investigating the armoured car robbery. They discover the accused's fingerprints on the back of the vehicle and a videotape showing him in the vicinity of the robbery. The accused is now charged with the Kingston armoured car robbery. He testifies at his trial. Can the Crown confront him with his earlier testimony? What if he testified at his bail hearing on the armoured car charge? Can the Crown cross-examine him at trial on this testimony?

Problem 3

The accused is charged with impaired driving. Prior to the accused's criminal trial, the victim launched a civil action against him. During the civil proceedings, the accused provided evidence pursuant to the civil obligation for a party to testify at his examination for discovery. The failure to testify is punishable through a finding of contempt. Can the Crown lead this discovery evidence at the accused's impaired driving trial? See *R. v. Nedelcu*, [2007] O.J. No. 1188 (S.C.J.).

KNUTSON v. REGISTERED NURSES' ASSN. (SASKATCHEWAN)
(1990), 90 Sask. R. 120, 1990 CarswellSask 195 (C.A.)

The issue was whether section 13 of the Charter of Rights and Freedoms applied to discipline proceedings under The Registered Nurses Act so that evidence given in criminal proceedings by the respondent nurse could not be subsequently used against her in discipline proceedings. When the respondent gave evidence at the criminal trial she did not invoke the provisions of section 5 of the *Canada Evidence Act* or the provincial counterpart to protect her against use of any of her evidence in subsequent proceedings.

SHERSTOBITOFF J.A. (VANCISE and WAKELING JJ.A. concurring):—

. . . .

The right protected by s. 13 is the right against use of incriminating evidence given a person in one proceeding to incriminate that person in subsequent proceedings.

. . . .

Accordingly, one can only incriminate oneself as defined by s. 13 in respect of matters which may be described as criminal, quasi-criminal, or proceedings with penal consequences.

. . . .

The disciplinary proceedings under review in this case are neither criminal nor quasicriminal.

. . . .

In this case, there is no liability to imprisonment or fine, and thus no possible element of punishment. There is no matter of public order or welfare in a public sphere of activity. The disqualification is an internal and private disciplinary matter imposed as part of a scheme for regulating an activity in order to protect the public. The respondent is entitled to apply for reinstatement at any time and has an appeal to the courts from an adverse decision, so that her expulsion is not permanent if she can show fitness to practice her profession. . . . [T]he result must be the same as in the related police discipline cases: a finding that there were no penal consequences, and thus s. 13 did not apply. The impugned evidence was therefore admissible.[185]

(iv) *Pre-trial Right to Silence: Charter section 7*

The issue in *Hebert*[186] was the admissibility of a statement by an accused who had been arrested on a charge of robbery. He gave the statement to an

---

185 See too *R. v. Jones*, 89 C.C.C. (3d) 353, 30 C.R. (4th) 1, [1994] 2 S.C.R. 229 (s. 13 not available at sentencing proceedings); *Martineau c. Ministre du Revenu national* (2004), 192 C.C.C. (3d) 129, 24 C.R. (6th) 207 (S.C.C.) (no s. 11(c) protection at Customs Act proceedings); and *R. v. D. (R.)* (2004), 182 C.C.C. (3d) 545 (Ont. S.C.J.) (s. 13 not available in perjury proceedings).

186 (1990), 77 C.R. (4th) 147 (S.C.C.).

undercover police officer placed in his cell after he had indicated that he did not wish to speak to the police. The Supreme Court of Canada unanimously decided that the statement had been obtained in violation of a breach of the right to silence under section 7 and had been properly excluded under section 24(2).

McLachlin J. delivered the majority judgment, with six justices concurring.[187] She found in the common law voluntary confession rule and in the privilege against self-incrimination, which granted the accused immunity from incriminating himself at trial, the essence of the right to silence:

> [T]he person whose freedom is placed in question by the judicial process must be given the choice of whether to speak to the authorities or not.

Consideration of other Charter rights suggested that the right to silence of detained persons under section 7 had to be broad enough to accord that person a free choice on the matter of whether to speak to the authorities. The most important function of the right to counsel was to ensure that the accused understood his rights, chief among which was his right to silence. The privilege against self-incrimination enshrined in sections 11(c) and 13 of the Charter would be diminished if a person were to be compelled to make statements at the pre-trial stage. The right of a detained person to silence under section 7 had to be viewed as broader in scope than the confession rule existing in Canada at the time of the adoption of the Charter. The right had to reflect the Charter's concern for individual freedom and the integrity of the judicial process, and permit the exclusion of evidence offensive to those values. On a "purposive approach" to the right to silence, the scope of the right had to be extended to exclude police tricks which would effectively deprive the suspect of the choice of remaining silent:

> To permit the authorities to trick the suspect into making a confession to them after he or she has exercised the right of conferring with counsel and declined to make a statement, is to permit the authorities to do indirectly what the Charter does not permit them to do directly. This cannot be in accordance with the purpose of the Charter.

McLachlin J. had earlier pointed out that *Rothman* had been decided after the majority ruling in *Wray* that a court had no power to exclude admissible and relevant evidence on the basis that the administration of justice would be brought into disrepute. Distinguished scholars and judges had criticized this approach and it could no longer be maintained under the Charter.

Justice McLachlin further determined that her approach was not one of an "absolute right to silence in the accused, capable of being discharged only by waiver." On the subjective approach to waiver defined in *Clarkson*[188] all statements made by detainees not knowingly made to a police officer would be excluded because the Crown could not establish waiver. The majority decided that the scope of the right to silence should not be extended this far.[189]

Madam Justice McLachlin further identified four limits to this newly recognized constitutional right to silence:

---

187   Dickson C.J., Lamer, La Forest, L'Heureux-Dubé, Gonthier and Cory JJ. Wilson and Sopinka JJ. gave separate concurring reasons.

188   [1986] 1 S.C.R. 383.

189   Both Sopinka and Wilson JJ. would have applied the accepted waiver standard.

1.   The police may question the accused in the absence of counsel after the accused has retained counsel:

> Presumably, counsel will inform the accused of the right to remain silent. If the police are not posing as undercover officers and the accused chooses to volunteer information, there will be no violation of the Charter. Police persuasion, short of denying the suspect the right to choose or depriving him of an operating mind, does not breach the right to silence.

2.   The right to silence applies only after detention:

> In an undercover operation prior to detention, the individual from whom information is sought is not in the control of the state. There is no need to protect him from the greater power of the state. After detention, the situation is quite different; the state takes control and assumes the responsibility of ensuring that the detainee's rights are respected.

3.   The right to silence does not affect voluntary statements to a cell-mate provided that person is not acting as a police informant or an undercover police officer.

4.   The right to silence is not violated where undercover agents observe the suspect and do not "actively elicit information in violation of the suspect's choice to remain silent."

Provincial courts have proved reluctant to extend the *Hebert* pre-trial right to silence to situations where the officer is identified. It has been held that non-coercive questioning prior to detention is no violation.[190] In *Smith*,[191] Mr. Justice Doherty for the Ontario Court of Appeal confirmed that a detained person has no absolute right to remain silent. The police are not absolutely prohibited from questioning a detained person and do not have to advise as to the right to remain silent. Where there is no section 10(*b*) right to counsel, as in the case of a motorist asked to perform sobriety tests under the Highway Traffic Act, the section 7 right to make an informed choice as to whether to speak to police required only that the police did not engage in conduct that effectively and unfairly deprives the detainee of the right to choose whether to speak. The Court held that section 7 had not been violated by two simple questions as to whether the motorist had been drinking and as to the quantity.

In *R. v. Orbanski*,[192] a 5-2 majority of the Supreme Court chose not to confront the right to silence issues in deciding that a motorist detained and asked questions as to alcohol consumption or asked to perform sobriety tests was not entitled to the right to counsel under s. 10(b) of the Charter.

Recent interpretations of the right to silence in the context of police questioning after the accused has been afforded an opportunity to consult counsel have turned on the following passage of McLachlin, J. in *Hebert*:

> [The] Charter requires that the suspect be informed of his or her right to counsel and be permitted to consult counsel without delay. If the suspect chooses to make a statement, the suspect may do so. But if the suspect chooses not to, the state is not

---

190   *Hicks* (1988), 64 C.R. (3d) 68 (Ont. C.A.), affirmed (1990), 54 C.C.C. (3d) 575 (S.C.C.). See too *Imeson* (1992), 13 C.R. (4th) 322 (Ont. Gen. Div.).
191   (1996), 46 C.R. (4th) 229 (Ont. C.A.).
192   29 C.R. (6th) 205, 196 C.C.C. (3d) 481, [2005] 2 S.C.R. 3.

entitled to use its superior power to override the suspect's will and negate his or her choice.[193]

The B.C. Court of Appeal determined in *K. (H.W.)*[194] that the section 7 right to silence was not breached by overriding the accused's choice not to speak where police asked the accused in a murder case whether he wished to take a breathalyser, after assuring the lawyer they would not be interviewing him. Because of the agreement with the lawyer, McEachern C.J.B.C., for the court, found this case close to the line between "fair and unfair treatment" but noted that the accused had chosen freely and voluntarily to say far more than was necessary to answer the question.[195] So too the B.C. court held there was no right to silence violation in *Ekman*.[196] The accused had indicated that he was only willing to answer questions with his lawyer present, but did so without his lawyer when the police advised him he had no right to the presence of a lawyer and the choice was his. There had been no confusion in the accused's mind as to his rights.

However, in *Otis*,[197] the Quebec Court of Appeal decided that the right to silence should be more meaningful. Although the court decided that the accused had sufficient, though limited, cognitive capacity to make choices Justice Proulx for the court decided that the continued police questioning, after he had asked them to stop four times, violated section 7. The police were not entitled to use their superior power to totally disregard the accused's desires and undermine his choice to remain silent. Once an accused has clearly stated he wishes to remain silent, the police cannot act as if there has been a waiver.

In *R. v. Roy* (2004), 15 C.R. (6th) 282 (Ont. C.A.) the accused was convicted of a murder of an 11-year-old girl lured from her home. On his conviction appeal the Ontario Court of Appeal dismissed the argument that his confession following an eight hour interrogation had breached his section 7 pre-trial right to silence. The Court held that he had not chosen not to speak as he had a game plan to answer some not all questions. For the Court, Doherty J.A. (Feldman and Macpherson JJ.A. concurring) however added *obiter*:

> [The] repeated assertion by a detained person during a lengthy interview that he does not want to speak to the police any further will provide strong and sometimes conclusive evidence that any subsequent statement was not the product of a free exercise of the detainee's right to choose whether to speak. The question is, however, a factual question to be decided on a case by case basis by the trial judge (at 187).[198]

Otis and *Roy* were not followed in the surprising and controversial ruling of a 5-4 majority of the Supreme Court in *R. v. Singh*[199] that in the context of interrogation by police the s. 7 pre-trial right to silence has been subsumed by the voluntary confession rule. We will fully consider this ruling later in chapter 6.

---

193 At para. 80.
194 (2000), 32 C.R. (5th) 359 (B.C.C.A.).
195 At para. 18.
196 (2000), 146 C.C.C. (3d) 346 (B.C.C.A.).
197 (2000), 37 C.R. (5th) 320 (Que. C.A.). See Guy Cournoyer, "*Otis*: The Quebec Court of Appeal Asserts a Meaningful Right to Silence Where a Suspect Says No to Interrogation" (2000), 37 C.R. (5th) 342.
198 See annotation by Guy Cournoyer in (2004), 15 C.R. (6th) 284.
199 [2007] 3 S.C.R. 405.

(v) *Principle Against Self-incrimination: Charter section 7*

Since *Hebert*, in a series of complex and split Supreme Court decisions, a majority position has emerged through the judgments of Chief Justice Lamer that within principles of fundamental justice guaranteed by section 7 there is a "principle against self-incrimination" wider than the pre-trial right to silence, the protections against compellability in section 11(*c*) and the privilege against self-incrimination in section 13. The Chief Justice put it best for the majority of the court in *P. (M.B.).*[200]

> Perhaps the single most important organizing principle in criminal law is the right of an accused not to be forced into assisting in his or her own prosecution. . . . This means, in effect, that an accused is under no obligation to respond until the state has succeeded in making out a *prima facie* case against him or her. In other words, until the Crown establishes that there is a "case to meet", an accused is not compellable in a general sense (as opposed to the narrow, testimonial sense) and need not answer the allegations against him or her.[201]

The Chief Justice saw the presumption of innocence and the power imbalance between the state and the individual as being at the root of the principle. In a later judgment, he describes the principle against self-incrimination in even broader terms:

> Any state action that coerces an individual to furnish evidence against him or herself in a proceeding in which the individual and the state are adversaries violates the principle against self-incrimination. Coercion means the denial of free and informed consent.[202]

This principle against self-incrimination or a "case to meet" is not merely an organizing principle of existing rules and principles but one that has the capacity to introduce new rules.[203] It is now seen to be the explanation of the recognition of a pre-trial right to silence in *Hebert*.

It also led the court in *B.C. Securities Commission v. Branch*[204] to create a doctrine of derivative use immunity and also a discretion to prevent the compellability of a witness who is (or may be) charged with an offence. Two officers of a company were served with summonses from the Securities Commission under the provincial Securities Act compelling their attendance for examination and requiring them to produce all records in their possession. When the officers failed to appear, the Commission sought an order from the court committing the officers for contempt. The officers applied for a declaration that the Act violated section 7 of the Charter. The Supreme Court decided that the

---

200 (1994), 29 C.R. (4th) 209 (S.C.C.). In *S. (R.J.)* (1995), 36 C.R. (4th) 1 (S.C.C.) Iacobucci J., speaking for four justices not including Lamer C.J., expressly adopted the principle of self-incrimination outlined by the Chief Justice in *P. (M.B.)*.

201 At 226.

202 *P. (M.B.)* at 41. This statement was adopted by La Forest J. for a unanimous Court in *Fitzpatrick* (1995), 43 C.R (4th) 343 (S.C.C.), although distinguished on the facts.

203 Iacobucci J. in *S. (R J.)* at 49.

204 (1995), 38 C.R. (4th) 133 (S.C.C.), where Sopinka J. and Iacobucci J. reached a consensus majority position not evident in the earlier 229-page inconclusively split decision in *S. (R.J.)* (1995), 36 C.R. (4th) 1 (S.C.C.). See further *Jobin* (1995), 38 C.R. (4th) 176 (S.C.C.) and *Primeau* (1995), 38 C.R. (4th) 189 (S.C.C.).

principle against self-incrimination required that persons compelled to testify be provided with subsequent derivative-use immunity in addition to the use immunity guaranteed by section 13 of the Charter. The accused would have the evidentiary burden of showing a plausible connection between the compelled testimony and the evidence later sought to be adduced. Once this was done, in order to have the evidence admitted, the Crown would have to satisfy the court on a balance of probabilities that the authorities would have discovered the impugned derivative evidence absent the compelled testimony. The court also decided that, in addition, courts can, in certain circumstances, grant exemptions from compulsion to testify. The crucial question was whether the predominant purpose for seeking the evidence is to obtain incriminating evidence against the person compelled to testify or rather for some other legitimate public purpose. That test was seen to strike the appropriate balance between the interests of the state in obtaining the evidence for a valid public purpose on the one hand, and the right to silence of the person compelled to testify on the other.[205]

Branch was distinguished by La Forest J. for the Court in *Fitzpatrick*,[206] in holding that section 7 did not prevent the Crown from relying on statutorily required fishing logs on a charge of overfishing. The Court held that the principle against self-incrimination should not be applied as rigidly as it might in the context of a purely criminal offence. Fishing logs were required from all commercial fishers as conditions of their license to assist in the routine administration of a regulated industry.

In *G. (S.G.)*,[207] the Supreme Court held 5-2[208] that the discretion to allow the Crown to reopen its case after the defence had begun to answer was extremely narrow and far less likely to be exercised, otherwise the section 7 right of an accused not to be conscripted would be compromised. The minority pointed to the fact the late evidence had been unforeseen, had not arisen through fault of the Crown and should be left to a determination of whether there was prejudice to the defence case.[209]

In *White*,[210] Iacobucci J. held for a 6-1 majority[211] of the Supreme Court that the section 7 principle against self-incrimination barred the admission of motor vehicle accident reports made under the compulsion of a provincial Motor Vehicle Act at a trial for failing to stop at the scene of an accident under section 252(1)(*a*) of the Criminal Code. To obtain this use immunity, the person who made the statement would have to prove compulsion on a balance of probabilities. The

---

205 This is further addressed by Cory J. (Iacobucci and Major JJ. concurring) in concurring reasons in *Phillips v. Nova Scotia (Commissioner, Public Inquiries Act)* (1995), 39 C.R. (4th) 141 (S.C.C.).

206 *Supra*, note 202.

207 (1997), 8 C.R. (5th) 198 (S.C.C.).

208 Per Cory J. (Lamer C.J., Sopinka, Iacobucci and Major JJ. concurring). McLachlin J. (L'Heureux-Dubé J. concurring) dissented on this point.

209 See comment by Delisle, "Annotation", (1997) 8 C.R. (5th) 204 in favour of the majority position.

210 (1999), 24 C.R. (5th) 201 (S.C.C.). See criticism of Steven Penney, "The Continuing Evolution of the s. 7 Self-Incrimination Principle: *R. v. White*" (1999), 24 C.R. (5th) 247 and the reply by Michael Plaxton, "An Analysis and Defence of Free Choice Theory: A Response to Professor Penney" (1999), 27 C.R. (5th) 218.

211 L'Heureux-Dubé J. dissented.

test was whether the declarant held an honest and reasonable belief that he or she was required by law to report the accident to the person to whom the report was given.[212]

Iacobucci J. restated the residual principle against self-incrimination in the following broad terms:

> It is now well-established that there exists, in Canadian law, a principle against self-incrimination that is a principle of fundamental justice under s. 7 of the Charter. [The] principle has at least two key purposes, namely to protect against unreliable confessions, and to protect against abuses of power by the state. There is both an individual and a societal interest in achieving both of these protections. Both protections are linked to the value placed by Canadian society upon individual privacy, personal autonomy and dignity. . . . A state which arbitrarily intrudes upon its citizens' personal sphere will inevitably cause more injustice than it cures.
>
> The jurisprudence of this Court is clear that [it] . . . is an overarching principle within our criminal justice system, from which a number of specific common law and Charter rules emanate, such as the confessions rule, and the right to silence, among many others.[213]

However he also added an important general caveat.[214] The fact that the principle against self-incrimination had the status of an overarching principle did not imply that it provided absolute protection for an accused against all uses of information compelled by statute or otherwise. The residual protections were specific, contextually-sensitive and required a balancing process. In some contexts, the factors that favoured the importance of the search for truth would outweigh the factors that favour protecting the individual against undue compulsion by the state.

The principle against self-incrimination has not caught fire in lower courts, but there are some signs of life. The Ontario Court had no difficulty in holding that the principle did not bar the admission of a guilty plea at a subsequent criminal proceeding.[215]

So too the B.C. Court of Appeal determined that the principle against self-incrimination did not bar the admissibility of information provided to Revenue Canada in a fraud prosecution.[216] The principle has not availed in the context of compelled testimony under the Mutual Legal Assistance in Criminal Matters Act given the evidentiary immunity provided.[217] On the other hand, the Quebec Court of Appeal excluded the evidence of an accused and his wife compelled at a fire commissioner's inquiry from the subsequent arson trial.[218]

---

212 At 230-232, applied in *Gibb* (1999), 30 C.R. (5th) 189 (Sask. Q.B.) (admitting statement made to parole officer after arrest).

213 At 219-220.

214 At 220-221.

215 *Ford* (2000), 33 C.R. (5th) 178 (Ont. C.A.). See too *Thompson* (2001),151 C.C.C. (3d) 339 (Ont. C.A.) (upholding offence of failing to provide roadside test).

216 *Wilder* (2000), 142 C.C.C. (3d) 418 (B.C.C.A.). See also *Graham* (1997), 121 C.C.C. (3d) 76 (B.C.S.C.).

217 *États-Unis c. Ross* (1995), 41 C.R. (4th) 358, (*sub nom. United States of America v. Ross*) 100 C.C.C. (3d) 320 (Que. C.A.), *U.K. v. Hrynyk* (1996), 107 C.C.C. (3d) 104 (Ont. Gen. Div.).

218 *Kabbabe* (1997), 6 C.R. (5th) 82 (Que. C.A.).

In *R. v. B. (S.A.)*,[219] the Supreme Court dismissed a number of Charter challenges to the D.N.A. warrant powers. In the course of this ruling Justice Arbour, speaking for the full Court, asserted that the principle against self-incrimination developed under section 7 of the Charter is of "limited application". Previously we saw that in *P.M.B.* the Court had described the principle as the "single most important organizing principle in criminal law" and one capable of growth. Growth is clearly now stunted. This may well come as a relief to lower court judges who have often been resistant to wide applications. Arbour J. sees the application of the principle as depending on context (that unruly horse), and hinging on consideration of factors of reliability and state abuse of no concern in the D.N.A. legislation.[220]

The Supreme Court later rejected a principle against self-incrimination challenge to investigative hearings under anti-terrorism provisions: see *Application under s. 83.28 of the Criminal Code*.[221] As a result of a vote in Parliament (159-124), the investigative hearing provision of the Criminal Code expired as of March 1, 2007.[222]

(vi) *No Adverse Inference from Pre-trial Silence*

Can guilt be inferred from pre-trial silence? Should it be? Can pre-trial silence impair credibility about a defence first raised at trial?

R. v. TURCOTTE
31 C.R. (6th) 197, 200 C.C.C. (3d) 289, [2005] 2 S.C.R. 519

The accused went to a police station and asked that a car be sent to the ranch where he lived and worked. According to the police evidence, he also told them to put him in "jail" although Turcotte denied making this statement but did admit that he could have said to "lock him up" to shift their focus from him to the investigation of the farm. Turcotte also told the police in response to a question that there was no danger to the officers or anyone else at the farm. Despite repeated questions from the police, he refused to explain why a car was necessary or what would be found there. He indicated there was a rifle in his truck. Officers found three victims at the ranch. All three died from axe wounds to the head. The accused was charged with three counts of second degree murder. At trial, the evidence against the accused was entirely circumstantial, including his conduct at the police station, fingerprints on two items at the farm and small blood stains from two of the victims found on his clothing. The accused admitted finding the victims, but denied killing them. With respect to the accused's refusal to respond to police questioning as to why they should go to the farm, the trial judge told the jury that they could not draw inferences of guilt or innocence from the accused's silence but that this silence could be considered as relevant to his state of mind. He later instructed the jury that it could be considered "post-

---

219 (2003), 14 C.R. (6th) 205 (S.C.C.).
220 See further David Stratas, "R. v. B. (S.A.) and the Right Against Self-Incrimination: A Confusing Change of Direction?" (2003), 14 C.R. (6th) 227.
221 (2004), 21 C.R. (6th) 82 (S.C.C.).
222 O'Neill and Mayeda, "Anti-Terrorism Measures Defeated" Montreal Gazette (28 February 2007) A12.

offence conduct," and that it was the only substantial evidence proving guilt. The jury returned a verdict of guilty on each count.

The B.C. Court of Appeal set aside the convictions and ordered a new trial. It held that no adverse inference should have been drawn from the accused's silence. The Crown appealed.

ABELLA J. (MCLACHLIN C.J.C, MAJOR, BASTARACHE, BINNIE, LEBEL, DESCHAMPS, FISH and CHARRON JJ. concurring): —

. . . .

The essence of the Crown's argument is that Mr. Turcotte's refusal to respond to some of the questions from the police can be relied on as post-offence conduct from which an inference of guilt can be drawn.

"Post-offence conduct" is a legal term of art. It is not meant to be a neutral term embracing all behaviour by an accused after a crime has been committed, but only that conduct which is probative of guilt. It is, by its nature, circumstantial evidence.

The more traditional designation of such conduct, "consciousness of guilt" evidence, was changed by this Court to "post-offence conduct" evidence in *R. v. White*, [1998] 2 S.C.R. 72, 125 C.C.C. (3d) 385, 161 D.L.R. (4th) 590. Major J. held, at para. 20, that use of the phrase "consciousness of guilt" should be discouraged because it might undermine the presumption of innocence or may mislead the jury. In *White*, at para. 19, Major J. provided a non-exhaustive list of conduct that is typically admitted as post-offence conduct evidence: flight from the scene of the crime or the jurisdiction in which the crime was committed; attempts to resist arrest; failure to appear at trial; and acts of concealment such as lying, assuming a false name, changing one's appearance, and hiding or disposing of evidence. In *White*, the post-offence conduct was the accused's running from the police to avoid arrest, the attempted disposal of one of the murder weapons, and fleeing the jurisdiction following the killing.

Although the terminology has been changed, the evidentiary concept has not. As with evidence of "consciousness of guilt", only evidence after a crime has been committed that is probative of guilt can be relied on as "post-offence conduct".

The first issue, therefore, is to determine whether the trial judge erred in designating Mr. Turcotte's refusal to answer some of the police questions as "post-offence conduct" capable of supporting an inference of guilt. This in turn requires a determination of whether Mr. Turcotte had the right to refuse to answer the police's questions. The Crown's dual argument is that no right to silence was engaged in this case, but that even if it was, Mr. Turcotte's conduct in going to the police station and answering some of the police's questions, showed that it was a right he chose to waive.

Under the traditional common law rules, absent statutory compulsion, everyone has the right to be silent in the face of police questioning. This right to refuse to provide information or answer inquiries finds cogent and defining expression in *Rothman v. The Queen*, [1981] 1 S.C.R. 640, 59 C.C.C. (2d) 30, 121 D.L.R. (3d) 578, per Lamer J.:

In Canada the right of a suspect not to say anything to the police . . . is merely the exercise by him of the general right enjoyed in this country by anyone to do whatever one pleases, saying what one pleases or choosing not to say certain things, unless obliged to do otherwise by law. It is because no law says that a suspect, save in certain circumstances, must say anything to the police that we say that he has the right to remain silent, which is a positive way of explaining that there is on his part no legal obligation to do otherwise. [Footnotes omitted; p. 683]

Although its temporal limits have not yet been fully defined, the right to silence has also received *Charter* benediction. In *R. v. Hebert*, [1990] 2 S.C.R. 151, 57 C.C.C. (3d) 1, the first decision from this Court recognizing it as a s. 7 right, an accused, who had been arrested and advised of his rights, refused to provide a statement to the police after consulting counsel. He was then placed in a cell with an undercover officer posing as a suspect under arrest. During the course of their conversation, the accused incriminated himself. The question before the Court was whether the statement to the undercover officer was admissible. Writing for the majority, McLachlin J. held that it was not admissible because it violated the accused's right to silence found in s. 7 of the *Canadian Charter of Rights and Freedoms*.

In addition to emphasizing the importance of providing protection from the power of the state, McLachlin J. founded the s. 7 right to silence in two common law doctrines: the confessions rule and the privilege against self-incrimination, explaining that both emerge from the following unifying theme:

[T]he idea that a person in the power of the state in the course of the criminal process has the right to choose whether to speak to the police or remain silent. [p. 164]

It would be an illusory right if the decision not to speak to the police could be used by the Crown as evidence of guilt. As Cory J. explained in *Chambers*, where the trial judge failed to instruct the jury that the accused's silence could not be used as evidence of guilt:

It has as well been recognized that since there is a right to silence, it would be a snare and a delusion to caution the accused that he need not say anything in response to a police officer's question but nonetheless put in evidence that the accused clearly exercised his right and remained silent in the face of a question which suggested his guilt. [p. 1316]

Although *Chambers* dealt specifically with silence after the accused had been cautioned, it would equally be "a snare and a delusion" to allow evidence of any valid exercise of the right to be used as evidence of guilt.

Moreover, as Doherty and Rosenberg JJ.A. explained in *R. v. B. (S.C.)* (1997), 36 O.R. (3d) 516, 119 C.C.C. (3d) 530 (C.A.), since, in most circumstances, individuals are under no obligation to assist the police, their silence cannot, on its own, be probative of guilt:

a refusal to assist is nothing more than the exercise of a recognized liberty and, standing alone, says nothing about that person's culpability. [p. 529]

Evidence of silence is, however, admissible in limited circumstances. As Cory J. held in *Chambers*, at p. 1318, if "the Crown can establish a real relevance and a proper basis", evidence of silence can be admitted with an appropriate warning to the jury.

There are circumstances where the right to silence must bend. In *R. v. Crawford*, [1995] 1 S.C.R. 858, 96 C.C.C. (3d) 481, for example, the Court was confronted with a conflict between the right to silence and the right to full answer and defence. Two men were charged with second degree murder after a man was beaten to death. At their joint trial, each blamed the other. Crawford, one of the accused, had not given the police a statement, but he chose to testify at trial in his own defence. His co-accused's counsel cross-examined him on his failure to make a statement to the police. This failure was negatively contrasted with the fact that his co-accused had given a full statement to the police at the earliest opportunity. Sopinka J., writing for the majority, held that a balance between the two competing rights can be achieved if the evidence of silence is admitted, but used only to assess credibility and not to infer guilt. Since the jury had been invited to infer guilt from Crawford's silence, the Court ordered a new trial.

Evidence of silence may also be admissible when the defence raises an issue that renders the accused's silence relevant. Examples include circumstances where the defence seeks to emphasize the accused's cooperation with the authorities (*R. v. Lavallee*, [1980] O.J. No. 540 (QL) (C.A.)); where the accused testified that he had denied the charges against him at the time he was arrested (*R. v. Ouellette* (1997), 200 A.R. 363, 119 C.C.C. (3d) 30 sub nom. *R. v. O. (G.A.)* (C.A.)); or where silence is relevant to the defence theory of mistaken identity and a flawed police investigation (*R. v. M.C.W.* (2002), 169 B.C.A.C. 128, 2002 BCCA 341, 165 C.C.C. (3d) 129).

Similarly, cases where the accused failed to disclose his or her alibi in a timely or adequate manner provide a well established exception to the prohibition on using pre-trial silence against an accused: *R. v. Cleghorn*, [1995] 3 S.C.R. 175, 100 C.C.C. (3d) 393.[223] Silence might also be admissible if it is inextricably bound up with the narrative or other evidence and cannot easily be extricated.

The Crown argued that any right to silence is engaged only when the accused comes within "the power of the state" and that the right has no relevance when the state has done nothing to use that power against the individual. This, with respect, makes the right's borders too confining. In general, absent a statutory requirement to the contrary, individuals have the right to choose whether to speak to the police, even if they are not detained or arrested. The common law right to silence exists at all times against the state, whether or not the person asserting it is within its power or control. Like the confessions rule, an accused's right to silence applies any time he or she interacts with a person in authority, whether detained or not. It is a right premised on an individual's freedom to choose the extent of his or her cooperation with the police, and is animated by a recognition of the potentially coercive impact of the state's authority and a concern that individuals not be required to incriminate themselves. These policy considerations

---

223 For a careful analysis of the traditional alibi exception see Doherty J.A. in *R. v. Wright*, [2009] O.J. No. 3550 (C.A.).

exist both before and after arrest or detention. There is, as a result, no principled basis for failing to extend the common law right to silence to both periods.

Nor do I share the Crown's view that by attending at the detachment and answering some of the police's questions, Mr. Turcotte waived any right he might otherwise have had. A willingness to impart some information to the police does not completely submerge an individual's right not to respond to police questioning. He or she need not be mute to reflect an intention to invoke it. An individual can provide some, none, or all of the information he or she has. A voluntary interaction with the police, even one initiated by an individual, does not constitute a waiver of the right to silence. The right to choose whether to speak is retained throughout the interaction.

At various points throughout the trial, the Crown, and the trial judge at the Crown's request, characterized Mr. Turcotte's silence in two ways: as post-offence conduct evidence (called "consciousness of guilt" evidence by the Crown), and as state of mind evidence rebutting his claim to be in shock and panic. Most troubling was the trial judge's final instructions on post-offence conduct. During this portion of his instructions, the trial judge told the jury that Mr. Turcotte's silence was post-offence conduct and zeroed in on his silence as the only relevant post-offence conduct. His invocation was: "[y]ou may decide that the only substantial evidence proving the guilt of Mr. Turcotte arises from his post-offence conduct".

Even before his detention at 10:06 a.m., Mr. Turcotte had no duty to speak to or cooperate with the police. He exercised this right by refusing to answer some of the questions put to him by the police, declining to explain why a car should be sent to the Erhorn Ranch and refusing to say what the police would find there. Although he answered some of the police's questions, when he did not answer others he was nonetheless exercising his right to silence.

This is significant in deciding whether evidence of his silence was admissible as post-offence conduct, that is, evidence that is probative of guilt. Conduct after a crime has been committed is only admissible as "post-offence conduct" when it provides circumstantial evidence of guilt. The necessary relevance is lost if there is no connection between the conduct and guilt. The law imposes no duty to speak to or cooperate with the police. This fact alone severs any link between silence and guilt. Silence in the face of police questioning will, therefore, rarely be admissible as post-offence conduct because it is rarely probative of guilt. Refusing to do what one has a right to refuse to do reveals nothing. An inference of guilt cannot logically or morally emerge from the exercise of a protected right. Using silence as evidence of guilt artificially creates a duty, despite a right to the contrary, to answer all police questions.

Since there was no duty on Mr. Turcotte's part to speak to the police, his failure to do so was irrelevant; because it was irrelevant, no rational conclusion about guilt or innocence can be drawn from it; and because it was not probative of guilt, it could not be characterized for the jury as "post-offence conduct".

Nor do I see how Mr. Turcotte's silence could be used as "state of mind" evidence from which guilt could be inferred. The Crown argued that Mr. Turcotte's silence negated his claim that his state of mind was one of shock and panic. It is clear from the Crown's closing argument that there was little difference between asking the jury to consider Mr. Turcotte's silence as evidence of his state of mind, and asking them to consider it as evidence of his guilty conscience. So, for example, during his closing argument the Crown argued:

> That may tell you something about the guilty mind of Mr. Turcotte at the time. But again, it doesn't show that he was in a state of shock or panic, but rather that he was thinking about what he said and chose to say what he wanted to say and didn't want to say.

In order to make this claim, it was necessary for the Crown to suggest that his silence was motivated by a different state of mind, namely his guilty conscience. Characterizing the silence as state of mind evidence was simply another way of arguing that the silence was post-offence conduct probative of Mr. Turcotte's guilt.

While not admissible as post-offence conduct or state of mind evidence, Mr. Turcotte's behaviour at the R.C.M.P. detachment, including his refusal to answer some of the police's questions, was, arguably, admissible as an inextricable part of the narrative. As previously indicated, no issue was raised about its admissibility either at trial or on appeal. But, having admitted his silence into evidence, the trial judge was obliged to tell the jury in the clearest of terms that it could not be used to support an inference of guilt in order to contradict an intuitive impulse to conclude that silence is incompatible with innocence. Where evidence of silence is admitted, juries must be instructed about the proper purpose for which the evidence was admitted, the impermissible inferences which must not be drawn from evidence of silence, the limited probative value of silence, and the dangers of relying on such evidence. The failure to give the jury this limiting instruction, particularly given the circumstantial nature of the Crown's case, was highly prejudicial.

Given the significance of the error, I agree with the Court of Appeal that the curative proviso is inapplicable and a new trial is required. I would dismiss the appeal.

At his new trial, Turcotte was convicted in a judge-alone trial. What seemed to satisfy the trial judge of Turcotte's guilt was his statement that no one would be in danger at the farm.[224]

After *Turcotte* it will be especially important to distinguish between the common law right to silence, on which the judgment turns, and the section 7 Charter pre-trial right to silence recognised in *Hebert*. The Court decided that the common law right to silence applies whether or not the accused was cautioned as to the right to silence, prior to arrest or detention and also that the doctrine of waiver applies. As to waiver, as you cannot waive something of which you are unaware, it would appear that the Court is asserting a common law right to

---

224 See *R. v. Turcotte*, [2006] B.C.J. No. 3631 (S.C.C.).

be advised of the right to silence, although it never says this expressly. In contrast, limits imposed on the Charter right to silence recognized in *Hebert* include that the right is only triggered on detention and that the doctrine of waiver does not apply.

The gains in *Turcotte* are not all in favour of accused. The Court indicates that evidence of silence is admissible in limited circumstances with an appropriate warning where the Crown can establish a real relevance and a proper basis. Justice Abella offers six examples. The sixth is "inextricably bound up with the narrative or other evidence and cannot easily be extricated." No authority is provided for this new exception. Resort to language of "admissible as part of the narrative" is notorious as a device to avoid evidential rules and principles. In this case, Abella J. remarks that the evidence of how the accused refused to answer the police may "arguably be admissible as part of the narrative." This may suggest that the Court was not unanimous on this point. Justice Abella did say that

> juries must be instructed about the proper purpose for which the evidence was admitted, the impermissible inferences which must not be drawn from evidence of silence, the limited probative value of silence, and the dangers of relying on such evidence. [para. 58].

Could a jury ever not use such evidence to draw an adverse inference from silence or lack of co-operation? If this exception is widely applied, the right to silence may be illusory, which is what the Court set out to avoid.

(vii) *No Adverse Inference from Trial Silence*

Should adverse inferences be drawn from an accused's failure to testify? Should there be a distinction between inferences that might flow from silence during the investigative process and inferences from silence at trial? The appropriateness of drawing such inferences, the fairness, must be judged separately. Many protections available to an accused at trial are not present during police questioning. At trial the accused will normally be represented by counsel. He will then know the charge against him and will have listened to and been able to challenge the evidence against him. The trial is in public and an impartial judge is present to ensure the accused's rights are safe-guarded and the hearing is conducted according to the rules of natural justice. There are certain procedural safeguards in place as to how he may be questioned if he decides to take the stand. Before the accused is called on to answer the judge will have decided that there is a case to meet; the trial judge will have decided that there is evidence upon which a reasonable jury properly instructed could return a verdict of guilty. Finally, it is almost certain that judges and juries will draw adverse inferences from the accused's silence at trial as they personally witness the accused's silence in the face of accusation; there is no need for evidence to be led as to the accused's silence.

We have seen in *Turcotte* that the Supreme Court has determined that normally no adverse inference should be drawn from the accused remaining silent before trial. The Supreme Court in some early cases suggested that different considerations apply to silence at trial given that the accused is represented, knows the case to meet due to disclosure and there are rules regarding the admissibility of evidence. It appeared to be clear from various Supreme Court dicta that adverse inferences can be drawn against an accused for not testifying in some circumstances. What those circumstances are was far less clear. In *Francois*,[225] McLachlin J. wrote for the majority that:

> subject to the caveat that failure to testify cannot be used to shore up a Crown case which otherwise does not establish guilt beyond a reasonable doubt, a jury is permitted to draw an adverse inference from the failure of an accused person to testify.[226]

In *Lepage*,[227] the Supreme Court divided 3-2 as to whether the trial judge had drawn an adverse inference from the accused's failure to offer an explanation for the presence of his fingerprints but was in agreement that such an inference could be drawn "once the Crown had proved a *prima facie* case".[228] Chief Justice Lamer in *P. (M.B.)*,[229] in describing the "principle against self-incrimination" for the Court, stated the following:

> Once the Crown discharges its obligation to present a *prima facie* case, such that it cannot be non-suited by a motion for a directed verdict of acquittal, the accused can be expected to respond . . . and failure to do so may serve as the basis for drawing adverse inferences. [Once] there is a "case to meet" which, if believed, would result in conviction, the accused can no longer remain a passive participant in the prosecutorial process and becomes — in a broad sense — compellable. That is, the accused must answer the case against him or her, or face the possibility of conviction.[230]

It would appear at this point that the Supreme Court had no objections to adverse inferences based on the accused's failure to testify provided that there is otherwise enough evidence to go to the jury.

However in *Noble* a 5-4 majority abruptly changed course and decided that normally an adverse inference should not be drawn from trial silence.

R. v. NOBLE
[1997] 1 S.C.R. 874, 6 C.R. (5th) 1, 114 C.C.C. (3d) 385

The manager of an apartment building found two young men in the parking area of his building, one of whom appeared to be attempting to break into a car with a screwdriver. When the manager asked the man for identification, he handed over an expired driver's licence. The manager testified that he thought the photograph on the licence accurately depicted the man in front of him in the garage and told the man that he could retrieve the licence from the police. The accused was eventually charged with breaking and entering and having in his possession an instrument suitable for the purpose of breaking into a motor vehicle. At trial, neither the manager nor anyone else could identify the accused, but the trial judge concluded that he as the trier of fact could compare the picture in the driver's licence with the accused in the courtroom and conclude that the

---

225 (1994), 31 C.R. (4th) 201 (S.C.C.).
226 At 210. La Forest J., Gonthier J. and Iacobucci J. concurred. Major J. (Sopinka J. and Cory J. concurring) dissented.
227 (1995), 36 C.R. (4th) 145 (S.C.C.).
228 Sopinka J. for the majority at 159, Major J. for the minority.
229 (1994), 29 C.R. (4th) 209 (S.C.C.).
230 At 227-228.

driver's licence accurately depicted the accused. He also was satisfied that the building manager would have carefully examined the licence at the time of the incident. The trial judge noted that the accused faced an overwhelming case to meet as a result of the licence, yet remained silent. In the trial judge's view, he could draw "almost an adverse inference" that "certainly may add to the weight of the Crown's case on the issue of identification". The accused was convicted on both counts. The Court of Appeal set aside the conviction and ordered a new trial. A 5:4 majority of the Supreme Court dismissed the Crown's appeal.

SOPINKA J. (L'HEUREUX-DUBÉ, CORY, IACOBUCCI and MAJOR JJ. concurring): —

. . . .

The right to silence is based on society's distaste for compelling a person to incriminate him- or herself with his or her own words. Following this reasoning, in my view the use of silence to help establish guilt beyond a reasonable doubt is contrary to the rationale behind the right to silence. Just as a person's words should not be conscripted and used against him or her by the state, it is equally inimical to the dignity of the accused to use his or her silence to assist in grounding a belief in guilt beyond a reasonable doubt. To use silence in this manner is to treat it as communicative evidence of guilt. To illustrate this point, suppose an accused did commit the offence for which he was charged. If he testifies and is truthful, he will be found guilty as the result of what he said. If he does not testify and is found guilty in part because of his silence, he is found guilty because of what he did not say. No matter what the non-perjuring accused decides, communicative evidence emanating from the accused is used against him. The failure to testify tends to place the accused in the same position as if he had testified and admitted his guilt. In my view, this is tantamount to conscription of self-incriminating communicative evidence and is contrary to the underlying purpose of the right to silence. In order to respect the dignity of the accused, the silence of the accused should not be used as a piece of evidence against him or her.

The Presumption of Innocence

The presumption of innocence, enshrined at trial in s. 11(d) of the Charter, provides further support for the conclusion that silence of the accused at trial cannot be placed on the evidentiary scales against the accused. . . . If silence may be used against the accused in establishing guilt, part of the burden of proof has shifted to the accused. In a situation where the accused exercises his or her right to silence at trial, the Crown need only prove the case to some point short of beyond a reasonable doubt, and the failure to testify takes it over the threshold. The presumption of innocence, however, indicates that it is not incumbent on the accused to present any evidence at all, rather it is for the Crown to prove him or her guilty. Thus, in order for the burden of proof to remain with the Crown, as required by the Charter, the silence of the accused should not be used against him or her in building the case for guilt. Belief in guilt beyond a reasonable doubt must be grounded on the testimony and any other tangible or demonstrative evidence admitted during the trial.

Some reference to the silence of the accused by the trier of fact may not offend the Charter principles discussed above: where in a trial by judge alone the trial judge is convinced of the guilt of the accused beyond a reasonable doubt, the silence of the accused may be referred to as evidence of the absence of an explanation which could raise a reasonable doubt. If the Crown has proved the case beyond a reasonable doubt, the accused need not testify, but if he doesn't, the Crown's case prevails and the accused will be convicted. It is only in this sense that the accused "need respond" once the Crown has proved its case beyond a reasonable doubt. Another permissible reference to the silence of the accused was alluded to by the Court of Appeal in this case. In its view, such a reference is permitted by a judge trying a case alone to indicate that he need not speculate about possible defences that might have been offered by the accused had he or she testified. . . . Such treatment of the silence of the accused does not offend either the right to silence or the presumption of innocence. If silence is simply taken as assuring the trier of fact that it need not speculate about unspoken explanations, then belief in guilt beyond a reasonable doubt is not in part grounded on the silence of the accused, but rather is grounded on the evidence against him or her. The right to silence and its underlying rationale are respected, in that the communication or absence of communication is not used to build the case against the accused. The silence of the accused is not used as inculpatory evidence, which would be contrary to the right to silence, but simply is not used as exculpatory evidence. Moreover, the presumption of innocence is respected, in that it is not incumbent on the accused to defend him- or herself or face the possibility of conviction on the basis of his or her silence. Thus, a trier of fact may refer to the silence of the accused simply as evidence of the absence of an explanation which it must consider in reaching a verdict. On the other hand, if there exists in evidence a rational explanation or inference that is capable of raising a reasonable doubt about guilt, silence cannot be used to reject this explanation.

. . . .

The principles to which I have referred which derive from ss. 7 and 11(d) of the Charter find ample support in recent case law of this Court. While earlier cases on the appropriate use of silence by the trier of fact are admittedly ambiguous, recent decisions are clear: silence may not be used by the trier of fact as a piece of inculpatory evidence. . . . In my view, these comments clearly indicate that it is not permissible to use the failure to testify as a piece of evidence contributing to a finding of guilt beyond a reasonable doubt where such a finding would not exist without considering the failure to testify. McLachlin J. stated that the failure to testify could not be used to "shore up a Crown case which otherwise does not establish guilt beyond a reasonable doubt". Major J. stated that "this lack of testimony cannot otherwise be used to strengthen the Crown's case where the Crown has fallen short of proving guilt". In my view, these statements indicate that silence cannot be used to take an unproven case to a proven case.

. . . .

There may, however, be confusion over the use of the words "adverse inference" in the above cases. Professor R. J. Delisle, in an annotation to *R. v. François* (1994), 31 C.R. (4th) 203, asked that if an adverse inference is permitted, what inference is relevant if it can only be drawn after guilt beyond a reasonable doubt has been proved? He stated at p. 204:

> The essence of a criminal trial is whether the Crown has established its case beyond a reasonable doubt. If a jury cannot use the failure to testify to assist in its determination of whether they are satisfied beyond a reasonable doubt, then pray tell what the permissible adverse inference does? For what else can the jury use it?

As set out above, silence is not inculpatory evidence, but nor is it exculpatory evidence. Thus, as in *Lepage*, if the trier of fact reaches a belief in guilt beyond a reasonable doubt, silence may be treated by the trier of fact as confirmatory of guilt. Silence may indicate, for example, that there is no evidence to support speculative explanations of the Crown's evidence offered by defence counsel, or it may indicate that the accused has not put forward any evidence that would require that the Crown negative an affirmative defence. In this limited sense, silence may be used by the trier of fact. If, however, there is a rational explanation which is consistent with innocence and which may raise a reasonable doubt, the silence of the accused cannot be used to remove that doubt. Thus, there are permissible uses of silence by the trier of fact. However, Delisle is correct in stating that, since these permissible uses only arise after the trier of fact has reached a belief in guilt beyond a reasonable doubt, the uses may be superfluous. I would therefore conclude that courts should generally avoid using the potentially confusing term "inference" in discussing the silence of the accused. "Inference" could be taken to indicate that the trier of fact used silence to help establish the case for guilt beyond a reasonable doubt, which is not a permissible use of silence. Indeed, because of the potential for confusion, discussion of the silence of the accused should generally be avoided. However, where silence is mentioned by the trial judge as confirmatory of guilt given the totality of the evidence, but not as a "make-weight", there is no reversible error. *Lepage* provides an example of such a situation.

. . . .

On a related point, I would add that nothing in s. 4(6) or in the analysis thus far prevents the trial judge from telling the jury that the evidence on a particular issue is uncontradicted. In such a circumstance, the judge is not instructing the jury to consider the failure of the accused to testify per se, but rather is simply instructing the jury to take note of the fact that no evidence had been led to contradict a particular point. Rather than inviting the jury to place the failure of the accused on the evidentiary scales, the judge is instructing the jury that it need not speculate about possible contradictory evidence which has not been led in evidence.

. . . .

In support of its contention that silence may be used to build the case against the accused, the appellant pointed to various appellate review cases involving s. 686 of the Criminal Code. Section 686(1)(b)(iii) is a curative provision; notwithstanding errors of law at the trial, if the court of appeal is satisfied that no miscarriage of justice occurred when the conviction was entered, the conviction will be upheld. In applying this curative provision, this Court has established that it is permissible for an appellate court to account for the silence of the accused. . . . Similarly, it has also been established that it is appropriate for an appellate court to account for the accused's failure to testify in assessing the reasonableness of the verdict under s. 686(1)(a)(i). . . . The appellant submitted that since it is permissible for appellate courts to consider silence in assessing the verdict, it must be permissible for the trier of fact to consider silence in reaching a verdict. In my view, the appellate review cases do not contradict the conclusion that silence may not be placed on the evidentiary scales, either by the trier of fact or by appellate courts. Rather, the cases hold that appellate courts, like triers of fact, may refer to the silence of the accused as indicative of the absence of an exculpatory explanation; silence is not inculpatory, but nor is it exculpatory. Nowhere do the appellate review cases outlined above explicitly state that silence may be used as a "make-weight" by the trier of fact, but there is wording that suggests that silence may be used simply in the limited sense of not providing an innocent explanation. . . . The appellate court, and the trier of fact, may consider the silence of the accused as failing to provide an innocent explanation for the existence of otherwise convincing inculpatory evidence.

. . . .

In any event, the principles generally governing appellate review are not necessarily identical to those governing the trial. At trial, the accused is presumed innocent under s. 11(d) of the Charter, but this section does not establish a presumption of innocence in other proceedings such as appeals. . . . In my view, the presumption of innocence does not operate with the same vigour in the context of an appeal of a conviction as it does at trial. After the guilty verdict has been entered, it is no longer incumbent on the Crown to establish guilt — that guilt having already been proved beyond a reasonable doubt — rather it is incumbent on the appellant to demonstrate an error at trial. In such a context, the presumption of innocence is not applied in the same manner as it is at trial. . . . Regardless of the use of silence by the appellate court in exercising its discretion to confirm the conviction or order a new trial, the conviction will not be reached on the basis of the silence of the accused, rather the presumption of guilt established by the guilty verdict will not be dislodged. Thus, even if the appellate review cases go farther than suggesting that silence may be accounted for by the court of appeal only in the limited sense of confirming the absence of innocent explanations, the principles applying to appellate review are not necessarily those that apply to a trial. At trial, which is the context with which the present appeal is concerned, not appellate review, the presumption of innocence and the right to silence are of paramount importance. . . . I leave for another day any final conclusion as to whether the appellate review cases were correct insofar as they implied that silence may be treated as a make-weight by an appellate court.

Alibi Cases

The appellant submitted that *Vézeau v. The Queen*, [1977] 2 S.C.R. 277, held that silence could be treated as a "make-weight". In *Vézeau*, this Court considered the significance of the failure to testify in the context of a defence of alibi. In that case, the defence was alibi, but the accused did not testify. In giving his instructions to the jury, the judge said that they could not draw any conclusion unfavourable to the accused from the fact that he had not testified. The majority of this Court held that, aside from the prohibition of comment on the failure of the accused to testify set out in the Canada Evidence Act, it was an error of law for the trial judge to instruct the jury that they could not consider the absence of testimony by the accused in assessing the alibi. Martland J. stated on behalf of the majority at p. 292 that:

> It was part of the appellant's defence to the charge that he could not have committed the offence because he was in Montreal when the murder occurred. Proof of this alibi was tendered by a witness who claimed to have been with the appellant in Montreal. The direction of the trial judge precluded the jury, when considering this defence, from taking into consideration the fact that the appellant had failed to support his alibi by his own testimony. The failure of an accused person, who relies upon an alibi, to testify and thus to submit himself to cross-examination is a matter of importance in considering the validity of that defence. The jury, in this case, was instructed that they could not take that fact into account in reaching their verdict.

In my view, *Vézeau* set out a narrow exception to the impermissibility of using silence to build the case against the accused at trial. It has clearly been recognized in other contexts that alibi defences create exceptions to the right to silence. . . . In my view, there are two reasons supporting the alibi exception to the right to silence pre-trial which apply also to the right to silence at trial: the ease with which alibi evidence may be fabricated; and the diversion of the alibi inquiry from the central inquiry at trial. I am therefore sympathetic to the view expressed in *Vézeau* that in the limited case of alibi, the failure of the accused at trial to testify and expose him- or herself to cross-examination on the alibi defence may be used to draw an adverse inference about the credibility of the defence. A second reason to permit such a limited exception to the right to silence at trial is that the alibi defence is not directly related to the guilt of the accused; as Gooderson put it, "[a]libi evidence, by its very nature, takes the focus right away from the area of the main facts". Rejecting the alibi defence does not build the case for the Crown in the sense of proving the existence of the required elements of the offence in question, but rather negatives an affirmative defence actively put forward by the accused. Using silence to inform the trier of fact's assessment of the credibility of the accused's affirmative defence of alibi simply goes to the alibi defence itself.

. . . .

On balance, it appears to me that the trial judge used the failure to testify as evidence going to identification which permitted him to reach a belief in guilt beyond a reasonable doubt. Indeed, he stated explicitly that the failure to testify "certainly may add to the weight of the Crown's case" and concluded by finding guilt on the basis of "those reasons", which appeared to include the discussion of the failure to testify. In light of these statements, when the trial judge stated that he "can be" satisfied on the identity issue prior to discussing the failure to testify, in my view he indicated that the evidence before him was consistent with proof of identity, and the failure to testify took belief in identity beyond a reasonable doubt.

. . . Given my conclusion that such reasoning constituted an error of law, I would dismiss the appeal and confirm the judgment of the Court of Appeal ordering a new trial.

LAMER C.J. (dissenting): —

According to Sopinka J. the silence of an accused can only be used by the trier of fact in two very limited senses. The accused's silence may: (1) confirm prior findings of guilt beyond a reasonable doubt; and (2) remind triers of fact that they need not speculate about unstated defences. With greatest respect, this misinterprets the case law. This Court and others have repeatedly held that when the Crown presents a case to meet that implicates the accused in a "strong and cogent network of inculpatory facts", the trier of fact is entitled to consider the accused's failure to testify in deciding whether it is in fact satisfied of his or her guilt beyond a reasonable doubt. . . . None of these early cases suggests that the accused should be compelled to testify or that the accused is anything other than presumed innocent until proven guilty. They merely recognize that when an accused is implicated or "enveloped" in a case of unexplained inculpatory circumstances, there are consequences to silence that trial judges, juries, and appellate courts alike may consider in reaching a verdict. This does not happen in every case. A trier of fact is entitled to draw adverse inferences only where there is a "damning chain of evidence" or more aptly a "strong and cogent network of inculpatory facts". This approach to adverse inferences has been expressly adopted and refined by this Court in a number of judgments in recent years, both before and after the advent of the Charter.

. . . .

Why, one might ask, has this Court commented so frequently on the effect of the accused's silence? Why has it arisen so often as an issue before this Court? The reason is simple: silence can be very probative. Consider, for example, a case of sexual assault where the victim describes her attacker as a man with a very unusual tattoo on the upper portion of his arm. Nothing allows the Crown to call the accused as its first witness, as it could do under an inquisitorial system of criminal justice. However, assuming the Crown, by adducing other evidence, establishes a case to meet (i.e. enough evidence to make a guilty verdict reasonable), would not every man wrongly accused who lacks the described tattoo roll up his sleeve in court to exonerate himself? . . . Recognizing that silence can be probative, this Court has said in the above-mentioned cases that it is a factor that both juries and appellate courts may properly consider.

. . . .

My brother Sopinka disagrees. He asserts that these cases mean only that the silence of the accused can confirm verdicts or at most serve as the basis to refuse to speculate about unstated defences. Nothing, he says, provides that silence can be used as evidence itself. With respect, I find Sopinka J.'s interpretation difficult to support. For one, an inference which merely confirms prior conclusions of guilt is superfluous. As Professor R. J. Delisle has commented:

> The essence of a criminal trial is whether the Crown has established its case beyond a reasonable doubt. If a jury cannot use the failure to testify to assist in its determination of whether they are satisfied beyond a reasonable doubt, then pray tell what the permissible adverse inference does? For what else can the jury use it? (Annotation to *R. v. François* (1994), 31 C.R. (4th) 203, at p. 204.)

Second, I find it illogical for the Court to say that silence may be used by judges and juries but only to the extent that it highlights the fact that the Crown's evidence remains uncontradicted. Uncontradicted by whom? To allow a trial judge to instruct the jury that the evidence remains uncontradicted is just a coded message to remind the jury that the accused has not led any evidence in his or her own defence. The jurisprudence clearly establishes that, once the Crown has proffered a case to meet, the silence of an accused itself can be used in determining whether an accused is guilty beyond a reasonable doubt. I believe that we should be straightforward and say so.

. . . .

With respect, I find it profoundly illogical to say that trial judges and juries must not weigh the silence of the accused on the evidentiary scales, but in reviewing whether their verdicts are reasonable appellate courts can assume that they did. . . . I simply cannot conceive how a trial verdict that is a miscarriage of justice can be cured by an appellate court pursuant to s. 686(1)(*b*)(iii) because we say that certain Charter rights no longer apply on appeal. I similarly cannot understand how a verdict that would ordinarily be considered unreasonable can magically become reasonable pursuant to s. 686(1)(*a*)(i) simply because the case has progressed from one level of court to another. If the role of a trier of fact is to have any meaning, appellate courts must undertake their statutory responsibility to review the fitness of verdicts and to cure trial errors on the same understanding of the silence of an accused. I cannot endorse a criminal justice system in which an accused's silence may be used to a greater extent by appellate judges than by triers of fact at the trial level. Otherwise the Court is effectively sanctioning what it says is prohibited — inviting both judges and juries to use silence as evidence, but asking them to keep it quiet.

. . . .

The act of drawing adverse inferences from the silence of an accused is not contrary to the accused's right of non-compellability or the presumption of innocence. This point becomes clear upon a proper understanding of the case to meet. If the Crown establishes a case to meet, such that its case cannot be non-suited by a motion for a directed verdict of acquittal, it has put forth, by definition, sufficient evidence upon which a jury, properly instructed, could reasonably convict. Put differently, when the Crown provides a case to meet, all of the evidence to sustain a conviction has been put forth by the Crown in keeping with its burden of proof. As Professor R. J. Delisle has argued:

> Some object that permitting an inference of guilt modifies the burden of proof. But query whether this is so. The prosecution has the burden of proving the accused's guilt beyond a reasonable doubt and the Crown will not have discharged that burden, if at all, until the end of the case after all the evidence has been heard. The defendant's silence may be treated as a piece of evidence in assisting the discharge of the Crown's burden, it may constitute part of the totality of the evidence, but that does not mean the burden of proof has been shifted.("Silence at Trial: Inferences and Comments" (1997), 1 C.R. (5th) 313, at pp. 318-19.)

. . . .

This approach to adverse inferences is more consistent with the letter and spirit of s. 4(6) of the Canada Evidence Act, R.S.C., 1985, c. C-5, than the approach endorsed by Sopinka J. Section 4(6) currently provides:

> 4.(6) The failure of the person charged, or of the wife or husband of that person, to testify shall not be made the subject of comment by the judge or by counsel for the prosecution.

This rule against commenting on the accused's failure to testify was originally created to ensure that neither the court nor the prosecution would draw unfair attention to the silence of the accused. It was not, however, intended to preclude triers of fact from drawing natural and reasonable inferences from his silence. Under s. 4(6), this Court has said on a number of occasions that a jury is "free to draw" and "frequently does draw" adverse inferences from the failure of the accused to explain. If adverse inferences themselves were impermissible, s. 4(6) would not merely prohibit "comment", it would prohibit the drawing of adverse inferences altogether.

. . . .

I question how Sopinka J.'s position can be reconciled with s. 4(6). Even though s. 4(6) does not prohibit adverse inferences, the intractable rule that emerges from the reasons of Sopinka J. is that no trier of fact can use the accused's silence as inculpatory evidence adding to the weight of the Crown's case. The reason for this rule, he suggests, lies in an accused's fundamental right of non-compellability and the presumption of innocence. However, if this Court is prepared to conclude that the fundamental Charter rights to silence and the presumption of innocence prohibit triers of fact from using the accused's silence as evidence, one would have thought that trial judges would be empowered, if not required, to say so. Similarly, if there are subtle, permissible uses to be made of an accused's silence, trial judges must be able to explain them. . . . I cannot reconcile Sopinka J.'s position with s. 4(6) of the Canada Evidence Act. Indeed his reasons indirectly challenge the constitutionality of s. 4(6), which has not been contested at this Court, but which was upheld by Cory J.A. (as he then was) at the Ontario Court of Appeal in *R. v. Boss* (1988), 46 C.C.C. (3d) 523. Other Commonwealth jurisdictions have not only endorsed the act of drawing adverse inferences from the silence of the accused, they affirm that such inferences do not alter the traditional notions of the burden of proof and the right to silence.

. . . .

In my view, the trial judge's use of the accused's silence was proper. Although he could have been more precise, Lemiski Prov. Ct. J. clearly found, without reference to the accused's silence, that the Crown had established an "overwhelming" case to meet. Then, given the network of inculpatory facts, or the "virtual outcry situation" as he referred to it, Lemiski Prov. Ct. J. properly inferred guilt from the silence of the accused. As I have gone to great lengths to discuss, having no doubt concluded that silence was probative in this case, the trial judge's inference was natural and reasonable. Moreover, given the existence of a case to meet, it was perfectly consistent with the respondent's right to silence and the presumption of innocence. For all of these reasons, I would allow the appeal.

LA FOREST and GONTHIER JJ. concurring: — I agree with the Chief Justice, except that I prefer not to comment on the constitutional validity of s. 4(6) of the Canada Evidence Act, R.S.C., 1985, c. C-5, an issue that is not before us.

MCLACHLIN J. dissenting: — I agree with the Chief Justice that this appeal should be allowed. I add only this. The difference between the positions adopted by Lamer C.J. and Sopinka J. turns on a different conception of the case to meet. . . . In summary, the matter must be viewed in two stages. The first question is whether the Crown has adduced evidence which, if believed, would support a conviction, i.e. prove guilt beyond a reasonable doubt. This is the case to meet. The second question is whether the trier of fact should believe the Crown's evidence. At this second stage, and only at this second stage, the judge or jury may consider the absence of evidence contradicting the Crown's case to meet, including the accused's failure to testify. Any conviction will be based on the Crown's unchallenged evidence. To say that an inference has been drawn from the accused's failure to testify is only to say that the Crown's evidence stands unchallenged. This does not violate the accused's right to silence or presumption of innocence.[231]

Witnesses are on a different footing from the accused. However, in *R. v. Jolivet*[232] the Supreme Court held that it will be a rare case when the trial judge

---

231 For annotations on *Noble*, see Delisle and Stuart (1997), 6 C.R. (5th) 5 and 8.
232 [2000] 1 S.C.R. 751.

can instruct the jury to draw an adverse inference from the failure of the Crown to call a witness and even more rare with respect to the defence.[233]

(viii) *Comments on Accused's Failure to Testify*

If triers of fact are not entitled to draw inferences tending to guilt should we talk about it openly? The judge in his reasons or the judge in his direction to the jury?

In *Griffin v. California*[234] the accused was convicted of murder. Both the judge and the prosecutor had commented to the jury on the accused's failure to testify. This was in accordance with the State's constitution. The United States Supreme Court, however, decided that this was violative of the Fifth Amendment to the U.S. Constitution as applicable to the states through the Fourteenth Amendment. The dissent argued:

> It is not at all apparent to me, on any realistic view of the trial process, that a defendant will be at more of a disadvantage under the California practice than he would be in a court which permitted no comment at all on his failure to take the witness stand. How can it be said that the inferences drawn by a jury will be more detrimental to a defendant under the limiting and carefully controlling language of the instruction here involved than would result if the jury were left to roam at large with only its untutored instincts to guide it, to draw from the defendant's silence broad inferences of guilt.[235]

The majority saw quite a difference:

> [Comment] is a penalty imposed by courts for exercising a constitutional privilege. It is said however that the inference of guilt from failure to testify as to facts peculiarly within the accused's knowledge is in any event natural and irresistible, and that comment on the failure does not magnify that inference into a penalty. What the jury may infer, given no help from the court, is one thing. What it may infer when the court solemnizes the silence of the accused into evidence is quite another.

The *Canada Evidence Act*[236] provides: "The failure of the person charged, or of the wife or husband of that person, to testify shall not be made the subject of comment by the judge or by counsel for the prosecution."

The first thing to notice about the Canadian provision is that our courts have decided that the comment is only prohibited in cases of trial by jury and when the comment is made in the presence of the jury. In *R. v. Binder*[237] Roach, J. wrote:

> I had always understood that the comment there prohibited was one made by either the Judge or Crown counsel to or in the presence of the jury. I still think so. Counsel for the appellant was unable to refer to any case in which it was held otherwise.

---

233 For a discussion of drawing adverse inferences from the failure of a party to call a witness in civil cases, see *Buksh v. Miles*, [2008] B.C.J. No. 1500 (C.A.).

234 380 U.S. 609 (1964).

235 *Ibid.*, at p. 621.

236 R.S.C. 1985, c. C-5, s. 4(6).

237 (1948), 92 C.C.C. 20 (Ont. C.A.); followed in *Pratte v. Maher*, [1965] 1 C.C.C. 77 (Que. C.A.), *R. v. Bouchard*, [1970] 5 C.C.C. 95 (N.B.C.A.), *Tilco Plastics Ltd. v. Skurjat*, [1967] 1 C.C.C. 131 (Ont. H.C.); affirmed [1967] 2 C.C.C. 196n (Ont. C.A.).

. . . .

> It is impossible to think of any other reason for prohibiting such a comment than its improper effect upon a jury.[238]

Perhaps such reasoning was born of a belief that in trials by judge alone the accused's failure to testify could not be magnified out of its proper proportion, since a trial judge is able to place it in its proper perspective.

The next thing to notice is that comment by an accused on his co-accused's failure to take the stand is not foreclosed by the section.[239] In *R. v. Crawford*[240] the accused and another were charged with second degree murder. The accused Crawford made no statement to the police. He testified at trial and blamed the other. He was cross-examined by the other's counsel on his failure to make any statements to the police. The other accused Creighton did not testify at trial. His version of the events was set out in a videotaped statement to the police on his arrest. The Crawford's lawyer said to the jury "an innocent man sitting in Creighton's seat would have gotten into that witness box and sworn that he was not guilty". Only Crawford appealed to the Supreme Court. The Supreme Court was then principally concerned with the extent to which one accused could use his co-accused's silence during the investigation to challenge the credibility of the co-accused's testimony in court. The language of the court, however, appears to accept that comment by one accused on the other's failure to testify was permissible. The court noted in passing that in *R. v. Naglik*[241] the Ontario Court of Appeal had held that neither section 11(*c*) of the Charter nor section 4(6) of the *Canada Evidence Act* prevented a co-accused's counsel from commenting on an accused's failure to testify. The Court of Appeal in *R. v. Crawford* concluded that: "[I]t was open to counsel for Crawford to comment upon the failure of Creighton to testify on his own behalf."[242]

The next thing to notice about section 4(6) is that there are comments and then there are comments. In *Avon v. R.*[243] the trial judge had said to the jury:

> The accused did not testify. Evidently, he could have done so. He is not obliged to do so. I must tell you immediately, . . . it is not because the accused did not testify that you should believe that he could be guilty. . . . Actually, you have merely the Crown's evidence. The defence did not call witnesses, and the accused did not testify: he did not have to. It is up to the Crown to prove its case.[244]

For the majority Fauteux C.J.C. wrote:

> I would say that the language used by [the trial judge] is a "statement" of an accused's right not to testify, rather than a "comment" on his failure to do so. In my opinion, the instructions complained of cannot be construed as prejudicial to the accused or such to suggest to the jurors that his silence was used to cloak his guilt.[245]

---

238 *Ibid.*, at pp. 24-25.
239 This appears also to be the approach in England. See *R. v. Wickham* (1971), 55 Crim. App. R. 199 (C.A.); but contrary to the approach in the United States: see *DeLuna v. U.S.*, 308 F.2d 140 (1962).
240 [1995] 1 S.C.R. 858.
241 (1991), 65 C.C.C. (3d) 272.
242 *R. v. Creighton* (1993), 20 C.R. (4th) 331, 348.
243 (1971), 21 D.L.R. (3d) 442 (S.C.C.).
244 *Ibid.*, at p. 445.
245 *Ibid.*, at p. 446.

In *R. v. McConnell* the accused were charged with possession of house-breaking instruments. They had offered an explanation to the police at the time but they did not testify. The trial judge told the jury:

> You are not to be influenced in your decision by either of the accused not going into the witness box and testifying, but the Court does point out that these explanations when made were not made under oath and it is not only for that reason alone, but for any other number of reasons that may occur to you, to decide if you will accept these explanations.[246]

The accused's appeals were dismissed and Justice Ritchie noted:

> [T]he language used by the trial Judge was taken not so much a "comment" on the failure of the persons charged to testify as a statement of their right to refrain from doing so, and it . . . should not be taken to have been the intention of Parliament in enacting s. 4(5) of the *Canada Evidence Act* to preclude Judges from explaining to juries the law with respect to the rights of accused persons in this regard.[247]

R. v. MILLER
(1998), 131 C.C.C. (3d) 141, 1998 CarswellOnt 4983,
21 C.R. (5th) 178 (C.A.)

The accused was charged with robbery. Identification was the main issue at trial. The Crown's case rested essentially upon the testimony of an eyewitness who was with the complainant at the time of the robbery and claimed to recognize the accused, someone she knew reasonably well, as one of the assailants. The accused did not testify, but advanced a defence of alibi through his parents. His conviction was reversed on appeal.

CHARRON J.A.:—

. . . .

Section 4(6) of the Canada Evidence Act provides as follows:

4(6). The failure of the person charged, or of the wife or husband of that person, to testify shall not be made the subject of comment by the judge or by counsel for the prosecution.

Notwithstanding this provision, the trial judge instructed the jury that they were entitled to draw an adverse inference from the failure of the appellant to testify in support of his alibi defence in these terms:

> An alibi is testimony which supports the accused's evidence that he did not commit the offence on trial because he or she was somewhere else at the time. Where the supporting evidence is led but the accused does not testify or submit himself to cross-examine on that evidence, the jury is entitled to draw the inference that the alibi is untrue. This is an exception to the general rule that every accused person is entitled to sit silent and require the prosecution to prove its case against if it can. A plea of not guilty is not the same as sworn testimony from the accused as to his whereabouts

---

246 [1968] 4 C.C.C. 257, 260 (S.C.C.).
247 *Ibid.*, at p. 263.

at the time of the crime. On this issue there is no testimony from the accused as to where he was at the time of the robbery in this case.

It is open to the jury, if you so decide, to draw an inference that because the accused did not testify, the testimony of the supporting witnesses, [the parents of the appellant], is not credible or, alternatively, not reliable. Nevertheless, you need not necessarily draw that inference. You are equally able to accept the evidence and thus accept the alibi.

Despite s. 4(6), the trial judge was of the view that, based on case law, he was entitled to charge the jury on the inference that could be drawn from the appellant's failure to testify. In *R. v. Noble* (1997), 114 C.C.C. (3d) 385 (S.C.C.), the Supreme Court considered the evidentiary significance of the failure of the accused to testify. Sopinka J., writing for the majority, held that a trier of fact, whether judge or jury, cannot draw an adverse inference from the silence of the accused. The accused's silence cannot be used as a piece of inculpatory evidence contributing to a finding of guilt beyond a reasonable doubt. The impermissibility of using silence as inculpatory evidence was held to be a principle flowing from the right to silence and the presumption of innocence. Sopinka J. did, however, recognize a limited exception to this principle in the case of alibi. He noted that it has been recognized in other cases that alibi defences create exceptions to the right to silence. The trial judge in this case, appears to have interpreted the carved out exception to the general rule, the alibi exception, as creating an exception to the rule of prohibited comment under s. 4(6). This is not so.

Section 4(6) of the Canada Evidence Act prohibits a judge from commenting to the jury on the failure of an accused to testify. From a reading of Noble in its entirety, it is clear that this is entirely separate and distinct from the question of when a trier of fact may draw an adverse inference from the failure of an accused to testify. One is a blanket prohibition against comments and the other is a general rule, with exceptions, as to what inferences can be drawn. In Noble, Sopinka J. made express reference to s. 4(6). He noted that s. 4(6) prohibits the trial judge from giving the jury instructions on inferences that cannot be drawn from the silence of the accused.

. . . .

He stated as follows (at 424-25):

. . . Section 4(6), whose validity is not at issue in the present case, prevents a trial judge from commenting on the silence of the accused. The trial judge is therefore prevented from instructing the jury on the impermissibility of using silence to take the case against the accused to one that proves guilt beyond a reasonable doubt. . . .

. . . .

Because of s. 4(6) and the absence of reasons, there is no practical way of preventing the jury from drawing an improper inference from silence. The fact that the jury is permitted to do so does not elevate the use of silence to a principle of law which should be extended to all triers of fact.

While Sopinka J. makes no further reference to s. 4(6), the same reasoning clearly applies to the alibi exception to the general rule. One has to conclude that, by reason of s. 4(6), "the trial judge is therefore prevented from instructing the jury on the [permissibility] of using silence to take the case against the accused to one that proves guilt beyond a reasonable doubt" in cases of alibi. The constitutional validity of s. 4(6) was not at issue in *Noble*. The principles set out by the court cannot serve to repeal s. 4(6).

———————————

On the authority of *Noble*, Canada has a constitutional standard that no adverse inference can be drawn from the accused's silence but a statutory rule in section 4(6) bars a trial judge from advising the jury not to do so. This appears to be so even if they were to ask "Is it true that the Supreme Court decided that a jury cannot draw an inference of guilt from the accused's silence?" For consistency, section 4(6) should be declared unconstitutional.

PROBLEMS

Problem 1

The accused is charged with break and enter of a computer store. The perpetrators entered the store by smashing the glass door. A vehicle resembling the one used by the perpetrators was stopped by the police approximately one hour after the robbery. The accused was in the car. Glass fragments were found on his shoes and in the vehicle. An expert testified that the fragments exhibited the same physical characteristics as the glass from the store. The accused did not testify. In his reasons for conviction, the trial judge stated:

> It is true that a man is not called upon to explain suspicious things, but there comes a time when, circumstantial evidence having enveloped a man in a strong and cogent network of inculpatory facts, that a man is bound to make some explanation or stand condemned. In the circumstances of this case, I am satisfied that the totality of the circumstantial evidence is such that I am satisfied beyond a reasonable doubt that the accused is guilty.

You are the Crown on appeal. What argument will you make to convince the Court of Appeal that the trial judge's reasons are not inconsistent with *Noble*? See *R. v. Baynham* (2003), 173 C.C.C. (3d) 68 (B.C. C.A.).

Problem 2

The accused is charged with selling drugs to an undercover officer. The accused does not testify. During deliberations, the jury asked the following question:

> Q. Can we draw any inference from the failure of the defendant to testify?

The trial judge responds as follows:

> And my answer will be quick. Section 4(6) of the Canada Evidence Act reads as follows:
>
>> The failure of the person charged . . . to testify shall not be made the subject of comment by the judge or by counsel for the prosecution.
>
> I think that is the section that binds me; and that is all I have to say, thank you.

Are there grounds for an appeal? How would you frame the issue? See *R. v. Trevor* (2006), 206 C.C.C. (3d) 381, 2006 CarswellBC 470 (C.A.).

Problem 3

The accused was charged with sexual assault. He did not testify. In his closing address to the jury, Crown counsel stated at the outset that the jury ought not to be "mesmerized" by the concept of reasonable doubt and that "reasonable doubt" did not mean "a speculative doubt conjured up by a timid juror to escape his or her duty." Then, after twice observing that the complainant's evidence stood uncontradicted, Crown counsel stated in reference to the accused's belief in consent: "But he didn't testify, so he can't be asked directly what he thought at the time or what he construed or what he knew." On appeal, the defence argued that the Crown counsel's closing address to the jury violated the prohibition in s. 4(6) of the *Canada Evidence Act* against commenting on the failure of the accused to testify. Rule. Compare *R. v. Biladeau* (2008), 63 C.R. (6th) 187 (Ont. C.A.)

(ix) *Reform*

Reform proposals in this area in Canada and elsewhere have been highly controversial.

In 1972, the Criminal Law Revision Committee in England recommended major changes. The Committee noted:

> The present law and practice are much too favourable to the defence. We are convinced that, when a prima facie case has been made out against the accused, it should be regarded as incumbent on him to give evidence in all ordinary cases. We have no doubt that the prosecution should be entitled, like the judge, to comment on his failure to do so. The present prohibition of comment seems to us wrong in principle and entirely illogical. It may be of little significance if there is no case against him or only a weak one. But the stronger the case is, the more significant will be his failure to give evidence. . . . As to what may be properly included in a comment, we have no doubt that . . . adverse inferences, such as common sense dictates, should be allowed to be drawn from the from the accused's failure to give evidence.[248]

The Committee felt so strongly that it recommended a procedure whereby the accused would be formally called on to give evidence so that his refusal would demonstrate to the jury that the accused had the right to give evidence but declined to do so.[249]

Professor Cross, who was a member of the Committee, afterwards defended the Committee's restrictions on the right to silence allowing for such inferences to be drawn as were seen to be proper. He agreed with the critics that the Committee had no empirical data to support the thought that the common law permitted too many wrongful acquittals and that he could not say that the

---

248 Criminal Law Revision Committee, *Eleventh Report on Evidence (General)*, Cmnd. 4991, s. 110.

249 In 1976 the Republic of Singapore adopted the recommendations of the Committee. See generally Yeo, "Diminishing the Right to Silence: The Singapore Experience" [1983] Crim. L. Rev. 89. Courts in Singapore inform the accused, after the prosecution has rested its case, that if they should "without good cause, refuse to answer any question, the court in determining whether you are guilty of the offence charged may draw such inferences as appear proper"; see *Haw Tua Tau v. Public Prosecutor*, [1981] 3 All E.R. 14, 18-19 (P.C.). It needs to be noted that jury trials were abolished in Singapore in 1969.

proposed change would lessen the total. But he argued it would at least rid the law of gibberish. The proposed changes would

> spare the judge from talking gibberish to the jury, the conscientious magistrate from directing himself in imbecilic terms and the writer of the law of evidence from drawing distinctions absurd enough to bring a blush to the most hardened academic.[250]

In 1975 the Law Reform Commission of Canada recommended an abolition of section 4(6). In their proposed Code of Evidence, which was never adopted, they provided:

> The accused in a criminal proceeding cannot be compelled to be a witness, but the judge, prosecutor and defence counsel may comment on his failure to testify and the trier of fact may draw all reasonable inferences therefrom.[251]

Nevertheless the Committee's and the Commission's proposals were resisted in England and in Canada. In 1981 the Royal Commission on Criminal Procedure rejected the suggestion for change. Although the Commission noted that objections to adverse inferences regarding silence at trial were not as objectionable as adverse inferences from silence at the investigative stage, still, in their view:

> Any modification to the present law of evidence which aimed at requiring the accused to answer a prima facie case established by the prosecution would be likely to weaken the initial burden of proof that the accusatorial system of trial places upon the prosecution.

In 1982 the Task Force Report on Evidence[252] in Canada recommended that the section prohibiting comment be retained and the jury be advised in neutral terms that the accused has the right to testify but that there is no obligation to do so.

In 1988 the English Parliament imposed restrictions on the right to silence in Northern Ireland.[253] The government maintained it was necessary in order to convict terrorists but the change affected persons charged with any offence. The Order adopted the recommendations of the Revision Committee and judges were required to warn accused that adverse inferences might be drawn if they chose not to testify; this warning is to be done in the presence of the jury.[254]

---

250 Cross, "The Evidence Report: Sense or Nonsense" [1973] Crim. L. Rev. 329 at 332-36.

251 The Code also proposed, s. 64(2), that no evidence of the accused's previous convictions could be introduced in attacking the accused's credibility unless the accused had first introduced evidence solely to support his credibility. The Task Force on Evidence, the "successor" to the Commission in recommending changes to the law of evidence, were unanimous in recommending the retention of the existing s. 4(6) forbidding comment by the judge or prosecutor.

252 Report of the Federal/Provincial Task Force on Uniform Rules of Evidence prepared for the Uniform Law Conference, 1982.

253 The Criminal Evidence (N.I.) Order cited in Jackson, "Curtailing the Right to Silence" [1991] Crim. L. Rev. 404.

254 Recognizing the certain change in the common law as a result of the Order, see *Murray v. D.P.P.* (1992), 97 Cr. App. R. 151 (H.L.). Professor Dennis notes the possibility of a challenge to the legislation as violative of the European Convention's guarantee to a fair trial which involves the privilege against self-incrimination; see Dennis, "The Criminal Justice and Public Order Act 1994" [1995] Crim. L. Rev. 4.

In 1993 the Royal Commission on Criminal Justice concluded that eliminating the right to silence would reduce the prosecution's burden of proof being convicted:

> Given the principle that the burden of proof should rest on the prosecution, it must be wrong for defendants who leave the prosecution to prove its case to be exposed to comment by either the prosecution or the judge to the effect that their failure to enter the witness box corroborates the prosecution case.[255]

The Commission believed that the directions then being given by judges were sufficient:

> The defendant does not have to give evidence. He is entitled to sit in the dock and require the prosecution to prove its case. You must not assume that he is guilty because he has not given evidence. The fact that he has not given evidence proves nothing, one way or the other. It does nothing to establish his guilt. On the other hand, it means that there is no evidence to undermine, contradict, or explain the evidence put before you by the prosecution. [However, you still have to decide whether, on the prosecution's evidence, you are sure of the defendant's guilt.][256]

Some months later, despite the Royal Commission's recommendation to the contrary, the Home Secretary announced his government's plan to seriously limit the right to silence.

The Criminal Justice and Public Order Act, 1994[257] allows U.K. judges and juries to consider a defendant's failure to testify as evidence of his guilt. The Act extended to England and Wales the reforms accomplished in Northern Ireland in 1988. By section 35, if the accused chooses not to give evidence or, having been sworn, refuses to answer questions, the judge or jury is entitled to draw such inferences as appear to them to be proper. The Act does not require that the judge formally call on the accused to give evidence.

As to what inferences are *proper*, Lord Mustill commented, with respect to the similar Northern Ireland legislation:

> Everything depends on the nature of the issue, the weight of the evidence adduced by the prosecution upon it . . . and the extent to which the defendant should in the nature of things be able to give his own account of the particular matter in question. It is impossible to generalise, for dependent upon circumstances the failure of the defendant to give evidence may found no inference at all, or one which is for all practical purposes fatal.[258]

This dictum emphasizes that it will be for the trial judge in each case to decide whether an inference is permissible.

(h) Compellability of Corporate Officers

R. v. AMWAY CORP.
[1989] 1 S.C.R. 21

---

255 Cmnd. 2263, s. 28.

256 *Ibid.*

257 The Criminal Justice and Public Order Act (Commencement No. 6) Order 1995 provided for the coming into force of the sections relating to inferences from the accused's silence on April 10, 1995.

258 *Murray v. D.P.P.*, *supra*, note 254, at p. 155.

In forfeiture proceedings brought by the government pursuant to the Customs Act, the government applied for an order under Rule 465(1) of the Federal Court Rules that Amway produce one of its officers for examination for discovery. The Federal Court of Appeal reversed the Trial Division's decision to grant the application. Amway argued that Rule 465 infringed section 11(*c*) of the Charter by requiring a corporate defendant to be examined for discovery.

SOPINKA J. (DICKSON C.J.C., MCINTYRE, LAMER, WILSON, LA FOREST, and L'HEUREUX-DUBÉ JJ. concurring): —

. . . .

Section 11(c) provides:

11. Any person charged with an offence has the right

. . .

(c)   not to be compelled to be a witness in proceedings against that person in respect of the offence;

In order to obtain the benefit of this section of the *Charter* the respondent must establish that it is:

(a) a person;
(b) charged with an offence; and
(c) a witness in proceedings against that person.

With respect to (a) it is neither necessary nor desirable in this case to decide that under no circumstances may a corporation avail itself of the provisions of s. 11. I am also prepared to assume without deciding that the proceedings in question are such that the requirement in (b) is satisfied. In my opinion, however, a corporation cannot be a witness and therefore cannot come within s. 11(*c*).

Pre-*Charter* cases . . . held that an officer of a corporation who testifies in criminal proceedings against the corporation, is the witness. This principle applied equally to an officer who is the directing mind of the corporation. . . .

. . . .

. . . It would be startling to suggest that the officer, if asked a question the answer to which tended to incriminate him, could not avail himself of s. 13 of the *Charter* and s. 5(2) of the *Canada Evidence Act*. If such protection is available, it must be because the officer is a witness. It is hard to rationalize that the officer is a witness and the corporation is a witness. There is only one witness under examination and that is the entity that swore the oath and that would be subject to a penalty for perjury. That is not to say that a witness must be one capable of taking an oath, but where the evidence is sworn evidence, it is my view that the *Charter* intended to protect the person who swore the oath.

. . . .

In my view, it would strain the interpretation of s. 11(*c*) if an artificial entity were held to be a witness. Such a metamorphosis could not be justified on the basis that the rules of evidence on an examination for discovery do not restrict the person testifying to personal knowledge. That person may answer questions based on belief as well as on information obtained from the corporation. There are many proceedings where witnesses are permitted similar latitude. I need only mention public inquiries and proceedings before administrative tribunals to illustrate the point. Traditionally, witnesses in these proceedings have been accorded the protection of s. 5 of the *Canada Evidence Act* (see, for example, *Di Iorio v. Warden of the Montreal Jail*, [1978] 1 S.C.R. 152). The mere fact that rules of evidence permit greater latitude in the source of the information which the witness imparts to the tribunal does not have the effect of transforming the source into a witness.

Applying a purposive interpretation to s. 11(*c*), I am of the opinion that it was intended to protect the individual against the affront to dignity and privacy inherent in a practice which enables the prosecution to force the person charged to supply the evidence out of his or her own mouth. Although disagreement exists as to the basis of the principle against self-incrimination, in my view, this factor plays a dominant role.

. . . .

Accordingly, I am in respectful disagreement with the Federal Court of Appeal that the respondent can obtain the benefit of s. 11(*c*). . . .

2. MANNER OF QUESTIONING

The chief source of information for the trier of fact is oral testimony elicited from witnesses called by the parties. The fact that the witnesses are chosen by the parties and may be prepared in advance by them has led to different rules regarding their manner of questioning dependent on who is putting the questions. The witness's description of the incident is first elicited by the party calling him in a process labelled examination-in-chief or direct examination. On the conclusion of direct examination, the adversary engages in cross-examination; the adversary is able to elicit further data concerning the incident from the witness and is also able to question the witness concerning his powers of perception and memory, to demand explicitness in his communication and to explore his sincerity, all in an attempt to challenge the accuracy of his first description. Following cross-examination the witness may be re-examined by the party who called him and permitted to explain or amplify answers given on cross-examination. Further opportunities to cross-examine and re-examine, all at the discretion of the trial judge, are possible.

(a) Leading Questions

A party calling a witness should not ask leading questions. One of the first instances of this rule's articulation provides a good illustrative characterization of the phrase "leading question," and at the same time demonstrates both the rule's justification as well as the frequent irretrievability of the harm done. In the *Trial of Thomas Rosewell*[259] the accused was indicted for High Treason.

---

259 (1684), 10 Howell's State Trials 147 (K.B.).

Witnesses against him had testified that in his preaching he had spoken against Charles I and Charles II as "two wicked Kings." The accused maintained that mention in his sermon of "two wicked Kings" was not concerning Charles I or his present majesty but rather was in reference to Kings referred to in the Book of Chronicles in the Old Testament, i.e., Ahab and his son Ahaziah, whose example he was using to expound on the 20th chapter of Genesis. To make his point the accused called a witness, Hudson, and the transcript reads:

L.C.J. Jeffries:	Come, here is your witness, what say you to him? . . .
Rosewell:	Pray Sir, as to the truth of the business; Did you hear me speak of two wicked Kings? That, my lord, came in, I say upon the second verse of the 20th of Genesis, which I then was expounding.
L.C.J.:	Nay ask him in general what he heard you say; and whether he heard you say anything of two wicked kings, and what it was.
Rosewell:	Ay, about Ahab, and Ahaziah his son —
L.C.J.:	Nay, nay, I must have none of those things, we must have fair questions put; for, as you see we will not admit the king's counsel to put any questions to the witnesses, nor produce any witnesses against you, that are leading, or not proper, so nor must you. But if you have a mind to ask him any questions, what he heard concerning two wicked kings generally, do so.
Hudson:	Upon the second verse he was then.
L.C.J.:	Of what chapter?
Hudson:	Of the 20th of Genesis.[260]

To describe the common law position it would be difficult to improve on the test of Mr. Justice Beck in *Maves v. Grand Trunk Pacific Railway Co.*[261]

> I find the general subject of leading questions dealt with in a most satisfactory way in Best on Evidence, 11th ed., 624 *et seq.* I quote, italicising what I wish to emphasize: —
>
> The chief rule of practice relative to the interrogation of witnesses is that which prohibits "*leading questions,*" *i.e.*, questions which directly or indirectly suggest to the witness the answer he is to give. The rule is, that *on material points* a party must not lead his own witnesses, but may lead those of his adversary; in other words, that leading questions are allowed in cross-examination, but not in examination-in-chief. This seems based on two reasons: first, and principally, on the supposition that the witness has a bias in favour of the party bringing him forward, and hostile to his opponent; secondly, that the party calling a witness has an advantage over his adversary, in knowing beforehand what the witness will prove, or, at least, is expected to prove; and that, consequently, if he were allowed to lead, he might interrogate in such a manner as to extract only so much of the knowledge of the witness as would be favourable to his side, or even put a false gloss upon the whole.
>
> I think a third reason may be added, namely, that a witness, though intending to be entirely fair and honest may, owing, for example, to lack of

---

260 *Ibid.*, at p. 190.
261 (1913), 14 D.L.R. 70, 73-77 (Alta. C.A.). And see Denroche, "Leading Questions" (1963-64), 6 Crim. L.Q. 21.

education, of exactness of knowledge of the precise meaning of words or of appreciation at the moment of their precise meaning, or of alertness to see that what is implied in the question requires modification, honestly assent to a leading question which fails to express his real meaning, which he would probably have completely expressed if allowed to do so in his own words.

. . . .

So that the *general* rule is that in examining one's own witness, not that no leading questions must be asked, but that *on material points* one must *not* lead his own witness but that on points that are *merely introductory and form no part of the substance* of the inquiry one *should* lead.

. . . .

A case which not infrequently arises in practice is that of a witness who recounts a conversation and in doing so omits one or more statements which counsel examining him is instructed formed part of it. The common and proper practice is to ask the witness to repeat the conversation from the beginning. It is often found that in his repetition he gives the lacking statement — possibly omitting one given the first time. This method may be tried more than once, and as a matter of expediency — so as to have the advantage of getting the whole story on the witness' own unaided recollection — counsel might pass on to some other subject and later revert to the conversation, asking him to again state it. But when this method fails, the trial Judge undoubtedly ought to permit a question containing a reference to the subject-matter of the statement which it is supposed has been omitted by the witness. If this method fails, then and not till then — that is when his memory appears to be entirely exhausted, the trial Judge should allow a question to be put to him containing the supposedly omitted matter. It will be, of course, for the jury, or the Judge if there be no jury, to draw a conclusion as to the truthfulness of the witness; although the permitting of a question in a certain form is largely — though I think not wholly — in the discretion of the trial Judge. I should think that, with regard to the class of leading question I have been considering, they should, in every case, be permitted after all the steps which appear to shew the witness' memory to have been exhausted have been taken. If not permitted, great injustice may result. If permitted, the jury or Judge acting as a jury, may, of course, as I have said, disbelieve the answer elicited.

The third reason suggested by Justice Beck for prohibiting leading questions in chief highlights a different kind of leading question from that which directly suggests an answer: a question may be so phrased as to assume within it the truth of some fact which remains controverted between the parties and a witness, not attuned to that fact, may inadvertently agree to its existence. An example would be "when did the accused stop spanking their child?" Another example, "what was the deceased doing when the accused shot her?", in a prosecution where the issue is the identity of the assailant, is equally objectionable as leading, or "misleading," as the witness may unwittingly testify to a fact concerning which he has no knowledge or which he has no wish to concede.

The common law, then, prohibits leading questions but provides exceptions to the general rule. A list of exceptions would include:

a)   for introductory, formal or undisputed matters;
b)   for the purpose of identifying persons or things;
c)   to allow one witness to contradict another regarding statements made by that other;
d)   where the witness is either hostile to the questioner or unwilling to give evidence;

e) where it is seen, in the trial judge's discretion, to be necessary to refresh the witness's memory;

f) where the witness is having difficulty communicating on account of age, education, language or mental capacity;

g) where the matter is of a complicated nature and, in the opinion of the trial judge, the witness deserves some assistance to determine what subject the questioner is asking about.

In exercising his discretion to allow leading questions the trial judge should, however, keep in mind the reasons for the rule canvassed above, and rule not according to a grocery list of exceptions but in accord with the underlying philosophy. The evidence we seek is that of the witness and not that of the questioner. Stating the rule in this open way is preferable, as one could never close the list of exceptions and the matter must be left to the trial judge's discretion. In determining whether a question suggests an answer, much will depend on the character, mood and bias of the witness, and the manner and inflection of the questioner, all matters to be determined in the particular case.[262]

Justice Beck, though admitting that the authorities were not quite clear on the point, suggested that, given the underlying rationale of the rule, the trial judge has a discretion to restrain the cross-examining party from using leading questions when the witness appears to favour him. If the judge does not restrain such leading questions the form of the question may nevertheless detract from the weight of the answer; comment thereon to the jury might be made, and perhaps counsel might be warned of this effect.

R. v. ROSE
(2001), 42 C.R. (5th) 183, 153 C.C.C. (3d) 225 (Ont. C.A.)

The accused was charged with trafficking in cocaine and possession for the purpose of trafficking. The charges arose as a result of police surveillance observations of an alleged drug transaction between the accused and B. B was observed entering a motor vehicle driven by the accused. The motor vehicle was on the fringes of an area known to the police for its high level of crack cocaine selling activity. Shortly after B entered the motor vehicle, the police stopped it. The accused was arrested. After the arrest, money and crack cocaine were found inside the vehicle. B was initially charged jointly with the accused. However, on the first date set for trial, B agreed to give a statement to the police and testify against the accused. It was the Crown's theory that the accused, at the time of his arrest, had just finished selling drugs to B. B testified in accordance with this theory. The accused testified that B was the trafficker and that he was merely an accommodation buyer picking up some drugs for a friend. The trial judge rejected the accused's evidence, found that the accused was the owner of the drugs located in the motor vehicle and that he was the one selling drugs to B on the occasion in question. The accused was convicted. Most of the grounds of appeal related to Crown counsel's conduct of the trial.

---

262 See *Reference re R. v. Coffin*, [1956] S.C.R. 191, 211 per Kellock, J.: ". . . while, as a general rule, a party may not either in direct or re-examination put leading questions, the court has a discretion, not open to review, to relax it whenever it is considered necessary in the interests of justice."

CHARRON J.A. (FELDMAN and MACPHERSON JJ.A. concurring): —

Proof of the Crown's Case Through the Use of Leading Questions

A leading question is one that suggests the answer. It is trite law that the party who calls a witness is generally not permitted to ask the witness leading questions. The reason for the rule arises from a concern that the witness, who in many instances favours the party who calls him or her, will readily agree to the suggestions put in the form of a question rather than give his or her own answers to the questions. Of course, the degree of concern that may arise from the use of leading questions will depend on the particular circumstances, and the rule is applied with some flexibility. For example, leading questions are routinely asked to elicit a witness' evidence on preliminary and non-contentious matters. This practice is adopted for the sake of expediency and generally gives rise to no concern. Leading questions are also permitted to the extent that they are necessary to direct the witness to a particular matter or field of inquiry. Apart from these specific examples, the trial judge has a general discretion to allow leading questions whenever it is considered necessary in the interests of justice.

The transcript in this case presents numerous transgressions of this rule by Crown counsel. The appellant relies mainly on the examination-in-chief of the Crown's main witness, Noel Beaudry. Several excerpts are reproduced below. The questions that are most offensive are highlighted.

> Q.   All right, and do you recall when — when and how you first met Mr. Rose?
>
> A.   No.
>
> Q.   And what's your connection with Mr. Rose?
>
> A.   What do you mean, connection?
>
> Q.   Well, what do you do with Mr. Rose?
>
> A.   I talk to him.
>
> Q.   What else do you do with him?
>
> A.   That's about it.
>
> Q.   Does he supply you with crack cocaine?
>
> A.   Sometimes.
>
> Q.   Now, my information is that the police had set up surveillance on yourself and on the 19th of August you got into a motor vehicle with Mr. Rose. The 21st of August you got into a motor vehicle with Mr. Rose.

At this point, defence counsel objected to the leading questions. Crown counsel maintained that his questions were not leading. His submission to the trial judge, in answer to defence counsel's objection, somewhat exemplifies the general approach Crown counsel adopted in questioning not only Beaudry, but all of the Crown witnesses:

> [Crown]: Well, this is information I have and I'm asking this witness to either confirm or deny it. If he confirms it, it will become a fact. If he denies it, it won't become a fact. I don't think it's leading at all. It's information I have and I'm asking him to confirm it or deny it. It's not suggesting the answer.

The judge ruled that the question was still incomplete and not objectionable at that point in time. He invited defence counsel to renew his objection if he so wished after hearing the whole question. Crown counsel continued to question the witness much in the same fashion and defence counsel did not renew his objection. Counsel for the appellant relies more particularly on the following excerpts from the examination-in-chief in support of his contention that Crown counsel proved his case through the use of leading questions:

> Q.   Mr. Beaudry, I started advising you that my information is that the police were conducting surveillance and on the following dates they saw you get into a motor vehicle which Mr. Rose was driving and those dates were August 19, August 21, September 4, and September 5. Did you, in fact, meet Mr. Rose on those dates?
>
> A.   If it's right there, I guess so. I don't mark it in a book, you know, it's just —
>
> Q.   You didn't mark it. How many times have you purchased crack cocaine from Mr. Rose? You don't have to give me an exact number, give your best estimate or you can give me a range.
>
> A.   Three, four times.
>
> Q.   Three or four times, and do you recall when those three or four times would have been?
>
> A.   No.
>
> Q.   Now, on the 6th of September — or the 5th of September, you were in an automobile with Mr. Rose and the police stopped that automobile?
>
> A.   Yeah.
>
> Q.   You remember that?
>
> A.   Yeah. I don't remember the date, but I remember when they stopped us.
>
> Q.   And there were police cars in front and back of Mr. Rose's car?
>
> A.   Something like that.
>
> Q.   And do you recall what kind of automobile Mr. Rose was driving or drives?
>
> A.   A black car.
>
> Q.   You don't know the make?
>
> A.   No.
>
> Q.   The license number? Has it been — all the times that you've purchased crack cocaine from Mr. Rose, has he been in the same motor vehicle?
>
> A.   Yeah.
>
> Q.   And that's the black car you just indicated?
>
> A.   Black car, yeah.
>
> Q.   Now, when the — on the 5th of September when the police officers stopped the motor vehicle, you were in Mr. Rose's automobile, were you not?
>
> A.   Yeah.
>
> Q.   Mr. Rose was in the automobile?

A.   Yeah.

Q.   Correct, and who was driving the automobile?

A.   Mr. Rose.

Q.   Mr. Rose, and you were in which seat, the front passenger seat?

A.   Yeah. The front seat.

Q.   Was there anyone else in the car?

A.   No.

Q.   All right, and what was your purpose for being in that automobile on that date and time, why were you there?

A.   To tell you the truth, I don't even know because it happened so fast. I didn't have time to say nothing or nothing, you know.

Q.   Well, were you going to purchase crack cocaine from Mr. Rose on that date?

A.   I guess I would have tried.

Q.   Did you have money with you?

A.   Yeah. Of course, it was my rent money, but . . .

Q.   Well, I — is it fair to say that every time you had gotten into Mr. Rose's automobile in the past you purchased crack cocaine from him?

A.   Maybe two out of three.

Q.   Two out of three. Did you have any crack cocaine with you at that time when you got into Mr. Rose's car on the 5th of September?

A.   No.

Q.   You had money with you though?

A.   Yeah.

Q.   Would you agree with me that it's — it seems that you were there to buy crack cocaine from him?

A.   I could have.

Q.   Other than meeting Mr. Rose to buy crack cocaine from him, have you and Mr. Rose ever done anything else together? Do you go to movies together, go to see friends together?

A.   No, we just went for coffee.

Q.   Coffee and when you go for coffee does that end up — is that when you have a conversation about whether —

A.   Sometimes.

Q.   — he has crack cocaine?

A.   Sometimes no. All depends.

Q.   How often would you have gone for coffee with Mr. Rose?

A.   I don't know. Four times, three times.

Q.   Okay, as many times as you've bought crack cocaine from him?

A.   Maybe a little bit less.

Q.   Now, when the police stopped the automobile they found some crack cocaine in the automobile?

A.   That's what they claim.

In my view, Crown counsel's questions to Beaudry were clearly suggestive of the answers. Indeed the entire examination-in-chief reads more like the cross-examination of a witness. This was highly improper particularly in these circumstances where Beaudry, as the trial judge himself stated in his reasons, was "the primary Crown witness" and the questions concerned crucial and contentious matters. The impropriety of Crown counsel's approach is further heightened by the fact that Beaudry's testimony, obtained as it was in return for a stay of the charges against him, was already highly suspect. The manner in which his testimony was elicited could only further undermine its probative value. Consequently, I am of the view that the trial judge erred in ruling against the defence's initial objection and further erred in failing to intervene when Crown counsel continued in this fashion. I do not view defence counsel's failure to renew his objection as an impediment to raising this ground of appeal. In view of the trial judge's failure to appreciate that Crown counsel's questions were indeed leading at the time the objection was made, defence counsel may well have thought that any further objection would be futile.

Virtually all of the incriminating evidence given by Beaudry was elicited through leading questions. Given the circumstances in which he agreed to testify against the appellant, this irregularity raises a real concern that the testimony was proffered, not for its truth, but for the purpose of meeting the expectations of the Crown and the police. The trial judge ultimately accepted some of Beaudry's evidence "as being cogent and vital". Consequently, the finding of guilt may be based, at least in part, on highly questionable evidence.

New trial ordered.

(b) Refreshing Memory/Past Recollection Recorded[263]

R. v. WILKS
(2005), 35 C.R. (6th) 172, 201 C.C.C. (3d) 11 (Man. C.A.)

The accused was involved in a car accident and was receiving income replacement benefits from an insurer. The case manager for the insurer met her and talked to her on the phone on several occasions. He took notes that were summaries rather than verbatim accounts of what was said. The contents of those notes were subsequently entered into a computer and the notes were destroyed. The case manager became suspicious of the accused and subjected

---

263   See generally, Maguire and Quick, "Testimony: Memory and Memoranda" (1957), 3 How. L.J. 1, and Newark and Samuels, "Refreshing Memory," [1978] Crim. L. Rev. 408. See also, *U.S. v. Riccardi*, 174 F. 2d 883 (3d Cir., 1949) per Kalodner, J.

her to video surveillance. The tapes showed her reporting was at variance with her actual physical condition. She was charged with fraud.

At her trial, the trial judge permitted the case manager to refresh his memory from the computer notes. During his testimony he frequently relied on his notes rather than his memory. The trial judge convicted. She appealed.

PHILP and FREEDMAN JJ.A. (KROFT J.A. concurring): —

Because this issue seemed to the court one of potential significance, we requested, and received from counsel, supplementary submissions on the issue. These submissions effectively highlighted the relevant legal principles, which may be briefly explained in the following way.

Witnesses often forget, and so it is permissible to use aids to assist the witness. The use of these aids will fall into one of two categories. They will either i) assist the witness by reviving his or her memory so that the witness, whose memory has been jogged by the aid, now has a present memory of the fact ("present memory revived"), or ii) be a record of the fact, previously made and now attested to as an accurate record ("past recollection recorded"). The distinction has been explained this way in Professor Alan W. Mewett, Q.C. & Peter J. Sankoff, *Witnesses,* vol. 1, looseleaf (Toronto: Carswell, 2004) (at 13-3):

> True cases of "present memory revived" involve a witness who has actually had his or her memory refreshed. "Past recollection recorded" is probably best viewed as an exception to the hearsay rule, whereby evidence of which a witness has no current recall can nonetheless be admitted for the truth of its contents as it was recorded at a time when the witness was able to verify its accuracy.

In the case of present memory revived, the aid is not evidence, but is simply a facilitative mechanism which becomes irrelevant once the witness has had his or her present memory revived by the use of the aid. In the case of past recollection recorded, there is no present memory, so it is the evidence of the past recollection, recorded usually in the form of notes or the like, that is admitted.

i) Present Memory Revived

There are few restrictions on the nature and use of testimonial aids which are used to revive a witness's memory. Mewett and Sankoff state (at 13-3ff):

> Anything may, in fact, jog a person's memory - a smell, a sound, some association, or something the witness is reminded he or she said on a previous occasion. In principle, the use of something said on a previous occasion in order to jog a person's memory is no different from the use of anything else; nevertheless, this proposition has not always been accepted, likely because . . . the courts have confused true cases of present memory revived with past recollection recorded.

In cases where the aid genuinely revives the witness's memory, the nature of the aid, its contemporaneity with the event and other issues relating to it are not relevant to the admissibility of the evidence. If reviewing a note jogs the witness's memory, then it is the memory, now articulated in testimony, which becomes the evidence of the witness.

ii) Past Recollection Recorded

Here matters are entirely different. Out-of-court evidence, such as notes, are admitted because facts once remembered have been forgotten. Whether viewed as an exception to the hearsay rule or as a separate rule of evidence, where such evidence is admitted for its truth, the criteria of necessity and reliability must be satisfied. As Mewett and Sankoff write (at 13-12.1):

> There is certainly a strong argument to be made suggesting that the doctrine was not designed to allow for the wholesale admission of complex statements, but rather to allow persons to supplement their oral evidence with records preserving obscure or intricate details that a person would not ordinarily remember. In these situations, reliability is assured by the contemporaneous nature of the recording as well as by the nature of the information recorded. Where the recollection involves a licence plate number or other "technical" detail, there is less worry about a subjective interpretation of words that cross-examination is designed to explore . . . [Where, however, it is the admissibility of a complex statement which is at issue] it makes sense to examine the hearsay criteria (reliability and necessity) to ensure that the evidence is not overly prejudicial to the accused. The past recollection recorded doctrine should not be utilized to ignore very real hearsay dangers.

One of the most recent, and a very clear, exposition of the principles applicable to this type of evidence was in the decision of the Supreme Court of Canada in *R. v. Fliss*, [2002] 1 S.C.R. 535, 2002 SCC 16. In *Fliss*, the accused freely confessed to an undercover police officer that he had killed a woman. This conversation was recorded and the next day the officer reviewed and corrected the transcript. The trial judge declared the tape and transcript inadmissible for reasons not relevant here, but admitted the officer's viva voce evidence which was basically a recitation of the corrected transcript. At the Supreme Court, the issue related to "the indirect' reading of the excluded transcript into evidence" (at para. 18).

Binnie J. (writing for the majority) said that the jury was entitled to hear from the officer about the conversation because the officer had a present recollection of the "gist" of the important elements of the discussion (which related to graphic details of the murder).

Binnie J. explained why even inadmissible evidence could be used to refresh memory (at para. 45):

> There is also no doubt that the officer was entitled to refresh his memory by any means that would rekindle his recollection, whether or not the stimulus itself constituted admissible evidence. This is because it is his recollection, not the stimulus, that becomes evidence. The stimulus may be hearsay, it may itself be largely inaccurate, it may be nothing more than the sight of someone who had been present or hearing some music that had played in the background. If the recollection here had been stimulated by hearing a tape of his conversation with the accused, even if the tape was made without valid authorization, the officer's recollection - not the tape - would be admissible.

But the problem in the case was that what went into evidence went well beyond the officer's current recollection. For example, "[t]he account of the murder was put into evidence word for word from the excluded . . . transcript" (at para. 55). This, said Binnie J., should not have been permitted (at paras. 60-61):

> . . . The officer was quite entitled to attempt to "refresh" his memory by an out-of-court review of the corrected transcript, but in the witness box his testimony had to be sourced in his "refreshed" memory, not the excluded transcript.

> In short, the problem with the corrected transcript as a stimulus to memory is not that it was itself inadmissible but that it failed to stimulate.

Futhermore, the testimony did not meet the standards applicable to "past recollection recorded" (at para. 63): Secondly, the officer's testimony does not qualify for admission as "past recollection recorded". This doctrine would apply only if the prosecutor could satisfy the four Wigmore criteria, usefully summarized by the Alberta Court of Appeal in *R. v. Meddoui* (1990), 61 C.C.C. (3d) 345, per Kerans J.A., at p. 352:

> The basic rule *in Wigmore on Evidence* (Chadbourn rev. 1970), vol. 3, c. 28, s. 744 et seq. provided:

> 1. The past recollection must have been recorded in some reliable way.

> 2. At the time, it must have been sufficiently fresh and vivid to be probably accurate.

> 3. The witness must be able now to assert that the record accurately represented his knowledge and recollection at the time. The usual phrase requires the witness to affirm that he "knew it to be true at the time".

> 4. The original record itself must be used, if it is procurable.

> And (at para. 64):

> . . . The admission of past recollection recorded but no longer remembered is an exceptional procedure and the conditions precedent to its reception should be clearly satisfied.

iii) *The Importance of the Two Rules*

We refer again to Mewett and Sankoff (at 13-13):

> . . . Failure to distinguish between a witness using something to refresh his or her present memory and a witness using something as a record of a past memory may result in a witness being refused permission to consult notes or other memory-jogging devices or, *conversely, being permitted to testify on the basis that his memory has been refreshed when it is clear that it is not the memory that is being refreshed, but an inadmissible record of past memory that is being introduced.* [Emphasis added]

It will be convenient to refer back (see paras. 9-10) to the ruling of the trial judge regarding the use by Unger of his notes. It is clear that they were to be used to jog Unger's memory, so that his present memory of the events at issue (i.e., his discussions with the accused) could be revived. The trial judge specifically rejected the applicability of the "past recollection recorded" principle. Yet, as is evident from the extracts of the transcript quoted earlier, Unger was, in respect of those matters at least, totally reliant on his notes. He had and demonstrated no present memory, and candidly said so. On these matters, he knew what was in his notes, and no more, only because they were in his notes. That is the classic situation of "past recollection recorded," as discussed in *Fliss*, yet that was not the basis on which Unger was permitted to refer to his notes. The present case illustrates clearly the differences in the two concepts. The failure to distinguish properly between them may result in the introduction of inadmissible evidence, which is an error of law. That is what happened here.

As noted above, before evidence which falls into the "past recollection recorded" category is admitted, the conditions precedent to its admission are to be clearly satisfied. When the notes do not revive memory, as here, the notes or the recitation of them become the evidence. The witness cannot be effectively cross-examined on his or her recollection, because he or she has no recollection of the event. That is why, for the notes or what is in them to become evidence, stringent rules apply.

On the other hand, as Professor David M. Paciocco & Professor Lee Stuesser, *The Law of Evidence*, 3rd ed. (Toronto: Irwin Law, 2002) explain, a witness whose past memory has been revived, say by notes, is subject to proper cross-examination on his testimony: "As original testimony, the information supplied by the witness can be cross-examined on as effectively as any other original testimony" (at p. 336).

The trial judge ruled that the notes were only to be used to refresh memory. However, if the circumstances relating to the notes and Unger's reliance on them did meet the rigorous standards for admissibility under the "past recollection recorded" rule, Unger's evidence as to what was in his notes would still have been admissible. For this to occur, however, each of the four rules outlined by Wigmore (see *Fliss*, above, at para. 27) must be satisfied. In our opinion, a review of the transcript discloses that the first and third rules were not met.

. . . .

In summary, there is insufficient testimony regarding how and when the notes were made and the Crown did not ask if they were a complete and accurate record of the discussions which they purport to summarize. The Crown did not establish definitively that the witness's memory was fresh when he made the notes, although Unger does say that the notes were made as he was talking to the accused. Further, at no point did the witness say expressly that he was certain that the notes were accurate when he made them. The most he said was that he attempted to take accurate notes. Threshold reliability was not established.

The trial judge inadvertently erred by allowing into the record the contents of Unger's notes under the guise of present memory revived. In so doing, evidence was let in that amounted to an unacceptable past recollection recorded. If Unger truly did not remember the events and facts about which he testified, and that seems to have been the case here, then his recitation amounted to inadmissible past recollection.

D) Applicability of Principles to this Case

The notes did not revive Unger's memory on the many matters dealt with in the notes on which he testified. The foundation for the use of the notes, purportedly to refresh his memory, fell short of what was required for that purpose. Although no precise formula need be followed, the substance of what is dealt with in the following extract from Thomas A. Mauet, Donald G. Casswell & Gordon P. Macdonald, *Fundamentals of Trial Technique*, 2nd Canadian ed. (Boston: Little Brown and Co., 1984), must be discernible from the evidence (at pp. 102-3):

A certain litany must be followed to establish the foundation for refreshing recollection . . . .

. . . .

The following elements must be demonstrated to establish a foundation for refreshing the recollection of a witness who is on the witness stand:

1. Witness knows the facts, but has a memory lapse on the stand.

2. Witness knows his report or other writing will refresh his memory.

3. Witness is given and reads the pertinent part of his report or other writing.

4. Witness states his memory has now been refreshed.

5. Witness now testifies what he knows, without further aid of the report or other writing.

None of these elements was established by the Crown's evidence. Moreover, at no time did Unger say (nor was he asked) that looking at his notes would jog his memory. He simply had carte blanche to refer to the notes, and it is obvious that in many respects he could do no more than read, or repeat, what was written. The problem in this case is that the notes did not refresh his memory. Unger's evidence reciting matters recorded in the notes was inadmissible.

The trial judge was clearly aware of the two legal principles. He noted that the weight and probative value of Unger's refreshed memory would be considered later. He did not do so. In his brief decision, he simply accepted Unger's evidence entirely, and effectively treated his recitation of his notes as evidence of the same quality as all the other evidence. With respect, he did not do what was nicely explained by Mewett and Sankoff (at 13-14):

... Ultimately, after his or her own observation of the witness and after assessing how the witness answers questions on oral examination and cross-examination, the trial judge will have to rule on whether the evidence of the witness can be received as present memory revived or rejected as an attempt to circumvent the rules relating to past recollection recorded.

So, in our opinion, the evidence derived from the notes should not have been admitted under the present memory revived principle. For the reasons given earlier, it also failed to meet the standards for admissibility under the present recollection recorded principle.

We conclude that what was in Unger's notes formed an essential part of the evidence warranting conviction. The notes were, therefore, critical to the Crown's case. Permitting the evidence to be part of the record was highly prejudicial to the accused. Without the notes, Unger's evidence would have been decidedly weaker and more equivocal. The evidence was critical because, by itself, the videotape was neutral. What was needed was the contrast provided by Unger's evidence.

The Crown referred to the failure by defence counsel to object to the use to which the notes were put, but the failure cannot make admissible evidence which is inadmissible. (*R. v. D.(L.E.)*, [1989] 2 S.C.R. 111, at 126-27; *R. v. D.C.B.* (1994), 95 Man. R. (2d) 220 (C.A.), at para. 14.)

Finally, the Crown suggested that "this might be a case where s. 686(1)(b)(iii) [of the *Criminal Code*] ought to be applied." Given what has been said above, it is not possible to conclude that, notwithstanding the error of law discussed above, no substantial wrong or miscarriage of justice has occurred.

The evidence of Unger could be no more probative if a new trial was held. In all the circumstances, we would allow the appeal and order the entry of a verdict of acquittal.

R. v. B. (K.G.)
(1998), 125 C.C.C. (3d) 61 (Ont. C.A.)

The accused was charged with second degree murder. At his first trial he was acquitted. The Crown's appeal to the Court of Appeal was dismissed. On the Crown's further appeal to the Supreme Court of Canada, the appeal was allowed and a new trial directed. At that trial he was convicted of the included offence of manslaughter. On appeal the accused argued that the trial judge erred in his consideration of the evidence of the mothers of two accomplices of the accused because, before testifying, they had refreshed their memories from statements each had given to the police some considerable time after the events about which they were testifying. The accused argued that the two mothers had little or no independent recollection of the subject events and that their evidence should have been given little or no weight. The mothers each acknowledged that they had refreshed their memories from statements that they had given to the police, two and one-half and three and one-half years after the meeting at which they said that the accused admitted killing the deceased. This is not a case where either witness drew a blank in the witness box and sought to refresh her memory from a previous statement. They refreshed their memories well before the trial.

OSBORNE J.A. (AUSTIN and GOUDGE JJ.A. concurring):—

. . . .

The trial judge meticulously reviewed the testimony of both Mrs. D. and Mrs. McD. before he accepted it and relied on it. He concluded that the fact that both witnesses had refreshed their memories from statements that they had given to the police could affect the weight of their evidence. Nevertheless, he found as a fact that both witnesses had an independent recollection of the relevant events and that their evidence was reliable. The evidence of both witnesses supports this conclusion. In the end, the trial judge confronted the defence position concerning the weight to be given to Mrs. D.'s and Mrs. McD.'s evidence by stating in his reasons for conviction:

It is the position of the defence that Mrs. D. and Mrs. McD. were honest but unreliable witnesses. The defence submits that Mrs. D. and Mrs. McD. should not have refreshed their memories from statements which were given to the police a substantial time, two and a half and three and a half years respectively, after the events. While I believe that it is permissible for a witness to refresh his or her memory out of court from notes which were not made contemporaneously with the events about which he or she is testifying it is equally clear that doing so can, and does, affect the weight to be given to the witness's evidence.

I see nothing wrong with either witness reviewing her police statement before testifying. There is also nothing wrong with a defence counsel attempting to determine in cross-examination whether Mrs. D. or Mrs. McD. had a present memory of events about which she testified. What triggers recollection is not significant. This was long ago made clear in 1814 in *Henry v. Lee* (1814), 2 Chitty 124, where Ellenborough L.C.J. said:

> If upon looking at any document he can so far refresh his memory as to recollect a circumstance, it is sufficient; and it makes no difference that the memorandum is not written by himself, for it is not the memorandum that is the evidence but the recollection of the witness.

There is a danger in allowing the phrase "refreshing memory" to apply to those cases where the witness has no present memory, but is able to state that she accurately recorded a past event. In such cases, the witness has no present memory. The evidence, to the extent there is any, is the past record. When a witness refreshes her memory from some external source or event, she has a present memory, albeit one that has been refreshed; how reliable and truthful her recollection is, will be determined by the trier of fact, as happened here.

. . . .

I see nothing wrong with the trial judge's approach to the evidence of Mrs. D. and Mrs. McD. He was alert to all factors that might bear upon the reliability of their evidence, including the fact that both had refreshed their memories from earlier statements that were not made contemporaneously with the events referred to in them. Clearly, the evidence given by Mrs. D. and Mrs. McD. was not their previous statements but their current recollection of the appellant's admission, as refreshed by their earlier review of their statements. Refreshing memory may take place before trial, as happened here, or in some cases, at trial. I would not give effect to this ground of appeal.

R. v. MATTIS
(1998), 20 C.R. (5th) 93 (Ont. Prov. Div.)

The accused was charged with trafficking in cocaine. The trial judge considered the evidence of the Crown and of the defence as to what had been observed prior to the accused's arrest.

BIGELOW J.:—

. . . .

Officers Peters and Berrill whose evidence was clearly crucial to the Crown's case both stated that they had made up their notes of the events separately. In cross-examination they both admitted that their notes with respect to that incident were identical save and except for some short forms of words used by Officer Peters in her notebook. Neither were able to provide any explanation for how this could have occurred.

. . . .

Obviously credibility is a major factor in this case. Mr. Rusonik argues that there are significant concerns with respect to the credibility of the police witnesses. As well Ms. Mattis has given evidence on her own behalf contradicting that of the police witnesses.

The only reasonable inference which can be drawn from the fact that the notebooks were identical is that one of the officers copied the notes of the other. In the recent decision of *R. v. Green*, [1998] O.J. No. 3598 (Ont. Ct. Gen. Div.). Malloy, J. commented on the importance of police officers preparing their notes independently:

> There are important reasons for requiring that officers prepare their notes independently. The purpose of notes made by a police officer is to record the observations made by that officer. The notes themselves are not admissible as evidence for the truth of their contents. An officer with relevant evidence to offer may testify at trial as to the act or observations made by him or her. However, that officer is not permitted to testify as to the information received from other officers for the purpose of proving their truth. Such evidence [is] hearsay and inadmissible.

> An officer's notes perform a valuable function at trial. It is usually many months, sometimes years, from the time of an occurrence to the time that the officer is called upon to testify at trial. Without the assistance of notes to refresh his or her memory, the evidence of the officer at trial would inevitably be sketchy at best. If the officer's notes are prepared without any indication of which is the officer's independent recollection and which is somebody else's recollection, there is every likelihood that that officer at trial will be "refreshing" his or her own memory with observations made by someone else. In effect, the officer will be giving hearsay evidence as if it was his or her own recollection rather than the observations of somebody else written into the notes without attribution.

The concerns raised by Malloy, J. are particularly relevant in the present case where it was clear that neither Officer Peters nor Officer Birrell had a clear recollection of the events and both were relying heavily on notes in giving their evidence.

Malloy, J. went on to comment on the effect of collaboration in the making of notes would have on the credibility of the testimony of police officers:

> The fact that officers have collaborated on their notes will always cause a trier of fact to give careful consideration to the reliability of that officer's evidence. There

will, however, be situations in which such collaboration, although not good police practice, will not undermine the testimony of the officers. The extent to which the collaboration renders the evidence of the officers' unreliable will depend on the circumstances of each case and the explanation given by the officers.

In the present case no explanation was offered as to how the notebooks could be identical. The obvious fact that the notebooks were copied combined with the lack of any explanation as to how this occurred and the lack of specific recollection by both officers has a significant impact on the reliability of the evidence. Absent confirmation of that evidence in material particulars, it would be unsafe to base a conviction on it.

. . . .

As indicated above absent confirming evidence, it would be dangerous to base of finding of guilt in this case on the evidence of Officers Peters and Birrell. . . . Accordingly, all three charges are dismissed.

There are ethical restraints on your ability as counsel to communicate with a witness during their testimony. For example, in Ontario, Rule 4 of the *Rules of Professional Conduct* provides:

4.04 COMMUNICATION WITH WITNESSES GIVING EVIDENCE

4.04 Subject to the direction of the tribunal, the lawyer shall observe the following rules respecting communication with witnesses giving evidence:

(a) during examination-in-chief, the examining lawyer may discuss with the witness any matter that has not been covered in the examination up to that point,

(b) during examination-in-chief by another legal practitioner of a witness who is unsympathetic to the lawyer's cause, the lawyer not conducting the examination-in-chief may discuss the evidence with the witness,

(c) between completion of examination-in-chief and commencement of cross-examination of the lawyer's own witness, the lawyer ought not to discuss the evidence given in chief or relating to any matter introduced or touched on during the examination-in-chief,

(d) during cross-examination by an opposing legal practitioner, the witness's own lawyer ought not to have any conversation with the witness about the witness's evidence or any issue in the proceeding,

(e) between completion of cross-examination and commencement of re-examination, the lawyer who is going to re-examine the witness ought not to have any discussion about evidence that will be dealt with on re-examination,

(f) during cross-examination by the lawyer of a witness unsympathetic to the cross-examiner's cause, the lawyer may discuss the witness's evidence with the witness,

(g) during cross-examination by the lawyer of a witness who is sympathetic to that lawyer's cause, any conversations ought to be restricted in the same way as communications during examination-in-chief of one's own witness, and

(h) during re-examination of a witness called by an opposing legal practitioner, if the witness is sympathetic to the lawyer's cause the lawyer ought not to discuss the evidence to be given by that witness during re-examination. The lawyer may, however, properly discuss the evidence with a witness who is adverse in interest.

PROBLEMS

Problem 1

The defendant is being tried for the theft of a quantity of household goods, the property of Ms. Farid. The defendant had been hired to move these goods from Ms. Farid's former residence to her new address and Ms. Farid maintains that some of her things never arrived. Ms. Farid has testified that as her chattels were being taken out of her house she made longhand notes and later, in anticipation of the trial, she copied these notes on her typewriter. The witness is being examined by the prosecutor:

Q.:	When you look at that typewritten sheet, does that refresh your recollection as to the items therein mentioned?
A.:	It does.
Q.:	In what way?
A.:	Well, every item here — for instance: "2 Chinese vases octagonal shape Satsuma," I remember.
Q.:	You remember these items individually as packed?
A.:	Individually, each one. I lived with these things, your Honour, I know them.
The Court:	You lived with them yourself?
A.:	I did.
The Court:	So when you look at that paper, it does refresh your recollection?
A.:	Absolutely.
Prosecutor:	Your Honour I tender in evidence as proof of the items removed from Ms. Farid's home this typewritten list.

Do you have any objection to make? Do you have any questions to ask? Suppose the typewritten copy had been made by the investigating officer from Ms. Farid's notes: any difference? See *R. v. Kearns,* [1945] 2 W.W.R. 477 (B.C.C.A.).

Problem 2

A witness to a hit-run collision recorded the licence number of the fleeing automobile. The witness advised the investigating officer, who made a notation in his note-book; the witness heard the officer correctly broadcast the licence number on the police radio but never looked at his notebook. At trial, the witness, having lost her own note, seeks to refresh her memory from the officer's notebook. How would you rule? Compare *R. v. Davey* (1969), 68 W.W.R. 142 (B.C.S.C.). See also *R. v. Hanaway* (1980), 63 C.C.C. (2d) 44 (Ont. Dist. Ct.) and *R. v. Lamb,* [2007] N.J. No. 239 (P.C.).

Problem 3

You are a Crown prosecuting a domestic violence case. Court ends for the day while you are still in the middle of your examination-in-chief of the complainant. That night, she is in your office for moral support. You would like to take the opportunity to discuss with her evidence that you have not yet covered. Can you?

Problem 4

Your client in a medical malpractice case is being examined for discovery by the defendant's lawyer. Before lunch, your client advises you that she would like to speak with you privately.

(c) Videotaped Statements by Children

VIDEO-RECORDED EVIDENCE

Evidence of victim or witness under 18

715.1 (1) In any proceeding against an accused in which a victim or other witness was under the age of eighteen years at the time the offence is alleged to have been committed, a video recording made within a reasonable time after the alleged offence, in which the victim or witness describes the acts complained of, is admissible in evidence if the victim or witness, while testifying, adopts the contents of the video recording, unless the presiding judge or justice is of the opinion that admission of the video recording in evidence would interfere with the proper administration of justice.

R.S., 1985, c. 19 (3rd Supp.), s. 16; 1997, c. 16, s. 7; 2005, c. 32, s. 23.

Evidence of victim or witness who has a disability

715.2 (1) In any proceeding against an accused in which a victim or other witness is able to communicate evidence but may have difficulty doing so by reason of a mental or physical disability, a video recording made within a reasonable time after the alleged offence, in which the victim or witness describes the acts complained of, is admissible in evidence if the victim or witness, while testifying, adopts the contents of the video recording, unless the presiding judge or justice is of the opinion that admission of the video recording in evidence would interfere with the proper administration of justice.

1998, c. 9, s. 8; 2005, c. 32, s. 23.

R. v. L. (D.O.)
[1993] 4 S.C.R. 419, 25 C.R. (4th) 285, 85 C.C.C. (3d) 289

The accused was charged with sexual assault alleged to have taken place between September 1985 and March 1988. Following a medical examination of the complainant, a 9-year-old girl, the police began their investigation in May 1988 and a videotaped interview of the complainant took place in August 1988. At the preliminary inquiry, the complainant testified before the court. At trial, the Crown sought to introduce the videotaped interview of the complainant pursuant to s. 715.1 of the Criminal Code. The accused sought a declaration that s. 715.1 was unconstitutional but the trial judge upheld the section. Following a *voir dire*, the videotaped interview was admitted into evidence and the accused was convicted. The Court of Appeal allowed the accused's appeal and declared s. 715.1 unconstitutional.

LAMER C.J. (LA FOREST, SOPINKA, CORY, MCLACHLIN and IACOBUCCI JJ. concurring):—

I have read the reasons of Justice L'Heureux-Dubé and concur in her result. It is my view that s. 715.1 of the *Criminal Code* . . . is a response to the dominance and power which adults, by virtue of their age, have over children. Accordingly, s. 715.1 is designed to accommodate the needs and to safeguard the interests of young victims of various forms of sexual abuse, irrespective of their sex. By allowing for the videotaping of evidence under certain express conditions, s. 715.1 not only makes participation in the criminal justice system less stressful and traumatic for child and adolescent complainants, but also aids in the preservation of evidence and the discovery of truth.

. . . As s. 715.1 neither offends the principles of fundamental justice nor violates the right a fair trial, it cannot be said to limit the rights guaranteed under s. 7 or 11(*d*) of the *Canadian Charter of Rights and Freedoms*. The respondent has failed to establish that s. 715.1 offends the rules of evidence against the admission of hearsay evidence and prior consistent statements. In addition, as there is no constitutionally protected requirement that cross-examination be contemporaneous with the giving of evidence, the respondent has failed to show that his fundamental right to cross-examine has been violated. The admission of the videotaped evidence does not make the trial unfair or not public, nor does it in any way affect an accused's right to be presumed innocent.

[L'Heureux-Dubé J., in a lengthy judgment, Gonthier J. concurring, also found section 715.1 to be not violative of the accused's Charter rights.]

R. v. F. (C.C.)
[1997] 3 S.C.R. 1183, 11 C.R. (5th) 209, 120 C.C.C. (3d) 225

The accused was charged with touching his six-year-old daughter for a sexual purpose. The police investigated the complaint the evening it was made and videotaped the complainant's statement describing the incident. At trial, the complainant was shown the videotape following her examination-in-chief. She confirmed that she made the statements on the videotape and that they were true. The trial judge ruled that the complainant had adopted the videotaped statement and admitted it as evidence pursuant to s. 715.1 of the Criminal Code. On cross-examination the complainant made statements which contradicted in part the videotaped statements. The Ontario Court of Appeal overturned the conviction and directed a new trial. The Court of Appeal held that the videotaped evidence that was later disavowed could not be considered as having been adopted under s. 715.1.

The judgment of the Court was delivered by CORY J.:—

. . . .

The appellate courts of Alberta and Ontario have given different meaning to the word "adopted". What constitutes the adoption of a videotape statement is the first and paramount issue that must be resolved in this appeal. The second is a consideration of what effect, if any, subsequent contradictory evidence of the complainant will have upon the admissibility of the videotape statement.

. . . .

It will be self-evident to every observant parent and to all who have worked closely with young people that children, even more than adults, will have a better recollection of events shortly after they occurred than they will some weeks, months or years later. The younger the child, the more pronounced will this be. Indeed to state this simply expresses the observations of most Canadians. It is a common experience that anyone, and particularly children, will have a better recollection of events closer to their occurrence than he or she will later on. It follows that the videotape which is made within a reasonable time after the alleged offence and which describes the act will almost inevitably reflect a more accurate recollection of events than will testimony given later at trial. Thus the section enhances the ability of a court to find the truth by preserving a very recent recollection of the event in question. . . . The important subsidiary aim of the section is to prevent or reduce materially the likelihood of inflicting further injury upon a child as a result of participating in court proceedings. This will be accomplished by reducing the number of interviews that the child must undergo and thereby diminish the stress occasioned a child by repeated questioning on a painful incident. Further, the videotaping will take place in surroundings that are less overwhelming for a child than the courtroom.

. . . .

Section 715.1 provides that a videotaped statement is admissible in evidence if the complainant "adopts the contents of the videotape" while testifying. What meaning should be attributed to that phrase? . . . . Black's Law Dictionary defines "adopt" as follows:

> To accept, appropriate, choose, or select. To make that one's own, property or act, which was not so originally.

Obviously the term "adoption" is capable of several meanings. However, in the context of s. 715.1 the proper interpretation should be one which accords with its aim and purpose. The Alberta and Ontario Courts of Appeal have taken different approaches to the adoption of videotaped evidence. In *R. v. Meddoui* (1990), 61 C.C.C. (3d) 345, the Alberta Court of Appeal found that a witness "adopted" her statement within the meaning of s. 715.1 when she recalled giving the statement and testified that she was then attempting to be honest and truthful. It was held that the complainant need not have a present recollection of the events discussed. The decision approved the use of the videotape as evidence of the events described, even if the complainant is unable to recall the events discussed in the tape which formed the basis for the charge. . . . In *R. v. Toten* (1993), 83 C.C.C. (3d) 5, the Ontario Court of Appeal rejected the *Meddoui* interpretation of "adopts" in favour of a narrower one. It was held that in order to adopt the contents of a videotaped statement, the child complainant must be able, based on a present memory of the events referred to in the videotape, to verify the accuracy and contents of the statement. The child must not only acknowledge making the statement but also the truth of its contents. In light of the clear aim and purpose of s. 715.1, I cannot accept the Ontario Court of Appeal position. . . . S. 715.1 has built-in guarantees of trustworthiness and reliability which eliminate the need for such a stringent requirement for adoption. Further, a lack of present memory or an inability to provide testimony at trial regarding the events referred to in the videotape as a result of the youthfulness and the emotional state of the complainant increases the need to consider the videotaped statement.

The test set out in *Toten* would prevent a child who has little, or no memory of the events from "adopting" the video and it would therefore be inadmissible under s. 715.1. However, it is precisely in this situation that the video is most needed. Children, particularly younger ones, are prone to forget details of an event with the passage of time. A videotape made shortly after the event is more likely to be accurate than the child's viva voce testimony, given months later, at trial. It is quite possible that a young child will have a recollection of going to the police station and making the statement and of her attempt to be truthful at the time yet have no memory of the unpleasant events. This is particularly true where the elapsed time between the initial complaint and the date of trial is lengthy. If effect is to be given to the aims of s. 715.1 of enhancing the truth-seeking role of the courts by preserving an early account of the incident and of preventing further injury to vulnerable children as a result of their involvement in the criminal process, then the videotape should generally be admitted.

. . . .

I recognize that the *Meddoui* approach to "adoption" gives rise to another problem. Specifically, a witness who cannot remember the events cannot be effectively cross-examined on the contents of his or her statement, and therefore the reliability of his or her testimony cannot be tested in that way. However, it was recognized in *R. v. Khan*, [1990] 2 S.C.R. 531; *R. v. Smith*, [1992] 2 S.C.R. 915, and *R. v. B. (K.G.)*, [1993] 1 S.C.R. 740, that cross-examination is not the only guarantee of reliability. There are several factors present in s. 715.1 which provide the requisite reliability of the videotaped statement. They include: (a) the requirement that the statement be made within a reasonable time; (b) the trier of fact can watch the entire interview, which provides an opportunity to observe the demeanor, and assess the personality and intelligence of the child; (c) the requirement that the child attest that she was attempting to be truthful at the time that the statement was made. As well, the child can be cross-examined at trial as to whether he or she was actually being truthful when the statement was made. These indicia provide enough guarantees of reliability to compensate for the inability to cross-examine as to the forgotten events. Moreover, where the complainant has no independent memory of the events there is an obvious necessity for the videotaped evidence. In *Meddoui*, it was recommended that in such circumstances, the trier of fact should be given a special warning (similar to the one given in *Vetrovec v. The Queen*, [1982] 1 S.C.R. 811) of the dangers of convicting based on the videotape alone. In my view, this was sage advice that should be followed.

. . . .

After the videotaped evidence has been admitted, any questions which arise concerning the circumstances in which the video was made, the veracity of the witness' statements, or the overall reliability of the evidence, will be matters for the trier of fact to consider in determining how much weight the videotaped statement should be given. If, in the course of cross-examination, defence counsel elicits evidence which contradicts any part of the video, this does not render those parts inadmissible. Obviously a contradicted videotape may well be given less weight in the final determination of the issues. However, the fact that the video is contradicted in cross-examination does not necessarily mean that the video is wrong or unreliable. The trial judge may still conclude, as in this case, that the inconsistencies are insignificant and find the video more reliable than the evidence elicited at trial. . . . Although each witness' credibility must be assessed, the standard which would be applied to an adult's evidence is not always appropriate in assessing the credibility of young children. This approach to the evidence of children was reiterated in *R. v. W. (R.)*, [1992] 2 S.C.R. 122, at pp. 132-34. There McLachlin J. acknowledged that the peculiar perspectives of children can affect their recollection of events and that the presence of inconsistencies, especially those related to peripheral matters, should be assessed in context. A skilful cross-examination is almost certain to confuse a child, even if she is telling the truth. That confusion can lead to inconsistencies in her testimony. Although the trier of fact must be wary of any evidence which has been contradicted, this is a matter which goes to the weight which should be attached to the videotape and not to its admissibility.[264]

Parliament has now extended section 715.1 to apply to all criminal offences.

The *Ontario Evidence Act* was amended to provide:

18.3(1) A videotape of the testimony of a witness under the age of 18 that satisfies the conditions set out in subsection (2) may be admitted in evidence, if the court is of the opinion that this is likely to help the witness give complete and accurate testimony or that it is in the best interests of the witness.

(2) The judge or other person who is to preside at the trial and the lawyers of the parties to the proceeding shall be present when the testimony is given, and the lawyers shall be given an opportunity to examine the witness in the same way as if he or she were testifying in the courtroom.

(3) Subsection 18.4(1) and section 18.5 apply with necessary modifications when testimony is being videotaped.

(4) If a videotape is admitted under subsection (1), the witness need not attend or testify and shall not be summoned to testify.

---

264 For critical commentary see Moore and Green, "Truth and the Reliability of Children's Evidence: Problems With S. 715 of the Criminal Code" (2000), 30 C.R. (5th) 148, who argue that overly generous court interpretations of reasonable time and adoption have raised significant threats to reliability.

(5) However, in exceptional circumstances, the court may require the witness to attend and testify even though a videotape of his or her testimony has been admitted in evidence.

(6) With the leave of the court, a videotape of an interview with a person under the age of 18 may be admitted in evidence if the person, while testifying, adopts the contents of the videotape.

(7) Subsection (6) is in addition to any rule of law under which a videotape may be admitted in evidence.

(d) Adoption

Outside of the s. 715.1 context, when does a witness adopt a statement given on an earlier occasion?

R. v. MCCARROLL
(2008), 2008 CarswellOnt 6022, 238 C.C.C. (3d) 404, 61 C.R. (6th) 353
(C.A.)

The accused was charged with second degree murder. The victim was beaten to death with a baseball bat during a fight between two groups of friends. Kidd was part of the accused's group of friends. The issue at trial was who dealt the fatal blow. In a videotaped statement and at the accused's preliminary inquiry, Kidd put the accused in possession of a baseball bat. At trial, she did not remember these details. She did say, however, that she told the truth at the preliminary inquiry. The trial judge instructed the jury that Kidd had adopted her statements. The accused was convicted. On appeal, the conviction was overturned. The Court of Appeal held that the trial judge had erred.

EPSTEIN J.A. (for the Court):

Did Kidd adopt her previous statement?

38 I agree with the appellant's argument that the trial judge erred in instructing the jury that Kidd adopted the contents of her prior statement given she had no present recollection of the events it described.

39 Where a witness adopts a prior statement as true, the statement becomes part of that witness' evidence at trial and is admissible for its truth: *R. v. Deacon* (1947), 89 C.C.C. 1 (SCC), at p. 4. The question becomes whether the witness adopts the prior statement "as being the truth as she now sees it": *R. v. McInroy* (1979), 42 C.C.C. (2d) 481, at p. 498. As this court said in *R. v. Toten* (1993), 83 C.C.C. (3d) 5 (C.A.), at p. 23, in order for a prior statement to be incorporated into trial testimony, or adopted':

> The witness must be able to attest to the accuracy of the statement based on their present memory of the facts referred to in that statement. In this sense, adoption refers to both the witness's acknowledgment that he or she made the prior statement and the witness's assertion that his or her memory while testifying accords with the contents of the prior statement.

See *R. v. Tat* (1997) 117 C.C.C. (3d) 481 (Ont. C.A.), at para. 28, and *R. v. Atikian* (1990) 62 C.C.C. (3d) 357 (Ont. C.A.), at p. 364.

40 The determination of whether the witness adopts all or part of the statement must be made by the trier of fact, in this instance, the jury. However, as a condition of admissibility the trial judge must be satisfied that there is an evidentiary basis on which the trier of fact could conclude that the witness adopted the statement. The witness must acknowledge having made the statement and, based on present memory of the events referred to in the statement, verify the accuracy of its contents.

41 Kidd did acknowledge having made the statement and did say that she was likely telling the truth when she made it. However, given her selective memory of the events surrounding Prebtani's death, Kidd was, at best, only able to vouch for the accuracy of the statement based on circumstances surrounding its recording. She could not continue to assert the truth of its contents: see *Toten* at p. 24.

42 The trial judge committed two errors by directing the jury that Kidd had adopted her statement. First, there was no evidentiary basis for that conclusion. Adoption was simply not possible in these circumstances. Second, even if there was an evidentiary basis, it was a matter for the jury to decide whether or not Kidd adopted what she said in her interview with the police as part of her trial testimony and imprinted it with her trial oath. The trial judge usurped a function that was within the exclusive purview of the jury.

43 On appeal, the Crown advanced three arguments that were not advanced at trial. First, what Kidd said was tantamount to adoption. Second, the statements could have been admitted under the hearsay exception for past recollections recorded. Third, under the principled approach to the admission of hearsay evidence the statement would have been admitted.

44 Before this court, the Crown submits that under an expanded notion of the concept of adoption, the portions of the videotaped statement were properly before the jury for the truth of their contents.

45 Relying on *R. v. C.C.F.* (1997) 120 C.C.C. (3d) 225 (SCC), the Crown argues that the application of the principled approach in cases involving prior videotaped statements where the witness is available for cross-examination has substantially modified the orthodoxy of the traditional cases.

46 While the principled approach to the law of evidence continues to cultivate changes in how the court receives evidence, particularly in relation to the reception of hearsay, I do not accept the Crown's submission that these changes have eliminated the need for an adult witness to have some recollection of the events contained in the statement.

47 At issue in *C.C.F.* were the requirements for the admissibility of a videotaped statement under s. 715.1 of the *Criminal Code*, R.S.C. 1985, c. C-46, a statutory exception to the hearsay rule that permits an out-of-court statement to be admitted at the trials of certain enumerated offences if the complainant is a child under the age of eighteen and if the video was made within a reasonable time following the

alleged offences. The court held that the word "adopts" in s. 715.1 should be given a meaning that advances the dual purposes of the section; to create a record of what is likely to be the witness' best recollection of the events and to reduce the harm to a child of further participation in court proceedings.

48 To this end the legislators incorporated several factors into the section to provide the requisite reliability that traditionally comes from the witness' adopting the statement under oath. First, the statement must be made at a time reasonably proximate to the events in issue. Second, the statement must describe the acts complained of. Third, the child must be given the opportunity to attest to the fact that he or she was trying to tell the truth when the statement was recorded. As made clear in *C.C.F.*, the fact that a child does not have a present memory of the events described is not a barrier to the admission of the statement. In such circumstances, the trier of fact must have an opportunity to watch the entire videotaped statement - providing an opportunity to judge the child's demeanour.

49 The decision in *C.C.F.* does not affect the law as it applies to the adoption of out-of-court statements of adults. Quite the opposite. It reinforces the importance of adopting a statement under oath. Cory J. for the court makes it very clear that the traditional tests for adoption still apply outside the s. 715.1 context - the guarantees of reliability built into s. 715.1 make the strict adoption test unnecessary in relation to the evidence of children: see *C.C.F.* at para. 40.

. . .

Appeal allowed and new trial ordered.

(e) Cross-examination

The purposes of cross-examination, its place in our adversarial system, its scope, and its control may perhaps best be appreciated by examining a few classic quotations:

Professor Wigmore:

> For two centuries past, the policy of the Anglo-American system of Evidence has been to regard the necessity of testing by cross-examination as a vital feature of the law. The belief that no safeguard for testing the value of human statements is comparable to that furnished by cross-examination, and the conviction that no statement (unless by special exception) should be used as testimony until it has been probed and sublimated by that test, has found increasing strength in lengthening experience.
>
> Not even the abuses, the mishandlings, and the puerilities which are so often found associated with cross-examination have availed to nullify its value. It may be that in more than one sense it takes the place in our system which torture occupied in the mediaeval system of the civilians. Nevertheless, it is beyond any doubt the greatest legal engine ever invented for the discovery of truth. . . . If we omit political considerations of broader range, then cross-examination, not trial by jury, is the great and permanent contribution of the Anglo-American system of law to improved methods of trial-procedure.[265]

---

265 5 Wigmore, *Evidence* (Chad. Rev.), s. 1367.

Professor McCormick:

> For two centuries, common law judges and lawyers have regarded the opportunity of cross-examination as an essential safeguard of the accuracy and completeness of testimony, and they have insisted that the opportunity is a right and not a mere privilege.[266]

Mr. Justice Dennistoun:

> Cross-examination is a powerful weapon of defence, and often its sole weapon. The denial of full opportunity to sift and probe the witnesses of the opposing side has always been regarded with extreme disfavour by British Courts of justice.
> Cross-examination may be insisted on for a number of purposes: First, to bring out facts as to which a witness has not been asked to testify, or is anxious to conceal; Second, to show that the witness is unworthy of belief; Third, to adduce facts in mitigation of sentence; Fourth, to adduce facts which in the case of a guilty person may minimize his offence and assist in the rehabilitation of his character.
>
> . . . .
>
> That full cross-examination of an opposite witness should be permitted by the trial Judge is well settled. The Judge may check cross-examination if it become irrelevant, or prolix, or insulting, but so long as it may fairly be applied to the issue, or touches the credibility of the witness it should not be excluded.[267]

Notice particularly that the cross-examiner is not confined to asking questions about matters in issue which arose in examination-in-chief. Notice as well that the trial judge has some discretion to control the questioning if it is unduly lengthy or insulting.[268] Aside from the trial judge's discretion there is an obligation on counsel as well to have concern for the limited time and resources available to the court and also to have some respect for the witness as a fellow human being. As Lord Sankey noted:

> It is right to make due allowance for the irritation caused by the strain and stress of a long and complicated case, but a protracted and irrelevant cross-examination not only adds to the cost of litigation, but is a waste of public time. Such a cross-examination becomes indefensible when it is conducted, as it was in this case, without restraint and without the courtesy and consideration which a witness is entitled to expect in a court of law. It is not sufficient for the due administration of justice to have a learned, patient and impartial judge. Equally with him, the solicitors who prepare the case and the counsel who present it to the court are taking part in the great task of doing justice between man and man.[269]

Well prepared and competent counsel should always have a purpose in mind in cross-examining. Not all cross-examination is destructive where the major aim is to impeach, i.e., to seek to destroy credibility. In many cases the aim is merely to use cross-examination for another purpose such as to clarify, pin the witness down, or elicit other evidence. So, for example, counsel who called the

---

266 McCormick, *Evidence*, 2d ed., p. 43.
267 In *R. v. Anderson*, [1938] 3 D.L.R. 317, 319-20 (Man. C.A.). And see *R. v. Roulette* (1972), 7 C.C.C. (2d) 244 (Man. Q.B.) and *R. v. Makow* (1973), 13 C.C.C. (2d) 167 (B.C.C.A.).
268 See *R. v. Shearing*, [2002] 3 S.C.R. 33.
269 *Mechanical & Gen. Inventions Co. v. Austin* (1935), 153 L.T. 153, 157 (H.L.) cited with approval in *R. v. Rowbotham (No. 5)* (1977), 2 C.R. (3d) 293 (Ont. Co. Ct.).

witness elicits three things in chief. Opposing counsel seeks to elicit three other things the witness observed, which material supports opposing counsel's case.[270]

Is counsel entitled to put a question on cross-examination although he is not then in a position to prove the same by other evidence? One can imagine the possible impact on a jury of repeated questions suggesting misconduct of some kind on the part of the witness even though such misconduct is denied. And yet there appears to be nothing illegal about such a practice. Lord Radcliffe in *Fox v. General Medical Council*[271] explained:

> An advocate is entitled to use his discretion as to whether to put questions in the course of cross-examination which are based on material which he is not in a position to prove directly. The penalty is that, if he gets a denial or some answer that does not suit him, the answer stands against him for what it is worth.

This position has been adopted in Canada.[272] In England, however, the Bar Council laid down ethical guidelines. Rule Four provides:

> Questions which affect the credibility of a witness by attacking his character, but are not otherwise relevant to the actual inquiry, ought not to be asked unless the cross-examiner has reasonable grounds for thinking that the imputation conveyed by the question is well founded or true.

R. v. LYTTLE
(2004), 17 C.R. (6th) 1, 180 C.C.C. (3d) 476, 2004 CarswellOnt 510, 2004 CarswellOnt 511 (S.C.C.)

The accused was charged with robbery, assault, kidnapping and possession of a weapon. The victim was brutally beaten by five men with baseball bats. The victim said he was assaulted so that his assailants could recover a $7,000 chain that they thought he had stolen. The accused alleged that the victim was hurt during a drug deal gone awry and accused him in order to protect associates in a drug ring. Early on in the investigation, the police believed that the offences were committed against the victim in the context of a drug deal. The victim had a drug conviction record and certain features of the offence suggested "drug gangsterism". At trial, the Crown refused to call as its own witnesses the officers who formed the early theory. The trial judge did not permit defence counsel to put the drug transaction theory to witnesses, unless she was prepared to call evidence in support of that theory. Defence counsel undertook to call two officers, and was permitted to cross-examine other witnesses on the drug theory. After the cross-examinations, counsel sought to resile from the undertaking to call the two police officers, attempting to preserve the accused's right to address the jury last. The accused was forced to call the officers, who confirmed that the drug theory had been an initial operating theory. The accused was not permitted to address the jury last and was convicted. The Court of Appeal found that the trial

---

270 See generally Younger, *The Art of Cross-examination* (Chicago: A.B.A., Litigation Section, 1976).

271 [1960] 1 W.L.R. 1017, 1023 (P.C.).

272 See *R. v. Bencardino* (1973), 15 C.C.C. (2d) 342 (Ont. C.A.) and *R. v. Racco (No. 3)* (1975), 23 C.C.C. (2d) 209 (Ont. Co. Ct.). But compare Haines J. in *R. v. Hawke* (1974), 3 O.R. (2d) 210, 229 (Ont. H.C.).

judge unduly constrained defence counsel's cross-examination, but applied the curative proviso in s. 686(1)(b) (iii) of the Criminal Code. The appeal by the accused from his conviction was allowed and a new trial ordered.

MAJOR and FISH JJ. for the Court: —

. . . .

The right of an accused to cross-examine prosecution witnesses without significant and unwarranted constraint is an essential component of the right to make a full answer and defence. Commensurate with its importance, the right to cross-examine is now recognized as being protected by ss. 7 and 11(d) of the Canadian Charter of Rights and Freedoms. The right of cross-examination must therefore be jealously protected and broadly construed. But it must not be abused. Counsel are bound by the rules of relevancy and barred from resorting to harassment, misrepresentation, repetitiousness or, more generally, from putting questions whose prejudicial effect outweighs their probative value. [Citations omitted.]

Just as the right of cross-examination itself is not absolute, so too are its limitations. Trial judges enjoy, in this as in other aspects of the conduct of a trial, a broad discretion to ensure fairness and to see that justice is done—and seen to be done. In the exercise of that discretion, they may sometimes think it right to relax the rules of relevancy somewhat, or to tolerate a degree of repetition that would in other circumstances be unacceptable.

. . . .

This appeal concerns the constraint on cross-examination arising from the ethical and legal duties of counsel when they allude in their questions to disputed and unproven facts. Is a good faith basis sufficient or is counsel bound, as the trial judge held in this case, to provide an evidentiary foundation for the assertion?

Unlike the trial judge, and with respect, we believe that a question can be put to a witness in cross-examination regarding matters that need not be proved independently, provided that counsel has a good faith basis for putting the question. It is not uncommon for counsel to believe what is in fact true, without being able to prove it otherwise than by cross-examination; nor is it uncommon for reticent witnesses to concede suggested facts—in the mistaken belief that they are already known to the cross-examiner and will therefore, in any event, emerge.

In this context, a "good faith basis" is a function of the information available to the cross-examiner, his or her belief in its likely accuracy, and the purpose for which it is used. Information falling short of admissible evidence may be put to the witness. In fact, the information may be incomplete or uncertain, provided the cross-examiner does not put suggestions to the witness recklessly or that he or she knows to be false. The cross-examiner may pursue any hypothesis that is honestly advanced on the strength of reasonable inference, experience or intuition. The purpose of the question must be consistent with the lawyer's role as an officer of the court: to suggest what counsel genuinely thinks possible on known facts or reasonable assumptions is in our view permissible; to assert or to imply in a manner that is calculated to mislead is in our view improper and prohibited.

In *Bencardino*, Jessup J.A. applied the English rule to this effect:

Whatever may be said about the forensic impropriety of the three incidents in cross-examination, I am unable to say any illegality was involved in them. As Lord Radcliffe said in *Fox v. General Medical Council*, [1960] 1 W.L.R. 1017 at p. 1023:

> "An advocate is entitled to use his discretion as to whether to put questions in the course of cross- examination which are based on material which he is not in a position to prove directly. The penalty is that, if he gets a denial or some answer that does not suit him, the answer stands against him for what it is worth."

More recently, in *R. v. Shearing*, [2002] 3 S.C.R. 33, 2002 SCC 58, 165 C.C.C. (3d) 225, 214 D.L.R. (4th) 215, while recognizing the need for exceptional restraint in sexual assault cases, Binnie J. reaffirmed, at paras. 121-22, the general rule that "in most instances the adversarial process allows wide latitude to cross-examiners to resort to unproven assumptions and innuendo in an effort to crack the untruthful witness". As suggested at the outset, however, wide latitude does not mean unbridled licence, and cross-examination remains subject to the requirements of good faith, professional integrity and the other limitations set out above.

A trial judge must balance the rights of an accused to receive a fair trial with the need to prevent unethical cross-examination. There will thus be instances where a trial judge will want to ensure that "counsel [is] not merely taking a random shot at a reputation imprudently exposed or asking a groundless question to waft an unwarranted innuendo into the jury box". See *Michelson v. United States*, 335 U.S. 469 (1948) at p. 481, per Jackson J. Where a question implies the existence of a disputed factual predicate that is manifestly tenuous or suspect, a trial judge may properly take appropriate steps, by conducting a voir dire or otherwise, to seek and obtain counsel's assurance that a good faith basis exists for putting the question. If the judge is satisfied in this regard and the question is not otherwise prohibited, counsel should be permitted to put the question to the witness.

As long as counsel has a good faith basis for asking an otherwise permissible question in cross-examination, the question should be allowed. In our view, no distinction need be made between expert and lay witnesses within the broad scope of this general principle.

Lyttle is an important decision on the scope of cross-examination and control by trial judges on counsel who abuse their position as officers of the court. The Supreme Court has announced a revised regime. The Court declares that cross-examination is permissible on unproven facts without evidentiary foundation subject only to good faith assurance from counsel.

The Court revises its earlier decision in *R. v. Howard*,[273] where Lamer J., for a 3-1 majority of the Supreme Court, held that

> It is not open to the examiner or cross-examiner to put as a fact, or even a hypothetical fact, that which is not and will not become part of the case as admissible evidence.

---

273 [1989] 1 S.C.R. 1337.

The Court in *Lyttle* claimed that the ratio of *Howard* had been "misunderstood and misapplied". According to Major and Fish JJ., Lamer J.'s remarks only applied to cross-examination on evidence that was otherwise inadmissible. In *Howard*, the Crown sought to cross-examine an expert on the significance of an inadmissible guilty plea by a co-accused. There was , held the Supreme Court in *Lyttle*, a "crucial difference" between cross-examination on inadmissible evidence and cross-examination upon unproven facts (para. 61). The Court concluded that, as long as counsel has a good faith basis for the question, cross-examination should be allowed and that no distinction is to be drawn between expert and lay witnesses within the broad scope of this general principle (para. 66).

Lyttle is a decision of enormous import for both civil and criminal trials. In seeking to balance the right to cross-examination and the need for judicial control against abuse by counsel, the Court clearly comes down on the side of favouring full cross-examination. It is of interest that the judgment is authored by two justices with substantial experience as trial counsel.

The Court could have been more forthright in its consideration of *Howard*. The Court essentially overruled *Howard* and should have said so. Justice Lamer's remarks were certainly clear and capable of broad application: see for example Proulx and Layton, *Ethics and Canadian Criminal Law*[274] and decisions referred to by the Supreme Court in *Lyttle*. *Howard* has been responsible for confusion and inconsistency.

Reasonable belief is the long accepted standard for cross-examination in the United Kingdom and was adopted by the B.C. Court of Appeal in *R. v. Wilson*.[275] **Is the *Lyttle* test of "good faith" any different? Will it prove difficult for trial judges to police the good faith standard especially given that it can be based on intuition and counsel may mount claims of privilege?** As a practical matter, most judicial control is still likely to be exercised by relying on the overriding discretion recognised in a line by the Supreme Court in *Lyttle* to exclude evidence where probative force is exceeded by prejudicial value. The Court does not say, as it did in *R. v. Shearing*,[276] that defence evidence should only be excluded where prejudicial effect substantially outweighs its probative value.

R. v. R. (A.J.).
(1994), 94 C.C.C. (3d) 168 (Ont. C.A.)

The accused was convicted of incest with his daughter and granddaughter, sexual assault and threatening. One of his grounds of appeal concerned the prejudicial effect of the cross-examination of the accused conducted by Crown counsel. He alleged Crown counsel had argued with and demeaned the accused in cross-examining him, inserted editorial comment and gave evidence while cross-examining him, called upon the accused to comment on the veracity of Crown witnesses and conducted an improper attack on the accused's character.

---

274 (Toronto: Irwin Law, 2001) at p. 677.
275 (1983), 5 C.C.C. (3d) 61 (B.C. C.A.).
276 (2002), 2 C.R. (6th) 213 (S.C.C.).

DOHERTY J.A. (OSBORNE and LASKIN JJ.A. concurring):—

. . . .

The Cross-examination of the Appellant

Counsel for the appellant submits that Crown counsel's cross-examination of the appellant resulted in a miscarriage of justice. He does not base this contention on any isolated feature of the cross-examination or any specific line of questioning, but contends that the overall conduct and tenor of the cross-examination was so improper and prejudicial to the appellant, that it rendered the trial unfair and resulted in a miscarriage of justice. This argument is becoming a familiar one in this court.

Crown counsel conducted an aggressive and exhaustive 141-page cross-examination of the appellant. She was well prepared and well armed for that cross-examination. Crown counsel is entitled, indeed in some cases expected, to conduct a vigorous cross-examination of an accused. Effective cross-examination of an accused serves the truth-finding function as much as does effective cross-examination of a complainant.

There are, however, well-established limits on cross-examination. Some apply to all witnesses, others only to the accused. Isolated transgressons of those limits may be of little consequence on appeal. Repeated improprieties during the cross-examination of an accused are, however, a very different matter. As the improprieties mount, the cross-examination may cross over the line from the aggressive to the abusive. When that line is crossed, the danger of a miscarriage of justice is very real. If improper cross-examination of an accused prejudices that accused in his defence or is so improper as to bring the administration of justice into disrepute, an appellate court must intervene.

After careful consideration of the entire cross-examination of the appellant in the context of the issues raised by his examination-in-chief and the conduct of the entire trial, I am satisfied that the cross-examination must be characterized as abusive and unfair.

From the outset of the cross-examination, Crown counsel adopted a sarcastic tone with the accused and repeatedly inserted editorial commentary into her questions. I count at least eight such comments in the first eight pages of the cross-examination. During that part of the cross-examination, Crown counsel referred to one answer given by the appellant as "incredible". She repeatedly asked the appellant if he "wanted the jury to believe that one too". When questioned as to how he met T., the appellant said he was told by a friend that a relative would be coming to see him, whereupon Crown counsel remarked "so I guess you were expecting some long lost cousin in the old country". After the appellant had described his reaction to being told by T. that she was his daughter, Crown counsel sarcastically said "gee, I guess everybody would react the way you did".

Crown counsel's approach from the very beginning of the cross-examination was calculated to demean and humiliate the appellant. She persisted in that approach throughout. For example, after the appellant said that he had allowed

T. to move in with him shortly after they had met, Crown counsel said "you are just a really nice guy". At another point, she said, "tell me sir, do fathers usually have sexual intercourse with their daughters". Still later, after the appellant had testified that his girlfriend had left him but had told him that she wished to come back, Crown counsel said "you just have all these women running after you wanting to come back".

These are but a few of a great many instances where Crown counsel used the pretence of questioning the appellant to demonstrate her contempt for him and the evidence he was giving before the jury. No counsel can abuse any witness. This self-evident interdiction applies with particular force to Crown counsel engaged in the cross-examination of an accused.

The tone adopted by Crown counsel is not the only problem with her cross-examination. Crown counsel repeatedly gave evidence and stated her opinion during cross-examination. She also engaged in extensive argument with the appellant. For example, when the appellant gave contradictory explanations in the course of cross-examination, Crown counsel announced "you were lying", and when the appellant questioned Crown counsel's description of T. as "your victim" Crown counsel replied "certainly she is". Still later, after Crown counsel had very effectively cross-examined the appellant as to when he had learned that T. was his daughter, she proclaimed "you are playing games with me, with this jury". She followed that comment with the admonition "let's try and be honest". In several instances, the cross-examination degenerated into pure argument between the appellant and Crown counsel. After one lengthy exchange, Crown counsel announced: "It is hard to keep up with you sir because you keep changing your story".

Statements of counsel's personal opinion have no place in a cross-examination. Nor is cross-examination of the appellant the time or place for argument.

Crown counsel also repeatedly called upon the appellant to comment on the veracity of Crown witnesses and to explain why these witnesses had fabricated their evidence. Crown counsel pursued this line of questioning in relation to at least four Crown witnesses. With respect to some of the witnesses, the questions were repeated at different points in the cross-examination. For example, Crown counsel asked the appellant whether J. had "totally fabricated that evidence" and then asked him "why that little girl totally fabricated that evidence". After Crown counsel had put the appellant in the position of calling four of the Crown witnesses liars, the trial judge intervened and suggested that the questions were improper. Crown counsel returned to that form of questioning on at least one occasion following the trial judge's admonition.

The impropriety of these questions cannot be doubted and Crown counsel in this court acknowledged that they were improper. Crown counsel submitted that although the questions were improper, they caused no prejudice. She observed, quite accurately, that the defence implicitly involved an assertion that the Crown witnesses and, in particular, T., had concocted the allegations against the appellant.

The nature of the defence advanced will impact on the harm, if any, caused by this type of questioning. Despite the defence advanced, I cannot say that the repeated resort to this technique, whereby the appellant was placed in the position of accusing others, did not prejudice him in the eyes of the jury. By means of these improper questions, Crown counsel was able to paint the appellant as a callous accuser ready to charge virtually everyone, including a terrified, emotionally distraught young child, with deliberately fabricating evidence against him. These improper questions also forced the appellant to offer explanations for the allegedly false testimony offered by the Crown witnesses. In the case of J. and T., the explanations only served to open further fertile grounds for cross-examination.

I am also driven to the conclusion that at many points in the cross-examination, Crown counsel conducted what amounted to an improper and potentially prejudicial attack on the appellant's character and lifestyle. Given the allegations, it was inevitable and essential that the jury learn something of the appellant's sordid lifestyle and character to assess the charges before them properly. The appellant's decision to testify also meant that his lengthy criminal record would be placed before the jury. These conditions created a real danger that the jury could convict based on their assessment of the appellant as a despicable and evil man, rather than on a finding that the Crown had proven any or all of the charges beyond a reasonable doubt. Crown counsel's cross-examination significantly increased this danger.

There are numerous instances in the cross-examination when the questions went beyond the bounds of relevancy and legitimate credibility impeachment and became an attempt to highlight the appellant's bad character and deviant lifestyle. The appellant was cross-examined about whether he had filed income tax returns. He was also questioned about the criminal records of his associates and about his attitudes, as "a former drug dealer", to T.'s use of prescription pills. Still later, Crown counsel asked the appellant about his respect "for the law and court orders". Crown counsel also cross-examined the appellant to show that he was sexually promiscuous and had no sense of responsibility to any of the women with whom he had been involved during his lifetime. At another point in the cross-examination, she referred to the appellant as "a jailhouse lawyer".

The appellant was also cross-examined about the paternity of C., T.'s young son. He denied that he was the father. Crown counsel then gave evidence to the effect that C. could not be adopted because it was believed that he was the product of an incestuous relationship. She then asked the appellant why he did not submit to a blood test so that the question of C.'s paternity could be cleared up and C. could become eligible for adoption. None of this had anything to do with the allegations against the appellant and could only serve to inflame the jury further against the appellant. Defence counsel at trial objected to the question on the basis that it had no evidentiary foundation. The trial judge upheld the objection on the basis of relevancy, however, Crown counsel persisted, asking:

> If you knew you weren't the father of this child, why didn't you ask to take a blood test to show you weren't?

Cross-examination on this issue continued for several more questions. I can see only one purpose to these questions. Crown counsel wanted to demonstrate that the appellant did not have the decency to take the steps necessary to make C. eligible for adoption.

Defence counsel (not Mr. Campbell) did, at a recess, suggest that some of Crown counsel's questions were bringing out "discreditable conduct not covered by the indictment". He referred specifically to the questions about the income tax returns. Crown counsel responded that counsel should object when the questions were asked "not some two hours later". The trial judge made no ruling and when the jury returned Crown counsel continued her cross-examination in the same manner. Crown counsel also asked the appellant on more than one occasion about conversations he had had with his lawyer. These questions were improper in that they invited the appellant to disclose privileged communications or risk appearing non-responsive to the questions. The questions were also totally irrelevant. Defence counsel did eventually object to this type of questioning and Crown counsel did not pursue it. Crown counsel did, however, continue to ask the appellant questions about whether he intended to call certain persons as witnesses. Crown counsel would know full well that such decisions were for counsel and not the appellant. It was unfair to ask the appellant questions which Crown counsel knew he could not answer.

It must be acknowledged that the appellant was a difficult witness and to some extent contributed to the tone of the cross-examination through his own attitude and refusal on several occasions to answer directly the questions put to him. The vast majority of what I have characterized as improper cross-examination was not objected to at trial. Both of these considerations are relevant when deciding the propriety and potential prejudicial effect of a cross-examination. The failure of counsel to object does not, however, give Crown counsel carte blanche at trial or immunize the cross-examination from appellate scrutiny.

Cases like this, where the allegations are particularly sordid, the complainants particularly sympathetic and the accused particularly disreputable, provide a severe test of our criminal justice system. It is very difficult in such cases to hold the scales of justice in balance and to provide the accused with the fair trial to which he or she is entitled. By her cross-examination, Crown counsel skewed that delicate balance. The cross-examination, considered in its totality and in the context of the entire trial, prejudiced the appellant in his defence and significantly undermined the appearance of the fairness of the trial.

. . . .

The cross-examination destroyed the necessary appearance of fairness in the trial and resulted in a miscarriage of justice. The strength of the Crown's case becomes irrelevant in determining the appropriate disposition and s. 686(1)(b)(iii) has no application. The miscarriage of justice lies in the conduct of the proceedings and not in the verdict arrived at by the jury. All of the convictions must be set aside and a new trial ordered on all of those charges.

(f) Duty to Cross-examine (Rule in *Browne v. Dunn*)

Aside from counsel's right to cross-examine there may at times be a duty to cross-examine.

R. v. McNEILL
(2000), 33 C.R. (5th) 390, 144 C.C.C. (3d) 551 (Ont. C.A.)

The accused was charged with numerous offences arising out of an alleged abduction of one C. One of people involved in the abduction, B, testified as Crown witness that he was retained by the accused to collect a drug debt from the victim, that he and the accused went to the victim's motel room for that purpose. The appellant testified and denied any involvement in the abduction.

MOLDAVER J.A. (McMURTRY C.J.O., and GOUDGE J.A. concurring): —

. . . .

Cross-examination of the Appellant on Defence Counsel's Failure to Pose Specific Questions to the Crown witness Bonello

In his examination-in-chief of the appellant, defence counsel asked whether the appellant had spoken to Bonello after the Cudney incident. The appellant answered in the affirmative and the following series of questions and answers ensued, without objection from Crown counsel:

Q.   And what did Mr. Bonello say about it?

A.   I was — I was probably a little aggressive with him at first, and he became aggressive right back saying that . . . you know . . . I told him that Bob Cudney — you did this for me; and he said: No, no, no, no. This was done for "killer". It had nothing to do with you.

Q.   For who?

A.   "Killer". I know that sounds a little bit cliché, but . . . as you heard other people testify . . . this is actually somebody's name.

Q.   Did you force the issue with Bonello?

A.   I wouldn't force any issue with Bonello. He just told me that it was Cud — or "killer's" beef and it had nothing to do with me.

For reasons unknown, defence counsel did not question Bonello about this conversation. He was obliged to do so under s. 11 of the Canada Evidence Act, R.S.C. 1985, c. C-5, if it was his intention to lead evidence of a prior statement inconsistent with Bonello's testimony. Had Crown counsel raised the appropriate objection, it would have been for the trial judge to decide whether the appellant should be permitted to testify about the purported conversation (see *R. v. P. (G.)* (1996), 112 C.C.C. (3d) 263 at pp. 278-87 (Ont. C.A.)).

Defence counsel's failure to question Bonello about the conversation did not go unnoticed by the Crown. No doubt, she was concerned that Bonello had not been given the opportunity to confirm, deny or explain it. To the extent she felt the matter was worth pursuing, in my view, the proper procedure would have been to raise the issue with the trial judge in the absence of the jury. That way, the trial judge could have determined whether her concern was valid and if so, what steps should be taken to remedy the situation. Regrettably, Crown counsel did not pursue this course. Instead, she chose to confront the appellant with the fact that defence counsel had not questioned Bonello about the purported conversation either at the preliminary hearing or at trial:

> Q.   The gentlemen that you named . . . that you said Bonello named as having been the whole cause of the Cudney incident; you said his name was "killer"?
>
> A.   He said it was "killer's gig", that he was involved with Cudney over, not me; "killer's gig".
>
> Q.   You were present at the preliminary hearing as well as at the trial of this matter, isn't that true?
>
> A.   Absolutely.
>
> Q.   You never heard Mr. Bolnello asked if it was "killer's gig" did you?
>
> A.   I never heard him . . . ?
>
> Q.   Anybody ask Bonello anything about "killer's gig", or if he said that to you?
>
> A.   No. I believe "killer" was mentioned somewhere in this. I think by Bob Cudney. I don't believe Bonello ever used his name. He may have but I don't recall off the top of my head.
>
> Q.   That was my point sir. You're telling us about a conversation that you had with Mr. Bonello, but no one ever suggested to Bonello that that conversation occurred, correct?

In my view, this line of questioning was improper because it was capable of leaving the jury with the impression that the appellant should be held responsible for what may have been a tactical decision or mere oversight on the part of defence counsel. As explained, defence counsel's failure to question Bonello about the purported conversation involved a breach of s. 11 of the Canada Evidence Act. That, however, is not the way the issue was presented to us. Rather, it was framed as a breach of the rule in *Browne v. Dunn* (1893), 6 R. 67 (H.L.). Accordingly, I propose to address that rule, primarily with a view to considering the options available when it is breached.

The rule in *Browne v. Dunn* was succinctly stated by Labrosse J.A. in *R. v. Henderson, supra*:

> This well-known rule stands for the proposition that if counsel is going to challenge the credibility of a witness by calling contradictory evidence, the witness must be given the chance to address the contradictory evidence in cross-examination while he or she is in the witness-box.

In *R. v. Verney* (1993), 87 C.C.C. (3d) 363 at p. 376 (Ont. C.A.), Finlayson J.A. outlined the purpose and ambit of the rule:

> *Browne v. Dunn* is a rule of fairness that prevents the "ambush" of a witness by not giving him an opportunity to state his position with respect to later evidence which contradicts him on an essential matter. It is not, however, an absolute rule and

counsel must not feel obliged to slog through a witness's evidence-in-chief, putting him on notice of every detail that the defence does not accept. Defence counsel must be free to use his own judgment about how to cross-examine a hostile witness. Having the witness repeat in cross-examination, everything he said in chief, is rarely the tactic of choice. For a fuller discussion on this point, see *Palmer and Palmer v. The Queen* (1979), 50 C.C.C. (2d) 193 at pp. 209-10, [1980] 1 S.C.R. 759, 14 C.R. (3d) 22 (S.C.C.).

While these decisions explain the rule and its underlying purpose, they do not address the options available to a party who feels aggrieved by the failure of his or her opponent to adhere to it. To that end, I offer these suggestions. In cases such as this, where the concern lies in a witness's inability to present his or her side of the story, it seems to me that the first option worth exploring is whether the witness is available for recall. If so, then assuming the trial judge is otherwise satisfied, after weighing the pros and cons, that recall is appropriate, the aggrieved party can either take up the opportunity or decline it. If the opportunity is declined, then, in my view, no special instruction to the jury is required beyond the normal instruction that the jury is entitled to believe all, part or none of a witness's evidence, regardless of whether the evidence is uncontradicted.

The mechanics of when the witness should be recalled and by whom should be left to the discretion of the trial judge.

In those cases where it is impossible or highly impracticable to have the witness recalled or where the trial judge otherwise determines that recall is inappropriate, it should be left to the trial judge to decide whether a special instruction should be given to the jury. If one is warranted, the jury should be told that in assessing the weight to be given to the uncontradicted evidence, they may properly take into account the fact that the opposing witness was not questioned about it. The jury should also be told that they may take this into account in assessing the credibility of the opposing witness. Depending on the circumstances, there may be other permissible ways of rectifying the problem. The two options that I have mentioned are not meant to be exhaustive. As a rule, however, I am of the view that they will generally prove to be the fairest and most effective solutions.

Returning to the issue at hand, Ms. Fairburn does not attempt to justify the impugned line of questioning. Instead, she submits that the trial judge's instructions to the jury were sufficient to overcome any prejudice occasioned to the appellant. The trial judge dealt with this issue in generalterms as follows:

> The procedure of cross-examination is a procedure I regard as one of fairness; a rule of professional practice. It is applicable where it is intended to suggest the witness is not speaking the truth on a particular point. The question, by the suggestion made, often sets the stage, as I have tried to indicate, for defence evidence to be led in support of the suggestion. If put to a witness in cross-examination, the witness has the opportunity to explain. If not put to the witness in cross-examination, but put later to other witnesses, the suggestion is then perhaps impossible to explain, and triers of fact can be left with the inference that the witness's story is untrue and the witness unworthy of credit . . . believability.

There is therefore the practice of cross-examining counsel to put to the witness all significant matters upon which they seek to contradict. I emphasize the words "all significant matters", as some matters may be so obvious as not to be of significance, and likewise some matters may be so insignificant or interrelated with other matters so as not to require a singling out, and the use of time that might be involved in that singling out.

It is for you to decide if there were any significant matters upon which crown witnesses were not cross-examined, which matters were put forward by other witnesses with a view to suggesting the particular crown witness was not worthy of belief. It is for you to decide if there were any such lapses or failure to cross-examine, and if so, what weight to be given to the particular evidence to be called for which there was no opportunity to explain.

In my view, these instructions were deficient in two respects. First, to the extent the jury understood them to relate to defence counsel's failure to question Bonello about the purported conversation, the trial judge left the jury with the impression that Bonello (and inferentially the Crown), was left in the impossible position of being unable to explain the conversation. With respect, that was both inaccurate and misleading. Had Crown counsel wished to have Bonello's explanation before the jury, she could have sought permission to have him recalled. There was nothing to suggest that Bonello was unavailable or that his recall would have posed any difficulty. As it is, she made no effort to do so. Accordingly, it was wrong to leave the jury with the impression that defence counsel's failure to question Bonello rendered it impossible for him to offer an explanation.

Second, although the jury was instructed on the use that could be made of defence counsel's failure to question Bonello, they were not told that the appellant should not be held responsible for what may have been a tactical decision or mere oversight on the part of his counsel.

The existence of the *Browne v. Dunn* issue was recognized by the Supreme Court in *Lyttle*. The Court decided it did not arise for decision in that case.

In recent years it has been increasingly clear that Canadian judges have wide discretion as to how to apply the so-called rule in *Browne v. Dunn*. There is now significant agreement that its application in criminal trials is a matter of discretion for trial judges. There is consensus that its application should be reserved for serious matters and that discretionary remedies include the possibility of recall (see Moldaver J.A. in *McNeill*, above) and careful judicial direction, although the courts emphasise there is no hard and fast legal rule.[277] As to judicial direction, Justice Borins, speaking for the Ontario Court of Appeal, in *R. v. Marshall*,[278] confirmed that this should not be in the nature of a special

---

277 See *R. v. Giroux* (2006), 207 C.C.C. (3d) 512 (Ont. C.A.) at 529 and *R. v. Carter*, (2005) 32 C.R. (6th) 1 (B.C. C.A.).

278 (2005), 201 O.A.C. 154, 200 C.C.C. (3d) 179 (Ont. C.A.).

instruction, should not invite the drawing of an adverse inference nor should it involve comments on counsel deficiencies. According to Borins J.A.:

> I think much of the detail in the judge's charge should have been limited to a simple direction that the failure to cross- examine...on the matters in issue could be considered in weighing the [accused's] evidence and did not necessitate an adverse inference in respect of the [accused's] testimony.[279]

Some courts have voiced concern that the rule's application in criminal trials may unduly jeopardise the presumption of innocence. In *R. v. Carter*,[280] the Court ordered a new trial where the trial judge did not attempt to rectify the Crown's error in asking the jury to draw an adverse inference against the defence for not properly confronting the complainants. The Court left open the question of whether such an error could ever be cured by a judge's direction. Judge Allen of the Alberta Provincial Court in *R. v. Melnick*[281] went further. He broke new ground in deciding that although there was a failure to confront on a significant matter, the breach was not so egregious as to require any judicial response. It may be that it is time for our courts to abandon a contentious rule derived from a civil case in the House of Lords more than a century ago.

A high profile context to consider the rule in *Browne v. Dunn* and the collateral fact rule is the 1995 O.J. Simpson case. One of the theories of the defence was that the lead detective planted the "bloody glove" at Simpson's estate. The defence suggested that he was motivated to do so by a racist intent. F. Lee Bailey pointedly asked Detective Fuhrman whether he had ever used the "n" word to describe African-Americans. He answered that he had never used the word in the past 10 years. The defence then called Laura McKinney, an aspiring screenwriter, who had interviewed Fuhrman for her screenplay about female police officers. In an audio-taped conversation, Fuhrman repeatedly used the "n" word and bragged about beating and torturing African-Americans. When Fuhrman was later asked at the trial whether he had planted or manufactured evidence in the Simpson case, he invoked his privilege against self-incrimination. **Did *Browne v. Dunn* require these questions be put to Fuhrman? Assuming the questions were not asked, would a judicial comment on the fact that the defence did not ask Fuhrman really add anything of value? Was the question about his use of the "n" word a collateral issue?**

(g) Collateral Facts Rule

Counsel is entitled in cross-examination to ask questions about matters relevant to the material issues in the case but is also entitled to ask questions about other matters that may be relevant to the witness's credibility. These questions are subject only to the discretion of the trial judge, who will take into account such considerations as time and fairness to the witness. The common law decided that considerations of economy of time, the danger of confusing the issues before the jury, and fairness to the witness who came prepared to testify

---

279 Para. 67.
280 (2005), 32 C.R. (6th) 1, 199 C.C.C. (3d) 74 (B.C. C.A.).
281 (2005), 32 C.R. (6th) 18 (Alta. Prov. Ct).

to matters framed by the suit, demanded a rule which obliged the cross-examiner to be content with answers given to collateral matters.

The "collateral facts rule" is simple to state but often difficult in its application. The rule forbids the introduction of extrinsic evidence which contradicts a witness's testimonial assertion about collateral facts. A witness is summoned to court to testify concerning the material facts involved in the suit. In cross-examination the witness may be asked questions concerning the description given in chief, and may also be asked questions that impact solely on the witness's credibility. If the questions regarding credibility are collateral, the cross-examiner must accept the answers given, and cannot lead other witnesses to contradict the first witness on such matters.

The rule is difficult in its application because of the difficulty in determining what is "collateral". The *Hitchcock* case is the classic exposition.

In *Attorney General v. Hitchcock* [282] the defendant was tried for a violation of the revenue laws. The Crown witness, who had testified to having observed the violation, was asked in cross-examination whether he had not earlier made a statement that the officers of the Crown had offered him a bribe to give that evidence. The witness denied having said so and defense counsel proposed to call another witness to testify that in fact such a statement was made.

An objection that such evidence was *collateral* and the witness could not thereby be contradicted was allowed and the evidence excluded. It was held that the ruling at trial was correct. Had the evidence been that the witness had made a statement that he had *accepted* a bribe the ruling would have been different as that would have reflected the possibility of bias. The Court saw testimonial factors, bias, interest, corruption, capacity to observe and remember and so forth, as matters "directly in issue before the Court" on which the witness may then be contradicted. Evidence of such matters are proveable independently of the contradiction; they have relevance apart from the simple fact of contradiction. There are then *two* classes of facts which are not collateral: facts which are relevant to a material issue, and facts relevant to a testimonial factor.[283]

Baron Rolfe explained:

> If we lived for a thousand years instead of about sixty or seventy, and every case were of sufficient importance, it might be possible, and perhaps proper, to throw a light on matters in which every possible question might be suggested, for the purpose of seeing by such means whether the whole was unfounded, or what portion of it was not, and to raise every possible inquiry as to the truth of the statements made. But I do not see how that could be; in fact, mankind find it to be impossible. Therefore some line must be drawn.[284]

---

282 (1847), 154 E.R. 38 (Exch. Ct.).

283 See 3A Wigmore, *Evidence* (Chad. Rev.), ss. 1004-05, and see *R. v. Shewfelt* (1972), 6 C.C.C. (2d) 304 (B.C.C.A.). Compare another approach to the collateral facts rule which renders all facts collateral which are not relevant to a material issue but recognizes exceptions for bias, interest, etc., see Sopinka and Lederman, *The Law of Evidence in Civil Cases* (1974), pp. 511 and 289, following the lead of Phipson, *Evidence*, 11th ed., pp. 660-61.

284 *Supra*, note 282, at pp. 44-45.

R. v. KRAUSE
[1986] 2 S.C.R. 466, 54 C.R. (3d) 294, 29 C.C.C. (3d) 385

Accused was questioned by police about a fatal stabbing and charged with murder. At the trial, on a *voir dire*, the answers of the appellant were held to be voluntary. The Crown made it clear that it did not intend to adduce the questions and answers in evidence-in-chief but that it would use them in cross-examination if the need arose. When appellant testified on his own behalf he gave evidence not only with respect to the circumstances surrounding the murder but also with respect of his involvement with the police during the murder investigation. Crown counsel cross-examined appellant about his statements to police and applied to call rebuttal evidence at the end of the defence case. The rebuttal evidence was to impeach the credit of appellant.

McIntyre J. (Dickson, C.J. and Beetz, Chouinard, Lamer, Wilson and Le Dain JJ. concurring): —

. . . .

The appellant, in addition to giving the evidence summarized earlier, also gave evidence of his involvement with the police during the investigation of the murder. The points of significance for our purposes in this case may be summarized, as follows:

He swore that:

1. It seemed to be a regular thing for the police to come. . . .

2. The police had suggested to him that if he did not tell them where he had sent Hutter to look for marijuana, they were going to "kick in the doors" of known drug dealers and tell them that the appellant sent Hutter there looking for marijuana.

3. The police showed him a photograph of the deceased when they first interviewed him on March 26, 1981.

4. He had not told the police officers that he had never dealt with Hutter in a dope deal, but rather that the statement was taken out of context and that he had told them that he had never dealt with Hutter prior to January, 1981.

In cross-examination the appellant was questioned extensively regarding his statements to the police. It was put to him that he had told the officers that he had never dealt with Hutter in a dope deal when he had told him where to go.. . . .Crown counsel in cross-examining an accused are not limited to subjects which are strictly relevant to the essential issues in a case. Counsel are accorded a wide freedom in cross-examination which enable them to test and question the testimony of the witnesses and their credibility. Where something new emerges in cross-examination, which is new in the sense that the Crown had no chance to deal with it in its case-in-chief (i.e., there was no reason for the Crown to anticipate that the matter would arise), and where the matter is concerned with the merits of the case (i.e., it concerns an issue essential for the determination of the case) then the Crown may be allowed to call evidence in rebuttal. Where, however, the new matter is collateral, that is, not determinative of an issue arising in the pleadings or indictment or not relevant to matters which must be proved for the determination of the case, no rebuttal will be allowed. An early expression of this proposition is to be found in *Attorney-General v. Hitchcock*, [1847] 1 Ex. 91, 154 E.R. 38, and examples of the application of the principle may be found in *R. v. Cargill*, [1913] 2 K.B. 271 (Ct. Crim. App*.); R. v. Hrechuk* (1951), 58 Man. R. 489 (C.A.); *R. v. Rafael* [1972] 3 O.R. 238 (Ont. C.A.); and *Latour v. The Queen*, [1978] 1 S.C.R. 361. This is known as the rule against rebuttal on collateral issues. Where it applies, Crown counsel may cross-examine the accused on the matters raised, but the Crown is bound by the answers given. This is not to say that the Crown or the trier of fact is bound to accept the answers as true. The answer is binding or final only in the sense that rebuttal evidence may not be called in contradiction. It follows then that the principal issue which arises on this branch of the case is whether the issues arising out of items 1, 2 and 3 are collateral in the sense described or relevant as going to a determinative issue in the case.

. . . .

There was one principal issue raised in this case, that is, did the appellant kill Hutter or did he not. Evidence bearing on that issue would be clearly material and admissible and in no way collateral. The evidence in respect of which rebuttal was allowed dealt in item 1 with the appellant's assertion that the police harassed him before his arrest. He said it seemed to be a regular thing for the police to come and "grab' him and take him down to the station. Item 2 dealt with further harassing and intimidating conduct on the part of the police, an alleged threat to put pressure on other drug dealers, telling them that the appellant had sent Hutter to them to get marijuana. Item 3 dealt with an allegation that during the course of the investigation the police had shown the appellant a gory photograph of Hutter's body. Were the points so raised material and relevant in deciding the issue — did the appellant kill Hutter?

. . . .

The evidence of the appellant reflected on the integrity of the police — though not on that of any police witness who gave evidence as part of the Crown's case-in-chief — but it did not touch upon the question of guilt or innocence. I am unable to say that the rebuttal evidence, which merely answered allegations made by the appellant and did not touch questions relating to his guilt or innocence, was relevant on that issue. The fact that evidence is introduced by the defence-in-chief does not make it a proper subject for rebuttal evidence unless it is otherwise relevant to a matter other than credibility: see *Cargill, supra*, and *Hretchuk, supra*. In my view, in agreement with Anderson J.A. in his dissent, the issues made the subject of rebuttal were collateral, as being neither material nor relevant on the issue of guilt or innocence. The Crown was entitled to cross-examine and did cross-examine the appellant on this matter. The Crown, however, was bound by the answers and was not entitled to call evidence in rebuttal.

_____

According to Professor McCormick:

> The classical approach is that facts which would have been independently provable regardless of the contradiction are not "collateral".[285]

McCormick goes on to describe three kinds of facts which meet this test. The first kind of facts which are independently provable are facts relevant to the substantive issues in the case. The second kind are not relevant to the substantive issues but are independently provable by extrinsic evidence to impeach the witness; among these facts are facts showing a bias or interest in the witness. The third kind of facts with respect to which the witness might be contradicted are facts about which the witness could not have been mistaken if he really saw what he claims to have seen; contradicting such a fact would "pull out the linchpin of the story."

Another approach is that of Professor Younger:

> We struggled with the problem in law school; we read an English case called Attorney General Hitchcock. You may not recall it because you may not have understood it. If you went back and read it today, you would not understand it. If you read it every day of your life until you die, you would not understand it; there is no meaning to it. The case is important only because it states what seems to be the prevailing rule with respect to the collateral/not collateral distinction: if the witness denies the prior inconsistent statement, the issue may or may not be collateral. Sometimes you may call another witness to prove the prior statement; sometimes you will not be able to call him. The real question is, when will it be collateral, and when will it not be collateral? The answer is simple: when it is important, it is not collateral. When it is unimportant, it is collateral. Ten thousand cases add up to that.[286]

When judges use the word "collateral" or the "collateral facts rule" this may be historical jargon for a ruling that the evidence is irrelevant or to be excluded under the discretion to exclude where the probative value is found to be exceeded by the prejudicial effect on the fact-finding process. Consider the use of "collateral" in the following case.

R. v. CASSIBO
(1982), 70 C.C.C. (2d) 498 (Ont. C.A.)

After trial by judge alone, the accused was convicted on four counts of incest. One of the grounds of appeal was whether there had been improper curtailment of the cross-examination of the complainants with respect to whether they had read a certain article on incest in a magazine.

MARTIN J.A:—

Another ground of appeal . . . on which we did not require argument from Crown counsel was that the trial judge had improperly curtailed cross-examination of the complainants with respect to whether they had read a certain article in a magazine on the ground that the cross-examination related to a collateral matter.

_____

285 McCormick, *Evidence*, 3d ed., p. 110.
286 *The Art of Cross-Examination* (1976).

Rosetta was asked in a cross-examination whether she had read in magazines about fathers having sexual relations with their daughters and she testified that she had not. She was then shown a magazine entitled "True Experience" being the November 1978 . . . issue containing a story captioned "My Daughter's Lies Sent My Husband to Prison!". She said that it probably belonged to her parents but she did not remember seeing it. The trial judge interjected, observing that surely this was cross-examination with respect to a collateral matter. He, nevertheless, permitted defence counsel to introduce the magazine as an exhibit. Darlene, in cross-examination, said that she did not remember seeing the magazine. In cross-examination, the mother of the girls, Elsie Cassibo, testified that she found the magazine in Darlene's bedroom after Darlene had left the family residence.

. . . .

Even if the cross-examination of Rosetta and Darlene with respect to the contents of the magazine related to a collateral matter, counsel is entitled to cross-examine a witness called by the opposite party with respect to collateral matters on the issue of credibility, but, as a general rule, cannot contradict the answers of the witness with respect to collateral matters by the evidence of other witnesses. The cross-examination with respect to whether Rosetta and Darlene had read the article in the magazine did not, however, relate to a collateral matter. The purpose of the cross-examination was to endeavour to show that they had fabricated their testimony with respect to their allegations against the appellant. The cross-examination accordingly did not relate to a collateral matter but related to the truthfulness of their testimony on the very issue before the court. . . . In the result, however, I do not believe that any prejudice was suffered by the appellant since defence counsel was permitted to cross-examine Rosetta and Darlene as to whether they had read the magazine and to elicit from Mrs. Cassibo that she had discovered the magazine in Darlene's room.

Sometimes, but not always, the evidence that counsel wishes to use to contradict amounts to proof of a statement by the witness that is inconsistent with their present testimony. Proof of previous inconsistent statements, we will see, is subject to the collateral facts rule.

PROBLEMS

Problem 1

In a civil suit for damages the plaintiff's witness has described the motor vehicle accident, which he attributed to the fault of defendant, and is now being cross-examined:

Q.:   Sir, you've testified that you observed this accident which occurred on July 12, 1987. Can you tell us how you happened to be at that location?

A.:   Well, yes, as a matter of fact. The accident occurred near the Exhibition Stadium and I was on my way to see a ball game there.

Q.:	Who was playing?
A.:	The Blue Jays and the Red Sox.
Q.:	And this was on July 12, 1987.
A.:	Yes.
Q.:	You're sure about that.
A.:	I'm sure.
Q.:	You're as sure about it as you are about all the rest of your evidence.
A.:	Yes, I am!
Q.:	Would it surprise you to know that on July 12, 1987, the Jays were in the middle of a road trip to the West Coast and that night they were playing a game in Seattle?
A:	It would surprise me very much. I'm certain the Jays were at Exhibition Stadium that night.
Q:	You're right about everything.
A:	This time I am. I saw the accident, your client was at fault and the Jays were in Toronto.
Counsel:	Your honour, I have no more questions of this witness. I do feel obliged to alert the Court and my friend that in presenting my client's case I intend to call evidence that on the evening in question the Toronto Blue Jays were in Seattle.
Counsel for Plaintiff:	Your honour, our position is that this matter of where the Blue Jays were playing is collateral to the real issue between the parties, which is who was at fault in the accident. Being collateral the rules of evidence preclude the calling of contradictory evidence. My friend must take the answer of the witness and live with it.

What is your ruling?

Problem 2

The accused was charged with fraud in connection with the operation of a travel agency. The accused gave evidence and was asked in cross-examination whether he had filed income tax returns over a period of years. The accused stated that he had done so except for two or three years when his books were under seizure by Crown authorities. The Crown proposes to call evidence to establish that the accused has not filed any income tax returns for a period of some ten years. The accused objects. Rule on the objection. See *R. v. Rafael* (1972), 7 C.C.C. (2d) 325 (Ont. C.A.). Would it affect your ruling if the accused's evidence had come out in examination-in-chief?

(h) Examination by Court and Order of Witnesses

The Court has, apparently, no power, of its own motion and without the consent of both parties, to direct further evidence to be given: . . . The parties, and not the Court, are *domini litis* in all civil proceedings. If a party comes into Court with an imperfect case, the proper penalty is dismissal.[287]

---

287 *Re Fraser* (1912), 26 O.L.R. 508, 521 (C.A.).

In a civil case the court has no power to call a witness,[288] but it may do so in a criminal case when it is seen as necessary in the interests of justice.[289] Apparently the interest of the state in securing truth in criminal matters, where the liberty of the subject is at stake, accounts for the difference; in civil trials, while truth is important, justice, in the sense that both litigants feel satisfied that *their* dispute, framed by *them,* was properly settled, is paramount. The power of the court to call witnesses in criminal cases is limited when the defence has closed its case. The prosecution is not entitled to split its case and therefore cannot call further witnesses after the defence has closed its case unless a matter has arisen *ex improviso*, which no human ingenuity could have foreseen.[290] It was seen to be wise to impose the same limitation on the judge's right to call witnesses to avoid injustice to the accused.[291]

In *Cook*[292] the accused had been convicted of assault causing bodily harm. The conviction had been based on the evidence of the complainant's girlfriend. The Crown did not call the complainant. The New Brunswick Court of Appeal held that the accused had a right to face his accuser. L'Heureux-Dubé J., speaking for the Supreme Court, disagreed. There was no duty upon the Crown to call witnesses, nor a more specific duty to call the complainant. How the case was presented by the Crown should be left to the Crown, absent proof of abuse in the exercise of discretion. The trial judge had also not erred in failing to call the witness himself. That discretion, held the Court, should only be exercised rarely and with extreme caution.[293]

Both in civil and criminal cases the court has the right to ask questions to clarify matters and to interrupt if it feels the witness does not understand. In exercising this right the court must be extremely cautious as it does not know as much about the case as does counsel and interference can have the opposite effect of that intended. In a now-famous dictum, Lord Denning has observed:[294]

---

288 See also *Fowler v. Fowler*, [1949] O.W.N. 244 (C.A.).

289 See cases collected in Newark and Samuels, "Let the Judge Call the Witness," [1969] Crim. L. Rev. 399. And see *R. v. Bouchard* (1973), 12 C.C.C. (2d) 554 (N.S. Co. Ct.), criticized in Stenning, "One Blind Man to See Fair Play: The Judge's Right to Call Witnesses" (1973), 24 C.R.N.S. 49. See also *R. v. Brouillard*, [1985] 1 S.C.R. 39; *R. v. Roberts* (1984), 80 Cr. App. R. 89 (C.A.); and *R. v. MacPhee* (1985), 19 C.C.C. (3d) 345 (Alta. Q.B.).

290 See *R. v. P. (M.B.)* (1994), 29 C.R. (4th) 209 (S.C.C.), where the court held it to be error to allow the Crown to reopen its case and recall witnesses after the accused had signalled he would be calling an alibi witness.

291 See *R. v. Harris*, [1927] 2 K.B. 587, 594 (C.C.A.). See also *R. v. Cleghorn*, [1967] 2 Q.B. 584 (C.A.) and *R. v. Morin* (1977), 40 C.R.N.S. 378 (Sask. Dist. Ct.). With respect to the Crown improperly splitting its case, see *John v. R.* (1985), 49 C.R. (3d) 57 (S.C.C.); *R. v. Krause* (1986), 54 C.R. (3d) 294 (S.C.C.) and *R. v. Scott* (1984), 79 Cr. App. R. 49 (C.A.). With respect to proper rebuttal see *R. v. Wood* (1986), 28 C.C.C. (3d) 65 (Ont. C.A.) and *R. v. Wagner* (1986), 50 C.R. (3d) 175 (Alta. C.A.). Regarding re-examination and re-cross-examination see *R. v. Tremblay* (1984), 17 C.C.C. (3d) 359 (Que. C.A.) and *R. v. Rochester* (1984), 13 C.C.C. (3d) 215 (Ont. Co. Ct.).

292 (1997), 1997 CarswellNB 125, 7 C.R. (5th) 51 (S.C.C.).

293 See also Lynn Iding, "Crossing the Line: The Case for Limiting Personal Cross-Examination by an Accused in Sexual Assault Trials" (2004), 49 *Crim. L.Q,* 69.

294 *Jones v. Nat. Coal Bd.*, [1957] 2 Q.B. 55, 63 (C.A.). For an example of descending into the arena see *R. v. Rhodes* (1981), 59 C.C.C. (2d) 426 (B.C.C.A.).

No one can doubt that the judge, in intervening as he did, was actuated by the best motives. He was anxious to understand the details of this complicated case, and asked questions to get them clear in his mind. He was anxious that the witnesses should not be harassed unduly in cross-examination, and intervened to protect them when he thought necessary. He was anxious to investigate all the various criticisms that had been made against the board, and to see whether they were well founded or not. Hence, he took them up himself with the witnesses from time to time. He was anxious that the case should not be dragged on too long, and intimated clearly when he thought that a point had been sufficiently explored. All those are worthy motives on which judges daily intervene in the conduct of cases, and have done for centuries.

Nevertheless, we are quite clear that the interventions, taken together, were far more than they should have been. In the system of trial which we have evolved in this country, the judge sits to hear and determine the issues raised by the parties, not to conduct an investigation or examination on behalf of society at large, as happens, we believe, in some foreign countries. Even in England, however, a judge is not a mere umpire to answer the question "How's that?" His object, above all, is to find out the truth, and to do justice according to law; and in the daily pursuit of it the advocate plays an honorable and necessary role. Was it not Lord Eldon L.C. who said in a notable passage that truth is best discovered by powerful "statements on both sides of the question"?: see *Ex parte Lloyd.* And Lord Greene M.R. who explained that justice is best done by a judge who holds the balance between the contending parties without himself taking part in their disputations? If a judge, said Lord Greene, should himself conduct the examination of witnesses, "he, so to speak, descends into the arena and is liable to have his vision clouded by the dust of conflict".

And in Ontario, Evans J.A. explained:

There is unquestionably a right to intervene for the purpose of clarification of the evidence, and when the case is highly technical the interventions may be more frequent. No doubt the trial Judge was actuated by the highest motives, but his zealous participation, irrespective of motive, unfortunately caused him to transgress and he lost sight of the issues raised by the parties and launched into an investigation on behalf of Canadian motorists.[295]

While the judge in criminal cases in Canada has no control over the order in which the accused calls his witnesses,[296] many provinces in Canada have enacted in rules of court governing civil cases a power in the court to require that the party be examined before other witnesses on his behalf.[297] Similarly, these rules permit the court to order the exclusion of prospective witnesses until required to give evidence, whether the witness is a party or not.[298] In criminal cases as well the court has an inherent authority to order the exclusion of witnesses but since the accused has the right to be present at his trial the exclusion order may not refer to him. If the accused does not testify first and so gains the advantage of listening to his witnesses being examined and cross-examined before going into the witness stand himself he risks a comment being made on his credibility.

---

295 *Phillips v. Ford Motor Co.* (1971), 18 D.L.R. (3d) 641, 663 (Ont. C.A.).
296 See *R. v. Smuk* (1971), 3 C.C.C. (2d) 457 (B.C.C.A.) and *R. v. Angelantoni* (1975), 31 C.R.N.S. 342 (Ont. C.A.).
297 See, *e.g.*, Ontario Rule 52.06(2).
298 *Ibid.*

R. v. P. (T.L.)
(1996), 193 A.R. 146 (Alta. C.A.)

The accused was convicted of robbery. She had called witnesses at the trial to established an alibi. The defence called the accused as its last witness and she denied any involvement in the robbery. The trial judge commented before the accused's cross-examination that her evidence would be given very little weight since all the other evidence in the case had been heard by the accused. A new trial was ordered.

O'LEARY J.A. (CONRAD and KENNY JJ.A. concurring):—

. . . .

There are two aspects of the trial which cause us concern about the manner in which the trial judge assessed the credibility of the witnesses and the evidence. The first arises from comments made by the trial judge after the appellant had been examined-in-chief but before she was cross-examined. After referring to the fact that the appellant had been called as the last defence witness, the trial judge said:

> It makes her evidence useless or shall we say I would give very little weight to the accused's evidence.

While it is true that in alibi cases, calling the accused out of order, that is, other than as the first witness, may, and quite frequently does, diminish the weight to be accorded to her evidence, it does not necessarily do so and certainly does not destroy entirely the credibility of that evidence. An accused is entitled to have his or her evidence heard in full and assessed in conjunction with all of the other evidence presented at the trial and in the light of the submissions of counsel. It is quite clear here that the trial judge committed himself to an adverse assessment of the evidence of the appellant in isolation and before hearing the conclusion of her evidence and before hearing the submissions of counsel.

In *R. v. Sherry*,[299] the accused was charged with impaired driving. A defence witness testified that he and not the accused had been driving. The trial judge interrupted cross-examination of that witness and suggested that the defence counsel review the perjury provisions of the Criminal Code with the witness before re-examination. The majority of the Ontario Court of Appeal found that the judge had prejudiced the witness and compromised the appearance of justice essential to a fair trial. The Supreme Court disagreed in a short judgement and substituted a conviction. **Which Court got this right?**

3. IMPEACHMENT

Professor McCormick has provided the outline for this section of the chapter:

> There are five main lines of attack upon the credibility of a witness. The first, and probably the most effective and most frequently employed, is an attack by proof that

---

299 3 C.R. (5th) 314, 110 C.C.C. (3d) 160, [1996] 3 S.C.R. 602.

the witness on a previous occasion has made statements inconsistent with his present testimony. The second is an attack by a showing that the witness is biased on account of emotional influences such as kinship for one party or hostility to another, or motives of pecuniary interest, whether legitimate or corrupt. The third is an attack upon the character of the witness. The fourth is an attack by showing a defect of capacity in the witness to observe, remember or recount the matters testified about. The fifth is proof by other witnesses that material facts are otherwise than as testified to by the witness under attack.[300]

(a) Prior Inconsistent Statements

Proof that the witness made an earlier inconsistent statement may be gained during cross-examination out of the mouth of the witness himself or, should the witness deny making the statement, by proof from other witnesses. Should the latter mode of contradiction prove necessary, the common law developed some limitations.

The common law limitation with respect to collateral facts was legislated in England, with respect to statements, in the mid-19th century and that legislation was copied in all common law jurisdictions in Canada. For example, the *Canada Evidence Act*[301] provides:

> **10.**(1) On any trial a witness may be cross-examined as to previous statements that the witness made in writing, or that have been reduced to writing, or recorded on audio tape or video tape or otherwise, relative to the subject-matter of the case, without the writing being shown to the witness or the witness being given the opportunity to listen to the audio tape or view the video tape or otherwise take cognizance of the statements, but, if it is intended to contradict the witness, the witness' attention must, before the contradictory proof can be given, be called to those parts of the statement that are to be used for the purpose of so contradicting the witness, and the judge, at any time during the trial, may require the production of the writing or tape or other medium for inspection, and thereupon make such use of it for the purposes of the trial as the judge thinks fit.
>
> (2) A deposition of the witness, purporting to have been taken before a justice on the investigation of a criminal charge and to be signed by the witness and the justice, returned to and produced from the custody of the proper officer shall be presumed, in the absence of evidence to the contrary, to have been signed by the witness.
>
> **11.** Where a witness, on cross-examination as to a former statement made by him relative to the subject-matter of the case and inconsistent with his present testimony, does not distinctly admit that he did make the statement, proof may be given that he did in fact make it; but before that proof can be given the circumstances of the supposed statement, sufficient to designate the particular occasion, shall be mentioned to the witness, and he shall be asked whether or not he did make the statement.

Cross-examination on a prior inconsistent statement can be a highly effective strategy to attack credibility. However it should be attempted with preparation

---

300 McCormick, *Evidence* (2d ed.), p. 66.
301 R.S.C. 1985, c. C-5, ss. 10 and 11; 1994, c. 44, s. 86.

and care. Most advocacy texts (see, for example Lee Stuesser[302]) identify four separate steps:

1. Anchor the contradiction by first confirming with some precision the witnesses's evidence in chief (e.g. "You testified this morning that the car was black. Is that correct"?)

2. Confront him with the fact that the witness made an earlier statement (e.g. "Do you recall speaking to the officer on the day of the accident and giving a signed statement?") If the witness denies making any statement it would have to be proved by calling the officer.

3. Highlight the contradiction (e.g. "In the statement you said the lighting was bad and you could not see the colour of the vehicle". Or have the witness read that passage out loud.)

4. Decide on a strategy:

   (i)   explore the contradiction to show this witness cannot be believed,

   (ii) leave that argument to counsel's final address or

   (iii) get the earlier statement admitted as the truth, either by getting the witness to adopt it as the truth or by making a successful *K.G.B.* application (to be considered later under Hearsay). Only in (iii) can the statement be entered as an exhibit.

Section 10 is concerned with written statements and section 11 with oral; contradictory proof is limited, as it was by the common law, to previous statements which are "relative to the subject-matter of the case."

By the common law,[303] impeachment by proof of a prior contradictory statement could only be done if preceded by a cross-examination of the witness as to the matter thereof. The common law requirement, now seen in the above legislation, saved time and energy, promoted fairness to the witness and eliminated surprise.

Another limitation imposed by the *Queen Caroline's Case* was described by Professor Wigmore as:

> a rule which for unsoundness of principle, impropriety of policy, and practical inconvenience in trials committed the most notable mistake that can be found among the rulings upon the present subject.[304]

The judges had advised in that case that a witness could not be asked any questions in cross-examination about previous written statements without first producing the writing to the witness and allowing him to read it. Acquainting the witness with the writing in advance was seen by the practising bar as severely blunting the effectiveness of cross-examination[305] and the rule was overturned by statute in England in 1854. The English Act was later copied in Canadian legislation: *Canada Evidence Act*, section 10, which is quoted above.

---

302 *An Advocacy Primer* (3rd. ed., 2005) pp. 293-297.

303 *Queen Caroline's Case* (1820), 129 E.R. 976 (H.L.).

304 4 Wigmore, *Evidence* (Chad. Rev.), s. 1259, p. 610.

305 Wonderful examples of the effectiveness of cross-examination when unhampered by the rule are given in Wigmore, *ibid.*, at pp. 617-26.

Counsel may cross-examine the witness as to whether the witness has ever described the incident differently without first alerting the witness that he has it in writing. The *Queen's Case* also required that the whole statement be read in if counsel used it in cross-examination. Notice that the legislation leaves it to the trial judge to determine in each case what use will be made of it.

When a witness at trial testifies that the car was black, while on an earlier occasion she had said it was white, there is clearly an inconsistency and the witness is open to impeachment by proof of the earlier statement. Suppose, however, that the witness who earlier stated the car was white now disclaims all knowledge of the car's colour. Professor McCormick states:

> A distinct but somewhat cognate notion is the view that if a party interrogates a witness about a fact which would be favourable to the examiner if true, and receives a reply which is merely negative in its effect on examiner's case, the examiner may not by extrinsic evidence prove that the first witness had earlier stated that the fact was true as desired by the inquirer. An affirmative answer would have been material and subject to be impeached by an inconsistent statement, but a negative answer is not damaging to the examiner, but merely disappointing, and may not be thus impeached. In this situation the policy involved is not the saving of time and confusion, as before, but the protection of the other party against the hearsay use by the jury of the previous statement.[306]

Is the situation different when the trial judge disbelieves the witness's present disclaimer?[307]

(i) *Impeaching One's Own Witness*

By a common law rule obscure in its origin,[308] a party was not permitted to impeach his own witness by attacks on his character. The rule may have been a lingering effect of the older form of trial by wager of law in which issues were decided by parties calling the requisite number of oath-helpers; these were partisan witnesses chosen by the party and it was unseemly for the party to later attack them should they disappoint him. As witnesses changed into their modern form the policy against impeachment was expressed in terms that a party calling a witness vouched for, or guaranteed his credit. Another, and perhaps better, theory advanced was that it was wrong to permit a party to coerce a certain story from his witness by holding, to the sure knowledge of the witness, ammunition in reserve for the destruction of the witness's character should he deviate. Buller J. wrote in the 18th century:

> A party never shall be permitted to produce general evidence to discredit his own witness; for that would be to enable him to destroy the witness if he spoke against him, and to make him a good witness if he spoke for him, with the means in his hands of destroying his credit if he spoke against him. But if a witness prove facts in a cause which make against the party who called him, yet the party may call other

---

306 McCormick, *Evidence* (2d ed.), p. 71.

307 Compare views of Farris, B.C.C.J. and Martland, J. in *McInroy and Rouse v. R.* (1978), 42 C.C.C. (2d) 481, 494-95 (S.C.C.). See further, *R. v. Fleet* (2001), 48 C.R. (5th) 28 (N.S. C.A.); and *R. v. Chretien*, [2009] O.J. No. 810 (S.C.J.) at paras. 24-28.

308 See 3A Wigmore, *Evidence* (Chad. Rev.), s. 896; Ladd, "Impeachment of One's Own Witness" (1936-37), 4 U. Chi. L. Rev. 69; and Bryant, "The Common Law Rule Against Impeaching One's Own Witness" (1982), 32 U.T. L.J. 412.

witnesses to prove that those facts were otherwise; for such facts are evidence in the cause, and the other witnesses are not called directly to discredit the first witness, but the impeachment of his credit is incidental and consequential only.[309]

An exception to the common law rule prohibiting impeachment or cross-examination at large arises where the witness is declared hostile. In *Reference Re R. v. Coffin*[310] the Supreme Court held that hostile means "not giving her evidence fairly and with a desire to tell the truth because of a hostile animus toward the prosecution."

Consider the approach to hostility taken by the following civil case.

ANDERSON v. FLYING SAUCER DRIVER-IN LTD.
(August 31, 2009), Doc 46818/05, [2009] O.J. No. 3617 (Ont. S.C.J.)

J.W. QUINN J.:—

Introduction

1 In the midst of conducting his direct examination of a witness in the trial of this matter, counsel for the plaintiff moved to have the witness declared hostile. The motion did not rely on a prior inconsistent statement but, instead, invoked what counsel submitted was the common-law jurisdiction of the court to declare a witness to be hostile on the grounds that the witness: held animosity toward, and feared prosecution by, the plaintiff; was loyal to the defendant; and, was testifying in a vague and unresponsive manner. The object of the motion was to permit counsel to cross-examine the witness, contrary to the near-antiquitous common-law rule prohibiting a party from impeaching his or her own witness.

. . . .

17 The next testimony came from Mr. Cunningham (who had been summonsed by the plaintiff). He entered the witness box and, upon being sworn, read a prepared statement:

> As the plaintiff, on January 26, 2001, threatened to sue me, I seek protection afforded to me by s. 9(2) of the Ontario Evidence Act [R.S.O. 1990, c. E.23, as am.], s. 5(2) of the Canada Evidence Act [R.S.C. 1985, Chap. C-5, as am.] and s. 13 of the [Canadian] Charter of Rights and Freedoms. Thank you, Your Honour.

. . . .

21 When the trial resumed at 10:00 a.m. the next day, Mr. Richard made an oral motion requesting that I declare Mr. Cunningham a hostile witness so as to permit cross-examination.

Discussion

22 The motion presumably was prompted by answers given by Mr. Cunningham that contradict the evidence of the plaintiff . . .

---

309 Buller's *Nisi Prius*, p. 297, quoted in *Wright v. Beckett* (1833), 174 E.R. 143, 144 (C.C.P.).
310 [1956] S.C.R. 191.

23 Every reported decision that counsel could unearth for their submissions dealt with declaring a witness adverse, under either s. 9(1) of the *Canada Evidence Act* or s. 23 of the *Ontario Evidence Act*, in the face of a prior inconsistent statement.[311]

24 Mr. Richard argued that: (1) Mr. Cunningham harboured animosity toward the plaintiff; (2) claiming the protection of the statutes shows, in the mind of Mr. Cunningham at least, a fear of prosecution; (3) Mr. Cunningham was still the insurance agent for the defendant and, therefore, had a disqualifying loyalty to the defendant; (4) the nature of Mr. Cunningham's testimony so far in the trial was vague and unresponsive so as to betray a bias against the plaintiff and it reflected a lack of reliability.

25 As part of the inherent jurisdiction to control its own process, and in those situations not involving the prior-inconsistent-statement provisions of the federal and provincial evidence acts, the court has the discretion to permit counsel to cross-examine his or her own witness (either as to a specific topic or in general) where it would be unfair not to do so. However, such unfairness must rise to the level of a failure of justice before the discretion should be exercised. To say that this would be a rare occurrence is borne out by the fact that neither Mr. Richard nor Mr. Argiropoulos could find a supporting case.

26 The reality of litigation is that sometimes a witness will be called to prove or corroborate a matter of evidence where it is known or suspected that the witness will also give damaging testimony on another point. For counsel, litigation is all about choices. Mr. Richard knew that Mr. Cunningham had also been summonsed by the defendant and that Mr. Argiropoulos, counsel for the defendant, had undertaken to call him as part of the defence (neither counsel had interviewed Mr. Cunningham). Yet, the choice was made to call Mr. Cunningham as part of the plaintiff's case. Associated with that choice was the foreseeable risk that Mr. Cunningham would give evidence contrary to the position of the plaintiff.

27 Where counsel has reason to believe that a witness will be hostile, the proper procedure is to hold a voir dire. Where the hostility arises, without warning, in the course of the testimony of the witness the court will consider the testimony already given by the witness, and, perhaps, slip into a voir dire for additional evidence. However, before doing any of these things, counsel requesting the finding of hostility must meet a threshold. Certainly, the mere fact that a witness seeks the protection of the two evidence acts and the Charter, by itself, is insufficient to declare a witness to be hostile. Neither is the fact that a witness may give, or gives, testimony unfavourable to the case of the summonsing party. Also, it is not enough to show that the witness has a business connection to the opposing party . . . Such a connection would go to the weight of the testimony. Finally, I respectfully disagree with the submission made by Mr. Richard that the

---

311 Although it is not entirely clear to me, I think that the term "adverse" should be restricted to situations falling within the two Evidence Acts, whereas "hostile" describes instances arising under the common law. The terms are not synonymous. A witness may be "adverse" without being "hostile."Here, we do not have such a statement.

testimony of Mr. Cunningham so far has been vague and unresponsive. The witness brought his file and seems to have made an effort to ensure that it was complete and he answered the questions put to him in an unremarkable manner. Mr. Cunningham has not shown, by his demeanour in the witness box or by his testimony, that he is being uncooperative, that he has a disregard for the trial process or that he is blatantly lying to thwart the plaintiff or at all.

Conclusion

28 The plaintiff has not met the evidentiary threshold needed to trigger the exercise of the common-law discretion permitting the impeachment of one's own witness. The motion is dismissed.

(ii) *Canada Evidence Act, s. 9(1)*

Section 9(1) reads:

Adverse witnesses

> **9.**(1) A party producing a witness shall not be allowed to impeach his credit by general evidence of bad character, but if the witness, in the opinion of the court, proves adverse, the party may contradict him by other evidence, or, by leave of the court, may prove that the witness made at other times a statement inconsistent with his present testimony, but before the last mentioned proof can be given the circumstances of the supposed statement, sufficient to designate the particular occasion, shall be mentioned to the witness, and he shall be asked whether or not he did make the statement.

The issues that have arisen under s. 9(1) include (i) the meaning of adverse (i.e. is it the same as hostile or is it broader to include unfavourable?); and (ii) what follows from a finding of adverse (i.e. does it permit cross-examination at large)? Only on the prior inconsistent statement? Or only proof that the earlier statement was made? These issues are addressed in the following case.

R. v. VIVAR
2004 CarswellOnt 5, [2004] O.J. No. 9 (S.C.J.)

The accused was charged with first degree murder. The Crown's theory was that the accused killed Gary Malo because Malo had been stealing drugs and money from two of the accused's gang associates. The Crown called Reyes to testify. The Crown applied to have Reyes declared adverse.

DAMBROT J.:

. . .

3 It is fair to say that to some extent the evidence of Mr. Reyes supports the Crown's case, and to some extent, it does not. For the most part, this comes as no surprise to the Crown and is consistent with a statement made by Mr. Reyes under oath to the police, and with his evidence at the preliminary inquiry.

4 Despite this, however, Crown counsel has brought an application under s. 9(1) of the *Canada Evidence Act*. He asks that I declare Mr. Reyes to be an adverse

witness, principally on the basis of thirteen alleged inconsistencies between his evidence at trial, and certain things said by him to Detective Sergeant Comeau at a meeting held with the witness and Crown counsel on January 29, 2003, shortly before the preliminary inquiry. The Crown relied on certain other items of evidence in support of a declaration of adversity, but I consider them to be of little moment. Crown counsel asks that he be permitted to conduct a cross-examination of the witness not only on the inconsistencies, but also at large.

. . .

6 I have reviewed each of the thirteen alleged contradictions with care. I am satisfied that some of them are not contradictions at all. In other cases, I am unable to tell if there is a contradiction because the answer recorded in the statement is ambiguous, perhaps because of the way the statement was recorded. . . .

7 At the same time, there are a few clear inconsistencies between the statement and the evidence at trial that relate to matters of significance.

ANALYSIS

[Dambrot J. was not satisfied that the January 29, 2003, statement was taken down verbatim to constitute a statement reduced to writing so as to permit cross-examination under s. 9(2). This is discussed in the next section.]

9 . . . [Section] 9(1) permits a party to make use of a prior inconsistent statement of that party's own witness made orally, but only after the trial judge finds the witness to be adverse. There has been controversy about the meaning of adverse, and continues to be such controversy outside of Ontario. In a long line of cases, it has been held that adverse means hostile. In Ontario at least, however, it is clear that the word has a broader meaning than hostile, by reason of the decision of the *Ontario Court of Appeal in Wawanesa Mutual Ins. Co. v. Hanes*, [1963] 1 C.C.C. 176, 28 D.L.R. (2d) 386, varied [1963] 1 C.C.C. 321 (S.C.C.). The effect of that decision was described by Martin J.A. in *Cassibo*, at pp. 514-6, as follows:

> In *Wawanesa Mutual Insurance Co. v. Hanes*, this court considered the interpretation of s. 20 of the *Ontario Evidence Act*, R.S.O. 1950, c. 119 (now R.S.O. 1980, c. 145, s. 23) which the court held was, in effect, the same as s. 9(1) of the *Canada Evidence Act*. The majority of the court held that "adverse" in s. 20 was not limited to hostility but also included a witness who, though not hostile, was unfavourable in the sense of assuming by his testimony a position opposite to that of the party calling him. The majority also held that in deciding whether the witness is "adverse" the judge may take into account a prior inconsistent statement made by the witness. . . .

10 In this case, having regard to the cases I have just referred to, I am satisfied that Mr. Reyes has proved to be a witness who is adverse to the Crown. I have no doubt that he made the prior statement alleged by the Crown, that it is inconsistent with his testimony at trial to some degree, and that Mr. Reyes is a witness who is unfavourable to the Crown in the sense of assuming by his testimony a position opposite to that of the Crown. While there is much in the

prior statement that is consistent with his position today, the inconsistencies exemplify what is apparent about Mr. Reyes: he is determined to the extent possible to avoid saying anything in his evidence that might strengthen the Crown's case against Mr. Vivar. He has been untruthful about some things, and forgetful about others, in furtherance of this endeavour. Whether this effort comes from fear, or friendship, I cannot say with certainty. But it is sufficient to make him an adverse witness.

11 The question then arises what rights this finding gives to the Crown. While the Crown claims an entitlement to cross-examine Mr. Reyes at large, and many of the cases, without any real analysis, seem to support this position, I do not think it is correct. Certainly the words of s. 9(1) do not hint at such a right. Section 9(1) says no more than that upon a finding of adversity, the trial judge has a discretion to permit the party that called the witness to prove the prior inconsistent statement. It may well be that permission to prove the statement of necessity includes the right to confront the witness with it, and cross-examine the witness about the inconsistency. Indeed one would think that confronting the witness with the statement should be a prerequisite to proving it. But there is no suggestion of a right to cross-examine at large.

12 The confusion may arise as a result of the differences in view about the meaning of the word adverse in s. 9(1). If it meant hostile in the traditional sense, as many courts have thought, then cross-examination upon a finding of hostility, which was permitted at common law, would logically be available after a finding of adversity under s. 9(1). But since in Ontario at least it does not have that meaning, then unless s. 9(1) supplants the common law, it would be illogical to think that a finding of adversity would bring the same rights to a party as would a finding of hostility. There is support in the leading cases for my approach. . . .

[Having reviewed several Ontario decisions, Dambrot J. continued:]

18 Accordingly, having declared that Mr. Reyes is adverse to the Crown, I will permit Crown counsel to confront Mr. Reyes with those portions of his statement of January 29, 2003 that I have concluded are inconsistent with his evidence at trial, and that I have enumerated, and, should Mr. Reyes not admit that he said what he is alleged to have said, I will permit the Crown to lead evidence that he did.

19 I have reached the conclusion, however, that Mr. Reyes is a witness who should not be declared to be hostile to the Crown. In Reference *Re Regina v. Coffin* (1956), 114 C.C.C. 1 at p. 24, Kellock J. expressed the view that a hostile witness is one that does not give his or her evidence fairly and with a desire to tell the truth because of a hostile animus towards the prosecution. In the case of Mr. Reyes, as I have already stated, I am of the view that he is a witness who is unfavourable to the Crown in the sense of assuming by his testimony a position opposite to that of the Crown. While I believe that his evidence has been largely truthful, he clearly has a desire not to be entirely fair in the giving of his evidence, and not to tell the complete truth. This flows from his determination, to the extent possible, to avoid saying anything in his evidence that might strengthen the

Crown's case against Mr. Vivar. I suspect that he takes this attitude out of fear of Mr. Vivar's associates, or perhaps out of friendship. But whatever the reason, I am unable to conclude that it flows from any hostility towards the prosecution.

20 Accordingly, although I will permit Crown counsel to cross-examine Mr. Reyes on certain inconsistent portions of his statement of January 29, 2003, I will not permit Crown counsel to cross-examine Mr. Reyes at large.

In the next case, a British Columbia court concluded that section 9(1) includes a right to cross-examine at large. The Court also considered whether there is any room left for the common law in light of section 9.

R. v. MALIK
(2003), 194 C.C.C. (3d) 572 (B.C. S.C.)

This application arose in the "Air India" bombing trial in British Columbia.

JOSEPHSON J.: —

Overview

The Crown applies for a declaration at common law that its witness, Inderjit Singh Reyat, is hostile, thus entitling it to cross-examine him. Mr. Reyat was previously charged with the offences contained in the indictment before the Court. On February 10, 2003, Mr. Reyat pleaded guilty to manslaughter and was sentenced.

The Crown does not rely on the statutory provisions set out in ss. 9(1) and 9(2) of the Canada Evidence Act, R.S.C. 1985, c. C-5 (the "Act").

The Position of the Crown

The Crown submits that a witness can be declared hostile at common law where it is shown that he does not give his "evidence fairly and with a desire to tell the truth because of a hostile animus toward the prosecution": *R. v. Coffin* (1956), 114 C.C.C. 1 (S.C.C.) at 24. Relying on *R. v. Cassibo* (1982), 70 C.C.C. (2d) 498 (Ont. C.A.), and *R. v. Haughton* (1983), 38 O.R. (2d) 536 (Ont. Co. Ct.), the Crown submits that the right to cross-examine one's own witness at common law exists independently of, and has not been abrogated by, s. 9 of the Act.

The Crown submits that Mr. Reyat demonstrated a consistent failure to tell the truth during his evidence in chief. While not pointing to any prior inconsistent statements, the Crown says his evidence is manifestly untrue, reflecting an intention to obfuscate, rather than impart, the truth. It submits that Mr. Reyat's lack of veracity was patently obvious with respect to a number of issues including the identity of "Mr. X", the particulars of the request by Talwinder Singh Parmar that he construct an explosive device, the nature of the device he constructed, the testing of this device, and his failure to question Mr. Parmar about his (Mr. Reyat's) own role in the events of June 22, 1985.

The Crown attributes Mr. Reyat's unwillingness to tell the truth to predisposition antithetical to the Crown based on both his identification with the perpetrators of the offences at issue and his perception that he has been victimized by the Crown over the past 15 years, as reflected in Mr. Reyat's application earlier in this trial to declare the Crown's actions an abuse of process.

Position of Mr. Malik and Mr. Bagri

Mr. Malik and Mr. Bagri characterize the Crown's application under the common law as novel and unprecedented. They submit that it is not grounded in either of the traditional bases; a prior inconsistent statement by the witness or a hostile demeanour or attitude in the witness stand. Mr. Reyat's evidence in chief was consistent with his previous statements to the police and the facts upon which the Crown accepted his guilty plea to the lesser charge of manslaughter. As such, it would be premature and inappropriate for the Court to make a finding with respect to Mr. Reyat's credibility without reference to the remainder of the evidence to be led at the trial.

They also submit that it is not open to the Crown to rely on the common law in this regard since it has been superseded by the statutory procedure set out in s. 9 of the Act: *R. v. T. (T.E.)* (1991), 3 B.C.A.C. 29 (B.C.C.A.); *R. v. Soobrian* (1994), 96 C.C.C. (3d) 208 (Ont. C.A.).

They submit that under either s. 9 of the Act or at common law, findings of adversity or hostility have been justified as necessary to neutralize or discredit unfavourable evidence that has taken the party calling the witness by surprise. Here, the witness testified in a manner consistent with what could reasonably be expected. Thus, there is no principled basis upon which to depart from ordinary rules of procedure.

Finally, while Mr. Malik recognizes the enormous public interest in determining who is responsible for the events of June 22, 1985, he submits that this trial is not the forum for a public inquiry or an investigative hearing.

Conclusion

The Crown, in urging the Court to sidestep s. 9 of the Act and go directly to the common law rule regarding hostile witnesses, points to the origins of that section as a mere procedural step in the common law process. While s. 9(1) does not expressly confer a right of cross-examination, that right has been judicially grafted onto it, not without some controversy.

The Crown could not identify any recent cases which have granted this common law declaration without reference to and reliance on s. 9. Only one case has been identified (*R. v. Haughton*, supra) which made this common law declaration, but that was over twenty years ago when the right to cross-examine under s. 9(1) may not have been clear and even then only subsequent to a cross-examination under s. 9(2). However, the common law rule, while appearing to have been completely abandoned, has not been issued a judicial or legislative death certificate.

Nonetheless, courts should exercise caution before leapfrogging legislation designed (as judicially interpreted) to set the boundaries of this right and embrace the pre-existing common law rule. Assuming the common law rule remains alive,

I would nonetheless decline to grant the application. The Crown must establish that the withholding of the truth flows from a hostile animus to the Crown. While not necessarily the only route, in nearly every case where such animus has been established, it has been accomplished by demonstrating that the witness' evidence is inconsistent with a prior statement. In other cases, the manner and demeanour of the witness in giving evidence has also been a factor.

In this case, Mr. Reyat's evidence is generally consistent with his statement to police upon his arrest in 1985. It is not significantly inconsistent with the Crown theory advanced in the 1990 trial and conviction of Mr. Reyat for the offence of manslaughter. It also formed the basis of the Crown's acceptance of Mr. Reyat's plea of guilty to manslaughter in the course of this trial. Further, it has not been suggested that the Crown was misled or had any misapprehensions regarding the general nature of what Mr. Reyat's evidence would be.

The Crown submits that the improbabilities contained in Mr. Reyat's evidence mount so high that his untruthfulness is manifest. Assuming that to be the case, under the common law rule, the Crown must also demonstrate that this untruthful evidence flows from a hostile animus towards the Crown. That, the Crown submits, can be inferred from various factors including his affiliation with certain cultural and religious groups.

Hostile animus is more than an interest at variance with that of the Crown. Mr. Reyat's manner and demeanour in the witness box displayed no such animus. Keeping in mind that Mr. Reyat's version of events has been roughly consistent since his arrest in 1985, a more reasonable inference is that his evidence flows from a desire for self-preservation by minimizing his criminal conduct and a desire to protect his companions in crime. If these motives were to be regarded as sufficient to infer a hostile animus to the Crown, that inference would follow in nearly every case where a witness offers evidence which can be demonstrated to be untruthful.

I respectfully decline to declare Mr. Reyat a hostile witness at common law.

(iii) *Canada Evidence Act, s. 9(2)*

In 1969, section 9 of the *Canada Evidence Act* was amended to include subsection 2:

> (2) Where the party producing a witness alleges that the witness made at other times a statement in writing, reduced to writing, or recorded on audio tape or video tape or otherwise, inconsistent with the witness' present testimony, the court may, without proof that the witness is adverse, grant leave to that party to cross-examine the witness as to the statement and the court may consider the cross-examination in determining whether in the opinion of the court the witness is adverse.[312]

The legislation was designed[313] to adopt the wisdom of the *Hanes* case into criminal matters and to thus allow the adversity, demanded by subsection 1, to

---

312　Now R.S.C. 1985, c. C-5; 1994, c. 44, s. 85.

313　See legislative history noted in Delisle, "Witnesses — Competence and Credibility" (1978), 16 Osgoode Hall L. J. 337 at 346.

be demonstrated not only by the witness's demeanour or bearing but also by cross-examination on an alleged prior contradictory statement. Notice that section 9(2) is confined to written statements or statements reduced to writing or recorded in some way.[314] The new legislation was interpreted,[315] however, as if it created a new and independent method for impeachment of one's own witness. The cross-examination mentioned in section 9(2) was intended to be in the absence of the jury since its purpose was to enable the court to determine whether the witness was adverse for the purposes of section 9(1). But given the judicial interpretation, it was noted:

> The cross-examination provided for in s. 9(2) must be in the presence of the jury. The purpose of that cross-examination is to attack the credibility of the witness in respect to the evidence already given. As the jury are the judges of credibility, it is obvious the cross-examination would be meaningless if conducted in their absence.[316]

Accordingly, the courts have worked out a code of procedure to be followed when section 9(2) is invoked:

> In my opinion, a procedure that would give effect to the legislation, and at the same time eliminate the possibility of any adverse effect upon the jury, would be as follows:
>
> (1) Counsel should advise the Court that he desires to make an application under s. 9(2) of the *Canada Evidence Act*.
> (2) When the Court is so advised, the Court should direct the jury to retire.
> (3) Upon retirement of the jury, counsel should advise the learned trial Judge of the particulars of the application and produce for him the alleged statement in writing, or the writing to which the statement has been reduced.
> (4) The learned trial Judge should read the statement, or writing, and determine whether, in fact, there is an inconsistency between such statement or writing and the evidence the witness has given in Court. If the learned trial Judge decides there is no inconsistency, then that ends the matter. If he finds there is an inconsistency, he should call upon counsel to prove the statement or writing.
> (5) Counsel should then prove the statement, or writing. This may be done by producing the statement or writing to the witness. If the witness admits the statement, or the statement reduced to writing, such proof would be sufficient. If the witness does not so admit, counsel then could provide the necessary proof by other evidence.
> (6) If the witness admits making the statement, counsel for the opposing party should have the right to cross-examine as to the circumstances under which the statement was made. A similar right to cross-examine should be granted if the statement is provided by other witnesses. It may be that he will be able to establish that there were circumstances which would render it improper for the learned trial Judge to permit the cross-examination, notwithstanding the apparent inconsistencies. The opposing counsel, too, should have the right to call evidence

---

314 See *R. v. Carpenter* (1983), 31 C.R. (3d) 261, 266 (Ont. C.A.). See *R. v. Daniels*, [1984] N.W.T.R. 311 (S.C.), that a transcript of a taped interview is not a statement reduced to writing.

315 *R. v. Milgaard* (1971), 2 C.C.C. (2d) 206 (Sask. C.A.); leave to appeal to S.C.C. refused (1971), 4 C.C.C. (2d) 566n (S.C.C.). The *Milgaard* view was specifically approved by the Supreme Court of Canada in *McInroy and Rouse v. R.* (1978), 42 C.C.C. (2d) 481.

316 *Ibid.*, at p. 222, per Culliton, C.J.S.

as to factors relevant to obtaining the statement, for the purpose of attempting to show that cross-examination should not be permitted.

(7) The learned trial Judge should then decide whether or not he will permit the cross-examination. If so, the jury should be recalled.[317]

Crown counsel often have to resort to sections 9(1) and (2) in domestic assault prosecutions where the unfortunate reality is that principal witnesses often recant in whole or in part from previous incriminating statements. The current practice is to first try and coax the witness back by asking the witness to refresh her memory by reading her prior statement. If she persists in contradiction the usual practice is to use the above *Milgaard* procedure for a section 9(2) application. If that is granted, many judges now allow cross-examination at large. However some would require a further section 9(1) application and some even a declaration of hostility at common law before such cross-examination is permitted. The effect of such applications is that the Crown is granted permission to cross-examine their own witness on a prior inconsistent statement. The procedure is similar to any cross-examination under sections 10 and 11 but the strategy here is not to destroy credibility but rather to try to get the witness to adopt the earlier statement as the truth. A new option is to make a *K.G.B.* application: see later under hearsay, which turns on criteria of necessity and reliability.

The B.C. Court of Appeal decided in *R. v. Glowatski*[318] that the s. 9(2) procedure may be bypassed in a trial before judge alone in favour of a *B. (K.G.)* application.[319]

PROBLEM

You are a Crown counsel prosecuting a serious domestic assault case before judge and jury. The committal to trial after a preliminary inquiry was on consent of the defence counsel. No evidence was heard. A week before the trial you interviewed the principal witness, Jane. She confirmed that on the day in question she was with the accused, Bob, in her apartment where the assault was alleged to have occurred. She admitted to having been in a common law relationship with him. Apart from that she was totally uncooperative and begged you to drop the charges as she is still with him and loves him. After a couple of minutes she walked out of the interview. You see this as a classic domestic assault case and wish to try for a conviction.

The arresting officer will testify that he answered a 911 call and arrived at the apartment to hear the sound of a fight, breaking glass and shouts. He broke the door down to find the complainant sobbing, clutching her side and with blood streaming down her face. The accused was sort of crouching over her and took a run at the officer. He was arrested but refused to answer any questions then or later. Another officer arrived on the scene and took Jane to hospital where she was treated for cracked ribs and received 10 stitches for a wound on her

---

317 *Ibid.* See *R. v. Williams* (1985), 44 C.R. (3d) 351 (Ont. C.A.); leave to appeal to S.C.C. refused 44 C.R. (3d) 351n where the finding of adversity can only be on the basis of a prior inconsistent statement, the *judge* must be satisfied that the statement was in fact made.

318 (2001), 160 C.C.C. (3d) 525, 47 C.R. (5th) 230 (B.C. C.A.).

319 See too *R. v. Fleet* (2001), 48 C.R. (5th) 28 (N.S. C.A.).

cheek. On her release from hospital she gave a signed statement to the second officer.

There were two earlier statements:

(a) an oral statement by Jane to the arresting officer on his entry to the apartment, "Please go easy on Bob. I love him and he did not mean to hit me that hard".

(b) a written statement signed by Jane to the second officer at the hospital in which Jane stated: "He got jealous when I spoke to another guy at a bar. When he is drunk he often gets moody. When we got back to the apartment he immediately picked up a large purple vase and smashed it over my head. He shouted at me "You bitch" and kicked me in the side. I am glad you guys rescued me. I am tired and I want to go to my mother's house".

You expect Jane to fully or partly recant from both statements at trial. Leaving aside the possibility of a *K.G.B.* application, plan your strategy in dealing with her as a witness in as much detail as you can.

(b) Bias

Witnesses are no longer barred from testifying because of some interest they may have in the outcome of the litigation. Feelings for or against a party, though making testimony less than impartial, are not grounds for exclusion. These matters, however, are fruitful areas of exploration for impeachment purposes. The types of facts from which partiality or hostility may be inferred are infinitely varied and little is to be gained by exploring those judicially recognized in the reports. The inference may be made from the witness's circumstances, for example a family or employment relationship with the party, or acts done by the witness, for example offering a bribe to another witness to testify falsely. Since such feelings betray emotional partiality which may impair the witness's testimonial qualifications, evidence of the same is not collateral and may be elicited in cross-examination of the witness *or* by extrinsic proof.[320]

If it is intended to impeach the witness by evidence of his prior conduct illustrating bias, it should be preceded by a cross-examination of the witness concerning the same.[321] If the witness admits his bias, that should be the end of it.

In *General Films Ltd. v. McElroy* [322] the Saskatchewan Court of Appeal noted:

---

320 See *A.G. v. Hitchcock* (1847), 154 E.R. 38 (Exch. Ct.). See an application of this in *R. v. Finnessey* (1906), 11 O.L.R. 338 (C.A.) and cases there cited.

321 Compare 3A Wigmore, *Evidence* (Chad. Rev.), s. 953 and McCormick, *Evidence*, 2d ed., p. 80. In the case of *A.G. v. Hitchcock, ibid*, Baron Alderson stated: "In [that case] it was held to be competent for the prisoner to shew that the witness had a spite against him. It was material to shew that the mind of the witness was not in a state of impartiality or equality towards the prisoner. The witness was asked the question in the first instance; but in that case I do not know that it might not have been proved independently of the question having been put to him, although, as I have before said, it is only just and reasonable that the question should be put."

322 [1939] 4 D.L.R. 543, 549 (Sask. C.A.).

... it is ... only when the witness had denied his bias or partiality that counsel is entitled to adduce evidence to contradict him. In this case the witness deVries had admitted enough upon his cross-examination to show that he was adversely affected towards the plaintiff. Thus he had acknowledged that he was acting for a rival concern, that he was doing all he could to take business away from the plaintiff, and that he was interested in the result of the case ... Having thus sufficiently established the state of de Vries' mind and feelings towards the litigation, I do not think that plaintiff's counsel should have been allowed to question Widdifield about what de Vries had said at their interview. Such evidence was objectionable ... because it raised collateral issues which tend to unduly complicate and prolong trials without adequate reason.

A recent recognition of our courts' preference for admitting the possibility of bias affecting credibility rather than a blanket exclusion occurred in *R. v. Dikah*.[323] In that case the accused were charged with trafficking in cocaine. All charges involved alleged sales of cocaine to a paid police agent identified as Agent 21. The accused sought a stay alleging that the terms of Agent 21's agreement with the R.C.M.P. rendered any proceedings based on his alleged purchases of cocaine from the accused an abuse of process or a breach of the accused's rights under section 7 of the Charter. The agreement provided that the agent could not anticipate full payment of his fees unless the R.C.M.P. were able, through the agent's assistance, to successfully investigate some or all of the subjects identified. The trial judge decided that this paragraph of the agreement invited corruption and prejudiced the informant from the beginning by inviting him to put a spin on his evidence and fabricate it so that charges could be laid and he could pocket more money. The trial judge stayed the proceedings, relying on section 24(1) of the Charter. The Crown appealed successfully. Justice Labrosse wrote:

To the extent that agents are paid to gather evidence, their testimony must be viewed by the trier of fact with a certain degree of suspicion. While an expectation of financial advantage may reduce the weight of a witness' testimony, it does not render such evidence inadmissible without more.

. . . .

The testimony of some paid agents may be untrustworthy but it cannot be said that, as a category, all paid agents cannot be trusted to tell the truth. To paraphrase Dickson J. [in *Vetrovec*], the construction of a universal rule singling out the testimony of paid police agents as unreliable would reduce the law of evidence to blind and empty formalism.[324]

R. v. GHORVEI
(1999), 29 C.R. (5th) 102, 138 C.C.C. (3d) 340,
1999 CarswellOnt 2763 (C.A.)

The accused was charged with trafficking in heroin, possession of heroin and breach of recognizance. A police officer testified that he saw the accused drive a third party to a location where the third party conducted a drug transaction.

323 (1994), 31 C.R. (4th) 105 (Ont. C.A.), affirmed (*sub nom. R. v. Naoufal*), [1994] 3 S.C.R. 1020.
324 *Ibid.*, at pp. 113-14.

The charge of possession of heroin related to drugs found in the accused's possession when arrested. On his appeal from conviction, the accused sought to introduce fresh evidence relating to the police officer's credibility in the form of the transcript of an unrelated trial involving another accused person in which the trial judge, upon hearing the police officer testify for the Crown on the accused's application to exclude evidence, rejected the police officer's testimony as false and concluded that the officer was a compulsive liar. The appeal was dismissed.

CHARRON J.A.:—

. . . .

In *Pappageorge*, Constable Nielsen testified for the Crown on the accused's application to exclude evidence under s. 24(2) of the Charter. At the conclusion of the hearing, the trial judge granted the accused's application and excluded the evidence. In his reasons, the trial judge indicated that he was not impressed with Constable Nielsen. He rejected his testimony as being "false" and concluded:

> "I find that this officer is a compulsive liar. I do not believe his evidence at all."

Counsel for the appellant submits that the trial judge in *Pappageorge* made a clear finding that Constable Nielsen had lied under oath and that, if that finding had been available at the appellant's trial for the purpose of cross-examining Constable Nielsen, it could reasonably be expected to have affected the result. Consequently, the appellant seeks to admit this fresh evidence on his appeal and seeks an order directing a new trial on the basis of that evidence. The authority to admit fresh evidence on appeal is found in s. 683(1) of the Criminal Code. This court can admit fresh evidence "where it considers it in the interests of justice" to do so. The criteria for the admission of fresh evidence are set out in the often cited case of *Palmer v. The Queen*.

The determining issue is whether the evidence could reasonably be expected to have affected the result at trial. Of course, it could only have had any effect on the result if it could have been used at trial to impeach Constable Nielsen's credibility. The question then becomes whether a witness can be cross-examined on a prior judicial finding that he has lied under oath. If the prior judicial finding that Constable Nielsen lied under oath had formed the basis of a conviction of perjury or of giving contradictory evidence, it is clear that he could have been subjected to cross-examination on that conviction and on its underlying facts. See s. 12 of the Canada Evidence Act. Constable Nielsen, as an ordinary witness and unlike an accused person, would also be subject to cross-examination on relevant discreditable conduct even if the conduct has not resulted in a charge being laid or in a conviction. See *R. v. Gonzague* (1983), 4 C.C.C. (3d) 505 (Ont. C.A.). In this case, the judicial finding in *Pappageorge* that Constable Nielsen's testimony was "false" and that he was "a compulsive liar" was not made in the context of proceedings concerning the truth or falsity of the testimony in question. Had the finding been made in the context of a prosecution for perjury or for the giving of contradictory testimony, Constable Nielsen would have been given an opportunity to respond to the accusation that he had lied under oath and the trial judge's finding would have been subject to the criminal standard of proof beyond a reasonable doubt. As the matter stands, the judicial finding in question is nothing more than a rejection of Constable Nielsen's testimony, albeit in very strong terms.

In my view, it is not proper to cross-examine a witness on the fact that his or her testimony has been rejected or disbelieved in a prior case. That fact, in and of itself, does not constitute discreditable conduct. I do not think it would be useful to allow cross-examination of a witness on what is, in essence, no more than an opinion on the credibility of unrelated testimony given by this witness in the context of another case. The triers of fact who would witness this cross-examination would not be able to assess the value of that opinion and the effect, if any, on the witness's credibility without also being provided with the factual foundation for the opinion. This case, in fact, provides a good example of the difficulties that would arise if such cross-examination were permitted because, in my view, once the finding is examined in the context of the whole record in *Pappageorge*, it becomes apparent that it is essentially unfounded and hence can provide no assistance in determining Constable Nielsen's credibility.

Upon considering the full transcript in *Pappageorge*, I am unable to find support for the trial judge's finding that Constable Nielsen is "a compulsive liar". I can only surmise that this statement is either the unfortunate result of judicial intemperance or that the trial judge's conclusion is based on extraneous considerations not properly before the court. I make the first supposition on the basis that the transcript reveals that the trial judge made a number of premature expressions of incredulity with respect to Constable Nielsen's testimony while he was testifying and before hearing the whole evidence. I make the latter supposition based on the fact that the trial judge stated in his reasons that he has "known [the officer] for years". It may well be that the trial judge was not impressed with this witness but his finding must nonetheless be based on evidence properly before him.

Further, the trial judge's finding that the officer's testimony was "false" does not appear to be reasonable on the basis of the record before him. I note in this regard that the trial judge also disbelieved most of Mr. Pappageorge's testimony, yet, in the end analysis, it is on the basis of that testimony that he finds Constable Nielsen's evidence to be "false." While it was certainly open to the trial judge on the evidence to reject the officer's evidence, I find little support for any clear and express finding that the officer's testimony was "false", or, in other words, that he has lied under oath.[325]

---

[325] See comment by Addario and Pratt, "The Ontario Court of Appeal Polishes Up Some Bad Apples" (1999), 29 C.R. (5th) 102 (Ont. C.A.). *Ghorvei* was applied in *R. v. Karaibrahimovic* (2002), 164 C.C.C. (3d) 431, 3 C.R. (6th) 153 (Alta. C.A.) involving the prior testimony of an expert.

(i) *Motives of Accused and Complainants*

R. v. JACKSON
[1995] O.J. No. 2471, 1995 CarswellOnt 3388 (C.A.)

THE COURT: —

The absence of any motive to fabricate an allegation is a proper matter for consideration in the course of the fact finding process. The trial judge's reasons indicate no more than that he did consider the absence of any motive to fabricate as one feature of the case. The reasons do not suggest that the trial judge placed any onus on the appellant to prove a motive to fabricate. Nor do we accept that, because the trial judge's finding that the appellant's story had no ring of truth followed directly upon his reference to the absence of a motive to fabricate, the former was the exclusive product of the latter.

In sexual assault cases or cases involving police violence, there is sometimes a civil lawsuit filed after criminal charges are laid. Courts often take this into account in assessing credibility. **Is there an argument that using civil remedies as a motive to lie in these contexts is unfair? How would you articulate it?**

R. v. ELLARD
(2003), 172 C.C.C. (3d) 28, 10 C.R. (6th) 189 (B.C. C.A.)

Ellard was convicted of second degree murder in the beating and drowning death of Reena Virk. A number of witnesses testified that Ellard admitted her involvement in the deceased's death. In her testimony, Ellard admitted being involved in the swarming of the deceased but not her killing. She further denied admitting such to the witnesses. Credibility was the central issue at trial. The Crown cross-examined Ellard and asked her to provide a reason why the witnesses would lie about the admissions. It was a prominent feature of her cross-examination. Ellard appealed on the grounds that this cross-examination was unfair. A new trial was ordered.

DONALD J.A. (LAMBERT and ROWLES JJ.A. concurring): —

Asking the accused about the veracity of a Crown witness has long been considered improper. The accused's opinion is irrelevant and the questioning could prejudice her and render the trial unfair. In his reasons for the majority in *R. v. Markadonis*, [1935] S.C.R. 657, 64 C.C.C. 41, Duff C.J. agreed with the minority judgment below and quoted with approval the following passage from that judgment at pp. 658-59: The prisoner gave evidence on his own behalf and on his cross-examination he was repeatedly asked in effect what his opinion was as to the veracity of several Crown witnesses. The questions were I think irrelevant and should not have been asked, and it appears surprising that they were not objected to. The answers to such questions might prejudice the accused before the jury, and I cannot conceive of any legitimate reason for asking them. It is a method of cross examination which I think is unfair and should not be resorted to nor allowed especially in a case like the present: *Regina v. Bernard* [(1858) 1 F. x F. 240, at 249; 40 Cyc. 2509.]; *McMillan v. Walker* [(1881) 21 N.B. Rep. 31.]; *North Australian Territory Co. v. Goldsborough Mort & Co.* [[1893] 2 Ch. D. 381, at 385.].

The potential prejudice arising from this form of questioning is that it tends to shift the burden of proof from the Crown to the accused. It could induce a jury to analyze the case on the reasoning that if an accused cannot say why a witness would give false evidence against her, the witness's testimony may be true. The risk of such a course of reasoning undermines the presumption of innocence and the doctrine of reasonable doubt. The mind of the trier of fact must remain firmly fixed on whether the Crown proved its case on the requisite standard and not be diverted by the question whether the accused provided a motive for a witness to lie. I refer in this regard to the words of Finlayson J.A. giving judgment for the Ontario Court of Appeal in *R. v. W.S.* (1994), 90 C.C.C. (3d) 242 (Ont. C.A.) at 252-54, leave to appeal to S.C.C. refused 93 C.C.C. (3d) vi:

> The Crown on appeal conceded that it was improper for the Crown at trial to demand an explanation from the appellant as to why the complainant would make up what counsel referred to as "this horrendous lie". There is no onus on an accused person to explain away the complaints against him or her. The trial judge should have resolutely rejected this approach. Instead he implicitly adopted it. He was favourably impressed with the complainant and the manner in which she testified and, consequently, he believed her. He then subtly shifted the onus to the appellant, as accused, to give some explanation as to why the complainant would lie. Why would she bring all this grief upon herself and risk jeopardizing the close relationship between the two families if it were not true? He also accepted that M. was necessarily lying to support her father. In this manner, the trial judge failed to properly apply the presumption of innocence, and to adequately found the conviction on the whole of the evidence. . . . . .
>
> The trial judge in the present case gave full reasons and he recited the evidence accurately. He also referred to the appropriate authorities. I cannot say that he misdirected himself in a material way. His overall approach to this particular case, however, was wrong. Instead of questioning the veracity and accuracy of the witnesses who, because of the nature of the charge, were called to support a negative, he should have been more critical of the complainant who put forward the affirmative that the offences took place: see *R. v. Norman*, [(1993), 87 C.C.C. (3d) 153 (Ont. C.A.)], at pp. 172-3. This is another example of the way the trial judge shifted the onus to the appellant in spite of the Crown's burden to prove all elements of the crime beyond a reasonable doubt. [Emphasis added.]

The nature of the prejudice was described in this way in *R. v. F. (A.)* (1996), 30 O.R. (3d) 470 (Ont. C.A.) at p. 471:

> The cross-examination of the appellant and his wife by Crown counsel was replete with improper questions. Both the appellant and his wife were asked time and again why the complainant would fabricate the allegations and were called upon to comment on the credibility of the complainant. These questions were not isolated instances but part of an obvious strategy that was both considered and deliberate. The prejudice to the appellant is obvious. Such questions put the parents of the

complainant in the invidious position of having to call their own daughter a liar. More importantly, these questions suggested that there was some onus on the appellant and his witnesses to provide a motive for the complainant's testimony. This kind of examination undermines the fundamental principle of the presumption of innocence. This court has repeatedly held that this type of cross-examination is improper. We think it is unfortunate that Crown counsel persist in this kind of unfair questioning in the face of the many judgments of this court that such questioning is improper. [Emphasis added.]

See also *R. v. Rose*, [2001] O.J. No. 1150 (QL) [reported 153 C.C.C. (3d) 225] where the Ontario Court of Appeal said at paras. 27-28:

> Further, this court has held repeatedly that it is improper to call upon an accused to comment on the credibility of his accusers: see, for example, *R. v. Cole*, [1999] O.J. No. 1647 (C.A.); R. v. F. (A.) (1996), 30 O.R. (3d) 470; *R. v. Masse* (2000), 134 O.A.C. 79 (C.A.); *R. v. Vandenberghe* (1995), 96 C.C.C. (3d) 371 (Ont. C.A.); *R. v. S. (W.)* (1994), 90 C.C.C. (3d) 242 (C.A.). Crown counsel did this repeatedly during the course of the cross-examination. Questions of this nature suggest that there is some onus on an accused person to provide a motive for the Crown witness' testimony and, as such, they undermine the presumption of innocence. Consequently, I must conclude that Crown counsel's cross-examination of the appellant further undermined the fairness of this trial.

As was held in *R. v. B. (R.W.)*, supra, whether there exists a motive to lie can be a relevant consideration in assessing the credibility of a witness. The defence in this case attempted to raise a reasonable doubt on the motive issue. But that did not justify the Crown's tactic in cross- examination. If the appellant herself had evidence of motive, her counsel would have led it from her in her examination in chief and she could have been properly challenged on that evidence in cross-examination. However, in persistently questioning her about motive when she gave no such evidence, the Crown placed her in the unfair position of either answering as she did or arguing her defence. It was for her counsel to develop the case for the defence and to present argument at the appropriate time.[326]

In *R. v. B. (L.)*,[327] on a charge of sexual assault, the trial judge stated that in considering the credibility of the various witnesses he was entitled to take motive into consideration. The judge then stated that the complainant had no motive for testifying to an untruth but the accused "of course, has a motive for not telling the truth, he does not wish to be convicted". This was found to be error as it displaced the presumption of innocence. Arbour J.A., for the court:

> The statement made by the trial judge went beyond the common sense consideration that witnesses may have, to different degrees, an interest in the outcome of the proceedings, and that this is a factor, among others, which the trier of fact may take into account in assessing credibility.

---

326 For a further discussion of the issue of raising the issue absence of motive to lie in sexual assault cases, see *R. v. L.(L.)* (2009), 96 O.R. (3d) 412 (C.A.).
327 (1993), 82 C.C.C. (3d) 189 (Ont. C.A.).

There are many ways in which a witness may have an interest in the case which may be viewed as affecting the weight that the trier of fact may want to place on the witness's evidence. The interest may be pecuniary, as is often the case for both the plaintiff and the defendant in a civil case. In a criminal case, the accused has an obvious direct interest in the outcome of his or her trial, but other witnesses may have a large stake, be it an emotional, a financial or even a penal interest in the trial in which they are mere witnesses. The degree to which the presence of an interest in the outcome may affect the assessment of the credibility of a witness varies with the circumstances of each case.

This court held in *R. v. Wood*, February 26, 1992 (unreported), that an accused's interest in the outcome of the trial may be a factor which a jury could legitimately take into account in determining the appropriate weight to place on the accused's testimony. The court referred to this process as common sense, and said that it was not rendered offensive by the trial judge referring to the accused having a "great interest" in the outcome of his trial. In *Wood*, the court observed that the trial judge was careful to warn the jury that, despite the accused's great interest in the outcome of his trial, "that doesn't mean that every accused person's evidence must be necessarily rejected because of an interest in the outcome". . . .

The impugned passage in the trial judge's reasons in this case, in my opinion, goes beyond the permissible consideration of the accused's interest in being acquitted, as one factor to be taken into account when weighing his testimony. It falls into the impermissible assumption that the accused will lie to secure his acquittal, simply because, as an accused, his interest in the outcome dictates that course of action. This flies in the face of the presumption of innocence and creates an almost insurmountable disadvantage for the accused. . . . If the trial judge comes to the conclusion that the accused did not tell the truth in his evidence, the accused's interest in securing his acquittal may be the most plausible explanation for the lie. The explanation for a lie, however, cannot be turned into an assumption that one will occur.[328]

A witness may be cross-examined on the fact that he or she is facing an outstanding charge where it is alleged that the witness's testimony is an attempt to seek favour with the Crown.[329]

(c) Character of Witness

(i) *Extrinsic Evidence*

In the early common law, a witness's credibility might be impeached by leading extrinsic evidence of his character. Witnesses who had personal knowledge[330] would give their opinion of the witness's character trait for veracity or mendacity. At times the witness would supplement his own knowledge with what he had heard about the witness,[331] but the real question was whether this witness would, based on his knowledge, believe the former witness on his oath.[332] In 1722 in *Layer's Case*[333] the defense called over twenty character witnesses

---

328 *Ibid.*, at pp. 190-91. Accord *R. v. Murray* (1997), 115 C.C.C. (3d) 225 (Ont. C.A.).
329 See *R. v. Titus* (1983), 2 C.C.C. (3d) 321 (S.C.C.); *R. v. Gassyt* (1998), 127 C.C.C. (3d) 546 (Ont. C.A.), leave to appeal refused (1999), 136 C.C.C. (3d) vi (S.C.C.) and *R. v. Chartrand* (2002), 170 C.C.C. (3d) 97 (Ont. C.A.).
330 See *O'Connor's Trial* (1798), 27 Howell's State Trials 1, 32.
331 See variety in examples transcribed in *Layer's Case* (1722), 16 Howell's State Trials 94.
332 See precedents collected in 7 Wigmore, *Evidence* (Chad. Rev.), s. 1982, note 3.
333 (1772), 16 Howell's State Trials 94.

to impeach the credit of the principal Crown witnesses, Lynch and Plunkett. As typical examinations we read:

Defence Counsel:	What character hath Mr. Plunkett?
Witness A:	I have known Mr. Plunkett several years, and that he was an idle, broken man, and a great liar, and not to be believed.
Counsel:	He would lye before and behind, I think you say?
Witness A:	Yes, he did.
Counsel:	Do you think he is to be credited, if he comes to give testimony against a person?
Witness A:	Upon my word I think he is not, but what he told me; because I have found him to lie backwards and forwards.
	. . .
Defence Counsel:	Is (Lynch) accounted an honest man, or a knave?
Witness B:	I will not trust him for anything.
Counsel:	The wiser you. Is he a man to be credited? Can you believe what he says?
Witness B:	I think I would not believe him.
Counsel:	You are right.
	. . .
Defence Counsel:	Is (Mr. Plunkett) a man as may be believed, even upon his oath, or not?
Witness C:	I must tell you, that I found him in so many mistakes about his own wife, that, by God, I would not take his word for a halfpenny. . . .
Counsel:	Go on, but don't swear by God anymore.

The witness's personal opinion was clearly receivable.

In later decisions we see the witness giving his opinion regarding credibility based on his knowledge of the earlier witness's reputation. For example, in *Mawson v. Hartsink* [334] the questions are

> Have you the means of knowing what the general character of this witness was?

> From such knowledge of his general character would you believe him on his oath?

In *R. v. Watson,*[335] however, the court held it to be satisfactory for the witness to simply state whether he would believe the witness on oath and that form of adducing evidence respecting credibility was later approved in *R. v. Brown & Hedley.*[336] Lord Goddard in *R. v. Gunewardene* [337] recognized the *Brown & Hedley* case as

> direct authority that a witness called to impeach the credibility of previous witnesses can express an individual opinion and is not confined to giving evidence of the latter's reputation.

---

334 (1802), 170 E.R. 656.

335 (1817), 2 Stark 116, 152.

336 (1867), L.R. 1 C.C.R. 70.

337 [1951] 2 K.B. 600 (C.C.A.). Compare *R. v. Rowton* (1865), 10 Cox C.C. 25, which surprised the profession (see 7 Wigmore, *Evidence* (Chad. Rev.), p. 210) by confining evidence of character of an *accused* to reputation and foreclosing opinion.

In *Masztalar v. Wiens*,[338] the plaintiff was injured in a motor-vehicle collision. In dismissing the action the trial judge said that the only reliable witness as to how the accident occurred was the defendant. After the close of the defence case, the plaintiff's counsel announced that he intended to call rebuttal evidence. He wished to call three witnesses who would testify that, based on their knowledge of the reputation of the defendant they would not believe him on his oath. The trial judge refused to allow counsel to call these witnesses, refused to allow counsel to make submissions on the issue, and refused to read the authorities which counsel asked him to consider. The Court of Appeal ordered a new trial. Justice Cumming, Locke J.A. concurring, wrote:

> From the very beginning of the modern law of evidence it has been permissible to call a witness to swear that a witness called for the opposing side cannot be believed on his oath. The practice is to ask the witness whether he knows the impugned witness's reputation for veracity and whether, from such knowledge, he would believe the impugned witness on oath.
>
> . . . .
>
> . . . This ancient rule has been much criticized. It was described by Lord Pearce as "not very logical," "not very useful," and by the editor of *Cross on Evidence*, 7th ed. (London: Butterworths) as "cumbersome," "anomalous," "unconvincing" and "very rare in practice" (at p. 319).
>
> It is fair to say, as well, that although of long standing, it has not been adopted in any decision clearly binding on this Court. Nor is it one which need be applied in every case. On the contrary, it is one which should rarely be invoked. It need not be abolished, but it should be retained to be sparingly applied only in the rare case where the interests of justice require it.
>
> . . . .
>
> Undoubtedly, there is a discretion, on proper grounds, to exclude otherwise legally admissible evidence, but in this case I cannot conclude, the record being silent in this regard, that the learned trial judge exercised his discretion to reject the proffered evidence for any acceptable practical or policy reason recognized as appropriate in the passages from *Morris* and *Corbett* to which I have referred. All we can see, from the record before us, is that he rejected it out of hand.[339]

McEachern C.J.B.C. offered:

> [T]rial judges have at least a discretion not to permit this kind of evidence to become legal clutter in a modern courtroom. I do not think it will be wise or necessary to purport to abolish the rule entirely, for there may possibly be circumstances where a judge would allow such evidence to be called. An example might be where a witness has earned a well-known reputation for mendacity through a course of conduct or dealings over a considerable period of time and such witness may be sprung upon a plaintiff who has not been able to obtain adequate instruction for cross-examination.[340]

The rule appears to still exist, though subject to frequent criticism. Justice G.A. Martin, in *R. v. Gonzague*,[341] held that the trial judge had erred in refusing

---

338 (1992), 2 C.P.C. (3d) 294 (B.C.C.A.).
339 *Ibid.*, at pp. 299-303.
340 *Ibid.*, at p. 308.
341 (1983), 34 C.R. (3d) 169 (Ont. C.A.).

to allow a witness to express their opinion as to the lack of veracity of another witness; the trial judge believed such an opinion could only be expressed when the impeaching witness had knowledge of the other's reputation for veracity. Justice Martin decided that the impeaching witness was not so confined, but expressed the view that such evidence had little weight. Perhaps a sound exercise of discretion, as proposed by Chief Justice McEachern, to foreclose such evidence on the basis of normally trifling value in comparison to the time taken up, is the solution.

R. v. CLARKE
(1998), 18 C.R. (5th) 219, 1998 CarswellOnt 3447, 129 C.C.C. (3d) 1 (C.A.)

On charges of forcible seizure, assault with a weapon, and possession of a weapon for the purpose of committing forcible seizure defence counsel proposed to call five witnesses to testify about the reputation of the accused and the complainant, who were members of the small Caribbean community in Trenton. The trial judge held that the witnesses would be permitted to give their opinions as to the reputation of the accused and the complainant in the community of Trenton. Further, defence counsel could impeach the credibility of the complainant by asking questions of the character witnesses. The trial judge gave instructions as to the use of the character evidence in the charge to the jury.

ROSENBERG J.A.: —

The rules of evidence respecting the admissibility of character evidence are not always logical or founded in good policy. In this Crown appeal, the court is invited to reconsider the rationality of one of the more anomalous rules.

In *R. v. Gonzague* (1983), 4 C.C.C. (3d) 505, this court held that established authority permits the following line of inquiry of a witness called by the defence to give evidence about the character of a Crown witness:

1. Do you know the reputation of the witness as to truth and veracity in the community in which the witness resides?

   If the answer is "yes" the questioning proceeds.

2. Is that reputation good or bad?

   If the answer is "bad" a final question is permitted.

3. From that reputation, would you believe the witness on oath?

On behalf of the Crown, Mr. Shaw submits that the rule permitting the third question should be abrogated. He also urges this court to reassess whether the defence should automatically be entitled to ask the first two questions without an assessment of the probative value of the proffered testimony. Finally, Mr. Shaw argues that in any event the charge to the jury in this case as to the use of the evidence was inadequate.

I agree with Mr. Shaw that it is time to reassess this rule. I would hold that a judge has a limited discretion to prevent counsel from asking the first two questions of a witness called to attack the credibility of another witness.

I would also hold that only rarely should the third question be permitted.

. . . .

Although evidence has some probative value, it is not necessarily admissible. Even if the evidence is not subject to some exclusionary rule, such as the hearsay rule, it may still be held to be inadmissible having regard to the particular circumstances of the case. Relevance cannot be determined in a vacuum but only on the basis of the particular issues raised in the trial. Thus, evidence that may be relevant to one issue may be irrelevant to another or may actually mislead the trier of fact on the second issue. The law of evidence therefore gives to the trial judge the task of balancing the value of the evidence against its potential prejudice. In a proper case, the judge has the power to exclude otherwise relevant evidence because the prejudicial effect of admitting the evidence outweighs its value. In *Seaboyer*, McLachlin J. clarified the test for exclusion of otherwise relevant evidence. She held that the judge has the power to exclude relevant evidence tendered by the Crown on the basis simply that its prejudicial effect outweighs its probative value. The power to exclude relevant defence evidence, however, is narrower and constrained by the fundamental tenet that an innocent person not be convicted, a tenet which now has constitutional protection.

. . . .

In my view, the prejudicial effect of the answer to the third question will almost invariably substantially outweigh its probative value. The form in which the evidence is presented tends to usurp the function of the jury and engages what I have referred to as the fifth counter-balancing factor. . . . While the defence witnesses may know the Crown witness' reputation for telling the truth in everyday affairs, for the reasons expressed earlier, their ability to predict the witness' behaviour in court is limited and entitled to no special deference. Where the outcome of the case depends upon the evidence of a single witness, an expression of opinion as to that witness' veracity is a comment on the ultimate issue. There is the risk that in some cases the jury will simply defer to the opinion of the character witness rather than embarking on the difficult task of examining the evidence and measuring it against the standard of proof beyond a reasonable doubt, on the theory that the character witness obviously knows the Crown witness and is in a much better position to determine the outcome of the case. Put another way, the ability of a character witness, who has not heard the evidence in the case, to predict whether another witness has told the truth under oath is very limited. The jury may, however, overvalue that opinion because the character witness knows the witness.

Accordingly, I would hold that the accused does not have the absolute right to ask the third question and that in most cases the trial judge would be justified in refusing to permit that question to be asked. I would adopt the holding by Cumming J.A. in *Masztalar v. Wiens* (1992), 10 B.C.A.C. 19 at 23 to the effect that while the rule need not be absolutely abolished it should be retained "to be sparingly applied only in the rare case where the interests of justice require it". To the extent that the decisions of this court in Gonzague and Taylor hold to the contrary, they should no longer be followed. There may be unusual circumstances where the reputation of the Crown witness is such that it is possible to more accurately predict the likelihood that the witness would lie under oath. In those cases, the answer to the third question may provide the jury with useful information. With a careful jury instruction the danger that this testimony will usurp the jury's function can be minimized.

With respect to the first two questions, in my view, the trial judge also has a discretion to exclude witnesses that would provide that evidence where the prejudicial effect would substantially outweigh its probative value. I should say, however, that in my view it would be an extremely rare case where a trial judge would be warranted in excluding the evidence. Unlike the third question, the first two questions do not invite answers that would have the tendency to usurp the jury's function. The reputation evidence is simply another piece of circumstantial evidence that the jury can use to assess the credibility of the Crown witness' story. I also do not think that this evidence has the same tendency to distract the jury from the main issue in the case, nor is it likely to create side issues.

The only serious problem about this defence evidence is whether the evidence will consume an undue amount of time. It seems to me that a trial judge has the discretion to limit the number of reputation witnesses called by the defence where the judge is satisfied that the prejudicial effect of calling an endless series of witnesses testifying to essentially the same fact substantially outweighs the probative value of this additional evidence. The judge will, however, wish to keep in mind that the Supreme Court in *Seaboyer* has held that the discretion to exclude relevant evidence must be exercised with extreme caution and that in most cases the better course would be to permit the defence to call all of those witnesses.

(ii) *Evidence Elicited on Cross-examination*

While extrinsic evidence of specific instances of misconduct was excluded the common law permitted cross-examination of the witness himself regarding the same. The reasons forbidding extrinsic evidence were seen to be not applicable; confusion was minimal as it ended with the question and answer and the witness was not unfairly surprised as he needn't meet other witnesses.[342] In 1746 the Lord Chancellor noted:

> The other party is at liberty to cross-examine him either to the matter of fact concerning which he had been examined, *or any other matter whatsoever* that shall tend to impeach his credit or weaken his testimony.[343]

The only limitation appears to be counsel's imagination, the restraint of ethical considerations and the trial judge's discretion to protect a witness from harassment when the relevance of the questioning is regarded as minimal.[344]

---

342 3A Wigmore, *Evidence* (Chad. Rev.), s. 981.

343 Hardwicke, L.C. in *Lord Lovat's Trial*, 18 Howell's State Trials 529, 651.

344 See, *e.g.*, the protection for a complainant in a rape prosecution in *Laliberte v. R.* (1877), 1 S.C.R. 117. Compare *R. v. Bradbury* (1973), 23 C.R.N.S. 293 (Ont. C.A.). See generally Stephen, *History of the Criminal Law* (1883), vol. 1, p. 433. Observe the breadth of cross-examination permitted in *R. v. Titus* (1983), 33 C.R. (3d) 17 (S.C.C.); *R. v. Gonzague* (1983), 34 C.R. (3d) 169 (Ont. C.A.) and *A.G. Que. v. Charron* (1984), 43 C.R. (3d) 240 (Que. S.C.).

Recall as well the discussion of the Supreme Court in *Lyttle*. Protection for two particular classes of witnesses deserves closer examination: accused persons and complainants in sexual assault cases (see above, Chapter 4, Character Evidence).

(iii)   *Accused as Witness*

The accused was rendered a competent witness in Canada in 1893. The statute which accomplished this contained no language which would afford him any protection from cross-examination over and above that available to the ordinary witness.[345] This was early recognized in the cases. In Quebec in 1893 Wurtele J.A. stated:

> When a person on trial claims the right to give evidence on his own behalf, he comes under the ordinary rule as to cross-examination in criminal cases. He may be asked all questions pertinent to the issue, and cannot refuse to answer those which may implicate him. Under the new law, which protects him from the effect of his evidence in proceedings subsequently brought, but does not do so in the case in which the evidence is given, he may be convicted out of his own mouth. He cannot be compelled to testify, but when he offers and gives his evidence he has to take the consequences.[346]

In Ontario in 1902, Osler J.A. noted:

> The right, and if such it can be called, the privilege, of the accused now is to tender himself as a witness. When he does so he puts himself forward as a credible person, and except in so far as he may be shielded by some statutory protection, he is in the same situation as any other witness, as regards liability to and extent of cross-examination.[347]

Nevertheless, after some uncertainty,[348] some courts have recognized that the accused who chooses to become a witness exposes himself to a greater possibility of prejudice than the ordinary witness. In *R. v. Davison*,[349] Martin J.A. described the accused's position:

> An accused who gives evidence has a dual character. As an accused he is protected by an underlying policy rule against the introduction of evidence by the prosecution tending to show that he is a person of bad character, subject, of course, to the recognized exceptions to that rule. As a witness, however, his credibility is subject to attack. If the position of an accused who gives evidence is assimilated in every respect to that of an ordinary witness he is not protected against cross-examination with respect to discreditable conduct and associations.

---

345 Compare the Criminal Evidence Act, 1898, 61 & 62 Vict., c. 36, s. 1(*f*) in England which forbade cross-examination of the accused regarding his record unless it was admissible as relevant to a fact in issue, the accused led evidence of his own good character or sought to impugn the character of the prosecutor or his witnesses or he has given evidence against a co-accused.

346 *R. v. Connors* (1893), 5 C.C.C. 70, 72 (Que. Q.B.).

347 *R. v. D'Aoust* (1902), 5 C.C.C. 407, 411 (C.A.).

348 See, *e.g.*, the judgment of Spence, J. in *Colpitts v. R.*, [1965] S.C.R. 739; and compare *Koufis v. R.*, [1941] S.C.R. 481 and *R. v. McLaughlan* (1974), 20 C.C.C. (2d) 59 (Ont. C.A.).

349 (1974), 20 C.C.C. (2d) 424 (Ont. C.A.). But compare *R. v. Bird* (1973), 13 C.C.C. (2d) 73 (Sask. C.A.).

If an accused could in every case be cross-examined with a view to showing that he is a professional criminal under the guise of an attack upon his credibility as a witness it would be virtually impossible for him to receive a fair trial on the specific charge upon which he is being tried. It is not realistic to assume that, ordinarily, the jury will be able to limit the effect of such a cross-examination to the issue of credibility in arriving at a verdict.

In my view the policy rule which protects an accused against an attack upon his character lest it divert the jury from the issue which they are called upon to decide, namely, the guilt or innocence of the accused on the specific charge before the Court, is not wholly subordinated to the rule which permits an accused who elects to give evidence to be cross-examined on the issue of his credibility. In this area of the law, as in so many areas, a balance has been struck between competing interests, which endeavours so far as possible to recognize the purpose of both rules and does not give effect to one to the total exclusion of the other.

Consequently, limitations are imposed with respect to the cross-examination of an accused which do not apply in the case of an ordinary witness.[350]

Accordingly it was held that while witnesses generally are open to cross-examination at large as to credit, an accused, aside from questions regarding previous convictions, should not be cross-examined with regard to previous misconduct or discreditable associations unrelated to the charge for the purpose of impeachment.

R. v. JONES
(1988), 66 C.R. (3d) 54, 44 C.C.C. (3d) 248 (Ont. C.A.)

The accused was charged that he sexually assaulted an eight-year-old child. The appellant testified on his own behalf and denied assaulting the complainant. He relied upon an alibi.

GOODMAN J.A.: —

. . . .

The appellant testified in his own behalf. At the very outset of his cross-

---

350 *Ibid.*, at pp. 441-42. This excerpt from *Davison* was quoted and applied in *R. v. Lawrence* (1989), 52 C.C.C. (3d) 452 (Ont. C.A.); the court allowed the accused's appeal from conviction of manslaughter arising out of the death of a child where the Crown had cross-examined accused to show that he was a "biker," drug dealer and welfare cheat. And see *R. v. Geddes* (1979), 52 C.C.C. (2d) 230 (Man. C.A.):.

.   The accused was convicted on a charge of criminal fraud. At trial the accused testified on his own behalf. In the course of the cross-examination the accused was asked questions regarding previous convictions of fraud and particularly was asked whether he had testified on his own behalf in the trial resulting in the seven convictions of fraud. The Court of Appeal held that the latter questions were improper because the jury was being invited to conclude that if the accused was not believed by the judge in the prior case, he ought not to be believed by the jury in this case. Huband J.A. said (at 238):

.   The question went beyond what is authorized by s. 12, and into an area which could only reflect on the character, rather than the credit of the accused. Crown counsel was attempting to convey the impression that, since the accused had not been believed at that trial, he should not be believed by the jury in the instant case.

examination the following questions were asked by counsel for the Crown and answers given by the appellant.

Q.   Have you ever been a paedophile in the past?

A.   No.

Q.   Have you ever received treatment as a paedophile?

A.   Yes, I did, once when I was incarcerated I received treatment after the sexual assaults I was convicted of.

The appellant had not led any evidence of good character in his own behalf. He had not put his character in issue. It was improper, therefore, for the prosecution to cross-examine him with respect to matters relating to his bad character. No objection was made by defence counsel at the time the evidence was given.

Counsel for the Crown took the position on this appeal that no substantial wrong was occasioned by the impugned cross-examination in that the accused's answer that he was not a paedophile was uncontradicted and it was an insignificant portion of the evidence which was not mentioned by the Crown in argument nor by the trial judge in his reasons. Unfortunately it is not possible to know what weight, if any, the trial judge gave to this evidence standing alone or in conjunction with other evidence as to the issues of commission by the appellant of the acts of assault alleged or credibility of the appellant. In the absence of a statement by the trial judge that he disregarded this evidence in reaching his conclusions, this court is left with the trial judge's assertion quoted above that he found the accused guilty on the basis of all of the evidence.[351]

If the accused is seen as entitled to protection from questions concerning misconduct not resulting in a conviction, should he similarly be entitled to protection against questions regarding convictions for offences which have trifling probative value on the issue of credit? If an accused is charged with assault and testifies in chief that he was acting in self-defence, should the prosecution be entitled to ask him concerning his six previous convictions for assault? Should accused with previous records be obliged to forego the witness-stand? Should the trial judge have a discretion to foreclose such questioning?

By the early 18th century it seems settled that evidence of specific acts of the witness to affect credibility was not receivable.[352] It was regarded as necessary to exclude the same, for otherwise there would be confusion of the issues and unfair surprise to the witness. When counsel in *Rookwood's Trial* in 1696 proposed to lead evidence of a witness's previous actions which though criminal had not been prosecuted, it was said:

Any man in the world may by this means be wounded in his reputation, and crimes laid to his charge that he never thought of, and he can have no opportunity of giving

---

351   And see *R. v. C. (W.)* (1990), 54 C.C.C. (3d) 37 (Ont. C.A.): on a charge of sexual assault the accused denied the incident. He was persistently cross-examined by the Crown who suggested he was a satanist and that members of that cult practised child abuse as part of their religion. The court decided the cross-examination created unfair prejudice which could not be cured by the proviso.

352   See *Layer's Case, supra*, note 331, at pp. 247 and 256, and *R. v. Rookwood* (1696), 13 Howell's State Trials 139, 209-11.

an answer to it, because he never imagined there would be any such objection. It is killing a man in his good name by a side-wound, against which he has no protection or defence.[353]

Defence counsel objected to what he perceived to be an anomaly:

> My lord, I cannot imagine why a man that has been guilty of any such crimes, and is not taken, should be of greater credit than a man that has been taken and punished. . . .
> I say it is the crime that renders a man infamous, and I do not know why a man that has had the good fortune not to be taken and punished for great crimes by him committed, should be in a better condition as to the credit of his testimony, than one that is taken and undergoes the punishment of law.[354]

The anomaly disappears when we recognize that the evidence is excluded not by reason of a lack of relevance but because of the policy considerations of consumption of time, confusion of issues and fairness to the witness. If the witness has been previously convicted, proof of the same was permitted to impeach[355] as those dangers normally presented by collateral issues were not present; the previous judgment is conclusive, thus not open to dispute and the witness is not surprised. When witnesses who were previously incompetent to testify because of a conviction for an *infamous*[356] crime, were statutorily made competent[357] in 1843 in England, legislation was soon introduced, continuing the common law attitude, to provide for proof of their previous convictions for impeachment purposes.[358] The English Common Law Commissioners recommended in 1853 that cross-examination regarding previous convictions should be restricted to "offences which imply turpitude and want of probity, and more especially absence of veracity — as for instance, perjury, forgery, obtaining money or goods under false pretences and the like." Unfortunately, the legislation that was actually introduced, and which was later copied in Canada to become our section 12, provided no limitation on the nature of the crime to be inquired into. Our section 12 provides:

> **12.**(1) A witness may be questioned as to whether the witness has been convicted of any offence, excluding any offence designated as a contravention under the Contraventions Act, but including such an offence where the conviction was entered after a trial on an indictment.

---

353 *Ibid.*, at p. 210, per the argument of the Attorney General accepted by the court.

354 *Ibid.*, at p. 211.

355 *Lord Castlemaine's Trial* (1680), 7 Howell's State Trials 1067, 1084 per Scroggs, L.C.J.

356 See 2 Wigmore, *Evidence* (Chad. Rev.), s. 520 for discussion of the meaning "infamous crimes."

357 In England in 1843, 6 & 7 Vict., c. 85. In Canada see *Canada Evidence Act*, R.S.C. 1985, c. C-5, s. 3, for an example of legislation removing such disqualification.

358 In the early 19th century there appears to be recognized in the cases a privilege in the witness to refuse to answer questions which might bring him into disgrace. While Professor Wigmore is unqualified (3A Wigmore, *Evidence* (Chad. Rev.), s. 980) that extrinsic testimony in the form of convictions was receivable to impeach, the issue is not entirely free from doubt. The Common Law Practice Commission in 1853 (quoted in 3A Wigmore, *Evidence* (Chad. Rev.), s. 984) described as the "better authorities" those which allowed the witness to refuse to answer or deny an earlier conviction and prohibited contradiction. Their "compromise" (Common Law Procedures Act, 1854, c. 125) would preserve the privilege but allow contradictory proof.

(1.1) If the witness either denies the fact or refuses to answer, the opposite party may prove the conviction.

(2)   The conviction may be proved by producing

    (a)   a certificate containing the substance and effect only, omitting the formal part, of the indictment and conviction, if it is for an indictable offence, or a copy of the summary conviction, if for an offence punishable on summary conviction, purporting to be signed by the clerk of the court or other officer having the custody of the records of the court in which the conviction, if on indictment, was had, or to which the conviction, if summary, was returned; and

    (b)   proof of identity.[359]

The precursor of section 12 was first enacted at a time when the accused was not a competent witness at his trial. When the accused was made a competent witness in England, in 1898, they recognized that the earlier legislation could affect him very differently than other witnesses. They recognized that a jury would find it difficult to confine their use of the previous record to credibility and, despite any limiting instructions from the judge, the jury might use the fact of the previous conviction as indicative of the accused's character and as directly relevant to whether he did the deed alleged at his present trial. That use was prohibited by the rule of evidence which forbade the introduction of the accused's character save in particularly limited instances. The possibility of this prejudicial impact increased dramatically, of course, if the previous conviction resembled the matter at hand. The legislation which made the accused a competent witness in England addressed this concern and provided that an accused who chose to become a witness could not be asked as to his previous record unless the accused had led evidence of his own good character or attacked the character of the prosecution's witnesses; see Criminal Evidence Act, 1898, 61 & 62 Vict., c. 36, section 1. When Canada made the accused a competent witness at his trial, *Canada Evidence Act*, S.C. 1892, c. 31, section 4, the legislators displayed no similar foresight and no such modification of the existing law occurred.

In Chapter 3 we saw the Supreme Court of Canada recognize in the *Corbett* decision that there was a discretion. The exercise of the discretion has been uneven and many, if not most, trial judges, unfortunately, will not exclude such questioning but there have been exceptions.

In *R. v. Bailey*,[360] the defence applied for an order to prohibit cross-examination of the accused on his record. Specifically the defence wanted the word "sexual" deleted from any reference to the accused's previous conviction for sexual assault with a weapon. Justice Zelinski granted the application as a matter of common sense. He wrote:

If I were about to enter into a transaction . . . the first thing that I would like to know, referable to the person I was dealing with, is whether or not that person had engaged

---

359 First enacted in 1869: An Act Respecting Procedure in Criminal Cases, 1869, S.C. 32 & 33 Vict., c. 29, s. 65. For a provincial counterpart see s. 22, *Ontario Evidence Act*, R.S.O. 1980, c. 145. Concerning the type of offence relevant to credibility compare *Street v. Guelph*, [1965] 2 C.C.C. 215 (Ont. H.C.) and *Clarke v. Holdsworth* (1967), 62 W.W.R. 1 (B.C.S.C.). See also *Morris v. R.* (1979), 6 C.R. (3d) 36 (S.C.C.) re juvenile offences; *R. v. Stratton* (1978), 42 C.C.C. (2d) 449 (Ont. C.A.) re foreign convictions; and *R. v. Boyce* (1974), 28 C.R.N.S. 336 (Ont. C.A.) re ability to ask witness regarding penalty.

360 (1993), 22 C.R. (4th) 65 (Ont. Gen. Div.).

in the very type of activity I was concerned about. This, of course, identifies as propensity. I think even more than wanting to know whether someone has passed a bad cheque or cheated in cards, one would like to know whether or not that person has done something of the very nature as the matter you are concerned with, again, propensity.

. . . .

Of course, in the exercise of discretion as indicated by La Forest J., the more similar the offence is to the subject matter of the charge, the better the reason, on principles of fairness, for excluding it. As he indicated, while it is commonplace to suggest that jurors are capable of understanding a direction that they must only use a prior conviction on issues of credibility, the likelihood is, based on the studies that he referred to, that this will not be the case and this should be realized.

. . . .

I specifically challenged [the Crown] on the fact that her objection to the deletion of the word "sexual" is nothing more than a desire on the part of the Crown to save that word because of its potential identification with the offence before the jury (notwithstanding the charge I must give them, that evidence that a person who has done this or similar, previously, as proven by a conviction, cannot be used as evidence that he is likely to be at it again).[361]

In *R. v. Saroya*[362] the accused appealed from his conviction of assault. He admitted hitting the victim on the head with a bottle of wine but he testified that he did so in order to break up a fight between the victim and another man. One of the issues was with respect to the disclosure of his criminal record which included a conviction for attempted murder. The trial judge in refusing the accused's request for protection against cross-examination on his criminal record, decided:

In the case at bar the accused has one prior conviction in 1988 for attempt murder. A man wears the chains he forges in life. A conviction is part of the accused's persona that he puts before the jury when he chooses to testify. I have considered all the factors pertaining to the exercise of discretion as set out in *Corbett*. In my view the accused would not be prejudiced by the admission of the prior conviction and in the interests of justice it should he admitted in evidence.[363]

The Court of Appeal decided:

The balancing exercise is a particularly difficult one in this case. The relevant factors point to both probative value and prejudice. The accused's prior record discloses a conviction for attempted murder in 1988, some four years prior to the trial at issue here. That was his only prior conviction. A conviction for attempted murder cannot be dismissed as having little probative value on the credibility of a witness. Although it is not a so-called offence of dishonesty, which may be probative of deception, attempted murder is such a serious offence that, in itself, it may be taken to indicate that the prospect of a conviction for perjury is unlikely to keep the witness in line. More significantly, it would be open to a jury to find, on all the relevant evidence, that the witness is unlikely to have more respect for the truth than he has shown for human life.

---

361 *Ibid.*, at pp. 67-68.
362 (1992), 18 C.R. (4th) 198 (Ont. Gen. Div.); affirmed (1994), 76 O.A.C. 25 (C.A.).
363 *Ibid.*, at p. 201 (C.R.).

On the other hand, of course, a conviction for attempted murder shows a capacity for violence against the person, and, on a charge of aggravated assault and assault causing bodily harm invites an inference of guilt through disposition. Not only is the offence for which the appellant was previously convicted very similar to the one that he was facing at trial, but, being of a more serious nature, it would logically support an inference that if the appellant once attempted to kill someone, he would not likely hesitate to commit the types of assaults that he was alleged to have committed.

. . . .

In the end, guidance comes from the *Corbett* decision. In that case, the majority of the Supreme Court ruled in favour of inclusion, in conformity with s. 12 of the *Canada Evidence Act*, of a prior murder conviction when the accused was facing a charge of first degree murder. Although the potential for prejudice was recognized as significant, the Supreme Court held that the potential prejudice could be displaced by a proper instruction to the jury about the impermissible use of the prior record. It is conceded that such proper instruction was given in the present case. As in *Corbett*, we are of the opinion that the deletion of the appellant's record would leave the jury with incomplete and therefore incorrect information about his credibility as a witness. To deprive the jury of that information in the present case, would hinder the jury's ability to correctly appreciate the facts. On balance, we think that the probative value of the appellant's criminal record of the question of his credibility as a witness outweighs the potential risk that the jury might use that prior conviction as evidence that the appellant is the type of person likely to have committed the offences with which he was charged.[364]

In *R. v. Brand* [365] the accused appealed from his conviction by a jury on a charge of trafficking in cocaine. The accused had made a *Corbett* application, submitting that the trial judge should edit the accused's record of criminal convictions. The accused had a very lengthy record which included convictions for crimes of dishonesty but concluded with three convictions for trafficking in narcotics. The trial judge declined to do edit the record holding that such was an exceptional departure from the general rule which should only be invoked when there is some exceptional unfairness. The Court of Appeal decided:

He was obliged to weigh and balance the risks for and against exclusion, bearing in mind the evidentiary value of previous convictions admitted pursuant to s. 12, and the fair trial of the accused. The three convictions in question had no probative value with respect to the appellant's credibility but were highly prejudicial. On the other hand, the balance of the record included offences that reflected on credibility. Viewed in this way, we think on the facts, this was a proper case to exclude the three convictions for trafficking. To do so would ensure that the jury had sufficiently complete and correct information about the appellant's credibility as a witness and would effectively remove the possibility of any unfairness by the introduction of the evidence in issue.[366]

In *R. v. Charland*,[367] the Supreme Court in a brief oral judgment refused to overturn the conviction of sexual assault where the Crown had been permitted to cross-examine the accused as to prior sexual convictions. This was a

---

364 *Ibid.*, at p. 28 (O.A.C.).
365 (1995), 40 C.R. (4th) 137 (Ont. C.A.).
366 *Ibid.*, at p. 140.
367 (1997), 12 C.R. (5th) 226 (S.C.C.). See criticism of P. Sankoff, "A Lost Opportunity to Clarify Corbett and the Use of an Accused's Criminal Record" (1997), 12 C.R. (5th) 228.

discretionary decision, held Cory J., and the jury had been charged as to the very limited use they could make of the evidence.

Despite *Charland* there has been a recent trend to exclude, particularly in the Ontario Court of Appeal. Consider, for example,[368] that Court's decision in *McFadyen*.

R. v. McFADYEN
(2002), 2 C.R. (6th) 344, 2002 CarswellOnt 125, 161 C.C.C. (3d) 252 (C.A.), leave to appeal refused (2002), 2002 CarswellOnt 3502, 2002 CarswellOnt 3503 (S.C.C.)

The accused was convicted by a jury on a charge of sexual assault. The sole ground of appeal was that the trial judge erred by dismissing the accused's *Corbett* application and permitting the Crown to cross-examine him on his criminal record. That record included a conviction for indecent assault in 1981 and convictions for sexual assault in 1984 and 1986. His defence at trial was that the sexual intercourse had been consensual. Credibility had been the central issue.

Per GOUDGE J.A. (ROSENBERG and FELDMAN JJ.A. concurring): —

. . . .

I recognize that the decision made on a Corbett application is a matter of discretion and that absent a clear error in the exercise of that discretion this court should not interfere in order to substitute its own view of how that discretion should have been exercised. See *R. v. P. (G.F.)* (1994),18 O.R. (3d) 1 at 5 (Ont. C.A.).

In my view, in this case the trial judge did make such an error. In essence, he admitted the appellant's record simply on the basis that the credibility of the complainant and the appellant would be a central issue at the trial. The Corbett process rather requires a weighing of the factors relevant to the prejudicial effect and the probative value of the previous convictions, against the backdrop that the general course of preference is to give the jury all the information, but at the same time give a clear direction as to the limited use they are to make of such information.

---

368 New trials were recently ordered on the basis that *Corbett* applications should have been allowed where the criminal record involved the very type of offence charged: *R. v. Brown* (2002), 6 C.R. (6th) 380, 166 C.C.C. (3d) 570 (Ont. C.A.) (drug trafficking) and *R. v. Madrusan* (2005), 35 C.R. (6th) 220, 203 C.C.C. (3d) 513 (B.C. C.A.) (robbery). A new trial was ordered in a manslaughter case where the accused had been cross-examined on a prior record for which he had been pardoned: *R. v. Bruha* (2006), 39 C.R. (6th) 384, 2006 CarswellNWT 13 (C.A.). For arguments that the *Corbett* discretion is insufficiently protective of accused, see Peter Sankoff, "*Corbett*, Crimes of Dishonesty and the Credibility Contest: Challenging the Accepted Wisdom on What Makes a Prior Conviction Probative" (2006), 10 Can. Crim. L. Rev. 215 and "*Corbett* Revisited: A Fairer Approach to the Admission of an Accused's Prior Criminal Record in Cross-examination" (2006), 51 Crim. L.Q. 400. See further, Sankoff, "The Search for a Better Understanding of Discretionary Power in Evidence Law", (2007) 32 *Queen's L.J.* 487.

In this case the balancing of these factors requires that the appellant's record be excluded because of its very significant prejudicial effect and its minimal probative value. In *R. v. Batte* (2000), 145 C.C.C. (3d) 498 at 516 (Ont. C.A.) Rosenberg J.A. said this:

> In *Corbett*, while Dickson C.J.C. disagreed with La Forest J. as to whether the record should be admitted, he accepted the factors that should be taken into account in the exercise of the judge's discretion. Among the most important factors enumerated by La Forest J. at pp. 740-44 are: the nature of the previous conviction, the remoteness or nearness of the conviction to the present charge, whether it is a conviction for a similar offence (in which case there is a greater risk of prejudice to a fair trial), and the nature of the defence attack on the Crown witnesses.

The previous convictions were all at least 14 years old at the time of the appellant's trial. The fact that since his convictions the appellant has apparently led a legally blameless life for a long period of time substantially diminishes the relevance these convictions may have for his credibility. Moreover, the prior convictions were for offences similar to the one for which the appellant was on trial. The Crown does not advance them as similar acts. The prejudicial effect of the appellant's record is markedly greater given that the convictions were for offences of a similar kind. Finally, the appellant's attack on the complainant's credibility was not based on any assertion that she had a bad character or a criminal record of her own. There was no need on this score to balance the picture for the jury as there was in Corbett. Thus, all of these factors weigh against the admission of the prior convictions. . . . I would therefore allow the appeal, set aside the conviction and order a new trial.[369]

HUTTON v. WAY
(1997), 105 O.A.C. 361, 1997 CarswellOnt 4692 (C.A.)

This was an appeal from an award of damages rendered by a jury. The appellant Hutton argued that the trial judge erred by admitting his criminal record into evidence. Hutton's record included convictions for sexual assault and possession of marijuana. The evidence was admitted as going to the credibility of Hutton's claim that he was unable to return to his employment as a counsellor at a treatment centre of adolescent boys due to the injuries he suffered. The defence argued that he did not return because he would have been dismissed due to his record. Hutton was not given any award for future loss of income and his wife and child received nothing on their Family Law Act claims.

Per FINLAYSON J.A. (CATZMAN and AUSTIN JJ.A. concurring): —

In my opinion, the trial judge erred in admitting into evidence the record of convictions for criminal offences committed by the appellant when he was a teenager. The convictions were for sexual assault on a female in 1976 and for dangerous driving and possession of marihuana in 1978. It is to be noted that

---

369 See generally Owen Rees, "The Jury's Propensity for Prohibited Reasoning: Corbett Revisited" (2002), 7 Can. Crim. L. Rev. 333. P.

none was for an offence of dishonesty or perjury. In aggravation of this criminal record was the evidence of a more recent charge for sexual assault on a female, a charge for which he was acquitted, when the evidence at trial demonstrated that he was not the assailant and was in fact innocent.

The basis of the admission of this evidence of a criminal record which is highly prejudicial was that the appellant, at the time of the accident, was employed at Bayfield House, a private residential treatment centre for problem adolescent boys. The appellant had undergone special training to equip himself for this job. On application, he was never asked if he had a criminal record and did not volunteer the fact. However, it was stated in evidence that a ministry initiative called for a review of all criminal records of employees in institutions such as Bayfield and that the disclosure of the fact of this criminal record would mean that he would have a remote chance of maintaining employment.

To justify the admissibility of the criminal record and this unsubstantiated accusation, it was said that the credibility of the appellant was in issue when he testified that he was unable to resume his employment at Bayfield after the accident because of his injuries. The respondent suggested that he resigned because he knew that his criminal record and the then outstanding charges would become known to Bayfield and his employment would be terminated.

In my opinion, the fact that the appellant might be terminated for reasons that had nothing to do with his qualifications or work record is not only speculative but irrelevant in a civil action for personal injuries. The nature and extent of his injuries had nothing to do with his early criminal record or his current charges for an offence of which he was innocent. The only result of this evidence was to paint the appellant as a sex offender and create a hostile environment for his claim.

As indicated, the stale dated criminal record of the appellant did not relate to offences involving fraud or dishonesty. While prima facie admissible under the Ontario Evidence Act, these convictions should have been excluded on the Corbett application brought by the appellant. The fact of an outstanding charge is not admissible under the Evidence Act under any circumstances and the grounds advanced at common law, while remotely relevant, are so prejudicial so as to outweigh what limited probative value the evidence had.

The verdict reflects a certain meanness of spirit. The appellant received general damages for his injuries which were at the lower end of the scale. He received no award for future loss of income although the verdict reflected past loss of income from the accident to trial (a period of four and one half years) and may have reflected future disability by awarding future rehabilitation expenses covering a six month period. The wife and child of the marriage received nothing under the Family Law Act despite the evidence concerning them that supported such claims.

The improper admission of the evidence as to the criminal record and the charge of sexual assault may well have coloured the quantum of the above awards. The relief would ordinarily be a new trial but, understandably, that is not the relief the appellant seeks. He relies strongly upon the inconsistencies in the answers given to the questions asked by the jury and submits that this court, "if it considers it just", should exercise its powers under s. 119 of the Courts of Justice Act, R.S.O. 1990, Ch. C. 43 and substitute its own assessment of the damages.

I think we should do just that with respect of those areas where inexplicably the jury made no award. Having in mind that the jury was inclined to award figures throughout which were at the lower end of the scale, I would amend the judgment to award the following damages:

(i)	future loss of income for six months	$12,500
(ii)	FLA claim of Leisa Hutton	5,000
(iii)	FLA claim of Caleb Hutton	1,000

Section 22 of the *Ontario Evidence Act* provides:

Proof of previous conviction of a witness

22. (1) A witness may be asked whether he or she has been convicted of any crime, and upon being so asked, if the witness either denies the fact or refuses to answer, the conviction may be proved, and a certificate containing the substance and effect only, omitting the formal part, of the charge and of the conviction, purporting to be signed by the officer having the custody of the records of the court at which the offender was convicted, or by the deputy of the officer, is, upon proof of the identity of the witness as such convict, sufficient evidence of the conviction, without proof of the signature or of the official character of the person appearing to have signed the certificate. R.S.O. 1990, c. E.23, s. 22 (1).

R. v. UNDERWOOD
[1998] 1 S.C.R. 77, 12 C.R. (5th) 241, 121 C.C.C. (3d) 117

The accused was charged with first degree murder. After the Crown closed its case, his counsel made a Corbett application to have the accused's lengthy criminal record excluded. The trial judge did not make a ruling at that time, but rather indicated that he would prefer to wait until the accused had given his testimony in chief. The accused elected not to testify. He was later convicted and his conviction was upheld by the Court of Appeal. On further appeal a new trial was ordered.

LAMER C.J.C.:—

. . . .

The question which the Court must answer in this case is whether it is an error of law to refuse to make a ruling on a *Corbett* application before the accused has elected to testify and been examined in chief. On the one hand, it would be very undesirable to force the trial judge to make a decision without all the relevant information. On the other hand, the accused must have an opportunity to make an informed decision whether to testify and, accordingly, should know as much as possible about the consequences of that decision in advance of having to make it. A balance must be struck between these two necessities. However, the balance must reflect that the ultimate goal of the procedural and substantive protections in the criminal justice system are to ensure that trials are scrupulously fair. Our criminal process is based upon the principle that before the accused calls evidence in his own defence, he must have knowledge of the case to be met. The extent to which his criminal record will be admissible against him will encompass part of that case. In this context, the case-to-meet principle suggests that the accused should have a right to make a Corbett application, and to know its outcome at the close of the Crown's case. It would be manifestly unfair to force an accused to engage in what the appellant describes as "russian roulette", or what Professor Delisle, in an annotation to *R. v. Hoffman* (1994), 32 C.R. (4th) 396, at p. 398, calls "blind man's bluff".

Although fairness requires that the ruling be made no later than the close of the Crown's case, there is always the possibility that the defence evidence will influence that trial judge's prior evaluation of the probative value and prejudicial effect of the criminal record. There are various ways of dealing with this problem. One is the possibility of making a preliminary ruling, subject to reconsideration if necessary. [But] imagine the possible unfairness that would arise if the accused takes the stand in reliance on a ruling that some or all of his prior convictions will be excluded, and that ruling is subsequently reversed.

In my view, the situation can be resolved by holding a voir dire before the defence opens its case. In this voir dire, the defence will reveal the evidence which it intends to call, either through calling witnesses, or through agreed statements of fact. The trial judge can then consider the factors set out in Corbett (the nature of the previous convictions, the time since the previous convictions, and any attacks made on the credibility of Crown witnesses) in the context of the defence evidence, and make a final ruling on the Corbett application.

I would emphasize that the purpose of this voir dire is not "defence disclosure". It creates no independent rights in the Crown, and, therefore should not be treated as an excuse for the Crown to deeply probe the case for the defence, as the defence is entitled to do to the Crown's case at a preliminary inquiry. The point to to provide the trial judge with the information he or she needs to make an informed decision, but the Crown has no right to require more than that. There may even be cases in which the trial judge believes he or she has sufficient information to make a decision without such disclosure, such as where the nature of the defence is fairly clear or has otherwise been disclosed (e.g. an alibi), or where the outcome of the application is readily apparent without this information. In those cases, disclosure need not be given.

. . . .

In summary, a *Corbett* application should be made after the close of the Crown's case. If the trial judge believes it to be necessary, a voir dire should be held in which the defence discloses what evidence it intends to call, so he or she can make a fully informed ruling on the application. This ruling may be subject to modification if the defence evidence departs significantly from what was disclosed. In this case, the trial judge refused to rule until after the appellant had testified, and in so doing, he erred.

In *Hewson v. R.*,[370] the court decided, 5:4, that an accused could be questioned as to a previous conviction though at the time of the questioning the conviction was subject to a pending appeal. In *Titus v. R.*,[371] the accused had been convicted of murder. The court granted him a new trial because the trial judge had precluded cross-examination by the defence of a Crown witness with respect to an outstanding murder charge preferred against that witness by the same police department that had laid the murder charge against the accused. The court decided that cross-examination of a Crown witness concerning an outstanding indictment against that witness was proper and admissible for the purpose of showing a possible motivation to seek favour with the prosecution.

In *R. v. Danson*,[372] the Crown cross-examined the accused as to an incident where he was found guilty of assault and given a conditional discharge. The trial judge treated the discharge as a conviction. The conviction was quashed. The court noted that an accused unlike an ordinary witness, cannot be cross-examined with respect to discreditable acts unrelated to the charge on the issue of credibility unless he puts his character in issue or is examined pursuant to section 12 ; an adjudication of guilt followed by the granting of a discharge is not a conviction.

In *Morris v. R.*,[373] the accused was found guilty on a charge of breaking and entering with intent. He appealed on the ground that the trial judge erred by allowing cross-examination of the accused as to his having been having been found guilty, under the Juvenile Delinquents Act, of offences, under the Criminal Code. The Supreme Court, 5:4, dismissed his appeal, saying the word "offence" as used in section 12 includes a delinquency consisting in a violation of the Criminal Code which is enforceable under the Juvenile Delinquents Act, and a finding of delinquency under that Act was equivalent to a conviction within the meaning of section 12. There are now conflicting authorities on whether a youth can be cross-examined on their youth record under s. 12.[374] **Which approach do you think is most consistent with the underlying protections given to young offenders under the *Youth Criminal Justice Act*?**

(d) Defects in Capacity of Witness

The cross-examiner is always entitled, subject to the trial judge's discretion, to attempt impeachment by questioning the witness's general capacity to observe, recollect and communicate, and his particular ability in the case under review. At times the witness may confess the possibility of error. In other instances the very incredibility of a fact deposed to on cross-examination will disclose such obvious error on one point as to cast doubt on the rest of his evidence. The witness's capacities may also be tested in front of the trier of fact by means of an experiment.

---

370 [1979] 2 S.C.R. 82.
371 [1983] 1 S.C.R. 259.
372 (1982), 35 O.R. (2d) 777 (C.A.). See also *R. v. Sark* (2004), 182 C.C.C. (3d) 530 (N.B. C.A.).
373 [1979] 1 S.C.R. 405.
374 See *R. v. Sheik-Qasim* (2007), 230 C.C.C. (3d) 531 (S.C.J.) [not allowed]; and *R. v. U. (D.A.)* (2008), 239 C.C.C. (3d) 409 (N.S. S.C.) [permitted].

May extrinsic evidence by introduced to prove the incapacity alleged?

If the witness testifies that he observed the incident under review clearly because there was then a full moon, then obviously his opponent should be able to introduce contradictory evidence of the moon's illumination on the evening in question to demonstrate that the witness's opportunity for observation was less than full. But if the extrinsic evidence is previous specific instances of error by the witness, should we analogize to specific instances of misconduct and foreclose, or to evidence of bias and receive? If we seek to test the memory of the witness by asking him questions concerning matters which occurred at the same time as the material event, though unconnected with it, can we lead extrinsic evidence to contradict? May we seek to establish by extrinsic evidence that the witness misperceived other matters at other times unconnected with the material issue? Can we enunciate a clear rule or can we do more than simply rest the decision with the discretion of the trial judge who can weigh the probative value towards impeachment against consumption of time, confusion of issues and fairness to the witness?

Is the situation different when the extrinsic evidence on capacity is medical evidence? May a medical witness give his opinion on veracity and state the reasons for his belief? In *R. v. Toohey*[375] the House of Lords analyzing that problem noted:

> This unreliability may have two aspects either separate from one another or acting jointly to create confusion. The witness may, through his mental trouble, derive a fanciful or untrue picture from events while they are actually occurring, or he may have a fanciful or untrue recollection of them which distorts his evidence at the time when he is giving it.
>
> The only general principles which can be derived from the older cases are these. On the one hand, the courts have sought to prevent juries from being beguiled by the evidence of witnesses who could be shown to be, through defect of character, wholly unworthy of belief. On the other hand, however, they have sought to prevent the trial of a case becoming clogged with a number of side issues, such as might arise if there could be an investigation of matters which had no relevance to the issue save in so far as they tended to show the veracity or falsity of the witness who was giving evidence which *was* relevant to the issue. Many controversies which might thus obliquely throw some light on the issues must in practice be discarded because there is not an infinity of time, money and mental comprehension available to make use of them.

and concluded:

> Human evidence shares the frailties of those who give it. It is subject to many cross-currents such as partiality, prejudice, self-interest and, above all, imagination and inaccuracy. Those are matters with which the jury, helped by cross-examination and common sense, must do their best. But when a witness through physical (in which I include mental) disease or abnormality is not capable of giving a true or

---

375 [1965] A.C. 595, 607-08 (H.L.) per Lord Pearce. See Moore, "Note — The Admissibility of Medical Evidence to Impugn the Reliability of a Witness," [1965] Camb. L.J. 176 and "Note, Psychiatric Evaluation of the Mentally Abnormal Witness" (1949-50), 59 Yale L.J. 1324. See also Hoski, "Use of Psychiatric Evidence as to Credibility of Witnesses in Criminal Trials" (1976), 3 Queen's L.J. 40. For Canadian cases following *Toohey* see *R. v. Dietrich* (1970), 1 C.C.C. (2d) 49 (Ont. C.A.) and *R. v. Hawke* (1975), 22 C.C.C. (2d) 19 (Ont. C.A.). Compare *R. v. Steinberg*, [1931] O.R. 222 (C.A.).

reliable account to the jury, it must surely be allowable for medical science to reveal this vital hidden fact to them. If a witness purported to give evidence of something which he believed that he had seen at a distance of 50 yards, it must surely be possible to call the evidence of an oculist to the effect that the witness could not possibly see anything at a greater distance than 20 yards, or the evidence of a surgeon who had removed a cataract from which the witness was suffering at the material time and which would have prevented him from seeing what he thought he saw. So, too, must it be allowable to call medical evidence of mental illness which makes a witness incapable of giving reliable evidence, whether through the existence of delusions or otherwise.

4. SUPPORTING CREDIBILITY

(a) General Rule Prohibiting

Speaking generally, evidence in support of credibility is not receivable unless and until credibility has been attacked. When the witness's character for truthfulness has been impeached by evidence of general reputation, opinion or specific instances of misconduct, the witness may be rehabilitated by evidence of good character, but not before.[376] It is not that the evidence of good character is irrelevant but rather that

> there is no reason why time should be spent in proving that which may be assumed to exist. Every witness may be assumed to be of normal moral character for veracity, just as he is assumed to be of normal sanity. Good character, therefore, in his support is excluded *until his character is brought in question* and it thus becomes worthwhile to deny that his character is bad.[377]

So too, if it is offered to show that the witness has previously made statements consistent with his present testimony:

> . . . when the witness has merely testified on direct examination, without any impeachment, proof of consistent statements is unnecessary and valueless. The witness is not helped by it; for, even if it is an improbable or untrustworthy story, it is not made more probable or more trustworthy by any number of repetitions of it. Such evidence would ordinarily be cumbersome to the trial and is ordinarily rejected.[378]

Again, it is not irrelevance to credibility that dictates rejection, but superfluity and consumption of time as the matter is simply not in issue. At times it is said that a prior consistent statement is excluded as in its self-serving nature resides the danger of fabrication as the witness is tempted to manufacture evidence for himself,[379] but the better view is as above, or, as seen in the language of the Privy Council:

---

376 See *R. v. Kyselka* (1962), 133 C.C.C. 103 (Ont. C.A.) rejecting psychiatric opinion in support of credibility. See also *R. v. Burkart*, [1965] 3 C.C.C. 210 (Sask. C.A.).

377 4 Wigmore, *Evidence* (Chad. Rev.), s. 1104 accepted in *R. v. Clarke* (1981), 63 C.C.C. (2d) 224, 233 (Alta. C.A.). See also *R. v. Martin* (1980), 53 C.C.C. (2d) 425 (Ont. C.A.).

378 4 Wigmore, *Evidence* (Chad. Rev.), s. 1124; note change from the 3d edition.

379 See, *e.g.*, Sopinka and Lederman, *Evidence in Civil Cases* (1974), p. 264 and cases there cited. And see Eyre, C.J. in *Trial of Thomas Hardy* (1794), 24 Howell's State Trials 199: Declarations are evidence against a prisoner and are not evidence for him, because the presumption upon which declarations are evidence is, that no man would declare anything

The purpose of such evidence of a witness's previous statements is and can only be to support his credit, when his veracity has been impugned, by showing a consistency in his account which adds some probative value to his evidence in the box. Generally speaking, as is well known, such confirmatory evidence is not admissible, the reason presumably being that all trials, civil and criminal, must be conducted with an effort to concentrate evidence on what is capable of being cogent and . . . it does not help to support the evidence of a witness who is the accused person to know that he has frequently told other persons before the trial what his defence was. *Evidence to that effect is, therefore, in a proper sense immaterial.*[380] [Emphasis added.]

In *Cross on Evidence*,[381] the rule is so justified:

[Sometimes] the reason given for the ban (sometimes loosely described as "the rule against narrative" or "the rule against self-corroboration") is the ease with which evidence of this nature can be manufactured. . . . A more convincing reason is that in an ordinary case, the evidence would be at least superfluous, for the assertions of a witness are to be regarded in general as true, until there is some particular reason for impeaching them as false.

The first Supreme Court of Canada case to address the common law rule against oath-helping involved the use of the polygraph. The Court also set out the general prohibition against leading prior consistent statements.

R. c. BÉLAND
1987 CarswellQue 14, 1987 CarswellQue 96, [1987] 2 S.C.R. 398, 36
C.C.C. (3d) 481, 60 C.R. (3d) 1

1 McINTYRE J. (DICKSON C.J., BEETZ and LE DAIN JJ concurring):—

This appeal involves the question of the admissibility in evidence in a criminal trial of the results of a polygraph examination of an accused person.

2 The respondents, Beland and Phillips, were charged with conspiracy to commit a robbery. The Crown led evidence to the effect that the respondents had conspired with one Grenier and one Filippone to rob an armoured truck. No robbery took

---

against himself, unless it were true; but that every man, if he was in a difficulty, or in the view to any difficulty, would make declarations for himself. Those declarations, if offered as evidence, would be offered, therefore, upon no ground which entitled to them to credit. That is the general rule.

380 *Fox v. Gen. Medical Council*, [1960] 3 All E.R. 225, 230. See also Cross, *Evidence* (5th ed.), p. 236. In *Notes to Pothier on Obligations*, quoted in *R. v. Giraldi* (1975), 28 C.C.C. (2d) 248 (B.C.C.A.), Evans notes: "In an ordinary case the evidence would be at least superfluous, for the assertions of a witness are to be regarded in general as true until there is some particular reason for impeaching them as false; which reason may be repelled by circumstances . . . either from the inherent nature and complexion of the evidence itself, or it may be indicated by the imputations actually thrown out in cross-examination or otherwise, by the opposite party." But see Martin J.A., in *R. v. Campbell* (1977), 38 C.C.C. (2d) 6, 18 (Ont. C.A.): "The narration by a witness of earlier statements made to other persons out of Court appears to be excluded . . . because of the general lack of probative value of such evidence, save in certain circumstances, in support of the credibility of the witness."

381 Tapper, ed., 7th ed (London: Butterworths, 1990), p. 281.

place because Grenier disclosed the conspiracy to the police. He later gave evidence for the Crown and his testimony was the only evidence which directly implicated the respondents in the conspiracy. The respondents gave evidence on their own behalf, denying any participation in the conspiracy and saying that the evidence of Grenier was false. Each respondent during his testimony said that he was prepared to undergo a polygraph examination. After completion of the evidence at trial the respondents made an application to the trial judge to reopen their defence, in order to permit each of them to take a polygraph examination and submit the results in evidence. This motion was refused by the trial judge who held that the results of such an examination were inadmissible in evidence, in accordance with *Phillion v. The Queen*, [1978] 1 S.C.R. 18. The respondents were convicted. An appeal to the Court of Appeal by the respondents succeeded. By a majority, the Court of Appeal granted an order reopening the trial and directing that the results of the polygraph examination be submitted to the trial judge, for a ruling as to their admissibility in light of all the circumstances revealed in the evidence: [1984] C.A. 443, 15 D.L.R. (4th) 89, 16 C.C.C. (3d) 462, 40 C.R. (3d) 193. The Crown appeals to this Court as of right under s. 621(1)(a) of the Criminal Code. The parties agree that the sole issue in this appeal is whether evidence of the results of a polygraph examination is admissible in light of the particular facts of this case.

· · ·

5 The leading case in this Court concerning the admissibility of polygraph evidence is *Phillion v. The Queen, supra*, in which it was held that such evidence should be rejected. Speaking for the majority, Ritchie J. expressed the view that such evidence offended the hearsay rule. . . .. Spence J., with whom Laskin C.J. concurred, wrote separate reasons in which he agreed that the evidence should be rejected, but he left open the question of whether in other circumstances the polygraph evidence might be admissible.

6 It was the suggestion of the possibility of a different result in other circumstances which was relied upon by the majority of the Court of Appeal to distinguish the *Phillion* case. As has been noted, *Phillion* did not give evidence himself but sought to rely on the evidence of the polygraph operator to place his story before the jury and lend it credibility. In the case at bar the two respondents each gave evidence at trial and now seek to invoke that of the polygraph operator to support their credibility.

General Rule Against Oath-helping

7 The Crown appellant argues that the admission of polygraph evidence offends the rule which prohibits a party from presenting evidence which has, as its sole purpose, the bolstering of the credibility of that party's own witnesses. This is sometimes referred to in the earlier cases as oath-helping. There does not appear to be any decision of this Court which has dealt specifically with the rule, but there is other substantial authority supporting it. The leading decision on this point in Canada is *R. v. Kyselka, s*upra. In that case, the three accused were

charged with the rape of a mentally retarded 16-year-old girl. The trial judge permitted the Crown to call a psychiatrist, who gave evidence that because of her low mental age the complainant lacked sufficient imagination to concoct a story. It was therefore likely that she would tell the truth in court. The accused were convicted. On appeal, Porter C.J.O., speaking for the court (Porter C.J.O., Kelly and McLennan JJ.A.), held that the evidence of the psychiatrist should not have been admitted as its sole purpose was to suggest that the complainant, because of her mental classification, was likely to be a truthful witness. He said, at pp. 107-8:

> While the credit of any witness may be impeached by the opposite party, *R. v. Gunewardene*, [1951] 2 All E.R. 290 at p. 294, there is no warrant or authority for such oath-helping as occurred in the circumstances of this case, reminiscent as it is of the method before the Norman Conquest by which a defendant in a civil suit or an accused person proved his case by calling witnesses to swear that the oath of the party was true. If this sort of evidence were admissible in the case of either party no limit could be placed on the number of witnesses who could be called to testify about the credibility of witnesses as to facts. It would tend to produce, regardless of the number of such character witnesses who were called, undue confusion in the minds of the jury by directing their attention away from the real issues and the controversy would become so intricate that truth would be more likely to remain hidden than be discovered. For these reasons this evidence was not admissible.

. . .

9 From the foregoing comments, it will be seen that the rule against oath-helping, that is, adducing evidence solely for the purpose of bolstering a witness's credibility, is well-grounded in authority. It is apparent that since the evidence of the polygraph examination has no other purpose, its admission would offend the well-established rule.

Rule Against Past Consistent Statements

10 The rule against oath-helping is also consistent in principle with other rules of evidence which in some degree may be said to overlap it and which are based on similar principles. An example is the rule against the admission of previous consistent statements of a witness. McWilliams, *supra*, discusses this rule, at p. 353, and refers to the frequently quoted words of Neville J. in *Jones v. South-Eastern and Chatham Railway* (1917), 87 L.J.K.B. 775 (C.A.), at p. 779, that:

> . . . statements may be used against a witness as admissions, but... you are not entitled to give evidence of statements on other occasions by the witness in confirmation of her testimony.

This was said in the context of a case where an injury was alleged to have been suffered by the plaintiff while at her work, and it was sought to adduce evidence of a statement she had made after the accident to a third party. . . . .

While [earlier cases and commentary] . . . .. suggest that the statements are excluded on the basis of hearsay and lack of probative value, another rationale for the rule has been noted, namely, that such statements could be too readily manufactured for use in later proceedings. In *R. v. Hardy* (1794), 24 St. Tr. 199, Eyre C.J. said, at pp. 1093-94:

> . . . the presumption . . . is that no man would declare anything against himself, unless it were true; but that every man, if he was in a difficulty, or in the view to any difficulty, would make declarations for himself.

11 The rule is generally expressed in relation to past consistent statements. In the case at bar, evidence would be given of statements made subsequent to the evidence given by the respondents at trial. In my view, however, this leads to no difference in principle. The concern is with consistent statements made out of court. The fact that they may be made after evidence has been given at trial would not change their probative value or reliability. In my view, the rule against admission of consistent out-of-court statements is soundly based and particularly apposite to questions raised in connection with the use of the polygraph. Polygraph evidence when tendered would be entirely self-serving and would shed no light on the real issues before the court. Assuming, as in the case at bar, that the evidence sought to be adduced would not fall within any of the well recognized exceptions to the operation of the rule—where it is permitted to rebut the allegation of a recent fabrication or to show physical, mental or emotional condition—it should be rejected. To do otherwise is to open the trial process to the time-consuming and confusing consideration of collateral issues and to deflect the focus of the proceedings from their fundamental issue of guilt or innocence. . . .

12 It is therefore my opinion that evidence of the results of a polygraph examination would clearly offend the rule against the admission of past or out-of-court statements by a witness. All of the considerations upon which the rule is based are as applicable to polygraph evidence as to other statements. The repetition of statements by another witness adds nothing to their weight and reliability. The ultimate decision as to the truth or falsity of the evidence of a witness must rest upon the exercise of the judgment of the trier of fact. This is as true of evidence of polygraph tests as of any other evidence. In the last analysis, the trier of fact must reach its conclusion on the basis of the evidence given by a human being in court. The evidence of the polygraph operator if heard by the trier of fact adds nothing to the earlier statement of the witness which is sought to be supported.

. . .

18 In conclusion, it is my opinion, based upon a consideration of rules of evidence long established and applied in our courts, that the polygraph has no place in the judicial process where it is employed as a tool to determine or to test the credibility of witnesses. It is frequently argued that the polygraph represents an application of modern scientific knowledge and experience to the task of determining the veracity of human utterances. It is said that the courts should welcome this device and not cling to the imperfect methods of the past in such an important task. This argument has a superficial appeal but, in my view, it cannot prevail in the face of the realities of court procedures.

19 I would say at once that this view is not based on a fear of the inaccuracies of the polygraph. On that question we were not supplied with sufficient evidence to reach a conclusion. However, it may be said that even the finding of a significant percentage of errors in its results would not, by itself, be sufficient ground to exclude it as an instrument for use in the courts. Error is inherent in human affairs, scientific or unscientific. It exists within our established court procedures and must always be guarded against. The compelling reason, in my view, for the exclusion of the evidence of polygraph results in judicial proceedings is two-fold. First, the admission of polygraph evidence would run counter to the well established rules of evidence which have been referred to. Second, while there is no reason why the rules of evidence should not be modified where improvement will result, it is my view that the admission of polygraph evidence will serve no purpose which is not already served. It will disrupt proceedings, cause delays, and lead to numerous complications which will result in no greater degree of certainty in the process than that which already exists.

20 Since litigation replaced trial by combat, the determination of fact, including the veracity of parties and their witnesses, has been the duty of judges or juries upon an evaluation of the statements of witnesses. This approach has led to the development of a body of rules relating to the giving and reception of evidence and we have developed methods which have served well and have gained a wide measure of approval. They have facilitated the orderly conduct of judicial proceedings and are designed to keep the focus of the proceedings on the principal issue, in a criminal case, the guilt or innocence of the accused. What would be served by the introduction of evidence of polygraph readings into the judicial process? To begin with, it must be remembered that however scientific it may be, its use in court depends on the human intervention of the operator. Whatever results are recorded by the polygraph instrument, their nature and significance reach the trier of fact through the mouth of the operator. Human fallibility is therefore present as before, but now it may be said to be fortified with the mystique of science. Then, it may be asked, what does it do? It provides evidence on the issue of the credibility of a witness. This has always been a collateral issue and one to be decided by the trier of fact. Is the trier of fact assisted by hearing, firstly from witness "A" that he was not present at the scene of the crime, and then from witness "B", a polygraph operator, that "A" was probably truthful? What would the result be, one may ask, if the polygraph operator concluded from his test that witness "A" was lying? Would such evidence be admissible, could it be excluded by witness "A", could it be introduced by the Crown? These are serious questions and they lead to others. Would it be open to the opponent of the person relying upon the polygraph to have a second polygraph examination taken for his purposes? If the results differed, which would prevail, and what right would there be for compelling the production of polygraph evidence in the possession of a reluctant party? It is this fear of turmoil in the courts which leads me to reject the polygraph. Like Porter C.J.O. in *Kyselka*, I would not wish to see a return to the method of pre-Norman trials where parties relied heavily upon oath-helpers who swore to their veracity. For a description of the role of the oath-helper in early

times, see W.S. Holdsworth, *A History of English Law* (7th ed. 1956), vol. 1, at pp. 305-8, and W.F. Walsh, *Outlines of the History of English and American Law* (1926), at pp. 99-100 (footnote II). I would seek to preserve the principle that in the resolution of disputes in litigation, issues of credibility will be decided by human triers of fact, using their experience of human affairs and basing judgment upon their assessment of the witness and on consideration of how an individual's evidence fits into the general picture revealed on a consideration of the whole of the case.

21 For the above reasons, and following *Phillion, supra,* I would allow the Crown's appeal. I would set aside the order of the Court of Appeal and confirm the conviction recorded at trial.

Wilson J. (Lamer J. concurring) (dissenting):—

I must respectfully disagree . . . that these rules present a basis for excluding the polygraph evidence and I will comment briefly on each.

(1) *The Rule Against Oath-helping*

Oath-helping or compurgation was, as I understand it, a method used to prove one's case in pre-Norman England. The accused in a criminal case or the defendant in a civil case could prove his innocence by providing a certain number of compurgators who would swear to the truth of his oath. The compurgators swore a set oath. If they departed from it in the slightest, the "oath burst" and the opposing party won. The practice fell into desuetude in the 13th Century.

The connection between oath-helping and the admissibility of polygraph evidence seems to me to be very tenuous. Oath-helpers were not required to have any knowledge material to the innocence or guilt of the accused. They merely recited a particular oath and their oaths were not subject to rebuttal. The polygraph operator, on the other hand, has subjected the accused to a number of tests. He reports on the results of these tests and gives his expert opinion as to whether the physiological reactions of the accused are similar to those of someone telling the truth. He is open to cross-examination on his technique, his assumptions, his interpretation of the data and the accuracy of the device. His evidence is only one of the many factors the jury will consider when assessing the credibility of the accused.

In what sense then can polygraph evidence be said to be similar to the medieval device by which the accused was guaranteed an acquittal if he could muster a sufficient number of compurgators? Any suggestion of similarity would, it seems to me, have to be based on the assumption that, despite the cross-examination of the polygraph operator, the calling of other operators to challenge erroneous statements by the original operator, and the delivery of a proper charge to the jury, the jury would automatically base its decision on the polygraph operator's testimony. I think this is an unwarranted assumption. I do not think we can make it even if my colleague's concern about the heightened weight that might be given to polygraph evidence because of the "mystique of science" has some validity. For reasons which will be given later I doubt that this concern is a valid one.

My own view would be that the rule against oath-helping is a curious point of legal history that has little bearing on the issue of polygraph admissibility. Oath-helping was a method of proving one's case that ante-dated the modern concept of trial by evidence. Polygraph evidence, on the other hand, fits squarely within the modern trial theory whereby witnesses are examined to ascertain the truth.

It is suggested, however, that oath-helping is the antecedent of a "well-established rule" against the admissibility of evidence adduced solely for the purpose of bolstering the credibility of one's own witness. A number of authorities are cited in support of the proposition that evidence may not be given in chief to bolster the credit of one's own witnesses but, if evidence is given to impeach their credit, rebuttal evidence may be given on that issue. It is noted, however, that the Canadian cases relied on in support of the rule are all cases in which the Crown was attempting to lead evidence-in-chief to bolster the credibility of a Crown witness. No Canadian case was cited where an accused was denied permission to do this. I have some concern, therefore, as to the scope of the "well-established rule" in Canada. I believe it would require an extension of the rule in this case to apply it to the respondents. Perhaps it should be applied to Crown and defence alike but this is not self-evident. Analogies certainly can be drawn from other areas of criminal evidence law to support a more permissive approach to evidence led by an accused. For example, in *R. v. Miller* (1952), 36 Cr. App. R. 169, an accused was permitted to call evidence against a co-accused which would have been inadmissible if called by the Crown. . . .

I am very mindful of the fact that the respondents in this case took the stand in order to deny their involvement in the conspiracy and that the only direct evidence implicating them was that of Grenier, a self-confessed conspirator. The Crown, through Grenier, was impugning the credibility of the respondents by saying that they were lying under oath. It was his word against theirs. The respondents were, in effect, responding to an attack on their credibility by the Crown by offering to take a lie detector test. Indeed, the Crown's whole case was that the respondents were lying and that the informer Grenier was telling the truth.

Section 577(3) of the *Criminal Code* provides that an accused is entitled, after the close of the prosecution's case, to make full answer and defence. It might be said that this is precisely what the respondents were attempting to do through the introduction of the polygraph evidence. . . .

(2) *The Rule Against Past Consistent Statements*

The second ground for exclusion of the polygraph evidence is that it infringes the rule against the admission of past consistent statements. The cases and authorities make it clear that these statements are excluded because they are at best irrelevant and at worst fabricated and self-serving. The irrelevance rationale has, it seems to me, little applicability to polygraph evidence. The argument that the mere repetition of a story has no bearing on the truth of the story is, of course, a convincing one. Polygraph evidence, however, is not merely evidence that the accused has said the same thing twice. It is expert evidence on how closely his physiological responses during the test correspond to those of someone telling the truth. It is, in my opinion, clearly relevant.

Nor am I persuaded that the evidence should be excluded on the ground that by "examiner shopping" and by engaging in practice tests the accused may be able to increase the likelihood of a "successful" test. Unless it can be established that polygraph tests are *per se* without probative value (and I do not think this has been or could be established), it would seem to me that the possibility of abuse should be a factor going to weight rather than to admissibility.

In 2009, Romeo Phillion's 1972 conviction for murder was set aside by the Ontario Court of Appeal[382] pursuant to a miscarriage of justice review under s. 696.3 of the *Criminal Code*. The Court of Appeal concluded that his initial trial was unfair because his counsel was unaware of evidence establishing an alibi for the offence.

The rule against oath-helping also applies to limit the scope of expert opinion evidence (the admissibility of which is discussed in the next chapter).We will also there return to *Beland* and *Phillion* respecting the admissibility of expert testimony.

(b) Exceptions

To the general rule excluding previous consistent statements, the common law recognized certain exceptions.

(i) *To Rebut Allegation of Recent Fabrication*

> If, in cross-examination, a witness's account of some incident or set of facts is challenged as being a recent invention, thus presenting a clear issue whether, at some previous time, he said or thought what he has been saying at the trial, he may support himself by evidence of earlier statements by him to the same effect. Plainly the rule that sets up the exception cannot be formulated with any great precision, since its application will depend on the nature of the challenge offered by the course of cross-examination and the relative cogency of the evidence tendered to repel it. Its application must be, within limits, a matter of discretion, and its range can only be measured by the reported instances, not in themselves many, in which it has been successfully invoked.[383]

R. v. STIRLING
2008 CarswellBC 506, 2008 CarswellBC 507, [2008] 1 S.C.R. 272, 54 C.R. (6th) 228, 229 C.C.C. (3d) 257

The judgment of the Court was delivered by:

1 BASTARACHE J.:— The appellant, Mr. Stirling, appeals his convictions on two counts of criminal negligence causing death and one count of criminal negligence causing bodily harm. The convictions arose out of a single-vehicle accident in which two of the car's occupants were killed and two others, including Mr.

---

382 See *R. v. Phillion* (2009), 241 C.C.C. (3d) 193 (Ont. C.A.).
383 *Fox v. Gen. Medical Council, supra*, note 380, at p. 230.

Stirling, were seriously injured. The primary issue before the trial judge was whether the Crown had established that the appellant, and not the other survivor of the accident, Mr. Harding, was driving the vehicle when the crash occurred. The trial judge ultimately concluded that Mr. Stirling was the driver. He based this finding on a number of pieces of evidence, including the testimony of Mr. Harding, who stated that Mr. Stirling had been driving.

2 During the cross-examination of Mr. Harding, counsel for the appellant questioned the witness about a pending civil claim he had launched against Mr. Stirling as the driver of the vehicle and about several drug-related charges against Mr. Harding which had recently been dropped. All parties agreed that this line of questioning raised the possibility that Mr. Harding had motive to fabricate his testimony and, following a voir dire, the judge admitted several prior consistent statements which served to rebut that suggestion.

3 The appellant argues on appeal that although the trial judge was correct in admitting the prior consistent statements for the purpose of refuting the suggestion of recent fabrication, he erroneously considered them for the truth of their contents. . . .

4 In my view, this appeal ought to be dismissed. Although the passages above contain some ambiguous comments about the use the trial judge made of the prior consistent statements, these remarks must be read in the context of the reasons as a whole. It is clear from this judgment that the trial judge was very aware of the limited use of the prior consistent statements, and he correctly instructed himself on this point repeatedly.

Analysis

5 It is well established that prior consistent statements are generally inadmissible (*R. v. Evans*, [1993] 2 S.C.R. 629; *R. v. Simpson*, [1988] 1 S.C.R. 3; *R. v. Béland*, [1987] 2 S.C.R. 398). This is because such statements are usually viewed as lacking probative value and being self-serving (*Evans*, at p. 643). There are, however, several exceptions to this general exclusionary rule, and one of these exceptions is that prior consistent statements can be admitted where it has been suggested that a witness has recently fabricated portions of his or her evidence (Evans, at p. 643; *Simpson*, at pp. 22-23). Admission on the basis of this exception does not require that an allegation of recent fabrication be expressly made—it is sufficient that the circumstances of the case reveal that the "apparent position of the opposing party is that there has been a prior contrivance" (*Evans*, at p. 643). It is also not necessary that a fabrication be particularly "recent", as the issue is not the recency of the fabrication but rather whether the witness made up a false story at some point after the event that is the subject of his or her testimony actually occurred (*R. v. O'Connor* (1995), 100 C.C.C. (3d) 285 (Ont. C.A.), at pp. 294-95). Prior consistent statements have probative value in this context where they can illustrate that the witness's story was the same even before a motivation to fabricate arose.

6 In this case, the parties do not dispute that the trial judge was correct to admit Mr. Harding's prior consistent statements. The cross-examination of this witness included questions about both a civil lawsuit he had pending against Mr. Stirling as the driver of the vehicle and the relationship between his testimony and criminal charges against him which had recently been dropped. Given these questions, it was appropriate for the judge to admit statements made prior to the launching of the civil suit and prior to the dropping of the charges because these statements, if consistent with the in-court testimony, could demonstrate that Mr. Harding's evidence was not motivated by either of these factors.

7 However, a prior consistent statement that is admitted to rebut the suggestion of recent fabrication continues to lack any probative value beyond showing that the witness's story did not change as a result of a new motive to fabricate. Importantly, it is impermissible to assume that because a witness has made the same statement in the past, he or she is more likely to be telling the truth, and any admitted prior consistent statements should not be assessed for the truth of their contents. As was noted in *R. v. Divitaris* (2004), 188 C.C.C. (3d) 390 (Ont. C.A.), at para. 28, "a concocted statement, repeated on more than one occasion, remains concocted"; see also J. Sopinka, S. N. Lederman and A. W. Bryant, *The Law of Evidence in Canada* (2nd ed. 1999), at p. 313. This case illustrates the importance of this point. The fact that Mr. Harding reported that the appellant was driving on the night of the crash before he launched the civil suit or had charges against him dropped does not in any way confirm that that evidence is not fabricated. All it tells us is that it wasn't fabricated as a result of the civil suit or the dropping of the criminal charges. There thus remains the very real possibility that the evidence was fabricated immediately after the accident when, as the trial judge found, "any reasonable person would recognize there was huge liability facing the driver" (Ruling on voir dire, June 21, 2005, at para. 24). The reality is that even when Mr. Harding made his very first comments about who was driving when the accident occurred, he already had a visible motive to fabricate—to avoid the clear consequences which faced the driver of the vehicle—and this potential motive is not in any way rebutted by the consistency of his story. It was therefore necessary for the trial judge to avoid using Mr. Harding's prior statements for the truth of their contents.

8 It is clear from the reasons of the trial judge that he was aware of the limited value of Mr. Harding's prior statements. Not only did he acknowledge that this witness had a motive to fabricate immediately after the accident occurred (and thus before any statements were made about who was driving), but he also stated explicitly, on several occasions, that he had not considered the statements for the truth of their contents . . .

. . .

10 . . . . [P]rior consistent statements have the impact of removing a potential motive to lie, and the trial judge is entitled to consider removal of this motive when assessing the witness's credibility.

11 Courts and scholars in this country have used a variety of language to describe the way prior consistent statements may impact on a witness's credibility where they refute suggestion of an improper motive. Both the Nova Scotia Court of Appeal and the Alberta Court of Appeal refer to the "bolstering" of the witness's credibility (*R. v. Schofield* (1996), 148 N.S.R. (2d) 175, at para. 23; *R. v. R. (J.)* (2000), 84 Alta. L.R. (3d) 92, 2000 ABCA 196, at para. 8), a term which is also used in the leading text of Sopinka, Lederman and Bryant, at p. 314. The Ontario Court of Appeal recently found that these statements are capable of "strengthening" credibility (*R. v. Zebedee* (2006), 211 C.C.C. (3d) 199, at para. 117), while the British Columbia Court of Appeal has referred to their ability to "rehabilitate" credibility (*R. v. Aksidan* (2006), 209 C.C.C. (3d) 423, 2006 BCCA 258, at para. 21). This Court has found that the statements can be admitted "in support of" the witness's credibility (*Evans*, at p. 643). What is clear from all of these sources is that [page280] credibility is necessarily impacted—in a positive way—where admission of prior consistent statements removes a motive for fabrication. Although it would clearly be flawed reasoning to conclude that removal of this motive leads to a conclusion that the witness is telling the truth, it is permissible for this factor to be taken into account as part of the larger assessment of credibility.

12 It is therefore not entirely accurate to submit, as the appellant contends, that prior consistent statements cannot be used to "bolster" or "support" the credibility of a witness generally. This argument attempts to insulate the impact of the prior consistent statements from the remainder of the credibility analysis and suggests that "general" credibility can somehow be hived off from the specific credibility question to which the statements relate. Such a fine parsing of the notion of credibility is impractical and artificial. Further, while it would clearly be an error to conclude that because someone has been saying the same thing repeatedly their evidence is more likely to be correct, there is no error in finding that because there is no evidence that an individual has a motive to lie, their evidence is more likely to be honest.

. . .

Appeal dismissed.

R. v. ELLARD
(2009), 2009 CarswellBC 1514, 2009 CarswellBC 1515, 67 C.R. (6th) 78, 245 C.C.C. (3d) 183 (S.C.C.)

ABELLA J. (for the Court):—

. . .

32 Certain exceptions have nevertheless developed in the jurisprudence. In particular, where a party has made an allegation of recent fabrication, the opposing party can rebut the allegation by introducing prior statements made before the alleged fabrication arose, that are consistent with the testimony at trial. The allegation need not be express. It is enough if "in light of the circumstances of

the case and the conduct of the trial, the apparent position of the opposing party is that there has been a prior contrivance" (*Evans*, at p. 643; see also *R. v. Simpson*, [1988] 1 S.C.R. 3, at p. 24).

33 To be "recent", the fabrication need only have been made after the event testified about (*Stirling*, at para. 5). A mere contradiction in the evidence is not enough to engage the recent fabrication exception. However, a "fabrication" can include being influenced by outside sources (*R. v. B. (A.J.)*, [1995] 2 S.C.R. 413). To rebut an allegation of recent fabrication, it is necessary to identify statements made prior to the existence of a motive or of circumstances leading to fabrication. In all cases, the timing of the prior consistent statements will be central to whether they are admissible.

. . .

42 As previously noted, because there is a danger that the repetition of prior consistent statements may bolster a witness's reliability, a limiting instruction will almost always be required where such statements are admitted. The purpose of such an instruction is to tell the jury that consistency is not the same as accuracy, and that the statements can only be used to rebut the allegation of recent fabrication, not to support the fact at issue or the general reliability of the witness. (See *R. v. Rockey*, [1996] 3 S.C.R. 829, per McLachlin J.; *R. v. Fair* (1993), 16 O.R. (3d) 1 (C.A.), at pp. 20-21; *R. v. Divitaris* (2004), 188 C.C.C. (3d) 390 (Ont. C.A.), at para. 31; *R. v. A. (J.)* (1996), 112 C.C.C. (3d) 528 (Ont. C.A.), at p. 533; and *R. v. Codina* (1995), 95 C.C.C. (3d) 311 (Ont. C.A.), at p. 330.)

43 Delineated exceptions to the generally stringent rule have emerged, some of which were canvassed in *R. v. Demetrius* (2003), 179 C.C.C. (3d) 26 (Ont. C.A.), at para. 22. These include situations where the defence itself relies on the prior statement, *R. v. S. (P.)* (2000), 144 C.C.C. (3d) 120 (Ont. C.A.), at paras. 62-63; where the prior statement was not offered as proof of the underlying fact, *R. v. G.M.*, [2000] O.J. No. 5007 (QL) (C.A.); or where the concern over self-corroboration and thereby bolstering the witness's reliability is not present, *R. v. Clark* (1995), 87 O.A.C. 178. (See also David M. Paciocco and Lee Stuesser, The Law of Evidence (5th ed. 2008), at p. 501.)

(ii) *Prior Identification*

When a witness at trial is asked to identify a person in the courtroom the surrounding circumstances may seriously weaken the weight of the identification. In a criminal trial for assault the identification as the assailant of the person in the prisoner's dock would have little force, as the trier of fact might naturally theorize that the witness is not giving his present recollection of the incident but rather that the witness is concluding from the accused's location that the police have arrested the proper person. As in the previous section, the circumstances of the case may cast doubt on the witness's statement and we therefore receive evidence of any prior identification made when such circumstances were not present; a close examination of the earlier circumstances will enhance or detract from the cogency of the present identification. Viscount Haldane, L.C., in the case of *R. v. Christie*,[384] described the process:

> Had the boy, after he had identified the accused in the dock, been asked if he had identified the accused in the field as the man who assaulted him, and answered affirmatively, then that fact might also have been proved by the policeman and the mother who saw the identification. *Its relevancy is to shew that the boy was able to identify at the time and to exclude the idea that the identification of the prisoner in the dock was an afterthought or a mistake.* [Emphasis added.]

The opportunity for an early identification when the incident is fresh in the witness's mind is not only for the witness's benefit. It is not satisfactory to the prisoner's interests that identification first occur at trial; he should be paraded with others of like characteristics and the witness obliged to "pick him out."[385]

The fact of the previous identification should be made known so that opposite counsel can, through cross-examination, explore the fairness with which that identification was conducted. The witness at trial may in truth be testifying only to his memory of the person he identified at the line-up parade and its surrounding circumstances deserve detailed exploration for the accused's own protection. If the police have used photographs in their investigation:

> There is always the risk that a witness may unconsciously substitute the clear impression gained by looking at a photograph for the perhaps hazy recollection of the face he is trying to recall, and his subsequent identification of the accused may be really the result of a mental comparison with the photograph instead of with the living person. The possibility of error arising from this cause is a thing of which the defence is entitled to take the fullest advantage, and an injustice might be done to the accused if the fact of photographs having been shown to witnesses were not disclosed.[386]

R. v. TAT
(1997), 14 C.R. (5th) 116, 117 C.C.C. (3d) 481, 1997 CarswellOnt 5434 (C.A.)

DOHERTY J.A.:

36 Clearly, the evidence of the prior descriptions given and the prior identifications made by the identifying witness constitute prior consistent statements made by that witness. Generally speaking, evidence that a witness made prior consistent statements is excluded as irrelevant and self-serving. However, where identification evidence is involved, it is the in-court identification

384 [1914] A.C. 545, 551 (H.L.).

385 See *R. v. Cartwright* (1914), 10 Cr. App. Rep. 219, 221 per Reading, L.C.J.: ". . . the prisoner was not put with a number of other men so that a witness might be able to identify this man as the guilty man. It would have been infinitely better had this been done." For a recent case regarding defective line-ups see *R. v. Faryna*, [1983] 1 W.W.R. 577 (Man. C.A.). See generally Brooks, *Study Paper of Law Reform Commission of Canada, Pretrial Eyewitness Identification Procedures*, 1984.

386 *R. v. Fannon* (1922), 22 S.R.N.S.W. 427 (C.A.) approved in *R. v. Harrison*, [1928] 3 D.L.R. 224 (B.C.C.A.). There is of course the unavoidable prejudice possibility flowing from the fact that the police had pictures of the accused to use.

of the accused which has little or no probative value standing alone. The probative force of identification evidence is best measured by a consideration of the entire identification process which culminates with an in-court identification: e.g. *R. v. Langille, supra*, at 555; *DiCarlo v. The U.S.*, 6 F.(2d) 364 at 369, per Hough J., concurring, (2d cir. 1925); *Clemons v. The U.S.*, 408 F. (2d) 1230 at 1243 (D.C. cir. 1968). The central importance of the pre-trial identification process in the assessment of the weight to be given to identification evidence is apparent upon a review of cases which have considered the reasonableness of verdicts based upon identification evidence: e.g. see *R. v. Miaponoose* (1996), 110 C.C.C. (3d) 445 (Ont. C.A.).

37 If a witness identifies an accused at trial, evidence of previous identifications made and descriptions given is admissible to allow the trier of fact to make an informed determination of the probative value of the purported identification. The trier of fact will consider the entirety of the identification process as revealed by the evidence before deciding what weight should be given to the identification made by the identifying witness. Evidence of the circumstances surrounding any prior identifications and the details of prior descriptions given will be central to that assessment.

We will return to the issue of *Tat* in the next chapter on the issue of whether a prior identification is hearsay.

(iii) *Part of Narrative*

R. c. DINARDO
[2008] 1 S.C.R. 788, 231 C.C.C. (3d) 177, 2008 CarswellQue 3452, 2008 CarswellQue 3451, 57 C.R. (6th) 48

The accused was charged with sexual assault and sexual exploitation of a person with a disability. The complainant was a 22-year-old woman who suffered from a mild mental disability. The accused was a taxi driver who picked up the complainant at a home for mentally challenged persons and drove her to another facility about 15 minutes away. The complainant alleged that the accused sexually assaulted her during the drive. The complainant spontaneously recounted these allegations to a teacher and several others on the day of the alleged assault.

The trial judge ruled the complainant competent to testify on a promise to tell the truth. The complainant's trial testimony was essentially consistent on the central parts of her allegations, but she gave confused and contradictory testimony on many points, including whether she knew what it meant to invent a story and whether she had in fact invented the allegations. The accused testified and denied the allegations.

The trial judge convicted the accused on both counts. In his reasons for judgment, the trial judge held that the contradictions in the complainant's testimony were not on important facts but only on details too unimportant to affect her credibility. He found that the complainant's testimony was corroborated by her repeated, consistent statements about the event. A majority of the Quebec Court of Appeal dismissed the appeal against conviction, and the accused appealed to the Supreme Court of Canada.

CHARRON J.A. (for the Court):—

. . .

36 As a general rule, prior consistent statements are inadmissible (*R. v. Stirling*, [2008] 1 S.C.R 272, 2008 SCC 10). There are two primary justifications for the exclusion of such statements: first, they lack probative value (*Stirling*, at para. 5), and second, they constitute hearsay when adduced for the truth of their contents.

37 In some circumstances, prior consistent statements may be admissible as part of the narrative. Once admitted, the statements may be used for the limited purpose of helping the trier of fact to understand how the complainant's story was initially disclosed. The challenge is to distinguish between "using narrative evidence for the impermissible purpose of 'confirm[ing] the truthfulness of the sworn allegation'" and "using narrative evidence for the permissible purpose of showing the fact and timing of a complaint, which may then *assist the trier of fact in the assessment of truthfulness or credibility*" McWilliams' *Canadian Criminal Evidence* (4th ed. (loose-leaf)), at pp. 11-44 and 11-45 (emphasis in original); see also *R. v. F. (J.E.)* (1993), 85 C.C.C. (3d) 457 (Ont. C.A.), at p. 476).

38 In *R. v. G.C.*, [2006] O.J. No. 2245 (QL), the Ontario Court of Appeal noted that the prior consistent statements of a complainant may assist the court in assessing the complainant's likely truthfulness, particularly in cases involving allegations of sexual assault against children. As Rouleau J.A. explained, for a unanimous court:

> Although properly admitted at trial, the evidence of prior complaint cannot be used as a form of self-corroboration to prove that the incident in fact occurred. It cannot be used as evidence of the truth of its contents. However, the evidence can "be supportive of the central allegation in the sense of creating a logical framework for its presentation", as set out above, and can be used in assessing the truthfulness of the complainant. As set out in *R. v. F.(J.E.)* at p. 476:
>
> > The fact that the statements were made is admissible to assist the jury as to the sequence of events from the alleged offence to the prosecution so that they can understand the conduct of the complainant and assess her truthfulness. However, the jury must be instructed that they are not to look to the content of the statements as proof that a crime has been committed.
> >
> > The trial judge understood the limited use that could be made of this evidence as appears from his reasons:
>
> [I]t certainly struck me while the fact that you go and tell somebody that you were molested doesn't confirm the fact that you were molested. I'm struck by the manner or the way it came out, tends to confirm [the complainant's] story - how they were reading this book, and how the thing came up about child sexual abuse.
>
> > In cases involving sexual assault on young children, the courts recognize the difficulty in the victim providing a full account of events. In appropriate cases, the way the complaint comes forth can, by adding or detracting from the logical cogency of the child's evidence, be a useful tool in assisting the trial judge in the assessment of the child's truthfulness. This was such a case. [Emphasis added; paras. 20-22.]

39 The Ontario Court of Appeal's reasoning in *G.C.* applies equally to the facts of this case. The complainant's prior consistent statements were not admissible under any of the traditional hearsay exceptions. Thus, the statements could not be used to confirm her in-court testimony. However, in light of the evidence that the complainant had difficulty situating events in time, was easily confused, and lied on occasion, the spontaneous nature of the initial complaint and the complainant's repetition of the essential elements of the allegations provide important context for assessing her credibility.

40 The Court of Appeal correctly concluded that the trial judge erred when he considered the contents of the complainant's prior consistent statements to corroborate her testimony at trial, noting in his judgment that [TRANSLATION] "there is a form of corroboration in the facts and statements of the victim, who never contradicted herself" (para. 68). I am unable to agree with the majority, however, that the accused suffered no prejudice from the trial judge's improper use of the statements. The trial judge relied heavily on the corroborative value of the complainant's prior statements in convicting Mr. Dinardo. He was clearly of the view that the complainant's consistency in recounting the allegations made her story more credible. Accordingly, I would also allow the appeal on this basis.

The appeal was allowed and a new trial ordered.

R. v. CURTO
(2008), 2008 CarswellOnt 1238, 230 C.C.C. (3d) 145, 54 C.R. (6th) 237
(C.A.)

Rosenberg J.A. (for the Court):—

. . .

31 The admissibility of prior consistent statements under the narrative exception to the general exclusionary rule has been discussed in a number of cases, usually in the context of admission of prior statements by child complainants and often in respect of historical assaults. See for example: *R. v. Ay* (1994), 93 C.C.C. (3d) 456 (B.C.C.A.); *R. v. B. (D.C.)* (1994), 91 C.C.C. (3d) 357 (Man. C.A.); *R. v. C. (G.)* (1997), 8 C.R. (5th) 61 (Ont. S.C.J.); *R. v. F. (J.E.)* (1993), 85 C.C.C. (3d) 457 (Ont. C.A.); and *R. v. B. (O.)* (1995), 103 C.C.C. (3d) 531 (N.S.C.A.). To determine whether the trial judge misused the evidence in this case, it is necessary to briefly consider the basis for admitting evidence of prior consistent statements.

32 As Hill J. explains in *R. v. C. (G.)* at para. 44, evidence of prior consistent statements by any witness is excluded as a general rule because the evidence is irrelevant and lacking in probative value. The evidence is "self-serving, self corroborative and superfluous". Put simply, the fact that a witness has on prior occasions said the same thing does not generally make his or her testimony any more truthful or reliable. However, there are exceptions to the rule against admission of prior consistent statements because in some circumstances, the evidence of prior consistent statements may in fact be probative of some issue in

the case. One example is to rebut an allegation of recent fabrication. See *R. v. Evans* (1993), 82 C.C.C. (3d) 338 (S.C.C.).

33 Another example is what the cases describe as narrative. The narrative exception is, in my view, essentially a convenient label for instances falling outside the traditional exceptions where the fact that the witness has made prior statements about the incident has some probative value. Finlayson J.A. considered the issue in *R. v. F. (J.E.)* at p. 472 in the context of the evidence of children:

> It seems to me that the court should look to narrative as an exception to the rule against the admission of previous consistent statements for a more hopeful approach to this vexing problem of the evidence of children in sexual assault cases. It must be a part of the narrative in the sense that it advances the story from offence to prosecution or explains why so little was done to terminate the abuse or bring the perpetrator to justice. Specifically, it appears to me to be part of the narrative of a complainant's testimony when she recounts the assaults, how they came to be terminated, and how the matter came to the attention of the police. [Emphasis added.]

34 The admissibility of prior consistent statements as part of the narrative will depend on the circumstances of each case. In *R. v. F. (J.E.)*, Finlayson J.A. stressed at p. 474 that the evidence was admissible only if it was necessary, for example, "to provide chronological cohesion and eliminate gaps". It will not always be necessary to know why or how the case came to the attention of the police and it will not always be necessary to fill in every gap in the chronology to understand the story and properly assess the witness's credibility.

35 The cases make it clear, however, that when prior consistent statements are admitted, the contents of those statements are not admissible for their truth. This limitation on the use of the prior statements helps to balance the probative value and prejudicial effect of the evidence. The probative value lies in the fact that the statement was made. The contents of the statement itself do not add to the probative value because, as I have said, mere repetition of a story on a prior occasion does not generally make the in-court description of the events any more credible or reliable. This limit on the use of prior consistent statements has been applied with particular rigour in jury trials, where it has been held to be reversible error for a trial judge not to warn the jury on the limited use of narrative statements. See *R. v. F. (J.E.)* at p. 476, *R. v. B. (O.)* at p. 542, and *R. v. Ay* at p. 473.

In her Criminal Reports annotations on *Stirling and Dinardo*, Professor Lisa Dufraimont suggests that the distinction between prior consistent statements to support the witness's credibility but not the truth of the contents is difficult to apply and problematic. **Do you agree with this criticism?**

Wood J.A., in *R. v. Ay*,[387] held that where prior consistent statements are admissible only the fact the statement was made is admissible, not the "specific contents". Similarly, MacPherson J.A., in *R. v. R.(A.E.)*,[388] held that "prior consistent statements should only be described in general terms and should not contain much detail". **Do these approaches make any sense?**

---

387 (1994) 93 C.C.C. (3d) 456 (B.C. C.A.).
388 (2001) 43 C.R. (5th) 340 (Ont. C.A.).

(iv) *Recent Complaint*

Until the beginning of the 19th century complaints of rape were received in evidence with little discussion of the underlying principles, their reception apparently justified simply by a tradition that had its roots in the early procedural requirement of the "hue and cry." In the 13th century the hazards of trial were great and it was adjudged that not every complaint would be sufficient to put the antagonist to his proof. Complaint witnesses, suitors, were demanded who would vouch for the plaintiff's cause:[389]

> It is not enough that the plaintiff should tell his tale: he must offer to prove its truth. . . . No one is entitled to an answer if he offers nothing but his bare assertion, his *nude parole.* The procedure in the Appeal of Felony is no real exception to this rule. The appellor alleges, and can be called upon to prove, fresh "suit" with hue and cry, so that the neighbourhood . . . is witness to his prompt action, to the wounds of a wounded man, to the torn garments of a ravished woman. It should not escape us that in this case, as in other cases, what the plaintiff relies on as support for his word is "suit." This suggests that the suitors . . . whom the plaintiff produces in a civil action have been, at least in theory, men who along with him have pursued the defendant.[390]

During the 19th century, we see the courts enunciating principles to explain the reception of this evidence which violated the then crystallized rule against previous consistent statements, and the most common principle announced is akin to the principle underlying the first two exceptions above discussed: the circumstances of a case may cast doubt on the witness's present description of the incident. If a woman had been raped it was assumed that it would be a very natural thing for her to then speak out, and the failure so to do would act to contradict her present accusation. If nothing was said at trial about the fact of an earlier complaint, the trier might then assume there was none and so reject her present testimony. Accordingly, if there was a complaint, evidence of it could be led to counter this assumption;[391] this might be done in chief without the necessity of any allegation of recent invention in cross-examination. During the 19th century the prosecutor was confined to proving the fact of the complaint, but in 1896, in *R. v. Lillyman,*[392] it was decided that the details of the complaint were also receivable:

> In reality, affirmative answers to such stereotyped questions as these, "Did the prosecutrix make a complaint" (a very leading question, by the way) "of something done to herself?" "Did she mention a name?" amount to nothing to which any weight ought to be attached; they tend rather to embarrass than assist a thoughtful jury, for they are consistent either with there having been a complaint or no complaint of the prisoner's conduct. To limit the evidence of the complaint to such questions and answers is to ask the jury to draw important inferences from imperfect materials, perfect materials being at hand and in the cognizance of the witness in the box. In our opinion, nothing ought unnecessarily to be left to speculation or surmise.

Although the details may be received, the complaint was not receivable for the purpose of proving its truth but solely to counter the influence of the assumption

---

389 See Thayer, *Preliminary Treatise on Evidence at the Common Law* (1898), pp. 10-16.

390 Pollock and Maitland, *History of English Law,* 2d ed. (1898), vol. 2, pp. 605-06.

391 See generally 4 Wigmore, *Evidence* (Chad. Rev.), s. 1134-39, discussing this principle and others.

392 [1896] 2 Q.B. 167, 177-78 (C.C.R.). Accord, *R. v. Thomas,* [1952] 4 D.L.R. 306 (S.C.C.).

that might otherwise flow from silence and so confirm, by the victim's conduct, her present testimony.[393]

Belying its origins, the exception during the 19th century was confined to complaints of rape by female complainants. In the 20th century the courts have extended the exception to cover the prosecution of other sexual offences,[394] whether the complainant was male or female.

In *Kribs v. R.*[395] Fauteux J. explained:

> The principle is one of necessity. It is founded on factual presumptions which, in the normal course of events, naturally attach to the subsequent conduct of the prosecutrix shortly after the occurrence of the alleged acts of violence. One of these presumptions is that she is expected to complain upon the first reasonable opportunity, and the other, consequential thereto, is that if she fails to do so, her silence may naturally be taken as a virtual self-contradiction of her story.
>
> . . . .
>
> ... by giving evidence of her conduct shortly after the alleged occurrence, the prosecutrix does not, in a sense, enhance or confirm her story any more than she does in reciting all that she did in resistance to the assault, but she rebuts a presumption and, in doing so, adds, for all practical purposes, a virtually essential complement to her story.

The courts held that if there was an absence of complaint at the first reasonable opportunity, the trial judge should charge the jury regarding the adverse inference they may draw against the complainant's credibility.[396]

In 1983 the Criminal Code was amended[397] to provide:

> **275.** The rules relating to evidence of recent complaint in sexual assault cases are hereby abrogated.

To describe the provision as ambiguous is understatement. Does it mean that evidence of recent complaint cannot be given?

R. v. O'CONNOR
(1995), 100 C.C.C. (3d) 285 (Ont. C.A.)

The accused was charged with touching for a sexual purpose a young girl who was a member of a church group of which he was the leader. The accused was tried by a judge sitting without a jury. The defence was that the allegations of sexual activity were fabricated. The Crown asked the complainant during

---

393 See Hawkins, J. in *R. v. Lillyman, ibid.*, at p. 170. See the difficulty experienced by Fauteux J. in *Kribs, infra*, note 421, seeking to distinguish these two uses. See also in *R. v. Thomas*, [1952] 2 S.C.R. 344, the court allowing the statement to be used to show consistency but denying its use as corroboration. If the complainant doesn't testify the complaint is naturally inadmissible: see *R. v. Cook* (1979), 9 C.R. (3d) 85 (Ont. C.A.) and *R. v. Brasier* (1779), 168 E.R. 202 (Crown Cases).

394 See the history of this development canvassed in *R. v. Lebrun* (1951), 100 C.C.C. 1 (Ont. C.A.). And see *R. v. Christenson*, [1923] 2 D.L.R. 379 (Alta. C.A.) per Beck J. suggesting the exception should operate in all crimes of violence, sexual or non-sexual.

395 [1960] S.C.R. 400, 405-06. And see *R. v. Boyce* (1975), 23 C.C.C. (2d) 16, 33 (Ont. C.A.).

396 See *Boyce, ibid.*, at p. 33.

397 S.C. 1980-81-82-83, c. 125, s. 19. See now R.S.C. 1985, c. C-46, s. 275.

examination in chief if she had told anyone of her relationship with the accused and received the answer that she had told a camp counsellor and her best friend. Defence counsel objected and stated that no allegation of recent fabrication had been made. The trial judge gave effect to that objection. In cross-examination, defence counsel asked the complainant whether she had told certain persons within a specified time-frame about the sexual acts. The complainant replied that she had not. The trial judge later allowed the camp counsellor to testify as to a complaint to her within three days of the time-frame relied on by the defence to support an adverse inference, and the complainant's stepmother and older sister were permitted to testify that the complainant had told them about the sexual relationship and that they agreed that the stepmother would inform the police.

The accused was convicted and appealed.

FINLAYSON J.A.:—

. . . .

The position of the defence that emerges from the record at trial and the argument on appeal is that the testimony of the complainant, to the extent that it recounted sexual abuse, had been made up out of whole cloth. The fabrication was said to be in no sense recent, but defence counsel did not designate its origin as being at any specific time. Put simply, the position is that since the defence had never alleged *recent* fabrication (as opposed to fabrication *ab initio*), the Crown was not entitled to lead any evidence under the rubric of recent fabrication, because no such allegation had been made. Therefore (the submission went) while it was permissible for the defence to demand of the complainant why she had not complained of these assaults to her sister Kelly on a particular day, the Crown was not entitled to bring out in reply, or at all, that she had complained three days later to her camp counsellor and still later to her sister and her stepmother.

In my opinion, this is being too clever by half. "Recent" fabrication is by definition a subset of fabrication generally. One may escape this implication by asserting a challenge to the complainant's credibility based on an allegation of fabrication *simpliciter*, but not when it is coupled with a charge that she had not divulged the fact of the sexual conduct to a person to whom the trier of fact would expect her to complain, *i.e.*, an absence of recent complaint. The law does not require that an allegation of recent fabrication be made explicitly: the court can look at all the circumstances of the case. . .

In this case the whole thrust of the cross-examination relating to Jenny Lamb and the sister Kelly was structured so as to establish the lack of an early complaint to someone whom the trial judge would expect a complaint to be made under the circumstances. The questions as to why no complaints were made were restricted as to person and to time but with the object of leaving the impression that there were no complaints whatsoever. As such, the questioning was designed to give rise to an inference that the complaint was formulated subsequent to the event recounted in her testimony at trial. It clearly implied what is, by any other name, an allegation of recent fabrication.

I am of the view that an allegation of recent fabrication is no more than an allegation that the complainant has made up a false story to meet the exigencies of the case. The word "recent" means that the complainant's evidence has been invented or fabricated after the events in question and thus is a "recent" invention or fabrication. . . .

. . . .

I conclude that the rulings of the trial judge were correct and his use of the statements elicited were in accordance with the principle that he could only rely on the facts of the complaints, not the truth of their contents, in assessing the credibility of the complaint.

. . . .

GOODMAN J.A.:—

. . . In my opinion, the evidence of the complaints made by the complainant to her sister Kelly, Cynthia Collins and Tanya Kronschnabl, in the circumstances of this case, was not admissible on the basis of the exception to the rule against prior consistent statements resulting from an allegation of recent fabrication but rather on the basis hereinafter set forth.

Prior to the 1983 amendment to the *Criminal Code* . . . , purporting to abrogate the rules relating to evidence of recent complaint . . . , the prosecution was permitted to elicit from the complainant evidence of a complaint of a sexual assault, made at the first reasonable opportunity, to support the credibility of the victim. After the 1983 amendment, the prosecution was no longer permitted to do so.

In my opinion, however, the amendment does not prevent defence counsel from cross-examining a complainant about the lack of recent complaint, but in doing so the door is opened to permit the Crown to adduce evidence of a prior complaint in order to rebut any adverse inference which might be drawn by the fact-finder from the silence alleged by the defence and to rebut the attack on the credibility of the complainant based on the lack of recent complaint.

In Sopinka, Lederman and Bryant, *The Law of Evidence in Canada*, 1992, it is stated at p. 317:

> It appears that the effect of the statutory amendment is that recent complaint evidence may not be led in anticipation of the adverse inference drawn from silence. However, defence counsel are not precluded from cross-examining a complainant about the lack of a prior complaint. If they do, they take the risk that the Crown may adduce a prior complaint to rebut the allegation.

And further at p. 318:

> . . . the ability of the defence to question a complainant on the absence or untimeliness of a complaint has had nothing to do in the past with the doctrine of recent complaint. One of the most common means of suggesting that a witness's testimony is fabricated is to allege failure to speak when it would have been expected, and this has always been recognized.

In the case at bar, defence counsel cross-examined the complainant in a manner which might leave the impression that she had never made a prior complaint or at the very least had not made a timely complaint to a person or persons to whom it was reasonable to expect that she would have complained. In that circumstance it was, in my opinion, permissible for the Crown to re-examine the complainant with respect to the reasons for the lack of complaint to the persons referred to by defence counsel in his cross-examination and to adduce evidence with respect to the prior complaints which had allegedly been made by the complainant prior to the complaint to the police.

. . . .

WEILER, J.A.:— I am in agreement with Finlayson J.A. that the effect of the cross-examination which was conducted by counsel for the defence gave rise to the inference that the complainant had fabricated her evidence after the events in question and, in addition, suggested that there was an absence of any complaint concerning the alleged assault prior to the complaint being made to the police. In these circumstances, I agree with him that it was appropriate for the trial judge to hear evidence of the complainant's meeting with her sister Kelly and the social worker, Cynthia Collins, as well as her complaint to Tanya Kronschnabl. I also agree with Goodman J.A. that the impression resulting from the cross-examination, that there was no complaint made of any sexual assault prior to the complaint to the police, would have made the complainant's evidence of her complaint to Kelly, Cynthia Collins, and Tanya Kronschnabl admissible, quite apart from any suggestion of recent fabrication.

5. DEMEANOUR AS GUIDE TO CREDIBILITY

Lord Devlin, recognized by all as a great trial judge, wrote:

> The great virtue of the English trial is said to be the opportunity it gives to the judge to tell from the demeanour of the witness whether or not he is telling the truth. I think that this is overrated. I would adopt in their entirety the words of Mr. Justice MacKenna:
>
>> I question whether the respect given to our findings of fact based on the demeanour of the witness is always deserved. I doubt my own ability and sometimes that of other judges, to discern from a witness's demeanour, or the tone of voice whether he is telling the truth. He speaks hesitantly. Is that the mark of a cautious man, whose statements are for that reason to be respected or is he taking time to fabricate? Is the emphatic witness putting on an act to deceive me, or is he speaking from the fullness of his heart, knowing that he is right? Is he likely to be more truthful if he looks me straight in the face than if he casts his eyes on the ground perhaps from shyness or a natural timidity? For my part I rely on these considerations as little as I can help.[398]

Empirical studies conducted by psychologists confirm Lord Devlin's point.[399] They usually stress that bodily movements and the sound of the voice are better

---

398 Lord Devlin, *The Judge*, 1979, p. 63.

399 See for example, Ekman and Fresein, "Detecting Deception from the Body or Face" (1974), 29 J. of Personality & Social Psychology 288; Ekman, *Telling Lies: Clues to Deceit in the Marketplace*, Politics and Marriage, Norton, (U.S. 1991), esp. pp. 287-92; Blumenthal, "A Wipe of the Hands, A Lick of the Lips: The Validity of Demeanour Evidence in Assessing

indicators than facial demeanour, but then only if the observer is acquainted with the normal mannerisms of the witness. Professor Ekman's empirical studies indicated that while U.S. Secret Service agents scored very well in accurately picking out liars, judges, trial lawyers, police, forensic psychiatrists and the FBI achieved at a level no better than chance![400]

And yet, the frailty of using demeanour as indicative of credibility, as accepted by Lord Devlin and seemingly established by the psychologists, is certainly at odds with dicta from most trial judges who in their reasons frequently use the same as indicating their acceptance or rejection of the testimony of witnesses. It is also at odds with the deference often paid by appellate courts who frequently say that although they have a transcript of what was said at trial they are disadvantaged in their assessment of the worth of testimonial evidence because they were not present when the testimony was given.

Has the time come for judges to reappraise their attitudes towards demeanour? How might that be done?

R. v. NORMAN
(1993), 26 C.R. (4th) 256, 87 C.C.C. (3d) 153 (Ont. C.A.)

The accused was charged with raping the complainant, then 13 years old, in 1973. The complainant alleged that she had forgotten the rape, and remembered it in fragments in the course of therapy sessions. The accused testified and denied any sexual contact with the complainant. The trial judge found that the complainant was a credible witness and the accused was convicted.

The judgment of the court was delivered by FINLAYSON J.A.:—

. . . .

The trial judge in this case seems to have determined credibility solely on the basis of the demeanour of the complainant and Mrs. Goebel. He said that he was impressed with the manner in which the complainant testified: she was straightforward and stood up well in cross-examination, and it appeared to him that she was not being vindictive. As for Mrs. Goebel, he said that she testified in an assured and straightforward manner and impressed him as a credible witness.

In *White v. R.*, [1947] S.C.R. 268 at p. 272, the senior Mr. Justice Estey discussed the issue of credibility. He said it is one of fact and cannot be determined by following a set of rules. He stated in part:

> It is a matter in which so many human characteristics, both the strong and the weak, must be taken into consideration. The general integrity and intelligence of the witness, his powers to observe, his capacity to remember and his accuracy in statement are important. It is also important to determine whether he is honestly endeavouring to

---

Witness Credibility" (1993), 72 Nebraska L. Rev. 1157, Stone, "Instant Lie Detection? Demeanour and Credibility in Criminal Trials" (1991), Crim. L. Rev. 821 and Loretta Re, "Oral v. Written Evidence: The Myth of the Impressive Witness" (1983), Aus. L.J. 679.

400 Hunter and Cronin, *Evidence, Advocacy and Ethical Practice* (Butterworths, 1995), p. 329.

tell the truth, whether he is sincere and frank or whether he is biased, reticent and evasive. All these questions and others may be answered from the observation of the witness' general conduct and demeanour in determining the question of credibility.

I do not think that an assessment of credibility based on demeanour alone is good enough in a case where there are so many significant inconsistencies. The issue is not merely whether the complainant sincerely believes her evidence to be true; it is also whether this evidence is reliable. Accordingly, her demeanour and credibility are not the only issues. The reliability of the evidence is what is paramount. So far as Mrs. Goebel is concerned, her evidence is inherently hard to credit, and should have been subjected to closer analysis. For the purposes of this case, I adopt what was said by O'Halloran J.A., speaking for the British Columbia Court of Appeal in *Faryna v. Chorny* (1951), 4 W.W.R. (N.S.) 171 at p. 174:

> The credibility of interested witnesses, particularly in cases of conflict of evidence, cannot be gauged solely by the test of whether the personal demeanour of the particular witness carried conviction of the truth. The test must reasonably subject his story to an examination of its consistency with the probabilities that surround the currently existing conditions. In short, the real test of the truth of the story of a witness in such a case must be its harmony with the preponderance of the probabilities which a practical and informed person would readily recognize as reasonable in that place and in those conditions.

O'Halloran J.A. pointed out later at p. 175 that "[t]he law does not clothe the trial judge with a divine insight into the hearts and minds of the witnesses."

In *R. v. S. (W.)*[401] Justice Finlayson repeated the thought and explained:

> I am not satisfied that a positive finding of credibility on the part of the complainant is sufficient to support a conviction in a case of this nature where there is significant evidence which contradicts the complainant's allegations. We all know from our personal experiences as trial lawyers and judges that honest witnesses, whether they are adults or children, may convince themselves that inaccurate versions of a given event are correct and they can be very persuasive. The issue, however, is not the sincerity of the witness but the reliability of the witness' testimony. Demeanour alone should not suffice to found a conviction where there are significant inconsistencies and conflicting evidence on the record.[402]

Moreover as Justice Saunders recognized in *R. v. P. (S.H.)*:[403]

---

401 (1994), 29 C.R. (4th) 143 (Ont. C. A.), leave to appeal refused (1994), 35 C.R. (4th) 402 (note) (S.C.C.).

402 *Ibid.*, at pp. 149-50.

403 (2003), 176 C.C.C. (3d) 281 (N.S. C.A.). Over-reliance on demeanour evidence has proved fatal in a number of appeals including *R. v. F. (J.)* (2003), 177 C.C.C. (3d) 1 (Ont. C.A.); *R. v. DeHaan* (2002), [2002] O.J. No. 430, 2002 CarswellOnt 229 (C.A.); *R. v. Owen* (2001), [2001] O.J. No. 4257, 2001 CarswellOnt 3852 (C.A.); *R. v. A. (R.H.)* (2000), [2000] O.J. No. 2610, 2000 CarswellOnt 2420 (C.A.); *R. v. Gostick* (1999), 137 C.C.C. (3d) 53 (Ont. C.A.); and *R. v. G. (G.)* (1997), 115 C.C.C. (3d) 1 (Ont. C.A.).

Reasons of intelligence, upbringing, education, race, culture, social status and a host of other factors may adversely affect a witness's demeanour and yet may have little bearing on that person's truthfulness.[404]

PROBLEM

Problem 1

The accused is charged with sexual assault. The complainant is Islamic and wears a veil. Prior to her testimony, the defence brings a motion for the trial judge to compel her to remove the veil so that he and the jury can assess her demeanour. Rule on the motion. See *R. v. S.(N.)*, [2009] O.J. No. 1766 (S.C.J.).

PROBLEM

Where could (should) objections be made in the following transcript? What contrary arguments might be made and how would you rule?

The plaintiff is suing defendant for damages arising out of a motor-vehicle accident. The plaintiff calls Joseph Smith to the stand:

Clerk:	You swear that the evidence to be given by you to the court and jury sworn, touching the matters in question, shall be the truth, the whole truth and nothing but the truth. So help you God.
Witness:	I'd rather not swear.
The Court:	Do you affirm?
Witness:	Yes.
The Court:	Fine, proceed.
Q.:	Your name is Joseph Smith?
A.:	Yes.
Q.:	You live at 2236 Princess Street in the city of Kingston?
A.:	Yes.
Q.:	You are employed as a police officer by the municipality of Metropolitan Kingston and have been so employed as a traffic officer for some 22 years and as such have investigated thousands of accidents?
A.:	Yes.
Q.:	You've given evidence in court on numerous occasions?
A.:	Yes.
Q.:	You're wearing a gold pin in your lapel —
A.:	It's my 20 year pin for good service to the force.
Q.:	Fine, thank you officer, now, on the evening in question you were standing on the corner of Princess and North Streets at about 4:12 p.m. when your attention was attracted by a loud noise?
A.:	Yes.

---

404 See also S.L. Johnson, "The Colour of Truth: Race and the Assessment of Credibility" (1996), 1 Mich. J. of Race & Law 261 and D. Opekokew, "A Review of Ethnocentric Bias Facing Indian Witnesses" in R. Goose et. al. (ed) Continuing Poundmaker and Riel's Quest (Purich Publishing: Saskatoon, 1994).

Q.:   Tell the court and the jury what you saw.

A.:   I saw a car driven by the defendant —

Q.:   You mean the person sitting beside my friend Mr. Jones?

A.:   Yes.

Q.:   Continue please.

A.:   I saw his car driving furiously down the street squealing its tires and without any regard for the safety of pedestrians who were already in the cross-walk.

Q.:   Then what happened?

A.:   Well, he mustn't have applied the brakes because he went straight through the cross-walk and ran down the plaintiff. I went over to see if I could help and the defendant got out of his car.

Q.:   How did he get out of his car?

A.:   What do you mean?

Q.:   In what manner did he exit?

A.:   He opened the driver's door and stepped out.

Q.:   Was there anything noticeable about his gait?

A.:   I'm sorry, I don't know what you're driving at.

Q.:   Was the defendant walking with any noticeable characteristic? — a sway, for example.

A.:   Oh yes, I remember now, he staggered as he walked and he brushed against the hood of the car as he came around to see the victim.

Q.:   Anything else?

A.:   Like what?

Q.:   Well, as a result of your observations did you decide to charge the defendant with any offence?

A.:   Yes, I charged him with impaired driving and he was later convicted.

Cross-Examination

Q.:   Why were you at the intersection of Princess and North Streets at 4:42 p.m.?

A.:   I live near there.

Q.:   And you just happened to be there when the accident occurred?

A.:   That's right.

Q.:   Don't you find that to have been just a little convenient?

A.:   I suppose it was for the plaintiff.

Q.:   Don't be smart with me, witness! I suggest to you that you didn't arrive at the scene of the accident until one-half hour after the accident had occurred.

A.:   No, sir.

Q.:   Would you care to think about that for a moment?

A.:   No — there's no need to —

Q.:   Suppose I told you that I'm prepared to call three witnesses to testify that you came running up to them at the scene and shouted "what happened?"

A.:   They'd be lying.

Q.:	Everyone lies but you? All right, let's move on. Isn't it true that you've been on a crusade against teenage drivers ever since your own wife was injured by one and that coloured your thinking about my client who happens to be a teenager?
A.:	No.
Q.:	Aren't you known at the precinct as an officer who keeps score of how many teenagers he tickets a day?
A.:	No.
Q.:	You hate teenagers don't you?
A.:	No.
Q.:	You think they shouldn't be on the road until they're 20 years old?
A.:	No.
Q.:	You think they're dangerous.
A.:	No.
Q.:	I have nothing further at this time but I reserve my right to further cross-examination at a later time.

6. CORROBORATION

(a) When Required?

The ecclesiastical and civil law systems of proof provided that a verdict could not be had on the strength of one witness's evidence. For most issues two witnesses were sufficient but in other cases a higher number might be required. In addition, particular witnesses, according to their inherent quality or weakness, would be assigned a particular numerical value, perhaps a quarter or half of a regular witness. The common law generally resisted attempts at any quantitative measurement of the evidence necessary to a finding and the testimony of a single witness was sufficient. Wigmore sees the common law resistance resident in the different nature of the tribunal there present, the jury. As the jury continued being entitled to act as witnesses themselves until the eighteenth century it would have been otiose for the judge to attempt to erect rules of a number.[405] The common law was interested then in the quality of the witnesses tendered and not their number. The judge was entitled to express his opinion regarding that quality, but it was always for the jury, on the basis of their assessment, to accept or reject the testimony. As Greenshields J. expressed it:

> On questions of fact the presiding Judge is entitled to express an opinion as to the value of testimony offered; he is entitled to give his opinion as to the credibility of any particular witness, always, however, making it reasonably clear to the Jury that it is not bound to accept his opinion with respect to the facts; that it is the province of the Jury, irrespective of the guiding opinion of the Judge, to find upon the facts, particularly to pass upon the guilt or innocence of the accused. The extent to which the trial Judge should dwell upon the facts is largely discretionary, and that discretion rests with the Judge, and will not, if fairly and judicially exercised, be interfered with by an Appellate Court.[406]

---

405 For the History of Rules of Number, see 7 Wigmore, *Evidence*, 3d ed., s. 2032.

406 *R. v. Gouin* (1926), 41 Que. K.B. 157 (C.A.). See, however, the criticism by O'Halloran, J.A. in *R. v. Pavlukoff* (1953), 10 W.W.R. 26, 40-44 (B.C.C.A.).

The one common law exception to the general rule was the crime of perjury. The crime of perjury had been normally prosecuted in the Court of Star Chamber and that court followed ecclesiastical procedures wherein two witnesses were required. When the Court of Star Chamber was abolished in 1641 the prosecution of perjury in the common law courts incorporated the long established practice of requiring two witnesses as an exception to its normal process. This practice is now reflected in Canada in section 133 of the Criminal Code, which forbids a conviction of perjury "on the evidence of only one witness unless the evidence of that witness is corroborated in a material particular by evidence that implicates the accused."[407] A number of other statutory exceptions to the general rule have been created dependent either on the issue being litigated or on the kind of witness tendered. In some instances corroboration is required for a verdict while in others a warning is required that it is unsafe to convict without corroboration but open to the trier to do so.

(i) *Treason*

By the Criminal Code[408] the offence of treason requires corroboration. The roots of this requirement can be traced to a statute of Edward VI in 1547[409] requiring two witnesses in treason trials. The legislators, mindful of the excesses of Henry VIII, apparently saw this as a device to protect themselves against future regal uses of the law of treason. Wigmore wrote:

> The object of the rule requiring two witnesses in treason is plain enough. It is, as Sir William Blackstone said, to "secure the subject from being sacrificed to fictitious conspiracies, which have been the engines of profligate and crafty politicians in all ages.[410]

(ii) *Forgery*

The Criminal Code provided that corroboration was required to convict of forgery.[411] The requirement was an historical accident. This requirement was initially imposed in the Forgery Act of 1869,[412] when it was decided to allow witnesses to testify in such matters though they were interested in the outcome of the litigation.[413] It was, then, an exhibit of the legislators' caution in moving in that direction. Notice that the requirement of corroboration was limited to cases of those witnesses who were interested persons. When the Criminal Code was enacted in 1892 that limitation was abandoned and corroboration was required regardless of the character of the witness. No intelligent reason can presently be advanced for the requirement and the section was repealed in 1994.[414]

---

407 See *R. v. Doz* (1984), 12 C.C.C. (3d) 200 (Alta. C.A.) and *R. v. Predy* (1983), 17 C.C.C. (3d) 379 (Alta. C.A.).
408 R.S.C. 1985, c. C-46, s. 47(2).
409 1 Edw. VI, c. 12, s. 22, discussed in 7 Wigmore, *Evidence* (3d ed.), s. 2036.
410 7 Wigmore, *Evidence* (3d ed.), s. 2037.
411 R.S.C. 1985, c. C-46, s. 367(2). See *R. v. Esposito* (1985), 24 C.C.C. (3d) 88 (Ont. C.A.); leave to appeal to S.C.C. refused 24 C.C.C. (3d) 88n.
412 32 & 33 Vict., c. 19, s. 54.
413 Parties could not testify until 1869: see the *Evidence Act*, S.O., 33 Vict., c. 13.
414 Criminal Law Amendment Act, S.C. 1994, c. 44, s. 24.

(iii) *Accomplices*

It is well recognized that an accomplice who testifies for the prosecution may be purchasing immunity for himself and this particular weakness in his testimony may need to be pointed out to the trier. During the 19th century it became a rule of practice. Lord Abinger wrote in 1837:

> It is a practice which deserves all the reverence of law, that judges have uniformly told juries that they ought not to pay any respect to the testimony of an accomplice, unless the accomplice is corroborated in some material circumstance. . . . The danger is, that when a man is fixed, and knows that his own guilt is detected, he purchases impunity by falsely accusing others.[415]

This rule of practice became a rule of law in this century;[416] and the judge was required

> to warn the jury of the danger of convicting a prisoner on the uncorroborated testimony of an accomplice or accomplices, and, in the discretion of the judge, to advise them not to convict upon such evidence; but the judge should point out to the jury that it is within their legal province to convict upon such unconfirmed evidence.[417]

Failure to warn would result in the conviction being overturned. The classic definition of corroboration, accepted as gospel by the Canadian courts, was given by Lord Reading in *R. v. Baskerville:*

> We must hold that evidence in corroboration must be independent testimony which affects the accused by connecting or tending to connect him with the crime. In other words it must be evidence which implicates him, that is, which confirms in some material particular not only the evidence that the crime has been committed, but also that the prisoner committed it.[418]

Some courts required the trial judge to also indicate to the jury what evidence in the case was capable of constituting corroboration and to confine the jury to a consideration of those matters when determining if corroboration existed.[419] The law in this area grew into a complexity[420] which belied its humble beginnings as an admirable practice of caution.

VETROVEC v. R.
[1982] 1 S.C.R. 811, 67 C.C.C. (2d) 1, 27 C.R. (3d) 304

The accused were two of several persons charged with conspiring to traffic in heroin. The principal evidence against the accused was given by an accomplice

---

415 *R. v. Farler* (1837), 173 E.R. 418, 419.

416 See *R. v. Baskerville*, [1916] 2 K.B. 658 (C.C.A.); *Davies v. D.P.P.*, [1954] A.C. 378 (H.L.). And see in Canada *R. v. Gouin*, [1926] S.C.R. 539 accepting the *Baskerville* direction as a rule of law.

417 *R. v. Baskerville, ibid.*, at p. 663. See *R. v. Chayko* (1984), 12 C.C.C. (3d) 157 (Alta. C.A.).

418 *Ibid.*, at p. 667.

419 See *R. v. Racine* (1977), 32 C.C.C. (2d) 468 (Ont. C.A.). The Supreme Court of Canada left this point open: see *Kirsch v. R.* (1982), 62 C.C.C. (2d) 86.

420 To see how complex see Branca, *Corroboration in Studies in Canadian Criminal Evidence* (1972), ed. by Salhany & Carter; and Maloney, *Corroboration Revisited, Studies in Criminal Law and Procedure* (1973, C.B.A). See also the book by Wakeling, *Corroboration in Canadian Law* (1977).

who testified that he met the accused in Hong Kong and that they supplied him with six pounds of heroin which he then brought into the United States where he again met with the accused, and then into Canada where he again met them. The trial judge directed the jury that it was dangerous to act on the uncorroborated evidence of the accomplice but that certain pieces of evidence indicating that the accused were in Hong Kong at the relevant time and other pieces of evidence referring to subsequent events and indicating that the accused were involved in drug trafficking were all capable of corroborating the accomplice. The accused were convicted. The appeal by the accused was dismissed.

DICKSON J.: —

. . . .

I would like to review and reassess general principles relating to the law of corroboration of accomplices. This is one of the most complicated and technical areas of the law of evidence. It is also in need of reform. Both the Law Reform Commission of Canada (Report on Evidence, s. 88(b) of the proposed Code) and the English Criminal Law Revision Committee (11th Report on Evidence 1972, Cmnd 4991, paras. 183-5), have recently recommended a drastic overhaul of the law of corroboration. The Evidence Code proposed by the Law Reform Commission of Canada would contain the following provision:

> 88. For greater certainty it is hereby provided that:
>
> . . . .
>
> (b) Every rule of law that requires the corroboration of evidence as a basis for a conviction or that requires that the jury be warned of the danger of convicting on the basis of uncorroborated evidence is abrogated.

. . . .

In the case of a jury charge in which a witness who might be regarded as an accomplice testifies, it has become not merely a rule of practice but a rule of law for the trial judge to warn the jury that it is dangerous to found a conviction on the evidence of an accomplice unless that evidence is corroborated in a material particular implicating the accused. The jury may convict in such circumstances but it is dangerous to do so. The judge must determine as a matter of law whether the witness might be an accomplice for the purposes of the rule. The jury must then decide whether he is in fact an accomplice. The judge explains the legal definition of "corroboration" with heavy reliance upon what was said by Lord Reading in *R. v. Baskerville*. The judge lists for the jury the pieces of evidence which are in his view capable of amounting to corroboration. Finally, they are told that it is for the jury to decide whether the evidence to which their attention has been directed does amount to corroboration, As the study paper of the Law Reform Commission of Canada "Evidence: Paper Study 11, Corroboration" dryly observes an "enormous superstructure ... has been erected on the original basic proposition that the evidence of some witnesses should be approached with caution".

The accused is in the unhappy position of hearing the judge draw particular attention to the evidence which tends to confirm the testimony the accomplice has given. Cogent prejudicial testimony is thus repeated and highlighted. For the jury this part of the charge can only be, in the words of Lord Diplock in *Director of Public Prosecutions v. Hester*, [1972] 3 All E.R. 1056 at p. 1075, "a frequent source of bewilderment". The task of a trial judge seeking to identify the evidence capable of amounting to corroboration is unenviable. Lord Reading in the Baskerville case said that it would be in high degree dangerous to attempt to formulate the kind of evidence which could be regarded as corroboration. It is also often a difficult and dangerous exercise identifying what pieces of evidence are capable of being corroborative. To take a simple example.

. . . .

In evaluating the adequacy of the law in this area, the first question which must be answered is a basic one: why have a special rule for accomplices at all? Credibility of witnesses and the weight of the evidence is, in general, a matter for the trier of fact. Identification evidence, for example, is notoriously weak, and yet the trial judge is not automatically required, as a matter of law, to instruct the jury on this point. Similarly, the trial judge is not required in all cases to warn the jury with respect to testimony of other witnesses with disreputable and untrustworthy backgrounds. Why, then, should we automatically require a warning when an accomplice takes the stand.

. . . .

Since the judge's instructions on this issue involve questions of law, numerous technical appeals are taken on the issue of whether a particular item of evidence is "capable" of constituting corroboration. The body of case-law is so complex that it has in turn produced a massive periodical literature. Moreover, the cases are difficult to reconcile. The Law Reform Commission of Canada has described the case-law in the area as full of "subtleties, variations, inconsistencies and great complexities": study paper 11, at p. 7. The result is that what was originally a simple, common-sense proposition — an accomplice's testimony should be viewed with caution — becomes transformed into a difficult and highly technical area of law. Whether this "enormous superstructure" (to use the description of the Law Reform Commission) has any meaningful relationship with the task performed by the jury is unknown.

. . . .

The law of corroboration is unduly and unnecessarily complex and technical. I would hold that there is no special category for "accomplices". An accomplice is to be treated like any other witness testifying at a criminal trial and the judge's conduct, if he chooses to give his opinion, is governed by the general rules. I would only like to add one or two observations concerning the proper practice to be followed in the trial court where as a matter of common sense something in the nature of confirmatory evidence should be found before the finder of fact relies upon the evidence of a witness whose testimony occupies a central position in the purported demonstration of guilt and yet may be suspect by reason of the witness being an accomplice or complainant or of disreputable character. There are great advantages to be gained by simplifying the instruction to juries on the question as to when a prudent juror will seek some confirmation of the story of such a witness, before concluding that the story is true and adopting it in the process of finding guilt in the accused as charged. It does not, however, always follow that the presiding justice may always simply turn the jury loose upon the evidence without any assisting analysis as to whether or not a prudent finder of fact can find confirmation somewhere in the mass of evidence of the evidence of a witness.

Because of the infinite range of circumstance which will arise in the criminal trial process it is not sensible to attempt to compress into a rule, a formula or a direction the concept of the need for prudent scrutiny of the testimony of any witness. What may be appropriate, however, in some circumstances, is a clear and sharp warning to attract the attention of the juror to the risks of adopting, without more, the evidence of the witness. There is no magic in the word corroboration, or indeed in any other comparable expression such as confirmation and support. The idea implied in those words may, however, in an appropriate case, be effectively and efficiently transmitted to the mind of the trier of fact. This may entail some illustration from the evidence of the particular case of the type of evidence, documentary or testimonial, which might be drawn upon by the juror in confirmation of the witness's testimony or some important part thereof. I do not wish to be taken as saying that such illustration must be carried to exhaustion. However, there is, in some circumstances, particularly in lengthy trials, the need for helpful direction on the question of sifting the evidence where guilt or innocence might, and probably will, turn on the acceptance or rejection, belief or disbelief, of the evidence of one or more witnesses. All of this applies equally in the case of an accomplice, or a disreputable witness of demonstrated moral lack, as, for example, a witness with a record of perjury. All this takes one back to the beginning and that is the search for the impossible: a rule which embodies and codifies common sense in the realm of the process of determining guilt or innocence of an accused on the basis of a record which includes evidence from potentially unreliable sources such as an accomplice.

[The Court, in the result, decided that in this case it would have been sufficient for the trial judge simply to have instructed the jury that they should view the testimony of the accomplice with great caution and that it would be wise to look for other supporting evidence before convicting the accused. However, since the trial judge did outline for the jury items of evidence he considered capable of corroborating the accomplice's testimony, the court examined this evidence to ensure that the accused were not prejudiced by the instruction. The Court decided that the evidence referred to by the trial judge was capable of corroborating the accomplice. In the result, the instructions by the trial judge did not prejudice the accused.]

R. v. KHELA
(2009) 62 C.R. (6th) 199 (S.C.C.)

The two accused, K and S, were tried jointly on charges of first degree murder. It was alleged that K paid two shooters to murder the victim, and that S helped to organize the killing. The case against K rested primarily on testimony from two members of a prison-based gang that K had hired the two shooters. Several women associates of these unsavoury witnesses also testified against K. The case against S rested mainly on the testimony of W, S's girlfriend at the time of the shooting, who claimed to have witnessed various incriminating acts and statements by S before and after the killing.

The two prison gang members were the subject of a *Vetrovec* warning. The trial judge stated that, given these witnesses' criminal backgrounds, it would be dangerous to convict on their evidence unless it was confirmed or supported by other evidence. The trial judge instructed the jury to look for some confirmation from somebody or something other than what the unsavoury witnesses had to say before relying on their testimony to convict. The trial judge noted that the jury might find some confirmatory evidence in the case, and that they should consider the evidence of the female associates in that regard, while remembering that the defence had labelled the female associates as liars. The female witnesses were not the subjects of a *Vetrovec* warning.

The issue before the Supreme Court was the adequacy of this unsavoury witness warning.

FISH J. (BINNIE, LEBEL, FISH, ABELLA, CHARRON, ROTHSTEIN JJ. concurring):

[11] The central purpose of a *Vetrovec* warning is to alert the jury to the danger of relying on the unsupported evidence of unsavoury witnesses and to explain the reasons for special scrutiny of their testimony. In appropriate cases, the trial judge should also draw the attention of the jurors to evidence capable of confirming or supporting the material parts of the otherwise untrustworthy evidence.

[12] Since the decision of this Court in *Vetrovec*, the very real dangers of relying in criminal prosecutions on the unsupported evidence of unsavoury witnesses, particularly "jailhouse informers", has been highlighted more than once by commissions of inquiry into wrongful convictions (see, for example, *The Commission on Proceedings Involving Guy Paul Morin: Report* (1998) and *The Inquiry Regarding Thomas Sophonow* (2001)). The danger of a miscarriage of justice is to be borne in mind in crafting and in evaluating the adequacy of a caution.

[13] The crafting of a caution appropriate to the circumstances of the case is best left to the judge who has conducted the trial. No particular set of words is mandatory. In evaluating its adequacy, appellate courts will focus on the content of the instruction and not on its form. Intervention on appeal will not be warranted unless a cautionary instruction should have been given but was not, or the cautionary instruction that was given failed to serve its intended purpose.

[14] No single formula can be expected to produce an appropriate instruction for every foreseeable — let alone *unforeseeable* — situation at trial. That is why we vest in trial judges the discretion they must have in fashioning cautionary instructions responsive to the circumstances of the case. Trial judges nonetheless seek, and are entitled to expect, guidance from this Court as to the general characteristics of a sufficient warning. I shall later outline in broad brushstrokes

a proposed template which, while not at all mandatory, will in my view be of assistance to trial judges without unduly fettering their discretion, and will reduce the number of appeals attributable to the present uncertainty regarding the governing principles.

[15] Read as a whole, and in the context of the trial, the charge to the jury in this case was adequate. Any shortcomings in the *Vetrovec* caution itself were compensated for in the remainder of the charge. I am satisfied that the jury would have understood that it could not convict the appellants on the basis of the evidence of the impugned witnesses unless they found elsewhere in the dance sufficient comfort that those witnesses were telling the truth.

[16] Accordingly, I would dismiss the appeals.

. . . .

[31] This Court, in *Vetrovec*, changed the law in relation to unsavoury witness warnings in two important ways. First, the Court held that trial judges, rather than attempting to "pigeonhole" witnesses as an "accomplices", ought instead to consider all of the factors that might impair their credibility and decide on that basis whether a special instruction is necessary. Second, the Court relieved triers of fact from applying the technical definition of corroboration and directed them instead simply to determine whether the "evidence properly weighed overcame its suspicious roots" (*Brooks*, at para. 69). Dickson J. held that there was no magic in the word corroboration, "or indeed in any other comparable expression such as confirmation and support" (*Vetrovec*, at p. 831).

[32] Dickson J. adopted this "common sense" approach having found the law of corroboration "unduly and unnecessarily complex and technical" (p. 830). This approach, while unburdening judges and juries of the technical requirements of corroboration, was not meant to imply that any and all evidence is capable of confirming the testimony of a potentially untrustworthy witness. As Major J. noted in *Brooks*, [t]his new approach, while a change, was not intended to prejudice the accused. It would not lessen the protection afforded the accused when faced with unsavoury witnesses. Equally, it was intended that the jury could view that evidence with more ease but not less scepticism than previously required. [para. 69]

[33] The relaxation of the corroboration rules in *Vetrovec* was not a signal that juries should be set "loose upon the evidence without any assisting analysis as to whether or not a prudent finder of fact can find confirmation somewhere in the mass of evidence" (*Vetrovec*, at p. 831). The trial judge retains the role of providing the jury with "the proper framework within which that credibility can be evaluated" (*Brooks*, at para. 130, *per* Binnie J.).

[34] Since *Vetrovec*, this Court and several appellate courts have provided guidance on the appropriate form and content of the "clear, sharp warning". In *Brooks*, Justice Major wrote (at para. 94) that while no particular language is required, "[a]t a minimum", the caution must focus the jury's attention specifically

on the inherently unreliable evidence. It should refer to the characteristics of the witness that bring the credibility of his or her evidence into serious question. It should plainly emphasize the dangers inherent in convicting an accused on the basis of such evidence unless confirmed by independent evidence.

[35] Speaking for himself and Justices Iacobucci and Arbour, Major J. also cited with approval (at para. 79) this passage from a commentary by Marc Rosenberg (now Rosenberg J.A.) on *Vetrovec* and its progeny:

> The judge should first in an objective way determine whether there is a reason to suspect the credibility of the witness according to the traditional means by which such determinations are made. This would include a review of the evidence to determine whether there are factors which have properly led the courts to be wary of accepting a witness's evidence. Factors might include involvement of criminal activities, a motive to lie by reason of connection to the crime or to the authorities, unexplained delay in coming forward with the story, providing different accounts on other occasions, lies told under oath, and similar considerations. It is not then whether the trial judge personally finds the witness trustworthy but whether there are factors which experience teaches that the witness's story be approached with caution. Second, the trial judge must assess the importance of the witness to the Crown's case. If the witness plays a relatively minor role in the proof of guilt it is probably unnecessary to burden the jury with a special caution and then review the confirmatory evidence. However, the more important the witness the greater the duty on the judge to give the caution. At some point, as where the witness plays a central role in the proof of guilt, the warning is mandatory. This, in my view, flows from the duty imposed on the trial judge in criminal cases to review the evidence and relate the evidence to the issues. ("Developments in the Law of Evidence: The 1992-93 Term — Applying the Rules" (1994), 5 *S.C.L.R.* (2d) 421, at p. 463)

[36] Though he arrived at a different result, Binnie J. agreed in *Brooks* (at para. 130) that what matters, in determining the need for a clear and sharp warning, is not the judge's personal opinion as to the trustworthiness of the witness, but whether there are factors which experience shows us as requiring "that the witness's story be approached with caution".

[37] In *Sauve*, at para. 82, the Ontario Court of Appeal set out a principled framework that will assist trial judges in constructing *Vetrovec* warnings appropriate to the circumstances of each case. That proposed framework, which I adopt and amplify here, is composed of four main foundation elements: (1) drawing the attention of the jury to the testimonial evidence requiring special scrutiny; (2) explaining *why* this evidence is subject to special scrutiny; (3) cautioning the jury that it is dangerous to convict on unconfirmed evidence of this sort, though the jury is entitled to do so if satisfied that the evidence is true; and (4) that the jury, in determining the veracity of the suspect evidence, should look for evidence from another source tending to show that the untrustworthy witness is telling the truth as to the guilt of the accused (*R. v. Kehler*, 2004 SCC 11, [2004] 1 S.C.R. 328, at paras. 17-19).

[38] While this summary should not be applied in a rigid and formulaic fashion, it accurately captures the elements that should guide trial judges in crafting their

instructions on potentially untrustworthy witnesses. The fourth component, of particular interest on this appeal, provides guidance on the kind of evidence that is capable of confirming the suspect testimony of an impugned witness.

[39] Common sense dictates that not all evidence presented at trial is capable of confirming the testimony of an impugned witness. The attribute of independence defines the kind of evidence that can provide comfort to the trier of fact that the witness is telling the truth. Where evidence is "tainted" by connection to the *Vetrovec* witness it can not serve to confirm his or her testimony (N. Harris, "*Vetrovec* Cautions and Confirmatory Evidence: A Necessarily Complex Relationship" (2005), 31 C.R. (6th) 216, at p. 225; *R. v. Sanderson*, 2003 MBCA 109, 180 C.C.C. (3d) 53, at para. 61).

[40] Materiality is a more difficult concept. In *Vetrovec*, the Court did away with the requirement that corroborating evidence implicate the accused. As Dickson J. noted, such evidence is not the only type capable of convincing a jury that a witness is telling the truth. In *Kehler*, the Court confirmed that evidence, to be considered confirmatory, does not have to implicate the accused. We maintain that position here.

[41] Individual items of confirmatory evidence need not implicate the accused. As Dickson J. explained in *Vetrovec*:

> The reason for requiring corroboration is that we believe the witness has good reason to lie. We therefore want some other piece of evidence which tends to convince us that he is telling the truth. Evidence which implicates the accused does indeed serve to accomplish that purpose but it cannot be said that this is the only sort of evidence which will accredit the accomplice. [p. 826]

[42] However, when looked at in the context of the case as a whole, the items of confirmatory evidence should give comfort to the jury that the witness can be trusted in his or her assertion that the accused is the person who committed the offence. Again in *Vetrovec*, Dickson J. thus noted, with respect to evidence capable of being confirmatory:

Deschamps J. dissented in part on the basis that the majority's opinion was part of a regrettable incremental return to the former formalism of the former law of corroboration.[421]

(iv) *Informers*

R. v. BROOKS
[2000] 1 S.C.R. 237, 30 C.R. (5th) 201, 141 C.C.C. (3d) 321

A 19-month-old child was found murdered in her crib wrapped in a green comforter. Only the accused and the child's mother had access to her on the

---

421 For comments on *Khela* see annotations in the Criminal Reports by Lisa Dufraimont and Michael Plaxton.

night of the murder. The Crown led evidence from two jailhouse informants, King and Balogh, who testified that the accused, while incarcerated, had admitted that he had killed the child to stop her crying. Both informants had lengthy criminal records of dishonesty. One unsuccessfully sought a lighter sentence in return for his testimony and had testified as an informant in a prior trial. The other had a history of substance abuse and a psychiatric history highlighted by suicide attempts, paranoia, deep depression and a belief in clairvoyant ability. Both had histories of offering to testify in criminal trials. The trial judge's jury charge did not provide a *Vetrovec* warning to the jury about the danger of relying on the informants' testimonies. Neither counsel requested a warning nor objected to the lack of a warning. The accused was convicted of first degree murder. The Court of Appeal set aside the conviction and ordered a new trial.

BASTARACHE J. (GONTHIER, and MCLACHLIN JJ. concurring): —

. . . .

It is my opinion that the decision not to give a *Vetrovec* warning was within the discretion of the trial judge and that the exercise of this discretion should not have been interfered with on appeal. I have reached this conclusion for the reasons I set out below.

In *Vetrovec*, Dickson J. held that a trial judge has the discretion, and not the duty, to give a clear and sharp warning to the jury with respect to the testimony of certain "unsavoury" witnesses. Dickson J. followed what he referred to as the "common sense" approach, moving away from "blind and empty formalism" and "ritualistic incantations". . . . This Court in *Vetrovec* deliberately chose not to formulate a fixed and invariable rule where "clear and sharp" warnings would be required as a matter of course regarding the testimony of certain categories of witnesses. Rather, where a witness occupies a central position in the determination of guilt and, yet, may be suspect because of a disreputable or untrustworthy character, a clear and sharp warning may be appropriate to alert the jury to the risks of adopting the evidence "without more". It is therefore within the trial judge's discretion to give a *Vetrovec* caution. . . . In exercising his or her discretion to warn the jury regarding certain evidence, the trial judge may consider, *inter alia*, the credibility of the witness and the importance of the evidence to the Crown's case. These factors affect whether the *Vetrovec* warning is required. In other words, the greater the concern over the credibility of the witness and the more important the evidence, the more likely the *Vetrovec* caution will be mandatory. Where the evidence of so called "unsavoury witnesses" represents the whole of the evidence against the accused, a "clear and sharp" *Vetrovec* warning may be warranted. Where, however, there is strong evidence to support the conviction in the absence of the potentially "unsavoury" evidence, and less reason to doubt the witness's credibility, the *Vetrovec* warning would not be required, and a lesser instruction would be justified. The trial judge's instruction with respect to the evidence of jailhouse informants must therefore be commensurate with the particular circumstances of the case. For example, the trial judge is not required to give a "clear and sharp" warning on the dangers of convicting on the impugned evidence where, in the circumstances, the trial judge believes that there is no such danger. Similarly, the trial judge may properly decline to give a warning if the warning may prejudice the accused's case rather than assist it. Provided there is a foundation for the trial judge's exercise of discretion, appellate courts should not interfere. Here, that foundation was established having regard to the credibility of the witnesses, the importance of their evidence and the failure to request a warning.

. . . .

To find that the trial judge's failure to provide a "clear and sharp" *Vetrovec* warning in the circumstances of this case amounts to an error of law runs counter to the spirit of *Vetrovec*, which affirmed a judicial discretion to provide warnings only in appropriate circumstances. Provided there is a foundation for the judge's exercise of discretion, appellate courts should not interfere. Here that foundation existed. For these reasons, I am unable to conclude that the failure of the trial judge to give a "clear and sharp" *Vetrovec* warning amounted to an error of law. I would allow the appeal accordingly and restore the conviction entered by the trial judge.

MAJOR J. (IACOBUCCI and ARBOUR JJ. concurring): —

. . . .

In my opinion, the trial judge ought to have given a *Vetrovec* warning. In its absence the charge was not the equivalent nor was it adequate. In the result it cannot be said that the verdict would necessarily have been the same and accordingly the appeal should be dismissed.

. . . .

In summary, two main factors are relevant when deciding whether a *Vetrovec* warning is necessary: the witness's credibility, and the importance of the witness's testimony to the Crown's case. No specific threshold need be met on either factor before a warning becomes necessary. Instead, where the witness is absolutely essential to the Crown's case, more moderate credibility problems will warrant a warning. Where the witness has overwhelming credibility problems, a warning may be necessary even if the Crown's case is a strong one without the witness's evidence. In short, the factors should not be looked to independently of one another but in combination.

Recommendations of the Kaufman Report

Since the decisions of this Court in *Vetrovec* and *Bevan*, the extreme dangers of relying on the use of "jailhouse informers" as witnesses in criminal prosecutions has been highlighted in the *Report of The Commission on Proceedings Involving Guy Paul Morin* (the "Kaufman Report") released in 1998 where the Honourable Fred Kaufman, C.M., Q.C., stated at p. 602:

> In-custody informers are almost invariably motivated by self-interest. They often have little or no respect for the truth or their testimonial oath or affirmation. Accordingly, they may lie or tell the truth, depending only upon where their perceived

self-interest lies. In-custody confessions are often easy to allege and difficult, if not impossible, to disprove.

and at p. 638:

> The evidence at this Inquiry demonstrates the inherent unreliability of in-custody informer testimony, its contribution to miscarriages of justice and the substantial risk that the dangers may not be fully appreciated by the jury. In my view, the present law has developed to the point that a cautionary instruction is virtually mandated in cases where the in-custody informer's testimony is contested.

Since the release of the Kaufman Report, the Ministry of the Attorney General of Ontario has revised its internal policies to reflect many of the Report's recommendations. New policies include the establishment of an "In-Custody Informer Committee", the function of which is to review the use of all in-custody informers in criminal trials to determine whether their use as a witness is in the public interest. The Ministry has also adopted into its Policy Manual the Kaufman Report's recommended list of factors to be considered in assessing an informer's reliability or lack thereof. The factors also serve as a useful guide to a trial judge when determining whether a *Vetrovec* warning is necessary.

. . . .

In my opinion the failure of the trial judge to give a *Vetrovec* warning was a misdirection of law. The question is then whether in light of all the evidence the test in *Bevan* is met. Would the result have necessarily been the same?

[Major J. then examined the other evidence in the case and concluded.]

There was evidence that implicated the accused but with a proper instruction regarding the testimony of the jailhouse informants it is difficult for me to preclude the possibility of a different result. I agree with the Court of Appeal and would dismiss the appeal and confirm the order for a new trial.

BINNIE J.: —

I agree with the result reached by Justice Bastarache, but I reach that conclusion by a different route. In my view, the evidence of the "jailhouse informants" in this case was tainted by a combination of some of the more notorious badges of testimonial unreliability, including the opportunity to lie for personal benefit, and the jury ought to have been given a clear and sharp warning to that effect. The trial judge erred in law in failing to give such a warning, as found by Justice Major and a majority of the Ontario Court of Appeal. At the same time, I differ, with respect, from the conclusion that this error of law requires a new trial. Given the other evidence against the respondent that was necessarily accepted by the jury in reaching their verdict of first degree murder, I think, with great respect to those of the opposite view, that there is no reasonable possibility that the verdict would have been different had the error of law not been made.

. . . .

[Binnie J. then reviewed the evidence and concluded.]

For these reasons, I conclude that the failure of the trial judge to give a *Vetrovec* warning was an error of law, but that there is no reasonable possibility the jury would have rendered a different verdict had the proper warning been given. The Crown bears a heavy onus in seeking the application of the curative provision of s. 686(1)(*b*)(iii) but, for the reasons given, it is my view that justice does not require a new trial on the particular facts of this case. The appeal should therefore be allowed and the respondent's conviction and sentence restored.

(v) *Primary Witnesses in Sex Cases*

In the early common law the testimony of the victim in the trial of a sexual offence was sufficient to support a conviction. In Hale, *Pleas of the Crown,* we read:

> The party ravished may give evidence upon oath and is in law a competent witness; but the credibility of her testimony, and how far forth she is to be believed, must be left to the jury, and is more or less credible according to the circumstances of fact that concur in that testimony. . . . It is one thing whether a witness be admissible to be heard; another thing, whether they are to be believed when heard. It is true, rape is a most detestable crime, and therefore ought severely and impartially to be punished with death; but it must be remembered that it is an accusation easily to be made and hard to be proved; and harder to be defended by the party accused, tho never so innocent.[422]

By 1925, however, the common law had come to demand a similar warning about the evidence of primary witnesses in sex cases as they had required respecting the evidence of accomplices. Hewart L.C.J. in *R. v. Jones* wrote:

> The proper direction in such a case [where the offence charged is a sexual offence] is that it is not safe to convict upon the uncorroborated testimony of the prosecutrix, but that the jury, if they are satisfied of the truth of her evidence, may, after paying attention to that warning, nevertheless convict.[423]

In Canada the Criminal Code was amended in 1954 to provide that with regard to five sexual offences (rape, attempted rape, sexual intercourse with a female under 14, sexual intercourse with a female between 14 and 16, and indecent assault on a female):

> . . . the judge shall, if the only evidence that implicates the accused is the evidence, given under oath, of the female person in respect of whom the offence is alleged to have been committed and that evidence is not corroborated in a material particular by evidence that implicates the accused, instruct the jury that it is not safe to find the accused guilty in the absence of such corroboration, but that they are entitled to find the accused guilty if they are satisfied beyond a reasonable doubt that her evidence is true.[424]

Glanville Williams sought to justify the instruction:

> There is sound reason for this, because sexual cases are particularly subject to the danger of deliberately false charges, resulting from sexual neurosis, fantasy, jealousy,

---

422 1680, Hale, L.C.J., *Pleas of the Crown,* 1, 633, 635 quoted in 7 Wigmore, *Evidence,* 3d ed., s. 2061.

423 (1925), 19 Cr. App. R. 40, 41.

424 See R.S.C. 1970, c. 34, s. 142.

spite, or simply a girl's refusal to admit that she consented to an act of which she is now ashamed. Of these various possibilities, the most subtle are those connected with mental complexes.[425]

In 1975 the Criminal Code provision was repealed and, after a period of uncertainty, it now seems settled that the common law requirement of a warning was not thereby revived.[426]

The Criminal Code continued to require corroboration prior to conviction for a number of other sexual offences: per section 139, sexual intercourse with the feeble-minded, incest, seduction of a female between 16 and 18 years of age, seduction under the promise of marriage, sexual intercourse with a step-daughter, seduction of female passengers on vessels, parent or guardian of female person procuring her defilement; per section 195, procuring;[427] per section 253 communicating venereal disease to another person;[428] per section 256 procuring a feigned marriage.[429] Wigmore described statutory requirements of corroboration in sex cases:

> The fact is that, in the light of modern psychology, this technical rule of corroboration seems but a crude and childish measure, if it be relied upon as an adequate means for determining the credibility of the complaining witness in such charges. The problem of estimating the veracity of feminine testimony in complaints against masculine offenders is baffling enough to the experienced psychologist. This statutory rule is unfortunate in that it tends to produce reliance upon a rule of thumb. Better to inculcate the resort to an expert scientific analysis of the particular witness' mentality, as the true measure of enlightenment.[430]

Notice that the requirements here imposed *forbade conviction* even if the trier of fact was satisfied of the accused's guilt beyond a reasonable doubt.

The neanderthal ideas and attitudes above described in this section have now been largely overcome, at least in our legislative provisions. In 1982 section 139 was repealed and section 246.4 enacted. Section 246.4 was later enlarged in 1988 and the counterpart section now provides:

> **274.** If an accused is charged with an offence under section 151, 152, 153, 153.1, 155, 159, 160, 170, 171, 172, 173, 212, 271, 272 or 273, no corroboration is required for a conviction and the judge shall not instruct the jury that it is unsafe to find the accused guilty in the absence of corroboration.

---

425 "Corroboration — Sexual Cases," [1962] Crim. L. Rev. 662.

426 See *R. v. Camp* (1977), 36 C.C.C. (2d) 511 (Ont. C.A.) and *R. v. Firkins* (1977), 37 C.C.C. (2d) 227 (B.C.C.A.); leave to appeal to S.C.C. refused (1978), 80 D.L.R. (3d) 63n. But compare *R. v. Riley* (1978), 42 C.C.C. (2d) 437 (Ont. C.A.) and *R. v. Curtis*, [1989] N.J. No. 84 (C.A.), regarding the need for caution when relying solely on the evidence of the complainant in a sexual assault case.

427 See now R.S.C. 1985, c. C-46, s. 212.

428 *Ibid.*, s. 289.

429 *Ibid.*, s. 292.

430 7 Wigmore, *Evidence*, 3d ed., s. 2061, p. 354. For a good critical note calling for the repeal of such statutory provisions see "The Rape Corroboration Requirement: Repeal Not Reform" (1972), 81 Yale L.J. 1365. See also Bienen, "A Question of Credibility: John Henry Wigmore's Use of Scientific Authority" (1983), 19 Cal. Western L. Rev. 235.

R. v. S. (F.)
(1997), 116 C.C.C. (3d) 435 (Ont. C.A.)

The accused was charged with sexual assault causing bodily harm.

FINLAYSON J.A. (WEILER and LASKIN JJ.A. concurring):—

The complainant's testimony was central to the case for the Crown. However, with the exception of her evidence with respect to the incidents at the motel, her testimony was unsupported by any independent confirmatory evidence. In my opinion this case did call for a "clear and sharp warning" in relation to the testimony of the complainant as called for in *Vetrovec*. Apart from the highly suspect account she gave of the Lake Wilcox incident, the complainant had a lengthy psychiatric history, the details of which were before the jury, and which included "flashback" recollections of certain events. Her past conduct also revealed a pattern of false statements of fact to her doctors.

(vi) *Unsworn Evidence of Children*

If a child is sworn as a witness the judge is directed to warn the jury to treat his evidence with caution much as he would warn them with respect to the testimony of accomplices. In *Kendall v. R.*,[431] Judson J. explained:

> The basis for the rule of practice which requires the Judge to warn the jury of the danger of convicting on the evidence of a child, even when sworn as a witness, is the mental immaturity of the child. The difficulty is fourfold: 1. His capacity of observation. 2. His capacity of recollection. 3. His capacity to understand questions put and frame intelligent answers. 4. His moral responsibility.

Section 586 of the Criminal Code forbade conviction "upon the unsworn evidence of a child unless the evidence of the child is corroborated in a material particular by evidence that implicated the accused." Provisions in the *Canada Evidence Act* and in most of the provincial Evidence Acts mirrored this requirement.[432] Notice again that findings were *prohibited* though the trier is satisfied beyond a reasonable doubt.

In 1988 section 586 (659) of the Criminal Code[433] and section 16(2) of the *Canada Evidence Act*[434] were repealed. While the requirement of corroboration for the unsworn testimony of children was dispensed with, the legislation did not, unlike the new section 246.4, say anything forbidding a cautionary warning. For many, unfortunately, the "wisdom" of *Kendall* will cause many judges and lawyers to continue to be distrustful of the evidence of children. The common sense displayed in *Vetrovec* mandates that we ought not to automatically characterize a witness's capacity for truth-telling depending on whether they belong to a particular class of people. No one should assume that all children are inherently suspect. The child witness should be treated like other witnesses, as an individual with whatever individual shortcomings or individual attributes that are there to be

---

431 (1962), 132 C.C.C. 216, 220 (S.C.C.).
432 See *Canada Evidence Act*, s. 16(2); *Ontario Evidence Act*, s. 18(2).
433 1987, c. 24, s. 15; see now R.S.C. 1985, c. C-46, s. 659; 1993, c. 45, s. 9.
434 1987, c. 24, s. 18.

observed. Rather than parroting such phrases as "Out of the mouths of babes can only come truth . . .", or "It is well known that children fantasize (have poor memories, lack perceptual abilities) . . ." we, as lawyers, need to become more aware of the social science literature and the empirical studies that have been done.

R. v. S. (W.)
(1994), 29 C.R. (4th) 143, 90 C.C.C. (3d) 242

The accused was charged with sexual interference. The complainant, who was 15 years old at the time of the trial, testified that the accused, her uncle by marriage, touched her for a sexual purpose up to 200 times between January 1988 and January 1990 when she stayed overnight as a guest of the accused's family at their farmhouse. The Court of Appeal found that there was a conflict in the evidence about when and in what circumstances the complainant slept downstairs, which was where the interference allegedly took place. The Court expressed a concern that the trial judge, having made a positive finding of credibility in favour of the complainant, did not appear to have given serious consideration to the possibility that, on the whole of the evidence, there was a reasonable doubt that the alleged acts did, in fact, occur.

FINLAYSON J.A.:—

. . . .

My concern in this case is that the trial judge, having made a positive finding of credibility in favour of the complainant, does not appear to have given serious consideration to the possibility that, on the whole of the evidence, there is a reasonable doubt that the alleged acts did, in fact, occur. I think that the words of Wood J.A. in *R. v. K. (V.)* (1991), 4 C.R. (4th) 338 (B.C. C.A.), another case involving the alleged sexual touching of a child, are appropriate to bear in mind, where he stated at p. 357:

> I have already alluded to the danger, in a case where the evidence consists primarily of the allegations of a complainant and the denial of the accused, that the trier of fact will see the issue as one of deciding whom to believe. Earlier in the judgment, I noted the gender-related stereotypical thinking that led to assumptions about the credibility of complainants in sexual cases which we have at long last discarded as totally inappropriate. It is important to ensure that they are not replaced by an equally pernicious set of assumptions about the believability of complainants which would have the effect of shifting the burden of proof to those accused of such crimes.

Galligan J.A. alluded to a similar danger in *R. v. J. (F.E.)* (1990), 53 C.C.C. (3d) 64 (Ont. C.A.) at pp. 67-68:

> While there is no scale upon which conflicting evils can be weighed, it should be remembered that revolting as child sexual abuse is, it would be horrible for an innocent person to be convicted of it. For that reason I think the courts must be vigilant to ensure that the zeal to punish child sexual abusers does not erode the rules which the courts have developed over the centuries to prevent the conviction of the innocent.

It is evident from his reasons that the trial judge was impressed with the demeanour of the complainant in the witness box and the fact that she was not shaken in cross-examination. I am not satisfied, however, that a positive finding of credibility on the part of the complainant is sufficient to support a conviction in a case of this nature where there is significant evidence which contradicts the complainant's allegations. We all know from our personal experiences as trial lawyers and judges that honest witnesses, whether they are adults or children, may convince themselves that inaccurate versions of a given event are correct and they can be very persuasive. The issue, however, is not the sincerity of the witness but the reliability of the witness's testimony. Demeanour alone should not suffice to found a conviction where there are significant inconsistencies and conflicting evidence on the record: see *R. v. Norman* (1993), 16 O.R. (3d) 295 at pp. 311-15 for a discussion on this subject.

The Supreme Court of Canada has addressed the issue of the assessment of the evidence of child witnesses in two leading cases dealing with allegations of sexual abuse: *R. v. B. (G.)* (1990), 56 C.C.C. (3d) 200 and *R. v. W. (R.)* (1992), 74 C.C.C. (3d) 134. In *R. v. W. (R.)*, McLachlin J. comments that there have been two major changes in recent years in the approach that courts should take to the evidence of young children. The first is the removal of the notion, found at common law and codified in legislation, that the evidence of children was inherently unreliable and therefore to be treated with special caution. The second is a new appreciation that it may be wrong to apply adult tests for credibility to the evidence of children. With respect to the second change, she cites Wilson J. in *R. v. B. (G.)* at pp. 219-220, where Wilson J. advocates a common sense approach when dealing with the testimony of young children and advises judges not to impose the same exacting standards upon them as upon adults. Wilson J. emphasizes that the courts should continue to carefully assess the credibility of child witnesses and she does not suggest that the standard of proof beyond a reasonable doubt should cease to apply in criminal cases in which young children have been victimized. In *R. v. W. (R.)*, McLachlin J. adds that we should not approach the evidence of children from the perspective of rigid stereotypes and we should adopt a "common sense" approach which takes into account the strengths and weaknesses characterizing the evidence offered in the particular case.

As I understand these two judgments, we must assess witnesses of tender years for what they are, children, and not adults. We should not expect them as witnesses to perform in the same manner as adults. This does not mean, however, that we should subject the testimony of children to a lower level of scrutiny for reliability than we would do adults. My concern is that some trial judges may be inadvertently relaxing the proper level of scrutiny to which the evidence of children should be subjected. The changes to the evidentiary rules were intended to make child evidence more readily available to the court by removing the restraints on its use that existed previously but were never intended to encourage an undiscriminating acceptance of the evidence of children while holding adults to higher standards. With respect, I think the case on appeal illustrates the latter approach.[435]

The Court allowed the appeal on the basis that the verdict was unreasonable. The Court recognized the authority of *R. v. W. (R.)*,[436] that an appellate court determining the reasonableness of a verdict is entitled, while giving due deference to the trial judge's advantaged position, to assess findings of credibility made in the court below. To similar effect, with the majority and minority of the appellate court assessing credibility quite differently, see *R. v. François*.[437]

In *R. v. W. (R.)*, McLachlin J. wrote:

> The repeal of provisions creating a legal requirement that children's evidence be corroborated does not prevent the judge or jury from treating a child's evidence with caution where such caution is merited in the circumstances of the case.[438]

In *R. v. W. (R.S.)*[439] Justice Twaddle for the Court developed this thought:

> Whilst the previously held views as to the unreliability of complaints in cases of sexual assault have now been discarded, it would be foolhardy to assume that the danger once feared in every case now exists in none. The rationale for the old rules of practice requiring corroboration was not grounded in stereotypical thinking alone.[440]

R. v. G. (A.)
(1998), 21 C.R. (5th) 149, 130 C.C.C. (3d) 30 (Ont. C.A.)

The accused was convicted of sexual assault. The complainant was a niece of the accused. She alleged that on three occasions between December 1986 and March 1988, the accused briefly touched and rubbed her vaginal area while she was fully clothed. The accused denied the assault and led evidence of a motive in the complainant to fabricate. The trial was held in 1996. On appeal the issue was whether the verdict was unreasonable. The majority voted to dismiss the appeal. In the course of his dissenting opinion, Justice Finlayson commented on his understanding of the positions of complainants and accused in sexual assault cases.

FINLAYSON J.A.:—

The trial judge failed to approach the complainant's evidence with the scepticism that it deserved in this case. There is not the remotest of supporting evidence that any sexual acts took place. The sexual acts are highly ambiguous coming as they do from an uncle and "godfather" to the young girl. Any form of "horseplay" could explain them. Giving the most generous interpretation to the acts as described by the complainant, they are hardly consistent with intent to commit a sexual assault. Even the trial judge noted that at the time of their

---

435 *Ibid.*, at pp. 148-51.
436 (1992), 13 C.R. (4th) 257.
437 (1994), 31 C.R. (4th) 201 (S.C.C.).
438 *Supra*, note 436, at p. 266.
439 (1992), 74 C.C.C. (3d) 1, 8 (Man. C.A.).
440 *Ibid.*, at p. 8.

occurrence, the complainant did not know what the touchings meant. The evidence is very much open to the construction that the appellant could have had some incidental contact with the girl that was entirely innocent.

There is no pattern of abuse here. The appellant must have had more than three opportunities to abuse the girl if he was of a mind to. No explanation is offered for the fact that the assaults simply ceased. On the darker side, the evidence is not inconsistent with the appellant's contention that the complainant had a motive to fabricate, given the appellant's concerns regarding her friendship with N.

Having had the advantage of reading the transcripts of many of what are termed "historical sexual abuse cases" that have come before this court over the last decade, I am concerned that this case does fit a pattern of allegations of sexual abuse that are initiated by ulterior motives. The complaints are usually of this vague and unsubstantiated nature. They are so stale dated and amorphous that it is impossible for the person accused to give a detailed rebuttal to them without arousing suspicion as to why his memory is so precise.

The defence also reveals a pattern. Faced with attempting to recall what must have been a non-event to any normal person, the accused seized upon a material discrepancy in the complainant's evidence and demonstrated objectively that the appellant's story cannot be true in a significant particular. In this case it was the red couch. [The complainant described the assaults as having occurred on a red couch in the basement. Evidence was led that the red couch didn't come onto the premises until well after the complained of incident.] The trial judge at no time stated that he disbelieved the appellant or the other witnesses on this issue (by way of a sidebar, he did not expressly disbelieve the appellant on any, of his evidence). His approach to the red couch evidence was to ignore its importance. He said:

> The complained of detail is this case of course relates to the where of the offence as recounted by a six or seven-year-old as opposed to the who, the who-did-it and what-was-done to her by him.

The criminal courts need a new gatekeeper. Parliament and the judiciary have radically eroded the traditional protection available to the accused in sexual assault cases. My comment does not reflect nostalgia. The changes were long overdue. However, the pendulum must not be allowed to swing too far in the other direction. As I had occasion to observe in *R. v. P. (M.B.)* (1992), 9 O.R. (3d) 424, affirmed [1994] 1 S.C.R. 555 at p. 433:

> In our efforts to protect those most deserving of protection, we must not neglect our traditional role as protectors of the rights of the accused to a fair trial.

The majority of sexual offences are now tried without a jury in the Ontario Court (Provincial Division). There is no preliminary hearing in which both the Crown and the defence can make some assessment of the reliability of the complainant's testimony. In any event, the safeguard of the exercise of prosecutorial discretion in weak cases has fallen victim to the catchword "zero tolerance". The former rules regarding corroboration have been abolished. Despite the obvious need in most cases for some supporting evidence, many judges pay lip service to this admonition. Distortions in the complainant's evidence are too often dismissed as the norm with children. The accused who testifies is granted no such leeway. The burden quickly shifts to him to explain his conduct. Reasonable doubt, the most fundamental concept of British justice, runs the risk of becoming a hollow invocation, rather than the shield against injustice it was meant to be.

There has to be a new gatekeeper and that person is the trial judge. He was not present in this case. The trial judge was prepared to convict the appellant on the flimsiest of evidence. This complaint should not have gone to trial, much less have led to a conviction. Where the trial judge convicts on evidence such as this record displays, the Court of Appeal has more than the right, it has the duty to interfere and, in the interests of justice, quash the verdict as unreasonable.

LABROSSE, BORINS JJ.A. concurring:— . . .

In applying the unreasonable verdict test the appellate court should show great deference to findings of credibility made at trial given the advantage possessed by the trial judge in hearing the evidence and observing the demeanour of the witnesses, I conclude that the trial judge's verdict is supported by the evidence and is not unreasonable, as conceded by counsel for the appellant. I cannot agree with the comments made by Finlayson J.A. with respect to sexual assaults, particularly those found in paragraphs 25 to 26 of his reasons.

With whom do you agree?

———————

(vii) *Miscellaneous Provisions*

A number of statutory provisions exist in provincial legislation which require corroboration for a finding. For example, provisions in a number of Evidence Acts demand corroboration in actions against estates of deceased persons,[441] and in actions by or against the mentally ill.[442]

(b) What is Corroboration?

The classic definition of corroboration given by Lord Reading in *R. v. Baskerville*[443] requires that the corroborative evidence be independent of the principal witness and implicate the accused, that is "confirms in some material particular not only the evidence that the crime has been committed, but also that the prisoner committed it." Many of the statutory provisions requiring corroboration have similar language: "upon the evidence of only one witness, unless the evidence of that witness is corroborated in a material particular by evidence that implicates the accused." It is in the application of this definition to the evidence in the particular case that trial judges have had great difficulty and "probably has given rise to more new trials being ordered by appellate courts than any other branch of the law of evidence."[444] It is difficult, if not impossible, to reconcile all

———————

441 See, *e.g.*, R.S.O. 1980, c. 145, s. 13; R.S.A. 1980, c. A-21, s. 12.
442 See, *e.g.*, R.S.O. 1980, c. 145, s. 14; R.S.N. 1970, c. 115, s. 15.
443 [1916] 2 K.B. 658 (C.C.A.).
444 Task Force Report on Uniform Rules of Evidence (1981), p. 428.

the reported decisions on the application of the definition but the Supreme Court has recently sought to explain.

R. v. B. (G.)
[1990] 2 S.C.R. 3, 77 C.R. (3d) 327, 56 C.C.C. (3d) 161

The accused was charged with committing an aggravated sexual assault on the complainant, a kindergarten student who was five years old at the time of the alleged offence. The complainant gave unsworn testimony at the trial. There was, then, a need for corroboration, pursuant to the legislation then in existence.

WILSON J. (L'HEUREUX-DUBÉ, GONTHIER, CORY and McLACHLIN JJ., concurring):—

. . .

Any review of the case law dealing with corroboration must begin with a discussion of *Baskerville*. . . .

It is the interpretation of [*Baskerville*] which seems to have caused confusion in recent years. . . .

[The Crown] submits that the *Baskerville* rule is open to two interpretations. The first, or narrow rule, sees corroborative evidence as independent evidence that itself implicates the accused. The second, and considerably broader interpretation, is that if the witness identifies the accused and the evidence of the witness is confirmed in some material particular, then there is corroboration in law of that witness's evidence. The Crown advocates the broader interpretation. However, in my view, support for the broader interpretation is not to be found in Lord Reading's judgment. He made it abundantly clear throughout his reasons that there had to be corroborative evidence as to a material circumstance of the crime <u>and</u> as to the identity of the accused in relation to that crime. In *Vetrovec*, Dickson J. shared this view, stating at p. 826:

> Prior to the judgment of Lord Reading, there had been controversy over whether corroborative evidence must implicate the accused, or whether it was sufficient if it simply strengthened the credibility of the accomplice. Lord Reading settled the controversy in favour of the former view.

In the years following *Baskerville* the narrow interpretation of the rule was approved in numerous decisions of this Court. One text writer has commented that this Court acted upon the narrow interpretation of the rule on at least fifteen occasions over a period of sixty years: see Schiff, *Evidence in the Litigation Process* (1988), vol. 1, at p. 613. . . . .

The Court [in *Vetrovec*] expressed a preference for a common sense approach rather than the overly technical approach in *Baskerville*. It found at least three problems with *Baskerville*. The first was that it confuses the reason behind the accomplice warning and prompts the courts to determine whether the corroborative evidence fits the definition rather than deciding whether there is evidence that bolsters the credibility of the accomplice. Secondly, because corroboration became a legal term of art the law in the area became increasingly complex and technical. Thirdly, and most importantly, the Court was of the view that the definition was unsound in principle. Dickson J. stated at p. 826:

With great respect, on principle Lord Reading's approach seems perhaps over-cautious. The reason for requiring corroboration is that we believe the witness has good reason to lie. We therefore want some other piece of evidence which tends to convince us that he is telling the truth. Evidence which implicates the accused does indeed serve to accomplish that purpose but it cannot be said that this is the only sort of evidence which will accredit the accomplice.

. . . .

It seems to me, therefore, that this Court has clearly rejected an ultra technical approach to corroboration and has returned to a common sense approach which reflects the original rationale for the rule and allows cases to be determined on their merits. . . .

I am, accordingly, in agreement with the Crown's position.

. . . .

Also in favour of the liberal interpretation [of the legislation requiring corroboration] are the presumptions that the law does not require the impossible and the legislator intends only what is just and reasonable. Since the only evidence implicating the accused in many sexual offences against children will be the evidence of the child, imposing too restrictive a standard on their testimony may permit serious offences to go unpunished and perhaps to continue. Moreover, it is reasonable to assume that the legislator did not intend an accused to benefit from the youthful age of his victim by placing unnecessary impediments in the way of prosecuting offences against small children.[445]

---

445 See further regarding what counts as corroborative evidence *R. v. Dhillon* (2002), 166 C.C.C. (3d) 262 (Ont. C.A.) and *R. v. Kehler* (2004), 19 C.R. (6th) 49 (S.C.C.).

Chapter 6

Exclusionary Rules

A. CHARACTER

Some would characterise the common law rules tending to exclude bad character evidence as an exclusionary rule. We chose to address character evidence in Part 4 as a test case for the basic precept of admitting relevant evidence subject to a discretion to exclude.

B. HEARSAY

> A picture of the hearsay rule with its exceptions would resemble an old-fashioned crazy quilt made of patches cut from a group of paintings by cubists, futurists and surrealists.[1]

1. THE RULE

(a) History

The hearsay rule was described by Professor Wigmore as "that most characteristic rule of the Anglo-American law of evidence — a rule which may be esteemed, next to jury trial, the greatest contribution of that eminently practical legal system to the world's methods of procedure."[2] It was not always thus, and it may assist our understanding of the rule's present day workings and justifications if we have some regard for its origin.[3]

Common law courts disapproved of hearsay evidence with increasing frequency throughout the seventeenth and eighteenth centuries. By the end of the eighteenth century, this disapproval hardened into an exclusionary rule in both civil and criminal practice.[4] The jury initially was not to decide issues on the basis of evidence produced in open court; its members were selected because they had knowledge of the facts. Insofar as their knowledge was imperfect it was their function to investigate and gather information from those who were

---

1 Morgan and Maguire, "Looking Backward and Forward at Evidence" (1937), 50 Harv. L.R. 909 at 921.
2 5 Wigmore, *Evidence* (Chad. Rev.), p. 28.
3 A full account is provided in 5 Wigmore, *Evidence* (Chad. Rev.), p. 1364. And see Morgan, "History and Theory of the Hearsay Rule", in *Some Problems of Proof under the Anglo-American System of Litigation* (1956), Columbia University Press, pp. 106-40.
4 See Langebin, *The Origins of Adversary Criminal Law* (New York: Oxford University Press, 2003) at 242.

knowledgeable. The members of the jury were witnesses from the community, selected by a public official, who then tried the case.[5]

> We must not think of them as coming into court ignorant, like their modern successors, of the cases about which they will have to speak. . . . Some of the verdicts that are given must be founded on hearsay and floating tradition. Indeed, it is the duty of the jurors, so soon as they have been summoned, to make inquiries about the facts of which they will have to speak when they come before the court. They must collect testimony; they must weigh it and state the net result in a verdict. . . . At the least a fortnight had been given them in which to "certify themselves" of the facts. We know of no rule of law which prevented them from listening during this interval to the tale of the litigants; indeed it was their duty to discover the truth. . . . Separately or collectively, in court or out of court, they have listened to somebody's story and believed it. . . . We may say, if we will, that the old jurors were witnesses; but even in the early years of the thirteenth century they were not, and were hardly supposed to be, eye-witnesses.[6]

Witnesses had been called before the jury during the 13th and 14th centuries but these were pre-appointed witnesses; witnesses who had agreed at the time of the transaction to support its credit if later called upon, for example, attesting witnesses to a deed. These witnesses joined with the jurors and conferred privately to make a finding; they did not, until the middle of the 14th century,[7] testify in open court, but rather assisted the jury members with their particular knowledge. Professor Thayer described it:

> In the earlier cases these witnesses sometimes appear to have been conceived of as a constituent part of the jury; it was a combination of business witnesses and community witnesses who tried the case, the former supplying to others their more exact information. . . . But in time the jury and the witnesses came to be sharply discriminated. . . . The charge to the jury is to tell the truth to the best of their knowledge, while that to the witnesses is to tell the truth and loyally inform the inquest, without saying anything about their knowledge; "for the witnesses," says Thorpe, C.J. in 1349, "should say nothing but what they know as certain, i.e., what they see and hear."

It was not until the latter part of the 15th century that ordinary witnesses as we know them today, casual witnesses as Bentham called them, began to testify in open court about disputed facts. It was a natural development that the same requirement of speaking to first-hand knowledge imposed on the pre-appointed witnesses should eventually be placed on the casual witness.

Though witnesses began informing the jury in the latter part of the 15th century, their importance was slight in comparison to the jury's informing itself. This gradually changed during the 16th and 17th centuries, at which time evidence presented in open court became the prime source of information for the jury. The jury ceased to be witness and became solely trier. Coincident with this development came the need for the exclusionary rules of evidence, as the jury

---

5 See generally, Thayer, "Trial by Jury and Its Development," in *A Preliminary Treatise on Evidence at the Common Law* (1898), Chapter 3.

6 Pollock and Maitland, *The History of English Law* (2d ed., 1898), Vol. 2, pp. 621-28.

7 See Thayer, *supra*, note 5 at p. 125.

was directed to rely only on what it learned publicly in court. There obviously had been little need for exclusionary rules when the jury was informing itself. The earlier prohibition against the pre-appointed witnesses speaking to second-hand information may have caused litigants and judges to be skeptical about the value of hearsay from these new witnesses, and while it was being received there was constant worrying over its worth, and agitation for reform. In 1552[8] the first statutory attempt at reform took place. Although it was confined to treason trials, it demanded the production of the accusers, if then alive, to confront the accused at the trial and maintain their earlier depositions. This requirement was a marked departure from the then normal criminal trial process wherein previously sworn depositions were routinely filed. The celebrated case of Sir Walter Raleigh's prosecution on an indictment for conspiracy to commit various treasons[9] illustrates the practice of the time, the narrow judicial construction given the statutory efforts at reform, and the arguments then being made for change. When Raleigh demanded his statutory right to be confronted with his accuser, Lord Cobham, he was refused:

Raleigh:	The Proof of the Common Law is by witness and jury: let Cobham be here, let him speak it. Call my accuser before my face, and I have done. . . . All this is but one Accusation of Cobham's, I hear no other thing; to which accusation he never subscribed nor avouched it. I beseech you, my lords, let Cobham be sent for, charge him on his soul, on his allegiance to the King; if he affirm it, I am guilty. . . . By the rigour and cruelty of the law (the Accusation) may be a forcible evidence.
Popham, L.C.J.:	That is not the rigour of the law, but the justice of the law; else when a man hath made a plain Accusation, by practice he might be brought to retract it again.
Raleigh:	Oh my lord, you may use equity.
L.C.J.:	That is from the King; you are to have justice from us. . . . This thing cannot be granted, for then a number of Treasons should flourish: the Accuser may be drawn by practise, whilst he is in person.
Gawdy, J.:	The Statute you speak of concerning two Witnesses in case of Treason, is found to be inconvenient, therefore by another law it was taken away.
Raleigh:	The common Trial of England is by Jury and Witnesses.
Warburton, J.:	I marvel, Sir Walter, that you being of such experience and wit, should stand on this point; for so many horse-stealers may escape, if they may

---

8 5 & 6 Edw. VI, c. 11, s. 12. "Which said accusers at the time of the arraignment of the party accused, if they be then living, shall be brought in person before the party so accused, and avow and maintain that which they have to say to prove him guilty." And, in (1554), 1 & 2 Phil. & Mar., c. 10, s. 11: Upon arraignment for treason the persons "or two of them at the least," who shall declare any thing against the accused "shall, if living and within the realm, be brought forth in person before the party arraigned if he require the same, and object and say openly in his hearing what they or any of them can against him.".

9 *Sir Walter Raleigh's Trial* (1603), 2 Howell's State Trials 1, 15-19.

not be condemned without witnesses. . . . My Lord Cobham hath, perhaps, been labored withal; and to save you, his old friend, it may be that he will deny all that which he hath said.

Raleigh: I know not how you conceive the Law.

L.C.J.:   Nay, we do not conceive the Law, but we know the Law.

Raleigh: Indeed, where the Accuser is not to be had conveniently, I agree with you; but here my Accuser may; he is alive, and in the house. Susanna had been condemned, if Daniel had not cried out, "Will you condemn an innocent Israelite, without examination or knowledge of the truth?" Remember, it is absolutely the Commandment of God: If a false witness rise up, you shall cause him to be brought before the Judges; if he be found false, he shall have the punishment which the accused should have had. It is very sure, for my lord to accuse me is my certain danger, and it may be a means to excuse himself. . . . Good my lords, let my Accuser come face to face, and be deposed.

L.C.J.:   You have no law for it.

Gradually, during the 17th century, the new ideas took hold and concern for the worth of hearsay yielded an exclusionary rule. In the beginning, only oral hearsay was inadmissible. Previously sworn depositions continued to be received, but the practice developed of insisting on the deponent's attendance at trial to confirm the truth of the deposition; over many years, public oral testimony of confirmation became more important than earlier written depositions. In time, earlier writing became receivable only to confirm that what the witness said at trial had always been maintained. With this development toward openness, to publicly presenting the evidence in the presence of the parties, there was increased reliance by the jury on the parties' efforts to inform. As the parties took greater control over what evidence would be presented, and challenged the worth of evidence presented by their opponent, the adversary system and the peculiarly English technique of cross-examination was fashioned. With these developments, the hearsay rule was born as a natural counterpart. Juries were to be informed by witnesses with personal knowledge, speaking on oath, publicly, in their presence and in the presence of the parties, and were to be open to cross-examination when they expressed themselves; if the evidence was otherwise it was to be excluded as hearsay.

Against this background, observe two cases which display the early stated reasons for the hearsay rule. In the trial of Braddon and Speke[10] in 1684, the accused seeks to lead evidence:

Jeffries,
L.C.J.:
            Does she know anything of her own knowledge?

Braddon: She can tell what she heard, my lord.

L.C.J.:   'Tis no evidence. . . . Where is the woman that told her? Why is not she brought?

Counsel for
Braddon: They say, she is so big with child she can't come.

---

10 *Re Braddon and Speke* (1684), 9 Howell's State Trials 1127, 1188-89.

L.C.J.:   Why, if that woman were here herself, if she did say it, and would not swear it, we could not hear her; how then can her saying be an evidence before us? I wonder to hear any man that wears a gown, to make a doubt of it.

And later, even though the out-of-court saying was a *sworn* deposition by one with personal knowledge, it was rejected if the party against whom it was tendered was unable to cross-examine the deponent. This other reason for the rule was insisted on in *R. v. Paine*,[11] in 1696. In a prosecution for criminal libel, it was sought to introduce against the accused the deposition of the person to whom the accused had allegedly published the libel. That person had been examined upon oath by the Mayor of Bristol but had since died. The accused objected that he had not been present at the examination and therefore had not been able to cross-examine. The Crown argued that the deposition ought to be received as there was assurance of trustworthiness in that "if such oath should be false, the party might be indicted for perjury." The report noted:

> The court thereupon sent the Puisne Judge to confer with the Justices of the Common Pleas; who returning, the Chief Justice declared, that it was the opinion of both Courts that these depositions should not be given in evidence, the defendant not being present when they were taken before the mayor, and so had lost the benefit of a cross-examination.

The rule is now settled law, and became a source of pride to the English lawyer, as we read in a note from 1730:

> The excellency therefore of our laws above others, I take chiefly to consist in that part of them, which regards Criminal Prosecutions: here indeed it may with great truth and justice be said, that we have by far the better of our neighbours, and are deservedly their admiration and envy.
>
> This might be made to appear in many particulars. In other Countries . . . the Witnesses are examined in private, and in the Prisoner's absence; with us they are produced face to face, and deliver their Evidence in open court, the prisoner himself being present, and at liberty to cross-examine them.[12]

(b) Reason for Rule

In Hawkins' *Pleas of the Crown* we read:

> It seems agreed, that what a Stranger has been heard to say is in Strictness no manner of Evidence either for or against a Prisoner, not only because it is not upon Oath but also because the other Side hath no opportunity of a cross-examination.[13]

While it is sometimes said[14] that the hearsay rule was fashioned out of a distrust for the lay juror's capacity to properly assess the worth of the evidence, the history noted above confirms Professor Morgan's view that the reasons for the rule given at the time by judges and commentators:

> . . . have to do with the credulity not of jurors but of witnesses. . . . Not one of them even suggests a peculiar incapacity of jurors to evaluate such evidence, and so long

---

11 (1696), 87 E.R. 584, 585 (K.B.).

12 Emlyn's Preface to the Second Edition of the State Trials, 1 Howell's State Trials, XXV.

13 Hawkins, *Pleas of the Crown* (1716), Book II, c. 46, s. 14 as noted by Morgan, *supra*, note 3 at p. 111.

14 See, *e.g.*, Ewaschuk, "Hearsay Evidence" (1978), Osgoode Hall L.J. 407.

as jurors could properly rely upon what they learned by inquiry or otherwise outside the presence of the court, any such suggestion would have bordered on absurdity.[15]

Nevertheless, distrust for the jury's capacity to adequately assess hearsay becomes an after-the-fact added justification. The trier of fact will be more assured of accuracy in his decision if descriptions of events are given in open court rather than through an intermediary. Trustworthiness of decision-making is enhanced for a number of reasons which may be grouped under two heads. First, the witness who speaks in open court is subject to a perjury prosecution should he lie; this witness who speaks in open court is encouraged to speak honestly and without exaggeration by the solemnity of the occasion and by the presence of the party against whose interests he speaks; the witness's manner of speaking, his demeanour, will be available for review by the trier of fact, who will thus be better able to evaluate his credibility. The second group of reasons resides in our adversary system and in the faith we repose in "the greatest legal engine ever invented for the discovery of truth"[16] — cross-examination. The description of a past event by a witness has resident within it the possibility of error due to at least four dangers.[17] The description may be defective because first, the witness did not perceive the incident accurately; second, the witness does not now remember the incident accurately; third, the witness's language describing the incident may be ambiguous or otherwise defective and the communication of his thoughts may therefore be misunderstood; fourth, the witness may be presently insincere in his account and wish to deliberately mislead the trier of fact. These four dangers may be guarded against by canvassing their existence through cross-examination which, of course, is only possible when the individual with the personal knowledge is present in the witness stand; the adversary may be greatly prejudiced if the description comes in through the relation of another who has no ability to aid in exposing possible defects in the declarant's perception, memory, communication or sincerity.

If we keep this background of history and reason in mind, we will be better able to deal with the ever recurring problem of identifying whether a particular piece of evidence is hearsay, and we should also be better able to construct arguments for and against the receivability of hearsay evidence in a particular case.

(c) Identifying Hearsay

Professor McCormick defined hearsay:

Hearsay evidence is testimony in court, or written evidence, of a statement made out of court, the statement being offered as an assertion to show the truth of matters asserted therein, and thus resting for its value upon the credibility of the out-of-court asserter.[18]

Notice particularly the closing lines of that definition, "resting for its value upon the credibility of the out-of-court asserter." Why is that a requirement?

---

15 Morgan, *supra*, note 3 at p. 112.
16 5 Wigmore, *Evidence* (Chad. Rev.), c. 1367, p. 32.
17 See the classic exposition by Morgan, "Hearsay Dangers and the Application of the Hearsay Concept" (1948), 62 Harv. L. Rev. 177.
18 McCormick, *Evidence*, 2d ed. (1972), p. 584.

Because, as we discussed above, the principal reasons for excluding hearsay evidence are the lack of the protective safeguards of oath and cross-examination, safeguards which are only necessary when the value of the evidence depends on the credibility of the asserter.

A sues B for failure to deliver lumber in accordance with their contract; B defends, denying the existence of any contract. A calls X to testify that he heard B unequivocally and unambiguously agreeing to deliver lumber to A on a certain date for a certain price. Clearly this is not hearsay, as we care not whether B was sincere in expressing his intention to accept the terms. The legal consequences of a valid contract are produced by the fact that B spoke the words, and the value of the words does not rest on the credibility of the out-of-court asserter.[19] Similarly, proof of statements constituting defamation would not offend the hearsay rule; the proponent of the evidence is obviously not attempting to prove the truth asserted within the statements.[20] Words accompanying actions often characterize the same, and if the substantive law has an objective test of intention, the words are receivable.[21] Statements made by suspects which are established as false during the course of a police investigation may be received as non-hearsay evidencing a consciousness of guilt.[22] The list of situations of relevant non-hearsay statements, and their variety, is limitless, and their identification is only eased when the purpose of the hearsay rule is kept in the forefront.

Identifying whether an out-of-court statement is hearsay or not is seen by many as a difficult exercise and various formulae of words have been used for the purpose. The best way to begin is to ask:

1. Who is the declarant? (i.e. who uttered the out-of-court statement?)
2. What does the statement assert?
3. What is the purpose of tendering the assertion?
4. If it is to prove the truth of the assertion, there is a hearsay problem.

One popular formula of words is problematic. Ask whether the statement is being tendered for its truth or tendered for the fact that the statement was made. Although this is perhaps a fair description, the formula frequently produces circumlocutions that confound. It is not unusual for counsel to seek an end run around the hearsay rule by insisting that he is not tendering the evidence for the purpose of establishing its truth but rather only for the purpose of establishing that the statement was in fact made. When counsel offers such in justification, the adversary should ask the proponent of the evidence to precisely articulate the relevance in the case resident in the fact that the statement was made. It will often be seen that the only relevance that can be found will reside in accepting the speaker's belief concerning an external event as accurate; the statement will be seen to be of value only if we assume its truth. The statement on close analysis will often be seen to be hearsay.

A better analytical technique for determining whether a statement is hearsay would be framed in terms of the underlying concern of the rule. As with the proper

---

19 See *Creaghe v. Iowa Home Mut. Casualty Co.*, 323 F. 2d 981 (10th Cir., 1963).
20 See *Dalrymple v. Sun Life Assur. Co.*, [1966] 2 O.R. 227 (C.A.); affirmed 60 D.L.R. (2d) 192n (S.C.C.).
21 See *Leeson v. Leeson*, [1936] 2 K.B. 156 (C.A.).
22 See *Mawaz Khan v. R.*, [1967] 1 A.C. 454 (P.C.).

application of all rules of evidence, it is wise to always keep in mind the purpose of the rule. Given the basis for the hearsay rule — the adversary's inability to cross-examine the person with knowledge of the event — we can then construct an analytical tool for identifying hearsay. If there are relevant, meaningful questions that the adversary might wish to ask of the person who made the out-of-court statement, then the out-of-court statement is hearsay; if there are no meaningful questions that can be put, the statement is not hearsay. To properly identify whether or not an out-of-court statement is hearsay keep in mind the reason for the rule.

An example from the cases might assist. In *Subramaniam v. Public Prosecutor*,[23] the accused had been convicted of unlawfully possessing ammunition contrary to Emergency Regulations in Malaya and was sentenced to death. His defence had been duress and he sought to relate conversations he had had with the terrorists who had threatened him; the trial court ruled this evidence was hearsay, and not admissible unless the terrorists were called. The Privy Council held that the trial judge was in error and noted:

> Evidence of a statement made to a witness by a person who is not himself called as a witness may or may not be hearsay. It is hearsay and inadmissible when the object of the evidence is to establish the truth of what is contained in the statement. It is not hearsay and is admissible when it is proposed to establish by the evidence, not the truth of the statement, but the fact that it was made. The fact that the statement was made, quite apart from its truth, is frequently relevant in considering the mental state and conduct thereafter of the witness or of some other person in whose presence the statement was made.

The Privy Council then noted that the value of the impugned evidence in this case did not rest on the credibility of the out-of-court asserter; the value of the evidence was in the fact of the statement having been made, since if believed by the accused it would support his defence of duress. The trier of fact would not be misled, nor the adversary prejudiced, by the absence from the witness stand of the terrorist-declarant. If the terrorist were called as a witness, what questions would adversary ask? Could adversary ask the terrorist if he was sincere when he treatened the accused? If he intended to communicate a threat? Surely these questions would be properly objected to as immaterial since the issue before the court was not the terrorist's state of mind but rather the accused's. Since it was the fact of the statement having been made that was relevant, the adversary would be protected and trustworthiness guarded by allowing the accused to testify; the accused is on oath and may be cross-examined regarding his sincerity, perception and memory concerning whether the statement was in fact made.

A more modern example may be seen in the case of *R. v. Dunn*.[24] On a charge of threatening, the Crown needed to establish that the interception of the telecommunication containing the threat was lawfully made. The wiretap

---

23 [1956] 1 W.L.R. 965, 970 (P.C.). Compare *R. v. Bencardino* (1973), 15 C.C.C. (2d) 342 (Ont. C.A.): a witness had denied being threatened and the court held that another might be called to testify that the same witness had earlier told him he had been threatened "because the evidence will be received not to prove the fact of intimidation but rather to prove [witness's] state of mind of fear." The court relied on *Subramanian*. Do you agree?

24 (1975), 28 C.C.C. (2d) 538 (N.S. Co. Ct.).

provisions of the Criminal Code [25] provide that an intercept is lawfully made if the recipient of the communication has consented to the interception. The prosecution sought to lead evidence of conversations between the police officer and the victim, by then deceased, in which the victim, the recipient of the telecommunication, had given her consent to the interception. The defence objected to this evidence as hearsay, the court agreed, and the evidence was ruled inadmissible. Fortunately, the court found the necessary consent by implication from other evidence, and later confessed its error in identifying the evidence as hearsay. The court had initially failed to recognize that the value of the evidence did not rest on the credibility of the out-of-court asserter. The police officer had been tendered to testify to an objective fact which he had observed, consent given, the relevance of which resided simply in its happening. The adversary was not prejudiced in being unable to cross-examine the complainant regarding what she meant by the words she uttered and the trier of fact could equally well decide, without her presence, whether the words uttered amounted to a valid consent.[26]

Understanding the purpose of the rule is essential to avoid errors in identification of out-of-court statements. Justice MacDonald described it very well:

> Essentially it is not the form of the statement that gives it its hearsay or non-hearsay characteristics but the use to which it is put. Whenever a witness testifies that someone said something, immediately one should then ask, "what is the relevance of the fact that someone said something". If, therefore, the relevance of the statement lies in the fact that it was made, it is the making of the statement that is the evidence — the truth or falsity of the statement is of no consequence: if the relevance of the statement lies in the fact that it contains an assertion which is, itself, a relevant fact, then it is the truth or falsity of the statement that is in issue. The former is not hearsay, the latter is.[27]

R. v. KHELAWON

[2006] 2 S.C.R. 787, 2006 CarswellOnt 7825, 2006 CarswellOnt 7826, 42 C.R. (6th) 1, 215 C.C.C. (3d) 161 (S.C.C.)

CHARRON J. (MCLACHLIN C.J., BINNIE, LEBEL, DESCHAMPS, FISH, and ABELLA JJ. concurring): —

Definition of Hearsay

At the outset, it is important to determine what is and what is not hearsay. The difficulties in defining hearsay encountered by courts and learned authors have been canvassed before and need not be repeated here: see *R. v. Abbey*, [1982]

---

25 Section 189.

26 On the same point the Ontario Court of Appeal properly noted that "consent was an issue of fact in these proceedings and could be proved like any other fact in issue": *R. v. Cremascoli and Goldman* (1977), 38 C.C.C. (2d) 212, 217 per Brooke, J.A. Curiously the Supreme Court of Canada was less than emphatic in its approval: "While I am inclined to agree with that statement, I do not consider it necessary to deal with the point:" (1979), 51 C.C.C. (2d) 1, 25, per McIntyre, J.

27 *R. v. Baltzer* (1974), 27 C.C.C. (2d) 118, 143 (N.S.C.A.).

2 S.C.R. 24, at pp. 40-41, *per* Dickson J. It is sufficient to note, as this Court did in *Starr*, at para. 159, that the more recent definitions of hearsay are focussed on the central concern underlying the hearsay rule: the difficulty of testing the reliability of the declarant's assertion. See, for example, *R. v. O'Brien*, [1978] 1 S.C.R. 591, at pp. 593-94. Our adversary system puts a premium on the calling of witnesses, who testify under oath or solemn affirmation, whose demeanour can be observed by the trier of fact, and whose testimony can be tested by cross-examination. We regard this process as the optimal way of testing testimonial evidence. Because hearsay evidence comes in a different form, it raises particular concerns. The general exclusionary rule is a recognition of the difficulty for a trier of fact to assess what weight, if any, is to be given to a statement made by a person who has not been seen or heard, and who has not been subject to the test of cross-examination. The fear is that untested hearsay evidence may be afforded more weight than it deserves. The essential defining features of hearsay are therefore the following: (1) the fact that the statement is adduced to prove the truth of its contents and (2) the absence of a contemporaneous opportunity to cross-examine the declarant. I will deal with each defining feature in turn.

Statements Adduced for Their Truth

The purpose for which the out-of-court statement is tendered matters in defining what constitutes hearsay because it is only when the evidence is tendered to prove the truth of its contents that the need to test its reliability arises. Consider the following example. At an accused's trial on a charge for impaired driving, a police officer testifies that he stopped the accused's car because he received information from an unidentified caller that the car was driven by a person who had just left a local tavern in a "very drunk" condition. If the statement about the inebriated condition of the driver is introduced for the sole purpose of establishing the police officer's grounds for stopping the vehicle, it does not matter whether the unidentified caller's statement was accurate, exaggerated, or even false. Even if the statement is totally unfounded, that fact does not take away from the officer's explanation of his actions. If, on the other hand, the statement is tendered as proof that the accused was in fact impaired, the trier of fact's inability to test the reliability of the statement raises real concerns. Hence, only in the latter circumstance is the evidence about the caller's statement defined as hearsay and subject to the general exclusionary rule.

Absence of Contemporaneous Cross-Examination

The previous example, namely where the witness tells the court what A told him, is the more obvious form of hearsay evidence. A is not before the court to be seen, heard and cross-examined. However, the traditional law of hearsay also extends to out-of-court statements made by the witness who does testify in court when that out-of-court statement is tendered to prove the truth of its contents. This extended definition of hearsay has been adopted in Canada: *R. v. B. (K.G.)*,

[1993] 1 S.C.R. 740, at pp. 763-64; *Starr*, at para. 158. It is important to understand the rationale for treating a witness's out-of-court statements as hearsay.

When the witness repeats or adopts an earlier out-of-court statement, in court, under oath or solemn affirmation, of course no hearsay issue arises. The statement itself is not evidence, the testimony is the evidence and it can be tested in the usual way by observing the witness and subjecting him or her to cross-examination. The hearsay issue does arise, however, when the witness does not repeat or adopt the information contained in the out-of-court statement and the statement itself is tendered for the truth of its contents. Consider the following example to illustrate the concerns raised by this evidence.

In an out-of-court statement, W identifies the accused as her assailant. At the trial of the accused on a charge of assault, W testifies that the accused is *not* her assailant. The Crown seeks to tender the out-of-court statement as proof of the fact that the accused did assault W. In these circumstances, the trier of fact is asked to accept the out-of-court statement over the sworn testimony of the witness. Given the usual premium placed on the value of in-court testimonial evidence, a serious issue arises as to whether it is at all necessary to introduce the statement. In addition, the reliability of that statement becomes crucial. How trustworthy is it? In what circumstances did W make that statement? Was it made casually to friends at a social function, or rather, to the police as a formal complaint? Was W aware of the potential consequences of making that statement, did she intend that it be acted upon? Did she have a motive to lie? In what condition was W at the time she made the statement? Many more questions can come to mind on matters that relate to the reliability of that out-of-court statement. When the trier of fact is asked to consider the out-of-court statement as proof that the accused in fact assaulted W, assessing its reliability may prove to be difficult.

Concerns over the reliability of the statement also arise where W does not recant the out-of-court statement but testifies that she has no memory of making the statement, or worse still, no memory of the assault itself. The trier of fact does not see or hear the witness making the statement and, because there is no opportunity to cross-examine the witness *contemporaneously* with the making of the statement, there may be limited opportunity for a meaningful testing of its truth. In addition, an issue may arise as to whether the prior statement is fully and accurately reproduced.

Hence, although the underlying rationale for the general exclusionary rule may not be as obvious when the declarant is available to testify, it is the same — the difficulty of testing the reliability of the out-of-court statement. The difficulty of assessing W's out-of-court statement is the reason why it falls within the definition of hearsay and is subject to the general exclusionary rule. As one may readily appreciate, however, the degree of difficulty may be substantially alleviated in cases where the declarant is available for cross-examination on the earlier statement, particularly where an accurate record of the statement can be tendered in evidence. I will come back to that point later. My point here is simply to explain why, by definition, hearsay extends to out-of-court statements tendered for their truth even when the declarant is before the court.

R. v. EVANS
[1993] 3 S.C.R. 653, 25 C.R. (4th) 46, 85 C.C.C. (3d) 97

The accused and a co-accused D. were charged with robbery of a Brinks truck and attempted murder. Witnesses were able to identify D. as one of the robbers. The robbers got into a waiting car, which was driven by a third person. The getaway car had been purchased two days earlier from a married couple. Neither the husband nor the wife was able to make a positive photographic or dock identification. Both testified however that the man who bought the car told them that he worked in chain-link fencing. The wife testified that the man said he had big dogs. The husband testified that the man said his dog was going to have pups. Other evidence showed that the accused had a large dog that was going to have pups and that he had been employed as a chain-link fencer. The purchaser of the vehicle matched the accused's physical and facial description. In addition, the accused's townhouse had been used as a hide-out by him, D. and another individual. A city map was found on the accused's kitchen table. On the map a route was traced from the mall to the point where the car was found abandoned.

The accused was convicted and his appeal was dismissed. He appealed further.

SOPINKA J. (L'HEUREUX-DUBÉ, GONTHIER, CORY and IACOBUCCI JJ. concurring):—

. . . .

The respondent argued that the statements are not hearsay because the fact that the appellant owned a large pregnant dog and had worked as a chain-link fence installer had been independently proved. This argument was apparently accepted by the Court of Appeal. The appellant argued that the statements are hearsay because they had no probative value unless assumed to be true. Each of these submissions is slightly off the mark.

The ultimate value of these statements was to prove that the appellant and the purchaser of the getaway car were one and the same person. There was independent proof that the appellant worked as a fencer, and that he owned a large pregnant dog. If the purchaser could be proved to have a large pregnant dog and have worked as a fence installer, this would suggest that the appellant was the purchaser. However, there is no proof that the purchaser owned a dog or worked as a fencer unless the statements made to the Boutets are assumed to be true. The statements cannot be used for the truth of their contents unless they are admissible under an exception to the hearsay rule.

That being said, the statements still have some probative value as non-hearsay. Quite apart from the truth of the contents, the statements have some probative value on the issue of identity. On the issue of identity, the fact that certain representations are made is probative as it narrows the identity of the declarant to the group of people who are in a position to make similar representations. The more unique or unusual the representations, the more probative they will be on the issue of identity. I emphasize that the statements are not being used as truth of their contents at this stage.

For example, if a declarant stated: "I have a tattoo on my left buttock which measures 1 centimetre by 1$\frac{1}{2}$ centimetres and resembles a four-leaf clover" and it was proved that the accused had such a tattoo on his left buttock, the identity of the group to which the declarant belonged would be narrowed to include the accused as the most likely person, and his family or intimate friends, who would be in a position to know this fact. The statement has probative value without assuming the truth of the statement because the mere fact that it was made tells us something relevant about the declarant that connects him to the accused.

. . . .

The admission of this kind of evidence is not hearsay because the only issue is whether the statement was made, and the veracity, perception and memory of the witness relating the statement can be fully tested by cross-examination. Since the truth of the declarant's assertion is not in issue, deprivation of the right to cross-examine the declarant, on which rejection of hearsay is premised, is of no consequence.

. . . .

[The Court then went on to consider whether the statements by the purchaser, if hearsay, were nevertheless admissible as admissions.]

In this case there was evidence that it was the appellant who made the statements to the Boutets. The trial judge should have considered whether this evidence proved on a balance of probabilities that the statements were in fact made by the accused. In this determination he could have relied on the fact that the statements to the Boutets were made. It would be a most unusual coincidence that the purchaser and the accused would each have these two characteristics in combination. If he ruled out coincidence, the trial judge was entitled to consider that this narrowed the group of persons who were in a position to make this statement to the accused or someone who knew this about the accused and had some reason to make the representation as if he were the accused. Considered in light of the other evidence to which I will refer, the most likely person to make the statement was the accused.

. . . .

McLACHLIN J. (MAJOR J. concurring), dissenting:—

. . . .

My colleague concedes that viewed one way, the statements in question are hearsay. However, he says they are admissible as a statement of facts identifying the speaker as X on the ground that the facts could have been known only to X or to a small group of people to which X belongs. . . .

The probative value of such statements depends on the proposition that the person to be identified, here the accused, is one of very few people who would be able to relate the information which was disclosed by the "speaker" (here the perpetrator of the crime). If many people could have made the statement, it loses its force as an indicator that the "speaker" or perpetrator of the offence is the accused. The case my colleague cites of a "speaker" who describes in detail an unusual tattoo on his left buttock — a tattoo which also, it turns out, is possessed by the accused — is an example in point. The statement identifies both the speaker and the accused as members of the very small group of persons who could have known about the tattoo. It would be highly unusual that a "speaker" would describe himself as having such a tattoo, and that a quite different person, the accused, would possess the same characteristic. Because this would be so extraordinary, there is a strong, although not conclusive, inference that they are one and the same person.

The same inference does not follow where the characteristic is one which anyone who cares to inquire may detect. Consider the case of a criminal who wishes to "finger" another for his crime. Knowing that the other person possesses a peculiar tattoo on his left buttock, such a person might indicate in the course of committing the crime that he, the perpetrator, possessed such a tattoo. If the evidence is that only very few people could have known of the tattoo, the inference, as noted above, is strong that the speaker and the person with the tattoo are one and the same. But if the evidence is that many people could have known about the tattoo, the inference is weak. Any one of those people, whether to shift the blame to another or for a variety of other reasons, might have mentioned it. It is for this reason that the cases in which this principle has been applied uniformly insist that the information related be information which only the accused could have known (*McCormick's* formulation) or which, at the very least, only a few people would have known. . . .

This brings me to the information said to identify the accused as the person who bought the getaway vehicle in the case at bar. The person who picked up the getaway vehicle gave the vendor the information that he worked as a chain-link fencer and owned a large pregnant dog. That was not information which only the perpetrator of the offence could have known. Indeed, it was not information which only a small group of people could have known. It was, on the contrary, information which could have been obtained by anyone who had cared to observe or inquire into the accused's affairs. Accordingly, it does not fall within the rule as stated by *McCormick*. . . .

Nor should it. A number of inferences may be drawn from the fact such a statement was made. One is that another chain-link fencer who owned a large pregnant dog (and there may be a number of such persons in a large city like Calgary) bought the car. Yet another inference is that the criminal, seeking to shift blame from himself to the accused Evans, went out of his way to tell the vendors falsely that he worked as a chain-link fencer and owned a large pregnant dog. Yet another is the inference which the trial judge drew — that the person who bought the getaway car and the accused Evans were one and the same person. The fact that the inference of identity is merely one of several plausible inferences which may be drawn from the statement renders it, on the authorities, inadmissible. It does not have the necessary probative value to support a conviction. The danger of an erroneous inference is simply too great.

. . . .

I would allow the appeal and direct a new trial.

Suppose the vendor of the getaway car in *Evans* saw that in the purchaser's truck there was a quantity of chain-link fencing material and that the purchaser also had with him a large pregnant dog. In such a case the vendor would be able to later describe in court what he had seen at the time of the purchase and that evidence, together with evidence that the accused before the court was a chain-link fencer and the owner of a large pregnant dog, would go a long way towards identifying the accused as the purchaser. Suppose the vendor of the getaway car was by himself during the transaction and later told his wife that the purchaser of their car was a chain-link fencer and the owner of a large pregnant dog. No one would suggest that the wife could later come to court and testify that the purchaser of their car was a chain-link fencer and the owner of a large pregnant dog. Her belief would be founded in hearsay. And yet in *Evans* that's exactly what was permitted. *Someone* told the vendor that he, the purchaser, was a chain-link fencer and the owner of a large pregnant dog and the Court decided that the evidence was admissible. The Court decided the vendor could testify to the character of the purchaser though the vendor only knew the same as the result of what was told to him by *someone*. As far as it being classified as an exception, i.e. an admission, where is the evidence that the statements were made by the accused. Without such evidence, we have a first-rate bootstrap operation.[28]

Is an out-of-court statement of prior identification a matter of hearsay?

R. v. TAT
(1997), 14 C.R. (5th) 116, 117 C.C.C. (3d) 481 (Ont. C.A.)

The accused T and L were charged with first degree murder and attempted murder. They were alleged to have entered a restaurant and opened fire at a particular table, killing one man and injuring two. The case for the Crown rested on the identification of L by Q and the identification of both accused by JT. At the trial Q testified that much of what he said during his interview with the police was based on things he had been told and not his own observations. He said that he had initially identified a photograph of L but had quickly reconsidered his identification and told the officers that he was wrong and that L was not one of the shooters. The trial judge held that the officer's evidence of Q's identification of L during the interview was admissible to prove that L was one of the shooters. The accused were convicted and appealed.

DOHERTY J.A. (LABROSSE and WEILER JJ.A. concurring):—

. . . .

In my view, and contrary to what I suggested in *R. v. T. (W.P.)* (1993), 83

---

[28] For a detailed criticism of *Evans* see Delisle, "*Evans*: Mixing Authenticity and Hearsay" (1993), 25 C.R. (4th) 62. See also an application of *Evans* in *R. v. Brown* (2003), 13 C.R. (6th) 317 (Ont. S.C.J.).

C.C.C. (3d) 5 (Ont. C.A.) the circumstances in which out-of-court statements of identification are admitted do not involve a hearsay use of the out-of-court statements. More importantly, the current jurisprudence does not recognize any hearsay exception which admits prior statements of identification where the maker of the statement denies making the previous identification and testifies that the accused are not the persons who committed the offence. For reasons I will develop, the admissibility of such statements as substantive evidence is governed by *R. v. B. (K.G.)*, *supra* and its progeny.

My review of the Canadian case law reveals two situations in which out-of-court statements of identification may be admitted. Firstly, prior statements identifying or describing the accused are admissible where the identifying witness identifies the accused at trial. The identifying witness can testify to prior descriptions given and prior identifications made. Others who heard the description and saw the identification may also be allowed to testify to the descriptions given and the identifications made by the identifying witness. . . . Clearly, the evidence of the prior descriptions given and the prior identifications made by the identifying witness constitute prior consistent statements made by that witness. Generally speaking, evidence that a witness made prior consistent statements is excluded as irrelevant and self-serving. However, where identification evidence is involved, it is the in-court identification of the accused which has little or no probative value standing alone. The probative force of identification evidence is best measured by a consideration of the entire identification process which culminates with an in-court identification. . . . Where a witness identifies the accused at trial, evidence of prior identifications made and prior descriptions given by that witness do not have a hearsay purpose.

· · · ·

The second situation in which out-of-court statements of identification have been admitted arises where the identifying witness is unable to identify the accused at trial, but can testify that he or she previously gave an accurate description or made an accurate identification. In these circumstances, the identifying witness may testify to what he or she said or did on those earlier occasions and those who heard the description given by the witness or witnessed the identification made by the witness may give evidence of what the witness said or did.

In *R. v. Swanston* (1982), 25 C.R. (3d) 385 (B.C. C.A.), the victim of a robbery testified that he had previously accurately identified the person who robbed him at a police line-up and at the preliminary inquiry. By the time of trial, the accused had changed his appearance and the witness could not be certain that the accused was the person who robbed him. . . . *Swanston* does not create an unqualified exception to the hearsay rule admitting prior identification evidence. *Swanston* recognizes that where the identifying witness testifies that he or she previously identified the perpetrator of the offence, evidence of out-of-court statements is admissible as original evidence to show who it was that the identifying witness previously identified. *Swanston* vividly demonstrates the difference between an out-of-court statement identifying the person who the identifying witness testifies committed the crime (a non-hearsay use of the evidence), and evidence of an out- of-court statement relied on as evidence that the person identified committed the crime (a hearsay use of the statement). *Swanston* does not support the admissibility of Constable Dobro's evidence as evidence of identification. Constable Dobro's evidence that Q previously identified Long as one of the shooters had no value as original evidence, absent evidence from Q linking the person said to have been previously identified by him to the person who committed the crime. No such link was established given that Q. denied both making the previous identification and testified that Long was not one of the shooters.

Justice Doherty went on to conclude that the evidence of the previous identification was not admissible under the principles enunciated in *R. v. B. (K.G.)*. While conceding that the necessity criterion had been met, the Court was not persuaded as to reliability. The statement was not made under oath or its secular equivalent, the jury did not have an opportunity to observe the demeanour of Q. when he made the statement or the circumstances surrounding the making of the statement, and Q. was not subject to cross-examination by counsel for the appellants at the time he made the statement.

In *R. v. T. (W.P.)*,[29] referred to in *Tat*, the accused challenged the constitutionality of s. 715.1 of the Criminal Code. That section provides for the admissibility of videotaped statements made by specified complainants in certain cases. Justice Doherty wrote for a five-person court. In the course of that opinion he wrote:

> The admission of prior consistent statements, referable to the identification of an accused by a witness, provides a good example of a judge-made exception to the rule against prior consistent statements. Judges have long recognized that an in-court identification has little probative value. Consequently, they admitted prior out-of-court statements made by witnesses which were consistent with their in-court identification. These earlier statements are admitted for the truth of their contents, to assist the jury in determining whether the accused was identified by the witness, and to assist in assessing the weight to be given to that identification.

It seems that Justice Doherty then saw prior statements of identification as hearsay but receivable when the witness made an in-court identification. He would then have to similarly conclude that statements of prior identification, made by a witness who cannot identify the accused at trial, but who testifies that he identified the accused earlier and was then satisfied that he was being truthful would similarly be classified as hearsay. To be fair, Justice Doherty acknowledges in *Tat* that his position now is not consistent with his earlier position taken in *T. (W.P.)*. Some would say he got it right the first time!

---

29 (1993), 83 C.C.C. (3d) 5 (Ont. C.A.).

R. v. STARR
[2000] 2 S.C.R. 144, 36 C.R. (5th) 1, 147 C.C.C. (3d) 449,
2000 CarswellMan 449, 2000 CarswellMan 450

The accused was charged with two counts of first degree murder in two shooting deaths. The Crown's theory was that the accused killed the deceased C in a gang-related execution, and that the deceased W was an unfortunate witness who was killed because she was in the wrong place at the wrong time. The two deceased were drinking with the accused at a hotel and left at the same time. The two deceased gave two acquaintances a ride home. Shortly after the murders, the police interviewed Ball, one of the acquaintances who had been driven home by the two deceased. The police showed B some photographs. At trial she had a hazy memory of seeing the photos and testified that she had pointed to one of three photographs shown to her and told the police that the person looked "kind of familiar". She did not testify at trial as to why the person in the photo shown to her shortly after the murders looked familiar, or where she had seen the person. She was not asked whether she had seen the accused on the night of the murder, and she did not testify that she had done so. She did not mention the accused in her testimony, or identify the accused in court, but did testify that nothing she had said in her conversation with the police was untrue. The trial judge permitted the Crown to call evidence from the two police officers who interviewed Ball, on the basis that this evidence was admissible pursuant to the prior identification exception to the hearsay rule. The police officers testified as to the description that Ball had given of the man she had seen talking to the deceased C on the night in question. The police officers testified that when Ball identified a photograph shortly after the murders, she stated that it looked like the man she had seen talking to the deceased C. This was a photograph of the accused. The police officers also testified that when they interviewed Ball again several days later, she again picked out the accused's photograph as being the person she had seen talking with deceased. The accused was convicted and his appeal to the Manitoba Court of Appeal was dismissed.

IACOBUCCI J. (MAJOR, BINNIE, ARBOUR and LEBEL JJ. concurring):—

. . . .

It is not necessary in this case to review the entirety of the "prior identification" exception to the hearsay rule. The narrow issue before this Court is whether hearsay evidence of an out-of-court identification by a trial witness is admissible where the witness does not testify at trial that she made the identification. On the particular facts of this appeal, Cheryl Ball testified at trial that she told police that one of the men in the photographs she was shown on August 23, 1994 "look[ed] kind of familiar", but she did not testify that she had seen the person at the Mohawk gas station or at the wheel of the car that followed Weselowski's station wagon to St. Norbert.

The scope of the "prior identification" exception to the hearsay rule was recently thoroughly canvassed in the lucid reasons of Doherty J.A. in *Tat, supra.* As Doherty J.A. sets out, there are two situations in which out-of-court statements of identification may be admitted for the truth of their contents. First, "prior statements identifying or describing the accused are admissible where the identifying witness identifies the accused at trial" (pp. 497-98). Second, such statements are admissible "where the identifying witness is unable to identify the accused at trial, but can testify that he or she previously gave an accurate description or made an accurate identification" (p. 500). In the latter circumstance, Doherty J.A. explained, "the identifying witness may testify to what he or she said or did on those earlier occasions and those who heard the description given by the witness or witnessed the identification made by the witness may give evidence of what the witness said or did" (ibid.).

In the present case, only the second branch of the "prior identification" exception could possibly be applicable to permit the admission of the police testimony under the exception, because Ball did not identify the appellant in court. However, in my opinion, the requirements of this second branch are not satisfied in the circumstances. Ball did not testify that she could not remember whether the appellant was the person whom she identified. She was not asked to compare the appellant with her recollections about the person she saw on the night of the murders. Accordingly, the underlying circumstances of necessity required to trigger the second branch of the traditional exception did not exist. Even aside from this point, the police evidence went far beyond the scope of the "prior identification" exception. Part of the rationale underlying the second branch of the exception is that the testimony that is being admitted to complement the testimony of the identifying witness does not truly constitute hearsay. If the witness can at least testify that at some point she made an accurate identification, then a police officer's testimony that he or she observed the identifying witness in the act of identification is original evidence that the identifying witness did indeed select a particular person, and that that person is the accused. However, for this rationale to apply, the identifying witness must confirm that the person he or she identified in the police officer's presence was the person who committed an act that is relevant in the immediate proceedings. The testimony of the identifying witness may thus have its own hearsay component, but this issue is beyond the scope of this appeal: see H. Stewart, "Prior Identifications and Hearsay: A Note on *R. v. Tat*" (1998), 3 Can. Crim. L. Rev. 61. The point is that the officer's testimony should merely state who the witness identified, once the witness has already testified to the identification itself, and why the identification is relevant to the case.[30]

PROBLEMS

Problem 1

For some reason the material issue is whether the plaintiff could speak on March 4, 1993. A witness is prepared to testify that on March 4, 1993, he heard the plaintiff say, "I can speak."

---

30 The *Tat/Starr* views on prior identification have caused confusion and division: see *R. v. Campbell* (2006), 207 C.C.C. (3d) 18, 2006 CarswellBC 502 (C.A.).

Hearsay?

Problem 2

The plaintiff claims that he entered into a contract with the defendant who agreed to sell his old car to the plaintiff for $500. The plaintiff wants to call a witness to testify that he heard the defendant say to the plaintiff, "I offer to sell you my old car for $500."
Hearsay? See *R. v. Cook*, [1986] 1 S.C.R. 144, 50 C.R. (3d) 96.

Problem 3

The witness is being examined in chief:

Q.:   Did you see the accident?

A.:   Yes.

Q.:   Who had the green light?

A.:   I can't remember. But I did tell my husband when I got home that day. He reminded me this morning.

Q.:   What did you tell him?

Hearsay?

Problem 4

The accused claims that he was still suffering the effects of provocation when he attacked the victim, Tom Jones. The accused wants to testify that his wife said to him, "Tom Jones assaulted me."
Hearsay?

Problem 5

In a paternity suit, the plaintiff offers evidence that the defendant sent the child a birthday card addressed "To my darling son."
Hearsay?

Problem 6

A witness to an accident observes the plate number of the offending vehicle, makes a note of it, and communicates the number to another, who in turn records it. At the trial the witness no longer has his note and cannot recall the number, but the other person is prepared to testify to the number related. What result? Compare *R. v. Davey* (1969), 6 C.R.N.S. 288; *Cattermole v. Millar*, [1977] Crim. L. Rev. 553 (Div. Ct.); and *R. v. Schantz* (1983), 34 C.R. (3d) 370 (Ont. Co. Ct.).

Problem 7

Defendant, a power tool manufacturer, was displaying his wares at a hardware exhibition. Plaintiff, a potential customer, while operating defendant's table saw, suffered the loss of two fingers for which he now brings suit. Defendant resists plaintiff's claim and maintains he was contributorily negligent. Defendant offers his employee to testify that shortly before plaintiff screamed the employee heard defendant shout "Put the guard down before operating the saw!" Objectionable? Could employee testify that defendant told him "I told that nitwit to put the guard down before operating the saw!" Could defendant testify "I told that nitwit to put the guard down before operating the saw!"

Problem 8

In a murder prosecution the defence is alibi and the time of the alleged killing is therefore very important. A Crown witness who observed the shooting is now testifying:

Crown:	And then what happened?
Witness:	Well, that's about it — two shots and the victim collapsed right there in the middle of Union Station.
Crown:	And can you tell us what time this occurred?
Witness:	It was exactly 2:15 p.m.
Crown:	And how do you know?
Witness:	I asked a passerby and he told me . . .
Objection:	Clearly hearsay, Your Honour.
Witness:	Well, I heard the conductor call out "All aboard for the 2:15 to Kingston".
Defence:	Same objection, Your Honour.
Witness:	So I looked up at the station clock.
Defence:	Same objection.
Witness:	And then I looked at my own Rolex wristwatch which the jeweller had checked for accuracy the day before.
Defence:	Your Honour, it's clear to me, and I trust it's clear to you, that there is no way this witness can nail down the time.
Crown:	Well perhaps my friend will tell me what would satisfy him.
Defence:	That's not for me to say. It's your case.

Problem 9

The accused is charged with break, enter and theft. The premises entered were those of a coin shop. The Crown has called a second-hand dealer who testifies that on the day of the break-in he purchased a quantity of coins which roughly matched the coins taken. The dealer cannot identify the accused as the seller of the coins but says the seller gave the name Sammy John, a Kingston address, and a social insurance number; this information was recorded in his dealer's log. The Crown notes for the court that the address and social insurance number are those of the accused before the court, John Samuel Benson. The defence argues the dealer's evidence is hearsay. See *R. v. Evans*, *supra*.

(d) Approaches to Hearsay

For many years courts in England and Canada were content to limit the admission of hearsay to slowly developed pigeon-hole exceptions which changed little over time. We shall see that Canadian courts have now developed a broad principled approach to admitting hearsay through criteria of reasonable necessity and circumstantial guarantees of reliability.

In *Myers v. D.P.P.*,[31] the majority of the House of Lords refused to create a new exception to the hearsay rule as there had not been a new exception created for some 90 years.[32] The accused had been prosecuted for conspiracy to receive stolen cars and it was necessary to establish that numbers on the cylinder blocks of the seized cars were the same numbers as on the blocks in the stolen cars. The prosecution sought to do this by introducing the business records of the manufacturer. The common law then recognized an exception to the hearsay rule for declarations made in the course of duty provided the declarant was deceased. The prosecution was unable to satisfy this condition as they were unable to identify the declarant who was but a single worker on a mass production assembly line. They tried to justify reception of the evidence on the basis of unavailability of the declarant, the consequent necessity of using the best evidence available, and assurances of trustworthiness arising from the circumstances in which the record was made. The majority insisted that the rule had become so fixed that only the legislature could create new exceptions to meet society's new needs and conditions.[33]

The law regarding hearsay can produce absurd results if it is slavishly and mechanically applied. As with any rule of evidence, we should always keep in mind the reason for the rule. If the reason for the rule is otherwise satisfied by the circumstances of a particular case the rule need not operate to exclude relevant evidence. The classic Canadian exposition of common sense in this area is seen in one of the first Supreme Court of Canada opinions choosing not to follow the House of Lords' lead.

In *Ares v. Venner*,[34] the Supreme Court of Canada faced the same question of deciding on the proper approach to hearsay. Plaintiff had suffered a broken leg while skiing. At the hospital Dr. Venner attended, reduced the fracture and applied a full-leg plaster cast. The trial judge received in evidence notes which had been made by the attending nurses. These notes described the plaintiff's toes as "blue," "bluish pink," "cool," and "cold," and were relevant to the issue of the doctor's negligence, as the trial court made the crucial finding that:

> The classic signs of circulatory impairment manifested themselves clearly and early.

The trial court described the usual medical practice in response to such signs and observed that the defendant had not followed such practice. The trial judge relied on a passage from Wigmore,[35] which argued for the admissibility of hospital records as an exception to the hearsay rule based on grounds of necessity and circumstantial guarantees of trustworthiness. Professor Wigmore had found the grounds of necessity in the "serious interference with convenience of hospital management," and the circumstances guaranteeing trustworthiness in the fact that they are made and relied on in affairs of life and death. The Alberta Court of Appeal ordered a new trial on the basis that the nurse's notes contained not just numerical data but observations expressed in opinions which would be fruitful areas of cross-examination. It also noted that one of Professor Wigmore's

---

31 [1965] A.C. 1001.

32 See *Sugden v. Lord St. Leonard's* (1876), 1 P.D. 154 (C.A.).

33 See the English response in the Civil Evidence Act, 1968, c. 64. Newark and Samuels, "Comment" (1968), 31 Mod. L. Rev. 668.

34 (1970), 14 D.L.R. (3d) 4 (S.C.C.).

35 6 Wigmore, *Evidence* (Chad. Rev.), s. 1707.

requirements for admissibility, grounds of necessity, was not satisfied here since the nurses had been subpoenaed by the plaintiff and were present throughout the trial. The Supreme Court of Canada restored the trial judgment.

Speaking for a unanimous court, Hall J. noted that there had been a long felt need for a restatement of the hearsay rule and that there were two schools of thought regarding how the change should come about — by legislative action or judicial action. He noted that in *Myers v. D.P.P.*, the learned Law Lords had split on the question of approach, with the majority agreeing to the need for reform but deciding it must be left to the legislature. Hall J. decided:

> I am of opinion that this Court should adopt and follow the minority view rather than resort to saying in effect: "This judge-made law needs to be restated to meet modern conditions, but we must leave it to Parliament and the ten legislatures to do the job."[36]

The court in *Ares v. Venner* recognized that the adversary was not prejudiced by the reception of the nurses' notes. If the nurses were in fact called they would have been allowed to "refresh their memory" by having regard to their notes and little would be gained by their attendance as they would ordinarily add little or nothing to the information furnished by the record. The notes were made by trained observers and that should satisfy any concerns regarding the hearsay danger of perception. The notes were made contemporaneously with the observation and so concern for the memory danger should be stilled. Sincerity of the declarant should not be a concern as the nurse was under a duty to record her observations accurately and discipline could flow from any mistakes. The court displayed a common sense, principled approach. The court was aware of the reason for the rule and why that reason was not applicable to the particular factual situation before it.

Another admirable display of common sense, this time from south of the border, comes from the pen of Circuit Judge Wisdom in the case of *Dallas County v. Commercial Union Assurance Co.*[37] The clock tower of the Dallas County Courthouse at Selma, Alabama collapsed on July 7, 1957. Damage to the courthouse exceeded $100,000. An examination of the debris showed the presence of charred timbers. Dallas County concluded that the char was evidence of lightning having struck and decided that a lightning bolt had hit the building causing the collapse. Dallas County carried insurance for loss caused by fire or lightning and claimed from their insurance company. The insurance company's engineers decided that the collapse was due not to lightning, but to structural weaknesses. In their view the char was the result of a fire that had occurred many, many years before. The case went to the jury on one issue: Did lightning cause the collapse of the clock tower? The jury found for the insurers and the County appealed, arguing that the trial judge erred in receiving into evidence a newspaper clipping dated June 9, 1901 describing a fire in the courthouse. Dallas County argued that the clipping was hearsay. Listen to Wisdom, J., dismissing the appeal:

> In the Anglo-American adversary system of law, courts usually will not admit evidence unless its accuracy and trustworthiness may be tested by cross-examination. Here, therefore, the plaintiff argues that the newspaper should not be admitted: "You cannot

---

36 *Supra*, note 34, at p. 16.
37 286 F. 2d 388 (5th Circ., 1961).

cross-examine a newspaper." Of course, a newspaper article is hearsay, and in almost all circumstances is inadmissible. However, the law governing hearsay is somewhat less than pellucid. And, as with most rules, the hearsay rule is not absolute; it is replete with exceptions. Witnesses die, documents are lost, deeds are destroyed, memories fade. All too often, primary evidence is not available and courts and lawyers must rely on secondary evidence. . . . There is no procedural canon against the exercise of common sense in deciding the admissibility of hearsay evidence. In 1901 Selma, Alabama, was a small town. Taking a common sense view of this case, it is inconceivable to us that a newspaper reporter in a small town would report there was a fire in the dome of the new courthouse—if there had been no fire. He is without motive to falsify, and a false report would have subjected the newspaper and him to embarrassment in the community. The usual dangers inherent in hearsay evidence, such as lack of memory, faulty narration, intent to influence the court proceedings, and plain lack of truthfulness are not present here. To our minds, the article published in the Selma Morning-Times on the day of the fire is more reliable, more trustworthy, more competent evidence than the testimony of a witness called to the stand fifty-eight years later.

For 20 years courts balked at applying *Ares v. Venner* in criminal cases. Then came *Khan*.

R. v. KHAN
[1990] 2 S.C.R. 531, 79 C.R. (3d) 1, 59 C.C.C. (3d) 92

The accused was charged with sexual assault. The alleged victim was three-and-a-half years old at the time of the assault. She attended with her mother at the office of the family doctor for a general examination of the mother and a routine examination of the child. The child was in the doctor's office, alone with the doctor, for five to seven minutes, while the mother undressed and put on a hospital gown. When the mother rejoined her child she noticed the child picking at a wet spot on her sleeve. The spot on the sleeve was determined to have been produced by a deposit of semen and, in some areas, a mixture of semen and saliva that had soaked through the fabric before it dried. The concentration of the mixture suggested to the forensic biologist that the substances were probably mixed before they were applied to the material. Fifteen minutes after they left the doctor's office, the mother and daughter had essentially the following conversation:

MRS. O.: So you were talking to Dr. Khan, were you? What did he say?

T.: He asked me if I wanted a candy. I said "Yes". And do you know what?

MRS. O.: What?

T.: He said, "Open your mouth". And do you know what? He put his birdie in my mouth, shook it and peed in my mouth.

MRS. O.: Are you sure?

T.: Yes.

MRS. O.: You're not lying to me, are you?

T.: No. He put his birdie in my mouth. And he never did give me my candy.

The mother testified that the word "birdie" meant penis to T. At the trial, T. was called as a witness. She was four years and eight months old. The trial judge ruled that she could not give evidence, sworn or unsworn. The trial judge also ruled that the child's statement to her mother was inadmissible hearsay and could not be adduced. The Ontario Court of Appeal held that the trial judge was wrong in not allowing the child to give unsworn evidence. The court also held that the statement to the mother should have been received as falling within the exception for spontaneous declarations. In the Supreme Court it was decided that the Court of Appeal was right in their determination of error regarding the child's right to testify but, while agreeing that the child's statement deserved to be received, the court decided the spontaneous declaration exception was not the appropriate route. Rejecting the Court of Appeal's approach, Madam Justice McLachlin, writing for the court, noted, regarding

> statements made by children to others about sexual abuse. Insofar as they are tied to the exception to the hearsay rule of spontaneous declarations . . . they suffer from certain defects. There is no requirement [of necessity].[38]

The court decided it would be more appropriate to adopt the more flexible and principled approach of *Ares v. Venner.* Madam Justice McLachlin, writing for the court, decided that where there were grounds of necessity and circumstances surrounding the making of the statement, the hearsay could come in.

McLACHLIN J.:—

. . . .

The hearsay rule has traditionally been regarded as an absolute rule, subject to various categories of exceptions, such as admissions, dying declarations, declarations against interest and spontaneous declarations. While this approach has provided a degree of certainty to the law on hearsay, it has frequently proved unduly inflexible in dealing with new situations and new needs in the law. This has resulted in courts in recent years on occasion adopting a more flexible approach, rooted in the principle and the policy underlying the hearsay rule rather than the strictures of traditional exceptions.

This Court took such an approach in *Ares v. Venner.* . . .

. . . .

[There are] two general requirements: necessity and reliability. The child's statement to the mother in this case meets both these general requirements. Necessity was present, other evidence of the event, as the trial judge found, being inadmissible. . . . The evidence also bore strong indicia of reliability. T. was disinterested, in the sense that her declaration was not made in favour of her interest. She made the declaration before any suggestion of litigation. And beyond doubt she possessed peculiar means of knowledge of the event of which she told her mother. Moreover, the evidence of a child of tender years on such matters may bear its own special stamp of reliability.

. . . .

These developments underline the need for increased flexibility in the

---

38 (1991), 79 C.R. (3d) 1, 11.

interpretation of the hearsay rule to permit the admission in evidence of statements made by children to others about sexual abuse. Insofar as they are tied to the exception to the hearsay rule of spontaneous declarations, however, they suffer from certain defects. There is no requirement that resort to the hearsay evidence be necessary. Even where the evidence of the child might easily be obtained without undue trauma, the Crown would be able to use hearsay evidence. Nor is there any requirement that the reliability of the evidence in the particular be established; hence inherently unreliable evidence might be admitted. Finally, the rule being of an absolute "in-or-out" character, there is no means by which a trial judge could attach conditions on the reception of a particular statement which the judge might deem prudent in a particular case, as, for example, the right to cross-examine the deponent referred to in *Ares v. Venner*, supra. In addition to these objections, it can be argued that to extend the spontaneous declaration rule as far as these cases would extend it is to deform it beyond recognition and is conceptually undesirable.

In Canada too, courts have been moving to more flexibility in the reception of the hearsay evidence of children, although not under the aegis of the spontaneous declaration exception to the hearsay rule.

. . . .

These cases point the way in the correct direction. Despite the need for caution, hearsay evidence of a child's statement may be received where the requirements of *Ares v. Venner* are met. The general approach is summed up in the comment of Wilson J. in *R. v. B. (G.)*, [1990] 2 S.C.R. 30 at 55 [Sask.]:

> In recent years we have adopted a much more benign attitude to children's evidence, lessening the strict standards of oath taking and corroboration, and I believe that this is a desirable development.

The first question should be whether reception of the hearsay statement is necessary. Necessity for these purposes must be interpreted as "reasonably necessary". The inadmissibility of the child's evidence might be one basis for a finding of necessity. But sound evidence based on psychological assessments that testimony in court might be traumatic for the child or harm the child might also serve. There may be other examples of circumstances which could establish the requirement of necessity.

The next question should be whether the evidence is reliable. Many considerations, such as timing, demeanour, the personality of the child, the intelligence and understanding of the child, and the absence of any reason to expect fabrication in the statement, may be relevant on the issue of reliability. I would not wish to draw up a strict list of considerations for reliability or to suggest that certain categories of evidence (for example the evidence of young children on sexual encounters) should be always regarded as reliable. The matters relevant to reliability will vary with the child and with the circumstances, and are best left to the trial judge.

In determining the admissibility of the evidence, the judge must have regard to the need to safeguard the interests of the accused. In most cases a right of cross-examination, such as that alluded to in *Ares v. Venner*, would not be available. If the child's direct evidence in chief is not admissible, it follows that his or her cross-examination would not be admissible either. Where trauma to the child is at issue, there would be little point in sparing the child the need to testify in chief only to have him or her grilled in cross-examination. While there may be cases where, as a condition of admission, the trial judge thinks it possible and fair in all the circumstances to permit cross-examination of the child as the condition of the reception of a hearsay statement, in most cases the concerns of the accused as to credibility will remain to be addressed by submissions as to the weight to be accorded to the evidence and submissions as to the quality of any corroborating evidence.

I add that I do not understand *Ares v. Venner* to hold that the hearsay evidence there at issue was admissible where necessity and reliability are established only where cross-examination is available. First, the court adopted the views of the dissenting judges in *Myers v. D.P.P.*, supra, which do not make admissibility dependent on the right to cross-examine. Second, the cross-examination referred to in *Ares v. Venner* was of limited value. The nurses were present in court at the trial, but, in the absence of some way of connecting particular nurses with particular entries, meaningful cross-examination on the accuracy of specific observations would have been difficult indeed.

I conclude that hearsay evidence of a child's statement on crimes committed against the child should be received, provided that the guarantees of necessity and reliability are met, subject to such safeguards as the judge may consider necessary and subject always to considerations affecting the weight that should be accorded to such evidence. This does not make out-of-court statements by children generally admissible; in particular, the requirement of necessity will probably mean that in most cases children will still be called to give viva voce evidence.

I conclude that the mother's statement in the case at bar should have been received. It was necessary, the child's viva voce evidence having been rejected. It was also reliable. The child had no motive to falsify her story, which emerged naturally and without prompting. Moreover, the fact that she could not be expected to have knowledge of such sexual acts imbues her statement with its own peculiar stamp of reliability. Finally, her statement was corroborated by real evidence. Having said this, I note that it may not be necessary to enter the statement on a new trial, if the child's viva voce evidence can be received as suggested in the first part of my reasons.

CONCLUSION

I would dismiss the appeal and direct a new trial.

———————————

In *Khan v. College of Physicians & Surgeons (Ontario)*,[39] the Ontario

———————————

39 (1990), 43 O.A.C. 130.

Divisional Court reviewed the decision of the College to revoke Dr. Khan's licence to practice. It was four years later and the child was now seven and a half years old. At the hearing by a panel of the Discipline Committee, T. testified and her mother was permitted to give the statement attributed to T. That hearing was after the Court of Appeal's judgment in the criminal prosecution and before the decision of the Supreme Court of Canada. Writing for the majority, O'Driscoll J. noted:

> [T]he precondition of "necessity" was absent and, therefore, the out-of-court statement by Tanya to her mother did not qualify as an exception to the rule against hearsay. . . . [C]ounsel for the respondent College submitted that because Tanya, in her evidence before the Discipline Committee, could not recall anything about "ejaculation", it was "necessary" to allow the mother to give the hearsay statement as truth of the facts contained therein. . . .
>
> Whatever may be the outside limit of the meaning of "necessity", in my view, it does not include shoring up and/or filling in aspects of the evidence of Tanya.[40]

The Court of Appeal disagreed. In *Khan v. College of Physicians and Surgeons (Ontario)*[41] Doherty J.A. decided:

> The fact that the child testifies will clearly impact on the necessity of receiving his or her out-of-court statement. Necessity cannot, however, be equated with unavailability. In *Khan*, McLachlin J. instructs us that necessary means "reasonably necessary" (at p. 546 S.C.R., p. 104 C.C.C.). In the context of cases involving an alleged sexual assault on a child, reasonable necessity refers to the need to have the child's version of events pertaining to the alleged assault before the tribunal charged with the responsibility of determining whether the assault occurred. In my view, if that tribunal is satisfied that despite the *viva voce* evidence of the child, it is still "reasonably necessary" to admit the out-of-court statement in order to obtain an accurate and frank rendition of the child's version of the relevant events, then the necessity criterion set down in *Khan* is satisfied: see Anne McGillivray, "*R. v. Laramee*: Forgetting Children, Forgetting Truth" (1991), 6 C.R. (4th) 325 at pp. 335-41.

In *R. v. Khan*,[42] the retrial following the Supreme Court's dismissal of the accused's appeal, the child T., now aged nine, testified. The Crown was invited to argue necessity but declined. She was cross-examined and discrepancies were pointed out between her evidence at the disciplinary hearing and her evidence at the trial. At the trial, for example, T. testified to the accused putting his penis in her mouth and the accused then wiping her chest with a kleenex. She had not mentioned the ejaculation at the disciplinary hearing. Pointing to this and other discrepancies, defence counsel submitted that it would be dangerous to convict upon T.'s evidence, relying on the rule of practice in *Kendall v. R.*,[43] that it is dangerous to convict on the evidence of a child even when the child had been sworn. The mother, while testifying at the trial about matters that she herself had witnessed, did not relate what T. had told her soon after leaving the doctor's office. The accused was convicted and sentenced to four years.

---

40 *Ibid.*, at p. 137.
41 (1992), 9 O.R. (3d) 641 (C.A.).
42 [1991] O.J. No. 637.
43 (1962), 132 C.C.C. 216 (S.C.C.).

R. v. SMITH
[1992] 2 S.C.R. 915, 15 C.R. (4th) 133, 75 C.C.C. (3d) 257

The judgment of the Court was delivered by

LAMER C.J.: — The principal issue raised by this appeal is the admissibility of hearsay evidence as part of the Crown's case in a murder trial, when the declarant is dead.

The Facts

The respondent was convicted of the murder of Aritha Monalisa King and was sentenced to imprisonment for life with no parole eligibility for thirteen years. Both the respondent and Ms. King were American citizens, ordinarily resident in Detroit. At the respondent's trial, the evidence showed that on August 6, 1986, the respondent picked up Ms. King at her mother's house in Detroit. Together, they drove across the border to Canada. The respondent spent the weekend of August 9 and 10 with Ms. King in a hotel in London, Ontario. Ms. King's body was subsequently discovered at approximately 1:30 a.m. on August 11, near a service station at Beechville, Ontario. The body was found lying on a sheet which may have come from the hotel where Ms. King and the respondent had spent the night. Certain fibres found on the sheet matched fibres from the clothing of the respondent and Ms. King. The body's arms had been cut off, and were never found.

The theory of the Crown was that the respondent was a drug smuggler who had travelled to Canada with Ms. King in order to obtain cocaine. The Crown hypothesized that the respondent had asked Ms. King to take the cocaine back to the United States concealed in her body, but that she had refused. According to the Crown, he then abandoned her at the hotel in London. However, he later returned to pick her up, and drove her to a place where he strangled her, cut off her arms to impede identification, and dumped her body.

In support of this theory, the Crown relied upon evidence of four telephone calls made by the deceased to her mother in Detroit at 10:21 p.m., 11:21 p.m., 11:54 p.m. and 12:41 a.m. on the night between August 10 and August 11, 1986. The first two telephone calls were traced to the telephone in Ms. King's room at the hotel in London. Ms. King's mother testified that in the first telephone call, her daughter said that Larry (the respondent) had abandoned her at the hotel in London and that she wanted a ride home. In the second call, Ms. King told her mother that Larry had still not returned. Her mother testified that she then telephoned from Detroit to a taxi company in London to attempt to arrange a ride home for her daughter. A taxi did arrive at the hotel, but refused to take Ms. King because the credit card that she had been using had been confiscated at the hotel.

The third call was traced to a pay telephone in the hotel lobby. Ms. King's mother testified that in this call her daughter told her that Larry had come back for her, and that she would not need a ride home after all. The fourth telephone call was traced to a pay telephone at the service station near which Ms. King's body was found. Ms. King's mother testified that in this call her daughter told her that she was "on her way".

In addition to these calls, there was evidence that a further telephone call had been made shortly after 1:00 a.m. on August 11 from a pay telephone at the service station near which Ms. King's body was later found. This call was traced to the respondent's residence in Detroit. There was no direct evidence as to who made this telephone call, or what was said. However, a witness at the service station testified that he had seen the respondent near the pay telephones at the service station around this time.

The Crown also led evidence from one Hope Denard, a woman who had travelled with the respondent from Detroit to Canada in the month prior to the murder. Ms. Denard testified that the respondent had asked her to smuggle illegal drugs back to the United States for him, and that when she refused, he drove her to Windsor and abandoned her at a restaurant.

The respondent did not testify at his trial, but set up a defence of alibi supported by the evidence of various witnesses who placed him in Windsor or Detroit at or around the time of the murder. Defence counsel did not object to the testimony by Ms. King's mother as to what her daughter told her in the first two telephone calls. Indeed, it was apparently the theory of the defence that the respondent actually did abandon Ms. King at the hotel in London, a hypothesis supported by the evidence of what Ms. King said in the first two telephone calls to her mother. However, the defence contended that after leaving Ms. King, the respondent returned to Detroit and did not return to the hotel, and therefore could not have been with her when she was murdered.

The respondent appealed his conviction to the Ontario Court of Appeal, which allowed the appeal and ordered a new trial. The Court of Appeal found that evidence as to what was said in the telephone calls made by Ms. King to her mother on the night of the murder was hearsay, and therefore was inadmissible unless it fell within some recognized exception to the hearsay rule. The Court of Appeal went on to decide that the evidence as to what was said by Ms. King in the first two telephone conversations was admissible under an exception to the hearsay rule, but only for the purpose of establishing her state of mind at the time when she made the calls, i.e., that she wanted to come home. The evidence as to what was said in the third telephone conversation, however, fell within no exception to the hearsay rule, and was therefore not admissible for any purpose.

The Court of Appeal concluded that the inadmissible hearsay evidence had been so gravely prejudicial to the respondent that it could not say that, had it not been admitted, the verdict would necessarily have been the same. Therefore, notwithstanding the failure of defence counsel to object to the evidence at trial, the Court of Appeal declined to apply the curative provision in s. 686(1)(b)(iii) of the *Criminal Code*, R.S.C. 1985, c. C-46, quashed the respondent's conviction, and ordered a new trial.

. . . .

[The Supreme Court decided that, while the exception to the hearsay rule invoked by the Crown would operate to allow the first two statements into evidence for the purpose of proving that the deceased wanted to return home, the third statement ("Larry has come back") would not have been admissible under that exception for any purpose at all. The court went on, however.]

. . . .

This, however, is not fatal to the appellant's case. This Court has not taken the position that the hearsay rule precludes the reception of hearsay evidence unless it falls within established categories of exceptions, such as "present intentions" or "state of mind." Indeed, in our recent decision in *R. v. Khan*, [1990] 2 S.C.R. 531, we indicated that the categorical approach to exceptions to the hearsay rule has the potential to undermine, rather than further, the policy of avoiding the frailties of certain types of evidence which the hearsay rule was originally fashioned to avoid.

. . . .

The criterion of "reliability"—or, in Wigmore's terminology, the circumstantial guarantee of trustworthiness—is a function of the circumstances under which the statement in question was made. If a statement sought to be adduced by way of hearsay evidence is made under circumstances which substantially negate the possibility that the declarant was untruthful or mistaken, the hearsay evidence may be said to be "reliable", i.e., a circumstantial guarantee of trustworthiness is established. The evidence of the infant complainant in *Khan* was found to be reliable on this basis.

The companion criterion of "necessity" refers to the necessity of the hearsay evidence to prove a fact in issue. Thus, in *Khan*, the infant complainant was found by the trial judge not to be competent to testify herself. In this sense, hearsay evidence of her statements was necessary, in that what she said to her mother could not be adduced through her. It was her inability to testify that governed the situation.

The criterion of necessity, however, does not have the sense of "necessary to the prosecution's case". If this were the case, uncorroborated hearsay evidence which satisfied the criterion of reliability would be admissible if uncorroborated, but might no longer be "necessary" to the prosecution's case if corroborated by other independent evidence. Such an interpretation of the criterion of "necessity" would thus produce the illogical result that uncorroborated hearsay evidence would be admissible, but could become inadmissible if corroborated. This is not what was intended by this Court's decision in *Khan*.

As indicated above, the criterion of necessity must be given a flexible definition, capable of encompassing diverse situations. What these situations will have in common is that the relevant direct evidence is not, for a variety of reasons, available. Necessity of this nature may arise in a number of situations. Wigmore, while not attempting an exhaustive enumeration, suggested at §1421 the following categories:

> (1) The person whose assertion is offered may now be dead, or out of the jurisdiction, or insane, or otherwise unavailable for the purpose of testing [by cross-examination]. This is the commoner and more palpable reason. . . .

> (2) The assertion may be such that we cannot expect, again or at this time, to get evidence of the same value from the same or other sources . . . . The necessity is not so great; perhaps hardly a necessity, only an expediency or convenience, can be predicated. But the principle is the same.

Clearly the categories of necessity are not closed. In *Khan*, for instance, this Court recognized the necessity of receiving hearsay evidence of a child's statements when the child was not herself a competent witness. We also suggested that such hearsay evidence might become necessary when the emotional trauma that would result to the child if forced to give *viva voce* testimony would be great. Whether a necessity of this kind arises, however, is a question of law for determination by the trial judge.

It is now necessary to apply these principles to the evidence in question in this case. In my opinion, the hearsay evidence of what Ms. King said to her mother in the first two telephone conversations on the night of her murder satisfied the criteria of necessity and reliability set out by this Court in *Khan*. In my view, this evidence falls within the same principles. Ms. King is dead, and will never be able to testify as to what happened on the night of August 10 to August 11, 1986. The relevant direct evidence is therefore unavailable. Ms. King's mother's evidence as to what her daughter told her on the telephone that night was clearly necessary, in the sense that there was no possibility that evidence of what was said could be adduced through the declarant.

Moreover, in respect of the first two telephone conversations, there is no reason to doubt Ms. King's veracity. She had no known reason to lie. In my view, the hearsay evidence relating to the first two telephone conversations between Ms. King and her mother could reasonably be relied upon by the jury, as the traditional dangers associated with hearsay evidence—perception, memory and credibility—were not present to any significant degree.

In my view, it would be neither sensible nor just to deprive the jury of this highly relevant evidence on the basis of an arcane rule against hearsay, founded on a lack of faith in the capacity of the trier of fact properly to evaluate evidence of a statement, made under circumstances which do not give rise to apprehensions about its reliability, simply because the declarant is unavailable for cross-examination. Where the criteria of necessity and reliability are satisfied, the lack of testing by cross-examination goes to weight, not admissibility, and a properly cautioned jury should be able to evaluate the evidence on that basis.

However, I arrive at a different conclusion in respect of the contents of the third telephone conversation ("Larry has come back and I no longer need a ride"). While, as in the case of the first two telephone conversations, the unavailability of the declarant to testify satisfies the criterion of necessity, the conditions under which the statement was made do not, in my view, provide that circumstantial guarantee of trustworthiness that would justify its admission without the possibility of cross-examination. On the evidence, I cannot say that I am without apprehensions that Ms. King may have been mistaken, or, indeed, might have intended to deceive her mother on this account.

The evidence at trial disclosed that after making the second telephone call to her mother, Ms. King was observed to leave the hotel and get into a taxi that her mother had arranged to pick her up. She attempted to negotiate a fare to Detroit, but the taxi would not take her because, at this stage, she no longer had a credit card. She was then observed to leave the taxi and proceed immediately to the telephone booth from which she made the third telephone call. It is not, therefore, unreasonable, to ask whether she actually had time to observe the respondent's return. It is at least possible that she was mistaken, and had simply observed a car which resembled the respondent's car. In any case, it does seem somewhat curious that she would make the statement, "Larry has come back and I no longer need a ride" before having spoken to the respondent to ascertain whether he proposed to allow her to continue to travel with him.

In my view, it is highly significant that it was suggested in the course of the previous telephone conversations that one Philip come to pick up Ms. King and drive her back to Detroit. She was vehemently opposed to this suggestion, and there was some evidence that Philip had assaulted her on a previous occasion. When faced with the choice between a ride home with a person for whom she apparently had a great dislike, and of whom she was quite possibly frightened, on the one hand, and with telling her mother that Larry would take her home, on the other, Ms. King might well have preferred the latter alternative.

Moreover, with all due respect, it must be recalled that Ms. King was travelling under an assumed name and using a credit card which she knew was either stolen or forged. She was, therefore, at least capable of deceit. It may have been that she decided to lie to her mother to conceal some aspect of her activities or circumstances, or, indeed, simply to allay her mother's fears.

I wish to emphasize that I do not advance these alternative hypotheses as accurate reconstructions of what occurred on the night of Ms. King's murder. I engage in such speculation only for the purpose of showing that the circumstances under which Ms. King made the third telephone call to her mother were not such as to provide that circumstantial guarantee of trustworthiness that would justify the admission of its contents by way of hearsay evidence, without the possibility of cross-examination. Indeed, at the highest, it can only be said that hearsay evidence of the third telephone call is equally consistent with the accuracy of Ms. King's statements, and also with a number of other hypotheses. I cannot say that this evidence could not reasonably have been expected to have changed significantly had Ms. King been available to give evidence in person and subjected to cross-examination. I conclude, therefore, that the hearsay evidence of the contents of the third telephone conversation did not satisfy the criterion of reliability set out in *Khan*, and therefore was not admissible on that basis.

To conclude, as this Court has made clear in its decisions in *Ares v. Venner, supra*, and *R. v. Khan, supra*, the approach that excludes hearsay evidence, even when highly probative, out of the fear that the trier of fact will not understand how to deal with such evidence, is no longer appropriate. In my opinion, hearsay evidence of statements made by persons who are not available to give evidence at trial ought generally to be admissible, where the circumstances under which the statements were made satisfy the criteria of necessity and reliability set out in

Khan, and subject to the residual discretion of the trial judge to exclude the evidence when its probative value is slight and undue prejudice might result to the accused. Properly cautioned by the trial judge, juries are perfectly capable of determining what weight ought to be attached to such evidence, and of drawing reasonable inferences therefrom.

In the result, therefore, I conclude that the hearsay evidence of what Ms. King told her mother in the first two telephone calls satisfied the criteria of necessity and reliability set out in *Khan*, and was properly admissible on that basis. While the contents of the third telephone call satisfied the criterion of necessity as well, the events surrounding the making of that call were not sufficient to provide that circumstantial guarantee of trustworthiness which would justify their admission without the test of cross-examination. The Crown did not appeal in respect of the fourth telephone conversation, and therefore I make no comment as to the admissibility of hearsay evidence of its contents, other than to say that, in the event of a new trial, it will be governed by the same principles.

[On Smith's new trial the accused was acquitted. During the jury's deliberations they came back with a question: We heard that there were three phone calls that night. Why could we hear the contents of the first two calls but not the contents of the third?]

R. v. KHARSEKIN
(1994), 30 C.R. (4th) 252, 88 C.C.C. (3d) 193 (Nfld. C.A.)

The accused, a seaman aboard a Russian trawler, was charged with second degree murder. The victim was the chief engineer of the ship. He suffered a stab wound in the right side of his neck. Shortly afterwards he attended the medical centre on the ship. The doctor inquired who had wounded him. The deceased said "I was wounded by the knife from the second electrical mechanic". Just after this statement, he became unconscious. About 15 to 20 minutes later he was revived. Approximately 30 to 35 minutes after he had regained consciousness, the maintenance mechanic, arrived at the medical centre and inquired who had stabbed him. The doctor said it was the second electrical mechanic. The maintenance mechanic asked "was it Kharsekin?" and the doctor asked the victim "Kharsekin, is that Kharsekin?" The victim nodded in agreement. The medical evidence was that the victim was fully conscious and understood the questions being asked. He died within minutes. The trial judge held that the replies of the deceased were hearsay and were not admissible under any of the exceptions to the hearsay rule. The accused was acquitted and the Crown appealed.

CAMERON J.A. (O'NEILL and MARSHALL JJ.A. concurring):—

. . . .

The trial judge held in this case that the decision of the Supreme Court of Canada in *Khan* should be confined to the circumstances illustrated by that case. In fairness to the trial judge, he did not, at that time, have the benefit of the decision of the Supreme Court of Canada in *R. v. Smith* . . . , which made it clear that the principle stated in *Khan* was not confined to cases of sexual assault on children. . . .

The respondent concedes that the victim's statements are relevant and meet the criterion of necessity. The person making the statement is dead and unable to give evidence. There is no evidence to suggest that anyone other that the deceased and his assailant were present at the time of the stabbing and there is no evidence of the same value from other sources. In respect of the test of necessity, the facts in this case are similar to those in *Smith* where the test was held to have been met.

The trial judge concluded and the respondent argues that the indicia of reliability should be the same as those for dying declarations. With respect, I cannot agree. The purpose of the development of the *Khan* approach was to adopt a new principled approach as opposed to the narrow rule bound approach of the past. *Khan* and *Smith* make it clear that there is no inviolable list of considerations for reliability. The factors relevant to reliability will vary from case to case. The fact that some courts have continued to analyze cases under the traditional exceptions to the hearsay rule before turning to a *Khan* approach does not limit the application of *Khan* . . . , nor would I conclude that the admissibility of the evidence here would require the criteria of "hopeless expectation of death" and "spontaneity".

In this case the deceased had a peculiar means of knowledge. Indeed, only he and the person who wounded him had that knowledge. Pedyura's wound and rapid loss of blood when he arrived at the medical centre indicate that the initial statement was made shortly after the wounding and the confirming statements within an hour of the first. There was little time to plan falsification and the medical evidence supports the position that the deceased knew what he was saying. The first statement was in response to a question but it was not a leading question.

There is physical evidence to indicate that there were blood stains on the respondent's pants consistent with that taken from the body of the deceased.

There is nothing in the circumstances to suggest a reason for the deceased to be untruthful. The tests enunciated in *Khan* and *Smith* were met. There was, in the words of Wigmore, circumstantial probability of trustworthiness and the statements were admissible.

Therefore in failing to admit the deceased's statements the trial judge made an error in law.

R. v. CASSIDY
(1993), 26 C.R. (4th) 252 (Ont. Gen. Div.)

The accused was charged with first degree murder. He admitted killing the victim and the issue was intent. The Crown sought to call hearsay evidence related to two areas. First, statements said to have been made by the victim close to the time of her death to the effect that the accused used the victim's credit card without her consent, and that the victim demanded her money back and threatened to go to the police. Second, statements made by the victim as to threats made by the accused to her. In each case, the statements were tendered for the purpose of establishing the truth of what was said in the statement.

GRAVELY J.:—

. . . .

The issues are necessity and reliability. In my opinion, the profferred evidence is relevant to the issue of intent which is central to the trial. The victim is dead and the test of necessity is met. As to reliability of the credit card utterances, Crown counsel suggested that the circumstances insure a high degree of reliability. Four different witnesses say the deceased said the same thing on the same day. All four witnesses gave the statement to the police on the same day separately and soon after the victim's death. All witnesses say the utterances of the victim were made within a couple of days of her death. The Crown also points out that the statements are partially corroborated by the admission of the accused that he did use the victim's credit card. Counsel suggests that even though the victim is not available for cross-examination it would be open to the accused to give evidence contradicting the statements and, in any event, a proper warning to the jury would guard against any potential unfairness.

. . . .

It is somewhat difficult to know how to apply the principles of *Smith* but some guidance is given in the treatment by Chief Justice Lamer of the third telephone call, and he said:

> On the evidence, I cannot say that I am without apprehension that Ms. King may have been mistaken or indeed might have intended to deceive her mother on this account. . . . I wish to emphasize that I do not advance these alternative hypotheses as accurate reconstructions of what occurred on the night of Ms. King's murder. I engage in such speculation only for the purpose of showing that the circumstances under which Ms. King made the third telephone call to her mother were not such as to provide that circumstantial guarantee of trustworthiness that would justify the admission of its contents by way of hearsay evidence without the possibility of cross-examination.

I understand that to mean that before letting in hearsay evidence a trial judge is required to conduct a search for hypotheses that could explain the evidence in a fashion inconsistent with reliability. The search must extend to the point of speculation. Only if that search fails can it be said that the evidence meets the test of substantial equivalence to the reliability afforded by cross-examination. . . .

The facts of this case are that the accused had been in a tumultuous emotional relationship with the deceased for some time. It is not unlikely that under the circumstances, the victim's objective judgment could be clouded or her statements made to friends or her family about the accused be exaggerated, immoderate or otherwise unreliable. These then, are not, in my opinion, the kinds of rather straightforward uncomplicated statements given in a situation where reliability is guaranteed as contemplated in *Smith* and in *Kahn* or indeed in their predecessor, *Ares v. Venner*. Without cross-examination here, defence counsel would be virtually powerless to deal effectively with those statements. On the other hand, if the victim had been alive and available for cross-examination, it is not difficult to imagine that defence counsel could have been successful in obtaining admissions which might have changed some of the facts alleged in the statements.

The criterion of reliability then has not been met and I find that all the hearsay statements tendered are not admissible.

What of recanted out-of-court statements? At common law we have seen that they are only admissible for credibility and can only be admitted to prove the truth if the recanting declarant now expressly adopts the contents as true. This all changed with *K.G.B.*

R. v. B. (K.G.)
[1993] 1 S.C.R. 740, 19 C.R. (4th) 1, 79 C.C.C. (3d) 257

The accused and three other young men were involved in a fight with two others. In the course of the fight, one of the four young men pulled a knife and stabbed one of the men in the chest and killed him. The four young men then fled the scene. About two weeks later, the accused's friends were interviewed separately by the police. With the youths' consent the interviews were videotaped. In their statements, they told the police that the accused had made statements to them in which he acknowledged that he had caused the death of the victim. The accused was charged with second degree murder. At trial, the three youths recanted their earlier statements. They said they had lied to the police to exculpate themselves from any possible involvement. The trial judge held that the witnesses' prior inconsistent statements could not be tendered as proof that the accused actually made the admissions. They were, per the orthodox rule, hearsay. They could only be used to impeach the witnesses' credibility by proving that on an earlier occasion the witnesses had in fact made statements inconsistent with their present testimony. In the absence of other sufficient identification evidence, the trial judge acquitted. The Court of Appeal upheld the acquittal.

LAMER C.J. (SOPINKA, GONTHIER, McLACHLIN and IACOBUCCI JJ. concurring): —

. . . .

The orthodox rule has been almost universally criticized by academic commentators. Their criticisms can be distilled into the assertion that the hearsay dangers on which the orthodox rule is based are ill-founded or non-existent in the case of prior inconsistent statements. Respecting the oath, commentators discount the significance of the oath in modern society. Stuesser, is representative in arguing that "[t]he unfortunate reality in our modern society is that the power of an oath must be discounted as a means of ensuring reliability for a statement." . . . However, I note that while the witness faces the legal consequences of violating an oath or solemn affirmation at trial, in most cases there is less incentive to be truthful when the statement is made, leading to a natural preference for the testimony at trial if the alternative is unsworn or unaffirmed testimony.

Critics also claim that the lack of opportunity for the trier of fact to observe the demeanour of the witness at the time the statement was made, and thus to assess credibility based on that demeanour, is overstated in its significance. They argue that the opportunity to observe the witness as he or she denies or professes not to remember making the statement can give the trier insight into the truthfulness of the recantation, and therefore also the truthfulness of the prior statement which is denied. This does not obviate the problem of ensuring that the witness's prior statement is fully and accurately reproduced for the trier of fact. Of course, both of these criticisms of the orthodox rule are reinforced when, as in this case, the prior statement is videotaped, allowing the trier of fact to observe the witnesses' demeanour and ensuring that an accurate record of the statement is tendered as evidence.

. . . .

The lack of cross-examination is the most important of the hearsay dangers, but perhaps also the most overstated in the context of prior inconsistent statements. By definition, commentators argue, the maker of the statement is present in court and amenable to vigorous cross-examination respecting his or her recollection, testimonial capacity and bias at the time of the making of the prior statement. As it is argued in McCormick on Evidence, supra, at p. 120:

> The witness who has told one story aforetime and another today has opened the gates to all the vistas of truth which the common law practice of cross-examination and re-examination was invented to explore. The reasons for the change of face, whether forgetfulness, carelessness, pity, terror, or greed, may be explored by the two questioners in the presence of the trier of fact, under oath, casting light on which is the true story and which the false.

. . . .

Furthermore, commentators observe, the witness's recantation has accomplished all that the opponent's cross-examination could hope to: the witness now testifies under oath that the prior statement was a lie, or claims to have no recollection of the matters in the statement, thus undermining its credibility as much as cross-examination could have.

. . . .

Finally, it is clear that the orthodox rule, in so far as it is based on the hearsay rule, has been undermined by the decisions of this Court in *Khan* and *Smith*. In *Smith*, I stated that the decision in *Khan* "should be understood as the triumph of a principled analysis over a set of ossified judicially created categories", and that that decision:

> . . . signalled an end to the old categorical approach to the admission of hearsay evidence. Hearsay evidence is now admissible on a principled basis, the governing principles being the reliability of the evidence, and its necessity.

I will return to *Smith* and the principled approach to the hearsay rule as it applies in the particular case of prior inconsistent statements, but it is important to note that any erosion of the categorical approach to the hearsay rule must influence the Court's consideration of the orthodox rule as one instance of that rule.

[The court then examined the role of stare decisis and decided: "The existing rule has been attenuated by developments in the law of hearsay and is somewhat, if not overly, technical, and reforming the rule would not directly expand the scope of criminal liability."]

. . . .

I am of the view that evidence of prior inconsistent statements of a witness other than an accused should be substantively admissible on a principled basis, following this Court's decisions in *Khan* and *Smith*. However, it is clear that the factors identified in those cases — reliability and necessity — must be adapted and refined in this particular context, given the particular problems raised by the nature of such statements. Furthermore, there must be a *voir dire* before such statements are put before the jury as substantive evidence, in which the trial judge satisfies him or herself that the statement was made in circumstances which do not negate its reliability.

. . . .

(1) Reliability

(i) The oath

It is undeniable that the significance of the oath has drastically changed since its introduction. Originally the oath was grounded upon a belief that divine retribution would visit those who lied under oath. Accordingly, witnesses were required to believe in this retribution if they were to be properly sworn and their evidence admissible. . . .

We no longer require this belief in divine retribution; in *Reference re Truscott*, [1967] S.C.R. 309, at p. 368, this Court stated in the context of child witnesses that the witness need only understand "the moral obligation of telling the truth". In this sense the oath can be said to have a changed significance, and if critics of the oath suggest only that its original supernatural force has disappeared, I agree with that observation.

. . . .

However, there remain compelling reasons to prefer statements made under oath, solemn affirmation or solemn declaration. While the oath will not motivate all witnesses to tell the truth . . . its administration may serve to impress on more honest witnesses the seriousness and significance of their statements, especially where they incriminate another person in a criminal investigation.

In addition to this positive effect on the declarant, the presence of an oath, solemn affirmation or solemn declaration will increase the evidentiary value of the statement when it is admitted at trial. First, it will mean that the trier of fact will not be asked to accept unsworn testimony over sworn testimony; instead, the trier will have the opportunity to choose between two sworn statements, and the trier's ultimate decision will not be made on the basis of unsworn or unaffirmed testimony. Similarly, should the prior statement be decisive, there is no danger of the accused being convicted solely on the basis of unsworn testimony.

Second, the presence of the oath during the making of the prior statement eliminates the explanation offered by many recanting witnesses, including one of the witnesses in this case: when confronted with the prior inconsistent statement, witnesses explain that it was not made under oath, and assert that the oath they took at trial persuaded them to tell the truth. This naturally privileges the trial testimony in the mind of the trier of fact. If both statements were made under oath, such an explanation can no longer be employed. Furthermore, since both statements cannot be true, the trier of fact has an indication of the low regard in which the witness holds the oath. Therefore, while it is true that the oath in itself has no power to ensure truthfulness in some witnesses, the fact that both statements were made under oath removes resort to the absence of an oath as an indicium of the alleged unreliability of the prior inconsistent statement.

The presence of an oath, solemn affirmation or solemn declaration will have yet another positive effect on the declarant's truthfulness and the administration of justice. A sworn prior statement will be highly persuasive evidence in any prosecution against the declarant related to false testimony (whether in the statement or at trial), and the knowledge that this evidence exists for this purpose should weigh heavily on the mind of one who considers lying in a statement, or recanting his or her prior statement to lie at trial.

Of course, the incentives provided by the declarant's exposure to prosecution under ss. 137, 139 and 140 in relation to the first statement, and his or her fear of a perjury prosecution in relation to testimony given at trial, will only be effective if these sanctions are made known to the declarant. For this reason, the witness should be warned by the person taking the statement that the statement may be used as evidence at a subsequent trial if the witness recants (thereby engaging s. 137), and also that severe criminal sanctions will accompany the making of a false statement. This warning should refer specifically to ss. 137, 139 and 140 of the Criminal Code, and repeat the elements of and sanctions for those offences. As does the formal swearing of the witness in the trial process, this warning and the administration of the oath should serve to bring home to the witness the gravity of the situation and his duty to tell the truth.

. . . .

However, I do not wish to create technical categorical requirements duplicating those of the old approach to hearsay evidence. It follows from *Smith* that there may be situations in which the trial judge concludes that an appropriate substitute for the oath is established and that notwithstanding the absence of an oath the statement is reliable. Other circumstances may serve to impress upon the witness the importance of telling the truth, and in so doing provide a high degree of reliability to the statement. While these occasions may not be frequent, I do not foreclose the possibility that they might arise under the principled approach to hearsay evidence.

(ii) Presence

Proponents of the orthodox rule emphasize the many verbal and non-verbal cues which triers of fact rely upon in order to assess credibility. When the witness is on the stand, the trier can observe the witness's reaction to questions, hesitation, degree of commitment to the statement being made, etc. Most importantly, and subsuming all of these factors, the trier can assess the relationship between the interviewer and the witness to observe the extent to which the testimony of the witness is the product of the investigator's questioning. Such subtle observations and cues cannot be gleaned from a transcript, read in court in counsel's monotone, where the atmosphere of the exchange is entirely lost.

All of these indicia of credibility, and therefore reliability, are available to the trier of fact when the witness's prior statement is videotaped. During the course of the hearing, counsel for the appellant screened a brief excerpt from the videotape of one of the interviews. In the main portion of the television screen is a medium-length shot of the witness facing the camera and seated across a table from the interviewing officer, showing the physical relationship between the two people. In one upper corner is a close-up of the witness's face as he or she speaks, capturing nuances of expression lost in the main view. Along the bottom of the screen is a line showing the date and a time counter, with the seconds ticking off, ensuring that the continuity and integrity of the record is maintained. The audio-visual medium captures other elements of the statement lost in a transcript, such as actions or distinctive motions which the witness demonstrates (as in this case), or answers given by nodding or shaking the head. In other words, the experience of being in the room with the witness and the interviewing officer is recreated as fully as possible for the viewer. Not only does the trier of fact have access to the full range of non-verbal indicia of credibility, but there is also a reproduction of the statement which is fully accurate, eliminating the danger of inaccurate recounting which motivates the rule against hearsay evidence. In a very real sense, the evidence ceases to be hearsay in this important respect, since the hearsay declarant is brought before the trier of fact.

Of course, the police would not resort to this precaution in every case; it may well be reserved for cases such as this, where a major crime such as murder is being investigated, the testimony of the witnesses is important to the Crown's case, and the character of the witnesses suggests that such precautions would be advisable. It is quite possible that such equipment would be available to police of given forces at a central location, and that such crucial though unstable witnesses will be taken to such locations to make their statements, or, where the statements have already been made, to repeat them in a form which may be substantively admissible should the witness recant.

In addition to an oath or solemn affirmation and warning, then, a complete videotape record of the type described above, or one which duplicates the experience of observing a witness in the courtroom to the same extent, is another important indicium of reliability which will satisfy the principled basis for the admission of hearsay evidence.

Again, it may be possible that the testimony of an independent third party who observes the making of the statement in its entirety could, in exceptional circumstances, also provide the requisite reliability with respect to demeanour evidence. I would only note at this point that there are many persons who could serve this function: police stations will have justices of the peace present or available, the witness may have his or her own lawyer present, and ss. 56(2)(c) and 56(2)(d) of the Young Offenders Act, R.S.C., 1985, c. Y-1, provide that a young person making a statement has a right of access to counsel, parents, or adult relatives. It will be a matter for the trial judge to determine whether or not a sufficient substitute for a videotape record has been provided to allow the trier of fact access to sufficient demeanour evidence to make the statement admissible.

(iii) Cross-examination

The final hearsay danger is the lack of contemporaneous cross-examination when the statement is made. The appellant is correct to concede that this is the most important of the hearsay dangers. However, in the case of prior inconsistent statements, it is also the most easily remedied by the opportunity to cross-examine at trial. This is a feature of prior inconsistent statements that conclusively distinguishes them from other forms of hearsay. . . .

Furthermore, unlike the oath and presence, it is the hearsay danger which is impossible to address outside of judicial or quasi-judicial processes. Whereas the police can easily administer a warning and oath, and videotape a statement in the course of a witness interview, it would restrict the operation of a reformed rule to judicial or quasi-judicial proceedings to require contemporaneous cross-examination, and thereby severely restrict the impact of a reformed rule. Consider the facts of the present case: when the three witnesses were interviewed by the police, no one had yet been charged with an offence. Who could have cross-examined the witnesses at that point? How could cross-examination have been effective before the case to be met was known? These and other practical difficulties in requiring contemporaneous cross-examination tip the balance in favour of allowing cross-examination at trial to serve as a substitute. Again, we must remember that the question is not whether it would have been preferable to have had the benefit of contemporaneous cross-examination, but whether the absence of such cross-examination is a sufficient reason to keep the statement from the jury as substantive evidence. Given the other guarantees of trustworthiness, I do not think that it should be allowed to be a barrier to substantive admissibility. Of course, it will be an important consideration for the trier of fact in deciding what weight to attach to the prior inconsistent statement, and it is likely that opposing counsel will stress the absence of such cross-examination to the trier of fact.

Therefore, the requirement of reliability will be satisfied when the circumstances in which the prior statement was made provide sufficient guarantees of its trustworthiness with respect to the two hearsay dangers a reformed rule can realistically address: if (i) the statement is made under oath or solemn affirmation following a warning as to the existence of sanctions and the significance of the oath or affirmation, (ii) the statement is videotaped in its entirety, and (iii) the opposing party, whether the Crown or the defence, has a full opportunity to cross-examine the witness respecting the statement, there will be sufficient circumstantial guarantees of reliability to allow the jury to make substantive use of the statement. Alternatively, other circumstantial guarantees of reliability may suffice to render such statements substantively admissible, provided that the judge is satisfied that the circumstances provide adequate assurances of reliability in place of those which the hearsay rule traditionally requires.

(2) Necessity

Prior inconsistent statements present vexing problems for the necessity criterion. The necessity criterion has usually been satisfied by the unavailable witness: in *Khan*, the child declarant who could not be sworn, and in *Smith*, the dead declarant. By definition, the declarant in the case of prior inconsistent statements is available at trial; it is his or her prior statement that is unavailable because of the recantation.

However, it is important to remember that the necessity criterion "must be given a flexible definition, capable of encompassing diverse situations" [see *Smith*]. Wigmore, vol. 5 (Chadbourn rev. 1974), § 1421, at p. 253, referred to two classes of necessity:

> (1) The person whose assertion is offered may now be *dead*, or out of the jurisdiction, or insane, or *otherwise unavailable* for the purpose of testing. This is the commoner and more palpable reason.
>
> . . . .
>
> (2) The assertion may be such that we cannot expect, again, or at this time, to get *evidence of the same value* from the same or other sources. . . . The necessity is not so great; perhaps hardly a necessity, only an expediency or convenience, can be predicated. But the principle is the same. [Emphasis in original.]
>
> . . . .

The precise limits of the necessity criterion remain to be established in the context of specific cases. It may be that in some circumstances, the availability of the witness will mean that hearsay evidence of that witness's prior *consistent* (the kind of statement at issue in *Khan*) statements will not be admissible. However, I am not prepared, at this point, to adhere to a strict interpretation that makes unavailability an indispensable condition of necessity.

In the case of prior *inconsistent* statements, it is patent that we cannot expect to get evidence of the same value from the recanting witness or other sources: as counsel for the appellant claimed, the recanting witness holds the prior statement, and thus the relevant evidence, "hostage". The different "value" of the evidence is found in the fact that something has radically changed between the time when the statement was made and the trial and, assuming that there is a sufficient degree of reliability established under the first criterion, the trier of fact should be allowed to weigh both statements in light of the witness's explanation of the change.

[The court then described the process that should be followed on the *voir dire* determining necessity and reliability.]

. . . .

Even where there has been a warning and oath administered, and the statement videotaped, or sufficient substitutes established, the trial judge will still have the discretion to refuse to allow the jury to make substantive use of the statement. Prior statements share many characteristics with confessions, especially where police investigators are involved. Proponents of the orthodox rule voice the concern that malign influences on the witness by police may precede the making of the statement and shape its content, in the same way that confessions may be suspect if coerced by police investigators. That is, it still may be the case that the oath and videotape, and the acknowledgement of the warning, were made under circumstances that make them suspect. For this reason, the test developed by this court for the admission of confessions is well suited to making a threshold determination of whether the circumstances under which the statement was made undermine the veracity of the indicia of reliability. . . . I would apply this test to prior statements. The trial judge must satisfy him or herself (again, in the majority of cases on the balance of probabilities) on the *voir dire* that the statement was not the product of coercion of any form, whether it involves threats, promises, excessively leading questions by the investigator or other person in a position of authority, or other forms of investigatory misconduct. I would add another element to the trial judge's inquiry to address situations where the first factor might be satisfied, but there are other aspects of police conduct which militate against rewarding that conduct by admitting the evidence. In *R. v. Rothman* (1981), 59 C.C.C. (2d) 30 at p. 74, 121 D.L.R. (3d) 578, [1981] 1 S.C.R. 640, I wrote that even if the *Ibrahim* test was satisfied to make a confession admissible, such a confession "shall nevertheless be excluded if its use in the proceedings would, as a result of what was said or done by any person in authority in eliciting the statement, bring the administration of justice into disrepute".

It must be stressed that the trial judge is not making a determination on the *voir dire* as to the ultimate reliability and credibility of the statement. As I have indicated, that is a matter for the trier of fact. The trial judge need not be satisfied that the prior statement was true and should be believed in preference to the witness's current testimony. This distinction is also derived from the law relating to confessions.[44]

New trial ordered.

R. v. U. (F.J.)
[1995] 3 S.C.R. 764, 42 C.R. (4th) 133, 101 C.C.C. (3d) 97

The accused was arrested for engaging in sexual activities with his 13-year-old daughter. In the interview with the investigating officer, the daughter said that her father had been having sexual intercourse with her on a regular basis. She said that the last time her father had had sex with her was the previous night. The officer then questioned the accused. He admitted that he had had sex with his daughter many times, described the same sexual activities she had described, and stated that the most recent intercourse had been the previous night.

---

44 For an excellent comment see Rosenberg, "*B. (K.G.)* — Necessity and Reliability: the New Pigeonholes" (1993), 19 C.R. (4th) 69. For general concerns with the approach see Rollie Thompson, "The Supreme Court Goes Hunting and Nearly Catches a Hearsay Woozle" (1995), 37 C.R. (4th) 282.

The accused was charged with a number of sexual offences. His statement to the police was admitted as Crown evidence through the testimony of two officers. The daughter said that although she admitted that she had made the allegations against the accused in her statement, the allegations of sexual assault were untrue. The accused testified that while he had made an inculpatory statement to the police, he denied its truth.

The trial judge invited the jury to compare the daughter's unadopted prior inconsistent statement with the accused's unadopted statement to the police in determining if the prosecution had established guilt. The Court of Appeal upheld the conviction on the theory that there was worth solely on the basis that the daughter had made the statement; the statement was not hearsay and therefore was admissible.

The Supreme Court took a different approach: the statement was hearsay but admissible under *B. (K.G.)*.

LAMER C.J. (SOPINKA, GONTHIER, CORY, IACOBUCCI and MAJOR JJ. concurring): —

. . . .

The Voir Dire

I set out the proper procedure for the *voir dire* in my reasons in *B. (K.G.)*. . . . After the calling party invokes s. 9 of the Canada Evidence Act, and fulfils its requirements in the *voir dire* held under that section, the party must then state its objectives in tendering the statement. If the statement will only be used to impeach the witness, the inquiry ends at this point. If, however, the calling party wishes to make substantive use of the statement, the *voir dire* must continue so that the trial judge can assess whether a threshold of reliability has been met. The necessity criterion need not be assessed as it is met whenever a witness recants. The first factor contributing to reliability is the cross-examination of the witness. If the witness provides an explanation for changing his or her story, the trier of fact will be able to assess both versions of the story, as well as the explanation. However, where a witness does not recall making an earlier statement, or refuses to answer questions, the trial judge should take into account that this may impede the jury's ability to assess the ultimate reliability of the statement.

If the additional indicia of reliability I specified in *B. (K.G.)* are present, an oath or affirmation following a warning of penal consequences for lying, and a videotape of the statement, the reliability assessment can be relatively easily made. If the reliability criterion is to be met, in rare cases, by the striking similarity between the statement being assessed and another statement which is already clearly substantively admissible, the trial judge must be satisfied on a balance of probabilities that there are striking similarities between the two statements, and that there was neither reason nor opportunity for the declarants to collude and no improper influence by interrogators or other third parties.

At this stage, the trial judge need only be convinced on a balance of probabilities that the statement is likely to be reliable, as this is the normal burden of proof resting upon a party seeking to admit evidence. The trial judge must also ascertain at this stage that the prior statement relates evidence which would be admissible as the witness's sole testimony.

I would also highlight here the proviso I specified in *B. (K.G.)* that the trial judge must be satisfied on the balance of probabilities that the statement was not the product of coercion of any form, whether involving threats, promises, excessively leading questions by the investigator or other person in a position of authority, or other forms of investigatory misconduct.

The trial judge at this stage is not making a final determination about the ultimate reliability and credibility of the statement. The trial judge need not be satisfied that the prior statement is true and should be believed in preference to the witness's current testimony.

If the trial judge determines that the statement meets the threshold reliability criterion and is thus substantively admissible, he or she must direct the trier of fact to follow a two-step process in evaluating the evidence. The trier of fact must first be certain that the statement which is being used as a reliability referent *was made*, without taking into account the prior inconsistent statement under consideration. Once the trier of fact is satisfied that the *other* statement was made, the trier of fact may compare the similarities between the two statements and, if they are sufficiently striking that it is unlikely that two people would have independently fabricated them, the trier of fact may draw conclusions from that comparison about the truth of the statements.

Finally, where the trial judge finds that the statement is not sufficiently reliable to be used substantively, it may still, of course, be used to impeach credibility or for the fact that it was made. In other words, the orthodox rule will still apply if the minimum reliability threshold is not met.

Application to This Appeal

In this case, the recanting witness was cross-examined in detail about her reasons for changing her story at a preliminary inquiry, on a *voir dire* under s. 9 of the Canada Evidence Act, and before the jury. She provided a comprehensive explanation for changing her story which could be assessed by both the trial judge and the jury and therefore eliminates the most important danger of hearsay evidence. The statements made by the accused and by his daughter contained both a significant number of similarities in detail and the strikingly similar assertion that the most recent sexual contact between the two had been the previous evening. As a *voir dire* was also held with regard to the accused's statement, there was also sufficient evidence presented to found a conclusion that the accused and his daughter had neither a reason nor an opportunity to collude, and that the accused was not improperly influenced by the police officers who took his statement. On the basis of all these factors, I conclude that her statement was, therefore, substantively admissible at trial.

The jury was not, of course, instructed in accordance with the procedures I have set out here. Nonetheless, the statements in question are so strikingly similar that I am satisfied that had the instruction been given, the jury would inevitably have been satisfied as to their reliability on the basis which I have outlined above.

In these circumstances, the absence of a specific instruction in this regard did not occasion any wrong or miscarriage of justice.

L'HEUREUX-DUBÉ J.: —

... I agree with the Chief Justice that, in the case at hand, the complainant's prior inconsistent statement was admissible for the purpose of comparison with the appellant's confession. However, unlike my colleague, I do not believe that the similarities between the two statements must be "striking" before the jury can be permitted to use the prior inconsistent statement for this purpose. In my view, so long as there are significant similarities between the two statements, as there clearly were in this case, a witness's prior inconsistent statement will be admissible for purposes of comparison with an accused's unadopted confession in order to assess the truth of that confession.

R. v. CHAPPELL
(2003), 15 C.R. (6th) 350, 172 C.C.C. (3d) 539,
2003 CarswellOnt 693 (C.A)

The accused appealed from his conviction on charges of assault causing bodily harm. Police had been called to Chappell's residence after a neighbour complained. They broke down the door when they heard struggling and fighting inside. Upon finding Chappell's wife in the bedroom, visibly injured, and noting broken glass on the floor, the officers arrested Chappell. The officers testified that the wife told them that Chappell had been beating her for several hours. They claimed that she was visibly frightened and did not want to co-operate in the laying of charges. She was taken to hospital, where she claimed that she had fallen down and that Chappell had not assaulted her. At trial, she testified to this effect. The Crown sought leave to admit the evidence of her initial statements to the officer as evidence of its truth. The trial judge allowed the evidence. The officer used notes to testify about her statements, as they had not been recorded. The trial judge found that this evidence, along with other circumstantial evidence, was sufficient to convict.

ROSENBERG J.A. (MOLDAVER and SIMMONS JJ.A. concurring):—

As I will discuss below, the full extent of the B.(K.G.) exception to the hearsay rule is not yet determined. The statements sought to be admitted in this case did not fall within the traditional strictures of that exception as set out in that case. ... In *R. v. B.(K.G.)*, Lamer C.J.C. explained when a prior inconsistent statement of a Crown witness may be admissible for its truth as an exception to the hearsay rule. He accepted that the court could admit hearsay evidence if it met the requirements of necessity and reliability. In the case of a prior inconsistent statement the necessity requirement could be met because the witness has recanted his or her prior version of events and thus that version is no longer available to the trier of fact.

As to reliability, Lamer C.J.C. held in *R. v. B.(K.G.)* at p. 288 that because "the focus of the inquiry in the case of prior inconsistent statements is on the

comparative reliability of the prior statement and the testimony offered at trial
. . . additional indicia and guarantees of reliability to those outlined in Khan and
Smith must be secured in order to bring the prior statement to a comparable
standard of reliability before such statements are admitted as substantive
evidence." Those additional indicia and guarantees of reliability focus on the
hearsay dangers of the absence of an oath and presence. The absence of
contemporaneous cross-examination, i.e. cross-examination at the time the
statement was made is usually adequately compensated for by the fact that, by
definition, the declarant is available at the trial for cross-examination. To
compensate for the absence of oath, Lamer C.J.C. held that the "best" indicia of
reliability is that the statement was taken under oath, solemn affirmation, or
solemn declaration and following the administration of a warning of the witness's
amenability to prosecution if it were discovered that the witness has lied (p. 291).
However, there may be situations in which the trial judge concludes that an
appropriate substitute for the oath is established and that notwithstanding the
absence of an oath the statement is reliable.

To address the hearsay danger arising from the fact that the trier of fact
cannot observe the witness when he or she made the prior inconsistent statement,
Lamer C.J.C. held at p. 293 that there should be a complete videotape record of
the statement. Again he held that it might be possible that the testimony of an
independent third party observing the making of the statement in its entirety "in
exceptional circumstances" could also provide the requisite reliability.

However, Lamer C.J.C. made it clear at p. 294 of *R. v. B.(K.G.)* that the
requirements were not to be applied mechanically and thus, "other circumstantial
guarantees of reliability may suffice to render such statements substantively
admissible, provided that the judge is satisfied that the circumstances provide
adequate assurances of reliability in place of those which the hearsay rule
traditionally requires". An example of these alternative circumstances is provided
by *R. v. U.(F.J.)* (1995), 101 C.C.C.(3d) 97 (S.C.C.) where the complainant
recanted from an allegation that her father, the accused, had sexually assaulted
her. The court held that although the complainant's statement was not taken under
circumstances that would have met the *R. v. B.(K.G.)* requirements it was
sufficiently reliable because of the striking similarity between the statement and
the accused's own statement to the police, provided that there was neither reason
nor opportunity for the declarants to collude and no improper influence by
interrogators or other third parties. While *R. v. U. (F.J.)* illustrates the flexibility
of the principled approach as applied to prior inconsistent statements, it also
shows the unusual circumstances that must exist before the *R. v. B. (K.G.)*
requirements can be wholly disregarded.

In this case, the only one of the *R. v. B. (K.G.)* requirements that was met
was the fact that the complainant was available for cross-examination. There was
nothing else, as the trial judge seemed to recognize, to bring the case within *R. v.
B. (K.G.)*. The statements were not videotaped or even audiotaped. It is not even
clear that there was an accurate record of the entire statement-taking process. The
three officers involved conceded that they did not purport to take down everything
that the uncooperative declarant was saying. There was no warning to the witness

of the consequences of lying. There was no independent third party to compensate for the fact that the trier of fact was not present when the statement was made.

The question then is whether there are other exceptional circumstances as in *R. v. U. (F.J.)* that would permit the trial court to admit the prior inconsistent statements for their truth. In *R. v. U. (F.J.)* Lamer C.J.C. held that neither that case nor *R. v. B. (K.G.)* should be read as foreclosing the possibility that other indicia of reliability might suffice, where the declarant is available for cross-examination. Thus, he said the following at para. 39:

> Cross-examination alone, therefore, goes a substantial part of the way to ensuring that the reliability of a prior inconsistent statement can be adequately assessed by the trier of fact. In *B.(K.G.)*, I wrote that prior inconsistent statements subject to cross-examination, made under oath and videotaped would be substantively admissible because each of the hearsay dangers would be addressed. I also, however, indicated that in certain particular circumstances a prior inconsistent statement could be admitted even in the absence of an oath and a video record, although not in the absence of cross-examination. In my assessment, this is one of the cases where there are sufficient circumstantial guarantees of reliability that the statement of the complainant ought to have been admitted for the truth of its contents.

And at para. 45:

> I anticipate that instances of statements so strikingly similar as to bolster their reliability will be rare. In keeping with our principled and flexible approach to hearsay, other situations may arise where prior inconsistent statements will be judged substantively admissible, bearing in mind that cross-examination alone provides significant indications of reliability. It is not necessary in this case to decide if cross-examination alone provides an adequate assurance of threshold reliability to allow substantive admission of prior inconsistent statements.

In the absence of findings of fact by the trial judge, this court is in no position to decide whether there are exceptional circumstances as in *R. v. U.(F.J.)*, that would allow the trial judge to make substantive use of any of Ms. Chappell's statements to the police. I therefore offer the following comments to assist the trial judge on the new trial, should the Crown choose to proceed to retry the appellant.

It seems to me that, at best, only the initial statement to Constable Hollett could possibly meet the threshold reliability requirement. Two factors that the trial judge could take into account in favour of admitting that statement for its truth are: (1) Ms. Chappell was available for cross-examination and it appears that defence counsel was able to effectively cross-examine her; and (2) although she disputes Constable Hollett's evidence about the circumstances under which the first statement was made, she concedes that his recollection of the content of that statement is correct.

Even so, it seems to me that the statement would only be available for substantive use if certain critical findings of fact were made in favour of the Crown. If contrary to the evidence of Constable Hollett, the statement was not spontaneous or Ms. Chappell was intoxicated, the statement would not be sufficiently reliable. The trial judge would also have to make a determination of how proximate the statement was to the alleged assault and whether Ms. Chappell's state of fear, as observed by Constable Hollett, was the result of the assault or something else, such as the actions of the police in breaking down her front door with an axe and arresting her husband at gunpoint. If the trial judge was satisfied that the statement was made under emotional pressure from the assault and without apparent motive to fabricate, the statement might be admissible for substantive use, provided that Ms. Chappell was available for effective cross-examination.

Appeal allowed; new trial ordered.

R. v. KHELAWON
[2006] 2 S.C.R. 787, 2006 CarswellOnt 7825, 2006 CarswellOnt 7826, 42 C.R. (6th) 1, 215 C.C.C. (3d) 161 (S.C.C.)

In 1999, C, a cook at a retirement home, found S, an 81-year-old resident of the home, badly bruised in his room. S told C that the accused, the manager of the home, had repeatedly punched him in the face and ribs the previous evening, had packed his belongings in garbage bags and had threatened to kill him if he did not leave the home by noon the next day. C took S to her apartment and cared for him for a few days. He later agreed to be seen by a doctor. The doctor testified that he found three fractured ribs and bruises consistent with S's allegation of assault but which also could have resulted from a fall. The next day, C took S to the police and S gave a videotaped statement repeating the allegation he had been beaten and threatened. The statement was not under oath but S answered "yes" when asked if he understood it was important to tell the truth and that he could be charged if he did not tell the truth. Medical records seized from the retirement home described S as depressed, aggressive, angry and paranoid, and revealed that he had been treated for paranoid psychosis and depression. A psychiatrist testified that S understood that it was important to tell the truth and had the capacity to communicate evidence. The defence argued that C had influenced S to complain out of spite because the accused had earlier terminated C's employment.

After the police arrested the accused they obtained further statements from other residents alleging assaults by the accused. The accused was charged with various counts of assaults against five complainants but, by the time of the trial, four complainants, including S and D, had died of causes unrelated to the alleged assaults and the fifth was no longer competent to testify. Only one complainant had testified at the preliminary inquiry. The central issue at trial was whether the complainants' hearsay statements should be received in evidence. The trial judge admitted some of the hearsay based in large part on the striking similarity between the statements. The trial judge ultimately found videotaped statements given by S and D to the police sufficiently credible to found convictions for aggravated assault and uttering a death threat in respect of S, as well as assault causing bodily harm and assault with a weapon in respect of D. The accused was acquitted on the remaining counts.

On appeal, a majority of the Ontario Court of Appeal excluded all of the hearsay statements and acquitted the accused on all charges. The dissenting judge would have upheld the convictions in respect of S. The Crown appealed as of right from the acquittals in respect of S and was denied leave to appeal from the acquittals in respect of D.

CHARRON J. (McLACHLIN C.J., BINNIE, LeBEL, DESCHAMPS, FISH, and ABELLA JJ. concurring):—

Hearsay Exceptions: A Principled Approach

It has long been recognized that a rigid application of the exclusionary rule would result in the unwarranted loss of much valuable evidence. The hearsay statement, because of the way in which it came about, may be inherently reliable, or there may be sufficient means of testing it despite its hearsay form. Hence, a number of common law exceptions were gradually created. A rigid application of these exceptions, in turn, proved problematic leading to the needless exclusion of evidence in some cases, or its unwarranted admission in others. Wigmore urged greater flexibility in the application of the rule based on the two guiding principles that underlie the traditional common law exceptions: necessity and reliability (*Wigmore on Evidence* (2nd ed. 1923), vol. III, _ 1420, at p. 153). This Court first accepted this approach in*Khan* and later recognized its primacy in*Starr*. The governing framework, based on*Starr*, was recently summarized in *R. v. Mapara*, [2005] 1 S.C.R. 358, 2005 SCC 23, at para. 15:

(a) Hearsay evidence is presumptively inadmissible unless it falls under an exception to the hearsay rule. The traditional exceptions to the hearsay rule remain presumptively in place.

(b) A hearsay exception can be challenged to determine whether it is supported by indicia of necessity and reliability, required by the principled approach. The exception can be modified as necessary to bring it into compliance.

(c) In "rare cases", evidence falling within an existing exception may be excluded because the indicia of necessity and reliability are lacking in the particular circumstances of the case.

(d) If hearsay evidence does not fall under a hearsay exception, it may still be admitted if indicia of reliability and necessity are established on a *voir dire*.

. . . . .

Constitutional Dimension: Trial Fairness

Prior to admitting hearsay statements under the principled exception to the hearsay rule, the trial judge must determine on a *voir dire* that necessity and reliability have been established. The onus is on the person who seeks to adduce the evidence to establish these criteria on a balance of probabilities. In a criminal context, the inquiry may take on a constitutional dimension, because difficulties in testing the evidence, or conversely the inability to present reliable evidence, may impact on an accused's ability to make full answer and defence, a right protected by s. 7 of the *Canadian Charter of Rights and Freedoms*: *Dersch v. Canada (Attorney General)*, [1990] 2 S.C.R. 1505. The right to make full answer and defence in turn is linked to another principle of fundamental justice, the right to a fair trial: *R. v. Rose*, [1998] 3 S.C.R. 262. The concern over trial fairness is one of the paramount reasons for rationalizing the traditional hearsay exceptions in accordance with the principled approach. As stated by Iacobucci J. in *Starr*, at para. 200, in respect of Crown evidence: "It would compromise trial fairness, and raise the spectre of wrongful convictions, if the Crown is allowed to introduce unreliable hearsay against the accused, regardless of whether it happens to fall within an existing exception."

As indicated earlier, our adversary system is based on the assumption that sources of untrustworthiness or inaccuracy can best be brought to light under the test of cross-examination. It is mainly because of the inability to put hearsay evidence to that test, that it is presumptively inadmissible. However, the constitutional right guaranteed under s. 7 of the *Charter* is not the right to confront or cross-examine adverse witnesses in itself. The adversarial trial process, which includes cross-examination, is but the means to achieve the end. Trial fairness, as a principle of fundamental justice, is the end that must be achieved. Trial fairness embraces more than the rights of the accused. While it undoubtedly includes the right to make full answer and defence, the fairness of the trial must also be assessed in the light of broader societal concerns: see *R. v. Mills*, [1999] 3 S.C.R. 668, at paras. 69-76. In the context of an admissibility inquiry, society's interest in having the trial process arrive at the truth is one such concern.

The broader spectrum of interests encompassed in trial fairness is reflected in the twin principles of necessity and reliability. The criterion of necessity is founded on society's interest in getting at the truth. Because it is not always possible to meet the optimal test of contemporaneous cross-examination, rather than simply losing the value of the evidence, it becomes necessary in the interests of justice to consider whether it should nonetheless be admitted in its hearsay form. The criterion of reliability is about ensuring the integrity of the trial process. The evidence, although needed, is not admissible unless it is sufficiently reliable to overcome the dangers arising from the difficulty of testing it. As we shall see, the reliability requirement will generally be met on the basis of two different grounds, neither of which excludes consideration of the other. In some cases, because of the circumstances in which it came about, the contents of the hearsay statement may be so reliable that contemporaneous cross-examination of the declarant would add little if anything to the process. In other cases, the evidence may not be so cogent but the circumstances will allow for sufficient testing of evidence by means other than contemporaneous cross-examination. In these circumstances, the admission of the evidence will rarely undermine trial fairness. However, because trial fairness may encompass factors beyond the strict inquiry into necessity and reliability, even if the two criteria are met, the trial judge has the discretion to exclude hearsay evidence where its probative value is outweighed by its prejudicial effect.

The Admissibility Inquiry

Distinction Between Threshold and Ultimate Reliability: A Source of Confusion

As stated earlier, the trial judge only decides whether hearsay evidence is admissible. Whether the hearsay statement will or will not be ultimately relied upon in deciding the issues in the case is a matter for the trier of fact to determine at the conclusion of the trial based on a consideration of the statement in the context of the entirety of the evidence. It is important that the trier of fact's domain not be encroached upon at the admissibility stage. If the trial is before a judge and jury, it is crucial that questions of ultimate reliability be left for the jury — in a criminal trial, it is constitutionally imperative. If the judge sits without a jury, it is equally important that he or she not prejudge the ultimate reliability of the evidence before having heard all of the evidence in the case. Hence, a distinction must be made between "ultimate reliability" and "threshold reliability". Only the latter is inquired into on the admissibility *voir dire*.

The distinction between threshold and ultimate reliability has been made in a number of cases (see, for example, *B. (K.G.)* and *R. v. Hawkins*, [1996] 3 S.C.R. 1043), but we are mainly concerned here with the elaboration of this principle in *Starr*. In particular, the following excerpt from the Court's analysis has been the subject of much of the discussion and commentary (at paras. 215 and 217):

> In this connection, it is important when examining the reliability of a statement under the principled approach to distinguish between threshold and ultimate reliability. Only the former is relevant to admissibility: see *Hawkins, supra*, at p. 1084. Again, it is not appropriate in the circumstances of this appeal to provide an exhaustive catalogue of the factors that may influence threshold reliability. However, our jurisprudence does provide some guidance on this subject. Threshold reliability is concerned not with whether the statement is true or not; that is a question of ultimate reliability. Instead, it is concerned with whether or not the circumstances surrounding the statement itself provide *circumstantial* guarantees of trustworthiness. This could be because the declarant had no motive to lie (see *Khan, supra*; *Smith*, supra), or because there were safeguards in place such that a lie could be discovered (see *Hawkins, supra*; *U. (F.J.), supra*; *B. (K.G.), supra*).
>
> . . .
>
> At the stage of hearsay admissibility the trial judge should not consider the declarant's general reputation for truthfulness, nor any prior or subsequent statements, consistent or not. These factors do not concern the circumstances of the statement itself. Similarly, I would not consider the presence of corroborating or conflicting evidence. On this point, I agree with the Ontario Court of Appeal's decision in *R. v. C. (B.)*(1993), 12 O.R. (3d) 608; see also *Idaho v. Wright*, 497 U.S. 805 (1990). In summary, under the principled approach a court must not invade the province of the trier of fact and condition admissibility of hearsay on whether the evidence is ultimately reliable. However, it will need to examine whether the circumstances in which the statement was made lend sufficient credibility to allow a finding of threshold reliability. [Underlining added.]

The Court's statement that "threshold reliability is concerned not with whether the statement is true or not" has created some uncertainty. While it is clear that the trial judge does not determine whether the statement will ultimately be relied upon as true, it is not so clear that in every case threshold reliability is *not* concerned with whether the statement is true or not. Indeed, in *U. (F.J.)*, the rationale for admitting the complainant's hearsay statement was based on the fact that "the only likely explanation" for its striking similarity with the independent statement of the accused was that "they were both telling the truth" (para. 40).

Further, it is not easy to discern what is or is not a circumstance "surrounding the statement itself". For example, in *Smith*, the fact that the deceased may have had a motive to lie was considered by the Court in determining threshold admissibility. As both Rosenberg J.A. and Blair J.A. point out in their respective reasons, "in determining whether the declarant had a motive to lie, the judge will necessarily be driven to consider factors outside the statement itself or the immediately surrounding circumstances" (para. 97).

Much of the confusion in this area of the law has arisen from this attempt to categorically label some factors as going only to ultimate reliability. The bar against considering "corroborating or conflicting evidence", because it is only relevant to the question of ultimate reliability, is a further example. Quite clearly, the corroborative nature of the semen stain in *Khan* played an important part in establishing the threshold reliability of the child's hearsay statement in that case.

This part of the analysis in *Starr* therefore requires clarification and, in some respects, reconsideration. I will explain how the relevant factors to be considered on an admissibility inquiry cannot invariably be categorized as relating either to threshold or ultimate reliability. Rather, the relevance of any particular factor will depend on the particular dangers arising from the hearsay nature of the statement and the available means, if any, of overcoming them. I will then return to the impugned passage in *Starr*, dealing more specifically with the question of supporting evidence since that reference appears to have raised the most controversy.

Identifying the Relevant Factors: A Functional Approach

Recognizing Hearsay

The first matter to determine before embarking on a hearsay admissibility inquiry, of course, is whether the proposed evidence is hearsay. This may seem to be a rather obvious matter, but it is an important first step. Misguided objections to the admissibility of an out-of-court statement based on a misunderstanding of what constitutes hearsay are not uncommon. As discussed earlier, not all out-of-court statements will constitute hearsay. Recall the defining features of hearsay. An out-of-court statement will be hearsay when: (1) it is adduced to prove the truth of its contents *and* (2) there is no opportunity for a contemporaneous cross-examination of the declarant.

Putting one's mind to the defining features of hearsay at the outset serves to better focus the admissibility inquiry. As we have seen, the first identifying feature of hearsay calls for an inquiry into the purpose for which it is adduced. Only when the evidence is being tendered for its truth will it constitute hearsay. The fact that the out-of-court statement is adduced for its*truth* should be considered in the context of the issues in the case so that the court may better assess the potential impact of introducing the evidence in its hearsay form.

Second, by putting one's mind, at the outset, to the second defining feature of hearsay — the absence of an opportunity for contemporaneous cross-examination of the declarant, the admissibility inquiry is immediately focussed on the dangers of admitting hearsay evidence. Iacobucci J. in *Starr* identified the inability to test the evidence as the "central concern" underlying the hearsay rule. Lamer C.J. in*U. (F.J.)* expressed the same view but put it more directly by stating: "Hearsay is inadmissible as evidence because its reliability cannot be tested" (para. 22).

Presumptive Inadmissibility of Hearsay Evidence

Once the proposed evidence is identified as hearsay, it is presumptively *inadmissible*. I stress the nature of the hearsay rule as a general exclusionary rule because the increased flexibility introduced in the Canadian law of evidence in the past few decades has sometimes tended to blur the distinction between admissibility and weight. Modifications have been made to a number of rules, including the rule against hearsay, to bring them up to date and to ensure that they facilitate rather than impede the goals of truth seeking, judicial efficiency and fairness in the adversarial process. However, the traditional rules of evidence reflect considerable wisdom and judicial experience. The modern approach has built upon their underlying rationale, not discarded it. In *Starr* itself, where this Court recognized the primacy of the principled approach to hearsay exceptions, the presumptive exclusion of hearsay evidence was reaffirmed in strong terms. Iacobucci J. stated as follows (at para. 199):

> By excluding evidence that might produce unfair verdicts, and by ensuring that litigants will generally have the opportunity to confront adverse witnesses, the hearsay rule serves as a cornerstone of a fair justice system.

Traditional Exceptions

The Court in *Starr* also reaffirmed the continuing relevance of the traditional exceptions to the hearsay rule. More recently, this Court in *Mapara* reiterated the continued application of the traditional exceptions in setting out the governing analytical framework, as noted in para. 42 above. Therefore, if the trial judge determines that the evidence falls within one of the traditional common law exceptions, this finding is conclusive and the evidence is ruled admissible, unless, in a rare case, the exception itself is challenged as described in both those decisions.

Principled Approach: Overcoming the Hearsay Dangers

Since the central underlying concern is the inability to test hearsay evidence, it follows that under the principled approach the reliability requirement is aimed at identifying those cases where this difficulty is sufficiently overcome to justify receiving the evidence as an exception to the general exclusionary rule. As some courts and commentators have expressly noted, the reliability requirement is usually met in two different ways: see, for example, *R. v. Wilcox* (2001), 152 C.C.C. (3d) 157, 2001 NSCA 45; *R. v. Czibulka* (2004), 189 C.C.C. (3d) 199 (Ont. C.A.); D. M. Paciocco, "The Hearsay Exceptions: A Game of 'Rock, Paper, Scissors'", in*Special Lectures of the Law Society of Upper Canada 2003: The Law of Evidence* (2004), 17, at p. 29.

One way is to show that there is no real concern about whether the statement is true or not because of the circumstances in which it came about. Common sense dictates that if we can put sufficient trust in the truth and accuracy of the statement, it should be considered by the fact finder regardless of its hearsay form. Wigmore explained it this way:

> There are many situations in which it can be easily seen that such a required test [i.e., cross-examination] would add little as a security, because its purposes had been already substantially accomplished. If a statement has been made under such circumstances that even a sceptical caution would look upon it as trustworthy (in the ordinary instance), in a high degree of probability, it would be pedantic to insist on a test whose chief object is already secured. [&1420, p. 154]

Another way of fulfilling the reliability requirement is to show that no real concern arises from the fact that the statement is presented in hearsay form because, in the circumstances, its truth and accuracy can nonetheless be sufficiently tested. Recall that the optimal way of testing evidence adopted by our adversarial system is to have the declarant state the evidence in court, under oath, and under the scrutiny of contemporaneous cross-examination. This preferred method is not just a vestige of past traditions. It remains a tried and true method, particularly when credibility issues must be resolved. It is one thing for a person to make a damaging statement about another in a context where it may not really matter. It is quite another for that person to repeat the statement in the course of formal proceedings where he or she must commit to its truth and accuracy, be observed and heard, and be called upon to explain or defend it. The latter situation, in addition to providing an accurate record of what was actually said by the witness, gives us a much higher degree of comfort in the statement's trustworthiness. However, in some cases it is not possible to put the evidence to the optimal test, but the circumstances are such that the trier of fact will nonetheless be able to sufficiently test its truth and accuracy. Again, common sense tells us that we should not lose the benefit of the evidence when there are adequate substitutes for testing the evidence.

These two principal ways of satisfying the reliability requirement can also be discerned in respect of the traditional exceptions to the hearsay rule. Iacobucci J. notes this distinction in *Starr*, stating as follows:

> For example, testimony in former proceedings is admitted, at least in part, because many of the traditional dangers associated with hearsay are not present. As pointed out in Sopinka, Lederman and Bryant, *supra*, at pp. 278-79:

> ... a statement which was earlier made under oath, subjected to cross-examination and admitted as testimony at a former proceeding is received in a subsequent trial *because the dangers underlying hearsay evidence are absent.*
>
> Other exceptions are based not on negating traditional hearsay dangers, but on the fact that the statement provides circumstantial guarantees of reliability. This approach is embodied in recognized exceptions such as dying declarations, spontaneous utterances, and statements against pecuniary interest. [Emphasis in original; para. 212.]

Some of the traditional exceptions stand on a different footing, such as admissions from parties (confessions in the criminal context) and co-conspirators' statements: see *Mapara*, at para. 21. In those cases, concerns about reliability are based on considerations other than the party's inability to test the accuracy of his or her own statement or that of his or her co-conspirators. Hence, the criteria for admissibility are not established in the same way. However, in cases where the exclusionary rule is based on the usual hearsay dangers, this distinction between the two principal ways of satisfying the reliability requirement, although not by any means one that creates mutually exclusive categories, may assist in identifying what factors need to be considered on the admissibility inquiry.

Khan is an example where the reliability requirement was met because the circumstances in which the statement came about provided sufficient comfort in its truth and accuracy. Similarly in *Smith*, the focus of the admissibility inquiry was also on those circumstances that tended to show that the statement was true. On the other hand, the admissibility of the hearsay statement in *B. (K.G.)* and *Hawkins* was based on the presence of adequate substitutes for testing the evidence. As we shall see, the availability of the declarant for cross-examination goes a long way to satisfying the requirement for adequate substitutes. In *U. (F.J.)*, the Court considered both those circumstances tending to show that the statement was true and the presence of adequate substitutes for testing the evidence. *U. (F.J.)* underscores the heightened concern over reliability in the case of prior inconsistent statements where the trier of fact is invited to accept an out-of-court statement over the sworn testimony from the same declarant. I will briefly review how the analysis of the Court in each of those cases was focussed on overcoming the particular hearsay dangers raised by the evidence.

. . . . .

Revisiting paras. 215 and 217 in Starr

As I trust it has become apparent from the preceding discussion, whether certain factors will go only to ultimate reliability will depend on the context. Hence, some of the comments at paras. 215 and 217 in *Starr* should no longer be followed. Relevant factors should not be categorized in terms of threshold and ultimate reliability. Rather, the court should adopt a more functional approach as discussed above and focus on the particular dangers raised by the hearsay evidence sought to be introduced and on those attributes or circumstances relied upon by the proponent to overcome those dangers. In addition, the trial judge must remain mindful of the limited role that he or she plays in determining admissibility — it is crucial to the integrity of the fact-finding process that the question of ultimate reliability not be pre-determined on the admissibility *voir dire*.

I want to say a few words on one factor identified in *Starr*, namely "the presence of corroborating or conflicting evidence" since it is that comment that appears to have raised the most controversy. I repeat it here for convenience:

> Similarly, I would not consider the presence of corroborating or conflicting evidence. On this point, I agree with the Ontario Court of Appeal's decision in *R. v. C. (B.)* (1993), 12 O.R. (3d) 608; see also *Idaho v. Wright*, 497 U.S. 805 (1990). [para. 217]

I will briefly review the two cases relied upon in support of this statement. The first does not really provide assistance on this question and the second, in my respectful view, should not be followed.

. . . .

Idaho v. Wright, 497 U.S. 805 (1990), is more on point. In that case, five of the nine justices of the United States Supreme Court were not persuaded that "evidence corroborating the truth of a hearsay statement may properly support a finding that the statement bears 'particularized guarantees of trustworthiness'" (p. 822). In the majority's view, the use of corroborating evidence for that purpose "would permit admission of a presumptively unreliable statement by bootstrapping on the trustworthiness of other evidence at trial, a result we think at odds with the requirement that hearsay evidence admitted under the Confrontation Clause be so trustworthy that cross-examination of the declarant would be of marginal utility" (p. 823). By way of example, the majority observed that a statement made under duress may happen to be true, but evidence tending to corroborate the truth of the statement would be no substitute for cross-examination of the declarant at trial. The majority also raised the concern, arising mostly in child sexual abuse cases, that a jury may rely on the partial corroboration provided by medical evidence to mistakenly infer the trustworthiness of the entire allegation.

In his dissenting opinion, Kennedy J., with whom the remaining three justices concurred, strongly disagreed with the position of the majority on the potential use of supporting or conflicting evidence. In my view, his reasons echo much of the criticism that has been voiced about this Court's position in *Starr*. He said the following:

> I see no constitutional justification for this decision to prescind corroborating evidence from consideration of the question whether a child's statements are reliable. It is a matter of common sense for most people that one of the best ways to determine whether what someone says is trustworthy is to see if it is corroborated by other evidence. In the context of child abuse, for example, if part of the child's hearsay statement is that the assailant tied her wrists or had a scar on his lower abdomen, and there is physical evidence or testimony to corroborate the child's statement, evidence which the child could not have fabricated, we are more likely to believe that what the child says is true. Conversely, one can imagine a situation in which a child makes a statement which is spontaneous or is otherwise made under circumstances indicating that it is reliable, but which also contains undisputed factual inaccuracies so great that the credibility of the child's statements is substantially undermined.

Under the Court's analysis, the statement would satisfy the requirements of the Confrontation Clause despite substantial doubt about its reliability. [pp. 828-29]

Kennedy J. also strongly disagreed with the majority's view that only circumstances surrounding the making of the statement should be considered:

The [majority] does not offer any justification for barring the consideration of corroborating evidence, other than the suggestion that corroborating evidence does not bolster the "inherent trustworthiness" of the statements. But for purposes of determining the reliability of the statements, I can discern no difference between the factors that the Court believes indicate "inherent trustworthiness" and those, like corroborating evidence, that apparently do not. Even the factors endorsed by the Court will involve consideration of the very evidence the Court purports to exclude from the reliability analysis. The Court notes that one test of reliability is whether the child "use[d] . . . terminology unexpected of a child of similar age." But making this determination requires consideration of the child's vocabulary skills and past opportunity, or lack thereof, to learn the terminology at issue. And, when all of the extrinsic circumstances of a case are considered, it may be shown that use of a particular word or vocabulary in fact supports the inference of prolonged contact with the defendant, who was known to use the vocabulary in question. As a further example, the Court notes that motive to fabricate is an index of reliability. But if the suspect charges that a third person concocted a false case against him and coached the child, surely it is relevant to show that the third person had no contact with the child or no opportunity to suggest false testimony. Given the contradictions inherent in the Court's test when measured against its own examples, I expect its holding will soon prove to be as unworkable as it is illogical.

The short of the matter is that both the circumstances existing at the time the child makes the statements and the existence of corroborating evidence indicate, to a greater or lesser degree, whether the statements are reliable. If the Court means to suggest that the circumstances surrounding the making of a statement are the best indicators of reliability, I doubt this is so in every instance. And, if it were true in a particular case, that does not warrant ignoring other indicators of reliability such as corroborating evidence, absent some other reason for excluding it. If anything, I should think that corroborating evidence in the form of testimony or physical evidence, apart from the narrow circumstances in which the statement was made, would be a preferred means of determining a statement's reliability for purposes of the Confrontation Clause, for the simple reason that, unlike other indicators of trustworthiness, corroborating evidence can be addressed by the defendant and assessed by the trial court in an objective and critical way. [References omitted; pp. 833-34.]

In my view, the opinion of Kennedy J. better reflects the Canadian experience on this question. It has proven difficult and at times counterintuitive to limit the inquiry to the circumstances surrounding the making of the statement. This Court itself has not always followed this restrictive approach. Further, I do not find the majority's concern over the "bootstrapping" nature of corroborating evidence convincing. On this point, I agree with Professor Paciocco who commented on the reasoning of the majority in *Idaho v. Wright* as follows (at p. 36):

The final rationale offered is that it would involve "bootstrapping" to admit evidence simply because it is shown by other evidence to be reliable. In fact, the "bootstrapping" label is usually reserved to circular arguments in which a questionable piece of evidence "picks itself up by its own bootstraps" to fit within an exception. For example, a party claims it can rely on a hearsay statement because the statement was made under such pressure or involvement that the prospect of concoction can fairly be disregarded, but then relies on the contents of the hearsay statement to prove the existence of that pressure or involvement: *Ratten v. The Queen*, [1972] A.C. 378. Or, a party claims it can rely on the truth of the contents of a statement because it was a statement made by an opposing party litigant, but then relies on the contents of the statement to prove it was made by an opposing party litigant: see *R. v. Evans*, [1991] 1 S.C.R. 869. Looking to *other* evidence to confirm the reliability of evidence, the thing *Idaho v. Wright* purports to prevent, is the very antithesis of "bootstrapping."

Turning to the case at bar, the Court decided that S's videotaped statement to the police was inadmissible. Although S's death before trial made his hearsay statement necessary, the statement did not meet concerns as to reliability. Since S had died before the trial, he was no longer available to be seen, heard and cross-examined in court. There was no opportunity for contemporaneous cross-examination. Nor had there been an opportunity for cross-examination at any other hearing. Although S was elderly and frail at the time he made the allegations, there is no evidence that the Crown attempted to preserve his evidence by application under ss. 709 to 714 of the Criminal Code. He did not testify at the preliminary hearing.

Obviously, there was no case to be made here on the presence of adequate substitutes for testing the evidence. There were no adequate substitutes here for testing the evidence. There was the police video — nothing more. There was also no case to be made on the inherent trustworthiness of the statement. S was elderly and frail. His mental capacity was at issue. There was also the possibility that his injuries were caused by a fall rather than an assault. The evidence of the garbage bags filled with S's possessions provided little assistance in assessing the likely truth of his statement — he could have filled those bags himself. C's obvious motive to discredit the accused presented further difficulties. The extent to which S may have been influenced in making his statement by this disgruntled employee was a live issue. S had issues of his own with the way the retirement home was managed. This was apparent from his rambling complaints on the police video itself. The absence of an oath and the simple "yes" in answer to the police officer's question as to whether he understood that it was important to tell the truth did not give much insight on whether he truly understood the consequences for the accused of making his statement. In these circumstances, S's unavailability for cross-examination posed significant limitations on the accused's ability to test the evidence and, in turn, on the trier of fact's ability to properly assess its worth.

The crux of the trial judge's finding that the evidence was sufficiently trustworthy was based on the "striking similarities" between the statements of the five complainants. The possibility that the presence of a striking similarity between statements from different complainants could well provide sufficient cogency to warrant the admission of hearsay evidence in an appropriate case. However, the statements made by the other complainants in this case posed even greater difficulties and could not be substantively admitted to assist in assessing the reliability of S's allegations.

This judgment on the hearsay rule is a tour de force. Justice Charron provides a detailed and instructive review of the current law of hearsay and in particular of the Court's principled approach which requires proof of necessity and reliability before hearsay evidence can be admitted. She takes us all back to first principles in rehearsing how hearsay should be identified and why judges should be mindful about admitting presumptively inadmissible hearsay.

In identifying a "functional" approach she emphasises the need for flexibility in the approach to the factor of reliability. She finds this largely reflected in the Supreme Court's jurisprudence, which she fully reviews. The most important change in the law comes at the end of this lengthy judgment when the Court expressly reversed *R. v. Starr* to the extent that it divided factors into categories relevant to threshold and those relevant to ultimate reliability and forbade consideration of evidence extrinsic to the making of the statement. As the Court recognises, without providing citations, most judges and commentators have found no wisdom in those quick and restrictive *obiter*. Laurie Lacelle in "The Role of Corroborating Evidence in Assessing the Reliability of Hearsay Statements for Substantive Purposes"[45] long ago pointed out that not allowing consideration of extrinsic evidence such as medical evidence of bruises would have a detrimental and undesirable effect on the prosecution of domestic assault cases where, for example, the complainant's out-of-court statement speaks of assault causing bruises but she has now recanted.

Of course, as the ruling in *Khelawon* on the facts demonstrates, the existence of corroborating physical evidence will not necessarily be determinative on the issue of sufficient reliability. So too the Court stresses in its ruling on the facts that just because there are striking similarities in other statements there is to be no "rigid pigeon hole" admission.[46] The catchword is case by case flexibility looking to all the facts. For those concerned by the length of pre-trial *voir dires*, it is noteworthy that in *Khelawon* itself it was agreed that the *voir dire* on the statements would determine the result at trial.

In passing, the Court confirms the ruling in *R. v. Mapara*,[47] on the relationship between traditional exceptions and the principled approach. *Starr* seemed to promise that there would be a thorough review of each existing exception to see whether the principled requirements of necessity and reliability were met. Here, the Court again accepts the *Mapara* ruling that traditional exceptions are presumptively valid. With the Court's own acceptance of the wide co-conspirator's exception in *Mapara*, there seems little likelihood that existing exceptions will be re-configured. The only change so far has been with respect to the present intention exception in *Starr*. On the other hand, where the exception is narrow, the principled approach may be available as an avenue to admission in an appropriate case.[48]

---

45 (1999) 19 C.R. (5th) 376.
46 See expressly at para. 45.
47 [2005] 1 S.C.R. 358, 195 C.C.C. (3d) 225, 28 C.R. (6th) 1.
48 See, for example, Hill J. in *R. v. West* (2001), 45 C.R. (5th) 307 (Ont. S.C.) who avoided the rigours of statutory business records requirements by going straight to the principled approach to admit a forensic report from an expert who was now deceased. See similarly, Romilly J. in *R. v. Larsen* (2001), 42 C.R. (5th) 49 (B.C. S.C.) respecting hospital records.

Motive to lie has played a central role in determinations of threshold reliability and will continue so after *Khelawon.*

R. v. BLACKMAN
2008 CarswellOnt 3722, 2008 CarswellOnt 3723, 232 C.C.C. (3d) 233,
[2008] 2 S.C.R. 298, 57 C.R. (6th) 12

The accused was charged with first degree murder of E. The Crown's theory was that the shooting was in revenge for E having earlier stabbed the accused. The Crown also alleged that in the months before the shooting, the accused and two other men unsuccessfully tried to kill E. Before the fatal shooting, E allegedly told his mother about the stabbing and attempt on his life. The trial judge admitted E's statement to his mother under the principled approach. The accused was convicted. The Court of Appeal dismissed his appeal. Justice Simmons dissented and would have ordered a new trial. The accused appealed to the Supreme Court. One of the issues before the Court was the relevance of an apparent absence of motive for E to lie to his mother.

CHARRON J. (for the Court):-

. . .

5.2.2 The Question of Motive

[39] Simmons J.A. was of the view that, much as in *Czibulka*, "the trial judge erred by founding his implicit conclusion that Ellison had no motive to fabricate on an absence of evidence of a motive to fabricate" (para. 106). In *Czibulka*, the Court of Appeal for Ontario overturned the accused's conviction for second degree murder based on the trial judge's failure to distinguish between an absence of evidence of motive and evidence of an absence of motive in his assessment of threshold reliability. Rosenberg J.A., in writing for the court, explained the distinction between the two concepts as follows (at para. 35):

It seems to me that it was fundamental to the trial judge's conclusion about reliability that the deceased had "no apparent motive to lie". In my view, however, since there was little or no evidence of the circumstances under which the letter was written, the trial judge had no evidence that the deceased had no motive to lie. The trial judge appeared to approach the question of fabrication by using the absence of evidence of fabrication to find that there was no evidence of a motive to fabricate. There was nothing in the circumstances to justify this approach. This was not a case like *Khan*, for example, where it was apparent from the circumstances as related by the mother that the declarant child had no motive to accuse the accused falsely. The absence of evidence of motive to fabricate is not the same as evidence of the absence of motive to fabricate. In fact, what evidence exists tells against the deceased having no motive to fabricate. [Emphasis added.]

[40] The court in *Czibulka* added that where there is no evidence of a motive to lie, motive "is in effect a neutral consideration" (para. 43).

[41] The distinction between an "absence of evidence of motive to fabricate" and "evidence of absence of motive to fabricate", if taken out of context, can be rather elusive. It is therefore important to consider the Court of Appeal's decision in *Czibulka* in context. First, there was "little or no evidence" before the court about the circumstances surrounding the writing of the letter by the deceased. In addition, the Court of Appeal was of the view that what evidence did exist supported the *opposite* conclusion on the question of motive. Therefore, the trial judge's finding that there was no motive to fabricate was held to be unreasonable and unsupported by the evidence. Second, the trial judge's decision on threshold reliability essentially *turned* on the finding that the deceased had no motive to lie in her letter about the accused's alleged abusive conduct. Therefore, since the decision on threshold reliability was without support in the evidence, the trial judge's error on motive was decisive on appeal.

[42] There is no doubt that the presence or absence of a motive to lie is a relevant consideration in assessing whether the circumstances in which the statements came about provide sufficient comfort in their truth and accuracy to warrant admission. It is important to keep in mind, however, that motive is but one factor to consider in the determining of threshold reliability, albeit one which may be significant depending on the circumstances. The focus of the admissibility inquiry in all cases must be, not on the presence or absence of motive, but on the particular dangers arising from the hearsay nature of the evidence. In *Czibulka*, the question of motive, in the circumstances of that case, was a very significant factor. If the deceased had a motive to lie about the accused abusing her, the contents of her letter could not be relied on for their truth. In other cases, motive may not feature so prominently.

[43] Here, the majority of the Court of Appeal concluded that, unlike in *Czibulka*, there was circumstantial evidence to support the inference that Mr. Ellison had no motive to lie to Ms. Freckleton. I agree with the majority's conclusion that, the trial judge considered the relevant factors in determining whether Mr. Ellison had a motive to fabricate, including the nature of the relationship between Mr. Ellison and his mother and the context in which the statements were made. Among other factors, the trial judge noted that this was a case of a "shot and wounded" son telling his mother about the circumstances surrounding the shooting, an incident she already knew about from independent sources. Mr. Ellison had nothing to gain by telling this story falsely to his mother. As the trial judge put it, "[i]f he wanted to mislead her the easiest thing would be to say it was a stranger who shot him, thereby minimizing his own blameworthiness from the stabbing." Also, if he wanted to lie to his mother in order to alleviate her fears, linking his shooting to his own stabbing would achieve the opposite. Hence, this was "hardly a factor that suggests unreliability and perhaps a factor that suggest[s] the opposite to some degree." The trial judge was further of the view that the statements were "contemporaneous enough, having regard to the unusual and attention-focusing nature of the event . . . to provide some measure of reliability." Finally, the trial judge held that "[h]aving regard to the code of silence testified to by Detective

Prisor, there is an inherent plausibility and logical consistency in telling his mother more about the identity of the shooters than he told the police." In my respectful view, Simmons J.A. placed too much emphasis on the distinction drawn in *Czibulka*, a distinction which has no application on the facts here.

[44] In distinguishing *Czibulka*, the majority also noted that there were other indicia of reliability present including, as noted by the trial judge, that the statements were against Mr. Ellison's interest. In my view, it cannot be said that the statements were against interest in the hearsay sense of the term. The statements would not satisfy the criteria of the traditional hearsay exception for declarations against interest. There is also no suggestion in the evidence that Ms.Freckleton was inclined to go to the police and report that her son had stabbed someone the summer before. That being said, however, I am not persuaded that the mischaracterization of this factor had any significant bearing on the trial judge's ruling.

. . .

Appeal dismissed.

In *R. v. Pasqualino*,[49] LaForme J.A. (Laskin and Rosenberg JJ.A. concurring) refused to declare a broad rule that hearsay statements uttered during the course of marital difficulties or imminent divorce proceedings are presumptively unreliable under the principled exception. The existence of a motive to lie was just one factor to consider when determining threshold reliability. There should be no broad rule of presumptive exclusion.

R. v. DEVINE
2008 CarswellAlta 784, 2008 CarswellAlta 785, 232 C.C.C. (3d) 1, 57 C.R.
(6th) 1, [2008] 2 S.C.R. 283

The accused was charged with robbery and assault causing bodily harm. The complainant (S) was allegedly assaulted by the accused a second time. S and P, a witness, refused to give a statement after the first assault but agreed following the second one, and both identified the accused as S's assailant. At trial, they recanted their identification. The trial judge admitted P's statement under the principled approach and convicted the accused (the Crown did not seek to introduce the complainant's statement because it was not videotaped). The Court of Appeal dismissed the appeal. The accused appealed to the Supreme Court.

CHARRON J. (for the Court):—

. . .

[25] Here, there was no contemporaneous cross-examination as in *R. v. Hawkins*, [1996] 3 S.C.R. 1043, but the *K.G.B.* requirements were found by the trial judge to have been complied with:

---

49 (2008) 233 C.C.C. (3d) 319 (Ont. C.A.).

the statement was videotaped and recorded, and before Ms. Pawliw gave her statement, a police officer explained the seriousness of making the statement, the possible consequences of giving a false statement, and administered a form of oath. These factors were identified in *K.G.B.* as the general attributes of in-court testimony that provide the usual safeguards of reliability (pp. 795-96).

In the words of *K.G.B.*, together with the availability of the declarant for cross-examination, these attributes bring "the prior statement to a comparable standard of reliability" such that the statement can be "admitted as substantive evidence" (p. 787).

[26] It is important to note that the availability of the declarant to be cross-examined will not necessarily tip the scales in favour of admissibility. In order for this factor to weigh in favour of admission, there must be a "full opportunity to cross-examine the witness" at trial (*K.G.B.*, at p. 796). As this Court explained in *R. v. U. (F.J.)*, [1995] 3 S.C.R. 764, at para. 46:

> The first factor contributing to reliability is the cross-examination of the witness. If the witness provides an explanation for changing his or her story, the trier of fact will be able to assess both versions of the story, as well as the explanation. However, where a witness does not recall making an earlier statement, or refuses to answer questions, the trial judge should take into account that this may impede the jury's ability to assess the ultimate reliability of the statement.

[27] For example, in *R. v. Post* (2007), 217 C.C.C. (3d) 225, 2007 BCCA 123, the accused pointed to the trial judge's finding that the *K.G.B.* factors were all present to support his argument that the witness's police statement should be admitted under the principled approach to hearsay. A unanimous Court of Appeal rejected this argument, noting that "it is clear that the most important of these three, namely the opportunity for cross-examination, existed only notionally because while Malloway was present in the courtroom, there was no real opportunity to test her account because of her inability to recall what she saw, or to say that what she had said previously was true" (para. 65). A similar conclusion was reached in *R. v. N. (T.G.)* (2007), 216 C.C.C. (3d) 329, 2007 BCCA 2. The Court of Appeal in that case concluded (at para. 17):

> In this case, any "full opportunity to cross-examine" was completely frustrated. There was no meaningful comparison between different accounts because Mason denied any knowledge of the facts, apart from a grudging concession that he had given a statement to the police, which he asserted was completely false.

[28] Here, although Ms. Pawliw recanted her identification of Mr. Devine at trial, there was a meaningful opportunity to test her evidence through cross-examination. Ms. Pawliw testified under oath that at the time she gave her statement, she was aware of the seriousness of the statement and told the truth to the best of her ability. The trial judge was able to assess the witness's demeanour, and gave a detailed account of her evasiveness and reluctance to identify Mr. Devine in the courtroom. He concluded by stating as follows (at para. 41):

> I have reviewed the manner of Ms. Pawliw giving evidence on the stand and compared it to the straightforward manner in which she described the incident, and Mr. Devine's

involvement, when she gave the KGB statement to the police. I conclude that she was trying to avoid identifying the accused from the witness stand and is trying to distance herself on the witness stand from any identification of the accused.

There is no reason to disturb the trial judge's finding in this regard.

. . .

Appeal dismissed.

What role does policy play in the principled approach? In *R. v. Couture*[50] the Supreme Court held that the principled approach to hearsay had to yield to the existing rules on spousal incompetency and compellability. Recall earlier from our discussion of spousal competence and compellability that in *Couture*, the accused's wife gave a statement to the police in which she recounted her husband's confession that he had murdered two women. The issue before the Supreme Court was whether the statements should have been admitted at trial under the principled approach. Necessity was met because she was not a competent witness for the prosecution. In an earlier case, the Court in *R. v. Hawkins*[51] had admitted hearsay evidence (i.e. her preliminary inquiry evidence) given by the accused's wife under the principled approach. The Court had to confront that case in *Couture*.[52] Justice Charron, writing for McLachlin C.J. and Binnie, LeBel and Fish JJ., held:

> From the outset, it can readily be appreciated that the circumstances surrounding the *creation* of the evidence in this case raise concerns about the spousal incompetency rule. Unlike the situation in *Hawkins*, in the present case the spouse's statements were given during the course of the marriage. While no issue respecting privileged communications made during the course of a marriage arises here and a spouse is at liberty to speak to the police, I agree with Mr. Couture's submission that, as a matter of principle, the taking of a statement by the police *for the express purpose of introducing it in evidence against the declarant's spouse* raises concerns about the spousal incompetency rule and its underlying rationales. The police in this case did not obtain a videotaped statement under oath in accord with the requirements set out in *B. (K.G.)* for the purpose of introducing it in evidence. Nonetheless, as noted earlier, Darlene Couture expressed serious concerns about the implications that giving a statement would have on her marriage (see para. 25). If this Court were to rule that statements made by spouses can be admitted at trial based solely on threshold reliability without further regard to the spousal incompetency rule, I agree with Mr. Couture's contention that this would encourage the institutionalized taking of spousal statements for the express purpose of introducing them at trial, a practice that would seriously undermine the preservation of marital harmony. This result would constitute a significant inroad on Parliament's policy choice to maintain the rule against spousal incompetency, a result not intended by the majority in *Hawkins*. For that reason, I would conclude that this factor alone is sufficient to distinguish this case from *Hawkins*. The operation of the principled approach to the hearsay rule would effectively thwart the spousal competency rule and, consequently, cannot provide a basis for admitting the evidence in this case.[53]

---

50 [2007] 2 S.C.R. 517.
51 [1996] 3 S.C.R. 1043.
52 *Supra*, note 50.
53 Para. 71.

Justice Charron further held that the statement did not satisfy threshold reliability because the declarant could not be cross-examined and her statement was neither under oath or videotaped. The appeal was allowed, statement excluded and a new trial ordered.

(e) Establishing Necessity

R. v. PARROTT
[2001] 1 S.C.R. 178, 39 C.R. (5th) 255, 150 C.C.C. (3d) 449

A mature woman with a mental disability was seen being put into the accused's car parked outside the psychiatric hospital where the woman resided. After conducting a search which lasted over seven hours, the police located the car, with the woman and the accused, in a remote area. Her shorts and underwear were in disarray. She had bruises and scratches on her body. The woman made out-of-court statements to the police constable who found her and to the doctor who first examined her. Pointing to her injuries, she communicated that the man in the car had done it. The accused was charged with kidnapping and sexual assault. The out-of-court statements were admitted. The accused was convicted of kidnapping, acquitted of sexual assault, but convicted of assault causing bodily harm. The majority of the Court of Appeal held that the trial judge erred in admitting the hearsay evidence when the complainant herself was available to testify and there was no expert suggestion that she would suffer any trauma or adverse effect by appearing in court. The curative proviso of the Criminal Code was applied to maintain the conviction with respect to kidnapping but the conviction with respect to assault causing bodily harm was quashed and a new trial was ordered. The Crown appealed against the setting aside of the assault verdict.

BINNIE J. (MAJOR, BASTARACHE, and ARBOUR JJ. concurring): —

This appeal tests the limits of the principled hearsay exception that allows the Crown in exceptional circumstances to lead the out-of-court evidence of a complainant at a criminal trial without having him or her present in court and available for cross-examination by the defence.

In this case, the complainant in a kidnapping and sexual assault case was a mature woman who had suffered since birth from Down's Syndrome. She was considered mildly to moderately retarded and had been in institutional care for almost 20 years. Expert evidence was called to establish that her mental development was equivalent to that of a three- or four-year-old child and that her memory of events was poor. Her response to even the simplest questions was said to be not very coherent. The complainant herself was never called into the presence of the trial judge so that these attributes could be verified even though she was available and there was no suggestion that she would suffer any trauma or other adverse effect by appearing in court. Instead the court received evidence of out-of-court statements that she had earlier made to the police and to a doctor.

. . . .

About 7:00 p.m. on July 15, 1994, the respondent drove to the Waterford hospital, a psychiatric hospital in St. John's, and was seen talking to a female resident of the hospital who then brought the complainant to his car. James Barry, a psychiatric nursing assistant at the hospital observed these events from a distance of about 200 feet. He shouted at the respondent and the female resident but neither of them acknowledged the shouts. Mr. Barry testified he saw the female resident grip the complainant, seat her in the car and lift her knees and shut the door. He saw the respondent reach over the seat and lock the door. The respondent was observed giving the female resident $20. Mr. Barry reported the incident to his supervisors who called the police. Despite a search effort it took over seven hours to find the complainant. When she was found, both she and the respondent were still in the same car, now located in a remote coastal area at about 2:35 the next morning.

. . . .

The complainant made statements to police at the time of her being found, as well as to the doctor who first examined her. She repeatedly pointed to her injuries and stated "Man did it, bad man, man in car, patient". Police also conducted a videotaped interview the following day. She was questioned for 15 minutes in the presence of two nurses who had known and worked with her. She was asked about the marks on her hands, arm and face to which, in halting broken sentences, she replied that a man "in handcuffs" did it and that he should be "put in jail". She said that it happened "last night" and that he was wearing glasses and a black hat. She also communicated the facts that he scratched her in the car and that he smacked her.

. . . .

Analysis

While in this country an accused does not have an absolute right to confront his or her accuser in the course of a criminal trial, the right to full answer and defence generally produces this result. In this case, unusually, the Crown precipitated an inquiry under s. 16 of the Canada Evidence Act not for the purpose of establishing the testimonial competence of "a proposed witness", namely the complainant, but to lay an evidentiary basis to keep her out of the witness box. Having satisfied the trial judge entirely through expert evidence that the complainant neither understood the nature of an oath nor could communicate her evidence, the Crown used the *voir dire* as a springboard to establish the admissibility of hearsay evidence of her out-of-court statements under the principles established in *Khan.*

. . . .

This procedure raises two distinct though related issues, firstly the admissibility of the expert evidence at the voir dire, and secondly the admissibility of the complainant's out-of-court statements at the trial. In my view, these issues ought to have been resolved in favour of the respondent, as held by the majority judgment of the Newfoundland Court of Appeal, for the following reasons:

1. The expert evidence was improperly admitted at the voir dire. Trial judges are eminently qualified to assess the testimonial competence of a witness. The trial judge, after all, was to be at the receiving end of the complainant's communication, and could have determined whether or not she was able to communicate her evidence to him. If she had been called and it became evident that the trial judge required expert assistance to draw appropriate inferences from what he had heard her say (or not say), or if either the defence or the Crown had wished to pursue the issue of requiring an oath or solemn affirmation, expert evidence might then have become admissible to assist the judge. At the time the expert testimony was called, it had not been shown that expert evidence as such was necessary, and the testimony of Drs. Gillespie, Morley and Parsons was therefore inadmissible: *R. v. Mohan*, [1994] 2 S.C.R. 9.

2. Consequently, the trial judge erred in ruling at the conclusion of the *voir dire* that the complainant's out-of-court statements would be admissible at trial. Having dispensed with hearing from the complainant, and the expert medical testimony having been improperly admitted, the trial judge had no admissible evidence on which to exercise a discretion to admit the complainant's out-of-court statements.

3. Even if the expert medical evidence were to be admitted, and accepting the trial judge's conclusion that the out-of-court statements were "reliable" under the first branch of the *Khan* requirements, the trial judge still erred in the circumstances of this case in finding the admission of out-of-court statements to be "necessary" without first hearing from the complainant.

. . . .

Whether a complainant "is able to communicate the evidence" in this broad sense is a matter on which a trial judge can (and invariably does) form his or her own opinion. It is not a matter "outside the experience and knowledge of a judge or jury" (*Mohan*, supra, at p. 23). It is the very meat and potatoes of a trial court's existence.

Necessity

In *Rockey*, supra, Sopinka J. (for the majority) held that because the evidence regarding the child witness' competence to testify was equivocal, the out-of-court statements were not admissible on this basis. However, he further found that there was uncontroverted evidence that the child would be traumatized by giving evidence and decided that the out-of-court statements were necessary for that reason.

The complainant in this case could have been examined before the trial judge in a format that would have attempted to put her at ease. The trial judge could have ensured that nothing, including questions put to her by opposing counsel, would be used to demean or embarrass her. It is possible that, as anticipated by Dr. Gillespie, the complainant might have been incoherent or otherwise unable to communicate whatever she recalled of the events in question. On the other hand, it is also possible that she might, as suggested by Dr. Morley, have been able to give "some account of what happened to her". In the absence of any suggestion of potential trauma or other exceptional circumstances, I think the respondent was entitled to have this issue determined on the basis of the evidence of the complainant rather than on the conflicting opinions, however learned, of her various doctors.

I accept that it was kinder to the complainant to excuse her from appearing at the trial. It is possible, as my colleague LeBel J. suggests at para. 12, that her appearance "would have served no real purpose". But we do not know this. What we do know is that there were very serious accusations made against the respondent. He was confronted with evidence of her out-of-court statements taken in his absence and on which, of course, he could not cross-examine. As a result of the trial, he was sentenced to three years and nine months in jail in addition to the time already served. Compassion for the complainant must be balanced against fairness to the respondent.

While the concept of necessity "must be given a flexible definition capable of encompassing diverse situations" (*R. v. B. (K.G.)*, [1993] 1 S.C.R. 740, at p. 796), it must nevertheless be established on the facts of each particular case. Wells C.J.N., in dissent, observed that the phrase "to communicate the evidence" in s. 16(1)(b) requires exploration of whether the witness is capable of perceiving events, remembering events and communicating events to the court. This is so, but absent special circumstances, the exploration should include hearing from the witness herself.

The *Khan* principles of necessity and reliability were recently applied by a divided Court in *F. (W.J.)*, [1999] 3 S.C.R. 569, where the hearsay evidence of a child complainant was admitted but not until after the child herself had entered the witness box and demonstrated an inability to answer questions about the events surrounding the sexual assault. Even at that, Lamer C.J. dissented on the basis that the trial court had not adequately pursued the reasons why the child appeared unable to provide her recollection of events.

In this case, we are asked to take *F. (W.J.)* one step further. There was no attempt to seek the evidence directly from the witness/complainant even though there was no suggestion that she would suffer adverse effects from appearing in the witness box. No other explanation was given for her non-appearance. The Crown simply decided to relieve the trial judge of the burden of making his own decision, and left him to pick among the competing versions of her testimonial competence offered up by the medical experts.

In my view, if the witness is physically available and there is no suggestion that he or she would suffer trauma by attempting to give evidence, that evidence should generally not be pre-empted by hearsay unless the trial judge has first had an opportunity to hear the potential witness and form his or her own opinion as to testimonial competence. I say generally because there may arise exceptional circumstances where a witness is available and not called and the out-of-court statements may be nevertheless admitted. The Court was careful not to close the door to this possibility in *R. v. Hawkins*, [1996] 3 S.C.R. 1043, at paras. 71-72; *B. (K.G.)*, supra, at pp. 798-99; and *Rockey*, supra, per McLachlin J., concurring in the result, at para. 23. Green J.A. recognized that possibility in the majority judgment in this case (p. 111). The point is that there are no circumstances put in evidence here that would justify such an exceptional procedure.

The Crown in written and oral argument makes several points in justification of the procedure that was followed. It says, first of all, that while there was no evidence that the complainant would suffer trauma, nevertheless the Court can infer the likelihood of something approaching trauma from the video and the nature of the events she was to be asked about. Her otherwise reclusive existence in the Waterford Hospital suggests an inability to cope with the outside world. The Crown submits that "it would have been simply a bit of a circus and a bit of a farce to have gone through the procedure of calling her as a witness simply to be complete in relation to form", and "[i]t would have been, in effect, almost marking her as an exhibit simply for the purpose of bringing her into the Court and showing her to all sides".

Few complainants can welcome a courtroom appearance in a sexual assault charge, but there is no reason to think this complainant was more vulnerable than others on this account. If there was an issue about trauma, it ought not to have been left to inference. Psychiatric evidence was called specifically to address the necessity of having the complainant testify in person, and none of the doctors raised the issue of potential trauma. The onus was on the Crown to meet the *Khan* criteria for the hearsay exception. It was clear that trauma to a potentially vulnerable witness is an important consideration. No such evidence was called.

Further, as Green J.A. pointed out, the Court should not be quick to leap to the assumption that a person with mental disabilities is not competent to give useful testimony. Trauma should not be presumed, not only because such a presumption would deprive the accused of the ability to observe and cross-examine the witness, but also because stereotypical assumptions about persons with disabilities should be avoided. For the same reason, I disagree with my colleague LeBel J. that we should assume that the complainant's appearance in the witness box would be demeaning or an "infringement . . . of her dignity and integrity" (para. 22). Persons with disabilities should not be underestimated.

. . . .

For these reasons the judgment of the Newfoundland Court of Appeal should be affirmed and the Crown's appeal dismissed.

LeBel J. (L'Heureux-Dubé and Gonthier JJ. concurring) dissenting: —

. . . .

A hallmark of the principled approach to hearsay is flexibility. In moving away from the categorical approach of the past to hearsay exceptions, the Court signalled in the last decade an intention to render the rules governing the reception of hearsay evidence more responsive to individual situations. . . . When dealing with young children or people with mental disabilities, this approach seeks to address the necessity and reliability required for the admission of the evidence while at the same time safeguarding the dignity and integrity of the complainants or witnesses.

. . . .

We are far from the strict approach to hearsay which prevailed in the past.

Perhaps the most important aspect of the broad account of necessity quoted above is the fact that "the categories of necessity are not closed". Trial judges now have a much broader discretion to admit evidence which would otherwise be considered as hearsay. This court should not attempt to confine this discretion into limited categories, but should rather content itself with stating broad principles to guide judges in the exercise of their discretion.

. . . .

In this context, the ruling of the trial judge was not a narrow one limited to the application of a test of mental competence as in s. 16 of the Canada Evidence Act, R.S.C. 1985, c. C-5. The trial judge's inquiry was much broader. It sought to examine the whole of the complainant's condition as mandated by our principled approach to hearsay and necessity as discussed above. In that regard, the trial judge did not simply express a preference for the views of one of the experts heard, Dr. Gillespie. Barry J.'s decision examined more broadly the victim's childlike mental condition or mental retardation and its impact on her potential testimony. This careful consideration of the condition of the complainant led the judge to decide that she was incapable (as opposed to the more narrow concept of "incompetence") of testifying. He then decided that the out-of-court statements in the video should be received into evidence, because they met the reliability and necessity tests.

. . . .

This Court has without exception assumed a posture of deference toward a trial judge's assessment of testimonial capacity. As McLachlin J. admonished in *Marquard*, "[m]eticulous second-guessing on appeal is to be eschewed." The majority of the Court of Appeal engaged in just such a re-evaluation of the record and interfered too readily with the trial judge's findings. The trial judge was in a superior position to assess the expert testimony, which obviously confirmed his own observation of the complainant's abilities during her interview with Sergeant Ryan. In my view, the trial judge's decision to admit the hearsay evidence manifests no palpable error.

I would accordingly allow the appeal and restore the respondent's conviction.

Once admitted, a trial judge must provide a careful warning to the jury on the use it can make of a hearsay statement. In *R. v. Pasqualino* the Ontario Court of Appeal held:

> 62 This court has also held that with regard to hearsay evidence admitted for the purpose of proving the truth of its contents under the principled exception, the trial judge's jury instructions must explain the increased risk that such statements may be unreliable, as well as the jury's obligation to determine the reliability and weight it will attribute to such evidence: see *R. v. Blackman* (2006), 215 C.C.C. (3d) 524 at para. 85, aff'd 2008 S.C.C. 37; *R. v. Warner* (1994), 94 C.C.C. (3d) 540 at 551; *R. v. A.(S.)* (1992), 76 C.C.C. (3d) 522 at 527-29. In *Blackman*, Justice Cronk stated, at para. 85, that instructions concerning hearsay admitted under the principled exception are adequate so long as they make clear to the jury "the need to determine whether the [s]tatements were made and, if made, the nature of their contents, as well as the imperative to evaluate the evidence of the [s]tatements carefully and in the light of all the other evidence at trial."

DODGE v. KANEFF HOMES INC.
[2001] O.J. No. 1141, 2001 CarswellOnt 1099 (S.C.J.)

Kaneff Homes had agreed that Dodge would act as the real estate broker for the sale of a subdivision. The parties agreed on the payment of commission. Dodge's estate alleged that the vice president of Kaneff entered into an oral agreement with Dodge prior to his death that the commission payable to Dodge would be increased. The estate proposed to introduce evidence from Dodge's wife, and the ex-wife of the vice-president of Kaneff and others to support the existence of the oral agreement.

Per PITT J.:—

. . . .

The plaintiffs allege that on or about July 18, 1996, Raymond Dodge struck an oral agreement with Andy Berzins, whereby the commission rate payable to the Plaintiff Corporation would be increased from 2% to 4%. Raymond Dodge, the spouse of the plaintiff Susan Dodge, died suddenly and unexpectedly of a heart attack on December 24, 1996. It is the plaintiffs' position that certain notes made by Raymond Dodge, conversations he had with family members and friends in the months preceding his death, and an allegation by the former spouse of Andy Berzins of a conversation she had with Andy Berzins, all confirmatory of Raymond Dodge's recollection of the agreement, ought not to be excluded simply because Raymond Dodge is not available to testify at trial.

. . . .

Counsel quickly conceded that the real issue emanating from the application of the "principled approach", . . . is the issue of reliability, since in the present case necessity is obvious.

. . . .

The defendants contend that the absence of an opportunity for meaningful, contemporaneous, sworn cross-examination of the out-of-court declarant (the deceased) regarding the truth of the specific statement sought to be admitted—which is the rationale for the exclusion of hearsay evidence—will cause them irreparable harm. . . . The defendants accordingly argue that a hearsay statement may be admitted only if it "is made under circumstances which substantially negate the possibility that the declarant was untruthful or mistaken."

The defendants further allege that not only have the plaintiffs failed to adduce the evidence necessary to meet their burden of establishing reliability, by not providing the surrounding circumstances in which the alleged statements were made, but that the record contains undisputed facts which by themselves render the hearsay statement unreliable. They offer as examples:

(a) The deceased's failure to refer to the alleged agreement in communications with the defendants;

(b) The deceased's failure to increase the price of homes before his death, such increases having been a part of the alleged agreement and the basis for sustaining the increased commission rates;

(c) The very allegation that the deceased had promised to increase the price of the houses, since real- estate agents in the normal course of events do not determine the price of homes.

(d) The apparent lack of consideration for the alleged increase in the commission rate.

The defendants are particularly concerned about the circumstances under which the deceased is alleged to have told his spouse of the agreement to increase the rates. Susan Dodge will testify that on the morning after the agreement was made, the deceased's first words to her were "I got my deal." He then indicated the difficulty he had had in the negotiation, and the negotiating strategy he used, from which inferences may be drawn about Ray Berzins' response and his final agreement. The defendants argue that the attempt to provide testimony about what Berzins said is a form of double hearsay and therefore should require a higher level of reliability.

. . . .

Another important issue raised by the defendant's falls under the rubric of the interest or lack thereof of the declarant. It emanates from a passage in *Kahn*, *supra*, in the judgment of McLachlin J. at p. 541. Her Ladyship referred to *Ares v. Venner*, [1970] S.C.R. 608 at 624, a seminal case on the hearsay exception for business records. Hall J. quoted from the reasons of Lord Pearce's dissent in *Myers v. Director of Public Prosecutions*, [1965] A.C. 1001 at pp. 1040-41:

> I find it impossible to accept that there is any "dangerous uncertainty" caused by obvious and sensible improvements in the means by which the court arrives at the truth. One is entitled to choose between the individual conflicting obiter dicta of two great judges and I prefer that of Jessel M.R. His dictum was as follows, 1 P.D. 154, 241: "Now I take it the principle which underlies all these exceptions is the same. In the first place, the case must be one in which it is difficult to obtain other evidence, for no doubt the ground for admitting the exceptions was that very difficulty. In the next place the declarant must be disinterested: that is, disinterested in the sense that the declaration was not made in favour of his interest. And, thirdly, the declaration must be made before dispute or litigation, so that it was made without bias on account of the existence of a dispute or litigation which the declarant might be supposed to favour."

I respectfully suggest that since Raymond Dodge could not have predicted his demise, he may fairly be viewed as a disinterested party, since his assertion that there was an amended agreement could not have been made with a view to advance his interest.

. . . .

Of the plaintiffs' arguments, I find two particularly persuasive. The first is that at this stage, I am concerned only with threshold reliability, as ultimate reliability and the weight attached to it are to be decided later. . . . The second argument, even more important in my view, is that courts have held there is some flexibility with respect to the admissibility of hearsay evidence in civil proceedings, where the ultimate burden of proof is only on a balance of possibilities.

As I said at the outset, the main purpose of this proceeding is the plaintiffs' desire to determine whether the hearsay evidence is admissible so that they can decide whether they should devote scarce resources to a full-scale trial. A passage from Sopinka, *supra* at p. 195 may be appropriately quoted here:

> Accordingly, there may be instances where the necessity is so great—such as where the declarant is dead — that some elasticity on the issue of reliability may be given. . . .

> Is the standard of proof to establish admissibility less in civil cases, where the ultimate burden of proof is only on a balance of probabilities and other considerations such as expediency and the crippling costs of litigation come into question? Adams J., in *Clark v. Horizon Holidays Ltd. [supra]* in considering a wrongful dismissal case, had regard to the general flexibility in respect to the admission of hearsay evidence in the determination of such disputes as follows:

>> This is a wrongful dismissal case where alternative dispute resolution systems abound. All of these forums freely admit hearsay evidence in the name of informality, expediency and the reduction of cost. Indeed, those systems have arisen in reaction to the austere formalism of courts. In my view, Khan and Smith signal willingness in the judiciary to design procedures and evidentiary rules to enhance the accessibility, and therefore, the relevance of our courts.

On balance, it is my view that Raymond Dodge's death should not by itself completely deprive his estate of an opportunity to vindicate a contractual right he may have had. I am also mindful that, apart from the notes, in each instance one of the parties to the discussions will be available for cross-examination.

After careful consideration of the defendants' concerns, I am nonetheless prepared to admit the proffered evidence, except for the typed notes and the testimony of the son-in-law.

———————————

2. EXCEPTIONS

Professor Wigmore[54] sought to provide us with a theory which would explain the various existing exceptions to the hearsay rule and to generate a principled approach to the creation of new exceptions. Having eliminated from the hearsay category admissions and former testimony, he finds first, that with each of the other exceptions there are circumstances surrounding the making of the statement which guarantee its trustworthiness and so dispense with the need for an oath and cross-examination, and second, that some grounds of necessity exist resident in the unavailability of the declarant or the inconvenience in

———————————

54 5 Wigmore, *Evidence* (Chad. Rev.), s. 1420.

requiring his attendance.[55] But his teacher, Professor Thayer, in his historical researches, suggests no single theory to explain the various exceptions. He notes[56] rather, that along with the development of the hearsay rule in the late 17th century:

> There came a large and miscellaneous number of so-called "exceptions." Some of these, in reality, were quite independent rules, whose operation was rather that of qualifications and abatements to the generality of this other doctrine; rules which were coeval with the doctrine itself or much older. . . . a number of the so-called "exceptions" to the hearsay prohibition came in under the head of written entries or declarations; they came in, or rather, so to speak, stayed in, simply because they had always been received, and no rule against hearsay had ever been formulated or interpreted as applying to them. Such things, continuing at the present day, are, e.g., the admission of old entries and writings in proof of ancient matters, written declarations of deceased persons against interest, and in the course of duty or business; and, to a limited extent, a merchant's own account books to prove his own case. So also of regular entries in public books, a matter probably never even doubted to be admissible in evidence.

Nevertheless, Professor Wigmore's justification of the exceptions has become accepted by many as a useful tool for evaluating the creation of new exceptions.[57] The exact number of existing exceptions is unclear and the subject of some debate in the writings. Clearly all are not of equal importance and it is sufficient if the student is simply generally aware of their existence; those exceptions which regularly occur will need some exploration.

(a) Admissions

(i) *Generally*

The orthodox view is to treat admissions as an exception to the hearsay rule although they do not share the normal attributes, necessity and circumstantial guarantees of trustworthiness, possessed by the others. This fact has led some to suggest that, though admissible, they would be better characterized as non-hearsay.[58] An admission is, very simply, a statement made by a party tendered by the opposing party; the plaintiff or defendant in civil cases and the accused in a criminal case.

A number of theories have been suggested to justify the reception of admissions.[59] For this exception only, grounds of necessity obviously do not exist and trustworthiness is not always present, as there is no requirement that the

---

55 See the criticism by Morgan that if this demonstration of the law of hearsay seems rational and consistent, it is only a "seeming", and that Wigmore's theory has sadly encouraged piecemeal rather than fundamental reform: *Some Problems of Proof under the Anglo-American System of Litigation* (1956), Columbia University Press, pp. 167-68.

56 *Preliminary Treatise on Evidence* (1898), pp. 519-22.

57 See, *e.g.*, *Ares v. Venner*, [1970] S.C.R. 608 and s. 45 (3) of the Uniform Evidence Bill.

58 See Federal Rules of Evidence, Rule 801, 28 U.S.C.A. and Advisory Committee Note; see also McCormick, *supra*, note 18 at p. 629; 4 Wigmore, *Evidence* (Chad. Rev.), s. 1048; and Strahorn, "A Reconsideration of the Hearsay Rule and Admissions" (1937), 85 U. Pa. L. Rev. 564.

59 See their examination in Pickard, "Statements of Parties" (1978), 41 Mod. L. Rev. 124 together with his own suggested theory.

declarant have personal first-hand knowledge.[60] An example of the difference in approach may be seen in the case of *R. v. Peacock*.[61] It is usually accepted that a witness is not permitted to testify to his own age since his knowledge in that regard must clearly be founded on what someone else has told him, i.e., it is hearsay.[62] In *Peacock*, however, it was allowed that a police constable might relate the accused's *extra-judicial statement* of his own age, as such was an admission.

The various theories advanced to justify reception are grounded in ideas of fairness, responsibility and the adversarial nature of our system. Professor Morgan has offered:

> The admissibility of an admission made by the party himself rests not upon any notion that the circumstances in which it was made furnish the trier means of evaluating it fairly, but upon the adversary theory of litigation. A party can hardly object that he had no opportunity to cross-examine himself or that he is unworthy of credence save when speaking under sanction of an oath.[63]

And Professor Maguire:

> Your own words or other actions have turned out helpful to your adversary; because you are their author, evidence of them is admissible against you.[64]

And finally Chafee:

> What is said by a party or a person closely linked with him in respect to the transaction at issue is considered of such especial value that the usual rules are simply disregarded. This attitude is easier to grasp when we remember that a trial is not an abstract search for truth, but an attempt to settle a controversy between two persons without physical conflict.[65]

Lower courts have differed as to whether admissions of parties should also be subject to the necessity and reliability determination.[66] In *Khelawon*, Justice

---

60 See *Stowe v. Grand Trunk Pacific Railway* (1918), 39 D.L.R. 127 (Alta. C.A.); affirmed 59 S.C.R. 665; *R. v. Schmidt*, [1948] S.C.R. 333; *R. v. Turner* (1910), 3 Cr. App. R. 103, 161; but see *R. v. Marshall*, [1977] Crim. L.R. 106. Compare *Bird v. Adams*, [1972] Crim. L.R. 174 (Div. Ct.) and *R. v. Chatwood*, [1980] Crim. L.R. 46 (C.C.A.). See discussion in Cross, *Evidence*, 5th ed., p. 521. But see *R. v. Rydzanicz* (1979), 13 C.R. (3d) 190 (Ont. C.A.); *R. v. O'Neill* (1976), 31 C.C.C. (2d) 259 (Ont. C.A.). There appears to be a requirement that when the admission is not based on first-hand knowledge the party-opponent must have expressed his belief in the same: see Phipson, *Evidence*, 12th ed., p. 683 and Cross, *Evidence*, 5th ed., p. 522.

61 (1968), 3 C.R.N.S. 103 (Ont. Co. Ct.).

62 See, *e.g., Anthony v. Charter*, [1933] 1 D.L.R. 684 (Alta. C.A.). But compare the enlightened judgment of *R. v. Lachappelle* (1977), 38 C.C.C. (2d) 369 (Que. C.A.). And see the statutory provision in s. 658(2) of the *Criminal Code*.

63 Morgan, *Basic Problems of Evidence* (1962), p. 266.

64 Maguire, *Evidence, Common Sense and Common Law* (1947), p. 143.

65 "Review of Wigmore on Evidence" (1924), 37 Harv. L. Rev. 513 at 519.

66 For example, see *R. v. Osmar* (2007), [2007] O.J. No. 244, 2007 CarswellOnt 339, 217 C.C.C. (3d) 174, 44 C.R. (6th) 276 (C.A.), leave to appeal refused (2007), 2007 CarswellOnt 4187, 2007 CarswellOnt 4188 (S.C.C.); *R. v. Terrico* (2005), 199 C.C.C. (3d) 126, 31 C.R. (6th) 161 (B.C. C.A.); *R. v. Connolly* (2003), 176 C.C.C. (3d) 292 (N.S. C.A.); and *R. v. Foreman* (2002), 6 C.R. (6th) 201, 169 C.C.C. (3d) 489 (Ont. C.A.).

Charron makes an enigmatic comment that seems to suggest that such an inquiry should not occur:

> Some of the traditional exceptions stand on a different footing, such as admissions from parties (confessions in the criminal context) and co-conspirators' statements: see *Mapara*, at para. 21. In those cases, concerns about reliability are based on considerations other than the party's inability to test the accuracy of his or her own statement or that of his or her co-conspirators. Hence, the criteria for admissibility are not established in the same way. [par. 63]

In all fairness, if the adversary chooses to introduce a statement by the party-opponent he must introduce all of the statement and not just the portion which favours him. As noted in *Capital Trust Co. v. Fowler:* [67]

> The law seems quite settled that, if an admission is used by one party, it must be used in its entirety, that is, everything must be read that is necessary to the understanding and appreciation of the meaning and extent of the admission. It is also equally established that, if a party uses an admission, he makes it evidence in the cause both as to himself and as to the opposition party in the litigation as well; but, if he desires to contradict or qualify any statement in it, he may do so. He can therefore give other evidence so to contradict or qualify it, but, if he does not see fit to do so, the whole of the admission remains as evidence in the cause for the benefit of both parties.

While a party may have the right to insist that his adversary introduce the entirety of a single narrative, this governing principle does not, of course, demand that adversary must introduce all statements or none. As Kaufman, J. said:

> A word of warning may be in order. The fact that the prosecution is obliged, where it chooses to offer in evidence a declaration made by the accused, to introduce the whole, and not just parts, does not mean that an accused can create self-serving evidence by writing out a statement and handing it to the police. [68]

R. v. PHILLIPS
[1995] O.J. No. 2985 (Ont. Gen. Div.)

McIsaac J.:—

The accused, Lenard Roy Phillips, is charged with the murder of Provincial Constable Eric Nystedt as a result of a stabbing incident which took place in the early morning hours of July 3, 1993 in a relatively isolated cottage area near Furnace Falls, in the County of Haliburton. Mr. Phillips fled the scene and was not arrested until noon of the same day. At that time, he was located hiding in a ditch off Highway #503 several kilometres from the scene of the stabbing. The arresting officers, P.C. DeVoss and P.C. McMaster initially advised him at gunpoint that he was being arrested for stabbing a peace officer. That advice was shortly changed to include the killing of an officer. His response at that time was "I guess I really did it this time." He was immediately advised of his rights to

---

67 (1921), 64 D.L.R. 289, 292 (Ont. C.A.).

68 Kaufman, *The Admissibility of Confessions* (1979), p. 287. See the adoption of this caution in *R. v. Jackson* (1980), 57 C.C.C. (2d) 154 (Ont. C.A.).

counsel and he received the standard primary and secondary cautions. The defence waives the voluntariness of these statements.

When he was placed into the police cruiser, he asked the arresting officers "So who's the guy I murdered?" P.C. McMaster advised him that he should not say anything further when he said "Can I ask another question?" He did not speak further to these officers other than advising them that he wished to call his mother once they arrived at the Coboconk O.P.P. detachment at 12:34 p.m. At that time, he was asked if he wanted to call a lawyer. That led to his speaking to counsel before he was turned over to the investigating officers at 1:16 p.m. During that interview which lasted until 2:55 p.m., Mr. Phillips advanced several theories that either justified his actions by way of mistaken self-defence or partially excused his actions due to the consumption of alcohol or drugs. He claimed amnesia for the stabbing of P.C. Nystedt, but admitted taking a swing at "someone."

Counsel for Mr. Phillips submits that the utterances shortly after noon and the answers given in theinterview that took place between 1:16 p.m. and 2:55 p.m. constitute one entire statement and if the former part goes before the jury then they must hear the second part as well. On the other hand, the Crown suggests that the doctrine of severability applies and the second interview should be excluded on the principle that it is self-serving and is in no way explanatory of the statements made to the arresting officers.

In *Wigmore on Evidence* (Chadbourn Rev.), v. VII, at p. 670, the following comments from *Steward v. Sherman* 5 Conn. 244, 245 (1824) are presented as authoritative on the issue:

> The past and future cannot thus be brought together in order to form an artificial identity. The law never intends that a party may make evidence for himself from his own declarations, but merely that the meaning of a conversation shall not be perverted by proof of a part of it only.

My review of the Canadian jurisprudence with these observations of Hosmer, C.J. As one can easily see, the opportunity for reflection militates against the admissibility of such self-serving evidence.

. . . .

In this case, the statement by the accused to the investigating officers took place at least one hour after his initial contact with the arresting officers. In fact, the recorded interview did not begin until 1:33 p.m. It is clear that not only was Mr. Phillips speaking to completely different police personnel, but he had also had ample time for reflection on what he was going to say. Most importantly, he had had the benefit of legal advice in the interim. In my opinion, this is sufficient in itself to destroy any nexus between the two statements. I am not satisfied that anything said to P.C. Harvey and P.C. Bowen was an "amplification, qualification or explanation" of what he had said to P.C. DeVoss and P.C. McMaster at the time of his arrest.

The statement made or adopted by the party is admissible against that party, and in a joint trial an admission is only evidence against the party who made it and the trier of fact must be warned of its limited utility.[69] There remains a large danger that the jury will not follow the limiting instruction when the confession of the co-accused implicates the other. Indeed the limiting instruction has been referred to as a "placebo," a "medicinal lie," "a kind of judicial lie,"[70] as it is practically impossible to follow.[71]

The underlying philosophy of admissions which makes admissions only evidence against their makers produces at times "curious, but perfectly logical"[72] results. An admission by the correspondent of adultery with respondent wife is evidence only against him:

> I am obliged to find . . . that there was no evidence that the wife has committed adultery with this co-respondent, but there is evidence that the co-respondent has committed adultery with the wife. It is perfectly logical; that decision means not that what is in effect the same act was committed by the one person but was not committed by the other, it means that it is proved against the one but it is not proved against the other. That is the basis on which the law is administered; cases are decided upon proof and not upon suspicion and hearsay evidence.[73]

In some of the cases we will see this exception characterized as "a declaration against interest." This phrasing is confusing as there is no requirement that the statement be "against interest" when made,[74] and with respect to it being "against interest" when tendered, Professor Wigmore has noted:

---

69 It is "an advisable practice" that the jury be immediately warned when a confession is received in a joint trial that it is not evidence against a co-accused: see *Schmidt v. R.*, [1945] S.C.R. 438; *Chote v. Rowan*, [1943] O.W.N. 646 (C.A.). See too *R. v. Parberry* (2005), 202 C.C.C. (3d) 337 (Ont. C.A.).

70 Remarks attributed to Learned Hand J. and Jerome Frank J. in *Bruton v. U.S.*, 391 U.S. 123 (1968); in that case the U.S. Supreme Court held that a limiting instruction was not sufficient in such a case as the accused was denied his Sixth Amendment right to confront witnesses. It appears, then, that in the U.S. the prosecutor must proceed in separate trials or not tender the confession. It is interesting to note another solution which appears to have been the law in England until 1830: see *R. v. Hearne* (1830), 172 E.R. 676 and *R. v. Clewes* (1830), 172 E.R. 678. In a reporter's note to the latter case we read: "The practice has been, in reading confessions, to omit the names of other accused parties, and where they are used to say 'another person' 'a third person' & etc." In the above two cases Littledale, J. ordered the witnesses to use the names mentioned in the confession of the co-accused as it was seen necessary that the whole be repeated; he later noted that he would "take care to make such observations to the Jury, as will prevent its having any injurious effect against the other prisoners; and I shall tell the jury that they ought not to pay the slightest attention to this letter, except so far as it goes to affect the person who wrote it." *R. v. Fletcher* (1830), 172 E.R. 691.

71 An infrequent but allied problem concerns the use of one accused's pleas of guilty against his co-accused. See *R. v. Lessard* (1979), 50 C.C.C. (2d) 175 (Que. C.A.) and compare *R. v. Vinette* (1974), 19 C.C.C. (2d) 1 (S.C.C.).

72 *Morton v. Morton*, [1937] P. 151, 153.

73 *Ibid.* at 154-55. See also for a similar result *Harris v. Harris*, [1931] 4 D.L.R. 933 (Ont. S.C.).

74 See, *e.g.*, *R. v. Mandzuk* (1945), 85 C.C.C. 158 (B.C. C.A.); but see also *Piche v. R.*, [1970] 4 C.C.C. 27 (S.C.C.). Admissions by accused in criminal prosecutions must also be established as "voluntary", and this aspect will be considered later. Note however that the statement is receivable, as an exception to the hearsay rule, as an admission, though it was exculpatory in nature when made. And see Phipson, *Evidence* (11th ed.), p. 673.

... in effect and broadly, *anything said by the party-opponent may be used against him as an admission*, provided it exhibits the quality of inconsistency with the facts now asserted by him in pleadings or in testimony. (This proviso never needs to be enforced, because no party offers thus his opponent's statement unless it does appear to be inconsistent.) [Emphasis added.][75]

R. v. STREU
[1989] 1 S.C.R. 1521, 70 C.R. (3d) 1, 48 C.C.C. (3d) 321

The accused was convicted of possession of stolen property having a value in excess of $200. He sold the property to a police officer, who had posed as a purchaser, for $125. The officer testified that the accused, during conversation leading to the sale, had admitted that the tires and rims belonged to a friend who had "ripped them off." In the absence of the accused's statement there would not be evidence, sufficient to meet the criminal standard of proof, that the items were in fact stolen.

SOPINKA J.: —

. . . .

The evidence at trial indicated that the appellant attempted to sell four tires and rims to a police officer who posed as a purchaser. The police officer testified to the following conversation with the appellant:

I ask him, referring to the wheels: What are these off of? And he replies: A Volkswagen Rabbit. And I ask: Oh, yeah. From the City here? And he replies: I don't know. My friend ripped them off. I ask: Well, where's the other ones? Harv replies: They're in my house. I reply: Oh, I see. Well, I'll give you twenty bucks apiece. And he replies: I can't let them go for that, they are my friend's wheels. I ask: How much did he want. And Harv replies: He priced them out at one hundred and thirty apiece. That's for the rims. I reply: I'm not paying that much. Just yesterday I bought a 1984 Datsun for $180.

. . . .

Harv replies: Well, I know they're hot and all but they're his tires. I reply: Let me talk to your friend then. Harv replies: I know he'll be mad at me if I only get that much.

The appellant and the police officer proceeded to a garage at the end of a lane near the appellant's home to complete the sale. The appellant expressed concern that they not be observed. The police officer further testified that he paid the appellant $125 for the tires and rims.

. . . .

In *R. v. O'Neill* (1976), 13 C.R. (3d) 193 (Ont. C.A.), the only evidence against the accused regarding the theft of a stereo and turntable — the subjects of the charge against her of unlawful possession — was her statement to the

---

police. In response to the question of whether she knew that the items were stolen the accused replied "yes". She then added that she had been given the items by a male friend.

The Court of Appeal followed *R. v. Porter*, [1976] Crim. L.R. 58, in finding that the hearsay statement of the accused was not proof that the items were stolen. The Court, at p.194, cited the editorial commentary following *R. v. Porter* with approval:

> It is one thing for the accused to admit facts of which he has personal knowledge and for an inference to be drawn from those facts that the goods are stolen. It is another thing for the accused to 'admit' facts of which he has no personal knowledge.

In *R. v. Rydzanicz* (1979), 13 C.R. (3d) 190 (Ont. C.A.), the accused was charged with having in his possession a quantity of stolen cigarettes. The accused stated to the police that he saw his friend Mike enter the shopping centre and come out with a whole shopping cart full of cartons of cigarettes. The accused added that he helped Mike put the cigarettes in the back of the truck. The accused also stated that he knew that the cigarettes were stolen when he saw Mike come out of the shopping centre.

The accused was acquitted at trial on the strength of *R. v. O'Neill, supra*. The Court of Appeal overturned the acquittal because the trial judge had overlooked the fact that the accused stated that he saw Mike go into the store and come out with a shopping cart full of cigarettes. The Court of Appeal, at p. 192, held that:

> That admission was based on the personal knowledge of the respondent, and constituted evidence of relevant fact in a chain of circumstances in support of an inference that the cigarettes were stolen.

Aside from the accused's stated belief, sufficient circumstantial evidence existed to support a finding that the goods were stolen. The Court of Appeal added that it is a question of fact whether the inference that the goods were stolen should be drawn by the trier of fact.

In *R. v. Elliott* (1984), 15 C.C.C. (3d) 195 (Alta. C.A.), the accused was charged with possession of certain roof panels, the property of person or persons unknown, knowing them to "have been obtained by the commission in Canada of theft" contrary to s. 312 of the *Criminal Code*. The items involved were worth approximately $1,300 although the accused testified that he paid $150 for them, having purchased them from an unknown person in a bar. He did not receive a sales slip for the goods and the police testified that the accused told them that because of the low price he paid he realized they were "hot". There was no evidence as to where the goods had been obtained or who their owner was. On appeal by the accused from his conviction, the appeal was allowed and an acquittal entered.

The majority held that it was clear that the element of theft can be proved by circumstantial evidence. In this case, the circumstantial evidence was not strong enough to support the inference that the goods were stolen:

Here the only evidence of theft is proof of purchase for far below value, at a bar, from a stranger, without a bill of sale. Certainly, this gives rise to the suspicion that the goods which are being sold were stolen. Certainly in a civil case a court could prove on a balance of probabilities that a theft had occurred but I am of the opinion that proof of theft beyond all reasonable doubt has not been established by these facts alone. There has to be more. [p. 201]

. . . .

Although they do not always make it clear, some of these authorities deal with the question relating to the use to be made of an admission based on hearsay as a matter of weight, and others, as a matter of admissibility. In deciding which position is correct, account must be taken of the decision of this Court in *R. v. Schmidt*, [1948] S.C.R. 333, a case that apparently was not drawn to the attention of the Court of Appeal and is not referred to in the factum of either party in this Court. . . .

. . . .

The rationale underlying the exclusion of hearsay evidence is primarily the inherent untrustworthiness of an extra-judicial statement which has been tendered without affording an opportunity to the party against whom it is adduced to cross-examine the declarant. This rationale applies equally in both criminal and civil cases. It loses its force when the party has chosen to rely on the hearsay statement in making an admission. Presumably in so doing, the party making the admission has satisfied himself or herself as to the reliability of the statement or at least had the opportunity to do so. The significance of this factor is evident in the decision of this Court in *Ares v. Venner*, [1970] S.C.R. 608, in which evidence was admitted as an exception to the hearsay rule where the party against whom the evidence was tendered had the opportunity to test the accuracy of the evidence.

I agree with the following statement in *Kitchen v. Robbins*, 29 Ga. 713 (1860), cited by 4 *Wigmore, Evidence*, s. 1053 (Chadbourn rev. 1972) for which I am indebted to McWilliams, *Canadian Criminal Evidence* (2nd ed. 1984), at p. 428:

> Are no admissions good against a party, unless founded on his personal knowledge? The admissions would not be made except on evidence which satisfies the party who is making them against his own interest, that they are true, and that is evidence to the jury that they are true.

Accordingly, once it is established that the admission was in fact made, there is no reason in principle for treating it any differently than the same statement would be treated had it been made in the witness box. In the latter case, if a party indicates a belief in or acceptance of a hearsay statement, that is some evidence of the truth of its contents. The weight to be given to that evidence is for the trier of fact. On the other hand, if the party simply reports a hearsay statement without either adopting it or indicating a belief in the truth of its contents, the statement is not admissible as proof of the truth of the contents.

. . . .

Turning to the admission in question in this appeal, it is impossible to read it as merely reporting a hearsay statement without more. Clearly the appellant was relying on the hearsay statement as being true. Either he accepted it as being true or at least believed it to be true.

. . . Any evidentiary weakness in the information on which the admission was based was a matter of weight and not admissibility. This was a matter for the trial judge who considered the statement along with other evidence and concluded that the accused was guilty beyond a reasonable doubt.

Appeal dismissed.

(ii) *Confessions*

At common law, all statements made by an accused to a person in authority (i.e. a comfession) are inadmissible unless the Crown can prove voluntariness beyond a reasonable doubt. The voluntary confessions rule is addressed separately in the next section (**C. Voluntary Confession Rule**).

(iii) *Statements Adopted by Party's Conduct*

If an accusation is directed to a party in circumstances in which it would be reasonable to expect a denial should the accusation be untrue, the party's failure to deny will be received against him as an implied admission.[76]

The classic expression of this appears in *R. v. Christie:*

> . . . the rule of law undoubtedly is that a statement made in the presence of an accused person, even upon an occasion which should be expected reasonably to call for some explanation or denial from him, is not evidence against him of the facts stated save so far as he accepts the statement, so as to make it, in effect, his own. If he accepts the statement in part only, then to that extent alone does it become his statement. He may accept the statement by word or conduct, action or demeanour, and it is the function of the jury which tries the case to determine whether his words, action, conduct or demeanour at the time when a statement was made amounts to an acceptance of it in whole or in part. It by no means follows, I think, that a mere denial by the accused of the facts mentioned in the statement necessarily renders the statement inadmissible, because he may deny the statement in such a manner and under such circumstances as may lead a jury to disbelieve him, and constitute evidence from which an acknowledgment may be inferred by them.[77]

It would not be reasonable to take a party's failure to deny as an implied admission if the accusation was made by a police officer. An accused does have, at least on detention, a right to silence,[78] and it would violate that right if adverse inferences were to be drawn from its exercise.[79] There should be evidence that the party heard and understood the statement, and that given his personal

---

76 See *R. v. Christie*, [1914] A.C. 545 (H.L.); *R. v. Stein*, [1928] S.C.R. 553.
77 *Ibid.*, at p. 554, per Lord Atkinson.
78 See above Chapter 5.
79 See *R. v. Chambers*, [1990] 2 S.C.R. 1293 and *R. v. Turcotte*, [2005] 2 S.C.R. 519.

characteristics, emotional condition, and situation, a reasonable person would deny. Given the condition of admissibility, the evidence ought not to be received unless the trial judge is first satisfied that there is sufficient evidence from which a jury might reasonably find an acknowledgment.[80] The House of Lords thought this was a salutary rule of practice and, while they were unwilling to constitute it a rule of law, the view is well expressed by the British Columbia Court of Appeal in *R. v. Harrison*:[81]

> But there is a rule of practice that, for fear of prejudice to the accused, in case it is not shown that he has accepted the statement, that such evidence should not be allowed in until a foundation has been laid for its admission by proof of facts from which, in the opinion of the presiding Judge the jury might reasonably draw the inference that the accused had so accepted the statement as to make it in whole or in part his own.

Given the great prejudice that could result from the jury hearing the accusation, it is better to ensure in advance that there is some evidence of acceptance rather than charging them later to disregard in the absence of acquiescence.

Given that oral statements in the presence of the party may be adopted by silence, does the same hold true for written statements? Is it "reasonable to infer" that the recipient by his silence admits the truth of the statement?[82]

Nevertheless there are of course certain relationships where there has been mutual correspondence over a period of time which would make it "reasonable to infer" that failing to reply was an admission of the truthful nature of the communication, and each situation must be evaluated according to its own circumstances. For example, it has been noted:

> When a tradesman makes out his statement of account for goods against, and sends it to, a person, and that person takes no objection thereto, such statement and the failure to object are some evidence that the goods were furnished for the credit of that person . . .
>
> . . .
>
> In mercantile matters where an account is rendered it was said as far back as 1741 in *Willis v. Jernegan:* "There is no absolute necessity that it should be signed by the parties who have mutual dealings . . . it is not the signing which will make it a stated account but the person to whom it is sent, keeping it by him any length of time . . . which shall bind him."[83]

---

80 See McCormick, *Evidence*, 2d ed. (1972), p. 653.

81 [1946] 3 D.L.R. 690, 696. For an example of the importance of ensuring a foundation in advance see *R. v. Hryn* (1981), 63 C.C.C. (2d) 390 (Ont. Co. Ct.).

82 Compare *Bessela v. Stern* (1877), 46 L.J.C.P. 467 (C.A.) with *Wiedeman v. Walpole* (1890), 24 Q.B.D. 537. See also *R. v. Edwards*, [1983] Crim. L.R. 539.

83 *Sarbit v. Hanson & Booth Fisheries (Canada) Co.*, [1951] 2 D.L.R. 108, 112 (Man. C.A.) [citation omitted].

(iv) *Statements Authorized by Party*

R. v. STRAND ELECTRIC LTD.
(1968), 2 C.C.C. 264 (Ont. C.A.)

MacKay J.A.:—

. . . .

The Crown witness, Mr. McMurray, a duly authorized inspector under the Act, stated that he knew Richards and that he knew Richards was the supervisor on the subcontract for Strand Electric Limited. McMurray's evidence then continued as follows:

Question: Now, Mr. McMurray, did you have some conversation with Mr. Richards?

Answer: I did.

Question: And were the facts that he told you at that time voluntary?

Answer: Yes.

Question: Now, did Mr. Richards indicate to you what use was being made of the scaffold in question, which is shown in exhibits 1 through 4 and about which my learned friend has made certain admissions?

Answer: Mr. Richards admitted that he was engaging men on the scaffold . . .

By the Court: Question: He was what?

Answer: He was using workmen — or — using the scaffold by workmen.

Mr. Glass: Question: Did he make any observations as to who was using the scaffold?

Answer: He did, sir.

Question: And what did he admit to you as to his observations?

Answer: That the Frank Ribes was employed by Richards —

Question: By whom?

Answer: By Strand Electric, I'm sorry. Could I refer to my notes.

Question: Yes. These are notes that were made at the time of your investigation?

Answer: At the inspection, yes, sir. He agreed that Frank Ribes was an employee of Strand Electric and he was fully aware of the condition of the scaffold.

Question: When you say "he", to whom do you refer?

Answer: Mr. Alfred Richards, the super for Strand Electric.

Question: And did he make any observations about Mr. Ribes or about the scaffold or the two of them in combination?

Answer: Just that he was on the stage at the time of the accident. He was within ten feet of the scaffold in question.

Question: And did he make any observations as to who was using the scaffold before the accident, sometime before?

Answer: No, no, sir.

Question: Did he tell you or did he make any admissions to you as to what Mr. Ribes was doing?

Answer: Yes. Mr. Richard had mentioned that he was in the process of installing a sling on the top member of the uppermost platform of the scaffold, using the uppermost platform of the scaffold to install this sling.

Question: And did he admit whether or not he was aware that Mr. Ribes was on this scaffold?

Answer: Yes.

Question: I beg your pardon?

Answer: He was fully aware that Mr. Ribes was on the scaffold.

I am of the view that the Court below was right in holding that a supervisor on the location of the work was a person with authority as agent and employee of the appellant to make the admissions he did and that such statements were admissible as evidence as against the appellant company.

I adopt the statement of the author of *Cross on Evidence*, 2nd ed., pp. 441-2, as being a correct statement of the law on this point. The statement in part is:

> Statements made by an agent within the scope of his authority to third persons during the continuance of the agency may be received as admissions against his principal in litigation to which the latter is a party. So far as the reception of admissions is concerned, the scope of authority is a strictly limited conception. It is sometimes said that the agent must be authorised to make the admission, but that is a confusing statement for no one expressly or impliedly authorises others to make informal admissions on his behalf which may be proved against him in subsequent litigation.
>
> A better way of putting the matter is to say that the admission must have been made by the agent as part of a conversation or other communication which he was authorised to have with a third party.

Cross then refers to the case of *Kirkstall Brewery Co. v. Furness R. Co.* (1874), L.R. 9 Q.B. 468, where the plaintiff claimed damages for loss of a parcel, and it was held that a statement made by the defendants' stationmaster to a policeman suggesting that the goods had been stolen by a servant of the defendants could be proved against the defendants.

McLENNAN J.A., agrees with MacKAY J.A.

LASKIN J.A. (dissenting):—

. . . .

An accused's admissions are, of course, properly receivable in evidence against him from the mouth of the person to whom they were made. The rationale of the hearsay rule is not involved in the reception of such evidence to prove the truth of what was admitted. Where, as here, the accused is a corporation, it is not the hearsay rule that controls the reception of an admission against it; the question to be determined is by whose admissions and on what matters is the corporation vicariously committed. Principles of agency as well as of evidence must be considered.

. . . .

Two propositions underlie the reception of an agent's admissions against his principal. There must, first, be proof of the agency; and, as the textbooks say, unless the alleged agent testifies himself to his agency, his assertions that he is an agent, offered through the mouth of another, are inadmissible because as hearsay they beg the question: see 4 *Wigmore on Evidence*, 3rd ed., p. 123; *Cross on Evidence*, 3rd ed., p. 442. Second, the admissions of the agent tendered against the principal must have been made to a third party within the scope of his authority during the subsistence of the agency: *Wigmore on Evidence, op. cit.*, p. 119; *Cross on Evidence, op. cit.*, pp. 441-2. The application of the second of these propositions has, in the cases, revealed a different attitude of the Courts to the authority of an agent to "act" on behalf of his principal and his authority to "speak" on behalf of his principal, as if speech or conversation was not itself an act. There may, indeed, be justification for viewing authority differently in the two situations, but some of the case law exhibits, in relation to the reception of admissions, the same formal requirement of authority that in earlier days limited the develpment of vicarious liability in tort; and see also *Restatement of the Law*, Agency, 2d, ss. 286, 288 (1958).

The concept of authority, taken literally, would exclude as against the principal any admission of an agent tending to show liability in tort or penal liability, unless the agent is shown to have been authorized to make admissions to charge his principal. It would be a rare case to find such authority in any express sense; and, in the result, the admissions would be receivable only to impeach the agent, if, being called as a witness by the principal, he gave evidence with which the admissions were inconsistent. Authority as between agent and principal has in respect of vicarious liability of the principal to third parties, been translated into an issue of the scope of the agent's duties or employment, and I would apply the same test in relation to admissions by an agent which are tendered in evidence against the principal. The fact that penal liability is involved in the present case does not, in my view, make the test inapplicable here.

The approach that I am supporting would still make it necessary to examine carefully the admissible evidence on the scope of an agent's duties or employment lest the principal be charged by an admission not properly receivable against him. Of course, the trier of fact would also have to determine whether the admission offered against a principal was made; and, as in other cases where evidence is formally admissible, weight would have to be assessed. I do not think, therefore, that the test of admissibility that I have indicated would unfairly prejudice a principal who is a party or an accused in a proceeding against him.

In the present case, the fact of agency as between the accused and Richards is not, as I understood the submissions that were made, contested. McMurray, the inspector, testified that Richards was the supervisor for the accused. It does not appear that he was thereby reporting an assertion by Richards himself but rather that this was something that the inspector knew otherwise. I should note, in connection with the inspector's duties generally, that under ss. 12 [am. 1962-63, c. 22, s. 6] and 13 [am. 1965, c. 19, s. 5] of the Act an inspector may enter premises and may require information from any person in relation to any project. Certainly, in the absence of contrary evidence, it is proper to find that Richards was in a relationship of agency with the accused.

I turn, therefore, to the question of the scope of Richards' duties. Here too there is the problem that a finding on this matter cannot be based on the declarations of the agent where it is sought to receive them in evidence as admissions against the principal. So far as the evidence before us goes, it shows only that Richards is a supervisor of the accused, but in what respect and with what responsibilities does not appear. At one stage in the course of proceedings, counsel for the accused referred to Richards as the superintendent of the accused on the site of the project, but there was no indication as to what this title imported, whether it had to do with the disposition of men or material or inspection of the course of the work or anything else.

. . . .

Returning then to the issue of the scope of Richards' duties, the fact is that there was no evidence as to what his function as supervisor involved. I cannot therefore find that the prosecution has established that any workman of the accused was ordered or put on the defective scaffold by an agent acting in the course of his duties for the accused.

Appeal dismissed.

Quaere whether the exception should be limited to statements made to a third party; do not reports made to the party itself carry sufficient guarantees of trustworthiness? As Professor McCormick notes:

> While slightly less reliable as a class than the agent's authorized statements to outsiders, intra-organization reports are generally made as a basis for some action, and when this is so, they share the reliability of business records. They will only be offered against the principal when they admit some fact disadvantageous to the principal, and this kind of statement by an agent is likely to be true. No special danger of surprise, confusion, or prejudice from the use of the evidence is apparent.[84]

To receive vicarious admissions is consistent with the philosophy which underlies the subject as a whole: fairness, responsibility and the adversarial nature of our system. Scope of authority is key. As recited in a U.S. decision:

> The test of admissibility should not rest on whether the principal gave the agent authority to make declarations. No sensible employer would authorize his employee to make damaging statements. The right to speak on a given topic must arise out of

84 McCormick, *Evidence*, 2d ed., p. 643.

the nature of the employee's duties. The errand boy should not be able to bind the corporation with a statement about the issuance of treasury stock, but a truck driver should be able to bind his employer with an admission regarding his careless driving. Similarly, an usher should be able to commit his employer with an observation about a slippery spot on the lobby floor.[85]

Having agreed that scope of authority governs, it is perhaps sufficient to agree with Professor Wigmore that:

> Upon the application of the principle to specific instances, it would be useless here to enter, for only the rules of the substantive law of agency are involved.[86]

One particular form of agency does deserve mention. In a partnership each partner, when acting within the scope of the partnership, is an agent for the other partners and for the partnership. Applying the above principle, then, statements made by a partner while conducting the firm's business are receivable as admissions against the partnership if the existence of the firm is independently established.

(v) *Statements of Person with Common Purpose*

A particular form of partnership, of course, is conspiracy, civil or criminal. Responsibility underlies the receipt of statements of co-conspirators, as

> the basal reason for admitting the evidence of the acts or words of one against the other is that the combination or preconcert to commit the crime is considered as implying an authority to each to act or speak in furtherance of the common purpose on behalf of the others.[87]

Professor Wigmore notes:

> A conspiracy makes each conspirator liable under the criminal law for the acts of every other conspirator done in pursuance of the conspiracy. Consequently . . . the admissions of a co-conspirator may be used to affect the proof against the others, on the same conditions as his acts when used to create their legal liability.[88]

The statements to be received must then have been statements made during the term of the conspiracy and in furtherance of it, and not simply a narrative describing it.[89] This preliminary condition of admissibility presents a problem, as it coincides with the very fact sought to be established. When this concurrence exists[90] it seems reasonable that the statements be received if there is *some*

---

85 *Rudzinski v. Warner Theatres Inc.*, 114 N.W. 2d 466, 471 (Wisc., 1962).

86 4 Wigmore, *Evidence* (Chad. Rev.), s. 1078, p. 170. As an example of common sense, see *Tesco Supermarkets Ltd. v. Nattrass*, [1972] A.C. 153 (H.L.) restricting company's vicarious liability to acts of senior management.

87 *Tripodi v. R.* (1961), 104 C.L.R. 1, 7 (Aust. H.C.).

88 4 Wigmore, *Evidence* (Chad. Rev.), s. 1079, p. 180.

89 See *R. v. Miller* (1975), 63 D.L.R. (3d) 193, 217-21 (B.C.C.A.) and *R. v. Lynch* (1978), 40 C.C.C. (2d) 7, 24 (Ont. C.A.) re the distinction.

90 See generally on this point Cross, *Evidence*, 5th ed., pp. 69-71.

other evidence of a conspiracy and indeed the trial judge in his discretion may even have to relax that requirement.[91]

The leading case on the co-conspirators' exception to the hearsay rule is *R. v. Carter*,[92] a case involving a conspiracy to import marijuana into Canada from the United States. The test set out in *Carter* was summarized by the Supreme Court in *R. v. Barrow*[93] as follows:

> 1. The trier of fact must first be satisfied beyond reasonable doubt that the alleged conspiracy in fact existed.
>
> 2. If the alleged conspiracy is found to exist then the trier of fact must review all the evidence that is directly admissible against the accused and decide on a balance of probabilities whether or not he is a member of the conspiracy.
>
> 3. If the trier of fact concludes on a balance of probabilities that the accused is a member of the conspiracy then he or they must go on and decide whether the Crown has established such membership beyond reasonable doubt. In this last step, only the trier of fact can apply the hearsay exception and consider evidence of acts and declarations of co-conspirators done in furtherance of the object of the conspiracy as evidence against the accused on the issue of his guilt.

The court also explained that in taking the first step the jury would not necessarily have to be satisfied beyond a reasonable doubt as to the identity of the persons involved in the conspiracy. It is entirely possible, and not uncommon, to be satisfied beyond a reasonable doubt on all the evidence that a conspiracy for the purposes alleged in the indictment existed while still being uncertain as to the identity of all the conspirators. The hearsay exception would have no application at this stage but could certainly be useful at the third stage, if reached, in satisfying the trier that the accused was a member of the alleged conspiracy. This exception is not confined, of course, to cases where the offence charged is conspiracy, but rather the underlying principle makes it applicable to any offence which has been committed pursuant to some common design.[94]

R. v. MAPARA
28 C.R. (6th) 1, [2005] 1 S.C.R. 358, 195 C.C.C. (3d) 225

The accused and C were charged with first degree murder. The victim was shot seven times in a car lot of a business owned by the accused. The Crown alleged a conspiracy to murder consisting of five people including the accused,

---

91 See 4 Wigmore, *Evidence* (Chad. Rev.), s. 1079, p. 187. And see *Ford v. Elliott* (1849), 154 E.R. 1132: "It is a mistake to say that a conspiracy must be proved before the acts of the alleged conspirators can be given in evidence. It is competent to prove insulated acts as steps by which the conspiracy itself may be established," as quoted by Hunt, "Evidentiary Rules Peculiar to Conspiracy Cases" (1973-74), 16 Crim. L.Q. 307 at 330. And see *R. v. Parrot* (1979), 51 C.C.C. (2d) 539, 548-49 (Ont. C.A.) where the court was satisfied that there was *prima facie* evidence that the offence charged was the result of a common design in which the appellant and Mr. Walden were participants. Accordingly, writings which constituted acts or declarations by Mr. Walden in furtherance of the common design were admissible against the appellant.

92 [1982] 1 S.C.R. 938.

93 (2003), 12 C.R. (6th) 185, 174 C.C.C. (3d) 301 (B.C. C.A.).

94 See cases cited in *R. v. Parrot, supra*, note 91.

C, B and W. The accused was alleged to have lured the victim to the parking lot. Following trial by judge and jury, the accused and C were convicted.

On appeal the main issue was whether the trial judge had wrongly admitted evidence of B that he had met with W at a gas station where W had told him that "the little guy," understood to be the accused, had a job for him. The issue was whether the Court should revisit the co-conspirators' exception to the hearsay rule set out in *R. v. Carter* in light of the principled approach to the hearsay rule set out in *R. v. Starr.*

McLACHLIN C.J.C. (BASTARACHE, BINNIE, ABELLA and CHARRON JJ. concurring): —

I first address the appellant's main argument - the co-conspirators' exception to the hearsay rule does not reflect the necessary indicia of necessity and reliability. In *R. v. Chang* (2003), 173 C.C.C. (3d) 397, the Ontario Court of Appeal, per O'Connor A.C.J.O. and Armstrong J.A., rejected this argument. The criterion of necessity poses little difficulty. As stated in Chang, "necessity will arise from the combined effect of the non-compellability of a co-accused declarant, the undesirability of trying alleged co-conspirators separately, and the evidentiary value of contemporaneous declarations made in furtherance of an alleged conspiracy" (para. 105).

The criterion of reliability requires closer scrutiny. The appellant raises the concern that co-conspirators' statements tend to be inherently unreliable because of the character of the declarants and the suspicious activities in which they are engaged.

A preliminary issue arises at this stage. The federal Crown argues that the co-conspirators' exception is not grounded in a concern for reliability, but rests rather on the reasoning that once it is established that the people concerned were involved in the same conspiracy, then the statements of one are admissions against all. Thus, "the rationale for the rule in Canada was grounded in principles governing admissions by party litigants": *Chang*, at para. 82. This exception is grounded in "a different basis than other exceptions to the hearsay rule. Indeed, it is open to dispute whether the evidence is hearsay at all": *R. v. Evans*, [1993] 3 S.C.R. 653, 85 C.C.C. (3d) 97, 108 D.L.R. (4th) 32, per Sopinka J., at p. 664. Sopinka J. went on to suggest that circumstantial guarantees of trustworthiness are irrelevant to the party admissions exception to the hearsay rule:

> The practical effect of this doctrinal distinction is that in lieu of seeking independent circumstantial guarantees of trustworthiness, it is sufficient that the evidence is tendered against a party. Its admissibility rests on the theory of the adversary system that what a party has previously stated can be admitted against the party in whose mouth it does not lie to complain of the unreliability of his or her own statements.

It follows on this reasoning that if the appellant was a co-conspirator with the witness, Binahmad, the appellant cannot be heard to complain that what he said to Binahmad was unreliable. Similarly, it is argued, he cannot complain about the unreliability of what a third co-conspirator, Wasfi, said to Binahmad. They were all plotting together, and what each says can be used against the other.

Having entered into a criminal conspiracy, the accused cannot in his defence rely on its very criminality and the unreliability of his co-conspirators.

The unique doctrinal roots of the co-conspirators' exception to the hearsay rule cannot be denied. However, as noted in *Chang*, "the fact that the co-conspirators' rule is grounded in those principles does not alter the fact that a statement that becomes admissible under the *Carter* process is hearsay and concerns about unreliability are very real" (para. 85). In this sense, the directive of *Starr* that the traditional exceptions should be examined for conformity with necessity and reliability remains pertinent.

I return, therefore, to the question of whether the co-conspirators' exception to the hearsay rule possesses sufficient circumstantial indicators of reliability. The *Carter* process allows the jury to consider a hearsay statement by a co-conspirator in furtherance of the conspiracy only after it has found (1) that the conspiracy existed beyond a reasonable doubt and (2) that the accused was probably a member of the conspiracy, by virtue only of direct evidence against him.

The appellant argues that *Carter* cannot satisfy the reliability requirement because it amounts to using corroborating evidence to bolster the reliability of hearsay declarations against the accused, contrary to *Starr*, per Iacobucci J., at para. 217.

I do not agree. The question is whether the first two stages of the *Carter* process provide circumstantial indicators of reliability that do not amount to simply corroborating the statements in issue. In my view, they do. Proof that a conspiracy existed beyond a reasonable doubt and that the accused probably participated in it does not merely corroborate the statement in issue. Rather, it attests to a common enterprise that enhances the general reliability of what was said in the course of pursuing that enterprise. It is similar in its effect to the res gestae exception to the hearsay rule, where surrounding context furnishes circumstantial indicators of reliability. The concern is not with whether a particular statement is corroborated, but rather with circumstantial indicators of reliability.

The evidence under the first two stages of *Carter* is not inherently corroborative of the hearsay statement, in the sense of confirming the truth of its contents. Indeed the evidence establishing the conspiracy and the accused's probable participation may conflict with the hearsay evidence subsequently adduced. More often than not, the trier of fact will find corroboration, rather than conflict, in the direct evidence implicating the accused. However, this ultimate use of the evidence should not be confused with its initial role in establishing threshold reliability. Here it is relevant with respect to the context of the hearsay evidence, and not to its contents. The use of the *Carter* approach in the present inquiry thus stays within the boundaries of threshold reliability, as explained in *Starr*.

In addition to these preliminary conditions, the final *Carter* requirement, i.e., only those hearsay statements made in furtherance of the conspiracy can be considered, provides guarantees of reliability in the more immediate circumstances under which the statement is made. "In furtherance" statements "have the reliability-enhancing qualities of spontaneity and contemporaneity to the events to which they relate" (*Chang*, at paras. 122-23). They have res gestae type qualities, being "the very acts by which the conspiracy is formulated or implemented and are made in the course of the commission of the offence" (*Chang*, at para. 123). This "minimizes the motive and opportunity for contrivance" (*Chang*, at para. 124). The characters' doubtful reputation for veracity is not a factor at this stage of the analysis. Rather, it is to be taken into account by the jury when assessing the ultimate reliability of such characters' statements.

In sum, the conditions of the *Carter* rule provide sufficient circumstantial guarantees of trustworthiness necessary to permit the evidence to be received.

This conclusion makes practical sense. First, the rule does not operate unfairly to accused persons. Indicia of reliability exist. In this way, unreliable evidence that is likely to mislead the jury can be excluded. It remains open to the accused to cross-examine the deponent, call contrary evidence, and argue the unreliability of the co-conspirators' evidence before the jury. Moreover, it is not unfair to expect people who enter into criminal conspiracies to accept that if they are charged, the evidence of their co-conspirators about what they said in furtherance of the conspiracy may be used against them. Finally, the hearsay rule is supplemented by the discretion of the trial judge to exclude evidence where its prejudicial effect outweighs its probative value, discussed below.

Second, the rule allows the Crown to effectively prosecute criminal conspiracies. It would become difficult and in many cases impossible to marshal the evidence of criminal conspiracy without the ability to use co-conspirators' statements of what was said in furtherance of the conspiracy against each other. To deprive the Crown of the right to use double hearsay evidence of co-conspirators as to what they variously said in furtherance of the conspiracy would mean that serious criminal conspiracies would often go unpunished.

Finally, to modify the *Carter* rule would increase delay and difficulties in trial procedure. Any approach that requires the trial judge to scrutinize the necessity and reliability of particular pieces of hearsay evidence in deciding its admissibility would undermine the efficiency of the traditional categories of exceptions to the hearsay rule and increase the number of voir dire. As stated in *Chang*:

> We are concerned that conspiracy trials, many of which are already complicated, may become more so if every time the Crown seeks to introduce co-conspirators' declarations, the trial judge is required to hold a *voir dire* to determine if there is compliance with the principled approach. We do not anticipate that will be the case. A *voir dire* addressing the principled approach should be the exception. It will only be required when an accused is able to point to evidence raising serious and real concerns about reliability emerging from the circumstances in which a declaration was made, which concerns will not be adequately addressed by use of the *Carter* approach. As a general rule, the presumption that evidence that meets the *Carter* requirements also meets the principled approach should obviate the need for a voir dire. [para. 132]

The appellant suggests simply that we make the *Carter* rule inapplicable to double hearsay evidence. However, the underlying rationale for doing so is that all hearsay evidence, even if it falls under an established exception, must be rejected if that particular piece of evidence does not meet the concerns of necessity and reliability. This implies a case-by-case vetting more resembling the ultimate reliability inquiry that is for the jury, than the threshold reliability inquiry relevant to admissibility.

I conclude that the co-conspirators' exception to the hearsay rule meets the requirements of the principled approach to the hearsay rule and should be affirmed.

The appellant also asks us to change the *Carter* rule to require the first two elements to be determined by the trial judge, rather than the jury, on the ground that allowing the jury to decide these elements renders the exception operationally unfair. While courts may adjust common law rules incrementally to avoid apparent injustice, they do so only where there is clear indication of a need to change the rule in the interests of justice. That is not established in this case. Indeed, the appellant's suggestion was considered and rejected in *Carter* precisely because of the danger that the jury might confuse the direct and the hearsay evidence against the accused and rely on the latter to convict the accused. The Court concluded that the three-stage approach was better suited to bring home to the jury the need to find independent evidence of the accused's participation in conspiracy. I would not accede to this request.

I conclude that the *Carter* rule stands and that the evidence in question was not excluded by the hearsay rule.

This leaves for consideration the argument that even if the co-conspirators' exception to the hearsay rule satisfies the need for indicia of necessity and reliability, this is one of those rare cases where evidence falling within a valid exception to the hearsay rule should nevertheless not be admitted because the required indicia of necessity and reliability are lacking in the particular circumstances of the case. The same considerations that lead to the conclusion that the co-conspirators' exception to the hearsay rule satisfies the requirements for indicia of necessity and reliability, are applicable here. Necessity is established, in the absence of direct evidence from the co-accused declarants. Indicia of reliability are found in the requirements of the *Carter* rule for a conspiracy proved beyond a reasonable doubt, membership of the accused in it on a balance of probability, and the rule that only statements made in furtherance of the conspiracy are admitted. It therefore becomes difficult to conclude that evidence falling under the *Carter* rule would lack the indicia of reliability and necessity required for the admission of hearsay evidence on the principled approach. In all but the most exceptional cases the argument is spent at the point where an exception to the hearsay rule is found to comply with the principled approach to the hearsay rule.

Is this such a case? Certainly there are frailties in the evidence of the co-conspirator. Wasfi arguably had a motive to lie, namely a desire to falsely implicate the appellant, so Binahmad would think the appellant's money would be used in the killing. According to the appellant, Wasfi had his own reasons to have Chand killed, namely to obtain vengeance for the alleged rape of his girlfriend and to eliminate a debt. He implicated the appellant because Binahmad knew he himself could not finance the contract killing. Finally, the evidence showed that Wasfi was in jail at the time when Binahmad testified that the discussion took place.

These concerns, with the exception of the discrepancy as to the date of the conversation, do not go beyond concerns already addressed in the analysis of whether the co-conspirators' exception complies with the principled approach to the hearsay rule. They are characteristic of any conspiracy. Any weaknesses go to the ultimate weight of the evidence, which is for the jury to decide. Nor does Binahmad's error on when the conversation took place merit rejection of the evidence. This problem is one of ultimate reliability that the jury can decide. The trial judge reminded the jury in his charge about this difficulty, in the context of highlighting the defence position that both Wasfi and Binahmad were completely unreliable characters.

It follows that the appellant has not established that the evidence to which he objects constitutes one of those "rare cases" where evidence falling within a valid exception to the hearsay rule fails, in the peculiar circumstances of the case, to satisfy the indicia of necessity and reliability necessary for the admission of hearsay evidence.

. . . .

I would dismiss the appeal and affirm the decision of the Court of Appeal.

LeBel J. (Fish J. concurring) delivered a concurring opinion.

———————————

The bottom line of *Mapara* is that the co-conspirators' exception and the *Carter* rules remain unaffected by *Starr*.

The minority's difference of opinion with the majority turns out to be limited to the majority's view that the trial judge should only intervene to assess necessity and reliability in highly exceptional cases. According to the minority, this set the bar too high. An inquiry should rather occur when the circumstances in which the evidence was obtained or given raise real and serious concerns as to reliability or necessity. In such cases, the trial judge should be required to scrutinize the evidence to ensure that it meets the criteria of the principled approach. However even the minority judges emphasise that a *voir dire* to assess the hearsay evidence will remain the exception.

When the majority in *Starr* called for existing hearsay exceptions to be reviewed according to the requirements of necessity and reliability, many writers, as the minority acknowledge, suggested that the complex and inherently circular co-conspirator's exception was a prime candidate for review and reform. The major problem is that it seems more consistent with *Starr* to have the issues of threshold liability and necessity determined by a trial judge at a *voir dire* before the jury hears the evidence.[95] David Layton, for example, points out that the co-

———————————

95 See especially the detailed analysis of David Layton, "*R. v. Pilarinos*: Evaluating the Coconspirators or Joint Venture Exception to the Hearsay Rule", (2002) 2 C.R. (6th) 293.

conspirator exception has been applied in many contexts other than conspiracy and is best named the joint venture exception. He addresses concerns about rationale, reliability and necessity, the issue of corroboration inherent in the rule, the lack of a *voir dire* and the reality of the doctrine's dangerous reliance on conditional relevancy. Layton notes that some trial judges have decided on the compromise approach of allowing the statements to be conditionally admissible during the Crown's case, with the trial judge making a final decision as to admissibility at the close of the Crown case[96] or holding that statements not in furtherance of the alleged common design are not admissible at stage one of the *Carter* test.[97]

These concerns and solutions were not directly confronted by the Supreme Court and are now water under the bridge. The trumping consideration for the majority is the need to ensure that conspiracy trials are "effective" and not unduly complicated by hearsay *voir dires*. That seems at odds with the concern of the majority in *Starr* to ensure that necessity and reliability criteria are taken seriously before the admission of any hearsay. Chief Justice McLachlin was a dissenter in *Starr* and appears to have found a new majority much more accepting of the status quo of existing categories of exception to the hearsay rule, including this one sometimes known as "the prosecutor's darling". In her comprehensive review of *Mapara* and critics of the co-conspirators' rule, Lisa Dufraimont concludes, however, that "the co-conspirators' exception, ..for all its flaws offers a stable and workable response to a problem that admits of no perfect solution".[98]

In *R. v. Simpson*[99] a new trial was ordered because the trial judge erred in admitting co-conspirator hearsay where necessity was not met because the declarant was available to testify and reliability was not met because of the manner of recording the statements. Lisa Dufraimont[100] suggests this ruling is more in keeping with the minority view in *Mapara*.

(vi) *Statements by Representative*

At common law:

> What a trustee says or does in the exercise of his duty is evidence against his beneficiaries. But what he says or does in other respects is not.[101]

What a person says may be received in evidence against him, no matter in what capacity he says it. If a person sues or is sued in a representative capacity, for example, trustee, executor or administrator, his statements are only receivable against the party he represents if the statements were made as part of the exercise of his representative capacity. This position is consistent with the general

---

96 See especially *R. v. Duncan* (2002), 1 C.R. (6th) 265 (Man. Prov. Ct.).

97 See *R. v. Pilarinos*, [2002] B.C.J. No. 1958, 2002 CarswellBC 1971, 167 C.C.C. (3d) 97 (B.C. S.C.). See too Marvin Bloos and Michael Plaxton, "A Co-conspirators' Exception to the Standing Rule Keeping Out Hearsay in Gang Trials" (2003), 47 Crim.L.Q. 286.

98 See "*R. v. Mapara*: Preserving the Co-conspirators' Exception to the Hearsay Rule", (2006) 51 Crim.L.Q. 169 at 197-198.

99 (2007) 53 C.R. (6th) 1 (Ont. C.A.).

100 C.R. annotation.

101 *New's Trustee v. Hunting*, [1897] 1 Q.B. 607, 611, per Vaughan Williams J.; affirmed [1897] 2 Q.B. 19, 28, 32.

principle that admissions are receivable only against their maker, but is modified to allow for their receipt when the interests of the declarant and the party are identical.

(vii) *Statements by those in Privity with Estate or Interest with Party*

At common law:

> . . . vicarious admissions may become receivable . . . by *privity* (or, identity) of *interest*, i.e., a relation which permits one person's rights, obligations, or remedies to be affected by the acts of another person, and thus also permits resort to such evidence as that other person may have furnished by way of admissions. This privity may be of two sorts, namely, privity of *obligation* and privity of *title*.[102]

An example may assist. *Woolway v. Rowe*[103] was a civil action for trespass wherein the defendant claimed that plaintiff's estate did not extend so far as to cover the property in question. Defendant offered to prove that when plaintiff's father owned the estate he had specifically disavowed any exclusive interest in it. This was objected to on the basis that plaintiff's father was present in court and might be called, and that therefore his earlier declarations were not admissible. The evidence was received and a rule for a new trial refused with the simple statement, "receivable on the ground of identity of interest."[104]

Professor Morgan wrote:

> The dogma of vicarious admissions, as soon as it passes beyond recognized principles of representation, baffles the understanding. Joint ownership, joint obligation, privity of title, each and all furnish no criterion of credibility, no aid in the evaluation of testimony.[105]

(b) Exceptions where Declarant or Testimony Unavailable (Have Necessity Requirement)

We will consider four common law exceptions under this heading: declarations against interest, dying declarations, declarations in course of duty and former testimony. At common law the declarant in each case needed to be deceased.

(i) *Declarations Against Interest*

The common law recognized an exception for a declaration made by a person concerning a matter within his personal knowledge which declaration when made was to the declarant's own prejudice. The "standard" requirements of a hearsay exception are satisfied by this definition. There are clearly grounds of necessity, as the declarant is unavailable, and there are circumstances guaranteeing trustworthiness resident in the thought that a person is unlikely to intentionally misstate a situation against his own position. The hearsay danger of insincerity is guarded against though the dangers in perception, memory and communications are not eliminated. Notice that "collateral matters mentioned"

---

102 4 Wigmore, *Evidence* (Chad. Rev.), s. 1076, p. 153.
103 (1834), 110 E.R. 1151.
104 *Ibid.*, at p. 1152 per Lord Denman, C.J.
105 "Admissions" (1937), 12 Wash. L. Rev. 181, 202.

are also receivable though they may not be against interest;[106] it appears to be accepted that the collateral matters draw their assurance of trustworthiness from the proximity to the statements against interest. Commenting on the basis for the exception, Hamilton, L.J. noted:

> The ground is that it is very unlikely that a man would say falsely something as to which he knows the truth, if his statement tends to his own pecuniary disadvantage. As a reason this seems sordid and unconvincing. Men lie for so many reasons and some for no reason at all; and some tell the truth without thinking or even in spite of thinking about their pockets, but it is too late to question this piece of eighteenth century philosophy.[107]

It seemed to be early settled that the interest affected must be a pecuniary or proprietary interest[108] but there have always been arguments for expanding the nature of the interest to include exposure to criminal liability.[109]

R. v. DEMETER
[1978] 1 S.C.R. 538, 38 C.R.N.S. 317, 34 C.C.C. (2d) 137

Accused was charged with murder. The Crown case was that accused had procured some unknown person to kill his wife. Accused sought to introduce evidence that a person unconnected with him had confessed to the murder of the wife.

MARTLAND J. (JUDSON, RITCHIE, PIGEON, DICKSON, BEETZ and DE GRANDPRÉ JJ. concurring):—

. . . .

The appellant sought to introduce evidence through the witness Dinardo that one Eper, who was apparently unconnected with the appellant, had confessed to the murder of the appellant's wife. Eper was an escaped convict, who had been serving a sentence for life at the time of his escape, and who had died prior to the trial. Dinardo was his friend and testified that he would not have given evidence implicating Eper in this murder if Eper had still been alive. The trial judge excluded the alleged confession as being hearsay evidence.

---

106 As an example see *Higham v. Ridgway* (1808), 103 E.R. 717, 721 (K.B.): to establish a child's date of birth the court received the midwife's account book evidencing receipt of payment for services (against interest) for delivery of a baby on a certain day (collateral matter).

107 See *Lloyd v. Powell Duffryn Steam Coal Co.*, [1913] 2 K.B. 130, 138 (reversed on other grounds [1914] A.C. 733 (H.L.)).

108 *Sussex Peerage Case* (1844), 8 E.R. 1034 (H.L.). See *Watt v. Miller*, [1950] 2 W.W.R. 1144 (B.C.S.C.), holding that a declaration admitting tortious liability is a declaration against pecuniary interest.

109 In a dissenting opinion in *Donnelly v. U.S.*, 228 U.S. 243, 278 (1913), Holmes, J. noted:

> The confession of Joe Dick, since deceased, that he committed the murder for which the plaintiff in error was tried, coupled with circumstances pointing to its truth, would have a strong tendency to make anyone outside a court of justice believe that Donnelly did not commit the crime . . . No other statement is so much against interest as a confession of murder; it is far more calculated to convince than dying declarations, which would be let in to hang a man.

. . . .

It has generally been accepted as the law of England since *The Sussex Peerage* case that the exception to the rule excluding hearsay evidence in respect of declarations made against interest is confined to statements made against pecuniary or proprietary interest and does not permit evidence of a statement by a deceased person against his penal interest.

The Court of Appeal . . . . held that, even if a declaration against penal interest was not necessarily inadmissible, the confession of Eper in question here was not a declaration against penal interest. The reason for so holding is stated as follows:

. . . .

> At the time of both the alleged declarations in question in this case Eper was an escaped convict under sentence of life imprisonment. In the result, he could not be sentenced to a consecutive sentence so that there could be no penal consequence for the crime admitted to which he was vulnerable. The completely uncertain effect on his prospects of parole in the event of another conviction is too remote and uncertain to be regarded as a penal consequence. In addition, at the time of the declaration to Dinardo he and Eper had been accomplices in crimes for many years and Dinardo, on his evidence, was acting as an accessory after the fact in assisting concealment of evidence of the crime declared. Dinardo testified he would not have given his evidence if Eper were alive.

The Court of Appeal enunciated a number of principles which would have to be applied in determining whether a declaration is against penal interest which, in its view, would have to be applied in addition to those applicable in determining whether a declaration is against pecuniary or proprietary interest. They are as follows:

1. The declaration would have to be made to such a person and in such circumstances that the declarant should have apprehended a vulnerability to penal consequences as a result.

2. The vulnerability to penal consequences would have to be not remote.

3. The declaration sought to be given in evidence must be considered in its totality. If upon the whole tenor the weight is in favour of the declarant, it is not against his interest.

4. In a doubtful case a Court might properly consider whether or not there are other circumstances connecting the declarant with the crime and whether or not there is any connection between the declarant and the accused.

5. The declarant would have to be unavailable by reason of death, insanity, grave illness which prevents the giving of testimony even from a bed, or absence in a jurisdiction to which none of the processes of the Court extends. A declarant would not be unavailable in the circumstances that existed in *R. v. Agawa*. [Ed. note: *Agawa* was a joint trial and one accused had given a statement exonerating the other.]

These furnish a valuable guide for consideration in the event that this Court should determine that a declaration against penal interest is not to be held inadmissible under the rule against the reception of hearsay evidence.

Finally, in *R. v. O'Brien*,[110] the Supreme Court of Canada agreed:

> The distinction is arbitrary and tenuous. There is little or no reason why declarations against penal interest and those against pecuniary or proprietary interest should not stand on the same footing. A person is as likely to speak the truth in a matter affecting his liberty as in a matter affecting his pocketbook.[111]

R. v. LUCIER
65 C.C.C. (2d) 150, 1982 CarswellMan 74, 1982 CarswellMan 152, [1982] 1 S.C.R. 28

The accused was charged with arson as a result of the destruction of his house by fire. The fire was actually set by a friend of the accused who was badly burned in the fire. He was interviewed in hospital by the police and admitted setting the fire and stated that he did so for the accused for $500. The accused's friend died shortly after this and the Crown sought to introduce his statements to the police as declarations against penal interest. The statements were admitted. An appeal by the accused from his conviction was dismissed by the Manitoba Court of Appeal. On further appeal by the accused to the Supreme Court of Canada, held, the appeal should be allowed and a new trial ordered.

RITCHIE J.: —

Having regard to the judgment of this Court in the Demeter and O'Brien cases, it must now be recognized that in a proper case statements tendered on behalf of the accused and made by an unavailable person may be admitted at trial if they can be shown to have been made against the penal interest of the person making them; but neither the two cases to which I have just referred nor any of the wealth of authorities cited in the Courts below apply such a rule to statements which have an inculpatory effect on the accused. On the contrary, wherever such statements have been admitted it will be found that they have an exculpatory effect. The difference is a very real one because a statement implicating the accused in the crime with which he is charged emanating from the lips of one who is no longer available to give evidence robs the accused of the invaluable weapon of cross-examination which has always been one of the mainstays of fairness in our Courts. In the present case the statements made by Dumont which were tendered by the prosecutor are obviously inculpatory of the appellant and in my opinion this is not a "proper case" for admitting them so that the learned trial Judge did err in permitting their introduction into evidence and I would accordingly allow this appeal on the first ground specified in the notice of appeal,

---

110 (1977), 76 D.L.R. (3d) 513 (S.C.C.).
111 *Ibid.*, at p. 518; the court, however, applying the requirements of the exception outlined by Hamilton, L.J. in *Lloyd v. Powell, supra*, note 107, held that the instant declaration was not knowingly made against the declarant's interest.

quash the conviction and direct a new trial in accordance with the alternative relief sought by the appellant.

R. v. KIMBERLEY
(2001), 45 C.R. (5th) 273, 157 C.C.C. (3d) 129,
2001 CarswellOnt 3161 (C.A.)

The victim was killed in the underground parking lot of her condominium building. The trial judge refused to admit statements of one Teed that he had done the killing. Teed committed suicide prior to the accused's trial. The accused were convicted of first degree murder.

DOHERTY J.A.: —

The British Columbia statements were tendered for their truth and were hearsay. Hearsay is normally inadmissible. At trial, counsel argued that the British Columbia statements were admissible either as declarations made against penal interest by a person who was not available to give evidence, or under the principled approach to the admissibility of hearsay evidence developed by the Supreme Court of Canada in a line of cases beginning with *R. v. Khan*. On appeal, counsel did not rely on the penal interest exception to the rule against the admission of hearsay evidence but focussed exclusively on the necessity/reliability analysis required by the principled approach. I agree with counsel's approach to the admissibility of the British Columbia statements. As Iacobucci J., for the majority, recently said in *R. v. Starr* (2000), 147 C.C.C. (3d) 449 (S.C.C.) at 534:

> Hearsay evidence may only be admitted if it is necessary and reliable, and the traditional exceptions should be interpreted in a manner consistent with this requirement.

The words of Iacobucci J. are particularly apt where the statement against penal interest is the "traditional exception" said to provide a ticket to admissibility. That exception was first recognized in *R. v. O'Brien* (1977), 35 C.C.C. (2d) 209 (S.C.C.). Unlike many of the older exceptions it has not congealed into a rule dependent upon the existence of certain predetermined factors. Instead, the exception as recognized in *R. v. O'Brien, supra*, at p. 216, depends on the existence of sufficient "guarantees of trustworthiness" to warrant the admission of the statement. The approach to the admissibility of statements against penal interest adopted in *R. v. O'Brien*, presaged the principled approach to the admissibility of all hearsay developed in later cases by the Supreme Court of Canada. Whether characterized as a statement against penal interest, or simply viewed as hearsay, the British Columbia statements were admissible only if the appellants established the separate requirements of necessity and reliability. The necessity inquiry mandated by the principled approach to hearsay is straightforward in this case. The admission of hearsay evidence is necessary where the declarant is unavailable to testify and the party tendering the hearsay statement is unable to obtain evidence of a similar quality from some other source. Teed killed himself prior to trial and was obviously unavailable to testify.

. . . .

The reliability requirement looks to threshold reliability and not the ultimate truth of the statements tendered. . . . Threshold reliability inquiry looks to the circumstances in which the out-of-court statements were made to determine whether those circumstances negate or at least ameliorate the dangers inherent in hearsay evidence to the degree that the jury can safely evaluate those statements and determine their ultimate reliability. . . . The hearsay dangers presented by Teed's British Columbia statements run the full gamut of the dangers associated with hearsay evidence. He was not under oath or any imperative to speak the truth. The statements were not videotaped so there was no basis upon which a jury could assess Teed's demeanour and, perhaps more importantly, the interaction between Teed and his questioners. There is nothing approaching a detailed summary, much less a verbatim record, of what was said by Teed and what was said to Teed in these interviews. Teed insisted that his conversations concerning the Warrick killing should not be recorded. The only record of what he said consists of brief notes made by the British Columbia investigators some time after the various interviews. In the absence of anything approaching a full and accurate record of what was said, it is virtually impossible to discern either the contents or the context of Teed's British Columbia statements. Finally, Teed was not subject to cross-examination when he made these statements. The appellants submit that the dangers outlined above are overcome by the fact that Teed's British Columbia statements amounted to a confession to a murder made to police officers. The appellants argue that Teed could fully expect serious penal consequences as a result of the British Columbia statements and that his willingness to make those statements gives them a high degree of reliability. The circumstance relied on to establish the reliability of Teed's British Columbia statements is the same as the rationale driving the penal interest exception to the exclusion of hearsay evidence. However, as explained in *R. v. O'Brien*, *supra*, at pp. 215-16, the rationale only operates where the statement is made in circumstances where the declarant apprehends an immediate vulnerability to penal consequences. A person who confesses a murder to police officers will usually apprehend that immediate penal consequences will flow from that confession. Teed was, however, in a very unusual situation. He fully intended to plead guilty to (another homicide in British Columbia) the Chwartacki homicide knowing that he would be sentenced to life imprisonment. Any consequences which might flow from his admissions concerning Dr. Warrick would not really alter his future or impose any additional penal consequences: *R. v. Demeter*. . . . In my view, Teed apprehended no additional penal consequences flowing from his British Columbia statements. Consequently, the fact that the statements amounted to confessions to murder made to police officers does not enhance the reliability of those statements.

In addition to finding that Teed did not apprehend penal consequences as a result of his British Columbia statements because of his intention to plead guilty to the Chwartacki homicide, the trial judge also found that Teed had motives to falsely admit responsibility in the Warrick homicide. According to the trial judge,

Teed was motivated by self-aggrandizement, a desire to manipulate the criminal justice system and a desire to improve his living conditions in the Kent Institution. The trial judge said:

> While most would consider confessing to a crime that carried a minimum punishment of imprisonment for life decidedly against their interests, it was of not great moment to David Teed who wanted to spend the rest of his life in prison, and did.

I accept the trial judge's finding that Teed had reasons to falsely confess to the Warrick homicide. Those motives to lie rendered the British Columbia statements all the more unreliable.

The trial judge's finding that the British Columbia statements were not against Teed's interests as he perceived them, but rather, promoted those interests, and that Teed had motives to falsely confess to Dr. Warrick's killing combined with the absence of any circumstance that would counter the hearsay dangers inherent in Teed's statements, compel the finding that the appellants did not demonstrate threshold reliability. While I could stop the analysis here, there are additional factors referred to by the trial judge and the Crown in argument that warrant some reference. As indicated above, the statements were not recorded when made. The absence of any video or even audio recording of the statements creates the reliability problems that I have referred to above. In this case, however, the statements were not recorded because Teed insisted that they not be recorded. It is obvious that Teed did not want a record of what he said to the British Columbia police concerning the Warrick homicide. His insistence that there be no record of those statements further undermines their reliability. Teed's various statements concerning the details surrounding the killing of Dr. Warrick were inconsistent in some material particulars. Inconsistency in itself may be some indicator of unreliability. More important to me is Teed's reaction when confronted with apparent inconsistencies between his statements and the actual circumstances surrounding the killing. For example, Teed initially told the British Columbia police that after he murdered Dr. Warrick, he left the building through the lobby. The physical evidence made it clear, however, that whoever killed Dr. Warrick left through the garage. When the British Columbia police (contrary to the instructions of the Toronto police) advised Teed that the killer had left through the garage, Teed simply changed his story and indicated that he had left through the garage. Teed's reaction to the apparent inaccuracies in his statements hardly inspires confidence in their reliability.

It is also significant in my mind that although Teed had willingly discussed the details of the Warrick homicide with the British Columbia investigators on many occasions, he refused to discuss the details with the Toronto police when they travelled to British Columbia in August 1991. The Toronto police, unlike their British Columbia counterparts, knew the details of the Warrick homicide. Teed was not prepared to discuss the details with those who were in a position to make an informed assessment of the truth of Teed's statements. This circumstance, like the others outlined above, heightens reliability concerns.

. . . .

The appellants also argued that where hearsay evidence is tendered by an accused, the court should take a more relaxed view of the prerequisites to admissibility. It is well established that although the rules of evidence generally apply equally to the Crown and defence, a trial judge can relax those rules in favour of the defence where it is necessary to prevent a miscarriage of justice: *R. v. Williams* (1985), 18 C.C.C. (3d) 356 (Ont. C.A.) at 372, 378; *R. v. Finta* (1992), 73 C.C.C. (3d) 65 (Ont. C.A.) at 200-203, affirmed (1994), 88 C.C.C. (3d) 417 (S.C.C.) at 527-28; *R. v. Folland* (1999), 132 C.C.C. (3d) 14 (Ont. C.A.) at 31-32. Those cases do not, however, invite an abandonment of the threshold reliability inquiry where hearsay evidence is tendered by the defence. As Martin J.A. said in *R. v. Williams, supra*, at p. 378:

> It seems to me that a court has a residual discretion to relax in favour of the accused a strict rule of evidence where it is necessary to prevent a miscarriage of justice and where the danger against which an exclusionary rule aims to safeguard does not exist. [Emphasis added.]

Where hearsay evidence cannot pass the threshold reliability standard, the "danger" which justifies the exclusionary rule is very much in existence. What the cases referred to above do recognize is that fairness concerns may sometimes militate in favour of admitting defence evidence. These concerns may tip the reliability/necessity analysis in favour of the accused. Fairness concerns could not assist the Crown were it to tender the same evidence: *R. v. Finta, supra*; *R. v. Folland, supra*. Similarly, due process concerns, particularly the concern that an accused have a full opportunity to confront inculpatory evidence presented against that accused, may operate against admitting hearsay evidence tendered by the Crown. That concern would not have any relevance if the same evidence was tendered by an accused. The kinds of concerns which can lead a court to admit hearsay evidence tendered by the defence when the same evidence would not be admitted if tendered by the Crown do not operate here. The appellants have failed to demonstrate that the circumstances surrounding the making of the British Columbia statements by Teed offer any basis for a finding that those statements are sufficiently reliable to warrant their admissibility. The admission of evidence of such inherently unreliable statements would hardly prevent a miscarriage of justice. Indeed, it could occasion a miscarriage of justice. For the reasons set out above, I agree with the trial judge's conclusion that the British Columbia statements could not clear the threshold reliability hurdle.

(ii) *Dying Declarations*

At common law a deceased's declaration regarding the cause of his death was receivable in a prosecution for his death provided there was evidence that when he made the declaration he entertained a hopeless expectation of death.[112]

---

112 Compare Cross, *Evidence*, 5th ed., p. 564.

The ground for this exception was detailed very early in the development of the rules of evidence:

> . . . the general principle on which this species of evidence is admitted is, that they are declarations made in extremity, when the party is at the point of death, and when every hope of this world is gone; when every motive to falsehood is silenced, and the mind is induced by the most powerful considerations to speak the truth; a situation so solemn, and so awful, is considered by the law as creating an obligation equal to that which is imposed by a positive oath administered in a Court of Justice.[113]

The assurance of trustworthiness from the circumstances will only flow if the declarant was aware of his state and the statement would be competent evidence by him in the stand. Chief Justice Duff in the Supreme Court of Canada described the duty of the trial judge:

> First of all, he must determine the question whether or not the declarant at the time of the declaration entertained a settled, hopeless expectation that he was about to die almost immediately. Then, he must consider whether or not the statement would be evidence if the person making it were a witness. . . . a declaration which is a mere accusation against the accused, or a mere expression of opinion, not founded on personal knowledge, as distinguished from a statement of fact, cannot be received.[114]

Because of the curious happenstance in our Criminal Code that criminal negligence causing death may be charged under that head or under the head of manslaughter, the declaration is receivable in a prosecution of the former crime as well as the latter.[115]

Given the assurances or trustworthiness resident in the requirements of the exception, it is difficult to see why the law does not go further and allow reception with respect to *any* charge arising out of the transaction. Indeed it is worth noting that the common law restriction to the use of dying declarations only in homicide cases was the result, as unfortunately is the case with many of our rules of evidence, of an historical accident. Until the nineteenth century, the exception operated both in civil and criminal cases. The source of the restriction appears to be a statement by East in his chapter on Homicide; in that chapter he noted that dying declarations were receivable in homicide prosecutions. By the next generation this statement had been interpreted to mean that dying declarations were *only* receivable in homicide prosecution.[116] Limiting receipt of the dying declaration to those cases where it concerns the *declarant's* death or injuries was described by Wigmore as an "irrational and pitiful absurdity of this feat of legal cerebration."[117]

---

113 *R. v. Woodcock* (1789), 168 E.R. 352, 353, per Eyre, C.B.
114 *Chapdelaine v. R.*, [1935] 2 D.L.R. 132, 136 (S.C.C.). With regard to the immediacy of the death expected see *R. v. Perry*, [1909] 2 K.B. 697 (C.C.A.) and *R. v. McIntosh*, [1937] 4 D.L.R. 478 (B.C.C.A.).
115 See *R. v. Jurtyn*, [1958] O.W.N. 355 (C.A.).
116 See 5 Wigmore, *Evidence* (Chad. Rev.), s. 1431. Against that background it is remarkable to consider the holding in *R. v. Schwartzenhauer*, [1935] 3 D.L.R. 711 (S.C.C.).
117 5 Wigmore, *Evidence* (Chad. Rev.), s. 1433.

(iii) *Declarations in Course of Duty*

General

Common law declarations of a deceased person were receivable as exceptions to the hearsay rule if they described the deceased's own activities, were made contemporaneously therewith and the deceased was then under a duty to record the same.[118] This common law exception is no longer as important as it once was, as the federal government and most of the provincial governments have enacted statutory provisions regarding business records; the exception, however, operates with respect to oral and written statements while the statutory provisions deal only with the latter. The exception has, however, been considerably broadened by the Supreme Court of Canada in *Ares v. Venner*.[119] The unanimous opinion of the court, delivered by Hall, J., concluded:

> Hospital records, including nurses' notes, made contemporaneously by someone having a personal knowledge of the matters then being recorded and under a duty to make the entry or record should be received in evidence as *prima facie* proof of the facts stated therein.[120]

The exception now does not demand that the declarant be deceased; indeed in this case the declarants, the nurses, were present in the courtroom but neither side wished to call them as their own witnesses. The common law exception required the declarant to be under a duty to do the act and under a duty to record it; in this case the nurses were under a duty to observe and to record their observations, and therefore their observations, clearly opinions, were receivable. The Alberta Court of Appeal in *Ares v. Venner* had seen these opinions as providing "fruitful areas for cross-examination,"[121] but despite that truth the court ordered them received. It is true that Hall, J. continued:

> This should, in no way, preclude a party wishing to challenge the accuracy of the records or entries from doing so. Had the respondent here wanted to challenge the accuracy of the nurses' notes, the nurses were present in court and available to be called as witnesses if the respondent had so wished.[122]

It is difficult to imagine, however, that the bold direction towards reform of the hearsay rule described by the court was only to be applicable when the declarants were present in the court. In the court's recent decision in *R. v. Khan*, *supra*, that position was specifically disavowed:

> I add that I do not understand *Ares v. Venner* to hold that the hearsay evidence there at issue was admissible where necessity and reliability are established only where

---

118 See Ewart, "Admissibility at Common Law of Records", [1981] Can. Bar Rev. 52.

119 [1970] S.C.R. 608. Accepted as authoritatively stating the common law position in Ontario in *R. v. Laverty (No. 2)* (1979), 47 C.C.C. (2d) 60, 64 (Ont. C.A.) per Zuber, J.A.: ". . . a declaration in the course of a business duty either in its classic form or as enlarged by *Ares v. Venner* . . ." and in *Setak Computer Services Corp. v. Burroughs Business Machines Ltd.* (1977), 15 O.R. (2d) 750, 755 (H.C.) per Griffiths, J.: "that case settles the common law in Ontario." But *contra* see *Exhibitors Inc. v. Allen* (1989), 70 O.R. (2d) 103 (Ont. H.C.) per Arbour, J.

120 *Ibid.*, at p. 626.

121 (1969), 70 W.W.R. 96, 105 (Alta. C.A.).

122 *Supra*, note 119, at p. 626.

cross-examination is available. First, the Court adopted the views of the dissenting judges in *Myers v. D.P.P.* which do not make admissibility dependent on the right to cross-examine. Second, the cross-examination referred to in *Ares v. Venner* was of limited value. The nurses were present in court at the trial, but in the absence of some way of connecting particular nurses with particular entries, meaningful cross-examination would have been difficult indeed.[123]

Business Records

The common law exception for declarations in the course of duty had been fashioned in the 19th century and, if narrowly interpreted, was clearly inappropriate to the business methods which had evolved by the middle of the 20th. The decisions in *Myers v. D.P.P.*[124] caused the legislature to act, both in England[125] and in Canada. In Ontario, for example, the McRuer-Common Committee reported that

the absurdity of the common law is forcibly exposed in *Myers v. D.P.P.* . . . the law of evidence with respect to the proof of the contents of records kept in the ordinary course of business is quite unrelated to modern scientific developments in the making and the keeping of records.[126]

At the federal level, the then Minister of Justice regretted the fact that Canadian courts were following the *Myers* decision and noted:

It is therefore apparent that the law in this country has fallen far behind the major changes which the computer age has brought to business methods. Frequently records are kept either entirely or almost entirely by mechanical means, and in such cases it may be difficult and perhaps impossible to produce a witness to testify to the facts of a particular case, as distinct from testifying about the mechanical system under which transactions or events are recorded. Even in the case of records kept manually it is frequently impossible to trace the person, assuming he is still alive, who made the entries originally in the business records. A useful source of evidence is thereby excluded from the courts. It is little wonder that intelligent laymen conclude that, far from being blind, the goddess of justice is looking the wrong way.[127]

Various provinces and the federal government brought in statutory provisions during the late 1960's to ease the introduction of business records as evidence. As an example the Ontario legislation, enacted in 1966, provided:

> **36.** [now s. 35] (1) In this section,
>
>   (*a*)   "business" includes every kind of business, profession, occupation, calling, operation or activity, whether carried on for profit or otherwise;
>
>   (*b*)   "record" includes any information that is recorded or stored by means of any device.
>
>   (2) Any writing or record made of any act, transaction, occurrence or event is admissible as evidence of such act, transaction, occurrence or event

---

123 (1990), 79 C.R. (3d) 1, 14 (S.C.C.).

124 [1965] A.C. 1001 (H.L.). On the topic of business records see generally, Ewart, "Documentary Evidence: The Admissibility of Documents under Sec. 30 of the Canada Evidence Act," [1979-80] Crim. L.Q. 189.

125 See Criminal Evidence Act, 1965, c. 20 and Civil Evidence Act, 1968, c. 64.

126 Report of the Committee on Medical Evidence in Civil Cases (1965), pp. 64, 77.

127 Hansard, Jan. 20, 1969, p. 4496.

if made in the usual and ordinary course of any business and if it was in the usual and ordinary course of such business to make such writing or record at the time of such act, transaction, occurrence or event or within a reasonable time thereafter.

(3) Subsection 2 does not apply unless the party tendering the writing or record has given at least seven days notice of his intention to all other parties in the action, and any party to the action is entitled to obtain from the person who has possession thereof production for inspection of the writing or record within five days after giving notice to produce the same.

(4) The circumstances of the making of such a writing or record, including lack of personal knowledge by the maker, may be shown to affect its weight, but such circumstances do not affect its admissibility.

(5) Nothing in this section affects the admissibility of any evidence that would be admissible apart from this section or makes admissible any writing or record that is privileged.[128]

The amendment to the *Canada Evidence Act*[129] provided in part:

29A. [now s. 30]

(1) Where oral evidence in respect of a matter would be admissible in a legal proceeding, a record made in the usual and ordinary course of business that contains information in respect of that matter is admissible in evidence under this section in the legal proceeding upon production of the record.

. . . .

(12) In this section "business" means any business, profession, trade, calling, manufacture or undertaking of any kind carried on in Canada or elsewhere whether for profit or otherwise, including any activity or operation carried on or performed in Canada or elsewhere by any government, by any department, branch, board, commission or agency of any government, by any court or other tribunal or by any other body or authority performing a function of government;

"record" includes the whole or any part of any book, document, paper, card, tape or other thing on or in which information is written, recorded, stored or reproduced. . .

Ironically of course the Supreme Court of Canada very shortly afterwards decided to follow the dissenting opinion in *Myers* and to reform judicially the hearsay rule to meet modern conditions.[130]

There is apparent conflict between the statutory provisions. The provincial legislation specifically makes lack of personal knowledge by the maker a factor which does not affect admissibility but only weight. The federal legislation has, as a precondition, the requirement that oral evidence of the matter recorded be admissible.

---

128 This *Ontario Evidence Act* provision (now R.S.O. 1990, c. E.23, s. 35) is based on a provision of the Commonwealth Fund Act, a proposal for reform drafted by Professor Morgan's Committee in 1927; see generally McCormick, *Evidence* (1972), p. 719.

129 S.C. 1968-69, c. 14, s. 4. See now R.S.C. 1985, c. C-5, s. 30.

130 *Ares v. Venner, supra,* note 119, discussed above. Alberta, the birthplace of the *Ares* decision, did not enact business records legislation, seemingly content with the judicial creation.

Does this mean that the maker of the record must have had personal knowledge of the event recorded?[131] Or does it simply mean that the record must have relevance to the matters in issue and that if *any* witness would be permitted to describe the matter recorded, the record, though double hearsay, is receivable?

R. v. MARTIN
(1997), 8 C.R. (5th) 246 (Sask. C.A.)

The accused was charged with six counts of defrauding the Wheat Board. The Crown's theory was that the accused dishonestly overstated the amount of wheat and barley he had on hand, causing the Canadian Wheat Board to advance him more money than it would otherwise have done and depriving it of the difference. The Crown sought to introduce evidence of average crop yields for the municipalities where the accused farmed. The Crown called the Director of the Statistics branch at the Saskatchewan Department of Agriculture and Food. Through him, the Crown sought to present to the jury tables of estimated crop yield averages produced by the Statistics Branch from data gathered by Statistics Canada from Saskatchewan farmers. The tables pertained to the rural municipalities where the accused farmed. The trial judge refused to admit the tables because they relied on hearsay information collected by Statistics Canada and no witness could testify as to its accuracy.

JACKSON J.A. (CAMERON and SHERSTOBITOFF JJ.A. concurring):—

. . . .

Subsection 30(1) of the Canada Evidence Act increased the likelihood of a Court admitting a business record without testimony as to the source of the information contained in the record. It puts forward only two qualifications for admission: (i) the evidence tendered must be "a record made in the usual and ordinary course of business;" and (ii) it must contain the same information "where oral evidence in respect of a matter would be admissible in a legal proceeding." But vestiges of the old law, which resisted the admissibility of documents except under strict circumstances, remained.

The principal issue concerned "double hearsay", i.e., information contained in a record which was given to the record keeper who has no knowledge of its accuracy.

Many of the provincial equivalents of s. 30(1) specifically require a court to overlook double hearsay. For example, s. 31(3) of The Saskatchewan Evidence Act, R.S.S. 1978, c. S-16 provides "[t]he circumstances of the making of a writing or record mentioned in subsection (2), including lack of personal knowledge by the maker, may be shown to affect its weight, but such circumstances do not affect its admissibility." The difference between the provincial and federal legislation appears to lessen the effectiveness of the latter.

---

131 Advancing this interpretation see Lederman, "The Admissibility of Business Records — A Partial Metamorphosis" (1973), 11 Osgoode Hall L.J. 373 at 394-95 and Mewett quoted in McWilliams, *Canadian Criminal Evidence* (1974), pp. 115-16.

Added to this, s. 30(6) of the Canada Evidence Act provides that a court may consider the circumstances in which the information was written to determine whether an provision of s. 30 applies. This lends further weight to the proposition that Parliament intended courts to exclude documents containing double hearsay.

Mr. Ewart (*Documentary Evidence in Canada*, Carswell, 1984) indicated early academic opinion leaned toward the view that s. 30 did preclude the admissibility of records containing double hearsay but the courts did not share that view. In fact, early cases held double hearsay documents to be admissible, as long as they met the twin requirements of s. 30(1), with little comment.

In *R. v. Anthes Business Forms Ltd.* (1975), 19 C.C.C. (2d) 394, aff'd 26 C.C.C. (2d) 349, aff'd 32 C.C.C. (2d) 207 (S.C.C.) the Ontario Court of Appeal considered the admissibility of corporate files which contained third party records showing details of certain transactions. As in the case at bar, the corporate files were developed from information received from someone who in turn had received it from yet another. Houlden J.A., speaking for the Court, said the files were admissible because they were records "made in the usual and ordinary course of business by the persons who prepared them, and oral evidence in respect of the matters contained in them would have been admissible" (see p. 369). Although the Supreme Court of Canada's brief reasons may represent concurrence with the result rather than with the reasons, Houlden J.A.'s statement is significant in that it focused only on the twin requirements of s. 30(1).

Similarly, in *R. v. Penno* (1977), 35 C.C.C. (2d) 266 the British Columbia Court of Appeal also admitted a written record of inventory numbers prepared by one person based on the information of another. The Court relied on *Ares v. Venner* and s. 30(1) of the Canada Evidence Act.

In *R. v. Grimba* (1978), 38 C.C.C. (2d) 469 (Ont. Co. Ct.), the Crown tendered expert fingerprint evidence to demonstrate that the fingerprints taken from the accused were the same as those on a fingerprint record obtained from the United States Federal Bureau of Investigation. The expert had not made the record and had no personal knowledge of its accuracy, but had been with the FBI for eleven years and described the FBI as serving as a repository for fingerprint records. The Court interpreted s. 30(1) to allow the admission of the records even though they contained double hearsay. Callaghan Co. Ct. J. stated (at p. 471):

> It would appear that the rationale behind [s. 30(1)] for admitting a form of hearsay evidence is the inherent circumstantial guarantee of accuracy which one would find in a business context from records which are relied upon in the day to day affairs of individual businesses, and which are subject to frequent testing and cross-checking. Records thus systematically stored, produced and regularly relied upon should, it would appear under s. 30, not be barred from this Court's consideration.

This passage characterizes s. 30(1) as providing a clear exception to the hearsay rules.

In *R. v. Biasi* (1982), 62 C.C.C. (2d) 304 (B.C.S.C.) Justice Paris had to decide whether a telephone company's "circuit card security documents" were admissible. Some of the information contained in the cards was provided by the

RCMP to the telephone company who then prepared them. With respect to their admissibility Paris J. ruled:

> Nor does the fact that when the record was made up the information was received from another party make the record inadmissible as being hearsay. The provisions of the Canada Evidence Act provide for the admissibility of such records as proof of the facts contained in them even if the record maker received his information from another party, as long as the facts recorded on the document would themselves be admissible in evidence.

Since the Ewart text was published, the Alberta Court of Appeal in *R. v. Boles* (1985), 57 A.R. 232 considered the admissibility of hotel records which confirmed the presence of some of the principal conspirators in India. Admissibility was questioned on the basis that the records contained double hearsay, i.e., presumably the information was given to the hotel management by its employees. Relying on each of the above authorities, the Court concluded that s. 30(1) renders admissible a document made in the ordinary course of business notwithstanding that it contains double hearsay. (See also *R. v. Ross* (1992), 92 Nfld. & P.E.I.R. 51 (Nfld. S.C.) where the Court confirmed the admissibility under s. 30 of written records prepared by a manager with information given to him by other employees.)

Turning to apply these authorities to the case at bar, the trial judge ought to have admitted the tables pursuant to s. 30 of the Canada Evidence Act. As Houlden J.A. said in Anthes, s. 30 makes admissible records made in the usual and ordinary course of business where oral evidence in respect of a matter would be admissible in a legal proceeding. The tables in this case were made in the usual and ordinary course of business of Sask. Agriculture and Food. Section 6 of The Department of Agriculture Act mandates the gathering of the statistics which are then used in the department's regular business of administering agricultural programs. Oral evidence would be admissible, but at some considerable cost and inconvenience. To call every farmer who had farmed for the applicable 15 year period in the two rural municipalities would be impossible. In this case, but for the ability to admit these tables, the information they contained would be lost to the court as occurred in this case. The Crown's witness was prepared to testify that the department used these statistics in its work and relied upon them. As Callaghan Co. Ct. J. said in *Grimba*, "records thus systematically stored, produced and regularly relied upon should not be barred from the courts' consideration."

The opening words of s. 30(6) appear to permit a consideration of weight to be made when the court considers admissibility. But if this means a court must reject a record because it contains double hearsay, it places documents prepared in the ordinary course of business in a fundamentally different category than documents admitted pursuant to the common law business duty exception. As indicated in *Ares*, weight is an issue to be addressed after the document is accepted as evidence. The circumstances in which the information was gathered or the record produced, or the lack of such evidence, may affect the weight to be given to it by the trier of fact, but it does not affect its admissibility.

As a general rule, documents made in the ordinary course of business are admitted to avoid the cost and inconvenience of calling the record keeper and the maker. As a matter of necessity the document is admitted. Proof that a document is made in the ordinary course of business prima facie fulfils the qualification that in order for hearsay to be admitted it must be trustworthy.

Section 30 would have accomplished little if the author of the data contained in a business record had to be called to testify. The complexity of modern business demands that most records will be composed of information gleaned by the maker from others.

The Ontario-type legislation allows records of "any act, transaction, occurrence or event" and the Canada Act permits records "in respect of a matter." Should records containing opinion be received? McCormick argues:

> In general, the opinion rule should be restricted to governing the manner of presenting courtroom testimony and should have little if any application to the admissibility of out-of-court statements. It would, however, be appropriate to recognize a discretionary power in the trial judge to exclude an entry if the form in which it was made render it so vague or speculative as to cause its probative value to be outweighed by the danger that it would mislead or confuse the jury . . . Sustaining an objection to counsel's question to a witness as calling for an "opinion" is usually not a serious matter since counsel can in most cases easily reframe the question to call for the more concrete statement. But to reject the statement of the out-of-court narrative of what he observed on the ground that the statement is too general in form to meet the courtroom rules of interrogation mistakes the function of the opinion rule and may shut-out altogether a valuable item of proof.[132]

In *Adderly v. Bremner*,[133] Brooke J. wrote:

> As to the question of the admissibility of the hospital record as proof of diagnosis, opinion or impression which are recorded in the hospital record at the time that the diagnosis was made or opinion or impression formed, I should think there is no doubt that the making of medical diagnosis is basic to the business of a hospital and it is made in the usual and ordinary course of that business. However, diagnosis is a professional opinion, and in my view it is not an act, transaction, occurrence or event within the meaning of the words in this section.[134]

Why? Recall that the judicially created business records exception, *Ares v. Venner*, allowed opinion regarding the colour of the toes!

R. v. L. (C.)
(1999), 138 C.C.C. (3d) 356, 1999 CarswellOnt 2700 (C.A.)

The accused was charged with three historical sexual offences in relation to his wife's sister who alleged that she became pregnant as a result of sexual

---

132 McCormick, *Evidence* (1972), pp. 41-42 and 721-22.

133 [1968] 1 O.R. 621 (H.C.).

134 *Ibid.*, at pp. 623-24. Followed in *Setak Computer v. Burroughs* (1997), 15 O.R. (2d) 750 at 761 (H.C.) and *Augustine v. Inco Ltd.* (2006), [2006] O.J. No. 2607, 2006 CarswellOnt 3952 (S.C.J.).

intercourse with the accused when she was 13 years of age, and that she had an abortion. The Crown entered medical records as an exhibit at trial. These had not previously been disclosed to the defence and defence counsel did not read the contents of the medical records which included a letter from a doctor which stated that the complainant's pregnancy resulted from a relationship with a 15-year-old male. The trial judge instructed the jury that this statement was hearsay and should be ignored. The complainant testified at trial that when she told the hospital staff that the accused was responsible for the pregnancy, she was told to leave the room while her mother remained.

The accused argued on his appeal that he had been denied effective representation. In support of this argument, the accused introduced evidence from the doctor who signed the letter, who explained that attendance at the teen clinic for an abortion would have involved multiple interviews by nurses and a doctor and that the complainant would have been separated from any accompanying adult in order to get at the truth of the matter. The doctor did not recall whether she had direct dealings with the complainant or whether she relied on notes made in the records by the professional interviewers for the purposes of her letter. The doctor also advised that if the complainant had in any interview mentioned the accused as being the father, there would have been a duty upon the interviewer to report it to the appropriate authorities including the police.

By the Court: —

We are of the view that the hospital records, including Dr. Cowell's letter, were admissible as business records made in the ordinary course of the hospital's business by those charged with the responsibility for making such records: see s. 30 Canada Evidence Act, R.S.C. 1985, c. C-5. See also *R. v. Monkhouse* (1987), 61 C.R. (3d) 343 (Alta. C.A.) where the Court stated at pp. 350-51:

> An even earlier modification of the common law rules may be seen in a decision in the Supreme Court of Canada in *Can. Atl. Ry. Co. v. Moxley* (1888), 15 S.C.R. 145 [Ont.]. That case held that the person originally recording the event need not himself have direct personal knowledge of the event recorded. It was held to be sufficient if the person who has a duty to do and record the act "causes" a record to be made by an agent. This case, too, was cited by Mr. Justice Hall in *Ares v. Venner*.

> . . . .

> These hearsay records are not to be accepted in evidence merely to avoid the inconvenience of identifying a witness or because many witnesses would be involved, or even because otherwise no evidence would be available. Rather, they can be admitted only if they have come into existence under circumstances which make them inherently trustworthy. Where an established system in a business or other organization produces records which are regarded as reliable and customarily accepted by those affected by them, they should be admitted as prima facie evidence.

Given the evidence of Dr. Cowell in cross-examination on her affidavit, it appears reasonable to conclude that it would be likely that the complainant would have been interviewed separately from her mother as to the identify of the father, especially when the interviewers were under a duty to report a case of this nature if the father were not indicated to be a 15-year-old youth. The separate interview was corroborated by the complainant in her 1998 police interview. However, it is unfortunate there is no longer available the original notes on which Dr. Cowell relied to make her statement that the complainant's "pregnancy result[ed] from a relationship with a 15 year old male of two years duration". Even if Dr. Cowell's letter is not regarded as a business record, hearsay evidence is admissible if the criteria of necessity and reliability have been met: See *R. v. Khan* (1990), 59 C.C.C. (3d) 92 (S.C.C.); *R. v. Smith* (1992), 75 C.C.C. (3d) 257 (S.C.C.); *R. v. Hawkins* (1996), 111 C.C.C. (3d) 129 (S.C.C.); *R. v. B. (K.G.)* (1993), 19 C.R. (4th) 1, 79 C.C.C. (3d) 257 (S.C.C.). We are of the view that it would be unrealistic to expect hospital personnel to recall the specific event in question, given that they would deal with teenage pregnancies and abortion requests on a daily basis and therefore the criterion of necessity is met. As a result of interviews, it appears that it was recorded (as distilled by Dr. Cowell in her ordinary course of business procedure in reviewing such records to provide the responsible committee at the performing hospital with the background information and reasons in support of the abortion) that a 15-year-old boyfriend had been the father. No one on the interview team would have any reason not to faithfully record what had been said; further no reason for anything contrary to that was conjectured. Falsely recorded information would be cause for disciplinary action and even possible criminal compliant. It would appear to us that the distillation of those records into a "one-liner", given Dr. Cowell's responsibilities in writing such a letter, would be reliable.

We are of the view that if appellant's trial counsel had been alert to the contents of Dr. Cowell's letter which would be of exculpatory assistance to the appellant, then counsel would have been justified in requesting an adjournment to interview Dr. Cowell and to obtain further information of the sort now sought to be introduced as fresh evidence. That he did not do so appears to be pure inadvertence as opposed to any tactical decision on the part of the defence. This difficulty was compounded by the trial Crown not giving disclosure of this letter well prior to trial and in fact by her merely putting it in as an exhibit with other hospital records at trial, plus the trial judge, without any debate by counsel, declaring to the jury that "some factual statement" in the letter was hearsay and should be ignored. While the trial judge appropriately drew the jury's attention to: "The issue is who fathered the fetus and that is what we are here to decide today" she closed off a material avenue of exploration. It appears that she ignored what a valuable tool that letter and its reference to the pregnancy being as a result of an extended relationship with a mid-teenager would be for the defence not only as a base for effective cross-examination but for the searching out of cogent evidence of clinic procedures to present the basis of a reasonable doubt. Given the nature of the charges and their apparent interrelationship, together with the effect pro (without the letter and other evidence) and con (with such evidence) upon the complainant's credibility and vice versa for the appellant's credibility, we are of the view that the appellant was prejudiced on all three counts by lack of effective counsel. Under these circumstances, while ordinarily the fresh evidence would have been available for the appellant to make use of at trial, his lack of effective counsel prevented that end. We are therefore of the view that the fresh evidence may be introduced as it is relevant to the issues at trial. This fresh evidence, when taken with the evidence available but deemed inadmissible at trial, could reasonably be expected to have affected the result when credibility was obviously the main issue at trial.

Appeal allowed; new trial ordered.

R. v. LARSEN
(2001), 42 C.R. (5th) 49, 2001 CarswellBC 931 (S.C.)

The accused was charged with first degree murder. The Crown applied for a ruling that an autopsy report and supplemental report were admissible in evidence. The initial report was prepared in 1978 and the pathologist who made it had died. He had deferred his decision on cause of death for 14 months, at which later time, in a supplemental report, he declared that the victim had died of asphyxiation. His conclusions accorded with at least two observations made by the pathologist at the scene. The accused contended that the evidence was inadmissible hearsay. The Crown contended that the reports were admissible as declarations made in the course of duty and in the alternative under the principled approach to the hearsay rule.

ROMILLY J.: —

. . . .

Before addressing admissibility under the principled approach, I shall first address the issue of whether the autopsy and supplemental reports were declarations made in the course of duty. As recently noted by the Nova Scotia Court of Appeal in *R. v. Wilcox*, [2001] N.S.J. No. 85, 2001 NSCA 45, this is a prudent approach because, among other reasons, the analysis of admissibility under a traditional exception will assist in the application of the principled approach.

Are the autopsy report and supplemental report admissible as declarations made in the course of duty?

In *R. v. Wilcox, supra*, at para. 49, the Nova Scotia Court of Appeal accepted the following passage from *R. v. Monkhouse*, [1988] 1 W.W.R. 725 (Alta. C.A.) as an accurate statement of the requirements for admissibility under the common law exception of declarations made in the course of duty:

> In his useful book, *Documentary Evidence in Canada* (Carswell Co., 1984), Mr. J.D. Ewart summarizes the common law rule after the decision in *Ares v. Venner* as follows at p. 54:
>
> > . . . the modern rule can be said to make admissible a record containing (i) an original entry (ii) made contemporaneously (iii) in the routine (iv) of business (v) by a recorder with personal knowledge of the thing recorded as a result of having done or observed or formulated it (vi) who had a duty to make the record and (vii) who had no motive to misrepresent.

The rationale for admissibility of such documents at common law was that the routine nature of their creation, the fact they are relied upon for business purposes and the absence of any motive to misrepresent the information recorded all provide circumstantial guarantees of trustworthiness: *R. v. Wilcox, supra*, at para. 67. A duty to create or maintain the document was also considered to provide a circumstantial guarantee of trustworthiness "based upon the assumption that a declarant would fear censure and dismissal should an employer discover an inaccuracy in the statement": Sopinka, Lederman and Bryant, *The Law of Evidence in Canada*, 2d (Toronto: Butterworths, 1999) at pp. 211-12.

On the basis of the above, I conclude the autopsy report dated October 20, 1978, is admissible under the common law exception of declarations made in the course of duty. Dr. Sturrock prepared the autopsy report shortly after conducting the autopsy and he had personal knowledge of the information in the report, having conducted the autopsy himself. Further, Dr. Sturrock was under a duty to make the record having been directed to conduct a post-mortem examination of the deceased by the coroner in accordance with the Coroners Act, S.B.C. 1975, c. 15. The making of an autopsy report is a routine procedure conducted by the medical practitioner who performs an autopsy. Further, Dr. Sturrock had no motive to misrepresent.

However, I conclude that the supplemental report dated December 19, 1979, is inadmissible under the common law exception of declarations made in the course of duty. I make this finding because the supplemental report, dated 14 months following the performance of the autopsy, fails the requirement of contemporaneousness.

In *R. v. Starr, supra*, at para. 155, the Supreme Court of Canada held that where a traditional exception to the hearsay rule conflicts with the principled approach, the principled analysis of necessity and reliability should prevail.

. . . .

In my view, this is not one of those rare cases where a traditional exception to the hearsay rule, specifically declarations made in the course of duty, fails the test of reliability and necessity under the new principled approach to the hearsay rule. . . . I therefore turn to consider whether the autopsy report and the supplement report are admissible under the principled exception to the hearsay rule.

. . . .

On the basis of the evidence adduced on the voir dire, I am satisfied the Crown has met the onus of establishing the threshold reliability of both the autopsy report and the supplemental report.

I am satisfied the circumstances surrounding the making of both the autopsy report and the supplemental report provide sufficient circumstantial guarantees of trustworthiness. I conclude that Dr. Sturrock had no motive to misrepresent the information recorded in either report. I also find that the duty of Dr. Sturrock to prepare both reports provides a circumstantial guarantee of trustworthiness. Finally, the testimony of Dr. Harris, in that it corroborated aspects of Dr. Sturrock's reports, also suggests the reports are reliable.

The autopsy report of Dr. Sturrock is admissible both under the common law exception of declarations made in the course of duty and under the principled approach to hearsay. The supplemental report, while not meeting the requirements for admission as a declaration in the course of duty, does meet the requirements of necessity and reliability and thus is admissible under the principled approach to hearsay.

Compare the approach of Justice Hill in *R. v. West*.[135] The Court applied the principled approach to hearsay to business records. Justice Hill explained his approach:

> Hearsay that does not fit within a traditional hearsay exception may nevertheless still be admissible if sufficiently necessary and reliable - the principled approach to hearsay of *Khan v. The Queen* (1990), 59 C.C.C. (3d) 92 (S.C.C.) and its progeny. In the clear majority of cases, the presence or absence of a traditional exception will be determinative of admissibility: *Starr v. The Queen* (2000), 147 C.C.C. (3d) 449 (S.C.C.) at 533 per Iacobucci J. In rare cases, the presumption of admissibility inherent in a recognized exception may give way in the face of application of the principled approach probing necessity and reliability.
>
> Given the qualified recognition of traditional hearsay exceptions, the question arises, on a case-to-case basis, whether to first measure the hearsay at hand against any relevant exception(s) apparently applicable or simply to proceed directly to the overarching principled analysis. Post *Starr*, the former approach recommended itself to the court in *Regina v. Wilcox*, [2001] N.S.J. No. 85 (C.A.), while the latter approach prevailed in *Regina v. Lauzon*, [2000] O.J. No. 3940 (C.A.). In this case, I have elected to apply the principled approach to the admission of hearsay with liberal reference to the traditional exceptions advanced by the Crown, and the past recollection recorded exception, to the extent the exceptions provide an explanatory or educative instruct as to peculiar factors of historical significance in the context of the type of evidence at issue here - written hearsay. In other words, attention to the modern approach to hearsay admissibility, as opposed to pursuit of the ancestral roots of the common law exceptions and pigeon-holing, recommends itself in the circumstances here.
>
> The principled approach to hearsay is not bound by the strictures of the Canada Evidence Act as it has been recognized in s. 36 of the Act that the statutory exceptions are in addition to, not in derogation of, any power to prove documents existing at law: *Regina v. C. (W.B.)* (2000), 142 C.C.C. (3d) 490 (Ont. C.A.) at 503 per Weiler J.A.; *Regina v. Monkhouse* (1987), 61 C.R. (3d) 343 (Alta. C.A.) at 347-8 per Laycraft C.J.A.

(iv) *Former Testimony*

At common law:

> Where a witness has given his testimony under oath in a judicial proceeding, in which the adverse litigant had the power to cross-examine, the testimony so given will, if the witness himself cannot be called, be admitted in any subsequent suit between

---

135 (2001), 45 C.R. (5th) 307 (Ont. S.C.).

the same parties, or those claiming under them, provided it relate to the same subject or substantially involve the same material questions.[136]

Grounds of necessity reside in the declarant's unavailability, and circumstantial guarantees of trustworthiness in the fact that the statement was given under oath and subject to cross-examination. Indeed, Professor Wigmore[137] would say that "if it has been already subjected to proper cross-examination, it has satisfied the rule and needs no exception in its favour." Nevertheless, the orthodox treatment is to characterize it as an exception, as the trier does not have the advantage of observing the evidence being given and tested on cross-examination.

In criminal cases a statutory embodiment of the common law rule presently appears in the Criminal Code:

715.(1) Where, at the trial of an accused, a person whose evidence was given at a previous trial on the same charge, or whose evidence was taken in the investigation of the charge against the accused or on the preliminary inquiry into the charge, refuses to be sworn or to give evidence, or if facts are proved on oath from which it can be inferred reasonably that the person

(*a*) is dead,
(*b*) has since become and is insane,
(*c*) is so ill that he is unable to travel or testify, or
(*d*) is absent from Canada,

and where it is proved that the evidence was taken in the presence of the accused, it may be admitted as evidence in the proceedings without further proof, unless the accused proves that the accused did not have full opportunity to cross-examine the witness.

(2) Evidence that has been taken on the preliminary inquiry or other investigation of a charge against an accused may be admitted as evidence in the prosecution of the accused for any other offence on the same proof and in the same manner in all respects, as it might, according to law, be admitted as evidence in the prosecution of the offence with which the accused was charged when the evidence was taken.

(3) For the purposes of this section, where evidence was taken at a previous trial or preliminary hearing or other proceeding in respect of an accused in the absence of the accused, who was absent by reason of having absconded, the accused is deemed to have been present during the taking of the evidence and to have had full opportunity to cross-examine the witness.

(4) Subsections (1) to (3) do not apply in respect of evidence received under subsection 540(7).

R. v. POTVIN
[1989] 1 S.C.R. 525, 68 C.R. (3d) 193, 47 C.C.C. (3d) 289

The accused was charged with murder. The Crown called a witness who was alleged to have been an accomplice in the commission of the offence. The

---

136 Taylor, *Evidence*, s. 464, as adopted in *Town of Walkerton v. Erdman* (1894), 23 S.C.R. 352.

137 5 Wigmore, *Evidence* (Chad. Rev.), s. 1370. See *R. v. Speid* (1988), 63 C.R. (3d) 253 (Ont. C.A.).

witness had testified at the preliminary inquiry and was cross-examined by counsel for the accused. He refused to testify at the accused's trial. The trial judge held that since the conditions set out in then section 643 of the Criminal Code had been met the evidence should be admitted. The accused was convicted and his appeal dismissed. He appealed further.

WILSON J. (LAMER and SOPINKA JJ. concurring):—

The main issue on this appeal is whether the admission at trial of previously taken evidence under s. 643(1) [now section 715(1)] of the *Criminal Code*, R.S.C. 1970, c. C-34, as amended, . . . violates an accused's rights under ss. 7 or 11(*d*) of the *Canadian Charter of Rights and Freedoms*. . . .

. . . .

What rights then does an accused have under s. 7 of the Charter with respect to the admission of previous testimony? It is, in my view, basic to our system of justice that the accused have had a full opportunity to cross-examine the witness when the previous testimony was taken if a transcript of such testimony is to be introduced as evidence in a criminal trial for the purpose of convicting the accused. This is in accord with the traditional view that it is the opportunity to cross-examine and not the fact of cross-examination which is crucial if the accused is to be treated fairly. As Professor Delisle has noted: Annotation (1986), 50 C.R. (3d) 195 at p. 196: "If the opposing party has had an opportunity to fully cross-examine he ought not to be justified in any later complaint if he did not fully exercise that right." . . .

. . . .

With respect to the appellant's submission that he was deprived of a fair trial under s. 11(*d*) of the Charter, I would conclude, for the reasons given above in reviewing his s. 7 claim, that this claim must also fail if his constitutional right to have had a full opportunity to cross-examine the witness on the earlier occasion was respected. . . .

. . . .

It is my view that the word "may" in s. 643(1) is directed not to the parties but to the trial judge. I believe it confers on him or her a discretion not to allow the previous testimony to be admitted in circumstances where its admission would operate unfairly to the accused. . . .

. . . .

What then is the nature and purpose of the discretion conferred in s. 643(1) which enables the trial judge not to allow the evidence in at trial even in cases in which the requirements of the section have been met? In my view, there are two main types of mischief at which the discretion might be aimed. First, the discretion could be aimed at situations in which there has been unfairness in the manner in which the evidence was obtained. Although Parliament has set out in the section specific conditions as to how the previous testimony has to have been obtained if it is to be admitted under s. 643(1) (the most important, of course, being that the accused was afforded full opportunity to cross-examine the witness), Parliament could have intended the judge to have a discretion in those rare cases in which compliance with the requirements of s. 643(1) gave no guarantee that the evidence was obtained in a manner fair to the accused. This would, of course, represent a departure from the traditional common law approach that the manner in which evidence is obtained, with a few well-established exceptions such as the confessions rule, is not relevant to the question of its admissibility but it would be consistent with the contemporary approach to the expanded requirements of adjudicative fairness. An example of unfairness in obtaining the testimony might be a case in which, although the witness was temporarily absent from Canada, the Crown could have obtained the witness's attendance at trial with a minimal degree of effort. Another example might be a case in which the Crown was aware at the time the evidence was initially taken that the witness would not be available to testify at the trial but did not inform the accused of this fact so that he could make best use of the opportunity to cross-examine the witness at the earlier proceeding. These kinds of circumstances related to the obtaining of the evidence on the earlier occasion might have been in the mind of the legislator as triggering the judge's discretion with respect to its admission at the trial.

A different concern at which the discretion might have been aimed is the effect of the admission of the previously taken evidence on the fairness of the trial itself. This concern flows from the principle of the law of evidence that evidence may be excluded if it is highly prejudicial to the accused and of only modest probative value. . . . How the evidence was obtained might be irrelevant under this principle.

. . . .

In my view, once it is accepted that s. 643(1) gives the trial judge a statutory discretion to depart from the purely mechanical application of the section, the discretion should be construed as sufficiently broad to deal with both kinds of situations, namely where the testimony was obtained in a manner which was unfair to the accused or where, even although the manner of obtaining the evidence was fair to the accused, its admission at his or her trial would not be fair to the accused. I would stress that in both situations the discretion should only be exercised after weighing what I have referred to as the "two competing and frequently conflicting concerns" of fair treatment of the accused and society's interest in the admission of probative evidence in order to get at the truth of the matter in issue. . . . Having regard to the reservations that have been expressed over the restrictive formulation of the common law discretion in *Wray, supra,* . . . I believe there is no need or justification for importing a similar restriction into the statutorily conferred discretion in s. 643(1). The protection of the accused from unfairness rather than the admission of probative evidence "without too much regard for the fairness of the adjudicative process" . . . should be the focus of the trial judge's concern.

It will follow that I cannot accept the hard and fast rule approach to this issue taken by the Manitoba Court of Appeal in *Sophonow, supra.* That court seems to suggest that the very importance of the evidence requires it to be excluded. . . . I believe that this proposition is at odds with the purpose of s. 643(1) in ensuring that evidence, even important and highly probative evidence, is not lost because of the unavailability of a witness at trial. . . .

In the case at bar I am of the view that the trial judge did not instruct himself properly as to the nature and scope of his discretion under s. 643(1). He stressed the high probative value of the evidence of someone who had been in the victim's home at the time the events occurred but failed, in my view, to give adequate consideration to possible unfairness to the accused arising from either the manner in which the evidence was obtained or the effect of its admission on the fairness of the trial. The Court of Appeal proceeded on the basis that the trial judge had no discretion other than the restrictive common law formulation in *Wray*. Neither court applied its mind to the question whether in the circumstances of this case the trial judge should have exercised his statutory discretion in s. 643(1) to exclude the evidence.

There can be no doubt about the fact that the decision whether or not to exercise the statutory discretion in this case would not have been an easy one. In favour of the admission of the evidence is the absence of any allegation that the manner in which Deschênes' testimony was obtained was unfair to the appellant. Moreover, the appellant's counsel exercised his right to cross-examine Deschênes at the preliminary inquiry and there was some cross-examination. There was also a measure of corroboration of Deschênes' testimony (so far as it purported Potvin as the culprit) by the testimony of Thibault at trial. Also favouring admission of Deschênes' testimony was the factor emphasized by the trial judge, namely its high probative value. The testimony purported to be an eyewitness account of the appellant beating and killing the victim. On the other hand, given the appellant's defence that he was a passive observer and that it was Deschênes, the unavailable witness, who did the actual beating and killing, the issue of Deschênes' credibility was obviously critical to the trier of fact's decision whether to accept or reject Deschênes' version of the events. Yet the jury had no opportunity to observe Deschênes' demeanour as an aid in assessing that witness's credibility.

This is not, however, a matter for this court to decide but rather a matter to be referred back to a trial judge properly instructed as to the nature and scope of his or her statutory discretion under s. 643(1).

. . . .

La Forest J. (Dickson C.J.C. concurring):— I have had the advantage of reading the reasons of my colleague, Wilson J. I agree with her conclusion and, apart from what follows, her reasoning as well. However, I take a different view of s. 643(1) of the *Criminal Code* and, in consequence, of the source of the discretion to exclude the evidence permitted to be adduced under that provision.

As I read s. 643, it is not directly addressed to the prosecution or the judge, although it has, of course, implications for how they perform their duties. The provision is directed at a certain type of evidence. It makes it admissible. The parties to a trial may, therefore, invoke the provision if they wish. But the provision does not provide that the evidence previously taken shall be accepted; it provides, rather, that it may be read as evidence. This leaves room for the operation of the ordinary principles of the law of evidence, including the rule that the trial judge may exclude admissible evidence if its prejudicial effect substantially outweighs its probative value: see *R. v. Corbett.* . . . The case most frequently cited for the discretion to exclude is *R. v. Wray,* . . . where it is referred to in a dictum by Martland J., but it is simply one of the fundamental postulates of the law of evidence.

As my colleague notes, some have interpreted Martland J.'s dictum as limiting the discretion solely to situations where the evidence is highly prejudicial to the accused and is only of modest probative value. I do not accept this restrictive approach to the discretion. As I noted in *Corbett, supra,* at pp. 433-6 C.C.C., pp. 736-40 S.C.R., this narrow view, which can be traced from a statement by Lord du Parcq in *Noor Mohamed v. The King,* [1949] A.C. 182 at p. 192, has now been rejected by the House of Lords: *R. v. Sang,* [1980] A.C. 402 (H.L.). That case, and others there referred to, make it clear that under English law, a judge in a criminal trial always has a discretion to exclude evidence if, in the judge's opinion, its prejudicial effect substantially outweighs its probative value. . . .

. . . As their Lordships make clear, the discretion is grounded in the judge's duty to ensure a fair trial. . . . I am in accord with their view of the nature of the discretion.

. . . [I]t is evident that the trial judge failed to properly instruct himself either about the existence of the discretion or, more likely, about its nature. He repeatedly stresses the relevance of the evidence without any consideration of its prejudicial character. This smacks of the restricted view of the discretion I have rejected. In my view, therefore, the trial judge failed to exercise the discretion which was incumbent upon him to ensure a fair trial.

The Manitoba Court of Appeal had decided in *R. v. Sophonow* [138] that there was a discretion in the trial judge to exclude previous testimony, as the statutory provision

> was never intended to apply to a crucial witness whose evidence could work an injustice to the accused if the jury were deprived of seeing his demeanour and his reaction to cross-examination. [139]

PROBLEM

At a sexual assault trial the accused was unrepresented. He was permitted to cross-examine the complainant for two days. The accused was convicted but on appeal the Quebec Court of Appeal ordered a new trial. At the new trial the complainant refused to testify on the basis the experience of the first trial had lead to depression and a suicide attempt. The Crown applies to have the evidence of the complainant at the first trial admitted to prove the truth. Would you as the judge admit the evidence? On what basis? Do different considerations apply to

---

138 (1986), 50 C.R. (3d) 193.
139 *Ibid.,* at p. 209.

admitting the transcript as distinct from the audio recording? See *R. v. Dégarie, No. 1* (June 28, 2001), (C.Q.) and *R. v. Dégarie, No. 2* (June 29, 2001), (C.Q.).

(c) Exceptions Not Dependent on Availability of Declarant (Have No Necessity Requirement)

(i) *Declarations as to Physical Sensation*

In *Gilbey v. Great Western Railway* [140] it was alleged that the deceased had suffered his injury on the job and that compensation from his employer was forthcoming. The trial court received in evidence statements made by the deceased to his wife not merely of his sensations but as to the cause of the injury. On appeal it was held, by Cozens-Hardy, M.R.:

> I do not doubt at all that statements made by a workman to his wife of his sensations at the time, about the pain in the side or his head, or what not — whether those statements were made by groans or by actions or were verbal statements — would be admissible to prove the existence of those sensations. But to hold that those statements ought to go further and be admitted as evidence of the facts deposed to is, I think, open to doubt; such a contention is contrary to all authority.

There have never been grounds of necessity, such as death or insanity of the declarant, attached to this exception but it is believed that there is "a fair necessity, in the sense that there is no other equally satisfactory source of evidence either from the same person or elsewhere."[141] Given these grounds of necessity the evidence

> is not to be extended beyond the necessity on which the rule is founded. Anything in the nature of narration or statement is to be carefully excluded, and the testimony is to be confined strictly to such complaints, exclamations, and expressions as usually and naturally accompany and furnish evidence of a present existing pain or malady.[142]

Circumstantial guarantees of trustworthiness are resident in the fact that the declarant, if anyone, should be able to perceive his own sensations or feelings; his declaration is of the moment and defects in memory are absent. Arising from the spontaneity of the declaration and lack of opportunity to fabricate there is some assurance of sincerity, though it is recognized that fabrication can occur. Though the statements under review need not be made to a physician, such declarations would carry the further assurance that the declarant is unlikely to mislead the person from whom he seeks assistance.

(ii) *Declarations as to Mental or Emotional State*

When a person's mental or emotional state is a material issue in the trial, then that person's statements evidencing the same may be received, and for the same reasons as recounted above justifying declarations as to physical

---

140 (1910), 102 L.T. 202 (C.A.); cited with approval by Middleton, J. in *Youlden v. London Guar. Co.* (1912), 4 D.L.R. 721 (Ont. H.C.); affirmed 12 D.L.R. 433 (Ont. C.A.).

141 6 Wigmore, *Evidence* (Chad. Rev.), s. 1714, p. 90. It is believed that his spontaneous declaration would be superior to his later recounting of the condition in the witness stand.

142 Per Bigelow, J. in *Bacon v. Charlton* (1851), 7 Cush. 586, as quoted in 6 Wigmore, *Evidence* (Chad. Rev.), s. 1718.

sensation. If at trial X's domicile is material, his earlier statement, "I plan to make Canada my home," is receivable to prove his intent, as we see that the hearsay dangers of communication, memory and perception are absent; in a suit for alienation of affections the wife-declarant's earlier statement of "I don't love you anymore" would similarly be receivable under this exception. Notice that these statements will be received though they were made before or after the moment that the state of mind was material; if the trier determines that a certain state of mind existed on Day 1 he will be able to reason that the same state of mind continued to exist to Day 5.

In a prosecution for murder, statements of the accused, "I'll blow his brains out," "I hate him," would also be receivable under this exception as evidence of intent, but since they also constitute admissions, and are receivable under that head, this exception is seldom canvassed. Of course, admissions are only received when tendered *against* the accused. If statements of the accused, "I never meant to do him harm," "I loved him," are tendered under this exception they would be met with the rebuke that they are self-serving and inadmissible on that ground. Self-serving evidence is excluded because of the danger that an accused might manufacture evidence; but to assume the falsity of the evidence is to beg the question. Professor Wigmore comments:

> Because [we say] this accused person *might* be guilty and therefore *might* have contrived these false utterances, therefore we shall exclude them, although without this assumption they indicate feelings wholly inconsistent with guilt, and although, if he is innocent, their exclusion is a cruel deprivation of a most natural and effective sort of evidence. To hold that every expression of hatred, malice and bravado is to be received, while no expression of fear, goodwill, friendship, or the like, can be considered, is to exhibit ourselves the victims of a narrow whimsicality, which might be expected in the tribunal of Jeffreys, going down from London to Taunton with a list of his intended victims already in his pocket, or on a bench "condemning" to order, as Zola said of Dreyfus's military judges.

> . . . There is no reason why a declaration of an existing state of mind, if it would be admissible against the accused, should not also be admissible in his favour, except so far as the circumstances indicate plainly a motive to deceive.[143]

In the above instances, the statements are tendered as evidence when state of mind is a material issue. A larger problem develops if the statements are tendered to evidence an existing state of mind which is not itself material but is relevant to a material issue: for example, in a murder prosecution, evidence of the deceased's statement "I want it all to end" indicating her intention to commit suicide as evidence that later she did perform the act; evidence of the deceased's statement that "I'm going to see Joe tonight and have it out with him" as evidence against Joe that the two fought later that evening. The authorities on this point are meagre and in conflict.[144] The classic "text-book" case in this area is *Mutual*

---

143 6 Wigmore, *Evidence* (Chad. Rev.), s. 1732, p. 160.
144 Contrast *R. v. Buckley* (1873), 13 Cox C.C. 293 and *R. v. Wainwright* (1875), 13 Cox C.C. 171. See also *R. v. Thomson*, [1912] 3 K.B. 19 (C.C.A.); *Cuff v. Frazee Storage & Cartage Co.* (1907), 14 O.L.R. 263 (C.A.); *R. v. Moghal* (1977), 65 Cr. App. R. 56; *Home v. Corbeil*, [1955] 4 D.L.R. 750 (Ont. H.C.); affirmed 2 D.L.R. (2d) 543 (Ont. C.A.). Recall *Sugden v. Lord St. Leonard's* (1876), 1 P.D. 154 (C.A.) and its view of the pretestamentary declaration. And see *Workman v. R.*, [1963] 1 C.C.C. 297 (Alta. C.A.); affirmed [1963] 2 C.C.C. 1 (S.C.C.).

Life Insurance Co. v. Hillmon.[145] The plaintiff sought to recover the proceeds from an insurance policy on her deceased husband. The insurance company resisted on the ground that the body found in Crooked Creek, Kansas was not that of Hillmon but that of his travelling companion, Walters. The disputed evidence consisted of letters written by Walters to his fiancee that he intended to go with Hillmon to Crooked Creek. The court held that the letters should have been received:

> The existence of a particular intention in a certain person at a certain time being a material fact to be proved, evidence that he expressed that intention at that time is as direct evidence of that fact as his own testimony that he then had that intention would be. After his death there can hardly be any other way of proving it, and while he is still alive his own memory of his state of mind at a former time is no more likely to be clear and true than a bystander's recollection of what he then said, and is less trustworthy than letters written by him at the very time and under circumstances precluding a suspicion of misrepresentation. The letters in question were competent . . . evidence that . . . he had the intention of going, and of going with Hillmon, which made it more probable both that he did go and that he went with Hillmon than if there had been no proof of such intention.[146]

The hearsay analysis is faultless; the hearsay dangers are minimized. True it is that "it was only a statement of intention which might or might not have been carried out"[147] but the problem that the declarant might not follow through with his intention is not a hearsay problem but rather a problem of relevance.

Suppose however that the declaration of mental state is a statement of belief in the declarant as evidence of some past act.[148] In *Shepard v. U.S.*,[149] a murder prosecution, the statement of the deceased was received as a dying declaration: "Dr. Shepard has poisoned me." On appeal, the conditions of that exception were found not to have been met and the prosecution sought to justify the evidence as indicating the deceased's state of mind which was then inconsistent with the defence of suicide. Cardozo J. wrote:

> There are times when a state of mind, if relevant, may be proved by contemporaneous declarations of feeling or intent. Mutual Life Ins. Co. v. Hillmon. . . . (other examples are then given) . . . The ruling in that case marks the high-water line beyond which courts have been unwilling to go. . . . Declarations of intention, casting light upon the future, have been sharply distinguished from declarations of memory, pointing backwards to the past. There would be an end, or nearly that, to the rule against hearsay if the distinction were ignored.[150]

---

145 145 U.S. 285 (1892).

146 *Ibid.*, at p. 295.

147 The reason given by Cockburn, C.J. in *R. v. Wainwright, supra*, note 144, at p. 172, for rejecting such a statement.

148 The problem is canvassed in Seligman, "An Exception to the Hearsay Rule" (1912-13), 26 Harv. L. Rev. 146; and see Maguire, "The Hillmon Case — Thirty-three Years After" (1925), 38 Harv. L. Rev. 709.

149 290 U.S. 96 (1933).

150 *Ibid.*, at p. 104. But compare *People v. Merkouris*, 344 P. 2d 1 (Cal. S.C., 1959); cert. den. 361 U.S. 943 (1960).

R. v. P. (R.)
(1990), 58 C.C.C. (3d) 334 (Ont. H.C.)

The accused was charged with murder. The Crown sought to introduce several statements said to have been made by the deceased to various Crown witnesses. These statements were said to be capable of demonstrating her state of mind. They would show her unhappiness and dissatisfaction with the relationship she had with the accused and her determination to end that relationship. The Crown alleged that the accused was motivated to kill the deceased because he was enraged and humiliated by her decision to leave him.

DOHERTY J.:—

. . . .

Relevant evidence can be defined as evidence having any tendency to make the existence of any fact that is of consequence to the determination of the action more probable or less probable than it would be without the evidence: . . . R. Delisle, "*Evidence Principles and Problems*", 2nd ed. (1989), pp. 9-11.

In the case at bar, relevance has two aspects. Are the statements relevant to the deceased's state of mind in that they permit one to draw a reasonable conclusion as to her state of mind? If so, is her state of mind relevant directly or indirectly to the fact in issue? . . . I have already indicated that the statements clear the first relevance hurdle.

Relevance is a matter of inductive logic requiring that the trial judge examine the proffered evidence in light of his own knowledge and understanding of human conduct: *McCormick, ibid.*, p. 544; *Delisle, ibid.*, p. 10. Relevance is situational and depends not only on the ultimate issue in the case (*e.g.*, identification), but also on the other factual issues which either of the litigants raises as relevant to the ultimate issue. Consequently, the deceased's mental state may bear no direct relevance to the ultimate issue of identification but it will none the less be relevant to that issue if it is relevant to another fact (*e.g.*, motive) which is directly relevant to the ultimate issue of identification.

. . . .

Assuming relevance, evidence of utterances made by a deceased (although the rule is not limited to deceased persons) which evidence her state of mind are admissible. If the statements are explicit statements of a state of mind, they are admitted as exceptions to the hearsay rule. If those statements permit an inference as to the speaker's state of mind, they are regarded as original testimonial evidence and admitted as circumstantial evidence from which a state of mind can be inferred. The result is the same whichever route is taken, although circumstantial evidence of a state of mind poses added problems rising out of the inference drawing process.

. . . .

Evidence of the deceased's state of mind may, in turn, be relevant as circumstantial evidence that the deceased subsequently acted in accordance with that avowed state of mind. Where a deceased says, "I will go to Ottawa tomorrow", the statement affords direct evidence of the state of mind — an intention to go to Ottawa tomorrow — and circumstantial evidence that the deceased in fact went to Ottawa on that day. If either the state of mind, or the fact to be inferred from the existence of the state of mind is relevant, the evidence is receivable subject to objections based on undue prejudice. . . .

An utterance indicating that a deceased had a certain intention or design will afford evidence that the deceased acted in accordance with that stated intention or plan where it is reasonable to infer that the deceased did so. The reasonableness of the inference will depend on a number of variables including the nature of the plan described in the utterance, and the proximity in time between the statement as to the plan and the proposed implementation of the plan.

The rules of evidence as developed to this point do not exclude evidence of utterances by a deceased which reveal her state of mind, but rather appear to provide specifically for their admission where relevant. The evidence is not, however, admissible to show the state of mind of persons other than the deceased (unless they were aware of the statements), or to show that persons other than the deceased acted in accordance with the deceased's stated intentions, save perhaps cases where the act was a joint one involving the deceased and another person. The evidence is also not admissible to establish that past acts or events referred to in the utterances occurred.

. . . .

A trial judge may, in his discretion, exclude evidence which is otherwise admissible where the potential prejudicial effect of that evidence outweighs its potential probative force. [Citations omittted.]

Prejudice can refer to several things. In the context of this case, it means the danger, despite instructions to the contrary, that the jury will use the evidence of the deceased's utterances for purposes other than drawing inferences and conclusions as to her state of mind and as to her subsequent conduct. In particular, the jury may infer from some of the utterances that Mr. P. was a tyrannical person, obsessed with controlling the deceased even to the extent of engaging in illegal and bizarre conduct. From that, they may infer that he is the sort of person who would kill someone who dared challenge his authority over that person. This line of reasoning, while not illogical, is not permitted: *R. v. D. (L.E.)*, *supra*, at p. 157.

The balancing process envisioned by the claim that prejudicial potential outweighs probative potential is no longer designed only to root out the most extreme cases where prejudicial potential is "grave" and probative value is "trifling": *R. v. Wray*, [1970] 4 C.C.C. 1 at p. 17. The onus, however, is on the accused to demonstrate that the balance favours exclusion of otherwise admissible evidence. Where the prejudice asserted rests in the potential misuse of the evidence by the jury, one's assessment of the jury's ability to properly follow directions will play a key role in determining whether the accused has shown that the balance favours exclusion. Views as to the jury's ability to follow the law rather than their instincts or prejudices differ. . . . I incline to the view that lawyers and judges tend to underestimate the intellectual power and discipline of juries.

R. v. STARR
[2000] 2 S.C.R. 144, 36 C.R. (5th) 1, 147 C.C.C. (3d) 449

The accused was charged with two counts of first degree murder. He was accused of shooting C and W by the side of a highway. C and W had been drinking with the accused in a hotel. C and W drove to a gas station. The accused also drove to that station. There G, a sometime girlfriend of C, angry with C because he was out with W rather than her, confronted C. G asked C why he would not come home with her. According to G, C replied that he had to "go and do an Autopac scam with Robert". She understood "Robert" to be the accused. The Crown's theory was that the killing was a gang-related execution perpetrated by the accused. W was an unfortunate witness who was killed simply because she was in the wrong place at the wrong time. The theory was that the accused had used an Autopac scam as a pretext to get C out into the countryside. The trial judge found that G's anticipated testimony regarding the scam was admissible under the "present intentions" or "state of mind" exception to the hearsay rule. The Court of Appeal, in a majority decision, upheld the accused's convictions.

IACOBUCCI J. (MAJOR, BINNIE, ARBOUR and LEBEL JJ. concurring): —

. . . .

The theory of the Crown at trial was that the killing of Cook was a gang-related execution perpetrated by the appellant. Weselowski was an unfortunate witness who was killed simply because she was in the wrong place at the wrong time. The theory was that the appellant had used an Autopac scam as a pretext to get Cook out into the countryside. Outside the Turskis' home, Cook got into the smaller car and drove it into the ditch, hitting telephone poles in an effort to damage the car. The appellant shot Weselowski twice in the head, then drove Weselowski's station wagon up the road to where Cook had stopped the smaller car in the ditch. When Cook entered the station wagon on the passenger side, the appellant shot him from the driver's seat three times in the head and three times in the chest. He then pushed Cook's body out of the vehicle and drove away, parking near his brother's house, where the appellant abandoned the station wagon.

. . . .

The Crown argued that the "state of mind" or "present intentions" exception to the hearsay rule applied to render Cook's statement to Giesbrecht admissible. This exception was most recently discussed in detail by this Court in *Smith*, supra, where it was recognized that an "exception to the hearsay rule arises when the declarant's statement is adduced in order to demonstrate the intentions, or state of mind, of the declarant at the time when the statement was made". Wigmore has argued that the present intentions exception also includes a requirement that a statement "be of a present existing state of mind, and must appear to have been made in a natural manner and not under circumstances of suspicion": *Wigmore on Evidence*, vol. 6 (Chadbourn rev. 1976), at para. 1725, p. 129. L'Heureux-Dubé J., at para. 63 of her reasons, denies that Wigmore's suggestion has ever been adopted in our jurisprudence. As I will discuss below, regardless of whether the present intentions requirement ever had such a requirement, the principled approach demands that it must have it now. I will therefore examine the admissibility of Cook's statement under the present intentions exception in light of that understanding.

. . . .

It is important to emphasize that even in "cases where the act was a joint one involving the deceased and another person", the hearsay is not generally admissible to show the intentions of a third party. I draw this conclusion for two reasons. First, I can find no support in Canadian jurisprudence for the proposition that statements of intention are admissible against someone other than the declarant, apart from the one comment by Doherty J. noted above. . . . Second, there are very good reasons behind the rule against allowing statements of present intention to be used to prove the state of mind of someone other than the declarant. As noted above, the central concern with hearsay is the inability of the trier of fact to test the reliability of the declarant's assertion. When the statement is tendered to prove the intentions of a third party, this danger is multiplied. If a declarant makes a statement about the intentions of a third party, there are three possible bases for this statement: first, it could be based on a prior conversation with the accused; second, it could be based on a prior conversation with a fourth party, who indicated the third party's intentions to the declarant; or third, it could be based on pure speculation on the part of the declarant. Under the first scenario, the statement is double hearsay. Since each level of double hearsay must fall within an exception, or be admissible under the principled approach, the mere fact that the declarant is making a statement of present intention is insufficient to render it admissible. The second level of hearsay must also be admissible.

The other two scenarios also clearly require exclusion. If the statement about joint acts is based on a conversation with a fourth party, then the statement is triple hearsay, or worse. If, on the other hand, it is based on pure speculation, then it clearly is unreliable and does not fit within the rationale underlying the present intentions exception. In conclusion then, a statement of intention cannot be admitted to prove the intentions of someone other than the declarant, unless a hearsay exception can be established for each level of hearsay. One way to establish this would obviously be the co-conspirator exception: see *R. v. Carter*, [1982] 1 S.C.R. 938; Sopinka, Lederman and Bryant, supra, at pp. 303-7. This is no doubt what Doherty J. was referring to in *P. (R.)*, supra, when he spoke of "cases where the act was a joint one involving the deceased and another person". Barring the applicability of this or some other exception to each level of hearsay involved, statements of joint intention are only admissible to prove the declarant's intentions.

. . . .

With great respect to the Court of Appeal, I conclude that the trial judge erred in admitting Cook's statement to Giesbrecht under the present intentions exception and, having admitted it, in not limiting its use by the jury, for three reasons. First, the statement contained no indicia of reliability since it was made under circumstances of suspicion; second, the trial judge failed to instruct the jury that the statement was only admissible as evidence regarding the intentions of Cook, not the appellant; and third, even if it had been properly limited, the evidence was more prejudicial than probative.

Turning first to the circumstances of suspicion, I agree with Twaddle J.A. that the statement lacked circumstantial guarantees of trustworthiness. As Twaddle J.A. noted, Cook and Giesbrecht had been romantically involved for almost two years. Cook had lived with Giesbrecht and her mother for a time, and had spent the night before his murder with Giesbrecht, after getting out of jail. Then, in the early morning hours of August 21, 1994, Giesbrecht observed Cook in the car of another woman, Darlene Weselowski. Giesbrecht testified that she thought Cook might try to "take off on her" if he saw Giesbrecht approaching the car, and she endeavoured not to be seen by Cook until she was close enough to talk to him. After an initial confrontation, Giesbrecht walked away into an alley behind the gas station, where Cook followed her. Their conversation ended in an argument because Cook was with Weselowski. She was angry at Cook for being with another woman, and asked him expressly why Cook would not come home with her rather than remain with Weselowski. It was at this point, and in this heated context, that Cook said he was going to engage in an Autopac scam with the appellant, who was sitting in a car nearby. Giesbrecht testified that it was unusual for Cook to discuss such business matters with her.

Twaddle J.A. found that the circumstances surrounding the making of the statement cast serious doubt upon the reliability of the statement. The possibility that Cook was untruthful could not be said to have been substantially negated. Twaddle J.A. relied, in particular, upon the fact that Cook may have had a motive to lie in order to make it seem that he was not romantically involved with Weselowski, and upon the ease with which Cook could point to the appellant, who was sitting nearby in a car but out of earshot, as being the person with whom he was going to do a scam. In my view, Twaddle J.A. was correct in finding that these circumstances bring the reliability of Cook's statement into doubt. The statement was made under "circumstances of suspicion", and therefore does not fall within the present intentions exception. The statement should have been excluded.

. . . .

Finally, I would exclude Cook's statement as more prejudicial than probative. The trial judge did not make a finding on the issue of reliability. His focus was upon the impermissible inferences that the jury might draw from otherwise admissible hearsay, and he regarded the primary prejudice to the appellant to be that the jury might infer that he was the type of person likely to commit insurance fraud. However, as noted above, this was not the primary source of prejudice. The trial judge erred by not considering whether "the prejudicial effect of the prohibited use of the evidence [i.e., the appellant's intentions] overbears its probative value on the permitted use [i.e., Cook's intentions]": *Watt's Manual of Criminal Evidence* (1999). The impermissible inferences that the jury might well have drawn from Cook's statement are that the appellant was in the car that followed Cook, that the appellant was alone in the car (since Cook referred only to the appellant), and that the appellant went with Cook as part of a plan to lure Cook to a secluded area and kill him. These were the specific impermissible inferences that the jury might have drawn in this regard — indeed, they are inferences that the Crown specifically invited the jury to draw — quite apart from the inferences that they might have drawn regarding his general criminality. In my view, Twaddle J.A. was correct in finding that the prejudicial effect of the admission of Cook's statement accordingly outweighed the statement's probative value. The statement ought to have been excluded on this basis as well.

PROBLEM

You are the trial judge in the trial of Jack, who is charged with first degree murder of K. K's body was found by the police in a shallow grave on the farm Jack managed and occupied.

At trial you have admitted into evidence a voluntary statement by the accused to the police, soon after the police found the body. Admissibility of this statement is not in issue. In that statement Jack admitted he was at the farm when K was shot but maintained that the shooting was by a neighbour, who has since left the country. In the statement the accused also admitted that he helped bury the corpse.

The Crown's case is that the accused persuaded K to come to the farm with $50,000 cash to do a drug transaction with a third party but that this was just a ruse to get him to the farm to rob and kill him. A number of evidentiary rulings arise during the course of the trial. With reference to appropriate authority, rule on the admissibility of the following evidence tendered by the Crown:

(a) A statement made by K to a friend shortly before K disappeared that "I am collecting a large sum of money to go to the farm where Jack and I are going to make a big time drug score".

(b) A recorded 911 call by the accused's wife, Jill, to police on the night of the killing "Come quickly I think my husband is going to shoot someone". The police answered the call to the farm within 10 minutes. Everything seemed calm and Jack assured them all was well. Jill denied that she had called the police. The next day the police found the body in the shallow grave. The voice on the 911 call is now identified to be that of Jill.

Compare *R. v. Harrison* (2001), 44 C.R. (5th) 120 (B.C. C.A.).

(iii) *Spontaneous Statements (Excited Utterances)*

Discretion in this area there must be, but it is best to have guidelines articulated for its exercise; when the guidelines are spelled out in terms of the exception's justification, we are even further advanced. The chief justification lies in the fact that the danger of insincerity is minimized as there has been no opportunity for the declarant to fabricate, and the memory danger is eliminated since the declaration is contemporaneous with the event. A difficulty, of course, remains in the danger of misperception, and deserves stressing when evaluating the worth of the statement: how often have we exclaimed about a situation and found ourselves later saying, "on second thought. . . ." The very fact that the event was startling and caused the viewer to be excited can impair his perceptual abilities.[151]

Establishing the preliminary condition of admissibility, that the declaration was in response to a startling event, can produce a problem. Can we look at the statement itself to determine the relationship? While it appears as a bootstrap operation it appears to be the better view that the statement can be regarded, in the discretion of the trial judge, along with other matters.[152]

R. v. BEDINGFIELD
(1879), 14 Cox C.C. 341

The accused was charged with murder. The accused was present with the deceased in the deceased's house. The deceased came suddenly out of the house with her throat cut. She said something, pointing backwards to the house. In a few minutes she was dead. In the course of the opening speech on the part of the prosecution it was proposed to state what she said. It was objected on the part of the prisoner that it was not admissible.

Cockburn C.J. said he had carefully considered the question and was clear that it could not be admitted and therefore ought not to be stated, as it might have a fatal effect. I regret, he said, that according to the law of England, any statement made by the deceased should not be admissible. Then could it be admissible having been made in the absence of the prisoner, as part of the res gestae but it is not so admissible for it was not part of anything done, or something said while something was being done, but something said after something done. Anything, he said, uttered by the deceased at the time the act was being done would be admissible, as, for instance, if she had been heard to say something, as "Don't, Harry!". But here it was something stated by her after it was all over, whatever it was, and after the act was completed.

It was submitted, on the part of the prosecution, that the statement was admissible as a dying declaration, the case to be proved being that the woman's throat was cut completely and the artery severed, so that she was dying, and was actually dead in a few minutes; but Cockburn C.J. said the statement was not

---

151 See Hutchins and Slesinger, "Some Observations on the Law of Evidence" (1928), 28 Col. L. Rev. 432 and Stewart, "Perception Memory and Hearsay", [1970] Utah L. Rev. 1 at 28 and Marshall, *Law and Psychology in Conflict* (1969), pp. 19-20.

152 *Ratten v. R.*, [1971] 3 All E.R. 801 (P.C.), discussed below in *R. v. Clark*.

admissible as a dying declaration, because it did not appear that the woman was aware that she was dying.

It was urged that the woman must have known it as she was actually dying at the time, but Cockburn C.J. said that though she might have known it if she had had time for reflection, here that was not so, for at the time she made the statement she had no time to consider and reflect that she was dying; there is no evidence to show that she knew it, and I cannot presume it. There is nothing to show that she was under the sense of impending death, so the statement is not admissible as a dying declaration.

[The statement was later reported to be "See what Harry has done!" In the result the jury nevertheless found him guilty based on the other evidence.]

R. v. CLARK
(1983), 35 C.R. (3d) 357, 7 C.C.C. (3d) 46 (Ont. C.A.)

On the accused's trial for murder, spontaneous utterances by the deceased made shortly after she had been injured by the accused when the accused in fact was still present including the words "Help, I've been murdered, I've been stabbed", were admitted as evidence of the truth of the facts stated. On appeal it was argued that the statements were improperly admitted.

DUBIN J.A. (MACKINNON A.C.J.O and CORY J.A. concurring): —

. . . .

The appellant married Mr. Ade in January, 1977. Their marriage was a somewhat stormy and unusual one, and they separated in November, 1977. The appellant testified that she was still very much in love with her husband and during the period of their separation frequently attended upon him with a view apparently of winning him back. The marriage was annulled in April, 1978, and shortly after Mr. Ade began to see the deceased Beverly Ade. The appellant was devastated when he became involved with another woman. She telephoned his office with such frequency that Mr. Ade asked the switchboard operator to stop passing on her calls to him although some calls did get through. She waited outside his place of work, would follow him to the bank, to the parking-lot or to the cafeteria where he was having lunch.

In December, 1978, Mr. Ade married the deceased. The appellant was observed on many occasions loitering in the area of the residence of Mr. Ade and the deceased. She continued to telephone and visited his office and scouted his premises and the area in which he lived.

. . . .

On the morning of July 7th she attended at the residence of the deceased. The appellant testified that she did so to recover two lawn chairs which had been left in Mr. Ade's garage and which, unbeknownst to her, had been given away by him prior to July 7th. . . . It was during that visit that Beverly Ade came to her death as a result of penetrating stab wounds to her heart, admittedly at the hands of the appellant. The deceased had one superficial wound to the back, one to the right side, ten front torso wounds and four wounds to her hands. ... The appellant's left hand was cut in three places.

The defence was self-defence and/or provocation. The appellant testified that she knocked on the door of the deceased's premises and told the deceased that she wanted the two lawn chairs. They attended at the garage but could not find the chairs. According to the appellant, the deceased said, "Howard's been over you a long time, just don't make anymore excuses." The appellant replied, "Don't be too sure." The appellant testified that as they came out of the garage the deceased gave the appellant a push and said "not to come around anymore". She stated that she then stood with her back to the garage door and with her eyes closed. When she heard footsteps, she opened her eyes and saw the deceased quite close holding a knife. The appellant was startled and afraid. She testified that she grabbed the knife with her left hand and pushed the deceased with the other. The deceased fell. As the appellant tried to run away, she tripped over the deceased and fell down. She was not sure whether she had hit the deceased but saw that her own hand was bleeding. She said that the deceased then grabbed her, and she felt that she was hanging on to the deceased near a chair which was near the garage entrance. She testified that she did not know that she had injured the deceased who was at that time sitting on the chair.

. . . .

Spontaneous exclamations

It was submitted that the learned trial judge erred in admitting certain of the evidence to be found in the testimony of Fawn Pitcher. On July 7, 1980, Miss Pitcher was staying with her aunt who resided across the street from the Ade residence. ... In order to appreciate the evidentiary issues raised as well as to indicate the over-all importance of her testimony in this case, I set out hereunder in some detail the relevant portions of Miss Pitcher's testimony:

Q.   Okay, just take it slowly and tell the jury please what it was that you heard please.

A.   Okay, I was in the back kitchen making my breakfast. It was around ten o'clock and I heard somebody calling for help. First I thought it was kids fooling around a pool. I was sort of annoyed at it and it kept up and I thought no, so I went outside and I realized it wasn't a child in a pool. I went out the back gate and I realized where the cries were coming from, across the road.

Q.   Fawn, could you tell me then what you saw and heard as you went across the street to find out what was going on?

A.   Okay, as I came out the back gate to my aunt's place and up her side lawn I saw a woman standing at the top of the driveway in the picture shown and she was yelling: "Help, help I've been murdered. I've been stabbed." And I didn't see anyone else around. I walked across the road, down through their ditch and up into the lawn and I saw the accused sort of agitated going back and forth towards the deceased. . . .

Q.   All right. Now, where was the accused lady when you first saw her?

A.   She was on the grass.

Q.   Yes.

A.   Near a clump of trees or tree and she was moving back and forth towards the deceased and then back on to the lawn again.

Q.   Okay. Did you see the accused lady right away?

A.   Not right away. Not when I first came out I only saw the deceased.

. . . .

Q.   You were then approaching and the jury has seen the angle that you were approaching on, just tell me what happened then as you approached?

A.   Okay, as I approached, I saw only the deceased and she was yelling, "Help I've been murdered, I've been stabbed." I crossed the road, went up onto the lawn of the other house and she seemed to see me then and she said, "Go call the police, go call an ambulance."

Q.   All right, now, what can you tell me about the appearance of the deceased lady at this time when she was saying these things to you?

A.   She seem to be very distressed. I couldn't see at first that there was any injury apparent until I crossed up into her lawn and as I got closer I saw a red circle on the right shoulder and just below her right shoulder.

. . . .

It was the submission by counsel for the appellant that the words spoken by the deceased, "Help I've been murdered, I've been stabbed" were inadmissible hearsay. No objection was taken by counsel at trial to the admissibility of that evidence, but if the evidence was in fact inadmissible and highly prejudicial, the failure to object is not fatal.

[The Court then reviewed *Bedingfield* and English and Canadian cases that had followed it over the years.]

It is to be noted that the admissibility of the statements under consideration in the foregoing cases was dependent upon whether they could be said to be part of the res gestae, a Latin phrase much criticized in *Wigmore on Evidence*, which will be presently commented upon. In order to fit into a res gestae test, the statement had to form part of the transaction or event and if not immediately contemporaneous was held to be outside the otherwise permissible exception to the hearsay rule.

The basis for the admissibility of a spontaneous exclamation, the label assigned by Wigmore to such statements, was considered and expanded upon in *Ratten v. Reginam*, [1971] 3 All E.R. 801. Ratten was charged with the murder of his wife. Her death had been caused by a wound from a shot-gun held by the appellant. His explanation was that the discharge was accidental and had occurred while he was cleaning his gun in the kitchen of his house. He was unable to explain how the gun from which the shot was fired had come to be loaded. He testified that he immediately telephoned for an ambulance and, shortly after, the police had telephoned him, at which time he asked them to come immediately. At about 1:15 p.m. on the day of the alleged offence, a telephone call was made from their premises. The telephone operator who answered had stated in evidence at trial:

> I plugged into a number [the appellant's number] . . . and . . . I opened the speak key and I said to the person, "Number please" and the reply I got was "Get me the police please".

The person on the telephone gave her address and hung up. The telephone operator testified that the person on the telephone was in a hysterical state and later added that the person on the telephone sobbed. The telephone operator advised the police of the call. The police telephoned the Ratten house and spoke to the accused. By this time the deceased had been shot.

Objection was taken to the admissibility of the evidence of the telephone operator on the ground that it was hearsay and that it did not come within any of the recognized exceptions to the rule against hearsay, but the objection was overruled. The issue was again raised on appeal on the premise that the trial judge properly instructed the jury that on the evidence they might find the telephone call was made by the deceased woman.

The Privy Council first held that the evidence of the telephone operator was not hearsay evidence but was admissible as evidence of a fact relevant to an issue.

Lord Wilberforce stated at p. 805:

> The mere fact that evidence of a witness includes evidence as to words spoken by another person who is not called is no objection to its admissibility. Words spoken are facts just as much as any other action by a human being. If the speaking of the words is a relevant fact, a witness may give evidence that they were spoken. A question of hearsay only arises when the words spoken are relied on 'testimonially', i.e., as establishing some fact narrated by the words. Authority is hardly needed for this proposition, but their Lordships will restate what was said in the judgment of the Board in *Subramaniam v. Public Prosecutor*, [1956] 1 W.L.R. 965 at 970:
>
> > Evidence of a statement made to a witness by a person who is not himself called as a witness may or may not be hearsay. It is hearsay and inadmissible when the object of the evidence is to establish the truth of what is contained in the statement. It is not hearsay and is admissible when it is proposed to establish by the evidence, not the truth of the statement but the fact that it was made.

He then proceeded, however, to deal with the admissibility of the evidence on the premise that it was put forth as evidence of the truth of the facts asserted by the statement, and on that premise concluded at pp. 806-7 as follows:

> Their Lordships, as already stated, do not consider that there is any hearsay element in the evidence, nor in their opinion was it so presented by the trial judge, but they think it right to deal with the appellant's submission on the assumption that there is, i.e. that the words said to have been used involve an assertion of the truth of some facts stated in them and that they may have been so understood by the jury. The Crown defended the admissibility of the words as part of the "res gestae", a contention which led to the citation of numerous authorities.

The expression "res gestae", like many Latin phrases, is often used to cover situations insufficiently analysed in clear English terms.

. . . .

The possibility of concoction, or fabrication, where it exists, is on the other hand an entirely valid reason for exclusion, and is probably the real test which judges in fact apply. In their Lordships' opinion this should be recognised and applied directly as the relevant test: the test should be not the uncertain one whether the making of the statement was in some sense part of the event or transaction. This may often be difficult to establish: such external matters as the time which elapses between the events and the speaking of the words (or vice versa), and differences in location being relevant factors but not, taken by themselves, decisive criteria. As regards statements made after the event it must be for the judge, by preliminary ruling, to satisfy himself that the statement was so clearly made in circumstances of spontaneity or involvement in the event that the possibility of concoction can be disregarded. Conversely, if he considers that the statement was made by way of narrative of a detached prior event so that the speaker was so disengaged from it as to be able to construct or adapt his account, he should exclude it. And the same must in principle be true of statements made before the event. The test should be not the uncertain one, whether the making of the statement should be regarded as part of the event or transaction. This may often be difficult to show. But if the drama, leading up to the climax, has commenced and assumed such intensity and pressure that the utterance can safely be regarded as a true reflection of what was unrolling or actually happening, it ought to be received. The expression "res gestae" may conveniently sum up these criteria, but the reality of them must always be kept in mind: it is this that lies behind the best reasoned of the judges' rulings.

And at p. 808:

These authorities show that there is ample support for the principle that hearsay evidence may be admitted if the statement providing it is made in such conditions (always being those of approximate but not exact contemporaneity) of involvement or pressure as to exclude the possibility of concoction or distortion to the advantage of the maker or the disadvantage of the accused.

It is clear in this case that the challenged evidence was tendered as evidence of the truth of that which was stated, and, thus, if admissible, as a true exception to the hearsay rule.

. . . .

[A]lthough what was stated by Chief Justice Robertson in *R. v. Leland*, [1951] O.R. 12, 98 C.C.C. 337, 11 C.R. 152, [one of the Canadian cases that followed the contemporaneity requirement of *Bedingfield*] appears to have been consistent with the then state of the authorities, it cannot, in my respectful opinion, now be viewed as an authoritative statement of the law. This case can, of course, be readily distinguishable from *Leland*, in that, it is apparent from the evidence of Miss Pitcher that the words attributed by her as having been spoken by the deceased were spoken while the event was still transpiring and, thus, contemporaneous with the unfolding events. But I would prefer to rest my judgment on a broader base as it is now apparent from the foregoing that the narrow test of exact contemporaneity should no longer be followed.

The circumstances, as outlined by Miss Pitcher, under which the words were said to have been spoken by the deceased were such as to exclude the possibility of concoction or distortion, and if Miss Pitcher's evidence were accepted by the jury, the words spoken, "Help I've been murdered, I've been stabbed" were evidence of the belief of the deceased as to what had occurred and evidence as to the truth of the facts stated by her as a true exception to the hearsay rule. . . . The words, "Go call the police, go call an ambulance", to which no exception was taken on appeal, were, of course, admissible as a verbal act and not as an exception to the hearsay rule.

For these reasons, I would reject the submission made by counsel for the appellant on this issue.

Recall that in *Khan* the Supreme Court decided that the spontaneous statement exception was not the proper basis for admitting the infant's statement to her mother. McLachlin J. noted that there was no necessity requirement and went on to admit it under the principled approach of necessity and reliability. Given *Starr's* requirement that existing exceptions be reviewed it may be that the exception of spontaneous exceptions is no longer available in Canada. If so is this unfortunate given the justification provided in *Ratten*, followed in *Clark*?

In *R. v. Andrews*,[153] the Law Lords decided, following *Ratten*, that *R. v. Bedingfield* "would not be so decided today".

———————

The common law has received, normally with the appellation *res gestae*, declarations of a present sense of belief concerning a contemporaneous event witnessed by the declarant. For example it was held in *R. v. Graham*[154] in a prosecution for possession of stolen goods:

> . . . the respondent's verbal statement made when the attache case was found, that he had never seen it before in his life, *being one which was immediately connected with the initial discovery of the stolen goods*, was properly admitted in evidence. Explanatory statements made by an accused upon his first being found "in possession" constitute a part of the *res gestae* and are necessarily admissible in any description of the circumstances under which the crime was committed. [Emphasis added.][155]

———————

153 [1987] A.C. 281.
154 (1972), 7 C.C.C. (2d) 93 (S.C.C.). See too *R. v. Grand-Pierre* (1998), 124 C.C.C. (3d) 236 (Que. C.A.), where "res gestae" is used as synonymous with spontaneous exclamations. Given that the contemporaneous requirement for spontaneous exceptions has been abandoned in *Clark* it would be wise to avoid that ragbag term.
155 *Ibid.*, at p. 99. Applied in a trial for possession of narcotics, *R. v. Risby* (1976), 32 C.C.C. (2d) 242 (B.C.C.A.); affirmed (1978), 39 C.C.C. (2d) 567 (S.C.C.). See also *R. v. Keeler*, [1977] 5 W.W.R. 410 (Alta. C.A.) and *Reference re R. v. Latta* (1976), 30 C.C.C. (2d) 208 (Alta. C.A.).

Notice that the presence of a startling event or excitement in the declarant is not necessary; contemporaneity is the key.[156] Professor Morgan offered the justification:

> A statement by a person as to external events then and there being perceived by his senses is worthy of credence for two reasons. First, it is in essence a declaration of a presently existing state of mind, for it is nothing more than an assertion of his presently existing sense impressions. As such it has the quality of spontaneity. . . . Second, since the statement is contemporaneous with the event, it is made at the place of the event. Consequently the event is open to perception by the senses of the person to whom the declaration is made and by whom it is usually reported on the witness stand. The witness is subject to cross-examination concerning that event as well as the fact and content of the utterance, so that the extra-judicial statement does not depend solely upon the credit of the declarant. Unless exact contemporaneousness is insisted upon, the first of these guaranties is partially lacking and the second is weakened.[157]

Considering this justification for the exception under review, and remembering the previous exception for declarations as to existing mental states, did the court in *Graham* accurately describe the statement as receivable because it was part of the *res gestae*?

Contemporaneity minimizes the hearsay dangers of perception and memory and sincerity is thought to be enhanced as the declarant does not have time for reflection and deliberation. For example, in *Graham*, while admitting the first statement, contemporaneous with the discovery, the Supreme Court of Canada ruled the accused's later statement inadmissible:

> . . . his written statement was not made contemporaneously with the discovery but rather after ample time had elapsed for reflection. In my view if this statement were to be admitted it would mean that any person accused of receiving stolen goods could, after due consideration, devise an explanation which might easily be true for the goods having been found in his possession and could thus avoid the necessity of presenting himself as a witness and be afforded the full benefit of his explanation without being subjected to cross-examination. Such an explanation is, in my view, inadmissible under the general rule in criminal cases that self-serving statements made by an accused cannot be introduced on the cross-examination of third parties because they cannot themselves be tested by cross-examination of the accused person who made them, and their introduction in such manner deprives the jury of the benefit of appraising his credibility from observing his demeanour.[158]

---

156   See *Jarvis v. London St. Ry. Co.* (1919), 45 O.L.R. 167, 173 (C.A.) per Middleton J., holding a statement inadmissible: "The truth is that the statement said to have been made by the conductor formed no part of the *res gestae*, it was a mere narrative or discussion anent a thing then past. . . . [T]o make the statement admissible, it must be an involuntary and contemporaneous exclamation made without time for reflection; it is because the statement is involuntary and contemporaneous that it is received. These characteristics are supposed to impart some indication of its veracity."

157   Morgan, "A Suggested Classification of Utterances Admissible as Res Gestae" (1922), 31 Yale L.J. 229, 236-37.

158   *Supra*, note 154 at p. 99 per Spence J.

C. VOLUNTARY CONFESSION RULE

1. COMMON LAW PRE-*OICKLE*

In the middle of the 16th century, statutes were enacted[159] requiring justices of the peace to take dispositions from all witnesses to felony, including the accused. The results of the inquisitorial examination of the accused were transmitted to the judge, and his deposition was read to the jury at the outset of the trial. At the trial as well the accused was frequently questioned by the judge. The practice of questioning an accused at trial diminished during the 17th century, and questioning pre-trial diminished during the 18th century. By 1700 questioning at trial had ceased and by the early 19th century the pre-trial examination by the justices was limited to the recording of any statements which the accused volunteered. This new practice of preliminary examination was embodied in statute form in 1848,[160] giving us the form of preliminary inquiry now provided for by the Canadian Criminal Code:

> Having heard the evidence, do you wish to say anything in answer to the charge? You are not bound to say anything, but whatever you do say will be taken down in writing and may be given in evidence against you at your trial. You must clearly understand that you have nothing to hope from any promise of favour and nothing to fear from any threat that may have been held out to you to induce you to make any admission or confession of guilt, but whatever you now say may be given in evidence against you at your trial notwithstanding the promise or threat.

Two reasons appear to account for the fall-off of judicial questioning. First, the development and growth of professional police lessened the need for an investigative role by the judicial officers,[161] and, second, the growth of the concept known as the privilege against self-incrimination.

Statements of accused obtained by police interrogation were freely admissible at trial as the admissions of a party. Until the late 18th century there does not appear to be any judicial rule foreclosing their receipt.[162] The courts, however, perhaps mindful of the conclusive nature of these admissions and the heavy consequences of a finding of guilt, erected a barrier to their reception, and demanded that admissions of accused persons have an additional assurance of trustworthiness: to be receivable in a criminal prosecution a confession had to be proved voluntary. In 1783 in *R. v. Warickshall*,[163] the accused was charged with possession of stolen goods. She had made a full confession of her guilt, and as a result the goods were found under her bed. The confession had been obtained by promises of favour and the court refused to admit it. Her counsel then argued

---

159 (1554), 1 & 2 Phil. & Mar., c. 13, s. 4; (1555), 2 & 3 Phil. & Mar., c. 10, s. 2. See 1 Stephen, *History of The Criminal Law of England* (1883), 237-38; and 4 Holdsworth, *History of the English Law*, 3d. ed. (1945), 529.

160 Jervis's Act, 11 & 12 Vict., c. 42. See now Criminal Code, s. 541.

161 See 1 Stephen, *History of Criminal Law, supra*, note 159, at pp. 194-200.

162 See generally regarding the history of confessions, 3 Wigmore, *Evidence* (Chad. Rev.), s. 817.

163 168 E.R. 234 (Crown Cases).

that as the fact of finding the stolen property in her custody had been obtained through the means of an inadmissible confession, the proof of that fact ought also to be rejected; for otherwise the faith which the prosecutor had pledged would be violated, and the prisoner made the deluded instrument of her own conviction.[164]

But the court held:

It is a mistaken notion, that the evidence of confessions and facts which have been obtained from prisoners by promises or threats, is to be rejected from a regard to public faith: no such rule ever prevailed. The idea is novel in theory, and would be as dangerous in practice as it is repugnant to the general principles of criminal law. Confessions are received in evidence, or rejected as inadmissible, under a consideration whether they are or are not entitled to credit. A free and voluntary confession is deserving of the highest credit, because it is presumed to flow from the strongest sense of guilt, and therefore it is admitted as proof of the crime to which it refers; but a confession forced from the mind by the flattery of hope, or by the torture of fear, comes in so questionable a shape when it is to be considered as the evidence of guilt, that no credit ought to be given to it; and therefore it is rejected. This principle respecting confessions has no application whatever as to the admission or rejection of facts, whether the knowledge of them be obtained in consequence of an extorted confession, or whether it arises from any other source; for a fact, if it exist at all, must exist invariably in the same manner, whether the confession from which it is derived be in other respects true or false. Facts thus obtained, however, must be fully and satisfactorily proved, without calling in the aid of any part of the confession from which they may have been derived; and the impossibility of admitting any part of the confession as a proof of the fact, clearly shews that the fact may be admitted on other evidence; for as no part of an improper confession can be heard, it can never be legally known whether the fact was derived through the means of such confession or not.[165]

During the 19th century, the judicial attitude toward confessions hardened and a great prejudice against them led to the general exclusion of confessions whenever the slightest hope of advantage or fear of prejudice had been held out. For example, in *R. v. Drew*,[166] it was held to be an inducement, rendering the confession inadmissible, to advise the accused:

... not to say anything to prejudice himself, as what he said I should take down, and it would be used for him or against him at his trial,

as, per Coleridge J.:

I cannot conceive a more direct inducement to a man to make a confession, than telling him that what he says may be used in his favour at the trial.

A few years later in *R. v. Harris*,[167] the accused is advised

that whatever he said would be ... used against him,

but the confession was rejected, as, per Maule J.:

---

164 *Ibid.*, at p. 234.
165 *Ibid.*, at pp. 234-35.
166 (1837), 173 E.R. 433 (N.P.).
167 (1844), 1 Cox C.C. 106, and see *R. v. Furley* (1844), 1 Cox C.C. 76. But, *contra*, see *R. v. Baldry* (1852), 169 E.R. 568 (C.A.).

The prisoner was told that *whatever* he said would be taken down and used against him. I cannot say that that did not induce him to say something which he thought might be favourable to him.

The courts began to develop an attitude that *all* police questioning of accused persons, after they had been taken into custody, was wrong. In *R. v. Mick,*[168] Mellor, J. grudgingly received the accused's statement, given following a proper caution, but admonished the police superintendent:

I think the course you pursued in questioning the prisoner was exceedingly improper. I have considered the matter very much: many Judges would not receive such evidence. The law does not intend you, as a policeman, to investigate cases in that way. I entirely disapprove of the system of police officers examining prisoners. The law has surrounded prisoners with great precautions to prevent confessions being extorted from them, and the magistrates are not allowed to question prisoners, or to ask them what they have to say; and it is not for policemen to do these things. It is assuming the functions of the magistrate without those precautions which the magistrates are required by the law to use, and assuming functions which are entrusted to the magistrates and to them only. The evidence is admissible, but I entirely disapprove of this way of obtaining it.

In *R. v. Gavin,*[169] Smith J. prevented the receipt of one accused's statement against other accused with the statement:

When a prisoner is in custody the police have no right to ask him questions. . . . A prisoner's mouth is closed after he is once given in charge, and he ought not to be asked anything.

The early English decisions were very protective towards the accused, and Lord Hailsham, discussing the confession rule, explained:

By the judiciary, though it ought not to be extended, it must by no means be whittled down. It bears, it is true, all the marks of its origin at a time when the savage code of the eighteenth century was in full force. At that time almost every serious crime was punishable by death or transportation. The law enforcement officers formed no disciplined police force and were not subject to effective control by the central government, watch committees or an inspectorate. There was no legal aid. There was no system of appeal. To crown it all the accused was unable to give evidence on his own behalf and was therefore largely at the mercy of any evidence, either perjured or oppressively obtained, that might be brought against him. The judiciary were therefore compelled to devise artificial rules designed to protect him against dangers now avoided by other and more rational means. Nevertheless, the rule has survived into the twentieth century, not only unmodified but developed, and only Parliament can modify it now from the form in which it was given classical expression by Lord Sumner.

The early English decisions in the 19th century were by no means unanimous, however,[170] and the courts appear uncertain as to whether the exclusion of confessions is based solely on considerations of reliability, or whether

---

168 (1863), 176 E.R. 376.
169 (1885), 15 Cox C.C. 656.
170 See, *e.g.*, Parke, B. in *R. v. Baldry* (1852), *supra*, note 167, at p. 574: ". . . I think there has been too much tenderness towards prisoners in this matter. I confess that I cannot look at the decisions without some shame when I consider what objections have prevailed to prevent the reception of confessions in evidence."

there is an ability to exclude when the questioning is viewed as improper because of a perceived conflict with the accused's privilege against self-incrimination. As late as 1914 in *Ibrahim v. R.*,[171] we see the House of Lords still struggling with the question. The accused in that case, a soldier in the Indian army, was charged with murder. Evidence was admitted at his trial that within 10 or 15 minutes of the murder, the accused being in custody of the guard, was addressed by his commanding officer: "Why have you done such a senseless act?" to which the accused replied "some three or four days he had been abusing me; without a doubt I killed him." Lord Sumner recognized the oft-quoted classic formula:

> It has long been established as a positive rule of English criminal law, that no statement by an accused is admissible in evidence against him unless it is shewn by the prosecution to have been a voluntary statement, in the sense that it has not been obtained from him either by fear of prejudice or hope of advantage exercised or held out by a person in authority. The principle is as old as Lord Hale.[172]

He noted that it was common ground between the parties that in the circumstances receipt of the statement did not breach the rule, but felt it necessary to consider the objection that receipt was foreclosed simply because the prisoner's answer was preceded by and made in answer to a question, and that the question was put by a person in authority and the answer given by a man in his custody. Lord Sumner reviewed the authorities and concluded:

> The English law is still unsettled, strange as it may seem, since the point is one that constantly occurs in criminal trials. Many judges, in their discretion, exclude such evidence, for they fear that nothing less than the exclusion of all such statements can prevent improper questioning of prisoners by removing the inducement to resort to it. This consideration does not arise in the present case. Others, less tender to the prisoner or more mindful of the balance of decided authority, would admit such statements, nor would the Court of Criminal Appeal quash the conviction thereafter obtained, if no substantial miscarriage of justice had occurred. If, then, a learned judge, after anxious consideration of the authorities, decides in accordance with what is at any rate a "probable opinion" of the present law, if it is not actually the better opinion, it appears to their Lordships that his conduct is the very reverse of that "violation of the principles of natural justice" which has been said to be the ground for advising His Majesty's interference in a criminal matter. If, as appears even on the line of authorities which the trial judge did not follow, the matter is one for the judge's discretion, depending largely on his view of the impropriety of the questioner's conduct and the general circumstances of the case, their Lordships think, as will hereafter be seen, that in the circumstances of this case his discretion is not shewn to have been exercised improperly.
>
> Having regard to the particular position in which their Lordships stand to criminal proceedings, they do not propose to intimate what they think the rule of English law ought to be, much as it is to be desired that the point should be settled by authority, so far as a general rule can be laid down where circumstances must so greatly vary. That must be left to a Court which exercises, as their Lordships do not, the revising functions of a general Court of Criminal Appeal.[173]

---

171 [1914] A.C. 599 (P.C.).

172 *Ibid.*, at p. 609. This formula, accepted as gospel in Canada today, was first accepted by our courts as "correctly stating the rule" in *Prosko v. R.* (1922), 63 S.C.R. 226.

173 *Ibid.*, at p. 614.

In 1966 in *Commissioners of Customs v. Harz*,[174] Lord Reid reviewed the authorities and concluded:

> I do not think that it is possible to reconcile all the very numerous judicial statements on rejection of confessions but two lines of thought appear to underlie them: first, that a statement made in response to a threat or promise may be untrue or at least untrustworthy: and, secondly, that *nemo tenetur seipsum prodere*. It is true that many of the so-called inducements have been so vague that no reasonable man would have been influenced by them, but one must remember that not all accused are reasonable men or women: they may be very ignorant and terrified by the predicament in which they find themselves. So it may have been right to err on the safe side.

The question was squarely put to the Supreme Court of Canada in *R. v. Wray*.[175] The accused was charged with murder. The accused gave a statement to the police which ended as follows:

Q.   What happened to the gun?

A.   I threw it in the swamp.

Q.   Where?

A.   Near Omemee.

Q.   Will you try and show us the spot?

A.   Yes.

Q.   Is there anything else you wish to add to this John?

A.   Not now thank you.

The accused directed the police to the area where the rifle was found and ballistic evidence matched the bullet from the victim's body to the gun. After a lengthy *voir dire* the trial judge ruled the accused's statement was involuntary and hence legally inadmissible.[176] The prosecution then wished to introduce into evidence the accused's involvement in finding the murder weapon and relied on *R. v. St. Lawrence* where McRuer C.J.H.C. had said:

> Where the discovery of the fact confirms the confession — that is, where the confession must be taken to be true by reason of the discovery of the fact — then that part of the confession that is confirmed by the discovery of the fact is admissible, but further than that no part of the confession is admissible.[177]

The trial judge purported to exercise a discretion to disallow this evidence and directed a verdict of acquittal. The Ontario Court of Appeal, while recognizing the validity of the *St. Lawrence* rule, declined to disturb his decision, saying:

> In our view, a trial Judge has a discretion to reject evidence, even of substantial weight, if he considers that its admission would be unjust or unfair to the accused or calculated to bring the administration of justice into disrepute, the exercise of such

---

174 [1967] 1 A.C. 760, 820 (H.L.).

175 (1970), 11 D.L.R. (3d) 673, 677 (S.C.C.).

176 For a detailed description of how the confession was obtained see Ontario L.R.C. *Report on Evidence* (1976), pp. 74-90.

177 [1949] O.R. 215, 228 (H.C.). Approved in *R. v. Myrby* (1975), 28 C.C.C. (2d) 395 (Alta. C.A.).

discretion, of course, to depend upon the particular facts before him. Cases where to admit certain evidence would be calculated to bring the administration of justice into disrepute will be rare, but we think the discretion of a trial Judge extends to such cases.[178]

The Supreme Court of Canada reversed and directed a new trial. Martland J. reasoned:

> This development of the idea of a general discretion to exclude admissible evidence is not warranted by the authority on which it purports to be based. . . . the exercise of a discretion by the trial Judge arises only if the admission of the evidence would operate unfairly. The allowance of admissible evidence relevant to the issue before the Court and of substantial probative value may operate unfortunately for the accused, but not unfairly. It is only the allowance of evidence gravely prejudicial to the accused, the admissibility of which is tenuous, and whose probative force in relation to the main issue before the Court is trifling, which can be said to operate unfairly.[179]

In a separate concurring opinion, Judson J. wrote:

> I agree . . . that we ought not to overrule *R. v. St. Lawrence.* This case reviews the law which has stood since *R. v. Warwickshall,* to the effect that even if a confession is inadmissible in evidence, nevertheless facts which become known by means of this confession may be proved on behalf of the prosecution. . . .
>
> The theory for the rejection of confessions is that if they are obtained under certain conditions, they are untrustworthy. This theory has no application whatever to incontrovertible facts, such as the finding of articles. . . .
>
> How are the facts relating to the discovery of the weapon to be put before the jury? The minimum in this case is the account of Wray's trip from Toronto in the company of police officers to a swamp 15 miles west of the scene of the crime and the search for and the discovery of the weapon under the direction of the accused.[180]

The Supreme Court here appears then to regard the policy underlying the confession rule as rooted solely in concern for trustworthiness; if the confession is confirmed as true by tangible evidence, there is no need to exclude.

The "rule" forecloses receipt of confessions unless they are "voluntary." What is the meaning of "voluntary"? The *Shorter Oxford Dictionary* defines voluntary as

(a) Of feelings, etc.: Arising or developing in the mind without external constraint; purely spontaneous.

(b) Of actions: Performed or done of one's own free will, impulse, or choice, not constrained, prompted, or suggested by another.

Clearly the courts are not using the word in this sense. In *Boudreau v. R.,*[181] Rand J. had written:

> . . . the rule is directed against the danger of improperly instigated or induced or coerced admissions. It is the doubt cast on the truth of the statement arising from

---

178 [1970] 2 O.R. 3, 4 (C.A.).

179 *Supra,* note 175, at pp. 689-90 (S.C.C.).

180 *Ibid.,* at pp. 692 and 695 [citations omitted]. Compare the attitude of the court in *R. v. Warickshall* (1783), 168 E.R. 234 regarding evidence of accused's involvement in the finding of facts. And see the English attitude in *R. v. Barker,* [1941] 3 All E.R. 33 (C.C.A.).

181 [1949] 3 D.L.R. 81, 88 (S.C.C.).

the circumstances in which it is made that gives rise to the rule. What the statement should be is that of a man free in volition from the compulsions or inducements of authority and what is sought is assurance that that is the case. The underlying and controlling question then remains: Is the statement freely and voluntarily made?

In *R. v. Fitton*,[182] Pickup C.J.O. interpreted this passage:

> In my opinion, the Crown does not discharge the onus resting upon it by merely adducing oral testimony showing that an incriminating statement made by an accused person was not induced by a promise or by fear of prejudice or hope of advantage. That statement of the rule of law is too narrow. The admissions must not have been "improperly instigated or induced or coerced": per Rand J. in *Boudreau v. The King, supra*. The admissions must be self-impelled, and the statement must be the statement of a man "free in volition from the compulsions or inducements of authority". The statement must be "freely and voluntarily made".

R. v. SWEENEY
(2000), 36 C.R. (5th) 198, 148 C.C.C. (3d) 247,
2000 CarswellOnt 3290 (C.A.)

The accused was charged with robbery, assault with a weapon, possession of a weapon for a purpose dangerous to the public peace and possession of a restricted weapon. The police had prepared a warrant to search the accused's family's home. A police officer told the accused that the police would "trash" his mother's home if he did not tell them where the weapon was located. The accused told the officer that the weapon was in a box in his mother's closet and drew a diagram. The police executed the warrant and found the weapon in the location indicated on the diagram. The trial judge held that the accused's statements to the police officer were induced and involuntary, but admissible on the authority of the rule in *R. v. St. Lawrence*. The accused was convicted and appealed.

ROSENBERG J.A.:

. . . .

I have reached the following conclusions concerning the appellant's appeal from conviction:

(a) Admitting the involuntary confession in accordance with the common law St. Lawrence rule violated the appellant's rights under s. 7 of the Charter.

(b) In view of the violation of the appellant's s. 7 rights, the entire confession should have been excluded under s. 24(2) of the Charter.

(c) The common law St. Lawrence rule must be modified in light of subsequent decisions of the Supreme Court of Canada to give the trial judge a discretion to exclude those parts of the confession confirmed by the finding of the evidence.

(d) It would only be in the most exceptional circumstances that a trial judge would be entitled to exercise a discretion in favour of admitting the involuntary confession and such circumstances do not exist in this case.

(e) Without the appellant's confession there is no evidence upon which a properly instructed jury could convict and the appeal must be allowed, the convictions quashed and acquittals entered.

---

182 [1956] O.R. 696, 714 (C.A.).

What is the definition of "person in authority"?

R. v. HODGSON
127 C.C.C. (3d) 449, 1998 CarswellOnt 3417, 1998 CarswellOnt 3418,
18 C.R. (5th) 135, [1998] 2 S.C.R. 449

The accused was charged with acts of sexual assault, alleged to have occurred when he babysat the complainant. The complainant did not tell anyone about the incidents for several years. When the allegations were revealed, the complainant, her mother, her father and her stepfather went to the accused's place of employment and confronted him. They all testified that the accused confessed to having sexually assaulted the complainant on several occasions, that the accused said he was sorry, and that he said he knew it would catch up to him. The complainant's mother went to call the police, and when she returned she struck the accused. At some point, the complainant's father held a knife to the accused's back in order to prevent the accused from leaving before the police arrived. The accused testified that he was stunned, shocked and upset by the confrontation, but that he was neither frightened nor threatened. The accused raised no objection to the admission of the confession evidence at trial.

The trial judge relied on this evidence and convicted the accused. The Ontario Court of Appeal dismissed the accused's appeal.

CORY J., (LAMER C.J.C., GONTHIER, McLACHLIN, IACOBUCCI, MAJOR and BINNIE JJ. concurring):—

. . . .

The basic issue in this appeal is whether the trial judge erred in failing to hold a *voir dire* of his own motion to test the voluntariness of certain out-of-court statements made by the accused before admitting them. In order to resolve this issue, it is appropriate to consider whether the confessions rule should continue to apply only to statements made to persons in authority, or whether it should be expanded so as to capture the out-of-court statements made by the accused in this case. It will therefore be helpful to begin by examining the history of the confessions rule generally, and the person in authority requirement in particular, in order to understand the purpose and function of the rule in the criminal law.

A. The Confessions Rule and its Relation to the Person in Authority Requirement

Evidence of a confession has always been accorded great weight by triers of fact. This is a natural manifestation of human experience. It is because of the tremendous significance attributed to confessions and the innate realization that they could be obtained by improper means that the circumstances surrounding a confession have for centuries been carefully scrutinized to determine whether it should be admitted. A confession is not excluded, however, simply because of the risk that a conviction may result, but because of the greater risk that the conviction will be unfairly obtained and unjust. The unfairness of admitting a confession has historically been addressed by a consideration of two factors. First, the voluntariness of the statement; and second, the status of the receiver of the statement, that is to say, whether the receiver was a person in authority.

. . . .

The person in authority requirement generally refers to anyone formally engaged in "the arrest, detention, examination or prosecution of the accused". This definition may be enlarged to encompass persons who are deemed to be persons in authority as a result of the circumstances surrounding the making of the statement. For the moment, however, let us consider the purpose of each of these factors as they pertain to the admissibility of statements of the accused.

. . . .

The person in authority requirement is properly seen as an integral component of the confessions rule. The emphasis on voluntariness has two main effects: it both avoids the unfairness of a conviction based on a confession that might be unreliable, and has a deterrent effect on the use of coercive tactics. This deterrent effect is properly focused upon the prosecutorial authority of the state, not the personal authority of private individuals. It cannot be forgotten that it is the nature of the authority exerted by the state that might prompt an involuntary statement. As Estey J. stated in Rothman, supra, at pp. 650-51, "their very authority might, by promise or threat, express or implied, produce a statement whether or not the accused was truly willing to speak". In other words, it is the fear of reprisal or hope of leniency that persons in authority may hold out and which is associated with their official status that may render a statement involuntary. The rule is generally not concerned with conversations between private citizens that might indicate guilt, as these conversations would not be influenced or affected by the coercive power of the state. This limitation is appropriate since most criminal investigations are undertaken by the state, and it is then that an accused is most vulnerable to state coercion.

On a practical level, the Crown would obviously face an overwhelming burden if it had to establish the voluntariness of every statement against interest made by an accused to any person. See the Law Reform Commission of Canada, Report on Evidence (1975), at p. 62. In particular, as the intervener the Attorney General of Canada notes, the elimination of the person in authority requirement would have serious consequences for undercover police work and for the admissibility of wiretap evidence, where the identity of the receiver of the accused's statement is often unknown. For example, if the Crown were to intercept a phone call between an accused and a confederate who is senior to him in a criminal hierarchy, the Crown would obviously have difficulty tendering the requisite evidence if it were forced to prove beyond a reasonable doubt that the statements were made "without fear of prejudice or hope of advantage". Moreover, all statements to undercover police officers would become subject to the confessions rule, even though the accused was completely unaware of their status and, at the time he made the statement, would never have considered the undercover officers to be persons in authority.

Practical considerations alone lead to the conclusion that the person in authority requirement should remain a part of the confessions rule. Yet there can be no doubt that there may well be great unfairness suffered by the accused when an involuntary confession obtained as a result of violence or credible threats of imminent violence by a private individual is admitted into evidence. . . . However, it is the sort of change which should be studied by Parliament and remedied by enactment. . . . Because of the very real possibility of a resulting miscarriage of justice and the fundamental unfairness of admitting statements coerced by the violence of private individuals, I would hope that the study will not be long postponed.

I would suggest that in circumstances where a statement of the accused is obtained by a person who is not a person in authority by means of degrading treatment such as violence or threats of violence, a clear direction should be given to the jury as to the dangers of relying upon it. The direction might include words such as these: "A statement obtained as a result of inhuman or degrading treatment or the use of violence or threats of violence may not be the manifestation of the exercise of a free will to confess. Rather, it may result solely from the oppressive treatment or or fear of such treatment. If it does, the statement may very well be either unreliable or untrue. Therefore if you conclude that the statement was obtained by such oppression very little if any weight should be attached to it." However, if a private individual resorts to violence or threatens violence after the statement has been made, this conduct will not as a general rule be a factor affecting the voluntariness of the statement and the suggested direction will not be needed.

B. Limits of the Person in Authority Requirement

31 It has been seen that the person in authority requirement is grounded in the underlying rationales for the confessions rule, and as a result it should remain part of the rule. Consideration must now be given as to who should come within the designation "person in authority".

32 "Person in authority" typically refers to those persons formally engaged in the arrest, detention, examination or prosecution of the accused: see *A.B., supra*, at p. 26. However, it may take on a broader meaning. Canadian courts first considered the meaning of "person in authority" in *R. v. Todd* (1901), 4 C.C.C. 514 (Man. K.B.). In that case, the accused made a statement to two men he believed to be fellow prisoners, but who were in fact acting as agents of the police. It was held, at pp. 526-27, that:

> A person in authority means, generally speaking, anyone who has authority or control over the accused or over the proceedings or the prosecution against him. . . . [T]he authority that the accused knows such persons to possess may well be supposed in the majority of instances both to animate his hopes of favour on the one hand and on the other to inspire him with awe, and so in some degree to overcome the powers of his mind. . . . [Emphasis added.]

Thus, from its earliest inception in Canadian law, the question as to who should be considered as a person in authority depended on the extent to which the accused believed the person could influence or control the proceedings against him or her. The question is therefore approached from the viewpoint of the accused. See also *R. v. Roadhouse* (1933), 61 C.C.C. 191 (B.C.C.A.), at p. 192.

33 The subjective approach to the person in authority requirement has been adopted in this Court. See *Rothman, supra,* at p. 663. The approach adopted by McIntyre J.A. (as he then was) in *R. v. Berger* (1975), 27 C.C.C. (2d) 357 (B.C.C.A.), at pp. 385-86 is, in my view, a clear statement of the law:

> The law is settled that a person in authority is a person concerned with the prosecution who, in the opinion of the accused, can influence the course of the prosecution. The test to be applied in deciding whether statements made to persons connected in such a way with the prosecution are voluntary is subjective. In other words what did the accused think? Whom did he think he was talking to? . . . Was he under the impression that the failure to speak to this person, because of his power to influence the prosecution, would result in prejudice or did he think that a statement would draw some benefit or reward? If his mind was free of such impressions the person receiving this statement would not be considered a person in authority and the statement would be admissible.

34 However, to this statement I would add that the accused's belief that he is speaking to a person in authority must also be reasonable, in the context of the circumstances surrounding the making of the statement. If the accused were delusional or had no reasonable basis for the belief that the receiver of the statement could affect the course of the prosecution against him, the receiver should not be considered a person in authority. Since the person in authority requirement is aimed at controlling coercive state conduct, the test for a person in authority should not include those whom the accused unreasonably believes to be acting on behalf of the state. Thus, where the accused speaks out of fear of reprisal or hope of advantage because he reasonably believes the person receiving the statement is acting as an agent of the police or prosecuting authorities and could therefore influence or control the proceedings against him or her, then the receiver of the statement is properly considered a person in authority. In other words, the evidence must disclose not only that the accused subjectively believed the receiver of the statement to be in a position to control the proceedings against the accused, but must also establish an objectively reasonable basis for that belief. For example, if the evidence discloses a relationship of agency or close collaboration between the receiver of the statement and the police or prosecution, and that relationship was known to the accused, the receiver of the statement may be considered a person in authority. In those circumstances the Crown must prove beyond a reasonable doubt that the statement was made voluntarily.

35 Over the years, the courts have determined when and in what circumstances a person will be deemed a person in authority for the purposes of the confessions rule. See, e.g., *R. v. Trenholme* (1920), 35 C.C.C. 341 (Que. K.B.) (complainant's father was held to be a person in authority where he has control over the prosecution of the accused); *R. v. Wilband*, [1967] S.C.R. 14 (psychiatrist is not a person in authority where he cannot control or influence the course of the proceedings); *R. v. Downey* (1976), 32 C.C.C. (2d) 511 (N.S.S.C.A.D.) (victim is a person in authority if the accused believed that the victim had control over the proceedings); *A.B., supra* (a parent is not, in law, a person in authority if there is no close connection between the decision to call the authorities and the

inducement to a child to make a statement); *R. v. Sweryda* (1987), 34 C.C.C. (3d) 325 (Alta. C.A.)(a social worker is a person in authority if the accused knew the social worker was investigating allegations of child abuse and believed it could lead to his arrest). These cases have not departed from the governing rule that defines a person in authority in relation to the accused's perception of the receiver's involvement with the investigation or prosecution of the crime nor have these decisions defined a person in authority solely in terms of the personal authority that a person might wield in relation to the accused. Moreover, in concluding that the receiver of the statement was a person in authority, the courts have consistently found the accused believed the receiver was allied with the state authorities and could influence the investigation or prosecution against the accused.

36 The important factor to note in all of these cases is that there is no catalogue of persons, beyond a peace officer or prison guard, who are automatically considered a person in authority solely by virtue of their status. A parent, doctor, teacher or employer all may be found to be a person in authority if the circumstances warrant, but their status, or the mere fact that they may wield some personal authority over the accused, is not sufficient to establish them as persons in authority for the purposes of the confessions rule. As the intervener the Attorney General of Canada observed, the person in authority requirement has evolved in a manner that avoids a formalistic or legalistic approach to the interactions between ordinary citizens. Instead, it requires a case-by-case consideration of the accused's belief as to the ability of the receiver of the statement to influence the prosecution or investigation of the crime. That is to say, the trial judge must determine whether the accused reasonably believed the receiver of the statement was acting on behalf of the police or prosecuting authorities. This view of the person in authority requirement remains unchanged.

37 Finally, something must be said about the respective burdens which must be borne by the accused and the Crown on a *voir dire* to determine whether a statement of the accused to a person in authority should be admitted. The Crown, of course, bears the burden of proving beyond a reasonable doubt that the statement was made voluntarily. However, in relation to the person in authority requirement, the evidence required to establish whether or not a person should be deemed a person in authority will often lie primarily with the accused. The accused therefore must bear some burden in relation to this aspect of the confessions rule. The burden should be an evidential and not a persuasive one. See, e.g., *R. v. Scott* (1984), 1 O.A.C. 397, at p. 399. John Sopinka, Sidney N. Lederman and Alan W. Bryant, in *The Law of Evidence in Canada* (1992), at pp. 56-57, explain the difference between the two burdens:

> The term evidential burden means that a party has the responsibility to insure that there is sufficient evidence of the existence or non-existence of a fact or of an issue on the record to pass the threshold test for that particular fact or issue. . . . In contrast, the term legal burden of proof means that a party has an obligation to prove or disprove a fact or issue to the criminal or civil standard. The failure to convince the trier of fact to the appropriate standard means that party will lose on that issue.

The evidential burden on an accused in a criminal case is described as follows (at p. 138):

> Where an evidential burden for an issue rests on the defendant in a criminal case, for example self-defence, the accused has the obligation to ensure that there is some evidence on the record to make it a live issue. The evidence necessary to satisfy an evidential burden may arise in the case for the Crown or the defence.

38 In the vast majority of cases, the accused will meet this evidential burden by showing the accused's knowledge of the relationship between the receiver of the statement and the police or prosecuting authorities. For example, the fact that the statement was made to a police officer who was in uniform or identified himself or herself as a peace officer will satisfy the accused's evidential burden in relation to the person in authority requirement. See, e.g., *Morris v. The Queen*, [1979] 2 S.C.R. 1041, at p. 1066. Once the accused satisfies this evidential burden, the ultimate burden of proof rests with the Crown. See R. *v. McKenzie*, [1965] 3 C.C.C. 6 (Alta. S.C.A.D.), at p. 28. In *R. v. Postman* (1977), 3 A.R. 524, at p. 542, the Alberta Supreme Court, Appellate Division held, correctly in my view, that where a witness is not prima facie a person in authority (in that case, a doctor), "it is open to defence counsel to challenge the prima facie case and require evidence to be given to determine the facts of the matter". Thus, once the defence discharges its burden and establishes that there is an evidential basis to the claim that the receiver of a statement made by the accused is a person in authority, the burden shifts to the Crown to establish beyond a reasonable doubt either that the receiver is not a person in authority, or, if this burden cannot be discharged, that the statement was made voluntarily.

39 The receiver's status as a person in authority arises only if the accused had knowledge of that status. If the accused cannot show that he or she had knowledge of the receiver's status (as, for example, in the case of an undercover police officer) or close relationship to the authorities (as in the case of persons acting on behalf of the state), the inquiry pertaining to the receiver as a person in authority must end. It is therefore appropriate to consider at the outset the reasonable belief of the accused. It may not be useful to have the trial judge undertake a full analysis of the objective relationship between the receiver of the statement and the authorities, as Justice L'Heureux-Dubé suggests (para. 83), only to have those findings vitiated if the accused is later found to have no knowledge of this relationship. In addition, it is important to recognize that focusing the trial judge's inquiry on the reasonable belief of the accused accords with the allocation of the burden of proof on the voir dire.

[Justice Cory then addressed the issue of when a trial judge is obligated to hold a *voir dire* where defence counsel does not object to the admissibility of the accused's statement.]

IV. Summary

48 Perhaps it may be of some assistance to set out in summary form the applicable principles pertaining to the admission of statements made by the accused to

persons in authority and some of the factors to be taken into consideration with regard to them.

1. The rule which is still applicable in determining the admissibility of a statement made by an accused to a person in authority is that it must have been made voluntarily and must be the product of an operating mind.

2. The rule is based upon two fundamentally important concepts: the need to ensure the reliability of the statement and the need to ensure fairness by guarding against improper coercion by the state. This results in the requirement that the admission must not be obtained by either threats or inducements.

3. The rule is applicable when the accused makes a statement to a person in authority. Though no absolute definition of "person in authority" is necessary or desirable, it typically refers to those formally engaged in the arrest, detention, examination or prosecution of the accused. Thus, it would apply to person such as police officers and prison officials or guards. When the statement of the accused is made to a police officer or prison guard a *voir dire* should be held to determine its admissibility as a voluntary statement, unless the *voir dire* is waived by counsel for the accused.

4. Those persons whom the accused reasonably believes are acting on behalf of the police or prosecuting authorities and could therefore influence or control the proceedings against him or her may also be persons in authority. That question will have to be determined on a case-by-case basis.

5. The issue as to who is a person in authority must be resolved by considering it subjectively from the viewpoint of the accused. There must, however, be a reasonable basis for the accused's belief that the person hearing the statement was a person in authority.

6. The issue will not normally arise in relation to undercover police officers. This is because the issue must be approached from the viewpoint of the accused. On that basis, undercover police officers will not usually be viewed by the accused as persons in authority.

7. If it is contended that the recipient of the statement was a person in authority in the eyes of the accused then the defence must raise the issue with the trial judge. This is appropriate for it is only the accused who can know that the statement was made to someone regarded by the accused as a person in authority.

8. On the ensuing *voir dire* the accused will have the evidential burden of demonstrating that there is a valid issue for consideration. If the accused meets the burden, the Crown will then have the persuasive burden of demonstrating beyond a reasonable doubt that the receiver of the statement was not a person in authority or if it is found that he or she was a person in authority, that the statement of the accused was made voluntarily.

9. In extremely rare cases the evidence adduced during a trial may be such that it should alert the trial judge that the issue as to whether the receiver of a statement made by an accused was a person in authority should be explored by way of voir dire. In those cases, which must be extremely rare in light of the obligation of the accused to raise the issue, the trial judge must of his or her own motion direct a voir dire, subject, of course, to waiver of the *voir dire* by counsel for the accused.

10. The duty of the trial judge to hold a *voir dire* of his or her own motion will only arise in those rare cases where the evidence, viewed objectively, is sufficient to alert the trial judge of the need to hold a *voir dire* to determine if the receiver of the statement of the accused was, in the circumstances, a person in authority.

11. If the trial judge is satisfied that the receiver of the statement was not a person in authority but that the statement of the accused was obtained by reprehensible coercive tactics, such as violence or credible threats of violence, then a direction should be given to the jury. The jury should be instructed that if they conclude that the statement was obtained by coercion, they should be cautious about accepting it, and that little if any weight should be attached to it.

Justice Cory then held that there was no evidence in the case that the family members of the complainant were persons in authority so as to trigger the trial judge's obligation to hold a *voir dire*:

V. Application to this Appeal

49 The appellant contends that the fact that the confession was made to the complainant and her immediate family should have alerted the trial judge to the need for a *voir dire* since they are capable of being persons in authority for the purpose of the confessions rule. It is true the complainant and her family members are capable of being persons in authority. Indeed, anyone is capable of being a person in authority where a person becomes sufficiently involved with the arrest, detention, examination or prosecution of an accused, and the accused believes that the person may influence the process against him or her. It does not follow that simply because it has been held, in the circumstances presented in other cases, that a family member was a person in authority, that the trial judge should have been alerted to the need for a voir dire. Virtually any category of person—parents of the accused, parents of the complainant, teachers, psychiatrists, physicians—may, in light of the particular evidence adduced, be considered to be a person in authority. As the respondent observed, to hold that the trial judge committed an error on the basis that the receiver of the confession is merely capable of being a person in authority is to require a *voir dire* (or waiver) for every statement against interest made by every accused person to anyone. It cannot be forgotten that it is the accused who is in the best position to demonstrate that the receiver of the statement was in his or her eyes a person in authority.

50 In this case, the evidence at trial did not disclose any evidence that was sufficient to trigger the trial judge's obligation to hold a voir dire. The confrontation at the appellant's workplace was first described by the complainant. She testified as to the events leading up to the confrontation. She stated (1) that her mother questioned her about whether she was pregnant and whether she had had intercourse; (2) that in the course of that conversation, she told her mother that the appellant had sexually assaulted her; (3) that her mother telephoned her father; (4) that she and her mother visited a walk-in clinic in Mississauga where it was confirmed that the complainant was pregnant (her boyfriend at the time was the father); (5) that the complainant, together with her mother, father, stepfather and cousin went to confront the appellant. The complainant then related, without objection by the defence, the statements made by the appellant. Thus, when the statements were admitted into evidence, there was nothing to suggest that the complainant or her family members had spoken to the police or anyone else in authority or were even considering making a complaint. Similarly, there was nothing to suggest that the appellant subjectively believed the complainant's family to have control over criminal proceedings. In those circumstances, the trial judge cannot be said to have committed an error by failing to hold a *voir dire* on his own motion.

Appeal dismissed.

Parliament has not acted on Justice Cory's recommendation. See also *R. v. Wells*[183] where the Court recognized a power to exclude a confession by an accused to a person not in authority obtained by oppression and violence.

2. REVISED APROACH IN *R. v. OICKLE*

R. v. OICKLE
[2000] 2 S.C.R. 3, 36 C.R. (5th) 129, 147 C.C.C. (3d) 321

During a police investigation into a series of fires, the accused agreed to submit to a polygraph. The test was audiotaped. The fires, which appeared to be deliberately set, involved four buildings and a car (which belonged to Oickle's fiancée). He was a member of the local volunteer fire department and had responded to each of the fires. The accused was informed of his rights to silence, to counsel, and his ability to leave at any time. He was also informed that while the interpretation of the polygraph results was not admissible, anything he said was admissible. At the end of the test, about 5:00 p.m., the officer conducting the test informed the accused that he had failed. The accused was reminded of his rights and questioned for one hour. At 6:30 p.m., a second officer questioned the accused and, after 30 to 40 minutes, the accused confessed to setting the fire to his fiancée's car and provided the police with a statement. He appeared

---

183 (2003), 12 C.R. (6th) 185, 174 C.C.C. (3d) 301 (B.C. C.A.).

emotionally distraught at this time. The accused was arrested and warned of his rights. At the police station, he was placed in an interview room equipped with videotaping facilities where he was questioned about the other fires. Around 8:30 p.m. and 9:15 p.m., the accused indicated that he was tired and wanted to go home. He was informed that he was under arrest and he could call a lawyer but that he could not go home. A third officer took over the interrogation at 9:52 p.m. He questioned the accused until about 11:00 p.m., at which time the accused confessed to setting seven of the eight fires. The accused was then seen crying with his head in his hands. The police then took a written statement from the accused. He was placed in a cell to sleep at 2:45 a.m. At 6:00 a.m., a police officer noticed that the accused was awake and asked whether he would agree to a re-enactment. On the tape of the re-enactment, the accused was informed of his rights and was advised that he could stop the re-enactment at any time. The police drove the accused to the various fire scenes, where he described how he had set each fire. The accused was charged with seven counts of arson. The trial judge ruled on a *voir dire* that the accused's statements, including the video re-enactment, were voluntary and admissible, and subsequently convicted him on all counts. The Nova Scotia Court of Appeal excluded the confessions and entered an acquittal.

IACOBUCCI J. (L'HEUREUX-DUBÉ, McLACHLIN, MAJOR, BASTARACHE and BINNIE JJ. concurring): —

This appeal requires this Court to rule on the common law limits on police interrogation. Specifically, we are asked to decide whether the police improperly induced the respondent's confessions through threats or promises, an atmosphere of oppression, or any other tactics that could raise a reasonable doubt as to the voluntariness of his confessions. I conclude that they did not. The trial judge's determination that the confessions at stake in this appeal were voluntarily given should not have been disturbed on appeal, and accordingly the appeal should be allowed.

In this case, the police conducted a proper interrogation. Their questioning, while persistent and often accusatorial, was never hostile, aggressive, or intimidating. They repeatedly offered the accused food and drink. They allowed him to use the bathroom upon request. Before his first confession and subsequent arrest, they repeatedly told him that he could leave at any time. In this context, the alleged inducements offered by the police do not raise a reasonable doubt as to the confessions' voluntariness. Nor do I find any fault with the role played by the polygraph test in this case. While the police admittedly exaggerated the reliability of such devices, the tactic of inflating the reliability of incriminating evidence is a common, and generally unobjectionable one. Whether standing alone, or in combination with the other mild inducements used in this appeal, it does not render the confessions involuntary.

. . . .

Two Elements of the Rule

As indicated by McLachlin J. . . . . in *R. v. Hebert*, [1990] 2 S.C.R. 151, there are two main strands to this Court's jurisprudence under the confessions rule.

One approach is narrow, excluding statements only where the police held out explicit threats or promises to the accused. The definitive statement of this approach came in *Ibrahim v. The King*, [1914] A.C. 599 (P.C.), at p. 609:

> It has long been established as a positive rule of English criminal law, that no statement by an accused is admissible in evidence against him unless it is shewn by the prosecution to have been a voluntary statement, in the sense that it has not been obtained from him either by fear of prejudice or hope of advantage exercised or held out by a person in authority.

This Court adopted the "*Ibrahim* rule" in *Prosko v. The King* (1922), 63 S.C.R. 226, and subsequently applied it in cases like *Boudreau v. The King*, [1949] S.C.R. 262, *Fitton*, supra, *R. v. Wray*, [1971] S.C.R. 272, and *Rothman v. The Queen*, [1981] 1 S.C.R. 640.

The *Ibrahim* rule gives the accused only "a negative right — the right not to be tortured or coerced into making a statement by threats or promises held out by a person who is and whom he subjectively believes to be a person in authority": *Hebert*, supra, at p. 165. However, *Hebert* also recognized a second, "much broader" approach, according to which "[t]he absence of violence, threats and promises by the authorities does not necessarily mean that the resulting statement is voluntary, if the necessary mental element of deciding between alternatives is absent". . . .

While not always followed, McLachlin J. noted . . . that this aspect of the confessions rule "persists as part of our fundamental notion of procedural fairness". This approach is most evident in the so-called "operating mind" doctrine, developed by this Court in *Ward*, supra, *Horvath v. The Queen*, [1979] 2 S.C.R. 376, and *R. v. Whittle*, [1994] 2 S.C.R. 914. In those cases the Court made "a further investigation of whether the statements were freely and voluntarily made even if no hope of advantage or fear of prejudice could be found": *Ward*, supra, at p. 40. The "operating mind" doctrine dispelled once and for all the notion that the confessions rule is concerned solely with whether or not the confession was induced by any threats or promises.

These cases focused not just on reliability, but on voluntariness conceived more broadly. None of the reasons in *Ward* or *Horvath* ever expressed any doubts about the reliability of the confessions in issue. Instead, they focused on the lack of voluntariness, whether the cause was shock (*Ward*), hypnosis (*Horvath*), or "complete emotional disintegration" (*Horvath*). Similarly, in *Hobbins v. The Queen*, [1982] 1 S.C.R. 553, at pp. 556-57, Laskin C.J. noted that in determining the voluntariness of a confession, courts should be alert to the coercive effect of an "atmosphere of oppression", even though there was "no inducement held out of hope of advantage or fear of prejudice, and absent any threats of violence or actual violence"; see also *R. v. Liew*, [1999] 3 S.C.R. 227, at para. 37. Clearly, the confessions rule embraces more than the narrow *Ibrahim* formulation; instead, it is concerned with voluntariness, broadly understood.

The Charter Era

The Charter constitutionalized a new set of protections for accused persons, contained principally in ss. 7 to 14 thereof. The entrenchment of these rights answered certain questions that had once been asked under the aegis of the confessions rule. For example, while the confessions rule did not exclude statements elicited by undercover officers in jail cells (*Rothman*, supra), such confessions can violate the Charter: see *Hebert*, supra, and *R. v. Broyles*, [1991] 3 S.C.R. 595.

In *Hebert*, McLachlin J. interpreted the right to silence in light of existing common law protections, such as the confessions rule. However, given the focus of that decision on defining constitutional rights, it did not decide the inverse question: namely, the scope of the common law rules in light of the Charter. One possible view is that the Charter subsumes the common law rules.

But I do not believe that this view is correct, for several reasons. First, the confessions rule has a broader scope than the Charter. For example, the protections of s. 10 only apply "on arrest or detention". By contrast, the confessions rule applies whenever a person in authority questions a suspect. Second, the Charter applies a different burden and standard of proof from that under the confessions rule. Under the former, the burden is on the accused to show, on a balance of probabilities, a violation of constitutional rights. Under the latter, the burden is on the prosecution to show beyond a reasonable doubt that the confession was voluntary. Finally, the remedies are different. The Charter excludes evidence obtained in violation of its provisions under s. 24(2) only if admitting the evidence would bring the administration of justice into disrepute: see *R. v. Stillman*, [1997] 1 S.C.R. 607, *R. v. Collins*, [1987] 1 S.C.R. 265, and the related jurisprudence. By contrast, a violation of the confessions rule always warrants exclusion.

These various differences illustrate that the Charter is not an exhaustive catalogue of rights. Instead, it represents a bare minimum below which the law must not fall. A necessary corollary of this statement is that the law, whether by statute or common law, can offer protections beyond those guaranteed by the Charter. The common law confessions rule is one such doctrine, and it would be a mistake to confuse it with the protections given by the Charter. While obviously it may be appropriate, as in *Hebert*, to interpret one in light of the other, it would be a mistake to assume one subsumes the other entirely.

The Confessions Rule Today

As previously mentioned, this Court has not recently addressed the precise scope of the confessions rule. Instead, we have refined several elements of the rule, without ever integrating them into a coherent whole. I believe it is important to restate the rule for two reasons. First is the continuing diversity of approaches as evidenced by the courts below in this appeal. Second, and perhaps more important, is our growing understanding of the problem of false confessions. As I will discuss below, the confessions rule is concerned with voluntariness, broadly defined. One of the predominant reasons for this concern is that involuntary confessions are more likely to be unreliable. The confessions rule should recognize which interrogation techniques commonly produce false confessions so as to avoid miscarriages of justice.

In defining the confessions rule, it is important to keep in mind its twin goals of protecting the rights of the accused without unduly limiting society's need to investigate and solve crimes. Martin J.A. accurately delineated this tension in *R. v. Precourt* (1976), 18 O.R. (2d) 714 (C.A.), at p. 721:

> Although improper police questioning may in some circumstances infringe the governing [confessions] rule it is essential to bear in mind that the police are unable to investigate crime without putting questions to persons, whether or not such persons are suspected of having committed the crime being investigated. Properly conducted police questioning is a legitimate and effective aid to criminal investigation . . . . On the other hand, statements made as the result of intimidating questions, or questioning which is oppressive and calculated to overcome the freedom of will of the suspect for the purpose of extracting a confession are inadmissible . . . .

All who are involved in the administration of justice, but particularly courts applying the confessions rule, must never lose sight of either of these objectives.

The Problem of False Confessions

The history of police interrogations is not without its unsavoury chapters. Physical abuse, if not routine, was certainly not unknown. Today such practices are much less common. In this context, it may seem counterintuitive that people would confess to a crime that they did not commit. And indeed, research with mock juries indicates that people find it difficult to believe that someone would confess falsely. See S. M. Kassin and L. S. Wrightsman, "Coerced Confessions, Judicial Instructions, and Mock Juror Verdicts" (1981), 11 *J. Applied Soc. Psychol.* 489.

However, this intuition is not always correct. A large body of literature has developed documenting hundreds of cases where confessions have been proven false by DNA evidence, subsequent confessions by the true perpetrator, and other such independent sources of evidence. See, e.g., R. A. Leo and R. J. Ofshe, "The Consequences of False Confessions: Deprivations of Liberty and Miscarriages of Justice in the Age of Psychological Interrogation" (1998), 88 *J. Crim. L. & Criminology* 429 (hereinafter Leo & Ofshe (1998)); R. J. Ofshe and R. A. Leo, "The Social Psychology of Police Interrogation: The Theory and Classification of True and False Confessions" (1997), 16 *Stud. L. Pol. & Soc.* 189 (hereinafter Ofshe & Leo (1997)); R. J. Ofshe and R. A. Leo, "The Decision to Confess Falsely: Rational Choice and Irrational Action" (1997), 74 *Denv. U. L. Rev.* 979 (hereinafter Ofshe & Leo (1997a)); W. S. White, "False Confessions and the Constitution: Safeguards Against Untrustworthy Confessions" (1997), 32 *Harv. C.R.-C.L. L. Rev.* 105; G. H. Gudjonsson and J. A. C. MacKeith, "A Proven Case of False Confession: Psychological Aspects of the Coerced-Compliant Type" (1990), 30 *Med. Sci. & L.* 329 (hereinafter Gudjonsson & MacKeith (1990)); G. Gudjonsson and J. A. C. MacKeith, "Retracted Confessions: Legal, Psychological and Psychiatric Aspects" (1988), 28 *Med. Sci. & L.* 187 (hereinafter Gudjonsson & MacKeith (1988)); H. A. Bedau and M. L. Radelet, "Miscarriages of Justice in Potentially Capital Cases" (1987), 40 *Stan. L. Rev.* 21.

One of the overriding concerns of the criminal justice system is that the innocent must not be convicted: see, e.g., *R. v. Mills*, [1999] 3 S.C.R. 668, at para. 71; *R. v. Leipert*, [1997] 1 S.C.R. 281, at para. 4. Given the important role of false confessions in convicting the innocent, the confessions rule must understand why false confessions occur. Without suggesting that any confession involving elements discussed below should automatically be excluded, I hope to provide a background for my synthesis of the confessions rule in the next section.

Ofshe & Leo (1997), *supra*, at p. 210, provide a useful taxonomy of false confessions. They suggest that there are five basic kinds: voluntary, stress-compliant, coerced-compliant, non-coerced-persuaded, and coerced-persuaded. Voluntary confessions *ex hypothesi* are not the product of police interrogation. It is therefore the other four types of false confessions that are of interest.

According to Ofshe & Leo (1997), *supra*, at p. 211, stress-compliant confessions occur "when the aversive interpersonal pressures of interrogation become so intolerable that [suspects] comply in order to terminate questioning". They are elicited by "exceptionally strong use of the aversive stressors typically present in interrogations", and are "given knowingly *in order to escape* the punishing experience of interrogation" (emphasis in original). See also Gudjonsson & MacKeith (1990), *supra*. Another important factor is confronting the suspect with fabricated evidence in order to convince him that protestations of innocence are futile: see *ibid.*; Ofshe & Leo (1997a), *supra*, at p. 1040.

Somewhat different are coerced-compliant confessions. These confessions are the product of "the classically coercive influence techniques (e.g., threats and promises)", with which the *Ibrahim* rule is concerned: Ofshe & Leo (1997), *supra*, at p.214. As Gudjonsson & MacKeith (1988), *supra*, suggest at p. 191, "most cases of false confession that come before the courts are of the compliant-coerced type". See also White, *supra*, at p. 131.

A third kind of false confession is the non-coerced-persuaded confession. In this scenario, police tactics cause the innocent person to "become confused, doubt his memory, be temporarily persuaded of his guilt and confess to a crime he did not commit": Ofshe & Leo (1997), *supra*, at p. 215. For an example, see *Reilly v. State*, 355 A.2d 324 (Conn. Super. Ct. 1976); Ofshe & Leo (1997), *supra*, at pp. 231-34. The use of fabricated evidence can also help convince an innocent suspect of his or her own guilt.

A final type of false confession is the coerced-persuaded confession. This is like the non-coerced-persuaded, except that the interrogation also involves the classically coercive aspects of the coerced-compliant confession: see Ofshe & Leo (1997), *supra*, at p. 219.

From this discussion, several themes emerge. One is the need to be sensitive to the particularities of the individual suspect. For example, White, *supra*, at p. 120, notes the following:

> False confessions are particularly likely when the police interrogate particular types of suspects, including suspects who are especially vulnerable as a result of their background, special characteristics, or situation, suspects who have compliant personalities, and, in rare instances, suspects whose personalities make them prone to accept and believe police suggestions made during the course of the interrogation.

. . . . .

Another theme is the danger of using non-existent evidence. Presenting a suspect with entirely fabricated evidence has the potential either to persuade the susceptible suspect that he did indeed commit the crime, or at least to convince the suspect that any protestations of innocence are futile.

Finally, the literature bears out the common law confessions rule's emphasis on threats and promises. Coerced-compliant confessions are the most common type of false confessions. These are classically the product of threats or promises that convince a suspect that in spite of the long-term ramifications, it is in his or her best interest in the short - and intermediate - term to confess.

Fortunately, false confessions are rarely the product of proper police techniques. As Leo & Ofshe (1998), *supra*, point out at p. 492, false confession cases almost always involve "shoddy police practice and/or police criminality". Similarly, in Ofshe & Leo (1997), *supra*, at pp. 193-96, they argue that in most cases, "eliciting a false confession takes strong incentives, intense pressure and prolonged questioning. . . . Only under the rarest of circumstances do an interrogator's ploys persuade an innocent suspect that he is in fact guilty and has been caught."

Before turning to how the confessions rule responds to these dangers, I would like to comment briefly on the growing practice of recording police interrogations, preferably by videotape. As pointed out by J. J. Furedy and J. Liss in "Countering Confessions Induced by the Polygraph: Of Confessionals and Psychological Rubber Hoses" (1986), 29 *Crim. L.Q.* 91, at p. 104, even if "notes were accurate concerning the *content* of what was said . . ., the notes cannot reflect the *tone* of what was said and any body language that may have been employed" (emphasis in original). White, *supra*, at pp. 153-54, similarly offers four reasons why videotaping is important:

First, it provides a means by which courts can monitor interrogation practices and thereby enforce the other safeguards. Second, it deters the police from employing interrogation methods likely to lead to untrustworthy confessions. Third, it enables courts to make more informed judgments about whether interrogation practices were likely to lead to an untrustworthy confession. Finally, mandating this safeguard accords with sound public policy because the safeguard will have additional salutary effects besides reducing untrustworthy confessions, including more net benefits for law enforcement.

This is not to suggest that non-recorded interrogations are inherently suspect; it is simply to make the obvious point that when a recording is made, it can greatly assist the trier of fact in assessing the confession.

The common law confessions rule is well-suited to protect against false confessions. While its overriding concern is with voluntariness, this concept overlaps with reliability. A confession that is not voluntary will often (though not always) be unreliable. The application of the rule will by necessity be contextual. Hard and fast rules simply cannot account for the variety of circumstances that vitiate the voluntariness of a confession, and would inevitably result in a rule that would be both over- and under-inclusive. A trial judge should therefore consider all the relevant factors when reviewing a confession.

(a) Threats or Promises

This is of course the core of the confessions rule from *Ibrahim*, supra. It is therefore important to define precisely what types of threats or promises will raise a reasonable doubt as to the voluntariness of a confession. While obviously imminent threats of torture will render a confession inadmissible, most cases will not be so clear.

As noted above, in *Ibrahim* the Privy Council ruled that statements would be inadmissible if they were the result of "fear of prejudice or hope of advantage". The classic "hope of advantage" is the prospect of leniency from the courts. It is improper for a person in authority to suggest to a suspect that he or she will take steps to procure a reduced charge or sentence if the suspect confesses. Therefore in *Nugent*, supra, the court excluded the statement of a suspect who was told that if he confessed, the charge could be reduced from murder to manslaughter. . . . Another type of inducement relevant to this appeal is an offer of psychiatric assistance or other counselling for the suspect in exchange for a confession. While this is clearly an inducement, it is not as strong as an offer of leniency and regard must be had to the entirety of the circumstances. . . . Threats or promises need not be aimed directly at the suspect for them to have a coercive effect. In *R. v. Jackson* (1977), 34 C.C.C. (2d) 35 (B.C.C.A.), McIntyre J.A. . . . offered, as examples of improper inducements, telling a mother that her daughter would not be charged with shoplifting if the mother confessed to a similar offence (see *Commissioners of Customs and Excise v. Harz*, [1967] 1 A.C. 760 (H.L.), at p. 821), or a sergeant-major keeping a company on parade until he learned who was responsible for a stabbing (see *R. v. Smith*, [1959] 2 Q.B. 35.

The *Ibrahim* rule speaks not only of "hope of advantage", but also of "fear of prejudice". Obviously, any confession that is the product of outright violence is involuntary and unreliable, and therefore inadmissible. More common, and more challenging judicially, are the more subtle, veiled threats that can be used against suspects. The Honourable Fred Kaufman, in the third edition of *The Admissibility of Confessions* (1979), at p. 230, provides a useful starting point:

> Threats come in all shapes and sizes. Among the most common are words to the effect that "it would be better" to tell, implying thereby that dire consequences might flow from a refusal to talk. Maule J. recognized this fact, and said that "there can be no doubt that such words, if spoken by a competent person, have been held to exclude a confession at least 500 times" (*R. v. Garner* (1848), 3 Cox C.C. 175, at p. 177).

Courts have accordingly excluded confessions made in response to police suggestions that it would be better if they confessed. However, phrases like "it would be better if you told the truth" should not automatically require exclusion. Instead, as in all cases, the trial judge must examine the entire context of the confession, and ask whether there is a reasonable doubt that the resulting confession was involuntary. . . . I agree that "it would be better" comments require exclusion only where the circumstances reveal an implicit threat or promise.

A final threat or promise relevant to this appeal is the use of moral or spiritual inducements. These inducements will generally not produce an involuntary confession, for the very simple reason that the inducement offered is not in the control of the police officers. If a police officer says "If you don't confess, you'll spend the rest of your life in jail. Tell me what happened and I can get you a lighter sentence", then clearly there is a strong, and improper, inducement for the suspect to confess. The officer is offering a quid pro quo, and it raises the possibility that the suspect is confessing not because of any internal desire to confess, but merely in order to gain the benefit offered by the interrogator. By contrast, with most spiritual inducements the interrogator has no control over the suggested benefit. If a police officer convinces a suspect that he will feel better if he confesses, the officer has not offered anything.

. . . .

In summary, courts must remember that the police may often offer some kind of inducement to the suspect to obtain a confession. Few suspects will spontaneously confess to a crime. In the vast majority of cases, the police will have to somehow convince the suspect that it is in his or her best interests to confess. This becomes improper only when the inducements, whether standing alone or in combination with other factors, are strong enough to raise a reasonable doubt about whether the will of the subject has been overborne. On this point I found the following passage from *R. v. Rennie* (1981), 74 Cr. App. R. 207 (C.A.), at p. 212, particularly apt:

> Very few confessions are inspired solely by remorse. Often the motives of an accused are mixed and include a hope that an early admission may lead to an earlier release or a lighter sentence. If it were the law that the mere presence of such a motive, even if promoted by something said or done by a person in authority, led inexorably to the exclusion of a confession, nearly every confession would be rendered inadmissible. This is not the law. In some cases the hope may be self-generated. If so, it is irrelevant, even if it provides the dominant motive for making the confession. In such a case the confession will not have been obtained by anything said or done by a person in authority. More commonly the presence of such a hope will, in part at least, owe its origin to something said or done by such a person. There can be few prisoners who are being firmly but fairly questioned in a police station to whom it does not occur that they might be able to bring both their interrogation and their detention to an earlier end by confession.

The most important consideration in all cases is to look for a quid pro quo offer by interrogators, regardless of whether it comes in the form of a threat or a promise.

(b) Oppression

There was much debate among the parties, interveners, and courts below over the relevance of "oppression" to the confessions rule. Oppression clearly has the potential to produce false confessions. If the police create conditions distasteful enough, it should be no surprise that the suspect would make a stress-compliant confession to escape those conditions. Alternately, oppressive circumstances could overbear the suspect's will to the point that he or she comes to doubt his or her own memory, believes the relentless accusations made by the police, and gives an induced confession.

A compelling example of oppression comes from the Ontario Court of Appeal's recent decision in *R. v. Hoilett* (1999), 136 C.C.C. (3d) 449. The accused, charged with sexual assault, was arrested at 11:25 p.m. while under the influence of crack cocaine and alcohol. After two hours in a cell, two officers removed his clothes for forensic testing. He was left naked in a cold cell containing only a metal bunk to sit on. The bunk was so cold he had to stand up. One and one-half hours later, he was provided with some light clothes, but no underwear and ill-fitting shoes. Shortly thereafter, at about 3:00 a.m., he was awakened for the purpose of interviewing. In the course of the interrogation, the accused nodded off to sleep at least five times. He requested warmer clothes and a tissue to wipe his nose, both of which were refused. While he admitted knowing that he did not have to talk, and that the officers had made no explicit threats or promises, he hoped that if he talked to the police they would give him some warm clothes and cease the interrogation. Under these circumstances, it is no surprise that the Court of Appeal concluded the statement was involuntary. Under inhumane conditions, one can hardly be surprised if a suspect confesses purely out of a desire to escape those conditions. Such a confession is not voluntary. . . . Without trying to indicate all the factors that can create an atmosphere of oppression, such factors include depriving the suspect of food, clothing, water, sleep, or medical attention; denying access to counsel; and excessively aggressive, intimidating questioning for a prolonged period of time.

A final possible source of oppressive conditions is the police use of non-existent evidence. As the discussion of false confessions, supra, revealed, this ploy is very dangerous. The use of false evidence is often crucial in convincing the suspect that protestations of innocence, even if true, are futile. I do not mean to suggest in any way that, standing alone, confronting the suspect with inadmissible or even fabricated evidence is necessarily grounds for excluding a statement. However, when combined with other factors, it is certainly a relevant consideration in determining on a *voir dire* whether a confession was voluntary.

(c) Operating Mind

This Court recently addressed this aspect of the confessions rule in *Whittle*, supra, and I need not repeat that exercise here. Briefly stated, Sopinka J. explained that the operating mind requirement "does not imply a higher degree of awareness than knowledge of what the accused is saying and that he is saying it to police officers who can use it to his detriment". I agree, and would simply add that, like oppression, the operating mind doctrine should not be understood as a discrete inquiry completely divorced from the rest of the confessions rule. . . . [T]he operating mind doctrine is just one application of the general rule that involuntary confessions are inadmissible.

(d) Other Police Trickery

A final consideration in determining whether a confession is voluntary or not is the police use of trickery to obtain a confession. Unlike the previous three headings, this doctrine is a distinct inquiry. While it is still related to voluntariness, its more specific objective is maintaining the integrity of the criminal justice system. Lamer J.'s concurrence in *Rothman*, supra, introduced this inquiry. In that case, the Court admitted a suspect's statement to an undercover police officer who had been placed in a cell with the accused. In concurring reasons, Lamer J. emphasized that reliability was not the only concern of the confessions rule; otherwise the rule would not be concerned with whether the inducement was given by a person in authority. He summarized the correct approach . . .:

> [A] statement before being left to the trier of fact for consideration of its probative value should be the object of a *voir dire* in order to determine, not whether the statement is or is not reliable, but whether the authorities have done or said anything that could have induced the accused to make a statement which was or might be untrue. It is of the utmost importance to keep in mind that the inquiry is not concerned with reliability but with the authorities' conduct as regards reliability.

Lamer J. was also quick to point out that courts should be wary not to unduly limit police discretion (at p. 697):

> [T]he investigation of crime and the detection of criminals is not a game to be governed by the Marquess of Queensbury rules. The authorities, in dealing with shrewd and often sophisticated criminals, must sometimes of necessity resort to tricks or other forms of deceit and should not through the rule be hampered in their work. What should be repressed vigorously is conduct on their part that shocks the community. [Emphasis added.]

As examples of what might "shock the community", Lamer J. suggested a police officer pretending to be a chaplain or a legal aid lawyer, or injecting truth serum into a diabetic under the pretense that it was insulin.

In *Hebert*, supra, this Court overruled the result in *Rothman* based on the Charter's right to silence. However, I do not believe that this renders the "shocks the community" rule redundant. There may be situations in which police trickery, though neither violating the right to silence nor undermining voluntariness per se, is so appalling as to shock the community. I therefore believe that the test enunciated by Lamer J. in *Rothman* is still an important part of the confessions rule.

. . . .

Application to the Present Appeal

Applying the foregoing law to the facts of this appeal, and having viewed the relevant video- and audiotapes, I find no fault with the trial judge's conclusion that the respondent's confession was voluntary and reliable. The respondent was fully apprised of his rights at all times; he was never subjected to harsh, aggressive, or overbearing interrogation; he was not deprived of sleep, food, or drink; and he was never offered any improper inducements that undermined the reliability of the confessions. As the Court of Appeal reached a contrary conclusion with respect to a number of these issues, I will address them in turn.

[The Court then analyzed the fact situation under a variety of heads: 1. Minimizing the Seriousness of the Crimes. 2. Offers of Psychiatric Help. 3. "It Would Be Better". 4. Alleged Threats Against the Respondent's Fiancée. 5. Abuse of Trust. 6. Atmosphere of Oppression. And finally, 7. The Use of the Polygraph Test.]

. . . .

Summary on Voluntariness

In summary, there were several aspects of the police's interrogation of the respondent that could potentially be relevant to the voluntariness of his confessions. These include the comments regarding Ms. Kilcup; the suggestions that "it would be better" for the respondent to confess; and the exaggeration of the polygraph's accuracy. These are certainly relevant considerations when determining voluntariness. However, I agree with the trial judge that neither standing alone, nor in combination with each other and the rest of the circumstances surrounding the respondent's confessions, do these factors raise a reasonable doubt about the voluntariness of the respondent's confessions. The respondent was never mistreated, he was questioned in an extremely friendly, benign tone, and he was not offered any inducements strong enough to raise a reasonable doubt as to voluntariness in the absence of any mistreatment or oppression. As I find no error in the trial judge's reasons, the Court of Appeal should not have disturbed her findings.

Arbour J.: —

I have had the benefit of the reasons of my colleague, Justice Iacobucci, on this appeal. With respect, I believe that there were improper inducements held out by the police officers who interrogated the respondent and that these inducements, considered cumulatively and contextually in light of the "failed" polygraph test, require the exclusion of the respondent's statements. Moreover, in my view the proximity and the causal connection between the "failed" polygraph test and the confession also compels this result. Accordingly, I would dismiss the appeal, set aside the convictions and enter acquittals on all counts. . . . Properly understood, this case involves two confessions obtained by the police following the "failure" of a polygraph test and a skillful interrogation which lasted nearly six hours. Repeated threats and promises were made. They were often subtle but in my view, against the backdrop of the polygraph procedure, they overwhelmed the free will of the respondent. These seemingly mild pressures make this case a difficult one in which to apply the confessions rule and demand an attentive appreciation of the full context in which the alleged voluntary, incriminating statements were made. I fully agree with the summary of the applicable law provided by Justice Iacobucci. . . . However, I take a different view of the proper legal characterization of what happened in the course of the many hours during which the respondent was interrogated and of the voluntary quality of his incriminating statements.

[Justice Arbour then analyzed admissibility under the heads of The Administration of the Polygraph Test, The Post-Polygraph Interrogation, Promise of Psychiatric Help, Minimization of the Seriousness of the Crimes, Threat to Interrogate the Accused's Girlfriend, and finally, as another basis for exclusion, Fair Trial Considerations.]

For these reasons I would dismiss the appeal, set aside the convictions and enter acquittals on all counts.

Academic comment on *Oickle* has been critical.[184]

The majority ruling in *R. v. Spencer*[185] makes it very clear that the police are to be given considerable leeway to offer inducements to obtain confessions without rendering a statement involuntary. Charged with robbery, the accused was very much concerned with whether his girlfriend would also be charged. The majority see the case as all about promises. The dissenters are persuasive in seeing the transcript as all about an implied threat to charge the girlfriend unless Spencer confessed. The police did not claim to have authority to offer leniency for his girlfriend but they certainly indicated they would speak to the Crown if he confessed.

Spencer and *Oickle* will encourage police to exploit emotions about possible prosecution against partners. *Oickle* says police may use polygraphs and lie about their accuracy. **Do you think that *Oickle* has resulted to view few judicial controls on interrogation?**

The community shock test is a very high hurdle for accused and does not apply to the s. 24(2) remedy of exclusion for Charter breaches. In the United Kingdom, judges under s. 76(2) of the *Evidence Act of 1984* have a discretion to exclude a confession where police interrogation methods are considered oppressive and not just where they shock the community. Under s. 76(5) oppression "includes torture, inhuman or degrading treatment or the use or threatened use of violence (whether or not amounting to torture)."

Trial judges who have relied on *Oickle* to exclude confessions have often done so by giving a very wide meaning to the category of oppression resulting in involuntariness. Regulation of police interrogation is one area where Parliament may have achieved a better balance than the courts. Under s. 269.1 of the *Criminal Code*, torture is an indictable offence punishable to a maximum of fourteen years. Torture is widely defined in s. 269.1(2) as:

> any act or omission by which severe pain or suffering, whether physical or mental, is intentionally inflicted on a person.

---

184 See Stuart, "*Oickle*: The Supreme Court's Recipe for Coercive Interrogation" (2001) 36 (5th) 188; Lisa Dufraimont, "The Common Law Confessions Rule in the *Charter* Era: Current Law and Future Directions" (2008) 40 *Supr. Crt. L. Rev.* 250; Dale Ives, "Preventing False Confessions: Is *Oickle* Up to the Task" (2007) *San Diego L. Rev.* 1; and Edmund Thomas, "Lowering the Standard: *R. v. Oickle* and the Confessions Rule in Canada" (2005) 10 *Can. Crim. L .Rev.* 69. See, too, Stuart, *Charter Justice in Canadian Criminal Law* (5th ed., 2010).
185 (2007) 51 C.R. (6th) 199 (S.C.C.).

Further, under subs. 4, a statement obtained by torture is inadmissible in any proceedings over which Parliament has jurisdiction.[186] This may be a vehicle for further judicial checks on police interrogation. It is also of note that the newest member of the Court, Justice Tom Cromwell, wrote in his lengthy opinion for the Nova Scotia Court of Appeal in *Oickle* that the confession had been obtained by oppressive methods and ought to be excluded.

3. THE PRE-TRIAL RIGHT TO SILENCE AND INTERROGATION

In *Oickle* the Supreme Court confined itself to the common law. What is the relationship between the pre-trial right to silence and/or principle against self-incrimination under section 7 of the Charter and the common law confessions rule?

R. v. OSMAR

[2007] O.J. No. 244, 2007 CarswellOnt 339, 217 C.C.C. (3d) 174, 44 C.R. (6th) 276 (C.A.), leave to appeal refused (2007), 2007 CarswellOnt 4187, 2007 CarswellOnt 4188 (S.C.C.)

The accused was convicted of first degree murder. Part of the police investigation involved use of the notorious "Mr. Big" strategy. The police created this fictitious organized crime organization and recruited the accused who was a suspect in two murders. The accused eventually had a meeting with the "Boss" who told him that he needed something on the accused in the event he would later want to leave the organization. The accused confessed to the two murders. He argued that the trick violated his right to silence and that the confession was involuntary.

ROSENBERG J.A. (GOUDGE, LA FORME JJ.A. concurring): —

[The Crown argued that since the accused was not detained, section 7 was not triggered (see earlier the discussion in *R. v. Hebert*). The Court of Appeal ultimately agreed relying on the Supreme Court decision in *R. v. McIntyre*. It did, however, address whether there would have been a violation of section 7 assuming that it was triggered.]

. . . Applying the contextual analysis set out in *White*, assuming I can do so free of the dictates of *Hebert* and *McIntyre*, does not lead me to conclude that the strategy employed by the police in this case violated s. 7. In doing so, I am conscious of the point made by Iacobucci J. at para. 48 of *White*: "In every case, the facts must be closely examined to determine whether the principle against self-incrimination has truly been brought into play by the production or use of the declarant's statement." Thus, it is not helpful to look at the Mr. Big strategy at large but rather as it was employed in this case.

---

186 See generally Donald Macdougall, "Torture in Canadian Criminal Law" (2005) 24 C.R. (6th) 74.

The context in this case does not violate the principles of fundamental justice. There was little, if any, coercion. The appellant was seeking employment in what he believed was an illegal enterprise. While he had been the subject of intense surveillance many months earlier, the overt surveillance had ceased. He claimed that he was unable to secure other employment but this is belied by the evidence that he had refused to follow up an offer of legitimate employment. The motion judge dismissed the claim that the appellant was effectively prohibited from finding employment because of the actions of the police. He also rejected the claim that the appellant was "inflicted with emotional and psychological trauma because of the intense surveillance".

I accept that the appellant and the police were in an adversarial relationship, but the appellant was not under "pronounced psychological and emotional pressure". The motion judge found to the contrary; that the appellant "displayed a composed and stable personality" during his interviews with the undercover officers.

Finally, this example of the Mr. Big strategy does not contain the elements of a real possibility of an unreliable confession because of abuse of power by a person in authority. There was no abuse of power. The appellant was presented with an opportunity to obtain employment in a criminal organization, but he was not threatened or intimidated. Even if it is possible to apply the White analysis to this case, the evidence and the findings of fact by the motion judge undermine any claim to a violation of s. 7.

[The Court then turned to *R. v. McIntyre* for guidance on the issue of detention and the common law confessions rule.]

Finally, it is necessary to consider the impact of *R. v. McIntyre*. The reasons of the Supreme Court of Canada are brief:

> The appellant argues that his statements made to undercover police officers after he had been released but while he was still the subject of a murder charge are inadmissible under ss. 7 and 24(2) of the Canadian Charter of Rights and Freedoms. We share the view of the majority that the accused was not detained within the meaning of *Hebert* and *Broyles*. Furthermore, the tricks used by the police were not likely to shock the community or cause the accused's statements not to be free and voluntary. The appeal is dismissed.

To understand the effect of *McIntyre* it is necessary to look at the facts as set out in the reasons of the New Brunswick Court of Appeal reported at (1993), 135 N.B.R. (2d) 266. The facts are sufficiently similar to the facts of this case that the holding is, in my view, binding on this court. McIntyre was arrested for a murder and while he was detained an undercover police officer was placed in his cell. The officer was unable to get McIntyre to talk and he was released. Five months later, the same officer set up a chance meeting with the accused and set in motion a Mr. Big-type operation. Thereafter the plot unfolded in much the same way as in this case. McIntyre was offered a job in an illegal operation on condition that he could prove he was able to kill if necessary. The undercover officers required proof from his past to show that he was capable of killing. At first he refused to answer but the officers continued to push him for answers and, when he realized that this was the only way of getting the job, he told the officers about the murder.

The issue of extending the *Hebert* doctrine to cases not involving detention was clearly before the court in view of the dissent of Rice J.A and particularly this portion of his reasons at para. 15:

> *Crown counsel argued before us that there was no violation of the rights guaranteed under the Charter in the present case because the appellant, once released, was no longer subject to the greater power of the State.* Being perfectly free to hang around with or to talk to the undercover officers, the situation was very different from detention where the prisoner cannot choose his cell mates. I am not impressed by this argument because in this case, the undercover officer succeeded in passing himself off as a criminal and ex-convict. This allowed him to gain Mr. McIntyre's trust by reason of having been placed in the latter's cell. *This ruse, having its beginnings during detention, was successfully continued afterward.* [Emphasis added.]

The entire court, including McLachlin J., sat on *McIntyre*. The issue of detention cannot be regarded as obiter in that case. I do not think it open to this court to reject the detention requirement for this aspect of the right to silence under s. 7. I would not give effect to the appellant's Charter argument.

(ii) The Common Law Arguments

The decision of the Supreme Court in *McIntyre* also directly meets the appellant's submission that the strategy employed in this case would shock the community. The facts in *McInytre* were certainly no worse than the circumstances of this case, yet the court held that "the tricks used by the police were not likely to shock the community". I should not be taken as holding that the manner in which the Mr. Big strategy is executed could never shock the conscience of the community and lead to exclusion on common law grounds. However, the facts of this case do not meet that test.

I would also not give effect to the other common law grounds. The argument that the prejudicial effect of the evidence outweighs its probative value depends on the theory that the inducement offered by the undercover officers produced an unreliable confession inconsistent with the known facts. The appellant also points out the additional prejudicial effect of admitting the confession because it necessarily places him in a bad light, as someone willing to consort with people he believes to be criminals and join them in their illegal activities. Counsel for the Crown and counsel for the appellant have carefully reviewed the facts relating to the murders and compared them to the details in the confessions. In my view, the statements have sufficient probative value that it was open to the trial court to admit them. The most striking aspect of the confessions is the appellant's identification of the probable murder weapon in the first killing. While the appellant testified that he received this information from the police, the prosecution witnesses denied passing on this information to him. This was an issue to be resolved by the jury.

I am also of the view that it was for the jury to decide whether in the context of a meeting where he was seeking work, the inducement of a job in an illegal operation would be sufficient to cause the appellant to falsely confess to past deeds. This was not a case of such extraordinary coercion that it can be said the statement is too unreliable to be received by the triers of fact, nor a set of facts they would be unable to assess.

The B.C. Court of Appeal determined in *K. (H.W.)*[187] that the section 7 right to silence was not breached by overriding the accused's choice not to speak where police asked the accused in a murder case whether he wished to take a breathalyser, after assuring the lawyer they would not be interviewing him. Because of the agreement with the lawyer, McEachern C.J.B.C., for the court, found this case close to the line between "fair and unfair treatment" but noted that the accused had chosen freely and voluntarily to say far more than was necessary to answer the question.[188] So too the B.C. court held there was no right to silence violation in *Ekman*.[189] The accused had indicated that he was only willing to answer questions with his lawyer present, but did so without his lawyer when the police advised him he had no right to the presence of a lawyer and the choice was his. There had been no confusion in the accused's mind as to his rights.

However, in *Otis*,[190] the Quebec Court of Appeal decided that the right to silence should be more meaningful. Although the court decided that the accused had sufficient, though limited, cognitive capacity to make choices Justice Proulx for the court decided that the continued police questioning, after he had asked them to stop four times, violated section 7. The police were not entitled to use their superior power to totally disregard the accused's desires and undermine his choice to remain silent. Once an accused has clearly stated he wishes to remain silent, the police cannot act as if there has been a waiver.

In *R. v. Roy*,[191] the accused was convicted of a murder of an 11-year-old girl lured from her home. On his conviction appeal the Ontario Court of Appeal dismissed the argument that his confession following an eight hour interrogation had breached his section 7 pre-trial right to silence. The Court held that he had not chosen not to speak as he had a game plan to answer some not all questions. For the Court, Doherty J.A. (Feldman and Macpherson JJ.A. concurring) however added *obiter*:

> [The] repeated assertion by a detained person during a lengthy interview that he does not want to speak to the police any further will provide strong and sometimes conclusive evidence that any subsequent statement was not the product of a free exercise of the detainee's right to choose whether to speak. The question is, however, a factual question to be decided on a case by case basis by the trial judge (at 187).[192]

---

187 (2000), 32 C.R. (5th) 359 (B.C. C.A.).

188 At para. 18.

189 (2000), 146 C.C.C. (3d) 346 (B.C. C.A.).

190 (2000), 37 C.R. (5th) 320 (Que. C.A.). See Guy Cournoyer, "*Otis*: The Quebec Court of Appeal Asserts a Meaningful Right to Silence Where a Suspect Says No to Interrogation" (2000), 37 C.R. (5th) 342.

191 (2004), 15 C.R. (6th) 282 (Ont. C.A.).

192 See annotation by Guy Cournoyer in (2004), 15 C.R. (6th) 284.

Those looking for these *obiter* to result in further judicial controls on police interrogation were shocked by the decision of a 5-4 majority of the Supreme Court in *Singh*.[193]

R. v. SINGH
(2007) 2007 CarswellBC 2588, 2007 CarswellBC 2589, 51 C.R. (6th) 199, 225 C.C.C. (3d) 103, [2007] 3 S.C.R. 405

The accused was charged with second degree murder after an altercation outside a pub resulted in a man's death. Several shots were fired and an innocent bystander was fatally shot by a stray bullet. There was no physical evidence linking the accused to the shooting, but the doorman and another eyewitness implicated the accused as the shooter.

The accused was arrested, properly cautioned and advised of his right to counsel, and he privately consulted with counsel. The accused was subsequently interviewed twice by a police officer while in detention. During these interviews, which were videotaped, the accused stated on numerous occasions that he did not want to talk about the incident, that he knew nothing about it, and that he wished to return to his cell. On each occasion, the officer either affirmed that the accused did not have to say anything or explained that he, the officer, had a duty or desire to place the evidence before the accused. In all cases the officer persisted in questioning the accused and confronting the accused with incriminating evidence. The officer testified that he intended to put the police case before the accused in an attempt to get him to confess, no matter what.

During the first interview, the accused did not confess but made incriminating statements, admitting that he had been in the pub on the night of the shooting and identifying himself in pictures taken from video surveillance inside the pub in question and another pub. The accused had asserted his right to silence 18 times before making these admissions.

At trial, the accused challenged the admissibility of the statements, arguing that they were involuntary and that they were obtained in violation of the accused's pre-trial right to silence under s. 7 of the Charter. The trial judge admitted the statements and the accused was convicted. The accused's appeal to the British Columbia Court of Appeal was dismissed. The accused appealed to the Supreme Court on the s. 7 issue.

A 5-4 majority dismissed the appeal.

Per CHARRON J. (McLACHLIN C.J., BASTARACHE, DESCHAMPS, ROTHSTEIN JJ. concurring):

. . . .

Mr. Singh contends that trial and appellate courts, including the courts below,

---

193 For critical comments on Singh see Timothy Moore and Karina Gagnier, "'You can talk if you want to': Is the Police Caution on the 'Right to Silence' Understandable?" (2008) 51 C.R. (6th) 233, and Dale Ives and Christopher Sherrin, "*R. v. Singh* – A Meaningless Right to Silence with Dangerous Consequences" (2008) 51 C.R. (6th) 250, but see, however, strong support from Suhail Akhtar, "Whatever Happened to The Right to Silence?" (2009) 62 C.R. (6th) 73.

have generally misinterpreted the holding in Hebert as an authoritative statement which permits the police to ignore a detainee's expressed wish to remain silent and to use "legitimate means of persuasion" to break that silence (p. 177). He contends that the British Columbia Court of Appeal in the case at bar went even further and effectively extinguished the s. 7 right to silence when it questioned the utility of conducting "a double-barrelled test of admissibility", stating that "[i]n the context of an investigatory interview with an obvious person in authority " the expansive view of the common law confessions rule adopted in Oickle "may leave little additional room" for a separate s. 7 Charter inquiry (para. 19). Mr. Singh therefore submits that the Court of Appeal proceeded on the basis of erroneous legal principles when it affirmed the trial judge's dismissal of his s. 7 Charter application.

Further, Mr. Singh invites this Court to enhance the protection afforded to detainees under s. 7 by adopting a new approach that would require police officers to inform the detainee of his or her right to silence and, absent a signed waiver, to refrain from questioning any detainee who states that he or she does not wish to speak to the police.

First, I reject the appellant's contention that this Court should change the law relating to the pre-trial Charter right to silence. The new approach advocated by the appellant ignores the critical balancing of state and individual interests which lies at the heart of this Court's decision in Hebert and of subsequent s. 7 decisions. I see no reason to depart from these established principles.

Second, I find no error in law in the approach adopted by the courts below. The Court of Appeal's impugned comment on the interplay between the confessions rule and s. 7 of the Charter merely reflects the fact that, in the context of a police interrogation of a person in detention, where the detainee knows he or she is speaking to a person in authority, the two tests are functionally equivalent. It follows that, where a statement has survived a thorough inquiry into voluntariness, the accused's Charter application alleging that the statement was obtained in violation of the pre-trial right to silence under s. 7 cannot succeed. Conversely, if circumstances are such that the accused can show on a balance of probabilities that the statement was obtained in violation of his or her constitutional right to remain silent, the Crown will be unable to prove voluntariness beyond a reasonable doubt. As I will explain, however, this does not mean that the residual protection afforded to the right to silence under s. 7 of the Charter does not supplement the common law in other contexts.

Finally, I see no basis for interfering with the trial judge's factual determinations concerning Sgt. Attew's conduct and its effect on the appellant's freedom to choose whether to speak to the police. I would therefore dismiss the appeal.

. . .

Although historically the confessions rule was more concerned with the reliability of confessions than the protection against self-incrimination, this no longer holds true in the post-Charter era. Both the confessions rule and the constitutional right to silence are manifestations of the principle against self-incrimination. The principle against self-incrimination is a broad concept which has been usefully described by Lamer C.J. as "a general organizing principle of criminal law" from which a number of rules can be derived.

. . .

What the common law recognizes is the individual's right to remain silent. This does not mean, however, that a person has the right not to be spoken to by state authorities. The importance of police questioning in the fulfilment of their investigative role cannot be doubted. One can readily appreciate that the police could hardly investigate crime without putting questions to persons from whom it is thought that useful information may be obtained. The person suspected of having committed the crime being investigated is no exception. Indeed, if the suspect in fact committed the crime, he or she is likely the person who has the most information to offer about the incident. Therefore, the common law also recognizes the importance of police interrogation in the investigation of crime.

Of course, the information obtained from a suspect is only useful in the elucidation of crime if it can be relied upon for its truth — hence the primary reason for the confessions rule, the concern about the reliability of confessions. The common law confessions rule is largely informed by the problem of false confessions. As noted in *Oickle*, "[t]he history of police interrogations is not without its unsavoury chapters" (para. 34). The parameters of the rule are very much tailored to counter the dangers created by improper interrogation techniques that commonly produce false confessions: see *Oickle*, at paras. 32-46. Further, a confession is a very powerful item of evidence against an accused which, in and of itself, can ground a conviction. One of the overriding concerns of the criminal justice system is that the innocent must not be convicted. Because it is recognized that involuntary confessions are more likely to be unreliable, the confessions rule requires proof beyond a reasonable doubt of the voluntariness of any statement obtained from an accused by a person in authority before it may be admitted in evidence, so to avoid miscarriages of justice.

Of course, not every involuntary confession is false. While the confession rule's primary concern is with reliability, it is well established that voluntariness is a broader concept. As this Court stated in *Oickle* (at para. 70): "Wigmore perhaps summed up the point best when he said that voluntariness is 'shorthand for a complex of values': *Wigmore on Evidence* (Chadbourn rev. 1970), vol. 3, § 826, at p. 351." These values include respect for the individual's freedom of will, the need for law enforcement officers themselves to obey the law, and the overall fairness of the criminal justice system: see *Oickle*, at paras. 69-70, citing *Blackburn v. Alabama*, 361 U.S. 199 (1960), at p. 207.

Therefore, the notion of voluntariness is broad-based and has long included the common law principle that a person is not obliged to give information to the police or to answer questions. This component of the voluntariness rule is reflected in the usual police caution given to a suspect and the importance attached (even before the advent of the Charter) to the presence of a caution as a factor in determining the voluntariness of a statement made by a person under arrest or detention: see *Boudreau v. The King*, [1949] S.C.R. 262; *R. v. Fitton*, [1956]

S.C.R. 958; and *R. v. Esposito* (1985), 24 C.C.C. (3d) 88 (Ont. C.A.). A common form of the police caution given to a person who has been charged with an offence is the following: "You are charged with... Do you wish to say anything in answer to the charge? You are not obliged to say anything but whatever you do say may be given in evidence." Therefore, the police caution, in plain language, informs the suspect of his right to remain silent. Its importance as a factor on the question of voluntariness was noted by this Court as early as 1949 in *Boudreau*:

> The fundamental question is whether a confession of an accused offered in evidence is voluntary. There mere fact that a warning was given is not necessarily decisive in favour of admissibility but, on the other hand, the absence of a warning should not bind the hands of the Court so as to compel it to rule out a statement. All the surrounding circumstances must be investigated and, if upon their review the Court is not satisfied of the voluntary nature of the admission, the statement will be rejected. Accordingly, the presence or absence of a warning will be a factor and, in many cases, an important one.

Although the confessions rule applies whether or not the suspect is in detention, the common law recognized, also long before the advent of the *Charter,* that the suspect's situation is much different after detention. (As we shall see, the residual protection afforded to the right to silence under s. 7 of the *Charter* is only triggered upon detention.) After detention, the state authorities are in control and the detainee, who cannot simply walk away, is in a more vulnerable position. There is a greater risk of abuse of power by the police. The fact of detention alone can have a significant impact on the suspect and cause him or her to feel compelled to give a statement. The importance of reaffirming the individual's right to choose whether to speak to the authorities after he or she is detained is reflected in the jurisprudence concerning the timing of the police caution. Rene Marin, in his text *Admissibility of Statements* (9th ed. (looseleaf)), at pp. 2-24.2 and 2-24.3, provides a useful yardstick for the police on when they should caution a suspect:

> The warning should be given when there are reasonable grounds to suspect that the person being interviewed has committed an offence. An easy yardstick to determine when the warning should be given is for a police officer to consider the question of what he or she would do if the person attempted to leave the questioning room or leave the presence of the officer where a communication or exchange is taking place. If the answer is arrest (or detain) the person, then the warning should be given.

These words of advice are sound. Even if the suspect has not formally been arrested and is not obviously under detention, police officers are well advised to give the police caution in the circumstances described by Marin. Of course, with the advent of the Charter, the s. 10 right to counsel is triggered upon arrest or detention. The right to counsel has both an informational and an implementational component. It seeks to ensure that persons who become subject to the coercive power of the state will know about their right to counsel and will be given the opportunity to exercise it so they can make an informed choice whether to participate in the investigation against them. Therefore, if the detainee has exercised his s. 10 Charter right to counsel, he will presumably have been informed of his right to remain silent, and the overall significance of the caution may be somewhat diminished. Where the suspect has not consulted with counsel, however, the police caution becomes all the more important as a factor in answering the ultimate question of voluntariness.

. . .

On the question of voluntariness, as under any distinct s. 7 review based on an alleged breach of the right to silence, the focus is on the conduct of the police and its effect on the suspect's ability to exercise his or her free will. The test is an objective one. However, the individual characteristics of the accused are obviously relevant considerations in applying this objective test.

Therefore, voluntariness, as it is understood today, requires that the court scrutinize whether the accused was denied his or her right to silence. The right to silence is defined in accordance with constitutional principles. A finding of voluntariness will therefore be determinative of the s. 7 issue. In other words, if the Crown proves voluntariness beyond a reasonable doubt, there can be no finding of a Charter violation of the right to silence in respect of the same statement. The converse holds true as well. If the circumstances are such that an accused is able to show on a balance of probabilities a breach of his or her right to silence, the Crown will not be in a position to meet the voluntariness test. ...

Mr. Singh takes particular issue with the leeway afforded to the police in questioning the detainee, even after he has retained counsel and has asserted his choice to remain silent. He submits that courts have erroneously interpreted the underlined passage above as permitting the police to ignore a detainee's expressed wish to remain silent and to use "legitimate means of persuasion". I say two things in response to this argument. First, the use of legitimate means of persuasion is indeed permitted under the present rule — it was expressly endorsed by this Court in Hebert. This approach is part of the critical balance that must be maintained between individual and societal interests. Second, the law as it stands does not permit the police to ignore the detainee's freedom to choose whether to speak or not, as contended. Under both common law and Charter rules, police persistence in continuing the interview, despite repeated assertions by the detainee that he wishes to remain silent, may well raise a strong argument that any subsequently obtained statement was not the product of a free will to speak to the authorities. As we shall see, the trial judge in this case was very much alive to the risk that the statement may be involuntary when a police officer engages in such conduct.

. . .

Despite Sgt. Attew's admitted intention to put parts of the police case against Mr. Singh before him in an effort to get him to confess, "no matter what", his conduct of the interview as evidenced on the videotape shows that in so describing his method his bark is much worse than his bite. In my respectful view, the trial judge's ultimate judgment call on this issue is supported by the record and is entitled to deference. Therefore, I see no reason to interfere with his ruling on admissibility.

It must again be emphasized that such situations are highly fact-specific and trial judges must take into account all the relevant factors in determining whether or not the Crown has established that the accused's confession is voluntary. In some circumstances, the evidence will support a finding that continued questioning by the police in the face of the accused's repeated assertions of the right to silence denied the accused a meaningful choice whether to speak or to remain silent: see Otis. The number of times the accused asserts his or her right to silence is part of the assessment of all of the circumstances, but is not in itself determinative. The ultimate question is whether the accused exercised free will by choosing to make a statement: *Otis*, at paras. 50 and 54.

Per FISH J. (BINNIE, LEBEL, ABELLA JJ. concurring) (dissenting):

The question on this appeal is whether "no" means "yes" where a police interrogator refuses to take "no" for an answer from a detainee under his total control. As a matter of constitutional principle, I would answer that question in the negative, allow the appeal and order a new trial.

. . . .

What is at stake, rather, is the Court's duty to ensure that a detainee's right to silence will be respected by interrogators once it has been unequivocally asserted, and not disregarded or insidiously undermined as an investigative "stratagem" (the trial judge's own word in this case).

The appellant, Jagrup Singh, asserted his right to silence unequivocally — not once, but eighteen times. Throughout his interrogation, Mr. Singh was imprisoned in a police lock-up. In the trial judge's words, he was "totally under the control of the police authorities", "[did] not have freedom of unescorted movement" and "relie[d] totally on his jailers for the necessaries of life" (Ruling on the voir dire, [2003] B.C.J. No. 3174 (QL), 2003 BCSC 2013, at para. 8). Powerless to end his interrogation, Mr. Singh asked, repeatedly, to be returned to his cell. Yet he was not permitted to do so until he capitulated and made the incriminating statements impugned on this appeal.

Mr. Singh's interrogator understood very well that Mr. Singh had chosen not to speak with the police. The interrogator nonetheless disregarded Mr. Singh's repeated assertions of his right to silence. It is undisputed that he did so "an effort to get [Mr. Singh] to confess, no matter what" (Ruling on the voir dire, at para. 34. . .).

In his relentless pursuit of this objective, the interrogator urged Mr. Singh, subtly but unmistakeably, to forsake his counsel's advice. I find this aspect of the interrogation particularly disturbing.

To the officer's knowledge, Mr. Singh had been advised by his lawyer to exercise his right to silence. The officer, with irony if not cynicism, discounted this "absolutely great advice" (his words) as something he too would say if he were Mr. Singh's lawyer. And he then pressed Mr. Singh to instead answer his questions — "to confess, no matter what".

Mr. Singh was thus deprived not only of his right to silence, but also, collaterally, of the intended benefit of his right to counsel. These rights are close companions, like glove and hand.

. . .

At the very least, the interrogator's conduct in this case "unfairly frustrated [Mr. Singh's] decision on the question of whether to make a statement to the authorities" (*Hebert*, at p. 186). Accordingly, the impugned statements, in the words of s. 24(2) of the *Charter*, were "obtained in a manner that infringed or denied" Mr. Singh's constitutional right to silence. And I am satisfied that authorizing their admission in the circumstances of this case would bring the administration of justice into disrepute. They should therefore have been excluded at trial.

In the trial judge's view, Mr. Singh's repeated assertions of his right to silence signify that "Mr. Singh successfully invoked his right to silence" (para. 36)...

Where continued resistance has been made to appear futile to one person under the dominance or control of another, as it was in this case, ultimate submission proves neither true consent nor valid waiver. It proves the failure, not the success, of the disregarded assertions of the right of the powerless and the vulnerable to say "no".

. . .

I take care not to be understood to have held that eighteen (a significant number in other contexts) is of any importance at all in determining whether a detainee's right of silence has been effectively undermined. On the contrary, I favour a purposive approach and find it unnecessary to decide whether eighteen times is too many or once is too few. Constitutional rights do not have to be asserted or invoked a pre-determined number of times before the state and its agents are bound to permit them to be exercised freely and effectively. A right that need not be respected after it has been firmly and unequivocally asserted any number of times is a constitutional promise that has not been kept.

Nothing in *Hebert*, or in any other decision of this Court, permits the police to press detainees to waive the *Charter* rights they have firmly and unequivocally asserted, or to deliberately frustrate their effective exercise. This is true of the right to counsel and true as well of the right to silence.

Justice Charron agrees with the British Columbia Court of Appeal that "[i]n the context of an investigatory interview with an obvious person in authority, the expansive view of the confession rule in *Oickle* may leave little additional room for s. 7" ((2006), 38 C.R. (6th) 217 (B.C.C.A.), at para. 19). With respect, I am of a different view.

The rationale of the enhanced confessions rule adopted in *R. v. Oickle*, [2000] 2 S.C.R. 3, 2000 SCC 38, like the rationale of its narrower predecessor, is distinct from the purposes served by the Charter. A confession may be "voluntary" under the common law rule and yet be obtained by state action that infringes s. 7 of the *Charter*. And s. 7 will be infringed where, as in this case, a police interrogator has undermined a detainee's "freedom to choose whether to make a statement or not" (*Hebert*, at p. 176). Flagrantly disregarded in this way, the detainee's "positive right to make a free choice" (*Hebert*, at p. 177), is neither "positive" nor "free".

. . .

Justice Charron finds that the expansion of the confessions rule in *Oickle* leaves no additional room for the operation of s. 7 in the context of an "investigatory interview" (paras. 8, 25). I agree with her that there is considerable overlap between the *Charter* protection of the right to silence and the common law confessions rule. Given their different purposes, however, they should remain distinct doctrines: To overlap is not to overtake.

Even under its broader formulation in *Oickle*, the common law rule remains principally concerned with the reliability of confessions and the integrity of the criminal justice system. The purpose of the Charter, on the other hand, is "to constrain government action in conformity with certain individual rights and freedoms, the preservation of which are essential to the continuation of a democratic, functioning society in which the basic dignity of all is recognized" (*Canadian Egg Marketing Agency v. Richardson*, [1998] 3 S.C.R. 157, at para. 57).

As this case illustrates, a purposive approach makes plain that the right to pre-trial silence under s. 7 of the *Charter* is not eclipsed by the common law confessions rule under *Oickle*. This asymmetry should not surprise. The Court has consistently held that the two doctrines are distinct. Lower courts have continued to apply them separately. And even upon expanding the common law rule in *Oickle*, the Court took care to explain that neither rule "subsumes the other" (at para. 31).

Justice Charron finds the reasons of Proulx J.A. in *Otis* "particularly instructive" on the issue that concerns us here. I agree. In Justice Proulx's words: [Translation] "The refusal of the investigator to respect the respondent's specific insistent request to end the interrogation constitutes a violation of the right to remain silent": *R. v. Otis* (2000), 151 C.C.C. (3d) 416 (Que. C.A.), at para. 43. And I think it especially instructive that Justice Proulx [Translation] "ruled that the confession should be excluded due to the breach of a right guaranteed by the Charter" (para. 57) rather than under the common law confessions rule — even though, in the particular circumstances of *Otis* (notably the "emotional disintegration" of the accused), he would have excluded the accused's statement under the confessions rule as well.

The Court held in *Hebert*, as we have seen, that the s. 7 right to silence "must be interpreted in a manner which secures to the detained person the right to make a free and meaningful choice as to whether to speak to the authorities or to remain silent" (p. 181). Under the *Oickle* test, as noted earlier, a statement is admissible at common law where the detainee had an operating mind and the confession did not result from inducements, oppression, or police trickery that would shock the community. Clearly, however, a confession that meets these common law standards does not invariably represent a "free and meaningful choice" for the purposes of the *Charter*. A choice that has been disregarded, and "unfairly frustrated" (*Hebert*, at p. 186) by relentless interrogation "an effort to get a detainee to confess, no matter what", is, once again, neither "free" nor "meaningful". And it is a choice not born of "legitimate means of persuasion" within the meaning of *Hebert* (at p. 177).

. . .

With respect, I am troubled by Justice Charron's suggestion that the ability of the police to investigate crime in Canada would be unduly impaired by the effective exercise of the pre-trial right to silence. In a similar vein, the respondent warns against its "massive and far-reaching consequences in the arena of police investigations" and the federal Director of Public Prosecutions, an intervener, submits that it would have "a devastating impact on criminal justice in Canada".

. . .

Potential witnesses are rightfully expected, as a matter of civic duty, to assist the police by answering their questions. As a matter of law, however, they may refuse to answer, and go on home. Prisoners and detainees, on the other hand, are by definition not free to leave as they please. They are powerless to end their interrogation. As explained in *Hebert*, this is why they have been given the right to counsel and its close relative, the right to silence.

Neither of these rights has been given constitutional protection on the condition that it not be exercised, lest the investigation of crime be brought to a standstill. On the contrary, the policy of the law is to facilitate, and not to frustrate, the effective exercise of both rights by those whom they are intended to protect. They are *Charter* rights, not constitutional placebos.

Moreover, we have no evidence to support the proposition that requiring the police to respect a detainee's right of silence, once it has been unequivocally asserted, would have a "devastating impact" on criminal investigations anywhere in this country.

For more than 40 years, it has been the law in the United States that where a suspect "indicates in any manner, at any time prior to or during questioning, that he wishes to remain silent, the interrogation must cease": *Miranda v. Arizona*, 384 U.S. 436 (1966), at pp. 473-74. And yet, as Wharton puts it, "[n]umerous studies in the years following this decision have concluded that *Miranda* had little impact on the ability of the police to obtain statements": Wharton's *Criminal Procedure* (14th ed. looseleaf), at p. 19-9.

. . .

Not everyone will agree with Wharton that *Miranda* appears to have had little effect on the ability of the police to obtain statements. There are, of course, conflicting assessments of the evidence as to its impact, but *Miranda* can hardly be said to have paralysed criminal investigations in the United States. And there is no evidentiary basis for suggesting that it would do so in Canada.

In any event, the success of this appeal does not depend on the importation of the *Miranda* rule into Canada. And I take care not to be misunderstood to suggest that *Miranda* either is now, or ought to be made, the law in Canada. Here, the right to silence, once asserted, is not a barrier to the admissibility of any subsequent pre-trial statement of a detainee or prisoner. Nor is there any requirement that interrogators obtain a signed waiver from detainees, as the appellant suggests there ought to be. On the other hand, in the words of Professors Delisle, Stuart and Tanovich, "once an accused has clearly stated he wishes to remain silent, the police cannot act as if there has been a waiver" (R. Delisle, D. Stuart and D. Tanovich, *Evidence: Principles and Problems* (8th ed. 2007), at p. 489).

In short, detainees who have asserted their right to silence are entitled to change their minds. As I have stated elsewhere, "[a]n initial refusal can later give way to a crisis of conscience, to an 'unconscious compulsion to confess' — or, simply, to a genuine change of heart": *R. v. Timm* (1998), 131 C.C.C. (3d) 306 (Que. C.A.), at para. 145. But they cannot be compelled to do so by the persistent disregard of that choice. As mentioned earlier, that is what happened here.

Finally, even in the absence of the required evidentiary foundation, I am prepared for present purposes to recognize that the work of the police would be made easier (and less challenging) if police interrogators were permitted to undermine the constitutionally protected rights of detainees, including the right to counsel and the right to silence — either by pressing detainees to waive them, or by "unfairly frustrat[ing]" their exercise (*Hebert* at p. 186). More draconian initiatives might prove more effective still.

Nonetheless and without hesitation, I much prefer a system of justice that permits the effective exercise by detainees of the constitutional and procedural rights guaranteed to them by the law of the land. The right to silence, like the right to counsel, is in my view a constitutional promise that must be kept. . . .

In her comment on *Singh*, Professor Lisa Dufraimont writes in part:

> Arguably, *Singh* provides insufficient protection for the right to silence. As long as the Charter protects the pre-trial right to silence, there is something unseemly about the Supreme Court jealously guarding the power of police interrogators to undermine a suspect's choice to remain silent. At the same time, the majority in *Singh* recognizes that persistent questioning of suspects who repeatedly assert their right to silence can result in the exclusion of the resulting statements under the voluntariness rule. Such a statement will be involuntary, and exclusion automatic, where it was not the product of the suspect's free will to speak to the authorities.

> Ultimately, then, there may be less separating the majority and the minority in *Singh* that one might initially suppose. Certainly the majority rejects the dissenters' suggestion that the police are obliged to stop questioning a detainee who clearly asserts the right to silence. However, the full court agrees that persistent questioning in the face of repeated assertions of the right to silence can render a statement inadmissible. The question whether the exclusionary remedy arises from the confessions rule or the s. 7 pre-trial right to silence is less important than the availability of the remedy itself.

The problem is that even *Oickle* is not just about voluntariness. Under *Oickle*, there is a freestanding discretion to exclude confessions obtained by tricks that shock the community. Why wasn't such a sustained effort by the police to override an assertion of the right to silence shocking? Justice Abella held for the Supreme Court in *R. v. Turcotte* that adverse inferences should not be drawn against someone who is silent at the pre-trial stage as it would be a "snare and delusion" to advise about the right to silence and then to turn around and use silence as a sign of guilt. Why isn't it a snare and delusion to say a suspect has the right to silence but allow police to ignore its exercise? *Singh* has suddenly reduced this to the very little s. 7 right to one that an undercover agent cannot elicit statements from a detainee by the functional equivalent of an interrogation. Certainly in *Singh* there is no mention of any s. 7 right to be advised of the right to silence where police are not undercover. Whether the accused received advice from the police or a lawyer (if there was one) is just a factor to be considered on the voluntariness inquiry. With the changed composition of the Court one can only hope that *Singh* will be reconsidered.

PROBLEMS

Problem 1

John Howard has asked you to represent him on an anticipated charge of robbery. He assures you that he had nothing to do with the incident but that he understands the police are looking to question him. Contact with the local police has confirmed your client's suspicion and you have resolved to surrender him at the station this afternoon. How should you advise your client regarding the questions which will be forthcoming? Can you demand that the police only question your client in your presence? Are statements receivable if they question him in contravention of your instructions? Compare *R. v. Dinardo* (1981), 61 C.C.C. (2d) 52 (Ont. Co. Ct.); *R. v. Allen*, [1977] Crim. L. Rev. 163. See also *R. v. Letendre* (1975), 25 C.C.C. (2d) 180 (Man. C.A.).

Problem 2

The accused John Bent was arrested and jointly charged with William Tell with robbery. During the course of the first interview at the police station Bent declined to answer any questions. Two hours later the investigating officer returned Bent to the interrogation room and showed Bent a statement, purportedly signed by Tell, in which Bent is described as the prime mover in the robbery with Tell playing only a subsidiary role. In fact Tell had not given a statement to the police and his signature to the document had been forged by the investigating officer. Bent reacted angrily, saying, "I didn't think he'd turn on me — I guess there really is no honour among thieves." Defence counsel has objected to receipt of Bent's statement. Rule on the objection.

Problem 3

The accused was charged with several sexual offences involving young boys. The accused made an inculpatory statement. The accused was convicted and has appealed. Argue the admissibility of the statement, based on the following transcript.

The investigating constable testified:

A.   I then approach Cyril and inform him that I would like to speak to him but I made it quite clear that if he didn't wish to speak to me he didn't have to, not without consulting his lawyer, that was made very clear. I told him I was investigating this incident, that I in my job wanted to clear it up. I wanted to get his side of the story down on paper.

Q.   Get his side of the story down. Did he express any desire to wait until a lawyer is called or until he saw a lawyer?

A.   None that I can recall.

Q.   Okay. Did you ever tell Cyril he had a problem that you wanted to help him with?

A.   Yes, I did. I stated that I believed what the children were saying was true and based on that I thought he had a problem and I wanted to help him by talking about it. I stated that in perhaps speaking about it he could better understand it. And also I made it quite clear that in speaking about it he would be helping us in our investigation as well.

Compare the differing views of Monnin C.J.M. and Huband J.A. in *R. v. Bird* (1989), 50 C.C.C. (3d) 89 (Man. C.A.).

Problem 4

The accused was charged with arson. At 5 a.m. the Calgary Fire Department responded to a fire at an up/down duplex. They found the accused on a couch in the basement apartment, roused him and carried him out. He was taken to hospital. His nose hair, eyebrows, eyelashes and hair were singed and he had soot in his mouth. He was alert and could answer all questions. Further investigation revealed that the cause of the fire was tampering with the gas supply. The police found a bag in garbage containers in the back alley which contained two wrenches and torn pieces of mail addressed to the accused. The accused was arrested on his release from hospital a day later.

Shortly after the arrest, after he had been read his Charter rights and had consulted his lawyer, the accused agreed to be interviewed by detectives. During the next two hours of interrogation, which was recorded, detectives suggested that his daughter would be caused mental anguish if the explanation was attempted suicide. The detectives tricked the accused in two ways: falsely telling the accused that they had found his prints on the circuitbreakers and that this was highly incriminating and fabricating that a neighbour had seen him place the tools in the garbage can. They also left the impression, which was false, that the neighbour was conspiring with the police to unfairly put fabricated evidence to the court. The accused finally made several incriminating statements. Should these statements be admitted under the *Oickle* tests?

Compare *R. v. Wiegand* (2003), 11 C.R. (6th) 356 (Alta. Q.B.).

Problem 5

The accused, Pinnock and Robinson, were charged with first degree murder. During the investigation the police employed an undercover officer to pretend to be an Obeahman, a spiritual advisor in some Caribbean cultures. The officer befriended the mother of one of the accused and thereby arranged to meet with the two accused numerous times and persuade them that, in accordance with the religious practices of Obeah, they needed to confide to him what they knew about the death of the victim. In this manner, he elicited inculpatory statements from the accused as well as investigatively helpful information. All of the meetings were audio and videotaped, and the Crown sought to admit the tapes into evidence. The accused sought the exclusion of the evidence on the basis that there was a violation of their freedom of religion rights, that the police tactic was a dirty trick, that there was a violation of their equality rights, and that the communications were privileged.

Compare *R. v. Welsh,* (2007) 51 C.R. (6th) 33 (Ont. S.C.) and see annotation by Stephen Coughlan, C.R. *ibid.* 35.

Problem 6

The accused was charged with second degree murder after a man was fatally attacked in the street outside the accused's apartment. The attack took place in the early morning hours, soon after intruders robbed and pistol-whipped the accused and his friends in the accused's apartment. When the accused was arrested soon after these events, his left hand was injured so seriously that he required surgery. In hospital after the events, an officer who was seizing clothing heard the accused comment that he felt like he was going to jail. This comment was not in the context of any conversation or in response to any question.

The accused was taken to the police station later the same day. That night, police interrogated the accused for four hours but the accused made no admissions concerning the victim's death. The accused was then left in his cell for several hours, but he got little sleep before being interrogated for a further two hours early the next morning. The accused was twenty years old and had little experience with the law. In six hours of interrogation, he asked to be returned to his cell to sleep and asserted his right to silence many times. Although he was in the police station for most of the day, the accused was not brought before a court within 24 hours of his detention, as required under the *Criminal Code.* In questioning the accused, the police made numerous inflammatory and unfounded accusations, including that the accused was an evil monster, a killer, a racist and that he had tortured the victim. During the second interview, the accused made several equivocal statements that might be considered admissions or confessions.

The Crown applied to have the statements admitted as evidence against the accused.

Compare *R. v. Taylor,* (2008) 63 C.R. (6th) 142 (N.B. Q.B.) and see CR annotation by Lisa Dufraimont.

Problem 7

The accused was charged with several offences in connection with a home invasion. He was interrogated by an RCMP officer after his arrest. The interrogation was video-recorded and resulted in a confession. The interrogation was a well-planned, well-orchestrated exercise. Prior to the interview, police prepared extensive briefing notes on, among other things, the props to be used and the moral themes to be developed during the interrogation. The interviewing officer went into the interrogation familiar with the alleged offences and believing the accused guilty. The interrogation lasted 2 hours 51 minutes, and the accused was allowed two bathroom breaks. The interviewing officer maintained a conversational tone and conducted the interrogation in a skilful and professional manner.

The accused was alert and willing to participate in the interrogation to some extent. However, in the course of the interview, he expressed a wish to remain silent more than 40 times. On 19 such occasions, the interviewing officer responded that he was happy to hear the accused's comment because it indicated that the accused was aware of his right to silence, whereupon the officer immediately continued the interrogation. The accused's express exercise of his right to silence became increasingly persistent throughout the interrogation but was always ignored. For a substantial period near the end of the interview, the accused said nothing other than repeatedly expressing his refusal to talk.

The Crown applies to have the record of the interrogation admitted into evidence. Admissible?

Compare *R. v. Reader*, (2007) 49 C.R. (6th) 301 (Man. Q.B.)

4. VIDEOTAPING OF INTERROGATIONS

Should Confessions be Videotaped?

R. v. MOORE-McFARLANE
(2001), 47 C.R. (5th) 203, 2001 CarswellOnt 4242,
160 C.C.C. (3d) 493 (C.A.)

The accused M and B were charged with robbery and other offences arising out of the armed robbery of a convenience store. M denied any involvement in the robbery. He testified that the police approached him in the vicinity of the robbery, drove him to the spot where they later claimed to have apprehended him, and arrested him for robbery. On a *voir dire* to determine the voluntariness of inculpatory statements allegedly made by M, M testified that he was hit in the jaw with a walkie-talkie by the police on the way to the station. When they arrived, the police waited in the car for 30 minutes before bringing M into the station. That delay was unexplained. The trial judge did not permit counsel for M to ask questions relating to the events prior to the actual interview. Counsel did not correct the trial judge's assumption that those events were not relevant to the issue of voluntariness. M also testified that he gave three audiotaped statements during the interrogation, although the police said that only one was made. He stated that his confession was false, that he had been coerced into giving the statement after being assaulted during the interrogation by members of the hold-up squad and that he was questioned while naked. M's statement was not videotaped, nor was the first half-hour of his interrogation by the police audiotaped. The trial judge ruled that the statements were voluntary. B also testified on the *voir dire* and denied any involvement in the robbery. He was pepper-sprayed by the police prior to his arrest at the scene of the robbery. The arresting officer testified that he advised the accused of his right to counsel and asked him if he wanted to contact a lawyer, to which B replied, "No, because my eyes are killing me." The arresting officer continued to question B while taking him to the hospital to get his eyes washed out. B responded to the questions and continued to complain about the effects of the pepper spray in his eyes. B testified that he was struck in the face after being placed in the police cruiser. The officer in charge at the police station testified that B had a cut lip when he arrived. Counsel for B began to cross-examine that officer on the issue of lost records of arrest, but the trial judge cut off that line of questioning. B was interrogated by two members of the hold-up squad. One of those officers testified that B stated, "You got us and the gun. I'm fucked. You know what you need to know." The interrogation was not videotaped. Counsel for B sought to cross-examine this officer on his knowledge of recent remarks by the judiciary, primarily directed at the hold-up squad, concerning the need to videotape interrogations. The trial judge interrupted counsel mid-sentence and instructed the officer that he did not need to answer that question. When counsel submitted that it was relevant to his cross-examination, the trial judge ruled that it was a matter for argument before him and not for the witness to answer. The officer confirmed that B was not given an opportunity to check the notes of the conversation for accuracy and that he was not asked to initial them. The trial judge ruled that the statements made by B and M were both convicted and appealed.

CHARRON J.A. (SHARPE and SIMMONS JJ.A. concurring): —

In my view, the evidence adduced on the *voir dire* with respect to the voluntariness of the statements allegedly made by each accused cannot reasonably support the trial judge's conclusion that the statements were voluntary except for one spontaneous utterance allegedly made by McFarlane upon his arrest with respect to lottery tickets found in his coat. All other statements should have been excluded. Since I am not satisfied that this is an appropriate case to apply the curative proviso, I would order a new trial.

. . . .

It is clear from the discussion in *Oickle* that both elements of the modern confessions rule, the absence of threats or promises and the principles related to the "operating mind", are closely related to the predominant concern for reliability. Since voluntary confessions are admitted as an exception to the hearsay rule, it should come as no surprise that concerns over the reliability of the evidence are at the root of the confessions rule. In turn, the reliability of the evidence is intrinsically connected to trial fairness, the second rationale for the confessions rule. . . .

. . . .

One of the main issues raised on these appeals is the police officers' failure to record the statements allegedly made by either appellant. Counsel for the appellants submit that there should be both a common-law and a constitutional obligation on the police to create a record, preferably by videotape, of all custodial interrogations and waivers of the s. 10(b) right to counsel. The appellants have noted some of the numerous decisions in Ontario where courts have either excluded confessions where the failure to videotape was deliberate or have strongly urged the recording of interrogations. [Citations omitted.]

The Crown submits that there should be no firm rule on the issue of recording. Crown counsel submits that the Supreme Court of Canada in *Oickle*, while commenting on the desirability of video records, was clearly reluctant to go further and impose an obligation on the police to make such records. . . . Crown counsel submits further that the appellants have confused issues of weight with issues of admissibility. Since it is for the trier of fact to determine the ultimate reliability of the statement, including whether it was in fact made, and the weight that should be attached to it, it is submitted that a failure to accurately or completely record an accused's statement should not render the statement inadmissible. I agree that there is no absolute rule requiring the recording of statements. It is clear from the analysis in both *Hodgson* and *Oickle* that the inquiry into voluntariness is contextual in nature and that all relevant circumstances must be considered. . . . However, the Crown bears the onus of establishing a sufficient record of the interaction between the suspect and the police. That onus may be readily satisfied by the use of audio, or better still, video recording. Indeed, it is my view that where the suspect is in custody, recording facilities are readily available, and the police deliberately set out to interrogate the suspect without giving any thought to the making of a reliable record, the context inevitably makes the resulting non-recorded interrogation suspect. In such cases, it will be a matter for the trial judge on the *voir dire* to determine whether or not a sufficient substitute for an audio or video tape record has been provided to satisfy the heavy onus on the Crown to prove voluntariness beyond a reasonable doubt.

The sufficiency of the record does not go exclusively to the question of ultimate reliability and weight as contended by the Crown. . . . And, in my view, the completeness, accuracy and reliability of the record have everything to do with the court's inquiry into and scrutiny of the circumstances surrounding the taking of the statement. Indeed, it is difficult to see how the Crown could discharge its heavy onus of proving voluntariness beyond a reasonable doubt where proper recording procedures are not followed. It is clear that, while determining the legal test of voluntariness is a question of law, its application to the evidence is a question of fact or of mixed law and fact. A trial judge's finding of voluntariness is entitled to deference in this court and should not be interfered with in the absence of legal error in determining the test, or overriding and palpable error with respect to the facts.

. . . .

The police officers' allegation that their notes contained a complete, albeit not verbatim, account of the conversation and of the events that transpired during the first part of the interview with McFarlane, between 11:50 p.m. and 12:22 a.m., raised a serious issue of credibility given the short conversation that was noted. The concern over the reliability of the record was further heightened by McFarlane's allegation that he had given three statements on tape, the third one alone finding its way into court because he had finally got it right. Finally, the officers' decision not to videotape the interview or audiotape the first part of the interview was a very important factor to consider. The mysterious loss of the arrest records that purportedly would have confirmed each appellant's waiver of his right to counsel raised another concern. The significance of this evidence was heightened in the circumstances of this case where little, if any, effort was made to create a reliable record.

. . . .

In the usual case, the new trial would include a *voir dire* to determine the admissibility of any alleged confession. However, in this case, it is my view that the evidence falls far short of meeting the test of voluntariness. Quite apart from any question of credibility of the appellants' testimony and the police officers' evidence on the *voir dire* on issues related to voluntariness, a matter that would require a determination by a trial judge, it is my view that the Crown cannot meet its heavy onus of proving voluntariness based on the evidence adduced in this case. The serious deficiencies alone in the overall recording by the police authorities of the events that transpired while the two appellants were in police custody on the evening in question militate against any reasonable finding that the statements were voluntary. I would therefore give effect to this ground of appeal, declare that the statements allegedly made by each appellant are inadmissible (with the exception of McFarlane's alleged utterance to May at the scene of the crime as noted earlier) and order a new trial.

R. v. WILSON
(2006), 210 C.C.C. (3d) 23, 39 C.R. (6th) 345, 2006 CarswellOnt 3749
(C.A.)

The accused was convicted of importing cocaine into Canada. He made an inculpatory statement to the arresting officer that was not audio or video-taped. The accused denied making the admission. On appeal, it was argued that the trial judge had erred in not warning the jury that the failure of the police to record the confession was an important factor in determining whether it was, in fact, made.

ROSENBERG J.A. (ARMSTRONG and ROULEAU JJ.A. concurring): —

In pre-charge discussions, trial counsel for the appellant asked that the trial judge instruct the jury in accordance with this court's decision in *R. v. Moore-McFarlane* (2001), 160 C.C.C. (3d) 493 at para. 65 that where "the police deliberately set out to interrogate the suspect without giving any thought to the making of a reliable record, the context inevitably makes the resulting non-recorded interrogation suspect". The trial judge held that *Moore-McFarlane* applies only at the admissibility stage and since she had held that the statement was admissible, the special instruction was not required. Unfortunately, the trial judge did not have the benefit of this court's later decision in *R. v. Swanek* (2005), 28 C.R. (6th) 93, which I will discuss later.

In the result, the trial judge gave the following instruction concerning the reliability of the appellant's statement to the police:

When Constable Mitchell says what Rohan Wilson said to him, you have to decide whether you believe Rohan Wilson made the statement or any part of it. Regardless of who the witness is, it is still up to you to decide whether you believe him. In deciding whether Rohan Wilson actually said these things or any of them, you should use your common sense. Take into account the condition of Mr. Wilson and of Constable Mitchell at the time of the interview. Consider the circumstances in which the interview took place. Bear in mind anything else that may make Constable Mitchell's story more or less reliable.

Whether a witness has recorded a conversation or taken notes about it does not itself determine how reliable that witness' testimony may be. It is, however, one of the things that you may consider in deciding whether or how much of the witness' testimony to believe.

Unless you decide that Rohan Wilson made a particular remark or statement, you must not consider it in deciding this case. Some or all of the statements may help Mr. Wilson in his defence. You must consider those remarks that may help Mr. Wilson along with all of the other evidence unless you are satisfied that he did not make them. In other words, you must consider all the remarks that might help Mr. Wilson even if you cannot decide whether he said them.

In my view, for the following reasons, this was not an adequate instruction. This court briefly dealt with this issue in *R. v. Swanek*. In that case, the accused argued, for the first time on appeal, that the trial judge should have directed the jury that it was dangerous to rely upon an unrecorded inculpatory statement that was not confirmed by other evidence. Doherty J.A. at para. 12, noted the concern with unrecorded oral statements:

Counsel makes the valid point that while those who are regularly involved in the criminal process are familiar with the historical unreliability of oral confessions attributed to persons in custody, a jury may well not appreciate that unreliability.

Thus, he held at para. 13 that in a proper case a special instruction should be given to the jury:

If the police failure to make a proper recording of an alleged inculpatory statement is in issue at trial, I think a trial judge should tell the jury that the failure to make a proper recording is an important factor for the jury to consider in deciding whether to rely on the police version of the alleged statement.

In *Swanek*, the court held that there was no error in failing to give the instruction since the failure to make a proper recording was not an issue at trial and no special instruction had been requested by the accused. That is not the case here: defence counsel raised the failure to videotape in his examination of the officers and asked the trial judge to give a special instruction. I note that in *Swanek* the concern was with an oral statement that was not signed by the accused and only reduced to writing in the officers' notebooks. However, given the uncontested evidence that the appellant was all but illiterate, nothing turns on the fact the statement in this case was signed. The point remains that because of the failure to audio or video record the circumstances or manner of obtaining the statement cannot be objectively assessed.

Most of the cases that have considered the issue of videotaping of statements have been concerned with the impact of the failure to videotape on admissibility. However, in my view, and for the reasons set out in *Swanek*, in appropriate circumstances, a special instruction should be given to the jury where the accused contests the accuracy of the non-recorded statement. Over a decade ago, Carthy J.A. in his concurring reasons in *R. v. Barrett* (1993), 82 C.C.C. (3d) 266 (Ont. C.A.) at 270, noted the central feature a confession can play in a criminal case and the importance of having an accurate record of what occurred: and he said this: "On this determinative issue of conviction the police force has, by its own choice in this case, denied the court the opportunity of an undeniable record of what led to the "conviction". Given the modest cost of videotape equipment, such critical evidence should not, in fairness, be restricted to sworn recollection of two contesting individuals as to what occurred in stressful conditions months or years ago. The evidence is admissible under our present rules, but everyone involved in the criminal justice system should make reasonable efforts to better serve its ultimate ends."

These concerns do not relate solely to voluntariness; they also relate to the jury's task in attempting to decide whether the accused confessed as alleged by the police. *Barrett* was overturned on appeal to the Supreme Court of Canada (1995), 96 C.C.C. (3d) 319, on the basis that the failure of the trial judge to give reasons for admitting the statement did not amount to an error of law. That decision does not take away from the common sense identified by Carthy J.A.'s reasons.

In *R. v. Oickle* (2000), 147 C.C.C. (3d) 321 (S.C.C.) at para. 46, Iacobucci J. held that a video or audio recording "can greatly assist the trier of fact in assessing the confession". The trier of fact, of course is concerned not solely with voluntariness but whether the statement was made and the truth of the contents of the statement. It must also be said that at the present time the failure to electronically record the statement does not itself render the statement inherently suspect. Iacobucci J. made that clear in *Oickle* at para. 46. To the same effect is the decision of the Manitoba Court of Appeal in *R. v. Ducharme* (2004), 182 C.C.C. (3d) 243 at para. 46:

> The difficulty is that until either the Supreme Court articulates or Parliament legislates the duties of the police and lays out a protocol to be followed, the common law definition of voluntariness will remain in effect. That being the case, it cannot be said that the failure to videotape or electronically record will automatically mean the exclusion of the evidence on a voir dire. [Footnote omitted]

Thus, there must be other circumstances before a trial judge would be entitled to give the special instruction sought in this case. One set of circumstances was identified in *R. v Moore-McFarlane* at para. 65: "where the suspect is in custody, recording facilities are readily available, and the police deliberately set out to interrogate the suspect without giving any thought to the making of a reliable record, the context inevitably makes the resulting non-recorded interrogation suspect". Admittedly, in that case, Charron J.A. was concerned with voluntariness, but for the reasons set out above the concern for accuracy that arises at the voluntariness stage also applies at the guilt or innocence stage.

In my view, it was open to the jury to find that the police deliberately set out to interrogate the appellant without giving any thought to the making of a reliable video or audio record. The jury should therefore have been instructed along the lines suggested in *R. v. Swanek* that this was an important factor to consider in deciding whether to rely on the officer's version of the statement.

The respondent submits that the jury would have understood the concern with the reliability of the written statement because both counsel in their jury addresses acknowledged the problem stemming from the lack of an audio or video recording. I do not accept that position. While defence counsel in his address did review the circumstances of the taking of the statement and pointed out that Constable Mitchell could have used the pocket recorder, he expressly told the jury that the legal effect of those circumstances would be explained by the trial judge:

> So he's in a room specifically designed to audio and video-record a confession or a statement generally and he chose not to use that. Now, why is that important? Now, Her Honour will suggest what the law says about that but the logical reason why, over time, we've moved from having them written to having them video, doesn't take a lawyer to explain that. Obviously a video statement is much more trustworthy than having to take someone's word for how this all happened and that wasn't utilized.

Unfortunately, after the jury addresses, the trial judge ruled that she would not give this special instruction. While Crown counsel also gave a fair recitation of the facts in her jury address, she invited the jury to draw the inference that had there been a recording it would simply have confirmed Constable Mitchell's version:

> It is trite to say that given the accused's version of events, it would be very nice at this trial to have a perfect video or audio record. Obviously we may not even have been here.

In any event, counsel's views on the law are no substitute for a proper legal direction from the trial judge. Given the central role played by the statement, I cannot be satisfied that the absence of a proper instruction did not prejudice the appellant's defence.

5. MIXED INCULPATORY AND EXCULPATORY STATEMENTS

Recall earlier the discussion of the requirement of the Crown to lead the entire statement including any exculpatory parts. How is the trial judge to instruct the jury on the weight to be given the inculpatory and exculpatory portions? United Kingdom courts favour a so-called *Duncan* instruction to the jury that

> the incriminating parts are likely to be true (otherwise why say them?), whereas the excuses do not have the same weight.

The Supreme Court has recently decided that such a direction would be dangerous and was not required.

R. v. ROJAS
2008 CarswellBC 2196, 2008 CarswellBC 2197, [2008] 3 S.C.R. 111, 236
C.C.C. (3d) 153, 60 C.R. (6th) 271

CHARRON J.:—

. . .

36 Exculpatory out-of-court statements made by an accused are also subject to the general exclusionary rule against hearsay. Where the accused testifies, such statements are generally inadmissible because they are viewed as self-serving and lacking in probative value. Where the accused does not testify, there is an additional rationale for excluding such statements. McIntyre J. explained it in *R. v. Simpson*, [1988] 1 S.C.R. 3, as follows (at p. 22):

> As a general rule, the statements of an accused person made outside court - subject to a finding of voluntariness where the statement is made to one in authority - are receivable in evidence against him but not for him. This rule is based on the sound proposition that an accused person should not be free to make an unsworn statement and compel its admission into evidence through other witnesses and thus put his defence before the jury without being put on oath and being subjected, as well, to cross-examination.

37 Of course, the general rule that excludes out-of-court exculpatory statements is not without exceptions. One such exception is relevant here - the mixed statement exception. Just as in England, it has long been established that where the Crown seeks to tender an accused's out-of-court statement which contains both inculpatory and exculpatory parts, it must tender the entire statement, and the exculpatory portions are substantively admissible in favour of the accused: *R. v. Hughes*, [1942] S.C.R. 517, at p. 521. Fairness to the accused is the obvious rationale for the mixed statement exception. The exception is also based on the more pragmatic consideration that it is often difficult to determine which parts of a statement are inculpatory and which parts are exculpatory.

38 In recognizing both the basis for admitting inculpatory statements and the exceptional admissibility of an accused's untested statements, the *Duncan* instruction, as such, accurately reflects the state of the law. In England, the instruction is also perceived as achieving the "right balance", as the House of Lords explained in *Aziz* (at p. 485):

> Moreover, I would reject the suggestion that the law as stated in *Sharp* is unduly balanced in favour of the defendants who do not testify. On the contrary, as was emphasised in *Duncan* and *Sharp*, a judge is entitled to comment adversely on the quality of the exculpatory parts of a mixed statement which has not been tested by cross-examination. The right balance has been found. [Emphasis added.]

Judges in Canada, as in England, are also entitled to comment on the evidence so long as they make it clear that factual issues are for the jury to decide: *R. v. Gunning*, [2005] 1 S.C.R. 627, 2005 SCC 27, at para. 27. The Crown therefore urges this Court to adopt the *Duncan* instruction in Canada.

39 With respect to the contrary position adopted by our English colleagues, I would not accede to the Crown's argument. In certain circumstances, it may be useful to explain to the jury why the law permits them to hear a particular piece of evidence where such instruction will assist them with their task. This may be the case, for example, where evidence is admitted for a limited purpose only. The jury may be more likely to comply with the limiting instruction if they understand the underlying rationale for the rule. In most circumstances, however, expounding the rationale for an evidentiary rule may only serve to confuse the jury unnecessarily or risk encroaching unduly upon their role as fact finders. For example, I can think of no principled reason to explain to a jury that they are hearing the accused's confession because the court is satisfied beyond a reasonable doubt that it was voluntarily made. Likewise, it would only risk encroaching unduly on the jury's domain to tell them that they are hearing a piece of similar fact evidence because, in the judge's view, the similarities with the offence are such that they "defy coincidence".

40 In the same way, I see little advantage in expounding for the jury the underlying rationale for the mixed statement exception. If only for the pragmatic reason that it is often very difficult to differentiate between admissions and excuses, I . . . conclude—- as did . . .the court below, that it is dangerous for the judge to instruct the jury in a manner that suggests that inculpatory and exculpatory statements ought to be weighed differently. Such "common sense" comments are better left to the advocacy of counsel (David, at para. 42). Therefore, I conclude that the *Duncan* instruction should not be adopted by Canadian trial courts.

. . . .

47 When viewed in context, I am satisfied that the *Duncan* instruction could not have misled the jury. It was clear from the charge that the burden of proof did not shift to Hugo or Miguel, that any exculpatory statement need only raise a reasonable doubt, and that the accused were entitled to the benefit of any such doubt. In commenting on the relative weight that may be attributed to the statements, the trial judge did not exceed his function. It was clear that the assessment of the reliability of the statements was left entirely with the jury. Accordingly, I agree with the Court of Appeal below that the *Duncan* instruction did not constitute reversible error in the context of this case.

48 Accordingly, for these reasons, I would dismiss the appeals.

D. *OPINION EVIDENCE AND EXPERTS*

1. OPINION RULE

The following hypothetical direct examination of a witness to an automobile accident illustrates the possible bewilderment that may be suffered by a lay witness when in the hands of a trial judge who believes in applying an opinion rule with the utmost rigour:

Q.   What happened then?

A.   The lady in the car that got hit stumbled out of her car and fell in a
                      faint.

Defence
Counsel: Move to strike the opinions of the witness. Let him state the facts.

The Court: Strike them out. The jury will disregard that answer. [To witness:]
                      You must state the facts and not your conclusions regarding them.
                      You can't give the jury your opinion as to *which* car got hit, *whose*
                      car it was, *how* the lady got out of the car or *why* she fell, if she did
                      fall, — you must state the facts.[194]

Thankfully the English and Canadian courts have not generally applied an
exclusionary opinion rule with such strictness and consequently we have had a
great deal less trouble with the rule than our American friends.

As suggested by Cowen and Carter:[195]

> The opinion rule has appeared to work in England only because it has been laxly
> applied.

The true scope of an opinion rule in the law of evidence can be properly
appreciated only with an awareness of the historical development in this area.
The early 18th century announcements of English courts, that witnesses must
speak to facts and not to opinion, when read in the context of that age, forbade
quite different testimony than is presently thought to be foreclosed by the opinion
rule. Samuel Johnson's Dictionary (1st ed., 1755) defined opinion as "Persuasion
of the mind without proof of certain knowledge . . . Sentiments, Judgment, Notion,"
and never referred to "opinion" in the sense of a reasoned conclusion from facts
observed.[196] Prior to the close of the eighteenth century there was no opinion
rule, as we know it today[197] and statements made at the time, an opinion: "[I]t is
mere opinion, which is not evidence"[198] were statements condemning testimony
by witnesses who had no personal knowledge of the event and so suffered from
the same lack of testimonial qualification as the witness who repeated hearsay.
What was being forbidden then were notions, guesses, conjectures; as phrased
by Professor Wigmore, they were statements demanding that "the witness must
speak as a knower, not merely a guesser."[199]

While judges and writers in Canada still mouth expressions that lay witnesses
cannot give their opinions but must state facts, the intrinsic impossibility of the
requirement has led in actual practice to the reception of opinion testimony from
witnesses who have personal knowledge. The opinion's reception is justified at
times as simply a "compendious mode of stating facts," or a "short-hand
rendering" or an application of the "congeries of circumstances rule" or "collective

---

194 See King & Pillinger, *Opinion Evidence in Illinois* (1942), p. 1.
195 Cowen and Carter, *Essays on the Law of Evidence* (1956), p. 164.
196 See King & Pillinger, *supra*, note 194 at p. 8.
197 See *Phipson on Evidence*, 11th ed. (1970), p. 504, noting that *Gilbert's Evidence* of 1726
    and Buller's *Nisi Prius* of 1767 make no mention of such rule with the first appearance of
    the same apparently in *Peake on Evidence* in 1801.
198 Lord Mansfield in *Carter v. Boehm* (1766), 97 E.R. 1162, 1168.
199 7 Wigmore, *Evidence* (Chad. Rev.), s. 1917.

fact rule."[200] On other occasions, the court simply recognizes that the opinion rule cannot be absolute. For example, in *R. v. German*,[201] in denying any injustice done by the reception of opinion testimony from lay witnesses respecting the defendant's intoxicated condition, Chief Justice Robertson noted:

> No doubt, the general rule is that it is only persons who are qualified by some special skill, training or experience who can be asked their opinion upon a matter in issue. *The rule is not, however, an absolute one.* There are a number of matters in respect of which *a person of ordinary intelligence may be permitted to give evidence of his opinion upon a matter of which he has personal knowledge.* Such matters as the identity of individuals, the apparent age of a person, the speed of a vehicle, are among the matters upon which witnesses have been allowed to express an opinion, notwithstanding that they have no special qualifications, other than the fact that they have personal knowledge of the subject matter, to enable them to form an opinion.[202] [Emphasis added.]

The Anglo-Canadian attitude to the opinion rule is justifiable on two bases: first, the impossibility of testifying only to facts and, second, the absence of any justification for totally excluding opinion testimony in the form of reasoned conclusions from witnesses without regard to their testimonial qualifications as observers of the event.

Regarding the impossibility of complying with the admonition to the witness that he must state facts and not opinion, it has been said:

> ... when our judge instructs the witness to "state the facts" it is as though he demanded that the witness fly by flapping his arms. The witness can't state facts and neither can the judge — facts are unspeakable and unstatable. We can't reproduce in language either reality or our perception of reality. All statements in language are statements of opinion, i.e. statements of mental processes or perceptions. So-called "statements of fact" are only more specific statements of opinion.[203]

---

200 See Tyree, "The Opinion Rule" (1955), 10 Rutgers L. Rev. 601. See also, *e.g.*, Baron Alderson in *Wright v. Doe d. Tatham* (1838), 7 E.R. 559 at p. 578: "... a compendious mode of putting one instead of a multitude of questions to the witness"; relied on in *Robins v. Nat. Trust Co.* (1925), 57 O.L.R. 46 in receiving the opinion of witnesses respecting testator's mental condition when he signed his will.

201 [1947] O.R. 395 (C.A.); relied on and followed on this point in *R. v. Pollock*, [1947] 2 W.W.R. 973 (Alta. Dist. Ct.) and *R. v. Nagy* (1965), 51 W.W.R. 307 (B.C. Co. Ct.); but *contra* see *R. v. Davies*, [1962] 1 W.L.R. 1111 (C.M.C.A.).

202 *Ibid.*, at p. 409. And see *Porter v. O'Connell* (1915), 43 N.B.R. 458 (C.A.) where the court held it admissible for the eye-witness to state, in answer to a question respecting the speed of defendant's horse at the time of the accident, "the horse was going that fast I don't think he could be pulled up immediately.".

203 King & Pillinger, *supra*, note 194 at p. 4. And see McCormick, *Evidence*, 2d ed., p. 23, discussing the doctrine that a witness must state facts not opinion: "This classic formula, based as it is on the assumption that 'fact' and 'opinion' stand in contrast and hence are readily distinguishable, has proven the clumsiest of all the tools furnished the judge for regulating the examination of witnesses. It is clumsy because its basic assumption is an illusion. ... There is no conceivable statement, however specific, detailed and 'factual', that is not in some measure the product of inference and reflection as well as observation and memory." See also for like statements, Maguire, *Evidence Common Sense and Common Law* (1947), p. 24 and 7 Wigmore, *Evidence* (Chad. Rev.), s. 1919.

Professor Thayer remarked:

> In a sense all testimony to matter of fact is opinion evidence; i.e., it is a conclusion formed from phenomena and mental impressions. Yet that is not the way we talk in courts or in common life. Where shall the line be drawn? When does matter of fact first become matter of opinion? . . . In the main, any rule excluding opinion evidence is limited to cases where, in the judgment of the court, it will not be helpful to the jury. . . . It is obvious that such a principle must allow a very great range of permissible difference in judgment; and that conclusions of that character ought not, usually, to be regarded as subject to review by higher courts.[204]

The second justification for the Anglo-Canadian attitude rests in Professor Thayer's premise that all that is logically probative is receivable unless excluded by a rule or principle of law.[205] If relevance is equated with logical probity and dictated not by law but by the common sense of experience, is it fair to say that the opinion of one who witnessed an accident that, for example, the plaintiff was driving too fast for the conditions of the road, is not logically probative of fault in the plaintiff? If it is accepted then that opinion is relevant,[206] it is clear that there must be some clear ground of policy to justify exclusion.[207] The theory has sometimes been put forward that to permit the reception of opinion testimony would be to permit the "usurpation of the jury's function."[208] Is this valid? To begin with, the trier of fact has the ability at all times to determine what evidence it will accept or reject and what weight will be given the same and is never bound to agree with the opinion expressed by the witness. The witness could never usurp the function of the trier of fact even if he or she wanted to.[209] Further, we do countenance the reception of opinion testimony from a class of witnesses whose opinions are the most likely to influence the trier of fact, the expert. Indeed, do we not want the expert to "usurp" the jury's function to a degree as we see the expert as more competent to perform that function?[210] It would appear that English and Canadian judicial decisions have received lay opinion evidence from those with personal knowledge when to do so would be helpful to the jury and to otherwise restrict the witness would unduly interfere with the normal manner of communication.

---

204 *Preliminary Treatise on Evidence* (1898), p. 524.

205 *Ibid.*, at p. 265.

206 See the criticism of Lord Goddard's view by Cecil Wright, *Case and Comment* (1943), 21 C.B.R. 653 at p. 658. And compare *Betterton v. Turner* (1982), 133 D.L.R. (3d) 289 (B.C.S.C.).

207 See Trautman, "Logical or Legal Relevancy — A Conflict in Theory" (1952), 5 Vand. L. Rev. 385.

208 See, *e.g.*, Phipson, *Evidence*, 11th ed., p. 504; *Carter v. Boehm*, *supra*, note 198, at p. 1168.

209 This justification for the opinion rule has been termed "empty rhetoric" by Professor Wigmore in 7 *Evidence* (Chad. Rev.), s. 1920.

210 See Cowen and Carter, *Essays on the Law of Evidence* (1956), p. 170. See also the majority holding in *R. v. Lupien* (1970), 71 W.W.R. 110 (S.C.C.), approving the reception of expert opinion on the "very thing" the jury had to decide because psychiatry had developed to the point that their views would be more competent.

GRAAT v. R.
[1982] 2 S.C.R. 819, 31 C.R. (3d) 289, 2 C.C.C. (3d) 365

21st December 1982. The judgment of the court was delivered by

DICKSON J.:—

This appeal [from 17 C.R. (3d) 55] raises the issue whether on a charge of driving while impaired the court may admit opinion evidence on the very question to be decided, namely, Was the accused's ability to drive impaired by alcohol at the time and place stated in the charge?

. . . .

At approximately 2:15 a.m. on the date in question, Constables Case and McMullen of the London City Police observed Mr. Graat's vehicle travelling at a high rate of speed. The constables followed for several blocks. They observed Mr. Graat's car weaving in the southbound lane, crossing the centre line on two occasions and driving on to the shoulder of the road on another occasion. When the vehicle turned left it straddled the centre line.

Both constables testified they noticed the smell of alcohol on the appellant's breath; both said Mr. Graat was unsteady on his feet, he staggered as he walked and had bloodshot eyes. At the police station Mr. Graat was observed by a Sergeant Spoelstra. The sergeant testified he smelled alcohol on the appellant's breath, the top part of his body was swaying and his walk was "kind of wavy".

Mr. Graat complained of chest pains. He told the police he suffered from a heart condition and asked to be taken to a hospital. The police complied. By the time Mr. Graat returned to the police station it was too late to taketwo breath samples because the two-hour time-limit for the taking of such samples had expired or was about to expire.

Mr. Graat testified he had had two drinks of gin between the hours of 3:00 p.m. and 7:00 p.m., and two glasses of wine with his dinner about 11:00 p.m. He said he and two friends, George Wilson and Vincent O'Donovan, were returning from a sailing party; he became tired. Wilson drove the car while he dozed in the back seat. The appellant resumed driving after Wilson had driven O'Donovan and himself home. Wilson testified that if he had thought Mr. Graat was not in a fit condition to drive he would have asked him to stay at his, Wilson's, house.

At trial Constable Case was asked the following questions and gave the following answers:

> Q. All right, now what, if any, opinion having made those observations, what if any opinion did you form regarding the accused man's ability to drive a motor vehicle?
>
> A. I formed the opinion that the accused's ability was impaired.
>
> Q. By?
>
> A. By alcohol.
>
> Q. You said the accused man's ability to what?
>
> A. To drive a motor vehicle was impaired by alcohol.

Constable McMullen was asked the following question:

> Q. Now officer when you were at the scene and having made the observations of the driving of the accused man, having observed him, having smelled the alcoholic beverage on his breath and observed him walk and observed him standing, observed him speaking to you what, if any, conclusion did you come to regarding his ability to drive a motor vehicle?
>
> A. It was in my opinion that the accused's ability to operate a motor vehicle was impaired by alcohol beverage.

Sergeant Spoelstra, the desk sergeant, gave similar evidence:

> Q. You saw him standing and you saw him walking. What, if any opinion, did you form regarding his ability to drive a motor vehicle?
>
> A. In my opinion the accused's ability was impaired by the use of alcohol to drive a motor vehicle.

. . . .

The trial judge preferred the evidence of the police witnesses to the evidence of Mr. Graat and Mr. Wilson. In particular, the judge relied on the evidence of Constable McMullen and Sergeant Spoelstra, policemen for 8 and 17 years respectively. Constable Case had only been a police officer for a few months, and had only charged two or three persons with impaired driving. The judge said he accepted the opinions of Officers McMullen and Spoelstra in reaching his conclusion that the accused's ability to drive was impaired: I'm of the view that I'm entitled to accept and I do accept the opinions of those two police officers on the issue of impairment as part of the totality of the evidence.

III

THE ONTARIO COURT OF APPEAL

The appellant sought leave to appeal to the Court of Appeal of Ontario and at that time the question was raised as to whether the trial judge had erred in law in relying on the opinion evidence of the two police officers that the appellant's ability to drive a motor vehicle had been impaired by alcohol.

The court dismissed the appeal, saying [p. 442] that the evidence was admissible under the exception to the rule excluding opinion evidence:

> . . . that permits non-expert opinion evidence where the primary facts and the inferences to be drawn from them are so closely associated that the opinion is really a compendious way of giving evidence as to certain facts — in this case the condition of the appellant.

This echoes the words of Parke B. in *Wright v. Tatham* (1838), 4 Bing. N.C. 489 at 543-44 (H.L.):

> . . . and though the opinion of a witness upon oath, as to that fact [testamentary capacity], might be asked, it would only be a compendious mode of ascertaining the result of the actual observation of the witness, from acts done, as to the habits and demeanour of the deceased.

. . . .

CONCLUSION

I have attempted in the foregoing to highlight the opposing points of view as reflected in some of the cases, texts, and reports of the law reform commissions.

We start with the reality that the law of evidence is burdened with a large number of cumbersome rules, with exclusions, and exceptions to the exclusions, and exceptions to the exceptions. The list of subjects upon which the non-expert witness is allowed to give opinion evidence is a lengthy one. The list mentioned in *Sherrard v. Jacob*, supra, is by no means exhaustive: (i) the identification of handwriting, persons and things; (ii) apparent age; (iii) the bodily plight or condition of a person, including death and illness; (iv) the emotional state of a person, e.g., whether distressed, angry, aggressive, affectionate or depressed; (v) the condition of things, e.g., worn, shabby, used or new; (vi) certain questions of value; and (vii) estimates of speed and distance. . . .

Except for the sake of convenience there is little, if any, virtue in any distinction resting on the tenuous and frequently false antithesis between fact and opinion. The line between "fact" and "opinion" is not clear.

To resolve the question before the court I would like to return to broad principles. Admissibility is determined, first, by asking whether the evidence sought to be admitted is relevant. This is a matter of applying logic and experience to the circumstances of the particular case. The question which must then be asked is whether, though probative, the evidence must be excluded by a clear ground of policy or of law.

There is a direct and logical relevance between (i) the evidence offered here, namely, the opinion of a police officer (based on perceived facts as to the manner of driving and indicia of intoxication of the driver) that the person's ability to drive was impaired by alcohol, and (ii) the ultimate probandum in the case. The probative value of the evidence is not outweighed by such policy considerations as danger of confusing the issues or misleading the jury. It does not unfairly surprise a party who had not had reasonable ground to anticipate that such evidence will be offered, and the adducing of the evidence does not necessitate undue consumption of time. As for other considerations, such as "usurping the functions of the jury" and, to the extent that it may be regarded as a separate consideration, "opinion on the very issue before the jury", Wigmore has gone a long way toward establishing that rejection of opinion evidence on either of these grounds is unsound historically and in principle. If the court is being told that which it is in itself entirely equipped to determine without the aid of the witness on the point then of course the evidence is supererogatory and unnecessary. It would be a waste of time listening to superfluous testimony.

The judge in the instant case was not in as good a position as the police officers or Mr. Wilson to determine the degree of Mr. Graat's impairment or his ability to drive a motor vehicle. The witnesses had an opportunity for personal observation. They were in a position to give the court real help. They were not settling the dispute. They were not deciding the matter the court had to decide, the ultimate issue. The judge could accept all or part or none of their evidence.

In the end he accepted the evidence of two of the police officers and paid little heed to the evidence of the third officer or of Mr. Wilson.

. . . .

A non-expert witness cannot, of course, give opinion evidence on a legal issue as, for example, whether or not a person was negligent. That is because such an opinion would not qualify as an abbreviated version of the witness's factual observations. An opinion that someone was negligent is partly factual, but it also involves the application of legal standards. On the other hand, whether a person's ability to drive is impaired by alcohol is a question of fact, not of law. It does not involve the application of any legal standard. It is akin to an opinion that someone is too drunk to climb a ladder or to go swimming, and the fact that a witness's opinion, as here, may be expressed in the exact words of the Criminal Code does not change a factual matter into a question of law. It only reflects the fact that the draftsmen of the Code employed the ordinary English phrase: "his ability to drive . . . is impaired by alcohol" (s. 234).

In short, I know of no clear ground of policy or of law which would require the exclusion of opinion evidence tendered by the Crown or the defence as to Mr. Graat's impairment.

I conclude with two caveats. First, in every case, in determining whether an opinion is admissible, the trial judge must necessarily exercise a large measure of discretion. Second, there may be a tendency for judges and juries to let the opinion of police witnesses overwhelm the opinion evidence of other witnesses. Since the opinion is admitted under the "compendious statement of facts" exception rather than under the "expert witness" exception, there is no special reason for preferring the police evidence over the "opinion" of other witnesses. As always, the trier of fact must decide in each case what weight to give what evidence. The "opinion" of the police officer is entitled to no special regard. Ordinary people with ordinary experience are able to know as a matter of fact that someone is too drunk to perform certain tasks, such as driving a car. If the witness lacks the relevant experience, or is otherwise limited in his testimonial capacity, or if the witness is not sure whether the person was intoxicated to the point of impairment, that can be brought out in cross-examination. But the fact that a police witness has seen more impaired drivers than a non-police witness is not a reason in itself to prefer the evidence of the police officer. Constables McMullen and Spoelstra were not testifying as experts based on their extensive experience as police officers.

There was some confusion about this matter in this case as appears from the following cross-examination of Mr. Wilson:

Q.   . . . And of course you've not and never have been a police officer. Do you agree or disagree with me? A. No. No.

Q.   You have never been a police officer? A. No.

Q.   And you're not in the habit of checking people as to the amount of alcohol that is consumed in order to make him impaired. Do you agree or disagree with me? A. I have to agree with you?

Q.   Yes. So you're really not in a position to tell us whether or not he was impaired or not impaired by alcohol. Do you agree or disagree with me? A. I was only . . .

Q.   . . . But of course you were in no position to judge as to whether or not he was impaired. Do you agree or disagree with me? A. I don't have any qualifications in that regard, I guess.

Mr. Wilson does not need any special qualifications. Nor were the police officers relying on any special qualifications when they gave their opinions. Both police and non-police witnesses are merely giving a compendious statement of facts that are too subtle and too complicated to be narrated separately and distinctly. Trial judges should bear in mind that this is non-expert opinion evidence, and that the opinion of police officers is not entitled to preference just because they may have extensive experience with impaired drivers. The credit and accuracy of the police must be viewed in the same manner as that of other witnesses and in the light of all the evidence in the case. If the police and traffic officers have been closely associated with the prosecution, such association may affect the weight to be given to such evidence.

The trial judge was correct in admitting the opinions of the three police officers and Mr. Wilson.

For the foregoing reasons, as well as for the reasons given by Howland C.J.O., I would dismiss the appeal.

Appeal dismissed.

2. EXPERT EVIDENCE

Toward the end of the 18th century what appears to be an exception to the general rule forbidding testimony by witnesses who had no personal knowledge of the facts at issue was established. Expert assistance had been furnished to the court from very ancient times but not in the form normally used today.[211] Special juries of experts were commonly used in the 14th century to resolve trade disputes,[212] and as early as 1353 we find the court summoning surgeons to give an opinion on whether a wound amounted to mayhem.[213] The court summoned the expert, and on considering his advice, then directed the jury respecting the major premise that could be used by them in determining the particular fact situation. With the change in the jury system to their being informed by witnesses

---

211 See generally Hand, "Historical and Practical Considerations Regarding Expert Testimony" (1901), 15 Harv. L. Rev. 40; see also Thayer, *Cases on Evidence*, 2d ed. (1900), at pp. 672-73 and Rosenthal, "The Development of the Use of Expert Testimony" (1935), 2 L. & Contemp. Prob. 403.

212 See Hand, *ibid.*, at pp. 41 and 42. For a more recent example of the empanelling of a special jury see *R. v. Anne Wycherley* (1838), 173 E.R. 486 a jury of married women impanelled to determine if the convicted defendant was with child, the jury "de vente inspiciendo."

213 *Anonymous*, Lib. Ass. 28, pl. 5 (28 Edw. III); see also *Buller v. Crips* (1705), 87 E.R. 793.

summoned by the parties rather than investigating themselves,[214] we find, toward the end of the 18th century, experts being called by the parties, testifying as witnesses, and so furnishing their assistance directly to the jury.[215] To justify this apparent exception to the long-standing rule that witnesses have personal knowledge, the courts reasoned that to receive the same was *necessary*.[216] The expert then could give his opinion on matters of science, though he had no personal knowledge of the event being litigated, where to do so would be *helpful* to the jury's decision-making; where the major premise or premises necessary against which the particular instance under review needs to be tested is lacking from the fund of knowledge possessed by the layman.

The expert's testimonial qualifications, just as those of lay witnesses, must be established before the trier of fact. It is for the trial judge in his discretion to rule whether the experiential qualifications of the witness have been made out,[217] and it is for the trial judge to rule whether the evidence will be helpful. As the state of the art varies with time so will the criterion of helpfulness. Professor McGuire wrote:

> The field of expertness is bounded on one side by the great area of the commonplace, supposedly within the ken of every person of moderate intelligence, and on the other by the even greater area of the speculative and uncertain. Of course both these boundaries constantly shift, as the former area enlarges and the latter diminishes. Only a few years ago it would have been necessary to take expert evidence on issues with respect to the operation of motor cars, airplanes, or radios which are now so completely inside the domain of popular understanding that such evidence would be rejected as superfluous. A century ago purportedly expert evidence on these topics would have been rejected as visionary.[218]

As the "speculative and uncertain" area changes, how should the court rule?

(a) Tests

R. v. MOHAN
[1994] 2 S.C.R. 9, 29 C.R. (4th) 243, 89 C.C.C. (3d) 402

The accused, a practising paediatrician, was charged with four counts of sexual assault on four of his female patients. Counsel for the accused sought to call a psychiatrist who would testify that the perpetrator of the offences alleged to have been committed would be one of a limited and unusual group of individuals, and that the accused did not fall within that narrow class because he did not possess the characteristics belonging to that group.

---

214 See generally Holdsworth, *A History of English Law*, 7th ed. (1856), vol. 1, pp. 332 *et seq.*, and *supra*, Chapter 8 — Hearsay.
215 See, *e.g.*, *Folkes v. Chad* (1782), 99 E.R. 589; (1783), 99 E.R. 686.
216 See note to *Carter v. Boehm* in *Smith's Leading Cases*, 13th ed., vol. 1, p. 560.
217 *Preeper v. R.* (1888), 15 S.C.R. 401.
218 *Evidence: Common Sense and Common Law* (1947), p. 30.

SOPINKA J.:—

. . . .

Admission of expert evidence depends on the application of the following criteria:

(a)   relevance;
(b)   necessity in assisting the trier of fact;
(c)   the absence of any exclusionary rule;
(d)   a properly qualified expert.

(a) *Relevance*

Relevance is a threshold requirement for the admission of expert evidence as with all other evidence. Relevance is a matter to be decided by a judge as question of law. Although prima facie admissible if so related to a fact in issue that it tends to establish it, that does not end the inquiry. This merely determines the logical relevance of the evidence. Other considerations enter into the decision as to admissibility. This further inquiry may be described as a cost benefit analysis, that is "whether its value is worth what it costs." See *McCormick on Evidence* (3rd ed. 1984), at p. 544. Cost in this context is not used in its traditional economic sense but rather in terms of its impact on the trial process. Evidence that is otherwise logically relevant may be excluded on this basis, if its probative value is overborne by its prejudicial effect, if it involves an inordinate amount of time which is not commensurate with its value or if it is misleading in the sense that its effect on the trier of fact, particularly a jury, is out of proportion to its reliability. While frequently considered as an aspect of legal relevance, the exclusion of logically relevant evidence on these grounds is more properly regarded as a general exclusionary rule (see *R. v. Morris*, [1983] 2 S.C.R. 190). Whether it is treated as an aspect of relevance or an exclusionary rule, the effect is the same. The reliability versus effect factor has special significance in assessing the admissibility of expert evidence.

There is a danger that expert evidence will be misused and will distort the fact-finding process. Dressed up in scientific language which the jury does not easily understand and submitted through a witness of impressive antecedents, this evidence is apt to be accepted by the jury as being virtually infallible and as having more weight than it deserves. . . . As La Forest J. stated in *R. c. Béland*, [1987] 2 S.C.R. 398, at p. 434, with respect to the evidence of the results of a polygraph tendered by the accused, such evidence should not be admitted by reason of "human fallibility in assessing the proper weight to be given to evidence cloaked under the mystique of science". The application of this principle can be seen in cases such as *R. v. Melaragni* (1992), 73 C.C.C. (3d) 348, in which Moldaver J. applied a threshold test of reliability to what he described as "a new scientific technique or body of scientific knowledge". Moldaver J. also mentioned two other factors, inter alia, which should be considered in such circumstances . . . :

(1)   Is the evidence likely to assist the jury in its fact-finding mission, or is it likely to confuse and confound the jury?

(2)   Is the jury likely to be overwhelmed by the "mystic infallibility" of the evidence, or will the jury be able to keep an open mind and objectively assess the worth of the evidence?

. . . .

(b) *Necessity in Assisting the Trier of Fact*

In *R. v. Abbey*, *supra*, Dickson J., as he then was, stated:

> With respect to matters calling for special knowledge, an expert in the field may draw inferences and state his opinion. An expert's function is precisely this: to provide the judge and jury with a ready-made inference which the judge and jury, due to the technical nature of the facts, are unable to formulate. An expert's opinion is admissible to furnish the Court with scientific information which is likely to be outside the experience and knowledge of a judge or jury. If on the proven facts a judge or jury can form their own conclusions without help, then the opinion of the expert is unnecessary. . . .

This precondition is often expressed in terms as to whether the evidence would be helpful to the trier of fact. The word "helpful" is not quite appropriate and sets too low a standard. However, I would not judge necessity by too strict a standard. What is required is that the opinion be necessary in the sense that it provide information "which is likely to be outside the experience and knowledge of a judge or jury". . . . As stated by Dickson J., the evidence must be necessary to enable the trier of fact to appreciate the matters in issue due to their technical nature. In *Kelliher (Village) v. Smith*, [1931] S.C.R. 672, at p. 684, this court, quoting from *Beven on Negligence* (4th ed. 1928), p. 141, stated that in order for expert evidence to be admissible, "[t]he subject-matter of the inquiry must be such that ordinary people are unlikely to form a correct judgment about it, if unassisted by persons with special knowledge." More recently, in *R. v. Lavallee*, *supra*, the above passages from *Kelliher* and *Abbey* were applied to admit expert evidence as to the state of mind of a "battered" woman. The judgment stressed that this was an area that is not understood by the average person.

As in the case of relevance, discussed above, the need for the evidence is assessed in light of its potential to distort the fact-finding process. As stated by Lawton L.J. in *R. v. Turner*, [1975] Q.B. 834, at p. 841, and approved by Lord Wilberforce in *Director of Public Prosecutions v. Jordan*, [1977] A.C. 699, at p. 718:

> An expert's opinion is admissible to furnish the court with scientific information which is likely to be outside the experience and knowledge of a judge or jury. If on the proven facts a judge or jury can form their own conclusions without help, then the opinion of an expert is unnecessary. In such a case if it is given dressed up in scientific jargon it may make judgment more difficult. The fact that an expert witness has impressive scientific qualifications does not by that fact alone make his opinion on matters of human nature and behaviour within the limits of normality any more helpful than that of the jurors themselves; but there is a danger that they may think it does.

The possibility that evidence will overwhelm the jury and distract them from their task can often be offset by proper instructions.

There is also a concern inherent in the application of this criterion that experts not be permitted to usurp the functions of the trier of fact. Too liberal an approach could result in a trial's becoming nothing more than a contest of experts with the trier of fact acting as referee in deciding which expert to accept.

These concerns were the basis of the rule which excluded expert evidence in respect of the ultimate issue. Although the rule is no longer of general application, the concerns underlying it remain. In light of these concerns, the criteria of relevance and necessity are applied strictly, on occasion, to exclude expert evidence as to an ultimate issue. Expert evidence as to credibility or oath-helping has been excluded on this basis. See *R. v. Marquard*, [1993] 4 S.C.R. 223, per McLachlin J.

(c) *The Absence of any Exclusionary Rule*

Compliance with criteria (a), (b) and (d) will not ensure the admissibility of expert evidence if it falls afoul of an exclusionary rule of evidence separate and apart from the opinion rule itself. For example, in *R. v. Morin*, [1988] 2 S.C.R. 345, evidence elicited by the Crown in cross-examination of the psychiatrist called by the accused was inadmissible because it was not shown to be relevant other than as to the disposition to commit the crime charged. Notwithstanding, therefore, that the evidence otherwise complied with the criteria for the admission of expert evidence it was excluded by reason of the rule that prevents the Crown from adducing evidence of the accused's disposition unless the latter has placed his or her character in issue. The extent of the restriction when such evidence is tendered by the accused lies at the heart of this case and will be discussed hereunder.

(d) *A Properly Qualified Expert*

Finally the evidence must be given by a witness who is shown to have acquired special or peculiar knowledge through study or experience in respect of the matters on which he or she undertakes to testify.

In summary, therefore, it appears from the foregoing that expert evidence which advances a novel scientific theory or technique is subjected to special scrutiny to determine whether it meets a basic threshold of reliability and whether it is essential in the sense that the trier of fact will be unable to come to a satisfactory conclusion without the assistance of the expert. The closer the evidence approaches an opinion on an ultimate issue, the stricter the application of this principle.

Application to This Case

I take the findings of the trial judge to be that a person who committed sexual assaults on young women could not be said to belong to a group possessing behavioural characteristics that are sufficiently distinctive to be of assistance in identifying the perpetrator of the offences charged. Moreover, the fact that the alleged perpetrator was a physician did not advance the matter because there is no acceptable body of evidence that doctors who commit sexual assaults fall into a distinctive class with identifiable characteristics. Notwithstanding the opinion of Dr. Hill, the trial judge was also not satisfied that the characteristics associated with the fourth complaint identified the perpetrator as a member of a distinctive group. He was not prepared to accept that the characteristics of that complaint were such that only a psychopath could have committed the act. There was nothing to indicate any general acceptance of this theory. Moreover, there was no material in the record to support a finding that the profile of a pedophile or psychopath has been standardized to the extent that it could be said that it matched the supposed profile of the offender depicted in the charges. The expert's group profiles were not seen as sufficiently reliable to be considered helpful. In the absence of these indicia of reliability, it cannot be said that the evidence would be necessary in the sense of usefully clarifying a matter otherwise unaccessible, or that any value it may have had would not be outweighed by its potential for misleading or diverting the jury. Given these findings and applying the principles referred to above, I must conclude that the trial judge was right in deciding as a matter of law that the evidence was inadmissible.

In the United States[219] a special evidentiary rule was set out in a federal appellate opinion in 1923 and despite criticism over the years it lasted until its repudiation by the United States Supreme Court in 1993.[220] That rule, which became known as the *Frye* test, demanded general acceptance in the scientific community before expertise could be admitted.[221] McCormick recommended:

> The traditional standards of relevancy and the need for expertise — and nothing more — should govern. This method for evaluating the admissibility of scientific evidence is the most appealing. It avoids the difficult problems of defining when "scientific" evidence is subject to the general acceptance requirement and how general this acceptance must be, of discerning exactly what it is that must be accepted, and of determining the "particular field" to which the scientific evidence belongs and in which it must be accepted.[222]

In 1975 the Federal Rules of Evidence were enacted by Congress. The impetus for these rules had been the United States Supreme Court and indeed the preliminary drafts were written pursuant to that Court's rule-making authority. It was only later that Congress involved itself in legislating the Rules. Rule 702 of the F.R.E. provides:

> If scientific, technical, or other specialized knowledge will assist the trier of fact to understand the evidence or to determine a fact in issue, a witness qualified as an

---

219 *Frye v. United States*, 293 F. 1013.
220 See Daubert, below, note 223.
221 For criticism in the U.S. see, e.g., Gianelli, "The Admissibility of Novel Scientific Evidence" (1980), 80 Col. L. Rev. 1197, and McCormick, "Scientific Evidence" (1982), 67 Iowa L. Rev. 879. The amount of writing on this issue was likened to "an academic cottage industry"; see Vu & Tamor, "Of Daubert, Elvis and Precedential Relevance" (1993), 41 U.C.L.A. L. Rev. 487, 491.
222 *McCormick on Evidence*, 4th ed. (1992) at p. 874.

expert by knowledge, skill, experience, training, or education, may testify thereto in the form of an opinion or otherwise.

This enactment caused many courts to disregard the *Frye* test. Finally, after 20 years of the rule's operation, the United States Supreme Court rejected the *Frye* test, saying it had been superseded by the F.R.E. rule.

In *Daubert v. Merrell Dow Pharmaceuticals Inc.*,[223] parents sued on their own behalf and on behalf of their children for birth defects. The plaintiffs maintained that these were due to the ingestion of Bendectin by the mother during her pregnancy. Bendectin was advertised as helpful to deal with morning sickness. The plaintiffs were unsuccessful in the lower courts. The trial court applied the *Frye* doctrine. The trial court granted summary judgment on the basis of an affidavit of a well-credentialed expert who deposed that having reviewed the literature, more than 30 published studies involving 130,000 patients, no study had found Bendectin to be a substance causing malformations in human fetuses. The plaintiffs did not contest this characterization of the published record regarding Bendectin. They responded with eight experts of their own, each with impressive credentials. They had concluded that Bendectin could cause birth defects. Their conclusions were based on animal studies; pharmacological studies of the chemical structure of Bendectin and the reanalysis of previously published, epidemiological, human statistical, studies. The trial court decided that scientific evidence was admissible only if the principle upon which it is based is sufficiently established to have general acceptance in the field to which it belongs. The court decided that the plaintiffs' evidence did not meet that standard. Given the vast body of epidemiological data concerning Bendectin, the court decided that expert opinion which was not based on epidemiological evidence was not admissible to establish causation. The epidemiological analyses were not admissible because they had not been published or subjected to peer review. The Court of Appeals affirmed holding that expert opinion based on a scientific technique is inadmissible unless the technique was generally accepted as reliable in the relevant scientific community.

The Supreme Court granted *certiorari* in light of sharp divisions among the courts regarding the proper standard. When *certiorari* was granted this was front page news in the United States and 22 amicus briefs were filed.[224] The court decided that the *Frye* test was superseded by the Federal Rules and general acceptance in the scientific community was not a prerequisite to admission of scientific evidence. The rejection of the *Frye* test does not mean however that a trial judge is deprived of authority to exclude expert testimony. Justice Blackmun for the court wrote:

> Nor is the trial judge disabled from screening such evidence. To the contrary, under the rules the trial judge must ensure that any and all scientific testimony or evidence admitted is not only relevant, but reliable.[225]

The court recognized that scientists typically distinguish between "validity": does the principle support what it purports to show?, and reliability: does application of the principle produce consistent results? The court was, however, at pains to

---

223 113 S.Ct. 2786 (1993).
224 See Imwinkelried, "Frye Is Dead" *Trial* (September 1993) 60.
225 *Supra*, note 223 at p. 2795.

point out that when they spoke of the need for reliability they were speaking of evidentiary reliability, i.e., trustworthiness, and that reliability would be based upon scientific validity.

The court recognized that it would be wrong to demand that the subject of scientific testimony be known to a certainty. To qualify as scientific knowledge however an inference or assertion must be derived by the scientific method. The trial judge is expected to assess whether the reasoning or methodology underlying the testimony is scientifically valid and whether that reasoning or methodology can properly be applied to the facts in issue. The court offered some observations as to how a trial judge might go about his task:

> [W]hether a theory or technique is scientific knowledge that will assist the trier of fact will [depend on] whether it can be and has been tested [and] whether the theory or technique has been subjected to peer review and publication. . . . The fact of publication, or lack thereof, in a peer-reviewed journal will be a relevant, though not dispositive, consideration. . . . [T]he court should consider the known or potential rate of error and the existence and maintenance of standards controlling the technique's operation. . . . Finally, "general acceptance" can yet have a bearing.[226]

Counsel for Merrell Dow Pharmaceuticals Inc. argued that abandoning the general acceptance test would result in a "free-for-all" in which juries would be confounded by irrational pseudoscientific assertions. The Court decided that alongwith the screening by the trial judge, the adversary system with vigorous cross-examination and presentation of contrary evidence were appropriate safeguards.

In *R. v. J. (J.-L.)* the Supreme Court expressly adopted the U.S. Federal Rules of Evidence approach to novel scientific evidence.

R. v. J. (J.-L.)
[2000] 2 S.C.R. 600, 37 C.R. (5th) 203, 148 C.C.C. (3d) 487, 2000 CarswellQue 2310, 2000 CarswellQue 2311

The accused was charged with sexual offences in relation to two boys who were between three and five years old. The Crown called evidence of statements made by one of the children to a foster mother, the foster mother's sister and a police officer. The statements suggested that the accused had engaged in anal intercourse with the child. The Crown also called medical evidence to support this allegation. The defence sought to call expert evidence from a psychiatrist to establish that in all probability a serious sexual deviant had inflicted anal intercourse on two children of that age, and that no such deviant personality traits were disclosed in the psychiatrist's testing of the accused. In evidence given on a *voir dire*, the expert testified that it was not possible to establish a standard profile of individuals with a predisposition to sodomize young children, but that such individuals frequently exhibit certain distinctive identifiable characteristics. The accused had been tested for these characteristics and excluded. In reaching this conclusion, the psychiatrist had evaluated the results of a series of general personality tests, and a plethysmograph test, which was directed to the accused's sexual preferences by exposing him to images and

---

226   *Ibid.*, at pp. 2796-97.

sounds of sexual activity, both normal and deviant, and measuring his physiological reaction through a gauge attached to his penis. The expert testified that if the subject had previously derived pleasure from a specific form of sexual activity, the pleasure was imprinted on the brain and may be re-stimulated on further exposure to pictures or sounds of similar activity. The accused was never confronted with specific images designed to replicate the offences alleged against him. The expert concluded that the accused had a normal profile with a preference for adult women and a slight attraction to adolescents, but exhibited no deviation with respect of boys in general or prepubescent boys.

The trial judge held that the expert's evidence was inadmissible. He acquitted the accused on charges relating to one boy but convicted the accused of having invited, counselled or incited the other child to touch the accused for a sexual purpose, and having engaged in an act of anal intercourse.

The Quebec Court of Appeal allowed the accused's appeal from his convictions and ordered a new trial. The majority held that the trial judge erred in excluding the psychiatrist's evidence.

BINNIE   J.   (L'HEUREUX-DUBÉ,   MCLACHLIN,   IACOBUCCI,   MAJOR, BASTARACHE and ARBOUR JJ. concurring):

. . . .

In this appeal we are required to consider aspects of the "gatekeeper function" performed by trial judges in the reception of novel scientific evidence.

. . . .

Expert witnesses have an essential role to play in the criminal courts. However, the dramatic growth in the frequency with which they have been called upon in recent years led to ongoing debate about suitable controls on their participation, precautions to exclude "junk science", and the need to preserve and protect the role of the trier of fact—the judge or the jury. The law in this regard was significantly advanced by Mohan. ... the course of Mohan and other judgments, the Court has emphasized that the trial judge should take seriously the role of "gatekeeper". The admissibility of the expert evidence should be scrutinized at the time it is proffered, and not allowed too easy an entry on the basis that all of the frailties could go at the end of the day to weight rather than admissibility.

. . . .

Mohan kept the door open to novel science, rejecting the "general acceptance" test formulated in the United States in *Frye v. United States*, 293 F. 1013 (D.C. Cir. 1923), and moving in parallel with its replacement, the "reliable foundation" test more recently laid down by the US Supreme Court in *Daubert v. Merrell Dow Pharmaceuticals, Inc.* 509 U.S. 579 (1993). While *Daubert* must be read in light of the specific text of the Federal Rules of Evidence, which differs from our own procedures, the U.S. Supreme Court did list a number of factors that could be helpful in evaluating the soundness of novel science:

(1) whether the theory or technique can be and has been tested;

Scientific methodology today is based on generating hypotheses and testing them to see if they can be falsified; indeed, this methodology is what distinguishes science from other fields of human inquiry.

(2) whether the theory or technique has been subjected to peer review and publication:

[S]ubmission to the scrutiny of the scientific community is a component of "good science", in part because it increases the likelihood that substantive flaws in methodology will be detected.

(3) the known or potential rate of error or the existence of standards; and,

(4) whether the theory or technique used has been generally accepted:

A "reliability assessment does not require, although it does permit, explicit identification of a relevant scientific community and an express determination of a particular degree of acceptance within that community."

Widespread acceptance can be an important factor in ruling particular evidence admissible, and "a known technique which has been able to attract only minimal support within the community," . . . may properly be viewed with skepticism.

Thus, in the United States, as here, "general acceptance" is only one of several factors to e considered. A penile plethysmograph may not yet be generally accepted as a forensic tool, but it may become so. A case-by-case evaluation of novel science is necessary in light of the changing nature of our scientific knowledge: it was once accepted by the highest authorities of the western world that the earth was flat.

The Supreme Court allowed the appeal and restored the convictions. The Court believed the trial judge had not erred in excluding the expert's evidence.

R. v. TROCHYM
[2007] S.C.J. No. 6, 2007 CarswellOnt 400, 2007 CarswellOnt 401,
43 C.R. (6th) 217 (S.C.C.)

T was charged with second degree murder of his girlfriend, H. Forensic evidence established that the killing had taken place in the early hours of a Wednesday morning but that the body had been repositioned some eight to twelve hours later. At trial, a neighbour, G, testified that early that morning or late Tuesday she heard a man banging on the door to H's apartment, demanding to be let in. Although she did not see the man, G testified she eventually heard the door open to admit him. Given the estimated time of death, it was likely that the man who entered the apartment at that time was the killer.

G also testified at trial that she saw the accused leaving H's apartment around 3:00 p.m. on Wednesday afternoon. In G's initial statements to police, she stated that she had seen T on Thursday afternoon, not Wednesday. It was only after undergoing hypnosis at the request of police investigators that G stated that she had seen T on Wednesday afternoon. The defence counsel objected to the admissibility of this post-hypnosis testimony. After a lengthy *voir dire* in which the evidence of three experts was considered, the trial judge ruled the evidence admissible and that weight would be a matter for the jury. Because of a tactical agreement between T's counsel and the Crown, jurors were not informed that G had been hypnotized, that she had initially told police she saw T on Thursday, nor did they hear expert evidence on the reliability of post-hypnosis testimony.

In support of its theory that the person who banged on the door was the accused, the Crown was permitted to call as similar fact evidence a former girlfriend, O. She testified that when she asked T to move out of her apartment at the end of a seven-year relationship, he had returned late that night or early next morning and had banged at her door, yelling profanities. T, who testified in his own defence, claimed that it was he who had ended the relationship with H that night and that when he left H's apartment at 12:30 a.m., she was still alive. He denied going back to her apartment on Wednesday, but admitted returning to the apartment building on that day to retrieve his car from the parking garage. T adduced evidence that he was at work at the time G claimed to have seen him leaving H's apartment on Wednesday afternoon. The jury convicted.

The Ontario Court of Appeal rejected the accused's appeal and confirmed his conviction. However, on further appeal, a 6-3 majority of the Supreme Court set aside the conviction and ordered a new trial. The majority held that the post-hypnosis evidence should not have been admitted and that this was not a case to apply the curative provision. The majority also found a reversible error in the admission of the similar fact evidence. Here we consider the Court's assessment of evidence induced by hypnosis.

DESCHAMPS J. (MCLACHLIN C.J., BINNIE, LEBEL and FISH JJ. concurring): —

. . . This case represents the first opportunity this Court has had to consider the admissibility of post-hypnosis evidence. The Court's framework for assessing novel science ensures that only scientific opinions based on a reliable foundation are put to the trier of fact (*J.-L.J.*, at para. 33), and the same principle applies to scientific techniques. Just as financial results contained in a report must be found to be prepared on the basis of a technique that has a reliable scientific foundation, post-hypnosis memories must be demonstrated to be sufficiently reliable before being put to the trier of fact. The "gatekeeper function" of the courts referred to in *J.-L.J.* (at para. 1) is thus as important when facts extracted through the use of a scientific technique are put to the jury as when an opinion is put to the jury through an expert who bases his or her conclusions on a scientific technique. As I will explain, the trial judge's error was to assume that post-hypnosis evidence is admissible provided that the *Clark* guidelines are followed. This is an error, both because the *Clark* guidelines themselves are insufficient and because post-hypnosis evidence does not meet the requirements of *J.-L.J.* I will consider both these points in turn.

a) *Problems with the Clark Guidelines*

In the case at bar, the trial judge assessed the reliability of the post-hypnosis evidence based on the factors set out in *R. v. Clark* (1984) 13 C.C.C. (3d) 117 (Alta. Q.B.). In that case, the accused was charged with two counts of first degree murder. He had no memory of the events until he was hypnotized. While there was no dispute that the accused had committed the acts with which he was charged, the issue at trial was his intent and mental capacity at the relevant time. Wachowich J. noted concerns regarding the use of hypnosis, but concluded that it would only be in an "extraordinary case" that a court would preclude a witness from testifying after having his or her memory stimulated by hypnosis (p. 123). However, he held that "the content of the hypnosis session is a proper subject for inquiry at the trial because it bears heavily on the credibility of the witness and the weight to be given his evidence" (p. 124). To this end, Wachowich J. set out a number of principles that should guide a hypnotist during a hypnosis session. These guidelines, he observed, would improve the reliability of evidence obtained under hypnosis.

Drawn from the American cases of *State v. Hurd*, 414 A.2d 291 (N.J. Sup. Ct. 1980) and *People v. McDowell*, 427 N.Y.S. 2d 181 (S.C. 1980), the *Clark* guidelines are as follows (*Clark*, at p. 125):

(1) The person conducting the hypnotic interview should be a qualified professional. . .

(2) The hypnotist must be independent of the party who requires his services. . .

(3) The hypnotist should be given only the minimum amount of information necessary to conduct the interview. . .

(4) The entire interview between the hypnotist and the potential witness should be recorded preferably on video tape. . .

(5) The interview should be conducted with only the hypnotist and the subject present. . .

(6) Prior to the actual hypnosis of the subject, the hypnotist should conduct a lengthy interview of the subject to determine his medical history including information about the present or past use of drugs. . .

(7) Prior to hypnosis, the hypnotist should elicit from the subject a detailed description of the facts surrounding the subject-matter of the hypnosis session, as the subject is able to recall them at that point in time.

(8) The hypnotist should pay careful attention to the form and manner of his questions, the choice of his words and the avoidance of body language so that he is not either intentionally or inadvertently providing the subject with information.

The *Clark* test has been adopted by a number of courts in Canada (see, e.g.: *R. v. Bernier*, [2004] Q.J. No. 11567 (QL) (Sup. Ct.); *R. v. Sanchez-Flores*, [1993] O.J. No. 4161 (QL) (Gen. Div.); *R. v. O'Brien* (1992), 117 N.S.R. (2d) 48 (S.C. App. Div.); and *R. v. Savoy*, [1997] B.C.J. No. 2747 (QL) (S.C.).

The guidelines are intended to limit the possibility of a hypnotist influencing, inadvertently or not, the persons being hypnotized, thereby tainting the witness's evidence. While they play an important role in limiting the possible exertion of influence during a hypnosis session, the guidelines are problematic in that they are based on an assumption that the underlying science of hypnosis is itself reliable in the context of judicial proceedings. Reliability is an essential component of admissibility. Whereas the degree of reliability required by courts may vary depending on the circumstances, evidence that is not sufficiently reliable is likely to undermine the fundamental fairness of the criminal process.

The probative value of post-hypnosis memories cannot be assessed without also inquiring into the reliability of the scientific technique that enabled them to arise.

. . . .

It should be noted that *Hurd*, which formed the basis for the *Clark* guidelines, has come to be revisited, in part as a result of the views expressed since then by Dr. Martin Orne, whose expert testimony had played a central role in that case. Dr. Orne subsequently warned that "hypnotically induced memories should *never* be permitted to form the basis for testimony by witnesses or victims in a court of law": *Burral v. State*, 724 A.2d 65 (Md. 1999), at p. 81 (emphasis in original). He was of the view that "there is a considerable risk that the inherent unreliability of information confidently provided by a hypnotized person may actually be detrimental to the truth-seeking process" (*State v. Moore*, 902 A.2d 1212 (N.J. 2006) at p. 1228). After reconsidering the inherent unreliability of post-hypnosis testimony, New Jersey joined the 26 states in the United States that limit the admissibility of post-hypnosis testimony. In New Jersey, post-hypnosis testimony is now generally inadmissible in a criminal trial (*Moore*, at p. 1213).

Since the *Clark* guidelines are derived from Dr. Orne's testimony in *Hurd*, it would be disturbing for this Court to blind itself to the subsequent developments in the American cases. With the basic reliability of post-hypnosis evidence increasingly in question, judicial approaches to such evidence have tended to shift from an assessment of the *weight* to be attributed to post-hypnosis testimony to whether it should even be admissible.

b) *The Court's Approach to Evidence Involving Science*

Not all scientific evidence, or evidence that results from the use of a scientific technique, must be screened before being introduced into evidence. In some cases, the science in question is so well established that judges can rely on the fact that the admissibility of evidence based on it has been clearly recognized by the courts in the past. Other cases may not be so clear. Like the legal community, the scientific community continues to challenge and improve upon its existing base of knowledge. As a result, the admissibility of scientific evidence is not frozen in time.

While some forms of scientific evidence become more reliable over time, others may become less so as further studies reveal concerns. Thus, a technique that was once admissible may subsequently be found to be inadmissible. An example of the first situation, where, upon further refinement and study, a scientific technique becomes sufficiently reliable to be used in criminal trials, is DNA matching evidence, which this Court recognized in *R. v. Terceira*, [1999] 3 S.C.R. 866. An example of the second situation, where a technique that has been employed for some time comes to be questioned, is so-called "dock", or in-court, identification evidence. In *R. v. Hibbert*, [2002] 2 S.C.R. 445, 2002 SCC 39, at para. 50, Arbour J., writing for the majority, stated that despite its long-standing use, dock identification is almost totally unreliable. Therefore, even if it has received judicial recognition in the past, a technique or science whose underlying assumptions are challenged should not be admitted in evidence without first confirming the validity of those assumptions.

. . . .

[The majority then applied the *J. (J.L.)* tests for a reliable foundation for novel science evidence.]

(i) Can the Technique Be Tested and Has it Been Tested?

Numerous references were made at trial and before this Court to studies on the use of hypnosis and to opinions of experts in the field. What is apparent from these sources is that the accuracy and effect of hypnosis are difficult to assess. While some laboratory studies suggest that hypnosis is not particularly effective in increasing the accuracy of memories, this may be a result of the laboratory setting itself. As Dr. Matheson, the Crown's expert, explained, what makes memories memorable are the emotional associations that give them meaning. Laboratory studies are largely abstract, and lack the emotional quality or meaning that normally attaches to "real life" memories. (A.R., at pp. 559-560) The findings of laboratory studies may not, therefore, be particularly applicable to the area of forensic hypnosis. However, it is significant that, despite their disagreement on other issues, all the experts in this case testified that while hypnosis can result in the subject's remembering a larger number of details, these will include both accurate and inaccurate information.

(ii) Has the Technique Been Subjected to Peer Review and Publication?

As noted, hypnosis is not a *new* technique. It was used in ancient times, and this case does not concern its usefulness as a therapeutic tool. What is in issue is its use for forensic purposes. While testifying at trial, the experts referred to a number of scientific articles and studies on hypnosis and memory. Moreover, legal commentators have discussed hypnosis extensively. Since it is the reliability of the technique in the judicial context that is in issue, these resources are useful for our purposes. Even the most superficial examination of these commentaries reveals that much of the substance of the testimonies of the experts heard at trial is supported by the abundant discussions found in the legal literature. The question whether the technique has been subjected to peer review and publication can thus be answered in the affirmative. Dr. Matheson cited the following study while testifying at trial in this case: Council on Scientific Affairs, "Scientific Status of Refreshing Recollection by the Use of Hypnosis" (1985), 253 *J.A.M.A.* 1918. It is also notable that many of Dr. Orne's publications have been cited by the courts, including the following: M. T. Orne, "The Use and Misuse of Hypnosis in Court" (1979), 27 *Int.'l J. Clinical and Experimental Hypnosis* 311; M. T. Orne et al., "Hypnotically Refreshed Testimony: Enhanced Memory or Tampering with

Evidence?" in*Issues and Practices in Criminal Justice* (January 1985), at pp. 5-27. Legal commentaries on the use of hypnosis in criminal trials have proliferated: B. L. Diamond, "Inherent Problems in the Use of Pretrial Hypnosis on a Prospective Witness" (1980), 68 *Cal. L. Rev.* 313; T. M. Fleming, "Admissibility of Hypnotically Refreshed or Enhanced Testimony", 77 A.L.R. 4th 927 (1990 & Supp. 2006); G. M. Shaw, "The Admissibility of Hypnotically Enhanced Testimony in Criminal Trials" (1991), 75 *Marq. L. Rev.* 1; G. F. Wagstaff, "Hypnosis and the Law: A Critical Review of Some Recent Proposals" (1983), *Crim. L. Rev.* 152; K. B. Evans, "Hypnotically Induced Testimony: Implications for Criminal Law in New Zealand" (1994), *N.Z.L.J.* 348; J. Harsel, "The Use of Hypnotically Enhanced Testimony in Criminal Trials" (1996), 20 *Melbourne U.L. Rev.* 897; D. R. Webert, "Are the Courts in a Trance? Approaches to the Admissibility of Hypnotically Enhanced Witness Testimony in Light of Empirical Evidence" (2003), 40 *Am. Crim. L. Rev.* 1301. It is noteworthy that the weaknesses of hypnosis are well known and uncontroverted. The experts differ not on the shortcomings themselves, but on the extent of their impact on the witness's ability to testify.

There is a general consensus that most individuals are more suggestible under hypnosis, that any increase in accurate memories during hypnosis is accompanied by an increase in *in*accurate memories, that hypnosis may compromise the subject's ability to distinguish memory from imagination, and that subjects frequently report being more certain of the content of post-hypnosis memories, regardless of their accuracy. In sum, while it is not generally accepted that hypnosis *always* produces unreliable memories, neither is it clear when hypnosis results in *pseudo-memories* or how a witness, scientist or trier of fact might distinguish between fabricated and accurate memories.

(iii) What is the Potential Rate of Error?

A recurring theme in the expert testimony at Mr. Trochym's trial and in the jurisprudence is that, while hypnosis may assist witnesses to recall additional detail, the medical community knows very little about how memory functions or what role hypnosis may have in recalling and/or altering memories. The general consensus appears to be that memory does not work like a tape recorder that can be played back but, rather, is constructive or additive. Remembering may therefore be a more creative mental process than it is usually understood to be. Given these gaps in scientific knowledge, the admission of post-hypnosis memories raises a number of concerns. The Crown's expert, Dr. Matheson, testified that "the general understanding is that if properly and professionally done you would probably get more information [through hypnosis], and that information will be a combination of accurate and inaccurate [information]" (A.R., at pp. 601-602).

The potential rate of error is linked to three factors. The first, and most significant, of these is the risk of confabulation, or the creation of hallucinated or false memories. Confabulation can result from the power of express or implied suggestions, or simply from a strong, unconscious desire to compensate for a lack of actual memory. It may also result from other causes that are unknown, because scientists know very little about memory. All three expert witnesses noted at trial that, while confabulation may also occur without hypnosis, a person's suggestibility is enhanced under hypnosis.

A second, and related, factor is that a person's critical faculty appears to be reduced while he or she is under hypnosis. As Dr. Pollock, one of two expert witnesses called by the defence, explained, a person who has a memory in the normal "waking state" will examine it and decide whether it is accurate and should be reported. A hypnotized person is more likely to report whatever comes to his or her mind. As a result, while hypnosis may help a witness recall an event in greater detail, this heightened recollection may simply contain both more correct and more false details. The greater number of *details* the witness remembers may therefore create the illusion that his or her memory has improved in *accuracy*.

Finally, experts express concern about the potential for "memory hardening", a process by which a person who has been hypnotized becomes increasingly, and unduly, confident in his or her memories. The exact cause of memory hardening is unknown but the phenomenon has been recognized. It is described as the "most consistent finding of all in studies on the various effects of hypnosis" (Shaw, at p. 12). This process is undetectable and seemingly irreversible. When combined with the possibility that memories have been tainted through confabulation, improperly phrased questions, or other unintentional influences, the danger that the accused will be denied a fair hearing becomes obvious.

At trial, Dr. Matheson observed that many of the concerns regarding post-hypnosis memories, such as confabulation and memory hardening, also apply to ordinary testimonial evidence. In admitting Ms. Haghnegahdar's post-hypnosis memories, the trial judge noted that if judge-made guidelines such as those set out in *Clark* can control any tainting that might occur during hypnosis, then post-hypnosis memories are no more, or less, accurate than ordinary eyewitness testimony.

With respect, I find this view problematic. Hypnosis introduces more sources of concern and a likelihood that existing fragilities of human memory will increase, tainting the reliability of the evidence. Furthermore, the frailties of human memory when unaffected by hypnosis are only just starting to become known; indeed, the fallibility of eyewitness identification has been a central concern in a number of inquiries into wrongful convictions. In his public inquiry into the wrongful conviction of Thomas Sophonow, for example, the Honourable Peter deC. Cory observed that most triers of fact have implicit faith in eyewitness identification and that this can be hazardous. He recommended, among other things, instructing the jury about the shortcomings of eyewitness identification and cautioning it that the vast majority of wrongful convictions have resulted from faulty eyewitness identification: *The Inquiry Regarding Thomas Sophonow: The Investigation, Prosecution and Consideration of Entitlement to Compensation* (2001), at pp. 33-34. While Justice Cory was specifically addressing ordinary memory, his recommendations make it all the more clear why a technique used to *enhance* memory must be approached with great caution.

(iv) Has the Technique Been Generally Accepted?

As indicated, there are differences of opinion in the scientific community on the acceptability of hypnosis for forensic purposes. This has resulted in some debate, in the courts of a number of jurisdictions, regarding the admissibility of post-hypnosis memories. In the United Kingdom, for example, post-hypnosis testimony has not been categorically excluded, although evidence of a witness who has been hypnotized can be excluded under s. 78 of the *Police and Criminal Evidence Act 1984* (U.K.), 1984, c. 60, on the basis that it would have an adverse effect on the fairness of the proceedings. For this reason, the Crown Prosecution Service warns Crown counsel to "advise the police to restrict the use of hypnotism to people who may be able to give them a lead on an investigation but who will not be called as witnesses" (online). In New Zealand and Australia, courts have permitted the admission of post-hypnosis evidence where certain safeguards have been met, resulting in such evidence being declared inadmissible in several instances: see *R. v. McFelin*, [1985] 2 N.Z.L.R. 750 (C.A.); *R. v. G.*, [1996] 1 N.Z.L.R. 615 (H.C.); and *R. v. Haywood* (1994), 73 A. Crim. R. 41, (S.C. Tasmania). Generally speaking, however, there has been very little discussion on the admissibility of post-hypnosis evidence in any of these three jurisdictions.

By contrast, courts have discussed the admissibility of post-hypnosis memories much more frequently in the United States. Two trends have developed. According to the first, the fact that a witness has been hypnotized goes to the weight of the testimony rather than to its admissibility. In *Harding v. State*, 246 A.2d 302 (1968), the Court of Special Appeals of Maryland held that the fact that only some of the victim's testimony was based on post-hypnosis recollections went to its probative value. As the psychology of memory has become better understood, however, some courts have developed a number of safeguards to guide the manner in which hypnosis sessions are conducted. This more rigorous framework is typified by *Hurd*, a decision that, as already mentioned, was one of the main sources of the *Clark* guidelines. Although setting a more rigorous standard than in *Harding*, the *Hurd* guidelines are typical of the approach under which admissibility is subject to the weight to be attached to the particular witness's post-hypnosis testimony.

The second trend is based on a view that hypnosis is fundamentally unreliable for the purposes of judicial proceedings and that post-hypnosis evidence should be excluded. In *People v. Shirley*, 723 P.2d 1354 (1982), the California Supreme Court held that the testimony of a witness who has undergone hypnosis to restore his or her memory of events is inadmissible "as to all matters relating to those events, from the time of the hypnosis session forward" (p. 1384). This means that a witness who has been hypnotized to restore his or her memory of an incident may not testify in relation to that incident, regardless of whether he or she made pre-hypnosis statements about it that would otherwise have been admissible. At least half of American jurisdictions now limit the admissibility of post-hypnosis evidence: *Moore*, at pp. 1220-22.

. . . .

In sum, it appears that the use of hypnosis in the judicial context has both supporters and opponents, but that the general tendency is to be extremely cautious in dealing with post-hypnosis evidence. This debate may continue until significant advances are made in the science of hypnosis, or until our understanding of human memory improves significantly. In *J.-L.J.*, Binnie J. mentioned, in addition to the factors discussed above, the importance of determining the impact of novel science on the trial process, and in particular of determining whether the value or utility of the evidence outweighs its potential costs in terms of the consumption of time, potential prejudice to the accused, and confusion caused to the trier of fact. For this reason, a judge should, in exercising his or her role as "gatekeeper", carefully scrutinize the admissibility of novel scientific evidence. While parties must be able to put forward the most complete evidentiary record possible (*R. v. Seaboyer*, [1991] 2 S.C.R. 577), admissibility will necessarily be circumscribed where the evidence may "distort the fact-finding process" (*J.-L.J.*, at para. 29). These concerns are highly relevant where hypnosis is used, because of the controversy surrounding the forensic use of the technique and the need to explain its shortcomings if it is in fact to be used.

c) *The Gap Between Clark and J.-L.J.*

When the factors set out in *J.-L.J.* are applied to hypnosis, it becomes evident that this technique and its impact on human memory are not understood well enough for post-hypnosis testimony to be sufficiently reliable to be used in a court of law. Although hypnosis has been the subject of numerous studies, these studies are either inconclusive or draw attention to the fact that hypnosis can, in certain circumstances, result in the distortion of memory. Perhaps most troubling is the potential rate of error in the additional information obtained through hypnosis when it is used for forensic purposes. At the present time, there is no way of knowing whether such information will be accurate or inaccurate. Such uncertainty is unacceptable in a court of law. Furthermore, while the *Clark* guidelines aid significantly in ensuring that the hypnotist and police make as few involuntary suggestions as possible, they afford no protection against external sources of influence or against the other problems associated with hypnosis, such as confabulation out of a desire to compensate for a lack of actual memory, an increase in detail without sufficient assurances that this new information will be accurate, and memory hardening.

. . . .

In sum, it is evident, based on the scientific evidence on record, that post-hypnosis testimony does not satisfy the test for admissibility set out in *J.-L.J.* While hypnosis has been the subject of extensive study and peer review, much of the literature is inconclusive or highly contradictory regarding the reliability of the science in the judicial context. Unless a litigant reverses the presumption on the basis of the factors set out in *J.-L.J.*, post-hypnosis testimony should not be admitted in evidence.

d) *Limited Use of Testimony Given by a Witness Who Has Undergone Hypnosis*

Some novel scientific techniques, such as polygraph examinations, that are inadmissible for evidentiary purposes may nevertheless continue to be useful for the investigation of offences. For example, while concerns about oath helping, character evidence and delay may prevent the use of polygraph results in court, these concerns do not preclude police officers from administering polygraph tests as an investigative tool: *R. v. Béland*, [1987] 2 S.C.R. 398.

The inadmissibility of post-hypnosis testimony does not mean that hypnosis may not be used for other purposes. However, investigators must be conscious of the potential consequences of hypnotizing a witness.

A trial judge may have to rule on a request to allow a witness to testify on topics in respect of which questions were <u>not</u> asked during the hypnosis session. The judge must then balance the risks inherent in the use of hypnosis against the search for truth. Although this testimony may be tainted by post-hypnosis memories and although the cross-examination of the witness may be impaired, the judge may be satisfied that the detrimental effects are outweighed by the probative value of the testimony. In such a case, the trial judge may consider it appropriate to allow evidence on topics that were not touched on during the hypnosis session to be put to the jury. However, if the judge considers that the evidence is so important that it has to be put to the jurors despite its potential shortcomings, those shortcomings have to be mentioned. The judge must then give proper instructions to the jury concerning the effect of hypnosis on the weight of the testimony. The rationale for requiring specific instructions even though a topic was not touched on in the session is that the impact of hypnosis on testimony is not limited to post-hypnosis recollection and that testimony on the topic in question is accordingly likely to affect the jury's assessment of the witness's testimony.

Where evidence on topics covered during the hypnosis session is concerned, however, the trial judge should not admit it even if the witness did not change his or her testimony while under hypnosis. In my view, it would be inconsistent with the inadmissibility rule to allow those parts of the testimony, since they are tainted by the inherent shortcomings of the technique of hypnosis.

. . . .

e) *Conclusion on Hypnosis*

The admission of Ms. Haghnegahdar's post-hypnosis testimony constitutes an error of law.

CHARRON J. concurred but expressed disagreement with the limits the majority placed on the use of testimony of a witness who has undergone hypnosis.

BASTARACHE J. (ABELLA and ROTHSTEIN JJ. concurring) (dissenting): —

. . . My concerns with the approach to hypnotically refreshed evidence that Deschamps J. advocates relate not only to her views on the admissibility of such evidence, but on the implications her decision will have on the admissibility of scientific evidence in future cases. In my view, the precedent set by permitting the appellant to succeed on this ground without his having adduced a sufficient evidentiary foundation for this challenge is, to say the least, troubling.

. . . .

Characterizing hypnosis as "novel science" by applying *R. v. J.-L.J.*, [2000] 2 S.C.R. 600, 2000 SCC 51, my colleague finds that hypnotically refreshed memories are, at least for now, presumptively inadmissible.

This ignored the fact that the technique has been used in Canada for almost 30 years, and has been employed in Canadian criminal investigations to assist in memory retrieval of both Crown and defence witnesses for similar amounts of time. The test for assessing the reliability of scientific evidence set out in *J.-L.J.* is not "new law" requiring that scientific methods, previously accepted as legitimate by our courts, must now be resubmitted for scrutiny under the *J.-L.J.* test.

. . . .

J.-L.J. was not intended, as my colleague appears to suggest, to set down a rigid formula where the results must be proved beyond a reasonable doubt before scientific evidence can be admitted. The factors from *Daubert v. Merrell Dow Pharmaceuticals Inc.*, 509 U.S. 579 (1993), adopted in *J.-L.J.* were designed to be flexible and non-exclusive. As noted above, similar factors to assist courts in assessing the reliability of scientific evidence have existed at common law long before *J.-L.J.* was decided. Well-established scientific methods accepted by our courts do not need to be systematically reassessed under *J.-L.J.* While my colleague suggests that not all previously accepted scientific techniques will have to be reassessed under *J.-L.J.*, her guidance that science which is "so well established" (at para. 31) need not be reassessed is so vague that it opens the door to most if not all previously accepted techniques being subject to challenge under *J.-L.J.*, without establishing a serious basis for the inquiry.

A further concern I have about Deschamps J.'s approach to *J.-L.J.* is that although she states that the standard it requires is 'sufficient reliability' (para. 33), her reasoning really reflects a standard of total consensus by members of the scientific community. She acknowledges that hypnosis has been the subject of significant study and peer review, as well as testing, yet, because there is not unanimity in the scientific community on the reliability of hypnotically refreshed memories, she would find this evidence inadmissible. In my view, this standard is more akin to the "general acceptance" test that this Court specifically rejected in *Mohan* in favour of the *Daubert* "reliable foundation" test, as stated in *J.-L.J.*, at para. 33.

. . . .

I fear that the high standard of reliability my colleague champions will result in the exclusion of far too much relevant and probative evidence.

Finally, I add that in order to come to the conclusion that hypnosis evidence does not meet the criteria of general acceptance, my colleague relies almost exclusively on the position of experts discussed in American cases. This is not a sufficient evidentiary foundation upon which to arrive at such a conclusion. However, this was the sole evidence the appellant advanced before this Court in support of his argument that it should adopt a general exclusionary rule towards hypnosis evidence.

. . . .

Deschamps J. would allow this ground of the appeal without a proper evidentiary foundation, thereby depriving the Crown of the right to present contrary evidence or to cross-examine the experts who maintain such a position.

....

It is only before this Court and the Court of Appeal that Mr. Trochym sought to challenge the long-standing admissibility rule. In order to properly challenge such a rule, however, he was required to present direct expert evidence on why the rule should no longer be accepted, not just some academic commentary supporting this position. No such evidence was presented. I have serious reservations about courts conducting personal research — and forming conclusions on the basis of such research — in areas that require expertise, like the sciences.

The concerns my colleague raises are not new and have been taken into account by trial judges in virtually every *voir dire* held to determine the admissibility of hypnotically refreshed memories. A review of Canadian hypnotically refreshed evidence cases reveals that when trial judges consider the admissibility of hypnosis evidence, they hear about the divergent opinions on the use of forensic hypnosis in the scientific community, including concerns regarding the dangers associated with hypnosis, such as suggestibility, confabulation and memory hardening, and they take these into consideration when deciding whether to admit the specific evidence.

. . . .

Perhaps a better evidentiary foundation in a future case may demonstrate that it is time for Canadian courts to reconsider the long-standing admissibility rule for hypnotically refreshed memories. That decision cannot be made in this case. For now, I would simply caution our courts not to encourage the practice of forensic hypnosis until better evidence is available regarding its value. However, I have not been persuaded at this point, on this record, that a complete exclusion of such evidence in all cases is appropriate, as this could deprive the trier of fact from hearing relevant, probative, and even sometimes critical evidence, to either the Crown's or defence's case in some instances. In my view, the admissibility of such evidence should always be made on a case-by-case basis. Here the evidence was highly relevant to the Crown's case and shown to be quite credible. In my view, the trial judge made no legal error in admitting it.

Recently in a major ruling in *Abbey,* the Ontario Court of Appeal announced a revised approach to the admission of expert opinion evidence. Consider whether it is consistent with the approach of the Supreme Court.

R. v. ABBEY
(2009), 2009 CarswellOnt 5008, 246 C.C.C. (3d) 301, 68 C.R. (6th) 201
(C.A.)

The accused was charged with first degree murder. The victim was killed in what the parties agreed was a gang-related shooting, and the only live factual issue at trial was the identity of the killer. The accused was a member of the Malvern Crew street gang. The Crown led evidence from three other Malvern Crew members implicating the accused in the shooting. The defence claimed that the accused had nothing to do with the shooting, and that the victim was actually killed by one or two of the Malvern Crew members who testified for the Crown.

The Crown sought to introduce at trial various items of evidence related to a teardrop-shaped tattoo that the accused had inscribed on his face some months after the shooting. This evidence included testimony from a sociologist with expertise in the culture of Canadian street gangs on the meaning of teardrop tattoos within that culture. The expert was prepared to offer an opinion, based on his research, clinical experience and familiarity with the relevant academic literature, that a teardrop tattoo on the face of a young gang member had three possible meanings:

1. The death of a fellow gang member or family member of the wearer of the tattoo;
2. That the wearer of the tattoo had served a period of incarceration in a correctional facility; or,
3. That the wearer of the tattoo had murdered a rival gang member.

The Crown's primary position was that the expert should be allowed to testify not only to the three possible meanings of a teardrop tattoo but also that a teardrop tattoo would mean that the bearer had killed a rival gang member in a hypothetical situation where the other possible meanings did not apply. As the defence had conceded that the other meanings did not apply to the accused, the effect of this evidence would be to establish that the teardrop tattoo on the accused's face signified that he had killed another gang member, who in the context of the case could only be the victim. The Crown's alternative position was that even if the expert should not be allowed to testify about this hypothetical, the expert should be allowed to identify the three possible meanings of a teardrop tattoo within street gang culture.

The trial judge excluded all the evidence from the expert and others concerning the meaning of the teardrop tattoo. He found that the expert's testimony was not sufficiently reliable to be admitted. The accused was acquitted and the Crown appealed.

DOHERTY J.A. (MACPHERSON and LANG JJ.A. concurring):

. . .

(a) Delineating the Scope of the Expert's Opinion

62 The admissibility inquiry is not conducted in a vacuum. Before deciding admissibility, a trial judge must determine the nature and scope of the proposed expert evidence. In doing so, the trial judge sets not only the boundaries of the proposed expert evidence but also, if necessary, the language in which the expert's opinion may be proffered so as to minimize any potential harm to the trial process. A cautious delineation of the scope of the proposed expert evidence and strict adherence to those boundaries, if the evidence is admitted, are essential. The case law demonstrates that overreaching by expert witnesses is probably the most common fault leading to reversals on appeal: see, for example, *R. v. Ranger* (2003), 67 O.R. (3d) 1 (C.A.); *R. v. Klymchuk* (2005), 203 C.C.C. (3d) 341 (Ont. C.A.); *R. v. K. (A.)* (1999), 45 O.R. (3d) 641 (C.A.), at paras. 123-35; *R. v. Llorenz* (2000), 145 C.C.C. (3d) 535 (Ont. C.A.), at paras. 33-40.

63 A determination of the scope of the proposed expert opinion evidence and the manner in which it may be presented to the jury if admissible will be made after a voir dire. The procedures to be followed on that voir dire are for the trial judge to decide. Sometimes the expert must be examined and cross-examined on the voir dire to ensure that the proposed evidence is properly understood. At the conclusion of the voir dire, the trial judge must identify with exactitude the scope of the proposed opinion that may be admissible. He or she will also decide whether certain terminology used by the expert is unnecessary to the opinion and potentially misleading: see *R. v. G. (P.)* (2009), 242 C.C.C. (3d) 558, at para. 16 (Ont. C.A.). Admissibility is not an all or nothing proposition. Nor is the trial judge limited to either accepting or rejecting the opinion evidence as tendered by one party or the other. The trial judge may admit part of the proffered testimony, modify the nature or scope of the proposed opinion, or edit the language used to frame that opinion: see, for example, *R. v. Wilson* (2002), 166 C.C.C. (3d) 294 (Ont. S.C.).

64 The importance of properly defining the limits and nature of proposed expert opinion evidence and the language to be used by the expert is one of the valuable lessons learned from the Inquiry into Pediatric Forensic Pathology in Ontario.7 That inquiry examined the forensic work of Dr. Charles Smith, who at the time was considered to be a leading pediatric pathologist in Ontario. The inquiry determined that, among other failings, Dr. Smith often went beyond the limits of his expertise when offering opinions in his testimony. His excesses were sometimes not caught by the court or counsel and, along with other shortcomings, led to several miscarriages of justice. Goudge J.A., the Commissioner, stressed the trial judge's obligation to take an active role in framing the scope and the language of the proposed expert opinion evidence. He observed at pp. 499-500:

> A final outcome from the admissibility process is a clear definition of the scope of the expertise that a particular witness is qualified to give. As discussed in the earlier

part of this chapter, *it will be beneficial to define the range of expertise with as much precision as possible so that all the parties and the witness are alerted to areas where the witness has not been qualified to give evidence. ... As I earlier recommended, the trial judge should take steps at the outset to define clearly the proposed subject area of the witness's expertise. At the conclusion of the voir dire, the trial judge will be well situated to rule with precision on what the witness can and cannot say.* These steps will help to ensure that the witness's testimony, when given, can be confined to permissible areas and that it meets the requirement of threshold reliability. [Emphasis added.]

. . .

(b) The Applicable Principles and a Suggested Approach to Admissibility

71 It is fundamental to the adversary process that witnesses testify to what they saw, heard, felt or did, and the trier of fact, using that evidentiary raw material, determines the facts. Expert opinion evidence is different. Experts take information accumulated from their own work and experience, combine it with evidence offered by other witnesses, and present an opinion as to a factual inference that should be drawn from that material. The trier of fact must then decide whether to accept or reject the expert's opinion as to the appropriate factual inference. Expert evidence has the real potential to swallow whole the fact-finding function of the court, especially in jury cases. Consequently, expert opinion evidence is presumptively inadmissible. The party tendering the evidence must establish its admissibility on the balance of probabilities: Paciocco & Stuesser at pp. 184, 193; S. Casey Hill et al., *McWilliams' Canadian Criminal Evidence*, 4th ed., looseleaf (Aurora, Ont.: Canada Law Book, 2009), at para. 12:30.10.

72 The increased reliance on expert opinion evidence by both the Crown and defence in criminal matters is evident upon even a cursory review of the reported cases. Sometimes it seems that a deluge of experts has descended on the criminal courts ready to offer definitive opinions to explain almost anything. Expert evidence is particularly prevalent where inferences must be drawn from a wide variety of human behaviour: see, for example, *R. v. McIntosh* (1997), 35 O.R. (3d) 97 (C.A.), at pp. 101-103, leave to appeal to S.C.C. refused *R. v. McCarthy*, [1998] 1 S.C.R. xii [leave sought by second appellant in McIntosh, Mr. McCarthy]; David M. Paciocco, "Coping With Expert Evidence About Human Behaviour" (1999) 25 Queen's L.J. 305, at pp. 307-308; S. Casey Hill et al. at para. 12:30.10; *R. v. Olscamp* (1994), 95 C.C.C. (3d) 466 (Ont. Ct. (Gen. Div.)), approved in *R. v. Lance* (1998), 130 C.C.C. (3d) 438 (Ont. C.A.), at para. 24; Ontario, *The Commission on Proceedings Involving Guy Paul Morin: Report, vol. 1* (Toronto: Queen's Printer, 1998), at pp. 311-24. As Moldaver J.A. put it in *R. v. Clark* (2004), 69 O.R. (3d) 321 (C.A.), at para. 107, a case involving the proposed expert evidence of a criminal profiler:

> Combined, these two concerns [giving expert evidence more weight than it deserves and accepting expert evidence without subjecting it to the scrutiny it requires] raise the spectre of trial by expert as opposed to trial by jury. That is something that must be avoided at all costs. The problem is not a new one but in today's day and age, with proliferation of expert evidence, it poses a constant threat. *Vigilance is required*

to ensure that expert witnesses like Detective Inspector Lines are not allowed to hijack the trial and usurp the function of the jury. [Emphasis added.]

73 Despite justifiable misgivings, expert opinion evidence is, of necessity, a mainstay in the litigation process. Put bluntly, many cases, including very serious criminal cases, could not be tried without expert opinion evidence. The judicial challenge is to properly control the admissibility of expert opinion evidence, the manner in which it is presented to the jury and the use that the jury makes of that evidence.

74 The current approach to the admissibility of expert opinion evidence was articulated by Sopinka J. in *Mohan*. Broadly speaking, *Mohan* replaced what had been a somewhat laissez faire attitude toward the admissibility of expert opinion evidence with a principled approach that required closer judicial scrutiny of the proffered evidence. After *Mohan*, trial judges were required to assess the potential value of the evidence to the trial process against the potential harm to that process flowing from admission.

75 The four criteria controlling the admissibility of expert opinion evidence identified in *Mohan* have achieved an almost canonical status in the law of evidence. No judgment on the topic seems complete without reference to them. The four criteria are:

- relevance;
- necessity in assisting the trier of fact;
- the absence of any exclusionary rule; and,
- a properly qualified expert.

76 Using these criteria, I suggest a two-step process for determining admissibility. First, the party proffering the evidence must demonstrate the existence of certain preconditions to the admissibility of expert evidence. For example, that party must show that the proposed witness is qualified to give the relevant opinion. Second, the trial judge must decide whether expert evidence that meets the preconditions to admissibility is sufficiently beneficial to the trial process to warrant its admission despite the potential harm to the trial process that may flow from the admission of the expert evidence. This "gatekeeper" component of the admissibility inquiry lies at the heart of the present evidentiary regime governing the admissibility of expert opinion evidence: see *Mohan*; *R. v. D.D.*, [2000] 2 S.C.R. 275; *J.-L.J.*; *R. v. Trochym*, [2007] 1 S.C.R. 239; *K. (A.)*; *Ranger*; *R. v. Osmar* (2007), 84 O.R. (3d) 321 (C.A.), leave to appeal to S.C.C. refused (2007), 85 O.R. (3d) xviii.

77 I appreciate that *Mohan* does not describe the admissibility inquiry as a two-step process. It does not distinguish between what I refer to as the preconditions to admissibility and the trial judge's exercise of the "gatekeeper" function. My description of the process as involving two distinct phases does not alter the substance of the analysis required by *Mohan*. In suggesting a two-step approach, I mean only to facilitate the admissibility analysis and the application of the Mohan criteria.

78 It is helpful to distinguish between what I describe as the preconditions to admissibility of expert opinion evidence and the performance of the "gatekeeper" function because the two are very different. The inquiry into compliance with the preconditions to admissibility is a rules-based analysis that will yield "yes" or "no" answers. Evidence that does not meet all of the preconditions to admissibility must be excluded and the trial judge need not address the more difficult and subtle considerations that arise in the "gatekeeper" phase of the admissibility inquiry.

79 The "gatekeeper" inquiry does not involve the application of bright line rules, but instead requires an exercise of judicial discretion. The trial judge must identify and weigh competing considerations to decide whether on balance those considerations favour the admissibility of the evidence. This cost-benefit analysis is case-specific and, unlike the first phase of the admissibility inquiry, often does not admit of a straightforward "yes" or "no" answer. Different trial judges, properly applying the relevant principles in the exercise of their discretion, could in some situations come to different conclusions on admissibility.

80 In what I refer to as the first phase, four preconditions to admissibility must be established, none of which were in dispute at trial:

- the proposed opinion must relate to a subject matter that is properly the subject of expert opinion evidence;
- the witness must be qualified to give the opinion;
- the proposed opinion must not run afoul of any exclusionary rule apart entirely from the expert opinion rule; and,
- the proposed opinion must be logically relevant to a material issue.

81 For the purpose of explaining the analytic distinction I draw between the preconditions to admissibility and the "gatekeeper" function, I need not address the first three preconditions. The relevance criterion, however, does require some explanation. Relevance is one of the four *Mohan* criteria. However, I use the word differently than Sopinka J. used it in *Mohan*.

82 Relevance can have two very different meanings in the evidentiary context. Relevance can refer to logical relevance, a requirement that the evidence have a tendency as a matter of human experience and logic to make the existence or non-existence of a fact in issue more or less likely than it would be without that evidence: *J.-L.J.* at para. 47. Given this meaning, relevance sets a low threshold for admissibility and reflects the inclusionary bias of our evidentiary rules: see *R. v. Clark* (1999), 129 C.C.C. (3d) 1 (Ont. C.A.), at p. 12. Relevance can also refer to a requirement that evidence be not only logically relevant to a fact in issue, but also sufficiently probative to justify its admission despite the prejudice that may flow from its admission. This meaning of relevance is described as legal relevance and involves a limited weighing of the costs and benefits associated with admitting evidence that is undoubtedly logically relevant: see Paciocco & Stuesser at pp. 30-35.

83 The relevance criterion for admissibility identified in *Mohan* refers to legal relevance. To be relevant, the evidence must not only be logically relevant but

must be sufficiently probative to justify admission: see *Mohan* at pp. 20-21; *K. (A.)* at paras. 77-89; Paciocco & Stuesser at pp. 198-99.

84 When I speak of relevance as one of the preconditions to admissibility, I refer to logical relevance. I think the evaluation of the probative value of the evidence mandated by the broader concept of legal relevance is best reserved for the "gatekeeper" phase of the admissibility analysis. Evidence that is relevant in the sense that it is logically relevant to a fact in issue survives to the "gatekeeper" phase where the probative value can be assessed as part of a holistic consideration of the costs and benefits associated with admitting the evidence. Evidence that does not meet the logical relevance criterion is excluded at the first stage of the inquiry: see e.g. *R. v. Dimitrov* (2003), 68 O.R. (3d) 641 (C.A.), at para. 48, leave to appeal to S.C.C. refused (2004), [2004] S.C.C.A. No. 59, 70 O.R. (3d) xvii.

85 My separation of logical relevance from the cost-benefit analysis associated with legal relevance does not alter the criteria for admissibility set down in *Mohan* or the underlying principles governing the admissibility inquiry. I separate logical from legal relevance simply to provide an approach which focuses first on the essential prerequisites to admissibility and second, on all of the factors relevant to the exercise of the trial judge's discretion in determining whether evidence that meets those preconditions should be received.

86 As indicated above, it was not argued that Dr. Totten's evidence did not meet the preconditions to admissibility. Nor is it suggested that it was not logically relevant to identity, a fact in issue. The battle over the admissibility of his evidence was fought at the "gatekeeper" stage of the analysis. At that stage, the trial judge engages in a case-specific cost-benefit analysis.

87 The "benefit" side of the cost-benefit evaluation requires a consideration of the probative potential of the evidence and the significance of the issue to which the evidence is directed. When one looks to potential probative value, one must consider the reliability of the evidence. Reliability concerns reach not only the subject matter of the evidence, but also the methodology used by the proposed expert in arriving at his or her opinion, the expert's expertise and the extent to which the expert is shown to be impartial and objective.

88 Assessment of the reliability of proffered expert evidence has become the focus of much judicial attention, particularly where the expert advances what is purported to be scientific opinion: see, for example, *Daubert v. Merrell Dow Pharmaceuticals Inc.*, 509 U.S. 579 (1993); *J.-L.J.* at paras. 33-37; S. Casey Hill et al. at para. 12:30.20.30; Bruce D. Sales & Daniel W. Shuman, *Experts in Court Reconciling Law, Science, and Professional Knowledge* (Washington, D.C.: American Psychological Association, 2005).

89 In assessing the potential benefit to the trial process flowing from the admission of the evidence, the trial judge must intrude into territory customarily the exclusive domain of the jury in a criminal jury trial. The trial judge's evaluation is not, however, the same as the jury's ultimate assessment. The trial judge is

deciding only whether the evidence is worthy of being heard by the jury and not the ultimate question of whether the evidence should be accepted and acted upon.

90 The "cost" side of the ledger addresses the various risks inherent in the admissibility of expert opinion evidence, described succinctly by Binnie J. in *J.-L.J.* at para. 47 as "consumption of time, prejudice and confusion". Clearly, the most important risk is the danger that a jury will be unable to make an effective and critical assessment of the evidence. The complexity of the material underlying the opinion, the expert's impressive credentials, the impenetrable jargon in which the opinion is wrapped and the cross-examiner's inability to expose the opinion's shortcomings may prevent an effective evaluation of the evidence by the jury. There is a risk that a jury faced with a well presented firm opinion may abdicate its fact-finding role on the understandable assumption that a person labelled as an expert by the trial judge knows more about his or her area of expertise than do the individual members of the jury: *J.-L.J.* at para. 25.

91 In addition to the risk that the jury will yield its fact finding function, expert opinion evidence can also compromise the trial process by unduly protracting and complicating proceedings. Unnecessary and excessive resort to expert evidence can also give a distinct advantage to the party with the resources to hire the most and best experts - often the Crown in a criminal proceeding.

92 All of the risks described above will not inevitably arise in every case where expert evidence is offered. Nor will the risks have the same force in every case. For example, in this case, I doubt that the jury would have difficulty critically evaluating Dr. Totten's opinion. There was nothing complex or obscure about his methodology, the material he relied on in forming his opinion or the language in which he framed and explained his opinion. As when measuring the benefits flowing from the admission of expert evidence, the trial judge as "gatekeeper" must go beyond truisms about the risks inherent in expert evidence and come to grips with those risks as they apply to the particular circumstances of the individual case.

93 The cost-benefit analysis demands a consideration of the extent to which the proffered opinion evidence is necessary to a proper adjudication of the fact(s) to which that evidence is directed. In *Mohan*, Sopinka J. describes necessity as a separate criterion governing admissibility. I see the necessity analysis as a part of the larger cost-benefit analysis performed by the trial judge. In relocating the necessity analysis, I do not, however, depart from the role assigned to necessity by the *Mohan* criteria.

94 It seems self-evident that an expert opinion on an issue that the jury is fully equipped to decide without that opinion is unnecessary and should register a "zero" on the "benefit" side of the cost-benefit scale. Inevitably, expert opinion evidence that brings no added benefit to the process will be excluded: see, for example, *R. v. Batista* (2008), 238 C.C.C. (3d) 97 (Ont. C.A.), at paras. 45-47; *R. v. Nahar* (2004), 181 C.C.C. (3d) 449 (B.C.C.A.), at paras. 20-21. Opinion evidence that is essential to a jury's ability to understand and evaluate material

evidence will register high on the "benefit" side of the scale. However, the ultimate admissibility of the opinion, even where it is essential, will depend on not only its potential benefit, but on the potential prejudice to the trial process associated with its admission.

95 In many cases, the proffered opinion evidence will fall somewhere between the essential and the unhelpful. In those cases, the trial judge's assessment of the extent to which the evidence could assist the jury will be one of the factors to be weighed in deciding whether the benefits flowing from admission are sufficiently strong to overcome the costs associated with admission. In addressing the extent to which the opinion evidence is necessary, the trial judge will have regard to other facets of the trial process -such as the jury instruction - that may provide the jury with the tools necessary to adjudicate properly on the fact in issue without the assistance of expert evidence: *D.D.* at para. 33; *R. v. Bonisteel* (2008), 236 C.C.C. (3d) 170 (B.C.C.A.), at para. 69.

. . .

(e) Assessing the Reliability of Dr. Totten's Opinion

(1) The *Daubert* Factors Are Not Applicable

104 During Dr. Totten's evidence and the argument following his evidence, the trial judge continually referred to the reliability factors identified in *Daubert*, the leading American authority, which is approvingly referred to in the Supreme Court of Canada's decision in *J.-L.J.* In numerous lengthy dialogues with Crown counsel, the trial judge repeatedly challenged the Crown to establish the reliability of Dr. Totten's opinion using the *Daubert* factors. Those factors include the existence of measurable error rates, peer review of results, the use of random sampling and the ability of the tester to replicate his or her results.

105 In his reasons for excluding Dr. Totten's evidence, the trial judge treated the evidence as advancing a "novel scientific theory" (para. 38) put forward to "scientifically prove that Mr. Abbey's tattoo means he killed Simeon Peter" (para. 92). Having set Dr. Totten's opinion up as a scientific theory, the trial judge then tested the reliability of that theory as if it had been put forward as the product of an inquiry based on the scientific method. The trial judge's reasons are replete with references to the absence of error rates (paras. 56-59, 62-64), the failure to use random sampling (paras. 56-59), the absence of peer review of Dr. Totten's conclusions (para. 78) and the absence of any attempt to replicate Dr. Totten's findings (para. 78). It is clear that the trial judge viewed the absence of the factors identified in *Daubert* as fatal to the reliability of Dr. Totten's evidence. He said at para. 78:

> . . . without evidence on the rate of error, a peer review of his conclusions, or the replication of his findings, I am not satisfied that Dr. Totten's conclusion is not flawed.

106 The extent to which the Daubert factors dominated the trial judge's reliability analysis can be seen in the following passage from his reasons (para. 56):

One of the problems with accepting his methodology is that the common *indicia* of reliable, replicable, scientific studies are not present (nor could they be according to Dr. Totten) in his qualitative research. In order to generalize and extrapolate Dr. Totten's findings, or use his theory as a diagnostic tool, *I should have some knowledge about the statistical probability of the accuracy of his conclusions. To that end, his conclusions should be tested by applying them to a random sample of the population of street gangs who wear teardrop tattoos to see if his conclusion can be falsified.* [Emphasis added.]

107 This passage mischaracterizes Dr. Totten's evidence as presenting a "theory" to be used as a "diagnostic tool". This language, taken from the leading authority of *J.-L.J.*, does not fit Dr. Totten's evidence. I also do not understand the meaning of the reference to "random samples of the population of street gangs who wear teardrop tattoos". The persons interviewed by Dr. Totten were randomly selected in the sense that he did not seek out particular gang members. They were not randomly selected in the sense that Dr. Totten specifically excluded persons who had a strong motive to mislead him. It may be that the trial judge was simply saying that Dr. Totten's conclusions could have been tested through additional interviews with more street gang members from different gangs all of whom had teardrop tattoos. One cannot disagree that interviews with more gang members who had teardrop tattoos would have assisted in weighing Dr. Totten's opinion. However, that process is not the same as the process of random sampling as that term is used in the application of the scientific method.

108 It is not surprising that Dr. Totten's opinion could not pass scientific muster. While his research, and hence his opinion, could be regarded as scientific in the very broad sense of that word, as used in *McIntosh*, Dr. Totten did not pretend to employ the scientific method and did not depend on adherence to that methodology for the validity of his conclusions. As his opinion was not the product of scientific inquiry, its reliability did not rest on its scientific validity. Dr. Totten's opinion flowed from his specialized knowledge gained through extensive research, years of clinical work and his familiarity with the relevant academic literature. It was unhelpful to assess Dr. Totten's evidence against factors that were entirely foreign to his methodology. As Professors Sales and Shuman put it in their text, *Experts in Court: Reconciling Law, Science, and Professional Knowledge*, at pp. 74-75: "[f]or non-scientific expert testimony, scientific validity is an oxymoron."

109 Scientific validity is not a condition precedent to the admissibility of expert opinion evidence. Most expert evidence routinely heard and acted upon in the courts cannot be scientifically validated. For example, psychiatrists testify to the existence of various mental states, doctors testify as to the cause of an injury or death, accident reconstructionists testify to the location or cause of an accident, economists or rehabilitation specialists testify to future employment prospects and future care costs, fire marshals testify about the cause of a fire, professionals from a wide variety of fields testify as to the operative standard of care in their profession or the cause of a particular event. Like Dr. Totten, these experts do not support their opinions by reference to error rates, random samplings or the

replication of test results. Rather, they refer to specialized knowledge gained through experience and specialized training in the relevant field. To test the reliability of the opinion of these experts and Dr. Totten using reliability factors referable to scientific validity is to attempt to place the proverbial square peg into the round hole.

110 Tested exclusively against the *Daubert* factors, much of the expert evidence routinely accepted and acted upon in courts would be excluded despite its obvious reliability and value to the trial process. However, *Daubert* does not suggest that the factors it proposes are essential to the reliability inquiry. Instead, *Daubert*, at p. 484, describes that inquiry as "a flexible one". This flexibility was subsequently emphasized in *Kumho Tire Co. v. Carmichael*, 526 U.S. 137 (1999). Unlike *Daubert*, *Kumho Tire Co.* did not involve an opinion, the validity of which relied upon the scientific method. The expert's opinion in *Kumho Tire Co.* depended in part on scientific principles but also upon the knowledge of the witness gained through his experience and training.

111 In *Kumho Tire Co.*, the court made it clear that, while all expert opinion evidence must demonstrate a sufficient level of reliability to warrant its admissibility, a flexible approach to the determination of reliability was essential. Some *Daubert* factors, e.g. error rates, are not germane to some kinds of expert testimony. The court observed at p. 150:

> ... In other cases, the relevant reliability concerns may focus upon personal knowledge or experience. As the Solicitor General points out, there are many different kinds of experts, and many different kinds of expertise. . . . *Daubert* makes clear that the factors it mentions do *not* constitute a "definitive checklist or test." ... We agree with the Solicitor General that "the factors identified in *Daubert* may or may not be pertinent in assessing reliability, depending on the nature of the issue, the expert's particular expertise, and the subject of his testimony. [Emphasis in original; footnote omitted.]

112 An example of the flexible approach to the assessment of reliability favoured in *Daubert* and *Kumho Tire Co.* is found in *U.S. v. Hankey*, 203 F. 3d 1160 (9th Cir. 2000), a case involving expert evidence regarding gangs. There, the prosecution offered expert opinion evidence through a long-time undercover police officer of the "code of silence" that operated within the culture of certain urban street gangs. After referring to *Kumho Tire Co.* and the need to assess reliability by indicia that are relevant to the particular expertise advanced, the court said at p. 1169:

> Given the type of expert testimony proffered by the government, it is difficult to imagine that the court could have been more diligent in assessing relevance and reliability. *The Daubert factors (peer review, publication, potential error rate, etc.) simply are not applicable to this kind of testimony, whose reliability depends heavily on the knowledge and experience of the expert, rather than the methodology or theory behind it.* [Emphasis added.]

113 Several Canadian trial courts have reached a similar conclusion and admitted expert evidence about various features of gang culture relevant to the particular

prosecution, see e.g. *R. v. Wilson*; *R. v. H.J.H.*, [2002] B.C.J. No. 3103 (S.C.); *R. v. Grant*, [2005] O.J. No. 5891 (S.C.); *R. v. Lindsay*, [2004] O.J. No. 4097 (S.C.).

114 The same caution against the inappropriate use of the *Daubert* factors to assess the reliability of expert opinion evidence can be found in Canadian commentary. Professor Paciocco has observed:

> Clearly it is inappropriate to consider all expertise as science, or to require all expertise to attain the scientific method. Some expert witnesses rely on science only in a loose sense. Actuaries apply probability theory and mathematics to produce decidedly unscientific results. Appraisers make subjective assessments of objective data, as do family assessment experts. Professionals testifying to standards of care within their profession are doing nothing scientific. Yet *Daubert spawned a jurisprudence that was fixated for a time with science. This led lower courts to commit two kinds of error.* First, it caused some lower courts to hold that the *Daubert* test and the gatekeeping role is confined to scientific expertise. Experts who were not scientists would not be subjected to the reliability inquiry prescribed by *Daubert. Second, it caused other courts to apply the criteria listed in Daubert in a wooden fashion, even to non-scientific forms of expertise.* Each of these two kinds of errors was caused by the failure to take context into account. [Emphasis added.]

115 Commissioner Goudge made the same point in his report at p. 493:

> Forensic pathology provides a good example of a discipline that has not traditionally engaged in random testing or determining rates of error. The reasons are obvious: testing and reproducibility cannot be used to verify a cause of death. *The forensic pathologist's opinion must instead rely on specialized training, accepted standards and protocols within the forensic pathology community, accurate gathering of empirical evidence, attention to the limits of the discipline and the possibility of alternative explanations or error, knowledge derived from established peer-reviewed medical literature, and sound professional judgment.* [Emphasis added.]

116 The trial judge mischaracterized Dr. Totten's opinion as involving a novel scientific theory. It was not scientific. It was not novel. And it was not a theory. Dr. Totten's opinion was based on knowledge he had acquired about a particular culture through years of academic study, interaction in various ways with members of that culture and review of the relevant literature. He spoke to the meaning, as he understood it from his knowledge, of certain symbols within that culture. Dr. Totten's evidence could no more be regarded as a "scientific theory" than would evidence from a properly qualified expert to the effect that wearing certain clothing in a particular culture indicates that the wearer belonged to a particular religious sect.

117 The proper question to be answered when addressing the reliability of Dr. Totten's opinion was not whether it was scientifically valid, but whether his research and experiences had permitted him to develop a specialized knowledge about gang culture, and specifically gang symbology, that was sufficiently reliable to justify placing his opinion as to the potential meanings of the teardrop tattoo within that culture before the jury: see David H. Kaye, David E. Bernstein & Jennifer L. Mnookin, *The New Wigmore, A Treatise on Evidence: Expert Evidence* (New York: Aspen, 2004), at para. 9.3.4.

(2) The Relevant Reliability Factors

118 In holding that the trial judge improperly attempted to use the specific Daubert factors in assessing the reliability of Dr. Totten's evidence, I do not suggest that the Crown was not required to demonstrate threshold reliability. That reliability had to be determined, however, using tools appropriate to the nature of the opinion advanced by Dr. Totten.

119 As with scientifically based opinion evidence, there is no closed list of the factors relevant to the reliability of an opinion like that offered by Dr. Totten. I would suggest, however, that the following are some questions that may be relevant to the reliability inquiry where an opinion like that offered by Dr. Totten is put forward:

- To what extent is the field in which the opinion is offered a recognized discipline, profession or area of specialized training?
- To what extent is the work within that field subject to quality assurance measures and appropriate independent review by others in the field?
- What are the particular expert's qualifications within that discipline, profession or area of specialized training?
- To the extent that the opinion rests on data accumulated through various means such as interviews, is the data accurately recorded, stored and available?
- To what extent are the reasoning processes underlying the opinion and the methods used to gather the relevant information clearly explained by the witness and susceptible to critical examination by a jury?
- To what extent has the expert arrived at his or her opinion using methodologies accepted by those working in the particular field in which the opinion is advanced?
- To what extent do the accepted methodologies promote and enhance the reliability of the information gathered and relied on by the expert?
- To what extent has the witness, in advancing the opinion, honoured the boundaries and limits of the discipline from which his or her expertise arises?
- To what extent is the proffered opinion based on data and other information gathered independently of the specific case or, more broadly, the litigation process?

120 The significance of testing the expert's methodologies against those accepted in the field was highlighted in *Kumho Tire Co.* at p. 152:

> The objective of that requirement [the gatekeeper function] is to ensure the reliability and relevancy of expert testimony. *It is to make certain that an expert, whether basing testimony upon professional studies or personal experience, employs in the courtroom the same level of intellectual rigour that characterizes the practice of an expert in the relevant field.* [Emphasis added.]

121 The study of cultural mores within particular communities or groups in a community is a well-recognized field of study within the broader academic and professional disciplines of sociology, criminology and anthropology. Dr. Totten's expertise in this particular field was acknowledged by all involved in this case. There was no challenge to the manner in which Dr. Totten gathered the relevant data. By that I mean it was not suggested that the information he looked to had not been accurately recorded and memorialized by those involved in the various studies. These three features of his evidence should have factored into the trial

judge's assessment of the threshold reliability of Dr. Totten's evidence. They were not.

122 Dr. Totten testified at length about the techniques and methods he used in his research to assemble and verify the information he ultimately drew on to advance his opinion. While acknowledging that he could not ensure that all the information he received from gang members was accurate, he explained the various methods used in an attempt to maximize the veracity of the information received. Dr. Totten testified that the methodology he followed was well established within his field of study and was entirely consistent with the methods used by others conducting the same kind of research. For example, Dr. Totten explained several ways in which the concept of peer review was used in his field. His studies were all peer reviewed using those techniques.

123 The trial judge, as he was entitled to do, made his own assessment of the effectiveness of some of the specific techniques used by Dr. Totten to enhance the reliability of the information he received in his studies. However, the trial judge should have taken into account in his threshold reliability assessment the unchallenged evidence that Dr. Totten's work was done in accordance with the established and accepted methodology used in his field. Dr. Totten, by employing "the same level of intellectual rigour" (*Kumho Tire Co.* at p. 152) when advancing his opinion in the courtroom that he and his colleagues used in the course of their practice, enhanced the threshold reliability of the opinion based on that work.

124 Two other factors not mentioned by the trial judge were potentially important to the reliability assessment. First, Dr. Totten drew his conclusions from data gathered in research studies that had no connection to this case. There was no chance that in gathering the relevant information, Dr. Totten sought, consciously or subconsciously, to lend his expertise to one side of the legal controversy. "Confirmation bias" was not an issue. It cannot be suggested that Dr. Totten set out to confirm an existing belief about the meaning of teardrop tattoos when he conducted his research. Dr. Totten's neutrality when he gathered the information he ultimately looked to form the relevant opinion distinguishes his evidence from that of experts who are sought out to generate information for the purposes of litigation, or those who come to a case with firmly held preconceived notions that place the expert firmly on one side of the controversy.

125 Second, neither the methodology used by Dr. Totten nor his opinion concerning the teardrop tattoos were complex or difficult for the layperson to understand and evaluate. I have no doubt that the methods Dr. Totten employed, the data those methods produced and his opinion based on those data could be critically evaluated and independently assessed by a jury. This was not rocket science.

126 I am satisfied that the factors outlined above, taken in combination, offer a firm basis upon which a trial judge could conclude that Dr. Totten's opinion, that the inscription of a teardrop tattoo on the face of a young male gang member carried one of three possible meanings within the urban gang culture, was sufficiently reliable to justify its admission.

. . .

[Justice Doherty also decided that the three Malvern Crew members who testified for the Crown should have been allowed to testify about the meaning of a teardrop tattoo in the gang culture in which they operated. All three would have stated that one meaning of such a tattoo is that the wearer had killed a rival gang member. The trial judge had treated this evidence as akin to expert evidence and excluded it on the basis that the grounds for the gang members' beliefs about the meaning of this symbol were unreliable. However, the Ontario Court of Appeal held that these witnesses were not put forward as experts; rather, their evidence was based on their knowledge gained from living within and being part of a particular group culture. The Court held that they should have been allowed to testify on that basis.]

. . . .

Appeal allowed, new trial ordered.

In her Criminal Reports annotation on *Abbey,* Lisa Dufraimont writes in part as follows:

> The new analytical framework proposed in *Abbey* improves on the *Mohan* test in several respects. First, based on the insight that *Mohan* test includes two very different kinds of criteria, Justice Doherty suggests that the pre-conditions to admissibility – a checklist of criteria that must be satisfied before the expert evidence can be admitted – should be separated from the discretionary cost-benefit analysis that lies at the core of the trial judge's gatekeeper function. One implication of this separation is that the relevance criterion that was unitary in *Mohan* is broken down under *Abbey*. Bare logical relevance is a pre-condition to admissibility that can be dispensed with as a preliminary matter. But the cost-benefit analysis associated with relevance in the *Mohan* sense – the question whether the evidence is worth what it costs – should be considered in the trial judge's exercise of discretion as gatekeeper.
>
> Another significant innovation in *Abbey* is the emphasis on the trial judge's duty, at a preliminary stage, to define the scope of the expert's evidence. Clearly Justice Doherty does not envision trial judges' gatekeeping role as a passive one of deciding which experts pass muster. Instead, he stresses the trial judge's role in shaping expert evidence by defining its limits and even, potentially, its language.
>
> Finally, *Abbey* provides useful guidance on how to assess the reliability of expert evidence that is not founded in the scientific method. Clearly, there is nothing to be gained by searching for error rates or random samples in disciplines where these trappings of the scientific method find no application. Justice Doherty's suggested approach to the reliability question is sensibly focussed on assessing expert opinion on the basis of the norms and methods appropriate to the particular subject matter and field of learning.

The Ontario Court of Appeal in *Abbey* has set out a new framework based on *Mohan* to be used in all cases including where the expert is giving evidence based not on the scientific method but rather on "specialized knowledge gained through extensive research, years of clinical work and . . . familiarity with the relevant academic literature." [at para. 108]

Justice Doherty infuses reliability as part of the gatekeeper stage of admissibility for all cases of expert evidence. This also reflects the *Report of the*

Goudge *Inquiry into Pediatric Forensic Pathology in Ontario.*[227] **Is this consistent with the Supreme Court trilogy? Is it now no longer necessary to determine whether the science or technique is novel?**

In *Mohan,* Justice Sopinka requires that the expert evidence be necessary. If the evidence of the gang members as to the significance of the teardrop was to be admitted as the Court of Appeal held, why was the evidence of the expert necessary?

Professor David Paciocco in "Unplugging Juke Box Testimony in an Adversarial System; Strategies for changing the Tune on Partial Expects"[228] suggests that the *Mohan* tests do not address the issue of bias directly enough. He calls for codes of conduct to recognise experts owe a special duty to courts of impartial advice and for exclusion after a *voir dire* if an opposing party can provide a realistic foundation that the testimony may be biased. **Do you agree with these suggestions? Does** *Abbey* **address some of his concerns?**

Do you think that *Abbey* **will result in the admission of more expert evidence?**

(b) Examples

Do you agree with the following applications of *Mohan* **and** *J. (J.-L.)***? Do you think that applying** *Trochym* **and/or** *Abbey* **would lead to a different and better result?**

We turn now to consideration of applications of *Mohan* and *J. (J.-L.).*

R. v. TERCEIRA
(1998), 15 C.R. (5th) 359, 123 C.C.C. (3d) 1 (Ont. C.A.)

The accused was convicted of murder. Hair, fibre, blood and DNA evidence which matched the accused was left on the floor at the attack site and on the victim's clothing. One of the main arguments on the appeal related to the admissibility of the DNA evidence and the instruction to the jury respecting it. The Supreme Court in an endorsement agreed with the courts below.

FINLAYSON J.A. (BROOKE and McKINLAY JJ.A., concurring):—

. . . .

DNA profiling is a comparatively new method of providing identification evidence for use in criminal cases. DNA evidence is used essentially for two purposes. The first use of DNA evidence is as evidence that the suspect's DNA "matches" the DNA found in blood, semen or tissue recovered at a crime scene. In this way, the DNA evidence serves an exclusionary purpose. In the absence of further qualifications, a "match" is no more than a failure to exclude a suspect's

---

227 (Toronto: Ontario Ministry of the Attorney General, 2008). See a full review by David Paciocco, "Taking a 'Goudge' out of Bluster and Blarney: an 'Evidence-Based Approach' to Expert Testimony", (2009) 13 *Can. Crim. L. Rev.* 135.

228 (2009) *Queen's L.J.* 565.

DNA from the crime scene. The debate at trial with respect to the determination of a match, as was the case during the trial of this matter, will often focus on the methodology used to determine a match. The second branch of the analysis of DNA evidence involves the application of population genetics. Probability statistics are introduced in an attempt to bolster the significance of a "match". The scientist determines, according to an established database of known DNA samples, the statistical likelihood that another individual person would have the same DNA pattern as that of the suspect. Simply stated, this second branch considers the statistical likelihood of a random DNA match. Cross-examination of the expert tendering DNA evidence serving this second purpose will usually focus on the methodology used to calculate the numbers reflecting the frequency of the DNA pattern. The DNA evidence in the present case was used by the Crown for the above two purposes.

. . . .

Both Crown and defence counsel on the DNA *voir dire* devoted a considerable portion of their submissions to a discussion of the standard to be applied in relation to the admission of novel scientific evidence. Crown counsel discussed the standard of "relevancy and helpfulness" as well as "relevancy and reliability". Defence counsel made submissions in favour of the adoption of the more restrictive "*Frye*" test articulated by the United States Supreme Court in *Frye v. United States*, 293 F.1013. Both counsel explicitly referred the trial judge to the decision in *R. v. Johnston* (1992), 69 C.C.C. (3d) 395, 12 C.R. (4th) 99 (Ont. Gen. Div.), wherein Langdon J. adopted a "reliability" standard. The trial judge characterized the defence position on the *voir dire* as urging "that the Crown has not produced sufficient evidence on the *voir dire* to support the reliability and admissibility of Pamella Newall's techniques in analysis". The foregoing demonstrates that the trial judge was aware that initial determinations of reliability would be required before the proposed DNA evidence could be proffered at trial. Moreover, the appellant concedes that the trial judge recognized that reliability was a preliminary finding of fact that would need to be made before the proposed DNA evidence was admissible.

. . . .

Relying upon the judgment of the Supreme Court of Canada in *R. v. Mohan*, counsel for the appellant submits that before the jury can be permitted to hear the evidence of DNA testing, the trial judge is required as a matter of law to conduct what he calls a "*Mohan* type hearing" in order to satisfy himself beyond a reasonable doubt as to the reliability of the evidence adduced by the experts for the Crown. By this counsel for the appellant suggests that the trial judge must satisfy himself as to the acceptance of the technology in the scientific community, the expertise of the Crown witnesses in that field, and the accuracy of the tests carried out pursuant to that technology, among other factors. All this to the criminal standard of proof. Then, and only then, can the same evidence be recalled for the consideration of the jury.

I have some considerable difficulty with this submission which, with respect, reflects a misreading of *Mohan*. In my opinion, the rules laid down by Sopinka J. in *R. v. Mohan* do not signify a departure from the common law rules relating to the admission of opinion evidence in a criminal trial, nor do they purport to do so. The four criteria for the admissibility of expert testimony are derived from case-law. . . . Prior to *Mohan*, when relevant expert opinion evidence has been proffered, Canadian courts focused on two factors in determining its admissibility: the special knowledge criterion and the expertise criterion. In *R. v. Abbey*, [1982] 2 S.C.R. 24 at p. 42, Dickson J. provided the following formulation of the "special knowledge" requirement for the admissibility of expert evidence:

> With respect to matters calling for special knowledge, an expert in the field may draw inferences and state his opinion. An expert's function is precisely this: to provide the judge and jury with a ready-made inference which the judge and jury, due to the technical nature of the facts, are unable to formulate. "An expert's opinion is admissible to furnish the Court with scientific information which is likely to be outside the experience and knowledge of a judge or jury. If on the proven facts a judge or jury can form their own conclusions without help, then the opinion of the expert is unnecessary (*R. v. Turner* (1974), 60 Cr. App. R. 80, at p. 83, per Lawton L.J.).

. . . .

It is to be observed that the word "reliable" is not listed among Sopinka J.'s four criteria. It is, however, discussed under "relevance" under his "cost-benefit analysis" as to whether expert evidence that is otherwise logically relevant may be excluded on the basis that its probative value is overborne by its prejudicial effect.

. . . .

In the appeal before this court the tension is between the probative value of the opinion evidence versus its prejudicial effect in the sense that its effect on the jury may be out of proportion to its reliability. *Mohan* stands as authority for the proposition that expert evidence which may be logically probative of an issue at trial may be nonetheless excluded in certain circumstances. Additionally, in light of the judicial reasoning from *Mohan*, since we are confronted with what was at the time of trial perceived to be a novel scientific theory or technique, we are concerned with the threshold issue of reliability, i.e., is the science itself valid. As I understand *Mohan*, with reference to the case in appeal, the requirement of a basic threshold of reliability as a pre-condition to admissibility is met where the trial judge is satisfied as to the reliability of DNA profiling as a novel scientific technique. Where the Crown and defence part company is with respect to the extent of the inquiry necessary to establish this pre-condition.

Our task is considerably narrowed by the concession of appellant's counsel that he is not suggesting that DNA profiling has not been found reliable in other jurisdictions. The appellant does not take issue with the microbiological aspects of DNA profiling. No general concern was raised at trial about the ability of the Centre of Forensic Science ("CFS") to extract DNA from biological substances and to isolate and remove regions on human chromosomes which are suitable for testing nor to determine whether any two samples were a "match" one to the other. Nor is counsel for the appellant suggesting that the process used by the CFS in this case, involving RFLP or "restriction fragment length polymorphism" analysis, is not an accepted methodology for DNA profiling. Rather, the complaint was that the DNA laboratory was only established by the CFS a few months prior to the testing in this case and there was no general acceptance of its specific methodology used to determine the statistical likelihood of a random match. The attack was not upon the technology of DNA profiling per se but upon the ability of the CFS, notably its principal expert Pamella Newall, to reliably utilize it. In addition, the appellant challenged the introduction of the probability figures as their prejudicial effect would exceed the probative value of presenting quantitative statements of random match probability as opposed to qualitative measures.

. . . .

The jury was given frequency numbers that ranged from one in 1,500 to one in 1.8 million. The appellant concedes the admissibility of qualitative expressions of match significance (such as "rare" or "common") without the specifics afforded by statistics where DNA evidence is admitted showing a match between the DNA found on the crime scene and the DNA of a suspect, counsel for the appellant objects simply to the admission of the numbers themselves. In this case, it would be difficult to translate the figures the experts were prepared to use into neutral language, but all that aside, why would the defence want to do so? The fact that there are competing figures which differ so radically should be before the jury for its assessment. The range of numeric frequency determined by the various experts was fertile ground for cross-examination. This is a classic case for the application of the language of Dickson C.J.C. in *R. v. Corbett*, [1988] 1 S.C.R. 670 at p. 692:

> The very strength of the jury is that the ultimate issue of guilt or innocence is determined by a group of ordinary citizens who are not legal specialists and who bring to the legal process a healthy measure of common sense. The jury is, of course, bound to follow the law as it is explained by the trial judge. Jury directions are often long and difficult, but the experience of trial judges is that juries do perform their duty according to the law. We should regard with grave suspicion arguments which assert that depriving the jury of all relevant information is preferable to giving them everything, with a careful explanation as to any limitations on the use to which they may put that information.

I do not believe that there should be an absolute prohibition against the introduction of specific match figures. The appellant correctly notes that the case-law reflects conflicting conclusions as to the admissibility of DNA probability statistics in this case, and it might be in others. I would leave the matter to the discretion of the trial judge in the particular case.[229]

---

229 *Terceira* was affirmed (1999), 142 C.C.C. (3d) 95 (S.C.C.) and applied in *R. v. Fisher* (2003), 18 C.R. (6th) 377, 179 C.C.C. (3d) 138 (Sask. C.A.).

R. v. McINTOSH
(1997), 117 C.C.C. (3d) 385 (Ont. C.A.)

The accused were convicted of various offences as a result of a robbery. The case for the Crown consisted primarily of three eyewitnesses. The trial judge refused to admit expert opinion evidence from a defence psychologist tendered on the issue of eyewitness identification. The psychologist had written extensively on the psychology of witness testimony and claimed that it was a specialty which he had pursued over the years. His evidence related to the frailties of eyewitness identification, including factors present at the time of the offence that would impair the witness' ability to make an accurate identification, the problem of cross-racial identification, the quality of memory recall for perceived events over different time spans, and the influence of "post-event information" on memory.

FINLAYSON J.A. (LABROSSE and AUSTIN JJ.A. concurring):—

. . . .

The general tenor of [the expert's] evidence is summed up in his own words:

> Well, the understanding of jurors, and how they perceive is what psychologists spend their lives doing. We hope to be able to assist the judge or the jury on the various levels and factors of what would lead to a good or a poor identification. It is not my job to decide whether or not that is the answer. All I can do is assist the trier in understanding, 'Here are the reasons why it could be a good identification or a poor one'.

I am astonished at the passivity of the Crown at trial and on appeal with respect to this type of evidence. At trial, Crown counsel contented himself with the early observation that the witness had said nothing that would convince him that a psychologist would know what information would be "probative" to the trial. However, he did not cross-examine Dr. Yarmey on his qualifications, or at all, and seemed to accept that the substance of his testimony was properly the subject-matter of expert evidence. On appeal, Crown counsel limited his argument to the submission that we should defer to the trial judge who rejected the evidence in the exercise of her discretion. He was careful, however, to state that there could be cases in which this evidence could be admitted.

This posture is not surprising given the reliance by the Crown on the "soft sciences" in other cases. In *R. v. Norman* (1993), 87 C.C.C. (3d) 153 (C.A.) the Crown introduced psychiatric evidence of child abuse accommodation syndrome which was misused by the trial judge and resulted in this court setting aside the conviction of the accused. In *R. v. Edwards* (1996), 105 C.C.C. (3d) 21 (C.A.) (leave to appeal to S.C.C. refused August 29, 1996) the Crown attempted unsuccessfully to introduce expert testimony in the form of affidavits to support two Crown appeals against sentences imposed upon the respondents following their pleas of guilty to charges of attempted spousal homicide. The affidavits were sworn by three persons with differing professional backgrounds. All three deponents, however, had written extensively on issues relating to spousal abuse. They advocated the need for greater public awareness and participation in dealing with this pressing social problem. This court dismissed the motion for fresh evidence, holding that it was of marginal relevance to the sentencing issue and smacked of special pleading.

In the light of the limited argument before this court on the matter, it is evident that this is not the case to engage in a full-scale analysis as to whether the type of evidence proffered by Dr. Yarmey is admissible in any circumstance. However, I do not intend to leave the subject without raising some warning flags. In my respectful opinion, the courts are overly eager to abdicate their fact-finding responsibilities to "experts" in the field of the behavioural sciences. We are too quick to say that a particular witness possesses special knowledge and experience going beyond that of the trier of fact without engaging in an analysis of the subject-matter of that expertise. I do not want to be taken as denigrating the integrity of Dr. Yarmey's research or of his expertise in the field of psychology, clearly one of the learned sciences, but simply because a person has lectured and written extensively on a subject that is of interest to him or her does not constitute him or her an expert for the purposes of testifying in a court of law on the subject of that specialty. It seems to me that before we even get to the point of examining the witness's expertise, we must ask ourselves if the subject-matter of his testimony admits of expert testimony. Where is the evidence in this case that there is a recognized body of scientific knowledge that defines rules of human behaviour affecting memory patterns such that any expert in that field can evaluate the reliability of the identification made by a particular witness in a given case? Paraphrasing freely from the definition of "science" in *The Shorter Oxford English Dictionary on Historical Principles*, it seems to me that before a witness can be permitted to testify as an expert, the court must be satisfied that the subject-matter of his or her expertise is a branch of study in psychology concerned with a connected body of demonstrated truths or with observed facts systematically classified and more or less connected together by a common hypothesis operating under general laws. The branch should include trustworthy methods for the discovery of new truths within its own domain. I should add that it would be helpful if there was evidence that the existence of such a branch was generally accepted within the science of psychology.

The definitive judgment on the admissibility of expert evidence in criminal cases is *R. v. Mohan* which was relied upon by both parties to this appeal. . . . I would caution courts to scrutinize the nature of the subject-matter of the expert testimony. Any natural or unnatural phenomenon may become the subject of an investigation conducted according to the scientific method. The scientific method requires the formation of a hypothesis, the testing of the hypothesis using reliable methodology, the examination of the results (usually with statistical analysis) and the formation of a conclusion. However, the fact that the testimony recites the application of the scientific method does not necessarily render the original object of study a matter requiring opinion evidence at trial.

As is implicit in what I have written above, I have some serious reservations as to whether the "Psychology of Witness Testimony" is an appropriate area for opinion evidence at all. I acknowledge that the subject is interesting and Dr. Yarmey's presentation is informative. I also applaud his evidence that he lectures on the subject to police officers. We should all be reminded of the frailties of identification evidence. However, I would have to be persuaded that the subject is a recognized branch of psychology. Even if it is, I do not think that it meets the tests for relevance and necessity set out in *Mohan*.

In the case in appeal, I think that I can deal with relevance and necessity together because they appear to overlap. This opinion evidence is noteworthy in that, unlike most expert psychological or psychiatric testimony, it is not directed to making the testimony of a particular witness more understandable to the trier of fact and therefore more believable (e.g., an explanation of repressed memory syndrome or battered spouse syndrome). This opinion evidence is directed to instructing the jury that all witnesses have problems in perception and recall with respect to what occurred during any given circumstance that is brief and stressful. Accordingly, Dr. Yarmey is not testifying to matters that are outside the normal experience of the trier of fact: he is reminding the jury of the normal experience.

Perhaps I can develop this point through illustration. I suggest that it would be a different situation if a Crown witness had demonstrated remarkable memory feats which would strike the normal juror as startling and therefore less capable of belief. In this hypothetical situation, expert evidence might be admissible to show that the witness is an autistic savant and that such exceptional memory feats are often associated with this syndrome. Or to deal with an example closer to the case at hand, Dr. Yarmey was prepared to testify as to the problems of "cross-racial identification": the perception that members of one race tend to think that members of another race "all look alike". Dr. Yarmey's research supports this popular perception and his opinion on the subject is hardly surprising. But before this opinion evidence could be outside the normal experience of the jurors, would he not have had to conclude that the perception was false and that a cross-racial identification problem did not exist?

This is not to say that a reminder as to cross-racial identification is not appropriate in a case where it is an issue. However, the argument that impresses me is that such a reminder from the trial judge is more than adequate, especially when it is incorporated into the well-established warnings in the standard jury charge on the frailties of identification evidence. Writings, such as those of Dr. Yarmey, are helpful in stimulating an ongoing evaluation of the problem of witness identification, but they should be used to update the judge's charge, not instruct the jury. I think that there is a very real danger that such evidence would "distort the fact-finding process".

More than that I am concerned that much of what Dr. Yarmey and those who support him are saying is that our jury system is not adequate to the task of determining the guilt of an accused person beyond a reasonable doubt where identification evidence is pivotal to the case for the Crown. Much of Dr. Yarmey's evidence might well give us pause to consider whether our present jury instruction is adequate to the task, but to admit such evidence in the particular case may foster apprehension in the timorous juror and give him or her an excuse for not discharging that juror's duty to the community that he or she has sworn to serve.

An additional problem is that this evidence introduces yet another potentially contentious issue into the trial. If the defence is entitled to call this opinion evidence, the Crown is entitled to rebut it. This means that the jury has to be instructed as how conflicts in the opinions of experts are to be resolved, and when resolved, as to the limited use of the evidence. The jury must also be told that to the extent that the opinion evidence contradicts anything said by the trial judge in his or her charge, the jury must reject the evidence and accept what is said by the judge. Would it not be simpler to have the trial judge give the instruction in the first place?

In the case in appeal, the trial judge had the benefit of hearing all of Dr. Yarmey's evidence and of listening to full argument as to its merits and admissibility. In the end, she appears to have had the same reservations as I do with respect to its quality. While she premised her ultimate refusal to admit the evidence upon the failure to meet the necessity test in *Mohan*, in the course of delivering her reasons she stated:

> I do not agree, based on the evidence I've heard from Dr. Yarmey, that the science has advanced that far away from the common experience of jurors.

To address the specific ground of appeal in this case, I am of the opinion that the manner in which the issue of identification was handled by the court (and by "court" I mean the trial judge and counsel for the Crown and the defence) was a model of fairness. The trial judge was correct in rejecting the proffered expert evidence. Her charge to the jury, following the very full closing arguments of all counsel, was exemplary. She impressed upon the jury the frailties of witness identification evidence generally and then, in considerable detail, she set out the identification problems as they applied to the particular facts of the case.

. . . .

We were referred to a number of cases from courts in the United States where expert evidence on identification has been accepted. We were also referred to *William Daubert v. Merrell Dow Pharmaceuticals Inc.*, 113 S.Ct. Rep. 2786 (1993), a decision of the United States Supreme Court which considered the admissibility of expert testimony generally under the Federal Rules of Evidence, Rule 702, 28 U.S.C.A. These cases must be approached with caution because the rules of court under consideration are dissimilar to ours. Moreover, juries in this jurisdiction receive significantly more assistance from the trial judge in their instruction than do juries in the United States. For this reason alone, expert testimony on matters which are covered by the jury instruction has less appeal. Our judges are not only encouraged to comment on the evidence, there are some cases in which they are obliged to do so.

This was such a case and the trial judge took full advantage of it. She was in a far better position than any witness or counsel to point out the frailties of the identification evidence, and her opinions, which she expressed, would have a very positive effect on the jury. She was also in a position to place these frailties in the context of the case for the Crown as a whole and she did that as well. This was not a "straight" identification case as counsel for the appellants submitted. After reading the complete charge of the trial judge on all of the evidence, I am left with no concern about the soundness of the verdict in this case. I would reject this ground of appeal.[230]

Given the findings of many inquiries and studies in Canada, the United States and England that identification evidence is a major cause of wrongful convictions[231] is it time to over-rule *McIntosh?*[232]

R. v. OLSCAMP
(1994), 35 C.R. (4th) 37, 95 C.C.C. (3d) 466 (Ont. Gen. Div.)

This was a ruling regarding the admissibility of expert evidence intended to be called by the Crown in support of the complainant's testimony that she had been sexually abused. Dr. W would testify if permitted that the girl displayed symptoms of a child who had been sexually abused.

CHARRON J.:—

. . . .

[D]efence counsel took serious issue at the hearing of this motion with both Dr. Wieland's personal qualifications and the validity of the theory being advanced. Consequently, Dr. Wieland testified for an additional three and a half days. Ultimately, the determinative question was not so much whether Dr. Wieland could give the proposed opinion evidence but whether anyone could do so having regard to the present state of knowledge in the field.

. . . .

The evidence is uncontroverted that this field of inquiry is a relatively recent one in the behavioural sciences. At the hearing of this motion, Dr. Wieland conceded that there is no existing valid profile of the sexually abused child. One article put to her in cross-examination appears to summarize well the existing state of knowledge in the field. Dr. Herbert N. Weissman in his article entitled

---

230 On the issue of the helpfulness of expert testimony on eye-witness identification, see Loftus and Doyle, *Eyewitness Testimony, Civil and Criminal*, 3d ed. (Lexis Law Publishing, 1997).

231 See for example Cory, P., The Inquiry Regarding Thomas Sophonow, "Recommendations", at http://www.gov.mb.ca/justice/sophonow/recommendations/english.html. See also the discussion of the admissibility of expert evidence in this context in D. Schermbrucker, "Eyewitness Evidence: The Role of Experts in the Criminal Courts" ADGN/RP-186 and S. Woller, "Rethinking The Role of Expert Testimony Regarding the Reliability of Eyewitness Identifications in New York" (2004), 79 New York Law School Law Review 323.

232 *McIntosh* was followed in *R. v. Woodard* (2009), 245 C.C.C. (3d) 522 (Man. C.A.), holding that the eyewitness expert had been rightly rejected as superfluous. A week earlier, a trial judge, Sinclair J., in *Henderson* (2009) 67 C.R. (6th) 132 (Man. Q.B.) admitted the evidence of such an expert. In his view, eyewitness evidence should be excluded where it only reminds jurors of what they already know but admitted where it lies outside common experience, overcomes myths or provides scientifically sound counterintuitive information. In her Criminal Reports annotation, Lisa Dufraimont applauds this test for deciding whether evidence of eyewitness experts should exceptionally be admitted.

"Forensic Psychological Examination of the Child Witness in Cases of Alleged Sexual Abuse" (1991), 61 Amer. J. Orthopsychiat., 48 states as follows at p. 52:

. . . .

> Mental health professionals may be called upon to give opinions as to whether abuse has occurred and whether harm exists as an element of abuse. Controversial methods associated with "profile validity" are sometimes applied, where the expert testifies as to the characteristics of abused children or the characteristics of child abusers. . . .
>
> The psycholegal literature illustrates the kinds of misconceptions that are common in this regard. Foremost among these is that there exists some form of valid, generally accepted profile of the child victim and of the child offender. There is none. . . .
>
> No reliable constellation of historical, demographic, personality, or other factors has been found that accurately characterizes either the child victim or the child offender. Neither is there any reliable psychological or physiological test or method for determining whether a child has been sexually abused or whether someone has committed an act of sexual abuse. . . .
>
> A diverse array of symptoms is found in a relatively small percentage of molested children, ranging from negligible distress to severe disturbance. Symptoms commonly mentioned include fear, anxiety, depression, anger, withdrawal, sexual preoccupation or precocity, and school and sleep difficulties. Symptoms, however, do not imply etiology, and no symptom constellation has been found sufficiently and substantially associated with sexual abuse so as to constitute a syndrome. All of the characteristics enumerated have also been found to be commonly present in child populations with no history of sexual abuse. Therefore, behavior assumed by some to be indicative of sexual abuse may in fact be so related, but may also be attributable to normal developmental variations, emotional or physical abuse, neglect, family conflict and parental discord, and modelling behavior imitative of adults observed in person or on videotapes or television.

. . . .

[The Court then reviewed much of the scientific literature in the field.]

The present state of knowledge in the field is such that the soundness and reliability of any expert opinion purporting to characterize behavioral symptoms as "consistent with sexual abuse" cannot be demonstrated. Indeed, if there is any consensus to be found among the experts, it is that there is no valid profile in existence which can enable one to identify a child who has been sexually abused. While the symptoms that have often been identified as "consistent with abuse" may indeed be related to the fact that a child has been sexually abused, the research shows that no single symptom or constellation of symptoms has been found to have any real discriminant validity, i.e., they do not serve to single out children who have been subjected to sexual abuse from children who have suffered some other kind of abuse or trauma or even from the general population of children.

. . . .

Expert opinion evidence about the general behavioural and psychological characteristics of child victims of sexual abuse has often been admitted in

Canadian criminal trials. The admissibility of this kind of evidence for certain purposes has been confirmed by a number of Canadian Courts of Appeal and by the Supreme Court of Canada: see *R. v. Marquard*; *R. v. B. (R.H.)*; *R. v. B. (G.)*; *R. v. F. (J.E.)*; *Khan v. College of Physicians & Surgeons (Ontario)*; *R. v. T. (S.)*; *R. v. C. (R.A.)*; *R. v. H. (E.L.)*; *R. v. Beliveau.* [Citations omitted.] It does not appear however that the validity of the very theory being advanced was contested in any of these reported cases. In this case, it was.

The Supreme Court of Canada recently has reiterated the governing principles for admissibility of expert opinion evidence in its unanimous judgment in *R. v. Mohan.* . . . Although the proposed evidence is certainly logically relevant to an issue in the case, its probative value, for the reasons set out earlier, is extremely limited. On the other hand, its prejudicial value can be overwhelming. This trial will turn on a question of credibility. Although a distinction can be made between evidence going to credibility alone and this kind of evidence admitted in support of the complainant's testimony, the line is a very fine one. The admission of evidence "[d]ressed up in scientific language" . . . in support of the complainant's testimony may well be given far more weight by the jury than it deserves and may even become determinative of the ultimate issue. The prejudicial effect of this evidence so far outweighs its low probative value that the matter cannot simply be left to be remedied by cross-examination and special instructions to the jury. The evidence should not be admitted.

Furthermore, it cannot be said that its admission is necessary for a proper verdict to be arrived at. While the proposed evidence is likely outside the experience and knowledge of the trier of fact, it is not yet within the experience and knowledge of the experts themselves with a sufficient degree of reliability to be useful. The expert's methodology and the validity of the theory advanced would become the central issue on trial and would consume most of the time and effort expended. The resulting cost to the trial process far exceeds any benefit that could be gained.

The proposed expert opinion evidence does not meet the test and is not admissible. Based on the present state of the art, the evidence could not be offered by any expert in the field.[233]

R. v. MARQUARD
1993 CarswellOnt 995, 1993 CarswellOnt 127, [1993] 4 S.C.R. 223, 25 C.R. (4th) 1, 85 C.C.C. (3d) 193

The accused was charged with aggravated assault on her 3 1/2 year-old grand-daughter. The allegation was that she put the complainant's face against a hot stove door as a way of disciplining her. In her unsworn testimony, the complainant testified that her "nana" had put her on the stove. The accused and her husband testified that they heard the complainant screaming and when they

---

233 Regarding how evidence rules ought to respond to syndromes, compare Raeder, "The Double-Edged Sword: Admissibility of Battered Woman Syndrome" (1996), 67 U. Col. L. Rev. 789 and Faigman, "The Syndromic Lawyer Syndrome" (1996), U. Col. L. Rev. 817.

arrived saw that she had burned herself trying to light a cigarette with a butane lighter. The defence called Dr. Mian to testify that the complainant had told hospital staff that she had been burned with a lighter. The Crown cross-examined Dr. Mian and elicited evidence about whether in her opinion, the complainant was telling the truth. The admissibility of this evidence was one of the issues before the Supreme Court.

MCLACHLIN J. (speaking for the Court on this point):

5. Expert Comment on the Credibility of the Child

47 The defence called Dr. Mian to prove that the child, upon arriving at Sick Children's Hospital, told the staff that she had burned herself with a lighter. The Crown, in cross-examination, elicited from Dr. Mian the opinion that the child was lying when she told her that she had burned herself with a cigarette lighter. She testified that it is quite common that children "will initially ... give the accidental explanation and later on will give us a story that is more consistent with her injury which is then put in a more convincing [manner] which we believe is the first disclosure of what actually happened." She also testified that even if the child's burn had looked like a lighter burn, she would have been suspicious of the child's story "because of the way the child said it...."

48 Dr. Mian went on to buttress her view that the child's actual explanation was a lie by reference to the behaviour of abused children:

> There's another reason [why children initially lie] which is that children who have been abused often feel that they are responsible for the behaviour that was done to them, for the injury that was inflicted on them.... Therefore if the care taker then takes them to the hospital and they're feeling that they did something wrong to elicit this punishment, they're certainly not going to want to tell the hospital staff that they did something wrong because they feel if my mom or whoever did this to me because of what I did, I wonder what these people who are strangers are going to do to me because of what I did.

The purport of this evidence was clear. Dr. Mian was of the view that the child was lying when she told the hospital staff that she had burned herself with a lighter, and that the child's second story—the one she told at trial—was the truth.

49 It is a fundamental axiom of our trial process that the ultimate conclusion as to the credibility or truthfulness of a particular witness is for the trier of fact, and is not the proper subject of expert opinion. This Court affirmed that proposition in *R. v. Béland, supra*, at p. 408, in rejecting the use of polygraph examinations as a tool to determine the credibility of witnesses:

> From the foregoing comments, it will be seen that the rule against oath-helping, that is, adducing evidence solely for the purpose of bolstering a witness's credibility, is well grounded in authority.

A judge or jury who simply accepts an expert's opinion on the credibility of a witness would be abandoning its duty to itself determine the credibility of the witness. Credibility must always be the product of the judge or jury's view of the diverse ingredients it has perceived at trial, combined with experience, logic and an intuitive sense of the matter: see *R. v. B. (G.)* (1988), 65 Sask. R. 134 (C.A.), at p. 149, per Wakeling J.A., affirmed [1990] 2 S.C.R. 3. Credibility is a matter within the competence of lay people. Ordinary people draw conclusions about whether someone is lying or telling the truth on a daily basis. The expert who testifies on credibility is not sworn to the heavy duty of a judge or juror. Moreover, the expert's opinion may be founded on factors which are not in the evidence upon which the judge and juror are duty-bound to render a true verdict. Finally, credibility is a notoriously difficult problem, and the expert's opinion may be all too readily accepted by a frustrated jury as a convenient basis upon which to resolve its difficulties. All these considerations have contributed to the wise policy of the law in rejecting expert evidence on the truthfulness of witnesses.

50 On the other hand, there may be features of a witness's evidence which go beyond the ability of a lay person to understand, and hence which may justify expert evidence. This is particularly the case in the evidence of children. For example, the ordinary inference from failure to complain promptly about a sexual assault might be that the story is a fabricated afterthought, born of malice or some other calculated stratagem. Expert evidence has been properly led to explain the reasons why young victims of sexual abuse often do not complain immediately. Such evidence is helpful; indeed it may be essential to a just verdict.

51 For this reason, there is a growing consensus that while expert evidence on the ultimate credibility of a witness is not admissible, expert evidence on human conduct and the psychological and physical factors which may lead to certain behaviour relevant to credibility, is admissible, provided the testimony goes beyond the ordinary experience of the trier of fact. Professor A. Mewett describes the permissible use of this sort of evidence as "putting the witness's testimony in its proper context." He states in the editorial "Credibility and Consistency" (1991), 33 *Crim. L.Q.* 385, at p. 386:

> The relevance of his testimony is to assist—no more—the jury in determining whether there is an explanation for what might otherwise be regarded as conduct that is inconsistent with that of a truthful witness. It does, of course, bolster the credibility of that witness, but it is evidence of how certain people react to certain experiences. Its relevance lies not in testimony that the prior witness is telling the truth but in testimony as to human behaviour. ...

> There are concerns. As the court stated in *R. v. J. (F.E.)*, [(1990), 53 C.C.C. (3d) 94, 74 C.R. (3d) 269, 36 O.A.C. 348 (C.A.)], and *R. v. C.(R.A.)* (1990), 57 C.C.C. (3d) 522, 78 C.R. (3d) 390, the court must require that the witness be an expert in the particular area of human conduct in question; the evidence must be of the sort that the jury needs because the problem is beyond their ordinary experience; and the jury must be carefully instructed as to its function and duty in making the final decision without being unduly influenced by the expert nature of the evidence.

52 The conditions set out by Professor Mewett, reflecting the observations of various appellate courts which have considered the matter, recommend themselves as sound. To accept this approach is not to open the floodgates to expert testimony on whether witnesses are lying or telling the truth. It is rather to recognize that certain aspects of human behaviour which are important to the

judge or jury's assessment of credibility may not be understood by the lay person and hence require elucidation by experts in human behaviour.

53 Had Dr. Mian confined her comments to expert evidence explaining why children may lie to hospital staff about the cause of their injuries, there could have been no objection to her evidence. She was an expert in child behaviour, and the evidence would arguably have been evidence needed by a lay jury to understand fully the implications of the witness's change in story. However, Dr. Mian went further. She clearly indicated that she personally did not believe the first story of the child, preferring the second version which the child told at trial. In so doing, she crossed the line between expert testimony on human behaviour and assessment of credibility of the witness herself. Moreover, the trial judge failed to instruct the jury that it was their duty to decide on the child's credibility without being unduly influenced by the expert evidence. In fact, the trial judge's statement that Dr. Mian gave "evidence as an expert in child abuse and relating to the truthfulness of the testimony of small children" actually reinforced the effect of the inadmissible evidence.

54 In my view, this error, considered with the others, requires that a new trial be directed.

R. v. D. (D.)
[2000] 2 S.C.R. 275, 36 C.R. (5th) 261, 148 C.C.C. (3d) 41

The accused was charged with sexual assault. The complainant alleged that the accused had sexually assaulted her when she was 5 to 6 years old. The complainant told no one about these events for two-and-a-half years. At trial, defence counsel cross-examined the complainant, who was ten years old at the time, on the lengthy delay in reporting the incidents and suggested that she had fabricated the story. The Crown called a child psychologist to testify that a child's delay in alleging sexual abuse does not support an inference of falsehood. During a *voir dire*, the psychologist gave a general explanation applicable to all children that delayed disclosure could occur for a variety of reasons and did not indicate the lack of truth of an allegation. The trial judge admitted the expert evidence and the jury found the accused guilty of sexual assault and invitation to sexual touching. The Court of Appeal held that the expert evidence should not have been admitted because it was neither relevant nor necessary. The guilty verdict was set aside for this and other reasons, and a new trial was ordered. The Crown appealed from the finding that the expert evidence was inadmissible but agreed that the order for a new trial was warranted based on the Court of Appeal's other reasons for setting aside the verdict.

McLACHLIN C.J. (L'HEUREUX-DUBÉ and GONTHIER JJ. concurring), dissenting:—

. . . .

During the *voir dire*, Dr. Marshall discussed delayed disclosure of child sexual abuse, based on his knowledge of the scientific literature in the area. He testified that there are many factors which can affect the timing of a complaint, including the relationship between the child and the abuser and the nature of the abuse. Some factors might discourage children from reporting abuse, such as embarrassment; fear of getting themselves or others into trouble; bribery or threats by the perpetrator; fear of being punished or sent away; disruption of the family; or fear that they would not be believed. Young children might also not fully comprehend what happened or not see anything wrong with the abuse.

Dr. Marshall also discussed the timing of allegations of abuse and its relevance to determining whether the abuse actually occurred. In his opinion, most sexual abuse is never disclosed, so one cannot assume that disclosure normally happens immediately. He testified that children disclose at various lengths of time after the event, so there is a continuum from immediate disclosure to delayed disclosure to no disclosure. When cross-examined by defence counsel as to whether the profile of a victim of abuse could be developed by reference to the timing of the complaint, Dr. Marshall stated "the fact of the delay . . . doesn't even enter into my thinking as to whether or not it happened. . . . [T]he research says that the length of time before a child reveals something is not diagnostic". The trial judge asked him to clarify what it means when delay is "not diagnostic", to which Dr. Marshall responded "[i]t proves nothing either way".

. . . .

The test for the admissibility of expert evidence was consolidated in *Mohan*. Four criteria must be met by a party which seeks to introduce expert evidence: relevance, necessity, the lack of any other exclusionary rule, and a properly qualified expert. Even where these requirements are met, the evidence may be rejected if its prejudicial effect on the conduct of the trial outweighs its probative value.

The application of the four *Mohan* criteria is case-specific. Determinations of relevance and necessity, as well as the assessment of whether the prejudicial effect of the evidence outweighs its probative value, must be made within the factual context of the trial. . . . The case-specific nature of the inquiry means that an appellate court cannot lay down in advance broad rules that particular categories of expert evidence are always inadmissible. Such a categorical approach would undermine *Mohan*'s requirement of a case-by-case analysis of the four applicable criteria.

It follows that we cannot say as a general rule that expert evidence on a child's delay in reporting sexual assault is always admissible. Nor can we say it is never admissible. We can only say that it may be admissible if the four *Mohan* criteria are satisfied and if the prejudicial impact of the evidence does not outweigh its probative value. The trial judge erred if he took the comments in *Marquard* as indicating as a matter of stare decisis that expert evidence on delayed disclosure always meets the necessity test. By the same token, it would be erroneous to say that such evidence can never be admitted, as the Crown submits the Court of Appeal suggested. Admissibility of expert evidence must be determined on a case-by-case basis in the factual context of the case as it develops.

Against this background, I turn to the issue of whether the *Mohan* criteria for admissibility were met in this case.

A. Relevance

The trial judge found Dr. Marshall's evidence relevant to a fact in issue — the significance of the child's delay in reporting. The Court of Appeal, by contrast, held that the evidence was not relevant to a fact in issue, but only to the complainant's credibility.

In my view, the trial judge was correct in finding that Dr. Marshall's evidence was relevant to a fact in issue at the trial. The trial turned on the credibility of the complainant. If her testimony was believed, the offence was proved as charged. If there was a reasonable doubt about her credibility, the case was not made out. The issue of delay was subsidiary to the complainant's credibility. The "fact in issue" was whether a child's delay in reporting sexual abuse suggests that the alleged abuse did not occur. The defence put that fact in issue by indicating that it would ask the jury to infer from the delay in reporting that the alleged events were not real occurrences but fabrications. According to the defence, the complainant "was not credible because she waited too long". That was the fact in issue. Dr. Marshall's evidence was relevant to that issue because he discussed reasons other than fabrication, such as fear of not being believed, that might explain why a child would delay reporting sexual abuse.

. . . .

The Court of Appeal reasoned that Dr. Marshall's evidence should be excluded because it represented "a blatant attempt to bolster the credibility of the only witness the Crown had to the alleged assault". Finlayson J.A. noted the principle, with which I agree, that the actual credibility of a particular witness is not generally the proper subject of opinion evidence: see *R. v. Béland*, [1987] 2 S.C.R. 398; *Marquard*, supra; *R. v. B. (F.F.)*, [1993] 1 S.C.R 697; *Mohan*, supra; *R. v. Burns*, [1994] 1 S.C.R. 656. This is known as the rule against oath-helping. In my view, Dr. Marshall's evidence did not violate that principle. In *Marquard*, supra, at p. 249, I noted that

> there is a growing consensus that while expert evidence on the ultimate credibility of a witness is not admissible, expert evidence on human conduct and the psychological and physical factors which may lead to certain behaviour relevant to credibility, is admissible, provided the testimony goes beyond the ordinary experience of the trier of fact.

. . . .

B. Necessity

When it comes to necessity, the question is whether the expert will provide information which is likely to be outside the ordinary experience and knowledge of the trier of fact: *Burns*, supra; *Mohan*, supra; *R. v. Lavallee*, [1990] 1 S.C.R. 852; *R. v. Abbey*, [1982] 2 S.C.R. 24; *Kelliher (Village of) v. Smith*, [1931] S.C.R. 672. "Necessity" means that the evidence must be more than merely "helpful", but necessity need not be judged "by too strict a standard": *Mohan*, supra, at p. 23. Absolute necessity is not required.

. . . .

The issue again may be put in simple terms: was there a sufficient basis for the trial judge to conclude that the issue of the child's delay in disclosure might involve matters beyond the ordinary knowledge and expertise of the jury? Was the evidence necessary to enable the trier of fact to properly dispose of the credibility issue? In answering this question, we must bear in mind that the trial judge is in the best position of determining the level of the jurors' understanding and what may assist them. In my view, there was an ample foundation for the trial judge's conclusion that Dr. Marshall's evidence went beyond the ordinary knowledge and expertise of the jury.

. . . .

Given the additional assistance that Dr. Marshall's testimony may have provided to the jury, I cannot conclude that the trial judge erred by failing to find that it was unnecessary because he could have given a jury warning. This is particularly so in view of the fact that the defence never raised this argument at trial. That said, the trial judge on the new trial should consider whether the expert's testimony is necessary to that trial in light of all the relevant circumstances, including the arguments of counsel and the possibility of a judicial instruction.

C. No Other Exclusionary Rule

The third criterion for admitting expert evidence is that it must not be excluded by the operation of any other rule. The only exclusionary rule raised here is the principle that an expert may not testify on the ultimate issue of credibility. As discussed earlier, this rule was not violated because Dr. Marshall testified on an issue that was subsidiary to the complainant's credibility. He did not express an opinion on whether her allegations were true or false. It was left for the jury to determine whether they accepted all, some or none of the evidence of the complainant.

D. Properly Qualified Expert

The final requirement for admissibility is that the expert be properly qualified. Neither the accused nor the Court of Appeal suggested that Dr. Marshall was not properly qualified to testify on the subject of delayed disclosure.

E. Probative Value Versus Prejudicial Effects

As with the other elements of the *Mohan* test, probative value and prejudicial effects are case-specific. The determinations made by the trial judge deserve appellate deference. In this case, Dr. Marshall's evidence brought relevant facts and opinions to the case that were not within the jury's knowledge and would not otherwise have been available to assist them. Dr. Marshall's qualifications were not questioned. His testimony was understandable and convincing. Taken together, these factors suggest that the expert evidence possessed considerable probative value.

The accused argues that the probative value of the evidence was outweighed by two important prejudicial effects: (1) that Dr. Marshall's evidence would neutralize a legitimate line of argument and interfere with his right of self-defence; and (2) that Dr. Marshall's evidence would distort the trial process through the undue weight the jury may place on expert evidence. The first alleged prejudicial effect does not withstand scrutiny. As the trial judge noted in his decision on the *voir dire*, admitting Dr. Marshall's evidence would not prohibit defence counsel from making its "common sense" argument that delay casts doubt on whether the alleged assaults occurred. The Crown's expert evidence merely countered that argument by providing evidence that it was contrary to the current consensus in the scientific community. Conflicting evidence and inferences are the natural product of the adversarial nature of the trial process. Each side seeks to bring evidence to support its arguments. Expert witnesses are subject to cross-examination to probe the validity of their evidence and the weight to be assigned to it. At the end of the day, the jury decides what they accept and what they reject. Evidence is neither inadmissible nor unfair simply because it contradicts an argument put by the other side.

The second prejudicial effect merits closer consideration. Low value expert testimony can distort the fact-finding process by taking a relatively simple issue, dressing it up in scientific language and presenting the trier of fact with a ready-made decision. The jury may be tempted to avoid engaging in serious consideration of the actual facts and instead rely on the apparent expertise of the scientist. In effect, the expert may usurp the domain of the jury. Trial judges must take this possibility into account in determining whether the prejudicial effect of expert evidence outweighs its probative value.

Part of this concern is addressed at the necessity stage: a party seeking to call expert evidence must show that the subject matter of the expert's opinion falls outside the likely range of knowledge and experience of the trier of fact. Nonetheless, that may not suffice. Even if expert evidence may assist the judge or jury, that benefit must be balanced against its costs. Can the expert address the issue in understandable terms? Is the judge or jury likely to take the expert's word as unchallengeable truth, or will the trier of fact be able to examine it critically? At the same time, the judge must not underestimate the ability of jurors to assess evidence; they may be quite capable of discerning whether scientific information is legitimate or not, as long as it is presented in accessible language.

The concern that the jury may be misled was not made out in this case. Dr. Marshall testified in a clear and straightforward manner. He avoided scientific terms which might obfuscate the issue and confuse the jury. His evidence was easy to understand and well within the ability of the jury to evaluate. Unlike some expert witnesses, Dr. Marshall did not rely on his credentials or "the mystique of science" to bolster his testimony: see *Béland*, supra, at p. 434. Nor did his testimony verge on advocacy. He neither explicitly nor implicitly commented on the complainant's credibility or the ultimate issue of the guilt or innocence of the accused. Defence counsel engaged Dr. Marshall in cross-examination and did not seem hindered by the scientific nature of the evidence. On the circumstances that prevailed in the trial below, I cannot conclude that the trial judge erred in holding that the probative value of Dr. Marshall's evidence outweighed its prejudicial effects.

MAJOR J. (IACOBUCCI, BINNIE and ARBOUR JJ. concurring):—

. . . .

I. General Approach to the Necessity Requirement

A. Standard of Necessity

The second requirement of the *Mohan* analysis exists to ensure that the dangers associated with expert evidence are not lightly tolerated. Mere relevance or "helpfulness" is not enough. The evidence must also be necessary.

I agree with the Chief Justice that some degree of deference is owed to the trial judge's discretionary determination of whether the *Mohan* requirements have been met on the facts of a particular case, but that discretion cannot be used erroneously to dilute the requirement of necessity. *Mohan* expressly states that mere helpfulness is too low a standard to warrant accepting the dangers inherent in the admission of expert evidence. A fortiori, a finding that some aspects of the evidence "might reasonably have assisted the jury" is not enough.

B. Dangers of Expert Evidence

In *Mohan*, Sopinka J. stated that the need for expert evidence must be assessed in light of its potential to distort the fact-finding process. A brief examination of the dangers associated with the admission of expert evidence is helpful to the analysis of this appeal.

A basic tenet of our law is that the usual witness may not give opinion evidence, but testify only to facts within his knowledge, observation and experience. This is a commendable principle since it is the task of the fact finder, whether a jury or judge alone, to decide what secondary inferences are to be drawn from the facts proved.

However, common law courts have since the 14th century recognized that certain exceptional issues require the application of special knowledge lying outside the experience of the usual trier of fact. Expert opinion evidence became admissible as an exception to the rule against opinion evidence in those cases where it was necessary to provide "a ready-made inference which the judge and jury, due to the technical nature of the facts, are unable to formulate" (*R. v. Abbey*, [1982] 2 S.C.R. 24, at p. 42).

Despite the emergence of the exception, it has been repeatedly recognized that the admissibility requirements of expert evidence do not eliminate the dangers traditionally associated with it. Nevertheless, they are tolerated in those exceptional cases where the jury would be unable to reach their own conclusions in the absence of assistance from experts with special knowledge.

Historically, there existed two modes of utilizing such expert knowledge as was available: first, to select jurors who by experience were best suited to deal with the facts before them, and second, to call experts as friends of the court rather than as witnesses for one side or the other. (See Learned Hand, "Historical and Practical Considerations Regarding Expert Testimony" (1901), 15 Harv. L. Rev. 40.) In this manner, the neutrality of the experts was assured. This notion has long disappeared and now the "professional expert witness" has emerged. Although not biased in a dishonest sense, these witnesses frequently move from the impartiality generally associated with professionals to advocates in the case. In some notable instances, it has been recognized that this lack of independence and impartiality can contribute to miscarriages of justice. (See, e.g., *The Commission on Proceedings Involving Guy Paul Morin* (Kaufman Report) (1998), at p. 172.)

The primary danger arising from the admission of any opinion evidence is that the province of the jury might be usurped by that of the witness. This danger is especially prevalent in cases of expert opinion evidence. Faced with an expert's impressive credentials and mastery of scientific jargon, jurors are more likely to abdicate their role as fact-finders and simply attorn to the opinion of the expert in their desire to reach a just result. The danger of attornment to the opinion of the expert is further increased by the fact that expert evidence is highly resistant to effective cross-examination by counsel who are not experts in that field. In cases where there is no competing expert evidence, this will have the effect of depriving the jury of an effective framework within which to evaluate the merit of the evidence.

Additional dangers are created by the fact that expert opinions are usually derived from academic literature and out-of-court interviews, which material is unsworn and not available for cross-examination. Though not properly admissible as evidence for the proof of its contents, this material generally finds its way into the proceedings because "if an expert is permitted to give his opinion, he ought to be permitted to give the circumstances upon which that opinion is based" (*R. v. Dietrich* (1970), 1 C.C.C. (2d) 49 (Ont. C.A.), at p. 65). In many cases, this material carries with it prejudicial effects which require special instructions to the jury (*Abbey*, supra, at p. 45).

Finally, expert evidence is time-consuming and expensive. Modern litigation has introduced a proliferation of expert opinions of questionable value. The significance of the costs to the parties and the resulting strain upon judicial resources cannot be overstated. When the door to the admission of expert evidence is opened too widely, a trial has the tendency to degenerate into "a contest of experts with the trier of fact acting as referee in deciding which expert to accept" (*Mohan*, supra, at p. 24).

. . . .

In my view, the content of the expert evidence admitted in this case was not unique or scientifically puzzling but was rather the proper subject for a simple jury instruction. This being the case, its admission was not necessary.

Distilling the probative elements of Dr. Marshall's testimony from its superfluous and prejudicial elements, one bald statement of principle emerges. In diagnosing cases of child sexual abuse, the timing of the disclosure, standing alone, signifies nothing. Not all victims of child sexual abuse will disclose the abuse immediately. It depends upon the circumstances of the particular victim. I find surprising the suggestion that a Canadian jury or judge alone would be incapable of understanding this simple fact. I cannot identify any technical quality to this evidence that necessitates expert opinion.

. . . .

A trial judge should recognize and so instruct a jury that there is no inviolable rule on how people who are the victims of trauma like a sexual assault will behave. Some will make an immediate complaint, some will delay in disclosing the abuse, while some will never disclose the abuse. Reasons for delay are many and at least include embarrassment, fear, guilt, or a lack of understanding and knowledge. In assessing the credibility of a complainant, the timing of the complaint is simply one circumstance to consider in the factual mosaic of a particular case. A delay in disclosure, standing alone, will never give rise to an adverse inference against the credibility of the complainant.

It was submitted that it is preferable to introduce the concept contained in Dr. Marshall's evidence to the jury by way of expert testimony rather than by judicial instruction. In my view, this argument is flawed. There is nothing to be gained from a cross-examination of the simple and irrefutable proposition advanced in this case by the expert. As well, there is no benefit to be derived from the added flexibility of expert evidence since the undeniable nature of the proposition does not lend itself to future advancements in knowledge and understanding.

A jury instruction, in preference to expert opinion, where practicable, has advantages. It saves time and expense. But of greater importance, it is given by an impartial judicial officer, and any risk of superfluous or prejudicial content is eliminated. In this appeal, the evidence presented by the expert was precisely what the jury would have been instructed by a proper charge. There is no difference of substance between the two.

See Nick Bala, "R. v. D. (DD): The Supreme Court and Filtering of Social Science Knowledge About Children"[234] and Nick Bala and Annelise Saunders, "Understanding the Family Context: Why the Law of Expert Evidence is Different in Family Law"[235] where it is suggested that the *Mohan* test needs to be applied less rigorously in family court. **Do you agree?**

R. v. TALBOT
(2002), 1 C.R. (6th) 396, 161 C.C.C. (3d) 256, 2002 CarswellOnt 63 (C.A.)

The accused was charged with three counts of sexual assault, three counts of anal intercourse, and 11 other sexual and non-sexual offences relating to three young boys. The evidence of the complainants was delayed, inconsistent, and marked by recantations. The Crown called a psychiatrist who testified that delayed or inconsistent disclosure and recantation were not unusual for child victims of sexual abuse, but that the nature of the disclosure by itself did not "tell us anything about the factual veracity of the disclosures that are ultimately made", and that it should not be seen as a certain indicator that a child has been sexually abused.

---

234 (2001), 36 C.R. (5th) 283.
235 (2003), 20 C.F.L.Q. 277.

Per LASKIN J.A. (GOUDGE and SIMMONS JJ.A. concurring): —

. . . .

The expert evidence

The Crown called two medical experts, Dr. Dirk Huyer, an expert in the medical aspects of child abuse. Dr. Huyer testified that anal penetration of a child is easier if the child has taken a muscle relaxant like Valium and Dr. Clive Chamberlain, a psychiatrist, who was qualified as an expert on the sexual abuse of children. On appeal the appellant challenges only the evidence of Dr. Chamberlain.

. . . .

The three complainants did not disclose the accused's sexual abuse immediately after it occurred. Instead, disclosure was delayed, at times inconsistent, and marked by recantations. The defence relied on the way the complainants disclosed the abuse to argue that their allegations were fabricated. Dr. Chamberlain was called by the Crown to explain to the jury that delayed or inconsistent disclosure and even recantation of claims of sexual abuse by child victims is not unusual. He testified that it is "a very commonly observed pattern of behaviour of kids who have been involved in sexual situations with adults" and he discussed the reasons for it. But he also cautioned that "this kind of disclosure on and off and recantation, I don't think that it, by itself, should tell us anything about the factual veracity of the disclosures that are ultimately made . . . it ought not to be seen as a certain indicator that a child has been sexually abused".

At trial, defence counsel did not object to the admissibility of Dr. Chamberlain's opinion evidence. On appeal, however, relying on the recent Supreme Court of Canada decision in *R. v. D. (D.)* (2000), 148 C.C.C. (3d) 41, the appellant submits that Dr. Chamberlain should not have been allowed to testify because his testimony did not meet the necessity criterion for the admissibility of expert evidence. The appellant also submits that, once admitted, the trial judge failed to properly instruct the jury on how they could use Dr. Chamberlain's evidence.

. . . .

Despite the holding in *D. (D.)* I would not give effect to the appellant's submission for two reasons. First, the expert evidence in *D. (D.)* differed materially from Dr. Chamberlain's evidence in this case. The expert evidence in *D. (D.)* related only to the significance of delay in disclosing sexual abuse allegations. As summarized by Major J., that expert testified that "the timing of the disclosure, standing alone, signifies nothing", at p. 64 [para. 59]. And the reason that delayed disclosure means nothing in and of itself is that, as a matter of law, no adverse inference can be drawn from a complainant's delay in disclosing the allegations. Major J. put it this way, at p. 66 [para. 63]:The significance of the complainant's failure to make a timely complaint must not be the subject of any presumptive adverse inference based upon now rejected stereotypical assumptions of how persons (particularly children) react to acts of sexual abuse: *R. v. M. (P.S.)* (1992), 77 C.C.C. (3d) 402 (Ont. C.A.) at pp. 408-9; *R. v. M. (T.E.)* (1996), 187 A.R. 273 (C.A.).

And further, at pp. 66-67:

> A delay in disclosure, standing alone, will never give rise to an adverse inference against the credibility of the complainant.

Because this principle forms a recognized part of Canadian law, one can easily understand why the Supreme Court found that the information offered by the expert in D. (D.) should have gone to the jury in the form of an instruction from the trial judge. No expert evidence was needed to establish that the delay in the complainant's disclosure did not by itself impair her credibility. The jury was not permitted to draw an adverse inference from this delay as a matter of law and the trial judge should have instructed them accordingly.

The present case is very different. Instead of dealing with the relevance of delayed disclosure "standing alone", Dr. Chamberlain testified to patterns of disclosure among sexual abuse victims, patterns that include not only delays in disclosure but also inconsistencies in disclosure and recantations. Although no adverse inference can be drawn from the mere fact that disclosure is delayed, the same cannot be said for inconsistent disclosures or recantations. Indeed, prior inconsistent statements are typically highly damaging to a complainant's credibility.

Thus, there is, quite rightly, no existing principle of law that would prevent a jury from drawing an adverse inference from inconsistent disclosures or recantations by a complainant. But the jury should be allowed to put these inconsistent disclosures and recantations in context. If, as Dr. Chamberlain testified, child victims of sexual abuse often make disclosures marked by delay, inconsistencies, and recantations, then expert evidence may be required to help the jury make an appropriate and informed determination of the complainant's credibility. Patterns of disclosure among sexual abuse victims do not form a part of the ordinary experience and knowledge of jurors. Expert evidence may well be necessary to help jurors draw the proper inferences, and I conclude that it was necessary in this case.

In the light of *D. (D.)*, it might have seemed preferable for the trial judge to have dealt with the relevance of delay in a jury instruction, and for the Crown to have limited Dr. Chamberlain's testimony to the patterns of disclosure involving inconsistencies and recantations. Accepting, however, that Dr. Chamberlain's evidence was necessary to help the jury understand the significance of the complainants' inconsistent disclosures and recantations, to restrict him from offering an opinion on the relevance of delayed disclosure would be unworkable. Dr. Chamberlain's evidence dealt with patterns of disclosure among sexual abuse victims; delays in disclosure form an integral part of those patterns. Dr. Chamberlain's testimony was properly admitted.

Second, even if Dr. Chamberlain's evidence should not have been admitted, its admission caused no substantial wrong. If necessary, I would therefore apply the proviso in s. 686(1)(b) (iii) of the Code. Although the Supreme Court of

Canada did not address the proviso in D. (D.) because it had already decided to allow the appeal on another ground, the majority reasons affirm that the jury is entitled to the information on delayed disclosure. The majority said simply that the information should come from the trial judge, not from an expert witness. Major J. stressed, at p. 67 [para.67], that an important advantage of a jury instruction over expert evidence is that the information "is given by an impartial judicial officer, and any risk of superfluous or prejudicial content is eliminated".

Here, though the information on disclosure patterns was given by an expert, Dr. Chamberlain's evidence was short, balanced and avoided any superfluous or prejudicial content. In both his examination-in-chief and his cross-examination he emphasized that neither late or inconsistent disclosure nor recantation proves that sexual abuse has occurred. If the admission of his evidence amounted to an error of law, the error did not cause a miscarriage of justice.

The appellant also contends that the trial judge did not properly instruct the jury on how they could use Dr. Chamberlain's evidence. I do not agree with this contention. The trial judge quite properly told the jury that if they accepted Dr. Chamberlain's evidence they could take it into account in assessing the credibility of the complainants, that is in determining whether the complainants fabricated their evidence. But the trial judge cautioned the jury at least three times that they could not use Dr. Chamberlain's evidence to conclude that sexual abuse had occurred. For example, in discussing Dr. Chamberlain's evidence, the trial judge told the jury:However, it is very important that you understand and accept that this evidence cannot be used as confirming that the complaints by young persons of sexual acts performed upon them by Mr. Talbot are in fact true, or are more likely to be true because their conduct fits the so-called pattern described by Dr. Chamberlain. Dr. Chamberlain said himself that the pattern of secrecy, helplessness, denial, disclosure and further denial should not tell you anything about the truth of the matters disclosed.

And later, in comparing Dr. Chamberlain's evidence with similar fact evidence, he repeated this caution: This evidence of Dr. Chamberlain's was admitted since it may help you, if you accept it, in understanding how one or more young persons might not complain about sexual abuse or might deny sexual abuse. To that extent, Dr. Chamberlain's evidence may help you to determine the credibility of young persons who now allege various sexual acts performed on them by Mr. Talbot after not complaining or, alternatively, after denying such sexual acts. Such evidence, expert evidence, may explain away a problem with credibility, depending on how you view that evidence. However, that expert evidence cannot be used to bolster or add to the credibility of a complainant, because it cannot be used to say that sexual abuse did, in fact, occur. It is thus distinct from similar fact evidence.

I would not give effect to this ground of appeal.

R. v. G.(P.)

(2009), 2009 CarswellOnt 123, 242 C.C.C. (3d) 558, 63 C.R. (6th) 301
(C.A.)

The accused was charged with several sexual offences against his four-year-old daughter. The complainant initially disclosed the abuse to her foster parents, and she later provided two videotaped statements to police. These out-of-court statements by the complainant were admitted for the truth of their contents. She did not testify at trial. An expert on child sexual abuse offered his opinion at trial that the complainant had been sexually abused but did not identify the accused as the abuser. The jury found the accused guilty and the accused appealed.

Juriansz J.A.:

Analysis

[14] The most helpful case regarding the admissibility and ambit of an expert's opinion as to whether a child has suffered sexual abuse is *Khan v. College of Physicians and Surgeons of Ontario* (1992), 9 O.R. (3d) 641 (O.C.A.). This case presents the opportunity to repeat and expand upon the principles stated in that case.

[15] *Khan v. College of Physicians and Surgeons of Ontario* arose out of disciplinary proceedings against Dr. Khan before the College of Physicians and Surgeons of Ontario for the sexual assault of a patient, then 3 1/2 years old. One of the issues on the appeal was whether the two expert witnesses who had testified at Dr. Khan's hearing had gone beyond the scope of what was permissible by giving their opinions on the ultimate issue to be decided by the tribunal. Doherty J.A. reviewed the law and stated the following general principles.

[16] First, expert evidence is not rendered inadmissible simply because it may bear on the very factual issue to be decided by the trier of fact. Second, an expert witness may not offer an opinion as to the veracity of any witness, except in very exceptional cases. Third, expert opinion as to what factual inferences or conclusions should be drawn from the evidence concerning the "behaviour and symptomatology" of a child is admissible even though it indirectly enhances the credibility of the child's evidence. Fourth, the trial judge may control the format in which the expert evidence is given by excluding an expert's conclusory statements where the expert is able to express the opinion in less conclusory terms without detracting from its accuracy.

[17] These principles, taken together, allow the Crown to present expert evidence that will assist the trier of fact while protecting the accused from the trier of fact placing undue weight on the expert's opinion. There exists, however, potential tension between the second and third principles. The second principle is that the expert is not permitted to express an opinion about the veracity of any witness. Despite this, the third principle states that the expert is permitted to offer an opinion (based on the child's "behaviour and symptomatology") that the child has been sexually abused even though it "indirectly enhances the credibility of the child's evidence."

[18] The third principle qualifies but does not annul the second principle. While the scope permitted an expert witness by the third principle is broad, the court should be vigilant in ensuring that the expert in expressing his or her opinions does not violate the second. As Doherty J.A. noted in *Khan v. College of Physicians and Surgeons of Ontario*, though there is strong value and need for evidence in cases of child sexual abuse, a trier of fact "[f]aced with the often intractable problem of trying to decide who is telling the truth in cases of alleged child abuse ... may seek refuge in the apparent security and objectivity of the expert's opinion evidence." Major J. made much the same observation in *R. v. D. (D)*, [2000] 2 S.C.R. 275 at para. 53, that there is a danger that "faced with an expert's impressive credentials and mastery of scientific jargon, jurors are more likely to abdicate their role as fact-finders and simply attorn to the opinion of the expert in their desire to reach a just result."

[19] Turning back to this case, I do not accept that the subject matter which Dr. Wehrspann addressed strayed outside the broad range permitted by the third principle. The scope of the child's "behaviour and symptomatology" is not narrowly limited to the psychological, social and physical traits. It includes the child's verbal behaviour. Verbal behaviour may include the fact that the child makes reports of being involved in sexual activity or that the child makes such reports without prompting. It may also include the particular vocabulary the child uses in making those reports.

[20] Dr. Wehrspann noted that the complainant was observed at the daycare [acting in a sexually inappropriate manner], and that she was indiscriminate in her attachments in that she would go up to anybody and make physical contact with them. In addition, Dr. Wehrspann's opinion was also based on his view of the complainant's verbal behaviour. It was important to his analysis that the complainant did report sexual activity, she made these reports without prompting, and that she described the sexual activity in age appropriate language. These are all matters of the complainant's "behaviour and symptomatology".

[21] Properly elicited expert opinion based on such matters is admissible even though it may indirectly enhance the credibility of the child witness or of the witnesses who testify about the child's disclosure. The problem here is that Dr. Wehrspann's opinions were not properly elicited and the effect of his evidence was to indicate his views of the veracity of the complainant and the foster parents.

[22] As noted, Dr. Wehrspann's opinion was primarily on his review of the Children's Aid Society's file that contained the reports of her foster parents to the Society. The only matters he could address directly were his observation that when he tried to talk to the complainant about her father she became fearful immediately and that she was too open and indiscriminate in her attachments to adults she did not know. His analysis, however, was based primarily on the material in the Children's Aid Society file, which included, notably, the reports from the complainant's foster parents, the veracity of which were disputed by the defence.

[27] Dr. Wehrspann's testimony clearly went beyond expressing an opinion based on the complainant's behaviour and symptomatology. His testimony would have left no doubt in the jury's mind that he believed the Crown's witnesses and disbelieved the appellant in arriving at his opinion that the complainant suffered sexual abuse. His testimony, in effect, directly addressed the credibility and reliability of other witnesses. As such it violated the second principle stated in *Khan v. College of Physicians and Surgeons of Ontario*. I would hold the trial judge erred in admitting it and that a new trial is necessary.

[28] This result could have been avoided had trial judge required that Dr. Wehrspann's testimony be elicited by hypothetical questions that incorporated all of the factual premises upon which his opinion was based. Properly framed hypothetical questions would have permitted Dr. Wehrspann to draw upon the foster parents' reports of the circumstances, manner and content of complainant's disclosure while leaving to the jury the task of deciding whether or not to believe them. This was especially important in this case as the defence attempted to implicate the foster father in the abuse and suggest that both foster parents helped concoct the allegations against him.

New trial ordered.

R. v. DIMITROV
(2003), 18 C.R. (6th) 36, 181 C.C.C. (3d) 554,
2003 CarswellOnt 5212 (C.A.)

H V was murdered in the garage attached to his home. The accused, a boarder in the house at the time, was convicted by a jury of second degree murder. The central issue at the accused's trial was the identity of the killer. Four people lived at the house at the time of the murder: the victim, his wife, F V, and two tenants, Tzenev and the accused. The position of the Crown at trial was that the deceased was killed by one of the persons living in the house and that that person was the appellant.

WEILER and GILLESE JJ.A. (ARMSTRONG J.A. concurring): —

. . . .

Did the trial judge err in admitting expert evidence of the barefoot impression in the Eagle Rock boots?

. . . .

Barefoot impression evidence must be carefully evaluated on a case-by-case basis to determine its admissibility. Based on the current state of the jurisprudence, such evidence may be admissible where there are distinctive features of the barefoot impression that can connect the footwear to the accused's feet, as in Légère. It may also be admissible to show that an accused person has not worn a particular pair of shoes or to eliminate persons as regular wearers of shoes. The fact, however, that an accused person's footprint is "similar to" the barefoot impression in a boot or shoe ought not to be admissible as positive identification.

As Sergeant Kennedy himself acknowledges, his research has not reached the stage where he can make a categorical identification from barefoot impressions.

. . . .

We would allow the appeal, set aside the verdict of guilt and order a new trial.

R. v. KLYMCHUK
(2005), 203 C.C.C. (3d) 341 (Ont. C.A.)

The accused was convicted of first degree murder of his wife. The accused was home when she was killed. He called 911 and reported that he had found his wife dead in their shed. In addition to relying on evidence of the accused's extra-marital affair as motive evidence, the Crown called an FBI expert to testify that the crime scene had been staged to look like a robbery. On appeal, the accused challenged the admissibility of this evidence.

DOHERTY J.A. (MOLDAVER and ARMSTRONG JJ.A. concurring): —

The admissibility of the expert evidence of "staging."

. . . .

This court has considered the admissibility of expert evidence that a crime scene was "staged" in *R. v. Ranger* (2003), 178 C.C.C. (3d) 375 (Ont. C.A.) and *R. v. Clark* (2004), 182 C.C.C. (3d) 1 (Ont. C.A.). In the present context, staging refers to a deliberate alteration of the crime scene by the perpetrator of the crime to mislead the police as to the identity of the perpetrator. The decisions in *Ranger* and *Clark* go a long way to resolving the admissibility of the expert evidence tendered in this case. The trial judge, whose reasons reflect a careful consideration of the issues before her, did not have the benefit of this court's reasons in either *Ranger* or *Clark*.

In *Ranger*, Charron J.A. distinguished between expert evidence of crime scene analysis offered to assist the jury in deciding what had happened at the crime scene (the WHAT question) and expert evidence based on crime scene analysis offered to assist the jury in deciding why a crime was committed (the WHY question), or who committed the crime (the WHO question). She observed at paras. 71 and 72:

> Crime scene analysis (which I find useful to label as the "WHAT" referred to earlier) results in many forms of expert opinion evidence that regularly meets the legal requirements for admissibility. A few examples readily come to mind: an expert's opinion in an arson case that a fire was not accidental but, rather, deliberately set; opinion evidence explaining the significance of blood splatters; a pathologist's opinion about the likely cause of death or of injuries observed on a deceased victim; an expert's opinion on how a motor vehicle accident happened. There are many more examples. *This kind of evidence assists the trier of fact in understanding WHAT the crime scene shows. The admissibility of that kind of evidence will usually turn on questions of relevance or the witness's particular expertise. Of course, issues may*

also arise under any other aspect of the Mohan test. However, the scientific basis for this kind of evidence is usually not contentious.

By contrast, attempts to adduce expert opinion evidence about WHY an offence was committed in a particular manner and, more particularly, about WHO is more likely to have committed the offence, that is, the kinds of evidence that I have labelled more particularly as criminal profiling, have generally not met with success, either in this jurisdiction or elsewhere. I will refer to some American and English jurisprudence later in this judgment. However, in so far as Canadian jurisprudence is concerned, the best example is *Mohan* itself [emphasis added].

In *Clark* at paras. 83 and 84, Moldaver J.A. applied the distinction drawn in *Ranger*. He characterized expert evidence addressed to the WHAT question as "crime scene reconstruction evidence". That evidence was potentially admissible if relevant and offered through a properly qualified witness. He characterized expert evidence aimed at answering the WHO or the WHY questions as "impermissible criminal profiling evidence".

The distinction drawn in *Ranger* and *Clark* between expert evidence based on crime scene observations and reconstructions on the one hand, and expert evidence based on assessments of the type or category of person who committed a particular offence on the other, is rooted in the established reliability of the former and the unproven nature of the latter. Expert evidence describing the type of person who would or would not engage in a particular criminal activity is admitted only in that narrow class of cases where psychiatric knowledge has advanced sufficiently to allow a qualified expert to testify that the crime in question would in all likelihood have been committed by a person with a particular mental makeup, or alternatively that a person with the accused's mental makeup would in all likelihood not have committed the offence. Psychiatric profiling evidence is admissible only if the profile relied on by the expert is sufficiently precise and detailed to provide a meaningful distinction between the group said to fit the profile and the rest of the population. The evidence must also demonstrate that the profile has been developed and confirmed through an application of proper scientific methodology: *R. v. Mohan* (1994), 89 C.C.C. (3d) 402 at 423 (S.C.C.); *R. v. J.(J.L.)* (2000), 148 C.C.C. (3d) 487 at 500-507 (S.C.C.).

The Court ordered a new trial as the expert had gone beyond an assessment of the crime scene and testified about possible motives for the murder and the relationship between the victim and her killer. For example, he testified that the killer knew the victim and had a motive for killing her, a profile that fit the accused.

R. v. OSMAR
44 C.R. (6th) 276, 2007 CarswellOnt 339 (C.A.)

ROSENBERG J.A. (GOUDGE and LaFORME JJ.A. concurring): —

The defence sought to call Dr. Richard Ofshe to testify before the jury about false confessions. I will briefly summarize his evidence as it was disclosed during a *voir dire*. Dr. Ofshe is a social psychologist who has spent many years studying police interrogation. He has consulted widely with law enforcement agencies and testified in courts in the United States. He has authored many books and articles, including articles in peer-reviewed journals. The works of he and his associate, Richard Leo, were cited with approval in the leading recent decision on the common law confessions rule, *R. v. Oickle* . . . He testified that it is generally accepted that false confessions can be caused by interrogation tactics using psychological techniques. There is no credible empirical research that has attempted to quantify the rate of false confessions. His own view is that it is a relatively rare but regularly occurring phenomenon. Dr. Ofshe has done no study of the Mr. Big strategy. It is not a strategy used in the United States or Great Britain.

The defence proposed to call Dr. Ofshe to testify principally about three matters. First, that there is a bias among lay people against the idea that someone who is indeed innocent might falsely confess. Second, he would testify about what motivates a person, including an innocent person, to confess to a person in authority. Third, he would testify about the way to evaluate whether or not a confession is false. I will briefly expand on these themes.

. . .

I agree with the trial judge's conclusion that Dr. Ofshe's evidence was not admissible in the circumstances of this case. What I say here should not be taken as a finding that this kind of evidence could never be admitted in other circumstances. I also intend to limit my analysis to whether the evidence meets the necessity requirement for admission of expert evidence. I tend to agree with the appellant that the trial judge may have taken too narrow a view of the possible relevancy of the evidence by focusing solely on its value in determining the appellant's credibility. Dr. Ofshe's evidence was broader than that and went to the question of the reliability of the appellant's statements to the undercover officers in the context of the Mr. Big strategy. This would have been an issue in the case, even if the appellant did not testify.

As is well known, in *Mohan*, Sopinka J., speaking for the court, held that the admission of expert evidence depends on relevance, necessity in assisting the trier of fact, the absence of any exclusionary rule and a properly qualified expert (p. 411). He described necessity in these terms at p. 413:

> What is required is that the opinion be necessary in the sense that it provide information "which is likely to be outside the experience and knowledge of a judge or jury": as quoted by Dickson J. in *R. v. Abbey, supra*. As stated by Dickson J., the evidence must be necessary to enable the trier of fact to appreciate the matters in issue due to their technical nature. In *Kelliher v. Smith*, [1931] 4 D.L.R. 102, at p. 116, [1931] S.C.R. 672 (S.C.C.), this court, quoting from *Beven on Negligence*, 4th ed. (1928), p. 141, stated that in order for expert evidence to be admissible, "[t]he subject-matter of the inquiry must be such that ordinary people are unlikely to form a correct judgment about it, if unassisted by persons with special knowledge".

In my view, the three areas about which Dr. Ofshe proposed to testify did not meet this test. In particular, given the particular circumstances, his evidence was not about matters on which ordinary people are unlikely to form a correct judgment.

I start with his evidence about the bias among lay people against the idea that someone who is indeed innocent might falsely confess. As I have said, unfortunately Dr. Ofshe did not explain the reason for this phenomenon. I suspect that it comes from the difficulty that lay people have in applying their own experience to the circumstances of police interrogation. While most people would understand how a person could come to admit to almost anything, true or false, under torture or physical coercion, they would find it hard to understand why someone would admit to a crime they did not commit and thus place themselves in greater legal jeopardy than they would encounter from simply tolerating the psychological coercion of interrogation. If that is the explanation, Dr. Ofshe's evidence would not be helpful to the jury since it was anchored in formal police interrogation. If there is some other explanation for this bias, it was not forthcoming from Dr. Ofshe.

Similar considerations apply to Dr. Ofshe's evidence concerning the manner in which interrogations are conducted and the motivators for false confessions. I repeat a portion of Dr. Ofshe's evidence quoted above: "The significant question would be what's the motivator that is being offered to elicit the compliance. If the motivator is strong, if there is a powerful inducement, then depending on the power of that inducement, the risk of possibly eliciting a false confession goes up." In this case, the motive for a possible false confession was obvious, as was the fact that there was no downside to confessing to men the appellant believed were criminals. There were no myths to be dispelled; Dr. Ofshe would simply be describing what was obvious from the testimony of the police officers and, indeed, from the appellant's own evidence. The jury did not require Dr. Ofshe's evidence to arrive at a correct conclusion on this issue. He did not purport to offer an opinion as to how powerful the inducement was in this case nor whether it could have led to a false confession.

The final theme of Dr. Ofshe's evidence was that the way to determine whether the confession was true or false was to compare it to the known facts about the killing. He would also testify about the risk from contamination. Dr. Ofshe's evidence would have been helpful on this issue, but, as the trial judge observed, helpfulness is not enough. The entire defence was focused on this very issue. The defence theory was that the details in the confession came from the police. The defence also pointed out that some details that the killer would have known about were not contained in the confession. The jury did not need help understanding this point. As Dr. Ofshe testified, this is a straight-forward element of police investigation.[236]

---

236 See similarly *R. v. Warren* ((1995), 35 C.R. (4th) 347 (N.W. T. S.C.) and *R. v. Bonisteel* (2008), 61 C.R. (6th) 64 (B.C. C.A.). In England expert evidence on false confessions is admissible: see *R. v. Fell* (2001), [2001] E.W.J. No. 1324 (C.A.). For an argument that *Osmar* does not absolutely preclude the admission of expert evidence as to the fallibility of a confession see Lisa Dufraimont, Annotation to Osmar, (2007) 44 C.R (6th) 278.

On August 2, 2006, following an investigation and review into the 1972 murder conviction of Romeo Phillion, the Minister of Justice ordered a reference to the Ontario Court of Appeal. The reference raised questions as to the admissibility as fresh evidence as to the non-disclosure of alibi and other evidence and expert opinion as to the reliability of the confession.

A majority of the Court (per Moldaver J.A. (Laskin J.A. concurring), Macpherson J.A. dissenting) quashed the conviction mainly on the basis of the non-disclosed alibi evidence.[237]

The Court of Appeal were asked to consider the admissibility of reports presented to the Minister prepared by a psychologist and by Dr. Gisli Gudjonsson. Dr. Gudjonsson, who examined Phillion in 2003, is a leading British expert on the psychology of false confessions. He has testified in over 700 cases worldwide. In the result the Court largely avoids the question because this expert evidence was held not to meet the test for fresh evidence as psychological evidence as to the reliability of the confession had in fact been lead at Phillion's original trial. However Justice Moldaver made a pointed comment as to the admissibility of such evidence:

> [The] admissibility of expert evidence on false confessions is anything but obvious and should be approached with considerable caution. Of particular concern is whether the proposed evidence reaches the level of scientific reliability required by Mohan to warrant its reception. That said, I want to be clear that, in cases such as this where the reliability of a confession is in issue, expert evidence regarding an accused's personality traits that is relevant to and probative of the issue will be admissible. [paras. 217-218]

Justice Moldaver had earlier noted that Dr. Gudjonsson had been cross-examined on his report before Justice Sharpe of the Ontario Court of Appeal in May, 2008, and had admitted that his opinion that Phillion's confession was probably false had gone beyond the limits of scientific evaluation. [para. 208]

The Ontario Court of Appeal has therefore once again, as previously in *Osmar,* left the door open to such evidence. The Court seems reluctant to follow the path of other countries and actually admit such expertise. For an argument that such expert evidence meets Canadian tests for reliability: see Timothy Moore and Cindy Wasser, "Social Science and Witness Reliability: Reliable Science Begets Reliable Evidence"[238]; and, see more generally Lisa Dufraimont, "Regulating Unreliable Evidence: Can Evidence Rules Guide Juries and Prevent Wrongful Convictions?"[239]

It is ironic that in 1972, the trial judge did admit expert evidence as to the reliability of Phillion's confession, with one of the experts even placing reliance on a polygraph test. On the appeal to the Supreme Court,[240] the Court held that evidence of the polygraph tendered by the defence had been properly excluded especially as the accused had chosen not to testify. This ruling was confirmed

---

237 See *R. v. Phillion* (2009), 65 C.R. (6th) 255 (Ont. C.A.).
238 (2006) 33 C.R. (6th) 316.
239 (2008) 33 *Queen's L.J.* 261.
240 *Phillion v. R.,* [1978] 1 S.C.R. 18.

by a 5-2 majority in *R. v. Beland*.[241] Wilson and Lamer JJ. in dissent sought to distinguish *Phillion* on the basis that Beland had testified. They rejected oath-helping and other concerns advanced by the majority.

R. v. MELARAGNI
(1992), 76 C.C.C. (3d) 78 (Ont. Gen. Div.)

Two police officers were charged following an incident in which Wade Lawson, an unarmed young African Canadian, was shot in the back of the head as he fled the scene in his car.

MOLDAVER J.:—

. . . .

The defence seeks to call expert evidence designed to rebut inferences which the jury might understandably choose to apply based upon their common everyday experience in life. The defence submits that there is a real risk that this jury will assume, absent the proposed evidence, that police officers are trained to react and do react in a cool, calm and deliberate fashion at all times, including situations of great stress, especially since stress is a regular component in the daily makeup of a police officer's existence. The defence submits that the jury would certainly be forgiven for asking questions such as, "How could a trained police officer miss his target by several feet at close range? How could a police officer think he had fired only two bullets when, in fact, he had fired four? How could a police officer possibly miss seeing his partner on the other side of a four and a half foot high motor vehicle if his partner was standing erect?"

The proposed evidence is sought to be tendered to dispell certain misperceptions that might exist in the minds of the jurors regarding these and other matters. While I have not received any evidence which would tend to confirm the existence of such misperceptions in the minds of the public, I cannot help but believe that the concerns expressed are real. As a society, we are generally unfamiliar through our common everyday experience as to just how police officers do react in situations of extreme stress and peril. What knowledge we do have is generally derived from Hollywood where police officers are for the most part portrayed as super human beings possessed of remarkable marksmanship skills with ice-water flowing through their veins. This perception, which I would describe as a myth, is one which the defence ought to be entitled to dispel. I am of the view that the proposed evidence is, therefore, not only relevant, but may well be helpful to the jury in dispelling the myth which I have described and in arriving at their ultimate decision in this case. Therefore, the evidence proposed by the defence is admissible.

The officers were acquitted. The verdict was one of the precipitating events that led to the decision by then Premier Bob Rae to set up an inquiry into systemic racism in the criminal justice system in Ontario.

---

241 (1987) 60 C.R. (3d) 1 (S.C.C.).

NASSIAH v. PEEL REGIONAL POLICE SERVICES BOARD
[2006] O.R.T.D. No. 18 (Ont. Human Rights Trib.)

The complainant alleged that she was the victim of racial discrimination during a police investigation of a purported theft from a Sears store. The Commission sought an interim ruling on the admissibility of expert evidence on racial profiling.

JOACHIM (MEMBER): —

Professor Norman Scot Wortley was called by the Commission as an expert witness on racial profiling in Canada to give opinion evidence of the nature of racial profiling in police investigations in general, and in this case, in particular. The Respondent objected both to Professor Wortley's expertise and to the necessity and relevance of his opinion evidence.

Professor Wortley gave evidence with respect to his qualifications before I made my order.

Professor Wortley has been an Associate Professor at the Centre for Criminology at the University of Toronto for five years; prior to that he was an Assistant Professor for five years. He holds a B.A., an M.A. and a Ph.D in Sociology. He has been personally involved in two large sociological studies into racial profiling in Canada and is currently completing work on a third. He was commissioned by the Kingston police for his current research to review information relating to race, age, etc. gathered during police stops over a period of one year.

. . . .

I am persuaded that Professor Wortley's credentials, detailed above, qualify him as an expert in racial profiling in the criminal justice system and in police investigation in Canada.

The Respondents argued that the evidence proposed to be given by Professor Wortley could be highly prejudicial as it is akin to propensity evidence or similar fact evidence. That is, evidence that racial profiling exists could be highly prejudicial. They relied on the case of *R. v. Handy* (2000) 48 O.R. (3d) 257, [2000] O.J. No. 1373. I am not persuaded that the case of *R. v. Handy*, supra which is a criminal law case dealing with the test for admission of similar fact evidence, is useful to my determination on whether to hear expert evidence.

In the criminal context, the Courts have stated (*R. v. Mohan*, supra [1994] 2 S.C.R. 9) that they will only admit expert evidence that meets the following criteria:

> 1. relevance 2. necessity in assisting the trier of fact 3. the absence of any exclusionary rule 4. the proper qualification of the proposed witness.

The Respondents argued that the expert evidence was not relevant or necessary in this case.

Since I am not bound by the formal rules of evidence applied in the criminal law context, I have also taken note of principles developed in human rights proceedings in particular. The Respondents relied on *Omoruyi-Odin v. Toronto*

District School Board, [[2002] O.H.R.B.I.D. No. 21], where the Tribunal declined to qualify certain witnesses as experts and refused to permit them to offer opinion evidence, in large part because the Tribunal determined that the proposed evidence was not relevant or necessary:

> [55] It was also proposed that Bernard proffer opinion evidence on the following topics: anti-Black racism in Canada and its manifestations in the workplace; the development and perpetuation of stereotypes and systemic barriers; and stereotypes directed against African Canadian men. None of these appear to be areas in which it is necessary that opinion evidence be adduced before the BOI, which is, after all, statutorily charged with and presumed to have the expertise to determine whether discrimination, including systemic discrimination, exists. Furthermore, it appears that this proposed evidence is all of a general or contextual nature in the sense that Bernard's views on these topics do not arise out of any examination of the circumstances obtaining in the Scarborough Board during the time covered by this Complaint.

The Respondents noted that in *Smith v. Canada Customs and Revenue Agency*, [2004] O.J. No. 3410 the Court did not permit Professor Wortley to testify on whether the Canada customs agent's actions amounted to racial profiling because he was not an expert on Canada customs enforcement practices. The Respondents argued that this is the same situation. Professor Wortley's evidence is not necessary. Nor is it relevant in that it is a general nature and not specific to the type of investigation at issue in this hearing. I note that in *Smith*, supra, Professor Wortley was qualified as an expert in racial profiling and permitted to testify about profiling in general.

Professor Wortley has not conducted any studies about the Peel police or the Greater Toronto police in particular. Also, Professor Wortley's research focuses primarily on police stops, which is not the situation in this complaint. However, Professor Wortley's research also focuses on the investigation by police after the initial stop, which may be analogous to the complaint before me.

The Respondents pointed out that in the case of *R. v. Brown*, [2003] 64 O.R. (3d) 161, a case involving racial profiling by the police, no expert evidence was needed. However, in that case the Crown conceded the existence of racial profiling, so the only issue was whether it had occurred in that case. I did not understand the Respondents to be conceding the existence of racial profiling in police investigations in Canada. At most, they agreed to a definition of racial profiling, not its existence.

I prefer the approach taken by the Nova Scotia Board in the case of *Johnson v. Halifax (Regional Municipality) Police Service*, [2003] N.S.H.R.B.I.D. No. 2 at paras. 92 and 93:

> ... With all due respect to the board, expertise in racism and expertise in discrimination are two different things. Racism is a social phenomenon, discrimination a legally prohibited act. Boards are presumed to possess a certain expertise in the law of discrimination and human rights, but do not necessarily possess expert knowledge in the practices and impact of racism beyond a basic understanding of their dynamics (though obviously a range of knowledge on these topics exists on the part of boards of inquiry). Racism takes many guises, exists in many different

environments and it is studied by a great variety of social scientists using various methodologies. A given board of inquiry is unlikely to be up to date on all this literature, and I would not wish to see *Omoruyi-Odin* cited as a way of cutting off recourse to expert evidence in discrimination cases. One method of providing this evidence to a board is of course simply to submit published works on the relevant matters, but works cannot be cross-examined.

. . . In my view, the actual context of the *Mohan* decision must be kept in mind in understanding where to draw the line between "helpful" and "necessary" evidence. *Mohan* was a criminal case where the rules of evidence are highly structured, partly because of a historic concern to ensure that unduly prejudicial evidence does not go before a jury. I note that with only one exception all the case authorities cited in *Mohan* are criminal cases, suggesting that the concerns relating to criminal trials were uppermost in the Court's mind. In any case, immediately after noting that the descriptor "helpful" sets too low a standard, Justice Sopinka went on to say at 429, "I would not judge necessity by too strict a standard. What is required is that the opinion be necessary in the sense that it provide information 'which is likely to be outside the experience and knowledge of a judge or jury.'" I have found that it satisfies this test for the reasons stated above. Expert evidence in discrimination cases can be statistically based, with an air of scientific validity, but often it is highly qualitative and uses the "softer" methodologies of the social sciences. This is clearly appropriate when we are dealing with the elusive but nonetheless powerful concept of human dignity that underlies human rights law. The often subtle nature of discrimination puts a high burden on complainants, and I would urge future boards not to be too quick to characterize proffered expert evidence as merely "helpful" and thus excluded.

. . . . .

In my view, while the standard remains "necessity," the assessment of "necessity" is somewhat lower in the context of a human rights hearing than in the context of a criminal proceeding. The "necessity" requirement must take into account the nature of human rights hearings and the often subtle nature of discrimination.

Regardless of the extent to which racial profiling has been raised in other cases, the Commission asserts that this is the first complaint before the Human Rights Tribunal in Ontario alleging racial profiling in a police investigation. I find that the proposed evidence would provide useful context about the meaning and existence of racial profiling (if any) in police investigations in Canada against which I can better understand the circumstances in which it may occur and the factors indicative of it. In that sense I find the proposed evidence to be relevant and "necessary" using the less strict standard appropriate for a human rights process.

The Respondents also relied on the human rights case of case of *Orughu v. Canada Border Services Agency*, 2004 CHRT 35 where Professor Wortley, although accepted as an expert, was not permitted to tender parts of his report because they were not necessary and Professor Wortley would be opining on the very issue before the Tribunal. Similarly, in *Smith v. Canada Customs, supra,* the Court did not permit Professor Wortley to testify on whether the custom agent's action amounted to racial profiling, because that was the very issue before the Court.

On that point, I find the comments of Justice Lane in the civil case of *Peart v. Peel (Regional Municipality) Police Services Board*, [2003] O.J. No. 2669 on the use of opinion evidence on racial profiling very useful:

> [23] If I find that the underlying 'facts' upon which Dr. Agard's opinion is based actually existed on December 1, 1997, then his evidence provides me with a basis for an inference that racial profiling was being practiced that day by one or both officers. That is the classic role of the expert: to provide the court with a ready-made inference based on scientific, medical, psychiatric, engineering or similar learning, which the court can draw if certain identified underlying facts are demonstrated to exist. . . . But the inference is one that the court draws. Dr. Agard's opinion is not a substitute for the court's own analysis of the evidence, taking account in so doing of the societal background and the description of the indicia of racial profiling which he has provided, to determine what the facts actually were on that day. Nor is the inference a mandatory one; it is available for the court to draw if the court is persuaded on the balance of probabilities that it is the more probable explanation for the events in question . . .

Regardless of Professor Wortley's opinion on whether factors in this case point to racial profiling, that is my decision to make, and I will not be unduly influenced by his opinion on that issue. Accordingly, I concluded that Professor Wortley was properly qualified, and that the evidence he proposed to give was relevant, necessary and not excluded by any other exclusionary rule.

The Human Rights Tribunal concluded that Ms. Nassiah had been the victim of racial profiling. She was awarded $20,000 and a number of systemic remedies were ordered. See *Nassiah v. Regional Municipality of Peel Services Board.*[242]

3. ULTIMATE ISSUE RULE

An issue which we find debated throughout the cases involving expert evidence involves the supposed problem of the expert giving opinion evidence on the ultimate issue. One would have thought that at this stage in our development of the law of evidence, a final disposition of such "problem" could have been made, but still we see this "red herring" being raised. To term this problem a "red herring" is not an original notion but rather conforms to Professor Wigmore's view of the ultimate issue rule as "one of those impracticable and misconceived utterances which lack any justification in principle."[243]

If the "ultimate issue" with respect to which opinion testimony was barred was narrowly construed to prohibit only expressions of opinion on issues which are mixed questions of fact and law, the rule would be justifiable on the general basis that opinion testimony ought to be received when it is necessary and helpful, and only then. An expression of opinion that involves the application of a legal

---

242 2007 HRTO 14 (CanLII).
243 7 Wigmore, *Evidence* (Chad. Rev.), s. 1921.

standard ought to be excluded as superfluous since a jury, properly instructed by the trial judge on the law, is as capable of applying the standard as the witness. As described by Bliss J.:

> No witness should be permitted to give his opinion directly that a person is guilty or innocent, or is criminally responsible or irresponsible, or that a person was negligent or not negligent, or that he had capacity to execute a will, or deed, or like instrument . . . But the reason is that such matters are not subjects of opinion testimony. They are mixed questions of law and fact. When a standard, or a measure, or a capacity has been fixed by law, no witness whether expert or non-expert, nor however qualified, is permitted to express an opinion as to whether or not the person or the conduct, in question, measures up to that standard. On that question the court must instruct the jury as to the law, and the jury must draw its own conclusion from the evidence. However courts have permitted both scientific and practical experts to express their opinion whether a certain method used, or course of conduct was a proper one.[244]

To perpetuate an ultimate issue rule framed any more broadly than this could exclude much that is helpful to a jury without any worthwhile justification; to say its reception would permit the jury's role to be usurped overlooks the fact that opinion evidence, like any other evidence, can always be rejected by the trier of fact.[245] In favour of the narrower view, the judgment of Aylesworth, J.A., in *R. v. Fisher*[246] is noteworthy. Speaking for the majority, he denied defendant's objection that the psychiatrist's opinion was inadmissible as dealing with the very point the jury had to decide by noting:

> . . . the basic reasoning which runs through the authorities here and in England, seems to be that expert opinion evidence will be admitted where it will be helpful to the jury in their deliberations and it will be excluded only where the jury can as easily draw the necessary inferences without it. When the latter is the situation, the intended opinion evidence is superfluous. . . .
>
> In some cases where opinion evidence has been rejected, the ground given is that the giving of the witness's opinion usurped the function of the jury. In other decisions it is said that the evidence tendered constituted an opinion upon the very point or issue which the jury had to decide. *An examination of these authorities, however, discloses, in my view, that the jury or the judge, in cases tried without a jury, would have had no difficulty in arriving at a proper conclusion in the absence of the tendered opinion and that this was the true ground for its rejection* . . .
>
> Where the opinion tendered involves what is a mixed question of law and fact, the opinion is not admissible. [Emphasis added.][247]

A broader formulation of the ultimate issue rule foreclosing other opinion testimony, over and above opinions respecting guilt or innocence, not only lacks justification but, in theory, is unworkable. The doctrines of relevance and

---

244 *Grismore v. Consol. Products Co.*, 5 N.W. 2d 646, 663 (Iowa, 1942). To similar effect, see *R. v. Fisher* (1961), 34 C.R. 320, 342 (Ont. C.A.), per Aylesworth, J.A.

245 See *Snow v. Boston & Maine R.R.*, 65 Me. 230, 231 (1875): "The reason for its exclusion given by counsel, that it would instruct the jury as to the amount of the verdict to be rendered, would seem to be a very good reason for its admission. *Instruction is what the jury want.* They would not be bound by it any more than by other testimony, but it would be more or less valuable in enabling them to come to a correct conclusion." [emphasis added]; noted in 7 Wigmore, *Evidence* (Chad. Rev.), s. 1921, p. 26.

246 *Supra*, note 244.

247 *Ibid.*, at pp. 340-43.

materiality dictate that *all* evidence given at a trial must be with respect to matters that are *necessary* to the prosecution or defence of the matter at issue. All testimony is then with respect to an ultimate issue in the sense that failure of proof with respect to anything necessary to a successful prosecution must yield an acquittal. In theory then, no expert, bound by the rules of relevancy and materiality, would be permitted to testify to *anything* under a broad formulation of the ultimate issue rule. In practice, of course, expert opinion testimony is received and the supposed ultimate issue rule which developed in the nineteenth century is seen, to be kind, as amorphous, and is applied or withheld with a great deal of discretion.

Finally, in *Graat v. R.*,[248] Howland C.J.O., for the court, concluded:

> In Canada the ultimate issue doctrine may now be regarded as having been virtually abandoned or rejected. Where evidence has been rejected on the basis of the doctrine, such rejection can be explained on other grounds. In some instances the opinion evidence should be rejected because the trier of fact, whether Judge or jury, is just as well qualified as the witness to draw the necessary inference. Accordingly, the non-expert testimony is superfluous, as it is of no appreciable assistance to the Judge or jury. . . . In the final analysis, even with the benefit of the expert's evidence the jury still has to make the final determination of the issue, so that the expert is not really usurping the jury's function.

R. v. BRYAN
(2003), 175 C.C.C. (3d) 285, 2003 CarswellOnt 2068 (C.A.)

The accused was convicted of possession of cocaine for the purposes of trafficking and possession of proceeds of crime. One ground of appeal dealt with the evidence of an expert witness.

Per GOUDGE J.A. (ABELLA and ARMSTRONG JJ.A. concurring): —

The appellant's third argument is that the Crown adduced evidence from a police expert witness that was inadmissible and prejudicial, since it went to the ultimate issue the jury had to decide. The evidence was called in relation to the two charges arising from July 18, 2001. On the first of those charges, the Crown alleged that the appellant had 2.96 grams of cocaine on his person at the time of his arrest and that this was for the purpose of trafficking. On the second charge, the Crown alleged that at the time of arrest the appellant was in possession of some $ 1,505 and that this was the proceeds of crime.

The appellant's defence to the first of these two charges was that he was not in possession of cocaine and that the police were mistaken. He did not assert that he had the cocaine for his own use or even that he was a user. His defence to the second charge was that while he was indeed in possession of the cash, there was an innocent explanation for this.

---

248 (1980), 55 C.C.C. (2d) 429, 443 (Ont. C.A.); affirmed (1982), 2 C.C.C. (3d) 365 (S.C.C.). See *R. v. Millar* (1989), 71 C.R. (3d) 78 (C.A.), on a trial of manslaughter of a nine-week-old baby, allowing the receipt of expert evidence that, considering the type and frequency of the injuries, the infant was the subject of "child abuse."

As part of its case, the Crown called the police officer and qualified him to give expert evidence relating to the business of trafficking in cocaine and the proceeds received therefrom. Defence counsel consented to the witness's expertise and objected to none of his evidence.

The witness testified in generic terms about the indicia that point to a possession of cocaine being for the purpose of trafficking as opposed to personal use. He was then asked to take as a given the evidence of the Crown in this case and provide his opinion about whether the possession of cocaine on those assumed facts was for trafficking or personal use. His opinion was that there was a very strong inference that somebody in these circumstances would be in possession for the purpose of trafficking. Similarly, his opinion as related to the second charge was that a very strong inference existed that the money in the person's possession would be the proceeds of crime.

The appellant does not quarrel with the generic evidence offered by the police expert, but says that his opinion assuming the facts alleged by the Crown in this case is inadmissible as it goes to the ultimate question for the jury.

I do not agree. The proper approach to the admission of expert evidence was set out in *R. v. Mohan*, [1994] 2 S.C.R. 9 S.C.C.. It laid out the four well-known criteria of relevance, necessity and assisting the trier of fact, the absence of any exclusionary rule, and a properly qualified expert.

In describing the necessity criterion, Sopinka J. made clear that there is now no general rule precluding expert evidence on the ultimate issue. At pp. 24-25, he said this:

> There is also a concern inherent in the application of this criterion that experts not be permitted to usurp the functions of the trier of fact. Too liberal an approach could result in a trial becoming nothing more than a contest of experts with the trier of fact acting as referee in deciding which expert to accept. These concerns were the basis of the rule which excluded expert evidence in respect of the ultimate issue. Although the rule is no longer of general application, the concerns underlying it remain. In light of these concerns, the criteria of relevance and necessity are applied strictly, on occasion, to exclude expert evidence as to an ultimate issue. Expert evidence as to credibility or oath-helping has been excluded on this basis: see *R. v. Marquard*, [1993] 4 S.C.R. 223, per McLachlin J.

Thus the simple answer to the appellant's third argument is that there is no general rule excluding expert evidence in respect of the ultimate issue. Moreover, there is no challenge to the contested expert evidence on the basis of the Mohan criteria. Indeed, in the circumstances of this case, the evidence would seem to easily satisfy those criteria.

4. EXPERT OPINION BASED ON HEARSAY

It is commonly said that an expert is confined to expressions of opinion based on facts proved at the trial, proved by the expert when he has had the advantage of personal observation of the facts at issue, or proved through the testimony of other witnesses, with the opinion elicited based on an assumption of their truthfulness using the device of hypothetical questions.[249] To this general proposition there has developed in Canada a seeming exception that, at least with respect to certain experts, an opinion may be expressed though based on facts not otherwise proved; i.e., where the basis for the expert's opinion consists partly of statements made to him prior to trial, and partly of where there are grounds of necessity in so proceeding or circumstances guaranteeing the trustworthiness of such statements.

R. v. JORDAN
(1983), 33 C.R. (3d) 394 (B.C. Co. Ct.)

WETMORE CO. CT. J.:—

The accused on arriving on a flight from Tokyo was searched at customs at the Vancouver airport. He was found in possession of narcotics. His statements to the customs officer confirm both the accused's knowledge of this substance in his luggage and that it was a narcotic. It appears that there was never specific mention of the word "heroin" in the conversation.

The indictment charges importing heroin in count 1 and possession of heroin for the purposes of trafficking in count 2.

The Crown first produced certificates showing the substance to be heroin. The Crown then produced the analyst for cross-examination. It is on the basis of this evidence that the defence says there is no reliable evidence that the substance is heroin.

Mr. Clark, a duly appointed analyst, explained the process of analysis used. In the final analysis the questioned substance in a gaseous state is subjected to a spectrometric comparison with a known standard of heroin. The spectrometric comparisons being identical, heroin is concluded as being the questioned substance. There is a further comparative study made of a standard graph prepared from scientific literature and the spectrophotomatic characteristics of the questioned substance. Again the points of comparison unite.

Mr. Clark testifies that he would not certify the questioned substance as heroin without a positive identity existing in *both* comparative studies.

In operating his apparatus the "known heroin" comes from the crime detection laboratory in Ottawa to the Vancouver laboratory. There, this "known standard" is again analyzed by the same process before use. This is done not by Mr. Clark necessarily but by other analysts in the Vancouver laboratory. He cannot say who did the actual analysis of the known standard prior to its use as the standard in making the comparisons with the exhibits in this case.

Defence counsel therefore argues that the opinion evidence of Mr. Clark is based upon hearsay evidence, which is not admissible, thus destroying the value of his opinion.

The argument is developed from the judgment of Dickson J. in *R. v. Abbey*, 29 C.R. (3d) 193 (S.C.C.). In that case the accused related several bizarre incidents

---

249 See, *e.g.*, Cross, *Evidence*, 5th ed., p. 446 and Phipson, *Evidence*, 11th ed., p. 507.

to the psychiatrist, which the doctor apparently accepted as truthful. The learned judge then dealt with the medical opinion as if those statements had been established as a fact. From pp. 208-14, Dickson J. discusses the problems of hearsay evidence and opinion evidence. He concludes [p. 214], "Before any weight can be given to an expert's opinion, the facts upon which the opinion is based must be found to exist."

It must be remembered that Dickson J. was dealing with a psychiatric opinion based upon facts which are unique to the particular inquiry. He was not commenting upon other types of information. For example, the psychiatrist's opinion in the final analysis is usually derived from three sources, the patient's comments, his own observations and experience, and the medical literature. Both the experience and medical literature elements involve a great deal of hearsay, but surely all knowledge need not be proved by primary research and observation. Indeed, if that were so, no scientific opinion beyond the most elementary could ever be forthcoming. There comes a time, after testing and observation, that some pragmatic conclusions legitimately arise which need no further verification from original sources.

With respect, I think that is the situation in the case at bar. If it had been established that either the spectrometric comparisons with the supplied "known source" or the published scientific journal graph had not all been consistent, a query may well arise which had not been settled by anything more reliable than hearsay evidence. That did not occur.

I can accept hearsay evidence as original evidence insofar as it relates to my evaluation of the expert's opinion. What I cannot do is accept, as proven for itself, the facts in that hearsay statement. What Mr. Clark really says is that in his opinion the fact that he compared the characteristics of this substance with two substances which he, for good reason, believed to be heroin standards satisfied him that the substance he was analyzing was heroin.

What I am then called upon to measure is my own judgment of his decision, that the conclusion was justified.

The standard is prepared in the crime detection laboratory for this specific purpose. It is then further checked for accuracy by analysts in the Vancouver lab. The standard graph from the scientific literature is likewise designed for this specific purpose. Using these techniques, Mr. Clark testifies to having done hundreds of tests of the same nature. Nothing in cross-examination suggests that observations of a suspicious nature relating to accuracy have ever occurred.

I conclude therefore that there is no reason to doubt the opinion of Mr. Clark that the substance involved in this case is heroin.

With respect to defence counsel, I think this sort of evidence is more analogous to such things as marine charts. Nobody suggests that those documents are inadmissible in proving depths of the ocean without calling the actual measurer and cartographer.

In dismissing the accused's appeal in *Jordan*, Anderson J.A. commented:

. . . In the case on appeal the analyst testified that the substance received from Ottawa and labelled "heroin" was tested by an analyst in his office. Such a course is perfectly proper. To call the analyst who made the test of the "known" sample is unnecessary. If such an analyst was called, it would, according to the argument of the appellant, be necessary for him to prove that the substance that he used for comparison purposes was heroin, and so on down the line. Such an argument, while logical, cannot be accepted because it would make scientific proof so ponderous and expensive that in reality the evidence of experts could never be used. In my view, the argument that the judgment in *R. v. Abbey*, [1982] 2 S.C.R. 24, applies to scientific tests of the kind under consideration here is unacceptable.[250]

R. v. LAVALLEE
[1990] 1 S.C.R. 852, 76 C.R. (3d) 329, 55 C.C.C. (3d) 97

On a charge of murder the accused relied on self-defence. The deceased was a man with whom the accused had been living for several years. The accused shot the deceased in the back of the head as he was leaving her room after he had assaulted and threatened her. A statement by the accused to police was introduced into evidence by the prosecution. In the statement the accused admitted the shooting. She told the police that the accused had threatened to kill her when the other visitors to their home left and that she was scared and thinking about all the other times that the accused had beaten her. The defence called a psychiatrist who testified with respect to the "battered-wife syndrome." He testified that the accused felt that unless she defended herself and reacted in a violent way that she would die. He testified that he had spoken to the accused and the accused's mother on several occasions and that he had read the accused's statement to the police and the police reports. Neither the accused nor the accused's mother testified at the trial. The accused was acquitted. An appeal was allowed and a new trial ordered on the basis that the trial judge did not adequately instruct the jury with respect to the evidence of the psychiatrist. The court changed the substantive law regarding self defence and allowed that lay juries needed the advice of experts to understand the woman's perspective; see, *supra*, Chapter 1. The following extract deals only with the expert's ability to rely on hearsay in coming to his opinion and the trial judge's instruction to the jury in that event.

WILSON J. (DICKSON C.J.C. and LAMER, L'HEUREUX-DUBÉ, GONTHIER and MCLACHLIN JJ. concurring):—

. . . .

The appellant did not testify but her statement made to police on the night of the shooting was put in evidence. Portions of it read as follows:

Me and Wendy argued as usual and I ran in the house after Kevin pushed me. I was scared, I was really scared. I locked the door. Herb was downstairs with Joanne and I called for Herb but I was crying when I called him. I said 'Herb come up here please.' Herb came up to the top of the stairs and I told him that Kevin was going to

---

250 (1984), 39 C.R. (3d) 50, 57 (B.C.C.A.).

hit me actually beat on me again. Herb said he knew and that if I was his old lady things would be different, he gave me a hug. OK, we're friends, there's nothing between us. He said 'Yeah, I know' and he went outside to talk to Kevin leaving the door unlocked. I went upstairs and hid in my closet from Kevin. I was so scared . . . My window was open and I could hear Kevin asking questions about what I was doing and what I was saying. Next thing I know he was coming up the stairs for me. He came into my bedroom and said 'Wench, where are you?' And he turned on my light and he said 'Your purse is on the floor' and he kicked it. OK then he turned and he saw me in the closet. He wanted me to come out but I didn't want to come out because I was scared. I was so scared. [The officer who took the statement then testified that the appellant started to cry at this point and stopped after a minute or two.] He grabbed me by the arm right there. There's a bruise on my face also where he slapped me. He didn't slap me right then, first he yelled at me then he pushed me and I pushed him back and he hit me twice on the right hand side of my head. I was scared. All I thought about was all the other times he used to beat me, I was scared, I was shaking as usual. The rest is a blank, all I remember is he gave me the gun and a shot was fired through my screen. This is all so fast. And then the guns were in another room and he loaded it the second shot and gave it to me. And I was going to shoot myself. I pointed it to myself, I was so upset. OK and then he went and I was sitting on the bed and he started going like this with his finger [the appellant made a shaking motion with an index finger] and said something like 'You're my old lady and you do as you're told' or something like that. He said 'wait till everybody leaves, you'll get it then' and he said something to the effect of 'either you kill me or I'll get you' that was what it was. He kind of smiled and then he turned around. I shot him but I aimed out. I thought I aimed above him and a piece of his head went that way.

. . . .

The expert evidence which forms the subject-matter of the appeal came from Dr. Fred Shane, a psychiatrist with extensive professional experience in the treatment of battered wives. At the request of defence counsel Dr. Shane prepared a psychiatric assessment of the appellant. The substance of Dr. Shane's opinion was that the appellant had been terrorized by Rust to the point of feeling trapped, vulnerable, worthless and unable to escape the relationship despite the violence. At the same time, the continuing pattern of abuse put her life in danger. In Dr. Shane's opinion the appellant's shooting of the deceased was a final desperate act by a woman who sincerely believed that she would be killed that night. . . .

Dr. Shane stated that his opinion was based on four hours of formal interviews with the appellant, a police report of the incident (including the appellant's statement), hospital reports documenting eight of her visits to emergency departments between 1983 and 1985, and an interview with the appellant's mother. In the course of his testimony Dr. Shane related many things told to him by the appellant for which there was no admissible evidence. They were not in the appellant's statement to the police and she did not testify at trial. For example, Dr. Shane mentioned several episodes of abuse described by the appellant for which there were no hospital reports. He also related the appellant's disclosure to him that she had lied to doctors about the cause of her injuries. Dr. Shane testified that such fabrication was typical of battered women. The appellant also recounted to Dr. Shane occasions on which Rust would allegedly beat her, then beg her forgiveness and ply her with flowers and temporary displays of kindness. . . . The appellant denied to Dr. Shane that she had homicidal fantasies about Rust and mentioned that she had smoked some marijuana on the night in question. These facts were related by Dr. Shane in the course of his testimony.

. . . .

In *Abbey, supra*, this Court addressed the bases upon which expert evidence that relies on hearsay is admissible. The accused in that case was charged with importing cocaine and his defence was insanity. The accused did not testify. A psychiatrist gave his opinion as to the sanity of the accused and, in the course of giving the basis for his conclusions, referred to incidents and hallucinations related to him by the accused for which there was no admissible evidence. The Crown submitted before this court that the trial judge "accepted and treated as factual much of this hearsay evidence" related to the psychiatrist. Dickson J. found that the point was "well taken". This was the preliminary finding on which the case was based and I think it is fair to say that the trial judge in the case at bar clearly did not make the same mistake as did the trial judge in *Abbey*. At pp. 411-2 of his judgment Dickson J. articulated the hazards inherent in admitting expert testimony based on hearsay:

> The danger, of course, in admitting such testimony is the ever present possibility, here exemplified, that the judge or jury, without more, will accept the evidence as going to the truth of the facts stated in it. The danger is real and lies at the heart of this case. Once such testimony is admitted, a careful charge to the jury by the judge or direction to himself is essential. The problem, however, as pointed out by Fauteux J. in *Wilband* resides not in the admissibility of the testimony but rather the weight to be accorded to the opinion. Although admissible in the context of his opinion, to the extent that it is second-hand his testimony is not proof of the facts stated.

> . . . .

> It was appropriate for the doctors to state the basis for their opinions and in the course of doing so, to refer to what they were told not only by Abbey but by others, but it was error for the judge to accept as having been proved the facts upon which the doctors had relied in forming their opinions. While it is not questioned that medical experts are entitled to take into consideration all possible information in forming their opinions, this in no way removes from the party tendering such evidence the obligation of establishing, through properly admissible evidence, the factual basis on which such opinions are based. Before any weight can be given to an expert's opinion, the facts upon which the opinion is based must be found to exist.

For present purposes I think the ratio of *Abbey* can be distilled into the following propositions:

1. An expert opinion is admissible if relevant, even if it is based on second-hand evidence.

2. This second hand evidence (hearsay) is admissible to show the information on which the expert opinion is based, not as evidence going to the existence of the facts on which the opinion is based.

3.   Where the psychiatric evidence is comprised of hearsay evidence, the problem is the weight to be attributed to the opinion.

4.   Before any weight can be given to an expert's opinion, the facts upon which the opinion is based must be found to exist.

In the case at bar the trial judge was clearly of the view that Dr. Shane's evidence was relevant. He would not have admitted it otherwise. As I stated above, in light of the evidence of the battering relationship which subsisted between the appellant and the deceased, the trial judge was correct in so doing.

With respect to the second point, the trial judge warned the jury generally that they could not "decide the case on the basis of things the witnesses did not see or hear", which would seem to include those matters which Dr. Shane neither saw nor heard. He then gave the marijuana smoking and the confirmatory evidence of the appellant's mother as two sources of information which were not evidence in the case. In my opinion, it would have been preferable if the trial judge had described the interview with the appellant as a source of inadmissible evidence, the marijuana smoking being an example of inadmissible evidence from that source. Nevertheless, I think the trial judge makes his meaning clear to the jury in the subsequent passage: "In terms of the matters considered by Dr. Shane he is left, therefore, with the deceased's [*sic* — he means accused's] statement, some supplementary information from the police report and his interpretation of the hospital records." The trial judge thus eliminates the interview with the appellant and his conversation with her mother as sources of admissible evidence. Elsewhere he reinforces the rule that the jury can only consider the admissible evidence. He refers to the hospital visits made by the appellant:

> Another evidentiary caution is necessary here. Mr. Brodsky, in his remarks, said, as he did in calling some of the evidence respecting hospital attendances that this is only a representative sample. He ought not to have said that. It is not evidence and must be completely disregarded by you. The only evidence before you are the eight attendances that you heard about and nothing else — eight attendances and nothing else.

The trial judge's instructions regarding the weight attributable to Dr. Shane's opinion also emphasize his distinction between admissible evidence and hearsay:

> *If the premises upon which the information is substantially based has not been proven in evidence, it is up to you to conclude that it is not safe to attach a great deal of weight to the opinion. An opinion of an expert depends, to a large extent, on the validity of the facts assumed by the evidence of the expert.*
>
> If there are some errors and the factual assumptions aren't too important to the eventual opinion, that's one thing. *If there are errors or matters not in evidence and those matters are substantial, in your view, in terms of the impact on the expert's opinion, then you will want to look at the value and weight of that expert's opinion very carefully.* It depends on how important you think the matters were that Dr. Shane relied on that are not in evidence. (Emphasis added.)

I agree with Huband J.A. that these instructions with respect to weight conform to this court's judgment in *Abbey*. The only complaint can be with the trial judge's attempt to distinguish admissible from inadmissible evidence. The trial judge was certainly not as clear as he might have been but I have no hesitation in finding that a retrial is not warranted on this account.

Given that Dr. Shane relied extensively on his interview with the appellant, the trial judge drew particular attention to the additional element of credibility that could affect the quality of Dr. Shane's opinion: "It is the position of the Crown that Dr. Shane's opinion stands or falls on the veracity of Lyn Lavallee because he relied so heavily and extensively on what she told him and the evidence contained in the statement, Exhibit 16. That's for you to decide." Later in the charge, he elaborates:

> Undoubtably [*sic*] she was a very important source, if not the major source, of his information. Dr. Shane agreed that if what she told him was erroneous, he would have to reassess his position.
>
> On cross-examination he reiterated that in his opinion her action was spontaneous to the moment to try to defend herself. The straw that broke the camel's back was the threat, 'When the others leave you're going to get it', even though similar statements had been made to her on other occasions. According to what she told him, the accused felt compelled to shoot.
>
> Based on the information he had in the interview, it was his opinion that the acts of the accused were impulsive and not premeditated. He disagreed with the Crown's suggestion that Lyn Lavallee took the opportunity when it presented itself.
>
> He conceded that patients had, on occasion, lied and misled him in the past.

The fourth proposition I have extracted from *Abbey* is that there must be admissible evidence to support the facts on which the expert relies before any weight can be attributed to the opinion. The majority of the Manitoba Court of Appeal appears to interpret this as a requirement that each and every fact relied upon by the expert must be independently proven and admitted into evidence before the entire opinion can be given any weight.

Dr. Shane referred in his testimony to various facts for which there was no admissible evidence. The information was elicited from his interviews with the appellant. It included the smoking of marijuana prior to the killing, the deterioration of the intimate relationship between the appellant and Rust, past episodes of physical and psychological abuse followed by intervals of contrition, the apparent denial of homicidal fantasies on the appellant's part, and her remorse after killing Rust.

If the majority of the Court of Appeal is suggesting that each of these specific facts must be proven in evidence before any weight could be given to Dr. Shane's opinion about the accused's mental state, I must respectfully disagree. *Abbey* does not, in my view, provide any authority for that proposition. The court's conclusion in that case was that the trial judge erred in treating as proven the facts upon which the psychiatrist relied in formulating his opinion. The solution was an appropriate charge to the jury, not an effective withdrawal of the evidence. In my view, as long as there is some admissible evidence to establish the foundation for the expert's opinion, the trial judge cannot subsequently instruct the jury to completely ignore the testimony. The judge must, of course, warn the jury that the more the expert relies on facts not proved in evidence the less weight the jury may attribute to the opinion.

On my reading of the record Dr. Shane had before him admissible evidence about the nature of the relationship between the appellant and Rust in the form of the appellant's statement to the police and the hospital records. In addition, there was substantial corroborative evidence provided at trial by Ezako, the emergency-room doctor who testified to doubting the appellant's explanation of her injuries. There was also the evidence of the witnesses on the night of the shooting who testified to the appellant's frightened appearance, tone of voice, and conduct in dealing with Rust. The evidence pointed to the image of a woman who was brutally abused, who lied about the cause of her injuries, and who was incapable of leaving her abuser. As Huband J.A. comments in dissent, if the trial judge erred at all, he was probably remiss in not mentioning the corroborative evidence of Ezako as buttressing the evidentiary foundation on which Dr. Shane premised his opinion.

. . . .

Where the factual basis of an expert's opinion is a mélange of admissible and inadmissible evidence the duty of the trial judge is to caution the jury that the weight attributable to the expert testimony is directly related to the amount and quality of admissible evidence on which it relies. The trial judge openly acknowledged to counsel the inherent difficulty in discharging such a duty in the case at bar. In my view, the trial judge performed his task adequately in this regard. A new trial is not warranted on the basis of the trial judge's charge to the jury.

I would accordingly allow the appeal, set aside the order of the Court of Appeal, and restore the acquittal.

. . . .

SOPINKA J. (concurring in the result):— I have read the reasons of my colleague Justice Wilson, and I agree in the result that this appeal must be allowed. I find it necessary, however, to add a few words concerning the interpretation of this Court's decision in *R. v. Abbey* (1982), 68 C.C.C. (2d) 394.

Abbey has been roundly criticized: see, *e.g.*, Schiff, *Evidence in the Litigation Process*, 3rd ed., vol. I, (1988), pp. 473-6, and Delisle, *Evidence: Principles and Problems*, 2nd ed. (1989), pp. 477-9. The essence of the criticism is that Abbey sets out more restrictive conditions for the use of expert evidence than did previous decisions of this court: *i.e.*, *City of St. John v. Irving Oil Co. Ltd.* (1966), [1966] S.C.R. 581; *Wilband v. The Queen*, [1967] S.C.R. 14, and *R. v. Lupien*, [1970] S.C.R. 263. Upon reflection, it seems to me that the very special facts in *Abbey*, and the decision required on those facts, have contributed to the development of a principle concerning the admissibility and weight of expert opinion evidence that is self-contradictory. The contradiction is apparent in the four principles set out by Wilson J. in the present case, *ante*, pp. 127-8, which I reproduce here for the sake of convenience:

1.   An expert opinion is admissible if relevant, even if it is based on second-hand evidence.

2.   This second-hand evidence (hearsay) is admissible to show the information on

which the expert opinion is based, not as evidence going to the existence of the facts on which the opinion is based.

3.   Where the psychiatric evidence is comprised of hearsay evidence, the problem is the weight to be attributed to the opinion.

4.   Before any weight can be given to an expert's opinion, the facts upon which the opinion is based must be found to exist.

The combined effect of Nos. 1, 3 and 4 is that an expert opinion relevant in the abstract to a material issue in a trial but based entirely on unproven hearsay (*e.g.*, from the mouth of the accused, as in *Abbey*) is admissible but entitled to no weight whatsoever. The question that arises is how any evidence can be admissible and yet entitled to no weight. As one commentator has pointed out, an expert opinion based entirely on unproven hearsay must, if anything, be inadmissible by reason of irrelevance, since the facts underlying the expert opinion are the only connection between the opinion and the case: see Wardle, "*R. v. Abbey* and Psychiatric Opinion Evidence: Requiring the Accused to Testify", 17 Ottawa L. Rev. 116 at pp. 122-3 (1984).

The resolution of the contradiction inherent in *Abbey*, and the answer to the criticism *Abbey* has drawn, is to be found in the practical distinction between evidence that an expert obtains and acts upon within the scope of his or her expertise (as in *City of St. John*,) and evidence that an expert obtains from a party to litigation touching a matter directly in issue (as in *Abbey*).

In the former instance, an expert arrives at an opinion on the basis of forms of enquiry and practice that are accepted means of decision within that expertise. A physician, for example, daily determines questions of immense importance on the basis of the observations of colleagues, often in the form of second or third-hand hearsay. For a court to accord no weight to, or to exclude, this sort of professional judgment, arrived at in accordance with sound medical practices, would be to ignore the strong circumstantial guarantees of trustworthiness that surround it, and would be, in my view, contrary to the approach this court has taken to the analysis of hearsay evidence in general, exemplified in *Ares v. Venner*, [1970] S.C.R. 608. In *R. v. Jordan* (1984), 11 C.C.C. (3d) 565 (B.C.C.A.), a case concerning an expert's evaluation of the chemical composition of an alleged heroin specimen, Anderson J.A. held, and I respectfully agree, that *Abbey* does not apply in such circumstances: see also *R. v. Zundel* (1987), 31 C.C.C. (3d) 97 at p. 146 (Ont. C.A.), where the court recognized an expert opinion based upon evidence ". . . of a general nature which is widely used and acknowledged as reliable by experts in that field".

Where, however, the information upon which an expert forms his or her opinion comes from the mouth of a party to the litigation, or from any other source that is inherently suspect, a court ought to require independent proof of that information. The lack of such proof will, consistent with *Abbey*, have a direct effect on the weight to be given to the opinion, perhaps to the vanishing point. But it must be recognized that it will only be very rarely that an expert's opinion is entirely based upon such information, with no independent proof of any of it. Where an expert's opinion is based in part upon suspect information and in part upon either admitted facts or facts sought to be proved, the matter is purely one of weight. In this respect, I agree with the statement of Wilson J., *ante*, p. 130, as applied to circumstances such as those in the present case:

> ... as long as there is some admissible evidence to establish the foundation for the expert's opinion, the trial judge cannot subsequently instruct the jury to completely ignore the testimony. The judge must, of course, warn the jury that the more the expert relies on facts not proved in evidence the less weight the jury may attribute to the opinion.

As Wilson J. holds, the trial judge's charge to the jury was adequate, and the appeal ought therefore to be allowed.

The dictum in *Abbey*,

> [b]efore any weight can be given to an expert's opinion, the facts upon which the opinion is based must be found to exist,

led some to believe that *all* the facts upon which an opinion was based had to be proved in evidence before the opinion could be given "*any weight*." In *Lavallee*, Madam Justice Wilson says the real ratio of *Abbey* was the fact that the trier there treated as true the facts as related to the psychiatrist. She decides that weight can be given to an opinion, although all the facts that form the basis of the opinion are not independently proved, provided that there is "some admissible evidence to establish the foundation for the expert's opinion" and provided that a careful warning is given to the jury that facts related to the expert which are not independently proved cannot be taken as true. There was admissible evidence in *Lavallee* to support the doctor's opinion and this made *Lavallee* notably different from *Abbey* where the opinion was based entirely on unproven hearsay. A judge should not tell the jury to completely ignore an opinion partially based on inadmissible evidence but rather it is the trial judge's duty to "warn the jury that the more the expert relies on facts not proved in evidence the less weight the jury may attribute to the opinion." The court does recognize, however, "the inherent difficulty in discharging such a duty in the case at bar." The doctor in *Lavallee* did testify that the accused was an important, if not the major, source of his information and that if what she had told him was erroneous he would have to reassess his position. He related to the trier much of what the accused had told him. A careful warning was therefore required by the decision in *Abbey* and, in the view of the Supreme Court, was provided; a view obviously not shared by the majority of the Manitoba Court of Appeal.[251]

The court recognized that the task for the trial judge is one of "inherent difficulty." This was an appellate decision looking back at the whole process and determining whether there ought to be a new trial. Aside from the inherent difficulty in charging a jury concerning the weight attributable to an expert's opinion when the factual basis for the same is "a melange of admissible and inadmissible evidence," there is also the danger that a jury might not follow the trial judge's limiting instruction and might treat as true the facts related by the expert as the basis for his opinion. In looking ahead, and seeking to avoid difficulties and

---

251 See *R. v. Lavallee* (1988), 65 C.R. (3d) 387 (Man. C.A.).

dangers, might a trial judge, following *Lavallee*, ensure, in the first instance, that the expert's opinion is confined to that which the expert is able to express based solely on admissible evidence which can be tested by the trier for trustworthiness? If there is no admissible evidence to support the opinion, for example if the opinion is based entirely on hearsay, the opinion, one assumes, must be inadmissible. As Justice Sopinka points out in his concurring opinion, there is no point in admitting an opinion which is entitled to no weight. It is irrelevant. For the trial judge to be able to confine the expert to an opinion based on admissible evidence he will need to know what that admissible evidence is. Could the trial judge direct that the expert give his opinion last, after all the other defence witnesses, including the accused if it is determined to call the accused, have testified?

The approach of Sopinka J. in *Lavallee* was adopted as the position of the full Court in *R. v. B. (S.A.)*[252] in which the Court upheld the constitutionality of D.N.A. warrant provisions.[253]

In *Worrall*, a manslaughter case, a very experienced trial judge, Watt J., noted this development and provided a clear summary of the current law.

R. v. WORRALL
(2004), 19 C.R. (6th) 213, 2004 CarswellOnt 669 (S.C.J.)

The accused was charged with unlawful act manslaughter in the death of his half-brother. It was alleged that he had injected a lethal dose of heroin or had given him a lethal dose to self-inject. The evidentiary issue was whether it was necessary to call technicians who had conducted tests as to whether the deceased had heroin in his blood.

WATT J.: —

It is well-established that, as a general rule, an expert may base his or her opinion on second-hand information. But when an opinion based on second-hand information is admitted, and the second-hand information is not otherwise established before the trier of fact, the weight of the opinion may recede accordingly. See, for example, *R. v. Lavallee*, [1990] 1 S.C.R. 852, 55 C.C.C. (3d) 97, 129-30 per Wilson J.

The nature of the second-hand information on which an expert may rely varies significantly. For example, a psychiatrist whose opinion is sought on an issue of criminal responsibility, or a toxicologist summoned to offer an opinion about a blood alcohol concentration will often rely on information provided on interview with an accused. On the other hand, experts in the physical sciences may rely on a variety of test results compiled by others in accordance with generally-accepted scientific principles.

In *R. v. Lavallee*, above, Sopinka J. drew a distinction between:

    (i) evidence that an expert obtains and acts upon within the scope of his or her expertise; and

---

252 (2003), 178 C.C.C. (3d) 193 (S.C.C.) at 217-218.
253 See too earlier in *Terceira* (in which the Court affirmed the decision of the Ontario Court of Appeal).

(ii) evidence that an expert obtains from a party to litigation about a matter directly in issue.

Where situation i, above, applies, the expert arrives at his or her opinion on the basis of forms of enquiry and practice that are accepted means of decision within that expertise.

Where the information on which the opinion is formed comes from the mouth of a party, or from any other source that is inherently suspect, we require independent proof of the information relied upon. See, *R. v. Lavallee*, above, at pp. 132-3 per Sopinka J.

And see, *City of Saint John v. Tans Oil Co. Ltd.*, [1966] S.C.R. 581; and *R. v. Abbey* (1982), 68 C.C.C. (2d) 97, 132 per Teeniest J.

. . . .

The distinction drawn by Sopinka J. in his concurring judgment in R. v. Lavallee, above, has been recently re-affirmed in connection with data compiled by others and used by experts in offering opinions on the results tense analysis. . . .

This case involves the testimony of experts, forensic toxicologists and pathologists, who reached their stated opinions, to a greater or lesser extent, on the basis of scientific tests and analyses carried out by others as directed by those skilled in the field. There is no suggestion that the tests were scientifically unsound or unwarranted. The principal complaint is that further tests could have been done or findings better quantified.

This is not a case where an expert obtained information from a party about a matter directly in issue, then expressed an opinion before the trier of fact based on that information, which was not otherwise and properly established.

In my respectful view it is consistent with established and binding precedent to conclude, as I do, that there was no necessity to call the technicians as witnesses to prove the test results on which all experts relied.

Accused convicted.

MIZZI v. DEBARTOK
(1992), 9 O.R. (3d) 383 (Ont. Gen. Div.)

THE COURT [DUNNET, J.]:— The plaintiff wishes to call William Franks as his first witness. This is a personal injury action involving closed-head injury, and the plaintiff indicates that he wishes to present the medical evidence of the doctors who assessed the plaintiff at the outset. The defence objects, and says that if the plaintiff is not called first, it would be difficult to cross-examine the doctors on hearsay evidence and without the evidence of the plaintiff to lay the proper foundation for opinion evidence put to the doctors.

The plaintiff contends that the court will be in a better position to understand the nature of the injury to the plaintiff if the expert evidence of the treating doctors is called first, as well as the evidence as to the functioning of the brain, the physical damage that occurred and the psychological consequences.

In my view the plaintiff is a key witness. He is claiming damages and should have the opportunity to tell his story however best he can at the outset of the trial.

As well, I find it is necessary for the court for the medical evidence to follow, and the plaintiff, if he is to be called, to be called at the outset of the trial.

Order accordingly.

5. EXAMINING EXPERT

(a) Hypothetical Questions

The reason for requiring the expert to provide the trier of fact with the basis for his opinion "is not a deduction from the opinion rule, but rests on the principle of testimonial qualifications that a witness's grounds of knowledge must be made to appear."[254] In a civil suit for negligence arising out of a motor vehicle accident, a witness is examined first respecting his past ability to observe the incident and his present ability to recollect and to communicate a description of the event. Without a demonstrated ability to observe and communicate, the witness's testimony is worthless. So, too, an expert's opinion, which rests always on certain premises of fact, must be directly coupled to those premises and both supplied to the jury.

The premises may be communicated by the same witness who expresses the opinion when the expert has had the opportunity of personal observation and so is able to recount, on request, the details observed forming the foundation of his opinion. It may be, however, that the factual premises are related by one witness and the opinion by another. Since it is the essential nature of an opinion that it is dependent on its premises, and since the premises can always be rejected by the jury whether testified to by the person giving the opinion or by another, it follows that all opinions in a sense are hypothetical. Is it necessary, therefore, that an expert testifying to an opinion based on personal observation must first state not only that he had an opportunity to observe, but also recount all the details of his observation, as premises, before being permitted to express his opinion?

To this Professor Wigmore answers:

> In academic nicety, yes; practically, no; and for the simple reason that either on direct examination or on cross-examination each and every detail of the appearance he observed can be brought out and thus associated with his general conclusion as the grounds for it, and the tribunal will understand that the rejection of these data will destroy the validity of his opinion.[255]

Where the expert is unable to supply from his own knowledge the details constituting his premises, then his opinion must be brought out by hypothetical presentation so that the jury will later be able to decide whether or not his opinion deserves acceptance after considering other testimony to its premises. As Professor Wigmore notes in describing "the orthodox and accepted theory of the hypothetical question":

---

254 7 Wigmore, *Evidence* (Chad. Rev.), s. 1927.

255 2 Wigmore, *Evidence* (Chad. Rev.), s. 675. See also Chadbourn, *Study Relating to the Uniform Rules of Evidence*, commissioned by the California Law Revision Commission, 1964, pp. 937-39. But see *R. v. Turner* (1975), 60 Cr. App. R. 80, 82.

The key to the situation, in short is that there may be two distinct subjects of testimony, — premises, and inferences or conclusions; that the latter involves necessarily a consideration of the former; and that the tribunal must be furnished with the means of rejecting the latter if upon consultation they determine to reject the former, i.e. of distinguishing conclusions properly founded from conclusions improperly founded.[256]

Phipson describes the English attitude in a similar way when he notes:

Where the issue is substantially one of science or skill merely, the expert may, if he has *himself* observed the facts, be asked the very question which the jury have to decide. If, however, his opinion is based merely upon facts proved by *others,* such a question is improper, for it practically asks him to determine the truth of their testimony, as well as to give an opinion upon it; the correct course is to put such facts to him *hypothetically,* but not *en bloc,* asking him to assume one or more of them to be true, and to state his opinion thereon; where, however, the facts are not in dispute, it has been said that the former question may be put as a matter of convenience, though not as of right.[257]

Where the expert is not speaking with personal knowledge, but basing his opinion on facts proved at the trial by other witnesses, then an expert cannot, where there has been conflict between the witnesses, be simply asked, "Having heard all the evidence led in this case, what is your opinion with respect to X?" As described by Ritchie J. in *Bleta v. R.:*[258]

. . . it is obviously unsatisfactory to ask him to express an opinion based upon the evidence which he has heard because the answer to such a question involves the expert in having to resolve the conflict in accordance with his own view of the credibility of the witnesses and the jury has no way of knowing upon what evidence he based his opinion.

On the other hand, the Supreme Court of Canada did recognize in *Bleta* the same relaxation of attitude to hypothetical questions noted by Phipson when the evidence led by the "fact-witness" is all one way; i.e., depending on the particular case the hypothesis on which the expert is proceeding may be so readily apparent to the jury as to permit the trial judge "in the exercise of his discretion in the conduct of the trial"[259] to dispense with the necessity of abiding the formal hypothetical question technique usually demanded.

(b) Use of Textbooks

R. v. MARQUARD
25 C.R. (4th) 1, [1993] 4 S.C.R. 223, 85 C.C.C. (3d) 193, 1993 CarswellOnt 127, 1993 CarswellOnt 995

The accused was charged with aggravated assault of her granddaughter as a result of the child having received a severe facial burn. The theory of the defence

---

256 2 Wigmore, *Evidence* (Chad. Rev.), s. 672; text quoted with approval by Ritchie J. in *Bleta v. R.,* [1965] 48 D.L.R. (2d) 139, 143 (S.C.C.). See also Maule J. in *M'Naghten's Case* (1843), 10 Cl. & F. 200, 207, 8 E.R. 718, 721.

257 Phipson, *Evidence,* 11th ed., p. 518.

258 [1965] 48 D.L.R. (2d) 139, 141; see also *R. v. Holmes,* [1953] 1 W.L.R. 686 (C.C.A.).

259 *Ibid.,* at p. 143. And see more recently *R. v. Swietlinski* (1978), 5 C.R. (3d) 324 (Ont. C.A.).

was that the burn had been caused accidentally by the child playing with a lighter. At the trial the child was permitted to give unsworn testimony after the trial judge conducted an inquiry into the child's ability to tell the truth. At trial, the Crown called a physician who had treated the child at the hospital and a physician who was an expert on burns. The defence called another physician from the same hospital who was an expert on child abuse and had been consulted by the admitting physician. The child-abuse expert was called by the defence to testify concerning a statement made by the child when she was initially admitted, and which statement was consistent with the theory of accident. This witness in cross-examination testified that the fact that the child acted maturely in dealing with her injuries suggested that she had been the victim of long-term abuse. In addition, the expert testified that children will initially give an accidental explanation and only later give a story that is more consistent with the injury, in a more convincing manner. The accused was convicted and her appeal to the Ontario Court of Appeal was dismissed.

Held: Appeal allowed and a new trial ordered.

[This case has been examined, *supra*, under Competence and also under Evidence in Support of Credibility. In the course of the judgment comments were made regarding the use of Learned Treatises.]

Per McLachlin J. (Sopinka J., Gonthier J. and Cory JJ. concurring):—

Cross-examination of Dr. Tenace

Dr. Tenace was a psychiatrist called by the defence. In the course of cross-examination, the Crown put a series of reports and case studies to him and read extensively from them. Dr. Tenace testified that he was unaware of many of these studies and, for the most part, did not accept their conclusions. None of the experts specifically adopted as authoritative the studies of which Dr. Tenace was unaware and with which he did not agree. Some of the material was very prejudicial. For example, by one "question", some three and one-half pages in length, the Crown introduced opinions regarding the memory of a child who had been put through an extended traumatic and abusive experience, which was described in detail. Moreover, the impression may have been left that Dr. Tenace's unfamiliarity with these unproven studies reflected a lack of expertise.

The proper procedure to be followed in examining an expert witness on other expert opinions found in papers or books is to ask the witness if she knows the work. If the answer is "no", or if the witness denies the work's authority, that is the end of the matter. Counsel cannot read from the work, since that would be to introduce it as evidence. If the answer is "yes", and the witness acknowledges the work's authority, then the witness has confirmed it by the witness' own testimony. Parts of it may be read to the witness, and to the extent they are confirmed, they become evidence in the case. This procedure was laid out in *R. v. Anderson* (1914), 22 C.C.C. 455, 16 D.L.R. 203, [1914] 5 W.W.R. 1052 (Alta. S.C.), and has been followed by Canadian courts: *Holland v. P.E.I. School Board Regional Administrative Unit #4* (1986), 59 Teeniest. & P.E.I.R. 6 at pp. 21-2 (P.E.I. S.C.); *Tans Limited v. Reed Tenus Limited* (1986), 70 B.C.L.R. 189 at p.

193 (B.C. S.C.).The Crown urged us to adopt the American approach to putting scholarly works to an expert witness. The American approach varies from jurisdiction to jurisdiction. Some jurisdictions require that the witness have acknowledged the authority of the work before it can be read into the record on cross- examination. Others, however, appear to allow the works to be put into the record on cross-examination where there is some proof of, or where the judge is prepared to take judicial notice of, the general authority of the work. Even this more liberal standard was not met in the case of the material put to Dr. Tenace. I am satisfied that expert evidence, introduced in the guise of cross-examination of Dr. Tenace without any proof that it constituted reputable authority, was inadmissible. It was also, as noted, prejudicial. This is yet another ground which suggests that a new trial must be ordered.

L'HEUREUX-DUBÉ J. (dissenting): —

. . . .

The law with respect to the admission of learned treatises into evidence has not been greatly altered since *R. v. Anderson* (1914), 22 C.C.C. 455, 16 D.L.R. 203, [1914] 5 W.W.R. 1052 (Alta. S.C.). Anderson requires that, in order for a learned treatise to be read into the body of evidence which the jury considers, it must first be adopted by the expert as authoritative. In this case, Dr. Tenace was unaware of the studies cited by the Crown, and of course, could not adopt them as authoritative.

There are a number of different views regarding the rules which should govern the admission of learned treatises. *Anderson* embodies a particularly strict approach: if a witness is asked about a text and expresses ignorance of it or denies its authority, no further use can be made of it by reading extracts of it into evidence. However, if the witness admits its authority, then he may be asked to explain any apparent differences between its opinion and his own: see Sopinka, Tannase and Tans, The Law of Evidence in Canada, *ibid.*, at p. 562.

By contrast, in many American jurisdictions, learned treatises may be put to considerably broader use. This explains the rationale behind the rule as follows: much expert testimony consists of information obtained from such sources and there are sufficient guarantees of trustworthiness to justify equating a learned treatise with the live testimony of an expert witness: Thins on Evidence (Thins rev. 1976), vol. 6, 1690-2. The hearsay exception to learned treatises under Rule 803(18) of the U.S. Federal Rules of Evidence, accordingly, permits such material to be read into evidence as long as it is called to the attention of the expert on cross-examination and its authoritativeness is reliably established. This may be done by the admission of the witness himself, by other experts who testify during the trial, or by judicial notice: J. W. Strong, ed., McCormick on Evidence, 4th ed. (1992), vol. 2, para. 321, at p. 351; see also, C. Tenace, "The Use of Learned Treatises in Canadian and United States Litigation", 24 U.T.L.J. 423 (1974).

I would be inclined to favour the American approach over Anderson, as it has the benefit of preventing the witness from foreclosing an inquiry into the depth or breadth of his or her knowledge by simply refusing to acknowledge a study. However, even if the law regarding the admission of learned treatises were not to be expanded in this way, while the examination in this case did not fall within the strict parameters of the rule in Anderson, no prejudice to the appellant arose from the cross-examination of Dr. Tenace considering the examination as a whole.

6. APPOINTMENT OF COURT EXPERTS

Since the 18th century, with the change from the use of court-appointed experts and special juries, to the use of experts called by the parties testifying as witnesses,[260] adverse criticism has been directed at the apparent partisanship displayed by experts. Too often, unfortunately, the criticism has been unfairly aimed at the expert and his profession, which is in no way responsible for the present system. Often, counsel does not seek the best expert to elucidate the matter in issue, but rather the best witness for his cause. Jessel, M.R. condemned this practice, saying:

> . . . I have, as usual, the evidence of experts on the one side and on the other, and, as usual, the experts do not agree in their opinion. There is no reason why they should . . . the mode in which expert evidence is obtained is such as not to give the fair result of scientific opinion to the Court. A man may go, and does sometimes, to half-a-dozen experts. . . . He takes their honest opinions, he finds three in his favour and three against him; he says to the three in his favour, Will you be kind enough to give evidence? and he pays the three against him their fees and leaves them alone; the other side does the same. It may not be three out of six, it may be three out of fifty. . . . I have always the greatest possible distrust of scientific evidence. . . . I am sorry to say the result is that the Court does not get that assistance from the experts which, if they were unbiased and fairly chosen, it would have a right to expect.[261]

It has been said that the role of the trier of fact in weighing such evidence is difficult and that it becomes impossible when two experts express diametrically opposed views. His decision turns out not on facts proved in evidence, but on which expert he believes. Spellman puts it this way:

> This presents a quandary which, except by coincidence, is remote from any concept of justice. The question at bar should be what is the proper conclusion to be drawn from recorded facts. By the nature of the case, no external criteria are available to the fact-finder to enable him to work his way out of the presented dilemma. Thus, strange as it may seem, the fact-finder, as to this phase of the litigation, is basing his finding on a conclusion as to *credibility*.[262]

---

260 See Hand, "Historical and Practical Considerations Regarding Expert Testimony" (1901), 15 Harv. L. Rev. 40; and Rosenthal, "The Development of the Use of Expert Testimony" (1935), 2 Law and Contemporary Problems 403.

261 On the hearing of a motion in *Thorn v. Worthing Skating Rink Co.* (1876), 6 Ch. D. 415n, as noted in *Plimpton v. Spiller* (1877), 6 Ch. D. 412, 416 (C.A.). But see *More v. R.*, [1963] S.C.R. 522, 537-38, where the court criticizes the trial judge's instruction to the jury for his "unwarranted disparagement" of the expert evidence: the trial judge had quoted extracts from Phipson, Taylor, and Lord Campbell to the same effect as the statement of Jessel, M.R. See, too, Overholser, *The Psychiatrist and the Law* (1952), pp. 106-14.

262 Spellman, *Direct Examination of Witnesses* (1968), p. 139.

A partial solution to the problem of inherent bias in an expert called by a party, may be a return to providing the necessary assistance through a court-appointed expert.[263] As the adversary system developed, the power of the trial judge to call witnesses of any kind declined, especially in civil cases. The view was favoured that the judge should determine the dispute on the basis of the issues raised by the parties and in accordance with the evidence they saw fit to introduce.[264] Whether there remains any inherent common law right in the court to appoint experts as assessors to assist the court on its own motion, is a matter of some doubt.[265] The technique followed in civil law jurisdictions is to permit the court to select experts to inform it of their opinion based on their own particular knowledge and experience.[266] Such experts are permitted not only to give their opinions, but also to conduct independent investigations for the purpose of preparing their written reports.[267] Under the federal criminal procedure in the United States, the trial judge is permitted to select an expert[268] in addition to the experts called by the parties. The court's expert may express his opinion and is not confined solely to the role of interpreter.[269] This practice forms the basis for Rule 706 of the Federal Rules of Evidence.[270] The question arises whether it is a desirable compromise with the civil law system, since the parties' experts are forced to testify in the face of the testimony of another expert who bears "the accolade flowing from a judicial appointment."[271] As DeParcq, commenting on a similar provision in the Uniform Rules, said:

> Although the rules purport to allow the parties to call other experts of their own, they might just as well save their money. The testimony of the court-appointed expert will be accepted as gospel, while any other expert testimony will be sound and fury, signifying nothing.[272]

---

263 See McCormick, "Some Observations Upon the Opinion Rule and Expert Testimony" (1945), 23 Texas L. Rev. 109, 130-36; and 2 Wigmore, *Evidence* (Chad. Rev.), s. 563. For statutory recommendations to such effect see *Uniform Rules of Evidence* (1953), Rules 59, 61; and *Model Code of Evidence* (1942), Rules 403-10. But see Levy, "Impartial Medical Testimony — Revisited" (1961), 34 Temple L.Q. 416.

264 See *Jones v. Nat. Coal Bd.*, [1957] 2 Q.B. 55 (C.A.); *Fowler v. Fowler*, [1949] O.W.N. 244 (C.A.); but seemingly *contra* in criminal cases: see *R. v. Harris*, [1927] 2 K.B. 587 (C.C.A.).

265 See *Phillips v. Ford Motor Co. of Can.*, [1971] 2 O.R. 637, 663 (C.A.).

266 See Hammelmann, "Expert Evidence" (1947), 10 Mod. L. Rev. 32; Ploscowe, "The Expert Witness in Criminal Cases in France, Germany and Italy" (1935), 2 Law and Contemporary Problems 504; and Schroeder, "Problems Faced by the Impartial Expert Witness in Court; The Continental View" (1961), 34 Temple L.Q. 378.

267 See *e.g.*, Quebec *Code of Civil Procedure*, R.S.Q. 1977, c. C-25, ss. 414-425. Compare also the position of assessors in admiralty cases at common law where expert evidence on matters within the sphere of the assessors cannot be led by the parties: see *Halsbury's Laws of England*, 4th ed., vol. 1, para. 443, at p. 283. For Canadian adoption of the English approach, see: *Montreal Harbour Comm. v. The Universe* (1906), 10 Ex. C.R. 305; and *Fraser v. Aztec* (1920), 20 Ex. C.R. 39.

268 See 2 Wigmore, *Evidence* (Chad. Rev.), s. 563.

269 See Beuscher, "The Use of Experts by the Courts" (1941), 54 Harv. L.R. 1105.

270 Fed. Rules Evid., Rule 706, 28 U.S.C.A. But see Wright, *Federal Practice and Procedure: Criminal*, pp. 229-33 to the effect that the rule in federal criminal cases is seldom used.

271 Per Hincks, J., in dissent in *Scott v. Spanjer Bros. Inc.*, 298 F. 2d 928, 933 (2d Cir., 1962).

272 DeParcq, "The Uniform Rules of Evidence: A Plaintiff's View" (1956), 40 Minn. L. Rev. 301, 334.

This may or may not be true, as the parties may feel that the court's appointed expert is in a preferred evidentiary position to one called by a party. In England, despite similar rules of the Supreme Court permitting the appointment of independent court experts on the application of the parties,[273] the power is seldom used. Lord Denning, M.R. commented in *Re Saxton:*

> . . . neither side has applied for the court to appoint a court expert. It is said to be a rare thing for it to be done. I suppose that litigants realize that the court would attach great weight to the report of a court expert: and are reluctant thus to leave the decision of the case so much in his hands. If his report is against one side, that side will wish to call its own expert to contradict him and then the other side will wish to call one too. So it would only mean that the parties would call their own experts as well. In the circumstances the parties usually prefer to have the judge decide on the evidence of experts on either side, without resort to a court expert.[274]

In 1970 the Law Reform Committee in England considered provisions for the appointment of court experts and concluded that the introduction of a "general 'court expert' system is not desirable."[275] The Committee concluded that its recommendations with respect to the simultaneous disclosure by the parties of experts' reports would obviate the need for court-appointed experts. It found the following objections to such a system compelling:

> [The exchange of experts' reports] we think, will eliminate the need for oral expert testimony except on matters upon which there is room for a genuine difference of expert opinion or where the expert's opinion has to be based upon facts which are in dispute between the parties and of which the true version will only be ascertained in the course of the hearing of the oral evidence of witnesses of fact. The role of a court expert in either type of case presents great practical difficulties. The first problem is the choice of expert. What voice are the parties to have in his selection if they are unable to agree upon who should be appointed? How is the judge to assess the validity of their objections to particular appointees nominated by the court? Next, how is the expert once appointed to inform himself of the facts upon which to base his report? If they are in controversy it would be for the judge to find the facts, not for the expert to hear and determine disputed matters of evidence. His report would have to await the judge's findings. The alternative of inviting him to report in advance on various hypotheses of fact would run the risk that the correct hypothesis, which would be known only at the conclusion of the evidence, had not been stated. Finally, there is the problem of the use to be made of his report. Plainly it would be contrary to our system of administering justice if it were final and conclusive on the matters of expertise with which it dealt, without giving to the parties an opportunity in open court to persuade the judge that it was wrong. Is the court expert to be called at the trial to be cross-examined by any party who wishes to do so? And, if so, are the parties to be entitled to call expert evidence in rebuttal?[276]

The Advisory Committee for the Federal Rules in the United States, on the other hand, wrote:

---

273 Rules of Supreme Court, 1982, Order 40, Rules 1-6.

274 [1962] 3 All E.R. 92, 95.

275 Seventeenth Report of the Law Reform Committee, *Evidence of Opinion and Expert Evidence*, Cmnd. 4489 (1970), p. 31, fn. 4.

276 *Ibid.*, at p. 8, s. 14. And see Report of the Ontario Attorney General's Committee on *Medical Evidence in Court in Civil Cases* (1965) reviewing the methods of appointing experts in other jurisdictions and rejecting the idea of selection of experts by the court.

The practice of shopping for experts, the venality of some experts, and the reluctance of many reputable experts to involve themselves in litigation, have been matters of deep concern. Though the contention is made that court appointed experts acquire an aura of infallibility to which they are not entitled, . . . the trend is increasingly to provide for their use. While experience indicates that actual appointment is a relatively infrequent occurrence, the assumption may be made that the availability of the procedure in itself decreases the need for resorting to it. The ever-present possibility that the judge may appoint an expert in a given case must inevitably exert a sobering effect on the expert witness of a party and upon the person utilizing his services.[277]

7. EXCHANGE OF EXPERTS' REPORTS

In 1965 the Ontario Attorney General's Committee on Medical Evidence concluded that, in actions involving personal injuries, an exchange of medical reports ought to be a prerequisite to calling medical testimony. They further recommended that to minimize the inconvenience to the medical profession these reports ought to be receivable in evidence without the necessity of calling the doctor as a witness. The *Ontario Evidence Act* was amended to create:

52.(1) In this section,

"practitioner" means,

(a) a member of a College as defined in subsection 1(1) of the *Regulated Health Professions Act, 1991*,

(b) a drugless practitioner registered under the *Drugless Practitioners Act*,

(c) a person licensed or registered to practise in another part of Canada under an Act that is similar to an Act referred to in clause (a) or (b).

(2) A report obtained by or prepared for a party to an action and signed by a practitioner and any other report of the practitioner that relates to the action are, with leave of the court and after at least ten days notice has been given to all other parties, admissible in evidence in the action.

(3) Unless otherwise ordered by the court, a party to an action is entitled, at the time that notice is given under subsection (2), to a copy of the report together with any other report of the practitioner that relates to the action.

(4) Except by leave of the judge presiding at the trial, a practitioner who signs a report with respect to a party shall not give evidence at the trial unless the report is given to all other parties in accordance with subsection (2).

(5) If a practitioner is required to give evidence in person in an action and the court is of the opinion that the evidence could have been produced as effectively by way of a report, the court may order the party that required the attendance of the practitioner to pay as costs therefor such sum as the court considers appropriate.[278]

---

277 Advisory Committee's Note, Fed. Rules Evid., Rule 706, 28 U.S.C.A., pp. 517-18.

278 S.O. 1968, c. 36, s. 2; now R.S.O. 1990, c. E.23, s. 52. The Committee's recommendations were first implemented by an amendment to the *Evidence Act* in 1966 (R.S.O. 1990, c. E.23, s. 52) and the Ontario Rules of Practice were altered accordingly (O. Reg. 207/66, s. 7). The relevant rule was held to be *ultra vires* in *Circosta v. Lilly*, [1967] 1 O.R. 398 (C.A.), since it effected a change in the substantive law. See also s. 657.3 of the Criminal Code.

Similar provisions exist in other provinces, though not always restricted to medical experts.

The Criminal Code now provides for an exchange of expert reports.

657.3 (1) In any proceedings, the evidence of a person as an expert may be given by means of a report accompanied by the affidavit or solemn declaration of the person, setting out, in particular, the qualifications of the person as an expert if

(a) the court recognizes that person as an expert; and

(b) the party intending to produce the report in evidence has, before the proceeding, given to the other party a copy of the affidavit or solemn declaration and the report and reasonable notice of the intention to produce it in evidence.

Attendance for examination

(2) Notwithstanding subsection (1), the court may require the person who appears to have signed an affidavit or solemn declaration referred to in that subsection to appear before it for examination or cross-examination in respect of the issue of proof of any of the statements contained in the affidavit or solemn declaration or report.

Notice for expert testimony

(3) For the purpose of promoting the fair, orderly and efficient presentation of the testimony of witnesses,

(a) a party who intends to call a person as an expert witness shall, at least thirty days before the commencement of the trial or within any other period fixed by the justice or judge, give notice to the other party or parties of his or her intention to do so, accompanied by

(i) the name of the proposed witness,

(ii) a description of the area of expertise of the proposed witness that is sufficient to permit the other parties to inform themselves about that area of expertise, and

(iii) a statement of the qualifications of the proposed witness as an expert;

(b) in addition to complying with paragraph (a), a prosecutor who intends to call a person as an expert witness shall, within a reasonable period before trial, provide to the other party or parties

(i) a copy of the report, if any, prepared by the proposed witness for the case, and

(ii) if no report is prepared, a summary of the opinion anticipated to be given by the proposed witness and the grounds on which it is based; and

(c) in addition to complying with paragraph (a), an accused, or his or her counsel, who intends to call a person as an expert witness shall, not later than the close of the case for the prosecution, provide to the other party or parties the material referred to in paragraph (b).

If notices not given

(4) If a party calls a person as an expert witness without complying with subsection (3), the court shall, at the request of any other party,

(a) grant an adjournment of the proceedings to the party who requests it to allow him or her to prepare for cross-examination of the expert witness;

    (b) order the party who called the expert witness to provide that other party and any other party with the material referred to in paragraph (3)(b); and

    (c) order the calling or recalling of any witness for the purpose of giving testimony on matters related to those raised in the expert witness's testimony, unless the court considers it inappropriate to do so.

Additional court orders

    (5) If, in the opinion of the court, a party who has received the notice and material referred to in subsection (3) has not been able to prepare for the evidence of the proposed witness, the court may do one or more of the following:

    (a) adjourn the proceedings;

    (b) order that further particulars be given of the evidence of the proposed witness; and

    (c) order the calling or recalling of any witness for the purpose of giving testimony on matters related to those raised in the expert witness's testimony.

Use of material by prosecution

    (6) If the proposed witness does not testify, the prosecutor may not produce material provided to him or her under paragraph (3)(c) in evidence without the consent of the accused.

No further disclosure

    (7) Unless otherwise ordered by a court, information disclosed under this section in relation to a proceeding may only be used for the purpose of that proceeding.

Note that there are statutory limits to the number of experts that can be called: 5 in the case of the *Canada Evidence Act*, s.7, subject to leave of the court, and 3 in the case of Provincial Evidence Acts.

Although the provisions for disclosure of experts' evidence may appear to be novel incursions into the adversary system, they are not without precedent. As early as 1782, in *Folkes v. Chadd*[279] Lord Mansfield permitted the reception of expert opinion evidence from scientists called by the parties. At the first trial, the opinion of Mr. Milne, an engineer, was received as to the cause of the decay of a harbour. The plaintiff obtained a verdict. However, a new trial was granted, on the ground that the defendants were surprised by the doctrine and reasoning of Mr. Milne, and the parties were directed to print and deliver over to the opposite side the opinions and reasonings of the engineers whom they meant to produce on the next trial, so that both sides might be prepared to answer them.

Against compulsory disclosure we have the remarks of Lord Denning:

> . . . the expert should be allowed to give his report fully and frankly to the party who employs him, with all its strength and weakness, and not be made to offer it beforehand as a hostage to the opponent, lest he take unfair advantage of it. In short, it is one of our notions of a fair trial that, except by agreement, one side is not entitled to see the proofs of the other side's witnesses.[280]

---

279 (1782), 3 Dougl. 157, 99 E.R. 589.
280 *Re Saxton*, [1962] 3 All E.R. 92, 95.

E. PRIVILEGE

1. PRIVILEGED COMMUNICATIONS

(a) Introduction

Evidentiary rules respecting privilege differ from the rules we have so far examined in that the earlier rules were, largely, designed to promote an approximation to truth; the rules we are about to examine clearly operate to restrict the search for truth and must, therefore, be justified by some other value. Rand, J. in *R. v. Snider*[281] wrote of privilege:

> It requires as its essential condition that there be a public interest recognized as overriding the general principle that in a Court of justice every person and every fact must be available to the execution of its supreme functions.

R. v. GRUENKE
[1991] 3 S.C.R. 263, 67 C.C.C. (3d) 289, 8 C.R. (4th) 368

The accused was convicted of first degree murder. The Crown's theory was that the accused had enlisted the aid of her boyfriend in the planning and commission of the murder, which she committed, to stop the victim's sexual harassment of her and to benefit from the provisions of his will. The evidence of the accused's pastor and the lay counsellor, which directly supported the Crown's theory, was ruled admissible at trial. The communications between the accused, the pastor and the lay counsellor took place when the lay counsellor, on hearing of the victim's death two days earlier, visited the accused. When the accused began speaking of her involvement in the murder, the pastor was called and the conversation continued. The accused unsuccessfully appealed her conviction.

LAMER C.J. (LA FOREST, SOPINKA, CORY, MCLACHLIN, STEVENSON and IACOBUCCI JJ. concurring):—

. . . .

This case requires the Court to consider whether a common law prima facie privilege for religious communications should be recognized or whether claims of privilege for such communications should be dealt with on a case-by-case basis.

. . . .

Given that the Wigmorean criteria (for privilege) play a central role in this case, I will set out the "test" below for ease of reference (Wigmore, *Evidence in Trials at Common Law*, vol. 8, McNaughton Revision, para. 2285):

(1) The communications must originate in a confidence that they will not be disclosed.

(2) This element of confidentiality must be essential to the full and satisfactory maintenance of the relation between the parties.

---

281 [1954] 4 D.L.R. 483, 486 (S.C.C.).

(3) The relation must be one which in the opinion of the community ought to be sedulously fostered.
(4) The injury that would inure to the relation by the disclosure of the communications must be greater than the benefit thereby gained for the correct disposal of litigation.

Analysis

Before delving into an analysis of the issues raised by this appeal, I think it is important to clarify the terminology being used in this case. The parties have tended to distinguish between two categories: a "blanket", prima facie, common law, or "class" privilege on the one hand, and a "case-by-case" privilege on the other. The first four terms are used to refer to a privilege which was recognized at common law and one for which there is a prima facie presumption of inadmissibility (once it has been established that the relationship fits within the class) unless the party urging admission can show why the communications should not be privileged (i.e., why they should be admitted into evidence as an exception to the general rule). Such communications are excluded not because the evidence is not relevant, but rather, because there are overriding policy reasons to exclude this relevant evidence. Solicitor-client communications appear to fall within this first category. The term "case-by-case" privilege is used to refer to communications for which there is a prima facie assumption that they are not privileged, i.e., are admissible. The case-by-case analysis has generally involved an application of the "Wigmore test", which is a set of criteria for determining whether communications should be privileged (and therefore not admitted) in particular cases. In other words, the case-by-case analysis requires that the policy reasons for excluding otherwise relevant evidence be weighed in each particular case.

Throughout these reasons, I will be using the terms "class privilege" and prima facie privilege to refer to the first category of communications and will generally use the term "case-by-case privilege" to refer to the second category of communications. I should note that some writers tend to use the term "privileged communications" or "privilege" only in relation to communications which are class-based or prima facie inadmissible. I will be using the term "privilege" in relation to both types of communications.

. . . .

Common Law, prima facie Privilege

A prima facie privilege for religious communications would constitute an exception to the general principle that all relevant evidence is admissible. Unless it can be said that the policy reasons to support a class privilege for religious communications are as compelling as the policy reasons which underlay the class privilege for solicitor-client communications, there is no basis for departing from the fundamental "first principle" that all relevant evidence is admissible until proven otherwise.

In my view, the policy reasons which underlay the treatment of solicitor-client communications as a separate class from most other confidential communications, are not equally applicable to religious communications. The prima facie protection for solicitor-client communications is based on the fact that the relationship and the communications between solicitor and client are essential to the effective operation of the legal system. Such communications are inextricably linked with the very system which desires the disclosure of the communication. In my view, religious communications, notwithstanding their social importance, are not inextricably linked with the justice system in the way that solicitor-client communications surely are.

. . . .

Having found no common law, prima facie privilege for religious communications, I will consider whether such communications can be excluded in particular cases by applying the Wigmore criteria on a case-by-case basis.

2. Case-by-Case Privilege

In *Re Church of Scientology and The Queen (No. 6)* the Ontario Court of Appeal recognized the existence of a "priest and penitent" privilege determined on a case-by-case basis, having regard to the Wigmore criteria. This approach is consistent with the approach taken by this Court in *Slavutych v. Baker*, and is, in my view, consistent with a principled approach to the question which properly takes into account the particular circumstances of each case. This is not to say that the Wigmore criteria are now "carved in stone", but rather that these considerations provide a general framework within which policy considerations and the requirements of fact-finding can be weighed and balanced on the basis of their relative importance in the particular case before the court. Nor does this preclude the identification of a new class on a principled basis. Furthermore, a case-by-case analysis will allow courts to determine whether, in the particular circumstances, the individual's freedom of religion will be imperilled by the admission of the evidence.

. . . .

Having found that religious communications can be excluded in particular cases where the Wigmore criteria are satisfied, I turn now to the question of whether the communications involved in this case satisfy the Wigmore criteria.

Application of the Wigmore Criteria

In my opinion, a consideration of the Wigmore criteria and the facts of this case reveals that the communications between the appellant, Pastor Thiessen and Janine Frovich were properly admitted at trial. In my view, these communications do not even satisfy the first requirement; namely, that they originate in a confidence that they will not be disclosed. Leaving aside the other components of the Wigmore test, it is absolutely crucial that the communications originate with an expectation of confidentiality (in order for those communications to be qualify as "privileged" and to thereby be excluded from evidence). Without this expectation of confidentiality, the raison d'être of the privilege is missing.

In the case at bar, there is evidence that Ms. Gruenke's communications to Pastor Thiessen and Ms. Frovich did not originate in a confidence that they would not be disclosed. The testimony of Pastor Thiessen and Janine Frovich indicates that they were unclear as to whether they were expected to keep confidential what Ms. Gruenke had told them about her involvement in the murder. As was stated by Twaddle J.A. in the Court of Appeal judgment at p. 300, "there was no evidence that the accused Gruenke made her admissions to them in the confident belief that they would be disclosed to no one". Ms. Gruenke did not approach Ms. Frovich and the Pastor on the basis that the communications were to be confidential. In fact, Ms. Frovich initiated the meeting and Ms. Gruenke testified that she saw no harm in speaking to Janine Frovich because she had already made up her mind to turn herself in to the police and "take the blame". In my view, the Court of Appeal accurately described these communications as being made more to relieve Ms. Gruenke's emotional stress than for a religious or spiritual purpose. I note that my view is based on the parties' statements and behaviour in relation to the communication and not on the lack of a formal practice of "confession" in the Victorious Faith Centre Church. While the existence of a formal practice of "confession" may well be a strong indication that the parties expected the communication to be confidential, the lack of such a formal practice is not, in and of itself, determinative.

The communications in question do not satisfy the first Wigmore criterion and their admission into evidence does not infringe Ms. Gruenke's freedom of religion. As I have stated above, whether an individual's freedom of religion will be infringed by the admission of religious communications will depend on the particular facts of each case. In the case at bar, there is no such infringement. I would dismiss the appeal.

L'Heureux-Dubé J., Gonthier J. concurring, agreed with the majority that the appeal should be dismissed, substantially for the reasons given. However, they would prefer, for utilitarian reasons, to recognize a class privilege for pastor-penitent communications. They concluded:

In my view, it is more in line with the rationales identified earlier, the spirit of the Charter and the goal of assuring the certainty of the law, to recognize a pastor-penitent category of privilege in this country. If our society truly wishes to encourage the creation and development of spiritual relationships, individuals must have a certain amount of confidence that their religious confessions, given in confidence and for spiritual relief, will not be disclosed. Not knowing in advance whether his or her confession will be afforded any protection, a penitent may not confess, or may not confess as freely as he or she otherwise would. Both the number of confessions and their quality will be affected. The special relationship between clergy and parishioners may not develop, resulting in a chilling effect on the spiritual relationship within our society. In that case, the very rationale for the pastor-penitent privilege may be defeated.

However, L'Heureux-Dubé J. and Gonthier J. decided that in the circumstances of this particular case, the communications did not originate in the confidence that they would not be disclosed and therefore the communications were not covered by such a privilege.[282]

Both Quebec and Newfoundland have legislated a class privilege for religious communications.[283]

Six years after the Supreme Court dismissed Gruenke's appeal, the Self Defence Review Committee which had been established to review cases of battered women convicted before *Lavallee* recommended that the Minister of Justice refer her case to the Manitoba Court of Appeal pursuant to section 690 of the *Criminal Code*. The issue was whether evidence surrounding her relationship with the deceased was admissible as fresh evidence on the issue of planning and deliberation. The Manitoba Court of Appeal concluded that the evidence was not admissible as fresh evidence.[284] The Supreme Court of Canada dismissed a further appeal.[285]

We will later further consider Wigmore's case-by-case approach and also the impact of the Charter. We first examine existing class privileges.

(b) Solicitor-Client Privilege

(i) *Generally*

> . . . the first duty of an attorney is to keep the secrets of his client.[286]

In the 16th and 17th centuries the "obligations of honour among gentlemen" were advanced as the basis for a general privilege from disclosure of communications made in confidence. Members of the legal profession qualified as gentlemen and, accordingly, from the earliest times they were permitted the objection.[287] By the end of the 18th century, this basis for a privilege was rejected by the courts as too obstructive to their search for truth, but a new rationale, pertinent only to the attorney, was established. The classic statement of the new rationale is that of Brougham, L.C. in *Greenough v. Gaskell*:

> The foundation of this rule is not difficult to discover. It is not (as has sometimes been said) on account of any particular importance which the law attributes to the business of legal professors, or any particular disposition to afford them protection, though certainly it may not be very easy to discover why a like privilege has been refused to others, and especially to medical advisers.
>
> But it is out of regard to the interests of justice, which cannot be upholden, and to the administration of justice, which cannot go on, without the aid of men skilled in jurisprudence, in the practice of the Courts, and in those matters affecting rights and obligations which form the subject of all judicial proceedings. If the privilege did not exist at all, every one would be thrown upon his own legal resources; deprived of all

---

282 For an application of *Gruenke*, see *R. v. Welsh* (2007), 51 C.R. (6th) 33 (Ont. S.C.J.).
283 See Newfoundland *Evidence Act*, R.S.N. 1990, c. E-16 s. 8; Quebec *Charter of Rights and Freedoms*, R.S.Q. 1977, c. C-12, s. 9. See generally H.R.S. Ryan, "Obligation of the Clergy Not to Reveal Confidential Information" (1990), 73 C.R. (3d) 217.
284 *R. v. Fosty* (1998), (*Reference re Gruenke*) 131 C.C.C. (3d) 72 (Man. C.A.).
285 *R. v. Fosty* [2000] 1 S.C.R. 836.
286 Per Gaselee, J., in *Taylor v. Blacklow* (1836), 132 E.R. 401, 406.
287 See *Berd v. Lovelace* (1576-77), 21 E.R. 33. See generally 8 Wigmore, *Evidence* (McNaughton Rev.), s. 2286.

professional assistance, a man would not venture to consult any skilful person, or would only dare to tell his counsellor half his case.[288]

And Jessel, M.R. later explained it as:

The object and meaning of the rule is this: That as, by reason of the complexity and difficulty of our law, litigation can only be properly conducted by professional men, it is absolutely necessary that a man, in order to prosecute his rights or to defend himself from an improper claim, should have recourse to the assistance of professional lawyers, and it being so absolutely necessary, it is equally necessary, to use a vulgar phrase, that he should be able to make a clean breast of it to the gentleman whom he consults with a view to the prosecution of his claim, or the substantiating his defence against the claim of others; that he should be able to place unrestricted and unbounded confidence in the professional agent, and that the communications he so makes to him should be kept secret, unless with his consent (for it is his privilege, and not the privilege of the confidential agent), that he should be enabled properly to conduct his litigation. That is the meaning of the rule.[289]

The privilege now belongs to the client, not the attorney, and protects him from the disclosure of any confidential communications made by him, or his agent, to his solicitor, or communications by the solicitor in response, while the client was engaged in seeking legal advice.

Consider the following views favouring and opposing the privilege. J.C. McRuer, in his Royal Commission Inquiry into Civil Rights,[290] justified the privilege:

Without the solicitor and client privilege the whole structure of our adversary system of administering justice would collapse, for the object of that system is that the rights of all persons shall be submitted with equal force to the courts. The only way that the imbalance between the learned and the unlearned, the wise and the foolish, can be redressed is that every man's case be brought before the courts with as nearly equal ability as possible. If a lawyer is to give useful service to his client, he must be free to learn the whole of his client's case. The basis of the privilege between solicitor and client is not, therefore, that the relationship is confidential but that confidentiality is necessary to insure that the public, with safety, may substitute legal advisers in their place instead of having to conduct their own cases and advise themselves.

But Jeremy Bentham argued against the privilege:

A counsel, solicitor, or attorney, cannot conduct the cause of his client" (it has been observed) "if he is not fully instructed in the circumstances attending it: but the client" (it is added) "could not give the instructions *with safety*, if the facts confided to his advocate were to be disclosed." Not with safety? So much the better. To what object is the whole system of penal law directed, if it be not that no man shall have it in his power to flatter himself with the hope of safety, in the event of his engaging in the commission of an act which the law, on account of its supposed mischievousness, has thought fit to prohibit? The argument employed as a reason against the compelling such disclosure, is the very argument that pleads in favour of it.[291]

---

288 (1833), 39 E.R. 618, 620-21 (Ch. Div.), approved in *Solosky v. R.* (1979), 50 C.C.C. (2d) 495, 506 (S.C.C.).

289 In *Anderson v. Bank of B.C.* (1876), 2 Ch. D. 644, 649 (C.A.).

290 Province of Ontario, Vol. 2, Report No. I (1968), at p. 819.

291 "Rationale of Judicial Evidence" (1827), 7 The Works of Jeremy Bentham, 475 (Bowring ed., 1842) quoted in 8 Wigmore, *Evidence* (McNaughton Rev.), s. 2291, p. 550.

DESCÔTEAUX v. MIERZWINSKI
[1982] 1 S.C.R. 860, 28 C.R. (3d) 289, 70 C.C.C. (2d) 385

The judgment of the court was delivered by

LAMER J.:—

A citizen who lies about his financial means in order to obtain legal aid is committing a crime. This appeal concerns the right of the police to be authorized by a search warrant to search a legal aid bureau and seize the form filled out by the citizen at his interview, for purposes of proving that this crime was committed. This issue raises several others, including, in particular, the scope of and procedures for exercising the authority to search lawyers' offices, in view of the confidential nature of their clients' files. This appeal will also give everyone an opportunity to note the deficiencies in the law in this area and the limited ability of the courts to compensate for them since their role is not primarily legislative.

. . . .

In the Superior Court

After the documents had been seized and sealed, Mr. Descôteaux and the legal aid bureau (Le Centre communautaire juridique de Montréal) presented to a judge of the Superior Court, District of Montreal, a motion for the issuance of a writ of *certiorari* requesting that the seizure be quashed on the grounds of nullity and requesting the Superior Court Judge to order the justice of the peace to return the sealed envelope and its contents to them.

The motion was dismissed, but the judge amended the wording of the warrant, stating that [translation] "the words 'other documents concerning this case' should be struck out and no longer regarded as forming part of the said search warrant".

The Superior Court Judge stated that he was of the view that solicitor-client privilege could be invoked as soon as confidentiality was threatened, "without waiting until the person or persons disregarding the privilege attempted to tender the information thus obtained as evidence". He found, however, that the documents seized were not privileged since they had been prepared before the solicitor-client relationship came into existence.

. . . .

In the Court of Appeal

The Court of Appeal adopted the conclusions of the Superior Court Judge, together with his reasons [16 C.R. (3d) 188]. To these Bélanger J.A. added on behalf of the court that in any event solicitor-client privilege could not have operated to protect the communication, since the latter was precisely what had been resorted to in order to mislead a representative of the legal aid bureau. On that matter, he stated the following (translation) [at p. 192]:

> In the case at bar the communications or documents that are alleged to be confidential are those referred to in the charge as having been used in the commission

of the offence in question. Apart from common law principles, they are no more privileged than if the same information and documents had been used to mislead the lawyer himself in order to fraudulently obtain his services on special terms. In either case I do not think that false communications made to the eventual victim who will have to bear the cost of the services are confidential in any way. In short, a communication made to a representative of the Commission des services juridiques [Legal Services Commission] is in no way confidential if it is an element of an offence committed to the latter's prejudice, since in such circumstances there is no confidentiality between solicitor and client.

I think that at this point I should state my findings in the case at bar; I shall give reasons for them later.

In my view, it was correctly decided that it is not necessary to wait for the trial or preliminary inquiry at which the communication is to be adduced or sought in evidence before raising its confidentiality.

. . . .

The right to confidentiality

It is not necessary to demonstrate the existence of a person's right to have communications with his lawyer kept confidential. Its existence has been affirmed numerous times and was recently reconfirmed by this court in *Solosky v. The Queen*, [1980] 1 S.C.R. 821 at p. 839, where Dickson J. stated:

> One may depart from the current concept of privilege and approach the case on the broader basis that (i) *the right to communicate in confidence with one's legal adviser is a fundamental civil and legal right, founded upon the unique relationship of solicitor and client*, and (ii) a person confined to prison retains all of his civil rights, other than those expressly or impliedly taken from him by law.

(Emphasis added.) There is no denying that a person has a right to communicate with a legal adviser in all confidence, a right that is "founded upon the unique relationship of solicitor and client" (*Solosky, supra*). It is a personal and extra-patrimonial right which follows a citizen throughout his dealings with others. Like other personal, extra-patrimonial rights, it gives rise to preventive or curative remedies provided for by law, depending on the nature of the aggression threatening it or of which it was the object. Thus a lawyer who communicates a confidential communication to others without his client's authorization could be sued by his client for damages; or a third party who had accidentally seen the contents of a lawyer's file could be prohibited by injunction from disclosing them. (I am dealing here generally with the effects of the right to confidentiality. In its present state, the rule of evidence, which I shall discuss later, would not prohibit a third party from making such a disclosure: see 8 Wigmore, *Evidence*, §2326, pp. 633-4 (McNaughton Rev. 1961.)

. . . .

There is no doubt that this right belonging to a person in his dealings with others, including the State, is part of our Quebec public law as well as of the common law.

Although we recognize numerous applications of it today, the right to confidentiality did not first appear until the 16th century, and then did so as a rule of evidence: see, *inter alia, Berd v. Lovelace* (1577), Cary 62, 21 E.R. 33; *Dennis v. Codrington* (1580), Cary 100, 21 E.R. 53.

The rule of evidence is well known; it has often been stated. This court referred to it again recently in *Solosky, supra.* That decision sets out the conditions precedent to the existence of the privilege, as well as its limits and exceptions. It should be pointed out that the substantive conditions precedent to the existence of the privilege, which the judges have gradually established and defined, are in fact the substantive conditions precedent to the existence of the right to confidentiality, the former being merely the earliest manifestation of the latter. There is no need to list those conditions exhaustively here or to review all the nuances that have been developed by the courts over the years. It will be sufficient to review them in broad outline and to emphasize certain aspects of particular relevance to this appeal.

The following statement by Wigmore (8 Wigmore, *Evidence*, §2292, p. 554 (McNaughton Rev. 1961)), of the rule of evidence is a good summary, in my view, of the substantive conditions precedent to the existence of the right of the lawyer's client to confidentiality:

> Where legal advice of any kind is sought from a professional legal adviser in his capacity as such, the communications relating to that purpose, made in confidence by the client, are at his instance permanently protected from disclosure by himself or by the legal adviser, except the protection be waived.

Seeking advice from a legal adviser includes consulting those who assist him professionally (for example, his secretary or articling student) and who have as such had access to the communications made by the client for the purpose of obtaining legal advice.

There are exceptions. It is not sufficient to speak to a lawyer or one of his associates for everything to become confidential from that point on. The communication must be made to the lawyer or his assistants in their professional capacity; the relationship must be a professional one at the exact moment of the communication. Communications made in order to facilitate the commission of a crime or fraud will not be confidential either, regardless of whether or not the lawyer is acting in good faith.

The substantive rule

Although the right to confidentiality first took the form of a rule of evidence, it is now recognized as having a much broader scope, as can be seen from the manner in which this court dealt with the issues raised in *Solosky, supra.*

. . . .

It is quite apparent that the court in that case applied a standard that has nothing to do with the rule of evidence, the privilege, since there was never any question of testimony before a tribunal or court. The court in fact, in my view, applied a substantive rule, without actually formulating it, and, consequently, recognized implicitly that the right to confidentiality, which had long ago given rise to a rule of evidence, had also since given rise to a substantive rule.

It would, I think, be useful for us to formulate this substantive rule, as the judges formerly did with the rule of evidence; it could, in my view, be stated as follows:

1. The confidentiality of communications between solicitor and client may be raised in any circumstances where such communications are likely to be disclosed without the client's consent.

2. Unless the law provides otherwise, when and to the extent that the legitimate exercise of a right would interfere with another person's right to have his communications with his lawyer kept confidential, the resulting conflict should be resolved in favour of protecting the confidentiality.

3. When the law gives someone the authority to do something which, in the circumstances of the case, might interfere with that confidentiality, the decision to do so and the choice of means of exercising that authority should be determined with a view to not interfering with it except to the extent absolutely necessary in order to achieve the ends sought by the enabling legislation.

4. Acts providing otherwise in situations under para. 2 and enabling legislation referred to in para. 3 must be interpreted restrictively.

The rule of evidence

The rule of evidence is formulated by Cross (*Cross on Evidence*, 5th ed. (1979), p. 282), as follows:

> In civil and criminal cases, confidential communications passing between a client and his legal adviser need not be given in evidence by the client and, without the client's consent, may not be given in evidence by the legal adviser in a judicial proceeding. . .

The rule of evidence does not in any way prevent a third party witness (I am referring here to someone other than an agent of the client or the lawyer) from introducing in evidence confidential communications made by a client to his lawyer. It is important to note, however, that before allowing such evidence to be introduced and in determining to what extent to allow it, the judge must satisfy himself, through the application of the substantive rule (No. 3), that what is being sought to be proved by the communications is important to the outcome of the case and that there is no reasonable alternative form of evidence that could be used for that purpose.

Confidentiality in the case at bar

In the case at bar the principal issue is to determine when the solicitor-client relationship, which confers the confidentiality protected by the substantive rule and the rule of evidence, arises.

The Superior Court Judge, as we have seen, was of the view that this relationship, and consequently the right to confidentiality, did not arise until the legal aid applicant had been accepted, that is, until the retainer was established.

When dealing with the right to confidentiality it is necessary, in my view, to distinguish between the moment when the retainer is established and the moment when the solicitor-client relationship arises. The latter arises as soon as the potential client has his first dealings with the lawyer's office in order to obtain legal advice.

The items of information that a lawyer requires from a person in order to decide if he will agree to advise or represent him are just as much communications made in order to obtain legal advice as any information communicated to him subsequently. It has long been recognized that even if the lawyer does not agree to advise the person seeking his services, communications made by the person to the lawyer or his staff for that purpose are none the less privileged: *Minter v. Priest*, [1930] A.C. 558; *Phipson on Evidence*, 12th ed. (1976), p. 244, para. 590; 8 Wigmore, *Evidence* §2304, pp. 586-7 (McNaughton Rev. 1961).

. . . .

Conclusion

In summary, a lawyer's client is entitled to have all communications made with a view to obtaining legal advice kept confidential. Whether communications are made to the lawyer himself or to employees, and whether they deal with matters of an administrative nature such as financial means or with the actual nature of the legal problem, all information which a person must provide in order to obtain legal advice and which is given in confidence for that purpose enjoys the privileges attached to confidentiality. This confidentiality attaches to all communications made within the framework of the solicitor-client relationship, which arises as soon as the potential client takes the first steps, and consequently even before the formal retainer is established.

There are certain exceptions to the principle of the confidentiality of solicitor-client communications, however. Thus communications that are in themselves criminal or that are made with a view to obtaining legal advice to facilitate the commission of a crime will not be privileged, *inter alia*.

The fundamental right to communicate with one's legal adviser in confidence has given rise to a rule of evidence and a substantive rule. Whether through the rule of evidence or the substantive rule, the client's right to have his communications to his lawyer kept confidential will have an effect when the search warrant provided for in s. 443 of the *Criminal Code* is being issued and executed.

Thus the justice of the peace has no jurisdiction to order the seizure of documents that would not be admissible in evidence in court on the ground that they are privileged (the rule of evidence).

Before authorizing a search of a lawyer's officer for evidence of a crime, the justice of the peace should refuse to issue the warrant unless he is satisfied that there is no reasonable alternative to the search, or he will be exceeding his jurisdiction (the substantive rule). When issuing the warrant, to search for evidence or other things, he must in any event attach terms of execution to the warrant designed to protect the right to confidentiality of the lawyer's clients as much as possible.

Applying these principles to the case at bar, I have arrived at the following conclusions.

First, all information contained in the form that applicants for legal aid must fill out is provided for the purpose of obtaining legal advice, is given in confidence for that purpose and, consequently, is subject to the applicant's fundamental right to have such communications kept confidential and, as such, is protected by the rule of evidence and the substantive rule.

It is alleged in the information laid that the communications made by Ledoux with respect to his financial means are criminal in themselves since they constitute the material element of the crime charged. This is an exception to the principle of confidentiality and these communications are accordingly not protected (this does not mean that we are expressing an opinion as to the validity of the allegations in the information). However, since the allegation concerns only the information dealing with the applicant's financial means, all other information on the form remains confidential.

Since the part of the form dealing with Ledoux's financial situation was as an exception admissible in evidence, the justice of the peace had jurisdiction to order its seizure.

For these reasons I would dismiss this appeal and refer the matter back to the justice of the peace, ordering him to deal with the envelope and its contents as stated above.

In response to *Descôteaux*, Parliament enacted section 488.1 of the Criminal Code which set out a detailed code of procedure to deal with search warrants issued to search lawyer's offices, striving to arrive at a procedure to protect against undue invasions of solicitor-client privilege. A series of Court of Appeal decisions and then finally the Supreme Court of Canada in *R. v. Lavallee*[292] decided that section 488.1 was insufficiently protective of solicitor-client privilege and therefore an unconstitutional violation of the Charter right to make full answer and defence.[293] The Supreme Court emphasised in *Maranda c. Québec (Juge de la Cour du Québec)*[294] that even where there is authorisation to search a lawyer's office the impairment of solicitor-client privilege must be as little as possible.

The rules of privilege prevent a client from being <u>compelled</u> by the state or third party to reveal a confidential solicitor-client communication. It is important

---

292 (2002), 167 C.C.C. (3d) 1 (S.C.C.).

293 For comment see M.C. Plaxton, "R. v. Lavallee, Rackel & Heintz: Jiminy Cricket Has Left The Building" (2002), 3 C.R. (6th) 253. See further *Festing v. Canada (Attorney General)* (2003), 172 C.C.C. (3d) 321 (B.C. C.A.) and *Maranda v. Richer* (2003), 15 C.R. (6th) 1, 2003 CarswellQue 2477, 2003 CarswellQue 2478. The Court has declared procedures to be applied in such cases pending any new legislation.

294 (2003), 15 C.R. (6th) 1, 178 C.C.C. (3d) 321 (S.C.C.).

to recognize that a lawyer's duty of confidentiality is broader than the privilege. It requires a lawyer, subject to a number of exceptions, to not disclose any information about the client obtained during the course of the relationship. This duty of confidentiality is enforced through the rules of professional conduct enacted by each provincial law society.

CANADA (PRIVACY COMMISSIONER) v. BLOOD TRIBE DEPARTMENT OF HEALTH

[2008] 2 S.C.R. 574, 2008 CarswellNat 2244, 2008 CarswellNat 2245

An employee with the Blood Tribe Department of Health was dismissed. At the time of her dismissal, her employee sought legal advice. Following her dismissal, the employee sought access to her file. She suspected that her employer may have collected inaccurate information. Her employer refused. She then brought an application under the relevant provisions of the *Personal Information Protection and Electronic Documents Act* (PIPEDA) to the Privacy Commissioner. The issue before the Supreme Court was whether the Commissioner could order production of documents protected by solicitor-client privilege. Writing for the Court, Justice Binnie held that the Privacy Commissioner, while an officer of Parliament and administrative adjudicator, has no jurisdiction to order disclosure as the position lacks the independence and authority of a court. In so holding, the Court provided a concise summary of the solicitor-client privilege.

BINNIE J. (for the Court):

. . .

IV. Analysis

9 Solicitor-client privilege is fundamental to the proper functioning of our legal system. The complex of rules and procedures is such that, realistically speaking, it cannot be navigated without a lawyer's expert advice. It is said that anyone who represents himself or herself has a fool for a client, yet a lawyer's advice is only as good as the factual information the client provides. Experience shows that people who have a legal problem will often not make a clean breast of the facts to a lawyer without an assurance of confidentiality "as close to absolute as possible":

> [S]olicitor-client privilege must be as close to absolute as possible to ensure public confidence and retain relevance. As such, it will only yield in certain clearly defined circumstances, and does not involve a balancing of interests on a case-by-case basis.
>
> (*R. v. McClure*, [2001] 1 S.C.R. 445, 2001 SCC 14, at para. 35, quoted with approval in *Lavallee, Rackel & Heintz v. Canada (Attorney General)*, [2002] 3 S.C.R. 209, 2002 SCC 61, at para. 36.)

It is in the public interest that this free flow of legal advice be encouraged. Without it, access to justice and the quality of justice in this country would be severely compromised. The privilege belongs to the client not the lawyer. In *Andrews v. Law Society of British Columbia*, [1989] 1 S.C.R. 143, at p. 188, McIntyre J.

affirmed yet again that the Court will not permit a solicitor to disclose a client's confidence.

10 At the time the employer in this case consulted its lawyer, litigation may or may not have been in contemplation. It does not matter. While the solicitor-client privilege may have started life as a rule of evidence, it is now unquestionably a rule of substance applicable to all interactions between a client and his or her lawyer when the lawyer is engaged in providing legal advice or otherwise acting as a lawyer rather than as a business counsellor or in some other non-legal capacity: *Solosky v. The Queen*, [1980] 1 S.C.R. 821, at p. 837; *Descôteaux v. Mierzwinski*, [1982] 1 S.C.R. 860, at pp. 885-87; *R. v. Gruenke*, [1991] 3 S.C.R. 263; *Smith v. Jones*, [1999] 1 S.C.R. 455; *Foster Wheeler Power Co. v. Société intermunicipale de gestion et d'élimination des déchets (SIGED) inc.*, [2004] 1 S.C.R. 456, 2004 SCC 18, at paras. 40-47; *McClure*, at paras. 23-27; *Blank v. Canada (Minister of Justice)*, [2006] 2 S.C.R. 319, 2006 SCC 39, at para. 26; *Goodis v. Ontario (Ministry of Correctional Services)*, [2006] 2 S.C.R. 32, 2006 SCC 31; *Celanese Canada Inc. v. Murray Demolition Corp.*, [2006] 2 S.C.R. 189, 2006 SCC 36; *Juman v. Doucette*, [2008] 1 S.C.R. 157, 2008 SCC 8. A rare exception, which has no application here, is that no privilege attaches to communications criminal in themselves or intended to further criminal purposes: *Descôteaux*, at p. 881; *R. v. Campbell*, [1999] 1 S.C.R. 565. The extremely limited nature of the exception emphasizes, rather than dilutes, the paramountcy of the general rule whereby solicitor-client privilege is created and maintained "as close to absolute as possible to ensure public confidence and retain relevance" (*McClure*, at para. 35).

11 To give effect to this fundamental policy of the law, our Court has held that legislative language that may (if broadly construed) allow incursions on solicitor-client privilege must be interpreted restrictively. The privilege cannot be abrogated by inference. Open-textured language governing production of documents will be read not to include solicitor-client documents: *Lavallee*, at para. 18; *Pritchard*, at para. 33. This case falls squarely within that principle.

As we will see in the next section (*(ii) Exceptions*), the privilege is not absolute, although *Blood Tribe* reveals how jealously guarded it is as a substantive organizing principle of our legal system and the rule of law. In the following case, the Supreme Court, applying its earlier decision in *Descoteaux*, set out a general "absolute necessity" test for when the privilege will be pierced. The issue was whether a judge could order disclosure of privileged records to a lawyer representing a client who sought production under the *Freedom of Information and Protection of Privacy Act* to enable the lawyer to make submissions on whether the records should be disclosed. The lawyer provided a non-disclosure undertaking.

GOODIS v. ONTARIO (MINISTRY OF CORRECTIONAL SERVICES)
2006 CarswellOnt 4077, [2006] 2 S.C.R. 32

ROTHSTEIN J. (for the Court):

. . .

15 The substantive rule laid down in *Descôteaux* is that a judge must not interfere with the confidentiality of communications between solicitor and client "except to the extent absolutely necessary in order to achieve the ends sought by the enabling legislation". In *Lavallee, Rackel & Heintz v. Canada (Attorney General)*, [2002] 3 S.C.R. 209, 2002 SCC 61, it was found that a provision of the *Criminal Code*, R.S.C. 1985, c. C-46, that authorized the seizure of documents from a law office was unreasonable within the meaning of s. 8 of the *Canadian Charter of Rights and Freedoms* because it permitted the automatic loss of solicitor-client privilege. That decision further emphasized the fundamental nature of the substantive rule. It is, therefore, incumbent on a judge to apply the "absolutely necessary" test when deciding an application for disclosure of such records.

. . .

17 Of particular significance is that the question of disclosure of solicitor-client privileged communications does not involve a balancing of interests on a case-by-case basis.

. . .

(3) Meaning of Absolute Necessity

20 Absolute necessity is as restrictive a test as may be formulated short of an absolute prohibition in every case. The circumstances in which the test has been met exemplify its restrictive nature. In *Solosky v. The Queen*, [1980] 1 S.C.R. 821, at p. 841, for example, it was found that subject to strict safeguards, mail received by an inmate at a penitentiary could be inspected to maintain the safety and security of the penitentiary. Similarly, in *McClure* [discussed in the next section], it was found that documents subject to privilege could be disclosed where there was a genuine danger of wrongful conviction because the information was not available from other sources and the accused could not otherwise raise a reasonable doubt as to his guilt.

21 While I cannot rule out the possibility, it is difficult to envisage circumstances where the absolute necessity test could be met if the sole purpose of disclosure is to facilitate argument by the requester's counsel on the question of whether privilege is properly claimed. Hearing from both sides of an issue is a principle to be departed from only in exceptional circumstances. However, privilege is a subject with which judges are acquainted. They are well equipped in the ordinary case to determine whether a record is subject to privilege. There is no evidence in this case that disclosure of records to counsel for the purpose of arguing whether or not they are privileged is absolutely necessary.

(4) Judicial Workload

22 It is suggested that the need to examine many records could place an undue burden on the reviewing judge. It is not obvious that disclosure to the requester's counsel will necessarily reduce that workload. In any event, there are techniques available to help reduce the volume of information that must be reviewed. At a minimum, for example, the 459 pages could be organized in categories that exhibit common characteristics relevant to the solicitor-client privilege. Nor do I see how an increase in judicial workload or other administrative considerations make absolutely necessary disclosure to the requester's counsel for the purpose of arguing the judicial review application. Convenience is not a reason to release information subject to a claim of solicitor-client privilege.

(5) Conclusion on Solicitor-Client Privilege

23 In sum, I agree with the Ministry that there is no justification for establishing a new or different test for disclosure of records subject to a claim for solicitor-client privilege in an access to information case.

24 I am of the respectful opinion that the Ontario courts were in error in permitting disclosure of all the documents in this case. The appropriate test for any document claimed to be subject to solicitor-client privilege is "absolute necessity". That test was not applied. Had it been, disclosure of all the records would not have been ordered.

25 I am mindful that openness of the court's process is a recognized principle. However, as with all general principles, there are exceptions. Records that are subject to a claim of solicitor-client privilege in an access to information case are such an exception. Absent absolute necessity in order to achieve the end sought by the enabling legislation, such records may not be disclosed. As stated, the evidence disclosed no such absolute necessity in this case.

Is there a litigation or work-product privilege in Canada? Is it accorded the same status as solicitor-client privilege? The following case is the first time the Supreme Court of Canada had occasion to answer these questions.

BLANK v. CANADA (MINISTER OF JUSTICE)
2006 CarswellNat 2704, 2006 CarswellNat 2705, 40 C.R. (6th) 1, [2006] 2 S.C.R. 319

Blank and a company were twice charged with regulatory offences. All of the charges were eventually quashed or stayed by the Crown. Blank and the company eventually sued the federal government for fraud, conspiracy, perjury and abuse of process. Blank sought all of the records pertaining to his prosecution. When his request was refused, he brought an application under the *Access Act*. The Minister of Justice claimed that the documents prepared for the dominant purpose of a criminal investigation were covered by litigation privilege. The Supreme Court was asked to determine whether some of the documents that fell within litigation privilege should be released if the original litigation that led to their creation had ended.

F<small>ISH</small> J. (for the majority):

. . .

1 This appeal requires the Court, for the first time, to distinguish between two related but conceptually distinct exemptions from compelled disclosure: the solicitor-client privilege and the litigation privilege. They often co-exist and one is sometimes mistakenly called by the other's name, but they are not coterminous in space, time or meaning.

2 More particularly, we are concerned in this case with the litigation privilege, with how it is born and when it must be laid to rest.

. . .

5 In short, we are not asked in this case to decide whether the government can invoke litigation privilege. Quite properly, the parties agree that it can. Our task, rather, is to examine the defining characteristics of that privilege and, more particularly, to determine its lifespan.

6 The Minister contends that the solicitor-client privilege has two "branches", one concerned with confidential communications between lawyers and their clients, the other relating to information and materials gathered or created in the litigation context. The first of these branches, as already indicated, is generally characterized as the "legal advice privilege"; the second, as the "litigation privilege".

7 Bearing in mind their different scope, purpose and rationale, it would be preferable, in my view, to recognize that we are dealing here with distinct conceptual animals and not with two branches of the same tree. Accordingly, I shall refer in these reasons to the solicitor-client privilege as if it includes only the legal advice privilege, and shall indeed use the two phrases—solicitor-client privilege and legal advice privilege—synonymously and interchangeably, except where otherwise indicated.

8 As a matter of substance and not mere terminology, the distinction between litigation privilege and the solicitor-client privilege is decisive in this case. The former, unlike the latter, is of temporary duration. It expires with the litigation of which it was born. Characterizing litigation privilege as a "branch" of the solicitor-client privilege, as the Minister would, does not envelop it in a shared cloak of permanency.

9 The Minister's claim of litigation privilege fails in this case because the privilege claimed, by whatever name, has expired: The files to which the respondent seeks access relate to penal proceedings that have long terminated. By seeking civil redress for the manner in which those proceedings were conducted, the respondent has given them neither fresh life nor a posthumous and parallel existence.

. . .

26 . . . The solicitor-client privilege has been firmly entrenched for centuries. It

recognizes that the justice system depends for its vitality on full, free and frank communication between those who need legal advice and those who are best able to provide it. Society has entrusted to lawyers the task of advancing their clients' cases with the skill and expertise available only to those who are trained in the law. They alone can discharge these duties effectively, but only if those who depend on them for counsel may consult with them in confidence. The resulting confidential relationship between solicitor and client is a necessary and essential condition of the effective administration of justice.

27 Litigation privilege, on the other hand, is not directed at, still less, restricted to, communications between solicitor and client. It contemplates, as well, communications between a solicitor and third parties or, in the case of an unrepresented litigant, between the litigant and third parties. Its object is to ensure the efficacy of the adversarial process and not to promote the solicitor-client relationship. And to achieve this purpose, parties to litigation, represented or not, must be left to prepare their contending positions in private, without adversarial interference and without fear of premature disclosure.

28 R. J. Sharpe (now Sharpe J.A.) has explained particularly well the differences between litigation privilege and solicitor-client privilege:

> It is crucially important to distinguish litigation privilege from solicitor-client privilege. There are, I suggest, at least three important differences between the two. First, solicitor-client privilege applies only to confidential communications between the client and his solicitor. Litigation privilege, on the other hand, applies to communications of a non-confidential nature between the solicitor and third parties and even includes material of a non-communicative nature. Secondly, solicitor-client privilege exists any time a client seeks legal advice from his solicitor whether or not litigation is involved. Litigation privilege, on the other hand, applies only in the context of litigation itself. Thirdly, and most important, the rationale for solicitor-client privilege is very different from that which underlies litigation privilege. This difference merits close attention. The interest which underlies the protection accorded communications between a client and a solicitor from disclosure is the interest of all citizens to have full and ready access to legal advice. If an individual cannot confide in a solicitor knowing that what is said will not be revealed, it will be difficult, if not impossible, for that individual to obtain proper candid legal advice.
>
> Litigation privilege, on the other hand, is geared directly to the process of litigation. Its purpose is not explained adequately by the protection afforded lawyer-client communications deemed necessary to allow clients to obtain legal advice, the interest protected by solicitor-client privilege. Its purpose is more particularly related to the needs of the adversarial trial process. Litigation privilege is based upon the need for a protected area to facilitate investigation and preparation of a case for trial by the adversarial advocate. In other words, litigation privilege aims to facilitate a process (namely, the adversary process), while solicitor-client privilege aims to protect a relationship (namely, the confidential relationship between a lawyer and a client).
>
> ("Claiming Privilege in the Discovery Process", in *Special Lectures of the Law Society of Upper Canada* (1984), 163, at pp. 164-65)

29 With the exception of *Hodgkinson v. Simms* (1988), 33 B.C.L.R. (2d) 129, a decision of the British Columbia Court of Appeal, the decisions of appellate courts in this country have consistently found that litigation privilege is based on a different rationale than solicitor-client privilege . . .

30 American and English authorities are to the same effect . . . . In the United States communications with third parties and other materials prepared in anticipation of litigation are covered by the similar "attorney work product" doctrine. This "distinct rationale" theory is also supported by the majority of academics . . . .

31 Though conceptually distinct, litigation privilege and legal advice privilege serve a common cause: The secure and effective administration of justice according to law. And they are complementary and not competing in their operation. But treating litigation privilege and legal advice privilege as two branches of the same tree tends to obscure the true nature of both.

32 Unlike the solicitor-client privilege, the litigation privilege arises and operates even in the absence of a solicitor-client relationship, and it applies indiscriminately to all litigants, whether or not they are represented by counsel: see *Alberta (Treasury Branches) v. Ghermezian* (1999), 242 A.R. 326, 1999 ABQB 407. A self-represented litigant is no less in need of, and therefore entitled to, a "zone" or [page333] "chamber" of privacy. Another important distinction leads to the same conclusion. Confidentiality, the sine qua non of the solicitor-client privilege, is not an essential component of the litigation privilege. In preparing for trial, lawyers as a matter of course obtain information from third parties who have no need nor any expectation of confidentiality; yet the litigation privilege attaches nonetheless.

33 In short, the litigation privilege and the solicitor-client privilege are driven by different policy considerations and generate different legal consequences.

34 The purpose of the litigation privilege, I repeat, is to create a "zone of privacy" in relation to pending or apprehended litigation. Once the litigation has ended, the privilege to which it gave rise has lost its specific and concrete purpose—and therefore its justification. But to borrow a phrase, the litigation is not over until it is over: It cannot be said to have "terminated", in any meaningful sense of that term, where litigants or related parties remain locked in what is essentially the same legal combat.

35 Except where such related litigation persists, there is no need and no reason to protect from discovery anything that would have been subject to compellable disclosure but for the pending or apprehended proceedings which provided its shield. Where the litigation has indeed ended, there is little room for concern lest opposing counsel or their clients argue their case "on wits borrowed from the adversary", to use the language of the U.S. Supreme Court in *Hickman*, at p. 516.

36 I therefore agree with the majority in the Federal Court of Appeal and others who share their view that the common law litigation privilege comes to an end,

absent closely related proceedings, upon the termination of the litigation that gave rise to the privilege. . .

37 Thus, the principle "once privileged, always privileged", so vital to the solicitor-client privilege, is foreign to the litigation privilege. The litigation privilege, unlike the solicitor-client privilege, is neither absolute in scope nor permanent in duration.

38 As mentioned earlier, however, the privilege may retain its purpose—and, therefore, its effect—where the litigation that gave rise to the privilege has ended, but related litigation remains pending or may reasonably be apprehended. In this regard, I agree with Pelletier J.A. regarding "the possibility of defining ... litigation more broadly than the particular proceeding which gave rise to the claim" (para. 89); see *Ed Miller Sales & Rentals Ltd. v. Caterpillar Tractor Co.* (1988), 90 A.R. 323 (C.A.).

39 At a minimum, it seems to me, this enlarged definition of "litigation" includes separate proceedings that involve the same or related parties and arise from the same or a related cause of action (or "juridical source"). Proceedings that raise issues common to the initial action and share its essential purpose would in my view qualify as well.

40 As a matter of principle, the boundaries of this extended meaning of "litigation" are limited by the purpose for which litigation privilege is granted, namely, as mentioned, "the need for a protected area to facilitate investigation and preparation of a case for trial by the adversarial advocate" (Sharpe, at p. 165).

. . .

42 In this case, the respondent claims damages from the federal government for fraud, conspiracy, perjury and abuse of prosecutorial powers. Pursuant to the *Access Act*, he demands the disclosure to him of all documents relating to the Crown's conduct of its proceedings against him. The source of those proceedings is the alleged pollution and breach of reporting requirements by the respondent and his company.

43 The Minister's claim of privilege thus concerns documents that were prepared for the dominant purpose of a criminal prosecution relating to environmental matters and reporting requirements. The respondent's action, on the other hand, seeks civil redress for the manner in which the government conducted that prosecution. It springs from a different juridical source and is in that sense unrelated to the litigation of which the privilege claimed was born.

44 The litigation privilege would not in any event protect from disclosure evidence of the claimant party's abuse of process or similar blameworthy conduct. It is not a black hole from which evidence of one's own misconduct can never be exposed to the light of day.

45 Even where the materials sought would otherwise be subject to litigation privilege, the party seeking their disclosure may be granted access to them upon

a prima facie showing of actionable misconduct by the other party in relation to the proceedings with respect to which litigation privilege is claimed. Whether privilege is claimed in the originating or in related litigation, the court may review the materials to determine whether their disclosure should be ordered on this ground.

46 Finally, in the Court of Appeal, Létourneau J.A., dissenting on the cross-appeal, found that the government's status as a "recurring litigant" could justify a litigation privilege that outlives its common law equivalent. In his view, the "[a]utomatic and uncontrolled access to the government lawyer's brief, once the first litigation is over, may impede the possibility of effectively adopting and implementing [general policies and strategies]" (para. 42).

47 I hesitate to characterize as "[a]utomatic and uncontrolled" access to the government lawyer's brief once the subject proceedings have ended. In my respectful view, access will in fact be neither automatic nor uncontrolled.

48 First, as mentioned earlier, it will not be automatic because all subsequent litigation will remain subject to a claim of privilege if it involves the same or related parties and the same or related source. It will fall within the protective orbit of the same litigation defined broadly.

49 Second, access will not be uncontrolled because many of the documents in the lawyer's brief will, in any event, remain exempt from disclosure by virtue of the legal advice privilege. In practice, a lawyer's brief normally includes materials covered by the solicitor-client privilege because of their evident connection to legal advice sought or given in the course of, or in relation to, the originating proceedings. The distinction between the solicitor-client privilege and the litigation privilege does not preclude their potential overlap in a litigation context.

50 Commensurate with its importance, the solicitor-client privilege has over the years been broadly interpreted by this Court. In that light, anything in a litigation file that falls within the solicitor-client privilege will remain clearly and forever privileged.

. . .

55 Finally, we should not disregard the origins of this dispute between the respondent and the Minister. It arose in the context of a criminal prosecution by the Crown against the respondent. In criminal proceedings, the accused's right to discovery is constitutionally guaranteed. The prosecution is obliged under *Stinchcombe* to make available to the accused all relevant information if there is a "reasonable possibility that the withholding of information will impair the right of the accused to make full answer and defence" (p. 340). This added burden of disclosure is placed on the Crown in light of its overwhelming advantage in resources and the corresponding risk that the accused might otherwise be unfairly disadvantaged.

56 I am not unmindful of the fact that *Stinchcombe* does not require the prosecution to disclose everything in its file, privileged or not. Materials that

might in civil proceedings be covered by one privilege or another will nonetheless be subject, in the criminal context, to the "innocence at stake" exception—at the very least: see *McClure*. In criminal proceedings, as the Court noted in *Stinchcombe*:

> The trial judge might also, in certain circumstances, conclude that the recognition of an existing privilege does not constitute a reasonable limit on the constitutional right to make full answer and defence and thus require disclosure in spite of the law of privilege. [p. 340]

57 On any view of the matter, I would think it incongruous if the litigation privilege were found in civil proceedings to insulate the Crown from the disclosure it was bound but failed to provide in criminal proceedings that have ended.

58 The result in this case is dictated by a finding that the litigation privilege expires when the litigation ends. I wish nonetheless to add a few words regarding its birth.

59 The question has arisen whether the litigation privilege should attach to documents created for the substantial purpose of litigation, the dominant purpose of litigation or the sole purpose of litigation. . . .

60 I see no reason to depart from the dominant purpose test. Though it provides narrower protection than would a substantial purpose test, the dominant purpose standard appears to me consistent with the notion that the litigation privilege should be viewed as a limited exception to the principle of full disclosure and not as an equal partner of the broadly interpreted solicitor-client privilege. . . .

. . .

62 A related issue is whether the litigation privilege attaches to documents gathered or copied—but not created—for the purpose of litigation. This issue arose in *Hodgkinson*, where a majority of the British Columbia Court of Appeal, relying on *Lyell v. Kennedy* (1884), 27 Ch. D. 1 (C.A.), concluded that copies of public documents gathered by a solicitor were privileged. McEachern C.J.B.C. stated:

> It is my conclusion that the law has always been, and, in my view, should continue to be, that in circumstances such as these, where a lawyer exercising legal knowledge, skill, judgment and industry has assembled a collection of relevant copy documents for his brief for the purpose of advising on or conducting anticipated or pending litigation he is entitled, indeed required, unless the client consents, to claim privilege for such collection and to refuse production. [p. 142]

63 This approach was rejected by the majority of the Ontario Court of Appeal in *Chrusz*.

64 The conflict of appellate opinion on this issue should be left to be resolved in a case where it is explicitly raised and fully argued. Extending the privilege to the gathering of documents resulting from research or the exercise of skill and knowledge does appear to be more consistent with the rationale and purpose of the litigation privilege. That being said, I take care to mention that assigning such

a broad scope to the litigation privilege is not intended to automatically exempt from disclosure anything that would have been subject to discovery if it had not been remitted to counsel or placed in one's own litigation files. Nor should it have that effect.

For a recent discussion of *Blank* and the issue of litigation privilege in the context of related criminal investigations, see *R. v. Basi* (2009), 244 C.C.C. (3d) 537 (B.C. S.C.).

(ii) *Exceptions*

Inadvertent Disclosure

AIRST v. AIRST
(1998), 37 O.R. (3d) 654, 1998 CarswellOnt 2630 (Gen. Div.)

During pre-trial proceedings in matrimonial case, it was ordered that a joint evaluation report be prepared in relation to certain assets. The husband was required to send a number of documents to the valuators. Included in the documents he sent were two letters from his lawyer that were privileged. The wife now claimed that privilege was lost and the letters should be admissible in evidence. It was agreed that the letters were inadvertently sent.

WEIN J.:

. . .

Case-law Relating to Waiver of the Privilege Upon Inadvertent Disclosure

The traditional common law approach, as set out in the English Court of Appeal in *Calcraft v. Guest*, [1898] 1 Q.B. 759, [1895-9] All E.R. Rep. 346 (C.A.), has been that the privilege is lost whether the disclosure is by accident or by design. This traditional approach has been adopted by the Supreme Court of Canada in *Descôteaux v. Mierzwinski*, [1982] 1 S.C.R. 860, 141 D.L.R. (3d) 592.

However, in the civil context, in cases where the disclosure is found to be inadvertent, more recent authority in this court and other courts has held that, Descôteaux notwithstanding, there is a discretion that may be properly exercised in favour of non-disclosure where the release of the documents or information has been found to be inadvertent: see *Unit Park Management Co. v. Nissan Canada Inc.*, [1997] O.J. No. 3265 (Gen. Div.), per Gans J.; ..[further citations omitted.]

The competing policy interests are obvious. The basic rationale behind the solicitor-client privilege is to permit people to speak frankly and openly with their solicitors. Inadvertent disclosure should not logically override the privilege in all cases, though there may be some level of obligation upon the solicitor and the client to take steps to ensure that their communications remain confidential.

Yet another important policy interest dictates that all relevant facts be disclosed, such that in a case where information has come to the knowledge of a third party, it may be contrary to public policy to allow the privilege to stand. For example, if a third party is in possession of information which contradicts evidence that may have been given in pre-trial disclosure or during a trial, it might be said to be improper to require the court to rule on that evidence without the benefit of weighing the contradictory material.

Certainly where the evidence is unlawfully or improperly obtained, the principle has emerged that a party may be restrained from introducing such evidence, at least in civil proceedings: see *Ashburton (Lord) v. Pape*, [1913] 2 Ch. 469, [1911-13] All E.R. Rep. 708 (C.A.). Under this line of authority, injunctive relief will be granted to restrain the use of confidential material obtained in such a manner. However, *Calcraft v. Guest*, supra, suggests that the material, if not so restrained, may be introduced in court. This conflict relating to resultant use appears dichotomous: see J. Sopinka, S.N. Lederman and A. Bryant, The Law of Evidence in Canada (Toronto: Butterworths, 1992) at pp. 672-77.

The more recent trend in the authorities is to permit the courts to enquire into the circumstances by which the privileged information has come to the attention of the third party. Where a third party has obtained the information by improper means, courts have held that the privileged information ought not to be disclosed. On the other hand, Charter principles, applicable in criminal cases, may override traditional approaches to the law of privilege.

In the criminal law context where Charter principles have overlaid a rights-based matrix onto the development of law, it has been fully recognized that interpretations of privilege and the scope of a waiver may be affected by Charter-based rights. So for example in *R. v. O'Connor*, [1995] 4 S.C.R. 411 at p. 431, 103 C.C.C. (3d) 1 at p. 15, it was noted that: "it must be recognized that any form of privilege may be forced to yield where such a privilege would preclude the accused's right to make full answer and defence" (per Lamer C.J.C and Sopinka J. dissenting on another point).

This principled approach to the law of evidence must clearly be given application in the civil law context: it has been acknowledged that the common law should develop in accordance with Charter principles and values, even though the Charter may not have direct application to the case: "ensuring that the common law of privilege develops in accordance with 'Charter values' requires that the existing rules be scrutinized to ensure that they reflect the values the Charter enshrines": see *M. (A.) v. Ryan*, [1997] 1 S.C.R. 157 at pp. 170-72, 143 D.L.R. (4th) 1, per McLachlin J.; see also *Hill v. Church of Scientology of Toronto*, [1995] 2 S.C.R. 1130 at paras. 93, 95, 121, 126 D.L.R. (4th) 129.

In this context, that principle dictates that the rigid approach embodied in *Calcraft v. Guest, supra*, must be modified to reflect the fairness approach developed in more recent cases.

General Conclusions

In balancing the competing interests in a case involving inadvertent disclosure, the court must exercise a discretion and determine the issue based on the particular circumstances. Factors relevant to the court's consideration will include the way in which the documents came to be released, whether there was a prompt attempt to retrieve the documents after the disclosure was discovered, the timing of the discovery of the disclosure and, sometimes, the timing of the application, the number and nature of the third parties who have become aware of the documents, whether maintenance of the privilege will create an actual or perceived unfairness to the opposing party, and the impact on the fairness, both actual and perceived, of the processes of the court.

In some cases of inadvertent disclosure there may be a limited risk that the information has become or will become widely known beyond the party to whom the disclosure was made. The information may not even have been fully released, as in cases where documents are released but not opened or read. In other circumstances, the balance may favour admission of the evidence, such as where the documents have come into the hands of the opposing party through the carelessness of the party claiming privilege, but not through any wrongdoing of the opposing party. In some such situations the failure to permit the introduction of the evidence could leave the party with a sense that the court was denying itself the opportunity to assess conflicting information on a material point, and consequently could negatively reflect on the public perception of the administration of justice. In other cases the information might have been so widely distributed that it would be futile as a practical matter to attempt to prevent its admission. In every case there must be a balancing of the relevant factors in the individual circumstances of the case, thus no hard rule can be laid down.

Findings in this Case

In this case, there is no issue that the disclosure was inadvertent. A review of the documents confirms that solicitor-client privilege would apply to all of the content of the documents. Notwithstanding that the content may in some way be relevant to the issues before the court, in my view the equities favour the holding that the privilege has not been lost in this case. The release of the documents was entirely inadvertent, apparently through the carelessness of a party of advanced years required to find documents relating to many years of transactions. The disclosure was limited in scope and restricted to one individual retained in a capacity that may be broadly construed as confidential. There has been no "public" disclosure of the documents. The content of the documents does not bear in any direct way on the third party's assessment of the material he was retained to review. The court's ability to assess the facts underlying the issues in the case will not be impaired by lack of disclosure. To the contrary, release of the solicitor-client instructions might well be seen, in this case, as giving the opposing party an unfair "windfall" advantage of revealing tactical approaches taken at one point in time by the other side. Given the timing of the discovery of the issue, well after both parties had testified, disclosure at this time is additionally problematic. All of these factors are relevant to my consideration.

Accordingly, in this case the letters will not be released to counsel for the wife. The court copies of the letters will remain sealed and are not to be opened without further court order.[295]

Public Safety – Future Harm Exception

SMITH v. JONES
[1999] 1 S.C.R. 455, 22 C.R. (5th) 203, 132 C.C.C. (3d) 225

The accused was charged with aggravated sexual assault on a prostitute. His counsel referred him to a psychiatrist hoping that it would be of assistance in the preparation of the defence or with submissions on sentencing in the event of a guilty plea. Counsel informed the accused that the consultation was privileged in the same way as a consultation with him would be. During his interview with the psychiatrist, the accused described in considerable detail his plan to kidnap, rape and kill prostitutes. The psychiatrist informed defence counsel that in his opinion the accused was a dangerous individual who would, more likely than not, commit future offences unless he received sufficient treatment. The accused later pled guilty to the included offence of aggravated assault. The psychiatrist phoned defence counsel to inquire about the status of the proceedings and learned that his concerns about the accused would not be addressed in the sentencing hearing. The psychiatrist commenced this action for a declaration that he was entitled to disclose the information he had in his possession in the interests of public safety. He filed an affidavit describing his interview with the accused and his opinion based upon the interview. The trial judge ruled that the public safety exception to the solicitor-client privilege and doctor-patient confidentiality released the psychiatrist from his duties of confidentiality and concluded that he was under a duty to disclose to the police and the Crown both the statements made by the accused and his opinion based upon them. The Court of Appeal allowed the accused's appeal but only to the extent that the mandatory order was changed to one permitting the psychiatrist to disclose the information to the Crown and police.

CORY J. (L'HEUREUX-DUBÉ, GONTHIER, McLACHLIN, IACOBUCCI and BASTARACHE JJ. concurring):—

. . . .

Dr. Smith reported that Mr. Jones described in considerable detail his plan for the crime to which he subsequently pled guilty. It involved deliberately choosing as a victim a small prostitute who could be readily overwhelmed. He planned to have sex with her and then to kidnap her. He took duct tape and rope with him, as well as a small blue ball that he tried to force into the woman's mouth. Because he planned to kill her after the sexual assault he made no attempt to hide his identity. Mr. Jones planned to strangle the victim and to dispose of her body in the bush area near Hope, British Columbia. He was going to shoot the

---

295 On the issue of inadvertent disclosure see further *Canada v. Chapelstone Developments Inc.* (2004), 191 C.C.C. (3d) 152 (N.B. C.A.).

woman in the face before burying her to impede identification. He had arranged time off from his work and had carefully prepared his basement apartment to facilitate his planned sexual assault and murder. He had told people he would be going away on vacation so that no one would visit him and he had fixed dead bolts on all the doors so that a key alone would not open them. Mr. Jones told Dr. Smith that his first victim would be a "trial run" to see if he could "live with" what he had done. If he could, he planned to seek out similar victims. He stated that, by the time he had kidnapped his first victim, he expected that he would be "in so deep" that he would have no choice but to carry out his plans.

. . . .

Just as no right is absolute so too the privilege, even that between solicitor and client, is subject to clearly defined exceptions. The decision to exclude evidence that would be both relevant and of substantial probative value because it is protected by the solicitor-client privilege represents a policy decision. It is based upon the importance to our legal system in general of the solicitor-client privilege. In certain circumstances, however, other societal values must prevail.

. . . .

Quite simply society recognizes that the safety of the public is of such importance that in appropriate circumstances it will warrant setting aside solicitor-client privilege. What factors should be taken into consideration in determining whether that privilege should be displaced?

There are three factors to be considered: First, is there a clear risk to an identifiable person or group of persons? Second, is there a risk of serious bodily harm or death? Third, is the danger imminent? Clearly if the risk is imminent, the danger is serious.

These factors will often overlap and vary in their importance and significance. The weight to be attached to each will vary with the circumstances presented by each case, but they all must be considered. As well, each factor is composed of various aspects, and, like the factors themselves, these aspects may overlap and the weight to be given to them will vary depending on the circumstances of each case. Yet as a general rule, if the privilege is to be set aside the court must find that there is an imminent risk of serious bodily harm or death to an identifiable person or group.

(a) Clarity

What should be considered in determining if there is a clear risk to an identifiable group or person? It will be appropriate and relevant to consider the answers a particular case may provide to the following questions: Is there evidence of long range planning? Has a method for effecting the specific attack been suggested? Is there a prior history of violence or threats of violence? Are the prior assaults or threats of violence similar to that which was planned? If there is a history of violence, has the violence increased in severity? Is the violence directed to an identifiable person or group of persons? This is not an all-encompassing list. It is important to note, however, that as a general rule a group or person must be ascertainable. The requisite specificity of that identification will vary depending on the other factors discussed here.

The specific questions to be considered under this heading will vary with the particular circumstances of each case. Great significance might, in some situations, be given to the particularly clear identification of a particular individual or group of intended victims. Even if the group of intended victims is large considerable significance can be given to the threat if the identification of the group is clear and forceful. For example, a threat, put forward with chilling detail, to kill or seriously injure children five years of age and under would have to be given very careful consideration. In certain circumstances it might be that a threat of death directed toward single women living in apartment buildings could in combination with other factors be sufficient in the particular circumstances to justify setting aside the privilege. At the same time, a general threat of death or violence directed to everyone in a city or community, or anyone with whom the person may come into contact, may be too vague to warrant setting aside the privilege. However, if the threatened harm to the members of the public was particularly compelling, extremely serious and imminent, it might well be appropriate to lift the privilege. All the surrounding circumstances will have to be taken into consideration in every case.

In sum, the threatened group may be large but if it is clearly identifiable then it is a factor — indeed an essential factor — that must be considered together with others in determining whether the solicitor-client privilege should be set aside. A test that requires that the class of victim be ascertainable allows the trial judge sufficient flexibility to determine whether the public safety exception has been made out.

(b) Seriousness

The "seriousness" factor requires that the threat be such that the intended victim is in danger of being killed or of suffering serious bodily harm. Many persons involved in criminal justice proceedings will have committed prior crimes or may be planning to commit crimes in the future. The disclosure of planned future crimes without an element of violence would be an insufficient reason to set aside solicitor-client privilege because of fears for public safety. For the public safety interest to be of sufficient importance to displace solicitor-client privilege, the threat must be to occasion serious bodily harm or death.

It should be observed that serious psychological harm may constitute serious bodily harm.

(c) Imminence

The risk of serious bodily harm or death must be imminent if solicitor-client communications are to be disclosed. That is, the risk itself must be serious: a serious risk of serious bodily harm. The nature of the threat must be such that it creates a sense of urgency. This sense of urgency may be applicable to some time in the future. Depending on the seriousness and clarity of the threat, it will not always be necessary to impose a particular time limit on the risk. It is sufficient if there is a clear and imminent threat of serious bodily harm to an identifiable group, and if this threat is made in such a manner that a sense of urgency is created. A statement made in a fleeting fit of anger will usually be insufficient to disturb the solicitor-client privilege. On the other hand, imminence as a factor may be satisfied if a person makes a clear threat to kill someone that he vows to carry out three years hence when he is released from prison. If that threat is made with such chilling intensity and graphic detail that a reasonable bystander would be convinced that the killing would be carried out the threat could be considered to be imminent. Imminence, like the other two criteria, must be defined in the context of each situation.

In summary, solicitor-client privilege should only be set aside in situations where the facts raise real concerns that an identifiable individual or group is in imminent danger of death or serious bodily harm. The facts must be carefully considered to determine whether the three factors of seriousness, clarity, and imminence indicate that the privilege cannot be maintained. Different weights will be given to each factor in any particular case. If after considering all appropriate factors it is determined that the threat to public safety outweighs the need to preserve solicitor-client privilege, then the privilege must be set aside. When it is, the disclosure should be limited so that it includes only the information necessary to protect public safety.

The disclosure of the privileged communication should generally be limited as much as possible. The judge setting aside the solicitor-client privilege should strive to strictly limit disclosure to those aspects of the report or document which indicate that there is an imminent risk of serious bodily harm or death to an identifiable person or group. In undertaking this task consideration should be given to those portions of the report which refer to the risk of serious harm to an identifiable group; that the risk is serious in that it involves a danger of death or serious bodily harm; and that the serious risk is imminent in the sense given to that word above. The requirement that the disclosure be limited must be emphasized. For example, if a report contained references to criminal behaviour that did not have an imminent risk of serious bodily harm but disclosed, for example, the commission of crimes of fraud, counterfeiting or the sale of stolen goods, those references would necessarily be deleted.

[In applying the criteria set out the majority found sufficient clarity, seriousness and imminence to satisfy the Public Safety Exception to Solicitor-Client Privilege.]

. . . .

Dr. Smith chose to bring a legal action for a declaration that he was entitled to disclose the information he had in his possession in the interests of public safety. However, this is not the only manner in which experts may proceed. Although it is true that this procedure may protect the expert from legal consequences, there may not always be time for such an action. In whatever action is taken by the expert, care should be exercised that only that information which is necessary to alleviate the threat to public safety is revealed.

It is not appropriate in these reasons to consider the precise steps an expert might take to prevent the harm to the public. It is sufficient to observe that it might be appropriate to notify the potential victim or the police or a Crown prosecutor, depending on the specific circumstances.

. . . .

The order of the British Columbia Court of Appeal is affirmed. . . . Dr. Smith seeks to recover his costs. He should not have them. This case raised the issue of when solicitor-client privilege can be set aside. It has been found that, because of the danger posed by Mr. Jones to the public, solicitor-client privilege, which Mr. Jones had every right to believe attached to Dr. Smith's report, was set aside. This case arises in the context of criminal proceedings and the result may well affect the sentence imposed on Mr. Jones. It would be unfair and unjust in the circumstances to impose the burden of costs on Mr. Jones and I would not do so.

MAJOR J. (LAMER, C.J. and BINNIE J. concurring) (dissenting):—

. . . .

In my opinion a limited exception which does not include conscriptive evidence against the accused would address the immediate concern for public safety in this appeal while respecting the importance of the privilege. I do not read Cory J.'s reasons as imposing that limitation. This approach will in my view foster a climate in which dangerous individuals are more likely to disclose their disorders, seek treatment and pose less danger to the public.

. . . .

I agree with Cory J. that the standard of a "clear, serious and imminent" danger is the appropriate test for disclosure of privileged communications. There are compelling public policy reasons for limiting disclosure to cases of clear and imminent danger. The record confirms that Mr. Jones only disclosed his secret plans because his lawyer had properly advised him that anything he said to Dr. Smith would be confidential. If Cory J. is correct in holding that, in cases where the necessity test is met, the privilege is overridden to the extent of allowing disclosure of self-incriminating evidence, the result might endanger the public more than the public safety exception would protect them.

If defence counsel cannot freely refer clients, particularly dangerous ones, to medical or other experts without running a serious risk of the privilege being set aside, their response will be not to refer clients until after trial, if at all. This could result in dangerous people remaining free on bail for long periods of time, undiagnosed and untreated, presenting a danger to society.

The chilling effect of completely breaching the privilege would have the undesired effect of discouraging those individuals in need of treatment for serious and dangerous conditions from consulting professional help. In this case the interests of the appellant and more importantly the interests of society would be better served by his obtaining treatment. This Court has recognized that mental health, including those suffering from potentially dangerous illnesses, is an important public good: see *M. (A.) v. Ryan*, [1997] 1 S.C.R. 157, at para. 27.

Although the appellant did not go to Dr. Smith to seek treatment, it is obvious that he is more likely to get treatment when his condition is diagnosed than someone who keeps the secret of their illness to themselves. It seems apparent that society will suffer by imposing a disincentive for patients and criminally accused persons to speak frankly with counsel and medical experts retained on their behalf.

As appealing as it may be to ensure that Mr. Jones does not slip back into the community without treatment for his condition, completely lifting the privilege and allowing his confidential communications to his legal advisor to be used against him in the most detrimental ways will not promote public safety, only silence. For this doubtful gain, the Court will have imposed a veil of secrecy between criminal accused and their counsel which the solicitor-client privilege was developed to prevent. Sanctioning a breach of privilege too hastily erodes the workings of the system of law in exchange for an illusory gain in public safety.

While I agree with Cory J. that the danger in this case is sufficiently clear, serious and imminent to justify some warning to the relevant authorities, I find that the balance between the public interests in safety and the proper administration of justice is best struck by a more limited disclosure than the broader abrogation of privilege he proposes. In particular, Cory J. endorses the trial judge's limitation of Dr. Smith's affidavit to those portions which indicate an imminent risk of serious harm or death. In the result, conscriptive evidence such as the accused's confession can be disclosed. In my opinion, the danger posed by the accused can be adequately addressed by the expression of that opinion by Dr. Smith without disclosing the confession.

. . . .

Courts are obligated to craft the narrowest possible exception to privilege which accomplishes this purpose. Accordingly, Dr. Smith should be permitted to warn the relevant authorities (i.e., the Attorney General and sentencing judge) that Mr. Jones poses a threat to prostitutes in the Vancouver area. However, Dr. Smith should only disclose his opinion and the fact that it is based on a consultation with Mr. Jones. Specifically, he should not disclose any communication from the accused relating to the circumstances of the offence, nor should he be permitted to reveal any of the personal information which the trial judge excluded from his original order for disclosure.

I agree with Cory J. that in rare cases where an individual poses an instant risk such that even an ex parte application to the court is not possible, the person reviewing the otherwise privileged information may issue a timely warning to the police. Otherwise, the scope and timing of disclosures should be dealt with by the courts on a case-by-case basis.

. . . .

I would allow the appeal without costs, confirm the entirety of Mr. Jones's communications to Dr. Smith to be privileged, but permit Dr. Smith to give his opinion and diagnosis of the danger posed by Mr. Jones.

Smith and Jones were aliases to keep matters confidential until the Supreme Court had ruled. Jones was in fact a man named Leopold and Dr. Smith was Dr. O'Shaughnessy, chairman of forensic psychiatry at the University of British Columbia. Leopold's sentence hearing proceeded after the Supreme Court's ruling. Dr. O'Shaughnessy now testified for the Crown. There had been plea negotiations for a reformatory sentence but now the Crown brought a dangerous offender application. The trial judge rejected that motion but imposed an 11 year sentence. On a further appeal the B.C. Court of Appeal held that Leopold should be declared to be a dangerous offender: *R. v. Leopold*.[296]

The future harm exception carved out by the Supreme Court is not limited to future crimes and includes serious psychological harm. **What is the significance of this broader approach to harm? Could a lawyer rely on *Smith v. Jones* to disclose that her client confessed to a crime for which another individual was convicted?**

Innocence at Stake Exception

R. v. McCLURE
[2001] 1 S.C.R. 445, 40 C.R. (5th) 1, 151 C.C.C. (3d) 321

The accused was a librarian and teacher at the school attended by J.C. in the mid-1970s. In 1997, the accused was charged with sexual offences against 11 former students. After reading about the accused's arrest, J.C. gave a statement to the police alleging incidents of sexual touching by the accused. His allegations were later added to the indictment. J.C. also brought a civil action against the accused. The accused sought production of J.C.'s civil litigation file to determine the nature of the allegations and to assess his motive to fabricate or exaggerate incidents of abuse. In his first ruling, the trial judge applied the *O'Connor* test and ordered the production of the appellant's civil litigation file for his review. In a second ruling, he granted the accused access to the file but ordered all references to quantum of settlement and fees deleted from the produced file. The trial judge ruled that certain matters of sequence were significant, and not available to the defence without access to J.C.'s file. The order granting access was stayed pending appeal. J.C., who was not a party in the criminal trial, was granted leave to appeal the order to the Supreme Court pursuant to section 40 of the Supreme Court Act.

---

296 (2001), 155 C.C.C. (3d) 251 (B.C. C.A.). For further discussion of *Smith v. Jones* and many of these issues see: D. Layton, "The Public Safety Exception: Confusing Confidentiality, Privilege and Ethics" (2001), 6 Can. Crim. L. Rev. 217; "R. v. Leopold: The Public Safety Exception and Defence Counsel as Confidential Informant" (2001), 43 C.R. (5th) 319 and A. Dodek, "The Public Safety Exception to Solicitor-Client Privilege: Smith v. Jones" (2000), 34 U.B.C.L. Rev. 292.

MAJOR J. (MCLACHLIN, C.J. and L'HEUREUX-DUBÉ, GONTHIER, IACOBUCCI, BASTARACHE, BINNIE, ARBOUR and LEBEL JJ. concurring):—

. . . .

There are two useful tests which help to identify when the right to make full answer
and defence will prevail over the need for confidentiality. While useful, neither test sufficiently addresses the unique concerns evoked by solicitor-client privilege and, as explained later, more is needed.

The first test originated in *O'Connor*, relative to procedures to govern production of medical or therapeutic records that are in the hands of third parties. Subsequently, Parliament codified the procedure in ss. 278.1 to 278.9 of the Criminal Code and its constitutionality was upheld in *R. v. Mills*, [1999] 3 S.C.R. 668. The *O'Connor* test and ss. 278.1 to 278.9 of the Criminal Code were created with the sensitivity and unique character of third party therapeutic records in mind. They focus on an individual's privacy interest and not the broader policy objectives underlying the administration of justice.

The other test is the innocence at stake test for informer privilege, see *Leipert*. This test details the circumstances under which the identity of an informer might have to be revealed. The value of reliable informers to the administration of justice has been recognized for a long time, so much so that it too is a class privilege. This explains why the high standard of showing that the innocence of the accused is at stake before permitting invasion of the privilege is necessary. Should the privilege be invaded, the state then generally provides for the protection of the informer through various safety programs, again illustrating the public importance of that privilege. The threshold created by the innocence at stake test comes the closest to addressing the concerns raised in this appeal as it is appropriately high. Both informer privilege and solicitor-client privilege are ancient and hallowed protections.

The Innocence at Stake Test for Solicitor-Client Privilege

In granting the respondent McClure access to the complainant's civil litigation file, the trial judge applied the *O'Connor* test for disclosure of confidential therapeutic records. With respect, this was an error. The appropriate test by which to determine whether to set aside solicitor-client privilege is the innocence at stake test, set out below. Solicitor-client privilege should be set aside only in the most unusual cases. Unless individuals can be certain that their communications with their solicitors will remain entirely confidential, their ability to speak freely will be undermined.

In recognition of the central place of solicitor-client privilege within the administration of justice, the innocence at stake test should be stringent. The privilege should be infringed only where core issues going to the guilt of the accused are involved and there is a genuine risk of a wrongful conviction.

Before the test is even considered, the accused must establish that the information he is seeking in the solicitor-client file is not available from any other source and he is otherwise unable to raise a reasonable doubt as to his guilt in any other way.

By way of illustration, if the accused could raise a reasonable doubt at his trial on the question of mens rea by access to the solicitor-client file but could also raise a reasonable doubt with the defence of alibi and/or identification, then it would be unnecessary to use the solicitor-client file. The innocence of the accused would not be at stake but instead it is his wish to mount a more complete defence that would be affected. On the surface it may appear harsh to deny access as the particular privileged evidence might raise a reasonable doubt, nonetheless, the policy reasons favouring the protection of the confidentiality of solicitor-client communications must prevail unless there is a genuine danger of wrongful conviction.

The innocence at stake test is applied in two stages in order to reflect the dual nature of the judge's inquiry. At the first stage, the accused seeking production of a solicitor-client communication must provide some evidentiary basis upon which to conclude that there exists a communication that could raise a reasonable doubt as to his guilt. At this stage, the judge has to decide whether she will review the evidence.

If the trial judge is satisfied that such an evidentiary basis exists, then she should proceed to stage two. At that stage, the trial judge must examine the solicitor-client file to determine whether, in fact, there is a communication that is likely to raise a reasonable doubt as to the guilt of the accused. It is evident that the test in the first stage (could raise a reasonable doubt) is different than that of the second stage (likely to raise a reasonable doubt). If the second stage of the test is met, then the trial judge should order the production but only of that portion of the solicitor-client file that is necessary to raise the defence claimed.

(1) Stage #1

The first stage of the innocence at stake test for invading the solicitor-client privilege requires production of the material to the trial judge for review. There has to be some evidentiary basis for the request. This is a threshold requirement designed to prevent "fishing expeditions". Without it, it would be too easy for the accused to demand examination of solicitor-client privileged communications by the trial judge. As this request constitutes a significant invasion of solicitor-client privilege, it should not be entered into lightly. On the other hand, the bar cannot be set so high that it can never be met. The trial judge must ask: "Is there some evidentiary basis for the claim that a solicitor-client communication exists that could raise a reasonable doubt about the guilt of the accused?"

It falls to the accused to demonstrate some evidentiary basis for his claim that there exists a solicitor-client communication relevant to the defence he raises. Mere speculation as to what a file might contain is insufficient.

That is then followed by a requirement that the communication sought by the accused could raise a reasonable doubt as to his guilt. This must be considered in light of what the accused knows. It is likely that the accused who, it must be remembered, has had no access to the file sought, may only provide a description of a possible communication. It would be difficult to produce and unfair to demand anything more precise. It is only at stage two that a court determines conclusively that such a communication actually exists.

The evidence sought should be considered in conjunction with other available evidence in order to determine its importance. It is the totality of the evidence that governs. However, when the accused is either challenging credibility or raising collateral matters, it will be difficult to meet the standards required of stage one.

Where an accused fails to show that the information sought could raise a reasonable doubt as to guilt, the solicitor-client privilege prevails.

(2) Stage #2

Once the first stage of the innocence at stake test for setting aside the solicitor-client privilege has been met, the trial judge must examine that record to determine whether, in fact, there exists a communication that is likely to raise a reasonable doubt as to the accused's guilt. The trial judge must ask herself the following question: "Is there something in the solicitor-client communication that is likely to raise a reasonable doubt about the accused's guilt?"

After a review of the evidence of the solicitor-client communication in question, the judge must decide whether the communication is likely to raise a reasonable doubt as to the guilt of the accused. In most cases, this means that, unless the solicitor-client communication goes directly to one of the elements of the offence, it will not be sufficient to meet this requirement. Simply providing evidence that advances ancillary attacks on the Crown's case (e.g., by impugning the credibility of a Crown witness, or by providing evidence that suggest that some Crown evidence was obtained unconstitutionally) will very seldom be sufficient to meet this requirement.

The trial judge does not have to conclude that the information definitely will raise a reasonable doubt. If this were the case, the trial would effectively be over as soon as the trial judge ordered the solicitor-client file to be produced. There would be nothing left to decide. Instead, the information must likely raise a reasonable doubt as to the accused's guilt. Also, upon reviewing the evidence, if the trial judge finds material that will likely raise a reasonable doubt, stage two of the test is satisfied and the information should be produced to the defence even if this information was not argued as a basis for production by the defence at stage one.

In determining whether or not the solicitor-client communication in question is likely to raise a reasonable doubt as to the guilt of the accused, the trial judge should consider that the communication in the solicitor-client file cannot be marginal but must be sufficient to establish the basis for its admission. It is the totality of the evidence then available that the trial judge considers in determining whether it is likely that the evidence can raise a reasonable doubt.

The difficulties described in successfully overcoming solicitor-client privilege illustrate the importance and solemnity attached to it. As described earlier, it is a cornerstone of our judicial system and any impediment to open candid and confidential discussion between lawyers and their clients will be rare and reluctantly imposed.

Application to the Case at Bar

In this case, the litigation file should not have been produced to the defence. With respect, the trial judge erred in using the earlier *O'Connor* test for the production of third party confidential therapeutic records to govern whether the litigation file should have been produced to the defence.

The first stage of the innocence at stake test for solicitor-client privilege was not met. There was no evidence that the information sought by the respondent McClure could raise a reasonable doubt as to his guilt. Even if the chronology of events in this case — i.e. lawyer, police, therapist, civil suit — was unusual, it does not justify overriding solicitor-client privilege. This "unusual" chronology does not rise to a level that demonstrates that the litigation file could raise a reasonable doubt as to guilt and so fails at the first stage.

In addition, the accused would be able to raise the issue of the complainant's motive to fabricate events for the sake of a civil action at trial from another source, simply by pointing out the sequence of events and the fact that a civil action was initiated.

The third party appellant, J.C., could not appeal the interlocutory order for production of his litigation file because he was not a party in the criminal trial. Instead, he applied directly to this Court pursuant to s. 40(1) of the Supreme Court Act for leave to appeal the final order ordering production of his litigation file. This avenue of appeal is unsatisfactory. The usual avenue for appeal should be to the court of appeal of the province. That court has broad powers of review and is the desirable forum for appeals of first instance. This appeal is not the first demonstration of the anomaly of a direct appeal of an interlocutory order to the Supreme Court of Canada. The only apparent method of resolving this problem is by legislative amendment.

The appeal is allowed and the order for production by Hawkins J. is set aside.[297]

One important refinement of *McClure* by the Supreme Court in *Brown* was the granting of use and derivative use immunity to the privilege holder. As Justice Major held:

> The invasion of solicitor-client privilege exposes the privilege holder to potential future liability, particularly in cases, such as the present one, that may involve a confession to a serious crime. . . .
>
> As described, solicitor-client privilege is a fundamental tenet of our legal system. Clients must be comfortable in making free and candid disclosure to their solicitors without fear that their communications will be later used against them. This principle should in no way be diminished by the limited disclosure allowed in *McClure*. The

---

297 For comments on *McClure* see Manson, "Annotation: *R. v. McClure*" (2001), 40 C.R. (5th) 1 and Layton, "*R. v. McClure*: The Privilege on the Pea" (2001), 40 C.R. (5th) 19. The Supreme Court considered further procedural issues on *McLure* applications in *R. v. Brown* (2002), 50 C.R. (5th) 1 (S.C.C.). See comment by David Layton, "*R. v. Brown*: Protecting Legal-Professional Privilege" (2002), 50 C.R. (5th) 37.

test established in that case provides for disclosure in the exceptional circumstance that it is necessary to prevent a wrongful conviction. . . . It should not be used to incriminate the privilege holder, who would have been protected but for the operation of *McClure*. . . .

This means that the privilege holder's communications and any evidence derived therefrom cannot be used in a subsequent case against the privilege holder. . . . Use and derivative use immunity should prohibit the Crown both from using the communications as direct evidence against the privilege holder and from using the communications to impeach the privilege holder if and when he is himself an accused.

In the next two cases which deal with the future crime/fraud and common interest exceptions, we will see the Supreme Court recognizing solicitor-client privilege in the context of Crown/police relationships and those between in-house counsel and their clients, including government agencies.

Future Crime/Fraud Exception

R. v. SHIROSE AND CAMPBELL
1999 CarswellOnt 949, [1999] 1 S.C.R. 565, 24 C.R. (5th) 365,
133 C.C.C. (3d) 257, 1999 CarswellOnt 948

As part of an undercover drug operation in Quebec, a number of police officers posing as large-scale hashish vendors contacted two potential groups of purchasers. Negotiations included showing the hashish to them. The operation was discussed with a Department of Justice lawyer and approved by two senior RCMP officers. Following their conviction, the accused brought a stay application alleging that the reverse-sting used by the police was unlawful and an abuse of process. The position of the RCMP was that they were acting in good faith based on the advice they had received. In support of their application, the accused sought to subpoena the Justice lawyer in relation to the communications with the police as to the legality of the reverse sting. The trial judge quashed the subpoena on the grounds that the communications were protected by solicitor-client privilege. The Court of Appeal dismissed the accused's appeal. On further appeal, the Supreme Court ordered a new trial and held that the legal advice should have been disclosed.

BINNIE J., speaking for the Court, held: —

. . . .

Existence of a Solicitor-Client Relationship between the RCMP Officers and Lawyers in the Department of Justice

The solicitor-client privilege is based on the functional needs of the administration of justice. The legal system, complicated as it is, calls for professional expertise. Access to justice is compromised where legal advice is unavailable. It is of great importance, therefore, that the RCMP be able to obtain professional legal advice in connection with criminal investigations without the chilling effect of potential disclosure of their confidences in subsequent proceedings. As Lamer C.J. stated in *R. v. Gruenke*, [1991] 3 S.C.R. 263, at p. 289:

> The prima facie protection for solicitor-client communications is based on the fact that the relationship and the communications between solicitor and client are essential to the effective operation of the legal system. Such communications are inextricably linked with the very system which desires the disclosure of the communication. . . .

See also *Smith v. Jones*, [1999] 1 S.C.R. 455, per Cory J., at para. 46, and per Major J., at para. 5. This Court had previously, in *Descôteaux v. Mierzwinski*, [1982] 1 S.C.R. 860, at p. 872, adopted Wigmore's formulation of the substantive conditions precedent to the existence of the right of the lawyer's client to confidentiality (Wigmore on Evidence, vol. 8 (McNaughton rev. 1961), sec. 2292, at p. 554):

> Where legal advice of any kind is sought from a professional legal adviser in his capacity as such, the communications relating to that purpose, made in confidence by the client, are at his instance permanently protected from disclosure by himself or by the legal adviser, except the protection be waived. [Emphasis and numerotation deleted.]

Cpl. Reynolds' consultation with Mr. Leising of the Department of Justice falls squarely within this functional definition, and the fact that Mr. Leising works for an "in-house" government legal service does not affect the creation or character of the privilege.

It is, of course, not everything done by a government (or other) lawyer that attracts solicitor-client privilege. While some of what government lawyers do is indistinguishable from the work of private practitioners, they may and frequently do have multiple responsibilities including, for example, participation in various operating committees of their respective departments. Government lawyers who have spent years with a particular client department may be called upon to offer policy advice that has nothing to do with their legal training or expertise, but draws on departmental know-how. Advice given by lawyers on matters outside the solicitor-client relationship is not protected. A comparable range of functions is exhibited by salaried corporate counsel employed by business organizations. Solicitor-client communications by corporate employees with in-house counsel enjoy the privilege, although (as in government) the corporate context creates special problems: see, for example, the in-house inquiry into "questionable payments" to foreign governments at issue in *Upjohn Co. v. United States*, 449 U.S. 383 (1981), per Rehnquist J. (as he then was), at pp. 394-95. In private practice some lawyers are valued as much (or more) for raw business sense as for legal acumen. No solicitor-client privilege attaches to advice on purely business matters even where it is provided by a lawyer. As Lord Hanworth, M.R., stated in *Minter v. Priest*, [1929] 1 K.B. 655 (C.A.), at pp. 668-69:

> [I]t is not sufficient for the witness to say, "I went to a solicitor's office." . . . Questions are admissible to reveal and determine for what purpose and under what circumstances the intending client went to the office.

Whether or not solicitor-client privilege attaches in any of these situations depends on the nature of the relationship, the subject matter of the advice and the circumstances in which it is sought and rendered. One thing is clear: the fact that

Mr. Leising is a salaried employee did not prevent the formation of a solicitor-client relationship and the attendant duties, responsibilities and privileges. . . .

Subject to what is said below, when Mr. Leising of the Department of Justice initially advised Cpl. Reynolds about the legality of a reverse sting operation, these communications were protected by solicitor-client privilege.

The "Future Crimes and Fraud" Exception

It is well established, as the appellants argue, that there is an exception to the principle of confidentiality of solicitor-client communications where those communications are criminal or else made with a view to obtaining legal advice to facilitate the commission of a crime. . . .

In this case, however, I think the RCMP did waive the privilege, as discussed below. The relevant solicitor-client communications that came within the scope of the waiver ought therefore to be turned over directly to the appellants without the need in the first instance of a two-stage procedure involving the trial judge.

. . . .

Waiver of Solicitor-Client Privilege

The record is clear that the RCMP put in issue Cpl. Reynolds' good faith belief in the legality of the reverse sting, and asserted its reliance upon his consultations with the Department of Justice to buttress that position. The RCMP factum in the Ontario Court of Appeal has already been quoted in para. 46. In my view, the RCMP waived the right to shelter behind solicitor-client privilege the contents of the advice thus exposed and relied upon. . . .

The scope of Crown-police privilege and in particular whether entrapment falls within the "innocence at stake" *McClure* exception to this privilege has been considered in a number of recent cases.[298]

Claims of Crown privilege including those of work product have succeeded in the face of disclosure requests in recent gangsterism trials.[299]

The Common Interest Exception

PRITCHARD v. ONTARIO (HUMAN RIGHTS COMMISSION)
2004 CarswellOnt 1885, 2004 CarswellOnt 1886, 19 C.R. (6th) 203, [2004]
1 S.C.R. 809

The appellant filed a human rights complaint against her employer, Sears Canada, alleging gender discrimination, sexual harassment and reprisal. The

---

298 See *R. v. Schacher* (2003), 179 C.C.C. (3d) 561 (Alta. C.A.) and *R. v. Castro* (2001), 157 C.C.C. (3d) 255 (B.C. C.A.); *R. v. Trang* (2002), 168 C.C.C. (3d) 145 (Alta. Q.B.) and *R. v. Chan* (2002), 168 C.C.C. (3d) 396 (Alta. Q.B.).
299 See Ian Carter, "Chipping Away at Stinchcombe: the Expanding Privilege Exception to Disclosure", (2002), 50 C.R. (5th) 332.

Ontario Human Rights Commission decided not to proceed with her complaint. She sought judicial review and brought a motion for production of all documents. One of those documents was a legal opinion provided to the Commission by in-house counsel.

MAJOR J. (for the Court):

. . .

Solicitor-client privilege has been held to arise when in-house government lawyers provide legal advice to their client, a government agency: see *R. v. Campbell*, [1999] 1 S.C.R. 565, at para. 49. In *Campbell*, the appellant police officers sought access to the legal advice provided to the RCMP by the Department of Justice and on which the RCMP claimed to have placed good faith reliance. In identifying solicitor-client privilege as it applies to government lawyers, Binnie J. compared the function of public lawyers in government agencies with corporate in-house counsel. He explained that where government lawyers give legal advice to a "client department" that traditionally would engage solicitor-client privilege, and the privilege would apply. However, like corporate lawyers who also may give advice in an executive or non-legal capacity, where government lawyers give policy advice outside the realm of their legal responsibilities, such advice is not protected by the privilege.

Owing to the nature of the work of in-house counsel, often having both legal and non-legal responsibilities, each situation must be assessed on a case-by-case basis to determine if the circumstances were such that the privilege arose. Whether or not the privilege will attach depends on the nature of the relationship, the subject matter of the advice, and the circumstances in which it is sought and rendered: *Campbell*, *supra*, at para. 50.

Where solicitor-client privilege is found, it applies to a broad range of communications between lawyer and client as outlined above. It will apply with equal force in the context of advice given to an administrative board by in-house counsel as it does to advice given in the realm of private law. If an in-house lawyer is conveying advice that would be characterized as privileged, the fact that he or she is "in-house" does not remove the privilege, or change its nature.

B. *The Common Interest Exception*

The appellant submitted that solicitor-client privilege does not attach to communications between a solicitor and client as against persons having a "joint interest" with the client in the subject-matter of the communication. This "common interest", or "joint interest" exception does not apply to the Commission because it does not share an interest with the parties before it. The Commission is a disinterested gatekeeper for human rights complaints and, by definition, does not have a stake in the outcome of any claim.

The common interest exception to solicitor-client privilege arose in the context of two parties jointly consulting one solicitor. See *R. v. Dunbar and Logan* (1982), 138 D.L.R. (3d) 221, *per* Martin J.A. at p. 245:

The authorities are clear that where two or more persons, each having an interest in some matter, jointly consult a solicitor, their confidential communications with the solicitor, although known to each other, are privileged against the outside world. However, as between themselves, each party is expected to share in and be privy to all communications passing between each of them and their solicitor. Consequently, should any controversy or dispute arise between them, the privilege is inapplicable, and either party may demand disclosure of the communication. . . .

The common interest exception originated in the context of parties sharing a common goal or seeking a common outcome, a "selfsame interest" as Lord Denning, M.R., described it in *Buttes Gas & Oil Co. v. Hammer (No. 3)*, [1980] 3 All E.R. 475 (C.A.), at p. 483. It has since been narrowly expanded to cover those situations in which a fiduciary or like duty has been found to exist between the parties so as to create common interest. These include trustee-beneficiary relations, fiduciary aspects of Crown-aboriginal relations and certain types of contractual or agency relations, none of which are at issue here.

The Commission neither has a trust relationship with, nor owes a fiduciary duty to, the parties appearing before it. The Commission is a statutory decision-maker. The cases relied on by the appellant related to trusts, fiduciary duty, and contractual obligations. These cases are readily distinguishable and do not support the position advanced by the appellant. The common interest exception does not apply to an administrative board with respect to the parties before it.

The appellant relied heavily on the decision of the New Brunswick Court of Appeal in *Melanson v. New Brunswick (Workers' Compensation Board)* (1994), 146 N.B.R. (2d) 294. In that case, the court ordered a new hearing based on a failure by the Workers' Compensation Board to observe procedural fairness in the processing of the appellant's claim. The court held that several significant errors were made at the review committee level, negating the review committee's duty to act fairly. Among these errors were the failure to provide the appellant with its first decision, the decision to turn the appellant's claim into a test case without her knowledge and partly at her expense, and the introduction of new evidence not disclosed to the appellant. For these reasons the court, in its *ratio*, concluded that "the taint at the intermediate level of the Review Committee has irrevocably blemished the proceedings" (para. 31). Other comments made by the Court of Appeal, pertaining to the production of legal opinions, were *obiter dicta*. The proper approach to legal opinions is to determine if they are of such a kind as would fall into the privileged class. If so, they are privileged. To the extent that *Melanson* is otherwise relied on is error.

C. *Application to the Case At Bar*

As stated, the communication between the Commission and its in-house counsel was protected by solicitor-client privilege.

The opinion provided to the Commission by staff counsel was a *legal opinion*. It was provided to the Commission by in-house or "staff" counsel to be considered or not considered at their discretion. It is a communication that falls within the class of communications protected by solicitor-client privilege. The fact that it was provided by in-house counsel does not alter the nature of the communication or the privilege.

There is no applicable exception that can remove the communication from the privileged class. There is no common interest between this Commission and the parties before it that could justify disclosure; nor is this Court prepared to create a new common law exception on these facts.

(c) Marital Communications

The English Evidence Amendment Act of 1853[300] made spouses of parties competent and compellable witnesses in civil proceedings; as discussed earlier, spouses had been incompetent at common law because of their supposed interest in the outcome of the litigation. The Act then went on to provide:

> Section 3. No husband shall be compellable to disclose any communication made to him by his wife during the marriage, and no wife shall be compellable to disclose any communication made to her by her husband during the marriage.

All Canadian jurisdictions have enacted identical or quite similar provisions. For example section 4(3) of the *Canada Evidence Act* reads:

> No husband is compellable to disclose any communication made to him by his wife during their marriage, and no wife is compellable to disclose any communication made by her husband during their marriage.

Notice, at the outset, that the privilege provided, unlike the case of solicitor-client communications, belongs to the recipient of the communication rather than to the communicant; "it is a mystery to me why it was decided to give this privilege to the spouse who is a witness."[301]

There is some dispute as to whether such a privilege ever existed at common law. Professor Wigmore maintains the privilege did exist but was seldom recognized since spouses of parties were incompetent as witnesses and it would be an exceptional case when such a communication would be otherwise admissible in proceedings to which neither was a party.[302] The courts, however, could find no authority for an earlier common law privilege and concluded that any protection from disclosure had to be found within the particular words of the statute.[303]

Notice that the legislation protects "*any* communication." Professor Wigmore suggests that this phrase should be construed in the spirit of the "correct principle" and the protection should be limited to *confidential* communications. He writes:

> The essence of the privilege is to protect *confidences* only. This is required by the very nature of this class of privileges. The purpose is to insure subjectively the

---

300 Commonly referred to as *Lord Brougham's Act.*

301 Echoing the words of Lord Reid in *Rumping v. D.P.P.* (1962), 46 Cr. App. R. 398, 409 (H.L.).

302 8 Wigmore, *Evidence* (McNaughton Rev.), s. 2333.

303 See *Rumping v. D.P.P., supra,* note 301; and *Shenton v. Tyler,* [1939] 1 Ch. 620 (C.A.) per Greene, M.R.

unrestrained privacy of communication, free from any fear of compulsory disclosure. It follows that if the communication is not intended to be a private one the privilege has no application to it.

. . . .

No justification for such an extension of the privilege has ever been attempted, and it must be supposed that this broad statutory phrasing originated in inadvertence. It is proper enough to maintain (as already noticed) that all marital communications should be presumed to be confidential until the contrary appears; but if the contrary appears, there is no reason for recognizing the privilege.[304]

The Canadian courts, however, have not seen fit to construe the language narrowly[305] and it is apparently available to *all* communications.

The legislation provides that "no husband" and "no wife" shall be compellable to disclose and if the privilege is solely based in statute, and that statute is literally construed, a widow or divorced spouse cannot claim the privilege. Greene, M.R. in *Shenton v. Tyler*[306] noted:

If my view is right that the only rule that exists is that contained in s. 3 of the Act of 1853, it remains to consider whether, under that section, upon its true construction, the privilege continues to exist after the marriage has come to an end. In my opinion it does not. The section in terms relates only to husbands and wives; and no principle of construction known to me entitles me to read into the section a reference to widowers or widows or divorced persons.[307]

It is noteworthy as well that the legislation does not forbid disclosure by the spouse testifying, that spouse is free to choose, nor does it forbid disclosure by third parties who intercept or overhear the communication. In *Rumping v. Director of Public Prosecutions*[308] the appellant had been convicted of murder. At his trial the prosecution had introduced a letter written by the accused to his wife which letter amounted to a confession. The appellant had given the letter to a fellow employee to post but instead it was turned over to the police. The appellant argued that aside from the statute there was a common law rule which forbade disclosure, but the absence of judicial authorities and the wording of the section convinced the House of Lords that the letter was properly receivable. In *R. v. Kotapski*[309] the accused, charged with armed robbery, had prepared for his lawyer a document giving an account of his movements and activities on the day of the robbery. Kotapski, having decided to retain different counsel, instructed his former lawyer to send a copy of the document to Mrs. Kotapski. During the execution of a search warrant of accused's residence the document was seized and at trial was tendered as evidence. Greenberg, J., relying on *Rumping v. Director of Public Prosecutions*, ruled the document was receivable in that

---

304 8 Wigmore, *Evidence* (McNaughton Rev.), s. 2336.

305 See, *e.g., MacDonald v. Bublitz* (1960), 31 W.W.R. 478 (B.C. S.C.).

306 *Supra*, note 301.

307 *Ibid.*, at p. 641. See also to like effect *R. v. Kanester*, [1966] 4 C.C.C. 231 (B.C. C.A.) per MacLean, J.A.; approved [1967] 1 C.C.C. 97n (S.C.C.); and *Layden v. North American Life Assur. Co.* (1970), 74 W.W.R. 266 (Alta. S.C.). Compare *R. v. Cooper (No. 1)* (1974), 19 C.C.C. (2d) 135 (Ont. H.C.) re incompetence surviving divorce, distinguishing *Shenton v. Tyler, supra*, note 303.

308 [1962] 3 All E.R. 256 (H.L.).

309 (1981), 66 C.C.C. (2d) 78, 81 (Que. S.C.)

even if [it] had been transformed into a matrimonial communication when it was sent by the accused's first attorney to Mrs. Kotapski, I have no choice but to admit it into evidence now that it is in the possession of the police, since the so-called privilege of s. 4(3) of the *Canada Evidence Act* avails only in favour of the recipient spouse, if he or she testifies.[310]

This attitude toward receivability of privileged communications through third parties is, of course, consistent with the treatment of solicitor-client communications, and may be justified by Professor Wigmore's analysis that it is up to the party to take the necessary precautions against being overheard.

With the advance in electronic eavesdropping techniques, is Wigmore's analysis sufficient?

In *Lloyd v. R.*[311] the accused, husband and wife, were convicted of conspiracy to traffic in narcotics. Telephone conversations between the spouses were intercepted by the police pursuant to an authorization granted under the Criminal Code, section 178.12,[312] and were received in evidence. The appellants argued that by the conjoint effect of section 178.16(5)[313] of the Criminal Code and section 4(3) of the *Canada Evidence Act*,[314] the intercepts were inadmissible. Those provisions read:

> 178.16(5) Any information obtained by an interception that, but for the interception would have been privileged, remains privileged and inadmissible as evidence without the consent of the person enjoying the privilege.

> 4.(3)   No husband is compellable to disclose any communication made to him by his wife during their marriage, and no wife is compellable to disclose any communication made to her by her husband during their marriage.

The majority in the British Columbia Court of Appeal ruled that while there was a privilege in a spouse to divulge or to refuse to divulge the information conveyed, that did not make the information privileged. Hinkson, J.A. wrote:

> In my view, it is not possible to equate the privilege attaching to a communication between solicitor and client with the privilege attaching to the spouse who is the recipient of a matrimonial communication. In the former case it is the information passing from client to solicitor, or *vice versa*, that is privileged. In the latter case the information conveyed is not privileged; the recipient spouse has a right to divulge or refuse to divulge the information conveyed. This right to choose what course to follow may be called a privilege but that does not make the information privileged in respect of which the right to choose is exercised. In short, it is a privilege attaching to a witness, not to the information. That distinction, it seems to me, is pointed up by the specific wording of s-s. (5).[315]

The majority in the Supreme Court of Canada held that this was too narrow a view and reaffirmed its earlier concurrence with the views of Moir J.A. in *R. v. Jean*:[316]

---

310 *Ibid.*, at p. 90. See also *R. v. Armstrong* (1970), 1 C.C.C. (2d) 106 (N.S.C.A.).

311 (1982), 64 C.C.C. (2d) 169 (S.C.C.).

312 See now R.S.C. 1985, c. C-46, s. 185.

313 *Ibid.*, s. 189(6).

314 R.S.C. 1970, c. E-10 [now R.S.C. 1985, c. C-5].

315 (1980), 53 C.C.C. (2d) 121, 130.

316 (1979), 46 C.C.C. (2d) 176 (Alta. C.A.); affirmed (1980), 51 C.C.C. (2d) 192n (S.C.C.).

So far as I am aware the only conversations to which s-s. (5) could apply are between solicitor and client and husband and wife. The subsection speaks of information that would have been privileged but for the interception. It seems to me that there was no information that was ever privileged *per se* because if the solicitor and client or husband and wife were overheard there was no privilege. What really occurred was a witness was able to decide whether or not the contents of certain communications were to be revealed. In a solicitor-and-client relationship the client could determine whether or not he would permit the conversation between himself and his lawyer to be revealed. The recipient of the conversation between spouses could decide if they would reveal the communication. In both cases if the party who had the right chose to exercise it the communication could be said to be privileged.

In my opinion, we must make the same sort of deductions to make sense of s-s. (5) of s. 178.16 of the *Code.* Parliament must be taken to have legislated sensibly and thus we must give s-s. (5) a sensible meaning. To do so it must be taken to mean that the so-called "privileged information" is that information that a person has a right not to reveal. Then, if it is intercepted by a wiretap or by other means dealt with in Part IV.1 of the *Criminal Code*, it is inadmissible by reason of s-s. (5) of s. 178.16. This follows from the philosophy of the "Invasion of Privacy" legislation which proceeds on the basis that these two types of information are private and if they are disclosed by a lawful intercept the information cannot be revealed in Court.

Here the wife had a right not to reveal what was said to her by her spouse during marriage. The conversation was overheard on a lawful interception. What was heard cannot be revealed where the wife does not choose to reveal it.[317]

In ruling on admissibility, should the courts distinguish spousal communications which discuss previous illegal acts and those which are plans for future illegal acts? If solicitor-client communications in furtherance of a criminal aim are not protected from disclosure, should marital communications be saved?[318]

In *R. v. St. Jean*[319] the accused was charged with incest and, pursuant to section 4(2) of the *Canada Evidence Act*, the wife was therefore "a competent and compellable witness for the prosecution without the consent of the person charged." An issue on appeal was whether the spouse could refuse to disclose communications made to her by her husband. For the Quebec Court of Appeal, Kaufman, J.A. ruled:

It seems to me that it would not make sense to make a spouse competent and compellable, only to put severe restrictions on the scope of his or her testimony. Take, for instance, the case of *R. v. Lonsdale*, where a husband was charged with the attempted murder of his wife. The Alberta Court of Appeal, in a clear and succinct opinion . . . held that in virtue of s. 4(4) of the Act the wife was a competent and compellable witness against the accused. No conversations between husband and wife appear to have taken place at the time of the incident, but supposing the husband, while pointing a gun at his wife, would have made certain remarks indicative of his intent to kill her, could it be seriously said that while the wife could describe her husband's actions she could not repeat his words? I think not.

---

317 *Ibid.*, at p. 187. For a recent application of *Lloyd*, see *R. v. Lam* (2005), 193 C.C.C. (3d) 567, 27 C.R. (6th) 373 (Alta. Q.B.).

318 Compare cases cited in 8 Wigmore, *Evidence* (McNaughton Rev.), s. 2338(7), 1982 supplement.

319 (1976), 32 C.C.C. (2d) 438 (Que. C.A.).

. . . .

> It might be said that to so hold would be to reduce the import of s. 4(3) of the Act. That may be so, but this section will still have its application in cases where a spouse is called by the defence, but even here it must be pointed out that the privilege is that of the witness and not the accused's.[320]

The Crown's appeal from accused's acquittal was accordingly allowed and a new trial was ordered. Prepare an argument on behalf of the accused for the Supreme Court of Canada.

R. v. ZYLSTRA
(1995), 41 C.R. (4th) 130, 99 C.C.C. (3d) 477 (Ont. C.A.)

Per CURIAM:—This appeal is from the appellant's conviction of sexual assault. The appellant did not testify. Defence counsel elected not to call the appellant's wife as a defence witness upon receiving a ruling from the trial judge relating to the manner in which she would be obliged to assert spousal privilege. The court received an outline of the testimony that the appellant's wife was prepared to give and it is obvious that it is highly relevant to the issues at trial.

. . . .

At the close of the Crown's case, counsel for the appellant asked the trial judge for an advance ruling as to whether this privilege could be asserted. He received a favourable ruling. The argument of the Crown on appeal notwithstanding, we are all of the view that the ruling was correct. The Crown relied upon the judgment of Kaufman J.A. of the Quebec Court of Appeal in *R. v. St. Jean* (1976), 32 C.C.C. (2d) 438. However, we prefer the reasoning of Moir J.A. of the Alberta Court of Appeal in *R. v. Jean* (1979), 7 C.R. (3d) 338, aff'd 51 C.C.C. (2d) 192 (S.C.C). . . . Section 4(3) is unambiguous and can be given its plain meaning without making it subject to any other subsection. It says simply that where a wife or husband is otherwise compellable or competent to give evidence, there is no compulsion to divulge communications with a spouse.

After receiving this favourable ruling, defence counsel asked for a ruling that the Crown not be permitted to ask questions of Mrs. Zylstra in cross-examination that would force her to assert the privilege in front of the jury. He submitted that the assertion of the privilege was not relevant to any issue in the trial, and that if the wife was obliged to rely upon it in the presence of the jury, the jury would invariably conclude that her husband had confessed to her his responsibility in the sexual assault. The trial judge refused to make such a ruling and stated that if the privilege was asserted, it must be before the jury.

Defence counsel then asked the trial judge to assure him that he would instruct the jury that the wife had a statutory right to invoke the privilege and that they were not to draw an inference adverse to her credibility from the fact that she exercised that right. The trial judge stated that he was not prepared to make

---

320 *Ibid.*, at pp. 441 and 444 [citations omitted].

any comment on this matter and stated that he was precluded from doing so by s. 4(6) of the Act.

. . . .

We do agree that if the privilege was asserted, it should be done in the presence of the jury. To proceed otherwise might have left the jury in some confusion by the failure of Crown counsel to pursue obvious lines of inquiry in cross-examination because they were not aware that the privilege had been asserted. We agree with the Crown on appeal that openness in the trial process is to be preferred. The Supreme Court of Canada has elected for this option when dealing with the problems of prior criminal convictions (*R. v. Corbett* (1988), 41 C.C.C. (3d) 385) and pre-trial publicity (*Dagenais v. Canadian Broadcasting Corp.* (1995), 94 C.C.C. (3d) 289). However, a special instruction is called for. We do not think that s. 4(6) has any application to a spouse who has testified. The Crown appears to concede this. It suggests the following in its factum:

> The jury ought then to be instructed with respect to the following points:
>
> (*a*)   *The privilege in s. 4(3) is a statutory privilege which all legally married witnesses are entitled to assert in a trial; and*
>
> (*b*)   The privilege is one that belongs to the witness, not the accused person, and, as such, the decision whether to assert or waive the privilege lies with the witness, not the accused.

In our opinion, the above represents a minimum requirement for a proper jury instruction. Whether or not the jury should be instructed that they can draw an adverse inference from the assertion of the privilege, we leave to another day. The trial judge should have a discretion as to what instruction is appropriate and we are not prepared to lay down a hard and fast rule in a case where no testimony was given.

The error on the part of the trial judge in stating that he was not prepared to make any comment to the jury in the event Mrs. Zylstra invoked the protection of s. 4(3) of the Act caused defence counsel to withdraw her as a witness. Crown counsel conceded on appeal that if we were of the opinion that some instruction was required, he could not rely upon the proviso in s. 686(1)(*b*)(iii) of the *Criminal Code*, . . . as standing in the way of a new trial. Accordingly, the appeal is allowed, the conviction below is set aside and a new trial is ordered.

In contrast there is no class privilege for communications between parent and child: *R. v. E. (T.K.).*[321]

In Ontario, section 11 of the *Ontario Evidence Act* has been amended to ensure that all married spouses, including same-sex spouses, get the benefit of marital privilege. It now reads:

Communications made during marriage

> **11.** A person is not compellable to disclose any communication made to the person by his or her spouse during the marriage, 2005, c. 5, s. 25(5).

---

321 (2005), 194 C.C.C. (3d) 496, 28 C.R. (6th) 366 (N.B. C.A.).

(d) Privilege for Without Prejudice Communications

MIDDELKAMP v. FRASER VALLEY REAL ESTATE BOARD
(1992), 71 B.C.L.R. (2d) 276 (B.C.C.A.)

The plaintiffs complained to the Director of the Competition Act about the defendant real estate board's conduct. The Director referred the matter to the Attorney General of Canada who proceeded against the board by way of information. There were lengthy negotiations. In the result there was a consent prohibition order in Federal Court. During the negotiations the board and the federal authorities exchanged numerous documents. In the plaintiffs' civil action against the board, the defendant board claimed privilege with respect these documents on the ground that they were exchanged on a without prejudice basis. An order to produce the documents was made. The defendant successfully appealed.

McEACHERN C.J.B.C. (PROUDFOOT, GIBBS AND HOLLINRAKE JJ.A. concurring):— Mr. Justice Locke has fully stated the facts of this case which I need not repeat. He bases his judgment upon an immunity equivalent to privilege arising out of the interest the public has in the settlement of disputes. While reaching the same conclusion I prefer, with respect, to base my judgment on slightly different grounds. . . .

I have no doubt that it is in the public interest, that parties to disputes should be free to negotiate *Competition Act* matters and other disputes freely, and without fear of later prejudice arising out of the steps taken during efforts to arrange settlements.

I am, however, hesitant to establish an immunity other than privilege because parties to negotiations, such as the appellant in this case, have no control over without prejudice communications once they are sent off to the other side, and documents of the kind in question in this case can easily find their way into the hands of strangers to the dispute being settled. There is no effective protection against the prejudice caused by such communications unless they are characterized as privileged.

. . . .

Considering the enormous scope of production which is required by our almost slavish adherence to the *Peruvian Guano* principle, the questionable relevance and value of documents prepared for the settlement of disputes, and the public interest, I find myself in agreement with the House of Lords that the public interest in the settlement of disputes generally requires "without prejudice" documents or communications created for, or communicated in the course of, settlement negotiations to be privileged. I would classify this as a " 'blanket', *prima facie*, common law, or 'class' " privilege because it arises from settlement negotiations and protects the class of communications exchanged in the course of that worthwhile endeavour.

In my judgment this privilege protects documents and communications created for such purposes both from production to other parties to the negotiations and to strangers, and extends as well to admissibility, and whether or not a settlement is reached. This is because, as I have said, a party communicating a proposal related to settlement, or responding to one, usually has no control over what the other side may do with such documents. Without such protection, the public interest in encouraging settlements will not be served.

. . . .

I would allow the appeal accordingly.

LOCKE J.A.:— This appeal deals with a litigant's obligation to produce certain documents for inspection prior to a civil trial when those documents were generated in negotiating the resolution of potential criminal charges against him.

. . . .

The trial judge examined the existing law at some length. He decided he was bound by previous authority in this court. He identified two competing issues: the promotion of negotiations leading to compromise, and the desirability of full discovery. He followed the case of *Derco Industries Ltd. v. A.R. Grimwood Ltd.* (1984), 57 B.C.L.R. 395, and ordered production.

. . . .

[There then follows a very thorough review of the jurisprudence in this area in other provinces and in England.]

This claim for protection from production of documents "without prejudice" is often considered to be one that the documents are "privileged" and the cases and writers on occasion classify it as a branch of this doctrine. This is no doubt satisfactory provided it is understood that the claim rests on a very different theoretical base than those other forms which arise because of the relationship between two parties which prohibits admission of their evidence at trial without the consent of the other: legal professional privilege, marital privilege, and concerning landlord and tenant as against disclosure of title deeds, by way of example. Those arise because society deems the relationships to be of such importance that it will not permit their sanctity to be undermined. The "privilege" with which we are concerned here deals not with a relationship but with competing legal interests, both of which are intrinsically meritorious. But as the doctrine we discuss is not a true "privilege" but really a rule of public policy, in my opinion papers leading up to a settlement, no matter how obtained, could not be produced in evidence at all.

Some of the difficulties of dealing with it as a "privilege" are dealt with in an article entitled " 'Without Prejudice' Communications — Their Admissibility and Effect" (1974), 9 U.B.C. Law Review 85, where the author D. Vaver has this to say at p. 107 of his dissertation:

> The undesirability of calling the "without prejudice" rule a "privilege" may also be pointed out in those cases where inadmissibility depends on irrelevancy and where the assertion of a privilege is an impossibility. Suppose that a motor accident arises involving A, B and C. A alleges that B is at fault and B alleges that C is at fault. C

compromises with B, but A sues B alone, claiming the accident was solely B's fault. B calls C to testify as to the fact of the offer of compromise. A is unable to object to the evidence on the grounds of privilege, for B and C alone can claim privilege. However, the evidence ought to be excluded on the grounds of irrelevancy, for a compromise *per se* is not evidence of an admission but merely implies a desire to buy peace. If the offer of compromise did contain an admission of liability by C and was thus admissible, "privilege" being waived by B and C, A could not prevent inclusion of the evidence. He could not claim privilege, since privilege is personal to the parties, and the evidence was clearly relevant. It may therefore be seen that there are good reasons for eschewing the use of the description "privilege" in the context of the "without prejudice" rule and for not considering the basis of the rule as one of "privilege".

. . . .

And so it is seen that the overwhelming current of authority is in favour of endorsing the protection from production with the aim of curtailing or shortening litigation. This has been the underlying object. I have laboriously canvassed all these cases to show that the principle has always been accepted from the earliest times. There has been much litigation, but it has all been to define the scope of the doctrine: Does it apply to arbitrations? Does it apply to opinion evidence? Does it apply to lawyers as well as clients? Does it apply when there has been a concluded settlement? And so on. Never has the principle, which is really one example of applying the principle of economy of means, been doubted.

In later times much intellectual powder has been expended in attempting to state the true theoretical basis for the doctrine. *Hoghton v. Hoghton* in 1852, *Underwood v. Cox* in 1912, one judge in *Schetky v. Cochrane* in 1918, *Scott Paper* in 1927, *Waxman* in 1968 and *Rush v. Tomkins* in 1988 have all placed it in the ground of public interest.

I agree with this. It has to my mind the immense advantage of enabling one to balance competing interests not on forms of words but on intrinsic strengths. One is enabled to apply principle to the kaleidoscope of circumstance.

The present case

. . . .

With all respect I cannot in law see one reason why this province, alone in the Commonwealth, should not recognize the overriding importance of this protection from the eyes of a third party. To refuse it is to inhibit and penalize one who wishes to settle. It is easy to envisage a building owner loath to compromise the minor claim of a small subcontractor, because of concern an admission of fact would be held against him in another major subcontractor's proceeding.

All the cases emphasize that no bars should be placed in the way of one who wishes to compromise, and to allow the production is by definition to inhibit. Such barriers to settlement should only be permitted if the other competing interest absolutely demands it.

. . . .

In my view, the guiding principle and one promising the greatest good for the greatest number of disputants is to shield these documents from production.[322]

In *British Columbia Children's Hospital v. Air Products Canada Ltd./Prodair Canada Ltée*,[323] a majority of the Court of Appeal took *Middelkamp* one step further and concluded that settlement privilege protected not only "without prejudice" communications made in furtherance of settlement but also the settlement agreements themselves. Justice Huddart dissented. In her view, a case by case determination of privilege should be applied.

R. v. PABANI
(1995), 89 C.C.C. (3d) 437

The accused was convicted of the second degree murder of his wife. The accused and his wife were married in late 1987. By June of 1988 she had moved out of the home because of marital discord and, it appeared, physical abuse by the accused. While the accused and his wife were separated, a mutual friend tried to assist them in reconciling their differences. Statements, in which the accused acknowledged having assaulted his wife previously, were admitted into evidence at trial. The accused argued that these statements should have been ruled inadmissible, on the basis that they were communications covered by the common law privilege pertaining to settlement talks in civil proceedings. The Court decided that the common law privilege was unavailable to the accused.

FINLAYSON J.A.:—

. . . .

In June of 1988, the wife moved out of the matrimonial home. Efforts were made, however, to mend the broken marriage. Through the mediation of a mutual friend, Muntaz Merali, the appellant and the deceased agreed to meet in the presence of their priest to discuss the future of their relationship. The priest was Nazim Ali Hirani who occupied the office of Moog, the most senior position of a priest in the Ismaili religion. . . .

Three meetings took place with the Moog and Mrs. Hirani at the Hirani home. Throughout, the wife placed four terms as pre-conditions to her return: first, the appellant would have to agree to cease the violence, on this she was adamant; second, the payment of the money owed by the appellant to his father-in-law would have to take place; third, the deceased's social insurance number would have to be returned to her; and fourth, the appellant's family would have to agree to stop speaking swahili in the wife's presence because this was a language she did not understand. The appellant agreed to all of these conditions. He implicitly conceded that there had been violence in the marriage, and although

---

322 See further *Gay (Guardian ad litem of) v. UNUM Life Insurance Co. of America*, [2003] N.S.J. No. 442, 2003 CarswellNS 419 (S.C. [In Chambers]).

323 (2001), [2003] B.C.J. No. 591, 2003 CarswellBC 614 (C.A.), leave to appeal allowed (2004), 2004 CarswellBC 121, 2004 CarswellBC 122 (S.C.C.).

it was not discussed in great length during the meetings with the Moog, the appellant pledged to discontinue this behaviour. The appellant had previously admitted to Merali that there had been violence in the relationship, but said that his wife had made too much of it.

The content of these meetings was allowed as evidence during the trial of the appellant.

. . . .

The law has always encouraged discussion between parties to civil litigation that is directed to settling their differences. To foster the resolution of these disputes, the parties are encouraged to speak freely and without the concern that statements will be used against them in the event that a settlement is not arrived at. . . . Additionally, in matrimonial disputes, the state is more interested in reconciliation than divorce and the rule as to privilege tends to promote the prospects of reconciliation. . . . There is, however, no such common law position recognized by the criminal law. The compromise of criminal charges has only recently been recognized within the structure of "plea bargaining". At common law, the settling for valuable consideration of felonies and the withdrawing or stifling of prosecutions for misdemeanours could amount to compounding those offences and become criminal offences themselves: see . . . the offence of compounding an indictable offence codified by s. 141. There does not, however, appear to have been any recognition by the criminal law of "without prejudice" statements outside of a plea bargaining structure. The law seems to be accurately summarized by Strong, *McCormick on Evidence*, 4th ed. (St. Paul: West Publishing, 1992), c. 25, para. 266, at p. 198:

> 266. *Compromise evidence in criminal cases.* The policy of protecting offers of compromise in civil cases does not extend to efforts to stifle criminal prosecution by "buying off" the prosecuting witness or victim. Indeed, such efforts are classed as an implied admission and generally admissible. The public policy against compounding crimes is said to prevail. On the other hand, the legitimacy of settling criminal cases by negotiations between prosecuting attorney and accused, whereby the latter pleads guilty in return for some leniency, has been generally recognized. Effective criminal law administration would be difficult if a large proportion of the charges were not disposed of by guilty pleas. Public policy accordingly encourages compromise, and as in civil cases, that policy is furthered by protecting from disclosure at trial not only the offer but also statements made during negotiations.

This policy would seem to have particular application in the case on appeal. It is true that so far as the matrimonial violence was concerned, any admissions by the appellant related to past misconduct which could amount to assault, but the appellant was not tried with respect to past misconduct, but rather was tried for the murder of his wife after an apparent reconciliation. I do not see on what basis he should be protected from utterances and conduct during the reconciliation process that are relevant to a subsequent criminal act of the magnitude of the one under appeal.

Accordingly, this ground of appeal must fail.

R. v. LAKE
[1997] O.J. No. 5447 (Ont. Gen. Div.)

The accused was charged with murder. R.C., a young person, was charged separately with the murder and was to be tried in Youth Court. R.C. was called by the Crown as a witness at the accused's trial. Although his testimony-in-chief supported some aspects of the Crown's case, in other more important respects, his testimony rebutted the Crown position. Among the applications made by the Crown was an application for a ruling that R.C.'s instructions to his lawyer were admissible at this trial.

McCOMBS J.:—

. . . .

In light of R.C.'s testimony the Crown seeks an order admitting for its truth, evidence as to what was said by R.C.'s lawyer to the Crown in the course of resolution discussions initiated by the defence. The Crown's motion is based on the argument that information allegedly conveyed to the Crown by R.C.'s counsel which was attributed to R.C. is not protected by privilege. Further, the Crown position is that the statements that the Crown alleges were attributed to R.C. by his lawyer at the resolution discussions meet the twin test of necessity and reliability, and are therefore admissible in evidence at this trial under the principled exception to the hearsay rule enunciated in *R. v. B. (K.G)*, supra, and related authorities.

Factual Background of the Motion

Crown counsel Mr. Loparco has advised me that Mr. Rotenberg, counsel for R.C., initiated resolution discussions with the Crown, and advised the Crown that if the charge of murder was withdrawn against R.C., he would be prepared to plead guilty to a charge of conspiracy to commit robbery on the following factual basis:

1. that R.C. had initially agreed to participate with Lake in the robbery of Tom Huston boots, then abandoned the agreement before the robbery.
2. that he went to the front door of the store while Lake was inside, and saw him "stabbing and stabbing" Louis Ambas.

Mr. Loparco further advises that the alleged offer to plead on that basis was rejected by the Crown.

. . . .

The position of the Crown is that if, in the course of resolution discussions, a lawyer attributes statements to his or her client, both the discussions and the statements are no longer protected by solicitor-client privilege. The Crown further asserts that although the law recognizes a further public interest privilege in protecting the confidentiality of resolution discussions, that privilege is not absolute, and must, in the circumstances of this case, give way to what is submitted to be a more important public interest: ensuring that criminal prosecutions are a search for the truth.

. . . .

There is a type of privilege recognized at common law. That privilege is related to the public interest in preserving plea negotiations as an essential component of the administration of justice. The privilege was recognized recently in *R. v. Bernardo* [May 10, 1994 (Ont. Ct. Gen. Div.), unreported], by LeSage, Assoc. C.J. (as he then was). He stated:

> I agree with the Crown's submissions that there should be a recognized privilege surrounding plea discussions vis-à-vis the accused and the Crown. There are many reasons in the nature of public policy that would suggest that such a privilege does exist or ought to exist in order to encourage Crown and defence to have full, frank, and private negotiations in criminal oases. I believe, as in civil cases, settlement negotiation privilege ought to exist. The rules of this court concerning pre-hearing conferences in criminal matters contemplate that those negotiations will normally occur in private and that they will remain confidential unless a resolution is achieved in which case the discussions would normally be disclosed in court. I am of the view that the public interest is well served by encouraging such frank and full discussions between counsel for the accused and counsel for the Crown. The saving to the public and the resulting benefit to the administration of justice in resolving cases that ought to be resolved is substantial.

. . . .

Recommendation 46 of the *Report of the Attorney General's Advisory Committee on Charge Screening, Disclosure, and Resolution Discussions* (1993) chaired by the Honourable G. Arthur Martin, also recognized the importance of resolution discussions as an essential component of the administration of justice. The recommendation provides:

> The Committee is of the opinion that resolution discussions are in essential part of the criminal justice system in Ontario, and, when properly conducted, benefit not only the accused, but also victims, witnesses, counsel, and the administration of justice.

The Martin Report recognizes that the integrity of the justice system requires that resolution discussions be encouraged. In my view that means that Counsel must be free to approach the Crown with a view to resolving cases, secure in the knowledge that nothing said in that context can be used to the detriment of their clients.

. . . .

In my view, a ruling favourable to the Crown in the circumstances of a case such as this would have a profound chilling effect upon resolution discussions, an essential component of the administration of justice, and would do irreparable damage to the public interest in the proper administration of justice. This public interest is of such importance that it must outweigh all other considerations. In the result, I conclude that the resolution discussions which took place in the circumstances of this case must remain privileged. The Crown's application must therefore be dismissed.

Can counsel ethically call his client at trial in circumstances where during the plea negotiations, counsel has advised the Crown that her client is prepared to plead guilty? In *R. v. Roberts*,[324] the accused was charged with first degree murder. Prior to trial, the Crown was prepared to accept a plea to second degree murder with the minimum period of parole ineligibility (i.e. ten years). The accused rejected the offer and he was convicted of second degree murder. At sentencing, the Crown sought a period of parole ineligibility of 20 years. The Court held resolution privilege prohibited counsel from introducing evidence of the Crown's original position on sentence.[325]

2. PUBLIC INTEREST IMMUNITY

(a) Statutory Provisions

Sections 37-39 of the *Canada Evidence Act* govern claims of public interest immunity. Section 37 applies where a "specified public interest" is asserted such as the identity of an informer privilege[326] or law enforcement investigative technique.[327] Section 38 applies where the immunity from production is sought to protect international relations, national defence or national security. Finally, s. 39 applies to confidences of the Privy Council or Cabinet.

Following the attacks of September 11, 2001, Canada moved quickly and passed its Anti-terrorism Act, S.C. 2001, c. 41 (Bill C-36) in December, 2001.[328] Bill C-36 amended sections 37 and 38 of the *Canada Evidence Act*. Generally speaking, Bill C-36 did not substantially alter the parameters of the balancing required to determine whether disclosure should be permitted. Under both sections 37(5) and 38.06(2), a judge is to determine whether the public interest in disclosure (usually the fair trial rights of the individual) outweighs the harm to a specified public interest or to international relations, national defence or security. However, there are some significant additions to the national defence and security section (i.e. section 38).[329] These include:

- an expansion of the kind of information that triggers scrutiny. Objections under the old section 38, for example, could only be made where it was alleged that disclosure *would* injure international relations or national defence or security. Under the new regime, objection can be made in relation to "potentially injurious information" which

---

324 (2001), [2001] A.J. No. 772, 2001 CarswellAlta 823 (Q.B.).
325 See also a discussion of this issue in *R. v. Larocque* (1998), 124 C.C.C. (3d) 564 (Ont. Gen. Div.); *R. v. Bernardo* (May 10, 1994), Doc. 247/94, [1994] O.J. No. 1718 (Gen. Div.) and *R. v. Steinhoff* (2003), 2003 CarswellOnt 6215, [2003] O.J. No. 3398 (C.J.).
326 See *R. v. Pilotte* (2002), 163 C.C.C. (3d) 225 (Ont. C.A.).
327 See *R. v. Richards* (1997), 115 C.C.C. (3d) 377 (Ont. C.A.).
328 Section 43 of Bill C-46 amends the *Canada Evidence Act*.
329 See J. Kalajdzic, "Litigating State Secrets: A Comparative Study of National Security Privilege in Canadian, U.S. and British Civil Cases" (2010), 41 *Ottawa L. Rev.* [forthcoming]; Cohen, *Privacy, Crime and Terror – Legal Rights and Security in a Time of Peril* (Toronto: Butterworths, 2005); and H. Stewart, "Public Interest Immunity After Bill C-36" (2003), 47 Crim. L.Q. 249 and P. Rosenthal, "Disclosure To The Defence After September 11: Sections 37 and 38 Of The Canada Evidence Act" (2003), 48 Crim. L.Q. 186.

is defined as *could* rather than would injure . . . and "sensitive information" defined as "information relating to international relations or national defence or national security that is in the possession of the Government of Canada, whether originating from inside or outside of Canada, and is of the type that the Government of Canada is taking measures to safeguard";[330]

- an obligation on both parties (including the defence)[331] to notify the federal Attorney General of the possibility that he or she or anyone else may disclose sensitive or potentially injurious information;[332]

- a power vested in the federal Attorney General to issue a certificate that prohibits disclosure of information in connection with a proceeding for the purpose of protecting information obtained in confidence from, or in relation to, a foreign entity or for the purpose of protecting national defence or national security.[333]

(i) *Section 38 – International Relations, National Defence or National Security*

CANADA (A.G.) v. RIBIC
(2003), 2003 CarswellNat 4708, 2003 CarswellNat 5043, 185 C.C.C. (3d) 129 (F.C.A.)

Nicholas Ribic is a Canadian citizen of Yugoslavian origin. During the civil war between Bosnian Serbs and Muslims, Ribic went to Bosnia and became involved in the Serbian war effort. On May 26, 1995, he and other individuals took three unarmed UN military observers, including a Canadian citizen, hostage at gunpoint and used them as human shields. The observers were shackled to Serbian ammunition bunkers that were the target of NATO air strikes. The hostages were detained for more than three weeks until their release was negotiated. Ribic was charged with hostage-taking under s. 279.1 of the *Criminal Code*. His trial took place in Canada following his extradition from Germany pursuant to s. 7(3.1) of the *Criminal Code*. Ribic's defences would include defence of property, self-defence and obedience to superior orders.

At his first trial, Ribic sought to call Witness A, a Canadian Intelligence officer for Bosnia-Herzegovina, and Witness B, an air-controller who was involved in directing NATO bombing targets. Both witnesses declared that their testimony might include "potentially injurious" or "sensitive" information concerning Canada's international relations, national defence or national security under s.

---

330 Section 38. In *O'Neill v. Canada (Attorney General)* (2006), 42 C.R. (6th) 63, 213 C.C.C. (3d) 389 (Ont. S.C.J.), Ratushny J. of the Ontario Superior Court struck down portions of the Security of Information Act concerning unauthorised release of secret information as vague, overbroad and not requiring fault. See "Annotation" by Steve Coughlan, C.R. *ibid.* The Federal Minister of Justice announced that an appeal of *O'Neill* was not in the public interest. For an application of s. 38.04 in the context of a terrorism trial, see *Canada (Attorney General) v. Khawaja* (2007) 52 C.R. (6th) 107 (F.C.A.). The Supreme Court decided that such a review of public interest immunity concerns was required by s. 7 of the Charter respecting an applicant captured by the United States forces, detained and charged with offences before military tribunals: *Khadr v. Canada (Minister of Justice,* (2008) 56 C.R. (6th) 255 (S.C.C.). See Benjamin Berger, "The Reach of Rights in the Security State: Reflections on *Khadr v. Canada (Minister of Justice)*", C.R. *ibid.* 268.

331 See *Canada (Attorney General) v. Ribic*, 185 C.C.C. (3d) 129, 2003 CarswellNat 4708 (C.A.).

332 Section 38.02.

333 Section 38.13.

38 of the *Canada Evidence Act*. Section 38 defines sensitive information as information relating to international relations, national defence or national security that is in the possession of the Government of Canada and that is of a type that the Government is taking measures to safeguard. As for potentially injurious information, it refers to information of a type that, if it were disclosed to the public, could injure international relations, national defence or national security.

The Attorney General of Canada received notice of these concerns from counsel pursuant to s. 38.01(1) of the *Canada Evidence Act*. The A.G. declined to authorize the disclosure of the witnesses' evidence. An application was brought in the Federal Court pursuant to s. 38.04 for an order for disclosure. In an effort to establish the relevancy and sensitivity of the evidence, an unusual (at least at that time unusual) procedure was adopted. The witnesses were examined under oath *in camera* by counsel designated by the federal government. Neither Ribic or his counsel, who did not have security clearance, were present. Counsel did, however, provide a list of questions to be asked. The questioning produced 550 pages of transcript. The A.G. subsequently agreed to disclose most of the evidence but refused to disclose other evidence.

In the Federal Court, Justice Blanchard prohibited the witnesses from testifying but authorized the introduction of the non-contested portions of the witnesses' transcript. He also ordered disclosure of certain contents of a videotape of some of the 1995 NATO bombing missions in Pale. However, he denied other parts of the videotape and prohibited Witness A from testifying about the videotape.[334]

Ribic appealed Justice Blanchard's order to the Federal Court of Appeal. He argued that his right to make full answer and defence demanded that the witnesses be permitted to testify without any vetting of their evidence.

LETOURNEAU J.A. (for the Court):

. . .

The role of the Trial Division on an application under section 38.04 of the *Act* for an order regarding disclosure of information

13 I should begin by saying that the appellant has not challenged the constitutional validity of the new legislation. Therefore, I am bound to take and apply the law as it stands. The Federal Court would be remiss of its duties under the *Act* if it were to endorse the appellant's philosophy of general disclosure based on mere relevancy, a philosophy which can only lead to and incite fishing expeditions. The Federal Court - Trial Division has been tasked with the difficult duty of balancing the competing public interests which, in this case, involve the protection of sensitive information and the protection of an accused's constitutional rights to a full answer and defence and to a fair trial. This is a function of the Trial Division which Blanchard J. understood well and performed with great care and full awareness of the issues at stake. A review of the transcripts of the hearing shows that he studiously and painstakingly considered each of the applicant's claims against disclosure before making his ruling.

---

334 Some of these facts come from Ribic's conviction appeal: see *R. v. Ribic* (2008), 63 C.R. (6th) 70 (Ont. C.A.).

14 As a general rule, a person charged with a criminal offence enjoys a qualified right to disclosure of all information relevant to his or her defence. The right is qualified in that it is subject to Crown's discretion and the law and rules of privilege: see *R. v. Stinchcombe*, [1991] 3 S.C.R. 326, at page 339. Where the information to be disclosed or sought to be obtained is sensitive information, a State privilege to confidentiality and secrecy is triggered and section 38 of the Act establishes the procedure by which the privilege is to be exercised and ultimately secured.

15 It is important to remind ourselves that proceedings initiated pursuant to section 38.04 of the *Act* for an order regarding disclosure of information are not judicial review proceedings. They are not proceedings aimed at reviewing a decision of the Attorney General not to disclose sensitive information. The prohibition to disclose sensitive information is a statutory one enacted by paragraph 38.02(1)(a) of the *Act* which reads:

> 38.02 (1) Subject to subsection 38.01(6), no person shall disclose in connection with a proceeding
>
> > (a) information about which notice is given under any of subsections 38.01(1) to (4);

* * *

The application to a judge of the Trial Division is an application whereby the judge is required to make an initial determination, i.e., to determine whether the statutory prohibition of disclosure should be confirmed or not: see subsection 38.06(3) which says that if the judge does not authorize disclosure, he or she shall, by order, confirm the prohibition of disclosure. In proceedings under section 38.04, the judge is required to make his own decision as to whether the statutory ban ought to be lifted or not and issue an order accordingly.

16 Where a judge of the Trial Division is seized with an application for an order regarding the disclosure of sensitive information, subsection 38.04(5) stipulates that he shall hear the representations of the Attorney General and, when required, those of the Minister of National Defence concerning the identity of the persons whose interests may be affected by the eventual order regarding disclosure as well as the persons who should be notified of a hearing, if any, on the matter. The judge may decide to hold a hearing in which case he shall decide who should be given notice and who may be given an opportunity to make representations.

17 The first task of a judge hearing an application is to determine whether the information sought to be disclosed is relevant or not in the usual and common sense of the *Stinchcombe* rule, that is to say in the case at bar information, whether inculpatory or exculpatory, that may reasonably be useful to the defence: *R. v. Chaplin*, [1995] 1 S.C.R. 727, at page 740. This is undoubtedly a low threshold. This step remains a necessary one because, if the information is not relevant, there is no need to go further and engage scarce judicial resources. This step will generally involve an inspection or examination of the information for that purpose.

The onus is on the party seeking disclosure to establish that the information is in all likelihood relevant evidence.

18 Where the judge is satisfied that the information is relevant, the next step pursuant to section 38.06 is to determine whether the disclosure of the information would be injurious to international relations, national defence or national security. This second step will also involve, from that perspective, an examination or inspection of the information at issue. The judge must consider the submissions of the parties and their supporting evidence. He must be satisfied that executive opinions as to potential injury have a factual basis which has been established by evidence: *Home Secretary v. Rehman*, [2001] H.L.J. No. 47, [2001] 3 WLR 877, at page 895 (HL(E)). It is a given that it is not the role of the judge to second-guess or substitute his opinion for that of the executive. As Lord Hoffmann said in *Rehman, supra*, at page 897 in relation to the September 11 events in New York and Washington, referred to in *Suresh v. Canada (Minister of Citizenship and Immigration)*, [2002] 1 S.C.R. 3, at paragraph 33:

> They are a reminder that in matters of national security, the cost of failure can be high. This seems to me to underline the need for the judicial arm of government to respect the decisions of ministers of the Crown on the question of whether support for terrorist activities in a foreign country constitutes a threat to national security. It is not only that the executive has access to special information and expertise in these matters. It is also that such decisions, with serious potential results for the community, require a legitimacy which can be conferred only by entrusting them to persons responsible to the community through the democratic process. If the people are to accept the consequences of such decisions, they must be made by persons whom the people have elected and whom they can remove.

19 This means that the Attorney General's submissions regarding his assessment of the injury to national security, national defence or international relations, because of his access to special information and expertise, should be given considerable weight by the judge required to determine, pursuant to subsection 38.06(1), whether disclosure of the information would cause the alleged and feared injury. The Attorney General assumes a protective role vis-à-vis the security and safety of the public. If his assessment of the injury is reasonable, the judge should accept it. I should add that a similar norm of reasonableness has been adopted by the House of Lords: see *Rehman, supra*, at page 895 where Lord Hoffmann mentions that the Special Immigration Appeals Commission may reject the Home Secretary's opinion when it was "one which no reasonable minister advising the Crown could in the circumstances reasonably have held".

20 An authorization to disclose will issue if the judge is satisfied that no injury would result from public disclosure. The burden of convincing the judge of the existence of such probable injury is on the party opposing disclosure on that basis.

21 Upon a finding that disclosure of the sensitive information would result in injury, the judge then moves to the final stage of the inquiry which consists in determining whether the public interest in disclosure outweighs in importance the

public interest in non-disclosure. The party seeking disclosure of the information bears the burden of proving that the public interest scale is tipped in its favour.

22 Balancing the competing interests at stake requires the application of a more stringent test than the usual relevancy rule. Otherwise, as evidenced by the appellant's position, relevant sensitive information would always be disclosed to the detriment of international relations, national defence or national security. It means in effect no balancing at all. This is what this Court said in the civil case of *Jose Pereira E Hijos, S.A. et al. v. The Attorney General of Canada*, [2002] F.C.J. No. 1658, 2002 FCA 470, where Stone J.A., in relation to former sections 37 and 38 of the Act, wrote at paragraphs 17 and 18:

> Thus, whether a question is relevant in the context of a section 37 and 38 determination is not to be viewed in the narrow sense of whether it is relevant to an issue pleaded, but rather to its relative importance in proving the claim or in defending it.

> I respectfully agree with the Motions Judge, at paragraph 28, that "the information which the plaintiffs seek to obtain will not establish a fact crucial to the plaintiffs' case". As I read his reasons, this was a significant factor in determining whether the importance of disclosure was outweighed by the importance of protecting the specified public interest.

The Court considered the factors enumerated in *R. v. Kahn*, [1996] 2 F.C. 316 (F.C.T.D.): the nature of the public interest sought to be protected by confidentiality, the seriousness of the charge or issues involved, the admissibility of the documentation and the usefulness of it, whether there were other reasonable ways of obtaining the information, whether the disclosure sought amounted to general discovery or a fishing expedition and whether the information will probably establish a fact crucial to the defence. Obviously, the last two factors impose a higher threshold than simple relevancy.

23 Counsel for the Attorney General submits that, when balancing in criminal law the State privilege to secrecy and confidentiality against the right to a full answer and defence, the test is even more stringent than the probability of establishing a fact crucial to the defence. He relies upon the decision of the Supreme Court of Canada in *R. v. Leipert*, [1997] 1 S.C.R. 281 in which the accused seeking disclosure of details of an informer telephone tip to the police was confronted with the rule of informer privilege. The accused's claim to disclosure was based on his right to full answer and defence: see also *R. v. Brown*, [2002] 2 S.C.R. 185, 2002 SCC 32 involving a solicitor-client privilege.

24 After a review of the importance to the administration of justice and the scope of the informer privilege, McLachlin J., as she then was, wrote for a unanimous Court at page 295:

> Informer privilege is subject only to one exception, known as the "innocence at stake" exception.

She went on to say at pages 295, 298 and 299 that "the only exception to the privilege is found where there is a basis to conclude that the information may be necessary to establish the innocence of the accused".

25 Not surprisingly, counsel for the appellant argue that this informer privilege falls in a different class and that the rationale governing its contents and application is not the same as the one invoked in the present case. Counsel for the Attorney General submits that whether it is informer privilege, solicitor-client privilege or State secrecy privilege, all these privileges are governed by the law and the rules of privilege. They are fundamental to the basic values that each one of them protects and promotes. So the information that they protect can only be disclosed when the innocence of the accused is at stake.

26 There is certainly a very important feature of the informer and the State secrecy privileges that is common to both. The informer privilege's purpose is to protect the safety and the security of the informer: part of the State secrecy privilege invoked in the case at bar aims at protecting the safety and the security of a whole nation. As Lord Hoffmann, previously cited, mentioned, the cost of failure can be high if matters of national security are ignored or taken lightly.

27 Be that as it may, it is not necessary in this case to determine whether the more stringent test developed in criminal law should apply although, in view of the important feature common to both privileges, I would be inclined to apply that test at least in respect of matters affecting national security or national defence. I am also sensitive to, and cannot ignore, the fact that prejudice to international relations may be of such a nature and magnitude as to compromise national security or defence. It appears that Blanchard J. applied the test developed in the civil case of *Pereira, supra*, which is more favourable to the appellant. For reasons that I will explain later, I will review his decision and the sensitive information at issue on that basis.

28 I cannot leave this topic without addressing two concerns other than an alleged violation of the appellant's right to full answer and defence that the new scheme, enacted to protect State secrecy privilege, raises with respect to persons charged with a criminal offence. The first one was alluded to briefly by counsel for the appellant in their submissions before us.

29 As the present case illustrates, the whole process leading to the determination of the State secrecy privilege compels an accused to reveal his defence and disclose information that supports that defence. As a general rule, there is no obligation to disclose imposed upon an accused in criminal law. In this regard, Sopinka J. wrote in *Stinchcombe, supra*, at page 333:

> In contrast, the defence has no obligation to assist the prosecution and is entitled to assume a purely adversarial role toward the prosecution. The absence of a duty to disclose can, therefore, be justified as being consistent with this role.

This absence of duty is consistent with the presumption of innocence and an accused's right to silence. Like any rule, it suffers some exceptions dictated at times by rules of expediency. For example, a defence of alibi must be disclosed in sufficient time and with sufficient particularity to enable the authorities to meaningfully investigate. Otherwise, an adverse inference can be drawn at trial by the trier of fact when weighing the alibi evidence: *R. v. Cleghorn*, [1995] 3 S.C.R. 175.

30 The legislative exception created in the present case by section 38 of the *Act* is justified by the need to balance competing interests and to offer an accused an appropriate forum for adjudication of the debated issue as well as for subsequent reviews. It is of fundamental importance to note that disclosure of the sensitive information that the appellant wants to rely upon is not made to the prosecution, but, under the seal of absolute confidentiality, to the Attorney General and a designated judicial forum where the matter will be decided in private. It is therefore not a disclosure which violates an accused's right to silence and the presumption of innocence in criminal proceedings. In addition, as the appellant requests in the present instance, this Court has the authority to issue an order that none of the information disclosed in the context of the section 38 process be released to the prosecution without the consent of the defence. In my view, sufficient and adequate guarantees are offered by the system which protect an accused's right not to disclose to the prosecution his defence.

31 The second concern relates to the presumption of innocence. An accused is not a compellable witness and, as mentioned by Sopinka J., supra, is entitled not to assist the prosecution. In other words, he has the right to remain silent and no adverse comment can be made on his silence: *R. v. Noble*, [1997] 1 S.C.R. 874; see also Cournoyer et Ouimet, *Code criminel annoté 2003*, Éditions Yvon Blais, Cowansville, 2002, pages 1329-1332. This is because the prosecution bears the burden of proving his guilt beyond reasonable doubt.

32 When balancing competing public interests in a case like this one where a person faces criminal charges, the judge must ensure that his order prohibiting disclosure does not result in his compelling the accused to take the stand to defend himself, thereby depriving him of the benefit of the presumption of innocence and of his right to remain silent. It is with this additional concern in mind that we have reviewed the orders of Blanchard J. regarding the vetted information, the prohibition to testify against witnesses A and B, and the form in which the information obtained from their testimony at the examination for discovery has been authorized to be disclosed.

Analysis of the judge's orders

33 . . . We are concerned here with an appeal pursuant to section 38.09.

a) The standard of review of the judge's orders

34 Subsection 38.06(2) that I reproduce hereafter is an empowering provision:

> 38.06 (2) If the judge concludes that the disclosure of the information would be injurious to international relations or national defence or national security but that

the public interest in disclosure outweighs in importance the public interest in non-disclosure, the judge may by order, after considering both the public interest in disclosure and the form of and conditions to disclosure that are most likely to limit any injury to international relations or national defence or national security resulting from disclosure, authorize the disclosure, subject to any conditions that the judge considers appropriate, of all of the information, a part or summary of the information, or a written admission of facts relating to the information.

* * *

35 As previously mentioned, section 38.02 of the *Act* enacts a general prohibition against disclosure. Subsection 38.06(2) authorizes the judge to disclose sensitive information, which would otherwise be kept secret, when the public interest in disclosure outweighs the public interest in non-disclosure. The use of the word "may" is not indicative of a discretion as counsel for the Attorney General suggests. It is indicative of an attribution of a power to derogate from a general prohibition to disclose privileged information. As this Court said in *Ruby v. Canada*, [2000] 3 F.C. 589, at page 623 (F.C.A.), quoting Thorson J.A. in *Falconbridge Nickel Mines Ltd. and Minister of Revenue for Ontario, Re* (1981), 121 D.L.R. (3d) 403, at page 408:

> In some contexts, of course, the word "may" is neither necessarily permissive nor necessarily imperative, but rather merely empowering. Its function is to empower some person or authority to do something which, otherwise, that person or authority would be without any power to do.

36 The power conferred by subsection 38.06(2) can be exercised when the conditions are met, that is to say in this case when the public interest in disclosure is greater than the public interest in keeping the information secret. The definition of the scope of the power involves a question of law. The scope of the power is determined by answering questions as to what is the subject of the power, who may exercise it, when, why, how and under what conditions. Thus, the decision which misconstrues or misconceives the "what", i.e., the competing interests, is legally an erroneous decision. The same is true of a decision which authorizes disclosure of sensitive information where the judge erroneously believed that the requisite legal conditions for disclosure are met when they are not. Such a decision extends the scope of the power beyond what is legally authorized. In the same vein, it is also an error of law to apply a wrong standard in balancing the interests at stake and, from there, to conclude that the conditions for the exercise of the power are met. All these decisions relating to the scope of the power are reviewable on a standard of correctness: see *Housen v. Nikolaisen*, [2002] 2 S.C.R. 185, 2002 SCC 33.

37 In exercising the power to authorize disclosure and before authorizing disclosure, the judge while bearing in mind the public interest in disclosure must ensure that the form of and conditions to disclosure are most likely to limit any injury to national security, national defence or international relations resulting from disclosure. The judge must resort to the means that are the least prejudicial to these interests. Parliament's intent is clear: any injury ought to be limited as

much as possible and appropriate measures ought to be taken to that end, that is to say measures that are most likely to produce that result.

38 The objective sought by Parliament in imposing this duty on the judge is paramount. It delimits the scope of the judge's power to authorize disclosure of sensitive information by imposing conditions for a lawful exercise of that power and issuance of the authorization to disclose. Thus, in my view, erroneous decisions as to the form of disclosure as well as to the conditions of such disclosure amount to errors in law as to the definition of the scope of the power. They too stand to be reviewed on a standard of correctness.

39 Having decided that the conditions to authorize disclosure of the sensitive information are met and, therefore, that an authorization to disclose will issue, the judge is given by subsection 38.06(2) the power to subject the authorization to disclose to "any conditions that he considers appropriate". The judge is invested by these terms with a wide discretion in the choice of conditions that can be attached to the authorization to disclose. The exercise of that discretion may be reviewed when the judge fails to act judicially or in conformity with the law. On the basis of these principles I now address the complaints made by counsel for the appellant against the judge's decision and orders.

b) The vetted information in the testimonies of the two witnesses at their examination for discovery

. . .

41 We have reviewed carefully the vetted information. Most of it falls into the category of information not relevant at trial. Some, as the judge pointed out, may be relevant in that it could assist the jury in putting into proper context the events leading to the hostage taking. However, that information is not necessary because, as the judge said at paragraph 26 of his decision, "there is sufficient information released to the applicant in the expurgated transcripts to inform the jury of the context in which the events leading up to the hostage taking and the hostage taking occurred". Moreover, the vetted sensitive information is neither necessary (*Leipert* test) nor crucial (*Pereira* test) to the defences raised by the appellant. We agree with the judge that, for the purposes of these defences, the expurgated transcripts reflect fairly the nature and substance of the testimony of the two witnesses and that the vetted information would not be helpful: see paragraph 27 of his decision. We have not seen anything in the vetted information which, because of its non-disclosure, would violate the presumption of innocence and compel the accused to testify.

c) The fairness of the process followed to balance the competing interests

42 The process followed in the present instance was unusual. It is certainly unusual for counsel to an accused to have two of their witnesses examined by another lawyer acting on their behalf. It is also unusual that this lawyer acting on their behalf be a counsel to the Attorney General who, in this case, instead of the

Attorney General for Ontario, leads the prosecution against their client. But "unusual" is not necessarily synonymous with "unfair". The process was dictated by urgency and necessity.

. . .

45 There is no magical solution when one is confronted with sensitive information and access to it is extremely limited for security reasons. A process similar to the one followed here was advocated by the House of Lords in *R. v. Shayler*, [2002] H.L.J. No. 11, [2002] 2 WLR 754 (HL(E)). At pages 786 and 799, Lord Hope of Craighead and Lord Hutton referred to the fact that the European Court of Human Rights has recognized the special problems posed by national security and the value attached to a process which ensures that disclosure is monitored by a judge. Lord Hutton also took into account the decision of the European Court in *Tinnelly & Sons Ltd. v. United Kingdom*, 27 EHRR 249 where the Court noted that "it had been found possible to modify judicial procedures in such a way as to safeguard national security concerns about the nature and sources of intelligence information and yet accord the individual a substantial degree of procedural justice". At page 800, he went on to state that "a possible course might be for the judge to appoint a special counsel to represent the interests of the person seeking disclosure". This is precisely what was done here to ensure that the appellant would obtain disclosure of all sensitive information that could be disclosed without unduly compromising national security, national defence or international relations. Creativity often carries their proponents into the realm of the unusual, as it did here, but I am satisfied that fairness accompanied them throughout their journey.

. . .

Conclusion

59 I am satisfied that the judge of the Trial Division committed no error in defining the scope of his power to order disclosure of the sensitive information at issue as well as the conditions which delimit it. The prohibition against the two witnesses to testify at the criminal trial was, in the circumstances, the only viable and efficient condition which would most likely limit any injury to national defence, national security or international relations.

60 Nor did, in my view, the judge err in defining the competing interests at stake and the test to be applied in balancing these interests. If he did err with respect to the balancing test, it is an error which was favourable to the appellant.

61 Finally, the process followed to monitor and review the disclosure of the sensitive information could, in hindsight, perhaps have been better, but it was not unfair given the time constraints that all the players were facing.

62 For these reasons, I would dismiss the appeal.

Ribic's first trial ended in a mistrial because of the Federal Court disclosure applications. He was convicted at a second trial and sentenced to three years.

His conviction occurred 79 months following his charge. His appeal was dismissed.[335] On appeal, Ribic again tried to challenge the disclosure process. In dismissing this ground, Justice Charron, for the Court, held:

78 Absent the Attorney General's authorization of or agreement to disclosure, a judge of the Federal Court is to determine disclosure requests. Unless the reviewing judge concludes that the disclosure of the information would be injurious to international relations, national defence or national security, he or she has the discretion to authorize the disclosure of the requested information (s. 38.06(1)).

79 However, where the reviewing judge concludes that the disclosure of the information would be injurious to international relations, national defence or national security, he or she is obliged to weigh the public interest in disclosure against the public interest in non-disclosure. If, after undertaking this balancing exercise and considering "the form of and conditions to disclosure that are most likely to limit any injury to international relations or national defence or national security resulting from disclosure", the reviewing judge concludes that the public interest in disclosure outweighs in importance the public interest in non-disclosure, the disclosure of the information may be authorized, in whole or in part (s. 38.06(2)). See also *Charkaoui v. Canada (Citizenship and Immigration)*, [2007] 1 S.C.R. 350, at para. 77.

80 The appellant does not challenge the constitutionality of the s. 38 statutory scheme. Nor do I understand him to dispute that the purpose of the scheme is to strike a balance between the need for protection of confidential information and the rights of the individual: *Charkaoui* at para. 77. Rather, the contentious issue is whether the Disclosure Process, and the Disclosure Rulings that flowed from it, violated the appellant's s. 7 *Charter* rights.

81 It is undisputed that the Disclosure Process was unusual in several respects. In the view of the Federal Court of Appeal, it was dictated by "urgency and necessity": FCA Decision at para. 42. . . .

82 Section 38 of the *CEA* was significantly amended by the *Anti-Terrorism Act*, S.C. 2001, c. 41, s. 43. We were informed that the Federal Court proceedings in this case were the first of their kind conducted under the amended legislation. As a result, some of the protective measures apparently now utilized under the amended s. 38 regime—e.g., the use of special counsel to serve as *amicus curiae* or as counsel on behalf of a disclosure applicant—were not yet employed. We were also advised that the Disclosure Rulings are the first rulings under s. 38 involving the disclosure of proposed defence evidence in a criminal trial.

83 Unquestionably, the method of examination of Witnesses A and B under the Disclosure Process was far from ideal, involving as it did a filter between the appellant's counsel and the witnesses and a proscription on the direct participation of the appellant's counsel in the examination process. That said, it is my opinion that the appellant cannot rely on a challenge to the fairness of the Disclosure Process itself to support his claim in this court that a stay of the prosecution should have been granted due to the alleged infringement of his s. 7 *Charter* rights. I say this for several reasons.

84 First, the parties acknowledge that the Disclosure Process was generated by the prevailing exigencies of time. . . .

86 Second, by renewing his attack on the fairness of the Disclosure Process before this court, the appellant seeks to relitigate issues that have already been judicially

---

335 (2008), 63 C.R. (6th) 70 (Ont. C.A.).

determined, with the expenditure of considerable judicial resources. At heart, this amounts to an impermissible collateral attack on the Disclosure Rulings that flowed from the Disclosure Process.

. . .

92 Accordingly, in the end, four judges of courts that are experienced in dealing with national security and national defence issues evaluated the fairness of the Disclosure Process and the nature and sufficiency of the information authorized for disclosure. They unanimously held that the information to be disclosed was fair and protective of the appellant's interests to the extent possible, given the nature of the information at issue, the defences sought to be raised by the appellant at his criminal trial, and the urgency of the situation. As I have said, leave to appeal that determination to the Supreme Court of Canada was refused.

(ii) *Section 39 – Confidential Cabinet Materials*

BABCOCK v. CANADA (ATTORNEY GENERAL)
[2002] 3 S.C.R. 3, 3 C.R. (6th) 1, 2002 CarswellBC 1576,
2002 CarswellBC 1577

On June 6, 1990, the Treasury Board of Canada set the pay of Department of Justice lawyers working in the Toronto Regional Office at a higher rate than that of lawyers working elsewhere. Vancouver staff lawyers brought an action contending that by failing to pay them the same salaries as Toronto lawyers the government breached their contracts of employment and the fiduciary duty toward them. During the proceedings, the Government filed an affidavit by Joan McCoy, an officer of the Treasury Board Secretariat. The affidavit stated that the rationale for the Order-in-Council authorizing the pay raise for Toronto lawyers was that lawyers in Toronto generally commanded higher salaries than lawyers in other parts of the country. Later in the proceedings, the government delivered a certificate of the Clerk of the Privy Council pursuant to section 39(1) objecting to the disclosure of various documents on the ground that they contain "information constituting confidences of the Queen's Privy Council for Canada". A majority of the Court of Appeal ordered production of the documents on the ground that the government had waived its right to claim confidentiality by listing some of the documents as producible and by disclosing selective information in the McCoy affidavit. The government appealed to the Supreme Court of Canada.

McLACHLIN C.J. (GONTHIER, IACOBUCCI, MAJOR, BASTARACHE, BINNIE, ARBOUR and LEBEL JJ. concurring):—

. . . .

IV. *Discussion*

A. *The Principles*

Cabinet confidentiality is essential to good government. The right to pursue justice in the courts is also of primary importance in our society, as is the rule of law, accountability of the executive, and the principle that official actions must flow from statutory authority clearly granted and properly exercised. Yet sometimes these fundamental principles conflict. How are such conflicts to be resolved? That is the question posed by this appeal.

The answer to the question lies in our understanding of Cabinet confidentiality. What is its purpose? What does it apply to? What is the process for claiming it? Once claimed, can it be relinquished or lost, and if so, how? These questions find their answers in an understanding of Cabinet confidentiality and the ambit and effect of s. 39 of the *Canada Evidence Act* that protects it.

(1) *The Function of Section 39 of the Canada Evidence Act*

Sections 37, 38 and 39 of the *Canada Evidence Act* deal with objections to the disclosure of protected information held by the federal government. Section 37 relates to all claims for Crown privilege, except Cabinet confidences, or confidences of the Queen's Privy Council; s. 38 pertains to objections related to international relations or national defence; and s. 39 deals with Cabinet confidences. Under ss. 37 and 38, a judge balances the competing public interests in protection and disclosure of information. Under s. 39, by contrast, the Clerk or minister balances the competing interests. If the Clerk or minister validly certifies information as confidential, a judge or tribunal must refuse any application for disclosure, without examining the information.

The British democratic tradition which informs the Canadian tradition has long affirmed the confidentiality of what is said in the Cabinet room, and documents and papers prepared for Cabinet discussions. The reasons are obvious. Those charged with the heavy responsibility of making government decisions must be free to discuss all aspects of the problems that come before them and to express all manner of views, without fear that what they read, say or act on will later be subject to public scrutiny: see *Singh v. Canada (Attorney General)*, [2000] 3 F.C. 185 (C.A.), at paras. 21-22. If Cabinet members' statements were subject to disclosure, Cabinet members might censor their words, consciously or unconsciously. They might shy away from stating unpopular positions, or from making comments that might be considered politically incorrect. The rationale for recognizing and protecting Cabinet confidences is well summarized by the views of Lord Salisbury in the *Report of the Committee of Privy Counsellors on Ministerial Memoirs* (January 1976), at p. 13:

> A Cabinet discussion was not the occasion for the deliverance of considered judgements but an opportunity for the pursuit of practical conclusions. It could only be made completely effective for this purpose if the flow of suggestions which accompanied it attained the freedom and fulness which belong to private conversations — members must feel themselves untrammelled by any consideration of consistency with the past or self-justification in the future. . . . The first rule of Cabinet conduct, he used to declare, was that no member should ever "Hansardise" another, — ever compare his present contribution to the common fund of counsel with a previously expressed opinion. . . .

The process of democratic governance works best when Cabinet members charged with government policy and decision-making are free to express themselves around the Cabinet table unreservedly. In addition to ensuring candour in Cabinet discussions, this Court in *Carey v. Ontario*, [1986] 2 S.C.R. 637, at p. 659, recognized another important reason for protecting Cabinet documents, namely to avoid "creat[ing] or fan[ning] ill-informed or captious public or political criticism". Thus, ministers undertake by oath as Privy Councillors to maintain the secrecy of Cabinet deliberations and the House of Commons and the courts respect the confidentiality of Cabinet decision-making.

At one time, the common law viewed Cabinet confidentiality as absolute. However, over time the common law has come to recognize that the public interest in Cabinet confidences must be balanced against the public interest in disclosure, to which it might sometimes be required to yield: see *Carey, supra*. Courts began to weigh the need to protect confidentiality in government against the public interest in disclosure, for example, preserving the integrity of the judicial system. It follows that there must be some way of determining that the information for which confidentiality is claimed truly relates to Cabinet deliberations and that it is properly withheld. At common law, the courts did this, applying a test that balanced the public interest in maintaining confidentiality against the public interest in disclosure: see *Carey, supra*.

In addition, many jurisdictions have enacted laws that modify the common law and provide a statutory process for determining what documents are protected and how claims to confidentiality may be challenged: see, for example, the *Ombudsman Act*, R.S.B.C. 1996, c. 340. The exercise of this statutory power is subject to the well-established rule that official actions must flow from statutory authority clearly granted and properly exercised: *Roncarelli v. Duplessis*, [1959] S.C.R. 121. The courts have the power and the responsibility, when called upon, to determine whether the certifying official has exercised his or her statutory power in accordance with the law.

Section 39 of the *Canada Evidence Act* is Canada's response to the need to provide a mechanism for the responsible exercise of the power to claim Cabinet confidentiality in the context of judicial and quasi-judicial proceedings. It sets up a process for bringing information within the protection of the Act. Certification by the Clerk of the Privy Council or by a minister of the Crown, is the trigger by which information becomes protected. The Clerk must certify that the "information constitutes a confidence of the Queen's Privy Council for Canada". For more particularity, s. 39(2) sets out categories of information that falls within its scope.

Section 39(1) permits the Clerk to certify information as confidential. It does not restrain voluntary disclosure of confidential information. This is made clear from the French enactment of s. 39(1) which states that s. 39 protection arises only "*dans les cas où*" (in the cases where) the Clerk or minister opposes disclosure of information. Therefore, the Clerk must answer two questions before certifying information: first, is it a Cabinet confidence within the meaning of ss. 39(1) and 39(2); and second, is it information which the government should protect taking into account the competing interests in disclosure and retaining confidentiality? If, and only if, the Clerk or minister answers these two questions positively and certifies the information, do the protections of s. 39(1) come into play. More particularly, the provision that "disclosure of the information shall be refused without examination or hearing of the information by the court, person or body" is only triggered when there is a valid certification.

If the Clerk or minister *chooses* to certify a confidence, it gains the protection of s. 39. Once certified, information gains greater protection than at common law. If s. 39 is engaged, the "court, person or body with jurisdiction" hearing the matter *must* refuse disclosure; "disclosure of the information shall be refused". Moreover, this must be done "without examination or hearing of the information by the court, person or body". This absolute language goes beyond the common law approach of balancing the public interest in protecting confidentiality and disclosure on judicial review. Once information has been validly certified, the common law no longer applies to that information.

This raises the issue of what constitutes valid certification. Two requirements are plain on the face of the legislation. First, it must be done by the Clerk of the Privy Council or a minister of the Crown. Second, the information must fall within the categories described in s. 39(2).

A third requirement arises from the general principle applicable to all government acts, namely, that the power exercised must flow from the statute and must be issued for the *bona fide* purpose of protecting Cabinet confidences in the broader public interest. The function of the Clerk under the Act is to protect Cabinet confidences, and this alone. It is not to thwart public inquiry nor is it to gain tactical advantage in litigation. If it can be shown from the evidence or the circumstances that the power of certification was exercised for purposes outside those contemplated by s. 39, the certification may be set aside as an unauthorized exercise of executive power: see *Roncarelli, supra.*

A fourth requirement for valid certification flows from the fact that s. 39 applies to *disclosure* of the documents. Where a document has already been disclosed, s. 39 no longer applies. There is no longer a need to seek disclosure since disclosure has already occurred. Where s. 39 does not apply, there may be other bases upon which the government may seek protection against further disclosure at common law: *Duncan v. Cammell, Laird & Co.*, [1942] A.C. 624 (H.L.), at p. 630; *Leeds v. Alberta (Minister of the Environment)* (1990), 69 D.L.R. (4th) 681 (Alta. Q.B.); *Sankey v. Whitlam* (1978), 142 C.L.R. 1 (Austl. H.C.), at p. 45. However, that issue does not arise on this appeal. Similarly, the issue of inadvertent disclosure does not arise here because the Crown deliberately disclosed certain documents during the course of litigation.

On the basis of these principles, I conclude that certification is generally valid if: (1) it is done by the Clerk or minister; (2) it relates to information within s. 39(2); (3) it is done in a *bona fide* exercise of delegated power; (4) it is done to prevent disclosure of hitherto confidential information.

It may be useful to comment on the formal aspects of certification. As noted, the Clerk must determine two things: (1) that the information is a Cabinet confidence within s. 39; and (2) that it is desirable that confidentiality be retained taking into account the competing interests in disclosure and retaining confidentiality. What formal certification requirements flow from this? The second, discretionary element may be taken as satisfied by the act of certification. However, the first element of the Clerk's decision requires that her certificate bring the information within the ambit of the Act. This means that the Clerk or minister must provide a description of the information sufficient to establish on its face that the information is a Cabinet confidence and that it falls within the categories of s. 39(2) or an analogous category; the possibility of analogous categories flows from the general language of the introductory portion of s. 39(2). This follows from the principle that the Clerk or minister must exercise her statutory power properly in accordance with the statute. The kind of description required for claims of solicitor-client privilege under the civil rules of court will generally suffice. The date, title, author and recipient of the document containing the information should normally be disclosed. If confidentiality concerns prevent disclosure of any of these preliminary indicia of identification, then the onus falls on the government to establish this, should a challenge ensue. On the other hand, if the documents containing the information are properly identified, a person seeking production and the court must accept the Clerk's determination. The only argument that can be made is that, on the description, they do not fall within s. 39, or that the Clerk has otherwise exceeded the powers conferred upon her.

As to the timing of certification, the only limits are those found in s. 39(4). Subject to these outer limits, it seems that information that falls within s. 39(2) may be certified long after the date the confidence existed or arose in Cabinet. At the same time, as discussed, if there has been disclosure, s. 39 no longer applies, since its only purpose is to prevent disclosure.

It may be that the Clerk or minister can withdraw a certification of Cabinet confidence under s. 39 of the *Canada Evidence Act*, on the theory that the power to certify must also include a power to decertify, as suggested by Southin J.A.; and that where a certification is made in error, for example, the Clerk or minister should be able to correct the matter. However, that issue does not arise here.

(2) *Waiver*

On the facts of this case, the concept of waiver in any ordinary sense of the term finds no place. As discussed, the Clerk or minister is not compelled to certify Cabinet confidences and invoke the protection of s. 39(1). However, if the Clerk or minister chooses to do so, the protection of s. 39 automatically follows. That protection continues indefinitely, unless: (i) the certificate is successfully challenged on the ground that it related to information that does not fall under s. 39; (ii) the power of certification of the Clerk or minister has otherwise been improperly exercised; (iii) s. 39(4) is engaged; or (iv) the Clerk or minister chooses to decertify the information. The clear language of s. 39(1) permits no other conclusion.

This is consistent with the fact that waiver does not apply at common law. A claim for confidentiality at common law cannot be contested on the ground that the government has waived its right to claim confidentiality. As Bingham L.J. observed in *Makanjuola v. Commissioner of Police of the Metropolis*, [1992] 3 All E.R. 617 (C.A.), at p. 623, "[p]ublic interest immunity is not a trump card vouchsafed to certain privileged players to play when and as they wish". Consequently, "public interest immunity cannot in any ordinary sense be waived" (p. 623). Issues of production pursuant to s. 39 of the *Canada Evidence Act* fall to be resolved by the Clerk or minister responsible for balancing the public interests. If a certificate is not properly filed, and documents are released, the Crown is precluded from claiming s. 39 protection. However, by releasing some documents, the Crown has not waived its right to invoke s. 39 over other documents.

It is argued that unless the broad power of waiver envisioned by the majority of the Court of Appeal is recognized, litigants opposing the Crown will be placed in the untenable position of being unable to rely on the Crown's production of documents, no matter how essential such documents are to their case or how late the Crown makes its claim to immunity. This concern is alleviated by the fact that s. 39(1) cannot be applied retroactively to documents that have already been produced in litigation; it applies only to compel disclosure.

The conclusion that waiver does not apply here makes it unnecessary to consider the issue of class waiver — whether disclosure of one document removes protection from all documents in the same class. However, the related issue of class disclosure of information must be addressed.

Section 39 protects "information" from disclosure. It may be that some information on a particular matter has been disclosed, while other information on the matter has not been disclosed. The language of s. 39(1) does not permit one to say that disclosure of some information removes s. 39 protection from other, non-disclosed information. If the related information has been disclosed in other documents, then s. 39 does not apply and the documents containing the information must be produced. If the related information is contained in documents that have been properly certified under s. 39, the government is under no obligation to disclose the related information.

This raises the concern that selective disclosure of documents or information may be used unfairly as a litigation tactic. The fear is that the Crown could choose to disclose only those documents which are favourable to its position and certify those documents which are detrimental. Selective disclosure designed to prevent getting at the truth would not be a proper exercise of the Clerk's or minister's s. 39 powers: *Roncarelli, supra.* Moreover, the ordinary rules of litigation offer protection from abuse. First, government witnesses may be cross-examined on the information produced. Second, the refusal to disclose information may permit a court to draw an adverse inference. For example, in *RJR-MacDonald Inc. v. Canada (Attorney General)*, [1995] 3 S.C.R. 199, the Attorney General's refusal to disclose information relating to an advertising ban on tobacco, led to the inference that the results of the studies must undercut the government's claim that a less invasive ban would not have produced an equally salutary result (para. 166, *per* McLachlin J.).

. . .

B. *Application of the Principles*

(1) *The Documents*

The government issued a s. 39 certificate for 51 documents. Twelve of these had been identified in its list of documents under "Part I: Documents to which there is no objection to production". Of these 12, a number appear to have been not only listed, but actually disclosed to the plaintiffs. The certificate also claimed confidentiality for five documents which were in the plaintiffs' possession or control and which the plaintiffs had listed as producible.

On the record before us, s. 39 certification applies to the 34 documents listed as not producible.

As discussed, s. 39 of the *Canada Evidence Act* does not apply to the government documents already disclosed. Nor does s. 39 apply to the five certified documents that were in the plaintiffs' possession or control. The documents were disclosed by the government in the context of litigation. The disclosure provisions of s. 39 therefore do not apply and these documents should be produced.

(2) *Information in the McCoy Affidavit*

The government claims protection from disclosure for the information contained in the affidavit of Joan McCoy, which was filed in support of the government's unsuccessful motion to transfer the plaintiffs' case from the Supreme Court of British Columbia to the Federal Court.

Of particular importance is Ms. McCoy's statement in para. 21 that: "The rationale for the Treasury Board's decision to increase rates for legal officers in the Toronto Regional Office was the rise in private sector salaries to levels well above those paid in the public sector during a period of rapid economic growth in the late 1980s". According to the McCoy affidavit, "[t]he escalation of external pay rates, matched to a large degree by increases for provincial lawyers as well, had impaired the ability of the Department of Justice to attract candidates for positions in the Law group in the Toronto Regional Office. It had also led to an increase in resignations from the federal Public Service as experienced legal officers, attracted by higher salaries, left for employment in the provincial government and the private sector in the Toronto area. The viability of the regional operation was imperilled by these losses and immediate action was required to stem the flow" (para. 21 of McCoy affidavit).

The plaintiffs take issue with this rationale and seek to cross-examine Ms. McCoy on her statement. The government refuses to permit the statement to be used in evidence and denies the right to cross-examine on the information contained in it.

When it filed the McCoy affidavit, the government chose to disclose the reason for the decision to pay the Toronto Law group more than other Law groups. The government disclosed that information to support the motion that the B.C. Supreme Court was not the appropriate forum for the case. Therefore, s. 39 cannot be invoked. The affidavit must be disclosed and Ms. McCoy may be cross-examined on its contents.

As to related information, if it has been voluntarily disclosed in other documents, then s. 39 does not apply and the documents must be produced. By contrast, the government is under no obligation to disclose related information contained in documents that have been properly certified under s. 39, but runs the risk that refusal may permit the court to draw an adverse inference.

C. *The Constitutionality of Section 39*

Because s. 39 applies to the undisclosed documents, it is necessary to consider the constitutional questions in this case. The respondents argue that s. 39 of the *Canada Evidence Act* is of no force or effect by reason of one or both of the preamble to the *Constitution Act, 1867* and s. 96 of the *Constitution Act, 1867*.

(1) *The Preamble to the Constitution Act, 1867*

The respondents in this case challenge the constitutionality of s. 39 and argue that the provision is *ultra vires* Parliament because of the unwritten principles of the Canadian Constitution: the rule of law, the independence of the judiciary, and the separation of powers. Although the unwritten constitutional principles are capable of limiting government actions, I find that they do not do so in this case.

The unwritten principles must be balanced against the principle of Parliamentary sovereignty. In *Commission des droits de la personne v. Attorney General of Canada*, [1982] 1 S.C.R. 215, this Court upheld as constitutional s. 41(2) of the *Federal Court Act*, the predecessor to s. 39, which permitted the government to claim absolute privilege over a broader class of confidences.

Recently, the Federal Court of Appeal considered the constitutional validity of s. 39 of the *Canada Evidence Act* in *Singh, supra.* On the basis of a thorough and compelling review of the principle of parliamentary sovereignty in the context of unwritten constitutional principles, Strayer J.A. held that federal Crown privilege is part of valid federal law over which Parliament had the power to legislate. Strayer J.A. concluded at para. 36:

> ... the rule of law cannot be taken to invalidate a statute which has the effect of allowing representatives of the Crown to identify certain documents as beyond disclosure: that is, the rule of law does not preclude a special law with a special result dealing with a special class of documents which, for long standing reasons based on constitutional principles such as responsible government, have been treated differently from private documents in a commercial law suit.

I share the view of the Federal Court of Appeal that s. 39 does not offend the rule of law or the doctrines of separation of powers and the independence of the judiciary. It is well within the power of the legislature to enact laws, even laws which some would consider draconian, as long as it does not fundamentally alter or interfere with the relationship between the courts and the other branches of government.

(2) Section 96 of the *Constitution Act, 1867*

A second constitutional question must be considered: whether Parliament's decision to limit superior courts from compelling disclosure of Cabinet confidences impermissibly invades the core jurisdiction of the superior courts?

There is no clear test for defining what is considered to be the "core jurisdiction" of a s. 96 court. In *Reference re Amendments to the Residential Tenancies Act (N.S.)*, [1996] 1 S.C.R. 186, Lamer C.J. stated at para. 56:

Section 96's "core" jurisdiction is a very narrow one which includes only critically important jurisdictions which are essential to the existence of a superior court of inherent jurisdiction and to the preservation of its foundational role within our legal system.

Citing *MacMillan Bloedel Ltd. v. Simpson*, [1995] 4 S.C.R. 725, the respondents argue that s. 39 impermissibly infringes on the core jurisdiction of a superior court because it interferes with courts' ability to control their own process. First, because the section operates to prevent a superior court from remedying an abuse of process, and second, because it denies evidence centrally relevant to the core factual questions in the litigation. The respondents contend that s. 39 deprives the judiciary of its role of review, a power which a superior court possesses under the common law of public interest.

As previously stated, there is a long common law tradition of protecting Cabinet confidences. In Canada, superior courts operated since pre-Confederation without the power to compel Cabinet confidences. Indeed, at the time of Confederation, no court had any jurisdiction regarding actions against the Sovereign: see *R. v. Eldorado Nuclear Ltd.*, [1983] 2 S.C.R. 551. Further, s. 39 has not substantially altered the role of the judiciary from their function under the common law regime. The provision does not entirely exclude judicial review of the determination by the Clerk that the information is a Cabinet confidence. A court may review the certificate to determine whether it is a confidence within the meaning provided in s. 39(2) or analogous categories, or to determine if the certificate was issued in bad faith. Section 39 does not, in and of itself, impede a court's power to remedy abuses of process.

I therefore conclude that there is no basis upon which to find that s. 39 of the *Canada Evidence Act* is unconstitutional.

V. *Conclusion*

I would allow the appeal in part, with costs to the respondents.

On the record before us, the documents certified but disclosed, including the McCoy affidavit, are no longer protected and may be used in the litigation. The plaintiffs may cross-examine on the McCoy affidavit. The remaining documents are protected by s. 39 of the *Canada Evidence Act*. These conclusions are made without prejudice to future applications in this case.

Most of the provinces in Canada have enacted legislation providing for immunity claims in proceedings where the Crown is a party. For example, the Proceedings Against the Crown Act in Alberta provides:

11. In proceedings against the Crown, the rules of court as to discovery and inspection of documents and examination for discovery apply in the same manner as if the Crown were a corporation, except that the Crown may refuse to produce a document or to make answer to a question on discovery on the ground that the production of it or the answer would be injurious to the public interest.[336]

---

336 R.S.A. 2000, c. P-25.

In addition, some provinces have enacted legislation regarding the procedure for immunity claims in suits between parties. For example, the *Ontario Evidence Act*[337] provides:

30.   Where a document is in the official possession, custody or power of a member of the Executive Council, or of the head of a ministry of the public service of Ontario, if the deputy head or other officer of the ministry has the document in his or her personal possession, and is called as a witness, he or she is entitled, acting herein by the direction and on behalf of such member of the Executive Council or head of the ministry, to object to producing the document on the ground that it is privileged, and such objection may be taken by him or her in the same manner, and has the same effect, as if such member of the Executive Council or head of the ministry were personally present and made the objection.

Where there is no specific statutory provision that is comparable to ss. 37-39 of the *CEA*, then the common law will apply to claims of immunity by the provinces. The leading case setting out the common law procedure is *Carey v. Ontario*[338] which dealt with Cabinet documents of the Ontario Legislature.

(b) Identity of Informers

An aspect of public interest immunity is the long-established rule that the identity of informers should be protected from disclosure; the information is not protected but only its source, unless disclosure of the former would disclose the latter. In the early case of *R. v. Hardy*, Eyre L.C.J. wrote:

It is perfectly right that all opportunities should be given to discuss the truth of the evidence given against a prisoner; but there is a rule which has universally obtained on account of its importance to the public for the detection of crime that those persons who are the channel by means of which that detection is made, should not be unnecessarily disclosed: if it can be made appear that really and truly it is necessary to the investigation of the truth of the case that the name of the person should be disclosed, I should be very unwilling to stop it, but it does not appear to me that it is within the ordinary course to do it.[339]

While informer privilege may have initially been recognized as existing only in criminal prosecutions, the Supreme Court of Canada has recently held it to be available in both criminal and civil proceedings.[340]

R. v. LEIPERT
[1997] 1 S.C.R. 281, 4 C.R. (5th) 259, 112 C.C.C. (3d) 385

The police received a Crime Stoppers tip that the accused was growing marihuana in his basement. The police walked the street outside the residence with a sniffer dog on four occasions and each time the dog indicated the presence of drugs. On one occasion a police officer smelt marihuana coming from the accused's house. He also observed that the basement windows were covered

---

337 R.S.O. 1990, c. E.23.
338 [1986] 2 S.C.R. 637.
339 (1794), 24 Howell's State Trials 199.
340 *Sol. Gen. Can. v. Royal Commn. Re Health Records*, (1982) 62 C.C.C. (2d) 173 (S.C.C.).

and one window was barred shut. The officer obtained a search warrant on the basis of the observations. The information to obtain the search warrant also disclosed that the officer had received a Crime Stoppers tip. The search warrant was executed and the accused was charged with cultivation of marihuana and possession of marihuana for the purpose of trafficking. At trial the accused obtained an order for disclosure of the document reporting the Crime Stoppers tip. The Crown had refused disclosure on the ground of informer privilege. The trial judge had attempted to edit out all references to the identity of the informer. The Crown asked to rely on the warrant without reference to the tip. The trial judge refused that request because the accused did not consent. The Crown ceased to tender evidence and the accused was acquitted. The British Columbia Court of Appeal quashed the acquittal and ordered a new trial. The accused appealed. The appeal was dismissed.

McLACHLIN J. (LAMER C.J.C., LA FOREST, SOPINKA, GONTHIER, CORY, IACOBUCCI and MAJOR JJ. concurring):—

. . . .

The trial judge was faced with two apparently conflicting rules. The first was the rule requiring disclosure to the defence of all information not clearly irrelevant or privileged. The second was the rule of informer privilege. The trial judge attempted to accommodate both rules by editing the tip sheet to remove information that could reveal the tipster's identity and ordering production of the balance of the tip sheet. I share the view of McEachern C.J.B.C. in the Court of Appeal that the trial judge's approach gave insufficient weight to both the importance of maintaining informer privilege and the danger of ordering disclosure of tip sheets containing details which, despite editing, may enable an accused person to identify the informant.

(a) The Importance of Informer Privilege

A court considering this issue must begin from the proposition that informer privilege is an ancient and hallowed protection which plays a vital role in law enforcement. It is premised on the duty of all citizens to aid in enforcing the law. The discharge of this duty carries with it the risk of retribution from those involved in crime. The rule of informer privilege was developed to protect citizens who assist in law enforcement and to encourage others to do the same. As Cory J.A. (as he then was) stated in *R. v. Hunter* (1987), 57 C.R. (3d) 1 (Ont. C.A.), at pp. 5-6:

> The rule against the non-disclosure of information which might identify an informer is one of long standing. It developed from an acceptance of the importance of the role of informers in the solution of crimes and the apprehension of criminals. It was recognized that citizens have a duty to divulge to the police any information that they may have pertaining to the commission of a crime. It was also obvious to the courts from very early times that the identity of an informer would have to be concealed, both for his or her own protection and to encourage others to divulge to the authorities any information pertaining to crimes. It was in order to achieve these goals that the rule was developed.

The rule is of fundamental importance to the workings of a criminal justice system. As described in *Bisaillon v. Keable*, [1983] 2 S.C.R. 60, at p. 105:

> The rule gives a peace officer the power to promise his informers secrecy expressly or by implication, with a guarantee sanctioned by the law that this promise will be kept even in court, and to receive in exchange for this promise information without which it would be extremely difficult for him to carry out his duties and ensure that the criminal law is obeyed.

In *R. v. Scott*, [1990] 3 S.C.R. 979, at p. 994, Cory J. stressed the heightened importance of the rule in the context of drug investigations:

> The value of informers to police investigations has long been recognized. As long as crimes have been committed, certainly as long as they have been prosecuted, informers have played an important role in their investigation. It may well be true that some informers act for compensation or for self-serving purposes. Whatever their motives, the position of informers is always precarious and their role is fraught with danger. The role of informers in drug-related cases is particularly important and dangerous. Informers often provide the only means for the police to gain some knowledge of the workings of the drug trafficking operations and networks. . . . The investigation often will be based upon a relationship of trust between the police officer and the informer, something that may take a long time to establish. The safety, indeed the lives, not only of informers but also of the undercover police officers will depend on that relationship of trust.

In most cases, the identity of the informer is known to the police. However, in cases like the instant one, the identity of the informer is unknown to everyone including the Crime Stoppers' agent who received the call. The importance of the informer privilege rule in cases where the identity of the informer is anonymous was stressed by the California Court of Appeal in *People v. Callen*, 194 Cal.App.3d 558 (1987). The court, in holding that the police have no duty to determine or disclose the identity of anonymous informers, stated at p. 587:

> Such an investigatory burden would not only be onerous and frequently futile, it would destroy programs such as Crimestoppers by removing the guarantee of anonymity. Anonymity is the key to such a program. It is the promise of anonymity which allays the fear of criminal retaliation which otherwise discourages citizen involvement in reporting crime. In turn, by guaranteeing anonymity, Crimestoppers provides law enforcement with information it might never otherwise obtain. We are satisfied the benefits of a Crimestoppers-type program — citizen involvement in reporting crime and criminals — far outweigh any speculative benefits to the defense arising from imposing a duty on law enforcement to gather and preserve evidence of the identity of informants who wish to remain anonymous.

Informer privilege is of such importance that once found, courts are not entitled to balance the benefit enuring from the privilege against countervailing considerations, as is the case, for example, with Crown privilege or privileges based on Wigmore's four-part test: J. Sopinka, S.N. Lederman and A.W. Bryant, *The Law of Evidence in Canada* (1992), at pp. 805-6. In *Bisaillon v. Keable*, supra, this Court contrasted informer privilege with Crown privilege in this regard. In Crown privilege, the judge may review the information and in the last resort revise the minister's decisions by weighing the two conflicting interests, that of maintaining secrecy and that of doing justice. The Court stated at pp. 97-98:

> This procedure, designed to implement Crown privilege, is pointless in the case of secrecy regarding a police informer. In this case, the law gives the Minister, and the Court after him, no power of weighing or evaluating various aspects of the public interest which are in conflict, since it has already resolved the conflict itself. It has decided once and for all, subject to the law being changed, that information regarding police informers' identity will be, because of its content, a class of information which it is in the public interest to keep secret, and that this interest will prevail over the need to ensure the highest possible standard of justice. Accordingly, the common law has made secrecy regarding police informers subject to a special system with its own rules, which differ from those applicable to Crown privilege.

The Court in *Bisaillon v. Keable* summed the matter up by asserting that the application of informer privilege "does not depend on the judge's discretion, as it is a legal rule of public order by which the judge is bound". In summary, informer privilege is of such importance that it cannot be balanced against other interests. Once established, neither the police nor the court possesses discretion to abridge it.

(b) Who May Claim Informer Privilege?

The privilege belongs to the Crown: *Canada (Solicitor General) v. Royal Commission (Health Records)*, [1981] 2 S.C.R. 494. However, the Crown cannot, without the informer's consent, waive the privilege either expressly or by implication by not raising it: *Bisaillon v. Keable*, supra, at p. 94. In that sense, it also belongs to the informer. This follows from the purpose of the privilege, being the protection of those who provide information to the police and the encouragement of others to do the same. This is the second reason why the police and courts do not have a discretion to relieve against the privilege.

The fact that the privilege also belongs to the informer raises special concerns in the case of anonymous informants, like those who provide telephone tips to Crime Stoppers. Since the informer whom the privilege is designed to protect and his or her circumstances are unknown, it is often difficult to predict with certainty what information might allow the accused to identify the informer. A detail as innocuous as the time of the telephone call may be sufficient to permit identification. In such circumstances, courts must exercise great care not to unwittingly deprive informers of the privilege which the law accords to them.

(c) The Scope of Informer Privilege

Connected as it is to the essential effectiveness of the criminal law, informer privilege is broad in scope. While developed in criminal proceedings, it applies in civil proceedings as well: *Bisaillon v. Keable*, supra. It applies to a witness on the stand. Such a person cannot be compelled to state whether he or she is a police informer: *Bisaillon v. Keable*, supra. And it applies to the undisclosed informant, the person who although never called as a witness, supplies information to the police. Subject only to the "innocence at stake" exception, the Crown and the court are bound not to reveal the undisclosed informant's identity.

Informer privilege prevents not only disclosure of the name of the informant, but of any information which might implicitly reveal his or her identity. Courts have acknowledged that the smallest details may be sufficient to reveal identity.

McEachern C.J.B.C. in the case at bar suggested that an "accused may know that only some very small circle of persons, perhaps only one, may know an apparently innocuous fact that is mentioned in the document". He noted: "The privilege is a hallowed one, and it should be respected scrupulously".

The jurisprudence therefore suggests that the Crown must claim privilege over information that reveals the identity of the informant or that may implicitly reveal identity. In many cases, the Crown will be able to contact the informer to determine the extent of information that can be released without jeopardizing the anonymity of the tipster. The informer is the only person who knows the potential danger of releasing those facts to the accused. The difficulty in this case is that the identity of the informer is unknown. Therefore, the Crown is not in a position to determine whether any part of the information could reveal his or her identity. This led the Crown in the case at bar to claim privilege for all of the information provided by the informer. The extension of privilege to all information that could identify an informant justifies this claim in the case of an anonymous informant.

(d) The "Innocence at Stake" Exception

Informer privilege is subject only to one exception, known as the "innocence at stake" exception. Lord Esher, M.R., described this exception in *Marks v. Beyfus* (1890), 25 Q.B.D. 494 (C.A.), at p. 498:

> If upon the trial of a prisoner the judge should be of opinion that the disclosure of the name of the informant is necessary or right in order to shew the prisoner's innocence, then one public policy is in conflict with another public policy, and that which says that an innocent man is not to be condemned when his innocence can be proved is the policy which must prevail.

In *Bisaillon v. Keable*, supra, this Court held (at p. 93):

> The rule is subject to only one exception, imposed by the need to demonstrate the innocence of an accused person.

As Cory J. stated in *Scott*, supra, at pp. 995-96:

> In our system the right of an individual accused to establish his or her innocence by raising a reasonable doubt as to guilt has always remained paramount.

In order to raise the "innocence at stake" exception to informer privilege, there must be a basis on the evidence for concluding that disclosure of the informer's identity is necessary to demonstrate the innocence of the accused: *R. v. Chiarantano*, [1990] O.J. No. 2603 (C.A.), per Brooke J.A., aff'd [1991] 1 S.C.R. 906. In *Chiarantano*, supra, the possibility that the information provided by the informer regarding the arrival at a residence of drugs later found in the possession of the accused might conflict with the evidence of the accused was held not to raise a basis for disclosure pursuant to the "innocence at stake" exception. The court held that the usefulness of the information was speculative and that mere speculation that the information might assist the defence is insufficient. If speculation sufficed to remove the privilege, little if anything would be left of the protection which the privilege purports to accord.

On the other hand, circumstances may arise where the evidence establishes a basis for the exception, as where the informer is a material witness to the crime or acted as an agent provocateur: see *Scott*, supra. Where such a basis is established, the privilege must yield to the principle that a person is not to be condemned when his or her innocence can be proved.

(e) Informer Privilege and the Charter

It has been suggested (although not by the appellant) that the Canadian Charter of Rights and Freedoms, as interpreted in *Stinchcombe*, supra, has introduced another exception to the informer privilege rule based on the right to full disclosure of documents in the Crown's possession in aid of the Charter guarantee of the right to make full answer and defence: D.M. Tanovich "When Does *Stinchcombe* Demand that the Crown Reveal the Identity of a Police Informer?" (1995), 38 C.R. (4th) 202. According to this argument, "innocence at stake" would no longer be the only exception to the informer privilege rule.

This argument rests on a right to disclosure broader than any which this Court has enunciated. In *Stinchcombe*, supra, the right to disclosure of Crown documents was expressly made subject to two conditions: relevance (to be interpreted generously as including all that is not clearly irrelevant) and privilege. The right to disclosure was not to trump privilege. Any doubt about its application to informer privilege was expressly negated:

> It is suggested that disclosure may put at risk the security and safety of persons who have provided the prosecution with information. No doubt measures must occasionally be taken to protect the identity of witnesses and informers. Protection of the identity of informers is covered by the rules relating to informer privilege and exceptions thereto.

. . . .

I find no inconsistency between the Charter right to disclosure of Crown documents affirmed in *Stinchcombe*, supra, and the common law rule of informer privilege.

(f) Informer Privilege and Challenges to Search Warrants

Where the accused seeks to establish that a search warrant was not supported by reasonable grounds, the accused may be entitled to information which may reveal the identity of an informer notwithstanding informer privilege "in circumstances where it is absolutely essential": *Scott*, supra, at p. 996. "Essential" circumstances exist where the accused establishes the "innocence at stake" exception to informer privilege. Such a case might arise, for example, where there is evidence suggesting that the goods seized in execution of the warrant were planted. To establish that the informer planted the goods or had information as to how they came to be planted, the accused might properly seek disclosure of information that may incidentally reveal the identity of the informer.

Absent a basis for concluding that disclosure of the information that may reveal the identity of the informer is necessary to establish the innocence of the accused, the information remains privileged and cannot be produced, whether on a hearing into the reasonableness of the search or on the trial proper.

(g) Judicial Editing

The ultimate issue on this appeal is whether the trial judge erred in editing the tip sheet to remove references to the informer's identity and in ordering the edited sheet disclosed to the appellant. In addressing this question, I have regard to the following propositions, discussed above. Informer privilege is of great importance. Once established, the privilege cannot be diminished by or "balanced off against" other concerns relating to the administration of justice. The police and the court have no discretion to diminish it and are bound to uphold it. The only exception to the privilege is found where there is a basis to conclude that the information may be necessary to establish the innocence of the accused. The scope of the rule extends not only to the name of the informer, but to any details which might reveal the informer's identity. It is virtually impossible for the court to know what details may reveal the identity of an anonymous informer. The same considerations apply on challenges to search warrants or wiretap authorizations.

These considerations suggest that anonymous tip sheets should not be edited with a view to disclosing them to the defence unless the accused can bring himself within the innocence at stake exception. To do so runs the risk that the court will deprive the informer of the privilege which belongs to him or her absolutely, subject only to the "innocence at stake" exception. It also undermines the efficacy of programs such as Crimestoppers, which depend on guarantees of anonymity to those who volunteer information on crimes.

. . . .

There may be cases where the informer and his circumstances are known, in which the court can be certain that what remains of an informant document after editing will not reveal the informer's identity. When, however, as in the case at bar, it is impossible to determine which details of the information provided by an informer will or will not result in that person's identity being revealed, then none of those details should be disclosed, unless there is a basis to conclude that the innocence at stake exception applies.

(h) Procedure

When an accused seeks disclosure of privileged informer information on the basis of the "innocence at stake" exception, the following procedure will apply. First, the accused must show some basis to conclude that without the disclosure sought his or her innocence is at stake. If such a basis is shown, the court may then review the information to determine whether, in fact, the information is necessary to prove the accused's innocence. If the court concludes that disclosure is necessary, the court should only reveal as much information as is essential to allow proof of innocence. Before disclosing the information to the accused, the

Crown should be given the option of staying the proceedings. If the Crown chooses to proceed, disclosure of the information essential to establish innocence may be provided to the accused.

(i) Application to the Case at Bar

The identity of the anonymous informer was protected by informer privilege. The police and the courts were bound to protect the identity of the informant from disclosure. Given the anonymous nature of the tip, it was impossible to conclude whether the disclosure of details remaining after editing might be sufficient to reveal the identity of the informer to the accused and others who might have been involved in this crime and seeking retribution. It follows that the statement should not have been edited and ordered disclosed to the defence. The informer's privilege required nothing short of total confidentiality. As it was not established that the identity was necessary to establish the innocence of the accused, the privilege continued in place.

. . . .

B. Did the Trial Judge Err in Declining to Allow the Crown to Delete the Reference the Informer from the Material in Support of the Warrant?

The trial judge declined to permit the Crown to withdraw the reference to the tip from the "Information to Obtain" and defend the warrant without reference to it. In his view, this could not be done unless the appellant consented. In my view, this was an error.

The issue before the trial judge was whether there were reasonable grounds for the issuance of the warrant. If the Crown wished to limit its defence of the reasonableness of the warrant and subsequent search to particular grounds, it was entitled to do so. At the end of the day, the task of the judge was to make a ruling on reasonableness on the basis of the information relied on by the Crown.

In the case at bar, the appellant has not brought himself within the "innocence at stake" exception. Therefore, the trial judge should have permitted the Crown to defend the warrant on the material in the "Information to Obtain" with the reference to the Crime Stoppers' tip deleted.[341]

NAMED PERSON v. VANCOUVER SUN
[2007] 3 S.C.R. 252

During his extradition proceedings, the appellant Named Person was granted an *in camera* hearing where he informed the judge that he was a confidential informer. He advised the Court that he wished to bring a stay application alleging that his Charter rights were violated. The judge asked for submissions on whether the proceedings should remain closed and sought the assistance of an *amicus*

---

341 For an application of the strict McLure "innocence at stake" exception to the context of police informers, see *R. v. Deol* (2006), 37 C.R. (6th) 335, 208 C.C.C. (3d) 167 (Man. C.A.).

curiae. A number of media outlets attended. They requested an order to review the documents prepared by *amicus curiae* upon an undertaking of non-disclosure. The application was granted. The Named Person and the Attorney General appealed to the Supreme Court.

BASTARACHE J. (for the majority):

. . . .

III. Analysis

15 At stake here are two important principles which seem fundamentally opposed. The principle of informer privilege provides an all but absolute bar against revealing any information which might tend to identify a confidential informer. The open court principle, on the other hand, provides that information which is before a court ought to be public information to the extent possible. How are these two principles to be reconciled? In order to answer this question, I will examine each of them in turn. The result of this exercise will be a model procedure to guide judges in similar situations.

A. Informer Privilege

16 Police work, and the criminal justice system as a whole, depend to some degree on the work of confidential informers. The law has therefore long recognized that those who choose to act as confidential informers must be protected from the possibility of retribution. The law's protection has been provided in the form of the informer privilege rule, which protects from revelation in public or in court the identity of those who give information related to criminal matters in confidence. This protection in turn encourages cooperation with the criminal justice system for future potential informers.

. . .

21 Thus a court does not have any discretion with regard to the privilege; a court is under a duty to protect the informer's identity. Indeed, the duty of a court not to breach the privilege is of the same nature as the duty of the police or the Crown.

22 It deserves emphasizing here that the rationale for the privilege's existence is not something that allows for weighing on a case-by-case basis the maintenance or scope of the privilege depending on what risks the informer might face. Informer privilege is a class privilege that always applies when it has been established that a confidential informer is present.

23 Once it has been established that the privilege exists, the court is bound to apply the rule. It is the non-discretionary nature of the informer privilege rule which explains that the rule is referred to as "absolute": see R. W. Hubbard, S. Magotiaux and S. M. Duncan, *The Law of Privilege in Canada* (loose-leaf), at p. 2-7. The Crown has a similar obligation: the privilege is "owned" by both the Crown and the informer himself, so the Crown has no right to disclose the informer's identity: *Leipert*, at para. 15.

24 This is a highly exceptional case. Usually, the informer is not a party to the proceedings, nor is he or she going to be a witness. The Crown will not be presenting his or her evidence. The confidential information is used by the police in its investigation, leading to evidence that will be presented in the usual way. The question of informer privilege is more likely to arise indirectly at trial, as when counsel seeks to cross-examine a Crown witness on whether he or she is or has been a confidential informer, or when a police officer is questioned on what led him or her to take a certain step and the officer invokes the informer privilege. Where such an informer reveals his or her identity, this would normally signify that he or she desires to waive the privilege. This could not have been the case in the present context however. Here, the Named Person came forth for the very purpose of enforcing the confidential informer agreement. The Extradition Judge was wrong in finding that the Named Person compromised the privilege by revealing his status. The Extradition Judge's decision on waiver is possibly due to the unusual circumstances of this case and the absence of clear precedent to provide guidance.

25 Moreover, the informer himself or herself cannot unilaterally decide to "waive" the privilege. The authors of *The Law of Evidence in Canada* write, at p. 883, that "[t]he privilege belongs to both the Crown and the informer and thus the informer alone cannot 'waive' the privilege and neither can a party to a civil proceeding": J. Sopinka, S. N. Lederman and A.W. Bryant, *The Law of Evidence in Canada* (2nd ed. 1999) (emphasis in original). Courts in the United Kingdom have found that a court may refuse to disclose an informer's identity even if he or she has explicitly requested disclosure: see *Powell v. Chief Constable of North Wales Constabulary*, [1999] E.W.J. 6844 (QL) (C.A.), and *Savage v. Chief Constable of Hampshire*, [1997] 1 W.L.R. 1061 (C.A.).

26 In addition to its absolute non-discretionary nature, the rule is extremely broad in its application. The rule applies to the identity of every informer: it applies when the informer is not present, where the informer is present, and even where the informer himself or herself is a witness. It applies to both documentary evidence and oral testimony: Sopinka, Lederman and Bryant, at pp. 882-83. It applies in criminal and civil trials. The duty imposed to keep an informer's identity confidential applies to the police, to the Crown, to attorneys and to judges: Hubbard, Magotiaux and Duncan, at p. 2-2. The rule's protection is also broad in its coverage. Any information which might tend to identify an informer is protected by the privilege. Thus the protection is not limited simply to the informer's name, but extends to any information that might lead to identification.

27 The informer privilege rule admits but one exception: it can be abridged if necessary to establish innocence in a criminal trial (there are no exceptions to the rule in civil proceedings). According to the innocence at stake exception, "there must be a basis on the evidence for concluding that disclosure of the informer's identity is necessary to demonstrate the innocence of the accused": *Leipert*, at para. 21. It stands to be emphasized that the exception will apply only if there is an evidentiary basis for the conclusion; mere speculation will not suffice: Sopinka,

Lederman and Bryant, at p. 884. The exception applies only where disclosure of the informer's identity is the only way that the accused can establish innocence: *R. v. Brown*, [2002] 2 S.C.R. 185, 2002 SCC 32, at para. 4.

. . .

29 For the sake of clarity, it is useful to pause here to explain the law regarding what were argued before us as some "other" exceptions to the informer privilege rule. As already noted, the only real exception to the informer privilege rule is the innocence at stake exception: *Leipert*. All other purported exceptions to the rule are either applications of the innocence at stake exception or else examples of situations in which the privilege does not actually apply. For example, situations in which the informer is a material witness to a crime fall within the innocence at stake exception: *R. v. Scott*, [1990] 3 S.C.R. 979, at p. 996. The privilege does not apply to an individual whose role extends beyond that of an informer to being an agent provocateur: *R. v. Davies* (1982), 1 C.C.C. (3d) 299 (Ont. C.A.); Hubbard, Magotiaux and Duncan, at p. 2-28. Similarly, situations in which s. 8 of the Charter is invoked to argue that a search was not undertaken on reasonable grounds may fall within the innocence at stake exception: Scott. Thus, as I noted, the only time that the privilege, once found, can be breached, is in the case of an accused raising the innocence at stake exception. All other so-called exceptions are simply applications of this one true exception: *Scott*, at p. 996; D. M. Paciocco and L. Stuesser, *The Law of Evidence* (4th ed. 2005), at p. 254.

30 In conclusion, the general rationale for the informer privilege rule requires a privilege which is extremely broad and powerful. Once a trial judge is satisfied that the privilege exists, a complete and total bar on any disclosure of the informer's identity applies. Outside the innocence at stake exception, the rule's protection is absolute. No case-by-case weighing of the justification for the privilege is permitted. All information which might tend to identify the informer is protected by the privilege, and neither the Crown nor the court has any discretion to disclose this information in any proceeding, at any time.

[The Court then reviewed the importance of the open court principle.]

C. Secrecy and Openness

38 What is being argued in this case is that the informer privilege rule is discretionary, and that judges have the power to determine, on a case-by-case basis, whether the courtroom should be closed to protect informer privilege.

39 This proposition cannot be accepted. The informer privilege rule is mandatory (subject only to the "innocence at stake" exception). To permit trial judges wide discretion in determining whether to protect informer privilege would undermine the purposes of the rule. Part of the rationale for a mandatory informer privilege rule is that it encourages would-be informers to come forward and report on crimes, safe in the knowledge that their identity will be protected. A rule that gave trial judges the power to decide on an ad hoc basis whether to protect informer privilege would create a significant disincentive for would-be informers to come

forward, thereby eviscerating the usefulness of informer privilege and dealing a great blow to police investigations.

40 Although a judge has no discretion not to apply the informer privilege rule, to ensure that the open court principle is respected, we must ensure that it retains the maximum effect possible by requiring that the informer privilege cover only that information which would in fact tend to reveal an informer's identity; all other information regarding the proceeding would continue to be information which should be published under the open court principle. It is clear therefore that an informer need simply indicate that it is necessary to proceed in camera. No reasons need be given at this point because the basis of the informer status is the very issue to be examined in camera at the first stage, i.e. at the stage where the privilege is to be found to be present.

41 In more practical terms, this will mean that a trial judge must have the authority to hold an entire proceeding in camera if informer privilege is found to be present; however, an entirely *in camera* proceeding should be seen as a last resort. A judge ought to make every effort to ensure that as much information as possible is made public, and that disclosure and publication are restricted only for that information which might tend to reveal the informer's identity.

. . .

D. The Procedure to Be Followed

[The Court set out the proper procedure to be followed where a claim of informer privilege is made. There should be a "first stage" hearing *in camera* to determine whether the privilege exists. Only the informant and Crown should appear. The judge determines, on a balance of probabilities, whether the individual concerned is a confidential informant. If such a determination is made, the privilege applies fully. *Amicus* may be appointed where the judge needs assistance in determining whether the facts establish that the person is an informant. A second hearing will occur where the judge will hear submissions from all interested parties on how the proceedings should occur in order to ensure openness and protection of the informant's identity.]

IV. Application to the Case at Bar

[The Court held that the trial judge had erred in following the procedure that he did. He should not have appointed an *amicus curiae* for the purpose of assisting him in determining the scope of the privilege or alerted the media. He should also have not provided privileged materials to the media or their counsel to make submissions.]

Appeal allowed. Order of the Extradition Judge set aside.

The issue of procedure was also addressed by the Supreme Court in *R. v. Basi*[342] where the Court held, in the context of an application for disclosure, that the trial judge had erred in allowing defence counsel to be present during the *in*

---

342 2009 SCC 52 (S.C.C.).

camera hearing even where counsel gave an undertaking of non-disclosure and confidentiality. *Basi* thus established an *ex parte* requirement for the first stage *in camera* hearing in cases where the identity of the informant cannot be otherwise protected. The Court further held that a trial judge should make all reasonable efforts to ensure that defence counsel can make meaningful submissions regarding what occurs in their absence including proposing questions to be put to the informant by the court.

Should individuals who allow the police to use their homes as location posts for surveillance be entitled to the same protection as police informers?[343]

3. CASE-BY-CASE PRIVILEGE

Wigmore recognized that to suppress relevant evidence and so inhibit the search for truth required a public interest weightier than the public's general right to everyman's evidence. He suggested then four conditions as necessary to the establishment of a privilege for confidential communications:

(1) The communications must originate in a *confidence* that they will not be disclosed.
(2) This element of *confidentiality must be essential* to the full and satisfactory maintenance of the relation between the parties.
(3) The *relation* must be one which in the opinion of the community ought to be sedulously *fostered*.
(4) The *injury* that would inure to the relation by the disclosure of the communications must be *greater than the benefit* thereby gained for the correct disposal of litigation.

Only if these four conditions are present should a privilege be recognized.[344]

In *Slavutych v. Baker* [345] the appellant appealed against his dismissal as a university professor. Slavutych had been asked for a confidential report on a colleague's suitability for tenure and this report was used against Slavutych to justify his dismissal; the actual charge against Slavutych was that he had in his report, made a "very serious charge on the flimsiest basis." A board of arbitration upheld the dismissal. The Supreme Court of Canada quashed the award of the arbitration board on the substantive law basis that a party who obtains information in confidence shall not be allowed to use it as a springboard for an action against the person who made the confidential communication. It was not necessary then for the court to consider the admissibility of the document as an evidentiary matter but, speaking for a unanimous court, Spence, J. measured the communication against Wigmore's criteria and concluded:

---

343 Compare *R. v. Lam* (2000), 148 C.C.C. (3d) 379 (B.C. C.A.) with *R. v. Thomas* (1998), 124 C.C.C. (3d) 178 (Ont. Gen. Div.). See also *R. v. Richards* (1997), 115 C.C.C. (3d) 377 (Ont. C.A.); *R. v. Meuckon* (1990), 57 C.C.C. (3d) 193 (B.C. C.A.) and R.W. Hubbard et. al., "Informer and Police Investigatory Privilege At The Preliminary Inquiry" (1999), 41 Crim. L.Q. 68 on the issue of privilege and police investigatory techniques.
344 8 Wigmore, *Evidence* (McNaughton Rev.), s. 2285.
345 (1975), 55 D.L.R. (3d) 224 (S.C.C.).

. . . considering this matter only an evidentiary one and under the doctrine of privilege as so ably considered in Wigmore the confidential document should have been ruled inadmissible.[346]

The court's lead, adopting Wigmore's criteria as a guide for the recognition of future privileged communications, has since been followed in a number of cases[347] as the courts seemingly agree with the observation of Laskin, C.J.C.:

What *Slavutych v. Baker* established is that the categories of privilege are not closed.[348]

———————

For a consideration of the *Slavutych* criteria see *R. v. Delong*.[349] The accused was charged with assaulting police. The question was whether the trial judge should have ordered production of statements given to police complaints investigators for use in the defence of the accused. The statements were those previously given by Crown witnesses to investigators on a complaint made by the accused to the Complaint Investigation Bureau of the Peel Regional Police, arising out of the same circumstances. The court decided that it was doubtful whether there was true confidentiality established by the informal understanding with the police association. Nor was the relationship one which needed to be "sedulously fostered." Finally, the court decided that it was not satisfied that under condition 4, the "injury" that would result to the relationship between the police officers and the Complaint Bureau had a social value that would outweigh the public interest in favour of the accused facing a serious criminal charge, of having the right to disclosure to enable him to make full answer and defence. The court

———————

346 *Ibid.*, at p. 229. In *Re Inquiry into the Confidentiality of Health Records in Ontario* (1979), 98 D.L.R. (3d) 704, 719 (Ont. C.A.), Dubin, J.A. echoed Spence, J.'s opinion and wrote: "The conditions set forth in that text are, in my opinion, the best test to date to determine whether the privilege contended for exists." On appeal to the Supreme Court of Canada, Laskin, C.J.C. wrote: "What *Slavutych v. Baker* . . . established is that the categories of privilege are not closed. . . . This Court, speaking through Spence J. in the *Slavutych* case, was of the opinion that the fourfold test propounded in 8 Wigmore *Evidence*, §2285, p. 527 provided a satisfactory guide for the recognition of a claim of privilege": (1981), 62 C.C.C. (2d) 193, 207 (S.C.C.).

347 See, *e.g.*, *Jones v. Crompton*, [1977] 4 W.W.R. 440 (B.C. S.C.), diary not prepared in a confidence not privileged; *Bergwitz v. Fast* (1979), 97 D.L.R. (3d) 65 (B.C. S.C.); reversed (1980), 108 D.L.R. (3d) 732 (B.C. C.A.), report by investigating committee of College of Dental Surgeons not privileged as "the injury that 'would enure to the relation by the disclosure' of the views of the investigating committee would not be 'greater than the benefit thereby gained for the correct disposal of litigation' "; *Smith v. Royal Columbian Hosp.* (1981), 123 D.L.R. (3d) 723 (B.C. S.C.), report of Credentials Committee privileged as all four criteria satisfied; *R. v. Littlechild* (1979), 108 D.L.R. (3d) 340 (Alta. C.A.), communication with official on legal aid application privileged as all four conditions satisfied; *Re Univ. of Guelph & C.A.U.T.* (1980), 112 D.L.R. (3d) 692 (Ont. H.C.), communications with university promotion and tenure committee privileged as all four conditions satisfied.

348 *Sol. Gen. Can. v. Royal Commn. Re Health Records, supra*, note 340, at p. 207. Compare Lord Hailsham in *D. v. N.S.P.C.C.*, [1978] A.C. 171, 230 (H.L.): "The categories of public interest are not closed, and must alter from time to time whether by restriction or extension as social conditions and social legislation develop."

349 (1989), 69 C.R. (3d) 147 (Ont. C.A.).

decided that the statements should have been produced and allowed the accused's appeal.

In *R. v. National Post*,[350] Justice Benotto applied the *Slavutych* test in the context of the relationship between a journalist and her source and concluded that the identity of the source was privileged where it was given pursuant to a promise of confidentiality. That decision was reversed by the Ontario Court of Appeal[351] on the basis that the source was needed to get at the truth of an allegation of forgery. The appeal is currently before the Supreme Court.

4. BALANCING CHARTER VALUES

The constitutional right to full disclosure has proved particularly controversial where relied upon by defence counsel to gain access to medical records of sexual assault complainants. The matter reached the Supreme Court in *O'Connor*[352] and *A. (L.L.) v. B. (A.)*.[353] The court in *O'Connor* announced a special procedure respecting discovery of medical records in the possession of third parties. The decision represents a fundamental broadening of the *Stinchcombe* right to disclosure of material in the Crown's possession or control to a right to discovery.

Through the judgment of Madam Justice L'Heureux-Dubé in *A. (L.L.) v. B. (A.)*, the court unanimously decided that production should not be determined by class or case-by-case privilege. According to L'Heureux-Dubé J., the creation of a class privilege in favour of private records in criminal law raised concerns relating to

(1) the truth-finding process of our adversarial trial procedure;
(2) the possible relevance of some private records;
(3) the accused's right to make full answer and defence;
(4) the categories of actors included in a class privilege; and
(5) the experience of other countries.

Carefully examining case law dealing with privilege and confidential information, including that relating to police informants, solicitor-client privilege and public interest immunity, she points out that the courts have consistently ordered production where necessary to establish innocence. While there was ground to recognize a case-by-case privilege along Wigmore lines for private records in some instances, such exceptions to the general evidentiary rule of admissibility and disclosure "should not be encouraged". The better approach was one of balancing competing Charter rights. L'Heureux-Dubé J. with La Forest, Gonthier and McLachlin JJ. concurring, saw the need to balance the accused's right to a fair trial and full answer and defence with the complainant's rights to privacy and to equality without discrimination. The majority through a joint judgment by Lamer C.J. and Sopinka J. with Cory, Iacobucci and Major JJ. concurring, determined that the accused's right to full answer and defence should be balanced against the complainant's rights to privacy under sections 7 and 8. However the majority, in not referring to a section 15 equality right for complainants, although it was fully argued, implicitly reject it.

---

350 19 C.R. (6th) 393, [2004] O.J. No. 178, 2004 CarswellOnt 173 (S.C.J.).
351 (2008) 56 C.R. (6th) 163 (Ont. C.A.).
352 (1996), 44 C.R. (4th) 1
353 (1996), 44 C.R. (4th) 91.

The court agreed that there should be a two-stage procedure but divided 5-4 as to the precise tests. For the majority Lamer C.J. and Sopinka J. decided that when the defence seeks information in the hands of a third party the onus should be on the accused to satisfy a judge that the information is likely to be relevant. In the context of disclosure, the meaning of relevance was whether the information might be useful to the defence. In the context of production, the test of relevance should be higher: the presiding judge must be satisfied that there is a reasonable possibility that the information is logically probative to an issue at trial or the competence of a witness to testify. While likely relevance was the appropriate threshold for the first stage of the two-step procedure, the majority determined that it should not be interpreted as an onerous burden upon the accused. A relevance threshold, at this stage, was simply a requirement to prevent the defence from engaging in speculative, fanciful, disruptive, unmeritorious, obstructive and time-consuming requests for production. The crux of the *O'Connor* regime is the determination by the majority that the first stage of establishing likely relevance had to be a low threshold as the accused might often be in a catch-22 situation where he was disadvantaged by arguing relevance of a document he had not seen. The majority in *O'Connor* disagreed with L'Heureux-Dubé J.'s position that such records would only be relevant in rare cases. They gave as examples of possible relevance records which may contain information about the unfolding of the complaint, the use of therapy to influence memory and information bearing on credibility. L'Heureux-Dubé J. thought the Charter mandated less, but she did not carry the day. Upon their production to the court, the judge should examine the records to determine whether, and to what extent, they should be produced to the accused. In making that determination, the judge must examine and weigh the salutary and deleterious effects of a production order and determine whether a non-production order would constitute a reasonable limit on the ability of the accused to make full answer and defence.

For the minority, L'Heureux-Dubé J. saw the first stage burden on an accused to demonstrate likely relevance as significant and, if it could not be met, the application for production should be dismissed as amounting to no more than a fishing expedition. The mere fact that the complainant had received treatment or counselling could not be presumed to be relevant to the trial as therapy generally focuses on emotional and psychological responses rather than being oriented to ascertaining historical truth.

There was a further difference of opinion as to the criteria at the production stage. Lamer C.J. and Sopinka J., for the majority, agreed with L'Heureux-Dubé J. that the following factors should be considered:

(1) the extent to which the record is necessary for the accused to make full answer and defence;
(2) the probative value of the record in question;
(3) the nature and extent of the reasonable expectation of privacy vested in that record;
(4) whether production of the record would be premised upon any discriminatory belief or bias; and
(5) the potential prejudice to the complainant's dignity, privacy or security of the person that would be occasioned by production of the record in question.

However, the majority departed from L'Heureux-Dubé J.'s further view that it was also necessary to balance two other factors:

(1) the extent to which production of records of this nature would frustrate society's interest in encouraging the reporting of sexual offences, and

(2) the acquisition of treatment by victims [and] the effect on the integrity of the trial process of producing, or failing to produce, the record, having in mind the need to maintain consideration in the outcome.

According to the majority the second factor was more appropriately dealt with at the admissibility stage and not in deciding whether the information should be produced. As for society's interest in the reporting of sexual crimes, the majority pointed to other avenues available to the judge to ensure that production does not frustrate the societal interests, such as publication bans and barring spectators.

The majority decided that quite different considerations should apply where records were in the possession of the Crown. In such cases the complainant's privacy interests in medical records would not have to be balanced. The Crown's disclosure obligations established in *Stinchcombe* were not to be affected. Concerns relating to privacy or privilege disappeared when the documents were in the Crown' s possession. If the records were in the possession of the Crown their relevance was to be presumed. It was unfair in the adversarial process for the Crown to have knowledge that was not shared with the accused. When the records had been shared with the Crown, an agent of the state, the records had become the property of the public to be used to ensure that justice was done. In deciding whether the complainant had waived any potential claim of privilege the waiver would have to be informed. There was to be an onus on the Crown to inform the complainant of the potential for disclosure. Any form of privilege would in any event have to yield where such a privilege precluded the accused's right to full answer and defence.

The majority opinion that privacy issues disappear where the medical records are in the possession of the Crown is utterly unconvincing and has been strongly criticized. Heather Holmes puts the problem well:

> This reasoning appears to assume a formal investigative dialogue by which relevant information is requested by the police or Crown and either provided or refused by the witness, with full opportunity for discussion of legal consequences. It cannot have been intended to apply to the hurly-burly of ordinary existence. A wide variety of material will make its way into the police or Crown files by accident, inadvertence, or because of an investigator' s less than perfect appreciation of relevance.

> Complainants who muster the considerable courage required for the bringing of criminal charges usually do so without counsel. The Crown prosecutor, as the lawyer tasked with presenting the complainant's report to the court, may appear to the complainant to be "her" lawyer. It is not unusual or unreasonable for a complainant to tacitly consider her relationship with the prosecutor to have a special, albeit undefined, legal status, that at the very least provides some basic protection of confidentiality. Waiver is a strained concept in this situation. See Holmes, "An Analysis of Bill C-46, Production of Records . . ." (1997), 2 Can. Crim. L.R. 71.

Even under *Stinchcombe* there is no absolute duty for the Crown to disclose. Disclosure is subject to determinations of relevance and privilege, both issues here predetermined against the Crown. The notion that the complainant no longer has a privacy issue in the records simply because they are in the possession of the Crown is extraordinary. What if they were stolen, given to the Crown by a therapist without the knowledge of the complainant or handed over to the police by the complainant on the basis that there would otherwise be no prosecution.

The minority, through L'Heureux-Dubé J., point out that the majority opinion is *obiter* as the appeal did not concern the extent of the Crown's obligation to disclose private records in its possession.

Following *O'Connor* the Parliament of Canada passed the comprehensive Bill C-46 to restrict the production of records in sexual offence proceedings.

In essence the legislation now contained in sections 278.1 to 278.9 of the Criminal Code in large measure reflects word for word the minority position of L'Heureux-Dubé J. in *O'Connor*. In particular:

1. The preamble asserts a section 15 equality right for women and children who are complainants in sexual cases.
2. Although the *O'Connor* likely relevance test is maintained, section 278.3(4) specifies ten assertions which are declared not sufficient on their own to establish that a record is likely relevant to an issue at trial or to the competence of a witness to testify.
3. Under section 278.5 a trial judge has to balance privacy and the interests of justice before deciding whether to order the production of a record for review by the court.
4. Under section 278.7 the trial judge may only order production to the accused on consideration of all seven factors listed by L'Heureux-Dubé, J. rather than the five adopted by the *O'Connor* majority.
5. Under section 278.2 the two-stage balancing process must be applied to records in the possession of the Crown.

In *Mills* a joint judgment by Justices McLachlin and Iacobucci holds constitutional the more comprehensive Parliamentary scheme for access to complainants' records in sexual assault cases, which had enacted the minority approach in *O'Connor*. Of the *O'Connor* majority, only Lamer, C.J. dissented in *Mills* and only on the issue of applying the balancing of complainants' rights approach to records in the possession of the Crown. Justice Cory chose not to participate before his retirement and Justices Iacobucci and Major no longer supported their earlier positions.

R. v. MILLS
[1999] 3 S.C.R. 668, 28 C.R. (5th) 207, 139 C.C.C. (3d) 321

McLachlin and Iacobucci JJ. (L'Heureux-Dubé, Gonthier, Major, Bastarache and Binnie JJ. concurring):—

. . . .

The law develops through dialogue between courts and legislatures: see *Vriend v. Alberta*, [1998] 1 S.C.R. 493. Against the backdrop of *O'Connor*, Parliament was free to craft its own solution to the problem consistent with the Charter. Turning to the legislation at issue in this appeal, we find it constitutional. It is undisputed that there are several important respects in which Bill C-46 differs from the regime set out in *O'Connor*, supra. However, these differences are not fatal because Bill C-46 provides sufficient protection for all relevant Charter rights. There are, admittedly, several provisions in the Bill that are subject to differing interpretations. However, in such situations we will interpret the legislation in a constitutional manner where possible: see *Slaight Communications Inc. v. Davidson*, [1989] 1 S.C.R. 1038, at p. 1078. By so doing, we conclude that

Bill C-46 is a constitutional response to the problem of production of records of complainants or witnesses in sexual assault proceedings.

. . . .

Like *O'Connor*, Parliament has set up a two-stage process: (1) disclosure to the judge; and (2) production to the accused. At the first stage, the accused must establish that the record sought is "likely relevant to an issue at trial or to the competence of a witness to testify" and that "the production of the record is necessary in the interests of justice" (s. 278.5(1)). Bill C-46 diverges from *O'Connor* by directing the trial judge to consider the salutary and deleterious effects of production to the court on the accused's right to full answer and defence and the complainant or witness's right to privacy and equality. A series of factors is listed that the trial judge is directed to take into account in deciding whether the document should be produced to the court (s. 278.5(2)). If the requirements of this first stage are met, the record will be ordered produced to the trial judge. At the second stage, the judge looks at the record in the absence of the parties (s. 278.6(1)), holds a hearing if necessary (s. 278.6(2)), and determines whether the record should be produced on the basis that it is "likely relevant to an issue at trial or to the competence of a witness to testify" and that its production is "necessary in the interests of justice" (s. 278.7). Again at this stage, the judge must consider the salutary and deleterious effects on the accused's right to make full answer and defence and on the right to privacy and equality of the complainant or witness, and is directed to "take into account" the factors set out at s. 278.5(2): s. 278.7(2). When ordering production, the judge may impose conditions on production: s. 278.7(3).

The respondent and several supporting interveners argue that Bill C-46 is unconstitutional to the extent that it establishes a regime for production that differs from or is inconsistent with that established by the majority in *O'Connor*. However, it does not follow from the fact that a law passed by Parliament differs from a regime envisaged by the Court in the absence of a statutory scheme, that Parliament's law is unconstitutional. Parliament may build on the Court's decision, and develop a different scheme as long as it remains constitutional. Just as Parliament must respect the Court's rulings, so the Court must respect Parliament's determination that the judicial scheme can be improved. To insist on slavish conformity would belie the mutual respect that underpins the relationship between the courts and legislature that is so essential to our constitutional democracy: *Vriend*, supra. . . .

Relationship Between the Courts and the Legislature Generally

A posture of respect towards Parliament was endorsed by this Court in *Slaight Communications*, supra, at p. 1078, where we held that if legislation is amenable to two interpretations, a court should choose that interpretation that upholds the legislation as constitutional. Thus courts must presume that Parliament intended to enact constitutional legislation and strive, where possible, to give effect to this intention. This Court has also discussed the relationship between the courts and the legislature in terms of a dialogue, and emphasized its importance to the democratic process. In *Vriend*, supra, at para. 139, Iacobucci J. stated:

> To my mind, a great value of judicial review and this dialogue among the branches is that each of the branches is made somewhat accountable to the other. The work of the legislature is reviewed by the courts and the work of the court in its decisions can be reacted to by the legislature in the passing of new legislation (or even overarching laws under s. 33 of the Charter). This dialogue between and accountability of each of the branches have the effect of enhancing the democratic process, not denying it.

See also Peter W. Hogg and Allison A. Bushell, "The Charter Dialogue Between Courts and Legislatures" (1997), 35 Osgoode Hall L.J. 75. If the common law were to be taken as establishing the only possible constitutional regime, then we could not speak of a dialogue with the legislature. Such a situation could only undermine rather than enhance democracy. Legislative change and the development of the common law are different.

. . . .

Courts do not hold a monopoly on the protection and promotion of rights and freedoms; Parliament also plays a role in this regard and is often able to act as a significant ally for vulnerable groups. This is especially important to recognize in the context of sexual violence. The history of the treatment of sexual assault complainants by our society and our legal system is an unfortunate one. Important change has occurred through legislation aimed at both recognizing the rights and interests of complainants in criminal proceedings, and debunking the stereotypes that have been so damaging to women and children, but the treatment of sexual assault complainants remains an ongoing problem. If constitutional democracy is meant to ensure that due regard is given to the voices of those vulnerable to being overlooked by the majority, then this court has an obligation to consider respectfully Parliament's attempt to respond to such voices.

Parliament has enacted this legislation after a long consultation process that included a consideration of the constitutional standards outlined by this Court in *O'Connor*. While it is the role of the courts to specify such standards, there may be a range of permissible regimes that can meet these standards. It goes without saying that this range is not confined to the specific rule adopted by the Court pursuant to its competence in the common law. In the present case, Parliament decided that legislation was necessary in order to address the issue of third-party records more comprehensively. As is evident from the language of the preamble to Bill C-46, Parliament also sought to recognize the prevalence of sexual violence against women and children and its disadvantageous impact on their rights, to encourage the reporting of incidents of sexual violence, to recognize the impact of the production of personal information on the efficacy of treatment, and to reconcile fairness to complainants with the rights of the accused. Many of these concerns involve policy decisions regarding criminal procedure and its relationship to the community at large. Parliament may also be understood to be recognizing "horizontal" equality concerns, where women's inequality results from the acts of other individuals and groups rather than the state, but which nonetheless may have many consequences for the criminal justice system. It is perfectly reasonable that these many concerns may lead to a procedure that is different from the common law position but that nonetheless meets the required constitutional standards.

We cannot presume that the legislation is unconstitutional simply because it is different from the common law position. The question before us is not whether Parliament can amend the common law; it clearly can. The question before us is whether in doing so Parliament has nonetheless outlined a constitutionally acceptable procedure for the production of private records of complainants in sexual assault trials.

. . . .

Tensions Among Full Answer and Defence, Privacy, and Equality

(a) Balancing Interests and Defining Rights

At play in this appeal are three principles, which find their support in specific provisions of the Charter. These are full answer and defence, privacy, and equality. No single principle is absolute and capable of trumping the others; all must be defined in light of competing claims. As Lamer C.J. stated in *Dagenais*, supra, at p. 877:

> When the protected rights of two individuals come into conflict . . . Charter principles require a balance to be achieved that fully respects the importance of both sets of rights.

. . . .

Whether or not all the rights involved are "principles of fundamental justice", Charter rights must always be defined contextually.

. . . .

(b) Nature of the Charter Principles

(i) Full Answer and Defence

It is well established that the ability of the accused to make full answer and defence is a principle of fundamental justice protected by s. 7. . . . Many of these principles of fundamental justice are informed by the legal rights outlined in ss. 8 to 14 of the Charter. . . . Our jurisprudence has recognized on several occasions "the danger of placing the accused in a 'Catch-22' situation as a condition of making full answer and defence". This is an important consideration in the context of records production as often the accused may be in the difficult position of making submissions regarding the importance to full answer and defence of records that he or she has not seen. Where the records are part of the case to meet, this concern is particularly acute as such a situation very directly implicates the accused's ability to raise a doubt concerning his or her innocence. As the Court stated in *R. v. Leipert*, [1997] 1 S.C.R. 281, at para. 24, "[t]his Court has consistently affirmed that it is a fundamental principle of justice, protected by the Charter, that the innocent must not be convicted". Where the records to which the accused seeks access are not part of the case to meet, however, privacy and equality considerations may require that it be more difficult for accused persons to gain access to therapeutic or other records.

That said, the principles of fundamental justice do not entitle the accused to "the most favourable procedures that could possibly be imagined": *R. v. Lyons*, [1987] 2 S.C.R. 309, per La Forest J., at p. 362. This is because fundamental justice embraces more than the rights of the accused. For example, this Court has held that an assessment of the fairness of the trial process must be made "from the point of view of fairness in the eyes of the community and the complainant" and not just the accused: *R. v. E. (A.W.)*, [1993] 3 S.C.R. 155, per Cory J., at p. 198. ... This spectrum of interests reflected in the principles of fundamental justice highlights the need to avoid viewing any particular principle in isolation from the others.

. . . .

Several principles regarding the right to make full answer and defence emerge from the preceding discussion. First, the right to make full answer and defence is crucial to ensuring that the innocent are not convicted. To that end, courts must consider the danger of placing the accused in a Catch-22 situation as a condition of making full answer and defence, and will even override competing considerations in order to protect the right to make full answer and defence in certain circumstances, such as the "innocence at stake" exception to informer privilege. Second, the accused's right must be defined in a context that includes other principles of fundamental justice and Charter provisions. Third, full answer and defence does not include the right to evidence that would distort the search for truth inherent in the trial process.

(ii) Privacy

Since *Hunter v. Southam Inc.*, [1984] 2 S.C.R. 145, this Court has recognized that s. 8 of the Charter protects a person's reasonable expectation of privacy. This right is relevant to the present appeal, as an order for the production of documents is a seizure within the meaning of s. 8 of the Charter [citations omitted]. Therefore an order for the production of records made pursuant to ss. 278.1 to 278.91 of the Criminal Code, falls within the ambit of s. 8.

. . . .

This Court has most often characterized the values engaged by privacy in terms of liberty, or the right to be left alone by the state. . . . This interest in being left alone by the state includes the ability to control the dissemination of confidential information. These privacy concerns are at their strongest where aspects of one's individual identity are at stake, such as in the context of information "about one's lifestyle, intimate relations or political or religious opinions".

. . . .

In fostering the underlying values of dignity, integrity and autonomy, it is fitting that s. 8 of the Charter should seek to protect a biographical core of personal information which individuals in a free and democratic society would wish to maintain and control from dissemination to the state. This would include information which tends to reveal intimate details of the lifestyle and personal choices of the individual. That privacy is essential to maintaining relationships of trust was stressed to this Court by the eloquent submissions of many interveners in this case regarding counselling records. The therapeutic relationship is one that is characterized by trust, an element of which is confidentiality. Therefore the protection of the complainant's reasonable expectation of privacy in her therapeutic records protects the therapeutic relationship.

. . . .

Given that s. 8 protects a person's privacy by prohibiting unreasonable searches or seizures, and given that s. 8 addresses a particular application of the principles of fundamental justice, we can infer that a reasonable search or seizure is consistent with the principles of fundamental justice. Moreover, as we have already discussed, the principles of fundamental justice include the right to make full answer and defence. Therefore a reasonable search and seizure will be one that accommodates both the accused's ability to make full answer and defence and the complainant's privacy right.

From our preceding discussion of the right to make full answer and defence, it is clear that the accused will have no right to the records in question insofar as they contain information that is either irrelevant or would serve to distort the search for truth, as access to such information is not included within the ambit of the accused's right. . . . The values protected by privacy rights will be most directly at stake where the confidential information contained in a record concerns aspects of one's individual identity or where the maintenance of confidentiality is crucial to a therapeutic, or other trust-like, relationship.

(iii) Equality

Equality concerns must also inform the contextual circumstances in which the rights of full answer and defence and privacy will come into play. In this respect, an appreciation of myths and stereotypes in the context of sexual violence is essential to delineate properly the boundaries of full answer and defence. As we have already discussed, the right to make full answer and defence does not include the right to information that would only distort the truth-seeking goal of the trial process. In *R. v. Osolin*, [1993] 4 S.C.R. 595, Cory J., for the majority on this issue, stated, at pp. 669 and 670:

> The provisions of ss. 15 and 28 of the Charter guaranteeing equality to men and women, although not determinative should be taken into account in determining the reasonable limitations that should be placed upon the cross-examination of a complainant. . . . A complainant should not be unduly harassed and pilloried to the extent of becoming a victim of an insensitive judicial system.

The reasons in *Seaboyer* make it clear that eliciting evidence from a complainant for the purpose of encouraging inferences pertaining to consent or the credibility of rape victims which are based on groundless myths and fantasized stereotypes is improper. The accused is not permitted to "whack the complainant" through the use of stereotypes regarding victims of sexual assault.

. . . .

When the boundary between privacy and full answer and defence is not properly delineated, the equality of individuals whose lives are heavily documented is also affected, as these individuals have more records that will be subject to wrongful scrutiny. Karen Busby cautions that the use of records to challenge credibility at large

> will subject those whose lives already have been subject to extensive documentation to extraordinarily invasive review. This would include women whose lives have been documented under conditions of multiple inequalities and institutionalization such as Aboriginal women, women with disabilities, or women who have been imprisoned or involved with child welfare agencies ("Discriminatory Uses of Personal Records in Sexual Violence Cases" (1997), 9 C.J.W.L. 148, at pp. 161-62).

These concerns highlight the need for an acute sensitivity to context when determining the content of the accused's right to make full answer and defence, and its relationship to the complainant's privacy right.

Summary

In summary, the following broad considerations apply to the definition of the rights at stake in this appeal. The right of the accused to make full answer and defence is a core principle of fundamental justice, but it does not automatically entitle the accused to gain access to information contained in the private records of complainants and witnesses. Rather, the scope of the right to make full answer and defence must be determined in light of privacy and equality rights of complainants and witnesses. It is clear that the right to full answer and defence is not engaged where the accused seeks information that will only serve to distort the truth-seeking purpose of a trial, and in such a situation, privacy and equality rights are paramount. On the other hand, where the information contained in a record directly bears on the right to make full answer and defence, privacy rights must yield to the need to avoid convicting the innocent. Most cases, however, will not be so clear, and in assessing applications for production courts must determine the weight to be granted to the interests protected by privacy and full answer and defence in the particular circumstances of each case. Full answer and defence will be more centrally implicated where the information contained in a record is part of the case to meet or where its potential probative value is high. A complainant's privacy interest is very high where the confidential information contained in a record concerns the complainant's personal identity or where the confidentiality of the record is vital to protect a therapeutic relationship.

With this background in mind, we now proceed to discuss the statutory provisions under attack.

. . . .

The Statutory Provisions

Section 278.3(4) lists a series of "assertions" that cannot "on their own" establish that a record is likely relevant. The respondent submits that on a plain reading, this provision prevents the accused from relying on the listed factors when attempting to establish the likely relevance of the records. This, he argues, interferes with the right to make full answer and defence by restricting what the judge can consider in determining whether the records must be produced to the defence. The legislation raises the bar for production, he asserts, making it difficult if not impossible for the accused to meet the likely relevance test of ss. 278.5 and 278.7. The respondent contends that it is unconstitutional to exclude the assertions listed in s. 278.3(4) as irrelevant.

This submission forgets that when legislation is susceptible to more than one interpretation, we must always choose the constitutional reading. See *Slaight*, supra, at p. 1078. This mistake leads the respondent to overstate the purpose and effect of s. 278.3(4). As has frequently been held, its purpose is to prevent speculative and unmeritorious requests for production [citations omitted]. It does not entirely prevent an accused from relying on the factors listed, but simply prevents reliance on bare "assertions" of the listed matters, where there is no other evidence and they stand "on their own".

The purpose and wording of s. 278.3 does not prevent an accused from relying on the assertions set out in subsection 278.3(4) where there is an evidentiary or informational foundation to suggest that they may be related to likely relevance. . . . The section requires only that the accused be able to point to case specific evidence or information to show that the record in issue is likely relevant to an issue at trial or the competence of a witness to testify, see *Leipert*, supra, at para. 21. Conversely, where an accused does provide evidence or information to support an assertion listed in s. 278.3(4), this does not mean that likely relevance is made out. Section 278.3(4) does not supplant the ultimate discretion of the trial judge. Where any one of the listed assertions is made and supported by the required evidentiary and informational foundation, the trial judge is the ultimate arbiter in deciding whether the likely relevance threshold set out in s. 278.5 and 278.7 is met. We conclude that s. 278.3(4) does not violate ss. 7 or 11(d) of the Charter.

. . . .

Both the majority and minority of this Court in *O'Connor*, supra, held that records must be produced to the judge for inspection if the accused can demonstrate that the information is "likely to be relevant": *O'Connor*, supra, at para. 19, per Lamer C.J. and Sopinka J., and at para. 138, per L'Heureux-Dubé J. The Court defined the standard of likely relevance as "a reasonable possibility that the information is logically probative to an issue at trial or the competence of a witness to testify". Although the majority recognized that complainants have a constitutional right to privacy it held that no balancing of rights should be undertaken at the first stage. This conclusion was premised on the finding that:

(1) to require the accused to meet more than the likely relevance stage would be to "put the accused in the difficult situation of having to make submissions to the judge without precisely knowing what is contained in the records"; and (2) there is not enough information before a trial judge at this initial stage of production for an informed balancing procedure to take place. To this end, the majority held that the analysis should be confined to determining "likely relevance" and "whether the right to make full answer and defence is implicated by information contained in the records". In contrast, the minority held that once the accused meets the "likely relevance" threshold, he must then satisfy the judge that the salutary effects of ordering the documents produced to the court for inspection outweigh the deleterious effects of such production, having regard to the accused's right to make full answer and defence, and the effect of such production on the privacy and equality rights of the subject of the records. L'Heureux-Dubé J. found that a sufficient evidentiary basis could be established at this stage through Crown disclosure, defence witnesses, the cross-examination of Crown witnesses at both the preliminary inquiry and the trial and, on some occasions, expert evidence. Parliament, after studying the issue, concluded that the rights of both the complainant and the accused should be considered when deciding whether to order production to the judge. In coming to this conclusion, Parliament must be taken to have determined, as a result of lengthy consultations, and years of Parliamentary study and debate, that trial judges have sufficient evidence to engage in an informed balancing process at this stage. . . . As a result of the consultation process, Parliament decided to supplement the "likely relevant" standard for production to the judge proposed in *O'Connor* with the further requirement that production be "necessary in the interests of justice". The result was s. 278.5. This process is a notable example of the dialogue between the judicial and legislative branches discussed above. This Court acted in *O'Connor*, and the legislature responded with Bill C-46. As already mentioned, the mere fact that Bill C-46 does not mirror *O'Connor* does not render it unconstitutional.

The question comes down to this: once likely relevance is established, is it necessarily unconstitutional that a consideration of the rights and interests of those affected by production to the court might result in production not being ordered? The answer to this question depends on whether a consideration of the range of rights and interests affected, in addition to a finding of likely relevance, will ultimately prevent the accused from seeing documents that are necessary to enable him to defend himself — to raise all the defences that might be open to him at trial. The non-disclosure of third party records with a high privacy interest that may contain relevant evidence will not compromise trial fairness where such non-disclosure would not prejudice the accused's right to full answer and defence.

Section 278.5(1) is a very wide and flexible section. It accords the trial judge great latitude. Parliament must be taken to have intended that judges, within the broad scope of the powers conferred, would apply it in a constitutional manner — a way that would ultimately permit the accused access to all documents that may be constitutionally required. Indeed, a production regime that denied this would not be production "necessary in the interests of justice".

. . . .

While this Court may have considered it preferable not to consider privacy rights at the production stage, that does not preclude Parliament from coming to a different conclusion, so long as its conclusion is consistent with the Charter in its own right. As we have explained, the Bill's directive to consider what is "necessary in the interests of justice", read correctly, does include appropriate respect for the right to full answer and defence.

This leaves the argument that the judge cannot consider the factors listed in s. 278.5(2) without looking at the documents. However, s. 278.5(2) does not require that the judge engage in a conclusive and in-depth evaluation of each of the factors. It rather requires the judge to "take them into account" — to the extent possible at this early stage of proceedings — in deciding whether to order a particular record produced to himself or herself for inspection. Section 278.5(2) serves as a check-list of the various factors that may come into play in making the decision regarding production to the judge. Therefore, while the s. 278.5(2) factors are relevant, in the final analysis the judge is free to make whatever order is "necessary in the interests of justice" — a mandate that includes all of the applicable "principles of fundamental justice" at stake.

Furthermore, contrary to the respondent's submissions, there is a sufficient evidentiary basis to support such an analysis at this early stage. This basis can be established through Crown disclosure, defence witnesses, the cross-examination of Crown witnesses at both the preliminary inquiry and the trial, and expert evidence, see: *O'Connor*, supra, at para. 146, per L'Heureux-Dubé J. As noted by Taylor J. for the British Columbia Supreme Court, "the criminal process provides a reasonable process for the acquisition of the evidentiary basis", *Hurrie*, supra, at para. 39. To this end, as the Attorney of British Columbia submitted: "Laying the groundwork prior to trial, or comprehensive examination of witnesses at trial, will go a long way to establishing a meritorious application under this legislation".

The nature of the records in question will also often provide the trial judge with an important informational foundation. For example, with respect to the privacy interest in records, the expectation of privacy in adoption or counselling records may be very different from that in school attendance records, see for example, *R. v. J.S.P.*, B.C. S.C., Vancouver Registry Nos. CC970130 & CC960237, May 15, 1997. Similarly, a consideration of the probative value of records can often be informed by the nature and purposes of a record, as well as the record-taking practices used to create it. As noted above, many submissions were made regarding the different levels of reliability of certain records. Counselling or therapeutic records, for example, can be highly subjective documents which attempt merely to record an individual's emotions and psychological state. Often such records have not been checked for accuracy by the subject of the records, nor have they been recorded verbatim. All of these factors may help a trial judge when considering the probative value of a record being sought by an accused.

As discussed above in the context of defining the right to full answer and defence, courts must as a general matter ensure that the accused can obtain all pertinent evidence required to make full answer and defence, and must be wary of the danger of putting the accused in a Catch-22 situation in seeking to obtain such evidence. Where there is a danger that the accused's right to make full answer and defence will be violated, the trial judge should err on the side of production to the court. We conclude that s. 278.5 is constitutional.

Once the first hurdle is passed and the records are produced to the judge, the judge must determine whether it is in the interests of justice that they be produced to the defence. Again the judge must be satisfied that the records are "likely relevant" and that production, this time to the accused, is necessary in the interests of justice. In making this decision, the judge must once again consider the factors set out in s. 278.5(2).

The respondent accepts that weighing competing interests is appropriate at this second stage of the analysis. However, the respondent contends that the requirement under s. 278.7(2), that the trial judge take the factors specified in paragraphs s. 278.5(2)(a) to (h) into account, inappropriately alters the constitutional balance established in *O'Connor*. Specifically, the respondent contends that ss. 278.5(2)(f) and (g) elevate the societal interest in encouraging the reporting of sexual offences and encouraging of treatment of complainants of sexual offences, to a status equal to the accused's right to make full answer and defence. This, he suggests, alters the constitutional balance established in *O'Connor*, where the majority specifically determined these factors to be of secondary importance to defence interests in any balancing of competing interests and better taken into account through other avenues. The respondent also contends that s. 278.5(2)(h) unfairly requires trial judges to consider the effect of disclosure on the integrity of the trial process. The respondent submits that this is a question going to admissibility.

These concerns are largely answered by the analysis advanced under s. 278.5(2), discussed at greater length above. Trial judges are not required to rule conclusively on each of the factors nor are they required to determine whether factors relating to the privacy and equality of the complainant or witness "outweigh" factors relating to the accused's right to full answer and defence. To repeat, trial judges are only asked to "take into account" the factors listed in s. 278.5(2) when determining whether production of part or all of the impugned record to the accused is necessary in the interest of justice, s. 278.7(1).

The respondent argues that the inclusion of the societal interest factors in ss. 278.5(2)(f) and (g) alters the constitutional balance established by the *O'Connor* majority. With respect, this argument is unsound. . . . As noted above, when preparing Bill C-46 Parliament had the advantage of being able to assess how the *O'Connor* regime was operating. From the information available to Parliament and the submissions it received during the consultation process, Parliament concluded that the effect of production on the integrity of the trial was a factor that should be included in the list of factors for trial judges to "take into account" at both stages of an application for production. Several interveners have interpreted this factor as requiring courts to consider, along with the other enumerated factors, whether the search for truth would be advanced by the production of the records in question; that is, the question is whether the material in question would introduce discriminatory biases and beliefs into the fact-finding process. We agree with this interpretation of the inquiry required by s. 278.5(2)(h) and believe it to be in keeping with the purposes set out in the preamble of the legislation.

By giving judges wide discretion to consider a variety of factors and requiring them to make whatever order is necessary in the interest of justice at both stages of an application for production, Parliament has created a scheme that permits judges not only to preserve the complainant's privacy and equality rights to the maximum extent possible, but also to ensure that the accused has access to the documents required to make full answer and defence.

LAMER C.J.:—

. . . .

While I agree with McLachlin and Iacobucci JJ.'s finding that Bill C-46 complies with ss. 7 and 11(d) of the Canadian Charter of Rights and Freedoms as it applies to the production of records in the possession of third parties, I take a different view of the legislative regime's approach to records in the hands of the Crown. In my opinion, Bill C-46's treatment of records that form part of the case to meet tips the balance too heavily in favour of privacy to the detriment of the accused's right to make full answer and defence.

Do you think there should be a presumption of constitutionality in Charter cases? What are the advantages and disadvantages of the new approach of dialogue and deference? What of Chief Justice Dickson's view in _Hunter v. Southam_ that the courts should be the guardians of the Constitution?

On the issue of equality, why was there no reference to the ten-part test for judging section 15 claims established in _Law v. Minister of Human Resources Development_,[354] by Iacobucci J. for a unanimous court, as recently as March, 1999 (later to be drastically simplified in _R. v. Kapp_?[355]

The essence of the _Law_ test is that there is in fact no Charter guarantee of equality per se. The guarantee is against discrimination within the meaning of section 15. This is set out in part 3 of _Law_ as follows:

---

354 [1999] 1 S.C.R. 497.
355 (2008) 56 C.R. (6th) 1 (S.C.C.)

(3) Accordingly, a court that is called upon to determine a discrimination claim under s. 15(1) should make the following three broad inquiries:

A. Does the impugned law (a) draw a formal distinction between the claimant and others on the basis of one or more personal characteristics, or (b) fail to take into account the claimant's already disadvantaged position within Canadian society resulting in substantively differential treatment between the claimant and others on the basis of one or more personal characteristics?

B. Is the claimant subject to differential treatment based on one or more enumerated and analogous grounds? and

C. Does the differential treatment discriminate, by imposing a burden upon or withholding a benefit from the claimant in a manner which reflects the stereotypical application of presumed group or personal characteristics, or which otherwise has the effect of perpetuating or promoting the view that the individual is less capable or worthy of recognition or value as a human being or as a member of Canadian society, equally deserving of concern, respect, and consideration?

The court in *Law* also requires careful identification of "one or more relevant comparators", discrimination on an enumerated or analogous ground and a consideration of context.

Is the comparator group in *Mills* all other victims of crime or is it male victims of sexual assault? It surely couldn't be the accused given that the context is a criminal trial where the issue is punishment rather than compensation. Is the violation discrimination by gender or age or is it an analogous ground because complainants in sexual assault cases have been discriminated against through myths and stereotypical views?

The implications of an enforceable section 15 claim for complainants in sexual assault cases is left unexplored. The policy issues are far wider than establishing privacy rights for therapeutic and other records of complainants. Can complainants now seek status to be represented throughout a sexual assault trial? How about rights to cross-examine the accused, to challenge the similar fact evidence rule or to reverse the presumption of innocence?

For an analysis that *O'Connor* applications were used almost always against female complainants see Karen Busby, "Third Party Records Cases Since R. v. O'Connor."[356]

Professor Stephen Coughlan, "Complainants' Records After *Mills*: Same as it Ever Was",[357] has suggested that a close reading of *Mills* is that, although the

---

356 (2000), 27 Man. L.J. 355. For critical comments on *Mills* see Stuart, "*Mills*: Dialogue with Parliament and Equality by Assertion at What Cost?" (2000), 28 C.R. (5th) 275 and Peter Sankoff, "Crown Disclosure After *Mills*: Have the Ground Rules Suddenly Changed?" (2000), 28 C.R. (5th) 285.

357 (2000), 33 C.R. (5th) 300.

language is deference to Parliament, the court has read in discretion at every point such that its regime still conforms to its earlier majority judgment in *O'Connor*. Accepting that there is reading down in *Mills*, this appears to place far too little emphasis on the raising of the bar at the first stage of production to the judge. Several courts have already decided that *Mills* has indeed raised that threshold test.[358]

The court in *Mills* certainly reads down the "insufficient grounds" section 278.3(4) which declares the long list of assertions which would not meet the likely relevant test. Pointing to words "on their own" the court holds this merely requires an evidentiary foundation. The court sees the purpose of the provision to be the prevention of speculative myths, stereotypes, and generalized assumptions about sexual assault victims and classes of records from forming the entire basis of an otherwise unsubstantiated order for production of private records. The problem, as Kent Roach points out, "Editorial on *Mills*"[359] is that only some of the prohibited assertions involve sexist rape myths. Those relating to credibility do not. The section requires only, holds the court in reading the section down, that the accused be able to point to case specific evidence or information to show that the record in issue is likely relevant to an issue at trial or the competence of a witness to testify. The court indicates one source of such an evidentiary base to be the preliminary inquiry. The difficulty here is that many sexual assault trials across Canada are now proceeded with, through Crown election, by way of summary proceedings where there is no preliminary (and no jury trial).

In such cases is it a good idea to encourage free-ranging and intrusive inquiries into the existence and type of records presumably necessitating adjournments where production is ordered?

The various other rulings in *Mills* on the records issues are supportable. This includes the acceptance by the majority of Parliament's view that the balancing of rights of complainants must also occur, in the absence of express waiver, where the records are in the possession of the Crown. We have seen that the majority ruling to the contrary in *O'Connor* was *obiter* and not persuasive in holding that privacy had necessarily been waived by complainants in such cases.

Subsequently the majority of the Supreme Court appears to have changed the balance again in favour of rights of accused. The context was a cross-examination of a diary in the possession of the accused as to why the complainant had not mentioned abuse by the accused.

R. v. SHEARING
[2002] 3 S.C.R. 33, 2 C.R. (6th) 213, 165 C.C.C. (3d) 225, 2002 CarswellBC 1661, 2002 CarswellBC 1662

The accused was charged with 20 counts of sexual offences alleged to have occurred between 1965 and 1989. The accused was the leader of a cult. He

---

358   See *Batte* (2000), 34 C.R. (5th) 197 (Ont. C.A.) (criticized by Joseph Wilkinson, *"Batte*: Raising the Defence Hurdle for Access to Third Party Records" (2000), 34 C.R. (5th) 257) and *M.(D.)* (2001), 37 C.R. 80 (5th) (Ont. S.C.J.) (denying access to a diary and counselling records because the evidentiary foundation was not laid at the preliminary inquiry).

359   (2000), 43 Crim. L.Q. 145.

preached that sexual experience was a way to progress to higher levels of consciousness and that he, as a cult leader, could be instrumental in enabling young girls to reach these higher levels. Two of the complainants were sisters who lived in a group home. One kept a daily diary for eight months in 1970. The day-to-day entries covered part of the 10-year period when she alleged sexual abuse by the accused. When the complainant left the group home her mother put some of her belongings in a cardboard box in the storage area shared with other residents. About 18 months later, after the accused had been indicted, another resident of the house opened the cardboard box, found the complainant's diary and gave it to the defence.

At trial, the defence sought to use the diary to contradict the complainant on the basis of entries arguably inconsistent with her evidence-in-chief, and by showing the absence of any entry chronicling physical or sexual abuse. The complainant objected and, at the *voir dire* into the admissibility of the diary, asserted a privacy interest. The trial judge permitted the accused to use the diary to cross-examine the complainant on entries the defence considered probative but did not permit cross-examination on the absence of any entries recording physical abuse by the complainant's mother or sexual abuse by the accused. The trial judge refused to allow cross-examination of the complainant's diary as to the fact there was no mention of the alleged abuse. The trial judge applied the *O'Connor* principles respecting production of therapeutic and other records of complainants. Justice Donald for the B.C. Court of Appeal approved the trial judge's decision and approach with these words:

> Mills has shifted the balance away from the primary emphasis on the rights of the accused. The decision requires a reconsideration of the position of the complainant, and in particular the equality rights of the complainant, so as to effectively guard against procedures which deny complainants equal access to and benefit of the law.

When the matter reached the Supreme Court, the Court divided 7-2 on this issue. The majority held that the trial judge ought to have allowed the cross-examination and ordered a new trial on the count for which the accused had been convicted.

Per BINNIE J. (MCLACHLIN C.J. and IACOBUCCI, MAJOR, BASTARACHE, ARBOUR and LEBEL JJ. concurring): —

. . . .

Limiting the Scope of Cross-examination

The critical importance of cross-examination is not doubted. The appellant stood before the court accused of crimes by numerous complainants but he was presumed to be innocent of each and every count. All of the alleged sexual misconduct, by its very nature, was in private. At trial, it was his word against the credibility of his accusers, individually and (by virtue of the similar fact evidence) collectively. If the complainants were untruthful about what happened in the privacy of their encounters, the most effective tool he possessed to get at the truth was a full and pointed cross-examination. The general principle was stated in *Seaboyer, supra*, per McLachlin J. at p. 611:

> Canadian courts, like courts in most common law jurisdictions, have been extremely cautious in restricting the power of the accused to call evidence in his or her defence,

a reluctance founded in the fundamental tenet of our judicial system that an innocent person must not be convicted. It follows from this that the prejudice must substantially outweigh the value of the evidence before a judge can exclude evidence relevant to a defence allowed by law.

It has been increasingly recognized in recent years, however, that cross-examination techniques in sexual assault cases that seek to put the complainant on trial rather than the accused are abusive and distort rather than enhance the search for truth. Various limitations have been imposed. One of these limits is the privacy interest of the complainant, which is not to be needlessly sacrificed. This was explored by Cory J. writing for the majority in *Osolin*, *supra*, at pp. 669 and 671, as follows:

> A complainant should not be unduly harassed and pilloried to the extent of becoming a victim of an insensitive judicial system. Yet a fair balance must be achieved so that the limitations on the cross-examination of complainants in sexual assault cases do not interfere with the right of the accused to a fair trial.
>
> . . . .
>
> In each case the trial judge must carefully balance the fundamentally important right of the accused to a fair trial against the need for reasonable protection of a complainant, particularly where the purpose of the cross-examination may be directed to the "rape myths".

I underline the reference to "rape myths" because in my view it is a concern about a potential revival of the shibboleth of "recent complaint" in sexual assault cases rather than a privacy concern as such, that lies at the heart of the trial judge's ruling.

In *Seaboyer*, the accused sought to cross-examine the complainant on her sexual conduct on other occasions to explain the "bruises and other aspects of the complainant's condition which the Crown had put in evidence". In *Osolin*, the accused sought to cross-examine a notation in the complainant's medical record of a concern she had expressed to her therapist that her attitude and behaviour may have influenced the accused to some extent. This case is different. The focus is not private information as such because, as stated, the trial judge allowed cross-examination by the defence on each of the specific diary entries the defence sought to utilize. The defence objection is to the restriction on its ability to cross-examine on the significance (if any) of what was not recorded. It is common ground that KWG's diary contains no references to beatings by the mother or to sexual abuse by the appellant.

The cogency of this line of questioning rested on the premise that if these assaults had happened, they would have been recorded, and because the events were not recorded,they did not happen. That, in the Crown's view, is where one of the "rape myths" surfaces. The trial judge agreed:

> In essence, [the appellant] wants to go to the jury and argue that the witness has made no "complaint", if I may use that word, to her private, confidential diary about the sexual assaults that she now testifies to.

. . . .

[Counsel for KWG] argues strongly that there is no probative value in a lack of complaint in these circumstances, and that to allow cross-examination and argument on the issue is premised upon a discriminatory belief or bias.

The trial judge's trade-off of permitting questions on actual entries but disallowing questions on the absence of entries was criticized in about equal measure by the appellant and the Criminal Lawyers' Association on the one hand, who thought it too restrictive on the defence, and on the other hand by the Crown and Women's Legal Education and Action Fund ("LEAF"), who thought it went too far against the complainant.

The Crown and LEAF took the position that KWG's diary was and remained her property, and that the appellant came into possession of it without colour of right. That being the case, the trial judge ought to have ignored the reality of the appellant's possession (a sort of constructive dispossession) and required the appellant to make anapplication for compelled production of documents under ss. 278.1 to 278.9, just as if KWG rather than the appellant had possession of it.

I will deal with these points in turn.

(1) Surprise Disclosure of the Diary

In her evidence-in-chief and in the initial cross-examination KWG committed herself to having experienced a profoundly unhappy childhood (a "chamber of horrors" is how the defence put it, somewhat sarcastically), lack of friends at school, prohibition on participation in extracurricular school activities, and not being allowed to wear ordinary teenager clothing. All of this was the background to alleged constant physical abuse by the mother and alleged sexual abuse by the appellant, the latter occurring mainly in the appellant's den at the Centre.

She was asked by the defence about the possible existence of a diary and she said she thought she had received one as a present at Christmas in her early teens, but had only made entries for two weeks or so.

At this point in the trial, counsel for the defence flourished KWG's original diary which she had not seen for 22 years, and announced that it contained day-by-day entries for a period of eight months (not the two weeks she had recalled) commencing January 1970, in the midst of the period of alleged abuse. It recorded what KWG herself described as "mundane" entries about schoolmates, participation in school functions, family outings to see films, Easter presents and some positive references to the appellant (e.g., "Stayed home from school today and had a nice talk with Ivon. He makes you want to work harder"). The defence wished to raise a doubt about the reliability and completeness of KWG's memory by contradicting her testimonywith what the defence viewed as inconsistent entries written under her own hand in the diary, and the omission of any entry chronicling physical or sexual abuse.

KWG's response to the surprise disclosure of her 1970 diary was to obtain a short adjournment, and to retain her own Counsel who argued that (1) the diary was the property of KWG and should be returned forthwith and (2) thereafter

1064   EXCLUSIONARY RULES

dealt with under the documentary production provisions of ss. 278.1 to 278.9 of the Criminal Code.

(2) Wrongful Possession of the Diary

KWG testified on the *voir dire* that she did "not at all" intend to give up her privacy rights. She was "appalled" and wanted the diary and all the copies returned to her as the defence had no right to "the little bit of privacy that [she] had". On cross-examination, KWG described the diary entries as "very mundane", "[b]ut it's still mine.... I don't understand what that has to do with anything. This is still mine. Whether it's mundane or exciting or boring, it's still mine". The trial judge found that KWG had never waived or abandoned her privacy interest in the diary and I agree with him.

The *voir dire* included a lengthy legal debate about whether KWG had or had not abandoned her property interest in her diary, and whether the appellant's possession of it amounted to conversion. I do not think KWG was illegally deprived of possession of the diary (unlike the Chinese restaurateurs whose safe containing private documents was stolen by thieves in *R. v. Law*, 2002 SCC 10). She simply left it behind in a common storage room with other possessions no longer required for day-to-day living. When her mother forwarded her possessions to her in 1995, the diary was not among them. When the diary fell into the appellant's possession 22 years after KWG left home, it was not a "wrongful" taking in any legal sense, although I agree with KWG that it underlined the extent of his unwelcome access to KWG's private life as a by-product of her mother's adherence to the cult.

I do not propose to pursue the property ownership debate. The issue for present purposes is not the "ownership of the diary" (which could be the subject of a civil cause of action) but the status of information contained within the diary. Return of the diary, as proposed by my colleague L'Heureux-Dubé J. at para. 161, would seem to me to shut the barn door after the horse had escaped. . . .

Our concern here is with the privacy interest not the property interest.

(3) Applicability of Sections 278.1 to 278.9 of the Criminal Code

Sections 278.1 to 278.9 on their face address the production not the use or admissibility of personal information, as stated by Parliament itself in the Preamble (S.C. 1997, c. 30):

> WHEREAS the Parliament of Canada recognizes that the *compelled production* of personal information may deter complainants of sexual offences from reporting the offence to the police and may deter complainants from seeking necessary treatment, counselling or advice;
>
> WHEREAS the Parliament of Canada recognizes that the work of those who provide services and assistance to complainants of sexual offences is detrimentally affected by the *compelled production* of records and by the process to compel that production;
>
> AND WHEREAS the Parliament of Canada recognizes that, while *production* to the court and to the accused of personal information regarding any person may be

necessary in order for an accused to make a full answer and defence, *that production may breach the person's right to privacy and equality and therefore the determination as to whether to order production should be subject to careful scrutiny*. . . . [Emphasis added.]

The text of ss. 278.1 to 278.9 that follows is consistent with such a purpose. Counsel for KWG at trial and LEAF before this Court, argued that the machinery of ss. 278.1 to 278.9 can be put into reverse, i.e., it contemplates taking documents already in the hands of the defence and restoring these to the complainant, thus requiring the defence to make a fresh application for the document just removed from its possession. In my view, this interpretation is unduly contrived and does violence to the statutory language.

(4) The Issue Here is Admissibility of Evidence, Not Production and Disclosure

The confusion between production (O'Connor) and admissibility (Osolin) took hold at an early stage of the *voir dire* in this case. Having rightly rejected the applicability of ss. 278.1 to 278.9 on the ground that there was no issue here of production or disclosure, the trial judge prefaced the opening of submissions on admissibility as "what I'll call an *O'Connor* application at this stage".

Although well aware of *Seaboyer* (1991) and *Osolin* (1993), the trial judge (and eventually the Court of Appeal) seems to have concluded that these earlier authorities had been overtaken by this Court's subsequent pronouncements in *O'Connor* (1995). I do not agree that *O'Connor* can substitute for *Osolin* or indeed that the two tests are equivalent or interchangeable.

The trial judge heard several days of argument from counsel for KWG as well as counsel for the prosecution and the defence on the use that would be made of KWG's diary in cross-examination before the jury. Much of this argument was directed explicitly to various dicta in *O'Connor, supra.* In his ruling on the permissible scope of the cross-examination, the trial judge "applied" the *O'Connor* principles. . . .

In my view, the trial judge erred in extrapolating the *O'Connor* test from the issue of production of information not previously disclosed to the defence and applying it to the admissibility (or use in cross-examination) before the jury of evidence already in the possession of the defence.

A simple "balancing of interests" test (*O'Connor, supra,* at paras. 129 and 150) cannot be equated to "substantially outweighs" (*Seaboyer, Osolin*). Under *O'Connor*, the default position is that the third party information is not produced to the defence. Under *Seaboyer* and *Osolin*, the default position is that the defence is allowed to proceed with its cross-examination. . . .

(5) The Proper Limits of Cross-examination

In *Seaboyer*, McLachlin J. noted that "our courts have traditionally been reluctant to exclude even tenuous defence evidence" (p. 607) and affirmed that the defence has a right to use evidence in its possession unless its prejudicial effect "substantially outweighs" (p. 611) its probative value. The reason for the different orientation is apparent. In the *O'Connor* situation, the accused is not entitled to disclosure, and seeks the intervention of the state to put aside the privacy of a third party complainant. In the *Seaboyer* situation, the state is asked by the complainant to intervene against the accused to deny him the use of information already in his possession. It is true that some of the same values must be weighed (e.g., full answer and defence, privacy, equality rights, etc.) but both the purpose and the context are quite different.

The issue for the trial judge here, therefore, was whether cross-examination on the diary would create prejudice to the complainant that "substantially outweighed" its potential probative value to the appellant, and in that regard whether cross-examination on the absence of entries recording abuse relied upon "rape myths" or the equivalent.

(6) KWG's Privacy Concerns

The fact KWG conceded that the diary contained "mundane" sorts of information is not, in my view, fatal to her wish to keep private the entries she did choose to record in her private diary, but the fact KWG freely acknowledged that her teenage diary was not written in any kind of confessional spirit does go to the weight of the privacy interest.

On this point, however, it is KWG not the appellant who might be expected to complain of the trial judge's ruling. He allowed the defence to put to KWG whatever entries it wished where specific entries arguably contradicted KWG on some of the statements she had made in her evidence-in-chief.

All that was left to explore was what she did not write down. Cross-examination on that point would be a high-risk tactic for the defence capable of generating some devastating answers, to put it mildly. However, the appellant considered pursuit of that point to be crucial to his defence.

(7) Omission of Entries Recording Abuse

We arrive then at the appellant's real grievance. He was not allowed to challenge the credibility of KWG based on the absence of any entries dealing with physical or sexual abuse in an important and relevant 8-month period in 1970.

In fact, the jury was never told the omissions existed.

The Crown contends that the effect of this restriction was marginal at best:

> The Respondent submits that the non-recording of an event is generally of much lower probative value than the recording of an event. If an event is recorded which a witness denies, that contradiction cries out for an explanation. Where an event is not recorded, however, that fact is not in itself logically inconsistent with the event having occurred.

The Crown's argument assumes the point in issue, of course. If we assume KWG intended a type of diary that would not be expected to contain entries recording abuse, the omissions would be irrelevant. It is that assumption, however, which the defence sought to explore in cross-examination.

The courts have recognized, no doubt belatedly, that certain techniques of cross-examination traditionally employed in sexual assault cases have distorted rather than advanced the search for truth. This case illustrates one of the problem areas. The omission to record some piece of information is only probative if there is a reasonable expectation that such a record would be made (*R. v. R.M.* (1997), 93 B.C.A.C. 81, at paras. 45-49; Wigmore on Evidence, Vol. IIIA (Chadbourn rev. 1970), at para. 1042). A pilot's log will record relevant flight information, because that is its purpose, but not what he or she had to eat for breakfast over the Atlantic Ocean. Hospital records will include medical observations but not what television station the patient happened to be watching that evening. What was objectionable about the defence approach here was that it overlooked (or perhaps resolutely resisted) the need to lay before the jury a rational basis for the inference it ultimately wished to draw, namely that the non-recording of a certain type of information was circumstantial evidence that the alleged abuse never happened.

The problem lies in the unspoken and unproven premise. KWG was obviously under no legal or other duty to record such observations. She clearly did not follow a regular practice of making such entries because no entries of any kind of abuse were made. All sides agree that the diary entries were "mundane". Why assume that a diary devoted to "mundane" entries would necessarily report on episodes of physical and sexual abuse? On what logical basis would such a non-record give rise to an inference of testimonial deficiency or fabrication? In the absence of some evidentiary basis for the premise that abuse ought to have been recorded, the result of allowing the cross-examination to proceed as proposed by the defence ("the entire contents are fair game") would be to allow the defence to go to the jury at the end of the trial and to point to the absence of entries in an effort to suggest—nod nod wink wink—that women and children who are sexually and physically abused do not suffer in silence, but must and do confide their inner hurt even if only to their private diaries.

(8) Legitimate Scope for Cross-examination

This does not turn persons accused of sexual abuse into second class litigants. It simply means that the defence has to work with facts rather than rely on innuendoes and wishful assumptions. This means, in turn, that the defence should not be prevented from getting at the facts. As L'Heureux-Dubé J. wrote in *O'Connor*, *supra*, at para. 124:

> Although the defence must be free to demonstrate, without resort to stereotypical lines of reasoning, that such information is actually relevant to a live issue at trial, it would mark the triumph of stereotype over logic if courts and lawyers were simply to assume such relevance to exist, without requiring any evidence to this effect whatsoever. [Emphasis in original]

At the time of the trial, KWG was a mature and well-spoken 42-year-old adult. She was (or had been) an airline stewardess. She was not a child in need of any special protection from the court. There were arguably some contradictions between her testimony as an adult and what she had written as a teenager 27 years before, as the trial judge recognized. These arguable contradictions nourished the defence argument that the diary (including omissions) provided a more accurate picture of events in 1970 than KWG's unaided recollection. I therefore do not, with respect, agree with my colleague L'Heureux-Dubé J. at para. 176 that cross-examination on such issues would serve "no legitimate purpose".

A witness's powers of recall and the reliability of his or her memory are important issues in a trial of events that took place 27 years previously.

(9) The Trial Judge's Ruling with Respect to the Absence of Entries

The trial judge's ruling was certainly understood by Donald J.A. in the British Columbia Court of Appeal, as based on *O'Connor*. He concluded that *Mills, supra*, following on *O'Connor, supra*, "casts a new light on the question of the complainant's privacy and supports the impugned ruling" (para. 83). Further, "Mills . . . shifted the balance away from the primary emphasis on the rights of the accused" (para. 93), and again, "[t]he majority in Mills emphasized the need to concentrate on the context in which the competing rights arise in order to strike the right balance in each case" (para. 94).

Mills, of course, dealt with the constitutional validity of the procedure set out in ss. 278.1 to 278.9 of the Criminal Code for the production of third party records. It did not purport to deal with the proper limits of cross-examination using evidence already in the possession of the defence. Moreover, even in terms of production of third party documents, I do not, with respect, agree that "*Mills* has shifted the balance away from the primary emphasis on the rights of the accused" (para. 93 (emphasis added)) because *Mills* itself affirms the primacy—in the last resort of the requirement of a fair trial to avoid the wrongful conviction of the innocent. *Mills* states in para. 94 that:

> where the information contained in a record directly bears on the right to make full answer and defence, privacy rights must yield to the need to avoid convicting the innocent.

I agree with Donald J.A. that the trial judge applied *O'Connor* to limit the defence cross-examination of the complainant but I do not agree, with respect, that this Court in *O'Connor* or *Mills* either intended to or did substitute a test intended for the production of third party documents to the quite different problem of imposing limits on cross-examination as laid down in *Seaboyer* and *Osolin*.

. . . .

The appeal is therefore allowed with respect to the counts pertaining to KWG but is dismissed with respect to the other convictions of the appellant, the validity of which is affirmed.

L'HEUREUX-DUBÉ J. (GONTHIER J. concurring, dissenting): — . . . I respectfully disagree that the defence should have been permitted to question KWG on the absence of reference to abuse in her diary. The reasons for my disagreement are twofold. First, the trial judge should have ordered the diary returned to KWG, its rightful owner, and required the appellant to seek production of it through the appropriate statutory channels. Second, even if the appellant had acquired the diary through the proper channels in the first place, the prejudicial effect of the proposed line of questions on the absence of entries substantially outweighs its probative value.

Like my colleague, however, I do not think it is necessary to dwell on the property ownership debate. Even if we assume, in the appellant's favour, that the diary came into his hands in a manner consistent with the statutory scheme, I believe both the trial judge and the Court of Appeal were nonetheless correct to prohibit the proposed line of cross-examination on the diary. . . .

The test for admissibility of defence evidence is whether the prejudicial effect of that evidence substantially outweighs its probative value: *R. v. Seaboyer*. . . . In weighing prejudicial and probative value, the trial judge must consider not only the accused's right to full answer and defence, but also the importance of the complainant's and other witnesses' privacy and equality rights, as outlined in *R. v. O'Connor* . . . and *R. v. Mills*. . . . The majority decision in *Osolin*, *supra*, clearly held that, similar to *O'Connor*, *supra*, and *Mills*, *supra*, the privacy and equality rights of the complainant as protected by the Charter should inform the trial judge's decision on whether to restrict the defence's cross-examination.

On this point, I disagree with my colleague that "the nature and scope of KWG's diary did not raise privacy or other concerns of such importance as to 'substantially outweigh' the appellant's fair trial right to cross-examine on the [absence of entries in the diary] . . . to test the accuracy and completeness of KWG's recollection of events 27 years previously" (para. 150). Instead, I believe that such cross-examination would introduce a high potential of prejudice. That possibility substantially outweighs the minimal probative value of questions concerning the absence of entries in the complainant's diary. . . .

Proper consideration of the complainant's equality rights also requires an appreciation of myths and stereotypes in the context of sexual violence: see *Mills*, *supra*; *O'Connor*, *supra*; *Osolin*, *supra*; *Seaboyer*, *supra*. Allowing questioning on the absence of the mention of sexual assault in the diary would be to endorse the same discriminatory beliefs that underlie the "recent complaint" myth. As I explained in *Osolin*, *supra*, at p. 625, the recent complaint myth "suggest[s] that the presence of certain emotional reactions and immediate reporting of the assault, despite all of the barriers that might discourage such reports, lend credibility to the assault report, whereas the opposite reactions lead to the conclusion that the complainant must be fabricating the event". Similarly, questioning the complainant as to why certain reactions are not present in her diary or why she did not "report" the incident by recording it in her diary, implies that the absence of such writings is support for the conclusion that she fabricated the events.

The rape myth of "recent complaint" has long been dismissed by this Court and, if used to draw a negative inference about the complainant's credibility, constitutes a reversible error: see *R. v. D.D.*, [2000] 2 S.C.R. 275, at para. 63. As this Court firmly explained in *Mills*, *supra*, at para. 90: "The accused is not permitted to 'whack the complainant' through the use of [such] stereotypes regarding victims of sexual assault." Oftentimes, merely posing a question that may be directed to myths and stereotypes in the sexual assault context is enough to distort the truth-seeking goal of the trial process because the prejudice derives from the innuendo imbedded in the question.

In summary, an application of the *Seaboyer/Osolin*, supra, test that cross-examination should be restricted if the prejudicial impact substantially outweighs the probative value, reveals that the trial judge and Court of Appeal in this case were correct to prohibit the particular line of questioning proposed by the defence. In applying this test, we must consider the accused's right to full answer and defence and the complainant's privacy and equality rights. In the case at bar, the prejudicial effect is very high, while the probative value is, at best, minimal. The diary is an intimate record of the complainant's life during that period of time and the proposed line of cross-examination would necessarily open up much of the diary's contents to scrutiny.

Besides constituting a wide-ranging violation of the complainant's privacy rights, the proposed cross-examination also has potential equality implications, as victims would naturally be loath to report sexual assaults if they feared that their entire private lives would be intensely scrutinized at trial. Given that a diary is an individualistic exercise, questioning a complainant on the failure to record a sexual assault is akin to questioning a complainant as to why she failed to raise a "hue and cry" immediately after the assault. As the proposed line of questioning is animated by a discriminatory belief, the prejudice is high and the potential probative value is very low, if anything. In addition, the defence has the benefit of getting evidence by directly cross-examining the complainant on her version of events, and thus does not require the additional evidence that would result from questioning the complainant on why she did not write about the assaults. Therefore, the evidence is neither relevant nor necessary for the accused to exercise his right to full answer and defence. A review of all of these factors strongly indicates that the trial judge and Court of Appeal were correct to prohibit the proposed line of cross-examination on the diary, as the potential prejudice substantially outweighs the probative value of such an exercise.

Has the majority in *Shearing* changed the balance between rights of accused and those of complainants in sexual assault cases the Court recognized in *Mills*? Is there now a hierarchy of rights where the right of an accused to full answer and defence trumps rights of complainants? Is L'Heureux-Dubé J. correct in suggesting that the majority ruling allowing cross-examination on the lack of mention of abuse in the diary wrongly revives recent complaint myths and stereotypes?[360]

The *Code* provisions for production of third-party records as interpreted in *Mills* apply only to sexual offences.

---

360 For comments see Stuart, "Shearing: Admitting Similar Fact Evidence and Re-asserting The Priority of Rights of Accused in Sexual Assault in Sexual Assault Trials" (2002), 2 C.R. (6th) 222 and "Zigzags on Rights of Accused: Brittle Majorities Manipulate Weasel Words of Dialogue, Deference and Charter Values" (2003), (20) Supreme Court L.Rev. 267-296.

In *R. v. McNeil*[361] Charron J., speaking for a unanimous Court, made it clear that the common law regime set out in *O'Connor* is applicable to applications for the production of third-party records for offences other than sexual offences *whether or not there is a privacy interest in the record*. The Court also provided welcome clarification of the distinction between an *O'Connor* application and an application under the statutory regime for sexual offences. The Court made clear that *O'Connor* applications are different from those under the statutory regime. First, the likely relevance standard serves a different purpose. Where a sexual offence is involved, the standard is intended to counter myths and stereotypes regarding sexual assault victims; in the case of *O'Connor* applications, it is intended only to screen out unmeritorious applications so as to avoid wasting valuable court time and resources. It reaffirmed that the likely relevance burden to be met to get courts to inspect third-party records had to be realistic. The accused could not be expected to identify the precise use to which the record would be put if counsel hadn't seen the record. Second, under the *O'Connor* regime, much more balancing of the interests of the accused and that of the third party occurs at the second stage of determining whether production to the defence should occur, rather than at the likely relevance stage under the statutory regime. Justice Charron finally streamlined the two-part inquiry for *O'Connor* applications with the remarks that the relevancy assessment will usually be largely determinative of the production issue (para. 30) and if the claim of likely relevance is borne out on inspection, the accused's right to full answer and defence will, with few exceptions, tip the balance in favour of allowing the application for production (para. 41).

Indeed, the Court further offered a simple test at the second stage: If the third-party record happened to be in the Crown's file, would there be any basis for refusing to disclose it under *Stinchcombe* disclosure obligations? If not, the record should be produced to the defence.

M. (A.) v. RYAN
[1997] 1 S.C.R. 157, 4 C.R. (5th) 220

McLachlin J. (La Forest, Sopinka, Cory, Iacobucci and Major JJ. concurring):—

After having been sexually assaulted by the respondent Dr. Ryan, the appellant sought counselling from a psychiatrist. The question on this appeal is whether the psychiatrist's notes and records containing statements the appellant made in the course of treatment are protected from disclosure in a civil suit brought by the appellant against Dr. Ryan. Put in terms of principle, should a defendant's right to relevant material to the end of testing the plaintiff's case outweigh the plaintiff's expectation that communications between her and her psychiatrist will be kept in confidence?

. . . .

---

361 (2009) 62 C.R. (6th) 1.

IV. General Principles

The common law principles underlying the recognition of privilege from disclosure are simply stated. They proceed from the fundamental proposition that everyone owes a general duty to give evidence relevant to the matter before the court, so that the truth may be ascertained. To this fundamental duty, the law permits certain exceptions, known as privileges, where it can be shown that they are required by a "public good transcending the normally predominant principle of utilizing all rational means for ascertaining truth": *Trammel v. United States*, 445 U.S. 40 (1980), at p. 50.

While the circumstances giving rise to a privilege were once thought to be fixed by categories defined in previous centuries — categories that do not include communications between a psychiatrist and her patient — it is now accepted that the common law permits privilege in new situations where reason, experience and application of the principles that underlie the traditional privileges so dictate: *Slavutych v. Baker*, [1976] 1 S.C.R. 254; *R. v. Gruenke*, [1991] 3 S.C.R. 263, at p. 286. The applicable principles are derived from those set forth in *Wigmore on Evidence*, vol. 8 (McNaughton rev. 1961), sec. 2285. First, the communication must originate in a confidence. Second, the confidence must be essential to the relationship in which the communication arises. Third, the relationship must be one which should be "sedulously fostered" in the public good. Finally, if all these requirements are met, the court must consider whether the interests served by protecting the communications from disclosure outweigh the interest in getting at the truth and disposing correctly of the litigation.

It follows that the law of privilege may evolve to reflect the social and legal realities of our time. One such reality is the law's increasing concern with the wrongs perpetrated by sexual abuse and the serious effect such abuse has on the health and productivity of the many members of our society it victimizes. Another modern reality is the extension of medical assistance from treatment of its physical effects to treatment of its mental and emotional aftermath through techniques such as psychiatric counselling. Yet another development of recent vintage which may be considered in connection with new claims for privilege is the Canadian Charter of Rights and Freedoms, adopted in 1982.

. . . .

The first requirement for privilege is that the communications at issue have originated in a confidence that they will not be disclosed. The Master held that this condition was not met because both the appellant and Dr. Parfitt had concerns that notwithstanding their desire for confidentiality, the records might someday be ordered disclosed in the course of litigation. With respect, I do not agree. The communications were made in confidence. The appellant stipulated that they should remain confidential and Dr. Parfitt agreed that she would do everything possible to keep them confidential. The possibility that a court might order them disclosed at some future date over their objections does not change the fact that the communications were made in confidence. With the possible exception of communications falling in the traditional categories, there can never be an absolute guarantee of confidentiality; there is always the possibility that a court may order disclosure. Even for documents within the traditional categories, inadvertent disclosure is always a possibility. If the apprehended possibility of disclosure negated privilege, privilege would seldom if ever be found.

The second requirement — that the element of confidentiality be essential to the full and satisfactory maintenance of the relation between the parties to the communication — is clearly satisfied in the case at bar. It is not disputed that Dr. Parfitt's practice in general and her ability to help the appellant in particular required that she hold her discussions with the appellant in confidence. Dr. Parfitt's evidence establishes that confidentiality is essential to the continued existence and effectiveness of the therapeutic relations between a psychiatrist and a patient seeking treatment for the psychiatric harm resulting from sexual abuse. Once psychiatrist-patient confidentiality is broken and the psychiatrist becomes involved in the patient's external world, the "frame" of the therapy is broken. At that point, it is Dr. Parfitt's practice to discontinue psychotherapy with the patient. The result is both confusing and damaging to the patient. At a time when she would normally find support in the therapeutic relationship, as during the trial, she finds herself without support. In the result, the patient's treatment may cease, her distrustfulness be exacerbated, and her personal and work relations be adversely affected.

The appellant too sees confidentiality as essential to her relationship with Dr. Parfitt. She insisted from the first that her communications to Dr. Parfitt be held in confidence, suggesting that this was a condition of her entering and continuing treatment. The fact that she and Dr. Parfitt feared the possibility of court-ordered disclosure at some future date does not negate the fact that confidentiality was essential "to the full and satisfactory maintenance" of their relationship.

The third requirement — that the relation must be one which in the opinion of the community ought to be sedulously fostered — is equally satisfied. Victims of sexual abuse often suffer serious trauma, which, left untreated, may mar their entire lives. It is widely accepted that it is in the interests of the victim and society that such help be obtained. The mental health of the citizenry, no less than its physical health, is a public good of great importance. Just as it is in the interest of the sexual abuse victim to be restored to full and healthy functioning, so is it in the interest of the public that she take her place as a healthy and productive member of society.

It may thus be concluded that the first three conditions for privilege for communications between a psychiatrist and the victim of a sexual assault are met in the case at bar. The communications were confidential. Their confidence is essential to the psychiatrist-patient relationship. The relationship itself and the treatment it makes possible are of transcendent public importance.

The fourth requirement is that the interests served by protecting the communications from disclosure outweigh the interest of pursuing the truth and disposing correctly of the litigation. This requires first an assessment of the interests served by protecting the communications from disclosure. These include injury to the appellant's ongoing relationship with Dr. Parfitt and her future treatment. They also include the effect that a finding of no privilege would have on the ability of other persons suffering from similar trauma to obtain needed treatment and of psychiatrists to provide it. The interests served by non-disclosure must extend to any effect on society of the failure of individuals to obtain treatment restoring them to healthy and contributing members of society. Finally, the interests served by protection from disclosure must include the privacy interest of the person claiming privilege and inequalities which may be perpetuated by the absence of protection.

As noted, the common law must develop in a way that reflects emerging Charter values. It follows that the factors balanced under the fourth part of the test for privilege should be updated to reflect relevant Charter values. One such value is the interest affirmed by s. 8 of the Charter of each person in privacy. Another is the right of every person embodied in s. 15 of the Charter to equal treatment and benefit of the law. A rule of privilege which fails to protect confidential doctor/patient communications in the context of an action arising out of sexual assault perpetuates the disadvantage felt by victims of sexual assault, often women. The intimate nature of sexual assault heightens the privacy concerns of the victim and may increase, if automatic disclosure is the rule, the difficulty of obtaining redress for the wrong. The victim of a sexual assault is thus placed in a disadvantaged position as compared with the victim of a different wrong. The result may be that the victim of sexual assault does not obtain the equal benefit of the law to which s. 15 of the Charter entitles her. She is doubly victimized, initially by the sexual assault and later by the price she must pay to claim redress — redress which in some cases may be part of her program of therapy. These are factors which may properly be considered in determining the interests served by an order for protection from disclosure of confidential patient-psychiatrist communications in sexual assault cases.

These criteria, applied to the case at bar, demonstrate a compelling interest in protecting the communications at issue from disclosure. More, however, is required to establish privilege. For privilege to exist, it must be shown that the benefit that inures from privilege, however great it may seem, in fact outweighs the interest in the correct disposal of the litigation.

At this stage, the court considering an application for privilege must balance one alternative against the other. The exercise is essentially one of common sense and good judgment. This said, it is important to establish the outer limits of acceptability. I for one cannot accept the proposition that "occasional injustice" should be accepted as the price of the privilege. It is true that the traditional categories of privilege, cast as they are in absolute all-or-nothing terms, necessarily run the risk of occasional injustice. But that does not mean that courts, in invoking new privileges, should lightly condone its extension. In the words of Scalia J. (dissenting) in *Jaffee v. Redmond*, 116 S. Ct. 1923 (1996), at p. 1941:

> It is no small matter to say that, in some cases, our federal courts will be the tools of injustice rather than unearth the truth where it is available to be found. The common law has identified a few instances where that is tolerable. Perhaps Congress may conclude that it is also tolerable. . . . But that conclusion assuredly does not burst

upon the mind with such clarity that a judgment in favor of suppressing the truth ought to be pronounced by this honorable Court.

It follows that if the court considering a claim for privilege determines that a particular document or class of documents must be produced to get at the truth and prevent an unjust verdict, it must permit production to the extent required to avoid that result. On the other hand, the need to get at the truth and avoid injustice does not automatically negate the possibility of protection from full disclosure. In some cases, the court may well decide that the truth permits of nothing less than full production. This said, I would venture to say that an order for partial privilege will more often be appropriate in civil cases where, as here, the privacy interest is compelling. Disclosure of a limited number of documents, editing by the court to remove non-essential material, and the imposition of conditions on who may see and copy the documents are techniques which may be used to ensure the highest degree of confidentiality and the least damage to the protected relationship, while guarding against the injustice of cloaking the truth.

It must be conceded that a test for privilege which permits the court to occasionally reject an otherwise well-founded claim for privilege in the interests of getting at the truth may not offer patients a guarantee that communications with their psychiatrists will never be disclosed. On the other hand, the assurance that disclosure will be ordered only where clearly necessary and then only to the extent necessary is likely to permit many to avail themselves of psychiatric counselling when certain disclosure might make them hesitate or decline. The facts in this case demonstrate as much. I am reinforced in this view by the fact, as Scalia J. points out in his dissenting reasons in *Jaffee v. Redmond*, that of the 50 states and the District of Columbia which have enacted some form of psychotherapist privilege, none have adopted it in absolute form. All have found it necessary to specify circumstances in which it will not apply, usually related to the need to get at the truth in vital situations. Partial privilege, in the views of these legislators, can be effective.

The view that privilege may exist where the interest in protecting the privacy of the records is compelling and the threat to proper disposition of the litigation either is not apparent or can be offset by partial or conditional discovery is consistent with this Court's view in *R. v. O'Connor*, [1995] 4 S.C.R. 411. The majority there did not deny that privilege in psychotherapeutic records may exist in appropriate circumstances. Without referring directly to privilege, it developed a test for production of third party therapeutic and other records which balances the competing interests by reference to a number of factors including the right of the accused to full answer and defence and the right of the complainant to privacy. Just as justice requires that the accused in a criminal case be permitted to answer the Crown's case, so justice requires that a defendant in a civil suit be permitted to answer the plaintiff's case. In deciding whether he or she is entitled to production of confidential documents, this requirement must be balanced against the privacy interest of the complainant. This said, the interest in disclosure of a defendant in a civil suit may be less compelling than the parallel interest of an accused charged with a crime. The defendant in a civil suit stands to lose money and repute; the accused in a criminal proceeding stands to lose his or her very liberty. As a consequence, the balance between the interest in disclosure and the complainant's interest in privacy may be struck at a different level in the civil and criminal case; documents produced in a criminal case may not always be producible in a civil case, where the privacy interest of the complainant may more easily outweigh the defendant's interest in production.

My conclusion is that it is open to a judge to conclude that psychiatrist-patient records are privileged in appropriate circumstances. Once the first three requirements are met and a compelling prima facie case for protection is established, the focus will be on the balancing under the fourth head. A document relevant to a defence or claim may be required to be disclosed, notwithstanding the high interest of the plaintiff in keeping it confidential. On the other hand, documents of questionable relevance or which contain information available from other sources may be declared privileged. The result depends on the balance of the competing interests of disclosure and privacy in each case. It must be borne in mind that in most cases, the majority of the communications between a psychiatrist and her patient will have little or no bearing on the case at bar and can safely be excluded from production. Fishing expeditions are not appropriate where there is a compelling privacy interest at stake, even at the discovery stage. Finally, where justice requires that communications be disclosed, the court should consider qualifying the disclosure by imposing limits aimed at permitting the opponent to have the access justice requires while preserving the confidential nature of the documents to the greatest degree possible.

It remains to consider the argument that by commencing the proceedings against the respondent Dr. Ryan, the appellant has forfeited her right to confidentiality. I accept that a litigant must accept such intrusions upon her privacy as are necessary to enable the judge or jury to get to the truth and render a just verdict. But I do not accept that by claiming such damages as the law allows, a litigant grants her opponent a licence to delve into private aspects of her life which need not be probed for the proper disposition of the litigation.

VI. Procedure for Ascertaining Privilege

In order to determine whether privilege should be accorded to a particular document or class of documents and, if so, what conditions should attach, the judge must consider the circumstances of the privilege alleged, the documents, and the case. While it is not essential in a civil case such as this that the judge examine every document, the court may do so if necessary to the inquiry. On the other hand, a judge does not necessarily err by proceeding on affidavit material indicating the nature of the information and its expected relevance without inspecting each document individually. The requirement that the court minutely examine numerous or lengthy documents may prove time-consuming, expensive and delay the resolution of the litigation. Where necessary to the proper determination of the claim for privilege, it must be undertaken. But I would not lay down an absolute rule that as a matter of law, the judge must personally inspect every document at issue in every case. Where the judge is satisfied on reasonable grounds that the interests at stake can properly be balanced without individual examination of each document, failure to do so does not constitute error of law.

VII. Application to This Case

The Court of Appeal declined to order production of Dr. Parfitt's notes to herself on the ground that they were unnecessary given that she would not be called to testify. It ordered the production of notes and records of consultations with the appellant, but under stringent conditions. While the Court of Appeal did not proceed on the basis of privilege, its orders are supported by the principles relating to privilege that I have attempted to set forth.

The interest in preserving the confidentiality of the communications here at issue was, as discussed, compelling. On the other hand, the communications might be expected to bear on the critical issue of the extent to which the respondent Dr. Ryan's conduct caused the difficulties the appellant was experiencing. A court, in a case such as this, might well consider it best to inspect the records individually to the end of weeding out those which were irrelevant to this defence. However, the alternative chosen by the Court of Appeal in this case of refusing to order production of one group of documents and imposing stringent conditions on who could see the others and what use could be made of them cannot be said to be in error. In the end, the only persons to see the documents in question will be the lawyers for the respondent Dr. Ryan and his expert witnesses. Copies will not be made, and disclosure of the contents to other people will not be permitted. In short, the plaintiff's private disclosures to her psychiatrist will be disclosed only to a small group of trustworthy professionals, much in the fashion that confidential medical records may be disclosed in a hospital setting. I am not persuaded that the order of the Court of Appeal should be disturbed.

VIII. Conclusion

I would dismiss the appeal with costs.

[L'Heureux-Dubé J. would have allowed the appeal and set aside the decision of the Court of Appeal. In conclusion she reasoned as follows.]

L'HEUREUX-DUBÉ J.:—

. . . .

The Court of Appeal in the present case allowed the appeal in part. It did so after attempting some balancing of the privacy interests of the plaintiff and the interests in a fair trial. Consequently, it withheld the notes made for diagnostic purposes and restricted the dissemination and reproduction of the records once produced. Nonetheless, it did not review the documents before ordering their production. In my view, such a process does not give due consideration to the appropriate balance of the Charter values engaged by the discovery procedures.

Indeed, in these particular circumstances, and given the nature of the damages claimed and the information sought by the defence, very little meaningful protection has been accorded to these private records. If plaintiffs in such cases know that the entire contents of their discussion with their therapists or any other private records may be revealed to the lawyers and expert witnesses of the defendant, they may very well be deterred from seeking civil remedies. Without anyone reviewing the documents to remove information which is private, irrelevant or of very limited probative value, an order of production constitutes a serious breach of privacy while affording potentially limited benefit to the defence. A hierarchy of Charter values has been created, one where the defence is greatly advantaged while the effect on the plaintiff may be highly detrimental. In striking an appropriate balance of Charter values, such a hierarchy is impermissible. The Court of Appeal's decision must, therefore, be revisited. While the Court of Appeal's general approach was correct and while it did not have the benefit of our judgments in *O'Connor* and *L.L.A.*, at the time its decision was rendered, the process it adopted is infirm.

As regards the first issue, that relating to the privileged nature of the communications between the appellant and Dr. Parfitt, I agree with McLachlin J. that a successful claim of privilege has clearly been established for the records which were exempt from disclosure. I also affirm the Court of Appeal's general conclusion that it had a broader discretion to control the process of discovery for the remaining documents to ensure that it not affect one of the parties unjustly.

The exercise of discretion upon which the order was based did not effect an appropriate balance of the Charter values of privacy, equality, and fair trial. By failing to screen private records in such cases, the court creates a hierarchy of Charter values, where interests in privacy and equality may be seriously affected for records or parts thereof which may provide very little if any benefit to the defence or be unnecessary to ensure the fairness of the proceedings. Procedures adapted to the context of discovery in civil proceedings from the principles developed by this Court in *O'Connor* are in order.

I would allow the appeal with costs. The decision of the Court of Appeal should be set aside, except as regards the notes which were not disclosed, and the matter remitted back to the Master for determination in a manner consistent with the foregoing reasons.

TABLE OF CASES

A

A. (L.L.) v. B. (A.) (1996), 44 C.R. (4th) 91 1044
A.G. v. Radloff (1854), 156 E.R. 366 224
A.G. Man. v. Manitoba Egg & Poultry Assn. (1971), 19 D.L.R. (3d) 169 (S.C.C.).....360
A.G. Que. v. Charron (1984), 43 C.R. (3d) 240 (Que. S.C.) 591
Abrath v. N.E. Ry. Co. (1883), 11 Q.B. 79 (C.A.) 51
Adderly v. Bremner, [1968] 1 O.R. 621 (H.C.) 769
Aguoine v.Galion Solid Waste Material Inc. (1998), 38 O.R. (3d) 161 (C.A.) 119
Airst v. Airst (1998), 37 O.R. (3d) 654, 1998 CarswellOnt 2630 (Gen. Div.) 977
Allen v. Hay (1922), 69 D.L.R. 193 (S.C.C.) 390
Anderson v. Bank of B.C. (1876), 2 Ch. D. 644 (C.A.) 960
Anderson v. Flying Saucer Driver-In Ltd., (August 31, 2009), Doc 46818/05, [2009]
    O.J. No. 3617 (Ont. S.C.J.) 569
Anderson v. Maple Ridge (District) (1992), [1993] 1 W.W.R. 172, 1992 CarswellBC
    250, 71 B.C.L.R. (2d) 68 (C.A.) 197, 288
Anonymous, Lib. Ass. 28, pl. 5 (28 Edw. III) 858
Anthony v. Charter, [1933] 1 D.L.R. 684 (Alta. C.A.) 733
Ares v. Venner, [1970] S.C.R. 608, 14 D.L.R. (3d) 4 .... 467, 678, 730, 739, 763, 941
Ashburton (Lord) v. Pape, [1913] 2 Ch. 469, [1911-13] All E.R. Rep. 708 (C.A.)..... 978
Attorney General v. Hitchcock (1847), 154 E.R. 38, 1 Ex. 91 (Exch. Ct.)   231, 557, 559,
    579
Augustine v. Inco Ltd., [2006] O.J. No. 2607, 2006 CarswellOnt 3952 (S.C.J.) 769
Avon v. R. (1971), 21 D.L.R. (3d) 442 (S.C.C.) 509

B

B.C. Securities Commission v. Branch (1995), 38 C.R. (4th) 133 (S.C.C.) 488
Babcock v. Canada (Attorney General), [2002] 3 S.C.R. 3, 3 C.R. (6th) 1, 2002
    CarswellBC 1576, 2002 CarswellBC 1577 1021
Bacon v. Charlton (1851), 7 Cush. 586 780
Bardal v. Globe & Mail Ltd., [1960] O.W.N. 253 (H.C.J.) 373
Bater v. Bater, [1950] 2 All E.R. 458 (C.A.) 54, 59, 142
Batte (2000), 34 C.R. (5th) 197 (Ont. C.A.) 1060
Belknap v. Meakes (1989), 64 D.L.R. (4th) 452 (B.C.C.A.) 214
Bentley v. Cooke (1784), 99 E.R. 729 456
Berd v. Lovelace (1577), Cary 62, 21 E.R. 33 .... 959, 963
Bergwitz v. Fast (1979), 97 D.L.R. (3d) 65 (B.C. S.C.); reversed (1980), 108 D.L.R.
    (3d) 732 (B.C. C.A.) 1043
Bessela v. Stern (1877), 46 L.J.C.P. 467 (C.A.) 741
Betterton v. Turner (1982), 133 D.L.R. (3d) 289 (B.C.S.C.) 853
Bird v. Adams, [1972] Crim. L.R. 174 (Div. Ct.) 733
Bisaillon v. Keable, [1983] 2 S.C.R. 60 1032
Blank v. Canada (Minister of Justice), 2006 CarswellNat 2704, 2006 CarswellNat 2705,
    40 C.R. (6th) 1, [2006] 2 S.C.R. 319 .... 968, 970
Bleta v. R., [1965] 48 D.L.R. (2d) 139 (S.C.C.) 946
Boardman v. Director of Public Prosecutions, [1974] 3 All E.R. 887 .... 199, 248
Bondholders Securities Corp. v. Manville (No. 2), [1935] 1 W.W.R. 452 (Sask.
    C.A.) 390
Boudreau v. R., [1949] 3 D.L.R. 81, [1949] S.C.R. 262 .... 802, 814
Brewster Transport Co. Ltd. and A.T.U., Local 1374 (1992), 26 L.A.C. (4th) 240 (Alta.
    Arb. Bd.) (Tettensor) 34
Brisson v. The Queen, [1982] 2 S.C.R. 227 114

British Columbia Children's Hospital v. Air Products Canada Ltd./Prodair Canada Ltée
    (2001), [2003] B.C.J. No. 591, 2003 CarswellBC 614 (C.A.), leave to appeal
    allowed (2004), 2004 CarswellBC 121, 2004 CarswellBC 122 (S.C.C.)......... 1005
Brouillard v. R. (1985), 16 D.L.R. (4th) 447 (S.C.C.)........................... 10
Brown v. Eastern & Midlands Railway Co. (1889), 22 Q.B.D. 391 292
Browne v. Dunn (1893), 6 R. 67 (H.L.)...553
Bruton v. U.S., 391 U.S. 123 (1968) 736
Buckingham v. Daily News Ltd., [1956] 2 All E.R. 904 (C.A.)...........................426
Buksh v. Miles, [2008] B.C.J. No. 1500 (C.A.) 508
Buller v. Crips (1705), 87 E.R. 793...858
Bunka v. R., [1984] 4 W.W.R. 252 (Sask. Q.B.)...............................156
Buttes Gas & Oil Co. v. Hammer (No. 3), [1980] 3 All E.R. 475 (C.A.)................995

C

C.J.A., Local 579 v. Bradco Construction Ltd. (1993), 102 D.L.R. (4th) 402
    (S.C.C.) 33
CTV Television v. The Queen [R. v. Hogg] (2006), 214 C.C.C. (3d) 70 (Man.
    C.A.)..384
Calcraft v. Guest, [1898] 1 Q.B. 759, [1895-9] All E.R. Rep. 346 (C.A.)................977
Can. Atl. Ry. Co. v. Moxley (1888), 15 S.C.R. 145 [Ont.]...................................770
Canada v. Chapelstone Developments Inc. (2004), 191 C.C.C. (3d) 152 (N.B.
    C.A.)..980
Canada (Attorney General) v. Khawaja (2007), 52 C.R. (6th) 107 (F.C.A.)........... 1010
Canada (Attorney General) v. Lameman, 2008 CarswellAlta 398, 2008 CarswellAlta
    399, [2008] 1 S.C.R. 372 118
Canada (Attorney General) v. Ribic, 185 C.C.C. (3d) 129, 2003 CarswellNat 4708
    (C.A.)... 1010
Canada (Privacy Commissioner) v. Blood Tribe Department of Health, [2008] 2 S.C.R.
    574, 2008 CarswellNat 2244, 2008 CarswellNat 2245 967
Canada (Solicitor General) v. Royal Commission (Health Records), [1981] 2 S.C.R.
    494.. 1033
Capital Trust Co. v. Fowler (1921), 64 D.L.R. 289 (Ont. C.A.)...........................734
Carey v. Ontario, [1986] 2 S.C.R. 637 .... 1022, 1030
Carter v. Boehm (1766), 97 E.R. 1162...................................851, 853
Cassell & Co. v. Broome, [1972] 1 All E.R. 801, [1972] A.C. 1027 (H.L.) 374
Castellani v. R., [1970] S.C.R. 310, 9 C.R.N.S. 111, [1970] 4 C.C.C. 287 ....345, 348
Catholic Children's Aid Society of Toronto v. L. (J.), [2003] O.J. No. 1722, 2003
    CarswellOnt 1685 (C.J.).. 35
Cattermole v. Millar, [1977] Crim. L. Rev. 553 (Div. Ct.) 676
Central Burner Service Inc. v. Texaco Canada Inc. (1989), 36 O.A.C. 239 (C.A.)...... 32
Chambers v. Murphy, [1953] 2 D.L.R. 705 (Ont. C.A.)....................................425
Chapdelaine v. R., [1935] 2 D.L.R. 132 (S.C.C.) 762
Chote v. Rowan, [1943] O.W.N. 646 (C.A.).....................................736
Chrysler Can. Ltd. v. U.A.W., Loc. 1285 (1983), 11 L.A.C. (3d) 415 (Palmer) 34
Circosta v. Lilly, [1967] 1 O.R. 398 (C.A.) 952
City of Saint John v. Tans Oil Co. Ltd., [1966] S.C.R. 581 944
City of St. John v. Irving Oil Co. Ltd. (1966), [1966] S.C.R. 581 940
Clark v. R. (1921), 61 S.C.R. 608... 53
Clarke v. Holdsworth (1967), 62 W.W.R. 1 (B.C.S.C.)...............................596
Clarkson, [1986] 1 S.C.R. 383...485
Clement (1830), 168 E.R. 980 129
Colpitts v. R., [1965] S.C.R. 739...592
Cominco Ltd. v. Westinghouse Canada Limited et al (1979), 11 B.C.L.R. 142.........198
Commission des droits de la personne v. Attorney General of Canada, [1982] 1 S.C.R.
    215.. 1028

Commissioners of Customs v. Harz, [1967] 1 A.C. 760 (H.L.) 801
Commonwealth Shipping Representative v. P. & O. Branch Service, [1923] A.C.
     191..354
Cook (1997), 1997 CarswellNB 125, 7 C.R. (5th) 51 (S.C.C.)............................563
Corbett v. R., [1988] 1 S.C.R. 670, 64 C.R. (3d) 1, 41 C.C.C. (3d) 385..... 185, 190, 202
Cowles v. Balac, (2006), 273 D.L.R. (4th) 596, 83 O.R. (3d) 660 (C.A.), additional
     reasons at (2006), 2006 CarswellOnt 7936 (Ont. C.A.), leave to appeal refused
     (2007), 2007 CarswellOnt 1359, 2007 CarswellOnt 1360 (S.C.C.) 23
Creaghe v. Iowa Home Mut. Casualty Co., 323 F. 2d 981 (10th Cir., 1963) 663
Cronk v. Canadian General Insurance Co. (1995), 25 O.R. (3d) 505 (Ont. C.A.) 178,
     372
Cuff v. Frazee Storage & Cartage Co. (1907), 14 O.L.R. 263 (C.A.) 781

D

D. v. N.S.P.C.C., [1978] A.C. 171 (H.L.) 1043
D.P.P. v. Boardman, [1975] A.C. 421..252
Dagenais v. Canadian Broadcasting Corp., [1994] 3 S.C.R. 835, (1995), 94 C.C.C. (3d)
     289.. 150, 1001
Dagle v. Dagle (1990), 81 Nfld. & P.E.I.R. 245 (P.E.I.C.A.)................................137
Daishowa Inc. v. Friends of the Lubicon (1998), 39 O.R. (3d) 620 (Ont. Gen. Div.)..360
Dallas County v. Commercial Union Assurance Co. 286 F. 2d 388 (5th Circ.,
     1961) 679
Dalrymple v. Sun Life Assur. Co., [1966] 2 O.R. 227 (C.A.); affirmed 60 D.L.R. (2d)
     192n (S.C.C.) 663
Daubert v. Merrell Dow Pharmaceuticals Inc., 113 S.Ct. 2786, 509 U.S. 579
     (1993) 864, 866
Davies v. D.P.P., [1954] A.C. 378 (H.L.) 635
Davis v. U.S., 160 U.S. 469 (1895)... 50
Deep v. Wood (1983), 143 D.L.R. (3d) 246 (Ont. C.A.) 225
Delgamuukw v. British Columbia, [1997] 3 S.C.R. 1010, 1997 CarswellBC 2358 409
DeLuna v. U.S., 308 F.2d 140 (1962)...508
Dennis v. Codrington (1580), Cary 100, 21 E.R. 53...963
Derco Industries Ltd. v. A.R. Grimwood Ltd. (1984), 57 B.C.L.R. 395................ 1003
Descôteaux v. Mierzwinski, [1982] 1 S.C.R. 860, 28 C.R. (3d) 289, 70 C.C.C. (2d)
     385 .... 961, 977, 992
Devgan v. College of Physicians & Surgeons (Ontario), [2005] O.J. No. 306, 2005
     CarswellOnt 342 (Div. Ct.) 218
Di Iorio v. Warden of the Montreal Jail, [1978] 1 S.C.R. 152..............................517
DiCarlo v. U.S., 6 F. 2d 364, 368 (2d Cir., 1925)..620
Director of Public Prosecutions v. Boardman, [1975] A.C. 421 257
Director of Public Prosecutions v. Jordan, [1977] A.C. 699 861
Director of Public Prosecutions v. Kilbourne...245
Dodge v. Kaneff Homes Inc., [2001] O.J. No. 1141, 2001 CarswellOnt 1099
     (S.C.J.) 729
Donnelly v. U.S., 228 U.S. 243, 278 (1913) 755
Draper v. Jacklyn, [1970] S.C.R. 92, 9 D.L.R. (3d) 264.................. 199, 209, 288, 421
Drew Brown Ltd. v. The Orient Trader (1972), 34 D.L.R. (3d) 339 (S.C.C.) 390
Dubois v. R., [1986] 1 S.C.R. 366 131
Duncan v. Cammell, Laird & Co., [1942] A.C. 624 (H.L.) 1024

E

Ekman (2000), 146 C.C.C. (3d) 346 (B.C.C.A.) 487
États-Unis c. Ross (1995), 41 C.R. (4th) 358, (sub nom. United States of America v.
     Ross) 100 C.C.C. (3d) 320 (Que. C.A.)..490
Exhibitors Inc. v. Allen (1989), 70 O.R. (2d) 103 (Ont. H.C.) 763

F

F. (W.J.), [1999] 3 S.C.R. 569 726
F.H. v. McDouggal, 2008 CarswellBC 2041, 2008 CarswellBC 2042, [2008] 3 S.C.R.
    41, 61 C.R. (6th) 1 53
FL Receivables Trust v. Cobrand Foods Ltd., 2007 CarswellOnt 3697, 2007 ONCA 425
    (C.A.)..120
Festing v. Canada (Attorney General) (2003), 172 C.C.C. (3d) 321 (B.C. C.A.) 966
Fitzpatrick (1995), 43 C.R (4th) 343 (S.C.C.) 488
Folkes v. Chad (1782), 99 E.R. 589; (1783), 99 E.R. 686............................859, 954
Fontaine v. Insurance Corporation of British Columbia, [1998] 1 S.C.R. 424 42
Ford (2000), 33 C.R. (5th) 178 (Ont. C.A.) 490
Fowler v. Fowler, [1949] O.W.N. 244 (C.A.) 563, 950
Fox v. General Medical Council, [1960] 3 All E.R. 225, [1960] 1 W.L.R. 1017 .... , 544,
    546, 607
Francois (1994), 31 C.R. (4th) 201 (S.C.C.) 498
Fraser v. Aztec (1920), 20 Ex. C.R. 39..950
Frye v. United States, 293 F. 1013 (D.C. Cir. 1923) 866, 894

G

G. (S.G.) (1997), 8 C.R. (5th) 198 (S.C.C.) 489
Galloway v. United States, 319 U.S. 372 (1943).. 80
Garton v. Hunter, [1969] 1 All E.R. 451 (C.A.)...405
Gay (Guardian ad litem of) v. UNUM Life Insurance Co. of America, [2003] N.S.J. No.
    442, 2003 CarswellNS 419 (S.C. [In Chambers]) 1005
General Films Ltd. v. McElroy, [1939] 4 D.L.R. 543 (Sask. C.A.).........................579
Gentles v. Toronto (City) Non-Profit Housing Corp., [2006] O.J. No. 1013, 2006
    CarswellOnt 1543 (S.C.J.) 225
Gibb (1999), 30 C.R. (5th) 189 (Sask. Q.B.)..490
Gilbey v. Great Western Railway (1910), 102 L.T. 202 (C.A.) 780
Goodis v. Ontario (Ministry of Correctional Services), 2006 CarswellOnt 4077, [2006] 2
    S.C.R. 32 ....968, 969
Gordon v. Gordon (1980), 23 R.F.L. (2d) 266... 33
Gosselin v. R. (1903), 33 S.C.R. 255...459
Graat v. R. (1980), 55 C.C.C. (2d) 429, 443 (Ont. C.A.); affirmed (1982), 2 C.C.C. (3d)
    365 (S.C.C.)..854, 931
Graham (1997), 121 C.C.C. (3d) 76 (B.C.S.C.) 490
Grand Central Ottawa Ltd. v. Ottawa (City) (1998), 39 O.R. (3d) 47 (Ont. Prov.
    Div.)...390
Greater Niagara Transit Commission v. A.T.U., Local 1582 (1987), 43 D.L.R. (4th) 71
    (Ont. Div. Ct.) 33
Greenough v. Gaskell (1833), 39 E.R. 618 (Ch. Div.) 959
Griffin v. California, 380 U.S. 609 (1964) 508
Gross v. Brodrecht (1897), 24 O.A.R. 687 (C.A.) 300

H

Hamstra v. BC Rugby Union, [1997] 1 S.C.R. 1092 210
Hanes v. Wawanesa Mutual Insurance Co., [1963] S.C.R. 154, [1963] 1 C.C.C. 321 ..57,
    142
Harris v. Harris, [1931] 4 D.L.R. 933 (Ont. S.C.)..736
Harrison v. Carswell, [1976] 2 S.C.R. 200 360
Haw Tua Tau v. Public Prosecutor, [1981] 3 All E.R. 14 (P.C.) 513
Hawkins v. U.S., 358 U.S. 74 (1958)..475
Hebert (1990), 77 C.R. (4th) 147 (S.C.C.)..484
Henry v. Lee (1814), 2 Chitty 124 531

Hersees of Woodstock Ltd. v. Goldstein (1963), 2 O.R. 81 (C.A.); leave to appeal to
     S.C.C. refused 359
Hewson v. R., [1979] 2 S.C.R. 82..604
Higham v. Ridgway (1808), 103 E.R. 717 (K.B.)..............................755
Hill v. Baxter, [1958] 1 Q.B. 277 51
Hill v. Church of Scientology of Toronto, [1995] 2 S.C.R. 1130, 126 D.L.R. (4th)
     129..978
Hiuser v. Hiuser, [1962] O.W.N. 220 (C.A.) 137
Hobbins v. The Queen, [1982] 1 S.C.R. 553....................................814
Hoch v. The Queen (1988), 165 C.L.R. 292 (Aust. H.C.)..................258
Hodgkinson v. Simms (1988), [1989] 3 W.W.R. 132 (B.C. C.A.).........973
Holland v. P.E.I. School Board Regional Administrative Unit #4 (1986), 59 Teeniest. &
     P.E.I.R. 6 (P.E.I. S.C.) 947
Home v. Corbeil, [1955] 4 D.L.R. 750 (Ont. H.C.); affirmed 2 D.L.R. (2d) 543 (Ont.
     C.A.)..781
Homolka v. Harris, [2002] B.C.J. No. 831, 2002 CarswellBC 821 (C.A.) 200
Horsburgh v. R., [1968] 2 C.C.C. 288 (S.C.C.) 432
Horvath v. The Queen, [1979] 2 S.C.R. 376.....................................814
Hosegood v. Hosegood (1950), 66 T.L.R. 735, 738 (C.A.) 128
Hunter v. Southam Inc., [1984] 2 S.C.R. 145.................................. 1051
Hutton v. Way (1997), 105 O.A.C. 361, 1997 CarswellOnt 4692 (C.A.) 600

I

Ibrahim v. R., [1914] A.C. 599 (P.C.).....................................800, 814
Irwin Toy Ltd. v. Quebec (Attorney General), [1989] 1 S.C.R. 927 ....146, 151

J

Jaffee v. Redmond, 116 S. Ct. 1923 (1996) 1074
Jardin Direct Inc. v. Floradin Florists Ltd., [2006] N.J. No. 195, 2006 CarswellNfld 200
     (T.D.)..291
Jarvis v. London St. Ry. Co. (1919), 45 O.L.R. 167 (C.A.)................796
Jobin (1995), 38 C.R. (4th) 176 (S.C.C.) 488
John v. R. (1985), 49 C.R. (3d) 57 (S.C.C.)....................................563
Johnson v. Bugera (1999), 172 D.L.R. (4th) 535 (B.C. C.A.) 286
Johnson v. U.S., 333 U.S. 46 (1948) 2
Jones v. Crompton, [1977] 4 W.W.R. 440 (B.C. S.C.)...................... 1043
Jones v. Nat. Coal Bd., [1957] 2 Q.B. 55 (C.A.) 2, 563, 950
Jordan (1984), 39 C.R. (3d) 50, 57 (B.C.C.A.) 934

K

K. (H.W.) (2000), 32 C.R. (5th) 359 (B.C.C.A.) 487
Kabbabe (1997), 6 C.R. (5th) 82 (Que. C.A.)...................................490
Kajala v. Noble (1982), 75 Cr. App. R. 149 (C.A.)...........................405
Kelliher (Village) v. Smith, [1931] S.C.R. 672...........................861, 908
Kendall v. R. (1962), 132 C.C.C. 216 (S.C.C.)...........................648, 684
Khadr v. Canada (Minister of Justice) (2008), 56 C.R. (6th) 255 (S.C.C.)............. 1010
Khan v. College of Physicians & Surgeons (Ontario) (1990), 43 O.A.C. 130..........683
Khan v. College of Physicians & Surgeons (Ontario) (1992), 9 O.R. (3d) 641
     (C.A.)...684, 917
Khan v. The Queen (1990), 59 C.C.C. (3d) 92 (S.C.C.) 774
Kirkstall Brewery Co. v. Furness R. Co. (1874), L.R. 9 Q.B. 468 743
Kirsch v. R. (1982), 62 C.C.C. (2d) 86..635
Knutson v. Registered Nurses' Assn. (Saskatchewan) (1990), 90 Sask. R. 120, 1990
     CarswellSask 195 (C.A.) 484
Koufis v. R., [1941] S.C.R. 481 592

Kribs v. R., [1960] S.C.R. 400...625
Kruger et al. v. The Queen, [1978] 1 S.C.R. 104...410
Kuruma v. R., [1955] A.C. 197 (East Africa P.C.)...................................203, 204

L

Laliberte v. R. (1877), 1 S.C.R. 117 591
Landolfi v. Fargione (2006), 79 O.R. (3d) 767 (Ont. C.A.)................................200
Latour v. The Queen, [1978] 1 S.C.R. 361 559
Laufer v. Bucklaschuk, [1999] M.J. No. 553, 1999 CarswellMan 565 (C.A.)...........122
Law v. Minister of Human Resources Development, [1999] 1 S.C.R. 497 1058
Layden v. North American Life Assur. Co. (1970), 74 W.W.R. 266 (Alta. S.C.) 997
Layer's Case (1722), 16 Howell's State Trials 94 586
Lazard Brothers & Co. v. Midland Bank Ltd., [1933] A.C. 289 (H.L.)...................390
Leblanc v. R., [1977] 1 S.C.R. 339 ....244, 292
Leeds v. Alberta (Minister of the Environment) (1990), 69 D.L.R. (4th) 681 (Alta.
    Q.B.)... 1024
Leeson v. Leeson, [1936] 2 K.B. 156 (C.A.)...663
Leland v. Oregon, 343 U.S. 790 (1952)... 50
Lepage (1995), 36 C.R. (4th) 145 (S.C.C.)..498
Levis (Ville) c. Tetreault, 207 C.C.C. (3d) 1, 36 C.R. (6th) 215, [2006] 1 S.C.R. 420,
    2006 CarswellQue 2911 52
Lloyd v. Powell Duffryn Steam Coal Co., [1913] 2 K.B. 130 (reversed on other grounds
    [1914] A.C. 733 (H.L.))...755
Lloyd v. R. (1982), 64 C.C.C. (2d) 169 (S.C.C.)..998
London Gen. Omnibus Co. v. Lavell, [1901] 1 Ch. 135 (C.A.) 425
Lord Audley's Trial (1631), 3 Howell's State Trials 401...................................461
Lord Castlemaine's Trial (1680), 7 Howell's State Trials 1067...........................595
Lord Lovat's Trial, 18 Howell's State Trials 529, 651 591
Lucas v. Williams & Sons, [1892] 2 Q.B. 113..406

M

M. (A.) v. Ryan, [1997] 1 S.C.R. 157, 4 C.R. (5th) 220 ....978, 984, 1071
M'Naghten's Case (1843), 10 Cl. & F. 200, 207, 8 E.R. 718...........................50, 946
MacDonald v. Bublitz (1960), 31 W.W.R. 478 (B.C. S.C.)................................997
MacMillan Bloedel Ltd. v. Simpson, [1995] 4 S.C.R. 725 1029
Makanjuola v. Commissioner of Police of the Metropolis, [1992] 3 All E.R. 617
    (C.A.).. 1025
Makin v. Attorney-General for New South Wales, [1894] A.C. 57 .... 244, 248, 250, 287
Maranda v. Richer (2003), 15 C.R. (6th) 1...966
Marchand (Litigation Guardian of) v. Public General Hospital Society of Chatham
    (2000), 51 O.R. (3d) 97 (C.A.) 17
Marcoux v. R. (1975), 24 C.C.C. (2d) 1 (S.C.C.) 480
Martineau c. Ministre du Revenu national (2004), 192 C.C.C. (3d) 129, 24 C.R. (6th)
    207 (S.C.C.)...484
Masztalar v. Wiens (1992), 2 C.P.C. (3d) 294, 10 B.C.A.C. 19 (B.C.C.A.) 588, 590
Maves v. Grand Trunk Pacific Railway Co. (1913), 14 D.L.R. 70 (Alta. C.A.).........518
Mawaz Khan v. R., [1967] 1 A.C. 454 (P.C.)..663
Mawson v. Hartsink (1802), 170 E.R. 656 587
McArthur v. Prudential Insurance Co. of America (1969), 6 D.L.R. (3d) 477 (Ont.
    H.C.)...225
McCutcheon v. Chrysler Canada Ltd., [1998] O.J. No. 5818, 1998 CarswellOnt 5091
    (Gen. Div.) 419
McFarlane v. Safadi (2004), 70 O.R. (3d) 599 (C.A.)...................................... 10
McGreevy v. Director of Public Prosecutions, [1973] 1 All E.R. 503 (H.L.)............. 91
McInroy and Rouse v. R. (1978), 42 C.C.C. (2d) 481 (S.C.C.) 568, 577

McQuaker v. Goddard, [1940] 1 K.B. 687, [1940] 1 All E.R. 471 (C.A.)...............358
Mechanical & Gen. Inventions Co. v. Austin (1935), 153 L.T. 153, 157 (H.L.)........543
Melanson v. New Brunswick (Workers' Compensation Board) (1994), 146 N.B.R. (2d)
    294..995
Meyers v. Govt. of Man. (1960), 26 D.L.R. (2d) 550 (Man. C.A.)........................426
Mezzo v. R. (1986), 52 C.R. (3d) 113 (S.C.C.)...84, 92
Michelson v. United States, 335 U.S. 469 (1948)..238, 546
Middelkamp v. Fraser Valley Real Estate Board (1992), 71 B.C.L.R. (2d) 276
    (B.C.C.A.)... 1002
Middlemiss v. Middlemiss, [1955] 4 D.L.R. 801 (B.C.C.A.)..............................137
Miller v. Min. of Housing & Loc. Govt., [1968] 1 W.L.R. 992 (C.A.) 34
Miller v. Min. of Pensions, [1947] 2 All E.R. 372 (K.B.) 53
Minter v. Priest, [1929] 1 K.B. 655 (C.A.) 992
Mitchell v. Minister of National Revenue, [2001] 1 S.C.R. 911, 2001 CarswellNat
    873...411
Mizzi v. Debartok (1992), 9 O.R. (3d) 383 (Ont. Gen. Div.) 944
Moge v. Moge, [1992] 3 S.C.R. 813..368, 374
Monks v. ING Insurance Co. of Canada (2005), 76 O.R. (3d) 146 (S.C.J.)..............200
Monteleone v. R., [1987] 2 S.C.R. 154, 59 C.R. (3d) 97, 35 C.C.C (3d) 193 98
Montgomery v. Graham (1871), 31 U.C.Q.B. 57 (C.A.) 402
Montreal Harbour Comm. v. The Universe (1906), 10 Ex. C.R. 305 950
Mood Music Publishing Co. v. De Wolfe Ltd., [1976] Ch. 119, [1976] 1 All E.R.
    763..199, 288
More v. R., [1963] S.C.R. 522..949
Morris v. R., [1979] 1 S.C.R. 405, 6 C.R. (3d) 36 ....596, 604
Morris v. R., [1983] 2 S.C.R. 190, 7 C.C.C. (3d) 97, 36 C.R. (3d) 1......... 159, 198, 254
Morton v. Morton, [1937] P. 151 736
Murray v. D.P.P. (1992), 97 Cr. App. R. 151 (H.L.) 514, 515
Mutual Life Insurance Co. v. Hillmon, 145 U.S. 285 (1892) 781, 782
Myers v. Director of Public Prosecutions, [1965] A.C. 1001 ....27, 678, 730, 764

N

Named Person v. Vancouver Sun, [2007] 3 S.C.R. 252 1037
Nassiah v. Peel Regional Police Services Board, [2006] O.R.T.D. No. 18 (Ont. Human
    Rights Trib.) 926
New's Trustee v. Hunting, [1897] 1 Q.B. 607; affirmed [1897] 2 Q.B. 19 753
Noor Mohammed v. R., [1949] 1 All E.R. 365, [1949] A.C. 182 (P.C.).... 204, 285, 421,
                                                                                779

O

O.P.S.E.U. v. Min. of Correctional Services (1984), 2 O.A.C. 351 (Div. Ct.)............ 34
O'Connor (1996), 44 C.R. (4th) 1.. 1044
O'Connor's Trial (1798), 27 Howell's State Trials 1..586
O'Neill v. Canada (Attorney General) (2006), 42 C.R. (6th) 63, 213 C.C.C. (3d) 389
    (Ont. S.C.J.).. 1010
Oakes (1986), 50 C.R. (3d) 1 (S.C.C.) 49
Omychund v. Barker (1744), 26 E.R. 15 (C.A.)..427
Ontario v. O.P.S.E.U. (1990), 37 O.A.C. 218..121
Operation Dismantle Inc. v. The Queen, [1985] 1 S.C.R. 441..............................203
Otis (2000), 37 C.R. (5th) 320 (Que. C.A.) 487

P

P. (D.) v. Wagg (2004), 184 C.C.C. (3d) 312 (Ont. C.A.)...................................208
P. (M.B.) (1994), 29 C.R. (4th) 209 (S.C.C.) 488, 498
Parke, Davis & Co. v. Empire Laboratories Ltd., [1964] S.C.R. 351 165

Peart v. Peel (Regional Municipality) Police Services Board, [2006] O.J. No. 4457, 43
    C.R. (6th) 175, 2006 CarswellOnt 6912 (C.A.) 44, 165
People v. Callen, 194 Cal.App.3d 558 (1987) 1032
People v. Collins, 438 P. 2d 33 (Cal. Sup. Ct., 1968) 210
People v. Jovanovic, 263 A.D.2d 182 (U.S. N.Y.A.D. 1st Dept.).......................... 344
People v. Zackowitz, 172 N.E. 466 (1930).. 296
Phillion v. R., [1978] 1 S.C.R. 18 .... 608, 924
Phillips v. Ford Motor Co. (1971), 18 D.L.R. (3d) 641, [1971] 2 O.R. 637 (C.A.)........ 2,
    564, 950
Phillips v. Nova Scotia (Commissioner, Public Inquiries Act) (1995), 39 C.R. (4th) 141
    (S.C.C.) 489
Piche v. R., [1970] 4 C.C.C. 27 (S.C.C.) 736
Pitre v. R., [1933] 1 D.L.R. 417 (S.C.C.)... 395
Plimpton v. Spiller (1877), 6 Ch. D. 412 (C.A.).. 949
Polgrain Estate v. Toronto East General Hospital (2008), 60 C.R. (6th) 67 (Ont.
    C.A.)... 210
Pollard v. Simon, [2009] B.C.J. No. 1258 (P.C.).. 209
Porter v. O'Connell (1915), 43 N.B.R. 458 (C.A.) 852
Powell v. Cockburn (1976), 68 D.L.R. (3d) 700 (S.C.C.) 135
Pratte v. Maher, [1965] 1 C.C.C. 77 (Que. C.A.) 508
Primeau (1995), 38 C.R. (4th) 189 (S.C.C.)... 488
Pritchard v. Ontario (Human Rights Commission), 2004 CarswellOnt 1885, 2004
    CarswellOnt 1886, 19 C.R. (6th) 203, [2004] 1 S.C.R. 809 993
Pritt v. Fairclough (1812), 170 E.R. 1391 239
Prosko v. R. (1922), 63 S.C.R. 226... 800, 814

Q

Que. (A.G.) v. Hamel (1987), 60 C.R. (3d) 174 (Que. C.A.); leave to appeal to S.C.C.
    refused (1988), 89 N.R. 80n 131
Quebec (Ministere du Revenue) v. Buffolino (2009), 2009 CarswellQue 3837, 66 C.R.
    (6th) 188 (C.Q.) 108
Queen Caroline's Case (1820), 129 E.R. 976 (H.L.) 567

R

R. v. A. (No. 2), [2001] 2 W.L.R. 1546 (H.L.) 332
R. v. A. (R.H.) (2000), [2000] O.J. No. 2610, 2000 CarswellOnt 2420 (C.A.).......... 630
R. v. A. (S.) (1992), 17 C.R. (4th) 233, 76 C.C.C. (3d) 522 (Ont. C.A.) 728
R. v. A. (W.A.) (1996), 3 C.R. (5th) 388, 112 C.C.C. (3d) 83 (Man. C.A.).............. 236
R. v. Abbey (2009), 2009 CarswellOnt 5008, 246 C.C.C. (3d) 301, 68 C.R. (6th) 201
    (C.A.)... 879
R. v. Abbey, [1982] 2 S.C.R. 24, 29 C.R. (3d) 193, 68 C.C.C. (2d) 97..... 452, 895, 908,
    911, 933, 935, 944
R. v. Abdi (1997), 116 C.C.C. (3d) 385, 11 C.R. (5th) 197 (Ont. C.A.).................. 402
R. v. Adam, [2006] B.C.J. No. 2615 (S.C.) 395
R. v. Adelman, [1968] 3 C.C.C. 311 (B.C.C.A.)...................................... 355, 359
R. v. Ah Wooey (1902), 8 C.C.C. 25 (B.C.S.C.).. 427
R. v. Akins (2002), 5 C.R. (6th) 400 (Ont. C.A.) 261
R. v. Alarie (1980), 28 C.R. (3d) 73 (C.S.P. Qué.) 37
R. v. Albright, [1987] 2 S.C.R. 383... 37
R. v. Algar, [1954] 1 Q.B. 279 (C.C.A.)... 466
R. v. Allen, [1977] Crim. L. Rev. 163.. 839
R. v. Alston (1985), 36 M.V.R. 67 (B.C.C.A.) 155
R. v. Amway Corp., [1989] 1 S.C.R. 21 515

R. v. Anderson (1914), 22 C.C.C. 455, 16 D.L.R. 203, [1914] 5 W.W.R. 1052 (Alta. S.C.) 947, 948
R. v. Anderson, [1938] 3 D.L.R. 317 (Man. C.A.)...543
R. v. Andrews, [1987] A.C. 281..795
R. v. Angelantoni (1975), 31 C.R.N.S. 342 (Ont. C.A.) 107, 564
R. v. Anne Wycherley (1838), 173 E.R. 486..858
R. v. Anstey (2002), 2 C.R. (6th) 203 (Nfld. C.A.) 343
R. v. Anthes Business Forms Ltd. (1975), 19 C.C.C. (2d) 394, aff'd 26 C.C.C. (2d) 349, aff'd 32 C.C.C. (2d) 207 (S.C.C.)...767
R. v. Appleby (1971), 3 C.C.C. (2d) 354 (S.C.C.) 136, 138
R. v. Arcuri, [2001] 2 S.C.R. 828, 44 C.R. (5th) 213, 157 C.C.C. (3d) 21 101
R. v. Armstrong (1970), 1 C.C.C. (2d) 106 (N.S.C.A.) 998
R. v. Arp, [1998] 3 S.C.R. 339, 20 C.R. (5th) 1, 129 C.C.C. (3d) 321 ....97, 256, 276
R. v. Ay (1994), 93 C.C.C. (3d) 456 (B.C.C.A.) 622, 623
R. v. B. (A.R.) (1998), 128 C.C.C. (3d) 457 (Ont. C.A.), affirmed (2000), 146 C.C.C. (3d) 191 (S.C.C.)...344
R. v. B. (C.) (1997), 118 C.C.C. (3d) 43 (Ont. C.A.)..292
R. v. B. (C.) (2003), 7 C.R. (6th) 3 (Ont. C.A.) 279
R. v. B. (C.R.), 55 C.C.C. (3d) 1, 76 C.R. (3d) 1, [1990] 1 S.C.R. 717 ..... 183, 251, 257, 349
R. v. B. (D.M.) (2005), 193 C.C.C. (3d) 409 (Ont. C.A.) 352
R. v. B. (F.F.), [1993] 1 S.C.R 697 908
R. v. B. (G.) (1988), 65 Sask. R. 134 (C.A.) 905
R. v. B. (G.) (1990), 56 C.C.C. (3d) 200, [1990] 2 S.C.R. 30 650
R. v. B. (G.), [1990] 2 S.C.R. 3, 77 C.R. (3d) 327, 56 C.C.C. (3d) 161 ..... 434, 654, 682
R. v. B. (H.S.) (2008), 235 C.C.C. (3d) 312 (S.C.C.) 69
R. v. B. (K.G.) (1998), 125 C.C.C. (3d) 61 (Ont. C.A.)......................................530
R. v. B. (K.G.), [1993] 1 S.C.R. 740, 19 C.R. (4th) 1, 79 C.C.C. (3d) 257........538, 693, 726, 771
R. v. B. (L.) (1993), 82 C.C.C. (3d) 189 (Ont. C.A.)..585
R. v. B. (L.) (1997), 35 O.R. (3d) 35, 9 C.R. (5th) 38, 116 C.C.C. (3d) 481 (C.A.)... 185, 220, 273
R. v. B. (R.T.) (2009), 63 C.R. (6th) 197 (Ont. C.A.) 280
R. v. B. (S.A.) (2003), 178 C.C.C. (3d) 193, 14 C.R. (6th) 205 (S.C.C.)...........491, 943
R. v. B. (S.C.) (1997), 10 C.R. (5th) 302, 119 C.C.C. (3d) 530 (Ont. C.A.) 493
R. v. B. (T.) (2009), 63 C.R. (6th) 197 (Ont. C.A.)..223
R. v. Bailey (1983), 32 C.R. (3d) 337 (Ont. C.A.)...466
R. v. Bailey (1993), 22 C.R. (4th) 65 (Ont. Gen. Div.) 596
R. v. Baksh (2005), 199 C.C.C. (3d) 201, 2005 CarswellOnt 3106 (S.C.J.) 351
R. v. Baksh, [2008] O.J. No. 538 (C.A.)..353
R. v. Baldry (1852), 169 E.R. 568 (C.A.)...798, 799
R. v. Ball, [1911] A.C. 47 (C.A.)...244
R. v. Baltovich (2008), 56 C.R. (6th) 369 (Ont. S.C.)..211
R. v. Baltzer (1974), 27 C.C.C. (2d) 118 (N.S.C.A.) 665
R. v. Barber, [1968] 2 O.R. 245 (C.A.) 33
R. v. Barker (1829), 172 E.R. 558 (N.P.)..301
R. v. Barker, [1941] 3 All E.R. 33 (C.C.A.)...802
R. v. Barsalou (1901), 4 C.C.C. 347 (Que. K.B.) 238
R. v. Bartleman, 55 B.C.L.R. 78, [1984] 3 C.N.L.R. 114, 13 C.C.C. (3d) 488, 12 D.L.R. (4th) 73 (C.A.)..357
R. v. Bashir, [1969] 3 All E.R. 692 (Q.B.) 301
R. v. Basi (2009), 244 C.C.C. (3d) 537 (B.C. S.C.)...977
R. v. Basi, 2009 SCC 52 (S.C.C.)...1041
R. v. Basken (1974), 21 C.C.C. (2d) 321 (Sask. C.A.).......................................300

R. v. Baskerville, [1916] 2 K.B. 658 (C.C.A.)..635, 653
R. v. Batte (2000), 34 C.R. (5th) 197 (Ont. C.A.)..279
R. v. Batte (2000), 145 C.C.C. (3d) 498, 34 C.R. (5th) 263 (Ont. C.A.)...........273, 600
R. v. Baynham (2003), 173 C.C.C. (3d) 68 (B.C. C.A.) 512
R. c. Bédard (2005), 38 C.R. (6th) 119 (C.Q.).. 23
R. v. Bedingfield (1879), 14 Cox C.C. 341 789
R. v. Béland, 1987 CarswellQue 14, 1987 CarswellQue 96, [1987] 2 S.C.R. 398, 36
    C.C.C. (3d) 481, 60 C.R. (3d) 1 ....607, 860, 908, 925
R. v. Beliveau (1986), 30 C.C.C. (3d) 193 903
R. v. Bencardino (1973), 15 C.C.C. (2d) 342 (Ont. C.A.)............................544, 664
R. v. Berger (1975), 27 C.C.C. (2d) 357 (B.C.C.A.) 129
R. v. Bernardo (May 10, 1994), Doc. 247/94, [1994] O.J. No. 1718 (Gen. Div.).... 1008,
                                                                                      1009
R. v. Betterest Vinyl Manufacturing Ltd. (1989), 52 C.C.C. (3d) 441 (B.C.C.A.)......405
R. v. Biasi (1982), 62 C.C.C. (2d) 304 (B.C.S.C.)...767
R. v. Big M Drug Mart Ltd., [1985] 1 S.C.R. 295 468
R. v. Biladeau (2008), 63 C.R. (6th) 187 (Ont. C.A.) 513
R. v. Billett (1952), 105 C.C.C. 169 (B.C.S.C.) 52
R. v. Binder (1948), 92 C.C.C. 20 (Ont. C.A.) 508
R. v. Bird (1973), 13 C.C.C. (2d) 73 (Sask. C.A.) 592
R. v. Bird (1989), 50 C.C.C. (3d) 89 (Man. C.A.) 840
R. v. Bisson (1998), 14 C.R. (5th) 1 (S.C.C.) 61
R. v. Blackman, [2006] O.J. No. 5041, 2006 CarswellOnt 8085, 215 C.C.C. (3d) 524
    (C.A.)..728
R. v. Blackman, 2008 CarswellOnt 3722, 2008 CarswellOnt 3723, 232 C.C.C. (3d) 233,
    [2008] 2 S.C.R. 298, 57 C.R. (6th) 12 718
R. v. Blake (2003), 68 O.R. (3d) 75, 181 C.C.C. (3d) 169 (C.A.) 274
R. v. Bleta, [1966] 2 O.R. 108 (C.A.) 389
R. v. Boardman, [1975] A.C. 421 (H.L.) 244
R. v. Boissonneault (1986), 29 C.C.C. (3d) 345 (Ont. C.A.)..............................107
R. v. Bonisteel (2008), 61 C.R. (6th) 64 (B.C. C.A.)...................................886, 923
R. v. Bordo, (Que. S.C.) (July 11, 2009)...474
R. v. Borg, [1969] S.C.R. 551 165
R. v. Boss (1988), 46 C.C.C. (3d) 523 507
R. v. Bouchard (1973), 12 C.C.C. (2d) 554 (N.S. Co. Ct.) 563
R. v. Bouchard, [1970] 5 C.C.C. 95 (N.B.C.A.)..508
R. v. Boucher, [2005] 3 S.C.R. 499...135
R. v. Bowles (1967), 60 W.W.R. 276 (Alta. Mag. Ct.) 461
R. v. Boyce (1974), 28 C.R.N.S. 336 (Ont. C.A.)..596
R. v. Boyce (1975), 23 C.C.C. (2d) 16 (Ont. C.A.) 625
R. v. Bradbury (1973), 23 C.R.N.S. 293 (Ont. C.A.)..591
R. v. Brand (1995), 40 C.R. (4th) 137 (Ont. C.A.) 598
R. v. Brasier (1779), 168 E.R. 202 (Crown Cases) 625
R. v. Bricker (1994), 90 C.C.C. (3d) 268 (Ont. C.A.) 243
R. v. Brooks, [2000] 1 S.C.R. 237, 30 C.R. (5th) 201, 141 C.C.C. (3d) 321............642
R. v. Brouillard, [1985] 1 S.C.R. 39 ....11, 563
R. v. Brown (1999), 27 C.R. (5th) 151, 1999 CarswellOnt 2443, 137 C.C.C. (3d) 400
    (C.A.)..240
R. v. Brown (2002), 6 C.R. (6th) 380, 166 C.C.C. (3d) 570 (Ont. C.A.) 599
R. v. Brown (2002), 50 C.R. (5th) 1, 162 C.C.C. (3d) 257 (S.C.C.).................. 36, 990
R. v. Brown (2003), 13 C.R. (6th) 317 (Ont. S.C.J.) 671
R. v. Brown & Hedley (1867), L.R. 1 C.C.R. 70...587
R. v. Broyles, [1991] 3 S.C.R. 595..815
R. v. Bruha (2006), 39 C.R. (6th) 384 (N.W.T. C.A.).......................................599

R. v. Bryan (2003), 175 C.C.C. (3d) 285, 2003 CarswellOnt 2068 (C.A.)...............931
R. v. Buckley (1873), 13 Cox C.C. 293..781
R. v. Budin (1981), 58 C.C.C. (2d) 352 (Ont. C.A.)...428
R. v. Buhay, [2003] 1 S.C.R. 631, 10 C.R. (6th) 205, 174 C.C.C. (3d) 97, 2003
    CarswellMan 230, 2003 CarswellMan 231 208
R. v. Buric (1997), 114 C.C.C. (3d) 95 (S.C.C.) 205
R. v. Burkart, [1965] 3 C.C.C. 210 (Sask. C.A.) 606
R. v. Burns, [1994] 1 S.C.R. 656...908
R. v. C. (R.A.) (1990), 57 C.C.C. (3d) 522, 78 C.R. (3d) 390 (B.C. C.A.).............905
R. v. C. (T.) (2005), 27 C.R. (6th) 94 (Ont. C.A.)...276
R. v. C. (W.) (1990), 54 C.C.C. (3d) 37 (Ont. C.A.) 594
R. v. Caccamo (1975), 29 C.R.N.S. 78 (S.C.C.) 210
R. v. Calderwood, [1995] B.C.J. No. 625, 1995 CarswellBC 2543 (C.A.)...............387
R. v. Cameron (1995), 96 C.C.C. (3d) 346 (Ont. C.A.)...................................297
R. v. Camp (1977), 36 C.C.C. (2d) 511 (Ont. C.A.)..647
R. v. Campbell (1977), 38 C.C.C. (2d) 6 (Ont. C.A.) 607
R. v. Campbell (2006), 207 C.C.C. (3d) 18 (B.C. C.A.)...................................675
R. v. Campbell, [1999] 1 S.C.R. 565 994
R. v. Candale (2006), 205 C.C.C. (3d) 167 (Ont. C.A.)...................................275
R. v. Cargill, [1913] 2 K.B. 271 (Ct. Crim. App.) 559
R. v. Caron (1994), 94 C.C.C. (3d) 466 (Ont. C.A.).................................442, 454
R. v. Carpenter (1983), 31 C.R. (3d) 261, 266 (Ont. C.A.)...............................577
R. v. Carter (2005), 32 C.R. (6th) 1 (B.C. C.A.) 555, 556
R. v. Carter, [1982] 1 S.C.R. 938 ....747, 786
R. v. Cartwright (1914), 10 Cr. App. Rep. 219...619
R. v. Cassibo (1982), 70 C.C.C. (2d) 498 (Ont. C.A.) 560
R. v. Cassidy (1993), 26 C.R. (4th) 252 (Ont. Gen. Div.) 691
R. v. Castro (2001), 157 C.C.C. (3d) 255 (B.C. C.A.) 993
R. v. Cerniuk (1948), 91 C.C.C. 56 (B.C.C.A.) 354
R. v. Chambers, [1990] 2 S.C.R. 1293...740
R. v. Chan (2002), 168 C.C.C. (3d) 396 (Alta. Q.B.) 993
R. v. Chappell (2003), 15 C.R. (6th) 350, 172 C.C.C. (3d) 539, 2003 CarswellOnt 693
    (C.A) 703
R. v. Charemski, 15 C.R. (5th) 1, [1998] 1 S.C.R. 679, 123 C.C.C. (3d) 225 ..... 92, 111,
                                                                                          116
R. v. Charland (1997), 12 C.R. (5th) 226 (S.C.C.)..598
R. v. Chartrand (2002), 170 C.C.C. (3d) 97 (Ont. C.A.)...................................586
R. v. Chatwood, [1980] Crim. L.R. 46 (C.C.A.) 733
R. v. Chaulk, [1990] 3 S.C.R. 1303, 2 C.R. (4th) 1, 62 C.C.C. (3d) 193 ......51, 145, 151
R. v. Chayko (1984), 12 C.C.C. (3d) 157 (Alta. C.A.).....................................635
R. v. Chenier (2001), [2001] O.J. No. 4708, 2001 CarswellOnt 4354 (S.C.J.) 204
R. v. Chiarantano, [1990] O.J. No. 2603 (C.A.), aff'd [1991] 1 S.C.R. 906 1034
R. v. Chretien, [2009] O.J. No. 810 (S.C.J.) 568
R. v. Christenson, [1923] 2 D.L.R. 379 (Alta. C.A.) 625
R. v. Christie, [1914] A.C. 545 (H.L.) 619, 740
R. v. Cinous, [2002] 2 S.C.R. 3, 49 C.R. (5th) 209 111
R. v. Clark (1974), 1 O.R. (2d) 210 (H.C.)..389
R. v. Clark (1974), 3 O.R. (2d) 716 (C.A.)..389
R. v. Clark (1983), 35 C.R. (3d) 357, 7 C.C.C. (3d) 46 (Ont. C.A.).................450, 790
R. v. Clarke (1981), 63 C.C.C. (2d) 224 (Alta. C.A.) 606
R. v. Clarke (1998), 18 C.R. (5th) 219, 1998 CarswellOnt 3447, 129 C.C.C. (3d) 1
    (C.A.)... 223, 239, 589
R. v. Clayton, [2007] 2 S.C.R. 725 362
R. v. Cleghorn, [1967] 2 Q.B. 584 (C.A.) 563

R. v. Clewes (1830), 172 E.R. 678..736
R. v. Cocchio, [2003] O.J. No. 780, 2003 CarswellOnt 767 (S.C.J.)......................243
R. v. Collins (2001), 160 C.C.C. (3d) 85, 2001 CarswellOnt 3462 (C.A.) 423
R. v. Collins, [1987] 1 S.C.R. 265 ....206, 815
R. v. Comiskey (1973), 12 C.C.C. (2d) 410 (Ont. Prov. Ct.) 461
R. v. Connolly (2003), 176 C.C.C. (3d) 292 (N.S. C.A.) 733
R. v. Connors (1893), 5 C.C.C. 70 (Que. Q.B.) 592
R. v. Cook (1979), 9 C.R. (3d) 85 (Ont. C.A.)..625
R. v. Cooper (1977), 74 D.L.R. (3d) 731 (S.C.C.)... 91
R. v. Cooper (No. 1) (1974), 19 C.C.C. (2d) 135, 51 D.L.R. (3d) 216 (Ont. H.C.).... 466,
                                                                                    997
R. v. Corbett, [1988] 1 S.C.R. 670, 41 C.C.C. (3d) 385 .... 202, 203, 448, 896, 1001
R. v. Coté (1972), 22 D.L.R. (3d) 353 (Sask. C.A.) 466
R. v. Cotroni (1977), 37 C.C.C. (2d) 409 (Ont. C.A.), affirmed (sub nom. Papalia v. R.)
    [1979] 2 S.C.R. 256, 45 C.C.C. (2d) 1, (sub nom. R. v. Swartz) 7 C.R. (3d) 185, 11
    C.R. (3d) 150 405
R. v. Couture, 2007 CarswellBC 1365, 2007 CarswellBC 1366, [2007] 2 S.C.R. 517, 47
    C.R. (6th) 1, 220 C.C.C. (3d) 289 ....458, 476
R. v. Crawford, [1995] 1 S.C.R. 858 509
R. v. Creighton (1993), 20 C.R. (4th) 331 509
R. v. Cremascoli and Goldman (1977), 38 C.C.C. (2d) 212 665
R. v. Crosby, [1995] 2 S.C.R. 912, 39 C.R. (4th) 315, 98 C.C.C. (3d)
    225..320, 326, 330
R. v. Curtis (1998), 14 C.R. (5th) 328, 123 C.C.C. (3d) 178 (Ont. C.A.).................153
R. v. Curtis, [1989] N.J. No. 84 (C.A.)...647
R. v. Curto (2008), 2008 CarswellOnt 1238, 230 C.C.C. (3d) 145, 54 C.R. (6th) 237
    (C.A.)..622
R. v. Czibulka (2004), 189 C.C.C. (3d) 199, 24 C.R. (6th) 152 (Ont. C.A.)..............712
R. v. Czipps (1979), 48 C.C.C. (2d) 166 (Ont. C.A.)..461
R. v. D. (D.) (2005), 203 C.C.C. (3d) 6 (B.C. C.A.)...221
R. v. D. (D.), [2000] 2 S.C.R. 275, 36 C.R. (5th) 261, 148 C.C.C. (3d) 41 ......906, 1069
R. v. D. (L.E.), [1989] 2 S.C.R. 111 .... 257, 272, 273
R. v. D. (R.) (2004), 182 C.C.C. (3d) 545 (Ont. S.C.J.)......................................484
R. v. D'Aoust (1902), 5 C.C.C. 407 (C.A.) 592
R. v. D'Souza (2004), 188 C.C.C. (3d) 386 (Ont. C.A.)...................................... 10
R. v. Daniels, [1984] N.W.T.R. 311 (S.C.)...577
R. v. Danson (1982), 35 O.R. (2d) 777 (C.A.)..604
R. v. Darrach (1998), 122 C.C.C. (3d) 225 (Ont. C.A.)..323
R. v. Darrach, [2000] 2 S.C.R. 443, 36 C.R. (5th) 223, 148 C.C.C. (3d) 97, 191 D.L.R.
    (4th) 539 .... 4, 323, 330, 333
R. v. Dass (1979), 47 C.C.C. (2d) 194 (Man. C.A.) 158
R. v. Davey (1969), 68 W.W.R. 142, 6 C.R.N.S. 288 (B.C.S.C.)....................534, 676
R. v. Davies (1982), 1 C.C.C. (3d) 299 (Ont. C.A.) 1040
R. v. Davies, [1962] 1 W.L.R. 1111 (C.M.C.A.)..852
R. v. Davis, [1999] 3 S.C.R. 759 112
R. v. Davison (1974), 20 C.C.C. (2d) 424 (Ont. C.A.)................................221, 592
R. v. DeGraaf (1981), 60 C.C.C. (2d) 315 (B.C. C.A.) 394, 395
R. v. DeHaan (2002), [2002] O.J. No. 430, 2002 CarswellOnt 229 (C.A.) 630
R. v. Dejong (1998), 125 C.C.C. (3d) 302, 16 C.R. (5th) 372 (B.C. C.A.)..............298
R. v. DeLong (1989), 47 C.C.C. (3d) 402, 69 C.R. (3d) 147 (Ont. C.A.) 297, 1043
R. v. Demeter, [1978] 1 S.C.R. 538, 38 C.R.N.S. 317, 34 C.C.C. (2d) 137.............755
R. v. Demetrius (2003), 179 C.C.C. (3d) 26 (Ont. C.A.) 618
R. v. Deol (1981), 58 C.C.C. (2d) 524 (Alta. C.A.)..450
R. v. Deol (2006), 37 C.R. (6th) 335, 208 C.C.C. (3d) 167 (Man. C.A.) 1037

R. v. Devine, 2008 CarswellAlta 784, 2008 CarswellAlta 785, 232 C.C.C. (3d) 1, 57
    C.R. (6th) 1, [2008] 2 S.C.R. 283..720
R. v. Dhillon (2002), 166 C.C.C. (3d) 262, 5 C.R. (6th) 317 (Ont. C.A.) ... 243, 292, 655
R. v. Dickins (1999), [1999] A.J. No. 331, 1999 CarswellAlta 267 (Q.B.) 204
R. v. Dietrich (1970), 1 C.C.C. (2d) 49 (Ont. C.A.) 605, 912
R. v. Dikah (1994), 31 C.R. (4th) 105 (Ont. C.A.), affirmed (sub nom. R. v. Naoufal)
    [1994] 3 S.C.R. 1020..580
R. v. Dimitrov (2003), 18 C.R. (6th) 36, 181 C.C.C. (3d) 554, 2003 CarswellOnt 5212
    (C.A.)..919
R. v. Dinardo (1981), 61 C.C.C. (2d) 52 (Ont. Co. Ct.)..839
R. v. Dinardo, [2008] 1 S.C.R. 788, 231 C.C.C. (3d) 177, 2008 CarswellQue 3452, 2008
    CarswellQue 3451, 57 C.R. (6th) 48 620
R. v. Dionne, 198 C.C.C. (3d) 159, 29 C.R. (6th) 32, [2005] 1 S.C.R. 665 131
R. v. Diu (2000), 144 C.C.C. (3d) 481, 33 C.R. (5th) 203 (Ont. C.A.)....................298
R. v. Divitaris (2004), 188 C.C.C. (3d) 390 (Ont. C.A.)..............................616, 618
R. v. Donald (1958), 121 C.C.C. 304 (N.B.C.A.)..405
R. v. Donovan (1991), 65 C.C.C. (3d) 511 (Ont. C.A.)...241
R. v. Downey, [1992] 2 S.C.R. 10, 13 C.R. (4th) 129, 72 C.C.C. (3d) 1 ....148, 150
R. v. Doz (1984), 12 C.C.C. (3d) 200 (Alta. C.A.) 634
R. v. Drew (1837), 173 E.R. 433 (N.P.) 798
R. v. Driscoll (1987), 49 Alta. L.R. (2d) 383; affirmed [1987] 6 W.W.R. 748
    (C.A.)..156
R. v. Driver (1984), 39 C.R. (3d) 297 (Ont. Dist. Ct.) 165
R. v. Drysdale, [1969] 2 C.C.C. 141 (Man. C.A.)..286
R. v. Dubois, [1985] 2 S.C.R. 350 481
R. v. Ducharme (2004), 20 C.R. (6th) 332, 182 C.C.C. (3d) 243 (Man. C.A.) 847
R. v. Dunbar (1982), 68 C.C.C. (2d) 13, 138 D.L.R. (3d) 221 (Ont. C.A.) 994
R. v. Duncan (2002), 1 C.R. (6th) 265 (Man. Prov. Ct.)......................................753
R. v. Dunn (1975), 28 C.C.C. (2d) 538 (N.S. Co. Ct.) 664
R. v. Dunn (1993), 22 C.R. (4th) 344 (Ont. C.A.) 242
R. v. Dunning, [1965] Crim. L.R. 372 (C.C.A.)...449
R. v. Duvivier (1991), 64 C.C.C. (3d) 20 (Ont. C.A.)...473
R. v. E. (A.W.), [1993] 3 S.C.R. 155 1051
R. v. E. (T.K.) (2005), 194 C.C.C. (3d) 496, 28 C.R. (6th) 366 (N.B. C.A.)........... 1001
R. v. Ecker (1995), 96 C.C.C. (3d) 161 (Sask. C.A.)...323
R. v. Edwards (1996), 105 C.C.C. (3d) 21 (C.A.)..897
R. v. Edwards Books & Art Ltd., [1986] 2 S.C.R. 713................................146, 362
R. v. Edwards, [1983] Crim. L.R. 539 741
R. v. Eldorado Nuclear Ltd., [1983] 2 S.C.R. 551 1029
R. v. Ellard (2003), 172 C.C.C. (3d) 28, 10 C.R. (6th) 189 (B.C. C.A.)..................583
R. v. Ellard (2009), 2009 CarswellBC 1514, 2009 CarswellBC 1515, 67 C.R. (6th) 78,
    245 C.C.C. (3d) 183 (S.C.C.)...617
R. v. Elliott (1984), 15 C.C.C. (3d) 195 (Alta. C.A.)..738
R. v. Elmosri (1985), 23 C.C.C. (3d) 503 (Ont. C.A.) 94
R. v. Escobar-Benavidez, 200 C.C.C. (3d) 287, [2005] 3 S.C.R. 386.....................221
R. v. Esposito (1985), 24 C.C.C. (3d) 88 (Ont. C.A.) 634
R. v. Evans, [1993] 3 S.C.R. 653..96, 668, 748
R. v. Ewanchuk, [1999] 1 S.C.R. 330, 131 C.C.C. (3d) 481, 22 C.R. (5th) 1......320, 331
R. v. F. (C.C.), [1997] 3 S.C.R. 1183, 11 C.R. (5th) 209, 120 C.C.C. (3d) 225 ...438, 536
R. v. F. (D.S.) (1999), 132 C.C.C. (3d) 97, 23 C.R. (5th) 37 (Ont. C.A.) 235
R. v. F. (J.) (2003), 177 C.C.C. (3d) 1 (Ont. C.A.)..630
R. v. F. (J.E.) (1993), 26 C.R. (4th) 220 (Ont. C.A.) 621, 622
R. v. F. (R.G.) (1997), [1997] A.J. No. 409, 1997 CarswellAlta 336 (Alta. C.A.)......443
R. v. F. (W.J.), [1999] 3 S.C.R. 569, 27 C.R. (5th) 169, 138 C.C.C. (3d) 1..............439

R. v. Fannon (1922), 22 S.R.N.S.W. 427 (C.A.) 619
R. v. Farler (1837), 173 E.R. 418 635
R. v. Farler (2006), 131 C.C.C. (3d) 134 (N.S. C.A.) 281
R. v. Farley (1995), 40 C.R. (4th) 190, 99 C.C.C. (3d) 76 454
R. v. Farrant, 4 C.C.C. (3d) 354, [1983] 1 S.C.R. 124, 32 C.R. (3d) 289...........234, 241
R. v. Faryna, [1983] 1 W.W.R. 577 (Man. C.A.) 619
R. v. Fatima and Khan, [2004] O.J. No. 6155 (S.C.J.) 349
R. v. Fehr, [2000] B.C.J. No. 2660 (S.C.J.), aff. [2000] B.C.J. No. 2660 (C.A.).......395
R. v. Felderhof (2003), 180 C.C.C. (3d) 498, 17 C.R. (6th) 20, 2003 CarswellOnt 4943
    (C.A.)... 14
R. v. Fell (2001), [2001] E.W.J. No. 1324 (C.A.)..923
R. v. Fellichle (1979), 12 C.R. (3d) 207 (B.C.S.C.) 461
R. v. Ferguson (1992), 70 C.C.C. (3d) 330 (P.E.I. T.D.) 156
R. v. Ferris (1994), 34 C.R. (4th) 26 (S.C.C.), affirming (1993), 27 C.R. (4th) 141 (Alta.
    C.A.)..195
R. v. Filippelli (2002), 12 C.R. (6th) 384, 169 C.C.C. (3d) 217 (Ont. C.A.).............. 37
R. v. Finnessey (1906), 11 O.L.R. 338 (C.A.) 300, 301, 579
R. v. Finta (1992), 73 C.C.C. (3d) 65 (Ont. C.A.), affirmed (1994), 88 C.C.C. (3d) 417
    (S.C.C.) 36, 761
R. v. Firkins (1977), 37 C.C.C. (2d) 227 (B.C.C.A.); leave to appeal to S.C.C. refused
    (1978), 80 D.L.R. (3d) 63n...647
R. v. Fisher (1961), 34 C.R. 320 (Ont. C.A.) 930
R. v. Fisher (2003), 18 C.R. (6th) 377, 179 C.C.C. (3d) 138 (Sask. C.A.) 896
R. v. Fitton, [1956] O.R. 696 (C.A.)...803
R. v. Fleet (2001), 48 C.R. (5th) 28 (N.S. C.A.)..568, 578
R. v. Fletcher (1830), 172 E.R. 691..736
R. v. Fletcher (1982), 1 C.C.C. (3d) 370 (Ont. C.A.), leave to appeal to S.C.C. refused
    (1983), 48 N.R. 319 (S.C.C.) 439, 453
R. v. Flis (2006), 205 C.C.C. (3d) 384 (Ont. C.A.) 229
R. v. Folland (1999), 132 C.C.C. (3d) 14 (Ont. C.A.).......................................761
R. v. Fontaine, 2004 CarswellQue 814, 2004 CarswellQue 815, 18 C.R. (6th) 203, 183
    C.C.C. (3d) 1 (S.C.C.)..115
R. v. Foreman (2002), 6 C.R. (6th) 201, 169 C.C.C. (3d) 489 (Ont. C.A.)..............733
R. v. Fosty (1998), (Reference re Gruenke) 131 C.C.C. (3d) 72 (Man. C.A.) 959
R. v. Fosty, [2000] 1 S.C.R. 836 959
R. v. François (1994), 31 C.R. (4th) 201 (S.C.C.) 501, 505, 651
R. v. Freng (1993), 86 C.C.C. (3d) 91 (B.C.C.A.) 155
R. v. Furley (1844), 1 Cox C.C. 76 798
R. v. G. (A.) (1998), 21 C.R. (5th) 149, 130 C.C.C. (3d) 30 (Ont. C.A.)................651
R. v. G. (G.) (1997), 115 C.C.C. (3d) 1 (Ont. C.A.) 630
R. v. G. (P.) (2009), 2009 CarswellOnt 123, 242 C.C.C. (3d) 558, 63 C.R. (6th) 301
    (C.A.)..880, 917
R. v. G. (S.), [2007] O.J. No. 1645 (S.C.J.) 344
R. v. G. (S.G.), 8 C.R. (5th) 198, [1997] 2 S.C.R. 716, 116 C.C.C. (3d) 193............221
R. v. Galarce (1983), 35 C.R. (3d) 268 (Sask. Q.B.) 405
R. v. Gardiner (1982), 68 C.C.C. (2d) 477 (S.C.C.) 37
R. v. Garner (1848), 3 Cox C.C. 175 819
R. v. Gassyt (1998), 127 C.C.C. (3d) 546 (Ont. C.A.), leave to appeal refused (1999),
    136 C.C.C. (3d) vi (S.C.C.) 586
R. v. Gavin (1885), 15 Cox C.C. 656...799
R. v. Geddes (1979), 52 C.C.C. (2d) 230 (Man. C.A.)......................................593
R. v. German, [1947] O.R. 395 (C.A.) 852
R. v. Ghorvei (1999), 29 C.R. (5th) 102, 138 C.C.C. (3d) 340, 1999 CarswellOnt 2763
    (C.A.)...580

R. v. Gibbons, [2009] O.J. No. 2295 (S.C.J.) 125
R. v. Gibson (2008), 55 C.R. 201 (S.C.C.) 135
R. v. Giraldi (1975), 28 C.C.C. (2d) 248, [1975] W.W.D. 166 (B.C.C.A.) 607
R. v. Giroux (1985), 38 Sask. R. 172 (Q.B.) 461
R. v. Giroux (2006), 207 C.C.C. (3d) 512 (Ont. C.A.) 555
R. v. Gladue, [1999] 1 S.C.R. 688 177
R. v. Glowatski (2001), 160 C.C.C. (3d) 525, 47 C.R. (5th) 230 (B.C. C.A.) 578
R. v. Gonzague (1983), 4 C.C.C. (3d) 505, 34 C.R. (3d) 169.............581, 588, 589, 591
R. v. Gosselin (1988), 45 C.C.C. (3d) 568 (Ont. C.A.) 155
R. v. Gostick (1999), 137 C.C.C. (3d) 53 (Ont. C.A.)...630
R. v. Gottschall (1983), 10 C.C.C. (3d) 447 (N.S. C.A.) 286
R. v. Gough (1985), 43 C.R. (3d) 297 (Ont. C.A.)..155
R. v. Gouin (1926), 41 Que. K.B. 157 (C.A.)...633
R. v. Gouin, [1926] S.C.R. 539..635
R. v. Graham (1972), 7 C.C.C. (2d) 93 (S.C.C.) 132, 795
R. v. Grand-Pierre (1998), 124 C.C.C. (3d) 236 (Que. C.A.)................................795
R. v. Grandinetti, 191 C.C.C. (3d) 449, [2005] 1 S.C.R. 27, 25 C.R. (6th) 1 292
R. v. Grant (2009), 66 C.R. (6th) 1 (S.C.C.) 206
R. v. Green, [1998] O.J. No. 3598 (Ont. Gen. Div.)..532
R. v. Griffin (2009), 67 (6th) 1 (S.C.C.) 96
R. v. Grift (1986), 43 Alta. L.R. (2d) 365 (Q.B.)...155
R. v. Grimba (1978), 38 C.C.C. (2d) 469 (Ont. Co. Ct.)......................................767
R. v. Grosse (1983), 9 C.C.C. (3d) 465 (N.S.C.A.); leave to appeal to S.C.C. refused 61
      N.S.R. (2d) 447n 238
R. v. Gruenke, [1991] 3 S.C.R. 263, 67 C.C.C. (3d) 289, 8 C.R. (4th) 368 ....955, 991,
                                                                                            1072
R. v. Gunewardene, [1951] 2 All E.R. 290, [1951] 2 K.B. 600 (C.C.A.)..................587
R. v. Gunning (2005), 29 C.R. (6th) 17 ....107, 849
R. v. H. (E.L.), [1990] N.S.J. No. 374 (C.A.)...903
R. v. H. (L.T.), [2008] 2 S.C.R. 739 97
R. v. H. (S.E.) (1994), [1994] B.C.J. No. 3057, 1994 CarswellBC 1721 (C.A.) 229
R. v. Hall (1987), 5 N.Z.L.R. 93 (C.A) 251
R. v. Hamilton (2003), 180 C.C.C. (3d) 80 (B.C. C.A.) 297
R. v. Hamilton, [2004] O.J. No. 3252, 2004 CarswellOnt 3214, 186 C.C.C. (3d) 129,
      241 D.L.R. (4th) 490, 22 C.R. (6th) 1 (Ont. C.A.).................................176, 383
R. v. Hanaway (1980), 63 C.C.C. (2d) 44 (Ont. Dist. Ct.)....................................534
R. v. Handy, [2002] 2 S.C.R. 908, 1 C.R. (6th) 203, 2002 CarswellOnt 1968, 2002
      CarswellOnt 1969, 164 C.C.C. (3d) 481..................................... 261, 289, 294
R. v. Hanemaayer (2008), 2008 CarswellOnt 4698, 234 C.C.C. (3d) 3 (Ont. C.A.)..... 85
R. v. Hardy (1794), 24 Howell's State Trials 199... 1030
R. v. Harrer, [1995] 3 S.C.R. 562, 42 C.R. (4th) 269, 101 C.C.C. (3d) 193 ....200, 204
R. v. Harris (1844), 1 Cox C.C. 106 798
R. v. Harris, [1927] 2 K.B. 587 (C.C.A.) 563, 950
R. v. Harris, [1997] O.J. No. 3560 330
R. v. Harrison (2001), 44 C.R. (5th) 120 (B.C. C.A.) 788
R. v. Harrison (2009), 66 C.R. (6th) 105 (S.C.C.) 207, 208
R. v. Harrison, [1928] 3 D.L.R. 224 (B.C.C.A.) 619
R. v. Harrison, [1946] 3 D.L.R. 690 741
R. v. Harvey (2001), 48 C.R. (5th) 247, 160 C.C.C. (3d) 52 (Ont. C.A.).................285
R. v. Hawke (1974), 3 O.R. (2d) 210 (Ont. H.C.)...544
R. v. Hawke (1975), 22 C.C.C. (2d) 19 (Ont. C.A.) 450, 605
R. v. Hawkins, [1996] 3 S.C.R. 1043, 2 C.R. (5th) 245, 111 C.C.C. (3d) 129....470, 709,
                                                                              720, 722, 726, 771
R. v. Hearne (1830), 172 E.R. 676..736

R. v. Hebert, [1990] 2 S.C.R. 151..813
R. v. Henry, [2005] 3 S.C.R. 609, 33 C.R. (6th) 215, 202 C.C.C. (3d) 449..............481
R. v. Hewitt (1986), 55 C.R. (3d) 41 (Man. C.A.) 165
R. v. Hill (1851), 169 E.R. 495 449
R. v. Hinchey, 111 C.C.C. (3d) 353, 3 C.R. (5th) 187, [1996] 3 S.C.R. 1128 221
R. v. Hodgson, 127 C.C.C. (3d) 449, 1998 CarswellOnt 3417, 1998 CarswellOnt 3418,
    18 C.R. (5th) 135, [1998] 2 S.C.R. 449..804
R. v. Hoffman (1994), 32 C.R. (4th) 396 603
R. v. Hoilett (1999), 136 C.C.C. (3d) 449 821
R. v. Holmes (1871), LR 1 CCR 334..334
R. v. Holmes, [1953] 1 W.L.R. 686 (C.C.A.)...946
R. v. Holmes, [1988] 1 S.C.R. 914..152
R. v. Howard and Trudel (1983), 3 C.C.C. (3d) 399, 1983 CarswellOnt 1332 (Ont.
    C.A.)..413
R. v. Howard, [1989] 1 S.C.R. 1357..414, 546
R. v. Hrechuk (1951), 58 Man. R. 489 (C.A.) 559
R. v. Hryn (1981), 63 C.C.C. (2d) 390 (Ont. Co. Ct.).......................................741
R. v. Hufsky (1988), 63 C.R. (3d) 14 (S.C.C.) 362
R. v. Humaid (2006), 37 C.R. (6th) 347, 208 C.C.C. (3d) 43 (Ont. C.A.)................194
R. v. Hunter (1987), 57 C.R. (3d) 1 (Ont. C.A.).. 1031
R. v. Hunter (2001), 155 C.C.C. (3d) 225, 45 C.R. (5th) 345, 2001 CarswellOnt 2164
    (C.A.)..195
R. v. Hurry (2002), 4 C.R. (6th) 358, 165 C.C.C. (3d) 182 (Alta. Q.B.)..................350
R. v. I.D., February 19, 2010..446
R. v. J. (F.E.) (1990), 74 C.R. (3d) 269, 53 C.C.C. (3d) 64 (Ont. C.A.) 649
R. v. J. (J.-L.), [2000] 2 S.C.R. 600, 37 C.R. (5th) 203, 148 C.C.C. (3d) 487, 2000
    CarswellQue 2310, 2000 CarswellQue 2311 865
R. v. J.S.P., Vancouver Registry Nos. CC970130 & CC960237, May 15, 1997, B.C.
    S.C.. 1056
R. v. J.T.S., [1997] A.J. No. 125 (C.A.) 259
R. v. Jackson (1977), 34 C.C.C. (2d) 35 (B.C.C.A.)..819
R. v. Jackson (1980), 57 C.C.C. (2d) 154 (Ont. C.A.) 734
R. v. Jackson (1984), 14 C.R.R. 248 (B.C. Co. Ct.) 41
R. v. Jackson, [1995] O.J. No. 2471, 1995 CarswellOnt 3388 (C.A.).....................583
R. v. Jahn, [1982] 3 W.W.R. 684 (Alta. C.A.)..389
R. v. Jarosz (1982), 3 C.R.R. 333 186
R. v. Jean (1979), 46 C.C.C. (2d) 176, 7 C.R. (3d) 338 (Alta. C.A.); affirmed (1980), 51
    C.C.C. (2d) 192n (S.C.C.)..998, 1000
R. v. Jeffrey (1993), 25 C.R. (4th) 104 (Alta. C.A.) 470
R. v. Johnson (1965), 49 C.R. 176 (N.S. S.C.) 298
R. v. Johnston (1992), 69 C.C.C. (3d) 395, 12 C.R. (4th) 99 (Ont. Gen. Div.)..........894
R. v. Jolivet, [2000] 1 S.C.R. 751...507
R. v. Jones (1925), 19 Cr. App. R. 40 646
R. v. Jones (1988), 66 C.R. (3d) 54, 44 C.C.C. (3d) 248 (Ont. C.A.) 593
R. v. Jones, 89 C.C.C. (3d) 353, 30 C.R. (4th) 1, [1994] 2 S.C.R. 229 484
R. v. Jordan (1983), 33 C.R. (3d) 394 (B.C. Co. Ct.).......................................933
R. v. Jordan (1984), 11 C.C.C. (3d) 565 (B.C.C.A.)...941
R. v. Junaid Khan (1987), 84 Cr. App. R. 44 (C.A.) 466
R. v. Jurtyn, [1958] O.W.N. 355 (C.A.) 762
R. v. K. (C.P.) (2002), 7 C.R. (6th) 16 (Ont. C.A.) 286
R. v. K. (S.) (1995), 99 C.C.C. (3d) 376 (Ont. C.A.)....................................... 90
R. v. K. (T.A.) (2006), 207 C.C.C. (3d) 547, 2006 CarswellBC 483 (C.A.) 401
R. v. K. (V.) (1991), 4 C.R. (4th) 338 (B.C. C.A.)...649
R. v. Kalevar (1991), 4 C.R. (4th) 114 (Ont. Gen. Div.)...................................428

R. v. Kanester, [1966] 4 C.C.C. 231 (B.C. C.A.); approved [1967] 1 C.C.C. 97n
   (S.C.C.) 997
R. v. Kapp (2008), 56 C.R. (6th) 1 (S.C.C.)...1058
R. v. Karaibrahimovic (2002), 164 C.C.C. (3d) 431, 3 C.R. (6th) 153 (Alta. C.A.)....582
R. v. Kearns, [1945] 2 W.W.R. 477 (B.C.C.A.)..534
R. v. Keeler, [1977] 5 W.W.R. 410 (Alta. C.A.) 795
R. v. Kehler (2004), 19 C.R. (6th) 49 (S.C.C.) 655
R. v. Kendall (1962), 132 C.C.C. 216 (S.C.C.)...426
R. v. Khan (2004), 189 C.C.C. (3d) 49, 24 C.R. (6th) 48 (Ont. S.C.J.) 47, 293
R. v. Khan, [1990] 2 S.C.R. 531, 79 C.R. (3d) 1, 59 C.C.C. (3d) 92 ....27, 467, 538, 680,
   687, 763
R. v. Khan, [1991] O.J. No. 637..684
R. v. Kharsekin (1994), 30 C.R. (4th) 252, 88 C.C.C. (3d) 193 (Nfld. C.A.)............690
R. v. Khela (2009), 62 C.R. (6th) 199 (S.C.C.)..638
R. v. Khelawon (2006), 42 C.R. (6th) 1, 215 C.C.C. (3d) 161 (S.C.C.) 665, 706
R. v. Kimberley (2001), 45 C.R. (5th) 273, 157 C.C.C. (3d) 129, 2001 CarswellOnt
   3161 (C.A.) 758
R. v. Kirk (2004), 188 C.C.C. (3d) 329, 22 C.R. 13 (6th) 231 (Ont. C.A.)..............273
R. v. Klymchuk (2005), 203 C.C.C. (3d) 341 (Ont. C.A.)...................................920
R. v. Knoshnow, [2005] A.J. No. 1812, 2005 CarswellAlta 1944 (Q.B.) 387
R. v. Kotapski (1981), 66 C.C.C. (2d) 78 (Que. S.C.).......................................997
R. v. Kowlyk, [1988] 2 S.C.R. 59...133
R. v. Krause, [1986] 2 S.C.R. 466, 54 C.R. (3d) 294, 29 C.C.C. (3d) 385 ....558, 563
R. v. Krausz (1973), 57 Cr. App. R. 466...300, 301
R. v. Krieger, 213 C.C.C. (3d) 303, 41 C.R. (6th) 201, 2006 CarswellAlta 1371, 2006
   CarswellAlta 1372 (S.C.C.)...107, 349
R. v. Krugel (2000), 31 C.R. (5th) 314 (Ont. C.A.)...221
R. v. Krymowski, [2005] 1 S.C.R. 101, 26 C.R. (6th) 207, 193 C.C.C. (3d) 129.......386
R. v. Kuhn (1970), 1 C.C.C. (2d) 132 (B.C. Co. Ct.)..354
R. v. Kuldip (1990), 1 C.R. (4th) 285 (S.C.C.) 481
R. v. Kyselka (1962), 133 C.C.C. 103 (Ont. C.A.)...606
R. v. L. (C.) (1999), 138 C.C.C. (3d) 356, 1999 CarswellOnt 2700 (C.A.) 769
R. v. L. (D.O.), [1993] 4 S.C.R. 419, 25 C.R. (4th) 285, 85 C.C.C. (3d) 289...... 11, 191,
   192, 438, 443, 535
R. v. L. (L.) (2009), 96 O.R. (3d) 412 (C.A.) 585
R. v. L. (R.I.) (2005), 29 C.R. (6th) 330, 197 C.C.C. (3d) 166 (B.C. C.A.).............194
R. v. Laba, [1994] 3 S.C.R. 965, 34 C.R. (4th) 360, 94 C.C.C. (3d) 385 149
R. v. Lachappelle (1977), 38 C.C.C. (2d) 369 (Que. C.A.)..................................733
R. v. Lai Ping (1904), 11 B.C.R. 102 (C.A.) 427
R. v. Lake, [1997] O.J. No. 5447 (Ont. Gen. Div.) 1007
R. v. Lalonde (1971), 5 C.C.C. (2d) 168 (Ont. H.C.)...6
R. v. Lam (2000), 148 C.C.C. (3d) 379 (B.C. C.A.)..1042
R. v. Lam (2005), 193 C.C.C. (3d) 567, 27 C.R. (6th) 373 (Alta. Q.B.)..................999
R. v. Lamb, [2007] N.J. No. 239 (P.C.)...534
R. v. Langmead (1864), 169 E.R. 1459...132
R. v. Larocque (1998), 124 C.C.C. (3d) 564 (Ont. Gen. Div.)............................1009
R. v. Larsen (2001), 42 C.R. (5th) 49, 2001 CarswellBC 931 (S.C.)................717, 772
R. v. Latimer, [2001] 1 S.C.R. 3..113
R. v. Lavallee (1988), 65 C.R. (3d) 387 (Man. C.A.) 942
R. v. Lavallee (2002), 167 C.C.C. (3d) 1 (S.C.C.) 966
R. v. Lavallee, [1990] 1 S.C.R. 852, 76 C.R. (3d) 329, 55 C.C.C. (3d)
   97 .... 163, 362, 365, 908, 935, 943
R. v. Laverty (No. 2) (1979), 47 C.C.C. (2d) 60 (Ont. C.A.) 763
R. v. Law, 2002 SCC 10, 160 C.C.C. (3d) 449, 208 D.L.R. (4th) 207 1064

R. v. Lawes (2006), 206 C.C.C. (3d) 15, 37 C.R. (6th) 301, 2006 CarswellOnt 1072
    (Ont. C.A.) 11
R. v. Lawrence (1989), 52 C.C.C. (3d) 452 (Ont. C.A.) 593
R. v. Lee Tuck (1912), 4 Alta. L.R. 388 (S.C.) 427
R. v. Lee's Poultery Ltd. (1985), 43 C.R. (3d) 289 (Ont. C.A.) 52
R. v. Leipert, [1997] 1 S.C.R. 281, 4 C.R. (5th) 259, 112 C.C.C. (3d) 385 .... 1030, 1050
R. v. Leland, [1951] O.R. 12, 98 C.C.C. 337, 11 C.R. 152 794
R. v. Leopold (2001), 155 C.C.C. (3d) 251 (B.C. C.A.) 986
R. v. Lepage, 95 C.C.C. (3d) 385, 36 C.R. (4th) 145, [1995] 1 S.C.R. 654 221
R. v. Lessard (1979), 50 C.C.C. (2d) 175 (Que. C.A.) 736
R. v. Letendre (1975), 25 C.C.C. (2d) 180 (Man. C.A.) 839
R. v. Levasseur (1987), 56 C.R. (3d) 335, 35 C.C.C. (3d) 136 (Alta. C.A.) 238
R. v. Levogiannis, [1993] 4 S.C.R. 475, 25 C.R. (4th) 325, 85 C.C.C. (3d) 327 .... 4, 438.
                                                                                    447
R. v. Lewis, 2009 CarswellOnt 7685, 2009 ONCA 874 (Ont. C.A.) 191
R. v. Liew, [1999] 3 S.C.R. 227 814
R. v. Lifchus, [1997] 3 S.C.R. 320, 9 C.R. (5th) 1, 118 C.C.C. (3d) 1 60
R. v. Lillyman, [1896] 2 Q.B. 167 (C.C.R.) 624
R. v. Litchfield, 86 C.C.C. (3d) 97, 25 C.R. (4th) 137, [1993] 4 S.C.R. 333 183
R. v. Littlechild (1979), 108 D.L.R. (3d) 340 (Alta. C.A.) 1043
R. v. Lonsdale (1973), 15 C.C.C. (2d) 201 (Alta. C.A.) 466, 469
R. v. Lorde and Johnson (1978), 33 N.S.R. (2d) 376 (N.S. Co. Ct.) 397
R. v. Lucier, 65 C.C.C. (2d) 150, 1982 CarswellMan 74, 1982 CarswellMan 152, [1982]
    1 S.C.R. 28 757
R. v. Lum, [1982] 3 W.W.R. 694 (B.C. Co. Ct.) 389
R. v. Lupien (1970), 71 W.W.R. 110, [1970] S.C.R. 263 .... 853, 940
R. v. Lynch (1978), 40 C.C.C. (2d) 7 (Ont. C.A.) 72, 746
R. v. Lyons, [1987] 2 S.C.R. 309 .... 203, 324, 1051
R. v. Lyttle (2004), 17 C.R. (6th) 1, 180 C.C.C. (3d) 476, 2004 CarswellOnt 510, 2004
    CarswellOnt 511 (S.C.C.) 18, 19, 544
R. v. M. (M.) (2003), [2003] O.J. No. 5949, 2003 CarswellOnt 6194 (S.C.J.) 292
R. v. M. (M.), [1999] O.J. No. 3943 (Ont. Sup. Ct.) 330
R. v. M. (P.S.) (1992), 77 C.C.C. (3d) 402 (Ont. C.A.) 915
R. v. M. (T.E.) (1996), 187 A.R. 273 (C.A.) 915
R. v. M. (T.E.), 114 C.C.C. (3d) 436, [1997] 1 S.C.R. 948, 6 C.R. (5th) 231 183
R. v. MacAulay (1975), 25 C.C.C. (2d) 1 (N.B.C.A.) 355
R. v. MacCormack (2009), 64 C.R. (6th) 137 (Ont. C.A.) 260
R. v. MacDonald (2000), 35 C.R. (5th) 130, 146 C.C.C. (3d) 525 (Ont. C.A.) 414
R. v. MacDonald (2008), 59 C.R. (6th) 339 (Ont. C.A.) 349
R. v. MacPhee (1985), 19 C.C.C. (3d) 345 (Alta. Q.B.) 563
R. v. MacPherson, [2005] B.C.J. No. 575, 2005 CarswellBC 610 (S.C.) 393
R. v. Madrusan (2005), 35 C.R. (6th) 220, 203 C.C.C. (3d) 513 (B.C. C.A.) 599
R. v. Mahalingan (2008), 61 C.R. (6th) 207 (S.C.C.) 261
R. v. Makow (1973), 13 C.C.C. (2d) 167 (B.C.C.A.) 543
R. v. Malik (2003), 194 C.C.C. (3d) 572 (B.C. S.C.) 574
R. v. Mallory (2004), 25 C.R. (6th) 182, 189 C.C.C. (3d) 345 (N.B. C.A.) 355, 387
R. v. Maloney (No. 2) (1976), 29 C.C.C. (2d) 431 (Ont. Co. Ct.) 402, 418
R. v. Malott, [1998] 1 S.C.R. 123, 12 C.R. (5th) 207, 121 C.C.C. (3d) 456 365
R. v. Mandzuk (1945), 85 C.C.C. 158 (B.C. C.A.) 736
R. v. Mann, [1971] 5 W.W.R. 84 (B.C.S.C.) 466
R. v. Mannion (1986), 53 C.R. (3d) 193 (S.C.C.) 481
R. v. Mapara, [2005] 1 S.C.R. 358, 195 C.C.C. (3d) 225, 28 C.R. (6th) 1. .... 717, 747
R. v. Marchand (1980), 55 C.C.C. (2d) 77 (N.S.C.A.) 461, 466
R. v. Marquard, 1993 CarswellOnt 995, 1993 CarswellOnt 127, [1993] 4 S.C.R. 223, 25
    C.R. (4th) 1, 85 C.C.C. (3d) 193 .... 440, 442, 862, 903, 932, 946

R. v. Marshall (2005), 201 O.A.C. 154, 200 C.C.C. (3d) 179 (Ont. C.A.) 555
R. v. Marshall, [1977] Crim. L.R. 106 733
R. v. Martin (1980), 53 C.C.C. (2d) 425 (Ont. C.A.).......................................606
R. v. Martin (1997), 8 C.R. (5th) 246 (Sask. C.A.) 766
R. v. Martin (2009), 64 C.R. (6th) 378 (Sask. C.A.)..472
R. v. Masterson (2009), 245 C.C.C. (3d) 400 (Ont. S.C.J.) 474
R. v. Mattis (1998), 20 C.R. (5th) 93 (Ont. Prov. Div.).....................................531
R. v. McCarroll (2008), 2008 CarswellOnt 6022, 238 C.C.C. (3d) 404, 61 C.R. (6th) 353
    (C.A.)...540
R. v. McClure, [2001] 1 S.C.R. 445, 40 C.R. (5th) 1, 151 C.C.C. (3d) 321.............986
R. v. McConnell, [1968] 4 C.C.C. 257 (S.C.C.)...510
R. v. McFadden (1981), 65 C.C.C. (2d) 9 (B.C.C.A.)..232
R. v. McFadyen (2002), 2 C.R. (6th) 344, 2002 CarswellOnt 125, 161 C.C.C. (3d) 252
    (C.A.), leave to appeal refused (2002), 2002 CarswellOnt 3502, 2002 CarswellOnt
    3503 (S.C.C.) 599
R. v. McGinty (1986), 52 C.R. (3d) 161, 27 C.C.C. (3d) 36 (Y.T.C.A.) 462, 469
R. v. McGovern (1993), 82 C.C.C. (3d) 301, 22 C.R. (4th) 359 (Man C.A.)............440
R. v. McIntosh (1997), 117 C.C.C. (3d) 385 (Ont. C.A.)...................................897
R. v. McIntosh, [1937] 4 D.L.R. 478 (B.C.C.A.) 762
R. v. McIntyre, [1963] 2 C.C.C. 380 (N.S.S.C.) 825, 826
R. v. McIver, [1965] 2 O.R. 475 (C.A.), affirmed (1966), 48 C.R. 4 (S.C.C.)............ 52
R. v. McLaughlan (1974), 20 C.C.C. (2d) 59 (Ont. C.A.)...................................592
R. v. McMillan (1975), 23 C.C.C. (2d) 160, 29 C.R.N.S. 191 (Ont. C.A.), affirmed 33
    C.C.C. (2d) 360, [1977] 2 S.C.R. 824..228, 292
R. v. McNamara (1979), 48 C.C.C. (2d) 201 (Ont. Co. Ct.) 461
R. v. McNamara (1981), 56 C.C.C. (2d) 193 (Ont. C.A.), affirmed 45 C.R. (3d) 289, 19
    C.C.C. (3d) 1, [1985] 1 S.C.R. 662.. 233, 241, 242
R. v. McNeil (2009), 62 C.R. (6th) 1 1071
R. v. McNeill (2000), 33 C.R. (5th) 390, 144 C.C.C. (3d) 551 (Ont. C.A.)..............552
R. v. McNicol, [1969] 3 C.C.C. 56 (Man. C.A.) 355, 359
R. v. McPherson (1980), 52 C.C.C. (2d) 547 (N.S.C.A.)...................................461
R. v. Meddoui (1990), 61 C.C.C. (3d) 345 537
R. v. Melaragni (1992), 73 C.C.C. (3d) 348 (Ont. Gen. Div.) 860
R. v. Melaragni (1992), 76 C.C.C. (3d) 78 (Ont. Gen. Div.)...............................925
R. v. Melnick (2005), 32 C.R. (6th) 18 (Alta. Prov. Ct) 556
R. v. Mensah (2003), 9 C.R. (6th) 339 (Ont. C.A.), leave to appeal refused (2003), 2003
    CarswellOnt 3640, 2003 CarswellOnt 3641 (S.C.C.) 211
R. v. Merz (1999), 140 C.C.C. (3d) 259 (Ont. C.A.) 221
R. v. Meuckon (1990), 57 C.C.C. (3d) 193 (B.C. C.A.) 1042
R. v. Mezzo, 27 C.C.C. (3d) 97, 52 C.R. (3d) 113, [1986] 1 S.C.R. 802 ......98, 102, 204
R. v. Mick (1863), 176 E.R. 376 799
R. v. Milgaard (1971), 2 C.C.C. (2d) 206 (Sask. C.A.); leave to appeal to S.C.C. refused
    (1971), 4 C.C.C. (2d) 566n (S.C.C.)..577
R. v. Millar (1989), 71 C.R. (3d) 78, 49 C.C.C. (3d) 193 (Ont. C.A.) 242, 249, 931
R. v. Miller (1998), 131 C.C.C. (3d) 141, 1998 CarswellOnt 4983, 21 C.R. (5th) 178
    (C.A.)...510
R. v. Mills, [1999] 3 S.C.R. 668, 28 C.R. (5th) 207, 139 C.C.C. (3d) 321 .... 987, 1047
R. v. Moghal (1977), 65 Cr. App. R. 56 781
R. v. Mohan, [1994] 2 S.C.R. 9, 29 C.R. (4th) 243, 89 C.C.C. (3d) 402 ....859, 932
R. v. Molnar (1990), 76 C.R. (3d) 125 (C.A.) 229
R. v. Monkhouse (1987), 61 C.R. (3d) 343, [1988] 1 W.W.R. 725 (Alta. C.A.)..770, 772
R. v. Monteleone, [1987] 2 S.C.R. 154, 35 C.C.C. (3d) 193.........................102, 204
R. v. Moore-McFarlane (2001), 47 C.R. (5th) 203, 2001 CarswellOnt 4242, 160 C.C.C.
    (3d) 493 (C.A.) 842, 845
R. v. Moore (1986), 30 C.C.C. (3d) 328 (N.W.T. T.C.) 464

R. v. Morden (1991), 69 C.C.C. (3d) 123 (B.C. C.A.) 344
R. v. Moreau (1986), 51 C.R. (3d) 209, 26 C.C.C. (3d) 359 (Ont. C.A.).................. 72
R. v. Morgan, (January 10, 2002), Flynn Prov. J., [2002] N.J. No. 15 (N.L. Prov.
    Ct.)...407
R. v. Morin (1977), 40 C.R.N.S. 378 (Sask. Dist. Ct.) 563
R. v. Morin (1995), 37 C.R. (4th) 395 (Ont. C.A.).. 73
R. v. Morin, [1988] 2 S.C.R. 345, 66 C.R. (3d) 1, 44 C.C.C. (3d) 193 .... 65, 70, 862
R. v. Morris (1978), 43 C.C.C. (2d) 129, [1979] 1 S.C.R. 405, 6 C.R. (3d) 36.........243
R. v. Mottola (1959), 124 C.C.C. 288 (Ont. C.A.)...480
R. v. Muir, [2008] O.J. No. 3418 (C.A.)...125
R. v. Mullins-Johnson (2007), 2007 CarswellOnt 6660, 50 C.R. (6th) 265, 228 C.C.C.
    (3d) 505 (C.A.) 7
R. v. Munoz (2006), 38 C.R. (6th) 376, 205 C.C.C. (3d) 70, 2006 CarswellOnt 673
    (S.C.J.) 76
R. v. Murray (1997), 115 C.C.C. (3d) 225 (Ont. C.A.) 586
R. v. Murray (2000), 144 C.C.C. (3d) 289, 2000 CarswellOnt 1953, 34 C.R. (5th) 290
    (S.C.J.) 19
R. v. Murrin (1999), [1999] B.C.J. No. 3131, 1999 CarswellBC 3051 (S.C.) 204
R. v. Myrby (1975), 28 C.C.C. (2d) 395 (Alta. C.A.) 801
R. v. N. (R.K.) (1996), 114 C.C.C. (3d) 40 (Ont. C.A.)...................................242
R. v. Nadeau (1984), 42 C.R. (3d) 305 (S.C.C.)... 63
R. v. Naglik (1991), 65 C.C.C. (3d) 272 509
R. v. Nagy (1965), 51 W.W.R. 307 (B.C. Co. Ct.)..852
R. v. National Post, 19 C.R. (6th) 393, [2004] O.J. No. 178, 2004 CarswellOnt 173
    (S.C.J.) 1044
R. v. Nealy (1987), 17 O.A.C. 164 (C.A.)..239
R. v. Nedelcu, [2007] O.J. No. 1188 (S.C.J.) 483
R. v. Nicholl, 25 C.R. (6th) 192, 190 C.C.C. (3d) 549, 2004 CarswellOnt 4289 (Ont.
    C.A.)...129
R. v. Nikitin (2003), 176 C.C.C. (3d) 225, 2003 CarswellOnt 2360 (C.A.)..............424
R. v. Nikolovski, [1996] 3 S.C.R. 1197, 3 C.R. (5th) 362, 111 C.C.C. (3d) 403........398
R. v. Noble, [1997] 1 S.C.R. 874, 6 C.R. (5th) 1, 114 C.C.C. (3d) 385.............498, 511
R. v. Noel, [2002] 3 S.C.R. 433 481
R. v. Norman (1993), 26 C.R. (4th) 256, 87 C.C.C. (3d) 153 (Ont. C.A.)..........629, 897
R. v. O'Brien (1977), 35 C.C.C. (2d) 209, 38 C.R.N.S. 325, 76 D.L.R. (3d) 513
    (S.C.C.) 757, 758
R. v. O'Connor (1995), 100 C.C.C. (3d) 285 (Ont. C.A.) 625
R. v. O'Connor, [1995] 4 S.C.R. 411, 103 C.C.C. (3d) 1......................324, 978, 1075
R. v. O'Neill (1976), 13 C.R. (3d) 193, 31 C.C.C. (2d) 259 (Ont. C.A.) 733, 737
R. v. Oakes, [1986] 1 S.C.R. 103, 50 C.R. (3d) 1, 24 C.C.C. (3d) 321 ....49, 138, 361
R. v. Oickle, [2000] 2 S.C.R. 3, 36 C.R. (5th) 129, 147 C.C.C. (3d) 321 812
R. v. Olscamp (1994), 35 C.R. (4th) 37, 95 C.C.C. (3d) 466 (Ont. Gen. Div.)..........901
R. v. Orbanski, 29 C.R. (6th) 205, 196 C.C.C. (3d) 481, [2005] 2 S.C.R. 3 486
R. v. Ortt, [1969] 1 O.R. 461 (C.A.)..128
R. v. Osmar (2007), [2007] O.J. No. 244, 2007 CarswellOnt 339, 44 C.R. (6th) 276
    (C.A.).. 733, 825, 921
R. v. Osolin, [1993] 4 S.C.R. 595 .... 112, 325, 330, 1052
R. v. Owen (2001), [2001] O.J. No. 4257, 2001 CarswellOnt 3852 (C.A.) 630
R. v. P. (G.) (1996), 112 C.C.C. (3d) 263 (Ont. C.A.) 552
R. v. P. (G.F.) (1994),18 O.R. (3d) 1 (Ont. C.A.)..599
R. v. P. (M.B.) (1992), 9 O.R. (3d) 424, affirmed [1994] 1 S.C.R. 555, 29 C.R. (4th)
    209..563, 652
R. v. P. (N.A.) (2002), 171 C.C.C. (3d) 70, 8 C.R. (6th) 186 (Ont. C.A.)..........234, 240
R. v. P. (R.) (1990), 58 C.C.C. (3d) 334 (Ont. H.C.) 783

R. v. P. (S.H.) (2003), 176 C.C.C. (3d) 281 (N.S. C.A.)..630
R. v. P. (T.L.) (1996), 193 A.R. 146 (Alta. C.A.) 565
R. v. Pabani (1995), 89 C.C.C. (3d) 437...1005
R. v. Paine (1696), 87 E.R. 584 (K.B.)..661
R. v. Palmer, [1970] 3 C.C.C. 402 (B.C. C.A.)..133
R. v. Palosaari (2004), 191 C.C.C. (3d) 228 (B.C. C.A.) 11
R. v. Parberry (2005), 202 C.C.C. (3d) 337 (Ont. C.A.) 736
R. v. Park, [1995] 2 S.C.R. 836...112
R. v. Parks, (1993) 24 C.R. (4th) 81 (Ont. C.A.)...376
R. v. Parnell (1995), 98 C.C.C. (3d) 83 (Ont. C.A.) 378
R. v. Parrot (1979), 51 C.C.C. (2d) 539, 548-49 (Ont. C.A.) 747
R. v. Parrott, [2001] 1 S.C.R. 178, 39 C.R. (5th) 255, 150 C.C.C. (3d) 449 ......442, 451,
                                                                                       723
R. v. Parsons (1977), 37 C.C.C. (2d) 497 (Ont. C.A.); affirmed (sub nom. Charette v. R.)
        (1980), 51 C.C.C. (2d) 350 (S.C.C.)...392
R. v. Parsons (1993), 84 C.C.C. (3d) 226, 24 C.R. (4th) 112 (Ont. C.A.) 292
R. v. Pasqualino (2008), 233 C.C.C. (3d) 319 (Ont. C.A.) 720, 728
R. v. Patterson (2003), 174 C.C.C. (3d) 193 (Ont. C.A.) 393
R. v. Paul (1998), 124 C.C.C. (3d) 1 (N.B. C.A.)...178
R. v. Pavlukoff (1953), 10 W.W.R. 26 (B.C.C.A.) 633
R. v. Peacock (1968), 3 C.R.N.S. 103 (Ont. Co. Ct.)..733
R. v. Penno (1977), 35 C.C.C. (2d) 266 (B.C.C.A.)...767
R. v. Perkins (2007), 51 C.R. (6th) 116 (Ont. C.A.)..387
R. v. Perrier, 22 C.R. (6th) 209, [2004] 3 S.C.R. 228, 188 C.C.C. (3d) 1, 2004
        CarswellBC 2116, 2004 CarswellBC 2117 281
R. v. Perry, [1909] 2 K.B. 697 (C.C.A.) 762
R. v. Peruta (1993), 78 C.C.C. (3d) 350 (Que. C.A.), leave to appeal refused, 81 C.C.C.
        (3d) vi (S.C.C.) 3
R. v. Pete (1998), 131 C.C.C. (3d) 233 (B.C. C.A.) 155
R. v. Peterffy (2000), 30 C.R. (5th) 297 (B.C. C.A.) 279
R. v. Peterson (1996), 106 C.C.C. (3d) 64, 27 O.R. (3d) 739, 47 C.R. (4th) 161 (C.A.);
        leave to appeal to S.C.C. refused [1996] S.C.C.A. no. 202, 109 C.C.C. (3d) vi,
        [1996] 3 S.C.R. xii...443
R. v. Phillion (2009), 241 C.C.C. (3d) 193 (Ont. C.A.)...............................614, 924
R. v. Phillips, [1995] O.J. No. 2985 (Ont. Gen. Div.)..734
R. v. Phillips, [2008] O.J. No. 4194 211
R. v. Pierce Fisheries Ltd., [1970] C.C.C. 193 (S.C.C.) 162
R. v. Pilarinos, [2002] B.C.J. No. 1958, 2002 CarswellBC 1971, 167 C.C.C. (3d) 97
        (B.C. S.C.)...753
R. v. Pilon (2009), 64 C.R. (6th) 356 (Ont. C.A.)...217
R. v. Pilotte (2002), 163 C.C.C. (3d) 225 (Ont. C.A.)......................................1009
R. v. Pleich (1980), 55 C.C.C. (2d) 13 (Ont. C.A.) 393
R. v. Pollock (2004), 187 C.C.C. (3d) 213, 23 C.R. (6th) 98 (Ont. C.A.) 293
R. v. Pollock, [1947] 2 W.W.R. 973 (Alta. Dist. Ct.) 852
R. v. Porter, [1976] Crim. L.R. 58 738
R. v. Potts (1982), 134 D.L.R. (3d) 227 (Ont. C.A.)..355
R. v. Potvin, [1989] 1 S.C.R. 525, 68 C.R. (3d) 193, 47 C.C.C. (3d) 289 .. 190, 192, 202,
                                                                                       775
R. v. Precourt (1976), 18 O.R. (2d) 714 (C.A.)...816
R. v. Predy (1983), 17 C.C.C. (3d) 379 (Alta. C.A.) 634
R. v. Priest (1996), 110 C.C.C. (3d) 289, 1 C.R. (5th) 275 (Ont. C.A.).............355, 387
R. v. Proctor (1991), 11 C.R. (4th) 200, 69 C.C.C. (3d) 436 (Man. C.A.)................347
R. v. Profit (1992), 16 C.R. (4th) 332, 85 C.C.C. (3d) 232 (Ont. C.A.)..................229
R. v. Profit, [1993] 3 S.C.R. 637, 24 C.R. (4th) 279, 85 C.C.C. (3d) 232 231

R. v. Proudlock (1979), 43 C.C.C. (2d) 321 (S.C.C.) 134
R. v. Pye (1984), 38 C.R. (3d) 375 (N.S.C.A.) 134
R. v. Quercia (1990), 1 C.R. (4th) 385, 60 C.C.C. (3d) 380 (Ont. C.A.) 100
R. v. Quinn (1975), 27 C.C.C. (2d) 543 (Alta. S.C.) 355
R. v. R. (A.E.) (2001), 43 C.R. (5th) 340 (Ont. C.A.) 623
R. v. R. (A.J.) (1994), 94 C.C.C. (3d) 168 (Ont. C.A.).....................................547
R. v. R.D.S. (1995), 18 Dal. L.J. 408..166, 175
R. v. R.M. (1997), 93 B.C.A.C. 81 1067
R. v. Racco (No. 3) (1975), 23 C.C.C. (2d) 209 (Ont. Co. Ct.)..........................544
R. v. Racine (1977), 32 C.C.C. (2d) 468 (Ont. C.A.)..635
R. v. Rafael, [1972] 3 O.R. 238, 7 C.C.C. (2d) 325 (Ont. C.A.) 559, 562
R. v. Raja, [2009] O.J. No. 3193 (S.C.J.)..125
R. v. Raviraj (1987), 85 Cr. App. R. 93 (C.A.) 132
R. v. Reader (2007), 49 C.R. (6th) 301 (Man. Q.B.) 842
R. v. Rennie (1981), 74 Cr. App. R. 207 (C.A.)..820
R. v. Rhodes (1981), 59 C.C.C. (2d) 426 (B.C.C.A.) 563
R. v. Ribic (2008), 63 C.R. (6th) 70 (Ont. C.A.) 1011
R. v. Richards (1997), 115 C.C.C. (3d) 377 (Ont. C.A.)........................... 1009, 1042
R. v. Riley (1887), 18 QBD 481..334
R. v. Riley (1978), 42 C.C.C. (2d) 437 (Ont. C.A.)..647
R. v. Riley (1992), 11 O.R. (3d) 151 (C.A.), leave to appeal refused [1993] 2 S.C.R.
    x 344
R. v. Risby (1976), 32 C.C.C. (2d) 242 (B.C.C.A.); affirmed (1978), 39 C.C.C. (2d) 567
    (S.C.C.) 795
R. v. Roberts (1984), 80 Cr. App. R. 89 (C.A.)..563
R. v. Roberts (2000), 31 C.R. (5th) 340 (Ont. C.A.)... 95
R. v. Roberts (2001), [2001] A.J. No. 772, 2001 CarswellAlta 823 (Q.B.) 1009
R. v. Robinson, [1996] 1 S.C.R. 683, 105 C.C.C. (3d) 97..............................113, 128
R. v. Rochester (1984), 13 C.C.C. (3d) 215 (Ont. Co. Ct.)................................563
R. v. Rodgers (2000), 144 C.C.C. (3d) 568 (Ont. C.A.) 292
R. v. Rodrigues (2007), 223 C.C.C. (3d) 53 (Yuk. C.A.)..................................221
R. v. Roher (1947), 89 C.C.C. 365 (Ont. C.A.)... 51
R. v. Rojas, 2008 CarswellBC 2196, 2008 CarswellBC 2197, [2008] 3 S.C.R. 111, 236
    C.C.C. (3d) 153, 60 C.R. (6th) 271 849
R. v. Rookwood (1696), 13 Howell's State Trials 139.....................................594
R. v. Rose (2001), 42 C.R. (5th) 183, 153 C.C.C. (3d) 225 (Ont. C.A.) 520
R. v. Ross (1992), 92 Nfld. & P.E.I.R. 51 (Nfld. S.C.)....................................768
R. v. Ross, [1980] 5 W.W.R. 261 (B.C. C.A.)..259
R. v. Rothman (1981), 59 C.C.C. (2d) 30, 121 D.L.R. (3d) 578, [1981] 1 S.C.R.
    640...208, 700
R. v. Roud (1981), 58 C.C.C. (2d) 226 (Ont. C.A.)...286
R. v. Roulette (1972), 7 C.C.C. (2d) 244 (Man. Q.B.) 543
R. v. Rowbotham (No. 5) (1977), 2 C.R. (3d) 293 (Ont. Co. Ct.)..........................543
R. v. Rowbotham, [1994] 2 S.C.R. 463 107
R. v. Rowton (1865), 10 Cox C.C. 25 ....231, 232, 237, 587
R. v. Roy (2004), 15 C.R. (6th) 282 (Ont. C.A.) 487, 828
R. v. Royal Bank, [1920] 1 W.W.R. 198 (Man. C.A.) 292
R. v. Ruzic, [2001] 1 S.C.R. 687..113
R. v. Ryan (1989), 49 C.C.C. (3d) 490 (Nfld. C.A.)..297
R. v. Rydzanicz (1979), 13 C.R. (3d) 190 (Ont. C.A.)................................733, 738
R. v. S-R (J.) (2008), 236 C.C.C. (3d) 486 (Ont. S.C.).....................................209
R. v. S. (F.) (1997), 116 C.C.C. (3d) 435 (Ont. C.A.) 648
R. v. S. (J.) (2008), 61 C.R. 282 (B.C. C.A.)..446
R. v. S. (J.H.), 2008 CarswellNS 270, 2008 CarswellNS 271, [2008] 2 S.C.R. 152, 57
    C.R. (6th) 79, 231 C.C.C. (3d) 302 64

R. v. S. (L.R.) (2005), 40 C.R. (6th) 180 (N.B. C.A.) 332
R. v. S. (N.), [2009] O.J. No. 1766 (S.C.J.) 631
R. v. S. (P.) (2007), 221 C.C.C. (3d) 56 (Ont. C.A.) 273
R. v. S. (R.D.), [1994] N.S.J. No. 629 (Fam. Ct.)...168
R. v. S. (R.D.), [1997] 3 S.C.R. 484, 10 C.R. (5th) 1, 118 C.C.C. (3d) 353..............166
R. v. S. (T.) (1995), 40 C.R. (4th) 1 (Sask. C.A.) 436
R. v. S. (W.) (1991) 6 C.R. (4th) 373 (Ont. C.A.)..386
R. v. S. (W.) (1994), 29 C.R. (4th) 143 (Ont. C. A.), leave to appeal refused (1994), 35
     C.R. (4th) 402 (note) (S.C.C.) 630, 649
R. v. S. (W.D.), [1994] 3 S.C.R. 521, 34 C.R. (4th) 1, 93 C.C.C. (3d) 1 ....66, 68
R. v. S.D.T. (1985), 33 M.V.R. 148 (N.S.C.A.)...155
R. v. Salituro, [1991] 3 S.C.R. 654, 9 C.R. (4th) 324, 68 C.C.C. (3d) 289, 1991
     CarswellOnt 1031, 1991 CarswellOnt 124...................................... 26, 467
R. v. Sandhu (2009), 63 C.R. (6th) 1 (Ont. C.A.) 221
R. v. Sang, [1980] A.C. 402 (H.L.) 779
R. v. Santeramo (1976), 32 C.C.C. (2d) 35 (Ont. C.A.)......................................155
R. v. Sark (2004), 182 C.C.C. (3d) 530 (N.B. C.A.)...604
R. v. Saroya (1992), 18 C.R. (4th) 198 (Ont. Gen. Div.); affirmed (1994), 76 O.A.C. 25
     (C.A.)...597
R. v. Sault Ste. Marie (City), [1978] 2 S.C.R. 1299 52
R. v. Sauve (1997), 13 C.R. (5th) 391 (B.C.C.A.) 344
R. v. Schacher (2003), 179 C.C.C. (3d) 561 (Alta. C.A.).....................................993
R. v. Schaffner (1988), 44 C.C.C. (3d) 507 (N.S.C.A.).......................................396
R. v. Schama (1914), 11 Cr. App. R. 45 132
R. v. Schantz (1983), 34 C.R. (3d) 370 (Ont. Co. Ct.) 676
R. v. Schell (2004), 20 C.R. (6th) 1 (Alta. C.A.) 475
R. v. Schmidt, [1948] S.C.R. 333 733
R. v. Schwartz, [1988] 2 S.C.R. 443, 45 C.C.C. (3d) 97.....................39, 52, 113, 116
R. v. Schwartzenhauer, [1935] 3 D.L.R. 711 (S.C.C.) 762
R. v. Scopelliti (1981), 63 C.C.C. (2d) 481 (Ont. C.A.) 216, 297
R. v. Scott (1984), 79 Cr. App. R. 49 (C.A.)..563
R. v. Scott, [1990] 3 S.C.R. 979.. 1032, 1040
R. v. Seaboyer, [1991] 2 S.C.R. 577, 7 C.R. (4th) 117, 66 C.C.C. (3d) 321 ......192, 303,
                                                                                          330, 467
R. v. Seck (2007), 52 C.R. (6th) 300 (Que. C.A.)...221
R. v. Shaw (1977), 36 C.R.N.S. 358 (Ont. C.A.)...354
R. v. Shearing, [2002] 3 S.C.R. 33, 2 C.R. (6th) 213, 165 C.C.C. (3d) 225, 2002
     CarswellBC 1661, 2002 CarswellBC 1662, [2002] S.C.J. No. 59 ..... 194, 276, 543,
                                                                               546, 547, 1060
R. v. Sheik-Qasim (2007), 230 C.C.C. (3d) 531 (S.C.J.) [Not Allowed] 604
R. v. Sherry, 3 C.R. (5th) 314, 110 C.C.C. (3d) 160, [1996] 3 S.C.R. 602...............565
R. v. Shirose and Campbell, 1999 CarswellOnt 949, [1999] 1 S.C.R. 565, 24 C.R. (5th)
     365, 133 C.C.C. (3d) 257, 1999 CarswellOnt 948....................................991
R. v. Shortreed (1990), 54 C.C.C. (3d) 292 (Ont. C.A.) 234
R. v. Shrimpton (1851), 5 Cox. C.C. 387..232, 240
R. v. Sillars (1978), 45 C.C.C. (2d) 283 (B.C.C.A.)...461
R. v. Simpson (2007), 53 C.R. (6th) 1 (Ont. C.A.)..753
R. v. Singh (2007), 2007 CarswellBC 2588, 2007 CarswellBC 2589, 51 C.R. (6th) 199,
     225 C.C.C. (3d) 103, [2007] 3 S.C.R. 405 ....487, 829
R. v. Smails, [1986] 2 All E.R. 928 (H.L.) 450
R. v. Smith, [1959] 2 Q.B. 35...819
R. v. Smith, [1988] O.J. No. 2551 389
R. v. Smith, [1992] 2 S.C.R. 915, 15 C.R. (4th) 133, 75 C.C.C. (3d) 257... 538, 685, 771
R. v. Smuk (1971), 3 C.C.C. (2d) 457 (B.C.C.A.) 564
R. v. Smythe (1980), 72 Cr. App. R. 8, 11 (C.A.)...129

R. v. Snelling, [1952] O.W.N. 214 (H.C.)..389
R. v. Snider (2006), 37 C.R. (6th) 61 (Ont. C.J.)...135
R. v. Snider, [1954] 4 D.L.R. 483 (S.C.C.)...955
R. v. Soares (1987), 34 C.C.C. (3d) 403 (Ont. C.A.)...298
R. v. Sodhi (2003), 179 C.C.C. (3d) 60 (Ont. C.A.)..210
R. v. Soikie, [2004] O.J. No. 2902, 2004 CarswellOnt 8840 (S.C.J).....................239
R. v. Sophonow (1986), 50 C.R. (3d) 193..779
R. v. Speid (1985), 46 C.R. (3d) 22 (Ont. C.A.)...286
R. v. Speid (1988), 63 C.R. (3d) 253 (Ont. C.A.)..775
R. v. Spence (1979), 47 C.C.C. (2d) 167 (Ont. C.A.) 158
R. v. Spence, 33 C.R. (6th) 1, [2005] 3 S.C.R. 458, 202 C.C.C. (3d) 1 376
R. v. Spencer (2007), 51 C.R. (6th) 199 (S.C.C.) 824
R. v. Squires, 171 C.C.C. (3d) 226, [2002] 4 S.C.R. 323.................................... 70
R. v. St. Jean (1976), 32 C.C.C. (2d) 438 (Que. C.A.) 999, 1000
R. v. St. Lawrence, [1949] O.R. 215, 228 (H.C.) 801
R. v. Stannard (1837), 173 E.R. 295 (N.P.) 228
R. v. Starr, [2000] 2 S.C.R. 144, 36 C.R. (5th) 1, 147 C.C.C. (3d) 449, 2000
    CarswellMan 449, 2000 CarswellMan 450 ....62, 674, 758, 785
R. v. Steane, [1947] 1 K.B. 997 (C.C.A.)...128
R. v. Stein, [1928] S.C.R. 553 740
R. v. Steinberg, [1931] O.R. 222 (C.A.) 450, 605
R. v. Steinhoff (2003), 2003 CarswellOnt 6215, [2003] O.J. No. 3398 (C.J.).........1009
R. v. Stillman, 113 C.C.C. (3d) 321, 5 C.R. (5th) 1, [1997] 1 S.C.R. 607... 183, 206, 815
R. v. Stinchcombe, [1991] 3 S.C.R. 326 2,1012
R. v. Stirling, 2008 CarswellBC 506, 2008 CarswellBC 507, [2008] 1 S.C.R. 272, 54
    C.R. (6th) 228, 229 C.C.C. (3d) 257 ....614, 621
R. v. Stoddart (1909), 2 Cr. App. R. 217 (C.C.A.)... 40
R. v. Stoddart (1987), 37 C.C.C. (3d) 351 (Ont. C.A.).......................................327
R. v. Stone, [1999] 2 S.C.R. 290 115
R. v. Straffen, [1952] 2 Q.B. 911 (C.C.A.) 244
R. v. Strand Electric Ltd. (1968), 2 C.C.C. 264 (Ont. C.A.) 742
R. v. Stratton (1978), 42 C.C.C. (2d) 449 (Ont. C.A.) 596
R. v. Streu, 48 C.C.C. (3d) 321, [1989] 1 S.C.R. 1521, 70 C.R. (3d) 1 737
R. v. Strickland, [2007] O.J. 517 (S.C.J.)..329
R. v. Suchard (1956), 114 C.C.C. 257 (S.C.C.) 132
R. v. Sussex Justices, Ex p. McCarthy, [1924] 1 K.B. 256.................................. 10
R. v. Suzack (2002), 141 C.C.C. (3d) 449 (Ont. C.A.).......................................293
R. v. Swanek (2005), 28 C.R. (6th) 93 (Ont. C.A.)...845
R. v. Swanston (1982), 25 C.R. (3d) 385 (B.C. C.A.)...672
R. v. Sweeney (2000), 36 C.R. (5th) 198, 148 C.C.C. (3d) 247, 2000 CarswellOnt 3290
    (C.A.)...803
R. v. Sweitzer, [1982] 1 S.C.R. 949 259
R. v. Swietlinski (1978), 5 C.R. (3d) 324 (Ont. C.A.)..946
R. v. T. (W.P.) (1993), 83 C.C.C. (3d) 5 (Ont. C.A.)....................................671, 673
R. v. Talbot (2002), 1 C.R. (6th) 396, 161 C.C.C. (3d) 256, 2002 CarswellOnt 63
    (C.A.)...913
R. v. Tarrant (1982), 63 C.C.C. (2d) 385 (Ont. C.A.) 229
R. v. Tat (1997), 14 C.R. (5th) 116, 117 C.C.C. (3d) 481, 1997 CarswellOnt 5434
    (C.A.)..540, 619, 671
R. v. Tatomir (1989), 51 C.C.C. (3d) 321 (Alta. C.A.).......................................402
R. v. Taylor (1988), 93 N.B.R. (2d) 246 (N.B.Q.B.) 394
R. v. Taylor (2008) 63 C.R. (6th) 142 (N.B. Q.B.) 841
R. v. Teerhuis-Moar (2009), C.R. (6th) (Man. Q.B.)...209
R. v. Temertzoglou (2002), 11 C.R. (6th) 179, 2002 CarswellOnt 4225 (S.C.J.) 329

R. v. Terceira (1998), 15 C.R. (5th) 359, 123 C.C.C. (3d) 1 (Ont. C.A.), affirmed [1999] 3 S.C.R. 866 .... 75, 893
R. v. Terrico (2005), 199 C.C.C. (3d) 126, 31 C.R. (6th) 161 (B.C. C.A.).............. 733
R. v. Therens, [1985] 1 S.C.R. 613 203
R. v. Thibert, [1996] 1 S.C.R. 37.. 113
R. v. Thibodeau, [1955] S.C.R. 646 352
R. v. Thomas (1998), 124 C.C.C. (3d) 178 (Ont. Gen. Div.) 1042
R. v. Thomas (2004), 26 C.R. (6th) 274, 190 C.C.C. (3d) 31 (Ont. C.A.)............... 280
R. v. Thomas, [1952] 2 S.C.R. 344, [1952] 4 D.L.R. 306 .... 624, 625
R. v. Thompson (1994), 90 C.C.C. (3d) 519 (Alta. C.A.) 473
R. v. Thomsen (1988), 63 C.R. (3d) 1 (S.C.C.)... 362
R. v. Thomson, [1912] 3 K.B. 19 (C.C.A.)... 781
R. v. Thurlow (1994), 34 C.R. (4th) 53 (Ont. Gen. Div.).................................... 450
R. v. Tierney (1982), 70 C.C.C. (2d) 481 (Ont. C.A.).. 241
R. v. Titmus (2004), 27 C.R. (6th) 77, 191 C.C.C. (3d) 468 (B.C.C.A.).................. 275
R. v. Titus (1983), 33 C.R. (3d) 17, 2 C.C.C. (3d) 321 (S.C.C.) 586, 591
R. v. Tolson (1864), 176 E.R. 488 (Surrey Assizes)... 396
R. v. Tombran, 31 C.R. (5th) 349, 142 C.C.C. (3d) 380, 2000 CarswellOnt 231 (C.A.).. 93
R. v. Toohey, [1965] A.C. 595 (H.L.)... 605
R. v. Toten (1993), 83 C.C.C. (3d) 5 537
R. v. Trang (2002), 168 C.C.C. (3d) 145 (Alta. Q.B.).. 993
R. v. Tremblay (1984), 17 C.C.C. (3d) 359 (Que. C.A.)..................................... 563
R. v. Trevor (2006), 206 C.C.C. (3d) 381, 2006 CarswellBC 470 (C.A.) 512
R. v. Trochym, [2007] S.C.J. No. 6, 2007 CarswellOnt 400, 2007 CarswellOnt 401, 43 C.R. (6th) 217 (S.C.C.) 286, 867
R. v. Truscott (2006), 213 C.C.C. (3d) 183 (Ont. C.A.) 243, 292
R. v. Turcotte, 31 C.R. (6th) 197, 200 C.C.C. (3d) 289, [2005] 2 S.C.R. 519 .....491, 740
R. v. Turcotte, [2006] B.C.J. No. 3631 (S.C.C.) 496
R. v. Turner (1816), 105 E.R. 1026.. 51
R. v. Turner (1910), 3 Cr. App. R. 103 733
R. v. Turner (1975), 60 Cr. App. R. 80 .... 895, 945
R. v. Turner, [1975] Q.B. 834 (C.A.)... 861
R. v. Turpin, [2005] B.C.J. No. 490, 2005 CarswellBC 871 (S.C.)....................... 234
R. v. U. (D.A.) (2008), 239 C.C.C. (3d) 409 (N.S. S.C.) [Permitted] 604
R. v. U. (F.J.), [1995] 3 S.C.R. 764, 42 C.R. (4th) 133, 101 C.C.C. (3d) 97.............. 700
R. v. Underwood, [1998] 1 S.C.R. 77, 12 C.R. (5th) 241, 121 C.C.C. (3d) 117 602
R. v. Valeanu (1995), 97 C.C.C. (3d) 338 (Ont. C.A.)....................................... 237
R. v. Vanegas (1987), 60 C.R. (3d) 169 (B.C.C.A.) 134
R. v. Vanezis (2006), 213 C.C.C. (3d) 449, 43 C.R. (6th) 116 (Ont. C.A.) 292
R. v. Varga (2001), 159 C.C.C. (3d) 502, 48 C.R. (5th) 387 (Ont. C.A.)................. 297
R. v. Verney (1993), 87 C.C.C. (3d) 363 (Ont. C.A.) 553
R. v. Vinette (1974), 19 C.C.C. (2d) 1 (S.C.C.) 736
R. v. Vivar, 2004 CarswellOnt 5, [2004] O.J. No. 9 (S.C.J.)............................... 571
R. v. Vrdoljak (2002), 1 C.R. (6th) 250 (Ont. C.J.)... 280
R. v. W. (D.), [1991] 1 S.C.R. 742, 3 C.R. (4th) 302, 63 C.C.C. (3d) 347 ....62, 64
R. v. W. (L.), 2004 CarswellOnt 4138, [2004] O.J. No. 4163 (C.A.) 222
R. v. W. (R.), [1992] 2 S.C.R. 122, 13 C.R. (4th) 257, 74 C.C.C. (3d) 134.......433, 539, 651
R. v. W. (R.S.) (1992), 74 C.C.C. (3d) 1 (Man. C.A.) 651
R. v. Wade (1994), 18 O.R. (3d) 33 (C.A.)... 209
R. v. Wagner (1986), 50 C.R. (3d) 175 (Alta. C.A.)... 563
R. v. Wainwright (1875), 13 Cox C.C. 171 781
R. v. Wang (2001), 153 C.C.C. (3d) 321 (Ont. C.A.) 204

R. v. Warickshall (1783), 168 E.R. 234..797, 802
R. v. Warren (1995), 35 C.R. (4th) 347 (N.W. T. S.C.).......................................923
R. v. Watkins (2003), 181 C.C.C. (3d) 78 (Ont. C.A.).......................................286
R. v. Watson (1817), 2 Stark 116 587
R. v. Watson (1996), 50 C.R. (4th) 245 (Ont. C.A.)....................................157, 215
R. v. Watson (2004), 191 C.C.C. (3d) 144 (Ont. C.A.) 11
R. v. Wayte (1983), 76 Cr. App. R. 110 405
R. v. Wells (2000), 141 C.C.C. (3d) 368 (S.C.C.) 177, 812
R. v. Welsh (1997), 120 C.C.C. (3d) 68 (B.C. C.A.) 426
R. v. Welsh (2007), 51 C.R. (6th) 33 (Ont. S.C.J.) 841, 959
R. v. West (2001), 45 C.R. (5th) 307 (Ont. S.C.) 717, 774
R. v. White, [1998] 2 S.C.R. 72, 16 C.R. (5th) 199, 125 C.C.C. (3d) 385................. 73
R. v. White, [1999] 2 S.C.R. 417, 24 C.R. (5th) 201, 135 C.C.C. (3d) 257 205
R. v. Whitman, 35 C.R. (6th) 12, 2005 CarswellBC 2678 (S.C.) 81
R. v. Whittle, [1994] 2 S.C.R. 914 814
R. v. Wholesale Travel Group Inc., [1991] 3 S.C.R. 154..................................... 52
R. v. Whynot (Stafford) (1983), 37 C.R. (3d) 198 (N.S.C.A.).............................164
R. v. Whyte (1988), 64 C.R. (3d) 123 (S.C.C.)...145
R. v. Wickham (1971), 55 Crim. App. R. 199 (C.A.) 509
R. v. Wiebe (2006), 205 C.C.C. (3d) 326 (Ont. C.A.).......................................430
R. v. Wiegand (2003), 11 C.R. (6th) 356 (Alta. Q.B.) 840
R. v. Wilcox, [2001] N.S.J. No. 85, 2001 NSCA 45 772
R. v. Wilder, [2002] B.C.J. No. 2110, 2002 BCSC 1333....................................394
R. v. Wilkes (1770), 4 Burr 2527 (H.L.)...183
R. v. Wilks (2005), 35 C.R. (6th) 172, 201 C.C.C. (3d) 11 (Man. C.A.) 524
R. v. Williams (1985), 44 C.R. (3d) 351, 18 C.C.C. (3d) 356 (Ont. C.A.); leave to appeal
    to S.C.C. refused 44 C.R. (3d) 351n...578, 761
R. v. Williams, [1998] 1 S.C.R. 1128...376
R. v. Wilson (1983), 5 C.C.C. (3d) 61 (B.C. C.A.) 547
R. v. Wilson (1999), 136 C.C.C. (3d) 252 (Man. C.A.).....................................242
R. v. Wilson (2006), 210 C.C.C. (3d) 23, 39 C.R. (6th) 345 (Ont. C.A.).................845
R. v. Wood (1982), 8 C.C.C. (3d) 217 (Ont. Prov. Ct.) 461
R. v. Wood (1986), 28 C.C.C. (3d) 65 (Ont. C.A.) 563
R. v. Woodard (2009), 245 C.C.C. (3d) 522 (Man. C.A.) 901
R. v. Woodcock (1789), 168 E.R. 352 762
R. v. Woodcock (2003), 177 C.C.C. (3d) 346, 14 C.R. (6th) 155 (Ont. C.A.)...........292
R. v. Worrall (2004), 19 C.R. (6th) 213, 2004 CarswellOnt 669 (S.C.J.).................943
R. v. Wray, [1971] S.C.R. 272, 11 C.R.N.S. 235, [1970] 4 C.C.C. 1, 11 D.L.R. (3d)
    673.. 159, 192, 204, 288, 784, 801, 814
R. v. Wright, [2009] O.J. No. 3550 (C.A.) 494
R. v. Y. (C.L.) (2008), 53 C.R. (6th) 207 69
R. v. Yaeck (1991), 10 C.R. (4th) 1 (Ont. C.A.) 298
R. v. Yebes (1987), 59 C.R. (3d) 108 (S.C.C.) 99
R. v. Z., [2002] 1 A.C. 483...261
R. v. Zebedee (2006), 211 C.C.C. (3d) 199 (Ont. C.A.) 617
R. v. Zeolkowski (1989), 50 C.C.C. (3d) 566 (S.C.C.)...................................... 36
R. v. Zundel (1987), 31 C.C.C. (3d) 97, 56 C.R. (3d) 1 (Ont. C.A.).................357, 941
R. v. Zundel (1990), 53 C.C.C. (3d) 161 (Ont. C.A.) 358
R. v. Zylstra (1995), 41 C.R. (4th) 130, 99 C.C.C. (3d) 477 (Ont. C.A.)...............1000
RJR-MacDonald Inc. v. Canada (Attorney General), [1995] 3 S.C.R. 199 1026
Ratten v. R., [1972] A.C. 378 (P.C.)..716
Ratten v. Reginam, [1971] 3 All E.R. 801..792
Rawdah v. Evans (February 1, 1995), Clarke J., [1994] O.J. No. 3322 (Gen. Div.)....225
Re Bell, [1946] O.R. 854 (C.A.) 137

Re Boyle (1983), 35 C.R. (3d) 34 (Ont. C.A.)..147
Re Braddon and Speke (1684), 9 Howell's State Trials 1127 660
Re C.A.S. Metro Toronto and N.H.B. (1980), 5 A.C.W.S. 66 (Ont. Prov. Ct.) 35
Re C.A.S., Metro. Toronto and R. (K.), [1983] W.D.F.L. 1320........................... 35
Re City of Toronto and C.U.P.E., Local 79 (1982), 133 D.L.R. (3d) 94 (Ont. C.A.);
    leave to appeal to S.C.C. refused 36 O.R. (2d) 386 33
Re Fraser (1912), 26 O.L.R. 508 (C.A.) 562
Re Inquiry into the Confidentiality of Health Records in Ontario (1979), 98 D.L.R. (3d)
    704 (Ont. C.A.)... 1043
Re Jennifer C. (1984), 39 R.F.L. (2d) 244 (Ont. Prov. Ct.) 35
Re Livingstone and R. (1975), 29 C.C.C. (2d) 557 (B.C.S.C.) 355
Re Northwestern Gen. Hosp. Bd. of Governors and Brown (1985), 52 O.R. (2d) 591,
    600 (Div. Ct.)... 32
Re Ont. Jockey Club (1977), 15 L.A.C. (2d) 273 (Schiff)................................. 34
Re Saxton, [1962] 3 All E.R. 92..951, 954
Re Univ. of Guelph & C.A.U.T. (1980), 112 D.L.R. (3d) 692 (Ont. H.C.) 1043
Read v. Lincoln (Bishop), [1892] A.C. 644 (P.C.)..357
Reference re Amendments to the Residential Tenancies Act (N.S.), [1996] 1 S.C.R.
    186... 1028
Reference re Anti-Inflation Act, 1975 (Canada), [1976] 2 S.C.R. 373....................360
Reference re R. v. Coffin, [1956] S.C.R. 191 ....520, 569
Reference re R. v. Latta (1976), 30 C.C.C. (2d) 208 (Alta. C.A.)........................795
Reference re R. v. Truscott (1967), 62 D.L.R. (2d) 545 (S.C.C.) 695
Regina v. C. (W.B.) (2000), 142 C.C.C. (3d) 490 (Ont. C.A.) 774
Regina v. Lauzon, [2000] O.J. No. 3940 (C.A.)...774
Regina v. Monkhouse (1987), 61 C.R. (3d) 343 (Alta. C.A.)..............................774
Regina v. Wilcox, [2001] N.S.J. No. 85 (C.A.)...774
Regina v. Wray, [1971] S.C.R. 272..199
Repouille v. U.S., 165 F. 2d 152 (2d Cir., 1947)..360
Robertson v. Edmonton (City) Police Service, [2005] A.J. No. 840, 2005 CarswellAlta
    949 (Q.B.)...226
Robins v. National Trust Co. (1925), 57 O.L.R. 46......................................852
Robins v. National Trust, [1927] A.C. 515 (P.C.)..135
Rock v. Canadian Northern Railway Co., [1922] 1 W.W.R. 496 (Sask. C.A.)..........292
Rodaro et. al. v. Royal Bank of Canada et. al. (2002), 59 O.R. (3d) 74 (C.A.)........... 79
Roman Catholic C.A.S. (Essex) v. H. (L.), [1987] O.J. No. 1845 (Ont. Fam. Ct.) 35
Ron Miller Realty v. Honeywell, Wotherspoon (1991), 4 O.R. (3d) 492 (Gen. Div.)   375
Roncarelli v. Duplessis, [1959] S.C.R. 121 1023
Rothman v. The Queen, [1981] 1 S.C.R. 640...814
Rudzinski v. Warner Theatres Inc., 114 N.W. 2d 466 (Wisc., 1962)......................746
Rumping v. D.P.P. (1962), 46 Cr. App. R. 398...996
Rumping v. Director of Public Prosecutions, [1962] 3 All E.R. 256 (H.L.)..............997

S

S. v. McC., [1972] A.C. 24 (H.L.) 137
S. (R.C.M.) v. K. (G.M.) 2005 CarswellSask 447, [2005] S.J. No. 443, 266 Sask. R. 31
    (Q.B.)...289
S. (R.J.) (1995), 36 C.R. (4th) 1 (S.C.C.)...488
Sankey v. Whitlam (1978), 142 C.L.R. 1 (Austl. H.C.)................................. 1024
Sarbit v. Hanson & Booth Fisheries (Canada) Co., [1951] 2 D.L.R. 108 (Man.
    C.A.)..741
Saxby v. Fulton, [1909] 2 K.B. 208 (C.A.)..391
Schmidt v. R., [1945] S.C.R. 438 736
Scott v. London and St. Katherine Docks Co. (1865), 159 E.R. 665 42

Setak Computer Services Corp. v. Burroughs Business Machines Ltd. (1977), 15 O.R.
    (2d) 750 (H.C.) 763, 769
Shenton v. Tyler, [1939] 1 Ch. 620 (C.A.) 996, 997
Sherrod v. Berry, 856 F.2d 002 (U.S. 7th Cir., 1988) 211
Sigeareak v. R., [1966] S.C.R. 645 355
Singh v. Canada (Attorney General), [2000] 3 F.C. 185 (C.A.).........................1022
Sir Walter Raleigh's Trial (1603), 2 Howell's State Trials 1 659
Slaight Communications Inc. v. Davidson, [1989] 1 S.C.R. 1038 1047
Slavutych v. Baker, [1976] 1 S.C.R. 254, 55 D.L.R. (3d) 224, 38 C.R.N.S. 30 1042,
                                                                                               1072
Smith v. Jones, [1999] 1 S.C.R. 455, 22 C.R. (5th) 203, 132 C.C.C. (3d) 225 ....980, 992
Smith v. Nevins, [1925] S.C.R. 619 135
Smith v. Rapid Transit Inc., 58 N.E. 2d 754 (Mass. Sup. Ct., 1945) 210
Smith v. Royal Columbian Hosp. (1981), 123 D.L.R. (3d) 723 (B.C. S.C.) 1043
Smith v. Smith, [1952] 2 S.C.R. 312 [B.C.]...142
Smith (1996), 46 C.R. (4th) 229 (Ont. C.A.)...486
Snow v. Boston & Maine R.R., 65 Me. 230 (1875) 930
Solicitor-General of Canada et al. v. Royal Com'n of Inquiry into Confidentiality of
    Health Records in Ontario et al. (1981), 62 C.C.C. (2d) 193 .... 1030, 1043
Solosky v. R. (1980), 50 C.C.C. (2d) 495, [1980] 1 S.C.R. 821.....................960, 962
St. Lawrence, [1970] 2 O.R. 3 (C.A.) 801
Stapleton v. R. (1952), 86 C.L.R. 358 (H.C.)..129
Starr v. The Queen (2000), 147 C.C.C. (3d) 449 (S.C.C.)..................................774
State v. Gallegos, 719 P.2d 1268 (N.M. 1986) 364
State v. Jalo, 557 P.2d 1359 (Or. Ct. App. 1976) 307
Stevenson v. Dandy, [1920] 2 W.W.R. 643 (Alta. C.A.) 402
Stowe v. Grand Trunk Pacific Railway (1918), 39 D.L.R. 127 (Alta. C.A.), affirmed 59
    S.C.R. 665..733
Street v. Guelph, [1965] 2 C.C.C. 215 (Ont. H.C.) 596
Subramaniam v. Public Prosecutor, [1956] 1 W.L.R. 965 (P.C.) 664
Sugden v. Lord St. Leonard's (1876), 1 P.D. 154 (C.A.).............................678, 781
Sussex Peerage Case (1844), 8 E.R. 1034 (H.L.) 755
Swadron v. North York (1985), 8 O.A.C. 204 (Div. Ct.)...................................426
Sweitzer v. R., [1982] 1 S.C.R. 949, 29 C.R. (3d) 97, 68 C.C.C. (2d) 193...............247

T

Tans Limited v. Reed Tenus Limited (1986), 70 B.C.L.R. 189 (B.C. S.C.)..............947
Taylor v. Blacklow (1836), 132 E.R. 401 959
Tesco Supermarkets Ltd. v. Nattrass, [1972] A.C. 153 (H.L.)............................746
Thompson v. R., [1918] A.C. 221...244
Thompson (2001), 151 C.C.C. (3d) 339 (Ont. C.A.) 490
Thomson Newspapers Ltd. v. Canada (Director of Investigation & Research) (1986), 30
    C.C.C. (3d) 145 (Ont. C.A.) 202
Thorn v. Worthing Skating Rink Co. (1876), 6 Ch. D. 415n 949
Tilco Plastics Ltd. v. Skurjat, [1967] 1 C.C.C. 131 (Ont. H.C.); affirmed [1967] 2 C.C.C.
    196n (Ont. C.A.) 508
Titus v. R., [1983] 1 S.C.R. 259..604
Toohey v. Metro. Police Commr., [1965] 1 All E.R. 506 (H.L.)...........................450
Toronto (City) v. C.U.P.E., Local 79, [2003] 3 S.C.R. 77..................................209
Town of Walkerton v. Erdman (1894), 23 S.C.R. 352.......................................775
Trammel v. United States, 445 U.S. 40 (1980) 469, 471, 475, 1072
Trial of Thomas Rosewell (1684), 10 Howell's State Trials 147 (K.B.)..................517
Triple A Invt. Ltd. v. Adams Bros. Ltd. (1985), 56 Nfld. & P.E.I.R. 272 (Nfld.
    C.A.)..426
Tripodi v. R. (1961), 104 C.L.R. 1 (Aust. H.C.) 746

Tsoukas v. Segura, [2001] B.C.J. No. 2418, 2001 CarswellBC 2562 (C.A.) 225

U

U.K. v. Hrynyk (1996), 107 C.C.C. (3d) 104 (Ont. Gen. Div.)............................490
U.S. v. Riccardi, 174 F. 2d 883 (3d Cir., 1949) 524
U.S. v. Sheppard, [1977] 2 S.C.R. 1067, 34 C.R.N.S. 207, 30 C.C.C. (2d) 424 ... 98, 105
Ullman v. U.S., 350 U.S. 422, 438 (1956) 478
Unit Park Management Co. v. Nissan Canada Inc., [1997] O.J. No. 3265 (Gen.
    Div.) 977
United Mexican States v. Ortega, [2006] 2 S.C.R. 120 105
United States v. Copeland, 369 F.Supp.2d 275 (E.D.N.Y., 2005) 63
United States v. Ferras, 39 C.R. (6th) 207, 209 C.C.C. (3d) 353, [2006] 2 S.C.R. 77..104
Upjohn Co. v. United States, 449 U.S. 383 (1981) 992

V

Varcoe v. Lee, 181 P. 223 (Cal. S.C., 1919) 369
Vetrovec v. R., [1982] 1 S.C.R. 811, 67 C.C.C. (2d) 1, 27 C.R. (3d) 304..........538, 635
Vézeau v. The Queen, [1977] 2 S.C.R. 277 503
Vriend v. Alberta, [1998] 1 S.C.R. 493 1047

W

Walkerville Brewing Co. v. Mayrand, [1929] 2 D.L.R. 945 (Ont. C.A.).................391
Walsh v. 1124660 Ontario Ltd. (2002), [2002] O.J. No. 4069, 2002 CarswellOnt 3026
    (S.C.J.) 17
Ward v. The Queen, [1979] 2 S.C.R. 30...260
Watt v. Miller, [1950] 2 W.W.R. 1144 (B.C.S.C.)..755
Wawanesa Mutual Insurance Co. v. Hanes, [1963] 1 C.C.C. 176, 28 D.L.R. (2d) 386,
    varied [1963] 1 C.C.C. 321 (S.C.C.) 572
Welstead v. Brown, [1952] 1 D.L.R. 465 (S.C.C.)...137
White (1999), 24 C.R. (5th) 201 (S.C.C.) 489
Wiedeman v. Walpole (1890), 24 Q.B.D. 537...741
Wilband v. The Queen, [1967] S.C.R. 14 940
Wilder (2000), 142 C.C.C. (3d) 418 (B.C.C.A.) 490
Willick v. Willick, [1994] 3 S.C.R. 670 371
Woolmington v. Director of Public Prosecutions, [1935] A.C. 462 (H.L.)..... 40, 49, 138
Woolway v. Rowe (1834), 110 E.R. 1151...754
Workman v. R., [1963] 1 C.C.C. 297 (Alta. C.A.); affirmed [1963] 2 C.C.C. 1
    (S.C.C.) 781
Wright v. Beckett (1833), 174 E.R. 143 (C.C.P.) 569
Wright v. Doe d. Tatham (1838), 7 E.R. 559 852
Wright v. Tatham (1838), 4 Bing. N.C. 489 855

Y

Youlden v. London Guar. Co. (1912), 4 D.L.R. 721 (Ont. H.C.); affirmed 12 D.L.R. 433
    (Ont. C.A.) 780
Yuill v. Yuill, [1945] 1 All E.R. 183, [1945] P. 15 (C.A.) 10

INDEX

Aboriginal Rights, 409

Accomplices, 635

Accused
Character evidence. *See under*
Character evidence
competence and compellability, 478
confessions. *See under* Confessions
failure to testify, 497
witness, as, 478

Adjudicative facts, 358

Administrative tribunals, 31

Admissions
confessions, *See* Voluntary Confession
Rule
conspiracy, 747
formal admissions, 345, 351
implied, 732
joint trials, 747
statements adopted by conduct, 740
statements adopted by silence, 732
statements authorized by party, 742
statements by trustees/executors, 753
statements of employees/agents, 732
statements of person with common
purpose, 795
theories justifying reception, 732

Adversary system, 1

Adverse witnesses, 568

Air of reality test, 111, 115

Applicability of laws of evidence, 31

Authentication, 391

Best evidence rule, 404

Bias, 2, 4, 166

Burdens of proof
air of reality test, 112
allocation
civil cases, 41
criminal cases, 49
choosing competing versions, 63
circumstantial evidence, 76, 79
confessions, 740
directed verdict. *See* Directed verdict
facts within knowledge of accused, 51

inferences, 76
insanity defence, 50, 154
measure of burden of persuasion, 53
civil cases, 53
criminal cases, 60
measure of evidential burden, 97
absence of evidence to contrary, 133,
147
air of reality, 111, 114
civil cases, 118
directed verdict, 98, 118
extradition, 104
impaired driving, 135
preliminary inquiry, 89, 98, 101
post offence conduct, 73
presumptions
false, 127
innocence, 138
true, 133
racial profiling, 44
reasonable doubt, 60, 62, 70
res ipsa loquitur, 42
rule in *Hodge's* case, 90
sentencing, 37
terminology, 39

Breathalyser, 135

Business records, 764

Character evidence
accused
See Criminal Record
assumptions, 223
disposition, 221
evidence of bad character, 228, 231
evidence of good character, 228
how to elicit evidence, 218
proof, 237
putting character in issue, 242
previous convictions. *See* Criminal
Record
reputation in community, 237
warnings, 242
civil cases, 218, 224
co-accused, 292
evidence of good character. *See*
Credibility, supporting
habit, contrasted, 213
impeachment of witnesses, and, 453
material issue, 221
propensity, 221
rebuttal, 240
relevant to fact in issue, 221
similar facts. *See* Similar Facts
third party, 292

victim, 296
    legislation to shield complainant,
        303, 318, 323
    self-defence, 297
    sexual asault, 298, 303, 318, 323
    warnings, 242

Charter of Rights and Freedoms
    balancing Charter values, 1044
    compellability, 479
    demonstrably justified reasonable limit,
        138
    insanity defence, 145
    presumption of innocence, 138, 145
    principle against self-incrimination, 488
    rape shield laws, 303
    records of third parties, 1044
    right to silence, 491, 497
    self-incrimination. *See* Self-
        incrimination
    trial by jury, 12

Children, evidence of, 437

Circumstancial evidence, 90

Civil actions. *See also* Negligence actions
    burden of proof, 41
    character, 224
    non-suit, motion for, 118
    presumptions, 133
    res ipsa loquitur, 42
    similar fact evidence, 286

Civility, 12

Codification, 25

Collateral facts rule, 556

Compellability. *See* Competence and
    compellability

Competence and compellability
    Accused, *See also* Self-incrimination,
        478
    children, 432
    corporate officers, 515
    immaturity, 432
    interest, 455
    mental capacity, 449
    oath/affirmation, 426
    spouses, 458

Confessions, 740
    expert opinion, 825
    recordings, 842

Confidential communications, 955, 1042

Consciousness of guilt, 73

Conspiracy, 747

Corporate officers, compellability of,
    515

Corroboration
    accomplices, 634
    children, 648
    defined, 653
    forgery, 634
    informers, 642
    perjury, 633
    sex cases, 599
    treason, 634
    Vetrovec warning, 635

Credibility, supporting, 606
    demeanour, 628
    exceptions
        allegation of recent fabrication, 614
        prior identification, 618
        recent complaint, 624
    oath-helping, 606
    rule prohibiting, 606

Criminal Record
    Canada Evidence Act, s. 12, 185, 592
    Corbett applications, 185, 593
    Criminal Code, s. 666, 220

Cross-examination
    Brown v. Dunn, 552
    duty, 552
    good faith, 542
    improper Crown, 536
    judicial control, 542
    purpose, 542

Crown privilege
    identity of informers, 1030
    statutory provisions, 1009

Declarations against interest, 754

Declarations in course of duty, 763

Defences
    Air of reality, 111, 115

Demeanour, 628

Demonstrative evidence, 412

Direct evidence, 81, 90

Directed verdict
civil cases, 118
test, 98

Disclosure, 3

Discretion
generally, 183
Charter, 185, 190, 195, 200, 205
probative value and prejudicial effect,
192, 261
reading in, 185
trial fairness, 200

DNA evidence, 75

Documents, 391, 402

Dying declarations, 761

Ethics, 14, 19
concealing evidence, 19
professional responsibility, 24

Evidence improperly obtained. *See*
Improperly obtained evidence

Exceptions to hearsay rule
Admissions. *See* Admissions
business records, 764
confessions, 740
declarant available, 780
declarant unavailable, 754
declarations against interest, 754
declarations as to mental/emotional
state, 780
declarations as to physical sensation,
780
declarations in course of duty, 763
dying declarations, 761
excited utterances, 789
former testimony, 774
hospital records, 764
past recollection recorded, 524
present sense impression, 674
spontaneous statements, 789

Excited utterances, 789

Excluding evidence. *See* Confessions,
Charter, 184, 200
Common law, 192

Expediency, 50

Expert witnesses
abuse 897, 913
appointment by court, 949
D.N.A., 76, 893
exchange of reports, 952
false confessions, 825
hearsay, opinion based on, 932
hypothetical questions, 945
identification, 897
learned treatises, 903
novel science, 865, 867
opinions on credibility, 906, 913
profile, 919
tests, 859
text books, use of, 946
ultimate issue rule, 929

Eye-witness identification, 81, 897

Fair trial, 200

Family matters, 33, 34, 289, 368

Formal admissions, 345

Former testimony, 190

Guilty plea, 345, 351

Habit and custom, 213

Hearsay rule
approaches, 677
child's out-of-court statements, 680
corroboration, 706
defined, 662
examples of non-hearsay statements,
662
exceptions. *See* Exceptions to hearsay
rule
history, 657
identifying hearsay, 662
necessity, 723
principled approach, 680, 706
prior identification, 619
prior inconsistent statements, 700
reasons for, 661
reliability, 665
reviewing exceptions, 747

Hodge's **case, rule in,** 90

Hostile witnesses, 568

Hypothetical questions, 945

Identification, 81

Impeachment of witnesses
    accused as witness, 591
    bias, 579
    capacity, 604
    character, 576
    experts, 906, 913
    impeaching one's own witnesses, 568
    previous convictions, 185, 593
    prior inconsistent statements, 380
    self-incrimination, 481

Inferences, 76

Insanity defence, 50, 154

Interest, compellability and, 455

Interrogations, videotaped, 842

Judge. *See* Trial Judge

Judicial notice
    adjudicative/legislative facts, 358
    boundaries of, 354
    Holocaust, 357
    law, of, 387
    legislative facts, 358
    legislative provisions, 387
    schools of thought, 354, 370, 376
    Spence tests, 376

Labour tribunals, 31

Leading questions, 517

Legislative facts, 358

Marital Communications, 996

Materiality, 162. *See also* Relevance

Medical privilege, 955

Mental capacity, competence and, 449

Multiple relevance, 164

Non-suit. *See* Directed Verdict

Oath/affirmation, 426

Oath-helping, 606

Opinion rule, 850. *See also* Expert
    Witnesses

Past recollection recorded, 524

Photographs, 395

Polygraph, 606, 812

Prejudicial, meaning, 192

**Pre-trial right to silence and
    interrogation,** 825

Present sense impression, 674

Presumption
    care and control, 136, 138
    conclusive, 133
    doctrine of recent possession, 129
    false, 127
    impaired driving, 134
    improper use of term, 133
    innocence, of, 138
    legitimacy, 138
    persons intend natural consequences of
        acts, 128
    proper use of term, 126
    testamentary capacity, 135
    true, 133

Previous consistent statements. *See*
    Credibility, supporting

Prior convictions
    civil cases, 595
    criminal cases, 185, 595

Prior inconsistent statements, 454

Prior testimony, 190

Privileges
    balancing Charter values, 1044
    case-by-case privilege, 1042
    class privilege, 955
    confidential communications, 955,
        1042

Crown privilege. *See* Crown privilege
marital, 996
police informants, 1030
records in possession of third parties,
    1044
religious communications, 955
self-incrimination. *See* Self-
    incrimination
solicitor-client privilege, 959
without prejudice communications,
    1002

Probative value, 192

Public interest immunity, 1009. *See*
    Crown privilege

Questioning of witnesses
collateral facts, 556. *See also*
        Impeachment of witnesses
cross-examination, 542
examination by court, 562
leading questions, 517
past recollection recorded, 524
refreshing memory, 524

Race
profiling, 44, 293
sentencing, 176

Rape. *See* Sexual offences

Real evidence
authentication, 391
best evidence rule, 404
demonstrative, 412
discretion to exclude. *See* Discretion
documents, 402
photographs, 395
recordings, 395, 842
videotapes, 395
views, 424

Recent possession, doctrine of, 129

Refreshing memory, 524

Relevance
materiality, 162
multiple, 164
social context, 165
tests, 157

Religious communications, 955

Reverse onus, 138

Res gestae, 789

Res ispa loquitur, 42

Right to silence, 491, 497

Rule in *Hodge*'s case, 90

Self-incrimination
Canada Evidence Act, 479
Charter of Rights, 481
comments re failure to testify, 508
derivative use immunity, 488
history, 478
no inferences from failure to testify,
    497
principle against self-incrimination, 488
right to silence, 491, 497
use immunity, 481

Sentence hearings, 39

Sexual offences
corroboration, 646
cross-examination on medical records,
    1044
motive of complainant, 583
opinions on credibility, 606, 906, 913
rape shield, 192, 318, 323
recent complaint, 499

Silence. *See* Right to silence

Similar fact evidence
civil cases, 286
collusion, 276
connection required, 241
gang cases, 281
general principles, 243, 251
Handy test, 261
Identity cases, 256, 281

Solicitor-client privilege, 959

Sources, 26

Spontaneous statements, 789

Spousal communications, 996

Spousal compellability, 458

Statements
Exculpatory, 848
Inculpatory, 848

Sufficiency, 97, 101

Trial Judge
bias, 2, 4, 165
civility, 14
comment on evidence, 11
discretion re cross-examination, 544
instruction to convict, 349
introduction of evidence, 176
interruptions by, 2, 562
right to call witnesses, 562

Tribunals, 31

Ultimate issue rule, 929

Videotapes, 191, 395, 842

Views, 424

Voluntary confession rule, 740
person in authority, 804
recording, 842

Without prejudice communications,
1002

Witnesses
adverse/hostile, 568
competence. *See* Competence and
compellability
corroboration. *See* Corroboration
exclusion of, 562
expert. *See* Expert witnesses
impeachment. *See* Impeachment of
witnesses
order of, 562
questioning. *See* Questioning of
witnesses
supporting credibility. *See* Credibility,
supporting